THE COMMENTARIES OF THE GREAT AFONSO DALBOQUERQUE, SECOND VICEROY OF INDIA

THE COMMENTARIES OF THE GREAT AFONSO DALBOQUERQUE, SECOND VICEROY OF INDIA

TRANSLATED FROM THE
PORTUGUESE EDITION OF 1774,
WITH NOTES AND AN INTRODUCTION,
BY

WALTER DE GRAY BIRCH, F.R.S.L.,

SENIOR ASSISTANT OF THE DEPARTMENT OF MANUCRIPTS IN THE BRITISH MUSEUM; MONORARY SECRETARY OF THE BRITISH ARCHAELOGICAL ASSOCIATION, ETC.

......."ut, quantum ad cognitionem pertinet rerum, etiam praeteritis saeculis vixisse videamur."—Quintilian, Instit. Orator., xii, 4.

Vol. I

GYAN

Published by

Gyan Publishing House
5, Ansari Road
Daryaganj, New Delhi-110002
Phone: 011-47034999, 9811692060
E-mail: books@gyanbooks.com

Distribution Network
gyanbooks.com
India, USA, Canada, UK, Australia, France

ISBN : 978-81-212-3261-6 (Set)
ISBN : 978-81-212-4805-1 (PB)
First Published, 1875

2nd Impression 2020

Printed at: Gyan Press, Delhi.

The
Commentaries of the Great Afonso Dalboquerque Vol. I
Author: Walter De Gray Birch

WORKS ISSUED BY

The Hakluyt Society.

THE COMMENTARIES OF THE GREAT AFONSO DALBOQUERQUE.

No. LIII.

Affonso de Albuquerque. 2º

COUNCIL

OF

THE HAKLUYT SOCIETY.

THE COMMENTARIES OF THE GREAT AFONSO DALBOQUERQUE,

SECOND VICEROY OF INDIA.

TRANSLATED FROM THE

PORTUGUESE EDITION OF 1774,

With Notes and an Introduction,

BY

WALTER DE GRAY BIRCH, F.R.S.L.,

SENIOR ASSISTANT OF THE DEPARTMENT OF MANUSCRIPTS IN THE BRITISH MUSEUM; HONORARY SECRETARY OF THE BRITISH ARCHÆOLOGICAL ASSOCIATION, ETC.

...... "ut, quantum ad cognitionem pertinet rerum, etiam praeteritis saeculis vixisse videamur."—QUINTILIAN, *Instit. Orator.*, xii, 4.

LONDON:

PRINTED FOR THE HAKLUYT SOCIETY.

M.DCCC.LXXV.

LIST OF CONTENTS.

INTRODUCTION.

"Que gloriosas palmas tecer vejo,
Com que victoria a fronte lhe coroa,
Quando sem sombra vãa de medo, ou pejo,
Toma a Ilha illustrissima de Goa!
Despois, obedecendo ao duro ensejo,
A deixa, e occasião espera boa,
Com que a torne a tomar; que esforço, e arte,
Vencerão a Fortuna, e o proprio Marte.

"Eis já sobre ella torna, e vai rompendo
Por muros, fogo, lanças, e pelouros,
Abrindo com a espada o espesso, e horrendo
Esquadrão de Gentios, e de Mouros:
Irão soldados inclytos fazendo
Mais, que Leões famelicos, e Touros,
Na luz, que sempre celebrada, e dina
Será de Egyptia Sancta Catharina."

Camões, *Lusiada*, x, 42, 43.

"What glorious *Palms* do I see weaving *There*,
With which his forehead Victory will crown
When without shadow or least touch of fear
He shall win Goa's Isle of bright renown!
But then (the *Storm* obeying) will not bear
So great a *Sayle*, and takes that *Bonet* down:
To reattempt the thing in fitter season.
Fortune and Mars fear *Valour* joyn'd with Reason.

"And (see) he does it; charges undismay'd
Through *walls*, through *Pykes*, through *Bullets*, and through *fire*:
Opens the quilted *Squadrons* with his *Blade*
Of Moors and Pagans knit in *Leagues* intire!
His gallant *Soldiers* in more blood shall wade
Then *Lyons* pin'd, *Bulls* prickt with love and Ire;
Upon the *Feast* (as pat as by designe)
Of Egypt's *Virgin Martyr*, Katherine.

Fanshaw.

There is no doubt that, to whomsoever the world may adjudge the pride and glory of first setting his

European foot in the East Indies, the Portuguese nation, when in the zenith of its energy and vitality, was the first to make use of the discovery, the first to bring the knowledge of these climes to a practical issue and to a fortunate result.

Among the illustrious band of noble heroes, whose chief pleasure it was ever

> "To scorn delight, and live laborious days",

performing their allotted part well, if we judge them according to the lights of their own times, perhaps a little fiercely, if rated by a more modern standard, never hesitating, for all that, to put their lives in jeopardy, or to relinquish them, provided only they might so best execute the commands and achieve the wishes of their Sovereigns in opening up new Channels of trade and commerce, new Tracts of Empire, in a word, new Worlds, stands pre-eminent the Great Afonso Dalboquerque, the Second Viceroy of Portugal in India, whose deeds of martial valour, whose intrepid spirit, whose kingly aptitude for supreme power, are now for the first time, from the original text, presented to the English reader in the English tongue.

Of the Biographical features of his Life, the text of these *Commentaries*, compiled by his natural son, Braz Dalboquerque (who, after the death of his father, assumed the name of Afonso), from the dispatches forwarded to the King Dom Emmanuel, forms the principal fountain of origin. From these the history of the illustrious warrior and navigator has been compiled with more or less accuracy for every Cyclopædia, and finds a place[1] in every Dictionary of Biography. A very great number of printed accounts of Afonso Dalboquerque's life also exist in works treating of Indian History, and they may be gleaned with profit for consideration and remembrance. It is my intention, in the Introduction of this present volume, to give some account of the two editions of the "*Commentarios*", viz., of 1576 and of 1774; a notice of two manuscripts which are deposited in the British Museum, Sloane MS., 197, and Additional MS., 20901; and a sketch of the character of our hero derived from the text of the "Commentarios" and other authorities. The principal points of his biography are given in the translated prefaces.

The edition of 1576, a fine copy of which is preserved in the Grenville Library in the British Museum, bears the following title:—

> "Commentarios | do Grande Afonso | Dalboquerque, capitam Geral | que foy das Indias Orientaes, | Em tempo do muito poderoso Rey dom | Manuel, o primeiro deste nome. |
>
> "Nouamente emendados & accrescentados pelo mesmo Auctor, | conforme ás informações mais certas que agora teue. |
>
> "Vão repartidos em quatro partes segundo o tempo dos | acontescimentos de seus trabalhos. |
>
> "Em Lisboa. | Com Licença impresso por Ioão de Barreira impressor del Rey | nosso senhor. Anno de 1576. | Com privilegio Real. |

This rare book is of quarto size, printed in a fine

[1] The best will be found in Hoeffer's *Nouvelle Biographie Générale*, Paris, 1855.

bold Roman pica type, leaded, and contains 578 pages of about 35 or 36 lines to a full page. In the numeration of the chapters of the First Part, chapter xvii has been, by inadvertence, made xix, and the error is continued throughout the First Part. A small slip, pasted on the fly-leaf at the beginning of the Volume, contains the following manuscript note, in the hand of the illustrious collector of this invaluable Library. The note is as follows :

"Alboquerque Commentarios. fo. Lisboa, 1576. This is an improved edition of the Commentaries of Alboquerque by his son, who had first edited them in 1557.

"Magni æstimatur hoc opus a Lusitanis, quippe quod e relationibus fide dignissimis haustum, haud vulgari prudentia et dexteritate compositum, historiæ et geographiæ Indiæ maxime inservire queat." *Meuselius*, ii, 2, 32.

"The first vol. of Lafitau Découvertes is translated from Alboquerque."

With regard to the statements in this note, I must confess that I have never been sufficiently fortunate as to see the first folio edition of 1557, nor do I know of any printed account of this work better than that contained in the biography of Affonso Dalboquerque the Second, which will be found among the prefatial matter translated and placed before the translation of the text. The second statement may be well endorsed by those who will give themselves the trouble or pleasure of reading the Commentaries, either in the original Portuguese, or in the present English translation. The third and concluding sentence of the note is entirely erroneous. Lafitau, in his excellent work entitled—"*Histoire des Découvertes et Conquestes des Portugais dans le Nouveau Monde. Par le R. P. Joseph François Lafitau de la Compagnie de Jesus. A Paris,* MDCCXXXIII"—undoubtedly made good use of these Commentaries, as indeed he was bound to do; but nothing can be more unfounded than the assertion that Lafitau's first volume is translated from Alboquerque. His history of the Discoveries of the Portuguese in India is a carefully written digest of the principal authors who have discoursed so fully and exhaustively on this subject, such as Barros, Osorio, Goes, Castanheda, etc.; and a mere translation of these Commentaries would have hardly sufficed to chronicle the extensive operations of this active nation in the Asian seas.

The other edition which I have occasion to mention is that of 1774, in octavo. The original title of this is thus given:—

> "Commentarios | do grande | Afonso | Dalboquerque | capitão geral | que foi | das Indias Orientaes | em tempo do muito poderoso | Rey D. Manuel | o primeiro deste nome | Parte I. | Lisboa | Na Regia Officina Typographica | Anno MDCCLXXIV. | Com Licença da Real Mesa Censoria, e Privilegio Real."

The First Part, that is Volume, contains 343 pages, of 30 lines to a full page. It relates to the first and second visits made by Afonso Dalboquerque to India, and the proceedings at Ormuz as far as the flight of the Captains, and the raising of the blockade by Afonso, who makes his way to Cananor and meets the Viceroy whom he is about to supersede.

The Second Part contains 285 pages. This volume

relates the circumstances with reference to the appointment of Afonso Dalboquerque as Viceroy, in the place of Dom Francisco de Almeida; and the events which took place during the interval of time from his arrival at Cananor early in December, A.D. 1508, and establishment in the Viceroyalty, until the taking of Goa for the first time.

The Third Part, of 289 pages, commences its narrative with the latter part of the year 1510, and contains the history of the second successful attempt upon Goa, and the events in connection with the extension of the Portuguese operations in Malacca, and concludes with the departure of Afonso Dalboquerque for the Straits of the Red Sea, in pursuance of his intention of conquering Ormuz and establishing the Portuguese rule in that part of Persia.

The Fourth and concluding Part, of 256 pages, is devoted to the arrival of Afonso Dalboquerque at Adem and places on that coast, his cruises to Calicut, Cananor, Cochim, Goa, and other ports, his operations at Ormuz, his death, and a genealogical sketch of his family. The account given in this place probably furnished materials to the author of the biographical account of Afonso Dalboquerque in the introductory matter before the text of the first part. The translation of this account follows this Introduction.

The present volume of the translation will be found to contain the whole of the First Part. A subsequent volume will be given to the Second Part, with an Introduction relating to the foundation, rise, progress, and decay of the Portuguese Empire in the Eastern

Indies; and some Bibliographical Notes in reference to the Indian Cycle of Portuguese Literature. These two prolific subjects could hardly be treated with that consideration to which they are entitled in the space at our command in this volume. I therefore shall limit my remarks to the character of Dalboquerque, and some reflections upon the study of the Portuguese Language. The Third and concluding Volume will contain the remainder of the translation, Parts III and IV, with an Appendix and Indices.

Before, however, entering upon the life of this great man, it will be profitable to call the reader's attention to two most valuable Manuscripts in the British Museum. The first[1] is in the Sloane Collection, No. 197, and consists of 423 large folios, written on paper, by the author, "Captain Pedro Barretto de Resende, Professed Knight of the Order of St. Benedict of Avis,[2] and a native of Pavia," in the year 1646.

The contents and great importance of the volume will be best gathered from its title, which is as follows:—

> "Livro do Estado da India Oriental Repartido em tres partes, a primeira Contem todos os retratos dos Vizorreis que tem avido no dito estado athe o anno de 634 com descripsoĩs de seus governos.
>
> "A Segunda parte contem as plantas das Fortalezas que há do cabo da boa esperança athe a fortalleza de

[1] Cf. the account of this MS. and its pictures, in the Hon. H. E. J. Stanley's *Three Voyages of Vasco de Gama*, p. ix (Hakluyt Society).

[2] A Military Order of Cistercians in Portugal, instituted by King Alphonso I, in the middle of the twelfth century, to commemorate the capture of Evora from the Moors.

Chaul e com larga descripçaõ de tudo ho que há em cada hũa das dittas fortalezas, Rendimento e gasto que tem, e tudo o mais que lhe toca.

"A terceira contem as plantas de todas as fortalezas que ha de Goa athe a China, com descripção da mesma forma, e Vão juntamente plantas de fortalezas que não são do estado que por estarem nas mesmas costas se puzerão por curiozidade.

"Feito pello capitão Po. Barretto de Resende, Caualleiro professo da Ordem de São Bento de Auis, natural de Pavia, Anno de 1646."

That is—

"Book of the State of Eastern India, divided into three parts; the first contains all the portraits of the Viceroys there have been in the said state, until the year [1]634, with accounts of their government.

"The second part contains the plans of the Fortresses that reach from the Cape of Good Hope to the Fortress of Chaul; and with a full description of everything there is in every one of the said fortresses, their Revenue and Expenditure, and all the rest that concerns them.

"The third contains the plans of all the fortresses that reach from Goa to China, with a description of the same kind; and with these are given plans of fortresses which do not appertain to the State, but they have been inserted out of interest because they are upon the same coasts.

"Made by Captain Pedro Barretto de Resende, Professed Knight of the Order of St. Benedict of Auis, a native of Pavia, in the year 1646."

This Manuscript claims a great interest from all who desire to extend their knowledge of the state of India in the early years of the seventeenth century, and it is well worthy of being printed hereafter by means of some such Society as the *Hakluyt*. It is only by the liberal action of this and kindred literary publishing societies that such great histories of bygone times can be reproduced and disseminated far and wide among those who delight in reading the original accounts of forgotten histories, and the exploits of their forefathers told in their own words. From this Manuscript (folio 11), I have obtained, by permission of the authorities of the British Museum, an Autotype permanent photographic facsimile of the portrait of Afonso Dalboquerque. This, in the original, is executed with thick body colours, and subscribed "Afonso de Albuquerque 2º," that is, *Afonso de Albuquerque, the Second (viceroy)*, by the same hand as that which wrote the text of the manuscript throughout. This portrait bears a great resemblance to most of the engraved portraits of the great Captain, and was in all probability copied from a panel painting at Goa in possession of the State, or in a collection belonging to the family of the Commander himself, although Barretto de Resende does not state the quarters from which he acquired the beautiful series of full-length portraits of the Viceroys, which adorns his Manuscript.

Folio 154 of this same Manuscript has furnished a map of part of the coast of Africa, of the coast of Arabia, and part of that of Persia. The entablature contains the following inscription :—

> "Petrus . Berthelot . primun . (*sic*)
> cosmographicum . Indiano
> rum . imperium . faciebat . &ct . 1635."

This inscription is written in a hand of the early seventeenth century at the left hand upper corner of the map. I am unable to obtain any information regarding this cosmographer, who claims in his title, given above, to have compiled the first complete map of the Indian Empire, several portions of which have been copied and placed in Pedro Barretto de Resende's Manuscript; but, as they are not noticed in the original List of Contents, I am inclined to think that they have been acquired and inserted subsequently by an owner of the volume.

The same manuscript affords, from folio 156, an opportunity of giving a plan of the island and fortress of Ormus, with the position of the adjacent islands of Lara or Larequa, and Queixome—places which are frequently alluded to in the text of the present volume.

Finally, I have extracted from folios 11 and 12 of this remarkable book the concise account of the principal episodes in the career of Afonso Dalboquerque; and as this has never, as far as I can gather, been printed, I need make no apology for its insertion in the present place:—

Afonso de Albuquerque 2º

Afonso de Albuquerque, filho segundo de Gonsallo de Albuquerque, senhor de Villa Verde, e de Dona Lianor de Menezes = Estaleyro Mor que foy del Rey Dom João Segundo: Primeyro guovernador da India, e segundo No guoverno della: Partio de Lisboa por Capitam mor de sinquo Naos em seis de Março de Mil quinhentos e seis como fica dito pera Andar De Armada Na boca do Estreyto do Mar Roxo e Costa de Arabia aonde andou e por Toda A Costa da Jndia athe que nas Naos do Anno passado lhe-Mandou El

Rey Dom Manoel A successão do governo da Jndia: que Dom Francisco De Almeyda lhe nam quis entregar sobre que ouve Tantos deferensas Entre Ambos que mandou Dom Francisco de Almeyda A Afonso de Albuquerque preso para Cananor aonde esteve athe chegar ho Marichal Dom Fernando Coutinho que passando do Cananor Levou Afonso de Albuquerque A Cochim e lhe entregou ho gouverno do Estado da Yndia do qual Tomou posse No fim De Outobro do anno de Mil quinhentos e Nove=guovernou seis annos=Tomou Goa Duas Vezes=A primeyra em desasete de fevereyro do anno de mil quinhentos e des=e Pella Nam poder sustentar por ser em prinsipio do Juverno e lhe faltar gente a Tornou a Larguar: e Esteve todo o Jnverno No Rio desde Ribandar athe pargim com suas Naos padessendo Jmmensos Trabalhos: E avendo grandes brigas com hos Mouros da Ilha de Goa e suas adyasentes de quem Teve muytas Vitorias Tomandolhe o Castello de Pargim e com a chegada das Naos do Reyno Tomou a Tomar Goa dia de sancta Catherina Vinte e sinquo de Novembro do mesmo anno de Mil quinhentos e des com grandissima Vitoria que Ouve dos Mouros e gentios: posto que Com perda de Algũs fidalgos: Tomou Malaqua em Julho de quinhentos E onze e a fortalleza de Ormus fes tributario O Rey das Ilhas de Maldiua Teue em Callecut aquella briga em que matarã ho Marichal Dom Fernando Coutinho=Mandou descobridores E Embayxadores a Malaquo=Fes Muyta gerra na Costa de Arabia No Tempo que nella Andou por Capitã Mor da Armada=foy sercar a Cidade de Adem No Estreyto do Mar Roxo=E yndo de fazer a fortalleza de Ormus fallesseo na barra de Goa: Em desaseis de Dezembro de Anno de quinhentos e quinze foy sepultado em Nossa Senhora da Serra que Elle fundou= E depois no Anno de mil quinhentos sesenta e seis forão seus Ossos Levados para Portugual: e postos na Capella Mor de Nossa Senhora da grassa que Elle avia mandado edificar.=

The equivalent of this in English is as follows:

Afonso de Albuquerque, Second Viceroy.

Afonso de Albuquerque, second son of Gonsallo de Albuquerque lord of Villa Verde, and of Dona Lianor de Menezes = Chief Equerry of the King Dom João the Second: Principal Governor of India, and second in the list of governors: He set out from Lisbon, as Chief Captain of five Vessels, on the sixth of March, 1506, as has been already related, to cruise with this squadron in the mouth of the Straits of the Red Sea [Straits of Babel Mandeb] and on the Coast of Arabia, whither he went, and along the whole Coast of India, until the King Dom Manoel conferred on him the appointment of Governor of India, sending word by the ships of the previous year. Dom Francisco de Almeyda was unwilling to give up the command to him, whereupon there arose so many differences between the two that Dom Francisca de Almeyda sent Afonso de Albuquerque a prisoner to Cananor, where he remained until the Marshal Dom Fernando Coutinho arrived there, and he, being on his way to Cananor carried Afonso de Albuquerque to Cochim and delivered to him the Government of the State of India, whereof he took possession at the end of October, 1509=He governed for six years=Twice he captured Goa=The first time on the sixteenth of February 1510 =And as he was unable to hold the city because the winter had commenced, and he was short of men, he had to evacuate it: and he remained the whole of the winter in the River from Ribandar to Pargim, in his ships, undergoing immense difficulties, and experiencing great hostilities from the Moors of the Island of Goa, and the adjacent places. Over these he gained many Victories, capturing from them the Castle of Pargim. And when a fleet arrived from Portugal he took Goa for the second time on the day of St. Catharine, the 26th of November, of the same year 1510, gaining a very complete Victory over the Moors and heathens, although it cost him the lives of several fidalgos.[1]

[1] See the extract from Camões at the commencement of this Introduction.

He took Malaca in July 1511, and the fortress of Ormus. He rendered the king of the Maldive Islands tributary [to Portugal]. He had in Callecut that disturbance in which they killed the Marshal Dom Fernando Continho=He sent explorers and Ambassadors to Malaca=He made many wars on the Coast of Arabia during the period that he held the post of Chief Captain of the Fleet. He set out to blockade the city of Aden in the Straits of the Red Sea. And as he was making his way to carry out the construction of the fortress of Ormus he died on the bar of Goa, on the 16th of December, in the year 1515. He was buried in the Church of Our Lady of the Heights, "Nossa Senhora da Serra", which he had founded. And afterwards, in the year 1576, his remains were transported to Portugal, and laid in the principal chapel of the Church of Our Lady of Grace, "Nossa Senhora da Grassa", which he had ordered to be built.

The Additional Manuscript 20901 was purchased by the Trustees of the British Museum at Lord Stuart de Rothesay's sale in June 1855 (Lot 2010). It is a quarto volume, on paper, measuring eleven inches by eight, of 230 folios, each containing about 26, 27, or 28 lines to a page, written in very confused chancery hands of the sixteenth century, evidently the work of two or more scribes. At fo. 202, some passages have been omitted and afterwards supplied in part from the mutilated leaf of the original.

The title of this manuscript is thus given in the sale catalogue prepared by Messrs. Sotheby and Wilkinson :—

2010. **INDIA. Historia do Descobrimento e primeiras Conquistas da India. Manuscript. An original Account of these Discoveries,** *written circa* 1516, *unfortunately wanting the first four chapters, and* *the name of the Author, whose style is more antiquated than that of J. de Barros, or Damiano de Goes.*

The note in Portuguese, written on a fly-leaf at the commencement of the volume, is given at p. 101, n., from which it appears that Manuel de Carvalho de Ataide gave the book to Freire, a well-known literary Portuguese, in the year 1714, and that it had at that time no binding, and was deficient in the beginning of the text. From an examination of the old pagination, it appears that seven folios are lost; portions of the folios 8, 9, 27, 28, 79, of the old arrangement, now folios 2, 3, 20, 21, 72, are also wanting; and the text ends abruptly, so that there is something wanting at the end which was in proper position when Freire acquired the volume by gift in 1714.

Folio 2 commences with these words:—"¶. Feitas assi estas cousas . . . . ."—the beginning of the text of Chapter 5. On folio 3*b* begins the first complete chapter, thus:—"¶ C°. 6. Como partiram de melinde e chegarã a Calecut, e do que hi passarom." The want of space prevents me from giving many of the headings of the succeeding chapters, but that of Chapter 9 helps to show the period of time embraced by this History. It is thus:—"¶. C°. Como p^r aluar'ȝ cabral partio de lixboa p^r capitam mor de xiiij vellas ꝑa a India, e do q̃ lhe socedeo." "How Pedralvarez Cabral set out from India as chief captain of fourteen sail, for India, and of what happened to him." This expedition set forth on the ninth of March, A.D. 1500.[1] In like manner, Chapter 12 is devoted to the account of the setting

[1] Brit. Mus., Add. MS., 20902, fo. 3.

out of João da Nova, with four sail, which was on the 15th of March, A.D. 1501.[1] Chapter 14 gives the account of the mission of Vasco da Gama, with twenty ships, in February and April, A.D. 1502.[2] Chap. 19 begins the narrative which is most closely concerned with the present volume. "C°. xix. Da partida daffonso Dalbuquerqȝ & ffᶜᵒ dalbuquerqȝ & Antonio de Saldanha." The Manuscript ends in the middle of Chapter 97, the title of which is as follows:—"Capitollo 97. Como sʳ a° dallbuquerque tornou a Reformar para hyr sobre guoa, e como fiz Rey em Cochym."

There is no doubt that this Manuscript, imperfect as it is, contains very valuable information respecting the period of which it treats, namely, from the earliest time of Portuguese power in India until the establishment of the capital of that power in Goa. It especially recommends itself to the members of the Hakluyt Society, as it appears to have been hitherto unpublished, and to contain new matter relating to a time and history of which the labours of that Society have taken so much cognisance. But the difficulty of deciphering the peculiarly formed handwriting will deter many from searching into its contents.

The reign of King John I witnessed a great extension of Portuguese naval enterprise,[3] which reached as far as the most southern point of the African continent. The first who actually doubled the Cape was Bertolameu

[1] *Ibid.*, fo. 4. [2] *Ibid.*, fo. 5.

[3] C. W. Koch, *An Historical View of the European Nations*, 3rd ed., London, *n. d.*, p. 81.—W. S. Lindsay, *History of Merchant Shipping*, 2 vols., 8vo. London, 1874.

Diaz, the Portuguese Admiral, who, from the difficulty of succeeding in his efforts, named this cape the "Stormy Cape", a name which the King, with prescient mind, changed into that of "Good Hope". Another Admiral, Vasco da Gama, extended the power of his country as far as India, landing at Calicut, on the Malabar coast, in 1498, early in the reign of King Manuel. Other navigators and commanders of this maritime nation, such as da Almeida, da Cunha, and de Castro, assisted in consolidating this European power in India and the parts east of the Cape of Good Hope. In the capture of Goa, Afonso Dalboquerque had ready to his hand a fortress almost impregnable, a splendid harbourage, a large and flourishing city and emporium of trade, placed in the very centre of the newly established Portuguese colonies. They found, indeed, not barren and uninhabited tracts of land, which required to be brought slowly into cultivation, and were alone amenable to an imported industry and stimulation, but powerful states and nations—rich, civilised, and teeming in abundance of wealth and luxuries, ready to fall without trouble into the hands of foreign invaders.

"There," says Koch, "nature and the industry of the natives produced or fabricated those articles of commerce and merchandise which have since become an object of luxury to Europeans, at least until the activity of the Venetians had furnished the inhabitants of this part of the world with them in such abundance as to make them be regarded as articles of absolute necessity. This circumstance was the reason why the

Portuguese never formed any other than mercantile establishments in India, which they erected on the coasts, without extending them into the interior. The working of the mines and the cares of agriculture were abandoned entirely to the natives.

"This era produced a total change in the commerce of the East. Formerly, the Venetians were the people that carried on the principal traffic to India. The Jewish or Mahometan merchants purchased, at Goa, Calicut, and Cochim, those and other productions of the East, which they imported into Syria by the Persian Gulf, and into Egypt by the Red Sea. They were then conveyed, by a laborious land carriage, either to Alexandria or Beyrout. Thither the Venetians repaired in quest of the luxuries of India; they fixed their price, and distributed them all over Europe. This commerce proved a vast source of wealth to these republicans; it furnished them with the means of maintaining a formidable marine, and of very often dictating the law to the other European powers: but, after the discovery of the new passage round the Cape, and the conquests of the Portuguese in India, the Venetians saw themselves compelled to abandon a traffic in which they could not compete with the Portuguese. This was a terrible blow to that republic, and the principal cause of its downfall. The Portuguese, however, did not profit by this exclusive commerce as they might have done: they did not, like other nations, constitute companies with exclusive commercial privileges; they carried it on by means of fleets, which the Government regularly despatched at fixed periods. In this manner, the commodities of the East were imported to Lisbon, but the indolence of the native merchants left to other nations the care of distributing them through the markets of Europe. The Dutch were the people that profited most by this branch of industry; they cultivated it with so much success, and under such favourable circumstances, that they at length succeeded in excluding the Portuguese themselves from this lucrative traffic, by dispossessing them of their colonies in the East."

Such were the conditions under which the great Dalboquerque lived, and in which he exercised his especial genius for widely spread conquest. Prompt, vigorous, decisive in his measures; not fiercer or more cruel than the spirit of the age in which he lived; impartial in his strictness and sense of honour, as we may well note in the incident relating to the death of Rodriguez Dias. This affair has been noted by all historians; and the Hon. H. E. J. Stanley, in his Preface to the *Three Voyages of Vasco da Gama*, p. xli, gives a translation of the account contained in Bishop Osorio's history. The same editor also mentions (at p. xlii, note) the narrative of Castanheda with relation to the same affair. There is no doubt that Dalboquerque felt compelled to make the fate of this unfortunate offender an example to the other Portuguese who were under his command in India, and whose laxity of discipline would have probably resulted in some disaster to the tenure of that power which he did all he could to extend. He was also too well aware, from events which had occurred in

Ormuz, that the enemy would not be behindhand in obtaining information respecting the true state of their Portuguese subjectors, and would lose no opportunity of encouraging insidiously any attempts to weaken the power of the Viceroy over his officers. To this must be attributed the apparent harshness of Dalboquerque on this occasion, for he felt that it was imperative on him to put a stop at once to acts of insubordination before they became too extensive for him to control. Camões, however, blames him, and speaks of this affair as the single blemish on his bright shield of glory.[1] The insubordination of the Captains when besieging Ormuz, and the consideration shown by Dalboquerque to the offenders, is a proof that he knew when to forget and forgive; and the cruelties practised on the Persians and Arabs were probably retaliations and the result of a conventional system of carrying on warfare in those regions, rather than a sort of gratuitous brutality invented and indulged in by the Portuguese conquerors. They themselves would, in all probability, have suffered much worse, had they had the ill fortune to experience any serious discomfitures.

An excellent exposition of the policy of Dalboquerque is given in the Voyages already quoted (p. lxii), whence we may conclude that the Viceroy's idea of reducing city after city, fortress after fortress, and state after state, establishing in their places fortified stations or factories along the coast, was weak in its conception, and led in the end to the too great dispersion of the imperial power, and rendered it unable to concentrate

[1] See page 107, note.

itself with sufficient rapidity, *élan*, and weight of arms. He indulged in the acquisition of a vast empire or rather coast line, but neglected the consolidation of the countries which lay beyond, and so left behind him a series of weak points which were sure to be recovered by those from whom he had wrested them, as soon as the native power and the native policy of patience could exert itself and spring back upon the invaders. The capture of Goa and formation of its city into the capital of the Portuguese empire in India is the most important act of Albuquerque's life, and he will ever be remembered by this deed, which by itself is sufficient to render eternal the memory of the man who conceived and executed such an onerous undertaking. From this invincible position nothing has yet availed to oust the Portuguese, who cling to it as the English clung to Calais, when every other spot of territory on the European continent had been torn from their hands.

There is no doubt that whoever will give some time and attention to the learning of Portuguese will find his labour amply requited by the advantages to be derived from the great mass of literature which the language possesses. The best idea of the proportions which this literature assumes—whether we incline more to admire the poetry, presided over by the immortal Camões, and the numerous aspirants to a share in his laurels, or whether we are more allured by the prose epics of Portugal's best days, when she was at the height of her power in India, and when she was promoting the extension of her rule in the Southern Continent of America—may be gathered from Bouterwek, and the Bibliotheca Lusitana. It is sufficient for me in this place to express an earnest desire that the critical study of the Portuguese language may soon become more extended among us, and a more cordial literary intercourse between England and Portugal established. This may be best accomplished by multiplying translations of standard works from one language into the other. This present volume of the Commentaries of the Great Afonso Dalboquerque, the Cæsar of Portugal, is the result of the operation of these sentiments in my own mind; and I shall feel that I have gained my desires and succeeded in my intentions, if the remarks here expressed may induce other students to follow in the footsteps of those who, like Fanshaw, Mickle, Lord Stanley, and others, have taken their delight in introducing Portuguese works to the English through the medium of translations, and thereby fostering a mutual interchange of literary and scientific progress. The true position of the English rule in India, the traditions it maintains, the point of view from which it is looked upon by the native races, can never be rightly understood until a better knowledge is acquired concerning the first impressions conveyed to, and made upon, the minds of the inhabitants by the first European nation which effected any extensive settlement among them. This fact alone, one out of many quite as pertinent which might be adduced, ought to convince us of the importance of examining the classical literary productions of a nation justly celebrated at all times for enterprise and military prowess.

I cannot close these introductory notes without putting on record my grateful recognition of services rendered me by Dr. W. Wright, Professor of Arabic in the University of Cambridge, who has kindly furnished me with the Arabic renderings of several names of persons and places mentioned in the text, and of more or less obscure derivation. To my colleague, Mr. G. F. Warner, my special thanks are due for aid willingly given in the revision of the translation throughout.

The Society is indebted to the Trustees of the British Museum for the permission to reproduce, by photography, the portrait of Afonso Dalboquerque from Pedro Barretto de Resende's Manuscript in the Sloane Collection.

London, November, 1875.

CHRONOLOGY OF PART I.

PAGE		
xxxvii.	Birth of Afonso Dalboquerque . .	A.D. 1453
xxxviii.	He accompanies the squadron of King Alfonso V to Otranto . . .	1480
xxxviii.	Takes part in the expedition to Graciosa	1489
2.	His first voyage to Asia . . .	[6] Apr., 1503
16.	Leaves Coulão for Cochim . .	12 Jan., 1504
17.	Leaves Cochim	25 Jan., 1504
18.	Doubles the Cape of Good Hope .	1 May, 1504
19.	Reaches Lisbon . . .	End of July, 1504
20, 21.	Accompanies Tristão da Cunha .	5 Apr., 1506
55.	Tristão da Cunha leaves Socotra for India	1 Aug., 1507
56.	Afonso Dalboquerque fits out his fleet	10 Aug., 1507
59.	Stands off Curia Muria . . .	13 Aug., 1507
132.	Lands at Ormuz	10 Oct., 1507
142.	Marks out the foundations for the fortress at Ormuz . . .	24 Oct., 1507
209.	Remonstrance of the disaffected captains to the Viceroy, against the operations at Ormuz . . .	13 Nov., 1507
170.	Letter of the captains to Afonso Dalboquerque	5 Jan., 1508

201. Afonso Dalboquerque takes up his quarters at the Cape of Guardafum . . . End of April, 1508

203. Anchors off S. Miguel . . . 15 May, 1508

210. Commission of inquiry into charges against Afonso Dalboquerque . 26 May, 1508

211. Arrival of a fleet of three vessels from Portugal at Cochim . . About the same time

213. Afonso Dalboquerque sets out for Ormuz . . . . . 15 Aug., 1508

256. Arrives at Cananor . . [December, 1508]

COMMENTARIES

OF THE

GREAT AFONSO DALBOQUERQUE.

COMMENTARIES

OF THE GREAT

AFONSO DALBOQUERQUE,

WHO WAS

CAPTAIN-GENERAL OF THE EAST INDIES

IN THE TIME OF THE VERY POWERFUL

KING D. MANUEL,

THE FIRST OF THIS NAME.

PART I.

LISBON:

IN THE ROYAL PRINTING OFFICE,

ANNO MDCCLXXIV;

With Licence of the Royal Board of Censors, and Royal Privilege.

TO THE MOST ILLUSTRIOUS

AND

MOST EXCELLENT LORD

SEBASTIÃO JOSÉ DE CARVALHO E MELLO,

MARQUEZ DE POMBAL,

PRIME MINISTER AND SECRETARY OF STATE

TO HIS MOST FAITHFUL MAJESTY

ETC., ETC., ETC.

DEDICATION.

Most Excellent Sir,

Nothing obtains more commonly among those men, whose spirits are not to be confined within the small limit of the sphere wherein either Nature or Fortune has placed them, than the employment of the greatest force, whereby they may overcome the obstacles which trammel them and reduce them to the condition of the many others over whom they desire to exercise superiority. Some by their deeds and virtues, yea and in spite of malice and envy, finally achieve an universal reputation, and having been encouraged by the good and rewarded with their deserts, repay what they have received by the great benefits they afford to the Public. Others, not aware of their powers, or perhaps estimating themselves at their own standard, yet being naturally ambitious, break through every impediment without any concern for what the better part of mankind thinks or says of them, solely interested in acquiring for themselves the goodwill and favour of those in whose authority and power they found the basis of the hopes of what they desire to obtain.

I, Most Excellent Sir, though far from placing myself among the few who belong to the first of these, certainly do not belong to the second class. Truth, zeal, fidelity, obedience, and the desire of serving as far as strength will permit me, have ever been the principal bases whereon I have established the little I have done that I may not be without merit. And what I have done, though but a little, Your Excellency was so good as to bring under the notice of the most Learned, the most Enlightened, and the most Generous of Monarchs, not only of Portugal but of the World. Thereupon Your Excellency further was pleased to consider me worthy of employment upon honorable works, and ennobled me and conferred such and so many benefits upon me as I had never expected to receive. Would then that I knew how to show in loud voice how much I owe to Your Excellency for the many and great favours that I have experienced at your hands. But since my genius is not able to soar so high, Your Excellency must permit me to call the whole World to witness this my confession, that never in time to come I may venture to speak in other than these terms without convicting myself of falsehood and without arriving at the lowest point of ingratitude.

This new Edition of the *Commentaries of the Great Afonso Dalboquerque*, containing the most illustrious Deeds of the Portuguese Nation—an uninterrupted plan of an excellent Government, and of a policy firmly grounded, and truly Christian—which shall serve as it were for a spur to the noble hearts of the Portuguese, recalling to their memory so many examples of bravery, of glory, and of virtue, that they may never lose sight of the grand deeds of eras more fortunate than their own: this, I say, is the work which I have the honour to present to Your Excellency, desiring your Excellency will permit it to go forth under your honourable name, to be restored to the light of the world. This work will cause me to be heard by all, for all with one accord reverence and admire your Excellency and take an interest in all that Your Excellency patronises, encourages, and sanctions. Thus not only by the natural impulse of my mind, which yet must always evince its gratitude, but even by the security of my honour and credit, I shall always be obliged to bear witness to this very truth. I am well aware that your Excellency, as the great Planet which imparts its light to the others, and receives from none, vivifies and exalts all with your benefits without searching for other recompense than you possess of yourself, seeing that you know how, and are able, to give felicity to so many. But among the immense number of those who have been protected by Your Excellency, though there are many whose willing duty it is to demonstrate their gratitude, yet there is the abominable example of others who have not so done: and these latter force the former even more than ever to give proofs of their goodness. Therefore it is, that apart from many reasons which compel me to free myself from so infamous a stain, I shall repeat here and for ever that by the hands of Your Excellency alone all the benefits, with which in the sight of the World I have been rewarded, have been conferred upon me.

To this, and this alone, I can attribute the accomplishing of my obligations. For to undertake to praise the magnanimity of Your Excellency, the sublime talents and heroic actions for the good of the State, of mankind, of the World, would be as it were to pretend to set a price upon them, whereas I cannot appraise them : for Your Excellency alone knows what you are and what you have done. And who is there who can be so presumptuous? If there be any who believes he can estimate your worth, let him reveal the little that he knows, and if he intend to make a panegyric upon your Excellency let him forsooth parade his audacity.

The Great Orator Tully used to say that the Roman Citizens after a time ceased to applaud Cæsar, for all the applause that was due to him "Obstupefactis hominibus ipsâ admiratione compressus erat, et eo prætermissus, quia nihil vulgare dignum Cæsare videri poterat." What reasons are there, that the Portuguese Nation and most learned men should not apply the same with respect to your Excellency?

I, truly, do so apply it. Therefore those who flatter themselves they possess the innate ability of pleasing the Public by becoming Panegyrists of Your Excellency will never seduce me with their example, and my respectful silence will be the greater proof of my admiration.

Yes, Most Excellent Sir, the great fame of your Excellency shall endure for ever, for the fruit of your more than extraordinary talents, and of your sublime Ministry, shall be experienced until the end of posterity. The World shall ever know by how much Your Excellency exceeded all in the most difficult art of governing People and rendering them happy. It shall admire your rare prudence in extirpating abuses, your great bravery in overcoming the greatest difficulties, your firm constancy in repressing the forces of those who for private interest, or by ignorance, or by malice opposed the good of the State. It shall confess, that Your Excellency was born to support the true Religion: to vindicate the inviolable prerogatives of Sovereigns: to civilize mankind and unite them within the bonds of the most perfect society: to extinguish vices: to cultivate virtues. These effects of the lofty comprehension and activity of Your Excellency shall ever be admired, as they shall ever exist; for all desire and protect that which they know to be useful.

Above all, Portugal will attribute the Epoch of its happiness and greatness to the time of the incomparable Ministry of Your Excellency. And what monuments shall it not have before it, to stimulate its voice and its recollection? A grand Capital, newly erected, and adorned with the most sumptuous edifices, after its destruction by an earthquake and fire, which overthrew it and reduced it to ashes: A Legislation founded upon the most solid principles, and dictated by reason and by Nature. Commerce, considered from the highest point of view, and increased and protected in spite of the envious and the jealous: Agriculture vindicated, encouraged, and established as the principal basis of riches: Industry animated: the Arts and Sciences cultivated: Manufactures introduced and at the same time brought to perfection. The kingdom garrisoned with impregnable forts, munitioned with troops in the highest state of discipline, and provided with all that is necessary to make it feared in war. The extermination of some men who put on an outward appearance of virtue, but were in reality impious, powerful with what they possessed, and by means of the dominion they usurped, united into one sole body the better to resist monarchs and peoples, being themselves disturbers of the government and of society. The immortal work, wherein in chronological order of consecutive facts is demonstrated with latest evidence the accumulation of the atrocities those hostile men practised ever since their admission into this Kingdom, and the insuperable necessity which there was of exterminating them. The recent and memorable foundation for the re-establishment of the Sciences, rejecting all that the barbarities of past ages had introduced into them, when the lights of truth and reason were yet obscured, planting the solid principles upon which they were to be established after reducing them by brevity, clearness, and method, entrusting the teaching of them to wise and renowned Masters, both native and foreign; and forming such a code of laws and statutes as were never before seen, which will serve as a model for the cultivation of studies to all enlightened nations. But why do I go on noting what the Portuguese and all the World will have ever before their eyes and will admire with awe? Such being the monuments which exist and which immortalise your Excellency, it is useless to bring them to remembrance. They speak for themselves, and in such a manner that the voice and force of eloquence yield to them.

No, Sir, I have neither praised nor pretended to praise Your Excellency. What I have hitherto said was the impetus of my unrestrained feelings, was the sign of my respect, was the liberty of my thoughts; or to speak more accurately was mistake, was error. But this error is committed by all, and so merits Your Excellency's forgiveness. Henceforth I must correct myself and I commence from this moment, keeping a profound silence. May God preserve Your Excellency many, many years for the glory of OUR MONARCH, for the happiness of the Kingdom, and for the honour of the Nation and the World.

Your Excellency's

Most obliged, obedient, and humble servant,

NICOLAO PAGLIARINI.

TO THE READER.

This Edition of the "Commentaries of the Great Afonso D'Alboquerque", which now comes forth from the press of this Royal Printing Office, is the third which has been made in Portuguese, and was reduced to four volumes from eight, for easier use, and for the convenience of readers. As regards the elegance of the impression, and the diligent care that it should be published without defects and errors, it will speak for itself. And as it is intended to issue in the same form other new editions of the more Classical Portuguese Authors, the printing of the "Decades of Asia" by the illustrious Historian João de Barros has been already commenced, and will be continued with the greatest diligence and application, so as to publish the whole work complete as rapidly as possible. In order to afford better information about these *Commentaries* and what they contain, it seemed convenient to introduce beforehand to the Reader what is said by *Diogo Barbosa Machado* in his *Bibliotheca Lusitana Historica, Critica, e Chronologica*, fol. tom. i., pag. 22, as follows:—

"D. Affonso De Albuquerque, surnamed the Great, by reason of the heroic deeds wherewith he filled Europe with admiration, and Asia with fear and trembling, was born in the year 1453 in the Estate called, for the loveliness of its situation, the Paradise of the Town of Alhandra, six leagues distant from Lisbon. He was the second son of Gonçalo de Albuquerque, Lord of Villaverde, and of D. Leonor de Menezes, daughter of D. Alvaro Gonçalves de Ataíde, Count of Atouguia, and of his wife D. Guiomar de Castro, and corrected this injustice of nature by climbing to the summit of every virtue, both moral and political. He was educated in the Palace of the King D. Affonso V, in whose palæstra striving emulously to become a rival of this African Mars, he set sail in the squadron commanded by this Prince in the year 1480, to succour King Fernando of Naples and repress the fury of the Turks who had invested Otranto, showing on this occasion that to reach heroic pitch, his bravery did not depend on the length of his service, but rather upon the liberality of Fortune toward him.

"Not less was the glory his arm acquired in the expedition sent out in the year 1489 for the defence of the fortress of Graciosa situated on the island which the river Luco makes close to the city of Larache, under the happy auspices of the King D. João II, to whom he was Chief Equerry. These two famous and successful enterprizes, one in Europe, and the other in Asia, were the fortunate prelude of the victories of which Asia was soon to be the theatre, whither he sailed on the sixth of April, 1503; and after having performed deeds superior to any other spirit but his own, he returned to Portugal more full of glory than spoils, of which covetousness has more share than bravery. Having for a second time ploughed the seas as Captain in a squadron of fifteen ships, in company with Tristão da Cunha, to continue the triumphs of which his sword was the arbiter, the King D. Manoel chose him Governor of India, of which he took formal possession on the fourth of November 1509. The prudent mind of the Monarch trusted that upon shoulders so robust as these the Empire would be able to remain impregnable to the violent irruptions of all the potentates of Asia.

"It seems difficult to believe the continued current of victory achieved by the arm of this invincible Hero, who, just as a thunderbolt launched from the sphere which his Sovereign had taken for his device, left no portion of all the

East, which did not experience the unfettered impulse of his destruction, reducing to ashes the cities of Brama, Orfação, Calicut, Pangim, and the numerous fleets of Meca, Adem, and Ormuz. On two occasions he was crowned with victory by the famous conquest of Goa, humbling the pride of the Hidalcão, on the second taking, in such a manner, that for a long time he lamented the fatal overthrow he suffered upon the walls of a place destined to be the head of the Portuguese Empire in Asia. What leafy palms and laurels did not his invincible arm obtain at the surrender of Malaca, whose heroic deed admiring fame made known by three thousand mouths of bronze,—glorious trophies of such a celebrated attack. It was less owing to the violence of his sword than to the respect in which his name was held, that the cities of Lamo, Mascate, Benastarim, Calayate, and the Islands of Camaram, Queixome, surrendered, as did also Homelião at the death of two nephews of the King of Larec.

"To avenge the hostilities shown by the formidable fleets of the King of Ormuz and the Hidalcão, he made use of two elements, fire and water, burning and sinking some ships at Cape Rosalgate, and others in the harbours of Adem and Calicut. The fame of the awe-striking actions, wherewith he had abased all the East, compelled the King of the Isles of Maldiva, Vengapor, and the Hidalcão to yield, and imploringly seek him as a Guardian of their territories, and in corroboration of their obedience they made themselves tributary to our Crown. He received different embassies from the Princes of Persia and Arabia, and from the Kings of Pegú, Bengala, Pedir, Sião, and Pacem, soliciting his friendship with generous donatives, for which he benignly thanked them, but generously rejected the presents.

"In order to preserve the State impregnable to the invasion of its enemies, he erected, with an expense equal to their magnificence, the Fortresses of Malaca, Ormuz, Calicut, Cochim, and Cananor, inscribed on whose stones his name is handed down to posterity under the glorious title of Founder of the Portuguese Empire of the East. Having concluded terms of peace with the kingdoms of Cambaia, Dabul, Onor, Baticalá as far as Cape Camorim, and with the Princes of China, Jaoa and Maluco, he felt his last sickness fall upon him when he was at Ormuz; and being desirous that Goa should be the setting, as it had so often been the rising, of his heroic labours, he set out so enfeebled, that at four leagues distance from the haven, he rendered his unconquerable spirit to its Creator, with evident signals of its destination, on the sixteenth of December 1515, after sixty-three years of age, and ten of government. He was shrouded in the cloak of the Military order of Sant-Iago, of which he was a *Commendador;* and as soon as his body arrived at the Quay of Goa, so lugubrious an uproar arose among the people that even the priests interrupted their ecclesiastical chants with tears and sighs.

"The natives, astonished to behold him with so long a beard, and having his eyes as it were open, asserted with superstitious credulity that certainly he was not dead, but God had called him to be General of his armies. He was borne to his grave covered with the Pall, and upon the shoulders of the principal persons of Goa, who buried him in the Church of Our Lady of the Heights, which he had himself erected in gratitude for the fortunate success he had experienced in the conquest of Malaca. At the deposition of his triumphant ashes the inhabitants assembled obsequiously with various offerings, hoping that he would be propitious to their supplications.

"After fifty-one years his remains were translated, according to the desire expressed in his will, to the Convent of Our Lady of Grace, belonging to the Religious Hermits of St. Augustine in this Court, whither his body was removed on the nineteenth of May, 1566, with the pomp befitting so great a Hero. In stature he was ordinary, his face long, and fresh-coloured, his nose aquiline, his aspect agreeable, and made venerable by the white beard which reached down to his waist. He was perfectly intimate with the Latin tongue, and as discreet when he spoke as when he wrote. He was loved and feared, without his benevolence degenerating into partiality or his correction into rigour. He observed truth religiously, naturally abhorred lying, and executed justice promptly. In so many battles both by sea and land he had frequently been wounded, bearing witness with his blood, that he had ever sought the place where danger was more certain. He was profusely generous, giving to the Captains the spoils obtained in so many victories, whereof he never reserved the least part for himself, for his desire was more for glory than for wealth. He always adhered to the utmost fidelity with his domestic enemies, and only brought his political sagacity to bear upon strangers.

"There were two actions suggested by the magnanimity of his heart which he determined to perform. One was to divert the channel of the Nile to the Red Sea, and prevent it from running through Egypt, thereby to render the lands of the Grand Turk sterile; the other to carry away from Méca the bones of the abominable Mafoma, that, these being reduced publicly to ashes, the votaries of so foul a sect might be confounded. His name will be eternally applauded by the voice of Fame, as it was in the thoughts of the greatest Monarchs, and by the pens of illustrious writers, for D. Fernando, King of Castile, praised him as an illustrious captain to Pedro Correa, the Ambassador of the King D. Manuel, and the Grand Turk to D. Alvaro de Sande, Captain of the Emperor Charles V.

"Of the authors who have mentioned him the first is Maffeo,[1] towards the end of the fifth book of his History of

[1] Johannes Petrus Maffei: *Historiæ Indicæ, cum Ignatii Loyolæ vita*, folio, Colon. Agrip., 1589 and 1593.

India. 'Prorsus invicti ad laborem, ac patientiam æque corporis, animique vir, et cum quolibet suæ ætatis Ducum, vel navalis scientiæ, vel expediti consilii magnitudine comparandus.'"

Faria,[1] *Asia Portugueza*, tomo i, Part II, cap. 10, n. 8: "Aquella espada con cuya punta se avia labrado el Scetro, que ElRey Dom Manoel tenia no con menor interez de sus rentas, que reputacion de sus armas."

Castanheda[2], *Historia do Descubrimento da India*, liv. III, cap. 155: "Esforcado e famoso Capitão...Em summa nenhuma virtude lhe falleceo para ser tão singular Capitão, como o foram os singulares, que ouve entre barbaros, Gregos, e Latinos."

Fr. Antonio de San Roman,[3] *Historia General de la India Oriental*, liv. II, cap. 9: "Dexò el Imperio dela India mui quieta en la devocion, y fidelidad delRey D. Manoel, y el exercicio de las armas quedò en su punto con su industria, y las cosas de la Religion en mucho augmento.

Brentan.[4] *Epitome Chronolog. Mund. ad annum* 1515: "Christianissimus Heros."

Mariz,[5] *Dialogos de Var. Hist.*, *Dialogo* 5: "Falleceo em tão claro nome de perfeito Governador, que não era facil a questão, que em seu louvor se movia, se resplandecia mais em suas excellencias o esforco de Alexandre, ou a sabedoria de Nestor; porque administrava a guerra como summo Emperador, e governava a Republica como perfeitissimo Magistrado."

[1] Manoel Severim de Faria: *Asia Portvgvesa*, 3 tom., folio, Lisbon, 1666-1675.

[2] Fernando Lopez de Castanheda: *Historia do Descobrimento & Conquista da India pelos Portugueses*, 8 livr., folio, Coimbra, 1552-1561. See also "The first Booke of the Historie of the Discouerie and Conquest of the East Indias enterprised by the Portingales, in their daungerous Nauigations, in the time of King Dom John, the second of that name. Translated into English by N. L. [*Nicholas Lichefild*], Gentleman." Quarto, London, 1582.

[3] Folio, Valladolid, 1603.

[4] Ignatius Brentano Cimarola: *Epitome Chronologica Mundi Christiani ab anno Nativitatis Christi usque ad sæculi decimi octavi annum vigesimum sextum inclusive deducta*, etc., folio, Augustæ Vindelicorum, 1727.

[5] Pedro de Mariz: *Dialogos de Varia Historia dos Reyes de Portugal*, quarto, Lisbon. 1674.

Sampayo,[1] in cap. 2, *Vitæ Beati Petri Eborensis:* "Insignis ille et immortali laude dignus, atque Heroum antiquorum numero meritissimo referri potest."

Barbuda,[2] *Emprezas Militares de Lusitanos,* fol. 156, v.: "Adqueriendo triunfos a su Patria, y ganando Coronas a su Rey."

Lafitau,[3] *Histoire des Découvertes et Conquestes des Portugais,* tom. i, pag. 520: "Dans la guerre il fut veritablement grand par la noblesse de ses projets, et la prudence avec laquelle il les exécuta. Dans le Conseil et dans l'action il paroissoit en lui deux hommes tous differens."

Osorius[4] *de Rebus Emmanuelis,* lib. 10: "Tanta namque erat humanitate præditus, ut utrum magis multi illius virtutem metuerent, an bonitatem amarent, esset explicatu difficillimum. Imprimis autem jus æquabile colebat, et fidem violatam acerrimè puniebat, neminique injuriam fieri patiebatur...Non erat alienus a litteris: et cum otium erat, lectione sacrarum præcipuè litterarum oblectabatur."

Thevet,[5] *Vies des Hommes Illustres,* p. 422: "Fondateur de la domination des Portugalois en Inde."

Franciscus de Santa Maria,[6] *Ceo aberto na Terra,* liv. III, cap. 67: "Na liberalidade, e magnificencia foi insigne, na constancia admiravel, na religião excellente, e em tudo Heróe da primeira grandeza, glorioso assumpto das trombetas da Fama."

Neufuille,[7] *Histoire Général de Portugal,* tom. ii, lib. VIII, p. 466:

[1] ? Christovam Ferreyra de Sampayo: *Vida, e hechos del Princepe Perfecto D. Juan Rey de Portugal II deste nombre*, quarto, Madrid, 1626.

[2] Luys Coello de Barbuda: *Empresas.* etc., quarto, Lisbon, 1624.

[3] For the entire title, see page v.

[4] D. Ieronimo Osorio: *De rebus Emmanuelis Regis Lusitaniæ virtute, et auspicio gestis libri duodecim*, folio, Lisbon, 1571; and many subsequent editions. See account of the author and his works in Diogo Barbosa Machado: *Bibliotheca Lusitana Historica*, etc., 2 vols., folio, Lisbon, 1741-1747, vol. ii, pp. 510, 515.

[5] André Thevet: *Vies des Hommes illustres*, folio, Paris [1584]; and 8 vols., quarto, Paris, 1671, etc.

[6] P. Francisco de Santa Maria: *O Ceo aberto na terra*, Historia das Sagradas Congregaçoens dos Conegos Seculares de S. Jorge em Alga de Veneza, e de S. João Evangelista em Portugal, folio, Lisbon, 1697.

[7] Jacques Le Quien de La Neufville: *Histoire*, etc., 2 tom., quarto, Paris, 1700.

"Ce grand homme, cet Albuquerque le Grand, aussi heureux, et redoutable pendant la guerre, que craint et reveré pendant la paix, fut regretté de plusieurs Princes qui avoient connu sa valeur, et toutes les nations qui avoient éprouvé sa clemence."

Telles,[1] *Historia da Ethiopia Alta*, liv. I, cap. 7, and liv. II, cap. 1.

Fr. Agostinho de Santa Maria,[2] *Sanct. Marian.*, tom. viii, liv. I, cap. 55.

Barros,[3] *Decada II, da Historia da India*, passim.

Damião de Goes,[4] *Chronica del Rey D. Manoel*, Part III, cap. 80.

Martin., *Compendio de las Historias de la India Oriental*, pp. 174-194.

Gabriel Pereira,[5] *Ulyssea*, Canto VII, 100:—

"Logo o famoso Affonso o mar cobrindo
De Náos, os Malabares affugenta,
Do grão Neptuno as ondas opprimindo,
Que de seu grave pezo já rebenta."

Macedo, *Ulyssipo*, Canto XII, 56:—

"Se quereis ver o Capitão mais claro,
Que a Fama conheceo, que vio a terra;
Vede a Albuquerque insigne archivo raro,
Que a disciplina militar encerra.
Quantas vezes o vejo, mais reparo
Neste grande varão raio da guerra;
Notai-o de vagar, que basta vê-lo
Para ficardes do valor modélo."

"The Commentaries of the heroic actions, performed in

[1] Manoel d'Almeyda: *Historia geral da Ethiopia Alta, ou Preste João, abreviada pelo Padre Balthezar Tellez*, folio, Coimbra, 1660.

[2] Fr. Agostinho de Santa Maria: *Sanctuario Mariano, e Historia das Imagens*, etc., *que se venerão em a India Oriental, e mais conquistas de Portugal, Asia, Inglaterra, Africa, e Ilhas Filipinas*, tom. 8, quarto, Lisbon, 1720.

[3] João de Barros: *Segunda Decada da Asia*, folio, Lisbon, 1553, and many subsequent editions, see *Bibliotheca Lusitana*, ii, 606.

[4] Damiam de Goes: *Chronica do felicissimo Rey D. Emmanuel, dividida em quatro partes*, folio, Lisbon, 1566-1567, and 1619.

[5] Gabriel Pereira de Castro: *Ulyssea, ou Lisboa edificada, Poema Heroico*, quarto, Lisbon, 1636.

the East by the great Albuquerque, written by his son, were compiled from the despatches which the same Albuquerque forwarded to the King D. Manoel, as the Author himself states in the Dedication of the said work to the King D. Sebastião, in these words :—

"'I have dedicated to your Highness these Commentaries, which I have collected from the originals themselves, written by the great Afonso Dalboquerque in the midst of his adventures to The King D. Manuel, your Great grandfather.'

"Hence proceeds the idea of some writers (and among them the very learned João Solorzano Pereira,[1] de Jure Ind. tom. i, liv. I, cap. 3, n. 48), that it is the work of the great Albuquerque himself. In addition to the despatches written by this Hero, which have served to form the Commentaries of his actions, there are printed herein the following compositions by himself:—

Two replies which he sent in answer to two letters from Cogeatar, Part I, chap. 62.

Reply to a letter from Lourenço de Brito, Captain of Cananor, Part II, chap. 3.

Instructions sent through Fr. Luiz, of the Seraphic Order, to the King of Narsinga, wherein he gave him an account of what had taken place in the conquest of Calicut, Part II, chap. 17.

Letter written to the Xeque Ismael, Part II, chap. 23.

Instructions given to Ruy Gomes for the Xeque Ismael, *ibid.*

Letter to the King of Ormuz, *ibid.*

Letter to Gopicaiça, Chief Alguazil of the King of Cambaya, Part II, chap. 46.

Letter written to Timoja, Chief Alguazil, and Captain of the Forces at Goa, and Lord of the Lands of Cintacora, Part II, chap. 49.

Letter to the Hidalcão, when he conquered Goa, Part III, chap. 4.

[1] Johannes de Solorzano Pereira: *Disputationes de Indiarum Jure*, folio, Madrid, 1629; and reprinted in 1653, 1659.

Instructions which he gave to Antonio de Miranda de Azevedo, with a present for the King of Sião, Part III, chap. 36.

Letter written to the [Portuguese] Monarch on the Twelfth of December, 1515, when on the point of death, wherein he recommends to his notice the promotion of his son, Part IV, chap. 45.

"This latter one also occurs in the Second Decade of Barros, lib. x, ch. 8; translated into Latin by Ozorio, De Rebus Emmanuelis, lib. x: into Castilian by S. Roman, Historia de la India, lib. II, ch. 9; and into French by Lafitau, Histoire des Conquestes des Portugais, tom. i, p. 516."

"AFFONSO DE ALBUQUERQUE,

Son of the celebrated Hero of whom the previous memoir treats, was not only an inheritor of his virtues and heroic actions, but also of his very name. He was born in the Quinta, which was the cradle of his great Father, close to the Town of Alhandra, situate upon the banks of the Tagus, in the year 1500. The name Braz, which had been given to him at his baptism, was altered into Affonso by desire of the King D. Manuel, for this Prince desired as well to perpetuate in the person of the son the memory of his illustrious progenitor, as to continue in him the remuneration due to such eminent merits; and of this he gave manifest proofs in appointing him captain of a ship of war in the fleet which conveyed the Infanta D. Beatriz when she proceeded to be betrothed to the Duke of Savoy, and in being instrumental in procuring his marriage with one of the most illustrious Ladies whom Portugal honoured. This was D. Maria de Noronha, daughter of D. Antonio de Noronha, First Count of Linhares, and private Scrivener to the King D. Manoel, and of Donna Joanna da Silva, daughter of Diogo da Silva, first Count of Portalegre; he also presented him with a pension of three hundred thousand reis. Not only the merits which he inherited, but his own as well, rendered him worthy even of higher rewards. He was endowed with a remarkable prudence, acquired by study of books, and by a constant practice of business, on which account the King D. João III appointed him Overseer of his Household, and herein he was as vigilant for the interests of his Prince as he was disinterested in his own private gain. His ability manifested itself in a great act of providence, when in the year 1569, being at the time President of the Senate of Lisbon, he availed himself of all practicable means to prevent the calamitous losses that were produced throughout the city by the pestilence, which with horrible voracity had as it were consumed many thousands of men; indeed the total extermination of such a frightful scourge was entirely due to his universal watchfulness. As a recreation from the duties which he performed, he constructed in the village of Azeitão a magnificent Quinta, planted with leafy woods and watered with winding streams, of whose pristine grandeur some remains have been preserved even to the present day. When full of years and virtuous deeds, he died at Lisbon in the year 1580, and was buried in the Parish Church of St. Simon, situate in the Town of Azeitão, wherein he founded two chapels, with the intention that each Chaplain should say every week four masses, for his soul, and those of his ancestors, his wife, his friends and enemies, and those who are undergoing penance in purgatory. He left an only daughter, named Dona Joanna de Albuquerque, who married D. Fernando de Castro. He composed—

> '1. Commentarios de Affonso Dalbuquerque, Capitão Geral, e Governador da India, colligidos por seu filho Affonso Dalbuquerque das proprias Cartas, que elle escrevia ao muito poderoso Rey Dom Manoel o primeiro deste nome, em cujo tempo governou a India.' 'Commentaries of Affonso Dalboquerque, Captain-General, and Governor of India, collected by his son Affonso Dalbuquerque from the original letters which he wrote to the all powerful King Dom Manoel, the first of this name, in whose time he governed India.'

"They are divided into four parts according to the periods of his labours. At the end is written the following passage:—

> 'These Commentaries of Afonso Dalbuquerque, Captain-General, and Governor of India, were printed in the city of

Lisbon by João de Barreira, Printer to the King, our Master. The impression was completed on the eve of St. Sebastian's day, the nineteenth of January, in the year fifteen hundred and fifty-seven, on which day the Prince D. Bastião, our Master, to whom this book is dedicated, completed the third year of his age. Fol.

"A second edition was issued in Lisbon, by the same printer, in 1576, fol. Translated into the French language in Paris by João Marnef, 1579.

"In the Cancionero, collected by Garcia de Rezende, there are some verses of Affonso de Albuquerque, at folios 169, 170, and 176, by which it appears he was as well versed in Poetry as he was in History.

'II. Tratado da Antiguidade, Nobreza, e Descendencia da Familia dos Albuquerques. MS.'

Treatise of the Antiquity, Nobility, and Genealogy of the Family of the Albuquerques. Manuscript.

"This work is mentioned by himself in the *Commentaries*, Part IV, chap. 50; and by the Padre Dom Antonio Caetano de Sousa[1] in the *Apparato á Historia Geral da Casa Real Portugueza*, p. 38, § 17.

"The following writers speak of the author and his work with well merited encomiums:—

Barros, *Decada II da India*, lib. x, chap. 8.
Maffeo, *Rerum Indicarum Historiæ*, lib. v, *in fine*.
Goes, *Chronica del Rey D. Manuel*, Part III, chap. 80.
Antonio de Leon,[2] *Bib. Orient.*, Tit. III.
Nicolaus Antonius,[3] *Bibliotheca Hispana*, tom. i, Part VI.
D. Luiz de Salazar De Cast. *Historia da Casa dos Sylv.*, Part II, lib. VI, chap. 13, § 3, n. 14.

[1] Antonio Caetano de Sousa: *Historica Genealogia da Casa Real Portugueza desde a Sua Origem atè o prezente*, etc., large quarto, Lisbon, 1735.

[2] Antonio de Leam Pinello: *Epitome de la Bibliotheca Oriental y Occidental Nautica, y Geografica*, quarto, Madrid, 1629; folio, Madrid, 1737.

[3] Nic. Antonius, *Bibliotheca Hispana*, folio, Rome, 1672.

Faria,[1] *Epitome das Historias Portuguezas*, Part IV, chap. 18.

João Soarez de Brito,[2] *In Theatro Lusitaniæ*, lit. A, n. 8.

Antonio Ferreiro,[3] in the *Poemas Lusitanos*, Elegy 6;

And the Padre Lafitau, *Histoire des Découvertes et Conquestes des Portugais*, tom. i, p. 521: "Il y paroît un grand amour de la verité, une grande modération, beaucoup de ménagement pour la personne des ennemis de son Père, et tant de modestie dans le détail des actions de ce Héros, qu'on peut dire que le portrait qu'il en fait, bien loin d'être outré, est beaucoup au-dessous de son original."

[1] Manoel Severim de Faria: *Epitome de las Historias Portuguesas*, quarto, Madrid, 1628.

[2] *Theatrum Lusitaniæ Litteratum, sive Bibliotheca Scriptorum omnium Lusitanorum*, folio, compiled in 1645, but (?) never printed.

[3] Antonio Ferreiro: *Poemas Lusitanos*, quarto, Lisbon, 1598.

TO THE

MOST HIGH AND ALL POWERFUL LORD,

THE

KING D. SEBASTIÃO, OUR LORD,

AFFONSO DALBOQUERQUE.

In the lifetime of the King D. João the Third, your grandfather, I dedicated to Your Highness these Commentaries, which I have collected from the actual originals written by the great Afonso Dalboquerque in the midst of his adventures to the King D. Manuel your great grandfather. And as I perceived, Most Serene Lord, that there was a great demand for them (in order that the remembrance of his labours should by no means perish), I determined to reprint them, correcting some things which I had written, and adding others, being now possessed of more correct information than I then had, which have induced me to undertake this work. I was moreover invited to do so, by a conversation which took place in the presence of your Highness, wherein when some Fidalgos, who were present, were praising certain of the great Captains whom the world had produced, Your Highness rebuked them, saying:—"Wherefore is the need of speaking of Captains when we have Afonso Dalboquerque in India." Had there been no other reason than this to reprint these Commentaries, this alone would have influenced me to do so, to the end that of such high-minded words, spoken by an invincible spirit like that of Your Highness, the remembrance might remain to glorify yet further the glorious victories which this excellent Captain gained over the Moors in the conquest of the Kingdoms of India. For me to desire in this place to treat of the praises he merited and of the many hardships he suffered, and as many others which he overcame with the greatness of his mind, would require another history greater than his own. I shall say no more than tell you what a Soldier said who always accompanied him in war. This man being very old, and staying in the City of Goa, when he reflected upon the disorder of Indian affairs, went with a stick in his hand to the chapel of Afonso Dalboquerque, and striking the sepulchre wherein he was lying buried, cried out:—"Oh! great Captain, Thou hast done me all the harm thou couldst have done, but I cannot deny that thou hast been the greatest conqueror, and sufferer of troubles, that the world has known: arise thee, for what thou hast gained is like to be lost!" These Commentaries ought not to have the less credit and authority from your Highness because I, who am his son, have collected them, than that which those of Cesar, writing of himself so many years ago, obtain throughout the world, seeing that in this rugged style of mine I narrate the truth of what took place.

TITLES

OF THE

CHAPTERS CONTAINED IN THIS FIRST PART.

WHEREIN IS CONTAINED HOW THE GREAT AFONSO DALBOQUERQUE WENT TO INDIA FOR THE FIRST AND SECOND TIMES; AND WHAT TOOK PLACE IN THE CONQUEST OF THE KINGDOM OF ORMUZ, UNTIL HE ARRIVED AT CANANOR.

PART I.

WHEREIN IS CONTAINED HOW THE GREAT AFONSO DALBOQUERQUE WENT TO INDIA FOR THE FIRST AND SECOND TIMES; AND WHAT TOOK PLACE IN THE CONQUEST OF THE KINGDOM OF ORMUZ, UNTIL HE ARRIVED AT CANANOR.

CHAPTER I.

How he went to India for the first time as chief captain of three vessels, and arrived at Cochim, and what further took place.

THE affairs of India being in such a state that they could not well be placed upon a firm footing, nor receive any settlement from the large fleets which the King D. Manoel kept sending thither every year, on account of the incessant war which was made upon the Portuguese who remained in Cochim,[1] and upon the king who was friendly to us, by the Çamorim,[2] who had been corrupted by the bribes of the

[1] 9 deg. 56 min. N., 76 deg. 15 min. E. See an early plan and description of this port and fortress in the "Livro do Estado da India Oriental", by Capitão Pedro Barreto de Resende, A.D. 1646. Sloane MS. in British Museum, 197, ff. 311-318.

[2] Zamorim or Samorim, the title which the Indians give to the King of Calicut on the Coast of Malabar. Anciently, a single prince was lord of all the coast from Goa to Cape Comorim, but *Samari Perymal*, after embracing the faith of Mahomet, desiring to end his days in peace in the city of Medina, divided his estates, namely, the kingdoms of Calicut, Cochim, Cananor, and Coulão, among his friends, on condition

Moorish merchants from Cairo living in Calicut,[1] which they were constantly giving both to him and to his Governors,—being fearful of losing their trade and sailing traffic if our people were established in the land:—at this time, and to remedy these troubles, the King D. Manoel determined to send to India the great Afonso Dalboquerque and Francisco Dalboquerque, the son of João Dalboquerque, his uncle, to build a fortress in Cochim for the shelter of the people and the storage of the merchandise he might send. And, in order to bring this about, he gave order that six vessels should be made ready, with soldiers, artillery, and munitions of war; for these, with the others which the Admiral was about to leave there, as he (Afonso) took them under his command, were sufficient. He relied also upon the peace and friendship which Pedralvarez Cabral, at the time of his departure for these kingdoms, had left established with the Kings of Cananor[2] and Cochim, and upon the presents and recommendations which he had sent him through his ambassadors who had accompanied him. And he gave the chief command of three of the ships to Afonso Dalboquerque, and of the other three to Francisco Dalboquerque. So, when all that was needful for the voyage had been prepared, they set sail from the port of Belem[3] in the early part of April, in the year fifteen hundred and three; and, although Afonso Dalboquerque had taken such pains to despatch his affairs that he was able to start first, yet he experienced such bad weather, and met with so many storms and calms on the voyage, that when he reached Cochim some days had

that the King of Calicut should be recognised as the chief sovereign, and gave to him the title of Çamorim; the signification of which is:—"Supreme Emperor and God upon earth." *Dom Raphael Bluteau*, Vocabulario Portuguez. Lisboa, 1720. Sub v. *Zamorim, Samorim.*

[1] 11 deg. 12 min. N., 75 deg. 48 min. E.

[2] See plan and description in P. Barreto de Resende's work, ff. 298-302.

[3] The Port of Lisbon, on the north bank of the Tagus and nearer to the sea.

elapsed since Francisco Dalboquerque had arrived with the ships of his company and three others which he had met with on the way. Now, since the Çamorim, at the departure of the Admiral for these Kingdoms, had renewed the war with the King of Cochim, and had made himself master of the island, in defence of which the Portuguese had suffered much trouble and even death, great was the joy and delight of all at the arrival of Francisco Dalboquerque. And the king went at once to see him, and, after having inquired respecting the King of Portugal, his brother, and respecting the voyage just made, gave him an account of his troubles, and of the cruel war which the Çamorim had made upon him after the departure of the admiral, and of the way in which he had made himself master of the island. Francisco Dalboquerque gave him his recommendations on the part of the King of Portugal, and bade him be of good cheer; for he hoped in God quickly to be avenged of his enemies, the king, his lord, having sent both himself and Afonso Dalboquerque, who was waiting behind, with fleet and soldiers to serve him in all he ordered. The interview at an end, the king returned to his own house, and Francisco Dalboquerque proceeded to discuss the business with Diogo Fernandez Correa, whom the admiral had left as factor, and with Lourenço Moreno and Alvaro Vaz, who were notaries, and with other principal persons who were there, and these gave him account of all that had passed, and said that it was very necessary for the credit of the Portuguese, and for the lading of the ships with the least trouble, that they should rid the Island of Cochim of certain Caimais[1] (who are principal lords of the kingdom), whom the Çamorim had in it with men for its defence.

This being agreed upon, Francisco Dalboquerque made

[1] *Kaimal*, a title of rank amongst the Nairs, and used by the inferior classes when addressing them, as—My lord, and the like.—*H. H. Wilson, Glossary of ... Terms ... of British India.* London, 1855.

ready with all his soldiers, and those that were in Cochim, as well as certain Naires[1] of the king, and on the following day before dawn set out in the boats *paraos*[2] and *caravelas*,[3] to fight the Caimais, who were unconcerned at what had taken place, and he attacked them so suddenly that he put them to flight. And having routed them, he went on pursuing them till he drove them out of the island, killing many Naires and two Caimais. Having thus freed the island of them, he withdrew his men to the boats, and re-embarked without meeting any resistance. And, on his arrival at Cochim, the king and his own people received him with great honour, praising him very much for what he had done. There, too, he found Afonso Dalboquerque, who had that day arrived in the morning with the ships of his company, and all the people on board safe and sound, and to whom the King of Cochim had already given an account of his misfortunes. And seeing that he always kept his spies that he might know his enemies' movements, he was immediately informed that the Naires, who had fled from the attack made by Francisco Dalboquerque, had shut themselves up in the Island of Repelim, and were making interest with the lord of it. And because the King of Cochim was much alarmed at the power of this Lord of Repelim, as this lord was always opposed to him, and he himself could not be entirely safe if he made a settlement in that island, he informed Afonso and Francisco Dalboquerque of it, and begged them very greatly that they would be pleased to drive him thence. Accordingly, as they intended to do nothing except the king's pleasure, that they might

[1] *Nayar*, commonly *Nair*, or *Nayr*. The name of the ruling caste in Malabar, professing to be *Sudras*, but bearing arms and exercising sovereignty.—*Wilson*.

[2] Parão, a small boat used for fishing and other purposes in India.—*Bluteau*.

[3] Caravela, a round boat with sails of lateen, of about two hundred tons burden.—*Bluteau*.

reckon the more upon his assistance as regarded the construction of the fortress, which they were about to discuss with him, they made ready with five hundred Portuguese, and, on the following day before dawn, set out in the boats along the river banks to attack the island. And, although at first when they entered they met with some resistance from a force of two thousand Naires and many gunboats, which the Çamorim had sent to reinforce it, our people engaged them with such vigour, that they overcame them, and put them to flight, killing the greater number of the Naires, and setting fire to the place. Having gained the victory, they returned to Cochim, where they were well received by the king, who gave them great thanks for the service they had rendered him in this affair. In this company there were also Duarte Pacheco and Pedro Dataide.

CHAPTER II.

How the great Afonso Dalboquerque and Francisco Dalboquerque, after the skirmish, had an audience with the king upon the building of the fortress, and what passed between them.

These victories having been obtained, as well as others which our people gained against the soldiers of the Çamorim, and the King of Cochim having been reinstated in all that they had taken from him, the great Afonso Dalboquerque and Francisco Dalboquerque determined that, before they turned their attention to lading the ships, they would speak with the king respecting the fortress, which, according to their orders, they had to erect in Cochim. And both of them told him that the chief reason why the Portuguese who remained there for his service had suffered so many troubles, wars, and deaths, was that they had not a stronghold wherein they might be safe from the vexations which the Moors of the land every day inflicted upon them, and from which he was in no way able to protect them; and also whereby they might be able to withstand the power of the Çamorim, and that by what had hitherto taken place, his Royal Highness could clearly perceive that they stood in great need of it. And the King D. Manoel, his lord, confiding in his friendship, and in what was due to his service, had sent to beg him that he would be pleased to grant a site close by the river, in which they might construct a stronghold for the safety of the Portuguese, who remained there, and for the safe stowing of the merchandise which might be sent from Portugal, for thereby his estate would be safer. The king heard this demand, and, although there were on the part of the governors and lords of the land, to whom he communicated the business, some obstacles against the granting it,—for they had been induced to oppose it by the Moorish merchants of the land, by means of bribes which they had given them, because they were unwilling that we should make a settlement in it,—yet to establish his estate the more safely, and to preserve the friendship of the King of Portugal, and also to keep the great profit which accrued to him from this commerce, he put aside all the hinderers, and was pleased to grant a site for the building of the fortress, where it now stands: and this was the first which was made in India. That the work might be quickly finished, the two Dalboquerques divided the labour of it between them, so as to shorten the time, and each commenced to erect the part which fell to his share. As they had no means of working stone and mortar, they desired the king to order wood to be given them, which he sent for at once in great abundance. The building was begun with some large palisades filled in with earth. And because Afonso Dalboquerque had to go to Coulão[1] to take in a cargo of spices, according to the orders

[1] See P. Barreto de Resende for plan and description of this port and

which he had from the King D. Manoel, that as soon as he arrived in India he should take cargo in Cochim to assist Coulão, whither he had already despatched two ships of his company, he laboured day and night with all his men in such a manner, that in a short time he completed his share of the fortress. Thenceforth, some differences arose between them respecting their rivalry at the work. Afonso Dalboquerque, on excuse of being annoyed with his cousin, began to be chary of his conversation with him, and on several occasions sent to tell him that, since the fortress was finished on his side, he begged he would graciously appoint some person to stay in it as captain until the king's wishes were known. Francisco Dalboquerque, according to his wont, would not appoint anyone. Afonso Dalboquerque, seeing these jealousies, which his cousin desired to make with him, forgetting that the King D. Manoel had given orders to both that they should make this fortress, ordered Padre Fr. Rodrigo, of the Order of St. Dominic, to be sent for, and told him that he had constantly sent to beg Francisco Dalboquerque to come to some mutual arrangement how it would be best to leave the fortress, and that he would never come to any terms about it, but rather chose to introduce speeches of little value in the present state of affairs, and that he himself wanted to go to Coulão to load his ships; for he had sent thither two ships of his squadron, and it was necessary to relieve the place; for he had advice that many ships had passed bound for Choromandel, and that he, as far as regarded his portion of the labour which he had expended upon the fortress, was anxious to cause a Mass to be celebrated, and then set out to load his ships, and that Francisco Dalboquerque might do as he

fortress, ff. 319-323. "A fortalleza de Coulam esta sita na Costa Braua de huma piquena Bahia No destreito do Reyno de Travancor Em Altura de Noue graos da banda do Norte Vinte e sinquo Legoas de Cochim pera o Sul."

pleased, and that it was his especial desire that he would undertake the Mass himself. Fr. Rodrigo was much troubled that differences should exist between men so honourable and so nearly related, and that, too, in a land wherein the affairs of Portugal had not yet been firmly established. So he went with Afonso Dalboquerque to the fortress and celebrated Mass; and, at the close of the service, they walked in procession through it, and called it the "Convent of Christ", because it was undertaken in a land annexed to the magistracy of these kingdoms and the first fortress which had been made in those parts. Francisco Dalboquerque, in order not to agree with him as regarded the share he had in the labour, called it "Alboquerque", and appointed as captain and officers whom he chose, whereat Afonso Dalboquerque felt much discontent, but put up with everything that it might not come to the knowledge of the Moors that there were differences between them. So, having taken his leave of the king, he made ready to leave and take in his cargo.

CHAPTER III.

How the great Dalboquerque arrived at Coulão, and what passed with the governors of the land.

When the great Afonso Dalboquerque was just ready to set out, a *parão* arrived from Coulão, and in it a servant of Antonio de Sá, the factor, with a letter from him, wherein he said that he had come on a good errand, for there was certain news that thirty ships had left Calicut bound for Choromandel.

Now since Afonso Dalboquerque had sent two ships on before him to get his cargo ready, as I have said, he was not at all pleased at this news, and hastened his departure the more, and in a short time arrived at Coulão, where he was very well received by the governors of the land, and by the Nambeadarim,[1] who is the principal governor. And because the King had gone into the interior of the country to war, which he was waging with the King of Narsinga,[2] they sent him the news immediately by means of men whom they had in relays, and in a few days he was informed of their arrival. The king, from his desire of our friendship, wrote to the Nambeadarim, and the rulers of the city, giving great thanks for the honour and hospitality which they had shown to Afonso Dalboquerque, and commanded them to do all that he asked and required, and to try all they could to induce him to establish a trade there. Although the governors, owing to the inducements and bribes of the Çamorim, were greatly opposed to this establishment, which the King wished our people to make in the land, yet he was so much feared that, without showing their discontent, they performed everything with more faithfulness than Afonso Dalboquerque had expected of them; and he forthwith established a factory house, with much merchandise, and all other things necessary to the quick despatch of the ships, whenever they came there to take in cargo. The peace having then been made, and sworn to by the King and his governors, Afonso Dalboquerque began to load his ships with pepper, at the price and weight which the admiral had fixed at Cochim. When the Çamorim heard of this new friendship and trade, which the King of Coulão desired to hold with the Portuguese, in order to hinder the good effect of this business, he sent his ambassadors to him, saying that he must beware what he was about, for the Portuguese were a very bad race, and if he admitted them into his land they would rise up against him. And he added that this

[1] *Nambudiri*, commonly pronounced and written *Namburi* or *Namboori*, a Brahman of the highest order in Malabar, also the name of the tribe or caste.—*Wilson*.

[2] *Narsingah*, 20 deg. 41 min. N., 85 deg. 4 min. E.

was the chief reason which had moved him to insist so strongly upon driving them out of India. And on this behalf he also went on to represent to him many other things to the same purpose, and sent large presents to the governors of the land, begging them to influence the King against giving a cargo to the Portuguese, or receiving them in his port. But all these artifices which the Çamorim used, in order to withstand our people, now that he could not effect anything by force of arms, because the land was very far from his, availed him nothing: for the King of Coulão was a man of such truthfulness that, in spite of all these arguments which the Çamorim advanced, he kept his word, and established his friendship with Afonso Dalboquerque. And he answered the Çamorim that he had received no injury or insult from the Portuguese, but rather was convinced that they were men of their word, and that unless it was their own fault, he would not withdraw from what he agreed upon. The Çamorim was not pleased at this reply, and was deeply annoyed that he was unable to destroy the King of Coulão, or hinder the Portuguese from carrying the pepper which was there from Cochim to Coulão, because all the inhabitants of the interior were heathen who were desirous of peace and friendship with our people. And in Calicut all were foreign Moors who endeavoured to drive us from India, from the fear they had that we should be masters of it, and they be ousted from their trade. When Afonso Dalboquerque knew how the Çamorim was trying to induce the King of Coulão to hinder our people from settling in the land, he determined from that time forward to trade more familiarly with the latter, and transact somewhat more liberally the trading of the merchandise, although in this respect he might exceed in some measure the orders which the King had given him, and this was the reason such confidence sprang up between our people and those of the country, that they might have all been taken for native Portuguese. The chief cause of this good fellowship was the absence of Moors in the land who could endeavour to procure dissension between us and the heathen, as they had done in Calicut.

At the time when Afonso Dalboquerque arrived at Coulão it was a very large city, peopled with heathen, with not a single native Moor in it, nor any foreigner except the brother of Cherinamercar of Cochim, who had gone thither just lately to reside. This city was a great seaport of merchants, and anciently had in it many merchants stopping there from all parts of India, principally from Malacca. And as it was a port sheltered from the wind on every side, the ships which go to India, as well as those which passed the Island of Ceilão[1] and Chale made their entrepôt there. In those days the Island of Ceilão was subject to it, and paid tribute to it, and it possessed all the land from Coulão to Chale, which is about sixty leagues, and the distance from Coulão to the Island of Ceilão is eighty leagues. The King of Coulão was a very honest man, and very gallant, and in the war which he carried on with the King of Narsinga, who had many soldiers, both horse and foot, he attacked him with sixty thousand archers and overcame him. Besides the Nambeadarim, who was the chief governor of the land, there were in the city thirty-six principal men who governed it, so that it was the best ruled city at that time in those parts.

CHAPTER IV.

How the ships from Calicut hove in sight of Coulão, and the great Afonso Dalboquerque prepared to fight them, and what took place thereupon with the governors of the land.

At this time, when the great Afonso Dalboquerque was taking in his cargo, as abovesaid, the ships from Calicut arrived in sight of ours, and they were in all thirty-nine sail,

[1] Ceylon. See P. Barreto, for plan of this island, ff. 342, 343.

twenty-eight from Calicut, and the rest from Cochim and Cananor. And as Afonso Dalboquerque was desirous of distressing the Çamorim as much as possible, to be avenged on him, he made up his mind to go and attack them, somewhat against the opinion of Antonio de Sá and the people in the fleet, and, not to lose any time, he slipped his cables, and set sail. When the Moors saw our ships putting off and coming to challenge them, they sent a *paráo,* to beg for peace. In the meanwhile, however, they chained their ships in groups of five each, and determined to fight us. And because the wind dropped, and Afonso de Alboquerque feared that the ships would avail themselves at night of the land breeze to stand out to sea, and get away without his wreaking his vengeance upon them, he sent Antão Garcia in his ship, which was small and a quick sailer, to take up a similar position. The Moors were made timid by this arrangement, and held another council, and all of them at night stood in to the port of Coulão, because our ships were a little on one side of it, at the mouth of a river. When Afonso Dalboquerque saw that the ships desired to make for the land, he sent word to the Nambeadarim and to the governors of the land, that those ships were from the Çamorim, chief enemy of the King of Portugal, his lord, and begged they would of their favour order them to be given up to him; for if this were not done, he determined to enter the port and burn them all, and go away without taking in any cargo there, or making any treaty of peace with them. The governors replied that they had written to the king, giving him an account of the affair, and the reply would not be delayed many days: and they begged him graciously, since the ships were sheltered in the port, whence they could not depart without permission, to await the king's message. Afonso Dalboquerque told them he was willing to do as they desired, provided they gave orders that the ship's sails should be taken away, to prevent their escaping at night.

This having been agreed upon, the Nambeadarim sent immediately to lay hold of the captains, masters, and pilots, and take bail for their good behaviour. A few days afterwards the message of the king to the Nambeadarim arrived, wherein he ordered that if the ships were willing to show obedience to the city governors, and discharge their merchandise there, the governors were to beg of Afonso Dalboquerque on his part not to injure them, for it was sufficient punishment that they could not leave the port without permission. Afonso Dalboquerque replied that it was his determination to burn them, and put all the Moors of Calicut to the sword, in revenge for the treason they had committed against the Portuguese, but since the king had reasons for not chastising them, he would not do anything except what he ordered. The governors sent immediately to discharge the ships of their freight, and there they remained until Afonso Dalboquerque left. And because he had been informed that some Moors had purchased much pepper in the interior, to evade the standard weight of Coulão, as long as he was there he made all the ships that passed, whether friendly or hostile, even if they sailed under the flag or papers of the admiral, put in to the port of Coulão, where they were searched by the governors of the land, who took from them whatever spices they carried, and sent it to the factory where our people and the natives traded.

CHAPTER V.

Of the treaty which the great Afonso made with the governors of the land respecting peace, before his setting out, and the rest that took place with the native Christians there, and his setting out for Cochim.

When all these affairs had been set in order, the great Afonso Dalboquerque thought fit to renew the treaty of peace which he had established with the governors, and went on shore; and, speaking with them in presence of the factor, Antonio de Sá, and the other Portuguese who were there with him, told them, that in the agreement of peace which they had made, it was arranged that the civil and criminal jurisdiction should be under the control of the native Christians, as it had always been hitherto; and that, therefore, before his departure he was desirous of leaving this so settled that after he was gone no differences should arise between one side and the other; and also that he might give an account of his conduct to the king his lord, as to the manner in which their affairs in that kingdom were settled; and that he earnestly desired and besought them that they would hold to this for good, because the person whom he should entrust with this office would be required at all times to do what the King of Coulão might order. The governors told him that they agreed to it, and they would acquaint the king of it when he arrived: and that he could entrust the office to whom he pleased, for all would obey him. Afonso Dalboquerque forthwith confirmed the jurisdiction before them all to the factor, Antonio de Sá, and commanded him to act in all things conformably to the counsel and opinion of the native Christians, and so not exceed the order whereby they had been governed of old. And all were pleased at the choice of Antonio de Sá, to whom he especially recommended the provision due to the Church. And the Christians of the land had to take care to govern and rule the church, which was called "Our Lady of Mercy". The native Christians said that two saints, who were buried there in two chapels, had made it in a miraculous manner. There were three altars, on which stood three crosses, the centre one of gold, the other two of silver. The Christians of the place had destined one of them for the King D. Manoel, and wishing to send the golden one, Afonso Dalboquerque told them he would only take a silver one, as a sign that there were Christians in that land who worshipped the Cross whereon our Lord Jesus Christ had suffered; for this was (as it were) the gold wherewith the King of Portugal would be most pleased; and when he arrived in Portugal the king should send them many ornaments for their church, as was the usual custom between Christians. They were highly delighted at this, and desired Afonso Dalboquerque to give them a picture of Saint James, and a bell, which he gave them immediately. And because it was necessary to leave there some person who might educate them in the rites of our Holy Faith, he desired Father Fr. Rodrigo, of the Order of St. Dominic, who had accompanied him, to remain there, and he consented, for the service of God. And he took such care during the days that he was there, that, with his teaching and good example, he converted many heathen to the faith of Jesus Christ, and baptised many Christians thirty and forty years of age, as they did not remember whether they had ever been baptised or not. When all these things had been settled, the native Christians came to Afonso Dalboquerque and told him that, as he was desirous of confirming to them their ancient customs, they begged him that he would graciously preserve for them another custom, to wit, that the Christians who had the management of the church, also should have in their keeping the seal and standard-weight of the city, which privilege the King of Coulão had taken from them for the fault and negligence of one of their number. And that these things might remain in the power of the Christians as heretofore, they relied much on his authority that he would speak to the Nambeadarin and the governors in order that they might regain possession of them, for the fault for which they had been deprived of them was of one man and not of all. Afonso Dalboquerque replied that what they requested had not entered into the treaty of peace, and the time was too short to begin new requests, for he was already on the point of sailing; but he would leave word with Antonio de

Sá, who was remaining behind as factor, that, when the King of Coulão returned from the war, he should speak with him on the subject, and beg it of him on the part of the King of Portugal. With this reply they were quite content, and he took his leave of them and of the governors of the land, and went on board. And he left them on the 12th of January, in the year 1504, and steered direct to Cochim to meet Francisco Dalboquerque, that they might set out both together for Portugal according to the orders of the King, D. Manoel. And when he arrived at Cochim he did not find him, nor any message about his future movements. So he provided the fortress with gunpowder, arms, and munitions of war, such as seemed to him necessary to fulfil his duty, and left there two *caravelas*, and the ship *Conception*, all well armed. And because some of the soldiers whom Francisco Dalboquerque had placed there to garrison the fortress were detained by force and against their will, he ordered them to be removed, and left others who of their own accord were willing to remain. And when this was done, he took leave of them all and set sail.

CHAPTER VI.

How the great Afonso Dalboquerque set out from Cochim to Cananor, and what took place till he arrived at Portugal.

When the great Afonso Dalboquerque had his ships already prepared, and had embarked to sail for Portugal, the factor came on board and told him that Francisco Dalboquerque had gone away to Cananor without taking any commodities, although he had frequently besought him to take some, for he had some ready within the fortress, and he begged Afonso earnestly that he would be pleased to perform this service for the king and take the commodities to Cananor, as he was to meet Francisco Dalboquerque there. To serve the king, Afonso Dalboquerque, although his ships were very much overburdened with cargo, took in all the cloves and cinnamon which the factor sent him; and leaving port, put in at Calicut, where he found Francisco Dalboquerque treating for peace; but without coming to any settlement, they set out in company and went away to Cananor, where Afonso Dalboquerque transferred to him all the cloves and cinnamon he carried. And because Francisco Dalboquerque had to complete the lading of the ships, and was getting on rather slowly, though the King D. Manoel had given orders that they should keep together, yet all the officers of the factory agreed that Afonso Dalboquerque should wait till the 20th of January, and, after that time was passed, should sail at once. When the 25th day of the month had come, and Afonso Dalboquerque saw that Francisco was not hastening the lading of his ships, he made up his mind to sail, and to wait no longer. Respecting the course he was to take there were many advices and opinions, but last of all they agreed that he should steer his course dirèct to Moçambique; and because that course was not very much frequented at that time, Afonso Dalboquerque carried with him a Moorish pilot from Cananor—against the opinion of all, who said that that Moor would bring misfortune upon him—but the Moor was so well acquainted with his trade, and knew the passage so well, that he carried him direct to Moçambique by a fair course without any accident, and there left him, receiving fifty *cruzados*[1] for his trouble. Then, without making any stoppage, he shaped his course direct for the Cape of Good Hope. And because Fernão Martinz Dalmada ran very short of water, they put in for water at S. Bras, and remained there for two days, working night and day all the

[1] Cruzado: a silver coin (formerly gold), now equivalent to 480 reis, or about two shillings English money, but probably worth much more relatively in the time of Dalboquerque.

time. While engaged on this business, they lost the boat of Afonso Dalboquerque, for it was utterly decayed. And there they found a letter, sealed up, and wrapped in a piece of waxed cloth, fastened upon a post, which stated that Antonio de Saldanha and the *Taforéa*,[1] and the ship from Setubal, had arrived there in the month of October. As soon as his ships had taken in water, Afonso Dalboquerque set sail, and shaped his course for the current of the Cape of Good Hope, and having fair weather, doubled it on the 1st day of May. When they had doubled the Cape, at the advice of the pilots they kept on their course till they were in ten degrees north latitude; and here they experienced great calms, so that some of the men fell ill. On the morning of St. John's Day they sighted Cape Darca, which is between the shallows of Arguim and Cenaguá; and because Afonso Dalboquerque's ship leaked very much, he determined, as he was in such proximity, to go in search of Cape Verde Island, and there refit his ships with what was required, for that was the nearest place. And, although the winds were contrary at this season, Our Lord so helped them that they sighted the island. And having run aground, the main-yard of Afonso Dalboquerque's ship was broken and the mainsail torn down, for they were beating up against the wind to catch sight of the island, and he anchored with foresail only flying, in the port of the beach of Santa Maria, with the other two ships of his fleet, all being now very deficient in cables, sails, and all other necessaries required for so long a voyage. For had Our Lord not miraculously carried them thither (as this was not the true navigation they had to make), they would have been swallowed up by the sea. So they were there for three days, and having repaired the ships in all that was wanted, and taken water and provisions for their voyage,

[1] A kind of large boat used in India for transport and carriage of horses.

they started for Portugal, and with favourable breezes, without touching at any other place, they arrived at Lisbon at the end of July in the said year 1504, where Afonso Dalboquerque was very well received by the King Dom Manoel, who paid him much honour and entertainment, evincing his great pleasure at the good success that had attended the voyage, and at the completion of the fortress of Cochim.

Francisco Dalboquerque, who stayed behind in Cananor loading his ships, as I have related, sailed on the 5th of February, and was lost on the way home with the other two ships under his command, without any one ever knowing where or how they were lost.

CHAPTER VII.

How the king, D. Manoel, sent Tristão da Cunha to India in the year '6, and Afonso Dalboquerque accompanied him in a fleet of fourteen sail, that they might erect the fortress of Çacotora.[1]

The great Afonso Dalboquerque having arrived at Portugal in July 1504, as I have said, and having informed the King D. Manoel of the state of affairs in India, how it was imperative that arrangements should be made to prevent the Moors, after the sailing of the ships to this kingdom, from again becoming lords of the coast of Malabar, and—being encouraged by the Çamorim—from continually causing great trouble to the Portuguese and the Kings of Cochim and Cananor who were friendly towards us, the king consulted with his council upon this business, and there were different ideas upon the subject. But at last he agreed to send a governor to remain for three years in India, with soldiers and armaments needful for the alleviation of the

[1] Socotora, 12 deg. 30 min. N., 53 deg. 45 min. E.

troubles our people were suffering. And as he had confidence in Tristão da Cunha the elder, that he would serve him well in this matter, he determined to send him there as governor. But when he and his fleet were ready to sail, in the year 1505, he fell ill with giddiness in the head, whereby he finally became blind. And when the king heard of this sudden accident, knowing that it was necessary at once to send succour to India that year, to encourage our people who remained there, he sent for D. Francisco Dalmeida to Santarem[1] to go in the fleet, and after arriving in India to assume the title of Viceroy. So, seeing that the fleet was now prepared in everything necessary, he went away at once. And the following year, 1506, he sent Tristão da Cunha, who was now well and restored to sight, with a fleet of fourteen sail, to further the business yet more, under orders that, in case he could not reach India that year, he should go into winter quarters in the island of Çacotorá, and make there a fortress for the Christians, who, as he was informed, dwelt therein, making an arrangement thereby that the fleet, which he had determined to send to the coast of Arabia and to Cape Comorim to put a stop to the sailing of the fleets which came from India to the straits with spices, should have there a sure harbour to winter in. And as the King, D. Manoel, saw that Afonso Dalboquerque, in his voyage to India in the year '3, as has been narrated, had served him well and had spirit and prudence for governing, he sent him in the company of Tristão da Cunha to remain on that coast as chief captain over six ships and four hundred men. And he gave him secret instructions that on the expiration of three years he was to be Governor of India, and the Viceroy, Dom Francisco Dalmeida, was to return to Portugal; and being at the time in Abrantes,[2] lest he should die of plague in the city of Lisbon, he sent him a flag of white

1 In Estremadura, Portugal, 39 deg. 14 min. N., 8 deg 40 min. W.

2 Also in Estremadura, 39 deg. 29 min. N., 8 deg. 11 min. W.

satin, with a twisted silk fringe, crimson and white, having a cross of Christus in the centre, of crimson satin, which he took back with him to Portugal, as I shall mention by-and-bye. On the completion of all these arrangements, as soon as Tristão da Cunha had made his fleet ready at Belem, which cost him great labour, owing to the prevalence of the plague in the city and the paucity of men to carry with him, he started on the morning of the 5th of April, and sailed at once straight over the bar with all his fleet, leaving Afonso Dalboquerque behind, who remained at Belem in the ship *Cirne*, of which he held the captainship, waiting for a pilot whom he had sent for from the king's officers, for his own pilot, João de Solis, had fled into Castile two days back for murdering his wife. But when he saw that they would not send him a pilot, trusting to his own great experience in sea matters, and to Diogo Fernandez Piteira, master of his ship, who had already made two voyages to India, and also to that which Tristão da Cunha told him, namely, that he would give him the best pilot there was in the fleet, except the chief pilot, he made up his mind not to wait any longer, and gathered together some people who remained on shore out of the other ships, whom the captains were unwilling to take on board as they came from Lisbon, and set sail the following day, the 6th of the month. And so with much delay he reached the chief captain, who was looking out for him, and after saluting him he told him that he had brought some people whom the captains had left on shore, and he begged him graciously to order their distribution throughout the ships, according to the arrangements agreed upon, for some had died, and his own company was so displeased that he was at his wits' end to know what to do, and he had ventured upon bringing them, out of the need there would some day arise for them in those parts whither they were proceeding. The chief captain answered that if he were hampered by them, why had he brought them on? And he would not give orders for their distribution, whereat Afonso Dalboquerque became very much displeased. And on their arrival at Biziguiche, he sent him a list of the people, who they were, by Pero Vaz Dorta, who sailed as factor of his fleet, begging him earnestly that he would order the captains to take them, as he had no more supplies than were sufficient for his own men. And he begged that he would supply him with the pilot whom he had promised him before they left Belem, for he had not brought one, neither had the king's officers supplied him with one. The chief captain replied that he was to send and put the people with their baggage on land, and then he would dispose them as it seemed best to him; and as to the pilot he had none, nor could he take one from the other ships to give him. Afonso Dalboquerque, being annoyed at this answer, gave orders to set the people on shore, and that Pero Vaz Dorta should inform the chief captain that among the people were some Fidalgos and persons of repute, and he did not think it fair to mingle them with the others and put them on shore, for he ought forthwith to see that they were distributed throughout the other ships. The chief captain dissembled with him and made no reply. And because during the days they remained there not a single person died nor fell sick in the whole fleet, the chief captain, owing to the frequent importunity of Afonso Dalboquerque, ordered that the persons who were in good health should be distributed throughout the ships, and that the sick should embark in the *caravela* that he had despatched for Portugal, which the king, Dn. Manoel, had sent in their company to bring back news of their welfare, for he had great fear of the great plague wherewith the fleet was attacked.

CHAPTER VIII.

How the chief captain, Tristão da Cunha, despatched the caravel to Portugal, and set out from Biziguiche: and what took place until he arrived at Moçambique.

The chief captain, Tristão da Cunha, being ready with his fleet to set sail from the port of Biziguiche, despatched the captain of the *caravela*, and wrote by him to the king, concerning the state all were in, and how on their arrival there the Lord had been pleased to stay the plague. The *caravela* having sailed, all the ships stood out to double the Cape of St. Augustine, but as it was now late in the season, and the winds contrary, and as they had to delay because of the chief captain's ship, which was a bad sailer, they were unable to double the Cape, and tacked again towards Guiné, wherein much time was spent. While they were making this latter run, so severe a storm broke over the fleet that the ships parted company, one from the other, and two days after collected together again, and shaped their course for St. Augustine's, all except the ship of Job Queimado, which was not to be seen. And they kept on their course, keeping back very often for the chief captain's ship. When Afonso Dalboquerque saw that time was wasted in waiting for this ship, and the other captains dared not say a word, he had an audience of the chief captain, and told him he could see that the principal reason why they could not double Cape St. Augustine was the constant waiting for his ship, and as the season was far advanced it was very doubtful whether they would get to India that year, and since he could not keep up with the rest they must leave him behind with another ship in his company, whichever he might select, while he himself set sail and kept on his voyage with the rest. The chief captain replied that if the king, D. Manoel, had entrusted him with the fleet, it was for his advantage, and therefore he would have them wait for his ship, as in it he carried his cargo. As Afonso Dalboquerque would lose much if he did not get to India that year, a few days afterwards he went again to beg the chief captain to let his ship go, which produced angry words between them, and with good reason, to which Afonso Dalboquerque made no reply, nor for the future was he minded to say any more with respect to the voyage. When the chief captain, a few days afterwards, perceived the mistake he had made, and that he lost more in not reaching India that year than he gained by making the fleet wait for his ship, and that all the masters and pilots, when they spoke with him, told him of it, he made up his mind to adopt a remedy. So when they were in the latitude of the Island of the Ascension, he hung out a square flag, and all the captains came on board immediately to know what he wished. The chief captain told them that he had resolved that they should all set their sails, and not wait for any one, but each make way with what speed he could, and wait for him at Moçambique. And when they were all in their course for doubling the Cape of Good Hope, as the morning broke they came in sight of land very extensive and very beautiful. When Afonso Dalboquerque saw it, he went and spoke with the chief captain, and told him that since it had not yet been discovered, they ought to make for it, and know what land it was. As this advice seemed good to the chief captain, he gave orders to work his ship to windward, so as to come up with it, and all the others did the same, and when the evening was come he shaped his course again as at first. This land proved to be some islands,[1] to which they gave the name of "Tristão da Cunha", as he was the first who discovered them. And sailing along past them just as the sun was on the point of setting, the wind began to blow so hard, and with so many showers, that the ships were unable to keep with the chief

[1] In the South Atlantic, 37 deg. 6 min. S., 12 deg. 2 min. W.

captain, and all separated from him, except Afonso Dalboquerque, who followed him, and they kept on their way together for some days, with a favourable wind. And one night they encountered such a great storm from the front that it separated them; and the ship of Afonso Dalboquerque was forced to lie to for seven watches[1] with great labouring, and refused to answer her helm.

But it pleased Our Lord that the weather cleared up, and they sailed all that night without seeing the light on board the admiral's ship, nor did they see the ship on the following morning. And Afonso Dalboquerque kept on that course, having doubled the cape, until he came in sight of the first islands, there he found Francisco de Tavora; and they sailed together for Moçambique, where they found a *caravela* which had started from Portugal many days after Tristão da Cunha, the captain of which told them that Lionel Coutinho had gone to Quiloa.[2] A few days afterwards, the chief captain arrived with the other ships (except that of Alvaro Telez, who doubled the Island of S. Lourenço[3] by the outer passage, and stood over to Melinde), and left there a letter for that captain in which he gave him orders to go and wait at the Cape of Guardafum; except also Rui Pereira, who went into a harbour in the Island of S. Lourenço, called Tanana, where he remained for some days, getting information about the land, as it was the first time of its being discovered, and from thence went on to Moçambique, taking with him two negroes, who went willingly with him of their own accord.

[1] *Sete relogios de mar.* A *relogio de mar* was a half-hour glass.

[2] On the African coast, 9 deg. S., 39 deg. 29 min. E.

[3] Now Madagascar, on the east coast of Africa.

CHAPTER IX.

How the chief captain, Tristão da Cunha, from the information which the negroes whom Rui Pereira brought gave him, determined to go and discover the Island of S. Lourenço.

The chief captain, having arrived at Moçambique, determined, as it was now too late to cross over to India, to fit out his fleet there, for making the passage to Çocotora, wherein the king, D. Manoel, had ordered him to build a fortress for the rallying of some Christians, who, as he was informed, were living in that island, that they might not be troubled by the Fartaquins and other Moorish vessels which went thither to take in water, when they passed through the strait of Meca. At this juncture, Rui Pereira arrived and told him that at the time of that storm, wherein he had parted from him, he went into a harbour of the Island Sn. Lourenço, and while he was casting anchor, two *almadias*[1] with some negroes came up to his ship as peaceful people, and showed him silver, wax, and cotton stuffs; and they told him that if he would go in they would trade with him, for there was much of these things in the land; and all this they said by signs, for there was no one in the ship who could understand them. But when he would have gone in to get more certain information about this, the pilot, master, and factor of the ship, made a great demand that he should not go in, but keep on the voyage towards Moçambique, for the ship belonged to them, and they were not obliged to discover new lands, and they furthermore promised to indemnify him. And hearing their demands, he had brought these two negroes, as they seemed intelligent men, and set sail. The chief captain was very much pleased with this news, because if it were true, he could load his ships there and return to Portugal; and he sent immediately for a

[1] *Almadia*, an almadc, or launch made of a single log.

native Moor of Quiloa, who was in Moçambique and was conversant (as he had information) with the language of the men, and bade him inquire of these negroes what there was in their land, and by what name it was called. They told him that their land was called Tananá, and that it contained much ginger, cloves, silver, and wax. Hereupon the chief captain ordered that Afonso Dalboquerque, and all the other captains, masters, and pilots of the fleet should be summoned, and informed them of all that had passed with the negroes, adding that he thought that, as they had to remain there some days, they ought to go and search for this port which Rui Pereira had discovered, and so he would have them point out which route he should take, for he was determined to go thither. The pilots and masters of the fleet were of opinion that he ought to explore this land on the northern side. Afonso Dalboquerque, as he was a mariner and understood navigation very well, perceiving that the masters and pilots were speaking in error, asked them why it was their opinion that the northern route should be chosen, since the island was not explored on that side, nor was there in the fleet a single person who knew how far the land stretched out on the northern side. The pilots and masters made no reply to this, for they had none to make, but adhered to what they had said. When Afonso Dalboquerque saw that they were unwilling to withdraw from their opinion, he would have nothing more to do with them in the matter. To end these differences, the chief captain begged him to tell him his opinion; he replied, that since this exploration was determined upon, it ought to be made from that southern part, whence Rui Pereira had come, for it was not good advice to explore new parts by an uncertain route, and the more so, as he had a pilot who could carry him, without any trouble, to the port which Rui Pereira had discovered, and which could be reached in six days sailing before the wind; and, further, in the present season it would be very difficult to double the point of the land of the Island, which was in twelve degrees north latitude, for the east winds were blowing, and the currents running fast, and much time would be spent in doubling it, and it was time that they were more in need of than anything else. And although in this advice there was no one who could contradict Afonso Dalboquerque's opinion, yet, since what he alleged did not agree with the chief captain's opinion, he was not satisfied with what he had told him, and was guided by the opinion of the pilots and masters. Not many days, however, elapsed before he perceived the mistake he had made; and when he was at length desirous of remedying it, he had wasted three months along the coast, suffering many hardships and perils without achieving anything.

CHAPTER X.

How the chief captain, Tristão da Cunha, got himself ready to go and explore the island, and what took place therein.

When the chief captain had settled what course he intended to take, he made ready, and left Moçambique at the beginning of November with all the ships under the command of Afonso Dalboquerque, and those of João Gomez, and Ruy Pereira, and Job Queimado; the last named having arrived but two days before, for he was left behind, having been separated from the fleet in the tempest which struck it at the turn of Cape St. Augustine. He related that he had steered for the Island of St. Thomas,[1] and thence made his way along shore as far as Moçambique; and in his course, sixty leagues in the sea from the river of Angola, he had found a very large island, uninhabited and thickly

[1] (?) On the coast of Guinea, 0 deg. 20 min. N., 6 deg. 40 min. E.

wooded. The chief captain having started, in a few days sighted the reef of St. Mary, which is a crown of sand in 17½ deg. of latitude, sixty leagues from Moçambique, which Afonso Dalboquerque discovered the first time he went to India, and all the fleet sailed by that reef, the pilots with their sounding leads in hand, in from eight to four and a half fathoms' depth; and coming upon this bottom, as it was night, they cast anchor. When morning broke they resumed their course, and so journeyed until they sighted land, and when close to land they put out their boats, and took a small *Zambuco*[1] with two Moors, whom they immediately carried before the chief captain, and these brought him to a place of the Moors, which was close by, and when they arrived there they disembarked. The Moors abandoned the place, and fled into the interior country, and our people followed them up, and killed some, whom they found hiding in the woods. And the chief captain ordered his men to keep together, and not go too far in, and they brought some women, whom he ordered to be set free. He then set the place on fire and embarked with all his people and sailed along the coast; and with the greatest precautions they could, they made for a bay which is called Lulangane: within which, at the distance of a bowshot from the mainland, they found an island, densely peopled, wherein the king had his residence, though his establishments and farms were on the mainland. And on commencing to explore the bay, because the people had not kept together, the chief captain gave orders that two boats with men should take up a position between the island and the mainland, and not suffer any Moors to pass over from the other side. And these being gone, he went with all the ships and anchored opposite the place, and disembarked with all

[1] "As naos, ou *Zambucos*, em que navegavão estes Mouros, nem tinhão cuberta (deck), nem pregadura (bolt-work)" Damião de Goes, 23, 2.—*Bluteau.*

his men. When the Moors saw the determination of our people, such a panic struck them, that, without fearing the boats, they came down to the beach to seek a means of crossing from the other side to the mainland, in *zambucos*, *almadias*, and some swimming; and such was the haste they made to cross, that the *zambucos*, and *almadias*, owing to the great rolling of the sea (by reason of the current of the water from a river which debouched there), upset, with all those on board, so that the sea was quite strewn over with dead men, women, and children. The chief captain attacked the place, and entering into it, found many Moors yet therein, with pikes and shields, waiting for him, and put them all to the sword. And after this engagement, he gave orders to sack the place, wherein they found many clothes, silver, and gold, for the ships from Melinde and Mombaça come thither to trade, and in exchange for these things bring slaves, and supplies: and such was the quantity of the rice that twenty ships could not carry it. The chief captain stayed there three days; and after all the ships had taken water and supplies, he embarked and went along the coast, intending to double the headland, wherein he wasted much time, without being able to double it, owing to the east winds and currents. In this course, he captured a Moor, who showed him cloves, and told him that there was much in the woods; the chief captain, however, was by this time so disgusted with their lying, that he attached no credit to the tale, and let the man go, and made his course with all the fleet for that part where Ruy Pereira had taken the negroes.

CHAPTER XI.

How the chief captain, Tristão da Cunha, returned along the coast, and all but perished, and what passed with the great Afonso Dalboquerque.

The chief captain having turned back along the coast, as he was unable to double the headland at S. Lourenço, as I have said, the two Moors whom he had taken at Lulangane carried him to a large bay, which is called Çada, entirely surrounded with tribes of Cafres, because the principal exchange of all places on the coast of Melinde, Mombaça, and Mogadoxo is established there. As soon as the fleet had cast anchor, the chief captain with all his men got into the boats, and made for the land, where he attacked two tribes, who were stationed along the coast. The Cafres, whose number reached about two thousand, armed with pikes, shields, bows, and arrows, although they at first showed the intention of preventing our landing, when they saw the determined spirit of our people, dared not wait, but fled into the woods. Now Afonso Dalboquerque, seeing the waste of time in discovering that island, and the great risk incurred by the fleet, although the chief captain had resented any remonstrance made to him, went to him and told him he ought to bear in mind that it was now the middle of January, and that all the time that might hereafter be spent in that exploration would be lost, and that they would be performing more service to the king by going to the Cape of Goardafum, and waiting for the ships which came from India through the straits with spices, and by building the fortress in Çocotora, according to the king's orders, than by going on to their own destruction in the way they were doing. And if, nevertheless, he would continue this new exploration, he desired permission to go to Çocotora, and on his way enlist all the ships, wheresoever he might find them, and take them with him. The chief captain, who was highly delighted with the prospect of exploring the whole of the Island of St. Lawrence, approved of this, and gave permission for him to go, and delivered over to him all the ships which came from Portugal, with orders to remain with him, and gave him, as well, authority over all the captains whom he might find on that coast, that they should obey him. Although Afonso Dalboquerque carried secret powers from the king, D. Manoel, sufficient for all he might wish to do, yet, to avoid any quarrelling which might arise, about which of the two had the greater authority, he took his commission from the chief captain. After this, the latter despatched Antonio de Saldanha to go to Moçambique, and take the command of the ship *Sanctiago,* and get it ready, for he intended to despatch it to Portugal, immediately upon his arrival. Afonso Dalboquerque, having taken his leave, collected his ships, and went straight to Moçambique, and on the road gave orders that Antonio do Campo should go to Quiloa, and request Lionel Coutinho, and the captain of the ship *Garça,* to take all the supplies they required and wait for him at Melinde. Six days after the departure of Antonio do Campo, Afonso Dalboquerque arrived at Moçambique, and began to set about the refitting of his ships, which he made ready in a short time, and then he left, steering for Melinde by a straight course, where he was to join the other captains, and to go together with them to the Cape of Guardafum. And being as far advanced as the Islands of Comoro[1], he came by night to see the chief captain. And when it was morning he struck his flag, and came up close to him, and went to pay his respects. The chief captain recounted to him the many misfortunes he had experienced since they had separated; how Ruy Pereira had been lost in some shallows, wherein he himself would

[1] The group of Comoro Islands, Africa, 11 deg. 30 min. S., 43 deg. 30 min. E.

also have perished, as it was at night, had it not been for the shouting which the sailors made when they touched the sand, and for the vigilance of his pilot, who, hearing the shouting, ordered the ship to be stopped, and miraculously turned and went out the same way he went in, for all in front was shallows. Afonso Dalboquerque returned with him thence to Moçambique, where they found João da Nova very ill, who had sailed last year for India, in the ship *Flor de la mar*, for Portugal, but he, in tacking to pass the Cape of Good Hope, had sprung a large leak, which forced him to put in at the Islands of Angoja, where he remained some days working to repair it. When he found it so large that he could not stop it, he had made his way to Moçambique, to wait for the ships which were coming from the kingdom, in hopes of some means of repairing his ship. The chief captain was very glad to see him, for he was a friend of his, and tried to get his ship repaired, and because the leak was at the step of the mast, and could not be mended without discharging the cargo, he bought a merchant ship, of which André Dias (who was afterwards Alcaide of Lisbon) was captain and factor, and ordered all the cargo of the *Flor de la mar* to be stowed in it, and gave the command of it to Antonio de Saldanha, and sent it to Portugal, and in company with it a ship of Fernão de Loronha, of which the captain was Diogo Mendez Correa. When he was on his course doubling the Cape of Good Hope, he discovered a very favourable watering place for the ships, before the Island of St. Elena[1] had been noticed. To this, he gave the name of the watering station of Saldanha, and it was here that the Cafres of the land murdered the Viceroy D. Francisco Dalmeida, when he touched there to take water on his way from India to Portugal.[2]

[1] St. Helena.

[2] This event took place on the 1st of March, 1510. For a biographical memoir and portrait of this Viceroy, see Barretto de Resende, in MS. Sloan. 197, fo. 9*b*:—"Foy morto pellos Cafres Na *agoada de Saldanha* o prim^ro^ de Março do anno mil quinhentos e des aonde aynde oje se dis estão seus ossos."

CHAPTER XII.

How the chief captain, Tristão da Cunha, left Moçambique with his fleet, and had an audience with the King of Melinde, and thence went to Angoja and destroyed it.

As soon as Antonio de Saldanha had sailed for Portugal, the chief captain began to repair his fleet, and furnish it with all necessaries, and when all was ready, he started one day at morning, and in a few days arrived at Melinde. When he had entered the harbour, with all his ships having their flags flying, they saluted the city, and anchored, and then he went on shore with all his captains to pay the king a visit, and, on the part of the King of Portugal, made him a present which he brought, and made offer of his service in all that he might demand of him, with many other offerings which he made. The king thanked him very much, and said that he was very thankful to the King of Portugal, his brother, for all the kind messages he had sent him, because he was his true servant and friend.[1] And on this account the Kings of Mombaça and Angoja were his chief enemies, and caused him much annoyance: therefore, he begged that, before the chief captain left those parts, he would take vengeance upon them, that they might know he enjoyed the friendship of the King of Portugal. The chief captain told him, that, since the principal reason of his coming thither was to preserve the ancient friendship which the King of Portugal had with him, he promised him before many days should elapse he should have news of the state his enemies were in. So he took his leave with great show of friendship, and embarked. And Afonso Dalboquerque, on taking his leave of the king, told

[1] Camões speaks of the king and the people of Melinde with praise:—

"Gente mais verdadeira, e mais humana,
Que toda a de outra terra atraz deixada."—*Lusiada*, ii, 74.

In stanza 82, Gama styles the king "Rei benino, . . . de peito sincero, humano, e raro".

him that the King of Portugal, his lord, had sent him with a fleet to conquer the kingdom of Ormuz, and all that coast of Arabia which had not yet been made known to our pilots; so he begged he would of his favour order three pilots, who had good knowledge of the navigation of those parts, to be given him that he might take them with him, and he would pay them well and treat them as his own subjects. The king ordered the governors of the city to give him the pilots whom he asked for, and whatever else might be necessary for the service of the King of Portugal, his brother. The governors gave him the three principal pilots of the country, who always sailed to those parts, and had good experience of all the harbours of that coast of Arabia. When all had taken their leave of the king, they embarked and set sail, and without putting into any port, they anchored in the bay of Angoja, and as soon as they had anchored, the chief captain sent Lionel Coutinho in his boat to shore to obtain information about the people who were in the place and about the fortress. The Moors, who were waiting on the beach, as soon as the boat drew near to shore, began to shoot arrows at it, and would not parley with our people. So Lionel Coutinho ordered the boat to be kept off, that the men might not be wounded, and informed the chief captain of what had passed. He, therefore, sent at once for the captains, and told them that he was determined to punish the King of Angoja because of the offences which he had done to the King of Melinde, as well as on account of the slight he had given to his message; so they should all get ready, and on the next day, before morning, should come on board his ship that they might go together and attack the place. When the hour was come, the captains came in their boats on board the flag-ship, and thereupon stood in towards land to attack the city. When the Moors saw the boats coming, they came and awaited them on the beach to prevent their landing. But the chief captain observed their determination, and desiring room for disembarking, ordered the bombardiers to fire at them with the small cannons that were in the boats. And the Moors, when they saw they were harassed by the shot, deserted the beach, and having retired together into the city, took their wives and children and as much baggage as they could carry on their backs, and fled into the interior of the country. As soon as the beach was clear, the chief captain disembarked with all the soldiers in two battalions, Afonso Dalboquerque in the van with part of the men, and himself in the rear with the royal flag. And as they met with no resistance when disembarking, they entered the city at once, and found it empty of people and moveables. So the chief captain, who perceived that there was nothing to be feared from any side, ordered the fleet to be furnished with supplies, of which there were plenty there, and gave permission to his men to sack the city, but to return quickly, for he was going to order it to be set on fire. And because at the time it was fired they were not yet returned, and were all scattered up and down in the houses sacking them, they would have been burned too, had it not happened just in the nick of time, that the wind blew from that part to which they were making their way; even when they desired to return, it was only with great difficulty that they managed to do so. As soon as all had returned to the ships, the chief captain ordered that the fleet should set sail, and sailed out of the harbour with the land breeze that was then blowing, and steered in a straight line for Braboa.

This city of Angoja is very large, peopled with Moors, who trade at Çofala, and all along that coast. There were no houses of stone and mortar in it except the king's mansions; it was entirely surrounded with many gardens and fruit trees, which made it very luxuriant; its bay was very good and afforded capital anchorage; it was not fortified, but situated on the edge of the sea. The king was a Moorish merchant, who came from abroad, but as he was very rich he had made himself lord of all that land.

CHAPTER XIII.

How the chief captain, Tristão da Cunha, proceeded to Braboa, and what passed there.

The fleet having set sail, the chief captain proceeded along the coast towards the City of Braboa; and as soon as they had all anchored on their arrival, seeing a great disturbance on the beach, he sent Lionel Coutinho in his skiff to shore, to find out with certainty what the Moors were about, but before the skiff reached shore, those who stood on the edge of the beach made signs to him not to come into the land. When Lionel Coutinho saw that the Moors were unwilling to parley with him, he returned to the ships, and informed the chief captain of the disposition in which he had found them. And he, being annoyed, because the king had refused to receive his message, ordered all the captains to be summoned, and gave them an account of Lionel Coutinho's proceeding with the Moors, and told them there were many men among them, and these very well armed; but for all this he was determined to attack the place, and risk all to destroy it, so they should make ready, and on the following day before daybreak come on board his ship that all might go together to attack the place. The Moors, who were stationed on the beach, seeing the commotion that was going on in the fleet, and the collection of boats around the flag-ship, (which appeared to them as it were of people determined to attack them), in order that they should not be taken by surprise, commenced to make themselves ready, and collected many men to prevent the disembarking of our men. They relied, too, on the sea, which broke upon the shore, (as it was a boisterous coast) and would overset them when landing and drown them all. The king being thus minded, there went to him by night two old Moors who had gone thither to live, having fled from Calicut disgusted with the war which the Çamorim kept waging with the Portuguese, and said to him: "Sire, thou art not well advised in desiring war with the Franks, over whom the Çamorim of Calicut, all powerful as he is, could never get the better in the war which he had with them, and thou oughtest to believe that there is no single king of all this coast so powerful as to be able to prevent them from landing in his territory whenever they desire, and leaving it full of blood, burning and destroying it as they did Angoja; and since this is so, we beg thou wilt deign to hear them, and make a reasonable truce with the chief captain of this fleet, and not hazard the loss of thy estate, and the destruction of all of us. But should their demands be so unreasonable that thy honour cannot grant them, then the business can be continually put off with fair words, for this is the season when the *vara* of Coromandel sets this way, as thou knowest, and if it should come when they are anchored there, all their fleet will be destroyed, and not one ship be saved, and by these means we shall all be revenged upon them, without thy estate being hazarded." The king was inclined to follow the Moors' advice, and thanked them deeply for their remembrance of him, and sent at once to convene the principal natives, who had recommended him to fight, and informed them of what the two Moors had said. And when they had thoroughly discussed the matter between themselves, it was agreed that they ought to follow the advice the Moors had given them. Therefore, before it was yet morning, the king sent a Moor in a boat with a white flag, to request the chief captain to come under a safe-conduct and arrange matters peaceably, and he went immediately on receipt of this message, and returned forthwith with the safe-conduct. And as soon as he had arrived, the king ordered one of the principal governors of the land to speak with the chief captain, and this (governor) told him that the king was very angry at the scanty welcome the Moors had given to his captain, whom he had sent thither, but as the offenders were many in number, he could not single out the guilty ones to have them punished, but he desired to have peace and friendship with the King of Portugal, and desired he would send word of what he wished, for all should be done. Tristão da Cunha replied that he was chief captain of the King of Portugal, who had sent him with the orders to make stern war against and destroy all the kings and lords who, unwilling to be friends and tributaries, were established along that coast which was of his conquering. And because the king of Angoja had not cared to be obedient to this, he had destroyed him; and so also he was determined to do with the king of Braboa, unless he was willing to obey the King of Portugal and pay him tribute; but if he was willing to be his vassal, he would serve him with that fleet against his enemies, just as he had done for the King of Melinde by reason of the great friendship which he also showed towards the King of Portugal, and by reason of the favour and honour shown to his captains who went to his port. The Moor returned to land with this reply, and related to the king, before all the principal men of the place who were with him, all that had taken place with the chief captain. And after long discussion which took place respecting this reply at which they were not pleased, the king sent again the same Moor to the chief captain to say, that to send to him for tribute was not desiring friendship with him, but seeking reasons for quarrelling if he did not grant what was demanded of him, for he had never been a tributary of any king, but rather on the contrary all those of that coast endeavoured to have him as their friend; yet, as this demand was something new, and could not be answered without consulting the chief men of the land, he begged him of his favour to wait for three or four days while he assembled all the merchants and arranged with them what could be done. The chief captain replied that he had other affairs to attend to, which the King of Portugal had ordered to be done, and therefore he could not wait so many days; so, if he desired to come to terms with him, he must send back an answer at once, and, if not, he should do what he had orders to do. The Moor returned with an answer, begging him greatly of his mercy to grant that extension of time which the king of Braboa, his lord, had sent him to ask; for it would not be fair, since all that population would have to pay the tribute, when once it had been agreed upon, that it should be done without the knowledge and consent of all. The chief captain, to be final with him, gave him another day, saying that if no reply came before night he should consider it as refused. The Moor went on shore and conveyed this message to the king, and on the following day, when the sun was already set, returned with a reply, and said that the king was willing to pay tribute, but could not determine how much it should be without first consulting the principal Moors of the land, and all the merchants, so he had ordered them to be summoned, and would send back word at once when they had arrived. The chief captain, seeing that the Moor who was employed on these messages went and came from side to side without bringing anything to an end, and that there was nothing but delay and lying on the part of the king, ordered him, when he had come with the last message, to be tied to a stake, showing that he was willing to make a treaty, and was determined to know the real reason why the king was unwilling to make an end of the business, for to reply *yes* or *no* there was need of but little time; and he warned him that he had better tell the truth, for if he lied, he would throw him into the sea with a cannon ball round his neck. The Moor, out of fear that he would carry his threat into effect, said: "Sir, thou art in front of this city where at this season of the year a wind arises which is called the *vara de Coromandel*, which comes from those parts so suddenly and so fiercely that if it were to come now, not a single vessel of your fleet could escape from certain destruction.[1] And it is from this hope, which we all support, that it will come every day, that the king carries on these delays with you." The chief captain, in fear of this event, ordered the Moor to be well treated, and made ready to attack the city on the morrow before daybreak.

CHAPTER XIV.

How the chief captain, Tristão da Cunha, went to attack the city of Braboa, and after its destruction sailed for Çocotora.

As soon as this parley was over between the chief captain and the Moor who carried the message, the chief captain at once informed the captains of all that had taken place, and said that his determination was, on the following day before dawn, to attack the city. He ordered them all, therefore, to get themselves ready, and, at the appointed time, come on board his ship, bringing small anchors and long cords with them in the boats, to leave as guides in the sea, that they might not be upset; for, as it was an open harbour, there was a great surf on the shore. The captains spent all the night in preparations, and, when the hour was come, went with their men on board the flag-ship; and, as soon as they had arrived, the chief captain stood in to shore two hours before daybreak, without sounding trumpets, lest they should be heard. The king, meanwhile, dreading that something or other had happened to delay the Moor whom he had sent, but who had brought back no answer, gave orders to watch the beach all night, so that our men

[1] *Vara de Coromandel*, a dangerous blast of wind that frequently arises without warning on the Coromandel coast.—*Bluteau*.

could not go so quietly but that they were perceived: and many Moors flocked to the shore at once, and did all they could to prevent our landing. And, because they were numerous and the sea very boisterous, our people experienced great difficulty in disembarking. Yet, for all that they were hurled along by the water and half dripping, they attacked the Moors so bravely, that many of them soon lay dead, and those who escaped from their sword fled towards the city. When the chief captain saw they were put to rout, he was unwilling to give those Moors who fled time to rally from the panic into which the sudden attack had cast them; so he ordered Afonso Dalboquerque to take the vanguard in charge and go in pursuit of them, which he accordingly did with the men he had with him. At the entrance into the city the Moors made a stand against our men, and killed about four or five, and wounded Antonio de Sá in the face with an arrow.

While this conflict with the Moors was taking place, the chief captain came up, and all together entered the city behind the fugitives; and women threw down stones from the terraces and wounded many. When the Moors had arrived at a large square containing a mosque, all had collected together and awaited our attack with the determination to resist to the death; and, as they were very numerous and the square large, our men, who were but few, were in danger of destruction. Directly news of this came to the boats, the mariners and bombardiers who had remained in charge of them, left them, and took leathern belts full of cases of gunpowder and of other firearms, and started off at full speed for the square where the chief captain was, and, with the powder in cases, lances, and firearms which they carried, made great havoc among the Moors. Our people, with this fresh succour, pressed so hard upon them that they turned their backs and fled on out of the city, in which none remained but women, who, laden with household goods, followed their husbands. And our people followed after them and came up with them, and killed many and took from them what they carried.

The chief captain, being fearful lest they should follow the Moors, who were flying pell-mell, too far, ordered Afonso Dalboquerque to recall his men and not permit any further pursuit. And when they were collected, the chief captain returned to the square, and set to work to attack the mosque, where they killed all the Moors who were within, and in entering it they wounded him in the leg with an arrow. At the end of this affair he took up his quarters in the square, and, after resting, he begged Afonso Dalboquerque to do him the favour to dub him knight; for he was desirous of receiving the honour from his hand there in that place, where the Moors had shed his blood. And forthwith all the people were collected in the centre of the square, and Afonso Dalboquerque dubbed him knight with the wonted ceremonies. After Tristão da Cunha had been dubbed knight, he, in his turn, conferred the same honour upon his son, Nuno da Cunha, and many other Fidalgos. And when these ceremonies were done, the chief captain went with all the rest to the palace of the king, which was very large and very beautiful, and into which, until then, he had permitted no one to enter. Within it he found much silver and much gold, many silk stuffs, and many other very rich things, and much money in *xerafins*,[1] all which he divided among the captains and noble persons of the fleet. Then, as it was getting time to embark, and also on account of the fear he had of the coming of the storm of which the Moor had told him, the chief captain ordered the recall to be sounded on the trumpets; and, after all the people had been gathered together, they set fire to the city in four parts, and it burned so fiercely, that it was a terrible thing to behold. Therein was burned much goods

[1] Silver pieces, of the value of 1s. 3d. sterling.

which our people had not time to bring away, inasmuch as the sea did not allow of their putting it on board so rapidly as the chief captain wished.

Braboa is a large city, with very good houses of stone and mortar. It is situated on the water's edge, and has no harbour: all is open coast, unprotected on all sides. It is peopled with the native Moors, who trade with Çofala and all along the coast. Thither, also, come the ships of Cambaia, laden with stuffs, and in this city the principal trade in them is carried on; for a very large river passes through it, which cuts the whole of the land, and does not run out to the sea: and, by means of this river, the merchants of this land sail to many parts, and go thence to a fair which is held in Manamotapa, which is the interior of Çofala, whither they bring these stuffs from Cambaia and Anfião, sandal-woods and rose-water and other merchandise, whereby they make much profit, and from thence take gold and other commodities: and all those in the interior are wont to navigate this river, and come to Braboa, which would be about half a league from the sea, and on account of this river the city has become so noble, and has many good buildings.

CHAPTER XV.

How the chief captain, Tristão da Cunha, left Braboa, and made his course direct for the island of Çocotora, and what happened there.

Having collected his ships, the chief captain set sail, and kept along this coast with all the fleet, intending to touch at Magadaxo. And, as it had been agreed the other day that they should attack the city, Afonso Dalboquerque went forward and anchored in front of it. But when the chief pilot of the fleet, by name Afonso Lopez Buraquinha, perceived that it was the intention of the chief captain to attack

Magadaxo,[1] and that much time would be spent (since he was well acquainted with the navigation of these parts, having gone thither already in company with Antonio de Saldanha), he went to him and told him that the monsoon of those parts was now nearly exhausted, and if he went any further on that course there would be no time left for him to double the shallows of St. Lazarus, which were distant fifty leagues,—but when they were doubled, the head-winds, which at that season blew off that shore, could not do him any injury, even if they were to come; for there was plenty of sea-room for tacking. The chief captain ordered the pilots, both Moors, and those of the fleet, to be summoned, and told them the opinion of his pilot; and, as all were agreed in this opinion, he ordered the course to be shaped towards Çocotora, and made signals to Afonso Dalboquerque to weigh anchor and follow him. And, without touching at other land, they went and anchored at Çoco, which is the principal port of that island, and where the population lives: and, with flags flying from all the ships in holiday trim, they saluted the place with artillery, as it was inhabited by Christians. But when the chief captain saw the fortress which the Moors had built there, surrounded with wall and barbican, and with a keep,[2] which was very different to the information which the king, D. Manoel, had received, he sent for Afonso Dalboquerque and all the captains of the fleet, to come to his ship; and he told them that the king, his lord, had ordered him to construct a fortress in that island, and to leave behind D. Afonso de Noronha, then present there, as captain of it, for the guard and protection of the Christians who had lived there since the time of St. Thomas, the king's desire being to extend the name of Our Lord throughout all the parts he had conquered; but

[1] In Zanguebar, 2 deg. 3 min. N., 45 deg. 13 min. E.

[2] *Torre de menagem*, the chief or highest tower in a castle, in which the constable or keeper of it professes fealty to his sovereign.—*Vieyra.*

because he found this fortress to exceed the information which his Highness had, he begged them to give their opinion as to what he should do in the case. All the captains told him that he ought to have an audience with the captain of the fortress, to know of him what he intended to do, and should he be unwilling to put himself under the obedience due to the King of Portugal, that then he ought to attack it and make an entry by force of arms. This advice seemed good to the chief captain, and he sent immediately Pero Vaz Dorta and Gaspar Rodriguez, interpreter, to land, to tell the captain that the King of Portugal had sent him with that fleet to make a fortress in that island, as he had been informed that it belonged to Christians, but he found it really possessed by Moors; so he begged and desired him to quit the fortress, and safe-conduct and passage should be given to him and all his people to go to their own land. But if he were unwilling to do so, he was determined to take the fortress from him by force, and leave not one Moor alive in it, for such were the commands of the King of Portugal his lord. The captain replied that they should say to the chief captain that neither he nor the Fartaquins, whom he had in his company, would die of fear, but by the sword, and he might do as he chose, for he on his part would not leave the fortress until all were dead, for this was the custom of the Fartaquins. When this determined reply was brought to the chief captain, he ordered Afonso Dalboquerque and the captains to be sent for, and gave them an account of it all. All agreed that the fortress should be attacked, and that Our Lord would help them, and tame the pride of the Moor, for although from without it appeared very strong, still it was so small that it would not possibly contain enough people to withstand the power of that fleet.

This having been agreed upon, because in the port of Çoco, where they were anchored, the sea was always boisterous, and a landing therein could not be effected without much trouble and risk, the chief captain determined to seek a harbour where they might disembark without trouble, and went in his boat with Afonso Dalboquerque along the shore, and found a creek near a palm-grove where the sea was more quiet, and although it was a little too far, they agreed to land there, and returned to the ships. And the chief captain immediately informed all the captains that they must get ready to go and attack the fortress before break of day, and disembark at that part by the palm grove, as the sea formed no convenient landing in the harbour wherein they were anchored, although it was nearer. When the great Afonso Dalboquerque came on board his ship, he ordered his nephew D. Afonso de Noronha to make ready his boat with forty musqueteers, and take with him a falconet and powder for it, and cannon balls, and two bombardiers, and a *cabria*,[1] and two sets of ladders to scale the wall of the fortress if necessary; and he would go in the ship's skiff with D. Antonio de Noronha, D. João de Lima, and D. Geronimo de Lima his brother, and other Fidalgos, following close upon their track.

All being ready, Afonso Dalboquerque went on board the flagship, and all made their way at once towards the palm grove, the chief captain with all his fleet in the vanguard, and Afonso Dalboquerque with his captains and men in the rear. The latter, however, perceiving that the sea there in the harbour was abating, and that he could disembark in front of the fortress as it was nearer, let his ship drop slowly down along the shore, paddling the oars upon the water, to see if the sea would clear up. When the captain of the fortress, who was watching to see our plan, perceived that the chief captain was going to occupy the palm-grove, where he had already a strong

[1] A vessel used for placing masts in ships, and for keeping men pressed for service in India.—*Bluteau*. In this passage it signifies a derrick.

stockade, which he had made during all that night, he sallied out of the fortress with a hundred men, and went straight to the stockade, to prevent our landing. As soon as Afonso Dalboquerque saw the captain leaving the fortress, and the sea abating, he ordered D. Afonso de Noronha to put into shore opposite it, and land at once, and he would follow him, and all landed together. But the captain, who was on his way to attack the chief captain, seeing that Afonso Dalboquerque remained behind him, and fearing lest he should take the gate of the fortress, and he himself have no place of retreat, left eighty men with a captain to defend the stockade, and he himself with twenty in his company returned to assist at the gate, lest it should be taken, and happened to fall in with D. Afonso de Noronha, who was on his way with his men towards it. And when these met there was a sharp skirmish with cutlasses and lances, and some of either party were wounded. And D. Afonso de Noronha engaged in fight with the captain, and coming to blows with cutlasses, had almost overcome him, when Afonso Dalboquerque came up with all the rest of his men and put an end to his life. When the Fartaquins beheld the death of their captain, they turned and fled away towards the fortress, and when they arrived our men killed eight of them, while the others went round the fortress and fled to the mountains. The Moors, who were upon a watch-tower, seeing our men close to the wall, began to throw down many corner pieces and stones, which harassed them much. And they struck Afonso Dalboquerque on the helmet with a corner-stone, so that he immediately fell to the ground in bad plight; but for all this he did not lose his senses, and ordered the men to close round, and sent Nuno Vaz de Castelo-branco to the boat to bring the shot and the derrick, and the sets of ladders, axes, and rams to break down the doors of the fortress. When Nuno Vaz brought the ladder, Afonso Dalboquerque ordered them to place it against the wall, and our men began to ascend, and the first was Gaspar Dias de Alcacere do Sal, who took up his flag, and Nuno Vaz de Castelo-branco, and the standard of Job Queimado and others who followed it. The Moors, seeing themselves invaded by us, without their being able to prevent it, gathered themselves into a tower which was close to the principal one; and when they deserted the watch-tower, Afonso Dalboquerque ordered the gates to be broken down with axes and rams, and all entered in by an earthwork, and went to the tower gate, where the Moors had gathered themselves, and then waited for the arrival of the chief captain who now returned with the Moors.

CHAPTER XVI.

How the chief captain, Tristão da Cunha, entered the fortress, and what took place when he arrived there.

The chief captain, Tristão da Cunha, by the palm-grove whither he went to disembark, had some slight difficulty with the Moors, who stoutly opposed his landing; but it was of little avail for them, because he fell upon them with such fury and force that they made but little resistance, and quitting the stockade, fled away towards the gate of the fortress, the chief captain following up behind them with his men, and killing many of them; and those who remained alive, seeing themselves cut off by Afonso Dalboquerque, who had already got in, turned round behind the fortress and saved themselves in the mountains. The chief captain, entering by the gate in the court-yard, found Afonso Dalboquerque at the foot of the tower, wherein the Moors were collected; and on his arrival he dispatched Nuno Vaz de Castelo-branco with four or five men to go and see if he could find entrance on any side to get up into it. And at the head of the courtyard they found a stone staircase, which was the entry to the tower, and going up by it, they came out upon the terrace of the tower, and there found a door which led to the lower story, which the Moors had barred in such a manner that no one could get in, and from the middle story, where they were, they kept shooting arrows with bad effect upon our men. The Fidalgos, who were there, perceiving themselves severely attacked by the Moors without being able to do them any injury in return, determined to risk an assault upon the door, in order to get in to them. And the first who attacked it was Don Antonio de Noronha; but when he would have gone up, a Moor came upon him with a sword, and would have cut his throat, had not Afonso Dalboquerque, happening to see the attempt, warded off the blow with his shield. The Moors, perceiving themselves invaded by the upper way of the terrace, retreated to the principal tower by a stairway, which led from one to the other, there not being at this time more than twenty-five in the fortress out of a hundred and fifty at the beginning of the attack, for the others were either dead or fled to the mountains. When they had retreated to the principal tower, they barred the doors and kept quiet, but the chief captain ordered it to be broken open immediately with rams; yet, because the stairway was so narrow that only one at a time could ascend by it, and the Moors could easily defend it, the chief captain desired, in order that they might not kill any of our men when entering this tower, to offer them terms. He thereupon told Afonso Dalboquerque and the other captains that those Moors were so obstinate, and our men so eager to kill them, that it would cost much time and trouble to get in at them; so it would be advisable to let them go without hindrance, for even if they were to kill all of them, no more honour would accrue to them than that they had already gained in taking the fortress. And because what the chief captain said was well received by all, he sent forthwith for Gaspar Rodriguez, the interpreter, to parley with the Moors at the door of the tower, and tell them their captain was dead, as indeed they well knew, and all those of his company, and that they were left alone; therefore he earnestly entreated them that they would think right to change their opinion and quit the fortress, and he would give them a safe conduct and passage for them to go to their land. The Moors replied that they were much obliged to the worthy chief captain for wishing to spare their lives, but that, in telling them of their captain's death, he had given them a sufficient reason for declining to receive the favour, for the Fartaquins were not accustomed to return alive to their land, and leave their captain dead on the field, especially when he was the son of their king, therefore he might do as he pleased, for they were not going to yield.

The chief captain, at this declaration of the Moors, sent João Freire, his page, and Nuno Vaz de Castelo-branco, and Dinis Fernandes, who was afterwards Chief Superintendent of India, Antonio Dinis de Setubal, and Pedralvares, page of the Count of Abrantes, to ascend to the terrace of the tower and see if by that way they could get in at the Moors. And the first who went up was João Freire, who, when leaping from the parapet of the tower to the terrace, was perceived by them, and they opened the door which led to the terrace, and seeing him by himself, fell upon him and killed him, and while they were killing him the others arrived. As soon as the Moors perceived them, they returned to their retreat in the story where they had been, and barred the door; and our men, seeing that they could not follow the Moors, made a hole in the terrace of the tower, and threw down stones and bricks which they took thence, and Nuno Vaz de Castelo-branco began to do them some injury with a cross-bow he had taken with him. Afonso Dalboquerque, excited with the shame they all incurred for having been there three hours without being able to enter a tower defended by four Moors, ordered two Biscay palisadoes to be brought from

E 2

his boat, and under the protection of these, carried by two soldiers, they began to mount bravely to the top of the stairway, those who could find room, and all the others followed them, being well plied with arrows and lances hurled at them. Even this, however, availed the defenders nothing to prevent our men from entering, and those who were upon the top of the terrace, when they saw the disturbance going on in the story, and the little door unprotected, broke it down and went down the stairway, and both one and the other party got in pell-mell among the Moors, and killed all without one escaping, and this at the cost of five or six of us killed and many wounded. One Moor, indeed, who surrendered, was taken prisoner, and of him Afonso Dalboquerque made much use on the Arabian coast, whither he went, for this Moor was a great pilot for that coast, and gave him a chart of all those parts of the kingdom of Ormuz, which a pilot, who was called Omar, when going thither had made, in whose company this man had sailed as mariner. The fortress was attacked at six o'clock in the morning, and finally taken at one o'clock in midday. Not much spoil was taken in it, for the Moors were of the frontier, but some supplies and arms were found, and swords bearing in Latin the inscription, "God help me." This victory having been won, on the morning of the next day the chief captain went with all the men in procession to a Moorish mosque; and as it was to be the principal church, they named it "Our Lady of the Victory", wherein Fr. Antonio do Loureiro, of the Order of St. Francis, said mass, and not without the tears of our men, to behold in a land so remote from Portugal the name of our Lord Jesus Christ reverenced in that house of abomination.

CHAPTER XVII.

Of the message which the chief captain, Tristão da Cunha, sent to the people of the land, and what passed with them, and how he finished the fortress of Çocotora, and sailed for India; and how the great Afonso Dalboquerque became chief captain of the fleet.

When the chief captain, Tristão da Cunha, was in possession of the fortress, he ordered a verbal proclamation to be made to the Christians who had fled away from a colony close by, entreating them to return, and give themselves no uneasiness, nor be scandalised at the destruction with which he had visited the Moors; for the principal reason of the King of Portugal's sending him to take that fortress and drive the Moors from the island, was to free them from these men's power, on account of the information which he had that they who dwelt there were Christians. Directly the natives received this message from the chief captain, knowing that his men were Christians, they came and cast themselves at his feet (having already thrown off the fear they formerly had), giving him many thanks for the favour he had done them in liberating them from the thraldom of the Fartaquins, who so tormented them that, not content with being lords over all their possessions, they had even taken away their wives and children to make Moors of them, and had done them many other injuries; but since God had brought him thither, and all were Christians, they begged he would deign to protect and defend them from such a bad set as these Moors were. The chief captain, with many loving words, consoled them, saying that the King of Portugal, his lord, had sent him thither out of love for them, and that he might make a fortress for their safety in that island, and that a captain and soldiers might be stationed there to defend them from the Fartaquins and ships of the Moors, who passed by thither to the straits (not knowing that the

Fartaquins had already made one), and begged them and recommended them especially ever to keep the peace and friendship with the Portuguese, and chiefly with those who were to stay behind in the fortress, and supply them with the supplies they might require. And since they were Christians, he begged they would kindly receive the doctrine of Christ, and learn the ceremonies of our Church, which they had already long ago forgotten, for the King of Portugal, his lord, with the desires he had of their salvation, ordered the Padre Fr. Antonio, who was there present with other religious men, to instruct them. This and much more to the point the chief captain said to them, whereat they became very happy, and promised him they would do all that he ordered; and from there they went with the Padre Fr. Antonio to their churches, where many, by his preaching and good example, were baptised.

This done, the chief captain ordered great quantities of stone and mortar to be collected, and set about the building of the fortress at once, and made such haste about it that in a short time it was finished; and when it was complete he named it "St. Michael", and committed the captainship of it to D. Afonso de Noronha, who came from Portugal, appointed by the king, D. Manoel, and he made Fernão Jacome, his brother-in-law, the chief alcaide (constable). And as the time for his departure to India was drawing near, he handed over to Afonso Dalboquerque six ships which the king, D. Manoel, had ordered to be given to him, with men, supplies, artillery, and all the rest that was necessary for him to remain as chief captain of all those parts (as the king's order constituted him), with obligations to provide that fortress with whatever it might require; of which ships the captains were Francisco de Tavora of the *Rey Grande*, Manuel Telez of the little one, Afonso Lopes da Costa of the *Taforea*, and Antonio do Campo of the small ship. And because the Comendador Ruy Soares, was to remain in his company, but had not yet arrived, the chief captain, Tristão da Cunha, left João da Nova, captain of the *Flor de la Mar*, in his stead, and as soon as Ruy Soares arrived, he was to sail away at once to India, with news of what Afonso Dalboquerque had done on the coast of Arabia, to take word to the king, D. Manoel. All this having been brought to an end, the chief captain took leave of the captain of the fortress, and of Afonso Dalboquerque, and of all the Fidalgos and knights who remained there (and this not without many tears on either side), and shaped his course for India with four ships on the first of August, in the year '7, and arrived there in safety, and there took in cargo and started to Portugal.[1]

Afonso Dalboquerque began to turn his attention to the affairs of the land, and divided the palm-groves, which the Moors had there, among the native Christians, and those which belonged to the mosque he now gave to the churches. And after the departure of Afonso Dalboquerque

[1] Here, for a while, we lose sight of this celebrated navigator. The Syren of Camões sings truly of him :—

> "Mas oh que luz tamanha, que abrir sinto,
> Dizia a nympha, e a voz alevantava,
> Lá no mar de Melinde em sangue tinto
> Das cidades de Lamo, de Oja, e Brava,
> Pelo Cunha tambem : *que nunca extinto*
> *Será seu nome em todo o mar*, que lava
> As Ilhas do Austro, e praias que se chamam
> De São-Lourenço, e em todo o Sul se affamam."
>
> *Lusiada*, x, 39.

> "O! what *new light* beginneth *there* to bud
> (The SIREN said, and rais'd her Voyce thereat)
> From the *Melindian* sea, dy'd with the blood
> Of LAMO, OCHA, BRAVA, all laid flat
> By great DE CUNIA; who through all the *Flood*
> Which laves the *Southern Isles* and *Shores* (but *That*
> Of MADAGASCAR chiefly) the wide mouth
> Of FAME shall fill, and threat the unknown *South*."
>
> *Fanshaw*, p. 201.

to Ormuz, our people remained in peace and friendship with the natives; but as the people of the island are by nature very malicious and treacherous, those Fartaquins who had escaped had very little trouble to urge them against our people, and arranged with the Christians of the land, who lived in these colonies remote from the fortress, to rise up against the Portuguese, telling them that the Franks had only built that fortress there to enslave them all, and take their land from them, and that they ought to revolt and not give supplies to the Franks, for it was now mid-winter, and not a season for them to be able to live without such supplies, and thus they all would perish. And they added that the Fartaquins would assist this undertaking, and procure from Fartaque many Moors to help them further. The natives, believing all this, set themselves to the work, and revolted, whence it happened that wars and commotions took place between them. And although the time was short, for the labour was continual, our people suffered much from famine, and from misfortune, until Afonso Dalboquerque returned to visit them, and provide them with supplies, according to his promise; and when he arrived, it was some days since our people had eaten anything but palm rind, and some goats which they took by force of arms.

CHAPTER XVIII.

How the great Afonso Dalboquerque, after Tristão da Cunha had sailed, made his fleet ready, and sailed with the intention of going to wait for the Moorish ships which came from India to the straits, and what happened thereupon.

As soon as the great Afonso Dalboquerque had put the affairs of the land in order, he wished immediately to set about fitting out his fleet, so as to sail at the new moon, which would be on the tenth day of August, for this was the time, as the Moorish pilots, whom he had brought from Melinde, said, that he might start for the coast of Arabia. So he ordered Pero Vaz Dorta, factor of the fleet, and João Estão, scrivener, to overhaul all the ships, and find out what supplies each one had on board, and from the information they acquired he understood that there were only fifteen days' supplies on board the fleet. When this was reported to Afonso Dalboquerque, he ordered a bread-room to be opened which was in his ship, and which he had caused to be carefully guarded, when he saw that Tristão da Cunha was not managing well in that voyage after he left Portugal, being fearful lest the delay should consume all, and he ordered the contents to be divided among all the captains, he himself taking his fair share, as each one of them did, for he did not wish that what was wanting to the others should abound with himself. When all was ready, and waiting the time for starting on the second of the month, such a great storm from the south-west struck them that all the ships were like to have been overset, and by stress of weather they broke all the cables they had, and the *Rey Grande* went nearly out of soundings, but by a miracle one cable held her. So Afonso Dalboquerque, finding himself by night in this misfortune, was very anxious, as he had not arranged with the captains what course they were to take, and whither they were to go and wait for him if the ships slipped their cables. And at once, in the night, while the storm was at its height, he ventured his skiff and wrote to the captains, that in case his sins deserved that any ship should break cables at that time, it was to make its way to, and wait for him at, the Islands of Curia Muria, and there all would take counsel respecting the course to be followed. And, with this message, he sent to each one a pilot of the Moors, whom he brought with him from Melinde. And it pleased Our Lord that when morning broke the weather cleared up, and the mariners had an opportunity of mending their cables. As soon as the day of departure was come, Afonso Dalboquerque summoned the captains and all the pilots, both Moors and Christians, and told them the time of setting out was come, and it would be well to discuss the route they were to take, whether by the Straits of Meca[1] or of Ormuz, or whether they should go at once to Dio and Cambaia, and in which part of these the fleet could be best supplied with supplies; for there was great need of them. These questions being brought before the assembly, and all the obstacles which were alleged being removed, it was agreed that, with the west winds then blowing, they should make for the Straits of Ormuz and take Mazcate, and there make up their minds what to do, and in that latitude of Çocotora, Fartaque,[2] and Dofar,[3] cruise about for eight days, watching the ships which at that season started from Barbara[4] and Zeilo,[5] and all the Red Sea, for Dio and Cambaia, and all the ports of Malabar.

This having been settled, all the ships set themselves in readiness, with their yards set and anchors apeak, and the great Afonso Dalboquerque took leave of D. Afonso de Noronha, his nephew, captain of the fortress, and of all the others who remained in it, and gave him an account of his intentions, and also told him the time when he hoped to return. And he sailed out of the port of Çoco on the tenth of August, in the year fifteen hundred and seven, taking the northern course by way of Fartaque and Dofar. And while they were in that water, in the narrow part of the Straits of the Red Sea, the wind and haze were so great that, not to strain the tackle, they stood a little more off to

[1] This appears to be an error for Mokhā, now called the Straits of Bāb-el-Mandel, "The Gate of Grief".

[2] Cape Fartak, on the coast of Arabia, 15 deg. 33 min. N., 52 deg. 10 min. E.

[3] Dafar or rather Zafār, near Mirbāt, 17 deg. 20 min. N., 54 deg. 30 min. E.

[4] Nearly opposite Aden.

[5] For Zeila.

catch sight of Curia Muria;[1] because it was not yet time to cruize in that latitude, as had been agreed upon; and even if they had sighted any ship, there was neither sea nor wind for chasing, by reason of the great danger they would run, and also because they were obliged to take this route, and much time was lost in it. And, sailing on in open order with that wind, on the thirteenth day of the month (August) they sighted a high land close to Curia Muria, which the Moors call Nooz,[2] and coasted along it until they had gone seven leagues from the islands; and, as the haze was very thick, they did not sight them, and it being now night, all returned to the open sea, to keep away from land. When morning came, they returned to stand in shore, but did not see land that day. The pilots made themselves out to be off Curia Muria, opposite a coast running N.E. and S.W. Afonso Dalboquerque hung out an ensign in his flag, and came to speak with them, and told them that in that latitude, which they were keeping, he could not be beyond Curia Muria; for, sailing by the rhumb of N.E., as they said, they would run aground upon the island: and what he said was not well received by the captains nor by the pilots, and that night they steered north, and he consented to obey the desires of the many. And so sailing on the night of the eve of Our Lady of August,[3] the watch of prime being just finished, Antonio do Campo, who was leading the way, found himself close in to land, with a strong wind and running sea, and fired two guns. As soon as Afonso Dalboquerque heard them, he ordered a signal to be made to the ships to turn back into the open sea, and all turned, the

[1] The Bay of Kuria Muria, on the Arabian coast, 17 deg. 30 min. N., 55 deg. 25 min. E. The island is in the same latitude, and 56 deg. 0 min. E longitude.

[2] Rās Nūs, or, according to Ritter, Rās Nosz.

[3] This would be the 14th of August, the eve of the Feast of the Assumption of the B. V. Mary.

pilots going on with the sounding lines in their hands; until they found they were out of soundings, and when they got there, he ordered them by signal to heave to, and all answered him, and he remained that night, with his lantern alight, lying to, and all the ships at his stern.

CHAPTER XIX.

How the great Afonso Dalboquerque, owing to his great need of supplies, shaped his course for the Straits of Ormuz, and arrived at Mascate.

The night being over, on the morning of the following day the great Afonso Dalboquerque sent word to his captains to steer straight to land and touch at Çalayate; for, on account of the great need of supplies throughout the fleet, he could not keep his intention of watching for the ships at that point; and also because the Moorish pilots told him that they considered that the ships had already gone by since the weather had been so bad, that if they had left Aden they would have finished their voyage in three days. And, with this determination, all steered to land, and three days afterwards sighted a point of land, which the Moors call Madrica,[1] and kept continually coasting along with due precaution, keeping close to land by day, and by night standing out to sea, to make their voyage with greater safety, until they came in sight of the Cape of Maceiras.[2] And, as they were coming one morning from the sea to the coast, the Moorish pilots did not recognise it; for some made themselves out to be on this side of the Cape of Resalgate,[3] and others on the further side, and they were perplexed to

[1] Madrica, elsewhere Madraka, now Cape Isolette.

[2] Perhaps now Ras el Jezirah, forming the lower point of the Gulf of Massera; but this point is the same as Madraka.

[3] Perhaps Ras el Had, 22 deg. 24 min. N., 59 deg. 49 min. E.

find the currents there very rapidly setting in towards the Straits of Ormuz: but, as the sea was calm and the wind improving every moment, the Moorish pilots ordered the ships to be drawn up as close as possible to the shore, and anchored in from twenty-five to fourteen fathoms of water; for, although the coast is full of hidden rocks, it is clear, and affords good anchorage: and all this land near the sea is barren and sandy, and the interior has very lofty and rugged mountain ranges. As soon as the Moorish pilots arrived here, they at once knew they were on this side of the Cape of Resalgate, and at the Maceira point. The fleet remained at anchor there that night; and when morning broke, the ship *Taforéa*, which was on the weather beam, fired two shots, and some went up the round top immediately to see what it was, and the man on the look-out said he saw three sails on the sea. Then Afonso Dalboquerque sent word to Antonio do Campo and Manoel Telez to set sail and see what those sails were: and, in case they should lose sight of the fleet, he told them to coast along, and they would find him at the Cape of Resalgate, for the Moorish pilot he carried knew the coast very well.

The two captains having started, Afonso Dalboquerque ordered the other ships to sail, and they anchored that day in the afternoon on this side of the Cape of Resalgate, which is a coast well shaded and clear, and of good anchorage; and while they were there, Antonio do Campo and Manoel Telez arrived with the intelligence that the ships which the look-out man saw were three fishing barques; but with the sea air they had seemed large sails; and, as the wind had dropped, they fled away by sailing and rowing. And they found there, in that port where they were that night, thirty or forty fishing ships, which come thither from the City of Ormuz,[1] Calayate, and all that coast to fish for *bonitos*[2] and

[1] See plan and description of Ormuz, in Resende's work, ff. 155-158.

[2] A kind of tunny.—*Bluteau.*

Albecoras;[1] for there is great traffic in these fish to many parts, just as in the tunny of Algarve; and they burned all these ships, and on the following morning set sail with a fair wind, and took the ships' boats with masts and sails, and towards evening arrived at the mouth of a large river which formed a great lagoon within it. And Afonso Dalboquerque ordered the master of the *Taforéa* to go in his boat along the shore, and see what sort of a place it was, and of what depth the river was; and he found five fathoms depth, and the water of the lake salt. Within it were four small *zambucos*, which they burned. From this point they kept coasting along, with sunken rocks, at twenty or twenty-five fathoms, and a clear bottom, until they arrived at a small village of straw huts, which the Moorish pilots said belonged to the fishermen, and by land along the coast went much people on foot or horse or camel, pacing along and following our fleet, which kept along the bank until in sight of the City of Calayate. And when just opposite the harbour, Afonso Dalboquerque ordered the captains to set their mainsails and be ready to sail, and to deck out the ships with flags and get all their artillery in order, and with their foresails and mizensails, and taking their boats up in front, to go and anchor in front of the city, and all did so with great pleasure and many cheers, but without sounding trumpets, for Tristão da Cunha had refused to give them any.

CHAPTER XX.

Of what the great Afonso Dalboquerque transacted with the governors of the city of Calayate on his arrival there.

As soon as the great Afonso Dalboquerque had arrived with his fleet at Calayate,[2] they employed all that afternoon

1 Evidently an Arabic word, cf. al-bákara, al-bākūra, an ox, or a cow. Vieyra calls this fish a kind of tunny.

2 Kalhāt, between Rās-el-Hadd and Muskat.

in repairing their ships; and, on the following morning, he sent a boat to shore, and in it Pero Vaz Dorta, factor of the fleet, and João Estão, scrivener, and Gaspar Rodrigues, interpreter. When they landed, the Moors, who at once collected on the beach, questioned them as to what they required and whence they had come. And Pero Vaz Dorta replied, through the interpreter, that the fleet before them belonged to the king D. Manoel, King of Portugal and Lord of the Indies, and that the chief captain, who came with it, desired to know what place this was, and of what kingdom and lordship. The Moors replied, that the name of the city was Calayate, and that it belonged to the kingdom of Ormuz, and if they required anything they would give it very willingly; and, with this reply which the Moors gave, Pero Vaz Dorta and João Estão returned, and acquainted Afonso Dalboquerque with what had taken place. On the following morning the Goazil[1] and rulers of the city sent him word to send two of his men to land; for they wished to send two of their men to confer with him. Afonso Dalboquerque sent two of his young men, and two honourable Moors came from land, and informed him on the part of the Goazil and rulers of the city, that whatever was required for his fleet they would willingly cause to be sent to him; for they desired to have peace and friendship with the King of Portugal, and they brought him a present of oranges, lemons, pomegranates, and fowls, and some sheep; but, because, for all these good words and the presents, much people were continually marching along the beach and through the city, armed and clothed like Turks, with bows, lances, swords, and cimitars (and on the bank they had a stockade with four mortars), Afonso Dalboquerque declined receiving the present, saying that he would not accept anything from those against whom he would have to declare war if they refused to be vassals of the King of Portugal, whose chief

[1] Or Guazil, a governor, from the Arabic wazîr. Cf. Alguazil, Sp.

captain he was, sent by royal command to the kingdom and city of Ormuz.[1] The Moors replied, that if he was on his way to Ormuz, this place was the door to it, and if he

[1] Camões makes the nymph utter the following prophetic sentiments, concerning the operations of Dalboquerque at Ormuz and Calayate:—

"Esta luz he do fogo, e das luzentes
Armas, com que Albuquerque irá amansando
De Ormuz os Parseos, por seu mal valentes,
Que refusam o jugo honroso, e brando:
Alli verão as sellas estridentes
Reciprocarse, a ponta no ar virando
Contra quem as tirou; que Deos peleja
Por quem estende a fé da madre Igreja.

"Alli de sal os montes não defendem
De corrupção os corpos no combate,
Que, mortos, pela praia, e mar se estendem
De Gerum, de Mascate, e Calayate:
Até que á forca só de braço apprendem
A abaixar a cerviz, onde se lhe ate
Obrigação de dar o reino inico
Das perlas de Barem tributo rico."

Lusiada, x, 40, 41.

I forbear to give Mickle's incorrect rendering of these stanzas; Fanshaw translates them thus:—

"This *light* is of those flames and glitt'ring *Arms*
Wherewith the stubborn PERSIANS of ORMUZE,
Spurning the *yoake*, and valiant to their harms,
Fierce ALBUQUERQUE afterwards subdues.
There shall be hissing *Shafts* (like living swarms)
Turned in the Ayre, their *shooters'* Helmets bruize;
That they may see, with eyes though ne're so dim,
How GOD will fight for *Them* that fight for *Him*.

"The MOUNTAINS then of SALT will not be able
To keep those *Bodies* from corruption,
Which on the *Coasts* shall lye out (miserable)
Of CALAYAT, MASCATE, and GERUN;
Until the easie *yoake* and honorable
They learn (with all their fierceness) to put on:
Forc't by the *Conquerours*, to pay to *them*
Rich Tribute of their *Pearles* of BAHEREM."

treated them well they would open it for him, and he could so enter the house, and since he was determined to go and visit the King of Ormuz, their Lord, he might make some agreement with him, but if no agreement were made, they would agree to be subject to the King of Portugal, and as his vassals they desired he would not desire to destroy them nor make war upon them. Afonso Dalboquerque ordered the captains to be summoned, and recounted this reply to them, which the rulers of the city had sent him, and it was unanimously agreed that if these men were willing to supply all the stores necessary for the fleet, from the great need there was of such, he ought to dissemble and give them a respite until he arrived at Ormuz, making a virtue of necessity, until he obtained his supplies.

This having been decided, Afonso Dalboquerque dispatched the Moors back with a fitting answer: and, as the rulers were very desirous of peace, from the fear they had of our fleet, being unprepared, they sent the Moors back again at once with sixty bags[1] of rice, and as many of dates, and thirty sheep, and other fresh provisions. But, as Afonso Dalboquerque did not know how affairs at Ormuz would turn out, he would receive nothing in the way of a present, and ordered payment to be made for all that was brought. The Moors were unwilling to receive payment, saying that the present which the rulers of the city had sent him was for a sign of friendship; for all were prepared to do whatever he might order, and therefore they could not take any payment; and if the King of Ormuz were unwilling to make peace, then they would render the city up to him. Nevertheless, Afonso Dalboquerque made them by force take payment, and ordered a safeguard to be made out for them in the name of the king, D. Manoel, to hold good until his arrival at Ormuz. And because this safeguard did

[1] *Fardos.* A *fardo* in India was equivalent to 42 pounds Portuguese. —*Vieyra.*

not cover the ships of strangers who were in the port, he ordered a ship of Aden, of about two hundred tons, which was there loading horses and dates, to be seized. When the master of the vessel perceived that his ship was taken, he applied to the Goazil, who was the governor of the city, begging him to do what he could to prevent his ship being carried off, and the Goazil sent word to Afonso Dalboquerque that, for the honour of the city he begged he would be graciously pleased to send back the ship, and he would give whatever he ordered. But Afonso Dalboquerque put him off with the excuse that he had given it to Gaspar Rodrigues, the interpreter, and if he chose to ransom it of him, well and good; he, for his part, was sorry it was out of his power to serve him, though he would send him to come to some agreement with the present owner of the ship. So Gaspar Rodrigues arranged with the master, and gave the price to the factor for expenses of the fleet.

Calayate is a city as large as Santarem, badly populated, with many old edifices, now destroyed. According to the information given to Afonso Dalboquerque by the Moors, it appears that the city was destroyed by Alexander, who conquered all that country. The sea beats against it, and the harbour is very good, and is situated at the foot of some lofty ranges; on the land side, a little distance from the city, there was a wall about the height of a lance, which comes down from the top of the mountains, and reaches to the sea; this was made by the citizens out of love for [peace with] the Moors of the interior, for they had come into collision with them on several occasions. The interior is under the rule of a king who is called the Benjabar, who has much cavalry. Around the city there is not a single tree, except a few palms close to some pools of water, whence they get drink; and all their supplies of corn, barley, maize, millet, and dates, come from the interior, for there is plenty of these products there. This port is a great entrepôt of shipping, which comes thither to take horses and dates to India. The King of Ormuz used to send there every year a noble Moor to be Goazil, who administered justice and made war and peace as he chose. And in the taxes and duties paid to the king, no one interfered except an eunuch, a servant of Cogeatar, and in all the places under the Kingdom of Ormuz he placed these eunuchs, his servants, who had charge of the revenue, and great obedience was shown to them throughout the land.

CHAPTER XXI.

How the great Afonso Dalboquerque left the city of Calayate, and went on to Curiate,[1] and took it by force of arms.

The supplies having been collected, the great Afonso Dalboquerque took his leave of the Moors, who kept to the agreement he had made with them, and started from the port on Sunday, the twenty-second of August, always keeping in sight of the coast, with the determination to leave no place in the whole of the land ignorant of what he could do to it; for he held it a most important part in his plan for getting possession of Ormuz, first to make himself master of all those places and ports which he might find along the coast, and to burn all their ships to prevent their assisting the king. And going along thus within sight of land, he told the Moorish pilots that he had a chart, made by a Moorish pilot named Omar, when he accompanied Vicente Sodré, and containing all the harbours, towns, and places of that coast, and in it was set down that five leagues from Calayate there was a port called Icce, and he desired they

[1] A little south of Muscat. See plan and description in Resende's work, ff. 113-115, "Descripsam da fortalleza de Curiate que he a Primeyra do Estreyto de Ormus Antes de Mascate."

would point it out to him, thinking it was a large place. So the pilots showed it to him, and it proved to be a river of fresh water, in which the ships entering the Straits of Ormuz go and take water, and our fleet passed in sight of it; and when close to Curiate they anchored rather far from land, as it was all low rocks, and Afonso Dalboquerque ordered Manoel Telez and Antonio do Campo to approach as close as they could to the land, bearing in mind to make allowance for the low tide, for it was then on the turn; and when they were anchored, they set themselves in sailing order and hung out all their flags, remaining there all that night, without any one coming from land to speak with them. So when they had consulted together as to what they should do, although different opinions were advanced, it was agreed to destroy the place. But as it was large, not to proceed blindly to attack it, the great Afonso Dalboquerque made up his mind to go along with his captains and reconnoitre the place, and settle the manner in which they should disembark, and they entered the captains' boats and steered for the river. When they came close to it, the Moors, who lined the beach, would not have any communication with them, and began to make many hostile gestures; and they had made at that part a stockade of wood, five palms in breadth, and packed in with earth, which guarded all the front of the place, and within it were placed four large mortars, and many archers, and others with long lances, guarding it. And lower down than this, they had made another on the edge of the water in shape of a bastion, surrounded with wood, and packed up with earth, of the same size as the other, and at high water it was entirely surrounded by water; for between the fort and the village was a creek or backwater, in which there were two gates, one opposite to the other, for them to assemble whenever it was necessary. When Afonso Dalboquerque beheld the stockade, and saw that the Moors were unwilling to communicate with him, but were determined to make a bold stand in their own defence, he ordered the falconets which were in his boat to be fired at them, and retired to the ships. The Moors also, on their part, began to fire at him with their mortars, and with many arrows. And because in this harbour there is a small island, so close to the land that at low water one can pass over dryshod to the place, and the Moors could not prevent the disembarking of our people for all the force they had there, Afonso Dalboquerque ordered Antonio do Campo to go at once, that very night, with a hundred men, to take this island and fortify himself therein.

All this having been set in order, at the appointed time the captains came in their boats on board the flagship to set out thence all together, and because just then the tide was at its lowest ebb, Afonso Dalboquerque determined to disembark somewhat below the town, that our men might reach land with less danger from the mortars at the stockades, and told his captains this, his [altered] plan, that each one might be aware of what he was about to do. And having arrived at the island wherein Antonio do Campo was posted, Afonso Dalboquerque changed his mind, and desired to attack the stations at that point with all his men in one battalion, as it was too small to be divided into two; for if he gained that fort wherein the Moors had all their strength and trust, the others, which were on the other side of the town, would yield without fighting. And this being so arranged, he told Antonio do Campo to be on the watch for him, and at the moment when he should attack the station, to attack the other side with all his men facing it, and fight fiercely with the Moors, for he hoped in Our Lord to overcome them, and thereby get possession of the city. So Antonio do Campo knowing what he was to do, Afonso Dalboquerque went along the river to disembark at the other part where he had agreed upon, and with all his people went on his way softly, and when close upon the station, a number of Moors came in view, who proceeded from the other side of a hill which overlooked the place, as though about to attack our men in flank. When Afonso Dalboquerque saw them, he sent Afonso Lopez da Costa, with sixty men, to go and take the hill for him and drive them down and return at once to the main body. Afonso Lopez da Costa attacked these Moors very bravely and worsted them, killing some, and returned forthwith to our men, and all together assaulted the stockade. Antonio do Campo, who was in momentary expectation of what Afonso Dalboquerque had told him, seeing our men fighting in the stockade, attacked the rear of the Moors, at the part where he had received instructions to fall on. The Moors, being attacked in front by our men, began to fire their artillery and many arrows, defending themselves for a long while, and wounded some soldiers of the company led by Antonio do Campo. When this furious artillery fire was over, our men fell on with such eagerness that, fighting on the top of the stockades, they entered with the Moors into the place, and pursued them for the distance of half a league, putting to the sword all the Moors, women and children, who were fleeing into the interior. And because the heat was great and our men by this time were very tired, Afonso Dalboquerque took a hill, and set up his standard, and remained there, sending word to Francisco de Tavora, Afonso Lopez da Costa, and Antonio do Campo, that when they saw it they should likewise set up their flags, at distances from each other, to restrain the men from following up the Moors; and he also ordered João da Nova and Manuel Teles to return to the place, and collect all the people who were scattered up and down in it, and finding some Moors, he put them all to the sword, and remained on that hill until vespers. And when he had collected all the men, he proceeded to the town, and ordered them to repair the stockades of the Moors, and fortified himself in them until the supplies had been collected, for there was great need of them; and he ordered his flag to be set up on the dome of the mosque, and ten men to be placed there to watch the surrounding country. And as soon as the supplies were collected, and as much spoil as they could carry away, he ordered the place to be set on fire, especially some houses in which the bulk of the supplies were, to prevent the Moors from making use of them; and the fire was so fierce that there was not a house, not a building, nor the mosque, which was one of the most beautiful ever seen, left standing. He ordered also that they should cut off the ears and noses of the Moors who were captured there, and then send them away to Ormuz to bear witness to their disgrace. In this place we captured twenty-five pieces of artillery and a great quantity of bows, arrows, lances, and other arms; and thirty-eight ships, great and small, were burned. When this was all over, he returned with all the captains to the ships, and each went to his own to make ready for the passage to Mascate on the following day.

Curiate is a large town, having its principal population on the edge of the coast on the inner side; it is rather straggling, and contained to all appearance about five or six thousand men. It is an entrepôt of many ships which come to export dates, of which both in the town and neighbouring country there is abundance; but because the harbour is rather rocky, and the sea runs with a strong current, they do not export horses, although many are bred in the land. There are very good pools of water which the inhabitants use for drinking purposes. Two very large ships were burned, which were on the stocks, all in repair and order to be launched; they belonged to a corsair who lived in the place.

CHAPTER XXII.

How the great Afonso Dalboquerque set sail from Curiate and went to Mascate, and what passed there.

When day broke, the great Afonso Dalboquerque ordered all the fleet to set sail, and in four days they arrived at the city of Mascate,[1] which is the principal port for all that coast; and on that day in the evening all the ships entered the port, with the exception of those of Manuel Teles and Francisco de Tavora, which remained outside because the breeze dropped. Directly they were all anchored, there came on board the flagship two noble Moors in an *almadia,* and as they were already aware of the destruction of Curiate, they told Afonso Dalboquerque that the rulers of the city had sent them to beg him to do it no injury, for they were willing to be vassals of the King of Portugal. Afonso Dalboquerque asked them whether they brought with them authority from the rulers and people of the city to treat. To this the Moors replied that they had not brought any written instructions, but it was sufficient that they were come thither according to order of the city; so he told them he could not make any answer until the two of his captains who remained outside had first come into port, but they might return to shore, and on the following morning return safely to him, and he would arrange with them all that the service of the King of Portugal, Lord of the Indies, required. The Moors being gone with this reply, now that Francisco de Tavora and Manuel Telez had come in, Afonso Dalboquerque ordered both of them to take boat and sound the harbour, how many fathoms depth there was between the ships and the shore, and to try to get a view of the position of the stockade which the Moors had made; and

[1] 23 deg. 29 min. N., 58 deg. 33 min. E. See plan and description of the fortress in Resende's work, ff. 116-123.

they went along the shore, after having sounded the bottom, and saw all very well. So having returned to the ships, they told him that the Moors had constructed in front of the town a wall of timber ten palms broad and twenty high, packed with earth, very strong, and on either side it had been carried up into two very high mountain ranges, which ran down into the sea, and made the whole very strong; and in this wall they had made some defences, like bulwarks, with many mortars of the size of our *camelos*[1] mounted on them, and that we could land at the foot of the wall at high tide. While Afonso Dalboquerque was discussing this with Francisco de Tavora and Manuel Telez, the two Moors, who had come the day before, came on board, with permit of the Rulers to treat for peace, and told him that the city desired to be obedient to the King of Portugal, and perform whatever he, the chief captain, might order on his part. Afonso Dalboquerque, after hearing what they had to say, ordered them out while he communed with the captains who were then with him, respecting the agreement to be made with the envoys, and having settled what reply to make, he called the Moors in and told them, that if the city was willing to obey the King of Portugal, and pay him yearly a fair and reasonable tribute, and supply himself with all supplies he might require when he arrived at Ormuz, he on his part would not make war upon them, but, on the contrary, would protect and defend them as vassals of the king, his lord. The Moors replied that the inhabitants of the city were content to become vassals of the King of Portugal, and to pay him every year the dues—and they were many—which they had hitherto paid to the King of Ormuz; and as to the demand of supplies for that occasion only they would give him all he needed. As Afonso Dalboquerque considered it below his dignity to haggle with them, he desired Antonio do Campo, Pero Vaz Dorta, and João Estão, scrivener to

[1] A sort of heavy gun or cannon used in the sixteenth century.

the fleet, to speak with the Moors outside, and tell them that with the conditions mentioned he would receive them into the friendship of the King of Portugal, but they must on their part give him abundance of supplies and fresh water, carried at their own cost to the city of Ormuz as long as he might remain there. After long discussion about these terms, the factor returned to Afonso Dalboquerque, to tell him the Moors were unwilling to give more than they had at first agreed for. This reply annoyed him very much, and he ordered them before him, and asked them in a somewhat passionate voice how they dared deny to the officers of the king their lord those things that they demanded, since they had but just then cast themselves at his feet, and told him they desired to be his vassals: let them go at once and tell the rulers of the city that next morning he would show them how Portuguese cavaliers chastised places which were unwilling to obey the King of Portugal and his chief captain. When the Moors perceived that Afonso Dalboquerque was angry, and cast them off without any kind of agreement being concluded, they were in a great fright, and threw themselves at his feet, begging him to pardon them, and they would do whatever he desired. So he sent them to talk with Antonio do Campo and with the factor. The Moors went out very dejectedly, and agreed to all that was asked; and, the agreement being concluded, they went on shore again very gladly, and at once set about bringing the supplies as long as day lasted; but when the morning came that Afonso Dalboquerque hoped would finish the work, they did not return, and no message came from land, but he was kept thus in suspense until midday, without being able to divine what change had taken place with affairs; but in order to know better what course to take, he went into his skiff with D. Antonio de Noronha, his nephew, and D. Jeronimo and others, and went along the shore unconcernedly, in order to better understand the matter, and see the position of their stockades. At the time he arrived at the shore the boat of Afonso Lopez da Costa was on the beach taking in water, and from the boatswain who was in it he heard that all that night there had been great joy, excitement, and shouts in the city, and it was rumoured that a captain had arrived with ten thousand men from the interior, armed with lances and shields, whom the Benjabar sent to the aid of the city, and that the news was confirmed by the common sailors, who were at the watering places taking in water. Afónso Dalboquerque told the boatswain to get the sailors together without exciting suspicion, and if it proved difficult for him to collect the barrels, to leave them. So the sailors who were at the watering places, perceiving the excitement of the Moors, and fearing they would be murdered by them, left some of the barrels behind, and assembled at the boat in great haste, and related to Afonso Dalboquerque the same news that the boatswain had given him; and he having seen everything very clearly, went to the *Taforéa*, which was nearest to the shore, and despatched Dinis Fernandez in his skiff to land, bidding him summon one of those Moors who had consented to the agreement for peace. When the Moors, who were going up and down along the beach, saw the skiff, they gathered about, intending to take it; but Dinis Fernandez, who was well acquainted with their treacherous ways, seeing them in a state of excitement, did not touch land, but returned to the ships with some of his mariners wounded by the arrows shot at them. Afonso Dalboquerque, seeing the shamelessness of the Moors, gave orders to Afonso Lopez da Costa, Antonio do Campo, and Manuel Teles, to take their ships as close up to the shore as they could, and let down warps from the stern into the sea, that they might haul upon them whenever it might be necessary, and then to bombard the city to annoy the Moors, for he was determined to attack them in the morning. The captains weighed anchor, and took up positions according to the directions they had received, and commenced firing with their artillery against the stockades, but did very little damage, as the wall was closely packed with earth. So, perceiving that from where they were they could do no good, they took up a new position opposite an entrenchment made by the Moors outside the wall, and containing two mortars, which was rather exposed to our fire; and directly the firing began, the Moors deserted the mortars and fled away. When Afonso Lopez da Costa saw that the entrenchment was deserted by the Moors, he thought he could capture the guns; so he went into his boat with his men, and went to attack the entrenchment and take them, and Antonio do Campo followed behind to defend him, if there was any need for it; but when they landed, the Moors, who came up to the rescue of the mortars, were so numerous, that if Afonso Dalboquerque had not happened to arrive in time to succour them, it would have gone ill with them all, and as it was, when he arrived, Afonso Lopez da Costa was wounded, with five men in his boat, by the arrows; so he caused them to be mustered, and after severely reprimanding them for having fought in that way, contrary to the orders he had given, he desired them not to cease firing against the stockades, for even if no injury were done, yet it dispirited the Moors who were therein.

CHAPTER XXIII.

How the great Afonso Dalboquerque, by advice of the captains, attacked the town of Mascate, and destroyed it, and what took place there.

All this being over, the great Afonso Dalboquerque summoned all the captains from their ships, and told them they all knew the civilities which he had interchanged with the rulers of that city of Mascate, and he was truly concerned at their unwillingness to adhere to the agreement he had made with them; and the principal reason that induced him to make this agreement was that the place was very well supplied with necessaries, and had a harbour excellently adapted to the protection of the ships passing that way on their voyage from India to Ormuz; and in case any need arose while they were in Ormuz, they could from this town obtain what supply was required; and for all that the place appeared strong, as they all might see, and populous, yet he was determined to attack and destroy it, for the rebellion they had made against him, relying on the power of our Lord, who was greater than all, and he begged they would tell him their opinion. The captains replied that in a matter so completely agreed upon and determined, there was nothing to advise about; he might do as he liked and they would follow him. Although Afonso Dalboquerque gathered from this reply that they did not think it advisable to attack the place, because its fortifications appeared very different to those of other towns which they had attacked, yet for all this he dissembled with them, and sent them back to their ships to prepare themselves, and ordered them to come on board his ship with all their men at the sound of his drum.

On the next day, while yet the morning star was shining, he ordered the signal to be made, and the captains embarked at once, and came on board the flag-ship, and thence all set out straight to shore, and Jorge Barreto went in Afonso Dalboquerque's boat with his men, and he himself alone in the skiff, settling with each one the part he was to perform. And because the place of entry differed from others, and there was much more danger in attacking it, and it behoved them to use all possible diligence, in order to overcome the Moors with the least risk of their own safety, he ordered Francisco de Tavora and Afonso Lopez da Costa to unite their forces and attack the stockades on the right hand side, and when these had gone in, to run along the wall and unite with himself who intended to force an entry on the left hand; and having entered the stockades, they would then enter the town, being united in one body, for there were not enough men for two battalions. When he had told them this, all touched land, and attacked the stockade with the greatest fury; and as at this time it was high tide, and our men had to land at the foot of the wall, the Moors commenced shooting arrows and throwing down stones from the top, so that our men had much difficulty in effecting a landing. But when they were on shore, Afonso Dalboquerque drew off the company he commanded, and proceeded to attack the stockades on the left, for there the greatest strength of the enemy lay; and at the same time, Afonso Lopez da Costa and Francisco de Tavora attacked the same on the right hand side, as had been previously settled. The Moors who were inside, for a long time defended themselves bravely, but our men, albeit with difficulty, forced an entrance, and killed many of them. Francisco de Tavora and Afonso Lopez da Costa, having thus entered the stations, not bearing in mind the orders Afonso Dalboquerque had given, with that vigour and impetus wherewith they had begun the fight, followed up the flying Moors until they drove them into a street in the town, where they put some to death; but as many came up to the rescue, they ran a risk of being destroyed, so they turned back and went along the wall, seeking Afonso Dalboquerque, who severely censured them for disobeying his orders to come and unite with his company. Then all formed into one battalion, and marched to the attack; but as the streets were very narrow, and the lances they carried very long, and as in their eagerness they strove to pass in front of each other, they began to fall into confusion, so that the Moors in this fray wounded many with arrows. Yet, with all this trouble, our men fell upon the Moors so fiercely that the captain, who came from the interior with his men to succour the town, when he saw himself assailed, turned and fled; and Afonso Lopez da Costa and Francisco de Tavora, who were in the van, went after him, Afonso Dalboquerque, with the rest of the men, being close behind, and they continued the pursuit a good stretch out of the city. Antonio do Campo, leaving Afonso Dalboquerque, in whose company he was, pursued a crowd of women who were retreating to the hills, and killed many of them; while João da Nova, because his own men were very much scattered, collected together a few and followed some Moors who were taking refuge in a valley below, and killed many, as well as women and children who were with them, without sparing any, so that one and all did great execution among them, and killed some of the principal Moors of the town, and among the number an eunuch, who governed under orders of the King of Ormuz. Finally, Afonso Dalboquerque came up to Francisco de Tavora and sent him into the country to collect all the men who were scattered abroad, while he waited; and when all were assembled, he returned to the city, and put all the Moors, with their women and children, found in the houses, to the sword, without giving any quarter. Inasmuch as our men were much distressed with the heat and the hard fighting, and had eaten nothing all day, and there were no more Moors to fear, he ordered the captain to collect them and take them out of the town to rest at some waterpools, where the inhabitants used to get water, setting, nevertheless, sentries to watch the movements of the enemy, and prevent any sudden surprise; and he sent thither some bags of dates, of which all partook and drank of the water, and remained there some time, until all had rested. Afterwards, he returned to the town, and ordered the captains to take stockades on the land side, and fortify themselves in them with barriers in the streets, and with mortars, that they might defend themselves from the Moors in case they were attacked, and to set fire to the neighbouring houses where the mariners were to take water for the ships, lest any Moors should secrete themselves in them and cause trouble when they went for it.

When everything had been thus set in order, he gave permission to sack the town, and told the captains that each one must take care to collect into his ship as large a quantity of provisions as possible, for they were going to a land where there would be urgent need of them; and that they must keep good watch in the stockades, both by day and by night, for the Moors were on the mountains and saw all they did, and if they were to observe any remissness, there was very little doubt but that they would attack them by night, for they had no lack of soldiers, since they could get as many as they wanted from the interior. Our men began the sacking on the eighth day they had been there, and found nothing to lay their hands on; but one day, as a soldier was entering a house, carrying a short heavy pike in his hands, he struck it by chance into the front wall of the house, and made a hole, whereby he entered in and found there much merchandise; for the Moors of the town, fearing lest the inhabitants of the interior should come and rob them, had each built a compartment inside his house, without door or windows, and filled it with much merchandise. As soon as this came to the knowledge of our soldiers, there was not a house left standing which they did not break into, wherein they found things of great value, and the obtaining them made them forget their past troubles. And when every one had collected all the spoils he had found, and the ships had been provided with supplies, Afonso Dalboquerque ordered the captains to allot to each man a turn of duty, that water might be carried to the ships without those being endangered who carried it; and seeing that there was great lack of barrels for water in the ships, for all were cracked with the great heat of the sun, he ordered the captains to collect all

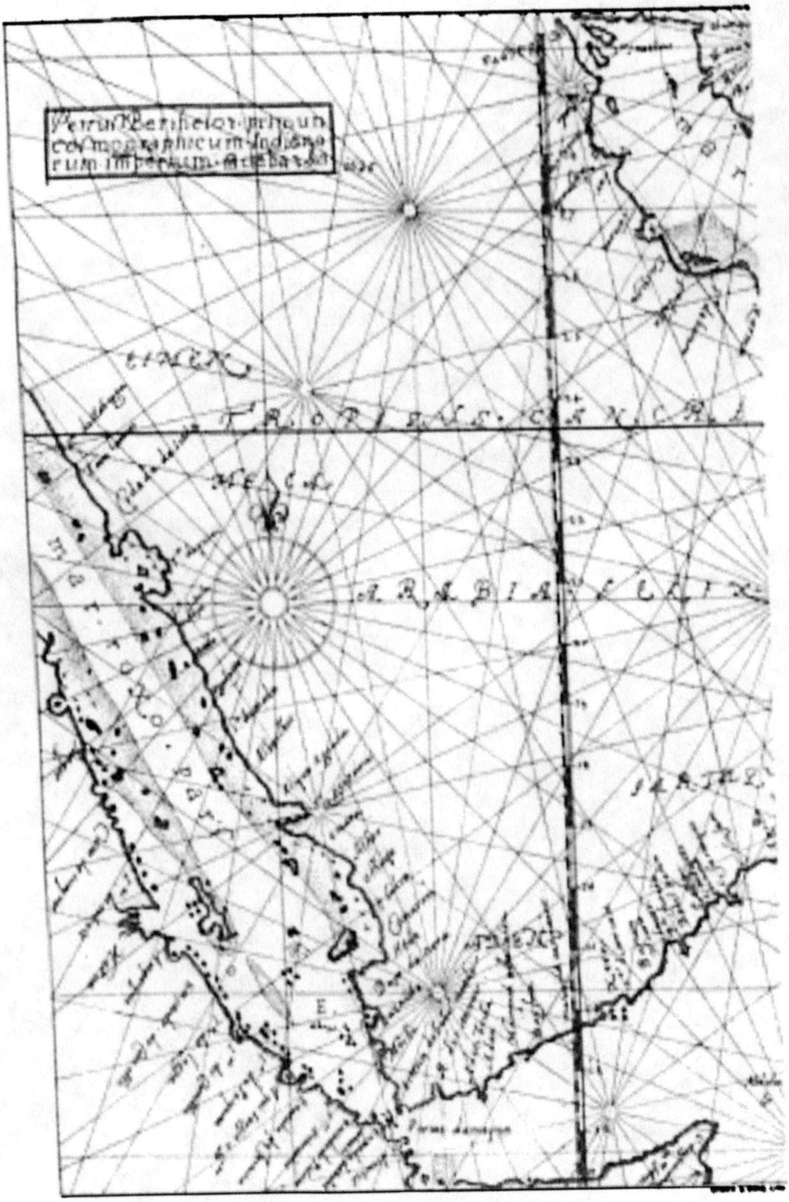

MAP OF

[British Museum, Sl

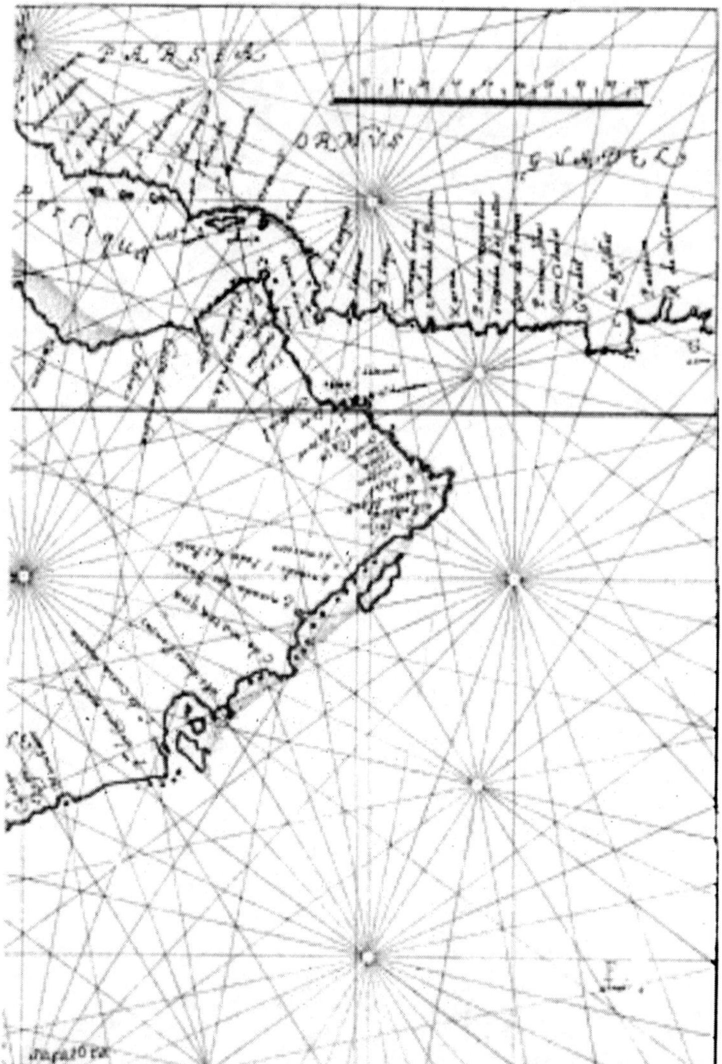

ARABIA.

ane MS. 197, *fo.* 154|

the wooden tanks which they found in the city (being used by the Moors in their ships for water), and those which were too large to pass through the hatches, he ordered to be placed on deck, for they were going to a country where they would make great use of them, and so, if it had not been for these tanks, our people would have had great trouble in sustaining themselves in Ormuz after getting there. When all was collected, Afonso Dalboquerque ordered them to fit out the ships with masts, yards, and shrouds, for there was great need of them. In this town there were taken many arms, bows, arrows, lances, and other weapons of iron of native workmanship, and much copper, thirty mortars, large and small, and much merchandise of every kind, which we burned, as we could not carry them away.

CHAPTER XXIV.

How the great Afonso Dalboquerque ordered the city of Mascate to be set on fire, and of the miracle which took place when the mosque was destroyed, and how he returned to the ships, and sailed away.

While the great Afonso Dalboquerque was ready on the bank with all his men to embark, a Moor descended from the mountains with a little white flag, and came up safely to him, and begged on the part of the rulers, since God had given him the city, and he had gained it like a brave cavalier, that he would be content to have killed their wives and children, and not burn the houses or the ships. Afonso Dalboquerque replied that for his part he was very sorry to see so noble a city destroyed, but it was their own fault, for they had broken the agreement which they had made with him, relying on the people who had come in from the interior, and, since this was so, they had no reason to demand anything of him; but if they desired to ransom the place, ships, and supplies yet remaining there, they might send him before noon next day ten thousand *xerafins*[1] of gold, and if they did not send the money by that time, he promised them he would leave nothing but dust and ashes, and that the people, whom they had on the mountains within sight of the place, might bear them news of its destruction. When the appointed hour was passed, he ordered the city to be set on fire, wherein were burned many provisions, and thirty-four ships in all, large and small, many fishing barks, and an arsenal full of every requisite for shipbuilding; and he ordered three gunners with axes to cut the supports of the mosque, which was a very large and beautiful edifice, the greater part of it being built of timber finely carved, and the upper part of stucco. When the supports had been cut through, and the gunners were about to go out, the building came down all at once upon them, so that Afonso Dalboquerque gave them up for dead; but, thanks to Our Lord, they came forth alive and sound, without a wound or a bruise, just as they stood when cutting the supports of the mosque. Our people were frightened, and when they saw them gave many thanks to Our Lord for that miracle which he had done for them, and set fire to the mosque, which was burned, so that nothing remained of it. Now, as our people had many Moors, men and women, prisoners, whom they did not expect to have any need of, and could not carry away, Afonso Dalboquerque gave orders that their ears and noses should be cut off, and that they should then be liberated. He then collected all his men, and went round the city to collect some soldiers who were wandering about at random for plunder, and came back to the beach to embark. As soon as the Moors, who were on the mountains, perceived that our people were about to gather themselves together, they began to

[1] A *xerafim* was worth three *tostões*, each valued at one hundred *reis*, therefore 10,000 *xerafins*=3,000,000 *reis*=3,000 dollars=£625.

descend, and Afonso Dalboquerque, observing their descent, remained where he was on the beach, with his flag flying for a good while, to see what they were about to do. When the Moors saw that he remained quiet, they came on more slowly. And our people, thanking God for the victory he had vouchsafed them, returned to the ships with great pleasure and contentment, firing frequently out of joy. And the Moors, noticing that our people were gone on board, descended the mountains in great haste, to see whether they could put out the fire which was raging in the city; but its fierceness was such that they dared not go in to quench it, being caused by the quantity of oil and molasses in all the houses.

Mascate is a large and very populous city, surrounded on the inner side with very large mountains, and on the seaboard it is close to the water's edge; behind, towards the interior, there is a plain as large as the square of Lisbon, all covered with salt pans, not that the tide reaches there, but the water which is produced therein is saltish, and converts itself into salt. Hard by there are many pools of fresh water, of which the inhabitants make use; and there are orchards, gardens, and palm-groves, with pools for watering them by means of wooden engines. The harbour is small, shaped like a horse-shoe, and sheltered from every wind; it is the principal entrepôt of the kingdom of Ormuz, into which all the ships that navigate these parts must of necessity enter, to avoid the opposite coast, which contains many shallows. It is of old a market for carriage of horses and dates; is a very elegant town, with very fine houses, and supplied from the interior with much wheat, maize, barley, and dates, for lading as many vessels as come for them. This city of Mascate is part of the kingdom of Ormuz, and the interior belongs to a king called the *Benjabar*, who had two brothers; between these [three] the land was divided, extending as far as Aden, and on the north reaching to the shore of the Persian sea, and from thence as far as the vicinity of Meca. The Moors call this interior the Island of Arabia, because the Persian Sea turns there opposite to the Red Sea in such a manner that this round land is surrounded entirely by sea, that is by the Red Sea and the Persian Sea. It is a very small land, and therefore the Moors call it the Island of Arabia. It had been all governed by a king called the *Benjabar*, and this man had three sons, to whom at his death he left the land to be divided, the eldest always retaining the title of *Benjabar*, as the father had done, and the other two acknowledging him as their lord. This *Benjabar* has dominion over Fartaque, Dofar, Calayate, and Mascate, and his boundary reaches to the land of the *Xeque* of Aden: the other two are situated on the coast of the Persian Sea, and one of them had taken from the King of Ormuz the Island of Baharem, where there is a pearl fishery, about five days voyage from the Island of Ormuz, and had also taken from him Catife, an island held originally by the King of Ormuz on the Arabian coast. In this land, which these lords hold, there are many horses, which the farmers breed for sale; there is also great abundance of wheat, maize, and barley, and great flocks and herds, and there are many who hunt with falcons about the size of our goshawks, and take by their aid certain creatures (*alimarias*), smaller than gazelles, training very swift hounds to assist the falcons in catching the prey.

CHAPTER XXV.

Of what took place between the great Afonso Dalboquerque and João da Nova, and how he set out from Mascate to the town of Soar,[1] and what passed with the governors of the land.

When the great Afonso Dalboquerque had returned to the ships with all the men, because he had been informed

[1] See the plan and description of the fortress of Soar, in Resende's work, ff. 133-136.

that João da Nova was determined to start off to India without permission, he ordered him to be summoned to his ship, and before all the captains who were present, told him that he had been informed that he was desirous of going off to India without leave, and deserting him in this war, when there was need of many more ships and men than were then available, and the more so, as his ship *Flor de la Mar* was so powerful that it alone was able to destroy all that coast, whereas he himself for his part was determined to set his face in the city of Ormuz, leaving first of all behind him all its towns destroyed, that no enemies might remain behind them. And although Afonso Dalboquerque had understood that the captains were in the league with João da Nova's intentions, as they were all getting so wearied with the war, yet he desired them to give him their advice on this matter. The captains told him that since he was determined to go to Ormuz and destroy every place that was unwilling to put itself under the King of Portugal, he ought to take with him not only the *Flor de la Mar*, but twenty ships if he had them there; and they said this because, if they had said the contrary, it would have been evident that they had counselled João da Nova to go. And with this advice of the captains, Afonso Dalboquerque received profession of obedience from João da Nova, and ordered him, under grave penalty, not to go away, but to continue to follow him; and he put up with everything without replying a word, for he was not innocent of the charge, and João Estão was instructed to draw up a notice of this, and lay it before the master and pilot. He then ordered the captains to return to their ships and weigh anchors, and sail along the coast, according to their usual custom. And as they sailed along, they passed by six desert islands, one in front of the other; and Afonso Dalboquerque, in order to make sure, ordered the pilots to keep to seaward of them, as it was night, and on the following morning they stood in closer to shore, not to pass by Soar, and the Moorish pilots said that Soar was further on. While they were in that latitude, a head wind struck them, and obliged them to make for land, and they anchored two leagues from it, and remained there all the night, and when it was morning they beheld a large and very beautiful town. Afonso Dalboquerque inquired of the Moorish pilots what the name of the place was, and they said that it was the fortress of Soar, and they dared not carry him to it, as it was very strong, and contained many men, both horse and foot, and if he was to be overcome there he would lay it upon them. But Afonso Dalboquerque replied that even although Soar were very strong, yet he would do to it as he had done to other places, and they themselves had better be careful, for in the chart which the pilot Omar had made, he had notice of all the places along the coast, and if henceforth they omitted any, he would order them all to be cast into the sea with cannon shot round their necks. He then ordered his anchor to be weighed, and stood as closely in to shore as he could with all the fleet, but as it was a rocky bottom, they anchored half a league from the place. When all the fleet had anchored, a Moor came at once from the place, and brought a message for Afonso Dalboquerque from the Alcaide of the fortress, and told him that the fortress before him belonged to the King of Ormuz, therefore he had better not make any intention of landing, nor think that he would do therein as he had done in other places by which he had passed, for they were in a position to defend themselves very differently. And as the Moor uttered this grand speech, those on shore began to parade the horse and foot soldiers, blowing trumpets and *anafijs*[1] without ceasing. Afonso Dalbo-

[1] A sort of (straight) Moorish trumpet.—*Bluteau; Vieyra.*

"Côos Anafijs os Mouros respondião".

Lusiada, ii, 106.

"Com toucas na cabeça, e navegando,
Anafis sonorosos vão tocando."—*Ibid.*, i, 47.

querque's reply was that the Moor might inform the Alcaide to beware what he was doing, for if he refused to put himself under the obedience of the King of Portugal, his lord, he might be certain that on the following morning he would be with him on shore, and take his fortress from him, and put him in chains. The Moor went away not very well pleased with this reply, nor were our party quite satisfied when they beheld so large a place, with a very strong fortress and so many people in it; but considering what had taken place in other parts, they relied on God Our Lord to help them. As soon as the Moor had gone off with the reply, Afonso Dalboquerque sent notices to the captains of what had passed with the Moor, and bade them make ready, each one bringing his ladder to scale the wall. He ordered also two guns to be prepared, and many axes and mattocks, and *alferces*,[1] and all the apparatus necessary for making a strong stockade, from which he could assail the fortress; so that in case they could not obtain immediate possession of it, they might yet be in such a position that they could assemble in the boats without endangering themselves, and this was so hastened on, that on the following day at noon all was ready and put into the boats. When on the point of setting out for the shore, three of the principal Moors of the place arrived with a message from the Alcaide and rulers of the land to Afonso Dalboquerque, telling him that they had of their own accord parted with two thousand horsemen and five thousand foot soldiers, whom the *Benjabar* had dispatched to assist them in defending his domain, for as they were not trustworthy, they were unwilling to admit them into their fortress, and since the King of Ormuz had not sent them the aid which they had requested of him, they had made up their minds to become vassals of the King of Portugal, and the Alcaide

[1] A provincial word, implying a sort of toothed or forked implement, "*Bidens*"; *Bluteau*.

was prepared to deliver up the fortress to him. Afonso Dalboquerque's reply was that they should say to the Alcaide and rulers of the city that he would accept the town and fortress in the name of the King of Portugal his lord; and that he was very glad to see that they had thought better of the message they had sent him, because of the grief it caused him to be obliged to destroy such a noble place as that was; but the accepting must be on condition of their paying reasonable tribute. The Moors were so dejected at seeing the apparatus which was ready in the boats to be taken to the attack of the place, that they no longer wished to protract the business, and told him that it was not necessary for them to return to land, as he could make whatever agreement he wished with them, since they brought a plenary commission from the rulers and Alcaide of the fortress.

CHAPTER XXVI.

How the great Afonso Dalboquerque sent a flag to the rulers of Soar, to be set up on a tower of the fortress as a signal of peace; and of the manner of its reception, and what further passed.

Inasmuch as the great Afonso Dalboquerque desired that there should be no delay in this affair, he determined forthwith to come to a final arrangement with the Moors, saying to them that as they were minded to become vassals of the King of Portugal, and put themselves under his orders, he was about to send them a flag of his royal arms, to be set up on the highest tower as a sign that they were his vassals; so it was necessary for them to go on shore, and tell the Alcaide and rulers of the place to come to the beach, with all the population, to receive it, and he would cause it to be taken thither. The Moors went away with this message, and Afonso Dalboquerque ordered Francisco de Tavora and Afonso Lopez da Costa to make ready their boats with gay flags flying, and their men equipped in the best armour they had, to escort the flag which was to go in his ship's boat; and he told D. Antonio de Noronha, his nephew, to prepare himself to accompany the flag to shore, and Jorge Barreto de Crasto, and Aires de Sousa Chichorro, and Duarte de Sousa de Portalegre, to bear it, with five men well appointed accompanying them, and João Estão, scrivener to the fleet, to make a note of everything that was done: and he instructed the captains that the persons who were to bear the flag were not to go on shore until certain Moors had been received into the boats as hostages, and that nobody was to enter the fortress except those whom he had ordered to take possession of it. When all this was arranged, the captains took their leave, and on reaching the land, they asked for six Moors to be detained in the boats, who were immediately delivered up; then Jorge Barreto, with the others of his company, disembarked, and the Alcaide and rulers, who were waiting on the beach with all the populace, received the flag with great delight, and began to march, the Alcaide of the fortress going in front, in very rich apparel, with a Turkish sword in his belt and a staff in his hand, clearing the way and striking the people, who were in crowds, on this side and that. When they arrived at the castle gate, Duarte de Sousa and the rest above-mentioned entered with the flag, and went and set it up on the highest tower, and when it was seen by the men on board the ships, they saluted it with all their artillery. And João Estão took possession of the castle for the King of Portugal, and closed the gates, without leaving any one in it, and a notarial account of all the proceedings was drawn up. This finished, all embarked again and released the Moors detained as hostages.

On the following morning the Alcaide of the fortress sent to Afonso Dalboquerque, desiring permission to enter therein, promising to obey the King of Portugal, and perform whatever he might command him. So Afonso Dalboquerque summoned the captains and some Fidalgos and noblemen of the fleet, and recounted this message to them, which the Alcaide had sent, asking them to give their advice as to what he had best do in the case. The greater portion considered that he ought to retain the fortress; for if he had a captain and some men in it, he would have, as it were, his foot upon the neck of all the coast. Afonso Dalboquerque replied, that when he found the fortress was so strong, he had determined to retain it; but, as he was resolved to go to Ormuz, and had neither ships nor men to detach for separate service, he had changed his mind, resolving to leave it in the hands of the Alcaide, and go away until he saw how affairs at Ormuz would turn out. And because this opinion of Afonso Dalboquerque was well received by all, he sent word to the Alcaide, that on condition of his continuing obedient to the King of Portugal, and becoming his vassal, he would give him the fortress. The Alcaide, anxious to come to the end of the matter, and regain his position as lord of the fortress, sent one of his servants forthwith with a message for Afonso Dalboquerque, telling him that he accepted the favour offered him; and, as the fortress now belonged to the King of Portugal, and he had revolted from the allegiance of the King of Ormuz, he hoped Afonso would make some provision respecting the pay of the men who were keeping guard there; for if they were not paid they would all desert. The representation made by the Alcaide seemed to Afonso Dalboquerque very reasonable, and he could in no way omit paying the men who were required there, as he had elected not to garrison the fortress with his own men; so he summoned the rulers of the place, and informed them that the yearly tribute due for the future from them was to go towards the payment and sustenance of the men whom the Alcaide required to keep guard over the fortress, just as they had hitherto paid to the King of Ormuz; and they must cause to be prepared a paper written in Arabic upon the agreement, signed by them, and by the Alcaide; while he, on his part, would execute a counterpart for them in the name of the King of Portugal, sealed with the royal seal of arms, and under these conditions he would receive them into the allegiance of the King of Portugal. The rulers hereupon went on shore, and summoned a meeting of all the people of the city and territory, and laid before them the demand made by Afonso Dalboquerque, and it was universally resolved to acquiesce in what was required of them. On the following day, therefore, in the morning, the paper was forwarded to him signed by all, together with a present of cows, sheep, and fowls, and he sent them a counterpart sealed with the seal of the King of Portugal, and to the Alcaide and to the two principal Moors of the place, some articles from Portugal. He ordered also Gaspar Rodrigues, the interpreter, to pay a visit to a captain of the *Benjabar*, who had remained there with thirty horsemen, when the others who had come to succour the fortress had been dismissed, in order to see our ships and the Portuguese, and he sent him a silver washing basin and a golden chain. When this had been done, leave was taken of the Alcaide, and the captains received orders to make all ready for departing on the following day.

The population of Soar is very large, the town being very beautiful and containing very good houses. There is a fortress of square shape, with six towers round it, having also over the gate two very large towers. The wall is of good height, and proportionately broad, placed close upon the coast in a large bay, which the coast there makes. The harbour has a very rocky bottom. Our ships were anchored in six fathoms, and from them to the shore it was over half a league. The fortress is so large that it requires more than a thousand men for its defence. They say they can isolate it with fresh water; for they have some close by. The situation of the fortress is very favourable, and when the tide is high the sea rises almost up to the wall. Within the fortress there were only the houses required for those who guard it. The houses of the Alcaide were very beautiful, he being a principal man from Ormuz, whom the late king ruined, and cast out of the city by reason of quarrels he had with one of his servants; yet for all that, he was a man well esteemed among the Moors as a cavalier. There would be about six thousand and upwards of inhabitants in the place, and five hundred cavaliers, the greater part of these armed with steel armour, covered with plates of iron, arranged after the manner of a roof tiled with slates, and they are strong enough to resist a shot from a cross-bow. The fore-quarters of the horses are similarly defended; their saddles are of Turkish style, rather high in the pommel; the stirrups also resemble those of the Turks; their spurs are pricks of iron or copper set in a plate fixed to the heel of the boot, and always so worn.

This place Soar contains more nobles than any other place along the coast. The land is more open from mountains towards the interior than the other places; its territory is very extensive, and all cultivated with wheat, maize, and barley, and as the country is thickly wooded, many cattle and horses are bred. The interior parts here are of the dominion of the *Benjabar*, and at peace with the King of Ormuz; and whenever any differences arise between them, and the people of the *Benjabar* attack them, they take refuge immediately in the fortress. The people of the interior are called the *Badens*,[1] and the greater portion of the horsemen are archers, but some carry lances and Turkish maces, while all the footmen go naked from the waist up; they wear hooded caps of felt, lances, and bucklers. The

[1] Badens, *i.e.*, *Bedaween*, or *Bedouins*, a term applied generally to the nomadic tribes of Arabia.

horses are Moorish, of a large kind, well shaped, and fleet. Great quantities of dates and maize are exported hence.

CHAPTER XXVII.

How the great Afonso Dalboquerque set sail from Soar, and went along the coast direct to Orfação, and how he took it.

Having taken his leave of the Alcaide and rulers of Soar, on the following morning the great Afonso Dalboquerque set sail, and proceeded direct to Orfação,[1] and that night kept well out to sea to avoid a large bay which the land makes there. On the next day, sailing thus along the coast, they sighted a small *zambuco*, which put off from one of the country houses lying along the beach; when he perceived it, Afonso Dalboquerque sent the boats after it to take it, but the *zambuco* sailed so fast that they could not come up with it and speedily lost sight of it. It was afterwards discovered that it went and informed Orfação of the approach of our fleet, and thereupon proceeded on its way to Ormuz direct. As they sailed then along the coast, they perceived a very large place, and the Moorish pilots from Melinde were not quite certain regarding the knowledge of the country; but a pilot whom Afonso Dalboquerque had taken on board at Çocotorá told him that the town in sight was Orfação, and in Omar's book it was so called. As soon as our fleet had arrived opposite the place, the small ships anchored close in to shore, but the large ones a little further out; and each one of them laid out two anchors, as the anchorage was not good. As they entered the harbour, the inhabitants made a great show with many men on foot and horse, and many camels, and

[1] Probably identical with the fortress, twelve leagues distant from Soar, called Corfacam by Pedro Barretto de Resende, who gives a plan and description of it, ff. 136-138.

there was a great excitement among them. Afonso Dalboquerque ordered the captains to make everything ready by night; for he was determined, in case the inhabitants did not come to put themselves in his hands, and make themselves tributary to the King of Portugal, to attack them on the following morning. All this time the people of the country, both on horse and foot, continued moving up and down the beach, with a great parade, skirmishing with one another, beating kettledrums *(atabaques)*, and giving their usual shouts, at one time making as if they would launch an *almadia* into the sea, at another drawing it back to shore, while the camels did nothing but go out of the town gate laden with stuffs towards the interior; and so the whole day passed until nightfall, without anyone coming from the shore to the ships.

As soon as night fell, Afonso Dalboquerque sent word to the captains that when they heard his drum beating, they should make all ready and prepare their boats. Two hours after midnight, to awaken them, he ordered the signal to be given, and the captains, being all prepared, came immediately on board the flagship, and as they approached it the morning broke, and all started in well-appointed order, straight for the place, wherein were many people: some on the wall towards the interior; many others on a hill overlooking the town; while some on horse and on foot continued to march up and down the beach. When our men arrived, they began at once to fire the mortars they had in the boats; and the Moors, fearful of our shooting, deserted the beach and gathered together into the town. As soon as the beach was clear, our men landed, and formed in two companies; in the vanguard went Francisco de Tavora, Afonso Lopez da Costa, and João da Nova, with some Fidalgos and Cavaliers of the fleet; in the rear, Afonso Dalboquerque with the other captains and the rest of the men. On coming up to the town, they attacked it in two places; and in front of Dalboquerque's company was Antonio de Noronha, his nephew, who followed up the Moors until he drove them through a gate; and when they got in, they left the small door open, and came to a hand to hand fight with lances. While this was going on, Afonso Dalboquerque came up; and, seeing D. Antonio de Noronha at the gate, cried out: "Ah! nephew, what a shame is this. Are you here too?" And, with these words, he covered himself with his buckler, and went in by the small gate, fighting the Moors with his sword; and he set himself with his back against the gate, and defended it until our men entered in a body, and there put many to death. By this time, Francisco de Tavora, with the other captains, had forced an entry at another part of the place, where they had killed many Moors. And when the survivors perceived that they were cut off on one side, and already worsted on the other, they took to flight, and our men pursued close upon their heels. And Afonso Lopez da Costa with his men in the front, and Antonio do Campo behind him, followed the Moors far up into a mountain, wherein they trusted to be in safety, by availing themselves of the stones as missiles; but the captains followed so closely upon them, that the Moors, not to injure their own men, left off hurling at ours. And because our men were enticed by the Moors to follow them, Afonso Dalboquerque hurried up with the men in his company, and collected them together, and returned with the united force again into the town, which was already deserted; and as he came near, he saw a band of Moors going out of the gate of the town wall, and he ordered Francisco de Tavora to intercept them, while he himself, with the other captains and men, followed him. So passing a palmgrove, which is situated just as one goes out of the place, Francisco de Tavora came up with some of the people who were fleeing, and spared no lives, and then returned to the position held by Afonso Dalboquerque, according to the orders he had received.

As soon as Francisco de Tavora was returned, Afonso Dalboquerque, perceiving that nevertheless the Moors made slow retreat, and were like tired people, unable to walk, dispatched Don Antonio de Noronha with eighty men, part carrying cross-bows and matchlocks, to pursue them and fall upon them fiercely, thinking to become thus possessed of all the spoils they carried, while he kept in sight, that he might render any assistance that might be required. As the Moors were now at some distance, D. Antonio followed after them at a brisk rate, and soon came up with those on foot, while those on horses, seeing the conflict between us and their comrades on foot, turned back to defend them, and wounded some of our men with arrows, among whom was Antonio Vogado, servant of the Constable, who was struck with an arrow in the face. But when the Moors on horseback perceived themselves evilly treated by our cross-bowmen and fusileers, they deserted their comrades and took to flight, and dared not come near us again. While, however, our men were thus engaged in fighting the Moorish horsemen with lances, those on foot had time to get a good distance away; so Don Antonio returned to the pursuit after them, and, when he came up with them, attacked them with lances, and put many to death, capturing women and children, and taking from them the spoils they were carrying. Afonso Dalboquerque, seeing that Don Antonio was proceeding in disorder, and that there was no more time for going forward, in consequence of the weariness of our men, sent word to him to hold back and return to where he was himself. And in Don Antonio's company were João Estão, Antonio de Sá, Pedralvares, Nuno Vaz de Castelobranco, Antonio Fragoso, Aires de Sousa Chichorro, Fernão Soarez, Lizuarte de Freitas, Antonio de Lis, João Teixeira, Antonio da Costa, Joane Mendez, and João Coelho, all honourable cavaliers, who at that time were not living with the king, but preferring rather to merit that honour by their own good service than for their fathers' or grandfathers' sakes, besides many others who fought right valiantly that day.

When all were united together, Afonso Dalboquerque ordered all the cattle to be collected which were wandering about in the plains, and the captains to take their stations on the wall to guard the place until he could collect the supplies that were so much needed. And while they were thus at their stations, many Moors came along the ridge of the mountain which leads over the wall, where Antonio do Campo had his station, slinging stones, and shooting many arrows; and as it was a place that our men could not well approach, being a very steep rock, Afonso Dalboquerque gave orders that five ship's cannons should be brought up and trained from the tower, which was close to the station held by D. Antonio do Campo, and with these they began to fire upon the Moors, who were scattered in front, and killed four or five, when the others, who saw that the artillery was too much for them, and that they had no protection on the mountain from the shot, assembled together with many others from the opposite side of the hill, and proceeded towards the pools just outside the town, and loosed some large stones down upon our people, who were just then getting water. The cross-bowmen and fusileers, who were stationed at the town gate to protect those who were engaged in supplying the ships with water, began to fire upon them, and knocked three or four of them down; so the Moors, seeing that they were hard pressed, retired that day and never came again. But on the following day, in the morning, there came three Moors, riding on horses and bearing a white flag, close to the place, demanding a safe conduct for themselves, under pretence of parleying with the captain of the fleet, but it seems that they did not want anything, for they never came again after the free pass had been accorded to them.

As soon as Afonso Dalboquerque got free from these

disturbances, and saw that the Moors were gone off together, he gave orders that the young men who had been captured there should be divided among the ships to work, and with them the captains began to collect what supplies were to be obtained, and these were very few. As for the old Moors who were of no use for work, he had their noses and ears cut off, and then let them go, so that all who had their lives spared were marked in this manner.[1] Among the Moors who had been captured here, Nuno Vaz de Castelo-branco took one, found in a house, who by reason of his extreme old age was unable to flee, and as he showed by his costume that he was an honourable man, Nuno desired to save him, and carried him before Afonso Dalboquerque, before whose feet he cast himself. Afonso ordered him to rise, asking him whom he was. The Moor replied that he was one of the three governors of the place, and being very old and unable to walk, his sons, to save their own lives, had left him in the open country and gone away, while he, to avoid the fury of the soldiers, had not ventured to wait where he was, but returned to the house wherein the cavalier had discovered him. Afonso Dalboquerque inquired of him respecting affairs at Ormuz, and he gave ample information about it, and related much of the past history of the kingdom, for he was very old and very well informed, praising the spirit of the Portuguese, and saying that he could not with truth deny that they were able to conquer the whole world, for having read the life of Alexander, who had conquered that country, he had not found that this

[1] For a native account of these brutalities, alleged to have been constantly practised by Europeans on the Malabar coast, the reader will do well to consult a work entitled "Tohfut-ul-Mujahideen", an historical work in the Arabic language; translated into English by Lieutenant M. J. Rowlandson, London, 1833. 8vo. At p. 103 is a section "Recounting some of the wicked acts of which the Franks were guilty". A copy of the Arabic text is in the British Museum (Additional MS., 22375).

hero's army had any superiority over that of the Portuguese. Afonso Dalboquerque was astonished when the Moor spoke of having read the life of Alexander, and asked him where he had read it, for he himself was well read, and well inclined to imitate his actions. The Moor then drew from his pocket a book[1] written in Persian, bound in crimson velvet, according to their fashion, and gave it to Afonso Dalboquerque, who indeed prized it more than anything else he could have given him, and accepted it, as it were, as a good omen respecting the determination he had formed of conquering Ormuz. He then gave orders that the Moor should be presented with a scarlet robe and some other Portuguese things, whereat he was greatly rejoiced; but much more so to find himself free, with his ears and nose entire. In this port they found no native or foreign ships, for all had fled as soon as news of our fleet reached them, and the merchants of Guzarat[2] had also gone inwards through the Persian straits, with their households and merchandise. And all the nights that our people spent in the place the Moors gave them so many alarms that they were tired to death, yet for all that they kept such a strict watch that the enemy could not have forced an entry, even if they had numbered ten thousand.

The captains having now laid in an ample supply of fresh water, not knowing how long it might be before they could get any more, as there was great scarcity of it at Ormuz, Alfonso Dalboquerque gave orders that they should collect their crews, and each one for himself set fire to the place, and when the fire began to seize upon the place, there was not a house nor a building left which would not fall to the ground. Thereupon they assembled on the beach and

[1] This was, without doubt, a copy of the well-known heroic poem by Nizāmī, entitled "Iskandar Nāmah", or the History of Alexander the Great. The author died about A.H. 607, or A.D. 1210.

[2] Gujarat (?).

embarked, giving many thanks to our Lord for the favour he had shown towards them.

Orfação is a large town of the kingdom of Ormuz, and contains very good houses; it is very strong on the land side, and the reason of it is this, that it was more fearful of being attacked by land than by sea. Many worthy merchants of Guzarat lived there. The town lies at the foot of a very high mountain, and on the land side it has a very strong wall, which is carried along to the sea; there are two islands within the harbour which improve it very much. In the interior are many estates with good houses, many orange trees, lemon trees, zamboa[1] trees, fig trees, palms, and all sorts of vegetables, and many water pools, which they use for irrigation; in the fields is much straw stubble, as in Portugal, and there are many maize fields. There were also many fishing barks, and many nets, all which were burnt; in the town there were also large stables for horses, and many straw lofts for their straw, for this port exports many horses to India. The country has a temperate climate and fine air. After passing this mountain, which overlooks the place, all the interior country is composed of large fields under cultivation and farms, and all this interior is under the dominion of the *Benjabar*, as the other parts are.

[1] Bluteau says of the Zamboa: "It is a kind of lime or citron tree, which yields a fruit of the shape of an orange, but much larger, and of a more deeply yellow colour. The taste of it resembles that of the orange, but insipid. It is called *Pomum Adami*, because it has on its rind the appearance of two bites, which the simplicity of the ancients imagined to be the vestiges of the impression which our forefather made upon the forbidden fruit, as though it had been reproduced upon this fruit for the remembrance of our disobedience. Others call it *Pomum Assyrium*, for they say that the first stock came from Assyria." The tree is probably one of the varieties of the *Citrus Medica* of Linnæus, with a pronounced warty base to the fruit. Vieyra calls the *Zamboa* a sort of pome citron, of a deep yellow colour. In Arabic the word is written *Zambūā* or *Zambōá*, according to Dozy, *Glossaire des mots Espagnols et Portugais*, p. 363.

CHAPTER XXVIII.

How the great Afonso Dalboquerque set out from Orfação to Ormuz, and what passed with the captains when the city came in sight.

The great Afonso Dalboquerque, having gone on board his ship, gave orders on the following morning to signal to the captains that they should weigh anchor and set sail; and while all were going on in this manner with a land breeze, a thunderstorm from the land struck them, and the wind dropped. So, because there was a violent current towards a bay which the land makes there, all the fleet re-anchored. And with this storm so much rain fell for the space of two hours that the water got in between the planks of the deck, which had opened by reason of the heat, and spoiled some provisions. They remained there all that night, and on the following morning the wind veered round to land, and they sailed along the shore as before. After two days they reached Cape Macinde,[1] and having doubled it in one day, by the afternoon they sighted two small islands, not inhabited, lying on the route to Ormuz; so when they were just opposite to them, a Moorish pilot (who had been taken on board at Orfação to be carried to Ormuz) advised Afonso Dalboquerque to order the sails to be furled, and all to remain with their foresails at most, for that night they would be off the island of Ormuz.[2] This

[1] Ras Mussendom, or Musandim. In Barretto's plan "Cabo de Monsandam".

[2] Ormuz, or Hormuz Island, 27 deg. 3 min. N., 56 deg. 26 min. E. See the plan and description in Pedro Barretto de Resende's MS., f. 155. A very interesting account of the doings of Afonso Dalboquerque at Ormuz may be gathered from Brit. Mus. Add. MS. 20901, which is a sixteenth century Portuguese MS., from the collection of Lord Stuart de Rothesay. The following account from the fly-leaf of this MS. will best show its importance:—

"Este Livro [me deu Manuel de Carvalho de Ataide no anno de 1714, o qual era . . . . (*erasures*) . . . . , e]se conservava sem pergaminho

same Moor related to Afonso Dalboquerque, when he found himself carried away to sea, that it was but ten days since he had come from Ormuz, and that the king was already aware of his approach, and had a large fleet to fight with him, and in the city many soldiers and many munitions of war. Afonso Dalboquerque was not pleased at this news, and commanded the Moor not to mention to any one what he had told him. The other Moorish pilots, whom Afonso Dalboquerque had brought from Melinde, advised him to go as before, and not shorten sail, for if he did he would not come in sight of Ormuz until next day.

The advice of these men was approved of by Afonso Dalboquerque, and he gave orders that the fleet should sail on as before, with all sails set, until midnight, when he ordered a gun to be fired four times, as a signal for striking sail, and all took in their mainsails and mizentopsails,[1] and as the sea was smooth, and the wind fair, they proceeded along with their foresails until the morning watch, when he

e com folhas menos no principio como está. He hua Historia do descobrimento e primeiras conquistas da India escrita na Lingua que naquelle tempo se falava, e com a má ortographia que os Portuguezes seguiam. Faltamlhe os primeiros quatro capitulos e o nome de seu autor; mas a marraçam, ainda que simples e de estilo antigo, parece sincera *e he muito mas antiga que Joam de Barros e Damiao de Goes* e chega so ate quando Affonso de Albuquerque conquistou Goa que foy no anno de 1510 e faleceu em Dezembro de 1515." Signed "Freire".

As I intend, on some future occasion, to publish this manuscript, or a translation of it, I merely in this place draw the attention of the reader to the arguments of two chapters, which deal with the present position of Afonso Dalboquerque and Portuguese affairs in Arabia:—

"Capitulo 77 (folio 166*b*). Como os nosos chegaram a villa de Orfacã e como os mouros a despuseram e se forã cõ suas Riquezas."

"Cap. 78 (*fo.* 167*b*). Como cheguaram há cidade de Ormuz e dos Recados q' houue amtre ElRey e o Capitão moor e da batalha q' houueram e como os Imiguos foram vemcidos e morttos muytos delles."

[1] A. Jal (*Glossaire Nautique*, Paris, 4to, 1848, p. 111) translates this passage thus:—"Quatre feux, qui étaient le signal pour amener les voiles, et tous se mirent alors sous une voilure nouvelle, composée de la grande voile et du contre-artimon."

ordered a sounding to be taken, and found himself in twenty-five fathoms, and hereupon he signalled to the other ships, to know in what depth they were, and all ordered soundings to be taken, and found the same depth, and thus they went along until two hours before morning, when they felt the land breeze, and in a short time the morning began to break, and they saw land clearly. Afonso Dalboquerque inquired of the pilots if the land he saw in front of him was the Island of Ormuz; but as it was yet dusk, they did not feel quite sure whether it was the Island of Ormuz, or of Lara, or of Queixome,[1] for all these three lie in a triangle. When, however, the morning was now cleared up, they recognised it as the Island of Ormuz, and the other two were in sight. Now, as the bottom was getting more shallow every moment, Afonso Dalboquerque became angry with the pilots, but they assured him that he had no cause for being alarmed at the lessening of the depth, for it was a shelving rock, and he would be able to anchor in the harbour in five fathoms. And as, when the sun rose, they were close upon the island, Afonso Dalboquerque conversed with the captains, and ordered them to go along the coast, and fly all their flags, and make ready all their artillery, and many weapons, and make all the men arm themselves, in order that, if anything should happen when they doubled the point, whence all the city could be seen, they might not be taken by surprise; and all made haste to be in readiness, and all the ships, one after the other, in order, doubled the point of the island.

Having doubled the point, when the captains beheld the greatness of the city, and the number of mounted men who were assembled on the beach, and many ships in the harbour well manned and armed, they became dismayed, and in that state of mind came alongside of Afonso Dalboquerque's

[1] These are called *Larequa* and *Queixome* on the Plan in Barretto de Resende's MS., f. 155. The Arabic names are *Lārek* and *Kishm*.

ship, and desired him to be cautious what he was going to meddle with, for that city was not like those others which he had destroyed, as many soldiers could be noticed on shore, and there were many ships, and these well armed, and in their opinion there might even be more than they yet saw, for many days had elapsed since news of his coming had reached Ormuz. He ought, therefore, they said, to take good advice in this business, and not come to any conclusion by himself alone, without taking the opinion of all of them. As Afonso Dalboquerque had been many days wearied by their importunities, he replied that he confessed it was a very serious undertaking, and one which required great caution; but as they were now got into the place, they wanted rather a good determined spirit than good advice. So he refused to hold any more conversation with them upon the subject, but he ordered Manuel Telez and Afonso Lopez da Costa to set their larger sails, and keep on sounding the depth. And if they found that the bottom did not become less than five fathoms, as the pilots had assured him, they were to anchor close to the Moorish ships, while he and the other captains would follow close upon them. Thus they all went and anchored close up to the Moorish ships, the small ships on the side of the land, and the great ships on the sea board. And as Antonio do Campo's ship was small, he ordered it to cast anchor close to his own ship, heading towards his ship; and told his master to cast an anchor and buoy it, so as to reach to a ship close to his own, which was the largest there was in the fleet. And when all the fleet had anchored, he ordered that a salute should be made to the city with all the artillery; and as it was now sundown, there was no more time for anything that day, except to make all taut, and all that night they kept a good look out. The shouting of the Moors, and the sounding of kettledrums and trumpets (*atabaques e anafis*) was so great that there was not a man who could hear what any other said to him.

CHAPTER XXIX.

Of the fleet which the King of Ormuz had in the harbour, and how it was arranged, and of the messages which passed between him and the great Afonso Dalboquerque.

As some days had elapsed since the king had received certain information of our fleet, and the destruction which the great Afonso Dalboquerque had wrought in all the places along the coast, he began to prepare himself to fight with him. For this end he gave orders to detain all the ships that came into the port of Ormuz, and added a force of sixty great vessels, into which he draughted off many soldiers and much artillery, with everything that was required for the undertaking. And among these great vessels there was one belonging to the King of Cambaya, called the *Meri*, of about one thousand tons burden, with many men and guns, and well equipped for its own defence; and another of the Prince of Cambaya, of six hundred tons, so well appointed that it required nothing from the king's magazine. And besides these ships there were in the harbour about two hundred galleons, which are long ships with many oars, but not very large, and they are armed with two large mortars in the prow, and packed with cotton bales, so high that the rowers are hidden from sight. There were also many *terradas*[1] (like the barques of Alcouchete) full of small guns and men wearing sword-proof dresses[2] and armed from head to foot, most of them being archers. All this fleet was rigged out with flags and standards, and coloured ensigns, and made a very beautiful appearance. The large ships were

[1] *Terradas*, or shore-boats. Barros (ii, 27, 4; 30, 1) uses the word to signify light rowing-boats employed in carrying supplies to Ormuz from the main land. The term is also applied to small boats for service in war.

[2] *Laudeis.* Bluteau quotes "hum laudel de laminas" *Barros*, ii dec., fol. 10, col. 3; and "laudeês de algodão," *id.* iii, 95, 2.

on the outside, and the galleons and *terradas* on the land side of the city, alternately arranged, the stem of one to the stern of the other; and in this order they had encompassed all our fleet. On shore, too, there were to all appearance along the beach fifteen or twenty thousand men, very brilliant with their arms, many of them on horses, and blowing their trumpets and *anafis;* and the shouting on land and on the ships was so great that one would think the world had come to an end.

As soon as Afonso Dalboquerque perceived the order in which the Moors had arranged their fleet, and that this time they meant fighting, he summoned his captains and inquired of them what he should do, and whereabouts he should commence, for his determination was, with the help of Our Lord, to fight the fleet, however great it might be, and risk his life and everything else for the honour and credit of the King of Portugal his Lord; and, therefore, he did not ask if he should do it, but how he should do it. And although there were many different opinions among the captains and the others, when they beheld themselves with a small fleet encompassed by so many ships, and were alarmed also at the great size of the city, and the numbers of soldiers it contained, so that they could no longer form any good counsel as to what they should do; nevertheless they agreed to fight, but first of all to communicate with the king to know his intentions.

Upon hearing this opinion expressed by the captains, Afonso Dalboquerque sent Gaspar Rodrigues, the interpreter, in the skiff to desire the captain of the ship *Meri,* which lay nearest to him, to give him a messenger by whom he could forward a message to the king; and the captain sent two, and made an offer of whatever else of which there was need. And by them Afonso Dalboquerque sent word to the king that he had come thither with the King of Portugal's fleet with the desire of serving him; and by reason of the tumult he observed among the men on board the ships, he desired to know whether there was to be peace or war between them. When the king had received this message, he forthwith forwarded the answer by an Armenian Moor, named Cogebeirame, who, upon entering the ship, found Afonso Dalboquerque and all the captains and nobles, armed, sitting on the quarter deck on benches covered with carpets, and all the rest of the fleet's company armed; and having made his obeisance (slightly disquieted) he said to Dalboquerque, "Sir Captain, the King of Ormuz hath heard thy message, and desireth to know of thee what thou wishest, and what thou comest to seek in this his port?" Afonso Dalboquerque answered him: "Say to the King of Ormuz, that the king D. Manuel, King of Portugal, and Lord of the Indies, desiring greatly his friendship, hath sent me to this his port to serve him with his fleet, and if the king be willing to become his vassal and pay him tribute, I will make peace with him and serve him in everything he shall command me against his enemies; but if he be unwilling, let him know that I will surely destroy all this fleet wherein he placeth his trust, and take his city by force of arms".

Cogebeirame took his leave with this reply, which was much reprehended by the captains, who said many things to their chief, as though they would chide him for replying so harshly to the king at a time when there was need of passing many compliments between them. But Afonso Dalboquerque, with his accustomed invincible spirit,[1] said to them, "Gentlemen, I am not the man to achieve so im-

[1] *Afonso Dalboquerque, com aquel animo invencivel que tinha*, etc. Camões, in several passages, alludes to the indomitable nature of Afonso Dalboquerque, as, for example:—

> "Albuquerque terribil, Castro forte,
> E outros, em quem poder não teve a morte."
>
> *Lusiada*, i, 14.

> "Mais estanças cantara esta Sirena
> Em louvor do illustrissimo Albuquerque,

portant an affair as this is with dissemblings and sentiments, but as a cavalier and great captain I will perform the duties entailed upon me by the orders I have received from the king our lord, and therefore fortune may incline whichever way she pleaseth, but I trust in the Passion of Jesus Christ in whom I place all my confidence, to break the spirit of these Moors and render their king tributary to the king, our lord, or they must take my head in their hands; and this is the best and soundest advice that in such a state and season as this we can take, for we are so placed that we can do nothing else; therefore let every one go to his ship and prepare himself, and when he hears one gun fired, let him up and do as he shall see me do." So Cogebeirame reached land, and recounted to the king all that had passed with Afonso Dalboquerque and how he had found him. And the king sent him immediately for Cogeatar and all the governors of the city, and related to them the reply brought by Cogebeirame, and the rest he had acquainted him of. Cogeatar, as he was the principal in the government, and the man upon whom all was dependent, said that the advice that the king ought to take in the business was to protract the affair as much as he could until the arrival of the fleet and soldiers sent for from the mainland, which could not possibly be later than the next day, as he already had information that they were on the other side; and they ought not, he said, to be frightened at the proud reply which the chief captain of that fleet had made to Cogebeirame, for it was to hide their fear by bragging, and he himself hoped to

Mas alembrou-lhe huma ira, que o condena,
Postoque a fama sua o mundo cerque.
. . . .
Se o peito, ou de cioso, ou de modesto,
Ou de usado a crueza fera e dura,
Co'os seus huma ira insana não refrea,
Põe na fama alva noda negra e fea."

Ib., x, 45, 47.

take alive all the Portuguese who were there, and make use of them in the war with the neighbouring people. This advice of Cogeatar was well received by all the governors; for by reason of the number of ships and men they had, they thought it would be great folly for our men to desire to fight with them.

So the king again sent Cogebeirame to Afonso Dalboquerque to say that he was highly delighted at his coming, because he wished to make a friendly treaty with the King of Portugal; but he desired to know, since he had determined to come to the port and make an arrangement for peace and friendship with him, wherefore he had destroyed his places that he had all along that coast, killing all the people that he found therein; for if he had received any insult from the rulers of these places, it was from him that he ought to have sought redress, instead of destroying them; and as for the tribute he had sent to demand, he would commune with his governors and officers of his revenues, and remit him the reply that they might agree upon. When Cogebeirame arrived with this reply, Afonso Dalboquerque sent forthwith a summons for the captains, and told them that they had many times complained of him behind his back that he did not give them any account of what he did, but now was an opportunity for them to advise him and reprehend him; for the reply sent to him by the king rather appeared to be dissembling than an agreement to give what was demanded, since he had made mention of the evil which his places had received at their hands. The captains replied that they had much reason to complain of him, for his coming to Ormuz had not been by their advice nor of their own will; but as they were now there, they would have to make some kind of convention with the king, because, by reason of the quantity of soldiers and ships which were in the port, they did not doubt but that they were very likely to be all undone, and since the agreement could be brought about without any trouble, they desired him as a great favour that he would use his best endeavours to arrange the affair peaceably.

Afonso Dalboquerque hereupon told them that he had not come thither to beg of the King of Ormuz, but to make war upon him if he were unwilling to become subservient to the King of Portugal, and that they had been there already three days, and all the rest of the time they might spend there without coming to any determination would be clearly a proof of their weakness. When this conversation with the captains was over, he told Cogebeirame to report to the king that he was very glad at the desire he had evinced for having peace with the King of Portugal his lord, for it would be better for him to do so; but this must be finally concluded without more words, and that as for his complaint that he had acted unreasonably in burning and destroying his places, the fault lay with his captains, who had endeavoured to deceive him, seeing that before he had made war upon them he had laboured hard for peace, and the proof of this was that he had not destroyed Soar and Calayate because those in command there chose peace. Cogebeirame returned with this reply, and as it was the policy of Cogeatar to protract this matter, he immediately sent Cogebeirame back again, begging Afonso Dalboquerque not to be annoyed at any delay there might be, for the king could not pay tribute without the advice and assent of all the lords of his kingdom, that there might not hereafter arise doubts about the payment; but that his men might come on shore safely and take fresh provisions and whatever else they required. This he did to gain some idea of the number of Portuguese in the fleet, for he was astonished at what Cogebeirame had reported as having witnessed in Afonso Dalboquerque's ship. As Dalboquerque, however, became more and more acquainted with the stratagems of Cogeatar, he told Cogebeirame to inform him that he had been there waiting for the king's ultimate reply three days, and desired him graciously to take good advice, and on the following day in the morning he would send him word of his future intentions; for unless an answer reached him, he assured him he would destroy his fleet, and afterwards capture the city by force of arms. And he dispatched the captains to their ships to make ready, and when they heard a gun shot, do as they saw him do.

CHAPTER XXX.

How the great Afonso Dalboquerque, seeing that the reply was put off, proceeded to attack the fleet which lay in the port of Ormuz, and defeated it.

Although the captains were not very well pleased at the reply sent by Afonso Dalboquerque to the king, yet having returned to their ships, they made ready their artillery and apparatus for assault, waiting for the signal which he had appointed. At the same time, the Moors, being alarmed at the consultations held in our ships, kept on hauling their cables, which were laid out in the direction of the city, to get further off from us. But as Afonso Dalboquerque perceived all that they did, he at once sent a message to the captains to go into their boats with armed men and splice their cables together, and lay them out with buoys close along the Moorish ships which were crowding away. The captains, though they were dismayed at the peril in which they found themselves, like brave and spirited cavaliers, set to work, and the master of the flag-ship, with fifty armed men, proceeded to place a grapnel upon the cutwater of the ship *Meri*.[1] The ship's captain, well aware of

[1] "Et le maître de la nef capitaine, avec 50 hommes armés, alla fixer un grappin dans la gorgère de la nef *Meri*." A. Jal, *Gloss. Naut.*, p. 792.

the reason for the king's delay, perceived the changed position of our ships, and called out from the quarterdeck to Afonso Dalboquerque not to be angered, for the reply would be sent very soon. And no less praise is due to the masters, pilots, and seamen, for, though fighting was not their profession, yet, being armed at all points, with great spirit and assiduity they carried out all the instructions given by the captains.

When Afonso Dalboquerque perceived the gleaming of the swords and waving of the bucklers, and other doings of the Moors on shore, who acted like people who cared nought for him, he understood by these signs that Cogeatar was determined to give him battle, and that there was no more time now for dissimulation, as they were now gotten into the place, but he would have to find some remedy for himself. He, therefore, made up his mind to attack the enemy before they received any of the expected succour, and put himself in order to make an assault on the fleet on the following day, unless a reply arrived, appointing the different commands of his ship to D. Antonio, his nephew, and Jorge Barreto de Crasto, D. Jeronymo de Lima and D. João de Lima, and all the remaining Fidalgos and king's officers in his ship. He ordered Nuno Vaz de Castelo-branco to take charge of the artillery and gunpowder, and advised the captains of the other ships to make similar arrangements, and remain in readiness and do whatever they saw him do. When morning broke, and Afonso Dalboquerque plainly saw that no message from the king was forthcoming, and that this delay meant war and not peace, he ordered a broadside to be fired. The bombardiers took aim so that with the first two shots they fired they sent two large ships which were in front of them, with all their men, to the bottom—one being the Prince of Cambaya's, the other that of Meliquiaz of Diu. Afonso Lopez da Costa, who was stationed on the land side,

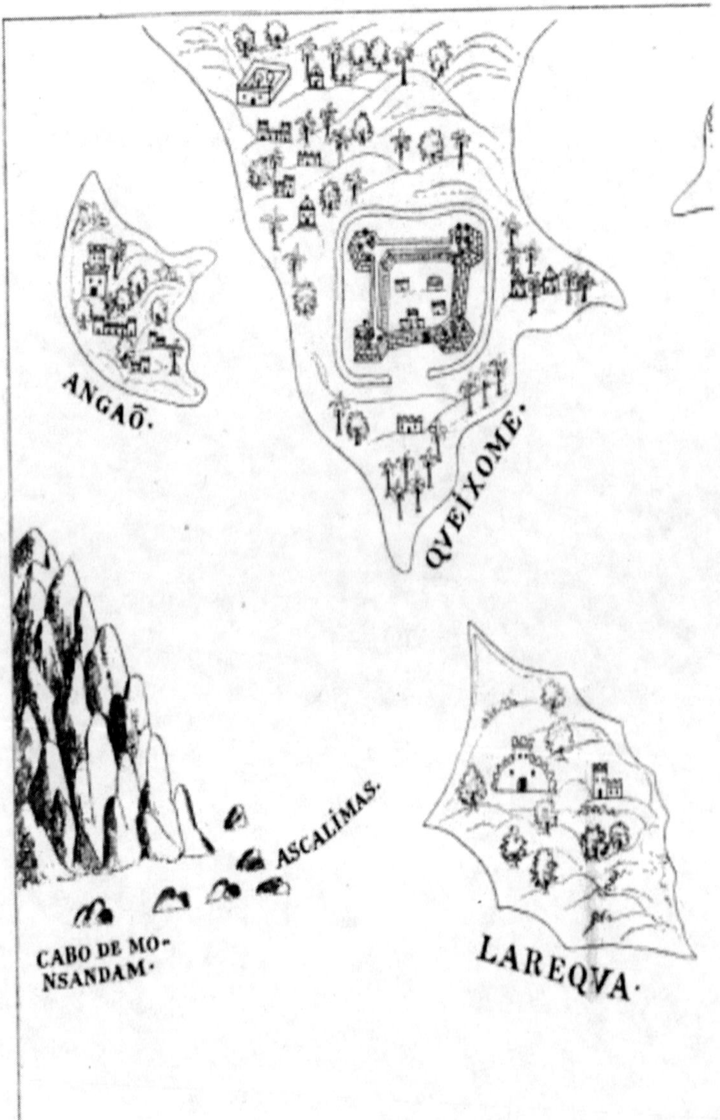

PLAN OF

[*British Museum, Slo*

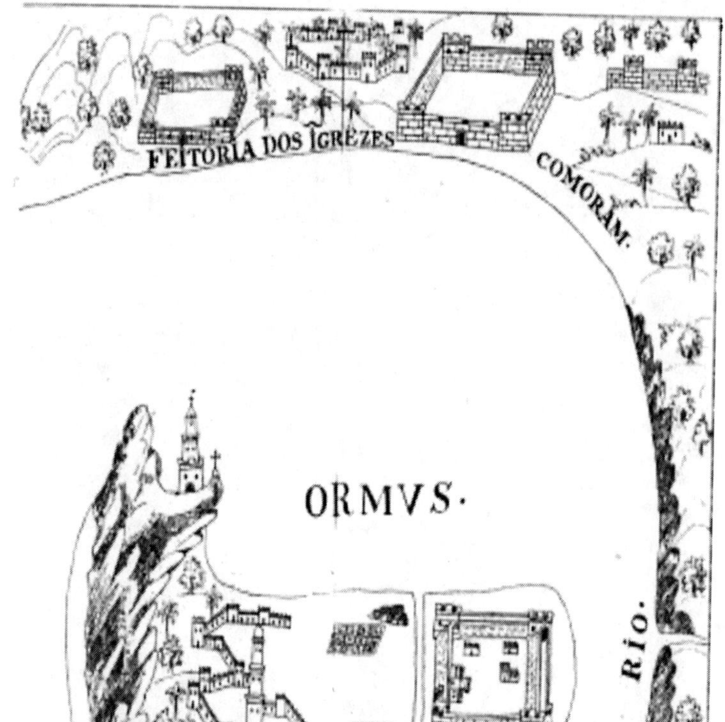

ORMUS.

ne MS. 197, fo. 156.]

vanquished and sent to the bottom some portion of the galleons and *atalaias*[1] which his artillery could reach. Manuel Telez, after having caused great slaughter upon some vessels, gave orders to let go a cable, which was laid out to the sea, and ran into a large vessel which lay close to him, and killed a part of the men in it, while the rest threw themselves into the sea, and those who were heavy-armed went down at once. João da Nova, too, with his artillery did great execution among the ships which lay along the piles; as did also Antonio do Campo and Francisco de Tavora among the galleons which had surrounded them, and all night long they kept on hooking their anchors together in order to catch the galleons in the middle of them. And although the Moors endeavoured to avenge themselves with their artillery, our men were so well fortified with their defences, that they did them no harm, except on the upper deck, and with their arrows they wounded some people.

The fight was so confused on this side and on that, both with artillery and arrows, that it lasted some time without either party seeing each other by reason of the smoke. As soon as this cleared off, Afonso Dalboquerque ordered in great haste to let go a cable which he had lying out seaward, and ran into the ship *Meri*, and killed many of its men with matchlocks and crossbows, and among them the captain (who was a principal man of Cambaya); and when Afonso saw the discomfiture of the king's fleet, and the unexpected victory which Our Lord had sent him, and the Moors throwing themselves into the sea from fear of our artillery, thinking, forsooth, that they could escape in that way by swimming, in order to repress them he left his ship and took D. Antonio with him in his skiff,

[1] *Atalaias.* Swift rowing boats used to accompany large vessels, and keep up their communications with the shore or the fleet. The Arabic signifies "a sentinel, a watch-tower". In this passage the word means "*guard-boats*". See Dozy, *Glossaire*, 209, 210.

and called out to the captains to take to their boats and follow up the victory. And the first captain who came up to him was Manuel Telez, and as his boat was the lighter for rowing, he got into it with his royal flag (which is now in the church of Our Lady of Grace), and proceeded, in sight of all our men, to set himself in the middle of the Moorish fleet, so as to be wherever he was required, and give orders to the captains respecting their proceedings, and there he remained without yielding, though well plied with arrows and gunshot. And he commanded Jorge Barreto de Crasto to get into his boat with Jorge da Silveira, Aires de Sousa Chichorro, Duarte de Sousa, Nicolao de Andrade, Nuno Vaz de Castelo-branco, and many other Fidalgos and king's officers with him, and go and attack the ship *Meri*, and if there were any men left in her, to put them all to the sword without sparing the life of any one.

So Jorge Barreto proceeded to attack the ship, and the first who entered was Gaspar Diaz de Alcacere do Sal, and as he boarded her they cut off his right hand, which immediately fell down there with the sword in its grasp, and Afonso Dalboquerque gave him of his possessions for life ten thousand reals pension. After him entered João Estão, scrivener to the fleet, who defended him from being killed, and Pero Gonçalvez, pilot, who received two such severe wounds that he had like to have died, and Nuno Vaz de Castelo-branco, who with his cross-bow wounded and killed many Moors, as long as his supply of arrows lasted. And after these all the others entered who came with Jorge Barreto, and three mariners from the flagship, and all united together fought with such spirit, that of sixty Moors who were left in the ship, unwilling to trust themselves to the sea, all lay dead stretched along the deck; and so the ship remained with the men whom Jorge Barreto left in it to guard it.

CHAPTER XXXI.

How the captains, after the taking of the ship *Meri*, followed up their victory, and of the havoc they made in the fleet, and how the great Afonso Dalboquerque proceeded to attack the jetty,[1] where he was wounded.

When Jorge Barreto had taken possession of the ship *Meri*, our men who were left in her began to use her artillery against the people of the city, who promenaded upon the beach, and did them much damage, while Jorge Barreto went to join D. Antonio, who was proceeding in the skiff of the flag-ship, and Francisco de Tavora, in his own boat, and all pursued some galleons, which were flying for safety to the island of Queixome; and with the artillery they had at hand, as well as with their matchlocks, they killed an innumerable multitude of Moors. In company with D. Antonio there were Francisco de Melo, Pero Gomez, Rui Diaz (sons of gentlemen of Alenquer), and Simon, eldest son of the Commendador of Almourol, James Teixeira, Duarte de Melo, Pedralvres Froes, and Antonio Vogado. These captains, after having routed the galleons and sent many of them to the bottom, went on towards the place where Afonso Dalboquerque was stationed, and he forthwith dispatched Antonio do Campo to go and take possession of a ship which was on the point of yielding; and with him went Nicolao Juzarte, his nephew, and Antonio Dabreu, and many others; and they fought with it a long time without being able to board it, for the Moors of the ship were Fartaquins, and made a stout defence.

[1] *Cerame*, a Malabar word for a kind of watch-tower made by erecting a flooring upon the standing trunks of four trees arranged in a square, over which is placed a roof of palm-leaves. Cf. "El-Rey de Calecut em seu Cerame."—*Barros*, i, 203, 2. In this chapter the word appears to be used for a kind of pier erected upon piles, and forming a kind of jetty, which latter word I have adopted in the translation of this chapter.

When Afonso Dalboquerque perceived them in this strait, he sent Afonso Lopez da Costa to their assistance, and he was accompanied by Antonio de Lis, son of Alvaro Gil de Lis, of Setuval, and Antonio de Azevedo, and Bras da Silva, his brother, and Alvaro Fernandes, page of the chapel to the king, and other gentlemen, who fought so well that they forced an entry into the ship, and killed a great number of the people in it, while some who could not stand against the fury of the attack cast themselves into the sea. João da Nova, who was close by them, seeing them in the sea, took to his boat with Fernão Soares, João Luis, servant to the king D. Manoel, and Antonianes, master of his ship, and all began to slaughter the Moors who were swimming, and killed many of them, while others were drowned; and thereupon he went to grapple with a large ship, wherein were many Moors who had not yet been exposed to our fire; and as he began to attack them, Francisco de Tavora arrived in his boat, and with him Manoel de Lacerda, D. João de Lima, Bastião de Miranda, Pero Dalpõe, Martin Vaz, Lopo Alvres, servant of the Constable, and Diogo Neto, and many men-at-arms. And so arriving alongside the ship, he on the one side and João da Nova on the other, they boarded her, and killed as many as they found in her, without sparing any lives. Afonso Dalboquerque, who was keeping a look-out over what was being done, perceived that some managed to escape by swimming, and ordered the captains to intercept them on the land side, and put all to the sword; and they did so, and gave life to none. So numerous in the sea were the Moors, who cast themselves out of the ships which the captains boarded, or belonged to the ships which our artillery had sunk, that as they could not find room to get off in the limited number of boats, and our soldiers were now fatigued with the carnage, they got away in large numbers by swimming.

At this period Cogeatar was advancing in a *parao*, well equipped, with its bulwarks covered with red cloths, and a half-round top on the masthead, inspired with the greatest fury of battle, encouraging his men to fight, and he carried with him many Turkish braves, their arms inlaid with silver and gold, and many archers, unknown to us until the last moment, when a Moor announced it to Afonso Dalboquerque, just as Cogeatar was already making for land after the defeat of his fleet. Thereupon he ordered the captains in their boats and Jorge Barreto de Castro to follow him to land, and attack the *parao* wherein he was. And when they came up with them, the Moors were so close to the houses that they cast themselves into the sea, and Cogeatar likewise with them, leaving behind in the *parao* many swords adorned with gold and silver, and *agomias*,[1] and brocaded vestments, and silk, all the spoil of the nobles, which our people took from him, and with it they returned to the place where Afonso Dalboquerque was. And when all were reunited, they returned again to the battle on the sea with the Moors who were swimming, and with lance thrusts and cuts they killed so many of them that, although, as they were tired of slaughter and unable to accomplish their whole purpose, some managed to escape, yet the sea was so tinged with blood that it was a fearful thing to look at.

The cabin boys and ships' servants, also, on their part, did nothing but thrust the bodies under water with grappling-hooks, and tear out their bowels, in such a manner that the slaughter was great among them; and there was one cabin boy who alone put to death eighty Moors. And inasmuch as all this took place along the water's edge, our people suffered much loss by reason of a jetty, which the king had made of wood, placed in the sea in front of the gates of the castle, with the artillery contained in it and with arrows.

[1] *Agomia*, a kind of poniard, like a scythe, used by the Moors.—*V.*

As soon as Afonso Dalboquerque observed that we were exposed to the artillery, he ordered his boat to be driven fiercely upon the jetty, determining, as soon as all the captains had assembled, to attack the castle; and there was not much doubt but that he would have entered it if all united, for the Moors were so full of fear at the rout they sustained, that there was but little to do to effect an entrance. But the captains had not been aware of his intentions, neither did Afonso Dalboquerque think it possible; but the victory and the rout of the enemy showed him what he could have done if all had arrived in time; yet with him none was found except Antonio do Campo, and both fought fiercely with the Moors who were placed upon the jetty; and with the guns that they carried in the boats they killed some of them at the castle gates, and these they saw dragged off at once into the fortress. The rowers in the boat wherein Afonso Dalboquerque was, on the return from the fight, launched it in such a manner that they drove the boat under the jetty, and there Afonso Dalboquerque was wounded, as were also Manoel Telez with an arrow-shot in the face, and Pero Vaz Dorta, and Jorge da Silveira and two bombardiers, and three or four more men; and in the boat of Antonio do Campo there were wounded himself and Antonio Dabreu and five mariners. And for all that these were then wounded, they fought so fiercely with the Moors that they drove them right through the castle gate, and in this all the captains assisted in their boats, and united together and disembarked, and marched along the city firing into all the houses. This battle, which our men had with the Moors on the sea, lasted from seven o'clock in the morning until three in the afternoon, and in it there perished an infinite number of Moors, and the gunners so managed that day (for Our Lord was thus pleased to help them) that there was not a single shot fired that did not send a ship to the bottom and put many men to death.

CHAPTER XXXII.

How the great Afonso Dalboquerque routed the fleet, and traversed the city, burning and destroying all the suburbs; and how the king sent two Moors in a ferry-boat to sue for peace.

Afonso Dalboquerque, not content with having routed and destroyed all the king's fleet, in order that nothing might remain undone, gave instructions to Afonso Lopez da Costa, Antonio do Campo, and D. Antonio de Noronha, to go in their boats and give chase to some guard-boats that were making off towards the mainland. And as they went favoured with the victory which Our Lord had given them, they pursued them, and sent all that they overtook to the bottom, and put to death all the people that were in them, and to others they set fire, and these went on burning over the sea, wherever the wind drove them, and it was a great sight to behold. And Afonso Dalboquerque, with the other captains, went along the beach, bombarding the suburbs, burning all the ships that were moored to the shore; and they approached so close that from the windows and terraces the enemy wounded some of the men with arrows and stones; and all the ships he met with in the sea, as they were collecting together to moor themselves to the land, he took and set on fire, putting all the people to death.

And as at this time there were some captains going about in disorder in their boats after this kind of fishing, he gave orders that a signal should be made for them to return to the place where he was, and all returned at once and came to land half a league from the city. As soon as Afonso Dalboquerque arrived he found Francisco de Tavora and João da Nova there, like persons of little prudence, with their men on land; and when he came up with them he told them that, as men to whom it was difficult and almost impossible to fight in that fashion they ought not to remain so carelessly on their enemy's land, without his permission, and commanded them to return at once to the boats, and ordered Afonso Lopez da Costa to disembark with his people, and go and take a hill whereon were large buildings and sepulchres of noble Moors, and to reconnoitre from thence all the country, and see what was going on there; and with him he sent certain gunners and other people to set fire to any ships they might meet with, and the houses in the vicinity. When Afonso Lopez da Costa had reconnoitred the country and saw that it was in a safe state, he set out from the hill along the side of the suburb with his people in sight of our boats, burning and destroying all he found; and Afonso Dalboquerque followed supporting him on the sea side along the shore, with all the captains, and from that point up to the city not a thing remained in the suburbs that was not burned, without any one offering resistance. And some Moors, who were minded to fortify themselves in some houses and defend them, died there, all being burned, while all the ground along was covered with people flying from the city to the mountains.

Cogeatar, finding all the fleet of the King of Ormuz routed, and his own bravado repressed, and fearing lest Afonso Dalboquerque should attack the city, now ordered a white flag to be raised upon the highest tower of the castle, in sign of peace. Afonso Dalboquerque, as he was going along the houses, perceived the flag, and rested on his oars at once and remained stationary, sending Afonso Lopez da Costa who was coming along the land, to collect his men; and as he was thus engaged, there arrived a ferry-boat with two Moors and a white flag, seeking peace; these Moors were natives of Ourão,[1] and had but a few days before arrived at Ormuz and brought news of the fleet which the king D. Manuel had sent to Turkey, wherein was the Count Prior as Captain-General, and by means of them the king of Ormuz sent word to Afonso Dalboquerque, that he put himself into

[1] ? Oran, the Arabic form is Wahrān.

his hands, and would deliver up the city to him, since he had taken possession of all the rest of his kingdom.

And as the sun was now gone down and the men had eaten nothing all the day long, Afonso Dalboquerque retired to his ships, and sent one of the Moors in the *almadia* to land with a message to the king, that before ever he would enter upon any business that the Moors had broached, he must send him ten principal Moors of the city as hostages, who without any more delay, on the following day at dawn, must come on board his ship, and he must know for a certainty that at the least attempt at deception he would order them to be cut in pieces and cast on shore. As soon as one of the Moors had set out with this message, Afonso Dalboquerque retired to his ships with all his men to rest after the labours of that day, and took with him the other Moor who was called Abedalá.[1] And when it was morning he sent word to the captains to come in their boats on board his ship, and they made their way to all the Moorish ships, which were at anchor without crews, and ordered them to be cut adrift, and to be set on fire. As the land breeze was blowing they drifted over the sea burning, so that it was a fearful thing to see it.

And as there were some ships which were among our fleet, and it was dangerous to set them on fire, Afonso Dalboquerque ordered them to be scuttled, and they sank to the bottom, after they had first taken out of them some of their contents for the use of the fleet. When this had been done he returned and they reassembled, and he told the captains that they must get ready, for if no reply from the king arrived before ten o'clock he was determined to attack the fortress and enter it by force of arms and take the king prisoner with all his governors. The captains retired to their ships, ill pleased with this determination of Afonso Dalboquerque; but they dared not to speak of it to him, and he went to his ship and sent for Abedalá and

[1] Abedalá, = Obaidallah, diminutive of Abdallah.

acquainted himself through him of the state in which the City of Ormuz lay, and asked him what was the reason that the king was unwilling to make peace and friendship with him. Abedalá told him that the king was a young man, and it was not his fault, but that Cogeatar, who was governor of the kingdom, had worked upon the king not to make any agreement with him, as he was quite certain of the victory when he saw the smallness of their fleet and fewness of the men; and that he had caused proclamation to be made throughout the city, that every Moor who killed a Portuguese should die for it, but they were to take them all alive, that he might by their means make war upon the *Benjabar*; and Cogeatar had summoned them on the day the fleet arrived, and inquired of them what manner of men the Portuguese were, and whether they were warlike, and what men they might bring in their fleet; and they told him that the Portuguese were reputed cavaliers beyond all the Christian and Moorish kings of those parts, and it was because they were so that the King of Portugal had gained possession of many places in the kingdom of Fez from the Moors; and upon hearing what they told him, Cogeatar began to threaten them greatly, but they answered him: "Sir, do not deceive thyself but believe me, if there is no sword there will not be any law of Mahomet."

And on the morning of the following day, the Moor who had accompanied Abedalá returned, and brought four principal Moors as hostages. Afonso Dalboquerque began to grow angry, and asked him why the king had not sent the ten Moors whom he had sent to demand. The Moor answered him that all the people of the city had fled or were dead, and, therefore, he had only sent four who were the chiefs of the land; and the king had said that if he were not content with this, he would come himself and deliver himself and all his household into his hands. Afonso Dalboquerque dissembled with him, and made no reply until he saw how the matter would turn out; but ordered all the captains, Fidalgos, and honourable men in the fleet to be summoned to his ship; and all being seated on the quarter-deck of the ship, which was very well adapted for this purpose, he caused the Moors to be brought before him, and one of them, who was the chief of the king's household, began to speak in this manner:

"The king of Ormuz, our lord, says, that in the affairs which have taken place between thee and him, which have produced so many ills, and the destruction of ships and men, he has no excuse to offer thee, for he is young, and has never entered into the troubles of war before now; and that evil counsels of his governors caused him to reject the peace and friendship which thou offeredst him, of which he is very sorry; and he would to God that this repentance of his had not cost him and his people and subjects so much as it has done. That this kingdom belongs to the King of Portugal, and he desires to deliver himself up into thy hands, and do all thou desirest, and he begs thee to have pity upon him and upon this people; and that thou wilt deal with him as a father with a disobedient son, who after his repentance pardons him; and that since this kingdom belongs to the King of Portugal, he hopes that thou wilt no longer desire to destroy this city, for it is in such a plight that there is not a house in it wherein are not felt troubles, deaths, and misfortunes. And Cogeatar, who is governor of the kingdom, and the rulers of the city, send to tell thee that they are thy slaves, and that the kingdom is thine, and they desire to be at thy command, and do all that thou wishest them to do." Afonso Dalboquerque ordered the Moors out without answering them, and consulted with the captains and Fidalgos who were there present what he should do in the matter, and all agreed that he ought to receive these offers, and that the Moors should remain in the ship until the business was settled with the king.

CHAPTER XXXIII.

Of the reply which the great Afonso Dalboquerque gave to the Moors; and how he sent Pero Vaz Dorta, factor, and João Estão, and Gaspar Rodrigues, interpreter, to land; and of what passed with the king and his governors.

The matter having been arranged in the manner I have mentioned, the great Afonso Dalboquerque ordered the Moors to be summoned, and told them before everybody that he was very desirous of serving the king provided he were willing to obey the King of Portugal, his lord, as he said he would; and, in order to put a finish to the matter, he would send Pero Vaz Dorta, factor of the fleet, to speak with the king, and he especially would desire them, until the man returned with the answer, not to be concerned at remaining there in the ship. The Moors replied, that he could do as he wished; for they had come of their own accord to do whatever he ordered them to do. Afonso Dalboquerque sent Pero Vaz Dorta to land, and João Estão, scrivener to the fleet, and Gaspar Rodrigues, the interpreter, with him, to tell the king and Cogeatar and the governors of the city, that he, in the name of the most high and mighty king D. Manuel, King of Portugal and Lord of the Indies, would receive the obedience which he had sent to offer; and that, until this was performed in the proper manner, he would hold his hand from continuing the war with him, so he begged they would conclude the matter forthwith, and not let there be pretences in this as there had been in past affairs. And after confiding this message to Pero Vaz in the presence of all, he withdrew with him apart, and told him to keep an eye unawares upon the disposition of the fortress and its entrances and exits, and notice how many men the king might have with him, and whether there were many pieces of artillery and arms, and in what order they were.

As soon as they were set out with this message, as Afonso Dalboquerque was not careless of the things which his duty required, and of the charge with which he was entrusted, and because he was not sure how this business would turn out, he at once commenced to provide himself with everything that was necessary to the attacking of the city, and ordered them to collect much timber from the Moorish ships to fortify themselves with palisades in whatever part of the city they might obtain a footing, and sent a watch to reconnoitre all round the island, lest any reinforcements of men, water, or provisions should come in from the mainland. Pero Vaz and João Estão went to land, and delivered the message to the king and to Cogeatar; and, as these were very desirous of peace, they forthwith dispatched the business. When Pero Vaz Dorta had returned with the reply, he said to Afonso Dalboquerque, in the presence of everybody, that the king sent to kiss his hands because he was willing to receive them for vassals of the King of Portugal, and accept their friendship, and he promised always to remain his faithful subject. And Cogeatar had sent word that he had been the slave of King Sargol, and now was his; and since the king had submitted to him and the land was his, he could do as he chose, and therefore he begged him of his grace to forgive him the punishment he rightly deserved for not coming the day before to submit himself: for he would swear by his faith that to such a course he never consented; but that the people and some Moorish merchant had made him do so, and if they were to blame at all in the matter, they should be well repaid for it. When Afonso Dalboquerque heard this reply of the king and Cogeatar, before ever he would take any steps in the matter with the hostages or with the Moors of Ourão, he withdrew with Pero Vaz and João Estão, and enquired of them concerning those things which he had desired them to notice. Pero Vaz Dorta told him that the king had about him some archers, and that the fortress within was strong and large, but that for its defence the King of Ormuz had need of more men than those whom they noticed about him, and that they noticed very good artillery of [gun]-metal, but small, and some other of iron; and that he had learned from some Moors, with whom he had spoken after taking his leave of the king, that his determination and that of all those who were with him, was to put themselves into their hands and do all he might command, and this he himself credited, as he found them very much broken down, like people who were conquered and overthrown.

At the receipt of this information from Pero Vaz and João Estão, Afonso Dalboquerque made up his mind to send the four Moors, whom he had detained as hostages, to shore, to prove whether in these words which the king and Cogeatar had conveyed to him, there lay any malice as in the other business now passed, as well as to show them his great confidence in them, making a virtue of necessity; for even were they to open the gates, and deliver up the city to him, our men were so few, that in the smallest house in Ormuz, wherein they could enter, there would not be more men than the enemy would be able to recognise, one from the other, and he hoped to remedy this by showing his confidence in the Moors, lest they should come to know how few men he had, and by remaining in his fleet he was more powerful and more completely master of the city. Having come to this inward conclusion, he liberated the hostages, and sent word by them to the king and Cogeatar that the factor would deliver his reply, and that, as regarded the allegiance which the king affirmed they were ready to make to the King of Portugal, his master, he would receive it in his name, and would pardon all that had occurred in the past war, as they were willing to be his vassals, and acknowledged the land to belong to the King of Portugal, and admitted that he might do within it whatever he pleased, therefore in this matter he would do whatever conduced most to the service of the king, his master; and, with this message he sent off the hostages.

Now, when the king saw them, not knowing the reason for Afonso Dalboquerque's releasing them after having demanded them with much pertinacity, he was not altogether satisfied at the reply which they brought him. So, on the following morning he sent them all four back again, to tell the chief captain that he would be vassal to the King of Portugal, and was ready to perform whatever was desired of him, and in the city and the whole of the kingdom he might command whatever was to the service of the King of Portugal, whose liegeman he was; and he again desired pardon for his past error, as he had committed it through evil counsel. When Afonso Dalboquerque considered the justness of the reply, he was desirous of seizing the opportunity, and sent off at once Pero Vaz Dorta to land with one of the four hostages, to tell the king that, as he was willing to become a loyal subject of the King of Portugal, his master, as he affirmed, he would leave him to exercise the government of the kingdom in his name, paying a reasonable yearly tribute for it, until he further determined some more serviceable plan. The king replied, that he looked up to him as to a father, and that the kingdom, the city, and all its revenues, were his, for he had gained them; so he could order to govern the city whomsoever he would, and to such an one he would immediately surrender the fortress, and deliver himself up into his hands, and he hoped he would not forget that, with great captains, to conquer was to forgive. And Cogeatar sent word to him, that he had been the slave of King Sargol, who had been King of Ormuz, as he had already sent word, and the king had always had great love for him, and had continually shown him many kindnesses, for the loyalty with which he had ever served him. But when he was *guazil* in Calayate, the Abyssinians who composed the guard of the king, who was son to King Sargol, revolted, and murdered their master treasonably, and plundered all his treasures, and remained in possession of the city; and when he came to know it, he had collected people from those parts of the kingdom, and came down to Ormuz and overthrew them, and put to death all those who were ringleaders of the treason, and set up for king this youth, who now reigned, to whom rightly pertained the succession to the kingdom, as he was of the royal lineage, being son of a blind king, who was there. Now, therefore, that he [Afonso] had obtained possession of the kingdom, he desired to remain in his service and do whatever he desired; but, if he would not permit it, he desired that he might be graciously permitted in his old age to go and live at Calayate, his native place, for there he desired he might end his days.

CHAPTER XXXIV.

How the great Afonso Dalboquerque arranged with the king the tribute which was to be paid, and how he demanded space in the city to erect a fortress.

At the receipt of these importunate justifications of the king and Cogeatar, Afonso Dalboquerque thought it a good opportunity to do the best he could for the service of the king, D. Manoel; and he made up his mind to desire the king [of Ormuz] to pay a certain tribute to him, and upon the settlement of this tribute, to send word, desiring space in the city to erect a fortress, because, with a fortress on land and his fleet on the sea, the affairs of Ormuz would remain in a more secure condition, and inconvenience and trouble would be avoided. On having come to this determination, his reply to the king and to Cogeatar, through the Moors, was that he thoroughly relied upon all they had told him, and he would ever preserve this confidence in them, from the love he had for the king; but they were to say to Cogeatar that he was much alarmed at his asking leave to retire to Calayate; for one of the principal reasons which had induced him to entrust the kingdom to their king was that he [Cogeatar] would have to govern it. If, however, this could not be so arranged, he would have to make some other disposition of it, and it must be on condition of paying some settled tribute every year to the King of Portugal, his master, towards the expense of a fleet which would have to cruise along that coast doing service for the King of Ormuz. Cogeatar sent word by the Moors to say that he would pay whatever was desired. Afonso Dalboquerque replied, that for all that he wanted to know what they could pay, and thereupon he would give his opinion. The king replied that he could not name any sum, but, as the whole kingdom was his, they would pay whatever he desired. When Afonso Dalboquerque perceived that the king was intending to make no offer, he sent him word by the factor and João Estão, that, since he left everything to his arbitration, it seemed to him, considering the greatness of the kingdom, and the nobility of the city, and the large sums which the custom house received, and the obligation which lay upon the King of Portugal to preserve and defend the kingdom from all his enemies—a thing which could not be done without great expenses—that he ought to pay thirty thousand *xerafins*,[1] every year as tribute, as well as to make good all the expenses which the fleet had incurred up to that day. The king, having considered the matter with Cogeatar and with his governors, replied, that the kingdom was quite ruined and impoverished, so that it was impossible to pay this tribute; but he begged very hard that he would be graciously pleased to accept six thousand *xera-*

[1] Trinta mil xerafins = £1875. See p. 110.

fins yearly, and five thousand towards the expenses of the fleet.

Afonso Dalboquerque summoned a meeting of the captains, and informed them what tribute the King of Ormuz proposed to pay, and asked them to decide for him whether to accept it. The captains began to give their opinions in favour of accepting the king's promised tribute, being firmly set in the desire they had that the affairs of Ormuz should not affect their departure for India, whereon they had set their hearts. So Afonso Dalboquerque dissembled with them, and told them to look well to what they said; for the kingdom of Ormuz was very large, and the trade of that city would increase more and more; and, as the kingdom now belonged to the king D. Manuel, his master, gained by force with his fleet, it would be unreasonable to let it off with so small a tribute, for even with thirty thousand *xerafins*, as he had originally demanded, he should not remain satisfied, so very valuable were the revenues of the kingdom. Nevertheless, the captains, in spite of all these arguments and others which he gave them, adhered to what they had said. And Afonso Dalboquerque, clearly perceiving that they desired to damage the business, no longer cared to ask their opinion about it, since, in spite of seeing that the king was willing to do all that was required by them of him, they advised that the kingdom should be delivered to him with such a small tribute. Yet, lest the matter should come to be known, and also that the governors of the land should be more willing to grant him space to make a fortress, which was what he desired more than anything else, he determined to fix for them a fair tribute, and to do this in such a manner, that there should always remain to the Kings of Portugal the right of increasing it whenever they chose, since the land was theirs, conquered by their captains and men with a great outlay of their treasure. So he sent word to the king that, on account of his desire to serve him, he was content that he should pay every year fifteen thousand *xerafins* of tribute to the king D. Manuel (provided he were willing to receive them), and to all his successors, and that he should give forthwith five thousand *xerafins* in hard cash (*mortos*) towards the expenses of the fleet; but that the merchandise coming from Portugal to the factory should be free of duty, and that bought by the Portuguese in Ormuz and in its ports should not pay more duty than that which the natives of the land paid. And, in addition to these conditions, he appointed others which seemed serviceable to the king, D. Manuel; and with them the king and Cogeatar and all the governors were quite content to receive the kingdom, and government of it, at the hands of Afonso Dalboquerque, in the name of the King of Portugal. And of this treaty they made two copies, the one in leaf-gold, of the size of a sheet of paper, made up like a book, written in Arabic, with letters engraved upon it, and its binding of gold, with three golden seals hanging appended by chains, namely, the seals of the king, of Cogeatar, his governor, and of the city; the other, by the king's desire, in Persian, which is the common language of the land, written on paper, with letters of gold and stops blue. Both these copies were sent by Afonso Dalboquerque, placed in silver caskets, to the king, D. Manuel, and the same ought to be in the Torre do Tombo,[1] unless by some carelessness they have allowed an antiquity like this, worthy of high remembrance, to perish. And Afonso Dalboquerque gave another copy to the same purpose to the King of Ormuz, written by João Estão, scrivener to the fleet, conformably to the power entrusted by the king, D. Manuel, to him in his instructions, signed by him, and sealed with the signet of the king's arms.

[1] The name of the Principal Repository of Public Records in Lisbon.

CHAPTER XXXV.

How the King of Ormuz sent to ask of Afonso Dalboquerque a flag to be placed on his palace in sign of peace, and what was done in the matter.

The agreement having been thus concluded, the king sent to ask Afonso Dalboquerque for a flag to place upon his palace in sign of peace and friendship; but, as there was no flag in the fleet which could be sent, he ordered the factor to go on shore and prepare one of white satin with a cross of *Christus*. And when it was finished, he sent word to the king by João Estão, that the flag was ready, and he might order Cogeatar and Rexnordim,[1] and the governors and officials of the city, and all the populace, to come down to the edge of the water to receive it with great rejoicings. He requested, too, that on that day no one should be permitted to work in the city, and that order should be given to get ready horses for the use of the captains, fidalgos, and servants of the king; and he told João Estão that when he had given this message to the king, he should make a hasty visit to the ships, and acquaint everybody that they were to come on board the flagship, to start thence with their boats very well equipped, and that he should tell the masters to deck out the ships with gay flags, and to see that the constables of the gunners gave directions for loading all the artillery, and, as soon as the flag reached land, to give the order to fire. He also commanded Jorge Barreto de Crasto to make himself ready to carry the flag.

When all was in trim, on one Monday morning early, on the tenth day of October, 1507, the captains came in their boats on board the flagship, and then and there Afonso Dalboquerque handed over the flag to Jorge Barreto, and

[1] This appears to be the Arabic "ar-raïs Nûr ad-dîn", or "er-reïs Nûr ed-dîn", "the Reïs, or chief, Nûr ed-dîn" (*i.e.*, the Light of the Faith).

told Pero Vaz Dorta and João Estão what part they were to play, and the order they were to maintain as they carried the flag to the city. So, having set out all together in the boats, with flags flying and covered with carpets, and firing shots from the prow, they came to land where were already awaiting them on the beach Cogeatar and Rexnordim, and the governors and principal men of the city, and the populace, with many horses for our men, well harnessed after their own fashion. And Jorge Barreto rode on in front of all, carrying the flag in his hands; and when he had raised it, then began at once the firing of artillery from the ships and boats. And when all were mounted they traversed the principal street of the town, and in front of all went all the people with many native musical instruments, shouting from time to time:—"Portugal, Portugal!" and, as the people were numerous, it seemed as if the world were come to an end, with their cries. Just behind the people came the flag, and Cogeatar, Rexnordim, and all the governors of the city, went close alongside of it, and the captains and fidalgos of the fleet followed; and in this order they passed through the principal street of the city, and turned into another straight to the palace, where the king was waiting for them on foot. Then all dismounted, and Jorge Barreto handed the flag over to the king, who gave it with his own hands to the governors to take, and thus they proceeded to place it on the loftiest tower of his palace; and when the vessels caught sight of it, they began again to fire off salutes of all their artillery.

And of this delivery João Estão prepared instruments, which the king, Cogeatar, and Rexnordim, with all the chief men of the city, signed: and the business having been thus concluded, the captains took their leave of the king, and proceeded to embark in their boats, and went on board Afonso Dalboquerque's vessel, and recounted to him all that had taken place, and the great triumph with which they had carried the flag through the city, whereat he was highly pleased, and rendered many thanks to Our Lord for permitting him to accomplish that matter according to his desires. On the following day the Moors sent to ask if he would permit them to take down the flag from the tower and take care of it. Afonso Dalboquerque gave his permission, and told them to take good care of it, because he hoped in God that under it he would have to assist the king in regaining many places and fortresses from the neighbouring kings who had always been at war with him. The king replied that he was the vassal of the King of Portugal, and this was sufficient to deter anyone from daring to trouble him. And because the document which João Estão had drawn up concerning the delivery of the flag had not been sworn to, Afonso Dalboquerque ordered him and Pero Vaz Dorta to proceed to the shore and tell the king, that he, and Cogeatar, and Rexnordim, and all the governors of the city, were to swear upon their Alcorão to keep and maintain all that they had signed; and the king was much pleased at this, and all were sworn accordingly, and João Estão prepared hereupon documents and letters testificatory, which Afonso Dalboquerque forwarded to the king, D. Manuel.

CHAPTER XXXVI.

How the great Afonso Dalboquerque had an audience with the king on the jetty, and what passed in these visits, and what took place with the sailors in the sea with the dead Moors, whose bodies floated on the water.

When the factor and João Estão had taken their leave of the king, after the documents had been sworn to, he informed them that he was very desirous of seeing Afonso Dalboquerque; and asked them to tell him on his part that he begged he would graciously send word where, and in what manner, he might see him. Afonso Dalboquerque sent word to him, saying that he also was very desirous of seeing him, and that there was no other place more suited for their interview than the jetty; for it was upon the sea, and was well adapted for their visit; but the rest could be arranged as he liked best. At this message from Afonso Dalboquerque, the king at once gave orders for his officers to make ready the jetty, which was all covered with many carpets, and around were carpeted benches, and there was a platform with two chairs of silk and cushions of the same suite. The day having been settled on which the audience was to take place, Afonso Dalboquerque ordered the captains to make themselves ready with their boats richly decorated, and all the fidalgos that there were in the fleet to accompany him; for it was in this manner that they had agreed Afonso Dalboquerque should go, as well as the king, with his governors and principal lords of his kingdom, who had come thither to serve him in the war. And when all were ready, Afonso Dalboquerque went on board his boat and the captains on board theirs, and all proceeded to the jetty, and when they touched it all the artillery of the ships was fired. As soon as the king was informed of the landing of Afonso Dalboquerque he came forth to receive him, accompanied by Cogeatar, Rexnordim, and all the others who were to be present.

Afonso Dalboquerque being now with the king, they treated each other with great courtesy, and thereupon sat down in the chairs, and the fidalgos and captains on the benches on the right hand, and Cogeatar, Rexnordim, and the lords who came with the king, on the benches on the left hand. At this time the king would be about the age of fifteen years, well fashioned, and of good appearance, rather short, dressed in a petticoat of crimson satin in the native costume, with a white cap upon his head, and a cloth girded around him, and a golden dagger, and a sceptre of gold in his hand with the head of crystal, set in gold. As soon as they were seated, Afonso Dalboquerque said to the king, through Gaspar Rodriguez, the interpreter, that he was much rejoiced to see him for the love which he bore him, and for the great obedience and respect which he had shown towards the affairs of the king, D. Manuel, his lord; and he begged graciously that he would always remain his loyal and true vassal, and thus acknowledge the benefit he had received from him in the king's name, seeing that he had restored to him the government of the kingdom and his estate as before. The king replied, that he was fully aware of the benefit which had been granted to him in the name of the King of Portugal, and he would always be his vassal, and remain in obedience under him; and after many speeches had passed, Afonso Dalboquerque, being desirous of taking his leave of the king, begged of Cogeatar and Rexnordim, and all the other lords, that they would be willing again in his presence to ratify and swear to the agreement they had made, for he also wished to be a witness of it; and they did so at once. This being completed, he took his leave of the king and all the lords, and proceeded to embark, and the king gave him a girdle of gold and a dagger ornamented with gold, and a horse very richly caparisoned, and two pieces of jewelled brocade, and to the captains and fidalgos he gave each a piece of silk. And from that time forward our people began to go backwards and forwards; for, up to that day, Afonso Dalboquerque had not permitted them to do so; and the king and all were so pleased that peace was concluded, seeing that the war had cost them so dearly, that they were happy to show all manner of politeness to the fidalgos and cavaliers who went on shore to amuse themselves, and they ordered that there should always be horses ready saddled for them to ride to the city.

At this time, eight days having already elapsed since the

battle on the sea, there appeared on the top of the water many dead bodies of those Moors who had cast themselves overboard on the day of the fight, as well as of many others who had died in the vessels at various parts. A cabin boy, who was in the boat of Antonio do Campo, seized hold of one with a boat-hook as it floated alongside, and as it seemed to him well clothed he began to strip it, and found on it money and a silver dagger. When the sailors of the other ships were aware of this, they set out in the boats about this part of the sea fishing for bodies, and stripped all those that they met with, and found on them money, short broadswords (*terçados*), poniards (*agomias*), mounted with gold, and silver, and jewels of people of quality and honour; and this went on for eight days, during which time the sailors made a good harvest. And on these dead Moors, who might be upwards of eighty in number, they found many arrows stuck into their bodies, of the wounds of which they had died, without having any other wounds of our weapons; for there was not in the whole fleet a single person who had a bow or any arrow, or knew how to make use of them.[1] It seems that Our Lord desired on that day to perform this miracle that he might show the captains, who shrank from engaging in this business, how certain a victory over their enemies they have who fight with true faith against infidels. And because the tide carried these corpses to shore, it caused to the inhabitants of the city a renewal of their past misfortunes; for some found there their sons, others their husbands and relations and friends, whom they proceeded to bury, with such great lamentations and weepings that it caused us great pain to hear them.

[1] Camões mentions this circumstance in the stanza already quoted at page 64.

CHAPTER XXXVII.

How the great Afonso Dalboquerque sent to beg of the king space in Ormuz to build a fortress, and what passed thereat, and how it was commenced where it now stands.

The assurances were now all settled on either side, and the tribute-money paid, as I have said; so Afonso Dalboquerque determined to erect a fortress in Ormuz, as without it, it seemed to him that the affairs of the kingdom could not be thoroughly safe. And having decided upon this, he sent word to the king by the factor, that the king, D. Manuel, his lord, had ordered him, in his written instructions, that when he had gained by conquest any place or city in those parts, he was to render it secure with a strong fortress, and bear in mind the treason and evildoings which the Kings of Calicut and Coulão had committed against his captains after an agreement of peace had been made and signed between them. Therefore, because he was desirous of avoiding these inconveniences, as well as of rendering the goods and people of the King of Portugal in the place more secure, he begged he would graciously take this in good part, and advise him where he should build this fortress. The king, being prompted by Cogeatar, replied that he excused his demand, for all belonged to the King of Portugal, and as for advising him whereabouts he might build it, in his opinion it would be best to do so in the island of Queixome or that of Turumbaque; for they were places where there was water. But if he desired to build it for the defence of Ormuz, it would be placed better in the port of Nabandé,[1] which was on the mainland, than in any other place. Now, although it was the intention of Afonso Dalboquerque to build it in Ormuz, where it now stands, yet, to dissemble with Cogeatar, and show him that he did not

[1] Perhaps Nobend, on the eastern coast of the Persian Gulf.

care to build it more in one place than another, he ordered Afonso Lopez da Costa with two armed boats, to survey the port of Nabandé, and gave him many stuffs from Cambaya to present to the principal merchants of the place. So Afonso Lopez da Costa set out, and on arriving at the port all the people of the country came down to receive him, with many earthen jars of water, melons, sweet apples (*maçans*), and other native fruits.

And after he had inspected the site, and divided the stuffs which he carried among those honourable men, he returned with his report to Afonso Dalboquerque, carrying him a present of fruits, which one of the honourable Moors of the place sent him; and he told him that the site of Nabandé was open sandy land, and close to the port there was three fathoms' depth of water, and from thence to Ormuz was about five leagues all shelving rock, which began at twenty fathoms and gradually diminished towards the port, and the water which the Moors used was removed a good distance from the sea-shore. On the day after Afonso Lopes da Costa had returned with this information respecting the port of Nabandé, there arrived D. Antonio de Noronha, who had been with two pilots to the island of Queixome to survey the port whence the Moors carried water to the city; and he told Afonso Dalboquerque that in the island there was a large place along the shore of the sea, in which the king had some houses, now old and tumbling down; and the water which was taken thence to Ormuz was from some wells which were some distance off from the shore, and all round the island was shelving rock of shallow bottom. While Afonso Dalboquerque was engaged in this discourse with D. Antonio, Cogebeirame arrived from shore, and told him that one league from the city of Ormuz there was a place called Turumbaque, and he ought to send some persons to survey it; for it might happen that he would be glad to construct the fortress there. And, although Afonso Dalboquerque was well aware that this Moor had been privately instructed in his part by Cogeatar, yet he dissembled with him and told him that he wished to go in person and look at the place. So, having sent off the Moor, he ordered Francisco de Tavora, Antonio do Campo, and Manuel Teles, to make ready to accompany him; and, on the following morning, they set forth early, and as they had a head wind, it cost them some trouble to arrive at Torumbaque, from which port the Cape of Maçandom is visible.

When Afonso Dalboquerque had now seen by himself and by the captains all the places which Cogeatar had offered him for the construction of the fortress, he gave an account of it to some persons in the fleet privately, whose honour he could trust, and whom he knew to be desirous of serving the king, D. Manuel, in everything. And having discussed the matter with them, and without giving any account of it to the captains (on whom he no longer had any reliance by reason of what had taken place with them), all came to the conclusion that, as they had to erect a fortress in those parts, it ought to be placed within Ormuz; for there it would be of more service to the King of Portugal when made than in the other places which Cogeatar had suggested. Having, therefore, made up his mind, Afonso Dalboquerque sent word by the factor to the king that he had caused an inspection to be made of all the places proposed to him for the site of the fortress, and by the information he had received concerning them, looking well at the conveniences and inconveniences likely to accrue to each, it appeared to him more useful that it should be erected on the point of Morona than in any other place; for, besides that it would be situated there between two good ports, one to the east and the other to the west, it would conduce greatly to the safety of his state to have the Portuguese very close to himself. The king gave an account of this message to his father the blind king, to Cogeatar, and to Rexnordim, and to the governors of the land, and as all were desirous of peace, they were well content with it; and he replied to Afonso Dalboquerque, that he was quite willing, from the desire he had of retaining his friendship, to give him the site he wished for to erect a fortress, and that he might send to commence the works as soon as he chose.

At this reply of the king, Afonso Dalboquerque was very much pleased, and sent word to Cogeatar that he should cause to be handed over to him all the masons there might be in the city, and everything else that might be required for the progress of the work, and servants in sufficient number; for he wished to commence it at once, and on his part he would pay whatever the king demanded. Cogeatar forthwith caused all the necessaries to be provided; and because enemies who are governed by force, if opportunity arise, scheme for their liberty, Afonso Dalboquerque was unwilling to put his whole trust in Cogeatar, and desired D. Antonio de Noronha, his nephew, to remain on land with eighty of the principal men in the fleet, for the security of the people engaged upon the work, and to keep along the shore two boats armed with artillery at the prow, which were to remain there always, close to the shore, ready to assist whenever there might be need of them. He ordered also to be moored there a *parao*, well covered over with an awning because of the heat, wherein he and all the other fidalgos and cavaliers might remain completing all the things necessary for the work, and he gave orders to Antonio do Campo to bring up his ship and anchor close to this *parao* to assist in all this. And that the men who were on land should not go by night about the city doing things at which the people might be scandalised, he enjoined upon D. Antonio that he was to go every night with all the men and sleep on the ship and on the *parao*, and keep a good look out from thence. He appointed, as master of this work, a gunner named Fernão Dalvarez, a good officer at the business, and arranged that the captains, two at a time, should take care to bring down stone from the quarry for the work.

When all these things had been settled, Afonso Dalboquerque went on shore with all the people of the fleet, and began to lay out the foundations of the principal tower on the twenty-fourth day of the month of October, in the year fifteen hundred and seven; and, as this tower was to be so high that one might from it have a view of all the mainland on the Persian side, he ordered the foundations to be laid very broadly, and in the same manner ordered them to set the walls of the fortress, to which he gave the name of "Nossa Senhora da Victoria" ("Our Lady of the Victory"). When once the work was begun, Afonso Dalboquerque made great haste to finish the tower, for his intention was, as soon as January was come, to go and take a view of the Red Sea, and he wanted to leave this tower finished up to the first story, that within it the Portuguese might defend themselves from all the men in Persia who could come, until his return to Ormuz. And in order that the workmen should do their duty with a better will, besides paying them every day that which Cogeatar had agreed on as their wages, he ordered that all who worked should be supplied with water and as many dates as they chose for nothing, and all were so pleased with this, that many came and laboured at the work without being sent by Cogeatar; and what with this, and what with the diligence which the captains and fidalgos showed in the service, the work began to increase very much in a short time. And he ordered that the principal portal of this tower should be made of three anchors of stone from the ship *Meri*, which was taken at that place, and the Moors would have given for them much money, but Afonso Dalboquerque was unwilling to give them up, but ordered them to be built up into the portal of the tower, that remembrance might remain for ever of the great victory gained there by the Portuguese.

CHAPTER XXXVIII.

How the great Afonso Dalboquerque made his fleet ready to go and take a view of the strait of the Red Sea, and of the reply he gave to Rexnordim concerning the tribute which the Ambassador of Xeque Ismael came to demand.

When the great Afonso Dalboquerque perceived the willingness and quiet with which the natives laboured at the work (which was not to be seen among the Portuguese, to many of whom it seemed a very unnecessary thing that the fortress should be built), in order the more to develop this friendly feeling with the native Moors, he ordered Pero Vaz Dorta, factor of the fleet, to take some of the houses in the city, wherein he was to collect all the merchandise which he brought, to begin the trade between us and the Moors, and he was to sell all the merchandise at a cheap rate, in order to attract them, through their cupidity, the more into friendliness towards us; and he gave him as scriveners, Pedralvarez, gentleman of the royal chamber, and Lizuarte de Freitas, and Antonio Fernandes Tassalho, servant of the Count of Villa Nova. And in order that the men who were on shore should always keep together to defeat the malicious designs of Cogeatar, he ordered the captains to prepare the mess for the men, according to their allowances, and each one was to have a man who should go and purchase all that was required, and this one could go about the city, having a written paper from the captain, but no other could go; and to execute all these things he made Martim Vaz an inspector, with twelve men, commanding him to take into custody every Portuguese who might be found without a permit in the city; and if he found any of those who had to go to market, with the writing of his captain, doing anything whereby the Moors might be scandalised, he was to seize him, and carry him before him for a sound flogging.

All these matters, then, being arranged in this order, as well as many others too tedious to narrate, Afonso Dalboquerque determined to careen all the ships of his fleet, and refit them with masts, yards, and shrouds, for all were worn out with the length of time that he had been in the sea; but as he did not put any trust in Cogeatar (inasmuch as, in the audiences he had with him, and in the completion which he had to give to all the arrangements that were necessary, he showed he did not deserve it), he instructed João Redondo, chief carpenter, not to lay up more than one ship at a time, and when that was finished and mended, and fitted with all that it stood in need of, to lay up another, so that if Cogeatar were to set in motion any treason, and they lost one ship, the others might remain to look after themselves. And, with foresight of this kind, carefully concealed, without letting anyone know it he proceeded in the work of repairing his ships and refitting them in all they required, just as if they were then setting out from Portugal; and simultaneously with this he ordered them to construct a galley *(fusta)* of eighteen banks of oars, meaning to avail himself of it on entering the strait of the Red Sea. And when he saw his fleet in this order, he had more happiness than at all the victories which he had gained in that kingdom against the Moors; for now that he had it thus repaired, he feared no longer the arrival of the fleet which was expected from Sal,[1] however great it might be.

Now, while he was prosecuting this labour, Rexnordim came to speak with him at the *parao* wherein he was, and

[1] *A vinda da Armada do Sal;* perhaps this last word, which I am unable to identify with any place in the neighbourhood of Persia, is an error of the editions for *Sul*, the South.

told him on the king's behalf, that from the opposite or further side of the mainland there had arrived a captain of Xeque Ismael, accompanied by horsemen, to demand the tribute which he was obliged to render to him every year; but knowing that he was there, building that fortress, he had not dared to proceed to Ormuz, but had sent from thence to demand the tribute from him; and he begged, therefore, he would tell him what he should do. Afonso Dalboquerque replied, that he might tell the king that this kingdom of Ormuz belonged to the King of Portugal, gained by his fleet and his men, and that he might know of a certainty that if any tribute should be paid to any other king, except the king D. Manoel, his lord, he would take the government of the kingdom and give it to someone who would not be afraid of the Xeque Ismael. He then sent to the ships for cannon-balls, guns, matchlocks, and grenades, and told him to say to the king that he might send all these to the captain of the Xeque Ismael, for that was the sort of money wherewith the King of Portugal had ordered his captain to pay the tribute of that kingdom that was under his mastery and command; he, for his part, would promise him, that as soon as the fortress was completed, he would enter the Persian straits and render tributary to the King of Portugal, his master, all the places which the Xeque Ismael held on that shore, and when he got there they might demand the tribute due from the King of Ormuz; for he would pay it to them in very good money.

As soon as Rexnordim had returned with this reply, it occurred to Afonso Dalboquerque that it would be necessary to content him and Cogeatar, and the three chief Moors with whom the king took counsel; for if these were contented and in his favour, as they were of the king's council, he would be able to get from him all he desired. So he made ready certain pieces of silver and red scarlet, and vermilion, and many rich cloths which he had taken from the prize ships, and some things he had brought from Portugal; and through João Estão, scrivener to the fleet, who carried the present, he sent word, saying he desired to be pardoned for sending so small a gift, for it was sent by one who had been on the sea for upwards of two years, but he had ventured to do it by reason of the great friendship which he had towards them. They received the gifts with great delight, and sent him many thanks for them.

CHAPTER XXXIX.

How the King of Ormuz sent word to Afonso Dalboquerque, saying that he desired to see the Portuguese musketeers fire a volley, and how it was done; and how Afonso Dalboquerque wrote to the Viceroy of India concerning the state of affairs in Ormuz, and what took place with the captains.

Rexnordím became so dejected at the idea of the boldness wherewith Afonso Dalboquerque had answered him, that as soon as he reached the king, they immediately prepared a guard-boat, wherein they sent a Moor with all those things sent by Afonso Dalboquerque, to be given to the captain of Xeque Ismael on his part; and the messenger was to undeceive him, and show him that they could not pay any tribute to Xeque Ismael, as the kingdom was in the possession of the King of Portugal. Six or seven days after this had taken place, the king sent word for Gaspar Rodriguez, the interpreter, and told him to say to Afonso Dalboquerque, his father, that he was very desirous of seeing his musketeers fire a volley, and graciously requested they might be sent to him some day. Now, as Afonso Dalboquerque was always on the alert against the evil desires and malice of Cogeatar, he sent round word to all the captains in their ships, to make ready two hundred and fifty crossbowmen and musketeers of the youngest and best drilled, and who knew very well how to fire; for he wished to show Cogeatar how much more power he had than what our men could have informed him of. For he was well aware of the coldness wherewith Cogeatar entered into the negotiations, as he was very sorry he had granted them a site for the construction of the fortress, since he had learned from the Portuguese with whom he conversed, that in the fleet there were very few men; and it was in this particular manner he desired to be more clearly informed of the truth.

Afonso Dalboquerque, perceiving these projects of Cogeatar all taking their origin from his accursed obstinacy, kept continually dissembling with him; yet, to comply with the king's wishes, he ordered some barriers to be erected along the wall of the fortress, and made them supply the crossbowmen and musketeers with all that was necessary for carrying out the design, advising also D. Antonio de Noronha, his nephew, who was on land, to look to them, and not permit anyone to fire except those who knew best how to do so. And when all was ready, he ordered Gaspar Rodriguez, the interpreter, to go and present these men to the king, and tell him that with these youths and many such others, whom the king, his master, would send him from Portugal, he hoped, with God's aid, to procure for him the restitution of all those places which his neighbours had taken from him. When the crossbowmen had reached the spot where the barriers had been placed, the king came down to see them from a terrace of his palace, and they fired so well, that they seemed masters of their business.

The king, after seeing them fire, took his leave of them, and sent word to Afonso Dalboquerque that he was highly pleased at the sight, and that for a long time he had not seen anything more to his liking; and he desired him of his favour, if he had not made any other arrangement respecting the ship *Meri*, to give him the refusal of her, and a pass that she might sail from Cambaya to Ormuz; for the city was so straitened, that it would be necessary to collect merchandise from one part after another to the customhouse, in order with the proceeds of it to be able to supply the expenditure that they had been put to. He also begged he would order to be returned to him some of his Moorish servants, who had been taken prisoners in the late war, and he would pay whatever ransom might be demanded for them. Cogeatar too sent word, begging of him another vessel, and some women and children, his servants, who were prisoners in possession of our men.

Afonso Dalboquerque ordered all these to be given to him, without receiving any payment in return, continually dissembling with Cogeatar, because he desired to finish the fortress. A Moorish captain of one of the ships belonging to the King of Onor, becoming informed of the liberality of Afonso Dalboquerque towards the king and Cogeatar, proceeded to speak to him, and told him that he was from the kingdom of Onor,[1] with which the Viceroy was at peace, as might be seen from two passes of D. Lourenço, his son, which he produced, and that at the time of his arrival at this port with his fleet, he (the captain) was discharging his cargo, but Cogeatar had taken his ship from him by force, and filled it with soldiers and artillery; and since he was in no blame, but had been forcibly deprived of it, as might be learned from Cogeatar, he begged as a favour that it might be ordered to be returned to him. And, although the Moor had but small right in what he begged, Afonso Dalboquerque wished to preserve inviolate the safe pass of D. Lourenço, and ordered the restitution to be made, and a safe pass that the ship might make the voyage; and by this Moor he forwarded a letter to the Viceroy, giving him an account of what he had done, and the determination he had come to, begging him at once to send reinforcement of men,

[1] Honore, or Honawar, in the Bombay Presidency, 14 deg. 17 min. N., 74 deg. 27 min. E.

small vessels, galleys, and munitions of war, and adding that he did not send this despatch by one of his own ships, by reason of the great need he had for them. Of this letter he gave a private relation to Antonio do Campo, who kept the secret so well that Cogeatar forthwith learned all about it, and all the things which he had sent to beg of the Viceroy, and all the other intentions he had. The captains also, and fidalgos of the fleet, because Antonio do Campo gave them to understand that in the letter there were many things prejudicial to them (though really not so), became very wroth with Afonso Dalboquerque; and because of the desires they entertained of going to India, already being wearied with the labours of that war, they began henceforth to do things which disgusted him.

CHAPTER XL.

Of the speech which the great Afonso Dalboquerque made to the captains upon the insubordination which they evinced; and of the complaints they made to him; and of some words that passed with them thereupon.

When the month of January was come, wherein the great Afonso Dalboquerque had determined to make his way to the Straits, the chief tower being already in a sufficiently forward state to be able to protect itself, and his fleet filled with all things necessary for the journey, he ordered Manuel Telez to load his ship with all the provisions that could be procured, to relieve the fortress of Çocotora on the way, and with some medicines and drugs for the sick. And he ordered the factor to purchase all the goods which Manuel Telez put down on a roll; which he did with great diligence, and laded the ship, and handed over everything to the master in the presence of the scrivener. When Afonso Dalboquerque had despatched the factor to set about this business, he went on shore to see the progress of the fortress, and the captains went immediately to him; and, as he had for some time past been aware that they murmured at the construction of the fortress, that he might be more certain of their intentions, he drew himself away along the shore with Manuel Telez, Francisco de Tavora, and Afonso Lopez da Costa, who were there, Jorge Barreto de Castro his cousin being also present, and said to them, that they now saw in what a state the affairs at Ormuz were situated, and he would beg them to tell him whether it was more serviceable to the king to finish the fortress or to sail for the Cape of Guardafum, for he had the fleet all ready and well prepared for the one course or the other.

The captains replied, that they were quite well aware of the state of affairs at Ormuz; but, nevertheless, in their opinion, it would be of more service to the king for them to make their way to the Cape of Guardafum, and lie in wait for the ships coming from India with spices for the Straits, than to stay building a fortress, which, as soon as it was left, would be taken by the Moors; and even if he left men in it they could not be sufficient in number to be able to defend it from the power of the King of Ormuz. Jorge Barreto, however, was of opinion that he ought to insure the safety of affairs at Ormuz, and complete the fortress which he had commenced; for it was a very important business in the service of the King of Portugal. Afonso Dalboquerque sided with this advice of Jorge Barreto, though he would not disclose to him any of his own intentions. And when Afonso Lopez da Costa perceived that Afonso Dalboquerque agreed with the opinion given by Jorge Barreto, he began to have angry words with him, and told him that this business was so important and of such weight, that it was imperative to set about it with slowness and circumspection; and since Antonio do Campo, and João da Nova were not present, he ought to send for them, and all being by, to arrange what should be done, because, in his opinion, it was bad policy to retain Ormuz. Afonso Dalboquerque dissembled with him, and walked away to the *parao*, where he had taken up his quarters now some time, without giving him a word in reply. Afonso Lopez da Costa, and Francisco de Tavora, and Manuel Telez, were so disheartened at this conversation, and at the small account Afonso Dalboquerque had made of them, that they proceeded to coalesce with João da Nova and with Antonio do Campo forthwith; and on the morning of the following day they sent him a written remonstrance (by no means necessary), whereat Afonso Dalboquerque was much annoyed; yet, from his urgent desire of completing the affairs at Ormuz, he dissembled with them, and destroyed the remonstrance without punishing them for it, as they deserved; but, with great forbearance, he sent word to them by João Estão that he begged they would so keep secret the state of affairs, that Cogeatar might not come to know of it, for they were at a point when it behoved them very much for the service of the King of Portugal to remain all of them of one mind and one will; for Cogeatar was so discreet, and possessed such means of obtaining information about everything, that he knew very well how much they desired to leave their enterprise there, and proceed to India, and that they had advised him not to construct the fortress; but that Cogeatar should not be made aware of their weakness, he ordered them to spread the report that all the differences that existed between them were because they were very angry at his not giving up to them the ships in which they had a share.

CHAPTER XLI.

How the captains made another remonstrance to the great Afonso Dalboquerque, and all signed it; and what he did thereupon, and what else passed with him.

The captains, upon intelligence that the great Afonso Dalboquerque had destroyed their remonstrance, in a few days' time, when he was in the principal tower, giving orders about some things necessary for the work, sent to him by Antonio Fernandes, scrivener of the ship commanded by Francisco de Tavora, another remonstrance, signed by all except João da Nova, who refused to sign. Afonso Dalboquerque, being angry with them and their conduct, took the remonstrance folded up, just as it was given to him, without reading it, and ordered it to be placed beneath a stone of the doorway of the tower, which was just then being laid, which the mariners ever afterwards named the "doorway of the remonstrances"; and the captains became so angry at this that from henceforth they laboured continually to find means to fall out with him; and all they talked about when they met together, was how to injure the progress of affairs at Ormuz, and they said that he was a traitor, and was constructing the fortress to elevate himself by its means, and make himself lord of the kingdom, and that it was all their own fault, since they had agreed that the fortress should be built, though it was very injurious to the king's interest, and that in the letter he had written to the viceroy (and of this Antonio do Campo was a true witness), he had sent word relating all sorts of evil stories about them, depriving them of their honourable character and services; and in these conversations they used to reprove João da Nova, asking him why he did not go off to India, as he was not under any obligation to remain. And, not content with these consultations which they held among themselves, each one of them in his own particular ship persuaded the seamen to take his part against Afonso Dalboquerque, affirming to them that he had robbed them of their share in the twenty thousand *xerafins* paid by way of tribute by the king; and that the king, D. Manoel, had given him written instructions in his orders, that of the first tribute which the conquered kings might pay, he was to give a share to every man in the fleet, but he had seized upon all of it for himself, in order to rise up in rebellion with the fortress as soon as it was completed, for he never intended to go back again to Portugal. When Afonso Dalboquerque became aware of these councils and consultations, by means of which the captains were labouring to procure all the men to rebel against him, and found that it was not sufficient to rouse their spirit for the business, to have told them frequently how well it would be to see in the windows of that fortress many ladies and bands of music, and to think of the great pleasure the king, D. Manoel, would experience when he knew that they had obtained possession of the kingdom of Ormuz, and built a fortress in it, thinking by these means he would excite in them a pleasure at the idea of helping them,—and because the chief reason at which they were dissatisfied with him was the letter which he had written to the viceroy, he ordered them to be sent for, and showed it to them, telling them they might see by it that it was not true what Antonio do Campo had told them, and he made to them many other justifying statements and explanations, as far as he could apologise, but they would receive none of them; but rather, like proud and overbearing men, gave him to understand in as many words, that that was not the letter, but he had written another. And they were so indignant at what Antonio do Campo had said of the letter, though it was not true, that Afonso Dalboquerque tore it up before them, and told them to write another of their own choice, and he would sign it; and so he parted from them, very much displeased at their refusing to accept his real exculpatory statements; and the principal in all this affair was Jorge Barreto, whom the others had already drawn quite over to their side. When Afonso Dalboquerque was departed, they ordered João Lopez, servant to Francisco de Tavora, to collect the pieces of the letter; and, although nothing more was written in it than an account to the viceroy of the then state of affairs at Ormuz, and how he had determined to maintain authority there, with a request that men, arms, and artillery might be sent him, they, perceiving this determination of Afonso Dalboquerque, agreed, as the matter was very important, not to go to India for three years, and to give up loading their holds, as they had arranged, and from thenceforth to plot all the more mischief against him.

CHAPTER XLII.

Of what the great Afonso Dalboquerque did with the masters, pilots, and all the other seamen whom the captains had incited to mutiny against him.

Now that the great Afonso Dalboquerque was aware that the captains had incited to mutiny all the men in their ships, principally masters, pilots, mariners, and gunners, who were the people of whom he made the most account, for they were always the best in the work upon the fortress, in order to remove all disaffection from them, he ordered all of them to be summoned, and showed them the instructions he carried from the king, D. Manoel, and told them that it had come to his knowledge how the captains incited them to anger against him, by saying that he had robbed them of their shares in the fifteen thousand[1] *xerafins*, paid as tribute by the King of Ormuz, and that by these instructions, as he demonstrated to them, they might see what the king's

[1] Twenty thousand, p. 153.

pleasure was in this matter, and he was not the man to appropriate anything except what belonged to himself, but that, on the contrary, he was willing to deposit as much as their claims would amount to with two responsible men, until the viceroy should decide the issue of the affair. But as they had been incited to mutiny by their captains, they would not accept any of his proposals, and began with loud voices and great tumult to cry out that they would not labour at the works, nor yet fight, as long as he refused to pay them their dues.

Afonso Dalboquerque replied to them very quietly, telling them that he excused their insubordination, and they must remember that they were Portuguese, and placed in the midst of enemies, very far from their own country, and that it would not do to have among them any feeling except profound peace and amicable feeling, for Cogeatar was very thoroughly cognisant of everything that took place in the fleet, and that they must not put any confidence in what their captains had advised them to do, for they were getting angry at the long war, and anxious to get to India, in order to fill up their cargoes; that what was their rightful due he would not withhold from them; that they ought to bear in mind how, contrary to the king's instructions, he had given them permission to make free booty in all the towns he had captured, whereby they had obtained great spoils, and had become very rich, besides having been always well treated by him, and having had their wages paid without any arrears; that if they felt galled at the labour the war involved them in, he himself was not exempt from this, yet he had done nothing herein beyond complying with the orders contained in the king's instructions; and that he desired them earnestly that they on their part would be willing so to serve him, as he had expected of them, and not by their fault ruin so great an enterprise as that they were now engaged upon, for this was the object for which they had set out from Portugal. Nevertheless, in spite of all these considerations, and more too, which Afonso Dalboquerque mentioned, they began to urge, without paying any attention to the matter in hand, that as there was no doubt that their share would be given to them, if justice were rendered, they would be content that Jorge Barreto, Afonso Lopez da Costa, and Antonio do Campo should decide the matter. To this Afonso Dalboquerque replied that the contents of his instructions having been determined upon and arranged by the king, his master, he was not going to lay them open to the decision of any one, but rather to perform them, according to the orders contained in the same, and it would be quite sufficient for them to have seen them to become convinced; but if, on the other hand, they fancied they were right in what they said, the viceroy was at hand to settle the matter, and he would be his own advocate before him; for he also, of all the money not due to the king, had his portion, and twenty-five shares. And now, being put out of temper, he took hold of a book in his hand, and said to them that he would swear by those holy gospels that he interpreted the commission in no other manner, neither had the king ordered that he should give a share of the tribute, paid by the kings they might conquer, to the men of the fleet.

Hereat all replied that he must give them their shares, and each captain should be responsible for his own men to return the shares to him if it was decided in his favour. Afonso Dalboquerque, being desirous to be more correctly informed who the captains were who had stirred up their men to this, temporised with them, and said he was quite willing to do what they asked him upon these conditions, provided also that each one brought a warrant signed by his captain, wherein he bound himself to this, and he would order the money to be paid at once. With this reply they departed, well pleased, to their own ships, and related to their captains all that had passed; but they could never succeed in getting from them the necessary warrant, and so the matter stood for the decision of the viceroy. This debate which Afonso Dalboquerque had had with the masters and pilots, being now brought to a close, he sent word to Francisco de Tavora to get ready to proceed to the quarry, for there was a lack of stone at the works, and it was his turn that day, and to come on the morrow to arrange with him to go thither in company; and as they had all sworn not to obey him, Francisco de Tavora went on in the morning without waiting for him, and Afonso Dalboquerque arrived a few hours later much annoyed, and, without saying a word to him, both walked up and down the beach while the boats took in their load. And while this was proceeding, Pero Vaz Dorta, the factor, arrived on horseback, coming from the city, and withdrew behind a rock to converse with Afonso Dalboquerque; and after they had conversed, on returning to the boats, he perceived Francisco de Tavora some distance off on the sea, steering for the city, so he ordered him to be signalled to stop, but he would not; and when he noticed this, he went on board, and went after him, and ordered a second signal to stop to be made to him, whereupon Francisco de Tavora, more out of shame than will, bade his men rest on their oars and wait.

CHAPTER XLIII.

Of what the great Afonso Dalboquerque did with Francisco de Tavora on leaving the quarry, and of the conversation he held with the captains after coming to land.

As soon as the great Afonso Dalboquerque came up with Francisco de Tavora, as he understood how the seed prospered which Antonio do Campo had sown in the hearts of all the captains, he could not restrain himself from coming to an explanation with him, so he said: "Sir Francisco de Tavora, I recommend you more courtesy when you next come with me than you have to-day shown me. How? Must you leave me between two rocks in the land of the enemy, and go away alone, and without my permission? I know well what punishment it is that you deserve, but I put up with it all because I must needs do so." Francisco de Tavora stood up on his feet, and, giving vent to oaths, said: "You shall not punish me, nor have you power to do so. Take your own vessel, and do as you like with it, for I promise you that if we set sail, I shall escape from you." And more words of this nature he said, to which Afonso Dalboquerque would not reply, but ordered him to return to his own vessel; and being mercifully inclined towards him, he told him he was a poor man, and lately married, and ought not to consent to enter into conspiracies with the other captains, for he would ruin himself with the king, D. Manoel. Francisco de Tavora, in a fume, told him he was richer than he himself, and wanted nothing from the king; that he was well aware that he wished him ill, because of the remonstrance that he had made; and that he would quit Ormuz and make his own way to the Cape of Guardafum, to perform the instructions contained in the king's order. Afonso Dalboquerque replied that he was much surprised at his saying that he wished him ill, because of the remonstrance made by them all, since he himself had announced to him that they were about to make it, and he had asked him if he would sign it, and he had replied, smiling, and without any emotion, that if what the other captains did pleased him, he would sign it. Francisco de Tavora, being ashamed at what was now retorted upon him, held his tongue, and made no reply; and, being now come to the shore, Afonso Dalboquerque took him with him on board his own vessel.

And because the captains were now thoroughly corrupted, and these proceedings were now for some time past well known throughout the whole city, and could no longer be remedied except by the sword of the king's justice, or by the patience of Job, he made up his mind to take some measures with them. So he summoned them to come before him, and told them that when the king, D. Manoel, had graciously appointed them to be captains of these ships, it was to the end that they should come and serve him in the enterprise at Ormuz in his company and fight under his flag, not to go fostering differences, as they were now doing with him, which indeed were very prejudicial to the interests of the king, as the King of Ormuz and Cogeatar knew full well; yet, from the moment of setting out from Çocotora until that very moment they had never given advice upon any subject but such as was opposed to the interests and honour of his highness, which he, for his part, had cared for with great judgment and much patience, which he had ever used towards them. And for all that the king had ordered him to take their advice, as they alleged, it was in his belief, that they, being what they appeared to be (that is, subordinate), would recommend him to do what seemed most to his interest, whereas they had counselled him to abandon so great an enterprise as the one they had in hand, and go frolicking about after prizes at the Cape of Guardafum, when, if they all had helped him like true Portuguese, he would have put the enterprise in the state in which it ought to be; but if, day after day, they meant to come after him with remonstrances, causing the people to be divided, and turning everything into confusion, as it now was (as Cogeatar well knew), he would not put up with it as he had hitherto done. He begged them, therefore, earnestly of their goodness to serve the king, all of them peaceably, for he would reward them for their services, and not to advise João da Nova to come to a rupture with him, or beg his permission to go to India; for they were all cognisant of the fact that as long as the present war continued it would not be to the king's interest to grant such a permission; and so they had themselves told him in a council he had held with them upon the very subject at Calayate. And if they were put out at the trouble they underwent at the continuation of the work upon the fortress, they could remain on board their ships and need not go to land, for he would hold them excused, for it was not so important but that he would be happier in letting it remain as it was, than in passing over all the rest they said and did every day against him. And in addition he would order them, on the behalf of the King of Portugal, their master, that not one of them should venture to land again without his permission, because, as the Moors were now disquieted at these events, if any misfortune arose, he would take care to know which captain had been there. This conversation being now over, as he was unwilling to hear any more of the feigned arguments that they continued to adduce, he dismissed them to their ships, and suspended Francisco de Tavora from the command of his vessel, because he had told him he meant to fly; and he appointed Diniz Fernandes de Melo in his place.

CHAPTER XLIV.

How four Christians fled from our fleet, and related to Cogeatar the disagreements that existed between Afonso Dalboquerque and the captains; and of the message he sent to him, and of the rest that ensued.

Inasmuch as it was part of the plan laid down by Cogeatar to study at all times to obtain information of all Afonso Dalboquerque's doings and intentions, he immediately became aware of the differences that had arisen between him and the captains, as well as of the remonstrances they had made to him. And at this very juncture four men deserted from the fleet, by whom he was better informed of all that was going on, and that Afonso Dalboquerque had determined, on his return from the straits (whither he was bent upon going), to establish himself in Ormuz, and break out into opposition with the aid of the fortress, as soon as it was completed, and that he was constructing it against the opinion of the captains, and without their advice, because the king, D. Manuel, had not given him any instructions to build a fortress in Ormuz. Cogeatar, having long repented of having granted a site for the fortress, became highly rejoiced at their making these assertions that the captains and men of the fleet were displeased at it, for it grieved his heart excessively to have consented to it; and their certifying him that Afonso Dalboquerque was minded to establish himself in Ormuz conduced in no small degree to his repentance, for, if this event were to come to pass, he would remain without any government, and Afonso Dalboquerque would be lord of the kingdom. Cogeatar, then, excited at the false news of this design on the part of Afonso Dalboquerque, gave an account of the affair to certain noble Moors who were admitted to his most intimate friendship, to gather from them what course he ought to pursue in regard to it. And having talked it over with them, after two days he sent word by Pero Vaz Dorta, the factor, to Afonso Dalboquerque, that the rulers of the land were coming to him every day with heavy complaints, asserting that the real reason why he was building that fortress was, that he might rise up in rebellion by its aid and destroy Ormuz; and should it be so he would not permit another stone to be put upon it.

Afonso Dalboquerque, enraged at this infamy, which the Portuguese had put upon him, replied that he was no corsair, neither had the king, D. Manuel, his master, sent him for any other object than to conquer that kingdom, which he had gained, and that Portuguese who possessed any feeling of honour were not in the habit of acting treasonably towards their king, and that he must not judge by the evidence of four runaways whom he had with him, and who were equally traitors to their God in deserting his Holy Faith as to their king, and that to destroy Ormuz, if he were so minded, he had no need of anything more than the fleet he then had with him, and that the fortress which he was building was not to serve as a means to enable him to break the treaty, as the captains gave him to understand, but rather to guard and defend Ormuz as a possession of the king, his master. And for all that Cogeatar sent this message, yet the work went forwards. The factor went on shore with this reply, and told Cogeatar all that Afonso Dalboquerque had said to him; and, as he, from what he heard from the captains, was desirous of a rupture with Afonso Dalboquerque, he told the factor to tell him that the king desired to send Rexnordim to converse with him upon certain important matters before the captains, and that he must arrange some place for the meeting. Afonso Dalboquerque sent back word that the best and safest place wherein they could meet was the fortress, and he would proceed thither and wait for Rexnordim that very afternoon. When the factor went with this reply, Afonso Dalboquerque, with all the captains, proceeded to the fortress and remained there a long time, until the factor returned and told him that Rexnordim would not come, for Cogeatar had repented of the message he had sent him, and that he had better not rely upon this man's words, for he noticed that he was so pleased at knowing of the differences that existed between him and the captains, that he would not fulfil any of his promised engagements; for, in the conversation he had held with him, he had discovered that the message which the king purposed to send by Rexnordim was, that he should get up at once out of the port with his fleet and be gone.

Afonso Dalboquerque was deeply incensed at the idea of this message which the king had intended to send him; for it was but a few days before, and when he was ready to pass on to the straits, that the king had sent him word by the very same Rexnordim not to go, for there was certain news that a great lord of the mainland, who was called the *Messará*, was preparing himself with a large fleet to fall upon the city, and as it was ruined and without men, it would be an easy matter to take it, and if he took it he would become master of the whole kingdom. To this he had replied that, although his voyage to the strait was imperative, inasmuch as the king, his master, had set it down in his instructions, yet he would do as he was desired; for, in the contract he had made with him in the king's name, he was bound to defend the kingdom as much as if it were his own possession. Now, as this message which the king was minded to forward to Afonso Dalboquerque was agreeable to the policy of the captains and to the remonstrances they had made, Afonso Dalboquerque clearly perceived that they were to blame for this disgraceful conduct of Cogeatar; and knowing this, he dissembled with them, and without saying anything to them, dismissed them to their own ships. He also sent word to Cogeatar through Gaspar Rodriguez, the interpreter, that from out the fleet of the King of Portugal, his lord, there were fled four Christians, whom he had arrested for punishment for certain crimes by them committed, and he desired, as a favour, that he would order them to be delivered up to him. Cogeatar told Gaspar Rodriguez that up to that moment he knew nothing whatever of them, but he would send and search for them, and if he found them, he would deliver them up to him immediately. Now, for all that Afonso Dalboquerque knew that Cogeatar had the Christians with him, yet he temporised with him, intending to complete the principal tower as far as the first story, to which work he gave great impetus. Nevertheless, after some days had elapsed, and he saw that the Christians were not forthcoming, he sent word that he especially begged they would send back his four men; for, as he was the chief captain of that fleet, he was obliged to give an account with the delivery of it and of the men to the king, his master; and he (Cogeatar) must remember that but a few days ago the king and he had taken an oath of implicit obedience to the King of Portugal, his master, and to thoroughly comply with the commands of him who represented his authority. Cogeatar replied that he need not distress himself, for his men were on the further side of the mainland, tied hand and foot, that he had sent them thither, and in five days' time he would send them back to him.

CHAPTER XLV.

How the great Afonso Dalboquerque, perceiving that Cogeatar would not deliver up the men, ordered the officers and men employed on the work, who were on shore, to be withdrawn, and of what else passed with the captains.

When the five days had elapsed which Cogeatar had required to send in search of the men, the great Afonso Dalboquerque sent him word by Gaspar Rodriguez that the time which he had sent to beg for instituting a search for his men was now gone by some days, and if they had arrived, would he send them back to him. Cogeatar told him that he had sent some of his servants to the mainland in search of the Christians, and that they had not come back and had done nothing, but he might tell the chief captain that he must return him one of his servants whom he had taken in reprisal, a man who knew the country very well, that he might despatch him in search of the men; for he was very diligent, and would set about this business in a different manner to anyone else, and then, in two days' time, he would send the fugitives back. Gaspar Rodriguez returned from the land with this reply, and informed Afonso

Dalboquerque that he perceived from the overbearing mien of certain Moors who were of the faction of Cogeatar, and also by the wording of his reply, that he would not deliver up the Christians to him, but was desirous of a rupture with him, and was fostering this delay with the intention of putting into practice some kind of treason which he had organised, for he had given orders that the entrances of two streets, which led to the houses where the factory of stone and mortar was situated, should be closed. Afonso Dalboquerque, being now advertised of this that Gaspar Rodriguez mentioned, and also to anticipate the malice of Cogeatar, determined to order a cessation of the work, and talked over the matter with João da Nova and the factor, who just then happened to be present with him in the *parao* close to the shore; and as they agreed in thinking it advisable, Afonso Dalboquerque, without further delay, issued orders to João da Nova to withdraw all the officers of the work, as well as the rest of the men who were going about the city, lest they should receive some affront from the Moors. So João da Nova proceeded forthwith to land, and caused all of them to withdraw to the *parao* so effectually, that before sunset there was not one left in the city.

When they were all withdrawn, Afonso Dalboquerque summoned the captains and certain fidalgos to his ship, and laid before the whole assembly what had passed with Cogeatar, and what Gaspar Rodriguez had told him, and desired them to tell him what to do, if Cogeatar still refused to deliver up the fugitives. The ensuing discussion of the matter ended in their agreeing that in the event of Cogeatar not delivering up the men, he ought to declare war against him and destroy Ormuz, if he were able to do so; and that he ought not to send back his Moor whom he had begged for, nor yet the others, as the king desired, for their whole conduct was a tissue of deceit and lies. But Afonso Lopez da Costa was of an opposite opinion, and said that, in spite of what the captains had alleged, it would be as well to send him his Moor, and so get a positive proof of their lies and deceptions; for it was always in his power to make war upon them whenever he liked. Afonso Dalboquerque sided with Afonso Lopez da Costa's idea, and sent to Cogeatar his servant, and granted him the days' grace he desired; and, in the meanwhile, he told the factor artfully to withdraw the factory and the men in it. When Cogeatar knew of the orders to withdraw the factory, and saw how Afonso Dalboquerque was always beforehand with him, he sent him word by Almaçá, on the king's behalf, begging him as a great favour not to order the factory to be withdrawn, for it would be a great scandal for the merchants, and he, on his part, would receive much annoyance thereby. Afonso Dalboquerque, in reply, asked how his royal highness could expect to have the confidence of the revenue of the king, his master, and his officers, if Cogeatar had ordered walls to be built across two streets which led to the factory, and refused to send him four vagabonds who had fled from his fleet, and for whom he had sent many times to seek; and, with this reply, he ordered João Estão to exhibit before him the documents they had ratified in his presence at the delivery of the kingdom, and to inform the king that he begged he would of his favour take great care in what he was about, and not fail from his word, nor desire to make war with the King of Portugal, his master, for it would be his ruin, but look well to those documents and the seals wherewith they were sealed, and not break the peace, which he had agreed upon with him in the name of the King of Portugal, for the kingdom of Ormuz could not be defended by force of arms, but only by prudence and good counsel. The king and Cogeatar would not look at the documents, saying that they were quite aware of their contents, and intended to comply entirely with them; for they were the subjects of the King of Portugal, and that they had taken all this trouble upon themselves out of charity towards the men who had deserted, but that they need not be alarmed, for they should be produced.

CHAPTER XLVI.

How Cogeatar sent word to the great Afonso Dalboquerque, asking for a safe conduct for the Christians, and how the captains sent him a remonstrance urging him not to make war against the city, and what further took place with them thereupon.

At the end of the two days which Cogeatar had required that he might send the Christians, Afonso Dalboquerque, who perceived they were not likely to come, sent him word by Gaspar Rodriguez, that he desired him earnestly to return his men, and not make any further delay, for he would not put up with it any longer. So Gaspar Rodriguez went to land, and delivered his messages to Cogeatar, who, after conversing with him for some time upon the subject, bade him inform the chief captain that he must send back certain Moors who had been captured in the destruction of the vessels, as they were his servants, and a written deed promising not to bring the deserters to justice, and then he would send them back at once, for he was not desirous of making war upon him, but of maintaining peace and friendship; for they were all vassals of the King of Portugal, and he would always continue in obedience to him; and thereupon he added many other words to the end that his deceitfulness might take effect. Gaspar Rodriguez returned with this reply, and told Afonso Dalboquerque that Cogeatar had caused the Christians to be exhibited to him, in very good trim, and to all appearance so well satisfied with themselves, that in spite of all the promises of Cogeatar, he would affirm that they would not be restored to him. For all that Afonso Dalboquerque was quite well aware of his tricks and lies, he continued to dissemble with him, for he was anxious to know from the fugitives who it was who had incited them to fly; and that nothing should remain untried, he sent Gaspar Rodriguez back again with the written deed which had been demanded of him for security, and desired to be informed where they should land the Moors, for he would send them back to him without delay.

As soon as Gaspar Rodriguez had set out with this message, Afonso Dalboquerque ordered João Estão to make his way quickly to all the ships and collect the Moors, who numbered about two hundred, and having embarked them in a *zambuco*, to bring them close to the shore, where he himself was in the *parao;* and as soon as they were there, he sent word to Cogeatar, that he had the Moors there, and he might now forward the Christians. Cogeatar replied that he might put them on shore, and send a captain to the jetty for the Christians because he would deliver them up there. Now, as Afonso Dalboquerque was on the alert with respect to this man's treacherous conduct, he sent D. Antonio de Noronha, his nephew, and João da Nova, with two hundred men, to draw up the Moors in order close to the fortress, tied one to the other, there to await a message from him; and he ordered Francisco de Tavora to proceed in a boat to the pier for the Christians, and Gaspar Rodriguez to go on in advance and tell Cogeatar that the Moors were on the land, and he must send the Christians to Francisco de Tavora, who had gone to the appointed place, to take them in charge. And, when Gaspar Rodriguez had been a long while gone, without returning with a reply, Afonso Dalboquerque despatched one of his servants to find out the cause of his delay, and he met him there on the way back. He told him that Cogeatar had detained him all that time without an answer, but he could not discover the reason of his doing so, and that he had seen the fugitives, clothed in the habit of the Moors, with their swords in their belts, very happy, like men who felt sure they would not be delivered up; and after much wrangling with him, he had told him that he ought to send the Moors back as a present to the king, that the business might proceed on a more favourable footing, and he would bid the Christians to be shown to Francisco de Tavora. Afonso Dalboquerque, enraged by this reply, sent word immediately to D. Antonio and João da Nova to put the Moors back again into the *zambuco*, for Cogeatar would not deliver up the Christians, and upon the jetty there was a great collection of archers, and he would come to their support with the rest of the men, lest, if Cogeatar were plotting some treachery, he should fall upon us unexpectedly.

When the Moors were all put on board the *zambuco*, Afonso Dalboquerque disembarked, and joined D. Antonio and João da Nova, and remained there a long time at the foot of the fortress, awaiting the decision of Cogeatar; and when all was quieted down, he returned with his men to the boats, and went on board his own vessel. No sooner had he arrived, than Antonio Fernandez, who was the bearer of the remonstrances (as I have before mentioned), put into his hands a written paper signed by all the captains, to the following effect:—"Sir, we do this in writing, because by word of mouth we dare not, as you always answer us so passionately; and for all that you, sir, have frequently told us that the king gives you no orders to take counsel with us, yet this business is of so great an importance, that we consider ourselves obliged to offer you our advice; did we not do so, we should be worthy of punishment. Now, because this war, in which you are now desirous of engaging, is very much opposed to the interest of the king, our lord, we consider that your worship ought to weigh well, before entering upon it, how little Cogeatar is to blame for objecting to have against all reason to pay down in ready money fifteen thousand *cruzados*[1] of revenue every year, contrary to the honour of such a large city and kingdom; yet, if notwithstanding all this, your worship is determined to prosecute the war, and break the peace and agreement which has been made with him, it is our opinion that you ought not to do so; for it would be more to the service of the king, our lord, if we were now to quit this city and temporise with Cogeatar, and in the course of the year return in strength in order to subdue it and confirm our hold upon it, than to destroy it for ever. And if, in spite of all we can say, your worship is bent upon entering into this war, see you that it be with all the circumspection and assurance that the fleet can command, in that it is more conducive to the interest of our said lord to obtain possession, and not to destroy the city now, since it can be destroyed at any time we please; because, in case of your worship's landing in Ormuz or at the city, we are determined not to go with you, nor enter into such a war, nor such designs, and that this may be known for certain, and we be not able to deny it hereafter, we all sign our names here: this day, the fifth of the month of January, in the year fifteen hundred and eight.

"*João da Nova.*
Antonio do Campo.
Afonso Lopez da Costa.
Francisco de Tavora.
Manuel Telez."

When Afonso Dalboquerque had perused this letter, he went on board Francisco de Tavora's ship, taking with him João Estão, scrivener to the fleet, and there summoned them all to him; and when they were assembled, he told them how Antonio Fernandez had handed him a writing signed

[1] The passage on p. 131, to which this refers, has the word *xerafins*; hence it would appear that the Portuguese *cruzado* and the Persian *xerafim* were equivalent.

by them all, which he had put away very carefully to show to the king, his lord; and since they had changed their mind from what they formerly advised him to do, and were now of opinion that it would not be well to destroy Ormuz, he desired them to tell him whether they would by word of mouth affirm the fact that they would not be with him in this war, as they in their writing had asserted; they ought, however, to remember that it was but two days ago, when discussing with him whether or not war should be made upon Ormuz, if Cogeatar would not deliver up the refugees, that they had counselled him to make war upon this man, and not rely any longer on his smooth and specious words, for they were all false, yet now he found them so altered, that he thought it must either be owing to their temper, or to something which he could not quite understand, for it was not the habit of cavaliers to shrink from the hardships of war, for the king, D. Manuel, with his usual confidence in them, had sent them in his company to conquer that kingdom, and they ought to consider very thoroughly what they said, for to refuse to obey him was to act in opposition to the king's power, which had been entrusted to him over them.

The captains' reply was that they had in truth counselled him to enter into war with Ormuz, in case that Cogeatar should not deliver up the deserters; yet after having told him so, they had taken thought in the matter, and come to the conclusion that it was very much to the interest of the king, our master, not to do so, and therefore he ought to put it off as long as he could, and temporise with Cogeatar, for the king, D. Manuel, had stated in the instructions he had given him, that all he did was to be upon their recommendation, which he, on his part, never would accept, but would keep acting as he chose, without giving them any account of it, and that it was on this account that each of them was mentioning the aggravations they had received from him. Afonso Dalboquerque, in answer to them, said they could not call troubles, brought about by war, aggravations, and even if they were, then was not the season to mention them, but rather they ought to finish the fortress and defend it, in spite of the Moors. And if the aggravations they mentioned were from his conduct, they had the viceroy in India, who would do them justice, and the king, D. Manuel, in Portugal, who would punish him; but, just then, what was far more to the interest of the king was, whether they would be with him in the war or not. Then Francisco de Tavora cried out that he would be with him, and do all he desired him to do; but the remaining captains declared they would do nothing else but what they had put down in their writing. João da Nova began to say that the reason the captains had come to that determination was because he had sent to withdraw the men from the city without their advice; and that since Cogeatar had admitted that they were all vassals of the King of Portugal, the pretext on which to found a war was taken away. Afonso Dalboquerque replied to him: "This is what you ought to have said to me when I sent you to collect the men, and not now, for I did it with your counsel and that of the factor." And without caring to hear any more from them, he dismissed them.

As soon as Afonso Lopez da Costa arrived on board his own ship, he summoned all his men together, and sought to hear from them if they remained in their original determination. All replied that they would die wherever their chief captain died. The colloquy over, Afonso Dalboquerque returned to his own ship, much annoyed at this obstinacy of the captains; and while he was thus in suspense, not knowing what course to take, Fernão Soares arrived and told him that the captains were very sorry on account of the writing they had sent him, and much more so at the words that had passed with him, and begged him very earnestly to do them the favour to forget it all, for their passion had blinded them, and all were ready to serve him in the war, and perform all that he might require of them.

CHAPTER XLVII.

How the great Afonso Dalboquerque determined to make war with Ormuz; and how the king's people, who were on guard at the watering stations of Turumbaque, were routed by ours.

As the great Afonso Dalboquerque had made up his mind to make war against the King of Ormuz, unless the fugitive Christians were delivered up, he desired, before commencing hostilities, to understand thoroughly the insubordination shown by the captains, and know whether the message they had sent him through Fernão Soares was real or merely complimentary; for if they were unwilling to remain in obedience to him, as they had asserted, he would provide other captains for the ships who would serve the king. He sent, therefore, João Estão, the scrivener to the fleet, to say on his behalf to Antonio do Campo, that he had certain charges to make against him, and he must resign his post as captain, and be taken into custody on board the flagship, and to say to the other captains, that since they were determined not to serve the king in the war, they must resign the command of their ships, and he would provide them with captains who would serve the king, and abide in obedience to him; and he told him also to make a legal statement of all that had passed with them.

When the captains perceived this determination of Afonso Dalboquerque, being ashamed of what they had entered upon, they told João Estão that they were very sorry for what they had said and done, and that they had sent to tell the chief captain this by Fernão Soares, and that they were prepared to serve him and be with him in this war he desired to enter upon. As Afonso Dalboquerque was now sure of the repentance of the captains, and as it was not the season now to punish their guilt, owing to the great need he had of them, he forgave them, and restored to them their captain-ships, with the exception of Antonio do Campo, whom he would not reinstate, as he was informed that he had been the ringleader of all these disturbances.

And, at the close of these conversations held with the captains, he desired them to approach the shore as closely as they could in their ships, and put out warps from their sterns that they might turn back whenever they wished, and with their artillery direct the fire in batteries against the king's fortress, and each one was to have alongside his ship a *parao* to screen them from the artillery which the Moors had on the fortress wall; he also ordered his master to bring his own ship as close as he could into shore on the side of the western harbour. The captains that day battered the city so furiously, that they killed many men in the fortress, and overthrew many houses throughout the city; while the Moors had their artillery trained so high, that at low tide it could not do any injury to the ships, for it passed over their head, and at high tide it struck the *paraos* with which they had screened themselves; and if they sunk any of these each captain would put another at once in its place.

Antonio do Campo, being ashamed at seeing the captains in their own ships fighting, and himself away from his, sent begging Afonso Dalboquerque to pardon his past errors and to restore him to his ship, that he might assist his comrades with it, and he would do all required of him. Now, at that very juncture there was a great lack of men, so that for all that Antonio do Campo had been the one who plotted these disturbances, he forgave him, and ordered the ship to be delivered up to him again; and he told the captains to go on with the attack upon the fortress upon the following day, which they did with such fury that the carriages of the larger guns, being all rotten, were split to pieces. When Afonso Dalboquerque knew of this, he ordered the ships to withdraw towards the sea, and ranged himself in order to prevent any supplies or water from entering the city, and surrounded the island in a circle with all the fleet, and ordered all the ships which were in the harbour under his safe pass to be burned, first of all requiring Cogeatar many times to surrender the deserters he had kept from him, and to bear in mind the agreement which he and the king had made when he delivered over to him the government of that kingdom in the name of the King of Portugal. And, owing to the blockade all round, there began to be in the city great want of supplies and of water, for these could not be procured from the mainland; and Afonso Dalboquerque knowing how short they were of provisions, ordered the circuit of blockade to be drawn in closer, and signified to the captains and all the men in the fleet that it was his determination not to raise the blockade until the king should deliver the city to him, and that he was no longer minded to proceed to the straits. Having agreed to this, he ordered Manuel Telez to make himself ready to transport the spoils they had collected to the fortress of Çocotorá; and on receipt of news on the way that any ships from Portugal were cruising along that coast, he was to visit the captains and order them, on the part of Afonso Dalboquerque, to proceed to his assistance, and he was also to bring back all the munitions of war he could find, for he had great need of them all.

When the people of the city saw that they were so surrounded, that from no direction could water be brought, which was what they felt most of all, the principal Moors collected together and went to the king, desiring him earnestly to provide a guard for the pools of Turumbaque, which were at the head of the island, lest the Portuguese should obtain possession of them, and from these the great lack of water could be supplied. The king immediately sent a captain, with men on horse and on foot, to remain on guard at the pools, and tents in which they could encamp.

When Afonso Dalboquerque was informed of this plan of the enemy, he sent by night a reconnoitring party; and having received intelligence of the order in which they were disposed, without any delay, he despatched D. Antonio de Noronha with one hundred men, and Francisco de Tavora and João da Nova with another hundred men, to attack them. These, when they were ready, went on board their boats and set out at nightfall; and on their arrival at the pools about two hours before daybreak, they immediately fell upon the Moors, who were thrown into confusion by the suddenness of the attack, and routed them, killing two of the king's principal captains, who had come with that guard, and many Moors, both infantry and cavalry; and they burned a few houses which stood there, and all the tents which they had taken thither for their accommodation. And when this was done they filled the pools with dead bodies of men, and horses, and camels, and betook themselves to their boats with this victory, and so returned to the ships, carrying with them two archers whom they there captured.

From these men Afonso Dalboquerque learned that some days ago the king, by the advice of the blind king and of the governors of the land, had made up his mind to rebel against him, and put to death all the Portuguese who were about in the city; for he was very sorry that he had ever granted them a place in which to construct the fortress; and that there was a great lack of water in the city, and Cogeatar, as he could not put confidence in anyone, kept the key of a cistern which would contain about eighty cubits,[1] and had a captain and company on guard over it.

[1] *Covados*, a measure used in Portugal, which contains three-quarters of a yard, or a Flemish ell.—*Vieyra.* Bluteau says that the *covado* corresponds to the lesser Roman cubit of one and a half feet, or three *palmos craveyros*, or standard palms, of which five go to the *vara*, or ell of three and one-third Portuguese feet.

Although the Moors who were on guard over the cistern were sure of support, as they were so near to the city, Afonso Dalboquerque, nevertheless, in order to disquiet them, made up his mind to attack them, and got himself ready with all his people, and set out from the ships before daybreak, and ordered Francisco de Tavora in the vanguard with forty men to attack, while he, with all the rest of the men, followed in reserve; and they fell upon the Moors so suddenly, that they put them at once to flight, and followed after them awhile, killing many Moors on foot, as well as their captain, who was on horseback; and Lopo Alvarez, who was the constable's servant, was the first who struck him with a lance. Many of our men were wounded with arrows, for the Moors on their horses fled away, and as they fled kept on shooting arrows against us, as we followed them in disorder. So Afonso Dalboquerque, being fearful lest a large force should sally out to succour them, ordered D. Antonio de Noronha to withdraw the men from the pursuit, and broke the gates of the cistern, and filled it full of corpses and dead horses, and with this victory returned to embark on board the boats, and made his way to the ships.

CHAPTER XLVIII.

How Cogeatar again ordered his people to clear out the pools of Turumbaque, and how the people whom he had appointed to guard them were discomfited by our men, and of further matters.

Two days had now elapsed since this skirmish, and there began to be a great want of water in the city, so that many children began to die of thirst, and they could provide themselves from no other quarter with dispatch, except from the wells of Turumbaque, because of the exceeding vigilance and care which the great Afonso Dalboquerque had employed in blockading the island. So Cogeatar determined to send secretly and clear out the pools; and with this view he dispatched a captain with some men on foot and on horse, and many camels and beasts to bring water immediately to the city. Now, as Afonso Dalboquerque had his sources of information respecting all the intentions of the king, to wit, Moors to whom he used to give many presents from his stock, he was immediately advised of this, and prepared Manuel Telez and Afonso Lopez da Costa, with one hundred and fifty men, to go and fall upon these men and cover up the wells again. The captains started at nightfall by sea, and arrived at the wells when morning was just breaking, and at once attacked the Moors; and, as these were not in careful array, they were routed, and, without making any resistance, took to flight, and our men pursued them, and killed many as they came up with them, and then returned in a body to the wells, and killed all the camels and beasts of burden which the Moors had there to carry water, and covered up the wells. When this was done they returned to the boats, and, betaking themselves to the ships, came upon Afonso Dalboquerque on his way towards them in boats to give them assistance, if it were necessary.

The captains recounted all that had taken place, and he praised their deed greatly, and the manner in which they had attacked the Moors. And he told them that he had been informed that opposite the wells there was a rising ground running down in a point towards the sea, whereon a fort might be built, which would hold both artillery and men, to oppose the enemy when carrying water thence to the city, and it would be well to survey the site, and see what could be done with it; for, if they could cut off that supply of water, the king would have of necessity to yield, for there were no means of provision, except with great trouble and risk of lives. Having come to this determination, they all returned, and proceeded to disembark in the harbour, and when they were about to mount the hill, they perceived mounted men coming from the city to succour a few archers who remained there after the late skirmish. Afonso Dalboquerque, as soon as he saw them, remained quiet with all his men, and ordered Afonso Lopez da Costa, D. Antonio de Noronha, Manuel Telez, and Jorge Barreto, to take up a front position among our men, and keep them back; and when they were all compactly united, he ordered D. Antonio, with one hundred men, to ascend the hill and attack the Moors; and he himself remained where he was on the beach, with the rest of the men, in sight of them.

D. Antonio achieved the ascent so valorously, that he fell upon the archers before the mounted men could get up, and, having put them to flight, pursued them along a valley which led to the mountains. The horsemen who had come out of the city, seeing our men disorganised in pursuit, began to attack them, and the archers, when they found themselves supported by the mounted men, faced about, and, joining their forces, attacked D. Antonio. As soon as Afonso Dalboquerque saw our men hard put to it with the horsemen, he sent orders to D. Antonio to return to the place where he himself was; and, as it was getting late, he commanded him, through Afonso Lopez da Costa, to retire at once, and with this decisive message he proceeded to withdraw down the course of the valley, in quick marching order. When the Moors perceived that D. Antonio was withdrawing his forces, they drew nearer to him; and D. Antonio, as soon as he found himself pressed in by the Moors, faced about and made them turn back, some archers being left stretched along the ground dead; and he thus returned to the beach where his uncle was stationed, the Moors following close upon him without any order, and killing a youth close beside Afonso Dalboquerque with an arrow-wound in the head. Dalboquerque, however, noticing that the Moors came on in disorder, commanded D. Antonio to fall upon them again with his people, and in this charge they killed three mounted Moors, who desired to outstrip the others, men well furnished with clothing and arms.

When the mounted men saw these were killed, they threw away their arms and the trappings of their horses to make less weight, and fled away towards the city. There were wounded in this skirmish D. Antonio (with seven arrows), Gonçalo Queimado, Nuno Vaz de Castelo-branco, and Antonio de Liz, and others; and they withdrew again. The archers, although they saw themselves deserted by the mounted men, rallied at the mouth of the valley with the intention of avenging themselves, and began to harass our party with flights of arrows, until Afonso Dalboquerque, annoyed at their importunity, told the captains to fall upon them, and they pursued them all along the valley upwards, and punished them so severely, that they no longer dared to attack us, but collected themselves together on a hill. And in this charge Afonso Lopez da Costa, Manuel Telez, Jorge da Silveira, Fernão Feijo, and João Rodriguez Pereira, were wounded. As he had now driven off the Moors from his party, Afonso Dalboquerque withdrew to the boats, and proceeded to the ships, without coming to any determination respecting the place which he had started to survey; and from two archers who were captured there he learned that one of the three horsemen whom they had killed was the son of Rexnordim, a very gallant man, who had come from Persia with an army to serve the king in this war, and for him they made so great an outcry in the city, that they could be heard in the ships. These three captains who were killed there paid dearly for the pride they had evinced in offering the king to protect the wells.

CHAPTER XLIX.

Of the message sent by the king to the great Afonso Dalboquerque, begging for peace, and the answer he gave, and what passed in the Island of Queixome on proceeding thither for water.

As soon as the great Afonso Dalboquerque had withdrawn to the ships, on obtaining this victory, it was announced to him that, after his departure to Turumbaque, two *almadias* had gone out by night to the mainland. Now, because he was desirous of knowing the whole reason of this trip, he ordered Duarte de Sousa, with two skiffs well furnished for any contingency, to go at once and wait for them at that part whence they had set out; and, as the *almadias* returned at night, they came unexpectedly upon Duarte de Sousa, who, directly that he caught sight of them, gave them chase, and before they touched land took them both, and proceeded with them to Afonso Dalboquerque. And from the Moors who were captured, he heard that Cogeatar, in consequence of the great lack of water in the city, sent swift-rowing *almadias* to Nabandé for it by night; for these could coast along more secretly than the *paraos*. When the Moors had told him of this, he ordered their noses and ears to be cut off, and that they should be put on shore, and their *almadias* burned; and from thenceforth he ordered a watch to be set upon the shore to put a stop to this device by which Cogeatar designed to get water. When the people of the city perceived this means of supply cut off, and that they were in great likelihood of perishing with hunger and thirst, many men assembled together, with their women and children, although it was night, and surrounded the king's palace, shouting loudly, and crying out, desiring him to take pity upon them and the troubles they were suffering in the death of their fathers, husbands, children, and relations, without any hope of aid coming to them from any quarter, and all because Cogeatar would not give up four Christians, who were worth nothing, and of whom they had no need. And further, they related many disasters which had taken place, so that it was grievous to hear them, and the cries were so loud that they were heard in the ships.

When the king perceived the troubles of his people, and the great need in which the city was placed, he concluded, with the advice of the blind king, to send and beg for mercy from the great Afonso Dalboquerque, and sent him word by Almaçá, a very confidential eunuch, that he was sorry for all that had taken place, and would swear to him, by his law, that the blame was none of his, and begged him earnestly to be graciously content with the destruction he had already done in the city, and he would do all that was desired of him. Afonso Dalboquerque replied, that if the king was desirous of making terms and peace with him, he ought first of all to order a surrender of the fortress of the King of Portugal, his master, and his men whom he had seized, and all the goods that remained in the factory, and to pay all the expenses incurred; and when all this had been satisfactorily settled, they could then deliberate in concert, for under any other consideration he would have no communications with him. So Almaçá returned with this reply to land, and the king, upon taking counsel upon the affair with the blind king and Cogeatar, and with the principal Moors of his government, answered that it was no use talking about the fortress, for he would not give it up, but he would give him as much money as he wished. Afonso Dalboquerque, on receipt of so haughty a reply, perceiving that it was due to the influence of Cogeatar, told Almaçá to inform the king that he had no need of money, nor desired anything further of him except the fortress, which belonged to the King of Portugal, gained with his men and fleet, and if he would not give it up to him, there was no use in speaking of any agreement; but he hoped that Cogeatar, who had caused him to send that reply, would some time or other repent of having advised him to do so.

Now, as Cogeatar knew that the captains were of opinion that war ought not to be made upon the king, he sent immediately by night to tell them at the ships, where they were close on shore, that he would have them to understand that the king had paid many compliments to their chief captain, and had offered him much money not to destroy their city, which was in obedience to the King of Portugal, even as they were all of them his vassals, but he would not accept it, and that therefore the king was minded to forward a ship with a message to the Viceroy of India, giving him an account of this unreasonable conduct towards him. Afonso Dalboquerque was immediately informed of this, that Cogeatar had communicated by night with the captains; but he dissembled with them, without punishing them as they deserved, until he could learn their further intentions, and went on with the war as before. And because the fleet was very much in want of water, he sent Antonio do Campo and Pero Vaz Dorta, the factor, to the port of Nabandé, to try whether by presents or money they could obtain any water, for the inhabitants of that harbour live by it, and carry it to Ormuz for sale. When they arrived there they found a captain of the King of Ormuz, with a company of men on guard over that port, who would have nothing to say to our party, nor permit the people to sell water to them for money. And Antonio do Campo, perceiving the determination of the captain, returned to the ships and related to Afonso Dalboquerque what had taken place, and he made ready at once to go in person to the Isle of Queixome, to obtain water by force, for this was the nearest point; and he took with him Antonio do Campo and Francisco de Tavora, with one hundred men, and *paraos*, and Moors who were accustomed to the business of carrying water to the city, and left João da Nova, with all the rest of the men, in charge of the ships during his absence.

When all was prepared, they set out at night, and reached the island before dawn. And before they disembarked, Afonso Dalboquerque ordered them to station sentries around the walls to keep a good look out over all the land afar off, and he bade Duarte de Sousa and the factor to take care and get the *paraos* loaded with water as rapidly as they could. When all this was set in order, he disembarked with all the party, and marched direct towards a place which was called Arbés, which was at some little distance from the seashore, and he ordered Jorge Barreto, with ten men, to ascend a lofty knoll, and keep watch over the land, while Antonio do Campo, with fifty men, went forward and attacked the place. As soon as Antonio do Campo arrived he made the assault without delay, and Afonso Dalboquerque, who was following up behiud him, did the same in another direction in company with Jorge Barreto, who had already come up, and they killed some Moors; and as the king had no garrison of men there, the Moors who came up, finding themselves badly used by our matchlocks, betook themselves to flight, and left the place.

When Afonso Dalboquerque saw that it was deserted, and that there was nothing more to be feared, he ordered all the provisions to be carried into the boats; and while they were proceeding with this booty, they heard a gun fired in their own direction, so he ordered the men to assemble together at once, for it seemed to him to be a signal for doing so, and proceeded with them all in a body straight to the shore. And when he arrived there Duarte de Sousa informed him that as he was taking in water he had seen a captain with thirty Moors and guns on camels, and he had withdrawn to the boats as soon as he caught sight of them, and kept clear of them; yet the captains had ordered the Moors to take down the guns from the camels, and commenced firing, but at the first shots, seeing our men coming up, the Moors had replaced the guns on the camels and withdrawn very rapidly. So Afonso Dalboquerque finished taking in water and set off, and on his arrival at the ships, was informed that João da Nova had gone by night in his skiff to land, to parley with the renegades and with some of the servants of Cogeatar, at which he was very angry, for it was without his permission, and he had left him in charge of the fleet in his name.

CHAPTER L.

Of what passed between the great Afonso Dalboquerque and João da Nova, when he would not go to Nabandé, whither he was ordered to go.

On the day following that on which Afonso Dalboquerque had returned to the ships, he sent word to João da Nova and Francisco de Tavora that he had news that a caravan coming from Persia towards Ormuz with supplies and other merchandise had arrived at the port of Nabandé, and they were to make ready with their men to go thither, but first to come on board his ship, that he might give them instructions in what they were to do. Francisco de Tavora, on receiving the message, made ready at once, and came on board the flagship at the appointed time; and as it was late, and João da Nova did not come, Afonso Dalboquerque sent to ask why he delayed, for Francisco de Tavora had been waiting many hours for him there; and João da Nova sent word to say that the delay was owing to the fact that the men of his ship would not accompany him, and he would not go by himself. Afonso Dalboquerque, being already annoyed at what he had done during his absence at the Island of Queixome, and enraged still further at this reply, went into his boat with João Estão, scrivener to the fleet, and a few men, and proceeded at this late hour of the night to João da Nova's ship; and on entering it, as he saw the men in an uproarious state, and an attitude of defiance, he dissembled, and bade João da Nova to cause them to embark in the boats, while he (João) went to the flagship. But he (as a man not altogether free from the blame) would not do so, and told him these men were unwilling to go and fight on land, for they were not under any obligation to do so, and if he desired them to go there, he ought to order that they should receive their share of the twenty thousand *xerafins* which the King of Ormuz had paid as tribute.

Afonso Dalboquerque told him that he would give him an answer upon this question as soon as he had ordered his men to embark. And although he reiterated his request very often, he always kept putting it off, on the ground that his men would not do so. Now, as Afonso Dalboquerque was well aware that it all arose from João da Nova and not from the men, he said to him:—"I have known for many days of the designs which you and the other captains are plotting, and have concealed it all, making always as though I did not know of them, for I desired to complete this fortress in peace, and you have all so acted that everything is likely to be lost. And not content with this, when I was in the Island of Queixome, leaving you by yourself with all my authority, in charge of this fleet, you went to land to parley with the besieged enemies, and with the men who fled from me, although you had not my permission to be able to do this. And this disobedience the men of your ship show towards me arises from your having incited them to mutiny against me, asserting that I have appropriated the share which belongs to them of the twenty thousand *xerafins* which the King of Ormuz has paid as tribute, and that the King of Portugal ordered me to divide the money in the instructions he gave me, though it is not so. And all this is done to the end, that I should quit this undertaking, for you all of you desire to make your way to India to take in full cargoes, being tired of the war, and not bearing in mind that this is an obligation required as much from you all as from me, and that it behoves us to give a good account to the king, our master, of this kingdom which we have gained. And it is very evident that Cogeatar suffers all these troubles and necessities without being willing to deliver up to me four Christians, because he well knows that you all advise me to leave off this war and be gone, but the king, our master, shall know whose fault it is."

João da Nova was not much pleased at these matters which Afonso Dalboquerque mentioned, and began to exculpate himself, and, as regards the inciting the men of his ship to mutiny, he desired him to ask them how many times he had reproved them, and tried to compel them to embark without their obeying; but what was mentioned about the cargoes was true, for when at Calicut they had begged his permission to depart and make their way to India, it was in order to load his ship and sail away to Portugal, in accordance with the order given to him by Tristão da Cunha at Çocotora so to do, in order to carry him back news before his departure of what he had done on this coast, and that if he chose to depart without his permission he would do so with impunity. And as João da Nova was of an obstinate and haughty spirit, he began to utter a number of silly things, and make a great outcry, in such a manner that the hubbub was so loud in the ship that the Moors, who were stationed on the walls of the city on the watch, commenced crying out loudly, and fired four shots of artillery, speaking much against Afonso Dalboquerque, as though they knew the reason for that noise and disturbance. And when he perceived these things, and that fair words were no longer of any avail, it appeared to him that for the credit of his person it would be more honourable to kill him there and then than to permit him to be disobedient, and he snatched a sword from a cabin boy whom he came across, and fell upon those who were the authors of this disturbance on the deck, and made them embark, and, approaching João da Nova, seized him by the neck, and bade him embark at once.

When the ship's company beheld Afonso Dalboquerque wrestling with João da Nova, there was not one who dared say anything more, and all set about embarking. João da Nova, finding himself arrested (in excuse for what he had done, although it was very dishonourable), pulled at his own beard, which he used to wear very long, and taking out some hairs, which he wrapped in a handkerchief, began to cry out in a loud voice: "I will betake me to the king, and in presence of his council will beg of him to do justice to these hairs of my beard which thou hast plucked out in payment, forsooth, for the service I have rendered in these parts of India." Afonso Dalboquerque replied sternly to him: "I never laid hands upon your beard, and even if I had plucked it all out by the roots for what you have done, and for having disobeyed me, not even for this will the king, our master, order my head to be cut off; but if I had treated you and the other captains according to the strict letter of my instructions, when you all began to damage our affairs at Ormuz, they would not be in the state in which they are now; but I bore with you with great patience, thinking that thus the king's interest would be better served, and this was what I was ever aiming at." And not caring to hold any more intercourse with him, he made him embark, and all the rest of the mutineers as well, and returned to his own ship very late at night; and on the following day he sent João da Nova in custody, upon his oath of allegiance, to the ship commanded by Francisco de Tavora, and told João Estão, the scrivener to the fleet, to hold an inquiry, in order to discover who was guilty of this mutiny.

The result of this inquiry was that the captain and all the

men were found to be so guilty that it was thought to be better counsel to forgive them, considering the times they had fallen upon, and the necessity there was of them, than to punish them as they deserved; and in order to wean the men from taking further part in the mutiny, he gave to each ten *xerafins* in part payment of what might accrue to his share in the twenty thousand *xerafins* of tribute, if it were found right that they should have it, and, if not, it was to be deducted from their pay; and he ordered them to return to the ship, and released João da Nova from custody, and returned him his captaincy, not caring to hear any more of his guilt, but leaving the punishment of it for the king to settle, although he had, in the instructions given to him, granted him power for all.

CHAPTER LI.

How the great Afonso Dalboquerque returned to the Island of Queixome with determination of taking water, and of the rout he made of the men whom the king had there for its defence.

Notwithstanding all these differences which the great Afonso Dalboquerque had every day with the captains, and which caused him much pains, yet he did not cease to seek a remedy by which to obtain water for his fleet, of which there was great need; and although in the Island of Queixome, which was close at hand, he could no longer obtain it without force of arms, because of the numerous forces which the king had sent there after the mutiny, for all this he had made up his mind to go there, and, before he set out, desired to be informed by the Moors, whom he had captured in Arbes, in what place the captains and men lodged whom the king had sent to keep guard over the wells. The Moors told him that the headquarters were in a large town called Queixome, and from it all the other settlements were supplied. Afonso Dalboquerque, upon receipt of this information, gave orders to João da Nova and Afonso Lopez to make ready with all their forces to accompany him, and to Antonio do Campo to provide the *paraos*, with Moors to beach them, in order to load with water, and he left Francisco de Tavora and Manuel Telez in charge over the ships.

So, when midnight was come, they set out, and arrived before Queixome so soon, that it was necessary to come to anchor until it was time to see where they could disembark; and when dawn began to appear Afonso Dalboquerque ordered the boats to make for the land, and disembarked with all the company, and told João da Nova and Afonso Lopez da Costa to take their division beforehand and march straight upon the place, and attack it without loss of time, and ordered Jorge Barreto, with fifty men, to attack it from the inner or land side, to draw off the Moors from collecting at any part, and they would thus all meet there; and after giving them these directions he set out with the remaining men, marching direct towards the place, to succour the captains. João da Nova and Afonso Lopez da Costa made such haste, that they arrived before Jorge Barreto at the head of the town, and attacked some large houses, wherein were three captains of the King of Ormuz, just in the act of mounting their horses, and some few bowmen. As soon as João da Nova and Afonso Lopez da Costa perceived there were people in the houses, they closed up with the doors and broke them in with axes, and got in along with them all in confusion; while Jorge Barreto, who by this time had come up, proceeded to attack them behind the houses, upon the top of the walls of some country houses. The Moors, now that the gates leading to the streets were broken open, assembled together in a courtyard and defended themselves there for some time without anyone being able to get in to them; but our men, being ashamed at the delay, attacked them with great vigour, and forced an entry. And, in the moment of getting in they wounded João da Nova, who was the first, and the *Meirinho*,[1] and steward of his ship, and killed one of his sailors; but our party revenged themselves amply, for they put the three captains to death who were getting on their horses to flee away, and all the bowmen who were with them.

All this was done so rapidly, and the fight was so well managed, that although Afonso Dalboquerque was stationed very close to these houses, wherein all this was going on, he did not hear anything that was passing inside; and when he entered the courtyard where our men were, and beheld so much blood and so many dead Moors, he began to be loud in his praises of the captains and all the rest of the people, and averred that he would be recompensed for all his services if the king, D. Manuel, his master, could have seen them fighting from those balconies. Then he went out again from the houses towards a terrace, and commanded Aires de Sousa, and Fernão Soarez, and the others, to mount upon the horses which were there and scour the country all round, and give no quarter to anyone they should meet. This they did, and put to death many Moors, as well as women and children, and collected all the cattle they could find, and returned to the place where Afonso Dalboquerque stood. And when they were come back he ordered that the horses should be killed, that the Moors might not make use of them, and had all the supplies carried into the boats, and returned with this victory to the ships; but he would not allow them to set the place on fire, for it was well supplied with all sorts of provisions, and he was in hopes that whenever the boats returned for water they might each time take away a little. He left Antonio do Campo in his ship on guard over the pools to protect those whom he might send for water; and as soon as he arrived at the ships

[1] The exact duty of this officer is not ascertained, but probably corresponded to that of the quartermaster or boatswain.

he ordered them to beach a *parao* full of the principal Moors who had been killed there, upon the coast of the city, and as these were honourable men and of great esteem, there was much lamentation made over them.

As soon as the *paraos* had discharged their supplies, Afonso Dalboquerque ordered Francisco de Tavora and Jorge Barreto to go to Queixome, where Antonio do Campo was stationed, to bring back all the water and supplies that they could get; and after they were started, Antonio do Campo's pilot arrived with intelligence for Afonso Dalboquerque, and gave him to understand that from the mast-head of his ship he could see many ships at sea coming up underweigh opposite the Island of Lara, and begged he would say what he had best do. Now, because it was but the day before that he had come from the place, and there was no news then of such a fleet, he could not make up his mind what it could be; and in order to make more sure of it he ordered them to bring before him two noble Moors whom he had captured in the island, and inquired of them what ships these might be. One of them told him that they must be some which Cogeatar had sent for from Julfar to proceed in them with the king and all his household to the same island, for there were no means of assistance at hand, as Cogeatar would not permit any more people to enter the city while he was there, in consequence of the great dearth of supplies and water that there was; and the other Moor said that so he thought also, for the night before they were captured, a servant of Cogeatar had passed by in great haste, and told him that he was going to Julfar with a message for the Guazil to send men and ships, but he did not know for what reason.

CHAPTER LII.

How the great Afonso Dalboquerque ordered Afonso Lopez da Costa and Manuel Telez to go and join Antonio do Campo, and attack the Moorish fleet, and how they left him and sailed away to India.

At this news, which the great Afonso Dalboquerque received of the arrival of these ships off the Island of Lara, he sent immediately that night a despatch to Afonso Lopez da Costa and Manuel Telez to go and unite with Antonio do Campo, giving them notice (from the information he had of the Moors captured in the Island of Queixome) of the fleet and the people in it, who they were; and so also he sent to tell Antonio do Campo how he ought to act in approaching the fleet to fight with it, and by Men Rodriguez, constable of the Gunners, the bearer of the despatch, he was to send back word how he fared, for if he were in want of assistance he would go in person with all the rest of the ships. As soon as the despatch was given to them, Manuel Telez and Afonso Lopez da Costa weighed anchor and stood over to the Island of Queixome, where Antonio do Campo was stationed, and gave him Afonso Dalboquerque's message, and then they all three agreed to proceed to attack the Moorish fleet; and as they sailed along, just beginning to espy a point of the island, directly the Moors caught sight of our vessels they slipped their cables and fled away by rowing and sailing, while our captains chased them for two leagues distance, but could not come up with them. And as it was now night they returned and anchored in the port of the island, where the Moorish fleet had been anchored, and from thence wrote, through Men Rodriguez, to Afonso Dalboquerque an account of what they had done, and how they were waiting his further orders for their future proceedings.

Men Rodriguez was no sooner arrived with this message when he was sent back to order Afonso Lopez da Costa and

Antonio do Campo, since the Moorish fleet had fled, to return and take up their original positions in the blockade of the city, and Manuel Telez to go and anchor close to the flagship, as the chief captain intended to send him to carry the supplies to the fortress of Çocotora, as he had told him. Men Rodriguez set about this at once, and proceeded forthwith to the Island of Lara, where all these captains remained, and on his arrival gave them this message, to which they replied that they were just then taking in water, but when they had taken in a sufficient quantity, they would return without delay to the stations appointed for them. Men Rodriguez returned, and on the way met with Francisco de Tavora and Jorge Barreto, coming from the Island of Queixome laden with water, and they gave him an old Moor, an inhabitant of the Island of Lara, whom they had captured there, to carry with him, and this man was a pilot who had fled to Cananor from Antonio de Saldanha, on his first voyage to India. On Men Rodriguez's arrival, he handed over the Moor to Afonso Dalboquerque, and told him how he had found all these captains walking along the beach, apart from the men, and how Afonso Lopez da Costa had said with great arrogance to him: "Tell our captain general that I say what sort of men are these for him to send them their shares of the fifteen thousand *xerafins* perfumed on board?"

Afonso Dalboquerque was not pleased at this that Men Rodriguez said, and asked the Moor what fleet that was, and what men there were in it. He told him there were sixty vessels, and they brought four thousand men under a captain named Xaquear, who came by order of Cogeatar to keep guard over all those watering places, in order that his men might not get their water there. After the lapse of two days, when Afonso Dalboquerque perceived that the captains did not proceed to take up their positions as he had ordered them, nor send any message, he sent Fernão Soarez in the boat of the *Flor de la Mar*, and Pero Gonçalvez, chief pilot, in the skiff of the *Cirne*, to go and seek for them, and tell them he was very much alarmed at not seeing them with their ships in the places he had assigned them. Fernão Soarez, on his arrival at the island, as he did not find them, put in to shore and seized a Moor, who told him that those three captains who used to be there had taken in water and furnished themselves with plenty of fresh salted and pickled meat in jars, and set sail, and steered towards the Cape of Maçandi.

Fernão Soarez returned with this information which he had obtained, and told Afonso Dalboquerque what had happened with the captains, and how the Moorish fleet was lying at anchor between the islands of Lara and Queixome. He was much annoyed at their desertion, leaving the Moorish fleet in a position to attack, and himself blockading so large a city with three ships, so that a fleet, however small it might be, could inflict much damage upon him. At so unexpected an event he remained in suspense for the space of six days, without knowing what to decide upon doing, and he was the more in doubt when he heard the great uproar made by the Moors in the city, like men who were aware of the desertion of the captains. On the one side he saw the city (owing to the great distress it suffered by hunger and thirst) surrendered if he did not raise the blockade; on the other side, he felt the great obligation he was under of supplying the fortress of Çocotora with supplies, of which it was in the utmost need, and which Manuel Telez had carried off on board his ship. After long consideration, however, he came to the conclusion that it would be safer conduct to raise the blockade, and proceed to the succouring of the fortress of Çocotora with what few supplies he had, and leave the affairs of Ormuz in the hands of God, for He would give him another opportunity, wherein He would be better able to assist him. So not without some grief at the idea of quitting Ormuz, he went on board the ship of João da Nova, and told him that his wish was now accomplished, seeing that Antonio do Campo, Afonso Lopez da Costa, and Manuel Telez had fled away to India, and that his own determination was to proceed to the succour of the fortress of Çocotora with some supplies, as Manuel Telez had carried away those placed on board his ship; and he bade him make ready, for he was to accompany him as far as Cape Recalgate, and from that point bear away to India.

João da Nova assured him that it was no pleasure to him if the captains had fled away from him, and that he had never joined with them in such a design; but, on the contrary, he thought they had done very wrong, and he begged he would have the kindness, as he had given him permission to set out for India, to enlarge the parole which had been demanded of him. Afonso Dalboquerque granted his request, and fitted out Pedralvarez, the constable's assistant, to accompany him, bearing letters for the viceroy, wherein he gave him an account of the flight of the captains, and how they had left him when on guard over the city, having certain intelligence that the Sultan's fleet was in Diu, making ready with the King of Cambaya to fall upon him, which intelligence he had gained from some Moors who were captured in a ship belonging to Ormuz, which came from Diu, Cogeatar having sent it thither to demand this assistance. And he begged his lordship that if these captains of his made their way thither, that he would give them that punishment which they so richly deserved, for leaving their captain general at such a juncture, and deserting from him. He gave permission also to Jorge Barreto, his cousin, to go, because he begged him to do so, and he commanded João Estão and João Teixeira (whose oath was taken upon the Holy Gospels) to commence a legal inquiry throughout the ships, concerning the flight of the captains, and after it had been taken, he sent it to Portugal, to D. Manuel, the king, that he might be certified how they had deserted him, and at what kind of season they had fled away; and he also gave permission to some of the men who held the king's commissions, to serve as officers and captains, and to all he ordered to be paid all that was their due with respect to their wages and allowances, that had been agreed upon up to that present time.

CHAPTER LIII.

How the great Afonso Dalboquerque set out towards Çocotora, and having arrived at the island, sent Francisco de Tavora to Melinde to seek for supplies, and what took place.

Afonso Dalboquerque was just on the point of sailing with all his ships in order, when two Moors came down close by our fortress, and began to make signals with a flag; and at sight of them he sent Aires de Sousa, João Estão, and Gaspar Rodriguez, the interpreter, to land, to see what they wanted. The Moors told them to say to the chief captain that the king was very desirous of retaining his friendship, and would do whatever he desired; but as for the four men, he could not return them to him, for they had now become his brothers. Afonso Dalboquerque, knowing that all this proceeded from some trickery and artfulness of Cogeatar, who would have discovered the diminution of the fleet by this time, replied that not once but often he had sent him word that he would make no arrangement with him, without he first of all delivered up to him his men; and now he would do so with worse will, since they had been made to abjure the faith of Jesus Christ in the mosques of Mahomet; but if he were to waive this demand, the king, his lord, would order his head to be cut off as soon as he arrived in Portugal; yet he would promise him (if our Lord only gave him a little longer life) that he would very quickly deprive him of the government of the kingdom of Ormuz, and would finish the fortress, which he now left only begun, and then he would requite him doubly for all the loss and damage which his fleet had received. He ordered also João Estão to notify all this to him in a formal manner, and prepare a public instrument containing an account of all that had happened up to that hour.

And for all that this declaration, which he ordered to be made to Cogeatar, appeared then to be a mere piece of pleasantry, nevertheless, in the second conquest of the kingdom of Ormuz he performed it all, causing him to refund him all the expenses he had been put to without any diminution. So Aires de Sousa went with this message to land, and, without entering into any further negotiations with them, returned; and on his arrival at the ships, Afonso Dalboquerque sent for Francisco da Tavora, and took his oath of allegiance, fearing that he was minded to desert, as I have before mentioned, and set sail with João da Nova in his company. But on reaching Çoá, he missed seeing the *Flor de la Mar* one morning, and, thinking that it had taken a different course, but would return to his company, he passed the whole day without seeing it; and as he did not see it on the following day, he came to the conclusion that it had sailed away to India also. And he was very much annoyed at João da Nova parting from him without mentioning it to him, after agreeing to bear him company as far as Cape Resalgate, and made his way straight to Çocotora; and being in the latitude of this cape, they had sight of a ship, and chased it all the day long, but lost sight of it at night, and continued their voyage. And as soon as they entered into the gulf, they captured a Moorish ship, which came from Mecca very rich: and twenty days after setting out from Ormuz, they came to anchor in the port of the island, and found that the captain of the fortress was very ill, and that the garrison were suffering from such want of provisions that they had nothing left to eat but palm leaves, and a fruit they found growing wild in the woods, four of them being already dead, and all the rest very ill. But on the arrival of Afonso Dalboquerque they became very much delighted, for he provided them with supplies, and all other things that were necessary for their sickness.

To Don Afonso (the captain of the fort) he gave an account of all that had taken place at Ormuz, and of the flight of the captains, and how Manuel Telez had carried away with him all the supplies and drugs which he had entrusted him with to bring to them; and in order to please the people still more, he gave them all a share in the contents of the ship which they had taken on their way, and ordered that they should be paid eight months' salary, which was due to them. And after all had been satisfied and contented, he set about giving orders for the repair of the boats which he carried, for they were now much injured by dryrot, and the ships too in some measure required some necessary repairs. As soon as all was in good trim, he despatched Francisco de Tavora, with money and merchandise, to go to Melinde and freight his ship with supplies, for the fortress had not sufficient for the men it contained; and he told him that after taking the supplies on board, he was to go and meet him at Cape Guardafum, bringing with him whatever vessels he might find in Melinde, to go into winter quarters in May at Çocotora.

Having come to this arrangement, they set sail, and Francisco de Tavora made his way towards Melinde, and Afonso Dalboquerque steered his course for the Island of Bedalcuria,[1] to cruise about there for a few days, because the Moorish pilots had informed him that the ships which made for Cape Guardafum would be more easily intercepted in that latitude than in any other. On his arrival at the port of the island, as soon as he had cast anchor, he

[1] Probably the island called Abd-el-Kury, between Socotra and Cape Guardafum.

ordered twenty men to be put on shore, with two Moors whom he had brought from Çocotora, and who were well acquainted with the language, in order to seize upon some native Moor, and they managed so well that they took six; and Afonso Dalboquerque ordered them, after they had been brought on board, to be asked about amber (for there is a great quantity of it on this island), and also whether any Moorish ships had passed by this course to India. Thereupon they showed him a piece of amber, of about one *marco*[1] by weight, and told him it was but a few days ago since a ship from India had touched there, and been wrecked by the east winds in that harbour, and the men had taken from the natives all the amber they had, and after constructing a small *zambuco* out of the timbers of the ship, had sailed away in it. The Moors of this island are a degraded people, and live in huts covered with seaweed; there are about forty inhabitants in the colony; they go about clothed in skins; they keep large flocks and herds; their food consists of fish, milk, and flesh; the land is very unhealthy.

And because the people began to grow sick at the time that they remained there, Afonso Dalboquerque changed the determination he had formed of staying there, and ordered the Moors who had been captured to be put on shore, and set sail, and proceeded to cast anchor within shelter of the Cape of Guardafum, and there he remained at anchor all alone, always keeping a man on the look out upon the summit of the high ground, which lies upon the front of the cape, and from which a view of Bedalcuria and of all the sea thereabouts may be had; and the Moors of a settlement which is there gave him all kinds of necessary provisions and water in exchange for clothes. Afonso Dalboquerque cruised about this parallel of Cape Guardafum from the fifteenth of January to the thirteenth day of May without seeing more than four ships, three of which escaped

[1] *Marco*, a weight equivalent to eight ounces.

him, for they caught sight of him from afar off, and had the advantage of the wind, and the one which he captured carried but little merchandise, and came from the Island of Diva, which is in the sea of Ceylon.

The people of this land are very domesticated, and Afonso Dalboquerque treated them very well; and from this cape, as far as the mouth of the straits, they have no king; they are armed with shields and Moorish swords; they have large herds of cattle and many camels, of which they make use. Throughout the interior there is plenty of myrrh, which they collect and sell, and in the mountains many trees, from which they obtain incense, which our people, in company with the Moors, went to collect very often, as long as they remained there: they use no money, and give nothing for money, but arrange their buying and selling by the interchange of cloth. From the Cape of Guardafum to Feliz there are three harbours—one is called Bendariçaa, the second Bendaraxaa, and the third Bendesymuçaa; all these three have fresh water close to the sea board, and each one has its lord, and right in front stand Feliz, Metee, Barbora jazira, and Barbora fiara, and nearest of all to the gates of the straits of the Red Sea, along the same coast lies Zeilajadit, and from thence to the cape of the strait there are no more stations.

CHAPTER LIV.

How, on the arrival of Francisco de Tavora at Cape Guardafum, the great Afonso Dalboquerque immediately despatched Fernão Gomez, together with the Moor whom Tristão da Cunha had left in Melinde, to go to the Preste, and how he set off towards Çocotora, and of what further took place.

The end of April was now come, when Francisco de Tavora arrived at the Cape of Guardafum, where the great Afonso Dalboquerque was stationed, and brought with him in his company Diogo de Melo and Martim Coelho, whom he found at Melinde, having come from Portugal; and while all three were in the latitude of Magadaxo, they captured a ship of Cambaya, laden with clothing, and after having stripped her of all she carried, they set her on fire. Afonso Dalboquerque was highly delighted at the arrival of Diogo de Melo and Martin Coelho, and divided with them the spoils of the prize ship; and after conversing upon the news from Portugal, Francisco de Tavora told him that at Melinde he had met the commander, Ruy Soarez, and had requested him to accompany him, for he was under an obligation to do so, and the other captains had gone their way to India, and in addition to this he had made him many other requisitions through his scrivener, but all the answer he got was that he was desirous of proceeding to the viceroy. He said, too, that he had also brought with him Fernão Gomez and the Moor whom Tristão da Cunha had left there under charge of the captain of Melinde, that they might be forwarded to Cape Guardafum, and thence proceed on the journey assigned them by the king; and Fernão Gomez had requested him to carry them with him since the captain had not put into execution what Tristão da Cunha had left with him to do so long ago.

Afonso Dalboquerque was much surprised when he saw them, for it was so long since they had set out that he thought they were by this time in Portugal; and he asked the Moor what road he intended to pursue, and by what means he purposed to return to Portugal. The Moor told him that his road lay through the interior of Barbora Zeila, and through the land of the Cadandin, a Moorish captain who was prosecuting a war with another captain of Preste João, for the one land is contiguous to the other; and that the caravan that went from Zeila to Preste João was always secure, for it enjoyed a safe guard from both, and his return to Portugal would lie through Tambocatu, and thence to

Arguin, along the river Çanaga,[1] for he had already made this journey. Afonso Dalboquerque ordered for each of them fifty *xerafins* for their expenses, for the Moor was unwilling to receive more, telling him that he could not carry with him a worse enemy than money: he also wrote for them a letter in Arabic, and another in Portuguese.

The Moor was very reserved and taciturn, and not altogether pleased with Fernão Gomez, for he was very talkative, and he was afraid he would let something slip from him, whereby they would be all lost, and he desired Afonso Dalboquerque would give him another companion, but he would not, as it had already been settled by Tristão da Cunha. And having set them on their way he ordered them to be carried in a boat by Nuno Vaz de Castelo-branco to land below Port Feliz, and from that point they commenced their journey, giving out to the native Moors that they were merchants who had lost their ship and merchandise, and they alone saved. After they were gone Afonso Dalboquerque still remained where he was at the cape with the other captains until the fifteenth of May, when the Moorish pilot told him that the monsoon for the ships was now passed, and if he was still of a mind to make a visit to Aden, as originally intended, he would not be able to return to winter quarters at Çocotora, for at that season the current sets towards the north, and it would be perfectly impossible for them to make the island. So with this report they weighed anchors, and set their sails, and without any thing of consequence taking place during the run, they came to anchor in front of the fortress of St. Miguel, with the determination of supplying it with the provisions they had on board, and from that place they meant to go and winter at Mascate. And because they found the people of the land had risen against the garrison, who had killed some of their

[1] This passage evidently relates to a route through Timbuctoo and along the course of the river Senegal.

men, he changed his plan, and remained here all that winter to see if he could pacify them, and ordered the factor of his fleet to see that he forwarded to the fortress all the supplies, and that none remained behind in the ships more than they would require for the voyage.

Then Afonso Dalboquerque, with the forces he had brought with him, began to wage war upon the natives, and these, after being thoroughly beaten, and paying the penalty due for the murder of our men, sent, desiring to make peace, and he received their petition, on consideration of their paying every year to the people in the fortress a tribute of six hundred head of sheep, and twenty cows, and forty bags of dates. Upon the conclusion of this agreement, and the return of all to the obedience of D. Afonso, the captain, he ordered his ships to be repaired and a *fusta* of fourteen banks of oars to be constructed to accompany him, for he was determined to pay a visit to Ormuz; and during this winter that he spent there, the storms were so violent and continuous that very often the ships were in great danger of being lost; and because the *Rey Grande* had very high castles, thereby running a greater risk of being lost than the other ships, it was necessary, according to the advice of the masters and pilots, to order them to be cut away. Francisco de Tavora was so much annoyed at this that he said to Afonso Dalboquerque that as he had ordered his ship to be cut down, he might give the command of her to any one he chose, for he for his part did not want her, and would sail no longer in her; and he grew very intemperate in his language about it. Yet, for all that these exhibitions of temper had been shown now for a long time, he would not give him any answer, and dissembled with him, though he had much reason to chastise him; for he had sent him to Melinde to search for provisions, but he omitted lading his ship with them, choosing rather to cruise about after prizes along that coast, and he brought back with him so few supplies, that when all the ships had been furnished with what they required of necessity for their voyage, there would not have been left a sufficiency for the people of the fortress for three months, had it not been for the dates, and other things which the natives were bound to deliver.

After three days Francisco de Tavora perceived that he was much to blame for the words he had spoken in such an unreasonable manner to Afonso Dalboquerque, and sent to ask his forgiveness through D. Afonso de Noronha, his nephew, and begged that he might be restored to his ship. D. Afonso Dalboquerque, however, replied that he was now quite disgusted with the bad behaviour of Francisco de Tavora, particularly after treating him so considerately as he had done, and as he had quitted his ship without any cause, he was not going to restore it to him, and as they were now on their way to India, the viceroy might give it back to him.

CHAPTER LV.

How Manuel Telez, Afonso Lopez da Costa, and Antonio do Campo, arrived in India and made depositions respecting the great Afonso Dalboquerque to the Viceroy: and of the inquiry which he ordered to be made in the matter.

Now, as these captains had come to the determination of leaving the great Afonso Dalboquerque many days before they actually did so, and meant to go to India to the viceroy, as soon as Men Rodriguez quitted the Island of Lara, they furnished their ships with water and supplies, and set sail, and arrived in a few days at Cochim; and when they had disembarked, all three proceeded together to the viceroy, and made before him a great outcry, exclaiming that the king, D. Manuel, had sent them in Afonso Dalboquerque's company to proceed with him to Cape Guardafum, and lie in wait for the ships that went to Meca laden with spices, but he had quitted this road and made his way to the coast of the kingdom of Ormuz, and cruised continually about there, contrary to the advice of them all, carrying on a perfectly unprofitable war; but, not content with this, he had begun to erect a fortress, although the king, D. Manuel, had not ordered him to do so; and they, when they saw how little to the interest of his majesty this was, and that he only did it of his own free will, had sent him a remonstrance, which he had answered with very evil words, for he was a very harsh sort of man, and very hasty, without bearing in mind the honour of his men; and as he would do nothing but insist upon the building of the fortress, they had made him a second remonstrance, to which he in like manner had not deigned a reply; and to show how much he despised them, and made light of what they said to him, although it was all in the interest of the king our lord, he had ordered the remonstrance to be placed beneath a gateway of the fortress, which was just being laid, as if, forsooth, his lordship intended to tread beneath his feet the remonstrance they had there presented to him, signed by themselves and by Francisco de Tavora, who was left behind in prison. They therefore begged his lordship that he would give orders to have depositions of all this taken down, as they had told it to him, by those heads of accusation which they there and then laid against him, and when the truth had been arrived at, that he would do them justice, and order their necessary papers to be made out for them to go to Portugal and demand from the king, D. Manuel, reparation for the injuries he had done to them, and for the shares of booty he had taken from them without being willing to pay them. And the viceroy ordered Gaspar Pereira, who acted in the capacity of secretary, to read him the requisition, which contained the following:—

"Of the remonstance and protestation which we, Afonso

Lopez da Costa, Francisco de Tavora, Manuel Telez, and Antonio do Campo, captains of the king our lord, make to the very honourable lord, Afonso Dalboquerque, our chief captain, you, João Estão, scrivener of this fleet, shall give us each one his copy, and more if it be necessary, for the king our lord, or for the lord viceroy. Whereas it is true that his Highness sent us in his company to these parts to construct a fortress in the Island of Çocotora, which the Moors had already made, and which we took from them by force of arms; and after completing it, we went to watch the straits of the Red Sea, that no ships should pass to Meca laden with spices; but since he has taken this city of Ormuz, and made it tributary to the king, our lord, and established in it a factory with great peace and mutual agreement, without any need of anything else, he, the chief captain, ought not to take upon himself to build a fortress, for it is very little to the interest of the king and loss of his material, and risk of the men and artillery remaining in it, in many respects and reasons which he, the chief captain, will not listen to. Nor yet does he heed a certain section of his instructions which says, that if he can build a fortress, he ought to build it in such a position and manner that it may be securely maintained and defended by the men left behind in it. And he ought to take especial care how far it is to the advantage of the king, our lord, and his estate, to build it thus. And the other reasons, in addition to these, we will lay before His Highness, or his Viceroy of India, if necessary. But he ought to bear in mind that the fortress of Çocotora was all this time standing with the greater part of its men ill, and with supplies for three months [only] counting from the time we left it, and the land contains no more supplies except those which may arrive there from abroad, and that there were yet remaining in it many Moors who certainly will endeavour to tamper with the Christians of the land, and incite them against our people, for these Christians, being angry at being robbed of their cattle against their will, for they live by them (and the Moors had never taken their cattle from them), will be inclined to side with them and keep in favour with them, whereby it may fall out that they will cause much trouble to our people. And this fortress, which he, the chief captain, is building here in Ormuz, cannot be completed so as to contain a guard of men and artillery within five months more; and if he, some time during this month of November, does not quit the place, he will not be able to do so for the whole of this year, for the monsoon, favourable for watching the Straits, will be past, and this would be very prejudicial to the interests of the king, our lord, and the fortress of Çocotora would run a great risk of being lost. Therefore, we do request him, on the part of the king, our lord, and of our lord, the Viceroy, that he will set out forthwith to supply the said fortress, according to the instructions given by his Highness, and thereafter enter the Straits of the Red Sea. And we do also request him, on the behalf of the said lord, that he will immediately send from here this ship, *Flor de la mar*, to the Lord Viceroy, in order to be renovated and not destroyed, inasmuch as the fleet which then remains is sufficient for the watch over the Strait, and in this ship the merchandise, tribute, and ambassadors can be forwarded, which he intends to send to the king, our lord; for it will be safer for anything to go from India than from here. And much more so, as with the merchandise and money he has received by way of tribute, this year the lading of the ships may be remedied (hitherto deficient), owing to the great failure of everything in India, which would be more to the service of the king, our lord, than to send it all to Portugal. And by João da Nova he can write of the condition wherein this city of Ormuz is, for his lordship to make such provisions thereupon as shall seem to him most beneficial to the affairs of his Highness; since,

in his instructions, since he orders him, that upon gaining possession of any kingdom, or any other thing whatsoever, he is to acquaint him immediately with the fact, that he may thereupon make such provision as shall seem best suited to his interest. But if he, the lord captain, be unwilling to perform all these things contained in this requisition, we hereby protest against all the losses, injuries, and diminutions of the material of our lord the king, and state that we are not liable to any blame, for we make this request in good time, whereby all may yet be made good. And of this, with the reply or without it (if he be unwilling to give a reply), you shall give us the said duplicates, with a similar copy of our reply if it be required. Signed and sealed by us in the port of the City of Ormuz, on the thirteenth of November in the year one thousand five hundred and seven."

CHAPTER LVI.

How the Viceroy, D. Francisco Dalmeida, after hearing the captains, ordered an information to be laid against the great Afonso Dalboquerque, and what took place with them on hearing the news which came to him from Portugal.

D. Francisco Dalmeida, upon considering the remonstrance and the articles which the captains had laid before him against the great Afonso Dalboquerque, ordered Gaspar Pereira, who acted as his secretary, to draw up an Act of accusation, and he prepared an ordinance which contained the following statement:—"I, D. Francisco Dalmeida, Viceroy of the Indies for the king my lord, command you, Gonçalo Fernandez, and Francisco Lamprea, public scrivener and judicial in these parts of India, and Pero Vaz, late scrivener of the caravel St. Jorge, and João Saramenho, receiver of the *defuntos*, that you all four open this inquiry (according to the depositions laid before you by Manuel Telez, Afonso Lopez da Costa, and Antonio do Campo) against Afonso

Dalboquerque, and prosecute the same by examination in order of certain articles which they will communicate to you; and Gonçalo Fernandez shall conduct the inquiry, and the other three of you be scriveners, and the four shall be always present at the taking down of the testimony. And as some of the witnesses are not present, all the testimony shall be taken upon oath before me, and the testimony which they require that is in Cananor shall be sent for and taken down there; and this inquiry shall be conducted in the house of Gonçalo Fernandez, inquisitor, wherein all that is done every day shall remain locked up in a chest with three keys of which each scrivener shall have one. And you four have now sworn upon oath in my presence, administered to you by Gaspar Pereira, to prosecute this inquiry well and diligently. Done in Cochim on the twenty-sixth day of the month of May. Gaspar Pereira drew this up in the year one thousand five hundred and eight.

"And furthermore I command that, if the witnesses make any additional statements beyond what is contained in the articles, to the advantage of the complainant's cause, you are to write them down; and if any witness (after having given his testimony) shall return and state that he remembers anything more, you are to write this likewise."

When the Viceroy had made an end of this dispatch concerning the remonstrance of the captains, he ordered Gaspar Pereira to deliver up all the papers to the scriveners and inquisitor who were charged with the execution of the suit, and in addition he ordered them to be supplied with a paper in seventy heads, drawn up by the said captains against Afonso Dalboquerque. What may one say hereupon concerning this affair? except that it was either hatred which the Viceroy felt against Afonso Dalboquerque, or else passion, which determined him to proceed in this hasty manner without hearing what he had to say for himself, and to receive articles against him laid by the captains who had deserted him, leaving their captain engaged in a war fighting day and night with arms always upon him, instead of reproving them for deserting him and flying to India, after he had rendered so large and powerful a kingdom obedient to the king of Portugal with so small a fleet; yea even to hold him in blame for the want of provisions experienced by the fortress of Çocotora, when all the while Manuel Telez was cruising about Cochim with his ship laden with those very provisions which Afonso Dalboquerque had ready to send to the fortress. I had much to say upon this matter, which I omit in order not to digress from the history.

About the period when this business was going on, there arrived from Portugal Fernão Soarez and Ruy da Cunha, in company with Jorge de Aguiar, who set out from this kingdom in the year '8 as chief captain of three vessels under orders from the king D. Manuel to join the fleet at Cape Guardafum and the coast of Ormuz with certain ships, when the great Afonso Dalboquerque was to become governor of India. And after the arrival of these two captains at Cochim, as the viceroy was sitting one day in the harbour with these *fidalgos* and cavaliers of India, João da Nova, Afonso Lopez da Costa, Antonio do Campo, and Manuel Telez being also present, he began to speak as follows:—"Gentlemen, in these ships before you letters have come for me, containing very favourable news for me, which the king our lord has sent, and the import of it is, that, having now finished my term of three years, I am to return to Portugal, and Afonso Dalboquerque will take my post in the government of India. Of a truth our Lord does me a great favour herein, for I am as it were quite dead to all that is going on in the world: and my sins have deserved that before my death I ought to see the troubles which I have seen." And so he went on saying many other things which signified to them the grief he had at the death of his son.

At this news, which the viceroy gave of his return to Portugal, all became very sad, especially João da Nova, and the captains who had fled away from the war at Ormuz. Antonio do Campo, who was always the ringleader in the quarrels that took place in Ormuz between Afonso Dalboquerque and the captains, thinking that hereby he would flatter the viceroy, as well as intending to incite those who were present against Afonso Dalboquerque, stood up and said: "Sir, in announcing that the king our lord orders your lordship to quit this land, and hand over its government to Afonso Dalboquerque, your Highness has stated in this how much it is to your liking, and I hope in God that, just as the affairs of India are governed by His hand, that so now He may show him in due time the error he is making herein, for I hold it for an undoubted fact that when Afonso Dalboquerque is known by the men in India who pass their lives favoured by the love and good deeds which your lordship shows towards them, and when they find how troublesome a man he is in his actions (of which we were witnesses during the time we were with him carrying on the war in Ormuz), there will not be a person in India who will not leave him, and depart to Portugal, and those who remain with him will do so more from compulsion than of their own free will. And as all this is so, your lordship ought not to persevere in your intentions of leaving the government of India, without first of all informing the king our lord, and sending him a written account of the things that Afonso Dalboquerque has done; for it is to be believed that if his Highness knew of them he never would have sent such a message." The viceroy told him that he could not do otherwise than depart and comply with the orders of the king his lord, as soon as Jorge de Aguiar came to land; and if India were to be lost the fault would lay at the hands of that man who had advised the king to order him to return, and to leave the government in the hands of Afonso Dalboquerque.

CHAPTER LVII.

How the great Afonso Dalboquerque set out from Çocotora to Ormuz, and arrived at Calayate, and what took place with the captain of the city.

As soon as he had provisioned the fortress of Calayate, as I have already mentioned, the great Afonso Dalboquerque made himself ready to go to Ormuz, and set out on the fifteenth day of the month of August with the intention of steering to the straits, and getting news of the viceroy, and of India, for it was now some time since he had heard of them; and then, after doing what he could on that coast, he meant to make his way to India. He gave an account of these intentions of his to D. Afonso de Noronha, his nephew, captain of the fortress, and also notified them to the captains in his company. Diogo de Melo, and Martim Coelho, as they were misinformed by Francisco de Tavora of the troubles the fleet had undergone in the conquest of the kingdom of Ormuz, and so were anxious to avoid the like, made a protest to Afonso Dalboquerque, which stated that they had come from Portugal to remain in the company of the viceroy, and were not under any obligation to him, and therefore they desired him to grant them the favour of a licence to sail away to India. He told them to show him their instructions, and because therein the king's order was contained that on arriving at the place where Afonso Dalboquerque was stationed they were to obey him, he obliged them to remain in obedience to him and ordered them, under penalty of death, to follow him, and not to quit his company, for they could see what a need he had of them after the flight of the captains, and he bade the scriveners of his ships to prepare papers upon this penalty which he had laid upon them.

When this business was ended, all set sail towards Cape

Resalgate, and when immediately opposite to Curiamuria (because they were too far out to sea) they held a council to steer towards the land, and stood about all day without getting a sight of it; and when night was come, Pero Gonçalvez, chief pilot, ordered them to alter their course and steer north-east. Afonso Dalboquerque, however, noticing that that course would be opposite to the way which he wanted to make by his chart, sent for him and all the pilots, and told him, that if, in the position and latitude wherein they then were, they were to sail along that point of the compass which he had said, viz., N.E., they would that night run aground, therefore he ought to take great care what he was about. But, as Pero Gonçalvez considered that in his particular business he knew better than anybody, he replied in anger, that since this was so he would give up the charge of the ship to him, and he might steer wherever he liked, and he himself would take his chart and compasses and throw them into the sea. Afonso Dalboquerque replied to him:—"Pero Gonçalvez, look to what you say; do not be put out, for I also know some little about this business, and it may be that the Holy Spirit speaks within me, for the course, which we must take, is that we should stand out to sea again, for if we continue in the course we are now going we shall run aground at the point of Madriçaa; but if you do not think with me, do as you please, for I well know what will happen."

Nevertheless, as Pero Gonçalvez was obstinate, he ordered the ship's course to be kept as before towards land and the others kept to the same course; and when the midnight watch was just begun the ship of Diogo de Melo, which was in advance of the others, fired a gun, and all were awakened. Afonso Dalboquerque ordered the lead to be cast at once, and they found themselves in four fathoms of water, as though they were close in to shore. As his own ship answered her helm very well, he ran very quickly to the tiller, and they all turned round to the seaward in a direct line as well as they could; and he called Pero Gonçalvez and said to him:—"I am the one who ought to throw my chart and compasses into the sea, for I trusted to your knowledge and not to my own; now from henceforward look well to what you do, and do not be wishing that our Lord should perform a miracle for us in delivering us from the danger to which we were exposed." And when the ship of Diogo de Melo made the signal, there was a large bank of rock, which the men-at-arms who were on the look out in the bow heard, with the sea breaking over it, and they called out to the mariners and asked them if it was land that they could hear, and in this doubt they remained, some inclining one way and some another, until at last they saw it was shallow water. So all that night they steered out to sea, and as soon as it was morning, they stood to the land again and made their way straight to Cape Resalgate. And, while they were prosecuting their voyage in this course, Afonso Dalboquerque held a council with the captains, and told them all to get ready with their armed forces, for it was his intention, at whatever hour of the day he arrived at Calayate, to attack the city and destroy it before any assistance could be rendered to it; and as soon as they came in sight of land all armed themselves, thinking that they would arrive that same day, but as the wind dropped they cast anchor and remained where they were that night, and on the following morning they set sail and cast anchor in the harbour. As soon as he had anchored, Afonso Dalboquerque sent D. Antonio de Noronha, his nephew, in the *fusta*, to the city, to see what people there were collected on the beach, and what ships there were in the harbour. When D. Antonio arrived close to the shore, an *almadia* with a few Moors came up alongside of the *fusta*, and brought four she-goats, and two baskets of lemons, and two more of pomegranates, their object being to find out who was the chief captain of these ships, for they were afraid lest it should be the great Afonso Dalboquerque. D. Antonio came with the *almadia* on board the flagship and found all the people already armed and ready to attack the city; and the Moor who brought the present, when he saw our men in such a warlike attitude, became very downcast. Afonso Dalboquerque inquired of him who the captain of the city was, and what men he had to garrison it, and the Moor told him that Xarafadin[1] was the captain, servant of Cogeatar, and very intimate with him, and that there were about two hundred bowmen as garrison. And, because while in Ormuz he had much knowledge about this Xarafadin, he sent D. Antonio to land, to inform him that the chief captain of the fleet had sent him to beg him earnestly that he would be pleased to go on board his own ship, warning him not to tell him who the captain was. So D. Antonio came to land and found Xarafadin on horseback on the beach with some Moors in his company; and he asked him after those whom he had sent in the *almadia* to the chief captain, and who the captain was, and whence they had come. D. Antonio told him that the Moors were waiting in the chief captain's ship for a present which he intended to give them, and they would soon come back, and that those ships came from Portugal by order of the king to assist another of his captains, who was cruising about that coast, called Afonso Dalboquerque, and that the chief captain of these ships had sent to desire that he would be pleased to pay him a visit, for it was very important that they should confer together. Xarafadin replied to him, that he would not go to his ship, but if he required anything from the city he might come to land with perfect safety.

[1] Probably the equivalent of the Arabic *Sharaf ed-deen*.

CHAPTER LVIII.

How the great Afonso Dalboquerque proceeded to attack the city of Calayate, and destroyed it, and what took place there afterwards.

On the return of D. Antonio with this reply, the great Afonso Dalboquerque commanded all the men to embark in the boats, and in the *fusta,* and permitted Francisco de Tavora to command his own ship's company for that particular day, to which indeed he had already appointed as captain, Diniz Fernandes, as chief mate, Diogo de Melo, and Martim Coelho, who had already Afonso Dalboquerque's commission. When they were ready they came on board the flagship to set out thence altogether; and the people of the city, seeing that the *almadia* did not return, and that our boats were collecting themselves together with the intention of going to land, began to take refuge in large numbers in the mountains. Afonso Dalboquerque let the Moors of the *almadia* go on their parole, and stood in straight for shore with all his people, and told Martim Coelho and Francisco de Tavora, that as soon as they disembarked they were to proceed at once to attack the city on the side near the mosque, which was close to the sea, while he with the rest of the men would enter by the other end.

And having arrived at the shore with this plan in view, our men began to fire with their guns, which they carried in the boats, to scatter the Moors who were stationed on the beach; and when they found themselves harassed by our artillery, they fled away in a body as quickly as they could to the city. Afonso Dalboquerque, now that the intention of the Moors had made him alter his original design, as soon as he disembarked, with all the forces united, entered the city along with the enemy in great confusion, passing through the gates into the inner part, and pursuing them through the streets until he had driven them out; and some who attempted to make a stand before our men were killed immediately there, and in this fight Payo Pereira and Diogo Camacho were wounded with arrows, as were also some other soldiers.

Having left the city, the Moors rallied about the distance of a cannon shot from the walls, and Afonso Dalboquerque, being anxious lest they should return and attack him because of the fewness of his men, ordered the captains to guard the gates of the city, and not permit our men to sack it, nor yet break their ranks until he should give his permission for them to do so, and all that night he patrolled the city from time to time with many men. When Xarafadin perceived that our men were so few in number (being ashamed of the feeble resistance he had made), he collected together three hundred Moors and came on to attack us. As soon as Afonso Dalboquerque saw what his intentions were, he sent word to the captains not to fall upon them, but suffer them to come up to the walls; and as soon as they were enticed up, he fell upon them with all his forces and put them to flight along a mountain range, and our crossbowmen and musketeers followed after them in pursuit and wounded many, and then returned and rallied. Xarafadin no sooner perceived that he was hard pressed by our musketeers, than he turned to rally the Moors and embodied himself with them; and Afonso Dalboquerque, to prevent them returning to attack him, sent down to the ship for four cannon and placed them upon the walls, and began to fire upon them. When Xarafadin saw the cannon, and that our men had guarded and defended the city for three days already, as if they had a mind to fortify themselves therein, and to sustain a siege, he withdrew to the mountains with all his army, and remained there until he could find out our intentions.

As soon as Afonso Dalboquerque found himself relieved from the attacks of the Moors, he gave orders to Diogo de

Melo, and D. Afonso de Noronha, to watch the gates of the city that led to the mountains, while he himself with Martim Coelho and a hundred men stationed themselves at the other gate which led to the beach, and he also ordered a look out to be placed in the tower of the mosque, to keep watch from thence upon the movements of the Moors. When the city had been disposed in this order he gave permission to all the remaining men to sack it; and after it had been sacked he ordered Francisco de Tavora to cause all those men to transport all the provisions and clothes they had seized to the ships.

The Xarafadin, upon perceiving that our men were engaged in removing the spoils they had taken, thinking also that they were all disbanded, came down from the mountains with five hundred men, and set to work to attack the gate where D. Antonio de Noronha and Diogo de Melo were stationed, and fought so fiercely with them that he got in by sheer force, and they proceeded to retire through some narrow streets in order to make in them a better stand against the superior number of the Moors. Directly the Xarafadin had forced an entry into the city, he divided his army into two batallions in order thereby to enclose our men; and Don Antonio and Diogo de Melo, seeing the Moors disposing themselves so as to cut off the retreat, shouted out to their men to wheel round. The sentry also who was stationed on the tower, when he saw the strait our men were in, began to shout out to our people that they must hasten up, for the Moors had entered the city; and Afonso Dalboquerque, hearing the sentry's shouts, proceeded with all speed to that part where our men were fighting. D. Antonio and Diogo de Melo, however, with their company which they had already rallied, turned upon the Moors, and attacked them at close quarters with such spirit, that by the time the vanguard of Afonso Dalboquerque's company came up with them our men were on the point of issuing out from the narrow streets in battle with the Moors, and from that point, up to the gate by which they had entered, they kept on pursuing them, and there killed many Moors, and took many arms which those who fled threw down in order to be less encumbered and to be the easier able to effect their escape.

As soon as Afonso Dalboquerque came up with them, and saw so many Moors defeated by so few men as there were in the company of D. Antonio and Diogo de Melo, he gave many thanks to our Lord for the great victory he had given us, and told them all when they were assembled together, that this indeed seemed the work of Portuguese cavaliers, and that the captains who had deserted him ought to be well ashamed at not participating in such a deed as this, when they came to know of the slaughter they had made, while the enemy were incomparably more numerous. Upon their defeat and expulsion from the city all the Moors drew up in view of our men, looking very sad (like men who had experienced a great loss), and among them stood Pedreanes Lamprea (one of the renegades who had deserted at Ormuz), with a helmet on his head, having escaped the day the city was entered, for they had not recognised him. In this action there were present D. Antonio de Noronha, Diogo de Melo, Aires de Sousa, Duarte de Melo, Pero Dalpoen, Lisuarte de Freitas, Antonio de Liz, Antonio Vogado, Lourenço da Silva, Antonio da Costa, Fernão Vaz, and João Teixeira, all honourable men, and of good family, and Simão Velho, Nuno Vaz de Castelo-branco, Antonio de Sá, James Teixeira, and Bertolameu Pessoa, servants of "Mestre Sanctiago," and Jorge Doria, Gentleman of the King's chamber, and Lopo Alvarez, and Martim Vaz, the constable's servants. All these men had their lances and swords dripping with blood, witnesses of what each one of them had done that day.

So Afonso Dalboquerque remained there that night with

all the men, two hundred and thirty Portuguese, and he ordered the captains each one to fortify himself in the houses he occupied, and to hold the boats ready equipped close at hand, and for no attack which the Moors might make upon them in the night were they to sally forth until it was broad daylight. And in this order they remained all night watching the city; and when it was morning he ordered sentries to be posted, and the men began to carry off the provisions and all the clothes which they had seized. As soon as all was collected Afonso Dalboquerque massed his men, and went down to the beach, and ordered fire to be laid to all the principal houses of the city, for in them the Moors had the greater portion of their supplies; and he also ordered the mosque to be fired, which the Moors took much to heart, for it was a very large building with seven naves, all lined with tiles, and containing much porcelain fastened upon the walls, and at the entrance to the gate a very large nave made with arcading, and above these was, as it were, a terrace looking towards the sea, all covered with tiles; the gates and roof of the mosque were all of elaborate masonry. And when it was set on fire it all fell to the ground, without anything remaining in it which was not burned.

They burned there twenty-seven ships, large and small, which lay in the harbour waiting for cargoes in order to sail away to different parts. When all this was done, Afonso Dalboquerque ordered them to cut off the ears and noses of all the Moors whom they had captured, and left them on the shore, and went on board the boats and proceeded to the ships, giving many thanks to our Lord for the favour he had shown him in giving him such a city gained without danger to our men with so small a force.

CHAPTER LIX.

Of the news which the Moor, who brought the gift, related to the great Afonso Dalboquerque, concerning India; and how he sailed from Calayate to the city of Ormuz, and what took place with Cogeatar.

On his arrival at the ship, Afonso Dalboquerque ordered before him the Moor who had brought him the present, and this man was very terrified both at the destruction which he had beheld done to his city, and also at not knowing what would become of himself and the others. And when he had him before him he inquired of him what news there was from India, and what state Ormuz was in, and what men there were there, and if the king had ordered anything to be done to the fortress which he had left just commenced. The Moor told him that Cogeatar had received certain information that the Portuguese fleet had fought in Chaul[1] with Mirocen, Captain of the Sultan of Cairo, and Meliquiaz, Captain of Diu, had assisted the latter with all his fleet to take a ship, and that they had killed the chief captain of the fleet, and that Ormuz was in great want of provisions, for no rice nor corn had come into it from the interior for two years. He said, too, that the Rustazes had rebelled against the king, and gone away with all their people, because Cogeatar had put out the eyes of one of their principal captains who was called Naçaradin, and ordered another called Tajadin to be cast into the sea. And that the sons of Rexnordim, *goazil* of the city, were banished from the kingdom, and he (Cogeatar) had taken from sundry merchants their goods, and had imprisoned Almaça (a very favourite captain of his own) because he was implicated in a conspiracy for putting him to death on account of the destruction and death of the people which had taken place

[1] Chowal, 18 deg. 35 min. N., 72 deg. 57 min. E., on the coast of the Bombay Presidency. See plans in Sloan. MS. 197, f. 230.

in the kingdom through his fault. And that he had made the Christians who had fled from the Portuguese turn Moors, and given them good marriages, and treated them very well for they had made him some very good metal cannons. And that in the fortress he had not done anything more than raise the principal tower and roof it over, and wall up the gate which led to the sea, and open another from the inner side of the terrace of the king's palace. And that in the city there was a great want of water, for the ships which transported it had been all burned in the late war, and on this account Cogeatar had ordered Xarafadin, his servant, to overhaul all that coast, and bring him all the *paraos* he could find for the service of the city. And that Cogeatar had information that the captains, who had deserted the Portuguese before Ormuz, were at Cochim, and had been very favourably received by the viceroy, and that in his opinion if he went to Ormuz with that fleet, considering the great need the city was in, it could not hold out for more than two months before it would surrender.

After Afonso Dalboquerque had heard this news, he gave permission for the Moor to return and take his companions with him and the present he had brought, for it was not his custom to receive anything from people with whom he was at war; and he desired him to excuse him for having detained him, saying that if he had done so it was in order that he might not go and give information to the captain how he found him prepared to attack the city, and that the city's destruction was owing to the fault of the governors of the land, for they had failed in executing the agreement which he had made with them when he passed by this place on his way to Ormuz, as they might see by the royal passport which he had given them in the name of the King of Portugal, his master. He ordered also the factor to give him two thousand *faluzes*[1] and some stuffs, and to the rowers

[1] *Fals*, Arab. (cf. φόλις. φόλλις, *Du Cange*), a small copper coin.

five hundred, and so they went away quite content. As soon as Afonso Dalboquerque had taken his leave of the Moor he ordered the captains to be convened, and gave them an account of all that had passed with him, and told them how he intended, in consequence of the leaky state of the *Cirne* and the *Rey Grande*, to steer away for India, and desired their opinion as to what he should do. All the captains were unanimously of opinion that if Ormuz was in such a necessitous condition as the Moor had told him, he ought to go and reconnoitre the place, for if it proved correct there was no doubt but that the king, on his arrival, would revert to the agreement which had been made, and there would then be a place and an opportunity for repairing his ships, and for providing the fortress of Çocotorá with supplies.

He considered the advice of the captains was very good, and bade them return to their ships and make ready to sail away on the following day; and when morning came they weighed anchor, and sailed along the coast, and came to anchor at a harbour called Tenij, and remained there for two days taking water at a large river which ran between two mountain ranges, jutting out, which formed a large lake close to the sea shore, all surrounded with palms and many other trees. And after having taken water they set sail, and without touching land again proceeded to cast an anchor all together opposite the city of Ormuz. Afonso Dalboquerque ordered all the captains to range themselves in such order as to effectually prevent any help of provisions and people from entering the city, since he intended not to stir thence until the city, surrendered, provided the ships did not make so much water as to cause him to alter his plan. When Cogeatar perceived our fleet, he issued immediate orders to clear the city of all the noncombatants, and to conduct them to the side of the main land, as well as all the *paraos* and vessels which he had for their use, in order that they might not be burned. Afonso Dalboquerque, being desirous of knowing the disposition in which Cogeatar had put the city, ordered the captains to endeavour to capture some one who knew the native tongue. And by means of a Moor, who was caught while fishing one night in an *almadia,* he learned that Cogeatar had constructed two very strong bulwarks on his fortress, with much artillery placed within them, and that five days before there had arrived at Ormuz two men and a Moor, who had escaped to him out of the ships in Calayate, and they had related to him the destruction of the city, whereat the king was much annoyed; and that these men had told him that the two captains who had accompanied him from Çocotora, had desired to go to the Viceroy in India, but he had brought them by force, and that the ships leaked so much that he would be obliged to discontinue the war, and make his way to India, and that the fleet contained very few people, and these were with him very much against their will, and in Portugal there was so much pestilence and hunger, that their king could not send him any assistance of men or ships that year; and that when Cogeatar knew of all this, he had ordered every native to procure a bow, a shield, and a sword, and provision of water for a month, and as he could not rely upon the people he had the keys of all the cisterns there were in the country; and that water was so dear at Ormuz, that a jar of it which in times of peace was worth ten pieces of money was now worth two hundred.

CHAPTER LX.

How a Moor put off from land in an *almadia* and went on board Martim Coelho's ship with two letters for the great Afonso Dalboquerque, without saying who had sent them, and of further proceedings.

Now that the great Afonso Dalboquerque had obtained this information of the state in which affairs at Ormuz were situated, he remained just where he was without sending any one to land, waiting for Cogeatar to make up his mind; and after three days' time two Moors together came out of our fortress and made signs with a flag. Afonso Dalboquerque ordered another to be hoisted at the yardarm of his ship and signals to be made to them to come on board, but they would not come, and on the following day they did just the same. And when the native Moors saw that they made no reply, they sent a Moorish fisherman in an *almadia* on board the ship of Martim Coelho, which was stationed on the other side of the city in the western harbour, with two letters, one from Cogeatar to Afonso Dalboquerque, and the other from the Viceroy to Cogeatar.

The letter for Afonso Dalboquerque was as follows:—

"Chief Captain,—Know thou that the Viceroy has written a letter for thee and for all the Portuguese captains, that ye make not any entry into the kingdom, islands, and lands of Ormuz; the same letter I have sent to thee, and thou hast not obeyed it, nor done what he commands; and he has written another letter to the king, Ceifadin, sealed with the King of Portugal's seals, and, for greater security, Gaspar, the interpreter, and the company, came to the beach and beheld the letter bearing the king's seal, and gave credence to the seal of their king, saying that it had a large quantity of red wax; now to this seal of thy king thou hast paid no attention, desiring, as it would seem, the destruction of the kingdom. Other two letters has he written in Persian, the one to the king, the other to me; both I send thee; read them, and return them to me, since thou carest nought for the commandment and seal of thy king. Cogeamir, whom the Viceroy has sent, and other people from Cananor, who are staying here, are surprised at all these things: and I shall write them all down, and shall despatch them in a small shallop[1] that the Vice-

[1] *Jelua*, a small vessel used in the Red Sea. Arabic *djelba*.—*Engelmann*, p. 276.

roy may know that thou art a traitor to the King of Portugal."

The Viceroy's Letter to Cogeatar.

"O, peerless, nobly-born one, of good fortune, principal commander, universal protector, great lord, and captain over all Alguazils and captains, most nearly allied of all to the dignity of king, acceptable to the Most High of all, perfect Lord Ataa![1] May God augment thy dignity! This thy friend, D. Françisco Dalmeida, Viceroy, sendeth submission, and offereth to kiss thy hands. It is good that there be such friendship between us, that thou mayest send a present every year to the king. I have released Negodaquiçar[2] with a hundred men of thy kingdom, all of whom I had captive, and thou wilt hear of it from them upon their arrival before thee: and the four ships which have come thence have told me that thou hast acted in all respects as a king should act, and hast not erred in any way, and afterwards the captain began to alter it all; and when the four ships perceived that the captain was in the wrong, they made their way to me, while he proceeded to Çocotora, whom I also shall chastise as the king shall appoint, that he may learn that wheresoever he shall receive honour, and give a writing on the king's behalf, he ought not to alter it, for the King of Portugal is not a liar, and it is necessary that his captain should not depart from his commands; but as he has departed from them, he shall receive his reward. The four ships say that they are not responsible for the war, but that the fault is on the captain's side. The first agreement that was made we will not retract, and thy friend-

[1] This word is evidently a misprint in the editions for *Atar*; and the phrase "*Lord Atar*" is here used as the translation of "*Cogeatar*", i.e., *Khojah*, Lord or Master. "*Attār*", a proper name.

[2] The first part of this word represents the Arabic and Persian *Nakhoda*, captain of a ship; the latter part is a proper name.

ship with the King of Portugal is in this state, as is also that of every one who is similarly minded. It is necessary, when thou receivest this letter, that thou come to me, to the end that I may know of it, if not, thou shall know of it. But the four ships, when they arrived here, brought many Moors, both old and young; yet I liberated them all because of the friendship we hold towards thee: and it is necessary that all the ships which desire to approach these parts take courage and be not dismayed, for if a single hair of them be injured, I shall become a traitor to the King of Portugal. Send quickly a ship with thy letters, for I am waiting for this, and there is nothing remaining to say, except that Negodaxemeçadin[1] kisses thy feet. He will soon be with thee, he knows somewhat about all this, thou must believe what he says, and there must not be any doubt in what he will do in conjunction with thee: he will do whatsoever thou wishest. I send thee seven letters in Portuguese for the ships which may come and go, and one under the seal of the King of Portugal; put thy trust in it: I write no more than this: peace and greeting."

And to the same effect came the other letter for the king Ceifadin,[2] and there was no difference between them, only where the one "kissed the hands of Cogeatar", the other "kissed the king's feet".

Reply of the great Afonso Dalboquerque to Cogeatar.

"I have seen a letter which came to me from this city, but it does not state who sends it to me; my answer to it

[1] This is the Portuguese rendering of *Nakhoda Shems-al-din*, or "*Sun of the Faith*". The same name (combined with the title of *Coje*, i.e., *Khojah*), *Coje-Cemeçadin*, occurs in Lafitau, p. 338, in A.D. 1544.

[2] For *Seif-al-din*, or "*Sword of the Faith*".

is, that I obey the letter and command of the Viceroy. Now, as in this letter I am ordered, in the event of the fifteen thousand *xerafins* of tribute not being paid over to me at the stipulated time, to do as shall appear best to me, and most serviceable to the interest of the king, I declare that I require thee, on the behalf of the said lord king and of the Viceroy of India, to pay them at the time which he commands; for I shall not stir hence until thou hast paid me, or until orders shall come from the Viceroy, commanding me to do otherwise. I do not make war upon thee, nor do I shoot upon thee with arrows and cannons as thy people have done upon me. These two letters, which have reached me, written in Persian, I do not believe are from the Viceroy, for they have not his signature; as for my letters which have my signature, take great care of them, for I shall not repudiate them at thy hands, as thou dost thine, and to this end omittest to sign them."

When Cogeatar perceived Afonso Dalboquerque made a specific claim upon him, he wrote this following letter to him, and signed it:—

"Chief captain Afonso Dalboquerque, with respect to that which thou hast written to me about, viz., that the two letters in Persian were not from the Viceroy, for they did not bear his signature, thou shalt know this:—The person who brought them is present, and I could not write of my own accord a letter in the name of the Viceroy. Since thou dost not believe them, return them to me, and I will send him an answer, and the letter which is in thy hand-writing with the Viceroy's signature. If the one in Persian is not his, whose is the other? This is nonsense that you say. With respect to the fifteen thousand *xerafins*, in the time of the re-establishing of the population of the kingdom, and when the maritime commerce is flourishing, it may be possible to pay something, but just now it is but one year since thou madest this destruction upon it, and wentest away until now, so that there has been no opportunity for obtaining it. When an opportunity was just presenting itself, thou hast again appeared before us and this news was reported everywhere, so that not a ship comes to trade with us. Thou verily desirest the destruction, not the reconstruction of this kingdom. Calayate, which is the last city left to the kingdom, thou hast sacked and destroyed, and carried away thence a hundred thousand *xerafins* and more; a hundred thousand *xerafins* make a good set-off against fifteen thousand; of all this destruction I intend to acquaint the Viceroy.

"For what thou has written, that thou wouldst not make war nor fire upon us, I do not thank thee for it; for what God willeth, that must come to pass: as for saying that thou wouldst not depart, and that thou heldest the sea, if thou profitest by remaining, remain by all means: in writing this, I write no evil; if your people read badly, this is another question. The Viceroy's letter, with thy handwriting, and with the king's seal, as thou hast readers from the king, order them to read them, that they may know the truth and the falseness. Respecting the four ships, of which thou hast written, that they fled away and acted treasonably, they have gone to the Viceroy, and behaved loyally in going to their captain, and performed their king's command, for they were witnesses that thou didst desire to destroy the kingdom, and all thy people are angered against thee; for if it were not so, they would not have combined at Calayate to speak ill of thee, neither would they have fled to the high ground, to the Arabians, if thou hadst been true and friendly to them. It is now a year since thou tookest tribute; then thou wentest away at once; but thou wast here five months before the war broke out. Whensoever I said to thee, thou oughtest to go, thou never wouldest go, but didst commence hostilities. Now, I address myself to the Viceroy; whatever may take place, to him I intend to relate it; for he, though absent, is my friend; but thou, who wast present here, and highly honoured by the king, yet at last becamest my enemy and didst not keep thy word, nor thy agreement, neither didst thou act as a father with his son; and now thou cruisest with thy boats along the waterside, not permitting people to enter with what God has provided for us. In men, in supplies, and in arms, we have no deficiency, and if thou dost not believe it, send a man who may see everything. I am not a liar. The messenger need not fear anything. My word is my bond; and in that thou sayest that thou dost not know who writeth to thee, my name is my signature, and hereto I have set my seal and signature."

I have given the translation of these letters here that it may clearly appear how much the Viceroy laboured to render futile all that the great Afonso Dalboquerque did, although there was much reason for him to give him every assistance, for he was the Viceroy of India.

Of the Reply which the great Afonso Dalboquerque sent to Cogeatar.

"Honoured Cogeatar,—I was much pleased to know that it was thou who wrotest to me, and I have thoroughly considered this letter thou hast sent me: and in respect to the two letters in Persian which the Viceroy has sent thee, and which thou hast forwarded me, I for my part never expected that the Lord Viceroy would give so much credit to some captains who deserted me in the war, and over whom I had as much authority as he has over those whom he has with him; and if thou desirest proof, I will send it thee, and then thou shalt know whether they have worked treason or not. I am well aware what kind of things they told thee, and how they procured thy rebellion against me, and planned that thou shouldest not restore me my men, on which all the peace and friendship between us was staked. These fugitives would not have fetched more than five *xerafins* each if they had been sold in the market-place of Ormuz; while I left for thee twenty servants of the king in the factory, under thy power and obedience, as well as the factory of the king, which was worth two hundred thousand doubloons. These thou mightest have taken from me without war if thou hadst wished, after my departure, hadst thou not taken from me these four fugitives before my very eyes, in order thereby to commence warfare, and rise up against me; and if thou hadst cared for them, thou wouldst not have confessed that thou hadst them, neither wouldst thou have said that thou wouldst restore them to me, neither wouldst thou have shown them to me; for hadst thou said that thou knewest nought of them, I should have then had no reason for making war upon thee. But what kind of obedience was that which thou hadst signed and sworn to the king, my master, and to his captains, if thou couldst yet take from me my people? and who could expect that thou wouldst pay him fifteen thousand *xerafins*, if thou tookest from him four runaways that were not worth ten? Thou art a captain, and therefore knowest how imperative it is upon such to give a good account of the men entrusted to them. I well know that my captains made thee do this, and thou shalt see them beheaded in the public square of Ormuz, for the King of Portugal, my master, has not conquered the Indies and whatever other places he has subdued, except by his captains prosecuting the war with their chief captain, and not working treason against him; and because Portuguese never yet so acted, thou shalt see what I say.

"And furthermore, in regard to the complaints which the Lord Viceroy makes against me in the two Persian letters (if they be true), taking as well done the actions of my captains, he ought to have remembered that I am the Captain-

General of the fleet of the king my master, and that the tribute, which he now sends to beg of you with honeyed words and high-sounding letters, this tribute I have made thee pay with my sword in hand, and thou thyself art hereof a true witness, for thou dost confess as much in the contracting papers, made between me and thy king, and on this account I trust in God that I shall not stir hence without the tribute, inasmuch as the viceroy so orders in his letter; because thou knowest that if I had not received this letter here, I should not have ventured to demand tribute of thee, but only my men (on whose account I began the war upon thee, by the advice of the captains, cavaliers, and servants of the king in my fleet, and of this even now I do not repent), and because thou holdest as leal and true the captains who deserted me in the war and fled from me, for all that they were minded as far as thou wert concerned to kill for thee those who were within thy house; and the house which I constructed, and which the captains led thee to suppose was for thy destruction, is this fleet, wherein I now am, and that which I made was for thy protection, for in times such as these (and there are many such as these in Ormuz) there is no reason that the men and factory of the king should be at the disposal of any who may conquer them, who would not indeed have been attacked, if it had been completed. As to what thou dost allege that my people are angry with me, and fly from me, when thou shalt see taking refuge with thee an honourable man, and a servant of the king, then believe this, but not two runaways, who escaped from prison, one of whom I had a good mind to sentence to the loss of his hands, and the other had incurred a flogging at the hands of the quarter-master, all the four whom thou hast deceived with specious words, in whom thou believedst all thy salvation was centred, these very men, to whom thou dost give such credence, were the beginning of all thy destruction, and I hope to God that they will not compass it.

"And as for what thou allegest, saying that I ought to have remained in peace and friendship for a year, and having received the tribute gone away directly, thou well knowest that I always endeavoured to repair my fleet, and was waiting for the season and trade wind, when the Straits of Meca can be navigated, which is at the commencement of the Ramadão,[1] for it was thither that the king commanded me to proceed, although I never divulged it to thee, nor to the captains nor to any one whomsoever, for it is the usual custom with chief captains to keep their instructions secret, that their enemies may not come to know what they intend to do, for if I had then mentioned the route I intended to take, in a few days Adem and Judá[2] would have been forewarned that I was on my way against them, according to the instructions given to me by the king, and with this end in view, I constructed the brigantine, which thou hast burned for me, for it was much wanted for such an expedition. And furthermore, if thou wilt be so good as to bear it in mind, the Noradin required of me on the king's behalf and on thine, that I would not depart thence, for the ships from Meçar were coming, and might possibly seize the city and hold it in possession; but I sent back word to him, that by the agreement I had made I was under the obligation to defend his kingdom, and that it only remained for the king to mention what he would have me to do.

"And to proceed yet further, what did Ormuz lose all the while I was stationed before her? Did the caravans cease to come, or did they not rather come more often? And the sailing ships also, if thou hadst not hindered them, would have come too. But on the contrary, by my establishing myself here the kingdom became more

[1] The Turkish month, of thirty days, corresponding to part of March and April, generally observed as a fast.

[2] Jidda, or Djeddah, the port of Mecca, lat. 21 deg. 30 min. N., long. 39 deg. 22 min. E.

and more secure and the common people grew rich. And thou well knowest that after I delivered it over to thee, I never meddled either in the administration of justice of the country, or in the government of the kingdom, but rather gave thee licence to order the arrest of my men if in the city they did not behave themselves with due propriety. Not a loaf was purchased without thy order, and if thou hadst set the price of it at a hundred *xerafins*, as much would have been paid, and so in the seed-pearl[1] and in everything else that was bought, all was paid as thou didst arrange. And I ordered nothing to be made in the city by the smith, the carpenter, the mason, the tailor, or by any other workman, without thy permission; wherein I demonstrated that I was more amenable to thy obedience than thou wast to mine. As for the house that I built, the king, and his father, and thou thyself gave me the site of it, and the foundation whereon I placed it, as I have proof of, under their signatures; and as for the stone and the workmen, whereby it was constructed, thou didst give them to me. Many a time did I send to ask thee if thou wert content at my building it, and thou didst answer yes. If thou wert not content, wherefore didst thou not say so, instead of taking my men from me, whereby thou hast fallen into disobedience and broken the contract? Yea, and as often as thou hast occasion to mention this war to the Viceroy, thou dost never tell him the reason of its commencement, which is a sign of guilt; and before such men thou hast to declare the whole of the affair. All this then will go before the king my master, and it will not seem very much to his interest that thou shouldst make Moors of his Christians.

"And in regard to thy statement that I have not kept the word and contract which I made with the king, nor

[1] *Aljofar*, cf. Arab., *jauhar*, *johar*; Pers., *gauhar*, *gohar*;—a jewel, or precious stone.—*Engelmann*, p. 145; *Bluteau*, vol. i, p. 260.

dealt with him as a father with a son, I have performed and maintained all that I agreed with him to do; and, if this is not so, do thou but leave him in free liberty to govern his kingdom, and I engage that he will make a recognition of the good service I have rendered him in delivering up the kingdom to him after that I had gained possession of it. Had he been free to act, and the kingdom governed by him, thou hadst not robbed me of my men nor rebelled against me; yet I hope in God yet to render him so many good offices, and to assist him in obtaining so many countries in Persia (captured according to his orders, and in obedience to the king my lord), that he may become the most powerful sovereign therein, for he deserves it because of his goodness, and because he is come of a line of kings. Again with regard to thy account that thou hast many supplies, arms, and soldiers, and art lacking in nothing, thou verily hast good need of them all; but for all these he who has overcome thee in thy prosperity will now also make thee do all that the Viceroy orders. And if thou dost not perform these orders, then shalt thou see whether the Portuguese cavaliers are disaffected with me or not, for there is not one among us this time who will corrupt the men's inclinations, only captains who with much spirit and good will are willing to die with their captain-general in the service of their king. And thou also art well aware that I know the Rustazes are against thee, because thou hast put out the eyes of the best captain and cavalier whom the King of Ormuz had, and Calcocejo,[1] who has many men, and whose orders in the land are always done, and Xeque Ale, too, are no longer under thy command. I know also what men thou hast with thee, and the intention wherewith thou hast sent Xarafadin to Calayate. And I am well informed where thou dost sleep, and what thou dost eat, and how thou dost live, and I know also that the house of Ormuz is upon a very weak founda-

[1] This name occurs as *Caecocejo* on p. 243.

tion, and must of necessity perish, if thou dost adhere to this path. I require thee once, twice, and three times to fulfil the command of the viceroy; and if thou hast aught to the contrary, show it to me and I will fulfil it entirely, according to the instructions of the king, my lord, given to me.

"If thou write to the viceroy, send him my letters, for to this end I send thee this one in Portuguese, signed and sealed with my signet; for when he hears both sides he will pronounce a better sentence. Yet again I tell thee that the cause of the war that has begun between me and thee is yet alive, and that no one from envy can put me down and hide me, for have I not already many a time told thee that I was no corsair but captain-general of the King of Portugal, an old man and a peaceable one, and that I have plenary instructions from him of which he will take from me account for all that I do? And as for what thou dost say that thou wilt speak with the viceroy for the future, and that whatsoever may happen thou wilt inform him of it, thou dost well herein and art right; for whenever I make war upon enemies it is in such a manner that it behoves them for their own sakes to go and beg for mercy of the king or of those who exercise his power. And since thou already hast begged mercy of him, I promise thee (unless thou dost comply with the order given in his letter) that thou shalt go yet again and beg it of him. In what is stated in the Persian letter about my not daring to go to him, but that I went indeed to Çocotora, know of certainty that I have fear of no one except of my king; but on the contrary I tell thee that the captain who knew both how to obtain this kingdom, and conquer a king in battle, and make him tributary to the King of Portugal, will be treated with great honour, let him go whithersoever he will, and the viceroy knows that I have performed my duty in proceeding to succour the fortress of Çocotora, as my king had ordered me, and that I had not now fled, had I not gone to seek for the supplies which the captains carried away from me when they departed, leaving thy fleet of seventy sail against me, although I commanded them to make for it and destroy it; but this they would not do, and well it was that it turned out so, since between thee and them there was such amity."

CHAPTER LXI.

How the great Afonso Dalboquerque recounted to the captains and principal men of the fleet all that had passed with Cogeatar, and of the message he sent him, and of the reply he made.

After the great Afonso Dalboquerque had sent this reply to Cogeatar, he ordered the captains to be summoned, with all the Fidalgos and principal men of the fleet, and gave them an account of all that had passed with Cogeatar; and after having read the letter which the Viceroy had written to him, he said to them that he begged them, as a favour, to consider the affair very carefully, and advise him as truly as they could, what steps he ought to take in the matter, for his judgment was insufficient for the understanding of the mode of dealing which the Viceroy desired to have with him. And he explained that the Viceroy had not been content with highly favouring the captains who had fled away from the war, and deserted him, permitting many insults to be perpetrated upon him, for the service of the king our lord; but that he even had written the letter before them to Cogeatar, praising him highly about his flight and returning to him the captive Moors, whom he had forwarded, though taken in fair war, together with many words of little credit to his person, and lightly esteeming his labours, as they had seen in this letter, all which was highly favourable to the Moors, but greatly to his own disadvantage. And since this was so, and he had no longer any hope of the Viceroy's assisting him in this undertaking, he had made up his mind to have no more disputes with Cogeatar, nor even to demand tribute from him, but to steer for India and come to the point face to face with the Viceroy. The captains, although they were deeply moved by the contents of the letter, and the slight estimation in which the Viceroy held Afonso Dalboquerque, yet, notwithstanding all this, they urged him to suffer it, and not to be put out, for all that he was on the eve of the journey; and they told him that he ought to send a declaration to Cogeatar, and notify to him the orders of the Viceroy.

Upon hearing this advice of the captains Afonso Dalboquerque suppressed the anger that he felt, and sent word to Cogeatar by Pero Dalpoem, and Gaspar Rodriguez, the interpreter, that the term appointed by the Viceroy for the payment of the tribute if it was wished to avoid the war, would end eight days therefrom; and if it were not paid by that time, that they would no longer care to demand tribute of him, but would insist on the return of the four Christians, whom he had taken from him, for the kingdom of Ormuz belonged to the King of Portugal, his lord, gained with his fleet, and would not be suffered to secede.

Cogeatar replied to Pero Dalpoem that he might tell the captain-general that he must undeceive himself, for neither to him nor to any other person whatsoever would he pay tribute, even if the Viceroy himself were to order him to do so. And, although Afonso Dalboquerque was very ill pleased with this reply, yet, because it had already been agreed by all that he ought not to make war upon him until the stated period had elapsed, he dissembled with him, and set about sending D. Antonio de Noronha, his nephew, to the Island of Queixome in the *fusta* and the boats, to obtain water, owing to the great need there was of it throughout the fleet. And as soon as it was all ready for them, he set out without delay by night, and arrived at the island by daybreak, and as he was on the point of landing, many people ran up to prevent him disembarking; but D. Antonio, with those whom he had with him, got to land by force of arms, and dispersed the natives, and reached the wells, but as he found them filled with rotten fish which the Moors had cast into them, he returned to the ships without carrying back any water.

Nevertheless, by reason of there being no supply of water throughout the fleet, and as the men were already beginning to suffer in consequence, and as none could be obtained from the Island of Queixome and from Nabande (these were the nearest) except with a large armed force, for Cogeatar had placed many soldiers there on guard over the wells, he again dispatched D. Antonio de Noronha in the *fusta* and boats, without loss of time to bring back water from the Island of Lara, and on the following day he returned with the *paraos* laden with it. On the arrival of D. Antonio, Afonso Dalboquerque sent Pero Dalpoem and Gaspar Rodrigues, the interpreter, to land, to inform Cogeatar that the term of the eight days, given to him to enable him to pay the tribute, was now past, and that now, in accordance with the warning already given, he was determined to do as he thought most service to the King of Portugal; therefore now he no longer desired tribute, but the men of his fleet, who had been taken from him, and he trusted in his friendship and in the treaty he had made with him when he delivered over the kingdom in the name of the King of Portugal, signed by the king, and sealed with his seal. But as for the tribute, he would be obliged to pay it; for the Viceroy would send and insist upon it, since he would take care about this, and so much friendship existed between them, and he could advise the king to look well after the preservation of the kingdom, and not seek its destruction by refusing to send back four runaways who would not be able to defend him from this attack.

Cogeatar, knowing that the king was not very well pleased with the war, desired to prevent Pero Dalpoem from giving him this message, yet for dissimulation's sake, gave place to it, and desired him to go before the king. Upon hearing the message, the king, who was anxious as to what reply he should make, cast his eyes upon Cogeatar, and said to Pero Dalpoem that he could not send back the four men, for they were now become Moors, and the law of their faith protected them; and after Pero Dalpoem had retired from the king's presence with this reply, Cogeatar told him to say to the captain-general, that the tribute, which the Viceroy had sent to demand, had been well paid by the destruction he had wrought in Calayate; and as he was constantly stationed in the harbour, seizing and destroying every thing that came to it, it was now two years since any dues had been received in the custom-house, and there was therefore no need of saying anything more. As for the four Christians whom he had sent to demand, the king had already replied upon this point, and if he was bent upon making war upon him because he would not yield them up, he might do as he pleased, for it would not hurt him in any way whether he stayed there a day, or a year, or a hundred years. He then summoned Cogeamir, the bearer of the Viceroy's letters, and told him, in the presence of Pero Dalpoem, that he was not going to decline paying the tribute, but that at present he had no means of paying it, but yet he was the servant of the King of Portugal, to whom the kingdom of Ormuz belonged, although the captain-general desired to destroy it; he therefore was to remember all these things and repeat them to the Viceroy when he returned to him; and he also told him many other lying words, full of deceit.

Pero Dalpoem made no answer, but took his leave, and Cogeatar managed that he should go forth through the gate of the castle, where he had ten metal pieces of ordnance,[1] as large and as well made as our own, and a large double-chambered mortar (*bombarda*), of the size of our *camelos*, all mounted on gun-carriages, as well as many other iron guns of good workmanship, which the renegades had made, planted upon a bulwark lately constructed there.

CHAPTER LXII.

Of the council which the great Afonso Dalboquerque held with the captains upon the reply of Cogeatar, and what they agreed upon, and the message which he sent to the Rustazes by some of their servants, and what further passed.

Upon the receipt of this reply of Cogeatar, so full of pride, the great Afonso Dalboquerque summoned the captains, fidalgos, masters, and pilots, and all the other people of the fleet, to make up their minds what to do; and all having assembled on board his ship, he recounted to them the message which Cogeatar had sent to him through Pero Dalpoem, and told them the disgust he felt in his soul at seeing how proudly Cogeatar had replied to his messages, a thing which he had never yet done until now, and only now because of the slight store which he perceived the Viceroy set upon him and upon all those who accompanied him in this war, to the service of the King of Portugal; and he explained how the captains who had deserted him, though he had been very intimate with them, had asked him whether he would make the voyage to India to save those ships which leaked so much, or rather continue to blockade the city until it surrendered; for he had certain

[1] "Falcões", falconets or howitzers.

information that it was in very great need of supplies and water, and that there had been great dissension among the inhabitants.

The captains and all the rest of the people, upon all these representations made to them by Afonso Dalboquerque, discussed this business, and, having carefully weighed everything, agreed that on condition that the leaks in the ships did not increase so as to render them liable to great risk of being unable to make the passage to India, they would remain there until the end of October, for until this time some ships might proceed thither from Portugal, on their arrival at Çocotorá, and this would be a great help in the matter. Having agreed upon this, Afonso Dalboquerque ordered the captains to set their ships in order round the city as before, and by night to cruise in the boats along the shore, each one on the watch, as chance might take them, to prevent any *paraos* from passing through the blockade to the city; and they made such diligence in this matter that they took many which approached, laden with supplies, and among them three, belonging to the captains of the Rustazes, who sailed from a place which was called Jáquem.

When Afonso Dalboquerque knew that the *paraos* belonged to them, he ordered them to be given up, and wrote to them through some of their servants who were in them, that if they were willing with their army to assist him in this war, he would pay them and supply them with rations; and when he had driven Cogeatar out of the city, would give up to them the government of the kingdom. The servants of the Rustazes went away, and gave the letters to Caecocejo,[1] who was the principal man amongst them; and, as the way was long, they consumed much time about it; so that when they returned with the reply, they found

[1] This name is spelled Calcocejo on p. 236.

Afonso Dalboquerque already determined to proceed to India.

The Caecocejo's reply was to the effect that he was highly pleased with possessing his friendship, and he was then engaged in making ready himself and all his relations to come and serve him in the war, for all were desirous of becoming vassals of the King of Portugal; and he would have him to know that as soon as he had arrived at Calayate, Cogeatar had caused them to be summoned, offering him many rewards, which he had, however, refused to accept. In addition to this reply, he sent a present of chickens, sheep, and pomegranates, and Afonso Dalboquerque sent him another of silk stuffs, and other things of great price, and wrote to him, thanking him greatly for his intention to come, but that he was very sorry that he could not wait for him, yet he hoped very shortly to return and take again in hand that enterprise, and then both together they would make war upon Ormuz.

Having dismissed these servants of the Rustazes, seeing that the water for the use of the men in the fleet (which was the source of more anxiety to Afonso Dalboquerque than anything else) was running very short in the ships, he ordered D. Antonio to go to the Island of Lara and fill the *paraos,* as he had done already some days ago. So Antonio set out and arrived at the island, and as he found it was already garrisoned with soldiers who had passed over from the Island of Queixome to guard the wells, he returned without taking in any supply. As soon as D. Antonio reached the fleet again, Afonso Dalboquerque made ready to proceed to the island in person, and sent Martim Coelho forward in his vessel, and he himself embarked in the *fusta* and in the boats with a large number of men, and followed after Martim Coelho. On arriving at the island, they disembarked, and proceeded to attack the Moors, and at once put them to rout, and made them quit the stations they held, and took many camels, she-goats, and cows, and uncovered the wells which the Moors had closed up, and loaded the *paraos* and boats with water and provisions. When this was done, Afonso Dalboquerque went back to the ships, leaving Martim Coelho in his vessel on guard over the wells; and, as long as he remained there, the Moors who were in the Island of Queixome did not dare pass over to the Island of Lara. And three days after his return to the ships he sent Diogo de Melo to the Island of Lara to tell Martim Coelho that he was to take in water, and go and cast anchor off the city, where he himself was stationed. Diogo de Melo went away without loss of time, and on reaching the island told Martim Coelho what Afonso Dalboquerque had ordered, so he took in water for himself, and weighing, went and anchored in the place where Diogo de Melo was stationed.

After Martim Coelho had taken up this new position, Afonso Dalboquerque ordered Pero Dalpoem and João Estão to go in his ship's skiff by night along the coast to see what our men (whom he had commanded to watch the city in the boats) were about; and while they were rowing up along the bank, a *parao* came close up to them, and not guessing what it could be, they proceeded to attack, though unprovided with arms, thinking that it was coming with supplies for the city; and as they boarded it they were all wounded with arrows, and because the affair took place of a sudden, they were so thrown aback that the Moors had opportunity to save themselves in the *parao*. Afonso Dalboquerque, thinking that it might be a stratagem of the renegades, who had advised Cogeatar to order archers to be placed on board the *paraos* which carried provisions to protect them, that very night ordered the boats, armed with soldiers, to take one, that he might learn from the Moors it would contain what this course of action proceeded from. And as our boats kept on going round the city all night, a *parao* with thirty archers came to close quarters with them and they took it without resistance, and carried it to the place where Afonso Dalboquerque was stationed. And from two Moors, whom he ordered to be put to the torture, he learned that the widow of King Cergol[1] had sent one hundred and fifty archers to the King of Ormuz, distributed in many *paraos*, that they might come more secretly, in order to assist him in the war, and that Cogeatar had ordered a fleet to be built at Julfar[2] to come and burn that of the Portuguese, and that a Persian caravan had arrived at the port of Nabande, wherein there came two captains of Xeque Ismael with five hundred archers, wearing high helmets, whom Cogeatar had sent for, giving a great sum of money that they might help him in the war, and these were only waiting for a safe passage to cross over.

CHAPTER LXIII.

How the great Afonso Dalboquerque informed Diogo de Melo of what news he had received concerning the fleet of Julfar, and went to Nabande, and fought with the captains of Xeque Ismael, and routed them.

As soon as the great Afonso Dalboquerque was informed of this fleet which was being prepared in Julfar, he wrote immediately to Diogo de Melo to be upon his guard and keep up his communications, lest they should fall upon him unawares; and in case so many ships should come that he would be unable to cope with them, he was to send him word at once, for he would come in person to help him.

[1] The king's name is given as *Sargol* in a former chapter.

[2] There are two places of the name of *Julfa*, but neither seem to have been likely places for building a fleet; one in 32 deg. 38 min. N., 51 deg. 52 min. E.; the other on the River Araxes, 38 deg. 57 min. N., 45 deg. 37 min. E.

And he told the other captains that he had news that two captains of the Xeque Ismael had reached Nabande, bringing men to reinforce the King of Ormuz, they must therefore make themselves ready, for he was determined to go thither and fight with them; and he ordered D. Antonio de Noronha to embark in his ship's boat with a portion of the men, while he, with the remaining portion, would go in the *fusta*. And lest the ships should be seen to be deserted by their companies in the sight of the city, and lest the renegades should perceive, by the absence of the ships' boats, that they were left empty (a stratagem these fellows themselves knew well enough how to practise), he agreed that this attack should be made at night, for the moon was very bright, and then they could return in time, that they might not be missed at the ships. He also posted several men to guard the ships, and left two gunners in each.

And having arranged all this, he embarked at once by night with all his men, and proceeded to join the other captains, who were already prepared; then they all together made their way straight to Nabande, where they arrived at midnight. They were, however, immediately discovered, and they heard a shouting as of many people, and, on coming nearer to land, the Moors gave another shout, which seemed to proceed from a smaller number of men. Afonso Dalboquerque, who was in the vanguard, as he did not hear any noise of people, thought they had quitted the place, and gone away; so he disembarked; but as soon as he put his feet on the ground, such a quantity of arrows were discharged at our men, without their perceiving from what quarter they were attacked (for it was night), that they could not stand to their quarters. Yet remaining with his men massed together in expectation of the arrival of the boats, and deeming it less danger to fall upon the Moors, than to wait while they wounded them all, he decided that he would attack them; and at this crisis the other captains came up, and as soon as they had landed their men, he started off and began to enter the place. Directly the Moors caught sight of him, they drew themselves up in a body close to the mosque, and there waited, while Afonso Dalboquerque, just as he was, in company with his men, fell upon them, and attacked them with so much fury, that at the first stroke they slew many, and thus having made good use of their lances, they came to close quarters with their swords upon the Moors on a sandbank which was hard by the place, and they fought, both one and the other side, with such vigour for a good space of time, that they made the sandbank so clear that it seemed more like the terrace of a palace than a bank of sand. And being in this critical position, which did not last very long, with the greater part of the men wounded, D. Antonio de Noronha came up from behind the mosque and fell upon the Moors, who, when they saw themselves out-flanked, took to flight. And just then arrived Francisco de Tavora, and Martim Coelho with his men, and pursued them for some time, disabling many of them, who, as they thus fled away, kept turning round to fight with our people and could not quite make up their mind to retreat. Afonso Dalboquerque, while it was still night, retained his position close to the mosque with his men in close order, and fearing lest those who pursued the Moors should straggle about, he ordered the captains to withdraw them and reinforce his men. And, as soon as they were united, they entered the place and passed up a street to attack a house wherein were the two captains of the Xeque Ismael, in the act of mounting their horses, with the servants, prepared for flight, and forcing their way in, they put every one of them to death, and returned immediately to the mosque, where there was another captain with a large body of men collected together to fortify themselves in it. It was, however, of no use for him to do so, for D. Antonio de Noronha, and Martim Coelho, and all the rest of the people, who followed them, proceeded to attack the mosque, and made an entry by force, and slew the captain, and all the people it contained, stripping them of their arms, and red helmets, and everything else they had, and then sallying out they began to sack the place. Afonso Dalboquerque, perceiving that the Moors of the land were beginning to assemble together, while he had but few men with him, for it was night, made his way back with the captains towards the shore, where the boats were stationed, that he might make use of the cannons if they attempted to attack him, and he ordered the town to be set on fire in four different places, and the drum to be beaten, that the people who were dispersed up and down, sacking the place, might know where he was. When our men heard the drum, each one made his way back towards that part where the drum was being beaten, with as much treasure as he could bring away; and when they had re-assembled, the Moors no longer dared to engage them, but withdrew to the opposite side of the place, and between us and them there was a marshy piece of ground, and there they remained, without being able to extinguish the fire in the place.

In this affair on that day there were in company with Afonso Dalboquerque the following persons:—Diogo Guisado and Gaspar Machado (of the royal household), Antonio de Sá, Bertolameu Pereira, Nuno Vaz de Castelo-branco, Antonio de Liz (pages of the Master of Sanctiago), João Coelho, Gonçalo Queimado, and Pero Gonçalvez (chief pilot); and they were all wounded with arrows. And with D. Antonio de Noronha there were Jorge da Silveira, Francisco de Melo, Duarte de Sousa, Bastião de Miranda, Antonio da Costa, Lisuarte de Freitas, João Estão, Nicoláo de Andrade, Antonio Fragoso, Pero Dalpoem, João Teixeira, Simão Velho, James Teixeira, Antonio Vogado, and many other honourable men. And with Francisco de Tavora there were, D. Jeronymo de Lima, D. João (his brother), Aires de Sousa, Lopo Alvarez, Martim Vaz, Antonio Fernandes (page of the Count of Villa Nova), Diogo Machado Dinis Fernandez (master of the *Cirne*), and many others. And with Martim Coelho there were, Antonio da Silva, Christovão de Magalhães (his brother), Paio Pereira, Pero de Sousa, Gaspar Vaz, Christovão de Azevedo (bastard brother of Martim Coelho). And these, one and all, fought upon that day so valiantly, and performed such an honourable feat (as it was against the Persians who in those parts are reckoned for the bravest men in the world), that I thought it right for the honour of their children, to make mention of their names in this place. And I thoroughly believe, that the Persians who escaped therefrom would give a better report of the bravery of the Portuguese in their land, than that which the captains who fled away from the war left behind them in Ormuz. And just as much as the flight of our captains was a source of marvel to the Xeque Ismael, so he very much praised this rout to which our men put his captains, for hereafter he tried very hardly to make friendly terms with Afonso Dalboquerque, and sent to visit him, but by the time his ambassadors had arrived at Ormuz Afonso had already started for India. The inhabitants of this place had not their wives nor their property in the place, for they lived in dread of what now happened to them, and the spoils that were taken came from those Persians who were stationed there, and consisted of money, clothing, arms, daggers mounted in gold and in silver, bows, arrows, and many horses, which they put to death, and they burned all the supplies for them, and all their munitions of war, which Cogeatar had stored there for transmission to Ormuz.

As soon as this affair was finished Afonso Dalboquerque withdrew with all his forces to the boats, and with rowing and sailing they laboured all the remainder of the night, so that they managed to reach the ships as morning dawned.

The men who had remained behind informed him that in the city during the whole of the night there had been a great disturbance, when they saw the fire at Nabande, and all that day was taken up in attending to the wounded, who were very numerous. On the following morning, Afonso Dalboquerque ordered Dinis Fernandez to go in the *Rey grande* to the Island of Lara, and take in water, and Diogo de Melo to take up this ship's position; and when the anchors had been weighed and he was sailing with his foresail set, a *parao* came from shore, rowing with all its power to reach the ship. Dinis Fernandez, thinking that it was bringing him some message, ordered the tacks to be let go, and waited for it. As soon as the Moors, who were in the *parao*, came up close to the ship, they fired a cannon at her. Afonso Dalboquerque, seeing the *parao* firing upon the ship, despatched with great haste in his boat D. Antonio, and Jorge da Silveira in his skiff, to go and cut off the return of the *parao* to the shore, with orders to run well in to the edge of the land, for it was low tide, and the artillery of the city was unable to injure them. When the Moors in the *parao* perceived that our boats pulled away from the ships, before they could cut them off, made for the land, and as our boats were now close upon them, they began to fire, with the artillery they carried, upon the people of the land who came down to the rescue, and made them keep off. D. Antonio and Jorge da Silveira, transported with great fury, wanted to land after the Moors; but Afonso Dalboquerque came up immediately in his *fusta*, and made them withdraw, for the Moors, who had rallied upon the alarm, were eight hundred archers and fifty horsemen, and our men were too few to attack them. And having got possession of the *parao* and the cannon which the Moors carried in it, they returned to the ships, and Dinis Fernandez made his way to the Island of Lara as he went.

CHAPTER LXIV.

How Diogo de Melo, who was stationed at the Island of Lara, was lost, and how the great Afonso Dalboquerque set out for India, and what took place until his arrival at the island.

While the great Afonso Dalboquerque was waiting for Diogo de Melo to bring his ship to anchor where the *Rey Grande* had been, Duarte de Melo, his brother, arrived in his boat, and told him that three days before Diogo de Melo had gone on board a small *zambuco*, which Manuel de Lacerda had captured laden with dates, and gone away with nine Portuguese and two Moors, but had never yet returned, nor did he know any news of them, but that the Moorish fleet which was fitting out at Julfar had arrived off the Island of Lara, and was now riding at anchor there. Afonso Dalboquerque, startled at this information which Duarte de Melo had given to him, immediately ordered D. Antonio de Noronha and D. Jeronymo de Lima to embark in the *fusta* and in his boat with men, and to go with Duarte de Melo, and see what it was that had happened. And he wrote a letter to Martim Coelho, bidding him weigh anchor and unite with them, that together they might attack the Moorish fleet which was lying off the Island of Lara, and do their best to obtain some information of Diogo de Melo, and go to his assistance, if by some chance he might happen to be in a place whence he could not come forth because of the Moorish fleet. As soon as the captains had started, they proceeded to unite with Martim Coelho, that all together might attack the Moorish fleet, which was lying at anchor, and this, directly it caught sight of our ships, weighed anchor and fled away under full sail and rowing.

D. Antonio, with the other captains, started in pursuit, but perceiving that they could not come up with them, they turned back and sailed all round the Island of Lara, to get any information they could concerning Diogo de Melo, and in this voyage they found in the sea six dead men, and recognised them as having belonged to his company; and as they sailed along the coast of the island they captured a small *parao*, with three or four Moors, and thereupon D. Antonio de Noronha parted with Duarte de Melo, sending him on with this news, and bidding him take with him the Moors whom they had just then taken. On the arrival of Duarte de Melo, Afonso Dalboquerque ordered the Moors to be put to the torture; and then they told him that, as their fleet lay at anchor off the Island of Queixome, a small *parao*, with some Portuguese in it, came up with it, and their captain proceeded to attack it, and it would not yield, so they sent it to the bottom; and as the Christians swam about in the water they killed them all, except one whom they took alive, and the captain sent him away at once to Cogeatar, and that the Portuguese boat, being heavily armed, sank. Afonso Dalboquerque was much grieved at this disaster, and asked Duarte de Melo how his brother could have acted in such a manner, when he had warned him over and over again about the fleet. Duarte replied, that his brother had been deceived by two Moors whom Manuel de Lacerda had taken captive in a *zambuco*, who had informed him that if he would release them, they would take him to a harbour where there were sundry *paraos* stationed, and he had been drawn into this trap by them, and given a deaf ear to all the remonstrances that had been made.

When Duarte de Melo had started off with this message, Martim Coelho weighed anchor, and proceeded to unite with Dinis Fernandez, captain of the *Rey Grande*, which was lying off the Island of Queixome, intending to wait for further instructions from Afonso Dalboquerque, while D. Antonio de Noronha remained in the vessel of Diogo de

Melo, and Jorge da Silveira in the *fusta*. After having taken in a supply of water, they proceeded to the city, and found Afonso Dalboquerque very much alarmed, as well by this disaster which had befallen Diogo de Melo, as also by the great leak in the *Cirne*, which was such that thirty Moors, working incessantly at the pump, could hardly keep it under with great labour; and in this state, so sudden a storm fell upon the ships, that they had like to have all been overset, but as it did not last very long, and the cables held firmly, they were saved. As soon as the storm was over, Afonso Dalboquerque, feeling himself without men, without a fleet, and but ill-assisted by the Viceroy, made up his mind to go to India; and without holding any more communication with Cogeatar, he set sail, and steered for the Island of Queixome, where Martim Coelho was stationed, with Dinis Fernandez, to take in water there, intending thence to make his way to India; but when he arrived there, as he did not see the *Rey Grande*, he asked Martim Coelho where she was. The captain replied that, on the last new moon, so fierce a storm had struck her, that they were nearly all lost, and Dinis Fernandez had let go the cables, and he, seeing him sailing away, had inquired of him whether he also should slip his cable? But Dinis Fernandez replied that, if his ship had strong cables he might remain where he was, for the weather would soon clear up, it was owing to the spring tides that the winds blew so, and he was going to steer for the other side of the island, to be sheltered from that wind, and as soon as the hurricane was over he would return.

Afonso Dalboquerque ordered all the pilots and masters to be assembled, and inquired of them what course the ship would take, and whether she would be lost? They all told him not to be alarmed, for Dinis Fernandez was so good a seaman, that he would give a good account of her; much more so as between those islands the sea was so smooth that the *almadias* were accustomed to go across from one side to the other without any danger. On hearing this that the pilots told him, Afonso Dalboquerque became a little more encouraged, but, nevertheless, he ordered Antonio de Noronha to go up a lofty hill which is on the island, whence all the sea round about can be perceived, taking with him some mariners, and to look about if he could see any vessel, and all those who went with him asserted that they saw a ship just doubling Cape Maçandi.[1]

D. Antonio having returned, and all being now supplied with water, they set sail, and doubling the Cape, took a ship of Guzarates,[2] which came from the Red Sea sailing for Cambaya, laden with silk stuffs, alum, and seed pearl, and some money. Afonso Dalboquerque ordered the pilot and master to be brought before him, and inquired of them if they had seen any large vessel in those parts belonging to his company. The pilot told him that, being at anchor behind the Cape, there came some fishing barques, returning from the open sea towards the shore, who told him that they were flying from a vessel of the Franks which was steering towards India. On receiving this information, he ordered the vessels to be stripped of all the merchandise they carried, and then to be set on fire, but he released the Moors, and let them go free, and then resumed his course, and without anything else taking place, came in sight of Angediva.

And after remaining there for three days he started again, and reached Cananor, where he found the Viceroy in company with the captains who had deserted him, and with the Commendador Rui Soarez, who, though under his orders, was yet not willing to put himself in the way of performing his obligations; and these had now

[1] See p. 101, Note 1.

[2] Gujerat, Gujurat, or Guzerat, a province of the Presidency of Bombay.

spent upwards of a year there, much favoured by the Viceroy, instead of being punished by him for their desertion, and for leaving Afonso in the war. And in a few days' time Dinis Fernandez arrived in the *Rey Grande* with all his ship's crew safe and sound. And for all that Afonso Dalboquerque felt it deeply, when he saw his captains in presence of the Viceroy unpunished, yet he dissembled, and delivered over to him the fleet and crews, paying them all that was due to them up to that hour, and gave him an account of the trouble he had had with the Moors and with the Christians, having spent two years and eight months in the sea, conquering the kingdom of Ormuz, as the king, Dom Manuel, his master, had ordered him, without experiencing any favour or help from the Viceroy during the whole of that period.

END OF THE FIRST PART.

THE COMMENTARIES OF THE GREAT AFONSO DALBOQUERQUE

PORTRAIT OF AFFONÇO DE ALBUQUERQUE.

FROM THE EDITION OF 1774.

THE COMMENTARIES OF THE GREAT AFONSO DALBOQUERQUE,

SECOND VICEROY OF INDIA.

TRANSLATED FROM THE

PORTUGUESE EDITION OF 1774,

WITH NOTES AND AN INTRODUCTION,

BY

WALTER DE GRAY BIRCH, F.R.S.L.

SENIOR ASSISTANT OF THE DEPARTMENT OF MANUSCRIPTS IN THE BRITISH MUSEUM; MONORARY LIBRARIAN OF THE ROYAL SOCIETY OF LITERATURE; MONORARY SECRETARY OF THE BRITISH ARCHAELOGICAL ASSOCIATION, ETC.

VOL. II

..."ut, quantum ad cognitionem pertinet rerum, etiam praeteritis saeculis vixisse videamur,"--Quintilian, Instit. Orator., xii, 4.

GYAN

Published by

GYAN

Gyan Publishing House
5, Ansari Road
Daryaganj, New Delhi-110002
Phone: 011-47034999, 9811692060
E-mail: books@gyanbooks.com

Distribution Network
gyanbooks.com
India, USA, Canada, UK, Australia, France

ISBN : 978-81-212-3261-6 (Set)
ISBN : 978-81-212-4806-8 (PB)
First Published, 1877

2nd Impression 2020

Printed at: Gyan Press, Delhi.

The Commentaries of the Great Afonso Dalboquerque Vol. II
Author: Walter De Gray Birch

THE COMMENTARIES OF THE GREAT AFONSO DALBOQUERQUE,

SECOND VICEROY OF INDIA.

TRANSLATED FROM THE

PORTUGUESE EDITION OF 1774,

With Notes and an Introduction,

BY

WALTER DE GRAY BIRCH, F.R.S.L.,

SENIOR ASSISTANT OF THE DEPARTMENT OF MANUSCRIPTS IN THE BRITISH MUSEUM; HONORARY LIBRARIAN OF THE ROYAL SOCIETY OF LITERATURE; HONORARY SECRETARY OF THE BRITISH ARCHÆOLOGICAL ASSOCIATION ETC.

VOL. II.

"Ut, quantum ad cognitionem pertinet rerum, etiam praeteritis saeculis vixisse videamur."—QUINTILIAN, *Instit. Orator.*, xii, 4.

LONDON:

PRINTED FOR THE HAKLUYT SOCIETY.

M.DCCC.LXXVII.

COUNCIL

OF

THE HAKLUYT SOCIETY.

The Right Hon. Sir DAVID DUNDAS, President.

Admiral C. R. DRINKWATER BETHUNE, C.B. } Vice-Presidents.
Major-General Sir HENRY RAWLINSON, K.C.B., F.R.S. } Vice-Presidents.

W. A. TYSSEN AMHURST, Esq.

Rev. Dr. G. P. BADGER, D.C.L., F.R.G.S.

J. BARROW, Esq., F.R.S.

Vice-Admiral Sir RICHARD COLLINSON, K.C.B.

Captain CRUTTENDEN.

EGERTON V. HARCOURT, Esq.

CHARLES GREY, Esq.

JOHN WINTER JONES, Esq., F.S.A.

R. H. MAJOR, Esq., F.S.A.

Sir CHARLES NICHOLSON, Bart., D.C.L.

Vice-Admiral ERASMUS OMMANNEY, C.B., F.R.S.

Captain PORCHER, R.N.

The Lord STANLEY of Alderley.

EDWARD THOMAS, Esq., F.R.S.

CLEMENTS R. MARKHAM, C.B., F.R.S., Sec.R.G.S., Honorary Secretary.

LIST OF CONTENTS.

CONTENTS.

INTRODUCTION.

Por terra jas o Emporio do Oriente,
Que do rigido Affonso o ferro, o raio
Ao grão Filho ganhou do grão Sabaio,
Envergonhando o Deos armipotente.

Cahio Goa, terror antigamente
Do Naire vão, do pérfido Malaio,
De barbaras Nações...ah! que desmaio
Apaga o Marcio ardor da Lusa Gente.

Oh Seculos de Heróes! Dias de Gloria!
Varões excelsos, que, a pesar da Morte,
Viveis na tradição, viveis na Historia!

"Albuquerque terrivel, Castro forte",
Meneses, e outros mil, vossa memoria
Vinga as injúrias, que nos fas a Sorte.

MANOEL MARIA DE BARBOSA DU BOCAGE, *Soneto* xxix.

IN the Introduction to the first volume of my translation of the COMMENTARIES OF THE GREAT AFONSO DALBOQUERQUE, I reserved for a future occasion some account of the foundation, rise, progress, and decay of the Portuguese Empire in the Eastern Indies, and some Bibliographical notes in reference to the Indian Cycle of Portuguese Literature, because these two great subjects could hardly be treated with due consideration in that volume. In the course of my remarks upon these points, which must necessarily be very limited even here, I shall incorporate a brief outline of the exploits of our hero Afonso Dalboquerque, so far as they are put before the reader now for the first time in their English form, that is, down to the first and unsuccessful attack upon the most important position ever held by the Portuguese in the great Indian Continent, viz., the fortress and Island of Goa, and to this I shall add some description of the settlement itself, gathered from such works as treat of this subject.

It was not until the final decade of the fifteenth century that the idea of a fourth quarter of the world, so long and so extensively prevalent among the ancients, began to be put to a crucial and practical test, in place of the visionary theories and unstable conjectures which those who had nothing better to adduce concerning this unseen and unknown world found so easy to multiply and disseminate. As we all know, the honour of the first finding belongs to modern navigators, and mainly, as well as primarily, to the great Christopher Columbus, whose researches in the necessary sciences and arts of the sailor led him irresistibly, and with all the greater force because they led him truly, to believe that the equilibrium of the terrestrial globe demanded incontrovertibly that there should be another continent or hemisphere lying to the westward, and as yet unknown to the civilised world. Of the discoveries which were the result of this great man's inductions—discoveries which were not brought about without an amount of depreciation and obstructiveness almost amounting to prohibition on the part of others, nor without self-denial and endurance on his own part which would have deterred many from a successful prosecution of them — there is no need to speak here, although indirectly they assisted the settlement of the Portuguese in India, because they stimulated and confirmed the intense desire for maritime investigations which had seized upon so many persons when they contemplated the good fortune which had at length attended the labours of doubling the Cape of Good Hope. I do not pretend to decide whether Columbus, who had acquired his skill in navigation among the Portuguese, and who, therefore, could not but be aware of that nation's long meditated design of discovering the naval road to India round the African coast, was, or not, actuated, as some have asserted, by any feeling of jealousy with respect to the then nearly discovered eastern passage to India, and desired to acquire, for a rival maritime power, a more easy and, as he thought, a shorter western passage, which had been rejected by the Portuguese, to the same places. At the very time that the Spaniards were carrying on their great works of discovery in the newly-found western hemisphere, the sister kingdom of Portugal, shut out from any solid participation in these conquests by the bull of Pope Alexander VI (who adjudged the countries lying to the west of an imaginary meridian line at the distance of four hundred and seventy leagues to the west of Cape Verd and the Azores to be the rightful possession of the King of Spain, while those lands only which when discovered should fall to the eastward of that great circle should belong to the Portuguese monarch), was busily engaged in extending her much anterior paths of discovery in the very opposite direction,[1] although Brazil fell, by virtue of accidental discovery in the year 1500 by the Portuguese commander Alvares Cabral as well as by the operation of this papal arbitrament.

In one very important point the springs which actuated and the machinery which directed Spanish and Portuguese maritime discovery and colonial enterprise differed. The former people, not given to commercial lines of thought, failed to observe the immense financial and political advantages which a well organised system of trade in the natural, nay, spontaneous products of their newly acquired territories offered to their native kingdom; the precious metal alone attracted their attention: the accursed greed of gold, solid mountains of which presented themselves to the over-excited imaginations and sanguine temperaments of a people by very nature prone to irritability and fierce excitements, occupied all their thoughts and prevented them from more generous and noble actions. Hence arose the soon exhausted working of mines, the introduction of foreign, generally negro, labour, the enslaving, persecution, and, finally, extermination of native tribes, the disastrous effects of which proceedings are felt to this very day in the American continents.

The Portuguese, on the other hand, were not so much impelled by the cupidity of gold, as by the ever increasing desire for commercial intercourse with their

[1] In 1497, the year before Columbus made the voyage which discovered the mouths of the River Oronoko, Vasco da Gama sailed on his first voyage to India.

newly made subjects: and next to the imposition of a tribute upon the inhabitants of districts, or petty kingdoms, added to the Lusitanian yoke, who were left in other respects to the free exercise of their own forms of government, the key-note of all the proceedings of this European power in the West and in the East, immediately upon obtaining a footing in places of apparent promise, is the acquisition of a factory--necessarily a strong house, fortress, or impregnable castle, wherein the few who were placed to manage the sales and purchases might, if necessity should arise, withdraw, for the preservation of their lives against the fury of whole armies arrayed against them.

Whatever may have been the first impulse which set men thinking of land beyond the Eastern seas, there is no doubt that the Portuguese naval expedition fitted out by Dom João I, King of Portugal, against the Moorish Princes of Africa—with the chivalrous intention of giving his sons an opportunity of exhibiting their prowess and dexterity, and of earning knightly honours—and brought to a successful issue by the capture of Ceuta in 1415, had such an influence upon one of the sons of that sovereign, Dom Henrique, Duke of Viseu, that he encouraged his countrymen in their nascent tastes for navigation,[1] maritime enterprises, and riparial exploration which had been thus inaugurated in so

[1] "He had already, in 1412, three years before the reduction of Ceuta, sent a ship to make discoveries on the Barbary coast. Cape *Nam*, as its name *(No)* implies, was then the *ne plus ultra* of European navigation; the ship sent by Henry, however, passed it sixty leagues, and reached Cape *Bojador*."—*Mickle.*

auspicious and happy a manner. Mr. Major's exhaustive work, entitled "The Life of Prince Henry of Portugal, surnamed the Navigator, and its Results...... with new facts in the discovery of the Atlantic Islands", London, 1868, is so well known and so universally accredited, that nothing need be here said respecting this scientific and enlightened prince by way of biography, beyond the fact that he established his abode at Sagrez, about a league and a half distant from Cape St. Vincent, a promontory at the western extremity of the province of Algarve, in the south of Portugal, and there ordered ships to be constructed at his own expense, and doubtless under his own superintendence, to which he afterwards appointed selected naval adventurers, who had been invited from all parts for this object, and despatched them to reconnoitre the far stretching coasts of the African continent. Hence fell to the genius of this organisation the practical discovery and colonisation of the islands of Madeira by Juan Gonsalez Zarco and Tristan Vaz in 1420 ; the Canary Islands in 1424 ; ceded or abandoned to Spanish claims[1] by a treaty in 1481 ; the Azores, discovered in 1449 by Gonçalo Vello, and colonised in 1431 ; and the Cape Verd Islands in 1460.

These discoveries, although infinitely inferior in point of value and historical interest to others which this

[1] In consequence of the statement that Jean de Bethencourt, or Jon de Betancour, a native of France, but in the service of the King of Castile, had in 1402 made a settlement in these islands, which had originally been discovered, it is said by some Biscayneers, about the year 1340.—*See* "The Canarian", Hakl. Soc., No. XLVI.

Portuguese nation, then in the summit of its splendour and renown, were so soon about to make, were not without their uses as incentives to that yearning spirit of extended journeys by sea which were destined to be promoted so extensively, and to render illustrious for ever the names of those who conceived them. For, although the reign of Alonzo V witnessed but little real progress in these discoveries, yet the reign of João II beheld the erection of a fort on the Gold Coast in 1481; the assumption of the title "Lord of Guinea" by the King; the operations of the Portuguese carried down to the lowest points of the African mainland; the Stormy Cape successfully doubled in 1486 by the Admiral Diaz; and the continent of India revealed to the prowess of Vasco da Gama.

The adventures of Vasco da Gama have afforded to the Portuguese Virgil, Luiz de Camões, the theme for one of the most beautiful epic poems ever written in any European language. Of prose, and, therefore, more circumstantial accounts of the hero's doings in those far off lands, perhaps the best, certainly the most accessible to English readers, is Lord Stanley's "Three Voyages", published by the Hakluyt Society in 1869, from the *Lendas da India* of Gaspar Correa, printed for the first time by the Lisbon Academy in 1858-63. This navigator was despatched with the command of a fleet of three vessels,[1] to follow up the mission of the

[1] See an illustration of one of them, the *San Gabriel*, commanded by Vasco da Gama himself, from an original picture in Lisbon, formerly in the possession of D. João de Castro, in Mr. W. S. Lindsay's *History of Merchant Shipping*, vol. ii, page 5.

two royal equerries, Pedro de Covilham, and Gonsalvo de Pavia, otherwise called Alonzo de Payva, whom the Portuguese King had dispatched secretly to "learn of many lands, and wander in many parts, because they knew many languages", for "in the year one thousand four hundred and eight-four, there came to Portugal the King of Benin, a Caffre by nation", from whom he "collected much information about India and its affairs, for he was very desirous to learn with much certainty that the King of it was Prester John, who was a Christian and the lord of great riches. Which information produced so great an impression upon the King's heart, that he became possessed with an earnest resolve to send and learn about and discover India."

We may safely leave the narrative of Vasco da Gama to the great poet of his own nation; and the reader who prefers them in an English form may gather some, even though faint, idea of style of the subject through the medium of the translations of quaint Fanshaw and Quillinan, or pompous Mickle. These, and Lord Stanley's Correa, in addition to a very excellent *resumé* in the second volume of Mr. Lindsay's *Merchant Shipping*, I fear must take the place of the old Portuguese historians whose works yet await translation into English. The main points in the "First Voyage of Vasco da Gama" may be taken succinctly thus, according to Correa:—He sails from Lisbon on the 25th of March, 1497, and, after a voyage of nearly five months, arrives at St. Helena Bay on the 18th of August, doubles the Cape, and enters rivers on the Eastern Coast in November, and sights the coast of

Natal on the 25th of December in the same year. In the early part of January, he enters the Rio dos Reis or Mercy River, where he stays a month to careen his ships, and one of them commanded by Nicolas Coelho was broken up. The two remaining vessels reached Mozambique at the end of March, where they remained for a space of about three weeks, leaving that country on Sunday, the 8th or 15th of April. The expedition reached Mombasa on the 21st, and Melinde on the 29th of the same month; and, after a long stay of three months, set sail and sighted the coast of India, at the Monte Dely, or Delielly, Rat Mountain, near Cananor, on the 26th of August. The first place on the Indian mainland touched by these navigators was Calicut, where they remained for seventy days, and from thence made their way to Cananor, Angediva, and Melinde, the latter place being reached on the 8th of January, 1499, marking the limit of the first voyage. The homeward journey commenced with the setting out from Melinde on the 20th of January; in it occurred the melancholy death of Paulo da Gama, the brother of Vasco da Gama, and Captain of the second ship, the *Sam Raphael*, and his burial at Terceira in the Azores at the end of August; and ends with the arrival at Lisbon on the 18th of September.

The incident of doubling the Cape of Good Hope—an incident of lasting honour to his nation—afforded to Camões an opportunity of introducing into the fifth canto of his Epic one of the finest passages to be met with in the whole cycle of Portuguese literature. I shall therefore venture, without any fear of wasting space in these pages, to introduce portions of the passage, in support of remarks, upon the value of studying the language, which I have made in my Introduction to the first volume.

37.

Porèm já cinco soes eram passados,
Que dalli nos partiramos, cortando
Os mares nunca d'outrem navegados,
Prosperamente os ventos assoprando:
Quando huma noite estando descuidados
Na cortadora proa vigiando,
Huma nuvem, que os ares escurece,
Sobre nossas cabeças apparece.

38.

Tão temerosa vinha, e carregada,
Que poz nos corações hum grande medo,
Bramindo o negro mar de longe brada,
Como se désse em vão n'algum rochedo.
O! Potestade, disse, sublimada!
Que ameaço divino, ou que segredo
Este clima, e este mar nos apresenta,
Que mór cousa parece, que tormenta?

39.

Não acabava, quando huma figura
Se nos mostra no ar, robusta e valida,
De disforme e grandissima estatura,
O rosto carregado, a barba esqualida,
Os olhos encovados, e a postura
Medonha e má, e a cor terrena e pallida,
Cheios de terra e crespos os cabellos,
A boca negra, os dentes amarellos.

40.

Tão grande era de membros, que bem posso
Certificar-te, que este era o segundo
De Rhodes estranhissimo colosso,
Que hum dos sete milagres foi do mundo:

C'hum tom de voz nos falla horrendo e grosso,
Que parece sahir do mar profundo:
Arrepiam-se as carnes, e o cabello
A mi, e a todos, só de ouvi-lo e ve-lo.

41.

E disse: O! gente ousada mais que quantas
No mundo commetteram grandes cousas,
Tu, que por guerras cruas, taes e tantas,
E por trabalhos vãos nunca repousas:
Pois os vedados terminos quebrantas,
E navegar meus longos mares ousas,
Que eu tanto tempo ha já que guardo, e tenho,
Nunca arados d'estranho, ou proprio lenho:

42.

Pois vens ver os segredos escondidos
Da natureza, e do humido elemento,
A nenhum grande humano concedidos
De nobre ou de immortal merecimento;
Ouve os damnos de mi, que apercibidos
Estão a teu sobejo atrevimento
Por todo o largo mar, e pela terra,
Que inda has de sobjugar com dura guerra.

43.

Sabe, que quantas naos esta viagem,
Que tu fazes, fizerem de atrevidas
Inimiga terão esta paragem,
Com ventos, e tormentas desmedidas:
E da primeira armada, que passagem
Fizer por estas ondas insoffridas,
Eu farei d'improviso tal castigo,
Que seja mór o damno, que o perigo.

* * * *

50.

Eu sou aquelle occulto e grande Cabo,
A quem chamais vós outros Tormentorio,
Que nunca a Ptolomeo, Pomponio, Estrabo,
Plinio, e quantos passaram, fui notorio:
Aqui toda a Africana costa acabo
Neste meu nunca vista promontorio,

Que para o polo Antarctico se estende
A quem vossa ousadia tanto offende.

51.

Fui dos filhos asperrimos da terra,
Qual Encélado, Egeo, e o Centimano :
Chamei-me Adamastor, e fui na guerra
Contra o que vibra os raios de Vulcano :
Não que puzesse serra sobre serra ;
Mas, conquistando as ondas do Oceano,
Fui capitão do mar, por onde andava
A armada de Neptuno, que eu buscava.

52.

Amores da alta esposa de Peleo
Me fizeram tomar tamanha empreza,
Todas as deosas desprezei do ceo,
Só por amar das agoas a princeza :
Hum dia a vi co'as filhas de Nereo
Sahir nua na praia ; e logo preza
A vontade senti de tal maneira,
Que inda não sinto cousa, que mais queira.

* * * *

56.

Oh que não sei de nojo como o conte !
Que, crendo ter nos braços quem amava,
Abraçado me achei c'hum duro monto
De aspero mato, e de espessura brava :
Estando c'hum penedo fronte a fronte,
Que eu pelo rosto angelico apertava,
Não fiquei homen não, mas mudo e quedo,
E junto d'hum penedo outro penedo.

* * * *

59.

Converte-se-me a carne em terra dura,
Em penedos os ossos se fizeram,
Estes membros que vês, e esta figura
Por estas longas agoas se estenderam :
Em fim, minha grandissima estatura
Neste remoto cabo converteram

Os deoses; e, por mais dobradas magoas,
Me anda Thetis cercando destas agoas.

37.

Five suns since we departed thence had set,
And smoothly wafted by a prosperous gale
We cleaved the seas where never nation yet
But ours had urged the exploratory sail;
When, as we watch'd one night, and not a threat
Of change disturb'd us, sure that all was well,
A cloud from overhead its shadow cast,
And densely lowering brooded o'er the mast.

38.

So heavily it gloom'd athwart our board,
A solemn fear to every heart it struck,
While from afar the blacken'd ocean roar'd
As if in thunder bursting on a rock.
"Oh what is this?" I cried, "Almighty Lord!
What threat divine? What new mysterious shock
Portend these howling waves, this sea difform?
For this is something greater than a storm!"

39.

While yet I spoke, what shape before us grew?
A mighty phantom in the air appear'd,
Uncouth, enormous, horrible to view,
With savage front and squalid length of beard,
And cavern'd eyes, and haggard earthly hue,
And evil scowl of thing that would be fear'd:
His tangled locks were thick with sand and slime,
And clots of ooze his hideous mouth begrime.

40.

So huge was he of limb, that I may swear
His bulk by that Colossus unsurpast
Which brought to Rhodes the wise of Greece, to stare
At one of earth's seven wonders. All aghast
We heard his voice that rent the trembling air,
A voice which seem'd from the abyss upcast:

To see, to hear, this monster on the deep,
Made the hair bristle and the flesh to creep.

41.

"O race the most audacious!" thus he spake—
"The world for measureless ambition knows,
You that for cruel warfare, and the sake
Of vain adventures ever shun repose;
Since those forbidden boundaries ye break,
And press along my seas your daring prows,
Seas by no keel for many a cycle plough'd,
So long 'twas mine to guard them and to shroud;

42.

"Since you are come to pierce the depths conceal'd
Of Nature, and the secrets of a tide
To mortal heroes never yet reveal'd,
Not even to those for prowess deified;—
Hear, then, from me the woes on flood and field
Prepared to scourge your rashness, and the pride
Of triumphs ye must reach with desperate hand,
For horror waits you both on sea and land.

43.

"Know that whatever ships hereafter brave,
Like yours, these fatal latitudes, shall find
A fierce antagonist in every wave,
A raging enemy in every wind.
And the first warlike force these waters lave
To it, on rough and boist'rous route inclined—
By me shall sudden punishment be dealt—
More than the danger shall the loss be felt.

* * * *

50.

"The Spirit of yon haughty cliff am I,
Called Cape of Storm by your precursor bold;
A headland in impassive mystery,
Enshrouded from geographers of old.
Here end the Afric shores that nearest lie
Unto the pole Antarctic,—shores controll'd
By that, my mountain throne so long occult,
Which you in your audacity insult.

51.

"My name was Adamastor; I was one
Of those gigantic brothers, born of Earth,
As vast Ægeon and Enceladon,
Who against the Lord of Thunder tried their worth
In battle: they Heaven's fortress would have won,
By piling hill on hill; but I went forth
To be their champion on the Ocean-plain,
And challenge Neptune on his own domain.

52.

"By love for Peleus' spouse, my fated scourge,
Was I to this wild enterprise suborn'd;
For her, the radiant Princess of the surge,
The goddesses of all the heaven I scorn'd.
One day I saw her from the wave emerge,
In nought but her own loveliness adorn'd,
Attended by the Nereids: from that hour
I felt—and yet I feel—her fatal power.

* * * *

56.

"Oh, how can I record my vile disgrace!
I found, instead of her whom I adore,
A crag encircled in my wild embrace,
A thorny cliff outstanding on the shore:
This was my prize angelic, face to face
I grappled with a mountain! Man no more,
But mute and passive, senseless with the shock
I stood, another rock against a rock.

* * * *

59.

"My living flesh obdurate earth became,
My bones a hard inexorable heap;
Head, trunk, and limbs, yet conscious to the shame,
A wall of rock, a wide and towering steep.
What once was Adamastor's giant frame
Is now the Storm-Cape, glooming o'er the deep;
So will'd the gods, and to torment me more,
The waves of Thetis dance about my shore."

Edw. Quillinan, 1853.

The Additional MS. 20,902 in the British Museum, which is entitled "Relação das Nâos e Armadas da India, Com os successos dellas, que se pudéram saber, para Noticia e instrucção dos Curiozos, e amantes da Historia da India," and was formerly in the possession of Lord Stuart de Rothesay, affords us a very succinct account of the first voyage of Dom Vasco da Gama; —this I give here in a literal translation, because it evidently incorporates into one historical sequence, and summarises, the principal events related in detail and at length by the Portuguese historians:—

"VASCO DA GAMA, CHIEF CAPTAIN, 1497.

"On[1] the second of June, 1497, there set out from Lisbon, in order to discover Oriental India, Vasco da Gama (the eldest son of Estevão da Gama, who was Comptroller *(veador)* of the household of the King Dom Affonso the Fifth, and of Dona Isabel Sodré, his wife), as chief captain of four ships; himself in the *São Raphael;* Paulo da Gama, his second brother,

[1] A marginal note in this manuscript says: "Another relation states that there set forth on the 8th of July Va[s]co da Gama in the ship *S. Gabriel;* Paulo da Gama, his brother, in the *S. Raphael;* Niculâo Coelho in the ship *Berrio;* Gonçalo Nunes in a ship with supplies; and that the people of this ship of Gonçalo Nunes, and the supplies which she carried, after having passed the Cape of Good Hope, beyond the *Agoada* of S. Bras, were divided by the others of the company; and after she had been stripped they set fire to her; and that Paulo da Gama's ship, returning to Portugal, went aground on the shallows between Quiloa and Mombaça, which are called [the shallows] of S. Raphael, on account of the ship, which was so named, and that the people were distributed between the two others of the company."

in the *São Gabriel;* Nicolâo Coelho in the *São Miguel.* Gonçalo Nunes was captain of a ship with supplies which, before reaching the Cape of Good Hope, they stowed away in the vessels, and he returned to this kingdom [of Portugal.] And the vessel *S. Gabriel*, wherein went Paulo da Gama, was taken to pieces to repair the others, because she was very much shaken, and could not continue her voyage in a river which is in the Cafre land beyond the Cape of Good Hope, that was named the *River of Mercy;* and Paulo da Gama was transferred to the ship of his brother, and the men were divided between the two, and thence they set out to follow up their voyage. And being at anchor at Moçambique, where the Xeque endeavoured to seize their ships by treachery, they disembarked on the Island of São Jorge, where the first mass on the further side of the Cape of Good Hope was celebrated. Thence they went to Quiloa and Mombaça, and the kings of all these islands endeavoured to treat them treacherously, but God suffered nothing thereof to take effect; and so to Melinde, where the King received them faithfully, and gave them pilots in whom they could trust, and these led them to Angediva, where they fought with the *fustas* of the Sabayo, Lord of Goa, over whom they obtained the victory. And from that place they proceeded to Calicut, where the Samorȳ planned much treachery against them that did not take effect. Thence they went to Cochim, where they were well received by the king, and in Cananor in the same manner, where they completed the lading of the two vessels and returned to this kingdom, and arrived at Lisbon in safety on the 18th of September, 1499. Paulo da Gama died of infirmity in the Island of Terçeira, in the city of Angra; he is buried there in the convent of São Françisco of the same city."

In continuation of this circumstantial account of the yearly naval expeditions of Portugal to the East, the same MS. relates the next proceedings as follows:—

"PEDRALVARES CABRAL, CHIEF CAPTAIN, 1500.

"Pedralvares Cabral set[1] out as chief captain of thirteen ships on the 9th of March, 1500. Captains, Sancho de Thoar, who on returning to Portugal was

[1] The marginal note says:—"Another relation states that the captains who set out with the chief captain were: Sancho de Toar, Simam de Miranda, Ayres Gomes da Silva (lost in a storm), Niculão Coelho, Nuno Leitam, Vasco de Atayde (lost in a storm), Bertolameu Dias (lost in a storm), Pero Dias his brother, Gaspar de Lemos, Luis Pires, Simão de Pina (lost in a storm), Pero de Atayde. And in the events which it narrates concerning the fleet, it states:—The tempest whereby the four ships mentioned above were lost, struck them in the crossing *(travessa)* to Brazil on their way to the Cape of Good Hope, whereby the ship of Simam de Miranda struck against that of Pero Alvarez Cabral, but miraculously was saved; and by reason of the same tempest Pero Dias was separated from the company of the others, and made his way to Magadaxo, hard by the Cape of Guardafuy, and on his return he met with Pedro Alvarez at Cape Verde, and Luis Pires arrived at Portugal; Sancho de Toar, on the return voyage to Portugal, was wrecked, by a high wind blowing dead against him, on a bank near the coast of Melinde, and after saving all his people, the ship was set on fire. Gaspar de Lemos returned from *Santa Cruz*, the land of Brasil, to this kingdom with the news of its discovery."

wrecked on a bank close to Quiloa, but he saved himself, with all his company and cargo; Simão de Miranda de Azevedo, Bras Matoso, Vasco de Attajde, were wrecked by a storm on the islands which were afterwards named those of Tristão da Cunha; Nuno Leitão da Cunha, Simão de Pina, Nicolâo Coelho, Pero de Figueiredo, Bartholameo Dias (who was also lost), Diogo Dias, Luiz Pi[re]z, Gaspar de Lemos, Andre G[onça]l[ve]z, who returned to the kingdom with six ships, namely, one which he took from Brazil, and five which he carried in his company, and the others were lost.

"This fleet discovered Brazil on the third of May, the day of the Exaltation of the Holy Cross *(Sancta Cruz)*, and for this reason they applied that same name to all that land. And in the same [year] factories were established in Cananor, Calicut, and in Coçhim, and officers were stationed in all of these places, except in Calicut, for in a tümult there the [people] killed the Factor Aires Correa, although the chief captain was there.

"And this fleet discovered Sophala, and the war continued to rage in Calicut; and in this fleet there went eight friars of São Françisco, who were the first religious that passed over to India; and for their custodian there went Frey Henrique, who was afterwards Bishop of Seita, chief inquisitor of this kingdom, and Archbishop of Bragua.

"Of these friars two suffered martyrdom in the rebellion at Calicut."

Encouraged by these discoveries, and nothing

daunted by the destruction which the winds and waves had exercised upon this large fleet, the Portuguese rapidly fitted out a new squadron of navigators, who eagerly set upon the work of prosecuting their voyages into unknown quarters; and accordingly we find the following mention, in the same manuscript, of—

"JOÃO DA NOVA, CHIEF CAPTAIN, 1501.

"João[1] da Nova, chief captain of four ships, set out on the 15th of March; Captains, Francisco de Novais, Fernão Pacheco, Misser Vineto, a Florentine: he returned to the kingdom with all his ships safely, and discovered, on his coming back, the Island of St. Illena,[2] which is in sixteen degrees south latitude, and on going out, the island which is called João da Nova,[3] which is in front of Moçambique."

The next year witnessed redoubled activity in the naval enterprise of the Portuguese, the principal event being the second voyage of Vasco da Gama to India in 1502, with a fleet of fifteen vessels, which, after having arrived safely at Mozambique, touched at

[1] The marginal comment relates:—"Another account reads as follows. The chief captain, João da Nova, Alcaide of Lisboa; Diogo Barboza, *Criado* of Dom Alvaro, brother of the Duke of Bargança; Françisco de Navaes; Fernam Vinet, a Florentine; and says that while they were in 8 degrees south latitude, they found an island which they named *Conceição* (*Conception Island*, now *Ascension Island*, 7 deg. 57 min. S. lat., 14 deg. 28 min. W.), and on returning to the kingdom they found that of *St. Elena.*"

[2] St. Helena, 16 deg. S., 5 deg. 38 min. W.

[3] Juan de Nova Island, in the Mozambique Channel, 17 deg. 10 min. S., 42 deg. 54 min. E.

Quiloa in July, and visited Melinde, Onor, Baticala, and Cananor. On the way to the last-mentioned place a horrid butchery of Moors, who were captured in a large ship of Calicut, coming from Mekkah to Mount Dely,[1] was carried out under the orders of the chief captain, Vasco da Gama himself.[2] This and other somewhat similar occurrences tarnish the bright shield of glory which that intrepid discoverer richly merits, and calls forth from Mr. Lindsay a well-timed indignation when he says, "Although[3] the first voyage of Da Gama may be read with satisfaction, no language can be found sufficiently strong to denounce his subsequent career, and especially his diabolical conduct towards the Moors and natives on his second expedition to India. And to that conduct, too faithfully adopted by his successors, may in a great measure be attributed the loss, as well as the gain, of the Portuguese Empire in the East." After establishing a factory at Cananor, Vasco da Gama departed for Calicut, which he bombarded; and here was perpetrated a second brutality, even more horrid than the former, and one which, for savage and bloodthirsty cruelty and extreme suffering, perhaps has no equal in the records of mediæval European history.[4] The details of this crime call to mind the refined tortures of the Chinese and Japanese, or the studied infliction

[1] See a plan, and sketch of Mount d'Ely, in Col. Yule's *Marco Polo*, vol. ii, pp. 362, 377.

[2] Lord Stanley's *Correa*, pp. 312-319.

[3] *Merchant Shipping*, vol. ii, p. 40.

[4] Lord Stanley's *Correa*, p. 331.

of mutilation and lingering death by the American Indians. The next places visited were Cochim, where a factor was appointed, and Coulam; after which, the fleet that had been hastily equipped by the natives at Calicut with the object of avenging the cruelties lately practised upon them, was successfully fought by the Portuguese, who made their way to Cananor: and strict regulations having been appointed for the safety and maintenance of the little factory established at this latter port under command of Vincente Sodré, the fleet set sail for Portugal on the 28th of December, 1502, and Vasco da Gama reached Lisbon, in completion of his second voyage, on the 1st of September, 1503.

Of this second voyage of Vasco da Gama, the simple narrative in the manuscript from which I have already quoted affords some useful names and dates. The translation of the paragraphs relative to this event is as follows:—

"DOM VASCO DA GAMA, ADMIRAL OF INDIA, 1502.

"Dom Vasco da Gama, chief captain of fifteen[1] ships, set out on the 10th of February for the second time. Captains, Dom Luiz Coutinho Ramiro, Gil F[e]r-

[1] A marginal note says:—"15 sail, and afterwards there were five more, because they could not go together; the 15 on the 10th of February, the 5 on the 1st of April.

"Another account states that the chief captain, D. Vasco da Gama, Admiral of India, set out with 20 sail and these captains, namely—Vicente Sodré, uncle of the Admiral, the brother of his mother (lost); Braz Sodré, his brother (lost); Alvaro de Atayde,

[nande]z de Sousa, Alvaro de Attayde, Vicente Sodré, Braz Sodré, Gil Matoso, Diogo F[e]r[nande]z Correa, Françisco da Cunha, Pedr' Affonço de Aguiar, Ruy de Castanheda, Antonio de Campo, Loppo Mendes de Vasconçellos; and of the *caravellas* Fernão Ro[dr]i-[gue]z Badarças, João Lopes Perestrelo, Antonio F[e]r[nande]z, Thomas de Cremona, João de Bonagracia, Italians, Loppo Dias; and in all there were fifteen vessels *(embarcações)*, for of the *Caravelas* there went as chief captain Dom Estevão da Gama; he set out on the 10th[1] of April, and there remained as chief captain of the sea Vicente Sodré, who was

a native of Algarve; Fernão Ro[dr]i[gue]z, Badarças, Antonio Fernandez, D. Luis Coutinho Ramiro, Francisco da Cunha, from the *Terceiras* Islands; João Lopez Perestrelo, P[edr]o Affonso d'Aguiar, Gil Matozo, Rûy de Castanheda, Gil Fernandez, Diogo F[e]r[nande]z Correa, Antonio do Campo; Estevão da Gama, son of Aires da Gama, cousin to the Admiral on the brother's side; Loppo Mendez de Vasconcellos, Thomas de Carmona: Loppo Dias, *Criado* of D. Alvaro, brother of the Duke of Bargança; João de Bonagraçia, an Italian.

The Admiral set out with the first fifteen sail on the 10th of February, his uncle Vicente Sodré going as chief captain of the first five of these fifteen, with the intention of remaining away from the rest of the fleet in India, for the protection of the factories which were to be established in Cananor and Cochim, and with the object of making his way in the summer to go and keep guard over the Straits of the Red Sea, and he carried with him the reversion to the post of the Admiral.

The last five of the twenty sail, because they could not be made ready in time to start with the Admiral, set out on the 1st of April, and Estevão da Gama was their chief captain. Vicente Sodré, and Bras Sodré, his brother, were wrecked in Curia Muria at the Cape of Guardafuy, while in company of the fleet.

[1] There is here an evident error produced by reading i° *(primeiro)*, as if it were 10 *(dez)*.

wrecked with his brother on the islands of Curia and Muria, which are in the straits of the Red Sea. In this year the King of Quiloa was made tributary. The chief captain returned to the kingdom with all his ships laden."

It is not many years since there was published a curious little work, in quarto, entitled "Calcoen (Calicut). Facsimile of a Dutch Narrative of the Second Voyage of Vasco da Gama to Calicut. Printed at Antwerp, circa 1504. With Introduction and Translation, by J. Ph. Berjeau." This book, unnoticed by both biographers and bibliographers, is preserved in the library of the British Museum. Although the name of the Great Navigator to India is not mentioned in it, yet the dates, events, and places recorded agree perfectly with the second voyage of Vasco da Gama to India round the Cape of Good Hope. According to the translator, it is a valuable narrative, and supplies a number of interesting details of the voyage which will be looked for in vain in Galvão, Ramusio, Castanheda, Faria, Barros, and others.

Of the Third Voyage of Vasco da Gama, in 1524, as Viceroy of India, little need be said here, as it occurred after the death of Afonso Dalboquerque.

In 1503, on the sixth of April, Afonso Dalboquerque set out on his first voyage to India, under circumstances narrated in the first chapter of the *Commentaries.*[1] In consequence of the opposition of the natives to the Portuguese factory at Cochim, lately established by his

[1] Vol. i, pp. 2, 3.

predecessors, which had been fostered by the Mahometans of Cairo living in Calicut, King Manoel determined to send Afonso Dalboquerque and his cousin Francisco Dalboquerque to erect a fortress in Cochim for the shelter of their fellow-countrymen and the protection of the merchandise. A fleet of six ships was fitted out, three being put under the command of Afonso, three under Francisco Dalboquerque. So eager were they to start, that Afonso left with his three before his cousin was ready, but contrary winds so retarded his progress, that Francisco Dalboquerque reached Cochim some days before him.

The King of Cochim received Francisco Dalboquerque with great demonstration of joy, and persuaded him to lose no time in falling upon the hostile force under the orders of the Çamorim, which he did with great success; and on the arrival of Afonso Dalboquerque, the united Portuguese forces attacked the neighbouring island of Repelim and drove out the lord or ruler of that place. After some demur, the King of Cochim permitted the commanders to commence the erection of a fortress made of palisades filled in with earth; in the work upon which the two cousins so eagerly laboured, that Afonso Dalboquerque had completed his portion first, and desired to sail away to Coulão to load spices, according to his instructions. But Francisco was piqued at this, and dissensions arose between them; and the portion which Afonso had completed was consecrated under the title of the "*Convent of Christ*", while Francisco entitled his "*Alboquerque*".

Afonso Dalboquerque, however, quickly proceeded

to Coulão, and began to take in his cargo; and the Çamorim did all that lay in his power to excite the king of this port against the foreigners in vain. While the lading was in progress, a fleet of thirty-nine vessels from Calicut hove in sight, whereupon Afonso slipped his cables and set out to fall upon the enemy's ships without giving them time to get ready to withstand him, but the ships chained themselves together in groups of five, and stood in to the river of Coulão, where they claimed the protection of the king, and, their cargoes being discharged, they were detained until after Afonso's departure.

After renewing the treaty of peace with this port, and confirming Antonio de Sá in his supreme office of factor, in accordance with the wishes of the native Christians, who sent a silver cross to the Portuguese King in token of their faith, Dalboquerque sailed away on the 12th of January, 1504, to meet his cousin Francisco at Cochim. But Francisco had already departed for Cananor, and Afonso, who delayed a little at Cochim to fill up his cargoes, caught up with him at Calicut, and the two sailed away in company to Cananor, intending to keep together for the return voyage.

The impatience of Afonso, however, and the tardy movements of Francisco, were ill-suited to each other, so Afonso left him on the 25th of January and steered straight across the Indian Ocean for Moçambique, and on reaching it, made his way for the Cape of Good Hope. Want of water forced the ships to put in for water at S. Bras, where Afonso's boat was lost. Here was found a letter sealed up and wrapped in a piece of waxed cloth, relating that Antonio de Saldanha had visited the spot in the previous October. The Cape was doubled on the return journey on the 18th of May, and the anchorage of Santa Maria at Cape Verde Island reached with great difficulties by reason of leakages and bad weather; and, finally, they arrived at Lisbon at the end of July, 1504, where the commander was received with much delight by the king. Francisco Dalboquerque did not complete his business in Cananor until the 5th of February, and, sailing on that day, was lost on his way home with the other two ships under his command, without anyone ever knowing where or how they perished.[1]

The manuscript of the "*Armadas*" gives these proceedings in somewhat altered form, and with some circumstantial additions :--

"AFFONSO DE ALBUQUERQUE, CHIEF CAPTAIN, 1503.

"Affonço de Albuquerque,[2] Chief Captain of three vessels, set out on the 6th of April. Captains: Pero Vaz da Veiga, Duarte Paçheco Pereira the Famous.

[1] See page xxxii, note 1.

[2] The margin reads:—"Another account relates that the Captain Affonso de Albuquerque went in the ship *Sant-Iago*; Duarte Pacheco Pereira, son of João Pacheco, in the ship *Conceição*; and that the third captain was Fernam Mīz de Almada, son of Vasco de Almada, Chief Alcaide of this town, and that the Captain Pero Vaz da Veiga went on the 14th of April with Francisco Albuquerque, but was always with one or the other.

"Francisco de Albuquerque went in the ship *Rainha (Queen)*, and was lost on coming back; Pero Vaz da Veiga of Monte Môr o Novo was also lost; Niculâo Coelho went in the ship *Fayal*—he returned to the kingdom with the rest, and he had already served under the Admiral (Vasco da Gama) in the discovery of India."

"In this same year there went another fleet, whereof was Chief Captain Francisco de Albuquerque; he set out on the 14th of April. Captains; Nicolas Coelho, Fernão Mīz de Almada; and the first fortress that was in Cochim was then made, of wood; and there remained for Chief Captain of the sea, Duarte Paçheco, who performed so many and such signal deeds of bravery, as are written in the Chronicles; and a factory was established in Coulão. On the return home to this kingdom Francisco de Albuquerque and Pero Vaz da Veiga were lost, but the others arrived safely.

"In May of this same year there set out as Chief Captain of another fleet, Antonio de Saldanha, who with Ruy Lourenço Ravasco went out to the kingdom to cruise about for prizes at the Cape of Guardafuy; and Diogo F[e]r[nande]z Pereira, who discovered Socotoraa, was a native of Setubal; and because he was a man accustomed to the sea, he also went in the capacity of Master of his ship.

"The six ships of the first two captaincies of the Albuquerques had to carry the cargo of spiceries, and the three of the captaincy of Antonio de Saldanha had to cruise about the mouth of the Red Sea, watching for the ships of the Moors from Meca.

"Francisco de Albuquerque and Pero Vaz de Veiga were wrecked on their return voyage to the kingdom.

"Diogo Fernandez Pereira proceeded to the island of Sacotorâ, which had not yet been discovered, and there he passed the winter.

"Antonio de Saldanha, on his return to Portugal, in a storm which he encountered in the latitude of the

Cape of Good Hope, broke his mast; yet without it he made his way to the island of St. Elena."

The year 1504 saw another Portuguese fleet, as was now become usual, fitted out for the Indian service, of which the following entry in the MS. quoted, gives the names of the ships and captains:—

"LOPO SOARES, CHIEF CAPTAIN, 1504.

"Loppo Soares, Chief Captain of 13 ships, set out on the 22nd of April. Captains: Pero de Mendoça, Leonel Coutinho, Tristão da Silva, Loppo Mendes de Vasconsellos, Loppo de Abreu da Ilha, Philipe de Castro, Pedro Affonso de Aguiar, Vasco da Siluejra, M[el] Telles Barreto, Afonso Lopez da Costa, Vasco Carvalho, Pero Dinis de Setuval; and they left M[el] Telles de Vasconsellos as Chief Captain of the Sea, who was the third Chief Captain of the Sea of India.

"Pedro Affonso de Aguiar received some damage from a tempest, by reason of his collision with the ship of Affonso Lopes da Costa."

P. Barreto de Resende, in his MS. (Sl. 197), gives a longer account of the doings of these early fleets.

In the following year, we find the celebrated, but unfortunate, Dom Francisco de Almeida, the immediate predecessor of Afonso Dalboquerque, was dispatched, under the following circumstances, as briefly narrated in the "*Armadas*".

"DOM FRANCISCO DE ALMEIDA, VICEROY, 1505.

"Dom Françisco de Almeyda, first Governor and Chief Captain of 14 ships and six *caravelas*, set out on the 25th of March. Captains: Dom Fernãodo de Eça, Lourenço de Brito, Dom Alvaro de Noronha, Pero F[e]rr[eir]a, Manoel Peçanha, Fernão Soares, Antão G[onça]l[ve]z, Diogo Correa, Ruy Freire, Vasco Gomes de Abreu, João da Nova, Lopo de Goes Henrriques, Bastião de Souza, Dioguo Serrão. Pero F[e]rr[eir]a and Loppo Sançhes were lost, and there was, as Chief Captain of the Sea, Dom Lourenço de Almeyda, the Viceroy's son.

"In the *caravelas* there were João Serrão, Alonso Bermundes, a Castilian *fidalgo*, Loppo Chanoca, Gonçalo de Payva, Antão Vaz, Lucas de Afonsequa, João Homem, a Cavalier. In this year was built the fortress of Quiloa, to which was given the name of *Sanctiago*, whereof the first captain was Pero F[e]rr[eir]a. And another fortress was built in Angediva, to which was given the name of *Sancta Christinha*, whereof the first captain was Manoel Peçanha. In this same year was built the fortress of Canonor of stone, whereof the first captain was Lourenço de Brito, and it was called *São Angelo*. And when these fortresses had been finished the Governor received the title of Viceroy.[1]

[1] The marginal note here is as follows:—Another relation. Dom Francisco de Almeida in the ship *Jesus*; Vasco Gomes de Abreu in *S. Gabriel*; Pedro Ferreira Fogaça in the ship *Bella*; João da Nova in the *Flor-de-la-Mar*; Ruy Freire, Fernão Soares, Sebastião de Sousa, Antão Gonçalvez (*Alcaide* of Cezimbra), Diogo Correa, Lopo de D's (Captain and Pilot), João Serram, D. Fernando de Sâ of Campo Mayor, Alonso Bermundes (a Castilian *fidalgo*), Lopó Sanches, Gonçalo de Paiva, Lucas da Fonseca, Lopo Chanoca, João Homem, Gonçalo Vaz de Goes, Antam Vaz. The first 12 of

"In this same year there set out another fleet[1] on the 18th of May, of which there went as Chief Captain of six ships Pero da Nhaya. Captains; Pero Barreto de Magalhães, Françisco da Nhaya, João Leite, João de Queiros, and Manoel Fernandez; and established a fortress and a factory-house in Sofalla, of which Pero da Nhaya was the First Captain.

the ships of this fleet had to return with the cargo of spiceries, and the rest to remain in the Indian fleet.

"Forty leagues on this side of the Line, the ship *Bella*, Captain Pedro Ferreira, sprang so large a leak that, not being able to stop it, she went to the bottom; but the people, and a great part of the cargo which was on deck, were saved, all being divided among the other ships.

"Lopo Sancho was caught in a tempest, and his ship began to leak, and because the leak could not be stopped, they ran her aground 40 leagues from Cape das Correntes, thus saving the people and timbers, whereof they made a *caravela*, which was afterwards lost."

[1] The marginal note here reads:—"6 sail on the 18th of May, Chief Captain Pero de Anhaya. Francisco de Anhaya in the ship *S. João*, etc. Three of these sail were to pass over to India to bring the cargo of spiceries, and the other three had to remain in charge of the coast of Sofalla, where Pero de Anhaia was to erect a fortress.

"Successes—Francisco de Anhaia, on his course along the coast of Sofalla as far as Quiloa, lost his vessel at Moçambique, when he desired to careen her *(querendo tiralo a monte)*.

"Pedro Barreto de Magalhães, on departing from Sofalla, lost the boat with the coffer of cash for the pepper cargo, and with it some of his men; and, on going out over the bar of Quiloa, lost his ship.

"João Leite, going out in a *proa* to catch fish, fell into the sea and was drowned.

"João de Queiros, wishing to take in water 60 leagues this side of Cape das Correntes, was murdered by the Cafres, with the master and pilot, and nearly all who were with him in the boat."

"Of these six sail, three had to go to India, and three to proceed to build the fortress of Sophalla.

"On the 8th of September, in the same year,[1] there set out Cide Barbudo and Pero Caresma to survey the land of the Cape of Good Hope, and discover if there were therein any men belonging to ships that had been lost. Of the ships of this fleet six returned with a cargo to the kingdom [of Portugal], and in them the Viceroy sent to the king an elephant, which was the first that ever came to this kingdom.[2] Another account calls Cide Barbudo—Cide Barboza."

There appears to be little difficulty in reconciling these statements with that of *Correa* and the *Commentaries*,[3] where it is expressly recorded that, in 1505 a great fleet was fitted out under the advice of Vasco da Gama, and in consequence of Afonso Dalboquerque's representation to the king, Tristão da Cunha[4] had been appointed Governor of India for three years; but the sudden attack of blindness which fell upon the newly-appointed Governor prevented his voyage, which

[1] The marginal note here reads :—"A°. 1505. Two sail in September to explore the land of the Cape of Good Hope as far as Sofalla, and part of those islands, to see if they could obtain information of Francisco de Albuquerque and Pero de Mendoça, who had disappeared in those latitudes."

[2] In this respect Portugal was far behind England, for Matthew Paris relates, under the year 1255:—"Missus est in Angliam quidam elephas, quem rex Francorum pro magno munere dedit regi Angliæ, cum in partibus esset Gallicanis. Nec credimus alium unquam visum fuisse in Anglia."—*Abbreviatio Chronicorum*, Ed. Madden, iii, 344. Before this, too, the Sultan had sent to the Emperor of Germany in 1229 an elephant.—*Ib.*, ii, 314.

[3] Vol. I, Chapter vii.

[4] Lord Stanley's *Correa*, p. 379.

fell to the lot of D. Francisco Dalmeida. "The rediscovery of the route to India", says Mr. Lindsay, in respect of this voyage of this Viceroy,[1] "by way of the Cape of Good Hope, proved an immense source of wealth to Portugal. The profits of her merchants on the products of the East were enormous, and for many years, as regarded the rest of Europe, this trade was kept a close monopoly. Lisbon then became the *entrepôt*, which the Italian republics had so long held, for the spices and other produce of India; and the palaces of her traders with that country, which still adorn, even amid their decay, and, in too many instances, their ruins, the banks of the Tagus, testify to the wealth of their original owners and occupants."

The tragic death of D. Francisco Dalmeida on the 1st of March, 1510, at the *Aguada de Saldanha*, has been more than once alluded to in these *Commentaries*, and some valuable notes in illustration of his biography, character, and policy in the East, may be read in Lord Stanley's Preface to Correa's *Voyages of Vasco da Gama*. As the *Commentaries* teach us, he appears to have exhibited (and perhaps with some reason) no slight amount of impatience and indignation at being superseded by Dalboquerque very shortly after his successful engagement with the fleet of the Rumes, or Turks, that is, the Mameluke Sultan of Egypt, in conjunction with that of the Kings of India in 1508, an event which may be read of at length in the principal works on Indian history that refer to the period.[2]

[1] Vol. ii page 44.

[2] See also an excellent biographical notice of this Viceroy by Ferd. Denis, in Hoeffer's *Nouv. Biogr. Univers.*, vol. i, p. 185.

During the Viceroyalty of Dalmeida, yearly expeditions took place, in consolidation of the Portuguese intercourse with their newly established Indian colonies. A fleet was sent in 1506, under Tristão da Cunha and Afonso Dalboquerque as joint Chief Captains. An independent notice of this voyage is thus given in the manuscript of the *Armados*.

"TRISTÃO DA CUNHA AND AFFONSO DE ALBUQUERQUE, CHIEF CAPTAINS, 1506.

"Tristão[1] da Cunha, and Affonso de Albuquerque, Chief Captains of 16 ships, set out on the 6th of

[1] Marginal notes. "16 sail on the 6th of March, whereof not one, in this year, owing to various circumstances, passed over to India."

"Another account reads:—Tristão da Cunha, and Affonso de Albuquerque, Chief Captains, set out on the 6th of March with 16 sail, whereof were Captains, Tristão da Cunha in the ship *Espirito S^to.*, Aluaro Tellez Baretto in *S. Vicente*, João Gomes de Abreu in the *Luz* (lost), Lionel Continho in the *Leitoa Nova* (Sucking Pig), Rûy Pereira, Rûy Dias Pereira, Job Queimado, Alvaro Fernandez, a cavalier from Alvito, João da Veiga, the foster brother of Tristão da Cunha, Tristão Roiz, page of the King's Chamber, Tristão Alvarez, Affonso de Albuquerque in *Flor-de-la-Mar*, Francisco de Tavora in *Rey Grande*, Manoel Tellez Barreto in *Rey Pequeno*, Afonso Lopes da Costa in the *S. Jorge Taforea* (transport), Antonio do Campo in the *Caravela Espirito S^to.*

"Of the first eleven ships which were to carry the cargoes of spiceries Tristão da Cunha was the Chief Captain; of the last five Affonso Dalbuquerque was the Chief Captain, with which he was to remain in position of a fleet on the coast of Arabia and mouth of the Red Sea Straits; with instructions that both these fleets, united into one body, should make for the island of Socotorá, and take a fortress from the Moors who were therein; and whereas this fortress did not turn out to be of the nature which our people expected it to be, namely that they could defend them-

March, 1506. Captains: Aluaro Telles Barreto, Job Queimado, João Gomez de Abreu, Leonel Continho, João Roïz Pereira, Tristão Alueres, João da Veiga, Aluaro Fernandez, Tristão Roïz. Aluaro Telles sailed in such a course as to fetch the Island of São Lourenço on the outer coast, mistaking this for the Cape of Guardafuy. João Gomez died on the voyage, and his ship was lost at Patê, which is an island on the coast of Melinde.

"In this voyage, Tristão da Cunha discovered the islands to which he gave his name, and thus they are called at the present day; and in this same year was constructed the fortress of Cochim, of stone, whereof the first Captain was Don Aluaro de Noronha, and it was called *Sancta Cruz.*

"By this fleet was built the fortress of Sacotorá, to which was given the name of *Sancthome,* of which Dom Affonso de Noronha was the first Captain; and the first monastery was made of the Order of São Fran-

selves in it, they built one of timber which they carried from the kingdom ready cut.

"Successes of this fleet. Alvaro Tellez, outside the Island of S. Lourenço, made his way to the Island of Samatra, thinking it was the Cape of Guardafuy.

"João Gomes de Abreu died on land in the Island of S. Lorenço, of illness, and his ship was lost in a creek close to Pate, the people saving themselves in another one. The rest of the sail, as well those of the Captaincy of Afonso Dalboquerque as also those of Tristão da Cunha, wintered; which Tristão da Cunha, on the tack from Brasil to the Cape of Good Hope, discovered the Islands which they now call after his name.

"Job Queimado, on his return journey to Portugal, was taken by the French."

cisco that was ever in India, and of it Frey Antonio de Loureiro was Guardian.

"The Chief Captain Tristão da Cunha made this fortress, and there Affonso de Albuquerque took leave of him, with five ships to make war upon Ormus; Captain Francisco de Tavora, Manoel Telles Barreto, Afonso Lopes da Costa, Antonio do Campo.

"And in this year the Viceroy dismantled the fortress of Angediva, in accordance with the King's commands, and built in Cochim the Castle of Çima; and Afonso Dalboquerque began to build the fortress of Ormus, to which he gave the name of 'Our Lady of the Victory' (Nossa Senhora da Victoria), and because the war broke out before it was finished, no captain was appointed to it this year.

"Of this fleet, four ships returned laden to the kingdom, for the others remained in India and in the war in Ormus."

The names and dates contained in the preceding extracts relating to this voyage, must be compared by the reader with corresponding statements in the text of *Commentaries of Afonso Dalboquerque*. In most cases the two will be found to agree; but there are, on the other hand, numerous points where discrepancies may be noted. According to the work before us, Afonso Dalboquerque's connection with India as Chief Captain commences with his advice to the King concerning the state of India in 1504. The King decided to send Tristão da Cunha in the position of Governor for three years. The fleet was ready in the following year, when the Governor-designate fell suddenly blind; an accident which led to the substitution of Dom Francisco Dalmeida as Viceroy. It does not appear that Dalboquerque had any active part in this expedition. But in 1506, Tristão da Cunha, being by this time happily restored to sight, was despatched with a fleet of fourteen sail, under orders to winter at the Island of Socotra in case of being unable to cross over to the Indian Continent. At Socotra a fortress was to be constructed for the relief and protection of the Christian inhabitants,[1] and for the safety of the Portuguese squadron about to be employed in blockading the Red Sea.

In this naval expedition Afonso Dalboquerque was associated as Chief Captain over six ships and four hundred men, and secret instructions were given to him that on the expiration of the Viceroy's term of office he was to succeed as Governor of India. Tristão da Cunha (page 21) sets out on the 5th of April, 1506, Alfonso Dalboquerque being delayed until the following day for want of a pilot. The captains met again off Biziguiche,[2] and stand off to double the Cape of St. Augustine, during which evolution a storm breaks over the fleet, the ships are scattered for two days, and on reassembling that of Captain Job Queimado was discovered to be missing.[3] When the fleet was in the

[1] Berjeau states that in 1502, at the time of the second voyage of Vasco da Gama, the island of Socotra was mainly inhabited by Greek Christians.

[2] Perhaps Bissagot's Island, between Bathurst and Sierra Leone.

[3] He rejoined the fleet, however, at Moçambique (vol. i, page 28), having met with an island "sixty leagues in the sea from the

latitude of Ascension Island, the Chief Captain gave orders for the fleet to separate and rendezvous at Moçambique, the usual point of departure across the Indian Gulf. And as they were all in a fair course to clear the Cape of Good Hope, an island hitherto unknown was seen, to which, in honour of the Commander of the expedition, the name of Tristão da Cunha was given. It does not appear by these *Commentaries* that any visit was made from the ships to the land on this occasion.[1]

river of Angola"; this island, which is described as very large, thickly wooded, and uninhabited, is perhaps Pinha Island.

[1] An interesting account of the present condition of this desolate island occurs in a description by Sir Wyville Thomson of some events observed by him during the voyage of the *Challenger*. As this is probably the latest recorded notice, it is worth while referring to it in this place:—"The sixteen or seventeen families who reside on the Island of Tristan da Cunha, have suffered so much from violent gales, that they now build their cottages of blocks of stone—a sort of soft volcanic tufa—of four or five feet square, in order to enable them to withstand these storms. The wind is sometimes so violent that these blocks, when being brought down from the quarry, are lifted bodily by the wind. As there is no mortar on the island, all the stones are dove-tailed into each other, and it is curious to see the people building these cottages. Very frequently wrecks occur on the island, and a number of large spars are picked up on the shore as the remains of lost vessels. The people take two or three of these spars, and, laying them up against the wall at a low angle, carefully grease them, and, by a method known to have been used in Assyria and ancient Egypt, they gradually move on rollers and slide up these blocks to the top of the wall, when they are fixed in their places. Tristan da Cunha is one of a little group of three islands, one of which is called Nightingale Island. It is covered with tussack grass seven, eight, or nine feet in height; and from the top of these tussacks grass springs about an inch and a half in height. The tussack grass becomes matted so as to form a very dense jungle, through which it is difficult to crush. Long avenues run between the tus-

Shortly afterwards, Moçambique was reached by Afonso Dalboquerque and Francisco de Tavora, the Chief Captain arriving a few days later on, with the remainder of the ships except that of Alvaro Mendez, who appears to have rounded Madagascar on the outer coast, contrary to the usual Portuguese navigation, and stood over to Melinde. At this point in the his-

sacks, covered with slippery wet clay, and on the ground are multitudes of penguins. These birds have millions of nests under the long grass, they keep the ground constantly wet, and it has the strongest possible smell of ammonia. It is impossible to pass a single yard along these avenues without crushing the young birds or the nests, while the old penguins all around make the most frightful din, and jag the leg of the traveller, their long sharp beaks drawing blood at every stroke. These penguins are a most extraordinary sight. They are perfectly tame, in the first place, because they do not know any reason for fear from proximity to man; and, secondly, because they have really no means of escape. They stand from one and half to two and a half feet in height. Their nests are little flat clay erections, about two inches in height. The bird lays one, sometimes two eggs, and sits on the nest upright. It is a singular sight to see the birds sitting on their eggs in the space between the tussacks. Some six or eight acres are covered with them. At certain times perhaps a thousand of these penguins come out from the various lanes and walk down to the sea. When they reach to the water they throw themselves down and squattle into it. The moment they are in the water they act just as if they were fishes. The grey groove in their backs is occasionally seen above the surface, but it is scarcely possible to imagine that they are birds—they look just like grey mullets. Having fished for a while, they return to their nests by a regular path, which is beaten as flat as a sheep walk. The whole is carried out by a regular system, the birds going to the sea by one path and returning by another. Sometimes they stand and have a talk for a while, apparently a regular chattering going on; then all of a sudden they stand at attention, and each proceeds to its particular nest."

tory of the expedition, it appears that Tristão da Cunha, persuaded by the information obtained by Rui Pereira (who had touched at the harbour of Tananá in Madagascar, and carried with him two natives to the rendezvous), determined to prosecute the exploration of the coast of that island. A descent was consequently planned upon a densely peopled island in the Mozambique channel—not identified by the writer of the *Commentaries*—the people put to the sword, and the place sacked.

After a delay of three days, spent in taking in water and supplies, Tristão da Cunha made an ineffectual attempt to continue his survey of the northern coast of Madagascar, and returned to the African coast at Çada, where he fell upon the inhabitants, according to his wont, and dispersed them. The policy of uncertainty and delay, which appears to have actuated the Chief Captain at this period, was very much opposed to the fiery and impatient spirit of Afonso Dalboquerque, who remonstrated with his superior officer in very decided tones, and eventually obtained permission to make his way to Socotra, and take his appointed fleet with him. On his way, he had hardly passed the Comoro Islands, when he heard of the wreck of Rui Pereira on a bank, and the narrow escape of Tristão da Cunha from the same fate. In consequence of this disaster, Dalboquerque rejoined his Chief Captain and returned with him to Moçambique, where they found João da Nova, the captain of the *Flor-de-la-Mar* on the homeward voyage,[1] who had put into

[1] See page xxx, note.

that port having sprung a leak at the step of the mast. It was found necessary to discharge the cargo of this ship (which was afterwards repaired and formed one of the fleet left with Dalboquerque) into a native vessel, that was forthwith dispatched home under command of Antonio de Saldanha, who on this voyage discovered the ill-fated watering place of Saldanha (now Saldanha Bay), where, in 1510, the Viceroy Dom Francisco Dalmeida was murdered by the inhabitants. Pedro Barreto de Resende adds, in his account of this event, somewhat mournfully, that the bones of the unfortunate Dalmeida are reported to be lying there to this day.

The reunited fleet proceeded to Melinde, and the friendly king was visited by the Chief Captain; the native potentate took advantage of the opportunity afforded him to request that the Portuguese forces might be directed against his neighbouring enemies the Kings of Mombaça and Angoja. This resulted in the attack, pillage, and destruction by fire of the latter city, and after some parley, a similar fate befell the city of Braboa, a little further on upon the same coast. At the fight which took place at this latter city Tristão da Cunha was wounded in the leg by an arrow, and in pursuance of his desire Afonso Dalboquerque dubbed him a knight, "in that place where the Moors had shed his blood".[1] After this episode, the fleet set sail and steered along the coast in a northerly direction, intending to touch at Magadaxo in Zanguebar; but in consequence of the advice of Afonso Lopez Bura-

[1] Perhaps in remembrance of the knighting of the sons of King João I, at the attack of Ceuta in 1415.—See above, page v.

quinha, the chief pilot, who had practical experience of the dangers attending the navigation of that locality, the course was altered, and the whole fleet stood in and anchored off Çoco, the principal port of Socotra. On arrival, it was found that a very strong fortress had been erected by the natives, who refused all overtures on the part of the fleet to render it up quietly. An attack was therefore organized, which resulted in the successful escalade of the stronghold, after seven hours' fighting, by Tristão da Cunha, who experienced an obstinate resistance on the part of the defenders, their resolute defence bringing about the complete destruction of all of their number except one. This individual was a pilot who gave Afonso Dalboquerque a Chart "of the kingdom of Ormuz" which had been made by another pilot named Omar. The mosque was consecrated to the religion of the conquerors on the following day, and dedicated to "Our Lady of the Victory"; the native Christians[1] encouraged and instructed by a priest who accompanied the fleet; and the Portuguese fortress completed and dedicated to St. Michael, Dom Afonso de Noronha being appointed Captain in charge.

The time was now approaching when Tristão da Cunha and Afonso Dalboquerque were to take separate

[1] Although there are now no traces of the Greek Christianity which then prevailed in the island of Socotra, a valuable account of it may be read in Col. Yule's *Marco Polo*, 2nd Edition, vol. ii, pp. 400-403. Degenerate forms of certain Christian ceremonies were there found side by side with heathen practices as late as the middle of the seventeenth century.

action in the Indian Seas. The former arranged the disposition of the forces, by committing to Afonso the chief captaincy of six well provided ships.

1. The *Cirne*, Flagship of the Chief Captain.
2. The *Rey Grande*, Captain Francisco de Tavora.
3. The *Rey Pequeno*, Captain Manuel Telez.
4. The *Taforea*, or Transport, Captain Afonso Lopes da Costa.
5. A Small Ship, Captain Antonio do Campo.
6. The *Flor-de-la-Mar*,[1] Captain João da Nova.[2]

This last ship, the *Flor-de-la-Mar*, was temporarily added to the fleet, pending the advent of the Comendador Ruy Soares, on whose arrival João da Nova was to sail away to India with the latest news of Afonso Dalboquerque's doings.

Having thus arranged the fleet, Tristão da Cunha shaped his course for India, with four vessels, on the 18th of August, 1507, and having arrived and laden his squadron with a suitable cargo, sailed away on the homeward voyage for Portugal.

Although the next naval expedition sent out from the mother kingdom did not in any way meet those of Tristão da Cunha or Afonso Dalboquerque, it is here fitting to turn to, and record, the mission of Chief Captain Jorge de Mello Pereira, whose fleet sailed in the year 1507, according to the following notice in the *Armadas da India*.

[1] Compare this list with that given on page xxxiv, note.

[2] "L'éternel compétiteur d'Albuquerque." *Ferd. Denis*, in Hoefer's *Nouv. Biogr. Univ.* s.v. *Almeida*.

"JORGE DE MELLO PEREIRA, CHIEF CAPTAIN, WITH 12 SHIPS, IN FOUR CAPTAINCIES, 1507.

"Jorge de Mello Pereira, Chief Captain, set out on the 12th, 13th, 15th and 20th of April. Captains Henrrique Nunes de Leão, Phelipe de Crasto, Chief Captain; Jorge de Crasto, Fernão Soares, Chief Captain; Ruy da Cunha, Gonçalo Carneiro, Vasco Gomes de Abreu, Chief Captain; Ruy de Brito Patalym, Ruy de Valadares, Loppo Crabr[a], Martym Coelho, Diogo de Mello; all these to build the fortress of Moçambique, whereof Vasco Gomez remained to be Captain.

While all these ships were wintering in Moçambique, the crews built the first fortress of stone and mortar, which they called *S. Gabriel*, the hospital, and church; and only Fernão Soares sailed away thence during the April monsoon, to India; and Henrrique Nunes de Leão returned thence to the Kingdom with the cargo of the ship *Leitoa*, which was lost at night at the island of Tristão da Cunha.[1]"

[1] Another account says:—"There set out 12 ships in four captaincies, etc.: Jorge de Mello Pereira, chief captain, in the ship *Belem*; Enrique Nunes de Leam, in *S. Antonio*; Fernão Soarez, chief captain; Rûy da Cunha, in *S. Gabriel*; Gonçalo Carneiro; Filippe de Castro, chief captain; Jorge de Castro, his brother; Vasco Gomes de Abreu, chief captain; Loppo Cabreira; Pedro Lourenço; Rûy Gonçalves de Valadares, in *S. Simam*; João Chanoca.

"The seven ships of the first three Captaincies had to carry the cargo of spiceries.

"The five of the last went as a guard over that coast of Melinde, whose chief captain, Vasco Gomes de Abreu, had to remain as Captain of Sofalla.

"Successes.—Of all these ships, not one passed this year to

The course of events here reverts to the text of the *Commentaries*, from which it will be easily perceived that now that Tristão da Cunha had sailed away to India, Afonso Dalboquerque was in the position of supreme head of Portuguese affairs on the Eastern Coast of Africa, and after settling the affairs of the land he prepared his ships and set out with the intention of cruising about to intercept the ships coming from India to pass into the Red Sea. A council was held under his direction, wherein it was decided that the fleet should steer for the Straits of Ormuz, take Mascate, and endeavour to capture any ships on their voyage from the African ports within the Red Sea bound for Dio, Cambaya, or the Malabar Coast.

On the 10th of August,—only ten days after the departure of Tristão da Cunha for shores further east,—the little squadron of six Portuguese ships sailed out of the port of Çoco, taking a northerly course, by way of Fartak and Zafār, in hopes of sighting the Bay of Curia Muria.[1] Want of necessary provisions compelled the commander to make for the Straits of Ormuz at the gates of the Persian Gulf, and put in at Kalhāt[2] on the

India, and in order to get rid of the confusion which was like to arise out of this upon those who were therein, they agreed to send Rûy Soares, Commendador of Rhodes, with a message to the Viceroy, which voyage he undertook, although it was very perilous. Anrrique Nunes de Leam returned from Moçambique to Portugal with the lading of the ship *Leitoa*, which could not proceed on account of its leaky condition."

[1] Some writers have sought to identify the Kuria Muria Islands with the Male and Female Islands described by Marco Polo.—See Col. Yule's 2nd Edition, vol. ii, p. 397.

[2] The *Calatu* of Marco Polo, ii, 448.

Arabian coast. The inhabitants of this city so readily agreed to all that was demanded of them, that it escaped the destruction which had been visited upon other less fortunate places; and, after re-victualling his fleet, Afonso Dalboquerque sailed away, intending to make for *Icce*, a site which he found to have been marked down in Omar's chart as distant five leagues from Calayate. This turned out to be a river, so the fleet proceeded to Curiate, a little below Mascate,[1] and burned it, and then to Mascate, where another scene in the fiery drama which proclaimed the progress of the destroyer was enacted; the operations of the Portuguese at this place being encouraged by the miraculous egress of the sapping party from the ruins of the mosque, which came down upon them just as they were about to quit it after cutting the supports.

At this period of their Arabian adventures, João da Nova, who throughout his career systematically opposed his superior officer, determined to sail away to India without waiting for Ruy Soares, *Commendador* [*of Rhodes*]. But Afonso Dalboquerque did not lack the voluntary information of those who were likely to be well-informed on the subject, and soon learned that it was the general opinion of all his captains that he was undertaking too much in attempting to besiege Ormuz by sea with so limited a number of ships.

The expedition next came in front of Soar, and stood in and anchored about a mile and a half from shore, but the readiness shown by the rulers of the city in accepting and admitting the demands made by

[1] See Col. Yule's *Marco Polo*, 2nd Edition, vol. ii, p. 448.

Afonso Dalboquerque upon the place, saved their town from imminent destruction by burning and the inhabitants from slaughter.

The next place visited by the conqueror was Orfação, or Corfacam, where, in the course of the proceedings consequent upon the defence of the place, a brutal mutilation of the "old Moors who were not fit for work" was perpetrated, in keeping with the cruel conduct of Vasco da Gama at Calicut during his second voyage in 1502, to which the attention of the reader has already been directed. Eventually the city of Orfação was fired, and the victorious fleet, setting sail in the midst of a violent thunderstorm, reached Ras Mussendom, where news was brought to Afonso Dalboquerque that "the King of Ormuz was already aware of his approach and had a large fleet to fight with him, and in the city many soldiers and many munitions of war".

This information resulted in shortening sail, with a view to a very cautious approach; but, notwithstanding this manœuvre, the fleet hove in sight of the island of Ormuz[1] on the following day, the little islands of Lārek and Kishm, or Larequa and Queixome as they are called in the narrative, being also within view of the little fleet of foreign adventurers. Among the vessels of war in the harbour of Ormuz, which were detained by the King, was the *Meri*, of Cambaya,—a ship of about one thousand tons burden.

The king, however, who had doubtless heard of the

[1] Some valuable notes on the situation of *Hormos* in Col. Yule, *Marco Polo*, ii, 450; View, in Correa's *Lendas*, Lisbon Acad. Ed., tom. ii, p. 439.

ruthless conduct of his visitors on former occasions, appears to have been by no means desirous of hazarding a conflict of naval power, and dispatched an Armenian Moor, named Cogebeiram, to negotiate terms of peace with Afonso Dalboquerque; but the terms offered by that spirited Captain were too severe for the king's acceptance, and after a short space of time, consumed in fruitless attempts at an adjustment, mutual preparations for hostilities were commenced. The Portuguese ships formed a semicircle outside the crowded body of native shipping in the harbour, and laying out cables, buoyed up at short intervals, prevented the enemy from breaking away and getting to sea. The *Meri* was grappled with and boarded, her crew overpowered and slaughtered, and her guns turned against the city itself, by Jorge Barreto, who took the ship.

The panic which seized the native seamen at this juncture was not quelled even by the presence among them of the Chief of their City—Cogeatar—who was compelled to quit his barge, and only saved his life by throwing himself into the sea close to the houses, when the Portuguese were on the point of capturing him. The consternation of the people on shore increased every moment, the carnage was now at its height, and was followed up in the way which appears to have become by this time, and for many years afterwards, almost conventional in the Indian Seas. "They[1] returned to the place where Afonso Dalboquerque was, and when all were reunited, they returned again to the

[1] Vol. i, p. 117.

battle on the sea with the Moors who were swimming, and with lance-thrusts and cuts they killed so many of them, that, although, as they were tired of slaughter and unable to accomplish their whole purpose, some managed to escape, yet the sea was so tinged with blood that it was a fearful thing to look at. The cabin-boys and ships' servants, also, on their part, did nothing but thrust the bodies under water with grappling-hooks, and tear out their bowels in such a manner that the slaughter was great among them; and there was one cabin-boy who alone put to death eighty Moors."

The only defence which could have protected the city of Ormuz against the foreigners was thus completely destroyed by an engagement which had lasted for eight hours, during which "there was not a single shot fired that did not send a ship to the bottom and put many men to death".[1] The dismantled and disabled ships were set on fire and cut adrift, and floating out to sea carried destruction with them in their unguided courses The victorious Afonso Dalboquerque landed, and set fire to the suburbs, thus filling up to the brim the ruin and desolation he had brought upon the city. Cogeatar, the Minister of Ormuz, lost no time in endeavouring to stay the hand of the infidel Franks, and sent two Moors (who had but recently arrived in Ormuz from Oran with news of a fleet sent

[1] It must not, however, be forgotten that many bodies were found afterwards mortally wounded by the arrows of their fellow men; a circumstance considered miraculous by the Portuguese, who declared the arrows were turned in their flight, but probably the result of adverse wind, or bad or distant aim.

from Portugal to Turkey under command of the Prior of Crato, as Chief Captain) to announce his unconditional surrender.

After some discussion, the amount of indemnity and of annual tribute was settled, a space within the boundary of the city was demanded for a Portuguese fortress, the kingdom formally restored to the king and his chief Cogeatar—who had shown a desire to retire to Calayate, his native place—and a treaty drawn up, in duplicate (Arabic and Persian), copies of which were sent home. On the 10th of October, the Portuguese flag was carried in procession through Ormuz, and planted on the loftiest tower of the Royal Palace.

All now seemed to be in good order; but Afonso Dalboquerque's desire of constructing a stronghold which should defy native treachery and all the advantages which superior numbers could wield against the resolute defence of a mere handful of men at bay within it, gave Cogeatar an opportunity of rousing his countrymen once more against their new masters. Nabandé or Nobend, was offered as a better site than any which the island of Ormuz could afford. This was found on examination to be unsuitable; another place, nearer to Ormuz,—Turumbaque—proved equally unfit, and eventually Afonso Dalboquerque determined to build his castle on the point of Morona, in Ormuz itself, looking towards the mainland, the place occupied by the square fortification in the plan given at page 112.

Under native labour and Portuguese superintendence, the work of construction rapidly progressed; the principal portal of the tower being cased with three stone anchors taken out of the *Meri*, a lasting memorial of the victory of the fleet, and of the disgrace of the defenders of the city. An attempt was made to encourage the merchants to trade with the ships, the ships themselves were careened and refitted one by one, and a *fusta* of eighteen banks of oars built for future service in the Red Sea. Meanwhile an Arab sheikh, Ismael, had arrived, to receive the yearly tribute paid to him by the King of Ormuz; and the matter having been reported to Afonso Dalboquerque, he threatened to deprive the king of his authority over the city if ever he should pay any future tribute to this or any other superior lord except only to the King of Portugal.

At this period of the Portuguese occupation of Ormuz, when Afonso Dalboquerque was contemplating an expedition to the Red Sea, an incident occurred which, although small in itself, led eventually to the abandonment of the hardly-won position. It arose in this way. Out of a feeling of magnanimity and a desire to let nothing delay the completion of the fortress, the Portuguese commander consented to restore the *Meri*, and some of the captives, to the king and Cogeatar. This liberal proceeding emboldened the captain of a merchant ship from Onor (Honowar), who had come into the port of Ormuz just before the engagement trusting to the security of a pass procured from Dom Lorenço Dalmeida, son of Dom Francisco Dalmeida the Viceroy, to beg restitution, for on the arrival of the hostile fleet Cogeatar had seized the Onor ship, which was discharging her freight, and converted her into a vessel of war. This was granted, a safe pass given to the captain to return to Onor, and a letter written by Afonso Dalboquerque to the Viceroy entrusted to his care, in which was set forth the whole Portuguese policy and the urgent need of reinforcements.

But there was a traitor in the fleet; for no sooner had Antonio do Campo, captain of one of the ships, obtained an idea of the contents of the communication thus made to the Viceroy, than Cogeatar was apprised of the information so given. Not content with this treachery, the other captains of the fleet were purposely irritated by the artful dissemination of matters prejudicial to their interest, which were falsely alleged to be proposed in this letter. This incensed them against their commander, and it was not long before they found opportunities to comport themselves with insubordination, and even to hold seditious meetings in which they discussed the lucrative advantages which they would obtain by a speedy abandonment of the works at Ormuz and a passage to India. The division of the prize money was another fruitful source of contention, and it was not until the extreme measure of depriving Francisco de Tavora of his captaincy and giving the command of his ship to another, that Afonso Dalboquerque, who had acted throughout this critical affair with great and exemplary forbearance, was able to regain some show of authority and command over his men.

In the midst of these internal dissensions four mariners deserted, and revealed to the willing ears of Cogeatar the disorder that was prevalent in the hostile ranks. This resulted in an endeavour on the part of that high functionary to retard the progress of the building by which the subjection of the natives would have been completed; and it was not long before the threatening aspect of affairs warned Afonso Dalboquerque to lose no time in withdrawing the persons employed upon that work to the ships, previous to a declaration of war against the king of Ormuz for not restoring the four fugitives whose surrender had been demanded in vain.

The successful accomplishment of the fortress of Ormuz was now a matter of great uncertainty. On the 13th of November 1507, the depositions of the disaffected captains were drawn up, in which it was alleged that Afonso Dalboquerque had neglected the fortress of Socotra, and omitted the opportunity of sending the *Flor-de-la-Mar* to India. On the 5th of January in the following year, a remonstrance signed by all the captains was handed to the commander, wherein they declared their intention of no longer co-operating with him in the siege. But Afonso Dalboquerque was unwilling to desist from his cherished scheme without a conflict. Skirmishes took place at the fresh-water tanks of Turumbaque, and at the watering place on the Island of Queixome or Kishm; the native forces were routed; and a *parao*, filled with the corpses of the principal Moors who had been killed in action, was sent drifting to shore towards the city, where the lamentations of the people were, without doubt, not unmixed with the horrible remembrance of the somewhat similar fate which had been meted out to the men of Calicut by a previous expedition from the same European nation.

It was not long after this wanton act of inhumanity had been perpetrated, before a large fleet was sighted off the island of Lara, and the three ships commanded by Antonio do Campo, Afonso Lopez da Costa, and Manuel Telez, were ordered to fall upon the Moorish vessels. The enemy, who turned out to be in great force—no less than four thousand men, in sixty ships under command of Xaquear—had been posted under orders from Cogeatar to dispute the possession of the watering stations, but they fled at the approach of the three Portuguese ships; and these in their turn took advantage of the opportunity, when they were not near the immediate observation of Afonso Dalboquerque, and sailed away for India, deserting their companions, who were thus left in but three ships in the presence of a very superior force, and between that force and a large and fortified city which was already beginning to show signs of surrender.

For six days the decision of the Chief Captain wavered, but at length he determined to abandon his position, and sailed away to Socotra, sending an account of the circumstances to the Viceroy by João da Nova in the *Flor-de-la-Mar*, one of the few ships yet in his company. On the way to Socotra a Mecca ship richly laden was captured, and on his arrival the island garrison was revictualled, and Franciso de Tavora, was dispatched, in the last ship, to Melinde for supplies, while Afonso Dalboquerque cruised about off the Cape of Guardafum.

At this period of the adventures of Afonso Dalboquerque, the spring months of the year 1508, a fleet was sent out from Portugal, as was now customary, to reinforce her distant colonies in the East. This was commanded by Jorge de Aguiar, and the brief record of its captains and its proceedings—as summarised in the MS. of the *Armadas da India*—introduces into the scenes in which Afonso Dalboquerque is the principal figure, several new names, and supplies some new details of information not contained in the *Commentaries*. The entry is as follows:

"JORGE DE AGUIAR, CHIEF CAPTAIN, 1508.

"Jorge de Aguiar,[1] Chief Captain of 8 ships, set out on the 9th of April. Captains Vasco Carvalho, Ruy da Cunha, João Roiz P[ereir]a, Alvaro Barreto, Tristão da Sylva, Gonçalo Mendes de Brito, Francisco Pereira Pestana. They wintered in Quiloa. These[2] eight ships for the cargo; and four small ones for the war

[1] For the Portuguese text of this passage, see page 31 of this volume.

[2] "Eight sail on the 9th April, and four more sail, others say 5. Another account is couched in this manner:—Jorge de Aguiar, chief captain, set out on the 9th of April with 13 sail, of which the captains were: Tristam da Silva; João Roiz Pereira, in the ship *Botafogo;* Vasco Carvalho; Alvaro Barreto, in the ship *Sta. Marta;* Francisco Pereira Pestana; Gonçalo Mendez de Brito; João Colaço; Diogo de Atayde; Duarte de Lemos da Trofa, in the *Sta. Cruz;* Vasco da Silveira; Pero Correa; Diogo Correa, his brother.

"Of these 17 ships, the first four, whereof Diogo Lopes de

against Ormus, of which Duarte de Lemos Datrofa was chief Captain. Captains João Colaço, Gonçalo da Sylveira, Diogo de Attajde, Pero Correa, and Diogo Correa. In this same year Diogo Lopez de Siqueira, Chief *Almotaçel* of the kingdom, sailed as chief Captain of four vessels on the 5th of April to go and explore, and conquer Malaca. Captains Jeronimo Teixeira in the ship *Sta. Clara*, Gonçalo de Souza, and João Nunes. He returned with all his ships safe to the kingdom."

At the end of April, Francisco da Tavora returned to the rendezvous at Cape Guardafum, bringing to Afonso Dalboquerque two captains in ships newly arrived from Portugal, and the news that the commendador Ruy Soares (who was under orders to join Afonso Dalboquerque) had gone on to the Viceroy.

Siqueira was chief captain, went to explore the island of S. Lourenço, and not finding therein the silver, cloves, and ginger, that it was reported to contain, they passed over to explore the island of Malaca.

"Of the 13 of the captaincy of Jorge de Aguiar, eight had to carry the cargo, and with the five remaining he, Jorge de Aguiar, had to keep guard over the coasts of Ethiopia and Arabia.

"On returning from Malaca to India, the ship *Santa Clara*, Captain Jeronimo Teixeira, struck upon a bank and foundered, and Diogo Lopez appointed him sub-captain of the ship of João Nunez.

"The ship of Gonçalo de Souza was burned because she had no crew to handle her.

"Jorge de Aguiar was lost by night on the islands of Tristão da Cunha.

"Francisco Pereira Pestana wintered in Quiloa, whither he went as captain."

He also brought Fernão Gomez and a Moor, who were to undertake a journey by land across the continent of Africa through the "land of Cadandin, a Moorish Captain who was prosecuting a war with another Captain of Prester John, for the one land is contiguous to the other", through Tambocatu (probably Timbuctoo), and thence to Arguin,[1] along the river Çanaga or Senegal—a journey which the Moor had already traversed.

Afonso Dalboquerque wintered at Socotra, repaired his ships, built a *fusta* of fourteen banks of oars, and, much to the disgust of her Captain, Francisco de Tavora, cut down the *Rey Grande*, which was too high out of the water for these stormy latitudes. In the meantime, the three fugitive ships arrived at Cochim, and their Captains laid their complaints before the Viceroy, the principal points being the Commander's neglect of reinforcing Socotra and his protracted operations before Ormuz; whereupon, at the Viceroy's order, a commission was appointed to inquire into the circumstances of the case, the text of the document being given in full, and dated on the 26th of May.

Not long after this time, the fleet[2] of Jorge de Aguiar, which has been already mentioned as setting out on

[1] A place of this name is marked on the maps of the coast between Cape Blanco and Cape Mirik, considerably to the north of the mouth of the Senegal, and therefore the route as laid down in the *Commentaries* has undergone some displacement, but we shall see further on how the travellers fared.

[2] The text of these *Commentaries* says *three* vessels—probably an error of *tres* for *treze (thirteen)*. The *text* of the *Armadas* mentions the names of fourteen captains; the *marginal note* mentions

the 9th of April, arrived. It was in this fleet that notice was sent out to the Viceroy to hand over the government of India to Afonso Dalboquerque, and to return to Portugal.

On the 15th of August, Afonso Dalboquerque set out from Socotra, not so much with the intention of renewing his attempt upon Ormuz as of observing the state of affairs, doing what he could towards the consolidation of the Portuguese power in those parts, and then rejoining the Viceroy in Cochim.

During the progress of the voyage, the fleet had a narrow escape from grounding opposite the Curia Muria Islands; but, at length, reached Calayate in safety, and lost no time in attacking the city, which made a stout defence under Xarafadin (*Sharaf Ed-Deen*), routing the defenders, sacking the place, and, finally, setting fire to the city and burning twenty-seven merchant ships that lay in the harbour. Not content with this, Afonso Dalboquerque, who appears on this occasion to have caught the spirit of Oriental cruelty, ordered the prisoners to be deprived of their ears and noses, and then he returned to his ships, "giving many thanks to Our Lord for the favour He had shown him in giving him such a city, gained without danger to our men, with so small a force."

The Commander now, for the first time, heard, from one of Cogeatar's Envoys, that the Portuguese fleet

thirteen,—that of Ruy da Cunha being omitted, although he is specially mentioned in conjunction with Fernão Soares, who does not appear to have held a captain's commission according to the *Commentaries*.

had routed the naval forces of the Mahometans, under Mirocem,—called by Camoēs Mir-Hocem[1]—and Meliquiaz—Melique Yaz—that affairs at Ormuz were in a critical state, and that his own fugitive Captains were with the Viceroy at Cochim. At the receipt of this startling intelligence the little fleet repaired to Ormuz, which was found to have been put into an improved state of defence; and, after some time spent in an angry correspondence full of fruitless complaints, recriminations and charges of little moment, Afonso Dalboquerque watered his fleet at the island of Lara, and determined to remain at anchor in sight of the city until the end of October, in hopes of a reinforcement of ships sent from Portugal to Socotra and dispatched to reinforce him from that island.

During this second blockade, a successful diversion was made by the Portuguese, in which a force of five hundred archers, sent to the assistance of Ormuz from the Xeque Ismael, was dispersed at Nabande; and all seemed favourable to the victors, when the disastrous loss of Diogo de Melo—who had joined Afonso from Melinde—off the island of Lara, changed once more the aspect of affairs; and a storm, which tried the seaworthiness of the nearly worn-out ships to the very utmost, compelled Afonso Dalboquerque again to abandon his intention of blockading Ormuz and to steer for India.

This voyage was safely accomplished, and the Chief Captain reached Cananor at the beginning of Decem-

[1] See vol. ii, pp. 112 and 113, note, for the passages relating to this event.

ber, where he found the Viceroy, the deserting Captains, the Commendador Ruy Soarez, and the fleet of Jorge de Aguiar. Dinis Fernandez, Captain of the *Rey Grande*, which had been missing for a little time previously, arrived a few days afterwards, and with this event the narrative of the First Part concludes.

The Second Part of the COMMENTARIES commences with the request made by Afonso Dalboquerque to the Viceroy that the office of Governor of India should be delivered up to him, according to the instructions sent out from Portugal in the fleet of that year. This demand gave an opportunity to the fugitive Captains to intrigue against their former Chief Captain with the Viceroy, who desired to remain in office; constant bickerings and quarrels arose between Dalboquerque and Dalmeida, which were for a while abated, while the latter was absent in an expedition against the *Rumes*, or so-called *Roman* Turks at Diu, but broke out afresh on his victorious return, Afonso Dalboquerque having, meanwhile, gone to Cochim, where the Viceroy celebrated his victory.

In the meantime, Diogo Lopez de Siqueira, who had set out from Portugal on the 5th of April, 1508, as Chief Captain of four ships bound for Malaca, arrived at Cochim, after a severe passage of nearly twelve months' duration. The Viceroy, who pretended that he desired to carry Afonso Dalboquerque back to Portugal with him, wished to appoint the newly arrived Diogo Lopez Chief Captain of India, but the latter declined the doubtful compliment, and was not long before he sailed away to prosecute his voyage. At length a final stroke was delivered by the Viceroy against his successor designate, by causing him to be arrested and imprisoned in the fortress of Cananor.

But the old proverb, that when things are at their worst they are sure to mend, was truly exemplified in the case of Afonso Dalboquerque. His case to all appearance was desperate, and had it not been for the indomitable spirit which formed so prominent a trait in his character, and which had already on several occasions of peril buoyed him up, and which did not even now desert him, he would have succumbed to the disgrace and indignity heaped upon his head at the very moment when he looked to enjoy the high reward which his sovereign had thought fit to bestow upon him for his fidelity and distinguished valour. His release was brought about by the arrival of his nephew, the Marshal Dom Fernando Coutinho, at Cananor, in the month of October, whose expedition is well and briefly set forth from the "*Armadas da India.*"

DOM[1] FERNANDO COUTINHO, MARSHAL OF PORTUGAL, 1509.

"D. Fernando Coutinho, Chief Captain of fifteen ships, set out on the 12th of March, Captains Francisco de Sá, etc., fifteen ships, containing three thousand men. In these ships orders went out that Afonso Dalboquerque was to govern India. Francisco de Sá was '*Vedor* da Fazenda do Porto'; Lionel Coutinho,

[1] For the original Portuguese text, see page 56, note.

son of Vasco Fernandez Coutinho, went in the *Flor da Rosa;* Ruy Freire, son of Nuno Fernandez Freire, in the *Garça;* Jorge da Cunha in the *Magdalena;* Rodrigo Rabello de Castelbranco in the *Santa Clara;* Bras Teixeira in the *Ferroa;* Francisco Marecos in the *S. Francisco,* etc.

"Of all these fifteen ships, that of Francisco Marecos alone did not pass over to India.

"The Marshal put Afonso Dalboquerque in possession of the Government of India, and Dom Francisco de Almeida embarked for the kingdom [of Portugal] in accordance with the orders of His Highness. After the departure of the Viceroy, the Governor and the Marshal went with all their fleet against Calicut, where they landed, and having destroyed and sacked the city, the Marshal and many Captains and soldiers were killed. At the end of this year the Viceroy delivered up the Government to Afonso Dalboquerque, and sailed away for the kingdom in three ships, and was killed by the Cafres at the watering place of Saldanha, etc."

Afonso Dalboquerque had been in confinement for three months when the Marshal opportunely arrived, and the latter, in obedience to his instructions, took him on, as Captain General of India, to Cochim, which port they reached safely on the 29th of October. On the 4th of November the Viceroy had a long conversation with the Marshal in reference to the dissensions between himself and Afonso Dalboquerque, and on the next day he surrendered the government into Dalboquerque's hands and embarked on board the *Garça,* which left India to carry him to Portugal on the 10th of the same month.

The affairs relating to the succession being now settled, the Marshal unfolded to his uncle the orders which he had received from the King to destroy the city of Calicut, one of the most important strongholds on the Eastern coast in the power of the Çamorim.[1] The King of Cochim created a diversion in favour of the Portuguese by stirring up war on the interior frontier of Calicut, and the Portuguese fleet was on the point of sailing when Vasco da Silveira arrived from Socotra, bringing an urgent request on the part of Duarte de Lemos, chief Captain of the Arabian coast, whose head-quarters were in that island, for new ships to replace his original fleet, which had fallen into decay. The unwelcome messenger was put off for a season, and seized the opportunity of accompanying the Portuguese fleet to Calicut, where he was killed; but on the conclusion of the affair at Calicut, Diogo Correa was dispatched in the same ship with reinforcements for Socotra, and news of the death of Vasco da Silveira, the destruction of Calicut, and the intention of Afonso Dalboquerque to come to Socotra on his way to the Red Sea in the course of the following summer. On the receipt of this intelligence, Duarte de Lemos appointed Pero Ferreira to the Captaincy of the Fortress, sent D. Afonso de Noronha

[1] For the treachery which the Portuguese under Vasco da Gama experienced here, and the severe punishment which that navigator visited upon the city, see Lord Stanley's *Correa*, chap xvii.

to India, and he himself returned to winter at Melinde.

Meanwhile, the combined fleet of twenty ships of war and a crowd of smaller vessels, with a force of two thousand Portuguese on board, set sail from Cochim on the 31st of December, 1509, and brought up in front of the Port of Calicut on the 3rd of January. On the following day the attack was made in the absence of the Çamorim, who was on the expedition which had been forced on him by the King of Cochim. It resulted in the entry of the city, the burning of the King's Palace, the ultimate retreat of the Portuguese before a strong reserve force, after slaying the *Catual*, the Governor of the city, two *Caimais* and three thousand native soldiers, and the death of ten or twelve of the principal men, including the Marshal Dom Fernando Coutinho, Vasco da Silveira, Gonçalo Queimado, the Governor's standard-bearer, and Manuel Peçanha (the officer appointed to succeed in case of the death of the Viceroy), who had much underrated the resistance of the inhabitants. Afonso Dalboquerque himself did not escape unhurt, for he was twice wounded in the shoulders by lances thrust at him by the enemy over the palisades. Thus repulsed, the fleet returned to Cochim, two *carauelas* being left behind to blockade the harbour.

Nothing daunted at the unsatisfactory result of this attack, Afonso Dalboquerque sent Frey Luis, a Franciscan Friar, to the neighbouring King of Narsinga, urging him to come down with a powerful force from the interior and co-operate with the maritime power of the Portuguese, promising in recompense for this aid to give a monopoly in the trade of horses[1] from Ormuz to the port of Baticala.

Two days after the departure of the Friar to Narsinga, and of Diogo Correa to Socotra as already noticed, two vessels of the fleet commanded by Diogo Lopez de Sequeira arrived with Nuno Vaz de Castelo Branco, who brought news of the treachery of the Malays, the arrest of Ruy de Araujo, the factor, and twenty men, the burning of two ships of the fleet, and the touching of his Chief Captain at Caecoulão, from which port they had made their way to Cochim, while the latter had taken a direct course homewards to Portugal.

The notes descriptive of the Province of Malabar and the customs of its inhabitants, which follow in the commentaries immediately after the text of the instructions to Fr. Luis, in respect of his journey to the Kingdom of Narsinga, are of course very superficial, yet they represent the matters which struck their observers most forcibly.

There are, however, two points which may be mentioned here. The first is the statement that the Brahmans "have knowledge of the Trinity and of Our Lady, whereby it appears that anciently they were Christians". With regard to the alleged Christianity which was observed in this and other districts of India, it must be borne in mind, that like all early travellers to that country, Afonso Dalboquerque, following the lead of

[1] For an account of the exportation of horses, see Col. Yule's *Marco Polo*, vol. i, page 88, note, and vol. ii, page 322, note.

Vasco da Gama, mistook the followers of Brahma and Buddha for Christians, because they worshipped the images of the Virgin and Child which were carried in the Portuguese ships. These idolaters probably saw in the Catholic images the representation of their own Blessed Lady, Maha Madja, holding in her arms her Son Shakya. Under the influence of the same sentiments, observing the similarity of the name of the Indian goddess, and the aureolæ or nimbi surrounding the heads of the mother and her son, the Portuguese on their part fell into the same mistakes when they beheld them in the native temples. Nevertheless, there were without doubt, in the time of Afonso Dalboquerque and early Portuguese discoverers, a certain but very moderate number of Nestorian Christians[1] on the great continent of India; a number far below the calculation of the Portuguese, whose enumeration of twenty-five thousand Christians and three hundred churches in one city alone (that of Coulão), and whose frequently recorded description of the refusal of these so-called Christians to consort with persons of another religious belief, clearly points to their mistaking[2] the highest caste of Indians for a people practising corrupt

[1] "In the Province of Malabar there are between Chetua (Chaitwa) and Coulão many Christians of the time of St. Thomas, and many churches"—page 79. See Col. Yule's *Marco Polo*, Book iii, chap. 18, "Discoursing of the place where lieth the body of St. Thomas the Apostle"; and chap. 22, "Of the kingdom of Coilum".

[2] A similar error was made by Afonso Dalboquerque with regard to the subjects of the Xeque Ismael.—See page 117.

forms derived from ancient knowledge of the details of Christianity.

The medicinal remedies (the other point to which the reader's attention should be directed) described in the text on p. 79, are so few and simple that it would appear, if the passage stood alone, that the Indians had a very imperfect acquaintance with the healing art; but this is an error arising from the superficial observation of the Portuguese. Anyone who will take the trouble to peruse the "Commentary on the Hindoo System of Medicine", by T. A. Wise, M.D., of the Bengal Civil Service, (8vo. Calcutta, 1845), or the first volume of the "Review of the History of Medicine", by the same author, will readily perceive that the Indians, who, like the ancient Egyptians, were a nation of druggists, possessed a very extensive pharmacopœia, and a general knowledge of anatomy, and that they performed important surgical operations with a scientific skill that is truly astonishing.

It was not long after the affair at Calicut, before Afonso Dalboquerque was ready to put into operation new and far wider schemes of conquest. On the 10th of February he set out from Cochim again, with a fleet of twenty-three vessels for Angediva, with the intention of going to Socotra, fulfilling his promise of reinforcing Duarte de Lemos and passing up the Red Sea, to destroy the fleet of the Grand Sultan, and having done this, to complete the fortress of Ormuz which had been left just commenced.

But the voyage was destined to be interrupted by a long delay of time spent in an undertaking, the magnitude and successful results of which were not at the time foreseen, although it now sheds lustre on the name of Afonso Dalboquerque, and the memory of that great commander is for ever connected with it. The fleet had only progressed as far as Mergeu, when Timoja — formerly a Hindoo corsair, but now self-raised to a position of great honour—a man completely in the interest of the Portuguese, visited the Governor, and dissuaded him from carrying out his intended voyage. He represented—a tale told to no unwilling ears — the political disorders at Goa, the intention entertained by the Mahometans of utilizing that naturally powerful position as a base of extensive operations, with a view to the expulsion of the Portuguese from India, the death of "the Çabaio," Lord of Goa, the youth and helplessness of "the Hidalcão" his son,[1] and urged Afonso Dalboquerque to take advantage of the opportunity presented to him and to seize the island. At first, Afonso Dalboquerque, with the tenacity which forms so strong a characteristic of the Portuguese nation, clung to his original scheme; but eventually, after convening a general meeting of all the Captains, *fidalgos*, and pilots of the fleet, he came to see the advantage of the situation, and brought up in front of Goa, while Timoja's men captured and took possession of the fortress of Cintacora; after which he conducted his fleet over the bar, and set to work to take soundings of the river.

This proceeding led to the storming and capture of the tower or castle of Pangij,—otherwise Pangim, and

[1] See further on, under the description of Goa.

now the site of the principal buildings of Portuguese Goa, as will be shown in the description of the island —which commanded the entrance to the bar. The fall of Pangij so disheartened the Moors, that they sent a message of surrender, which Afonso Dalboquerque accepted on conditions of all the Rumes and Turks (known to be within the city) being delivered over to him as prisoners. Melique Çufegurgij, the Governor of the city, however, having learnt by experience the inevitable fate of torture, mutilation and death, that was in store for these people if they fell into the power of the Portuguese, dismantled the fortress and fled away with the proscribed men, to avoid the performance of so heinous an act of treachery to those who had been his allies.

At this part of the text of the *Commentaries*, a brief description "of the site and foundation of the city of Goa" occurs, to which I shall revert hereafter, comparing it with the account given by Cottineau de Kloguen, who appears to have devoted considerable time and special attention to the history and topography of the island. The notice of the reader must, however, be directed to the consideration of one important change of native custom in this island which is alleged to have been brought about by the victorious Portuguese. The horrible East Indian custom of burning widows, which, to his lasting credit, Afonso Dalboquerque prohibited at Goa, (see vol. ii. p. 94), has been written of from almost every point of view, and it would be difficult to find anything new to record here concerning this inhuman custom. There is, however, in the *Journal of the Royal Asiatic Society* (vol. ix, part i, 1876) recently published, a very remarkable and circumstantial account of the hideous conventionalities in connection with these revolting practices, obtaining in a part of Asia where Brahminism flourishes vigorously, which appears to me to exhibit the newest, the most faithful, and the most painful picture of these self-inflicted tortures that has ever been penned. It occurs in "*An Account of the Island of Bali*," by R. Friederich, and the portions to which I would especially call attention are these :—

"The *burning of widows* has attracted most attention from Europeans. Wonder is expressed at the great number of women sacrificed in this way in former times. It cannot surprise us to see so many women burnt, particularly since the women who offer themselves gain the highest distinction, and the sacred writings from the *Parvas* (divisions of the *Mahâbbârata*) downwards represent this act as praiseworthy and almost necessary. That in India but one wife follows her husband in death, is naturally explained by the fact that very few Hindoos have more than one wife. But little is yet known of the burning of widows among the princes of India, and as but few independent princes now exist who are worshippers of Siva, the silence on this subject is easily accounted for. . . . . The names given to the burning of widows are *Satia*[1] and *Bela*. *Satia is the burning of a wife who*, from a platform erected for the purpose, *throws herself into the same fire with her husband, committing suicide with the creese at the same time. Bela*, on the contrary, *is the burning of a wife who is burnt in a separate fire*, not with her husband, *jumping into it alive*, without using the creese. This latter method is not thought so much of, but is the more common. The words *Satia* and

[1] *Suttee.*

Bela, are Indian—*Satia* is *truth, fidelity*; the wife who dies in this way is *Satiawati*, a true faithful woman, who has performed in all things her duty to her husband. *Bela* is *retaliation*, or rather the Sanskrit *welâ*, *sudden and easy death*. This is rendered clear by the way in which it takes place; and further by the fact that the sacrifice of the followers of a prince defeated in war, who then die together in an *amok* is also called *Bela*, . . . and the women who sacrifice themselves are indeed, as a rule, slaves, for they are mostly from the fourth caste—the *Sudras*—at least all the concubines are; but their immolation is voluntary. From the moment that they declare themselves ready to be burnt alive, they are holy persons; they enjoy all the honours of the Pitaras. They may no longer tread the ground, but must always be carried. Offerings are even made to them, and all their wishes are satisfied. Nevertheless, the successor of the deceased simply regards such concubines as the servants who will be required by his father after his cremation. The women themselves are excited by religious ideas; a female priest always accompanies them till the moment of death, and describes to them, in glowing colours, the happiness of life in *Swarga*, the rise to a higher caste, and how they will thereby become the lawful wives of the deceased. To these deceptions must be added the honour and the advantages which the woman's relations expect to receive from the prince's successor; the men of her family have a claim to offices. They are, therefore, the only persons who sometimes use means of compulsion to prevent the women from retracting. They accompany the victim of the family; they keep up the fire, and, if the woman hesitates, tip up the plank on which she stands above the fire, so that she falls in against her will. These cases, however, are of rare occurrence. Deception of the imagination and the use of opium have generally made the victims quite indifferent, and they jump into a fire as if it were a bath.

"Eight days after the death of a prince or noble, his

wives are asked whether any of them wish to follow him into the fire, those who then state their willingness are accepted, and, during the interval before the cremation, are shown the above honours. They cannot easily change their minds; the opposition of their relatives, and the shame which would attach to them, as well as the deceptions of the priests, hold them back. The women who may wish to give in their names after the period of eight days are not accepted, perhaps in order to avoid the appearance of compulsion. The women who have offered themselves to be burned, lead thenceforward a life of pleasure and enjoy much greater honour than they ever knew before. This again is a reason why they should not change their minds during the interval, sometimes a long one, before the cremation."

Mr. Friederich then goes on to relate the details of a cremation of which he was an eye-witness. He says:

"On the 20th December, 1847, the Prince of Gianyar was burnt. The corpse was followed by *the three wives* (concubines) who became *Belas.* A procession went before them as before the body. They, like the body, were seated in the highest storeys of the *Bades.*[1] After the body of the prince had arrived at the place of cremation, the three *Belas,* in their *Bades*—each preceded by the bearers of the offerings destined for her, with armed men and bands of music[2] were conducted to the three fires.

[1] The funeral pyres. The *Bade* "rests on a basis of bamboo, concealed by handsome hangings, under which the bearers place themselves, to move this structure along. On this foundation there is a pyramid of wood-work or bamboo, in from three to eleven stories."

[2] This agrees with the account in the *Commentaries,* Part II, chapter XX. "Tinham por costume, que se algum Gentio morria, a mulher se avia de queimar por sua vontade; e quando hia a este sacrificio, era com grandes festas, e tangeres, dizendo que queria ir acompanhar seu marido ao outro Mundo; e a que isto não fazia, era lançada dantre as outras, e ficava ganhando por seu corpo pera

"Their *Bades* were also turned round three times and were carried round the whole place of cremation. The women were then carried down steps from the *Bades*, and up the steps of the places erected for their cremation. These places consisted of a square of masoury three feet high, filled with combustibles, which had been burning since the morning, and threw out a glowing heat; the persons appointed to watch them fed the fire, and at the moment when the women leaped down, poured upon it a quantity of oil and arrack, so that it flared up to a height of eight feet, and must have suffocated the victims at once. Behind this furnace stood an erection of bamboo, in the form of a bridge, of the same width as the square of masonry, and about forty feet long and from sixteen to eighteen feet high; steps of bamboo led up to it in the rear. In the centre there is a small house, affording a last resting place to the victim, in which she waits until the ceremonies for her husband are finished, and his body has begun to burn. The side of the bamboo scaffold nearest to the fire is protected by a wall of wet Pisang-stems. Upon the bridge lies a plank smeared with oil, which is pushed out a little over the fire, as soon as the time for the leap draws near. At first there is a door at the end of the bridge, and this is not removed till the last minute. The victim sits in the house on the bridge, accompanied by a female priest and by her relatives. They all speak to her of the happiness which she will now shortly enjoy with her husband. She then makes her toilet; her hair especially is combed, the mirror used, and her garments newly arranged. She arrays herself exactly as she would for a feast. Her dress is white, her breasts are covered with

as obras do pagode, de que era freguez; e como Afonso Dalboquerque tomou o Reyno de Goa, não consentio que dali por diante se queimasse mais nenhuma mulher; e posto que mudar costume seja parelha de morte, todavia ellas folgáram com a vida, e diziam grandes bens delle, por lhes mandar que se não queimassem."—See page 94.

a white *slendang*; she wears no ornaments, and after all the preparations to which it has been subjected, her hair at the last moment hangs quite loose. When the corpse of the prince was almost consumed, the three Belas got ready; they glanced one towards another, to convince themselves that all was prepared, but this was not a glance of fear, but of impatience, and it seemed to express a wish that they might leap at the same moment. When the door had been opened, and the plank smeared with oil and pushed out, each took her place on her plank, made three *sembahs* by joining her hands above her head, and one of the bystanders placed a small dove (*titiran*) upon her head. When the dove flies away, the soul is considered to escape. They then immediately leaped down. There was no cry in leaping, no cry from the fire, they must have been suffocated at once. One of the Europeans present succeeded in pushing through the crowd to the fire, and in seeing the body some seconds after the leap; it was dead, and its movements were caused merely by the combustion of the materials cast upon the flames. On other occasions, however, Europeans have heard cries uttered in leaping, and in the first moments afterwards.

"During the whole time, from the burning of the prince till the leap of the victims, the air resounded with the clangour and noise of the numerous bands of music. The soldiers had drawn up outside the square, and contributed to the noise by firing off their muskets. Besides these some small cannon were discharged. There was not one of the 50,000 Balinese present who did not show a merry face, no one was filled with repugnance and disgust, except a few Europeans, whose only desire was to see the end of such barbarities. The Balinese look upon this cremation simply as the consummation of their religious and domestic duties. No one sees any cruelty in it. Yet, as the all powerful priests attach little importance to it for their own caste, with their aid the diminution and abolition of these human sacrifices among the other castes might be effected. The priests' interest in maintaining it is, alas! a monetary one; and therefore no help can be expected from them."

If Afonso Dalboquerque really succeeded in suppressing at Goa scenes such as these, it goes a great way towards the redemption of his character from the charge of cruelty which has been made against him by reason of his conduct at Ormuz, and on other occasions.

On the day after the flight of the Captain of Goa, the Portuguese fleet, except the large ships,[1] which were prudently anchored just outside the bar, steered to the city—containing a force of a thousand Portuguese, and two hundred men of Malabar. Afonso Dalboquerque went in procession to the Castle, where the keys of the fortress were delivered to him, inspected the Palace and Arsenals, and took possession of the wives and children of the fugitive Rumes and Turks. Immediately afterwards, he rewarded and dismissed the Cananor ships, which had accompanied him, on their appointed voyage, and dispatched Timoja to destroy the Castle of Banda, a neighbouring stronghold still in possession of the Turks. But, before the expedition arrived at the Castle, the Turks fled away, and the Hindoos, who were friendly to the Portuguese, were allowed to hold it, on promise of obedience. Similar proceedings took place at the neighbouring fortress of Condal.

But Afonso Dalboquerque strongly felt the urgent necessity of fortifying the position which he had so gloriously won, before the enemy, who had recoiled

[1] The names of these were *Sancta Clara*, *Cirne*, *Flor-de-la-Mar*, and *Flor da Rosa*.

before him, should have time to regain courage and concentrate their vastly superior numbers against him. Foundations for a fortress of very imposing strength were laid, and a turn of work allotted to every one; and, after some demur on the part of the Governor of India, who probably distrusted the old Hindoo corsair after all, Timoja was appointed chief *Alguazil* of the Kingdom of Goa, in the name of the King of Portugal, on condition of his paying a yearly favour or tribute of one hundred thousand cruzados.

On the fall of Goa, two ambassadors—the one from the Xeque Ismael, the other from the King of Ormuz, who were in the city with the object of enlisting the power of the Hidalcão against the Portuguese—had an audience of the victorious Governor. To the former, who demanded in vain the introduction of the laws and currency of the Xeque into the territory of Goa, an envoy was promised; and no time was lost in fitting out Ruy Gomez,—a Portuguese of position at home, who had come to India under some kind of banishment—and the Xeque's ambassador, in two ships, with a letter from Afonso Dalboquerque to Xeque Ismael, announcing his intention of revisiting Ormuz very soon, offering terms of an alliance, and with special and minute instructions for the conduct of the Portuguese envoy and his interpreter. Ruy Gomez also carried a letter from Dalboquerque to the King of Ormuz. But, on arriving at this city, Cogeatar, who had succeeded in his policy against the Portuguese, ill-treated the messenger, and procured his death by poison, so that the intended communication with the Xeque Ismael was never carried out.

When this Embassy had set out, Afonso Dalboquerque sent Francisco Pantoja to visit Afonso de Noronha, the Captain of Socotra, with a shipload of supplies, and a letter to Duarte de Lemos, explaining the delay which had befallen the fleet. On his way, the messenger, Pantoja, captured a Cambay ship of six hundred tons—the *Meri*—bound for Mecca, which he took into Socotra. There he found Duarte de Lemos with four ships, waiting for the arrival of Dalboquerque, Pero Ferreira acting as Captain of Fort S. Miguel, and D. Afonso de Noronha already set out since last April to India.

Duarte de Lemos was greatly irritated by this second procrastination of much-needed succour; he laid hands upon the *Meri* prize, claiming her as captured within the limits of his jurisdiction; and leaving Pero Ferriera in charge, took Francisco Pantoja and the prize away to Cananor, and, arriving on the 31st August, found Afonso Dalboquerque had returned thither from Goa just shortly before him.

In the meantime, Afonso Dalboquerque set himself to the task of consolidating his position at Goa. The annual revenue, which was originally paid by the inhabitants to their native rulers, had been 150,000 *xerafins*, and though this had been doubled under the rule of the Çabaio, it was now again fixed at the first sum above mentioned. Tanadares, or receivers of taxes, were appointed under the arrangements of João Alvarez de Caminha, from among Portuguese and Hindoos of suitable position; and a new Portuguese coinage of gold, silver, and copper, in accordance with the necessities of the currency, issued, the coins of the Çabaio being withdrawn from circulation. Supplies were collected from all parts, the *xabandar*—or superintendent of the coast—enjoined to look to the collection of horses and other importations, and Francisco Serrão dispatched at the beginning of winter, early in April 1510, to carry news to Cochim of the capture of Goa, and to take back stores. But by this time information began to reach the Governor that the Hidalçao was preparing for an early attempt to regain his lost territory; and the captains were commencing to murmur against the hardships and toil to which they were subjected. Yet out of a desire to complete the fort, Afonso Dalboquerque put up with all, and contented himself with reprimanding the chief instigator of the disaffection.

The first indication of the overwhelming forces that were about to be massed against the small Portuguese army was conveyed in a letter from Mandaloy, the friendly chief of Condal, to Afonso Dalboquerque, informing him of overtures made to the Hidalcão by the chiefs of Pervaloy, Sanguiçar, and Carrapetão, districts adjacent to Goa on the interior side. Accordingly Jorge da Cunha and sixty horsemen, together with Menaique and Melique Çufecondal, two native captains, and 4,000 native troopers, were dispatched with a large detachment to co-operate with Mandaloy; a squadron of three vessels commanded by Diogo Fernandez de Bejá being also told off for the same purpose. The detachment had not, however, crossed over from the Island of Divar (or Divarij) to the mainland when news reached Jorge da Cunha of the arrival of the advanced guard of Hidalcão in the neighbouring districts of Banda and Condal. When this had been reported to Afonso Dalboquerque another smaller detachment was sent out under the guidance of Diogo Fernandez, and twelve horsemen, with Mirale in command of one thousand Canarese peons; and marching in the darkness of the night, this force came up suddenly with the vanguard of the Hidalcão's troops, and was so utterly dispersed that half the number of the peons were lost, the remainder making their way back with difficulty to Goa.

By this movement, although it entailed a loss of men who could be ill spared, Afonso Dalboquerque had at length obtained definite news of the position of the enemy, who was found to be advancing towards Benastarim; Jorge da Cunha was recalled and the friendly Bersoré, king of Garçopa, who declared himself ready to fight for the Portuguese, was encouraged to hold himself in readiness for the enemy. The strong places of the Island of Goa were now inspected by the Governor; Benastarim, Old Goa (the ancient city), the passes of Augij, Gondalij, and Agacij reinforced; the whole floating strength reviewed under D. Antonio de Noronha; and the *xabandar*, being found guilty of unpermitted communication with the enemy, put to death. By the time that all these preparations had been effected, the Hidalcão had conducted his forces as far towards the Portuguese as the suburb of Benastarim, where Garcia de Sousa shot down some of the outposts and set fire to a mosque which they held;

and not long after, three deserters, a Cretan, an Albanian, and a Russian, reached the Portuguese lines.

Negociations thereupon commenced with the mission of João Machado, a Portuguese, and a Venetian whose name is not recorded, two foreigners in the service of the Hidalcão; these declared the strenuous efforts of the Hidalcão to recover possession of the island, and the readiness of the inhabitants to co-operate with any chance accession of native forces against the Portuguese. Afonso Dalboquerque, however, refused to evacuate Goa on any account, and Baldrez, a Portuguese hostage in the camp of the Moors, reported, on his return, their extensive arrangements for an attack on the island, in the course of which they were prepared to sacrifice a million of men. Timoja himself confirmed the information which had been obtained from the sources already mentioned, and advised Afonso Dalboquerque to shut up the head men, women, and children, not only of the Moors but of the Hindoos as well, a proceeding which was inaugurated by the incarceration of Timoja's own family among the first. No other harm appears to have been offered to these persons than incarceration; but the wives and children of the Rumes, who were absent in the enemy's camp, were taken for slaves, as an example of vengeance visited upon the subjects of the Grand Sultan of Cairo.

A stockade was erected by Garcia de Sousa at Benastarim; the pass of Augij reinforced with native troops; a general inspection made by Afonso Dalboquerque throughout the island; Melique Çufecondal imprisoned for improper communication with the enemy; and Diogo Fernandez de Beja, on his return from Condal, where he had manoeuvred in support of Jorge da Cunha, dispatched to the assistance of D. Antonio de Noronha, whose special duty was to defend the island from any attempted crossing *en masse*, and principally at the pass of Augij, where Timoja's contingent was posted. The friendly Mandaloy made a diversion against the Hidalcão with four thousand men, overran the passes, cut off the enemy's supplies, and wrote to Timoja that he would fall upon the Hidalcão in concert with any attack made by the Portuguese.

But, notwithstanding the great exertions made by the Portuguese to retain possession of the Island of Goa, their unabated vigilance and intrepid valour were outweighed by the vastly superior numbers of native warriors hurled against them. On the night of Friday, the 17th May, 1510,—the depth of the Indian winter—three hundred Turks crossed over at Augij[1] on rafts, unperceived by the Portuguese lookouts, and a second detachment of seven hundred were in the act of crossing when they were discovered, and the artillery from the fleet, under command of D. Antonio, very quickly dispersed and destroyed them. In the meantime, however, another body of two thousand Turks crossed over a lagoon of mud and weeds, overcame the resistance offered to their progress by Jorge da Cunha and Timoja's captain Menaique, and with their num-

[1] The chapter heading, page 154, reads *Agacij*, by a typographical error of the Portuguese Edition, in place of *Augij*.

bers augmented by the addition of some of Timoja's men who fraternised with them, ran to Benastarim, where they compelled Garcia de Sousa to withdraw to Goa, and finally proceeded to Gondalij, where Francisco de Sousa Mancias and Francisco Pereira Coutinho retreated in like manner on the approach of the enemy in such great force.

The Moorish inhabitants of Goa were by this time in a violent state of excitement, and rose up against the Portuguese; and Afonso Dalboquerque, after dispatching Diogo Fernandez to the assistance of Jorge da Cunha, who with difficulty was making his way to safer quarters with the main body, caused the city to be set on fire in four places, and fell upon the enemy with the sword, without giving quarter to any. Timoja himself nearly fell a victim to the Moors, but he was rescued, and all withdrew to the fortress, with a loss of thirty Portuguese killed and as many wounded, leaving to the Hidalcão possession of the burning walls of the great city of Goa, and the disfigured corpses of an uncounted number of his soldiers and subjects.

At first, it was the intention of the Governor of India to withstand a siege in the fortress of Goa—the great strength of which the writer of the *Commentaries* contrasts with the fortifications of Rhodes—yet on reflection that upon the safety of the fleet the maintenance of all his Indian possessions depended, and not without misgivings with regard to the fidelity of his captains—a bitter lesson which he had learnt at Ormuz under circumstances somewhat like the present—he decided to withdraw to his ships and drop down the river to Pangij. This movement was carried out on Friday,[1] 20th of May, 1510, after embarking all the stores and provisions, and the natives he had in his power, decapitating Melique Çufecondal and a hundred and fifty principal Moors, hamstringing the horses in the stables, and burning the arsenal. The captains endeavoured by every means in their power to compel Afonso Dalboquerque to sail away over the bar of Goa, and no amount of reasoning had any effect with these malcontents until the wreck of the *St. John*, which had been ordered to cross over, convinced even the most sceptical of the fruitlessness and foolhardiness of such an attempt at that season. In the meantime, the enemy, who had posted a strong force in the castle of Pangij which commanded the anchorage, began to harass the fleet; and the report of the shortness of provisions, which had reached the Hidalcão through two deserters, revived a hope in that chief that the Portuguese would be driven to come to terms; but Afonso Dalboquerque rejected all overtures, and feeling that the position of Pangij must be carried at all hazards, organised an attack which resulted in a successful entry of that fortress on the 14th June, and a slaughter of upwards of two hundred and fifty Turks and peons.

A report that the Hidalcão was preparing a fleet, induced Afonso Dalboquerque to send a reconnoitring party, which unfortunately terminated in the mortal wounding of his nephew D. Antonio de Noronha,

[1] The 20th May, 1510, fell on a Monday.

while attempting to launch a galeot that was found on the stocks in the dockyards by this expedition. This young captain, full of promise of military renown, died shortly afterwards on the 8th of July.

The Hidalcão did not, however, cease his endeavours to arrange terms with the Portuguese, but without achieving any diplomatic success, although Afonso Dalboquerque honoured the noble Mahometan Plenipotentiary Mostafacão with a reception due to his rank, and accorded to him a private interview, where the offer of Cintácora in lieu of Goa was made to, and rejected by, the Portuguese Commander, followed by an implied proposal to yield up Goa itself, if Timoja were delivered into the hands of the Turks. But this was a proposition which Afonso Dalboquerque dismissed with well merited rebuke and indignation. It was during the time that the Portuguese fleet was riding at anchor withinside the bar, that the affair of Ruy Diaz occurred, which has been brought forward so prominently in reference to the character of Afonso Dalboquerque. Divested of its sensational aspects, the case appears plainly enough to resolve itself into a flagrant instance of insubordination, and illicit communication with the enemy; for there is no doubt that the Moorish women, whom the unfortunate man was in the habit of visiting, were likely to tamper with him to compass their own liberty, and the destruction of the hostile fleet—and this at a time when affairs were in a most critical and unsatisfactory situation, an element which added considerably to the gravity of the offence. Sharp and sure as was the retributive punishment meted out to the offender, an example was needed to reduce the extensive and growing discontent and rebellious spirit which was rife among the officers; and there is little doubt that the fate of this person not only operated beneficially upon the disorderly dispositions of these men, but also that it was the means of preserving the whole party from a planned and inevitable destruction, had the matter not been found out in time.

Not long after this event, the prevailing sickness and want of all kinds of provisions forced Afonso Dalboquerque—much against his will, for he had set his mind on regaining possession of the Island of Goa—to dispatch D. João de Lima to Angediva, and Timoja to Onor for supplies, in the middle of July. But they could not get over the bar, and on the 21st of the same month, when, wearied with the importunities of his men, his whole fleet stood over to the bar, Afonso found the little squadron still at anchor, waiting for deeper water and better weather. In the meantime the enemy mustered in great strength at Bradez (or Bardes) and harassed the fleet with artillery, which drove it to return and reoccupy its old anchorage in the river; and it was not until the end of the month that João de Lima and Timoja were able to get over the bar, and sail for their respective destinations.

After the departure of these captains, redoubled pressure was put upon the Governor, who at length, on the 16th of August, passed over the bar with the remainder of his fleet and directed his course for Angediva. On that very day he sighted a fleet which had been sent out from Portugal under Diogo Mendez de Vasconcellos, particulars of which, from the MS. *Armadas da India*, are given at page 196.

"DIOGO MENDEZ DE VASCONCELLOS, CHIEF CAPTAIN, 1510.

"Diogo Mendez de Vasconçellos, Chief Captain of four ships, set out on the 12th of March to go and conquer Malaca;—Captains Balthazar da Sylva, Pero Caresma, Misser Serniche, Master-at-Arms. And in the same year there set out as Chief Captain of three *caravelas*, João Serrão: Captains Pero da Sousa, Gaspar Cão; and this was to go and explore the Island of São Lourenço, and establish therein a factory, which was not carried out.[1]

"In the same year Gonçalo de Siqueira, Chief Captain of seven ships, set out on the 16th March,[2] Captains Lourenço Moreno, João de Aveiro, Jorge Nunes de Leão, Lourenço Lopez, Manoel da Cunha, who was lost close by Moçambique, and Diogo Lobbo d'Alualade.

"Diogo Mendes de Vasconselos did not complete his voyage to Malaca in accordance with the Royal

[1] "João Serrão, Chief Captain of three sail, or *caravelas*, set out in the month of August, 1510. Another account calls Pero de Souza Payo de Souza, and does not record the name of the other captain, but only says that he was a cavalier of the king's household."

[2] "Manoel da Cunha was the son of Tristão da Cunha,—he was lost. Jorge Nunes de Leou went in the ship *Sta. Anna*. João de Aveiro, because he was well qualified in the art of the sea, served also as pilot to the ship *S. Sebastian*, in which he sailed. Manoel da Cunha was lost, with all his people, close to Moçambique. Gonçalo de Siqueira, on the return journey to Portugal, wintered in Moçambique, and arrived in the year 'twelve."

instructions, because the Governor Afonso Dalboquerque prevented him.

"Of these fourteen ships the first four, whereof Diogo Mendez de Vasconsellos was Chief Captain, was to go to Malaca to establish the trade there. The seven of which Gonçalo de Siqueira was Chief Captain were to go and carry the cargo of spiceries. The three of which João Serrao was Chief Captain, were sent by the King to explore the Island of S. Lourenço, and to establish a trade in ginger with the natives in the port of Matatana."

On the 17th of August, the united fleets of Afonso Dalboquerque from Goa, and of Diogo Mendez de Vasconcellos from Portugal, anchored off Angediva; but without loss of time all proceeded to Onor two days afterwards. At this latter port Bras Vieira, the Portuguese *Tanadar* of Cintácora, was found, having saved himself from molestation, when Goa was retaken, by a timely flight. Timoja was also found here, and this chief imparted to Afonso Dalboquerque the latest information of doings in Goa,—that three days after the departure of the Portuguese fleet, the Hidalcão had commenced removing his forces, and the inhabitants of the lands conterminous to Goa had revolted and massacred the Moorish *Tanadars*.

On the 26th of August, Afonso Dalboquerque and Diogo Mendez reached Cananor, where news was received that a large force had set forth from Suez to reinforce Goa. This determined Afonso Dalboquerque to exercise a discretionary power undoubtedly vested in the Governor of India, and to strengthen his forces by temporarily diverting the fleet of Diogo Mendez de Vasconcellos, which was destined for Malaca, from that adventure, to go with him to Goa.

A ceremonious interview was then held with the King of Cananor, and the formal delivery to him of the keys of the Portuguese fortress made—the King handing them back again immediately to the Portuguese captain. Two days afterwards, Duarte de Lemos arrived from Socotra with Francisco de Pantoja, and the prize ship *Meri*, respecting the disposal of which they were at variance. Duarte de Lemos brought disappointing intelligence of the supposed fate of the Governor's nephew, D. Afonso de Noronha, who had sailed in the *Sancta Cruz* for India in the previous April, and had been heard of no more. But almost immediately afterwards an ambassador from the King of Cambaya[1] brought a letter to Afonso Dalboquerque from the shipwrecked party detailing the loss of their ships by a storm at Nabande, a Guzarate port, and another letter from Gopicaiça, Chief *Alguazil* of the King of Cambaya, to Afonso Dalboquerque, the receipt of which offended Duarte de Lemos, who considered that Cambaya lay within the limits of his jurisdiction. From this time forward Duarte de Lemos, Jeronymo Teixeira, and Francisco de Sá intrigued against their chief.

Afonso Dalboquerque replied to the missive in amicable terms, the letter being dated from Cananor,

[1] For an early account of Cambaya, with useful notes, see Col. Yule's *Marco Polo*, vol. ii, page 389.

on the 16th of September; and organised two detachments of three vessels each, under Simão Martinz and Garcia de Sousa, to cruise about and intercept vessels coming from the Red Sea to India. Diogo Mendez de Vasconcellos was by this time become very desirous of going on to Malaca, and a council was held in which the advantages for his remaining with the Governor in order to co-operate in the projected expedition to Goa were discussed and adopted. On the 8th of September, Lourenço Moreno arrived from Portugal, in advance of the fleet of Gonçalo de Siqueira, of which his ship formed part, as already mentioned; and he was dispatched to conclude a treaty with the rulers of Baticalá, and to carry a letter to Timoja at Onor, advising him to be ready to take part in the second attack on Goa.

The cruise of Simão Martinz resulted in the capture of a Mecca ship bound for Calicut, in which were two Castilian Jews, from whom the interesting news was obtained that the Grand Sultan would not be able to attend to Indian Affairs for the present year on account of internal dissensions, and that they had met Fernão Gomez[1] at Suakim *en route* for Judá. Some particulars of the ensuing adventures of these two Jews are also recorded at this place in the text.

On the 16th of September, Gonçalo de Sequeira arrived at Cananor, bringing orders from Portugal for the return of Duarte de Lemos and the incorporation of his fleet and men with those already under Afonso Dalboquerque. A meeting was held wherein it was

[1] See above, page lvii.

decided that a combined effort should be made to regain possession of Goa; and in consequence of a communication from the friendly King of Cochim, the Governor left Duarte de Lemos as Vice-Governor at Cananor, and proceeded to Cochim with all his forces on the 22nd of September, arriving four days later on, and establishing the newly acceded king on the throne of his late uncle, in accordance with the Indian law of succession.[1]

At Cochim another deliberation was held, which appears to have been on the 10th of October, 1510, according to the Preface to Lord Stanley's *Correa*, page xxi, where the text of the original document in the Torre do Tombo is translated, and the opposition of the celebrated Magellan to the plans of the Governor indicated. This council discussed the advisability of the crews of the ships of burden going to the fight at Goa, while their cargoes were completed at Cochim, and from the document we gather the following names of those present at the council, nearly all, if not quite all of whom were comprised in the list of Alboquerque's fleet against Goa:—Nuno Vaz, captain of the ship captured from the Rumes; Antonio da Costa, of *Rey Pequeno;* Duarte da Silva, of the Great Galley; Simão Martins; Dom João de Lima, of the *S. Maria d'Ajuda;* Sebastião de Miranda, of the Little Galley; Fernão de Magalhães; Jeronimo Teixeira of the *S. Maria do Campo;* Jorge da Silveira; Francisco de Sousa, of the *Boa Ventura;* Manuel da Cunha; Garcia de Sousa, in the *Santa Clara;* Francisco Cor-

[1] See pages 77, 78.

vinel in the *Sant Jago;* Lourenço de Paiva; Antonio Real, chief alcalde of Cochim; and Gonçalo de Sequeira.

The last named Chief Captain was adverse to the proposal of taking the ships of burden to Goa, but Afonso Dalboquerque, who had already determined to let nothing delay his enterprise, declared his intention of starting with those who chose to go with him voluntarily; and proceeded to Cananor, where he found Lourenço, who had returned from Baticalá, where he had been unable to settle the terms of the projected treaty, and with news of the preparations of Timoja and the King of Garçopa for co-operating in the attack on Goa. This second part of the *Commentaries* concludes with the dispatch of Lourenço Moreno to Cochim, and of Duarte de Lemos as Chief Captain of seven ships to Portugal with the rare freight of three elephants as an offering to the king.

The beginning of Afonso Dalboquerque's career is thus in these volumes for the first time presented to the English reader in the form of a literal translation from the Portuguese *Commentaries*, the present volume bringing down the events of his life to the repulse at Goa, and the eve of the second and successful attack. The details of the attack, the consolidation of Portuguese power in the city as a capital of that nation's Indian Empire, the capture of Malaca, the taking of the fortress of Ormuz, Dalboquerque's battles and wars on the Arabian coast, his preparations for settling the factory and Portuguese fortress at Ormuz, and his death on shipboard at the bar of Goa on the 16th December, 1515, form the leading themes of the concluding parts of the work, and it would be premature to dilate upon these subjects on this occasion.

The principal events in the history of Portuguese India subsequent to the death of this great Governor must be told here in very few words, for the reigns of Emmanuel and João III have been described by many writers as the golden age of Portuguese India; the reigns of Sebiastião and Philip II, the silver age; and subsequent reigns down to the loss of Cochim, when a fatal blow was dealt once and for ever to Portuguese rule in India, the age of wars. During the rule of Lopo Vas de Sampayo, the governor appointed in 1526, parts of the Moluccas, Mangalor on the Malabar Coast, and the island of Maim or Bombay, were taken possession of by the Portuguese; and in 1529, Nuno da Cunha succeeded as Governor. He took the cities of Baçaim and Damão from Bahadur Shah, King of Guzerat, and afterwards the fortress and Island of Diu. In 1539, Estevão da Gama was Governor of Goa. He is illustrious for his successful expedition into the Red Sea, penetrating to Mount Sinai, where, at the Shrine of St. Catherine, patroness of Goa, he caused himself and his companions to be knighted. The celebrated João de Castro, the history of whose deeds requires a separate treatment at the hands of the Hakluyt Society, was Governor of Goa in 1545. His great fame rests upon the relief of Diu, when João de Mascarenhas,[1] the governor of that fortress, was besieged.

[1] There is an unpublished life of this hero among the Altamira MSS., in the British Museum.—Add. MS., No. 28,460.

On the resumption of the siege of Diu by the King of Cambaya, D. João de Castro inflicted upon that potentate a disastrous defeat, and conquered the whole kingdom of Diu in 1547. The life of this great man has been carefully written by Jacinto Freyre de Andrada, and an English translation of this valuable literary work would be worthy to be issued under the auspices of the Hakluyt Society, which has done so much towards the elucidation of the doings of the Portuguese both in the Old World and the New. During the Viceroyalty of Luiz de Ataide (1568), Goa was besieged by Ali Idalshaw or Hidalkhan, King of Bijapoor.

The close of the sixteenth century is memorable in the history of Portuguese India for the endeavour to reconcile the heretical Syrian Church of Travancore to Rome.[1] During the Viceroyalty of João de Silva Telles de Menezes, Goa was attacked by the Dutch, and from this time the decline of Goa became a matter of a few years; Cochim and the settlements of the coast of Malabar falling to the same nation between 1662 and 1666.

The causes of the decay of Portuguese power in India, and indeed throughout the East, where at one time they were all powerful, are too manifold to be

[1] The chief authorities, according to Mr. Tolbort (whose work will be described further on), are:—Gouvea, *Jornada do Arcebispo de Goa;* D. Fr. Aleixo de Meneses, *As Terras de Malabar;* Geddes, *History of the Church of Malabar;* La Croze, *Histoire du Christianisme des Indes;* and other works by Hough, Lee, Howard, and Day.

explained at length in this place. This fall of power was principally induced by the neglect of the merchants properly to provide for the markets of Europe, a work which, although vitally necessary to the maintenance of their position, was left to other more enthusiastic, and by this time more political, nations. Hence arose the powerful competition of Spain, Holland, England, France, and Denmark, all of which countries entered into mercantile relations with India and America. In the first voyage round the world, in 1519, the Portuguese Magalhães, in Spanish service, discovered the only other possible route to India, through the Straits justly named after him, where he visited the Moluccas and Philippines, and in that latter group he met his death in 1521. Spain occupied the fruitful Philippine Islands in 1564, and before the sixteenth century closed, the English, after despairing of the achievement of finding a north-east or north-west passage, doubled the Cape of Good Hope, and by this act initiated their present proud position in the continent of India.

By means of this great accession of commerce throughout Europe, the maritime power of the European nations gradually assumed more powerful proportions, arts and manufactures were stimulated, poor countries became rich, and in improved commerce were found at length the only resources for adding to the strength and influence of empires, and the only means of carrying out imperial plans of aggrandisement and extension. The most powerful rival, and the one that did the most to cast down the paramount

Lusitanian supremacy in the East, was Holland; for while England was struggling for that political freedom without which the English merchant service could not exercise any vital functions, the Dutch, who had passed through this political trial, and had already erected their kingdom into a free republic, were the real masters of the sea. The middle of the sixteenth century beheld them in the height of their maritime glory, and their vessels in every quarter of the world; and at this period, although the British navy showed some signs of improvement, the East India Company were hardly able to cope with the Portuguese and Dutch in India. "And it was feared that the Company would not, in their commercial operations, be able to contend successfully with the formidable Dutch and Portuguese monopolies which had been established in the East; and though Portugal and Spain were then beginning to decline from the exalted position they had so long held, Holland, in possession of public liberty and a wise system of commerce, was in the zenith of her commercial and maritime greatness."[1]

But if, as some have declared, the natives of India rejoiced when the overwhelming forces of Holland shattered the ascendancy of the Portuguese in the East, at any rate, the people of India, in their freedom from the yoke of their former masters, found little cause to congratulate themselves upon the change of oppressors. The Portuguese found themselves ousted from the Japan trade in 1638, and surrendered Ceylon in 1658; while at the same time the Dutch colonies at

[1] W. S. Lindsay, *History of Merchant Shipping*, ii, 173, 174.

the Cape of Good Hope were most conveniently situated as a place of rendezvous for their eastward-bound shipping, the extent and character of which contrasted favourably with that of any other maritime nation at this time. The reader who would read a lucid exposition of the struggles of the English against the Dutch, who, after overcoming the Portuguese, and maintaining by their maritime superiority a long sustained ascendancy in India, were forced in turn to yield before our advance, must be referred to Mr. Lindsay's work, which I have already had occasion to quote on more than one occasion.

The history of the island fortress of Goa, which the fearless bravery of Afonso Dalboquerque wrested from the native powers, led by Adilshaw or Idalkan (or as the writer of the *Commentaries* always calls this prince "O Hidalção," the Hidalcão), is naturally very much mixed up with the general history of the Portuguese possessions in the East (of which it was, and is, the capital), but it may be well made out by the student of Indian topographical antiquities, from the very full and lucid description given by Pedro Barreto de Resende in the Sloane MS. 197, folios 244-276,[1] a work which I have frequently consulted during the work of translating the text of the *Commentaries*.

The best work solely devoted to the history of Goa is that written by the Rev. Denis Louis Cottineau de Kloguen, who was a native of Nantes. His desire for a knowledge of the world made him quit his country for England and America. His stay in the

[1] Including notices of Bardes and Mormugam.

former of these places was not long comparatively with the latter, where he resided in the city of Baltimore for the period of ten years. From America Cottineau returned to France; he soon however left, and proceeded to the Isle of Bourbon, in which place he resided for several years, and was admitted a member of the Philotechnical Society. He afterwards set out for the Island of Bombay, where he resided for a long while, and became one of the members of the Bombay Auxiliary of the Royal Asiatic Society. In this place he commenced and completed in French, his native language, a history of India, from the earliest times down to the year he wrote; as also the work on Goa, from which I shall give some extracts. Shortly before his demise, he proceeded overland to Madras, with an intention of going thence to Calcutta, both which Presidencies he was anxious to see before he should leave India and return to France for the last time, which it was in his contemplation to do; but worn out with the travels he had performed in countries whose climates are so prejudicial to European health, he died on the 11th of February, 1830, at Karrical, a French settlement about a hundred and seventy-eight miles distant from Madras.

The title to Cottineau de Kloguen's work is as follows:

> "An Historical Sketch of Goa, the Metropolis of the Portuguese Settlements in India; with an Account of the present state of that celebrated City, and of the surrounding Territories under its immediate Jurisdiction, collected from the most authentic sources, and

> Undertaken and dedicated to His Excellency The Honorable Major-General Sir John Malcolm, K.C.B., and K.L.S., and the Members of the Bombay Auxiliary of the Royal Asiatic Society, by the late Reverend Denis L. Cottineau de Kloguen, Honorary Member of the same Society, of the Madras Literary Society, and of the Philotechnical Society of the Island of Bourbon, Madras; Printed for the Proprietor, by William Twigg, at the Gazette Press, 1831."

The book commences with a section devoted to the history of Goa, and contains the following interesting passage with regard to the authorities consulted :

"I have taken care, of course, to consult the original authors as much as possible, but unfortunately I found still much wanting in my researches. In the first place the earthquake which destroyed Lisbon, having been the cause of the loss of many ancient books and records, orders were issued to have a great part of those extant in the colonies, and chiefly in Goa, transported to Europe. Subsequent to this, the dark policy of the Marquis of Pombal, the Prime Minister of King Joseph, assisted by the misguided prelate whom he had raised to the see of Goa, despoiled anew the library of the Archbishopric of its most valuable books and manuscripts; and many of those that remain have been partially destroyed by those insects so prejudicial to books and libraries in India.

* * * * *

"§ i. *Historical Sketch of the Town, &c.*—We find the first mention of Goa in Ferishta's history of the Deccan, under the reign of Mujahid Shaw, the 3rd Emperor of the Bhamani dynasty, who began his reign in 1374. Goa is said to have been a seaport, appertaining then, as it did for near a century afterwards, to the kings or roys of Beejanuger.

"We know by tradition transmitted by the natives to the first Portuguese settlers, that the Hindoo religion was then the only one professed in the island. In 1469, according to the same author, Mullek-ul-Tijur Khaje Jehan, general Vizier and Prime Minister of Shumse or Mahomet II, the 13th Bhamani Emperor of the Deccan, took the island of Goa from Humrajee, regent of Beejanuger, who governed that kingdom during the minority of the sons of Severoy. The Deccanese monarch ordered great rejoicings on this occasion, and rendered great honours to his Minister. At his request he gave the government of the new conquered place to Kishwer Khan, one of his officers who had distinguished himself in the conquest. Three years after, Perkna, Rajah of Belgoan, at the instigation of the regent of Beejanuger, came to retake Goa; but the Sultan of the Deccan marched in person in its defence, and having attacked Belgoan, forced the Rajah to retire in order to defend his capital. In 1479, according to Antonio de Sousa in his *Oriente Conquistado*, Miguel Oum, at the head of the Mahometans of Onor, persecuted by the Rajah of that place, who was tributary to Beejanuger, retired to Goa, under the protection of the Deccanese Sovereign, who professed the same religion. It is then that Goa was built in its present place; for before that period the town stood near two miles to the southward, about the centre of the island, and nearer to the southern shore. Of that first town there remain at present but some wretched hovels around the parochial church of St. Andrew, but the spot is still known by the appellation of *Old Goa*, which modern travellers have, of late, improperly applied to Goa itself. This new town, built by the Moors or Mahometans on the N. shore of the island, opposite to that of Divar, soon became a very flourishing place by the excellence of its harbour; but it was not very extensive, according to the Dutch traveller Linschoten, who tells us that in 1583, when he arrived in Goa, the walls thereof were still standing, though the gates had been pulled down to facilitate the communication with the new built part of the city. He informs us that the walls of Goa, built by the Mahometans, were defended by a dry ditch, but he does not describe the exact extent of the ancient town; he only says that in his time it was twice larger. However, from what he and other travellers say, and from my own observations on the spot, I suppose that its length along the shore from E. to W. was from the old Custom House, the palace of the Governor, and the convent of St. Cajetan, to the small inlet that still separates Goa from the suburb of St. Peter or Pannely, including therefore not only the arsenal, but the College of St. Bonaventure, which latter must have been built on the ruins of the ancient walls. Towards the S. the town must have been bounded by the mountain of the Rosary, and the other rising ground back of the convent of *Bom-Jesus* and the present Bazaar. According to this supposition, which appears the most plausible, the city must have been hardly three-quarters of a mile in length, and not a quarter in breadth. Soon after the migration of the Moors, the empire of the Deccan having undergone a new division of government by the advice of Mulek-ul-Tijur, Goa fell to the lot of Fukhir-ul-Moolk; but in 1486 a certain officer named Bahadur Gelauce, got the command of the town by intrigue and violence. In 1495, that usurper having been slain in a battle against Mahmood, Emperor of the Deccan, the government was given to one Mullek-Eia-al-Moolk, whose son and successor, bearing the same name, acknowledged himself, in 1497, the vassal of Adilshaw or Idalkhan, as the Portuguese call him, but who had since 1489 declared himself King or Sultan of Bijapoor, though he still nominally acknowledged the supremacy of the Deccanese monarch. Such was the state of Goa, when Vasco de Gama landed at Calicut, with the first Portuguese fleet that had yet appeared in India. When the Admiral was about to return to Portugal, a Polonian Jew, giving himself out for an Italian, and Prime Minister to Zabajo, King of Goa, came to offer him the alliance of his master; but he was found out afterwards to be a spy and an impostor, and was taken to Portugal, where he embraced the Christian religion, and having had Gama himself for his godfather, took the name of Gaspar de Gama. The story of this Jew is certain, and this circumstance, related by the Portuguese, seems to contradict the account of Ferishta; but besides that the Jew, having been an impostor, might have said what he pleased, and given any name to the pretended King of Goa, it is not impossible that the Portuguese authors have disfigured the name, according to their custom, and that the king in question was either Mullek-Eia-al-Moolk, or Adilshaw himself, whom they call afterwards actually King of Goa, as they also call him King of Balagate ; even as they describe the Sultan of Ahmednugur King of Chowl, and that of Guzerat King of Cambay. The truth is that Adilshaw, or Idalkhan, particularly desired the residence of Goa ; and state reasons alone prevented him from transporting the seat of his Government thither from Bijapore. This predilection, the affluence of the Mahometans, and the liberty of commerce, greatly augmented the prosperity of Goa, and determined the great Alfonso de Alboquerque to undertake the conquest of that important place, and make it the metropolis and emporium of his countrymen in the East."

The second section consists of a "chronological table of the Viceroys and Governors of Goa and Portuguese India . . . with the most memorable events in each administration". The biographical sketches of João de Castro, Constantine de Braganza, Pedro de Mascarenhas, under whose period the Portuguese experienced great losses, and Emanuel de Saldanha de Albuquerque, Count of Ega, in this portion of the work, are worthy of notice.

The third section contains "Religious establishments, proceedings, and documents concerning the erection of the episcopal, and afterwards the archiepiscopal, see of Goa, the chronology of its bishops and archbishops, its provincial councils, the erection of its religious buildings and religious institutions." This part is also arranged in order of chronology, and notices the causes of the adoption of St. Catherine, virgin and martyr, as the patroness of Goa ; the foundation of the convent of the Franciscan Observantines, the first spiritual pastors in Goa, and that of the Dominican church of "Our Lady of the Rosary". In 1515, Pope Leo X erected the bishopric of Funchal, in Madeira, to comprehend within its diocese all Portuguese possessions beyond the seas; Pope Clement VII made this an archiepiscopal or metropolitan see in 1533; and in 1534, Paul III erected the bishopric of Goa, to embrace all the territory held by Portugal from the Cape of Good Hope to the extreme East, and to form a diocese subject to the Archbishop of Madeira; but this latter, with its suffragans of Angra, Goa, etc., soon became a simple bishopric, forming part of the Ecclesiastical Province of the Archbishop of Lisbon. The doings of the Church, the Jesuits, and other missionaries—especially St. Francis Xavier--in Goa, are minutely chronicled by the author in this part of the work.

The fourth section embraces a "Topographical and statistical description of the city and island of Goa in their present state, as likewise of the two Provinces of Salsette and Bardes, and of the new surrounding provinces." Of the actual extent and the state of Goa, Cottineau de Kloguen says: "The present city, improperly called *Old Goa* by foreigners, was built on the northern shore of the island that bears its name, and which is also called *Tissuary*, or improperly a river, but which is in fact an arm of the sea, separating the island, on the south, from the peninsula of Bardes and the islands of Charão and Divar on the north. The city is directly opposite this last-mentioned island, and, of course, by more than one-half nearer to the eastern than to the western extremity of the Island of Goa. Its centre is about six miles distant from the ocean. Its length from E. to W. is about 1¼ miles, not including the suburbs of Dowji [or Daujim], on the E. and of St. Peter or Pannely on the W. It extends in breadth from the shore or quay up to the top of the hill on which the church of Luz is situated, about ¾ of a mile, presenting, therefore, an extent of 3¾ sq. m. . . . . The whole road between Goa and the new capital Pangi is wholly bordered with houses. Goa never had any walls on the E. and S.; those that begin in the suburb of Little Dowji, and which extend along the E. shore of the island were extended by the Viceroy Antonio de Noronha (1564-1568), their founder, to defend the weak part of the island, and never were considered as the ramparts of the city. . . . One coming from Pangi, and seeing afar off the numerous churches of Goa with their towers and spires, and the handsome and neat houses of Pannely, would really think that he is going to enter a superb metropolis; but he is strangely disappointed as soon as he approaches, finding himself suddenly transported into the midst of a desert."

After describing the statistics of the five parishes; the population, which is given about 3,200 inhabitants;

the civil edifices; the Church of St. Catherine, erected into a Cathedral in 1534; the collegiate and parish churches; the inquisition (suppressed in 1812), and the ecclesiastical courts, the author proceeds to notice the various convents and religious orders, of Franciscans, Jesuits, Dominicans, Augustinians, Carmelites, Theatins of St. Cajetan of Thienna, and others which flourish in the island of Goa; and the section concludes with an account of Pangi and the neighbouring villages, viz., Ribandar, between Pangi and Pannely; St. Agnes, west of Pangi; the island of Chorão, opposite to Ribandar; that of Divar, S.E. of Chorão; that of Jua, N.E. of Divar; and that of Combarjua, to the S. of Jua; Salsette, a province or peninsula, S. and S.E. of Goa; Bardes province, extending from N. to S. along the coast, to the N.W. of the island of Goa; and other seven new provinces of later formation. The fifth and concluding section is devoted to the "State of the Population, Government, Religion, Public Instruction, Revenues, Commerce, and Manners of the Inhabitants at the present time", with some interesting remarks on the different castes existing in the colony. It is unnecessary to allude further to that portion of the work which does not concern the period of Afonso Dalboquerque.

A very useful addition to the history of Goa, by way of supplement to that of Cottineau de Kloguen, is a paper "On the Portuguese Settlements in India", by T. W. H. Tolbort, Esq., of the Indian Civil Service, printed in the "Proceedings of the Asiatic Society of Bengal" for June 1874. In this the principal points of historical interest concerning the three existing settlements of Damau, Diu, and Goa, are briefly described. Of Goa Mr. Tolbort writes :

"The changes since Cottineau's time are not so great as might have been expected. The buildings in Old Goa are mostly of laterite, and the damage caused by each year's monsoon must be considerable; still, many of the ruins are well preserved. Three miles up the river, is the church of the *Reis Magos*. Beyond this is New Goa or Panjim, which was an important suburb even in ancient days, and which supplanted Goa as the capital in 1765. One of its churches, I believe that of N. S. da Conceição, stands on an elevation overlooking the town. It appears to have been built in the beginning of the 17th century, as it contains inscriptions as early as 1654. *In the principal square is a statue of Albuquerque.* This statue, now black with age, was removed to Panjim from Old Goa in 1810. In Pyrard's time it stood in front of the church '*da Serra*' near that '*da Misericordia*'. The figure is that of a man rather below middle height, with a long beard, his elbows stretched out and his hands resting in front. . . . . *Goa Velha* must not be confounded with the ruins of the Portuguese city known to us as *Old Goa*. It is the site of a yet more ancient city occupied by Hindús and Muhammadans in times long prior to Portuguese conquest. . . . . The distance from Panjim to Goa itself is about six miles. The road crosses a bridge built by the Count of Linhares in 1634, and then traverses a causeway about two miles long, having the shore of the estuary, or *Rio de Goa*, on the left, and an expanse of marshy meadow land on the right. The causeway was built in 1771. At the end of this causeway is the village or suburb of Ribandar, then that of Pannely, and then Goa. Goa, however, provided wind and tide are favourable, is more easily and pleasantly reached from Panjim by water. . . . . A road leads from the landing place to [the principal] gateway, all that remains standing of the Viceroy's palace, founded in the first instance by Albuquerque himself. Over the gateway is a statue of Vasco da Gama, erected by his grandson in 1600."

Then follow some valuable notes of the various edifices in the city, with their dates of erection, and principal monumental inscriptions, and the treatise concludes with notices of Baçaim and Cochim, "two places renowned in early Portuguese history, though now held by the English."

I now propose to direct the attention of the reader to some concluding remarks concerning the bibliography of Portuguese-Indian literature. These must necessarily be very brief, because I have already exceeded the limits to which I am here restricted.

The period of Portuguese power in India—upwards of two centuries and a half if taken from the voyage of Vasco da Gama to the Dutch conquest of Cochim—naturally afforded an ample field for the historiographers of the Lusitanian nation, and consequently we find the *Bibliotheca Lusitana Historica, Critica, e Chronologica*, of Diogo Barbosa Machado, printed at Lisbon in two folio volumes in 1741-1747, filled page after page with the names of authors and titles of works devoted to this prolific and nationally interesting subject.[1] But it is not my desire to treat of these,

[1] A very useful paper on this subject (which I have followed in my remarks on these authors), entitled "Authorities for the History of the Portuguese in India", by T. W. H. Tolbort, Esq., B.C.S., will be found in the *Journal of the Asiatic Society of Bengal*, vol. xlii, Part I, 1873, pp. 193-208. This article contains notices of a large number of works touching the history of India, and deserves a place among the existing bibliographies of that country.

but rather to indicate, in a chronological order, the principal and most valuable authors, leaving it to the reader who desires more specific information to consult the great work just mentioned. Barros in his monumental work, the *Decades of Asia*, gives a succinct account of the Portuguese discoveries before the memorable voyage of Vasco da Gama. The oldest writer of the general history is *Gaspar Correa*. His work, entitled *Lendas da India*, was compiled about the year 1561, but was not printed until 1858-1864, when the Royal Academy of Lisbon issued it in three quarto volumes. This work,—from which the Hon. H. Stanley (now Lord Stanley of Alderley) translated the *Three Voyages of Vasco da Gama*, for the Hakluyt Society—has been considered very useful, and second only in veracity and importance to the *Decades* of Barros; and as a full account of the author and his works will be found in the *Voyages* mentioned above, it is unnecessary to repeat it here. Correa went to India about 1512, and there served under Afonso Dalboquerque; and from that period to 1550 it may be considered that he was moving about as an eyewitness of, and not unfrequently taking part in, the events he undertakes to describe; the parts descriptive of previous doings of the Portuguese having been derived in some measure from a manuscript work by João Figueiroa, a Portuguese priest who accompanied Vasco da Gama. Correa's work, as printed by the Lisbon Academy, contains the following illustrations which serve to elucidate the history of Afonso Dalboquerque, (1) a Portrait of Afonso, as frontispiece to tom. ii; (2) View of Mallaqua, tom. ii, pt. 1, p. 250; (3) Portuguese Fortress of Calequu or Calicut, p. 330; (4) Adem, p. 342; (5) Coullam, p. 394; (6) Ormuz, p. 439; (7) Judá, p. 494; (8) Ceilam, p. 541; (9) Portrait of Diogo Lopes de Sequeira, p. 555; (10) View of Cananor, tom. iii, p. 17; (11) Challe, p. 438; (12) Diu, p. 625; and (13) Basaim, p. 689.

Place appears to be required here for the manuscript *Historia do Descubrimento e Primeiras Conquistas da India*, which has been described in the Introduction to vol. i, pp. xiii-xv, and p. 101 of the *Commentaries*.

The next author for the general history is João de Barros. He is not known to have visited India, but the opportunities of his official position in the Lisbon India Office peculiarly fitted him for this work, which is entitled *Dos Feitos que os Portugueses Fizerão no Descobrimento e Conquista dos Mares e Terras do Oriente. Decadas* i-iii, iv (incomplete). It was first printed in folio at Lisbon in 1552, and again in 1628 and 1777; and is generally admitted to be the best authority upon the matters to which it relates. D. Barbosa Michado records several subsequent editions.[1]

Of Diogo de Couto, whose history overlaps and continues that of João de Barros, Mr. Tolbort writes: "De Couto[2] served in India, and though his portion of the history is not considered equal to that written by Barros, it is the best we have for the latter half of the sixteenth century. The fourth Decade by Barros comes down to the death of Nuno da Cunha in 1539, but as this Decade had not appeared when De Couto com-

[1] *Bibl. Lus.*, ii, 606.

[2] Page 194.

menced his continuation, he began twelve years earlier, bringing the continuation down to 1600. The joint history of De Barros and De Couto consists of twenty-four octavo volumes, there being, for the reason above stated, a duplicate account of the twelve years comprised in the governments of Lopo Vaz de Sampayo and Nuno da Cunha." The title of De Couto's continuation of Barros, is *Decada Quarta da Asia, dos feitos que, etc.*, as given above: printed in folio at Lisbon in 1602; the 5th and 6th Decade, 1612; the 7th [8th, 9th, 10th],[1] 1616; and five books of the 12th Decade, in Paris, 1645. From Faria y Sousa it appears that there is a MS. continuation of De Couto's work by Antonio Boccaro. Diogo de Couto wrote other works of minor import, and among these orations to incoming viceroys; a life of the celebrated Captain D. Paul de Lima; and a treatise entitled the *Soldado Pratico*, in which he exposes the causes of Portuguese decadence in India, in the shape of a dialogue between a soldier and a viceroy. A complete digest of this will be found in the Introduction to Lord Stanley's *Correa*, pp. lxvii, *et seq.* There is a work in the British Museum Library, entitled *Observações sobre as Principaes Causas da Decadencia dos Portuguezes na Asia*, 4to, Lisbon, 1790, which is the same as that called the *Soldado Pratico* in the previous sentence.

Fernão Lopez de Castanheda, the next general historian in this series, visited India in 1528, and is said

[1] These three decades in MS., in the British Museum copy.

to have travelled over all the districts of that empire under Portuguese domination, with the desire of obtaining correct information for his literary labours. Castanheda's work is entitled *Historia do Descobrimento & Conquista da India pelos Portuguezes.* It consists of eight books, and was published in folio at Coimbra, 1551-1561; the narrative running down to the first siege of Diu in 1538, and so covering nearly the same space of time as the previous work of João de Barros. Mr. Tolbort states that Castanheda intended to publish ten books, but the last two seem to have been suppressed because they reflected upon some powerful people of the Portuguese Court. But from a list furnished to him by Senhor da Cunha Rivara, secretary to the Portuguese Government at Goa, it appears that this work is brought down to the year before the commencement of publication. The first book of Castanheda appears to have been translated into French by Nicholas de Grouchy, and published in 8vo. Anvers, 1554; and the same book was again printed in quarto at London in 1582, in form of an English translation—the first English translation of any work of this series of authors—by a "gentleman" named Nicholas Lichefeld under the title of *The First Booke of the Historie of the Discouerie and Conquest of the East Indias, enterprised by the Portingales, in their daungerous Nauigations, in the time of the King Dom John the second of that name.* It is to be desired that the time may not be far distant when English translations of all these original histories shall have been prepared and printed.

The next name on this list of Indian historians[1] is that of a foreign Jesuit, Johannes Petrus Maffei, whose work (in Latin) is entitled *Historiæ Indicæ, cum Ignatii Loyolæ vita.* This was printed in folio at Cologne in 1589, and again in 1593. It is believed to be based on the work of Barros, and is carried down to 1557, being divided into sixteen books, with an appendix of four books of *Epistolæ Indicæ*, or selected letters from India. Maffei was, also, the author of the *Rerum a Societate Jesu in Oriente gestarum Volumen*, 8vo. Colon. 1574.

The Benedictine Fr. Antonio de San Roman followed apparently in the footsteps of Maffei. His work is thus entitled *Historia General de la India Oriental.* It was printed in form of a folio at Valladolid in 1603.

Another work,[2] also in the Spanish language, is that of Luys Coello de Barbuda, with the title of *Emprezas Militares de Lusitanos*, in quarto, printed at Lisbon in 1624.

The *Livro*[3] *do Estado da India Oriental* by Captain Pedro Barreto de Resende, in 1646, from which much assistance has been acquired during the progress of this translation, has been fully described in the Introduction to vol. i, pp. vii-xiii.

The next author is Faria y Sousa, or Manoel Severim de Faria; the work being entitled *Asia Por-*

[1] Titles of the works of Maffei, and their various editions and translations form No. 11, 11*bis*, of M. Léon Pagès' *Bibliographie Japonaise*, which will be noticed further on.

[2] Omitted by Mr. Tolbort.

[3] Also omitted by the same writer.

tuguesa, and beginning at the early voyages is carried down to 1640. It was printed in three volumes of folio size at Lisbon in 1666-1675, and has been also published in Spanish. Mr. Tolbort describes an English translation from the Spanish text in 1695. The description of China by Faria y Sousa is founded on the *Memoirs* of Semedo, and is valuable for the history of the China mission. M. Severim de Faria was the author of many other historical works; his *Africa Portuguesa* was translated into English by Captain John Stevens, three volumes, 8vo, London, 1695.

The last of the general historians is the Reverend Father Joseph Lafitau, a Jesuit like his literary predecessor Maffei. His Portuguese researches are entitled *Histoire des Découvertes et Conquestes des Portugais dans le Nouveau Monde.* It was published at Paris in two volumes in 1733, and is a very interesting and well written work, but does not pretend to give any great amount of detail.[1]

After the consideration of these comprehensive writers, it is very necessary to put on record the titles of some bibliographical and other works which treat of Indian matters incidentally, or of special subjects and particular events.

I am not aware of the existence of any work partaking solely of the nature of a *Bibliotheca Indica*, but the best Bibliographies for the prolific subject of European rule in India are the following: D. Barbosa

[1] In the Introduction to Vol. i, I have considered Grenville's statement that the first volume of Lafitau is translated from the *Commentaries* of Afonso Dalboquerque.

Machado's *Bibliotheca*, to which already references have often been made. The classified indices in this book greatly augment its literary value for reference and research. A very large portion of it, however, consists of notices of historical works, both manuscript and printed, which are unfortunately not available beyond the limits of the native libraries of Portugal.

Raphael Savonarola's work entitled *Universus Terrarum Orbis scriptorum Calamo delineatus, hoc est, Auctorum fere omnium qui de Europæ, Asiæ, ... regnis, etc. . . . scripserunt . . . . uberrimus elenchus, etc.*, and published with the name of the author arranged as an anagram, *Alphonsi Lasor a Varea*, Patavii, 1713, two vols., folio, contains notices of the titles of a large number of early books treating upon the prolific subject of India—travels, voyages, and histories. The titles are given under the names of the places to which they refer. The work is adorned with several copper-plate engravings of cities and towns, from an old collection of maps, plans, and views originally published about the year 1600. Among these may be mentioned Calechut, vol. i, p. 219; Canonor, vol. i, p. 226; Goa, vol. i, p. 452; and Ormus, vol. i, p. 94, which illustrate the period of the *Commentaries*.

One of the most comprehensive Bibliographical works that belong to this class is the *Bibliothèque Universelle des Voyages, ou Notice complète et raisonnée de tous les Voyages anciens et modernes dans les différentes parties du monde, etc.* Par G. Boucher de la Richarderie, in six vols. 8vo, Paris, 1808. The portions which relate to India are contained in the

Ie. Partie. § ii, Navigations et Voyages chez les anciens (vol i, p. 15).
§ iv, 1. Voyages faits en Orient dans le moyen âge (vol. i, p. 32).
§ iv, Collections de Voyages (*ib.* p. 55).
§ vi, Voyages autour du monde (*ib.* p. 107).
§ viii, 2, 3, 5, 6, 7, 9, Voyages dans différentes parties du monde (*ib.* p. 179, etc.)

IVe Partie. § vi, Description des Indes Orientales. Voyages faits dans ce pays (vol. v, p. 1, etc.)

The *Bibliothèque Asiatique et Africaine, ou catalogue des ouvrages relatifs à l'Asie et à l'Afrique qui ont paru depuis la Découverte de l'imprimerie jusqu'en* 1700, by H. Ternaux-Compans, 8vo, Paris, 1841, consists of many hundred references and titles of books, arranged in chronological order, and exhibits an untiring labour on the part of the compiler. Its usefulness would perhaps have been greater if the Bibliography of the two great continents of Asia and Africa had been kept separate, or printed in different type, to catch the eye of the reader.

I have not been able to inspect a copy of the *Bibliothèque Géographique*, by M. Le Breton, in seventy-two volumes, 18mo, published in Paris, 1802-1807; from the title it would appear to be useful for matters relating to Indian Bibliography.

Mention must also be made of the *Bibliographie Japonaise, ou Catalogue des Ouvrages Relatifs au Japon, qui ont été publiés depuis le XVe Siècle jusqu'à nos jours;* rédigé par M. Léon Pagès, ancien Attaché de Légation, large quarto, Paris, 1859. Although this most useful book is specially devoted to Japanese history, it contains a vast number of entries relating to Portuguese India; Japan, like that continent, being connected with Portugal by the exertions of the Jesuits and other propagandist missionaries, by the fame and labours of St. Francisco Xavier, and by the zeal of travellers and traders. Hence the books which treat of the one, in many cases do not fail to throw some light upon the other empire. The works included in the chronological series commence with Marco Polo[1] in 1496, and are arranged in order of chronology, with an appendix of "Documents Manuscrits", and a "Table Analytique" of names and subjects.

In the text, prefixed to the *Royal Illustrated Atlas of Modern Geography,* will be found comprehensive classified lists of (i) Collections and Histories of Voyages and Travels, p. 5; (xxiii) Voyages and Travels in Asia, p. 65; and (xxiv) Voyages and Travels, etc., in

[1] I am happily enabled to add the description of one MS. of *Marco Polo,* which has been, by some accident omitted in both editions by Col. Yule:—1871, vol. ii, p. 449, and 1874, vol. ii, p. 517. This is a Latin copy of quarto size, on vellum, of the fourteenth century, ending abruptly towards the end of Book III, chap. xvii, at the words—"ne possint ab homine vel a bestia". It has been in the British Museum since April 1853, when it was purchased at Baron Walckenaer's sale at Paris, lot 3385; and is now numbered, Additional MS. 19513, folios 85 to 132.

India, pp. 68-78, by Dr. N. Shaw, Secretary to the Royal Geographical Society. The entries relating to India are especially numerous, and are useful because they are brought down to a more modern period than that which limits other catalogues. At the same time it is to be remarked that Dr. Shaw has failed to give the correct title to the first edition of the *Commentaries of Afonso Dalboquerque* (p. 68, col. 1).

The entries in the new General Catalogue of Printed Books in the British Museum ; the Classed Catalogue of Manuscripts in the British Museum ;[1] the Catalogue of the Library of the East India House ; the Classified Catalogue of Books of the Royal Geographical Society, p. 229, published in 1871 ; and many other catalogues of similar institutions, must be carefully examined by the student who desires to perfect

[1] The principal classes are :—

INDIA, History of, Vol. iii, p. 455.
„ Portuguese, *ibid.*, p. 457.
„ Topography of, Vol. lviii, p. 385.
„ Travels in, *ibid.*, p. 117.
„ Transactions with Great Britain, Vol. vii, pp. 197, 277.
„ Army of, Vol. l, p. 557.
„ Religious Houses in the Indies, Vol. lxxix, p. 217.
„ Voyages to, Vol. lviii, p. 175.
„ Church History of, Vol. v, p. 135.

There is a very fine collection of forty volumes of Portuguese papers in the British Museum, entitled *Collecçam authentica de todas as Leys, Regimentos, Alvaras, e mais Ordens que se expediram para a India desde o estabelecimento destas conquistas, etc.*, 1518-1758 (Add. MS., 20861-20900). They are followed by fourteen other volumes of papers and miscellaneous documents of great importance in the History of Portuguese India.

his appreciation of the enormous quantity of literary materials existing of which the prolific subject of India has been the inspiration and the theme.

I am indebted to Mr. C. H. Coote, of the Map Department of the British Museum, for the substance of the following notes respecting the MS. Portolano from which the map of India, reproduced to face page 1, is redrawn.

Among the notable acquisitions of the Map Department of the British Museum, recorded in vol. 52 of the Parliamentary Papers for 1873, is a Portuguese MS. Portolano of the sixteenth century, the execution of which is of unusual beauty. This MS. is the work of Fernão Vãz Dourado, and the date of 1573 has been assigned to its production. This date, from internal evidence, appears to be correct, and if so, the MS. is a copy of one prepared three years earlier by the same hand. Barbosa Machado[1] records that the original manuscript was made in Goa in 1571, and that in his time (1747) it was preserved in the monastery of the Carthusians at Evora. It would appear that at some period between 1747 and 1812 the work was removed to the Academia Real da Marinha de Lisboa.

The learned Antonio Ribeiro dos Santos, although the existence and place of deposit of the original MS. were apparently known to him, arrived at the erroneous conclusion—probably through a misreading of Barbosa Machado—that it was afterwards printed.[2] It is

[1] *Bibl. Lusitana*, ii, 64.

[2] "O qual se Estampou em Goa em 1571, fol." *Mem. da Litterat. Portug.*, viii, Pt. I, p. 187.

hardly necessary to mention that this is an error. The original MS., which is generally known in Portugal under the name of the *Carte du Cartuxa*, is minutely described in the *Dictionnaire Historico-Artistique du Portugal*, par le Comte A. Raczynski (p. 73), as follows: "Le frontispiece de cet atlas est divisé perpendiculairement en deux parties égales. Un *Ecce Homo* occupe le côté droit; à gauche sont les armes des *Costa*, avec ce titre en portugais: Mappamundo que fez Fernão Vas Dourado fronteiro nestas partes que trata de todos os reinos, terras, ilhas, que ha na redondeza da terra, com suas derrotas e alturas per esquadria. Em Goa, 1571. Autour de ce frontispiece on lit encore en latin: Universalis et integra totius orbis Hydrographia ad verissimam Lusitanorum traditionem descriptio, Ferdinandus *(sic)* Vaz Dourado cosmografo auctore, in civitate Goa, anno 1571."

A later writer[1] informs us that the beautiful frontispiece above mentioned has disappeared from the National Archives of Lisbon, and in this respect the original compares unfavourably with the copy in the British Museum, of which the title is somewhat different: "Universalis et integra totius orbis Hidrographia ad verissimam Luzitanorum traditionem descripcio. Ferdinãdo Ṽz. Este livro fes Fernão Vãz Dourado." A comparison of the copy in the British Museum with the collation of the original afforded us by Da Silva enables us to realise their differences without difficulty. In the place of the lost frontispiece of

[1] Da Silva, *Diccionario Bibliographio Portuguez*, Supp., tom. ix, p. 221.

the original MS., containing the title in Portuguese on the one side and the *Ecce Homo* on the other, the Museum copy exhibits on the verso of the first folio, the Royal arms of Portugal, and on the recto of the following leaf, a representation of the Martyrdom of St. Sebastian, beautifully illuminated in charming colours by a Portuguese artist, and perhaps one of the finest specimens of the miniature painter's art to be found in any Portuguese manuscript. This picture was in all probability intended as a delicate act of homage to the reigning monarch Dom Sebastião. The original appears to have consisted, at a former period, of twenty sheets bound in folio, including title-page, sixteen charts, oue table of cosmographical rules, and two of nautical calendars;—whereas the Museum copy contains twenty-one sheets, viz., the title, seventeen charts, the table of rules, and two sheets of nautical calendars, apparently calculated for four years, ending in leap-year 1576. The rules in the Museum copy contain a table of feasts which coincide exactly with those for 1573, and this, with the allusion to the King Dom Sebastião in the frontispiece, points conclusively to the correctness of the date assigned to it. Barbosa Machado alludes to a copy of the work of Vaz Dourado in the library of José de Faria, the learned secretary to Dom Pedro II, *circ.* 1690, but of this copy no trace is known, unless perchance that in the British Museum be the very one.

With regard to the author himself little is known. According to the author, Antonio Ribeiro dos Santos, Fernando Vaz Dourado was born probably in the first quarter of the sixteenth century, at Goa; he is described in his own work as "*fronteiro* nestas partes"; and by Barbosa Machado as "igualmento perito no exercicio das armas, como versado na Geografia", a fact which no one will dispute. In addition to these meagre notices of the first cosmographer of the Indies, there is a notice in the *Archivo*[1] *Portuguez Oriental* relating to Fernão Vaz of Goa in 1584, and if this refers to the above, which is very doubtful, it would bring the life of the author well down towards the close of the sixteenth century.

The portrait of Afonso Dalboquerque, which is placed as a frontispiece to this book, forms the frontispiece of vol. i of the 8vo. edition of the *Commentaries* of 1774. It has been reproduced by the autotype process with permission of the trustees of the British Museum from the copy preserved in the library.

The portrait of Dom Francisco Dalmeida and the plan of Goa are derived from the same valuable MS. of Pedro Barreto de Resende from which I obtained that of Afonso Dalboquerque, given as frontispiece in the first volume of my translation, and the map of Arabia by P. Berthelot[2] at page 80; and my thanks

[1] Fascic. v, p. 1075.

[2] Pierre Berthelot, a barefooted Carmelite monk, whose name in religion was Denis de la Nativité, was born at Honfleur in 1600. After having followed the career of a pirate, he was received with distinction at Goa, and was nominated in 1629 first pilot to a Portuguese fleet sent to defend Malacca (Sumatra) against the King of Achim, who was besieging the town. His bravery won for him the post of Cosmographer Royal of the Indies, a title which he justified in revealing in his divers voyages the shores of the

are due to the trustees of the British Museum for permission to reproduce these also by photography.

There is an interesting map of Goa, in the possession of T. W. H. Tolbort, Esq., of the Bengal Civil Service, to whom I am indebted for the kindness shown by offering the use of it for this work, which bears the following title:

> "Mappa do Territorio Portuguez de Goa, mostrando tambem os principaes lugares de Sattari. Tudo examinado e visto debaixo da immediata Superintendencia do Tenente Jas. Garling de Madrasta pelos Annos de 1814. Corrigido e separado em Provincias por C. S. R. Nunes."

The lower space of the map is filled with statistical information[1] of great value, but, as it appertains to a period far more recent than that of Afonso Dalboquerque, I should be hardly justified in inserting these notices in this place. The scale to which the map is drawn is two miles to an inch—*duas Milhas por polegada.*

The modern map of Goa and the Portuguese de-

country that he visited. Berthelot, with the Portuguese ambassador, was massacred at Achim by the inhabitants on the 27th of November, 1638.—Frère, *Manuel de Bibliographie Normande*, vol. i, p. 336. Paris, 1850-60. 8vo.

[1] See also, Brit. Mus. Add. MS., 14382, ff. 112, 113. Some useful *Notices of the Portuguese Territories of Goa* are to be found in the British Museum Add. MS., 14384, ff. 19-40, written early in the present century; and there are also two large volumes respectively entitled a *Memoir Descriptive and Illustrative of the Map of the Portuguese Territories Dependent on Goa, surveyed in* 1811-1812, *by Lieut. J. Garling*, MS. 14385; and a *Collection of Statistical Tables of the Portuguese Territories in India*, 1776-1833, MS. 14386.

pendencies may be best studied from the survey (four miles to an inch) made by Lieutenant-Colonels Neil Campbell and G. Boyd and their staff, and published by John Walker, geographer to the Hon. East India Company, May 31st, 1852.

CHRONOLOGY OF PART II.

PAGE		A.D.
1.	Afonso Dalboquerque arrives at Cananor	At the beginning of December, 1508
1.	Requests to be received as Governor of India	A few days afterwards
4.	Reaches Cochim	14 Dec., 1508
11.	Meeting of Afonso Dalboquerque and Jorge Bàrreto	24 Dec., 1508
16.	D. Francisco Dalmeida, Viceroy of India, having routed the Rumes, visits Cananor and Cochim	8 March, 1509
123.	D. Afonso da Noronha sails away from Çacotora to India	April, 1509
34.	The Viceroy summons a Council to deliberate respecting the appointment of Afonso Dalboquerque to be Governor .	Monday, 15 May, 1509
49.	Death of João da Nova, at Cochim . .	July, 1509
46.	D. Fernando Coutinho, Marshal of Portugal, [having set out from Portugal on the 12th March, 1509, *see page* 56 *note*] arrives at Cananor, and carries Afonso Dalboquerque with him to Cochim	29 Oct., 1509
47.	The Marshal pays a visit to the Viceroy with respect to the affairs of Afonso Dalboquerque	Saturday, 4 Nov., 1509
48.	The Viceroy surrenders the government of India to Afonso Dalboquerque, and embarks	Sunday, 5 Nov., 1509

48. The Viceroy sails for Cananor in the ship *Garça* . . . . . . 10 November, 1509

52. Determination of Afonso Dalboquerque and the Marshal to destroy Calicut Beginning of Dec., 1509

63. They set out from Cochim . . . 31 Dec., 1509

63. And arrive at Calicut . . . . . . 3 Jan., 1510

64-71. The attack made, the Marshal killed and Afonso Dalboquerque wounded . . 4 Jan., 1510

" After burning the city of Calicut the Portuguese withdraw to Cochim . . . 5 Jan., 1510

80. Afonso Dalboquerque sets out from Cochim for the Red Sea with twenty-three ships 10 Feb., 1510

84. Alters his course, and bears down upon the Castle of Cintácora . . . . . 25 Feb., 1510

88. A Council deliberates upon the proposed enterprise to attack Goa. . . . [27 Feb., 1510]

88. D. Antonio de Noronha, nephew of Afonso Dalboquerque, sounds the bar of Goa . 28 Feb., 1510

48. The Viceroy murdered at the watering-place of Saldanha . . . . . . [1 March, 1510]

89. Capture of the fortress of Pangij . [1 March, 1510]

196. Note. [Diogo Mendez de Vasconcellos sets out from Portugal with a fleet for Malaca 12 March, 1510]

119. Letter of Afonso Dalboquerque to the King of Ormuz announcing the capture of Goa 20 March, 1510

133. Francisco Serrão dispatched from Goa to Cochim to carry news of the fall of the city, and to take back supplies . Beginning of April

137. Arrival of the Hidalcão's advanced guard at Banda and Condal, reported . . 23 April, 1510

155. The Hidalcão enters Goa through the pass of Agacij . . . . 17 May, 1510

164. Afonso Dalboquerque withdraws his forces from Goa, and anchors in the river . . . 20 May, 1510

176. The Portuguese renew their attack on Pangij, and succeed . . . . . . 14 June, 1510

180. Death of Don Antonio de Noronha, nephew of Afonso Dalboquerque.

188. Execution of Ruy Dias.

192. Afonso Dalboquerque orders João de Lima to prepare to sail for supplies . . . 15 July, 1510

193. Afonso Dalboquerque attempts to sail out over the bar of Goa . . . About 21 July, 1510

199. Afonso Dalboquerque sails away to Anjadiva 16 Aug., 1510

199. Arrival of Diogo Mendez de Vasconcellos with a fleet of five ships from Portugal . . 16 Aug., 1510

200. The combined fleets anchor off Anjadiva . 17 Aug., 1510

201. Anchor off Onor . . . . 19 Aug., 1510

202. And arrive at Cananor . . . . 26 Aug., 1510

124. Duarte de Lemos and Francisco Pantoja arrive at Cananor from Çacotorá . . . 31 Aug., 1510

224. Arrival of Lourenço Moreno from Portugal at Cananor . . . . 8 Sept., 1510

215. Letter from Afonso Dalboquerque to the Chief Alguazil of Cambaya . . . . 16 Sept., 1510

233. Arrival of Gonçalo de Sequeira at Cananor . 16 Sept., 1510

237. Afonso Dalboquerque sets out with all his forces to Cochim . . . . 22 Sept , 1510

237. Reaches Cochim, and visits the King . . 26 Sept., 1510

COMMENTARIES

OF THE GREAT

AFONSO DALBOQUERQUE,

WHO WAS

CAPTAIN-GENERAL OF THE EAST INDIES

IN THE TIME OF THE VERY POWERFUL

KING D. MANUEL,

THE FIRST OF THIS NAME.

PART II.

LISBON:

IN THE ROYAL PRINTING OFFICE,

ANNO MDCCLXXIV;

With Licence of the Royal Board of Censors, and Royal Privilege.

TITLES

OF THE

CHAPTERS CONTAINED IN THIS SECOND PART.

WHEREIN ARE CONTAINED THE DEALINGS OF THE GREAT AFONSO DALBOQUERQUE WITH THE VICEROY: AND WHAT HE DID AFTER BEING INVESTED WITH THE GOVERNMENT OF INDIA, UNTIL THE FIRST TAKING OF GOA.

CHAPTER LI.

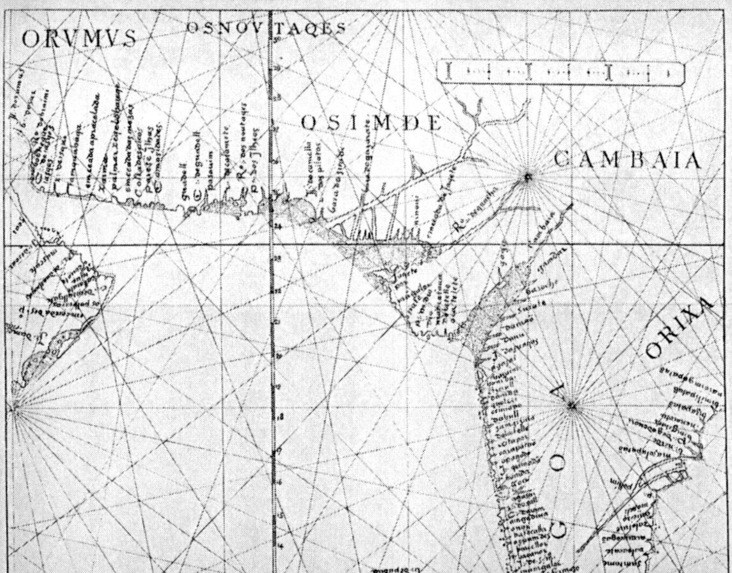

MAP OF INDIA.

[*British Museum, Portolano of Fernão Vaz Dourado, circ.* 1570.]

PART II.

WHEREIN ARE CONTAINED THE DEALINGS OF THE GREAT AFONSO DALBOQUERQUE WITH THE VICEROY: AND WHAT HE DID AFTER BEING INVESTED WITH THE GOVERNMENT OF INDIA, UNTIL THE FIRST TAKING OF GOA.

CHAPTER I.

How he arrived at Cananor at the beginning of December, in the year fifteen hundred and eight: and required the Viceroy to deliver up to him the government of India, as the king D. Manuel ordered in his instructions, and what took place thereupon.

The great Afonso Dalboquerque, on his arrival at Cananor, as I have mentioned, found the Viceroy there making his fleet ready to go and seek the *Rumes*, who were at Diu; and as the Viceroy had already learned by Fernão Soares and Ruy da Cunha, captains in the fleet of Jorge de Aguiar (who had arrived but a few days before), that the King D. Manuel had ordered him to return that year to Portugal, leaving Afonso Dalboquerque as Governor of India, he was not much pleased with his arrival, nor was the other, either, pleased at seeing how good a treatment the captains who had deserted him at Ormuz had experienced at the hands of the Viceroy; and thenceforward great dissensions began to grow up between them.

After the lapse of some days, Afonso Dalboquerque went to see the Viceroy, and told him, in the presence of Fernão Soarez and Ruy da Cunha, that since the King D. Manuel had ordered him to proceed to Portugal, and all the letters and official documents came directed to himself, as Governor of India, he desired that he would hand the office over to him, according to the King's instructions, for they were already at the beginning of December, which was the proper time to start, and he had the ship *Betlem*, wherein he could make the voyage with great comfort, and six other ships to convoy her. The Viceroy replied that the period of his government would terminate in January next, and that when it was so terminated then he would deliver it over to him. When Afonso Dalboquerque perceived that this was the intention of the Viceroy, he would not have any more words with him, but returned to his own house and sent Antonio de Sintra, who acted as his secretary (Gaspar Pereira having remained behind, sick, at Cochim), to show him the powers and diplomas he held from the King D. Manuel, fastened up and sealed just as they had been brought. These Antonio de Sintra opened at the desire of Afonso Dalboquerque, for the superscriptions stated that they were to be opened whenever he wished; and being thus opened, he carried them before the Viceroy, who, after having read them, told Antonio de Sintra he had done very wrong in opening these provisions without first of all informing him, and Afonso Dalboquerque had greatly erred in the request he had preferred in the presence of Fernão Soarez and Ruy da Cunha; he must therefore inform him the best thing he could do would be to fasten them up again, and so keep them in secret until his return from Diu.

Antonio de Sintra delivered this message, and told his master that if it were necessary to fasten up all those documents again, he would do so in such a manner that they would seem as though they had never been opened. Afonso Dalboquerque said to him:—"If this is so, then, Antonio de Sintra, it is not the first time you have done such a thing; I am not the kind of man to fasten up again the powers and diplomas of the King, whereby he orders me to govern India, after they have been opened. Tell the Viceroy that since the disposition of the fleet rests with me, as I am Governor of India, he must deliver it over to me, that I may go in search of the *Rumes*." The Viceroy sent word to him, saying that he himself was already prepared and determined to prosecute that expedition, but he (Afonso) was to remain where he was in Cananor, or go to Cochim and rest awhile from his past labours; but as soon as he returned he would deliver the office up to him, according to the King's instructions. Afonso Dalboquerque replied that he would not have time to go and return within the year, so as to be able to go back to Portugal; but that if he was determined to stay in India he might govern the country, so long as he handed over to him the fleet, that he might have charge of it.

The Viceroy, being weary of these constant messages, said to Antonio de Sintra: "That will do very well for the present," and gave him no other reply. On the following day, in the morning, Lourenço de Brito, Captain of the Fortress of Cananor, paid a visit to Afonso Dalboquerque, having been instructed by the Viceroy, and in course of conversation began telling him not to trouble himself with requisitions, nor even to talk about such things, for the men were very desirous that the Viceroy should retain the command; if he pushed the matter very hardly, and put it to the vote of the captains, all would incline to this opinion; and this he told him, as he said, out of a desire to serve him and be his friend, for he desired there should be no differences between him and the Viceroy. Afonso Dalboquerque replied that as he had not asked him for any advice, he might keep it to himself, for he had taken plenty of counsel with the powers and diplomas of the King, D. Manuel, which he had with him; his own advice to the Viceroy was to conform to these documents, and not make use of go-betweens.

When this had taken place, and Afonso Dalboquerque perceived that the Viceroy would not deliver India to him, but that the captains who fled away and left him in the war with Ormuz did many discourteous acts towards him, being encouraged to them by the Viceroy; in order to avoid these and similar unpleasantnesses, he proceeded to embark in the ship *Cirne*, which had brought him from Ormuz, and sailed away for Cochim. And in consequence of the leaky condition of the ship, he was almost cast away on the voyage, but reached the place on the fourteenth of December, and remained on board for five days, waiting until some houses for his occupation could be found. On his arrival, Gaspar Pereira, Rui de Araujo, and the other officers of the factory, came to see him, and after giving them an account of what had passed with the Viceroy in Cananor, he exhibited to them the powers and diplomas he held from the King D. Manuel, to be Captain-General of India, telling them he did not show these deeds of the King to force obedience from them, but to let them feel quite sure that he had demanded of the Viceroy that he should yield up the command and government of India and hand it over to him, according to the orders of the King D. Manuel, for he did not wish to be the cause of any faction: for already some people had come to him in Cananor and advised him to call himself Captain-General of India, but he would not do so, to avoid party differences; but he would swear to them that he had experienced such treatment at Cananor that he feared to encounter dishonourable outrage, or even death, at their hands.

When Afonso Dalboquerque departed, the Viceroy, fearing lest he should send complaints to the King by the ships which would make the voyage to Portugal that year, wrote to the Prior do Crato, his brother, to unite with the Baron and with the Governor D. Alvaro de Castro, and all three speak to the King, and tell him that his stay in India was caused by all the captains and noblemen requesting him not to leave, for if Afonso Dalboquerque remained as governor there, the Moors would immediately revolt against us, and therefore he had not delivered over to him the command until his Highness should be informed of what was going on, and forthwith arrange what should be most advantageous to his interest; as for the evil that Dalboquerque had done in the kingdom of Ormuz, Afonso Lopez da Costa (who was sent specially for this purpose) could give him a true account, as could also Gaspar Rodriguez, the interpreter, who would state that Ormuz was lost to them by reason of his fault and bad government. The Viceroy sent Manuel Fragoso with these letters to Cochim in the *fusta*, which had brought Nuno Vaz from Ormuz; and wrote to Gaspar Pereira that he earnestly desired he would take care to let no differences arise between Afonso Dalboquerque and Jorge Barreto, for he did not know whether they were friendly; and that, to avoid scandal, he would not give him quarters in the fortress, but let him have the best houses in the town to occupy (provided they were not in the possession of João da Nova), and he would proceed to send him some notice of the faults laid to the charge of Afonso Dalboquerque, to show him them; and he was to endeavour to persuade him to appropriate everything he could get possession of in the way of pay and goods, when he was Chief Captain of India, for he had desired to offer him this course of action, only he had not dared to do so when he saw how proudly he carried himself, though he had no cause for it. Afonso Dalboquerque, also, for his part and in his own manner, wrote to the King, sending him the affidavits he had ordered to be made out concerning the flight of the captains, and begged him to punish them. The King D. Manuel was so angry at this desertion of the captains that, on the arrival of Afonso Lopez da Costa, he ordered him immediately to be imprisoned in his castle, and would have had him executed for it, if he had not got off through the powerful influence of his friends.

CHAPTER II.

How Gaspar Pereira carried the appointments, which the Viceroy gave him, to the great Afonso Dalboquerque, and of the reply he received.

When the days had elapsed which Afonso Dalboquerque spent in the flagship, waiting while they emptied the houses of Gonçalo Fernandez, wherein he was to lodge, he went on shore; and Gaspar Pereira went immediately to see him, and told him that the Viceroy, previous to his departure from Cananor to Diu, had sent him some drafts of charges made against him, which he would show him, and if he would give him permission to lay them before him, or serve them upon him, he would do so; but if not, they could remain where they were until the arrival of the Viceroy, for he himself had nothing to do in the matter except as a messenger. Afonso Dalboquerque bade him give them to him, for he had come from Cananor so tired of his dealings with the Viceroy that unless they contained anything to alarm him he would prepare to answer them.

The first charge was that he had delayed sending to him to give up his power which the King had given him, through Antonio de Sintra, in Cananor, and making the request to him which he had made in the presence of Fernão Soarez and Ruy da Cunha, Captains of the King. Afonso Dalboquerque replied that he did not comprehend why he should be so alarmed at the request, when he so often told him that the King had written to him to return to Portugal and deliver over the government of India to himself; what was much more astonishing to him was that he should come to Cananor and find him determined not to deliver it over to him, as he had done.

The second charge was that he had quitted Çocotora without the King's order, and made his way to India, though he had written to him, through Tristão da Cunha, that his Highness ordered him to take great care of the place, and for this reason he had omitted to send any necessary supplies thither. Afonso Dalboquerque answered that on arriving at Cananor he had stated that the reason of his coming was because the weather did not permit any other voyage, for in the months of November and December one could not run from Ormuz to the Island of Çocotora, as the winds were south-east and the weather very rough: another thing, also, which forced him to come to India was the quantity of water which the *Rey Grande* and the *Cirne* made, lest they should be lost; and, moreover, the time was now come wherein the King had ordered him to receive the government of India. And since he demanded so strict an account of what he had done, he first ought to have taken an account from the captains who had deserted their posts in the war, and from Manuel Telez, who had carried off the supplies entrusted to him for carriage to the Fortress of Çocotora in his ship; but these captains he retained in favour before his eyes. And though he desired very often to give an account of himself in Cananor, yet the Viceroy would never listen to him or look at his instructions, because in them the King commanded him that if no clause in them bore upon a particular state of affairs, in that case he was to do as would be most advantageous to his interest; and if he was not pleased with his coming to India without the King's orders, how could he, on his part, be pleased with the Viceroy's stay in India and unwillingness to deliver up to him the government of it, not caring to follow his orders and instructions? As for the letter he had forwarded to him through Tristão da Cunha, it was to hand, as well as another, wherein he gave him an account of the flight of his captains, begging him to send back ships and men and other captains; wherein, also, he gave him an account of the state in which he then was; to this one never yet had he seen any reply, nor had he assisted him, as he was obliged to do by virtue of his position as Captain-General of the Indies; but, on the contrary, he had seen his (the Viceroy's) letters to the King and Cogeatar, making use of very dishonourable expressions respecting his own person, holding his labours as of little value, extolling the actions of the captains, and stating his good reception of them.

The third charge made against Afonso Dalboquerque was that he had blockaded Ormuz and prohibited all communications during the period protected by the safeguard which he had himself agreed upon, and Cogeatar had sent the document to demonstrate this fact to him, but he would not return it to him again. To this Afonso Dalboquerque replied that it was true that during this protected period he had surrounded the Island of Ormuz, and not permitted any one to enter or leave the place, for he was obliged to do so for the safety of his own men and his fleet, and to remain there waiting for the succour and aid of the King D. Manuel, for in the letters which he had found in Ormuz, on his return from Çocotora, directed to Cogeatar, he had indeed perceived how much help he was likely to give him. Gaspar Rodriguez, the interpreter, was a true witness to a letter which Cogeatar had shown him, sealed with the arms of the King of Portugal, which was of no other import than to destroy all his labours, and spoke of himself as if he were a corsair, banished from the kingdom. When Cogeatar perceived how little value was set upon him, like a cunning man, he understood how matters lay, and knew how to take advantage of the opportunity; and it was not a thing likely to terrify him that some members of his company were telling him that he had done imprudently to humour him, since the captains who had deserted him with the complaint that they were not satisfied with the way the war was carried on, and that he had ordered them to fill up their freights, had come to be well treated by him; and those who had protected him and accompanied him in all his troubles and fortunes, like very true and faithful cavaliers, had found their prospects unimproved and their cargoes not laden. And if Cogeatar wished to reap the advantage of this armistice which he (Alboquerque) offered him, he, on his part, as was reasonable to expect, would be insured by Cogeatar; but he would desire that Cogeatar would keep to the arrangement, and he desired him to stop the discharge of arrows, for he was Chief Captain of the King of Portugal, in whose name the armistice had been entered into.

The fourth charge was that Cogeatar had sent, desiring of him a mutual order and assignation for an interview, and that he would not grant it. Afonso replied that he did not remember whether he had sent it him or not, and even if it were so, it was not right that it should have been given, for the order was for himself, concerning his proper duty according to circumstances, and that he had to give account to the King D. Manuel of what he had done, because he acted under his directions. And above all, he had given him a translation, signed and sealed, and an account of the manner in which his order had been received. Because, if perchance the ships and men sent thither by the King D. Manuel to help him had gone to seek him according to the orders promulgated when he first left Portugal, they would have known, on arriving at Ormuz, of the events that had taken place there.

The fifth charge was that he had taken a slave away from a Moorish merchant of Ormuz against his will. Afonso Dalboquerque replied that this was not so, but that a caravan of merchants had come from Persia to Ormuz, and a Moor brought in company with him a Christian youth from Ruxia, who, on seeing our ships, fled, and managed to reach them, and the Moor had demanded the surrender of the youth, but he was unwilling to give him up, because he was a Christian and he would not return with him, but for all that he had not remained in slavery, and it was not likely that such a man as he (Afonso Dalboquerque) was, would enslave a youth who had put himself under his protection under the name of a Christian.

And because Gaspar Pereira, besides these statements, told Afonso Dalboquerque other things which the Viceroy had ordered him to say by word of mouth—one of which was that he was to pay him all due to him for the time he was in India—Afonso Dalboquerque replied that he should make answer to the Viceroy that at the Court of the King of Portugal, whither both of them were proceeding, there was no place for tricks and artifices to entice him to sell his honour and personal dignity, but that he trusted, with God's help, to perform such services in those parts for the King, our Lord, whereby he might merit the favours of other titles more noble than that of Viceroy.

After Afonso Dalboquerque had replied to all those points above described, he ordered Gaspar Pereira to be called, and, in the presence of Ruy de Araujo and André Diaz and the other officers of the Factory at Cochim, who were with him, he gave him the answers, telling him that he was very much alarmed for him, since he had gathered, from the letters which the King had written to him, in his capacity of Secretary of India, wherein he ordered the Viceroy to return to Portugal, and him (Afonso) to remain as Governor, that he had so much dread that he was unwilling to perform the commands contained in the letters of his Highness, and that since the Viceroy would not deliver the government of India over to him, it was not for him to take it by the sword, but conformably to the orders of the King, his lord. Gaspar Pereira informed him that he had no doubt that the Viceroy would yield up the government on his arrival at Diu, for he had often expressed his intentions of doing so before the officers who were there; and if the Viceroy would not obey the King's orders, he himself would resign his office, and let who would have it, and serve only under him.

CHAPTER III.

Of certain things which passed at Cochim, between the great Afonso Dalboquerque and Jorge Barreto: and of the letter which Lourenço de Brito, Captain of Cananor, wrote to him, and of the reply which was sent to him.

Ten days after the great Afonso Dalboquerque had arrived at Cochim, Jorge Barreto, captain of the fortress, because the Viceroy had written to desire there should be no disagreements between them, went to his house to visit him. Now he had married a daughter of Fernão Dalboquerque, brother of Afonso Dalboquerque, and had been well treated by him, and gained both goods and other favours; but, not bearing this in mind, he had thrown his weight into the party of the Viceroy, always informing him of whatever he chose about Afonso, and always depreciating his merits. On this account, despiting his affairs, Afonso did not receive him graciously, and, when he was taking leave, sent word to him by a clerk that he begged him very much of his goodness not to trouble to have much conversation with him, nor to visit him, for he was his deadly enemy, and spoke ill of him, but when they should happen to meet in the streets of the place, he would make a show of courtesy towards him.

Jorge Barreto was ill pleased with the message, and went to Gaspar Pereira and related it to him, and told him that after this as he was going in to the church where Dalboquerque was attending mass he desired to speak with him, but he turned his eyes on the ground and made as though he had not perceived him. And he added that he was determined to go to the Factory to require the officials to draw up a statement of all these doings, to the end that the Viceroy, at his coming, should know the conduct of Afonso Dalboquerque.

In pursuance of advice which the Viceroy had given him, that he should mollify him in such a manner as to prevent any differences arising between them, Gaspar Pereira betook himself to Afonso Dalboquerque, and after relating the complaints laid against him by Jorge Barreto, told him that he did not consider the service of the king promoted by these differences, and that his being governor of India ought to be enough for him to put up with all this, and that they should reserve their disagreements until they reached Portugal; and he begged him to go and inspect the fortress (which he had not entered since his arrival) in order that the natives of Cochim should not say: "Wherefore would the captain-general not set his foot in the fortress, nor speak with the captain thereof?" Afonso replied that he would not have any converse with Jorge Barreto nor speak to him, because he held this resolve to be for the king's service on many accounts, for he was not only content, while at Ormuz, to be privy to the flight of the captains, but also when before the Viceroy he had done and said all that he could against him. And that as for stating that he had been unwilling to speak with him in the church, he would swear upon the Gospels (and here he laid his hand on a book beside him) that he did not observe him. As for speaking to him whenever they chanced to meet, this he would do, but other conversation there should not be between them. And in order to withdraw himself from these disagreements, he had given orders to the master and mariners of the *Cirne* that all should lay their complaints in person before Jorge Barreto, for he was Captain of Cochim, and he for his part did not intend to have anything to do with the matter.

On the conclusion of this affair, while Gaspar Pereira

and Antonio Real, Patrão Mór, and Ruy de Araujo, were standing on the bank, Jorge Barreto came up on horseback, and said to them that Afonso Dalboquerque had told Manuel Peçanha not to speak to him for it was against the good of the king's service, and that whoever listened to it would think all the evil in the world of him; and he begged them to be so gracious as to draw up a formal statement of these disturbances in order that the Viceroy might know what kind of unity there was between them; for he for his part had always been very loyal and served his king very well, and if ever at any hour he found himself in Portugal, he would ask whether or not it was to the service of the king to speak to him. Gaspar Pereira went away forthwith to Afonso Dalboquerque, and desired him earnestly to consign these differences to the devil, for there was no object to be gained by them, and they only gave occasion for gossip. And he replied that if he really thought so he might order them to get his brigantine ready for the passage to Cananor, in order that he might stay there out of sight of Jorge Barreto, and out of hearing of all these troubles.

When Gaspar Pereira discovered that Afonso Dalboquerque was annoyed by his desiring to patch up a friendship with Jorge Barreto, he betook himself to his own house, and said no more in the matter. And within the space of two days, they forwarded a letter of Lourenço de Brito, Captain of Cananor, to Afonso Dalboquerque, wherein he stated that he begged him of his favour to be very circumspect in his intercourse with the natives of Cochim, for he would assure him that in all the world he had never seen such a bad set of peeple; and he would have him also to know that nothing could be done or said in Cochim without the Viceroy being informed of it wherever he went. But in Cananor, where he was, he congratulated himself every morning when he rose, and begged God to preserve him from the bickerings and quarrellings of Cochim; and that he should not worry himself about things that had passed between him and the Viceroy at Cananor, for he hoped all would turn out well, and he would serve him (Afonso) well in India. And so he went on saying many other things very different to what he had said before the Viceroy, and begged he would tear up this letter without delay.

Reply of the Great Afonso Dalboquerque to Lourenço de Brito.

"I beg you of your favour to put your trust in me, for my experience and intelligence never wrecked a venture; and well do I believe that they report another thing now about me in India, but I forgive them all, for time and place compels them to do what they are doing. But before the King, our lord, with whom rests the reward of our services, all must speak the truth, and then shall be known all that has been done and is to be done in India. Think not that the country, or the customs of it, can avail to injure the powers which I hold from the King, our lord, because the noble spirit which I possess and my weighty knowledge easily dissipate all these differences, and I apply to all of them this verse of David, when he says: '*Si*[1] *Deus adjutor mihi, non timebo quid faciat mihi homo?*' Nevertheless, Sir, have no concern for me, but rather have it for the captains of the King, our lord, who hold their commissions and letters-missive of his Highness directed to me, wherein he holds me for his Captain-General in these parts of India, yet they are unwilling to obey me, although I presented myself in person at proper time, when the Viceroy had six vessels in freight and a strong monsoon to enable him to set out. And bear in mind that you showed me your letter, and I do not fail to remember the favour which you offered to do for me,

[1] Psalm cxviii, 6, *Dominus mihi adjutor*, etc. "The Lord is on my side; I will not fear: what can man do unto me?" [Ps. 118, 6.]

when the Viceroy was about to start for Diu, which was that I should remain behind as your Castellan while you went with him. Just so now, Sir, the advice and sufferance, which there in Cananor I had in these matters, I shall not fail to appreciate, now that I am here placed in a hut of straw, with the title of Càptain-General of these parts, as the King, our lord, calls me to-day in Portugal; and do you, Sir, believe that since all these things could hardly make any impression upon me when I was in Cananor, little power ought these mischief-makers to have over me in this land, where they are always repeating: 'Here he said good of the Viceroy, there he said bad of him.' These ceremonious speeches will not be found to proceed from me, nor is there anyone who dares to bring news to my inn, because this courtesy was ever mine, as well by nation as by creation; in this last I have nothing to say, for we all desire to serve the King. This is what I know in this hermitage, wherein I rest all day and all night; and with respect to what you say in desiring me to keep secret your communication to me, your letter was torn up immediately, without relating anything about it to anyone."

And with this letter they gave to Afonso Dalboquerque another from Pero Fernandez Tinoco, wherein he said that he ought not to rely on the promise of the Viceroy to hand over India when he returned from Diu, because after his departure to Cochim he had held a council with his captains, his friends, and retainers, and agreed not to deliver it up, but to send him (Afonso) to Portugal by the first opportunity of a fleet.

CHAPTER IV.

How the Viceroy, D. Francisco Dalmeida, after routing the Rumes, set out from Diu, and arrived at Cananor with Lourenço de Brito, and so on to Cochim: and of what took place with the great Afonso Dalboquerque on his arrival.

After the Viceroy had destroyed the fleet of the Rumes, he set sail and made his way to Cananor, where he received letters from Jorge Barreto, containing much bad news of the great Afonso Dalboquerque, and from Gaspar Pereira and Ruy de Araujo. And because Lourenço de Brito, Captain of the fortress, was the one who fomented these disturbances, he also, on his part, began to be in an ill-humour, and told him many things against Afonso Dalboquerque, having, it may be, forgotten the letter which he had written to him. The Viceroy, who had been informed of everything they told him had taken place, without making any stay, set forth, and reached Cochim on the eighth day of the month of March, in the year one thousand five hundred and nine, with determination of not rendering up to Afonso Dalboquerque the government of India, being urged to this by the captains who had fled from the war at Ormuz, and by others of their way of thinking. On receiving intelligence of the arrival of the Viceroy, Afonso Dalboquerque summoned before him the officers of the Factory and Gaspar Pereira, and told them that as the Viceroy was now arrived, he desired to make a requisition for the formal delivery of India to himself, which they, as officers of the King, might present to him. And just as they were all thus engaged, and Afonso Dalboquerque was writing the requisition with João Estão, news was brought that the Viceroy was coming down the river in the galley which he had captured from the Rumes. So the officers, as they were obliged to go and receive him, proceeded all together to the bank, and got into the boat with Jorge de

Melo, to accompany him. When the Viceroy saw them, he got out of the galley and went into the boat with them, and disembarked close to the fortress, where there were awaiting him all the clergy, drawn up in a procession, and Jorge Barreto, Captain of Cochim, with many people. So Afonso Dalboquerque left the requisition which he was drawing up, and, accompanied by some persons who were taking a meal with him, proceeded to receive the Viceroy, and stood a long while on the beach awaiting his landing. But he, as soon as he landed, made as though he did not see him, and went up at once directly towards Jorge Barreto, and embraced him, and paid many compliments both to him and to the others who were standing by.

Afonso Dalboquerque did not fail to notice the little count the Viceroy made of him, so he took hold of him by a tag of his brocaded over-dress, and said: "Ah, Sir, here I am; see me!" The Viceroy turned round to him, and begged pardon for not having seen him, and without saying another word began to walk on; and so they all went in procession to the church, and Master Diogo preached, greatly lauding the victory the Viceroy had achieved over the Rumes. When the Service came to an end, the Viceroy proceeded to the fortress, in company with the captains and men who were there, and just as he reached the gate Afonso Dalboquerque said to him: "Sir, seeing that God has given you so complete a victory, and you have avenged the death of your son with so much honour, and there is no more to do in the matter, I beg you of your grace let there be no differences between us, but deliver to me the government of India by these provisions which I here hold from the King, our lord; and trust me that I shall not allow it to be lost, as my enemies would make you believe, for even now in Cananor I sent the papers for your inspection by Antonio de Sintra but you would not look at them, and sent me word advising me to seal them up again."

While this conversation was taking place, Gaspar Pereira, whom the Viceroy had sent for, arrived, and Afonso Dalboquerque said to him: "Gaspar Pereira, as you are my scrivener, I require you, on the part of the King, our lord, to notify to the Lord Viceroy and to all the captains, fidalgos, and men here present these provisions, which here I deliver to you, whereby the King, our lord, commands the Lord Viceroy to deliver up to me India, and to set forth on the back of the papers an instrument containing his assent thereto or refusal, as the case may be." When Afonso Dalboquerque had made an end of saying these words, the Viceroy turned his back upon him, saying: "You have no scrivener dependent on you where I am," and without further reply betook himself indoors; and Gaspar Pereira, with the instructions given to him by Afonso Dalboquerque, went in behind the Viceroy, and so did many others; and they began to laugh and quarrel over his requisition. And João da Nova, who was one of them, began to say to the Viceroy that he would do well if he sent him loaded with irons to Portugal, for he was a fool, who knew not what he said; and that he, on his part, knew very well who it was that was advising him to walk in these silly ways, pointing all these hints at Gaspar Pereira.

CHAPTER V.

How the Viceroy behaved towards Gaspar Pereira and Ruy de Araujo and the other officers of the Factory, with regard to the interview which he had held with the great Afonso Dalboquerque.

After the Viceroy had remained for a while conversing of the affairs in which he had been engaged at Diu, he dismissed the meeting, and remained behind with Ruy de Araujo, André Diaz, Pedromem, Antonio de Sintra, and Gaspar Pereira, officers of the King, and Jorge de Melo, whom he desired to stay with him; and then he began to say: "Now that we are alone, I would like to talk a little about that which was said to me by that foolish Afonso Dalboquerque, who is so impertinent that he would not allow us to take any rest, nor reach home, but immediately that I disembarked said that I gave him a bad reception, and made a disturbance, which you all heard, styling Gaspar Pereira his scrivener. You can well see hereby with how little reason it is that he demands that I should deliver over to him the government of India, and is unwilling to talk sensibly about it. As for the blame of this, it rests with the King, who favours this foolish fellow, and therefore let him look to the consequences. And the wonder is, that you, Gaspar Pereira, when he styled you his scrivener, did not laugh nor nudge with your elbows those who stood beside you, and call him senseless; but as you did not do so, but received from him those papers that you have now in your hands, and did not undeceive him there and then that he was not to be governor of India, all this is a sign that you are agreeable to his doings, and that it is true that you and Ruy de Araujo are advising him to do all these things, although I could not have believed it if I had not been certified of it in Cananor. But be sure that this business shall not be cured with herbs[1] and ointments, but with cold iron; for it is a case of treason and rebellion against the King our Lord and his Viceroy in India." And then with increased passion he stood up erect on his feet, and taking hold of his uniform, said: "Gaspar Pereira, I vow to God, by this uniform, with which I have been invested, that if you carry on with this business any further, I will order you to be loaded with irons, and dragged along this beach; and as for the foolish Afonso Dalboquerque, I shall punish him thoroughly, if he says any more about it. So give him back his papers to take care of, for I will not look at them. And I vow to God that

[1] *Malvas*, mallows.

I will forthwith imprison any man, even though he be one of the best in India, who sides with his statements and demands."

The dismay the Viceroy produced was so great, that all the officers were trembling with fear; but Gaspar Pereira, as he was put out, took no notice of his passion, and said to him: "Wherefore does your Lordship treat these matters as if I had more to do with them than these other officers who are present? It seems as though you would mix me up in them, whereas I am only here as the officer whose duty it is to exhibit these instructions of the King our Lord, which Afonso Dalboquerque has given to me, to your Lordship." The Viceroy replied: "How is it then, that you consented that he should call you his scrivener?" Gaspar Pereira answered: "As your Lordship appears determined to argue to your own disadvantage,[1] I shall tell you. The King our Lord made him his Captain-General of India on the expiration of the time of your Lordship's rule, and me he made his secretary, and writes to me to that effect and to your Lordship as well, and in his instructions he says the same, and on this account your Lordship is wrong to reprove me for allowing him to style me his scrivener."

The Viceroy replied: "It will be as God pleases. I know not in good faith, for the King does not know what he is ordering, nor does he know what the true position of India is; let all the captains assemble, and then we shall know how this will turn out; for I will not deliver India to a madman who will hurl her into destruction." Gaspar Pereira said to him: "I know nought of all this, that is for your Lordship to determine about; all I have to do is to obey him whom the King our Lord shall order me to obey; and do you, who understand it better than I do, and have to give an account of it, do as you think fit." The Viceroy replied: "Deuce

[1] *Que isto quebre polo mais fraco*, literally, *that this should break where it is the weakest*.

take me, Gaspar Pereira; but you understand this better than I do or anyone else, and now I am not surprised except at the conduct of Ruy de Araujo, who is here before me, because he has done all the good he could to Afonso Dalboquerque, and is set up in opposition to me as well." Ruy de Araujo replied: "What have I done to your Lordship? or in what have I acted ungratefully for the kindness and honour which you have bestowed upon me? For I never spoke against you, nor is there anything to my knowledge in which I have acted against your interests. I came to assist at your reception on the beach, on your arrival; I would have kissed your hands, as of my superior, but you were unwilling to see me. But I well know that this does not spring from your Lordship; it is the doing of Jorge Barreto, who wishes me ill on account of a demand I have made upon him to desist from building a ship which he was desirous of constructing for himself contrary to the orders of the King, at a time when your Lordship was at Diu."

The Viceroy said: "You go the wrong way to work,[1] for all that you came to receive me, I would that you all had cat's-tails on your heads, like little imps; and I have found you very sullen, like men who were sorry to see me; for I can tell at once, when they pass by, by the way they put their feet on the ground, who they are who wish me well, and who they are that wish me ill." And by this time he was so much annoyed at the mention of Jorge Barreto, that he made use of very bad expressions and was all but laying hands on the speaker. But Ruy de Araujo, who was a man of good judgment, went out by the door, and betook himself home without another word.

Although the great Afonso Dalboquerque, in putting up with all these expressions which the Viceroy spoke against

[1] *Nao vai ella por hi.* The full expression is *Nao vai por ahi o gato ás filhozes.* "This is not the way the cat goes to her kittens," a proverbial and colloquial phrase. See *Vieyra.*

him, gained more honour than in the trouble which he had taken in the conquest of the kingdom of Ormuz, nevertheless it would have seemed right to me to remind the Viceroy, had he been alive, of the many acts of friendship which his great-great-grandfather had experienced at the hands of Gonçalo Lourenço de Gomide,[1] the great-grandfather of Afonso Dalboquerque, when he was private scrivener to the King D. João, of good memory, and very influential with him. I could say much upon this matter, but as he is dead, I must go on with the history, and leave to those who shall read it, to judge by the exploits of Afonso Dalboquerque whether or not the Viceroy was right in asserting that he was unfit to govern India.

CHAPTER VI.

Of what passed between the Viceroy and Gaspar Pereira, and of the message sent by the Viceroy through him to the great Afonso Dalboquerque; and how he gave an account to the officers of the Factory at Cochim, and to Jorge de Melo and the rest of the captains of what had happened with regard to the pepper; and of the doings of Anchecala with them, in the Factory.

Now, because the Viceroy was but little pleased with this interview which he had with Gaspar Pereira and the other officers of the Factory, after the lapse of three days he sent for him, and in the presence of Jorge Barreto told him that on the late occasion of conversing with him respecting the impertinences of Afonso Dalboquerque, he (Gaspar) had made use of some expressions, as though he wished him ill, and to these he (the Viceroy) had not then cared to reply because the house was full of people; but since his three years of government of India were finished (as had been alleged), why had he accepted the offices which he had given him to fill with him? Gaspar Pereira said to him: "I, sir, wish you no ill; as for these offices, you have given

[1] See his pedigree in Lansd. MS. 189, fo. 581b.

them to me without my asking you for them, when Afonso Dalboquerque was yet in Ormuz, and your Lordship used sometimes to say to me that when he arrived you would have forthwith to deliver up to him the government of India; and you used to laugh at those who advised you not so to yield the government to him; and your Lordship may remember that when Tristão da Cunha arrived here, they told you that Manuel Fernandez (who had accompanied him from Portugal) asserted that Afonso Dalboquerque had been appointed to the succession in India, on the expiration of the three years' service of your Lordship; and you replied to him who reported this to you, that you did not care whether you delivered the succession to Afonso Dalboquerque, or to a bird in the sky, provided that you had the King's orders. If this be so, in what have I erred in performing these duties to which your Lordship has appointed me?"

The Viceroy replied: "These are very fine speeches, which have no practical meaning; but how would you have me surrender so important a post as the government of India to a fool who would drive the country to destruction? There is Martin Coelho, and others with him, who even advised me to arrest him and send him in irons to Portugal." To this Gaspar Pereira answered: "These very men who gave you this advice go about saying, behind your Lordship's back, that more honour would accrue to you if you surrendered the command on Afonso's arrival here, than that which you gained by your victory over the Rumes. But since there is so much discord in this matter, I beg your Lordship to let me go, and as for the offices to which you have appointed me, give them to some one else, for the end of all this will be that the King will be sure to reward you both, while I shall be left to atone for all these differences. Yet I think that the person who busies himself with these scandalous tales would be doing far more service to the King if he would remind your Lordship that there is no pepper for loading the ships, in order that some provision for procuring it may be made. As it is, the officers of the King of Cochim, when they are asked for it, say there is none, and give no hopes of there being any."

When Jorge Barreto heard the allusions which Gaspar Pereira made, he replied: "How is it possible that we can have any pepper if Afonso Dalboquerque, Gaspar Pereira, and Ruy de Araujo advise the King not to deliver it, unless your Lordship surrender the government of India to Afonso Dalboquerque and retire to Portugal. This is the true reason why the pepper does not come, and not that which Gaspar Pereira states." The Viceroy was angry at this which Jorge Barreto said, and sent word to Afonso Dalboquerque by Gaspar Pereira to be prudent enough to abstain from showing any more to any one the powers and letters patent he had received from the King D. Manuel, and to make no more remonstrances with him, and not to call himself Captain-General of India; but that he might, if he chose, call himself captain of the ship *Cirne;* and from that day henceforth not to hold any more meetings in his house, for information had been laid that some of those men who frequented his table spoke much that was ill of the Viceroy.

And in addition he summoned the officers of the factory at Cochim, and Ruy de Araujo, and told them how Gaspar Pereira had stated that there was no pepper in the factory, nor expectation of getting any, and how he understood that all this arose from the foolishness of Afonso Dalboquerque, who had set himself up in his house with two men, one of whom he styled factor, and the other scrivener, and was paying them wages with the money he had brought with him from Ormuz. "For he wants", said the Viceroy, "to show the Indians that there are two of us chief captains, a thing very prejudicial to the service of the king, and worthy of punishment as a case of treason. But in truth it is I myself who am to blame, for I used to allow him to approach me every day, and associate with me, as others do who are much worthier than he is. The reason I do not now allow it is that I cannot possibly endure him, and I am irritated when I see him before me, for he is so imperious, and addresses me so cavalierly, that I cannot bear it, and all he speaks of is his services, and his honour, and the estimation due to his person. Now since this dissension between me and him is the cause of the pepper not arriving at the factory for the loading of the ships, I have summoned you here to give me your advice how to proceed in the matter."

Gaspar Pereira and Ruy de Araujo exclaimed that they had nothing to say in the business, but that his Lordship should obtain information of the truth of it, and proceed to do what he thought most to the service of the King our Lord. However, André Diaz, Antonio de Sintra, and Diogo Pereira thought that he ought to order him to deliver immediately to the King's factory all the merchandise and money which he had brought from Ormuz. Acting on this advice, the Viceroy sent word to Afonso Dalboquerque, by Diogo Pereira, to order all that had been brought from Ormuz to be delivered over to André Diaz, who acted as factor, and if anything were owing to him he would give order for its payment in the King's factory, for there must not be two factories nor two captains-major.

Afonso Dalboquerque replied to Diogo Pereira that he held no more money than was due to him for his salary and expenses. And since he had acquired possession of it with his lance in his hand, and had issued orders for the payment of fifteen thousand *cruzados* of wages to the men who had accompanied him, it was not very unreasonable that he should also pay himself out of the same fund. The Viceroy replied that it was quite right that he should be paid his dues, but the factor of his fleet was to proceed at once to give in his accounts to the officers of the King, and disburse no more payments. Afonso Dalboquerque, was annoyed at these messages, and said to Diogo Pereira: "Say to the Viceroy, let the factor make up his accounts, for all the good this will procure will be the punishment of him who goes about with these lying tales."

Now since these dissensions which had sprung up between them[4] were of public notoriety, a *Naire*[1] who was scrivener of the revenue of the King of Cochim, by name Anchecala, came to the factory where all the officers of the King had assembled; and after conversing about the cargo of pepper, told them that these matters of difference between Afonso Dalboquerque and the Viceroy seemed to the people on land to be in a bad state. And, he added, the King of Cochim, his lord, was one day talking to him on many subjects, and had said that he thought the Portuguese were opposed in opinion one with the other, but up to that time he had always believed that they were all of one accord, and perfectly obedient to the commands of their king. For the one thing the people of Malabar were most surprised at, and which caused them the most consternation, was the implicit obedience which the Portuguese tendered to their king, although they were so far distant from him; seeing that he had been told that even if a cabin boy were to arrive with a commission of the King of Portugal, every one would obey him. But now he observed so many differences among them, that all those on land were astonished, for they saw Afonso Dalboquerque put into a house, and the Viceroy making but little account of him, and that this thing ought not to be; but rather they ought to be great friends, and unanimous for the proper performance of the service of the King of Portugal: yet

[1] For explanation of this word, see Vol. i, page 4.

the Viceroy had sent word to him by Gaspar da India[1] that he did not intend to go back to Portugal, whereat he was much surprised, for the King D. Manuel, his brother, had written to him informing him of the Viceroy's recall and the appointment of Afonso Dalboquerque to be governor of India. Therefore he had made up his mind to send some ambassadors to Portugal to inform the King of all that was passing, and that the king, his lord, was much annoyed at the treating of Afonso Dalboquerque so ill before them all, and at the evil reports that were in circulation respecting him.

At this, André Diaz, who was there present, began to excuse the Viceroy's conduct; saying, that he was not to be blamed for the disturbances that had arisen with Afonso Dalboquerque, for the captains and all the people of India were unwilling to agree that he should return to Portugal, in so far as concerned the service of the king. But Anchecala, having concluded the business for which he had come, took his leave of the officers and went away; while André Diaz went to see the Viceroy, and repeated to him all that Anchecala had said before the officers in the factory. The Viceroy was greatly surprised at it, and said, "Does not the little he-goat of the King of Cochim know that I will order him to be taken back to that island, and will make him a *Caimal*[2] again as he used to be? and as for the he-goat of Candagora, I will punish him thoroughly well according to his deserts, for it is by him that this one is advised to talk in this manner". And with this show of anger he sent orders to Afonso Dalboquerque that he should not stir forth out of his house, nor hold any communication with the king, nor with his officers.

[1] This is probably *Gaspar Rodriguez*, the interpreter, who occurs frequently in Vol. i. The first edition also reads *Gaspar da India*.

[2] For the signification of this word, see Vol. i, page 3.

CHAPTER VII.

How Francisco de Tavora, owing to some words he had with Jorge de Melo Pereira concerning the great Afonso Dalboquerque, sent him a challenge, and what took place thereafter; and of the arrival of Diogo Lopez de Sequeira in India.

Jorge Barreto and João da Nova were so desirous that the Viceroy should stay in India, for they were the prime movers of this scheme, that they tried every means in their power to move the people to wrath against the great Afonso Dalboquerque. And they kept on going about from house to house, saying to the men that they ought to bear in mind how much they were indebted to the Viceroy, and how much more fitted than Afonso Dalboquerque he was to be Governor of India, and that the Viceroy had assured them that he was determined on no account to deliver up the government, as, indeed, they would soon see, and as things were in this state they ought not to frequent Afonso's house, nor eat with him, for they would thereby be ruining themselves.

Now inasmuch as Francisco de Tavora had been much angered at the Viceroy, and spoke very ill of him, because of injuries he had received at the hands of Jorge Barreto, who wished him harm (for in Ormuz he (Jorge) had stated to Afonso Dalboquerque that the captains had been advised to desert by him), Jorge Barreto did all he could to become reconciled with him, because he feared that as he (Francisco de Tavora) was on friendly terms with Jorge de Melo (who was a great friend of Afonso Dalboquerque, and constantly went to his house), he would be able to reckon him as a friend, and one who would go against the Viceroy. And in order to foster yet further this friendliness, the Viceroy was persuaded to permit Francisco da Tavora to repair his ship, and showed him some marks of kindness, for this was the principal cause of his complaints.

When Francisco da Tavora found that the Viceroy was favourable to him, and had given him instructions for getting his ship repaired, he imagined that Afonso Dalboquerque no longer was likely to obtain the government of India, as the others had indeed told him, so he began to circulate ill reports concerning him, in order to ingratiate himself still further with the Viceroy. Some time afterwards, one day when Jorge de Melo happened to be in Francesco da Tavora's house at night, conversing on current events, and saying that he considered it wrong of the Viceroy to give out openly that he would not return to Portugal, and that he would not deliver India into the hands of Afonso Dalboquerque (and this too in the presence of Fernão Perez de Andrade), Francisco de Tavora said to him: "Sir, you ought not to speak ill of the Viceroy, nor defame him." Jorge de Melo replied, "I never spoke ill of the Viceroy; and if you assert that I spoke ill of him, I must tell you that you do not speak the truth. But on the contrary, you yourself have oftentimes told me that you wished him ill, because he would not give you permission to repair your ship, and also because he had an enmity against you for not deserting from Ormuz when the other captains deserted. This is the truth, but now it seems you have changed sides, which is not the part of an honest man and a cavalier."

Hereupon many angry words passed between them, and next day, in the morning, Francisco da Tavora sent to Jorge de Melo a written challenge by the hands of Fernão Perez de Andrade. And when Fernão had arrived at Jorge de Melo's house, and had just given him the writing from Francisco de Tavora, there came in, close behind him, a servant of the Viceroy, who had been sent to summon Jorge de Melo before him, for he had been informed of all that had taken place, and understood that Francisco de Tavora had done this by the advice of every one, and thought that Jorge de Melo would attend to the Viceroy's summons, and not go to the duel, but remain thereby deprived of honourable satisfaction. But Jorge de Melo saw through the affair, and told the servant to return, for he would follow at once. And as soon as the servant had departed, he took a sword and a cloak,[1] and, accompanied by one of his servants, he made his way to the rope-yard, which was the place that Francisco de Tavora had appointed for the meeting.

When he had reached the appointed spot, he sent word twice to Francisco de Tavora that he was waiting there, and begged him not to delay. But meanwhile Antonio de Sintra had arrived at Francisco de Tavora's house, and summoned him to the Viceroy's, and after they got there, the Alcaide major went to seek for Jorge de Melo at the rope-yard, where he yet remained, and took him prisoner, and as they went in at the gate of the castle the Viceroy said to him :—"I promise you, Jorge de Melo, that you shall pay me for what you have said and for what you have done." He then ordered them to shut him up in the keep,[2] with fetters on his feet, and not allow any one to speak with him. When Afonso Dalboquerque heard of the imprisonment of Jorge de Melo, he went to the Viceroy, and begged him of his kindness to liberate him, and make them two friends again. But the Viceroy replied that the time was not yet come for this, for he would first of all have to issue a commission of enquiry, and then visit with justice the one who should be found to be in fault.

Afonso Dalboquerque, as soon as he understood this, was unwilling to speak any more for the liberation of Jorge de

[1] *Bedem*, a Moorish word, according to Bluteau and the dictionaries, but I am unable to identify it with any Eastern word of allied meaning.

[2] *Torre de menagem.* See Vol. i, p. 45.

Melo; but ten days afterwards there arrived Diogo Lopez de Siquiera, who came from Portugal as chief captain of four ships, and at his request the Viceroy ordered Jorge de Melo to be set at liberty, and made them friends again. This Diogo Lopez the King D. Manuel had sent to discover Malaca,[1] but he reached Cochim in very distressed condition, for after he had set out he never sighted the land again. And having brought his interview with the Viceroy to an end, and given him an account of all that the King ordered to be done, he went away to his house, accompanied by Jorge Barreto and Antonio do Campo, who began to say many things that were ill of Afonso Dalboquerque, and how thoroughly determined all the people of India were not to consent that he should be their governor, and how they, on their part, would advise him, as friends, if he wished to get well through his business, to take care not to make any show of friendship towards Afonso Dalboquerque, and not even to venture to his house.

Three days afterwards, the Viceroy sent for Diogo Lopez de Siquiera, and in the presence of Jeronymo Teixeira told him that he was especially gratified at his arrival at this juncture of events, for he had made up his mind to go to Portugal, taking Afonso Dalboquerque along with him (as it was not good for the King's service that he should become governor of India), and that he, Diogo, should remain as chief captain of India, until the King D. Manuel should provide for this matter as he thought best. But Diogo Lopez very politely thanked him for this kind mark of

[1] "Neste mesmo anno [1508] foy Diogo Lopez de Siqueira, Almotaçel moor de Reino, por Capitão mor de quatro Nauios, a çinco de Abril para Ir, descobrir, e Conquistar, Malaca: Capitães Jeronimo Teixeira (na não *Sta. Clara*), Gonçalo de Souza, e João Nunes.—E Voltou Cô todas as Naos a Saluamento ao Reyno."—British Museum, Additional MS., 20902, fo. 11 (but for another account of the expedition, see fo. 11*b*). Afonso Dalboquerque subjected Malaca to the Crown of Portugal, as will be seen further on.

favour he sought to bestow upon him, but all the same declined to accept any charge which the king had not laid upon him, and he hinted that if the Viceroy really sought to do him a favour, it would be in despatching him at once to prosecute the voyage appointed to him by the king.

The Viceroy did not really intend all this that he put forward, but only desired to gain over Diogo Lopez, and have him on his side, so he took no more steps to press on him the acceptance of the government, but ordered him to repair his ships, and gave him pilots, and all that was necessary for him in great abundance for his voyage. While on his part Diogo Lopez de Siquiera, in order to keep in good favour with the Viceroy, commenced from that time forward to withdraw himself from the conversation of Afonso Dalboquerque, and to exculpate the captains for their desertion.

CHAPTER VIII.

Of the requisition which Jorge Barreto and João da Nova, in accordance with the opinion of some of the captains, made to the Viceroy D. Francisco Dalmeida, that he should not deliver the government of India to Afonso Dalboquerque, and of the counsel they all took upon this matter.

For all that the Viceroy would have been glad to remain in India, nevertheless, he was in dread that the King D. Manuel would not receive him favourably, so he was ever seeking for means whereby he might let him know how great the service was that he was performing in retaining his government. And although by means of the Prior of Crato,[1] his brother, he had already essayed this, one day,

[1] Crato, or Ocrato, near Portalegre, contains a castle and a Royal Priory, which is the largest and richest house of the Order of Malta, or Knights Hospitallers, in the whole of Portugal. See Juan Alverez de Colmenar, "*Les Delices de l'Espagne et du Portugal;* and Zedler's *Uni-*

when he was talking with Jorge Barreto and João da Nova, he said to them that they could see very well how India stood in great risk of being lost if Afonso Dalboquerque remained therein; but yet he, for his part, could do nought else than return to Portugal and obey the mandates of the King his Lord, unless the captains and all the people of India made him a formal request that he should not go. For he dreaded lest the king of Cochim, by reason of the hatred which he had towards him, and by reason of the kindliness which he evinced for Afonso Dalboquerque, should write to the king of this business which had taken place from a different point of view.

Thereupon João da Nova and Jorge Barreto, who were the principal ones who wove this web, combined themselves with Antonio do Campo, André Diaz, Diogo Pereira, Antonio de Sintra, and Diogo Pirez (who was governor to D. Lourenço), and arranged a requisition for presentation to the Viceroy. And when they had drawn it up, they both of them went about from house to house to the captains and fidalgos, and showed it to them, and begged them to sign it, since they knew that Afonso Dalboquerque was a man of great inaptitude, and covetous, and of no sense, and one who knew not how to govern anything, much less so great a charge as the Empire of India. And after that many had so signed the document (in order that this requisition might go with better credit before the King D. Manuel), they made their way to the King of Cochim, and took with them Antonio de Sintra, and told the king to look well after his own interests, for Afonso Dalboquerque was in the habit of corresponding with the Çamorim, and had promised to make peace with him directly after being appointed Governor of India, and to establish in Calicut a factory house.

versal Lexicon. The Priors or Grand-Priors were usually of royal birth or noble family, and possessed not only great ecclesiastical power but a considerable amount of political influence.

They told the king, in addition, that the captains and all the people of India, by reason of the dread they felt at all these matters, and likewise by reason of what was due to their service, had prepared a requisition to the Viceroy, begging him not to leave India, and that they desired him earnestly of his graciousness that he on his part would deign to be favourable to this their business, for in all the country there could not be found any one who with better reason than himself ought to condole with them at the turn the King of Portugal's affairs had taken.

To them the King of Cochim made answer that he did not intend to do such a thing, because it did not appear that it would be to the service of the King of Portugal to do so: but on the contrary he thought it wrong of the Viceroy not to resign the government of India to Afonso Dalboquerque, in accordance with the commands of the King of Portugal. It was not long before the Viceroy was informed of the replies of the King of Cochim, and thereupon he sent word to Afonso Dalboquerque that the officers of the factory were complaining that the king was unwilling to send any pepper to the scales, out of love for him; and, therefore, he (Afonso) must take care not to send any more messages to the king. And so Afonso Dalboquerque, in order not to give occasion for quarrelling, withdrew himself from all communication with the king. And now that João da Nova and Jorge Barreto had completed their documents, on a Monday, the fifteenth day of May, in the year fifteen hundred and nine, the Viceroy commanded that all the captains of India, and the fidalgos, who were in Cochim, should be called to a council. Some of these captains were inimical to Afonso Dalboquerque, because he had accused them of the weakness they had shown in letting D. Lourenço, his chief captain, be dashed to pieces, especially Diogo Pirez, D. Lourenço's governor.

It was on the occasion of this calamity that D. Lourenço,

when he saw Diogo Pirez going down the river in the galley (according to the relation afterwards given by Alvaro Lopez, master of his ship, who was then taken captive), said to him:—"O thou traitor of a Jew, get thee far away from me, for I promise thee that if I escape from this, since I have been deceived with thee, before my father, I will kill thee with my fists, for thou couldst have assisted me with the galley, but thou wouldst not."

There were present also at this meeting the captains who had fled from Ormuz, and Antonio de Mendonça, Manuel Peçanha, and Diogo Lopez de Siqueira. When all were met together, Jorge Barreto, who was the one on whom it devolved to open the business, stood up and declared that these lords who were present there requested him with one accord, not to deliver India to Afonso Dalboquerque until his Highness should be informed of the wickedness and tyrannies that he had committed in the kingdom of Ormuz, as could be seen set out in the articles which they there and then laid before the Viceroy, together with the formal requisition.

Hereupon the Viceroy ordered the immediate reading of the text of the requisition and the articles, before all, by Antonio de Sintra. And when they had been read, he told them that it was their duty to observe carefully the matter into which they were entering, because that business was of great importance. And if he were to do that which they desired of him, they on their part would have to write to the king that they had advised him so to do; for his Highness had confided the state of India to their forethought and sense. "And principally," he added, "let Senhor Manuel Peçanha, who is here present, look to it; for the King our Lord orders that if I die, he is to remain governing India, therefore it properly falls upon him to see to these matters."

As soon as the Viceroy had uttered these words, Manuel

Peçanha exclaimed:—"Sir, we cannot consent to your lordship going to Portugal; for it is no service to the king to yield the government of India to Afonso Dalboquerque, for the reasons that are specified in this requisition. And, inasmuch as we are all in a state of great concern, it is most probable that, if your lordship goes, all will have to go in your company. This I state publicly, for I do not pretend to anything more here beyond the service due to the king." So Manuel Peçanha made an end of his arguments, and all agreed that the Viceroy ought not to go to Portugal, but to govern India until the King our Lord should be informed of all this, and ordain what seemed most befitting for his service. And notwithstanding that there were many persons in this council who had uttered evil words against Afonso Dalboquerque, and signed the requisition, yet when they went out they became aware of their errors, and sent to ask his forgiveness; for they had done this, they said, out of dread of dishonouring the Viceroy. Yet I cannot admit this as any excuse for them, seeing that the state of the king, however far off it may be, should never be a single hour removed from its obedience to him, and from his disposal, even at the cost of life, much less threats and dishonour.

When the Viceroy had arranged this in the manner he liked best, he gave orders to Antonio de Sintra to draw up an indictment against Afonso Dalboquerque from these articles, which were in number ninety-six; he wrote, too, to Cogeatar, if he had any complaints to make against Afonso Dalboquerque, to send some person who should come and prefer the accusation, for he would see that justice was done. As soon as the indictment had been drawn up, the Viceroy commanded Antonio de Sintra to keep it in his possession, and well taken care of until the arrival of the ships from Portugal, when there would be an opportunity of conferring with the chief captain concerning the best course to be pursued.

But Afonso Dalboquerque became aware of their doings, and knew that the Viceroy was desirous of ensnaring him in some difficulties, so in order that they should not lay anything to his charge without sufficient reason, he adopted as a very safe one, the precaution of not venturing out of his house, and of leading that kind of life which he could most quietly pass in the service of the king. And I thoroughly believe that had he not done so, it would not have been possible to avoid a great revolt in India; but his endurance was so great, that there was not a single person who heard him speak ill, or even complain, of those whom he had reason to reproach, because of their former friendship with him, for having signed the requisition, nor yet for having said that he was unable to govern India. And it was well-known after he became captain-general, what he did and how he carried on the government. But it is to be believed that a man so honourable and so much a cavalier as the Viceroy (had he been at that time alive), must have been much grieved at having given so much dishonour and so many affronts as he did, by evil counsel, to this great captain.

CHAPTER IX.

Of the events which took place after the council, and how the Viceroy gave orders for the apprehension of João de Christus, Friar of the Order of St. Eloy, and what happened thereupon.

Now that it had been determined by all the fidalgos and captains that the Viceroy should not go to Portugal, but remain in the government of India, thenceforth many men took upon themselves the boldness of showing all the discourtesy they could towards Afonso Dalboquerque, with the object of doing or saying something or other whereby they could calumniate him. But he saw through the conspiracy which they had entered upon, to the prejudice of his honour in order to curry favour with the Viceroy; and, therefore, began to withdraw himself from conversation with them. And when several days had elapsed, during which he had not gone out of doors, one day, in the morning, he went out to the shore, accompanied by his servants (for now no one ventured to be seen in his company) to look at the ship *Cirne*, which was undergoing repair. And as he passed by the door of Antonio do Campo's house, Jorge Barreto and Fero Barreto, who were in the house, came to the window and began to mock him with disgusting noises, and called out "Jew!" and "traitor!" But Afonso Dalboquerque kept on his way without replying to them, and after spending some time on the shore, he returned home by another way.

Jorge Barreto, Pero Barreto, and Antonio do Campo were, however, not content with the endurance of Afonso Dalboquerque, so they all three made their way to the shore, but by the time they reached it he had already gone away; and then they commenced saying that if they had found him there, they would have broken his head for him; for he was, they said, so vain and so ill-bred, that he would not speak to Jorge Barreto, but had said that it was against the king's service to speak to him, yet he would be made to pay for this that he had said. Hereupon, Garcia de Sousa, who happened to be within hearing of this affair (he was an honest fidalgo and kept himself aloof from all these disturbances), reproved them very strongly for the expressions which they used, and went straightway to the Viceroy, and said to him:—"Sir, you have always shown me much regard, and bestowed on me great honour, and I shall ever owe you service for it, as I rightly should; and not only on this account, but also because it is proper for your service, I have to tell you of something which has just taken place before me on the shore, which does not appear right to me." And then he related to him all that Jorge Barreto, Pero

Barreto, and Antonio do Campo had said to [and about] Afonso Dalboquerque; and how João da Nova and Antonio de Sintra were in the habit of passing every night by his door, singing verses upon him which were very discourteous. "And when your lordship was in Diu," he added, "Jorge Barreto ordered them by night to wound his men; and Francisco de Tavora, when a page of Afonso Dalboquerque passed by him without taking off his cap, took the page and kicked him frequently, and pulled his hair. And they do all these things out of an idea that thereby they are doing you a service, but it may be that your lordship has no knowledge of it, so I tell you that you may order them to be very well punished for it."

The Viceroy said that he was very much obliged to him for this information, and that he did not know of their deeds, for Afonso Dalboquerque was such a miserable fellow that there was no one who cared for him, yet he had already sometimes told João da Nova that he was a foolish chatterer, and that he could not countenance him in such proceedings, but he would soon provide about the matter. Yet the Viceroy had so little intention of chastising them, that three days afterwards, when Jorge Barreto was proceeding on horseback to the castle, he came upon Afonso Dalboquerque's purveyor in the road, and told him to go back. But when the man would not, alleging that he had permission from the Viceroy to go thither, he said to him:—"You goat, will you not do what I command you?" And then he got down off his horse, and beat him several times with a stick, and carried him before him up to the house of the magistrate *(Meirinho)*, and ordered him to be placed in gaol. When the Viceroy knew this he ordered the man to be released; but yet he did not reprove Jorge Barreto for what he had done.

And notwithstanding that everybody was intimidated, and did not dare to utter any complaints against the Viceroy's doings, nevertheless, when some noblemen were found in the house of João de Christus (a brother of the order of Saint Eloi, and of very virtuous life), they were much surprised that the Viceroy did not reprove him. João de Christus, who was an upright man, remarked:—"I really believe that India cannot endure long with all this uproar, for Jorge Barreto, who is the deadly enemy of Afonso Dalboquerque, assaults his purveyor and gets off without either punishment or reprehension of it." Diogo Rodriguez, the scrivener of the ship *Flor de la mar*, who happened to be present, heard this, and went to João da Nova (thinking to give him a capital opportunity for exercising his ill-will), and repeated to him all that João de Christus had said.

Immediately thereupon, João de Nova made his way to Jorge Barreto, and then both proceeded to the Viceroy, and related the matter to him; and began to demonstrate to the Viceroy that if João de Christus on the occasion of Jorge Barrato cudgelling a villain (even though he were Afonso Dalboquerque's purveyor), could say that by reason of such things India would be ruined, this could not be so said unless the speaker knew for certain that Afonso Dalboquerque had resolved upon some such act of treason as to seize the fortress and put Jorge Barreto to death: and therefore his lordship ought to issue immediate orders for the apprehension of João de Christus, and keep him in irons until he should confess the truth, for he was very friendly towards Afonso Dalboquerque, and never went out of doors. The Viceroy received favourably all this that they said against Afonso Dalboquerque, and without any further enquiry into the allegations, but solely on the report of these men, ordered the immediate arrest of João de Christus, and loaded him with irons, and put him in a cellar in the fortress, and allowed no one to have any communication with him.

CHAPTER X.

How the great Afonso Dalboquerque, upon hearing of the apprehension of João de Christus, went to speak with the Viceroy in his behalf: and how the Viceroy gave orders to take Afonso Dalboquerque and carry him to Cananor, and raze to the ground the houses wherein he lived.

As soon as the news of the imprisonment of João de Christus was known in Cochim, all gave themselves up for dead, for they could not divine the reason of his imprisonment. But Afonso Dalboquerque, who did not know all of these uproars, proceeded to the Viceroy's, and begged him very earnestly of his kindness to give orders for the release of João de Christus, for he was so good a man that he could not believe that there was anything in him for which he should deserve that imprisonment.

The Viceroy replied very dryly that he should let justice take her course, for the Vicar-General would take good care to order his release, provided that in the indictment which was to be laid against him he should find no cause of blame; as for himself he knew nothing about it. Afonso Dalboquerque replied:—"Sir, I do not understand this justice of yours, apprehending, indeed, João de Christus without any reason, when he is a very virtuous man, and yet not ordering the hanging of Domingos Pousado, for I know very well that he was yesterday caught in the act of stealing two hundred cruzados, but as he was in Antonio do Campo's house, nothing is said about him."

The Viceroy could not bear to be spoken to about these men, so he rejoined that many had complained of him (Afonso) also for the insults he had visited upon them at Ormuz, and on the way there; but he had never spoken about the matter to him, to ask him the reason of such conduct. Afonso Dalboquerque replied, that all the harm he had done was to execute justice upon those who deserved it, and let him look to his instruction, and therein he would see that there was no appeal from one appellate jurisdiction to another, but only to the king, who up to that hour had delegated that superior power to no one. The Viceroy, who had now become enraged, answered, that he (Afonso) did not understand what justice was, nor knew how to exercise it; but that he (the Viceroy) understood it, for he was not so much a Viceroy, but a King, so long as he held that office, as indeed the traitorous rascal, Gaspar Pereira, could inform him. Afonso Dalboquerque retorted that he had reached the age of sixty years, and had lived till then without the advice of Gaspar Pereira, and how could it be that he thought he required such advice now more than ever. But if he, the Viceroy, was what he represented himself to be, why did he not order him to be hanged, since he had the power to do it?

The answer of the Viceroy to this was, that after the victory which Our Lord had given him over the Rumes, he had continually dissembled his anger with him, and did not wish to punish him, but would carry him to Portugal, where the king would order his execution as a traitor. When Afonso Dalboquerque perceived that the Viceroy did not intend to liberate João de Christus, he took his leave, for he did not wish to commit himself in any words with him, and returned to his house. And so soon as he had gone, the Viceroy gave orders for placing a strong guard over the fortress of Cochim, remembering what Jorge Barreto[1] and João de Nova had told him, and for issuing several proclamations to the effect that no one should carry arms neither by day nor by night, excepting only his servants, and the captains, and some persons specially licensed to do so; and he also ordered the arrest of Gaspar Pereira and

[1] See the genealogy of Jorge Barreto in the British Museum, Lansdowne MS. 189, fol. 506, entitled "Livro das Linhagês de Portugal, ordenado por Dõ Antonio de Lima P[erei]ra, anno 1620".

Ruy de Araujo, and their solitary confinement, loaded with irons, in the fortress, and no one to talk with them; and he also ordered the houses in which they had lived to be thrown down, and razed to the ground.

And as the intention of these men was to eject Afonso Dalboquerque from Cochim, thinking that they could effect this by means of his confessor, Francisco, a Friar of the Order of Avis,[1] they went to him and told him that if he would say how Afonso Dalboquerque had desired to put Cogeatar to death, and raise himself up in rebellion at Ormuz, that they on their part would prevail upon the Viceroy to show him some marks of favour, and give him substantial rewards for so doing. Friar Francisco replied to them that he knew nothing more of Afonso Dalboquerque than that he saw how very well he served the king, and captured towns and places in the kingdom of Ormuz, and he would say so to the Viceroy, if they liked. So, as they could get nothing from Friar Francisco to turn to advantage in their hands, they prevailed on the Viceroy to order the arrest of Duarte de Sousa,[2] who was a fidalgo indeed, but poor, and had come from Portugal in banishment, accompanying the fleet of Afonso Dalboquerque, and had remained in his company during the conquest of the kingdom of Ormuz, and served him so well that Afonso Dalboquerque remitted his

[1] See vol. i, Introduction, p. vii, note 2.

[2] "Duarte de Sousa, filho segundo bastardo do Comendador mor Gonçallo de Sousa, foi Comendador do Mogadouro da ordem de Chr[is-t]o, e houve bastardos Ruy de Sousa, Gonçallo de Sousa, João de Sousa, Manoel de Sousa, Cri[stin]a de Sousa, *etc.* Este Duarte de Sousa pellos tempos poderia ser aquelle que servio na India em tempo de VizoRey Dom Francisco de Almeida em que foi Castigado por aconselhar a A[fons]o de Albuquerque, indo suçeder naquelle Governo, que o tomasse por forsa contra vontade do dito VizoRey".—British Museum, Additional MS. 28460, folio 146*b*.

"Duarte de Sousa, . . . irmão de Fernão de Sousa, Comendador mor, . . . houve bastardos Ruy de Sousa, e Gonçalo de Sousa, que morrerão na India Solteyros," *etc.*—Brit. Mus., MS. Lansdowne 189, folio 65*b*.

banishment, and ordered the employment both of him and of a son he had, at a certain salary. Now since this Duarte de Sousa lived at Afonso Dalboquerque's table, and served him, and João de Nova never could entice him away from this allegiance, they imputed to him the design of putting the Viceroy to death, although he was perfectly innocent of it, and arrested him, and put him to the rack.[1]

When João de Nova and Jorge Barreto perceived that neither by means of Friar Francisco, nor yet by means of Duarte de Sousa, they could give effect to the plot they were embarking in, they entered into a conspiracy with Antonio do Campo, who was well versed in the language of Malabar, and concocted a letter from the Prince of Calicut to Afonso Dalboquerque, and his reply to him, inserting in it all the malicious things they required to say, and managed with great secrecy that the two documents should fall into the hands of the Viceroy. And the Viceroy, as soon as he saw the letters, being concerned at what was therein contained, ordered the arrest of Afonso Dalboquerque; and immediately, that very day, he was embarked on board the vessel of Martin Coelho, who had orders to carry with him none but three servants for his attendance, and to deliver him over to Lourenço de Brito, captain of the fortress, who was to place him in the tower, and keep a good guard over him.

On the departure of Martin Coelho, the Viceroy gave orders for throwing down the houses which Afonso Dalboquerque had occupied, and took out of them everything that was found there, which produced great consternation in the king of Cochim and the *Ñaires*, for he said that it was a case of treason, and very necessary for the good of the king of Portugal's estate that he should punish Afonso Dalboquerque with rigour. And as by this time Diogo Lopez de Sequeira was now ready with his fleet to set out

[1] *Dar tratos*, literally, to give (one) a treat.

for Malaca, and as Garcia de Sousa was to go in his company as captain of one of the ships, the Viceroy ordered that Ruy de Araujo and Nuno Vaz de Castelo-branco should be delivered over to them, to be taken in their charge to Malaca, and thence to proceed with Diogo Lopez de Sequeira[1] to Portugal, as they were implicated in these matters concerning Afonso Dalboquerque.

CHAPTER XI.

How D. Fernando Coutinho, Marshal of Portugal, arrived at Cananor, and carried with him the great Afonso Dalboquerque, to govern India.

The affairs of India were in the state which I have described, when the Marshal D. Fernando Coutinho arrived at Cananor, having set out from the kingdom of Portugal as chief captain of a fleet of fifteen sail. And in Cananor the Marshal, who proceeded to take up his quarters the

[1] "Diogo Lopez de Sequeyra filho segundo deste Lopo Vaz [de Sequeyra] foy Alcayde Mor do Landroal, e Almotaçe Mor (*i.e.*, Chief Magistrate of the Markets) d' ElRey Dom João o 3°. E foy Governador da India, e casado com Dona Maria Freyre, filha de N°. Francisco Freyre de Beja, que elle quizera matar por dizerem fizera adulterio com Christovão Freyre seu Primo com Irmão quando foy a 1ª vez a India", *etc.*—Brit. Mus., MS. Lansdowne 189, f°. 588*b*. The following remarkable incident is related of his voyage in 1518:—"Na paragem do Cabo da Boa Esperança hum peixe deu huma encontrada na naô de D. João de Lima, que cuidarão alguñs no estremecer, que ella fez, que dera em algum penedo, e acudindo logo â bomba, parecendo, que a naô devia fazer agoa, acharão que nam fazia mais, que a ordinaria, e dando depois em Cochim pender â naô acharamlhe metido no Costado hum focinho de peixe, que seria do Comprimento de dous palmos, e meyo agudo na ponta, preto e duro â Maneira de Corno das alimarias, a que os Gregos chamam Rhinoceros, e os Indios Ganda, somente tinha esta peixe huma differença, que a Crespidam de sua superficie era â maneira de groza de ferro tam dura, que o limava, como faz huma lima de dura tempera."—Brit. Mus., Additional MS. 20902, f°. 21. The same account is given in other words in Barretto de Resende's work, the Sloane MS. 197, f°. 15.

very day he landed with Lourenço de Brito, found the great Afonso Dalboquerque, who had already been confined there for three months by order of the Viceroy.

Afonso Dalboquerque was much pleased at the arrival of the Marshal, for besides that he was his nephew, he felt certain that on his coming the dissensions which had arisen between himself and the Viceroy would come to an end, and he recounted to him all the insults that had been shown to him, and all the rest that had happened to him. The Marshal, because his time was short, in which to perform what had been appointed for him to do before his departure for Portugal, was unwilling to be delayed, and proceeded to embark on the following morning, taking with him Afonso Dalboquerque, in obedience to his commands, as Captain-general of India; for it was to Afonso Dalboquerque, as his governor of India, that the King D. Manuel had ordered the Marshal to deliver all the provisions and specie which he carried. And the Marshal told Lourenço de Brito, that he, for his part, could not perceive where the faults of Afonso Dalboquerque lay, for the Viceroy to be obliged to arrest him, and to refuse to deliver up the government of India to him.

Lourenço de Brito replied that all he knew about it was, that the Viceroy had sent him to be kept in custody, and to be carefully guarded, and if the Viceroy had done thereby anything which he should not have done, the king must take account of this from him. When this conversation was at an end, the Marshal took his leave of Lourenço de Brito, and set out and reached Cochim on the twenty-ninth day of October; and on his arrival the Viceroy commanded Antonio de Sintra to pay him a visit. And this Antonio, as soon as he boarded the vessel and beheld Afonso Dalboquerque, became quite beside himself with astonishment. But after paying the visit to the Marshal, he began talking about other matters, and said unadvisedly to Afonso Dalboquerque, that the Viceroy had now become aware that the letter alleged to have been written by him to the Prince of Calicut was a forgery. He (Afonso) was unwilling to reply to him, for he well knew that Antonio de Sintra had been a party to this fraud.

Then Antonio de Sintra took his leave of the Marshal, and returned with a message for the Viceroy. But the captains and fidalgos, who had signed the requisition, so soon as they were informed that the Marshal brought with him Afonso Dalboquerque, and obeyed him as Captain-general of India, became beside themselves, and knew not how to make up their minds for any further action. Nevertheless, Afonso Dalboquerque, with his accustomed inviolable serenity and frankness of spirit forgave them, as will be shown further on. And on the following morning both (the Marshal and Afonso Dalboquerque) disembarked, and the Viceroy came down to the shore to receive them, accompanied by all those who were of his party; for the whole of the other party were unwilling to accompany him. And in this manner all proceeded to the church, and when the service was over, the Viceroy retired to the fortress, and the Marshal and Afonso Dalboquerque to the houses which had been appointed for their occupation. And on that very night there arrived Lourenço de Brito in a *caravela*,[1] making this journey to visit the Viceroy, to know how the Marshal would manage with him, and also to arrange for his voyage, for he was determined to go with him back to Portugal, and not remain in India with Afonso Dalboquerque.

And it was on a Saturday morning, the fourth day of November, that the Marshal went to the fortress to pay a visit to the Viceroy, and had a long conversation with him on many subjects in relation to the dissensions that he had with Afonso Dalboquerque; and tried all in his power to reconcile them again, but he could never prevail upon

[1] See vol. i, page 4, note 3.

Afonso Dalboquerque to let him effect his purpose. And although the Viceroy held a power from the king to retain the government of India until his departure, yet when he observed the uproars that the people made, he surrendered the government of India to Afonso Dalboquerque in order that he should not be troubled with any ill messages, and to avoid having any further annoyance about him. And then he embarked on the Sunday following, which was the fifth day of the month of November, and there he remained on board, arranging for his departure until the tenth day of the same month, when he left for Cananor, in the ship *Garça* (i.e. *Heron*), wherein he intended to make the voyage to Portugal, telling the captains who were to convoy him to proceed at once to follow him up closely, for it was his intention to make the journey from Cananor.

Thereupon Jorge de Melo Pereira, captain of the ship *Betlem* (i.e. *Bethlehem*), on hearing this order of the Viceroy, went to the Marshal and told him that he could not, for anything in the world, go in the company of the Viceroy, who was ill disposed towards him, and had had him in custody, since he feared that he would maltreat him on the way, and therefore he would much prefer to wait and go with him (the Marshal). The Marshal went to the Viceroy, and informed him of the demur which Jorge de Melo made to going in his company, and begged him graciously to forget and forgive past matters, and to be pleased to take him with him, for he would be a good companion; and so indeed it turned out, for at the watering-place of Saldanha, where the Viceroy was murdered,[1] there was not a relative nor a friend who behaved with greater kindness to him than did Jorge de Melo. The Viceroy took with him Jorge Barreto, Antonio do Campo, and Manuel Telez, and many other men of noble rank, whom they induced to go by putting them in great dread of remaining behind with Afonso Dal-

[1] See vol. i, page 33, note 2.

BRIT. MUS., SLOANE MS. 197, FOLIO 9.

P. BARRETO DE RESENDE'S PORTRAIT OF

D. FRANCISCO DALMEIDA.

boquerque. There is much that I could write about this; but, in order to avoid scandalising the living, I will be silent about what I know concerning the dead. And João da Nova, who was the one who walked in these disturbances with Jorge Barreto, died at Cochim in the month of July in the year 'nine, so reduced in circumstances that he had no one to care for him; but Afonso Dalboquerque forgot all that he had been guilty of towards him, and only held in memory that this man had been his companion in arms, and had helped him in all the troubles connected with the conquest of the kingdom of Ormuz like a cavalier, and ordered him to be buried at his expense, with the usual display of torches, and himself accompanied the body to the grave, clad all in mourning, a thing the Viceroy would not have done. These are the rewards which the world gives to him who does not do what he ought to do.

As soon as the Viceroy had sailed for Cananor, the King of Cochim came to pay a visit to Afonso Dalboquerque and to the Marshal; and when the formalities of the visit had passed, the Marshal said to the King, that he begged his royal Lordship very earnestly to command his officers to get ready fifteen thousand *quintals* of pepper which were required for loading the cargoes of the ships, for the Viceroy had told him that he could load them all with pepper for them if he pleased. The King said that he would have been very happy to serve him if he could, but it was impossible for him to have so much pepper, because in the year just passed there had been so slack a guard kept on that coast, that six vessels of Calicut had sailed, loaded with pepper, for the Straits of Meca;[1] and other ships, which took in the same cargo in Coulão and Caecoulão,[2] had sailed for

[1] See vol. i, page 58, note 1; and the "Portus da mequa" on the map in vol. i, at page 80.

[2] *Caecoulão* is the *Calecoulan* of Pedro Berthelot's chart, MS. Sloane 197, fo. 164; and the *Kayan Koulam* of modern maps of India, in Tra-

Choramandel. And this, he averred, was the truthful reason why he had no old pepper. And he added that it was not right for André Diaz and Antonio de Sintra to tell him (the Marshal), on the part of the Viceroy, in the presence of many persons, that he was unwilling to forward pepper to the factory because Afonso Dalboquerque had given him a hundred *cruzados* by way of a bribe, threatening him that unless the pepper were at once forthcoming, another king would be set up in his place, who was the friend of the Çamorim, and would make peace with him. And that he (the King) could not believe him to be capable of such an action as this piece of villainy which the Viceroy had threatened to do if the ships were not laden, and that quickly; for, apart from the service he would be doing to the King his brother, it was not likely that he would care to lose six thousand *cruzados*, which would come to him as dues out of the transaction, for the sake of a hundred *cruzados* of bribe which Afonso Dalboquerque was stated to have given him.

The Marshal told him not to be dismayed, for this was a way of speaking which the officers affected, but the Viceroy ought not to send such messages as that he complained of, for all of them were his vassals, and the King his lord had ordered them all to obey him. At this reply of the Marshal the King of Cochim was quite contented, and took leave of him, and of Afonso Dalboquerque, undertaking on his part to spare no trouble in forwarding all the pepper there could be found to the scales.

vancore, Madras Presidency, 9 deg. 10 min. N., 76 deg. 31 min. E., on the coast a little to the north of Coulão, Quilon, or Collum.

CHAPTER XII.

How the Marshal told the great Afonso Dalboquerque that the King D. Manuel gave orders for the destruction of the City of Calicut, and of what passed in this matter.

When this interview which the Marshal held with the King of Cochim had come to an end, because his object was to destroy Calicut before he set out for Portugal, in order not to lose any time on the following day, he summoned to his house Gaspar Pereira, Secretary of India, and told him privately that the King had trusted greatly in him, and ordered him in his instructions to destroy Calicut before his departure, if it should seem good to Afonso Dalboquerque, and therefore he begged him graciously to be minded to help him in the matter (for if this project were to fail, he would not have come to India on any account, seeing that his ancestors were never mere merchants), and that up to this time Afonso Dalboquerque had not mentioned the matter to any one, although Manuel Peçanha, if the reports that were in circulation at Cochim were true, had attempted to sound him on the subject very often, making light of the matter. And he added that he, Gaspar, must obtain knowledge of Afonso Dalboquerque's opinion; and if he should appear to have doubts, he must remove them, for there were some persons who would make him believe that Afonso Dalboquerque would disapprove of the plan.

Gaspar Pereira told him that it could not be that there would be any opposition, for he, Afonso, had always evinced a hearty good will towards the destruction of Calicut, and he was sure Afonso Dalboquerque would reward him for the intelligence when he announced it, and therefore he would not shrink from mentioning the matter to him, and for his part he would do all he could to be of use in every way;

yet, he said, he would beg him earnestly to proceed cautiously and slowly in the affair, taking advice from all persons who had any good understanding of it, for it was not such a light thing as Manuel Peçanha would have them to suppose. When this interview was over, Gaspar Pereira made his way to Afonso Dalboquerque's house, and recounted to him what had passed between himself and the Marshal; and, as Afonso Dalboquerque was anxious to gratify the Marshal in all things, one day, when he was in his house, and Gaspar Pereira present before them, he told him (being anxious to remove from the Marshal's mind that suspicion he had of his aversion to the enterprise) that he was there ready to obey him, and with regard to the Calicut business he had nothing to say against it; for, from the first occasion of his coming to India, he had become so wearied with the Çamorim,[1] that there was nothing he would undertake with greater pleasure than the destruction of Calicut; that this is what he must believe of him, and not what the reports said of him.

The Marshal replied, that since he was agreed to do him that favour, it must be done forthwith, for it was now the beginning of December, and it was necessary that some time should remain, when the business was over, for loading the ships, because the King D. Manuel had ordered him in his instructions to effect the destruction of Calicut before his departure. Afonso Dalboquerque said there was no need of instructions in this case, for it was sufficient for him that it was the desire of the Marshal, and much more was he willing to enter upon it as the King had written to him respecting it; but it would be as well, he said, that an account of the proposed operations should be laid privately before certain people before it was laid openly before the consideration of all. The Marshal quite agreed with this proposal, and they consulted with Manuel Peçanha, and

[1] See vol. i, page 1.

with others, and all passed a favourable opinion concerning it.

Having thus arranged the preliminaries, in order to proceed more cautiously and artfully in the matter, Afonso Dalboquerque gave orders to Lionel Coutinho and to Bras Teixeira, who were just ready with two ships to go to Baticalá[1] to bring cloves for the ships' cargoes, to make their way to Onor,[2] and announce to Timoja that he, Afonso, was getting himself ready with the Indian fleet, and with merchant vessels, to fall upon Goa, before they went off to Portugal; and that he would ask him for permission to be granted for Lionel Coutinho to enter the river in order to ascertain its depth; and that if he, Timoja, were able to come to Cochim to consult with the Marshal, so much the better, but if not, at any rate he was to hold himself in readiness to be with him in that expedition.

Then the two captains set sail, and Lionel Coutinho had audience with Timoja, and delivered the message he had received. Timoja replied that he should assure the captain-general that he was not prepared just then to make a journey to Cochim; and that, as for the river of Goa, there was no need for any one to see it, for he himself had seen it, and that was sufficient, and that Goa was alone without any garrison, and all the inhabitants in dreadful apprehension of the Portuguese; and that he, the Marshal, could take the city into his own hands whenever he liked to come; and that he himself would be in readiness with his men to co-operate with him in the affair; and he added that the Viceroy had put many affronts upon him, but he lived in hopes that the time would come when he could ask Afonso Dalboquerque to remove them, for he had always been a loyal servant of the King of Portugal, and in so serving him had received many losses, and never any satisfaction for them.

[1] Baticalá, a fortress on the coast of Malabar, about thirty leagues from Goa.—*Cam. Lus.*, *index*.

[2] See vol. i, page 148, note 1.

CHAPTER XIII.

How the great Afonso Dalboquerque and the Marshal gave the King of Cochim an account of their intended expedition to Calicut; and of the council they held with the Captains thereupon.

Two days after the departure of the captains, the great Afonso Dalboquerque and the Marshal paid a visit to the King of Cochim and gave him an account of this their determination, and told him how the King D. Manuel had ordered the destruction of Calicut. And they desired him earnestly that he would be willing to go in person with his army to help them in this enterprise, and attack some place in the interior, where the Çamorin would be forced to go to the rescue. But if he could not so go, at least he should write to some lord of the mountainous country, who was on amicable terms with him, to carry out such a manœuvre. And because they had no certain information of the internal condition of Calicut, after that it was currently reported in Cochim that an expedition was being got ready against the city, they begged him greatly of his favour to despatch certain Brahmins secretly to find out where the Çamorin was, and what sort of army he had, and if he had made any preparation of defence near the landing-place.

The King lauded very highly the determination at which the captains had arrived, for all the dissensions that existed between himself and the Çamorin were owing to the great friendship which he showed towards the King of Portugal. And he said he would forthwith send and find out the condition that everything was in. But as for going himself, they ought not to ask that of him, for Gaspar da India knew very well that he went there for four or five months every year, and hereby expended all the revenues which he obtained from Cochim, and that the waters were still very extensive, and the rivers could not be passed, but nevertheless he would write to certain lords, his vassals and friends, to commence the war in the interior frontier country.

Afonso Dalboquerque and the Marshal were convinced by the arguments of the king, and begged him to supply them with twenty *paráos*, to be used in disembarking the soldiers. The King gave them with good will, and also offered them many *catures*[1] and men if they were required, and then took his leave of them, and went to his own house, and wrote immediately to certain lords of the mountainous country recounting to them the determination at which all had arrived; and he ordered also two Brahmins, honourable men, in whom he reposed great confidence, to proceed to Calicut and obtain information of the state of the city, and the extent of its army. These Brahmins, by reason of their religious profession, can go through all these parts, from one kingdom to another, without anyone demanding of them whence they come, or what they want.

And when the King had gone back to his house, Afonso Dalboquerque summoned all the captains and the fidalgos that there were in the fleet, in order to give them an account of this business. These were the following: D. Antonio da Noronha, Lionel Coutinho, Manuel Peçanha, Pedrafonso de Aguiar, Ruy Freire, Gomez Freire, Francisco de Sousa Mancias, Jorge da Cunha, Francisco de Sá, Francisco Corvinel, Fernão Perez de Andrade, Simão de Andrade (his brother), Jorge da Silveira, Manuel de Lacerda, Bastião de Miranda, Antonio da Costa, Duarte de Melo, Francisco Pereira Coutinho, Simão Martinz, Gonçalo Dalmeida, Gaspar da India who was the Interpreter, and Gaspar Pereira the Secretary.[2]

[1] *Catur*, a sort of small man-of-war.—*Vieyra.*

[2] Several of these captains had come in the fleet of fifteen sail, with Dom Fernando Coutinho the Marshal, from Portugal in this year 1509, as may be gathered from the following passage in a manuscript already quoted, which also relates in brief terms the principal exploits of the Marshal, and the manner of his death:—

And when all had assembled together, before entering into the debate, the Marshal drew himself apart with Afonso Dalboquerque, and in the presence of Gaspar Pereira told him that the King, his lord, had ordered in the instructions that the affair at Calicut was to be carried out, provided that he, Afonso, approved of the design (as he had indeed already intimated to him); and therefore he

"Anno de 1509. Dom Fernando Coutinho, mariçhal de Portugal, Capitão moor de quinze naos, partio a doze de Março: Capitães Francisco de Sá, Bastião de Souza d'Elvas, Leonel Coutinho, Ruy Freire, Jorge da Cunha, Francisco de Sousa Mancias, Rodrigo Rabello de Castello branco; Braz Teixeira, Jorge Lopes Bixorda Armador, Francisco Coruinel armador, Fernão Juzarte, Gomez Freire, Francisco Marecos que sò não pasou à India.

"15 Vellas a 12 de Março, em que levou tres mil homens.

"Nestas naôs foy ordem a Affonso de Albuquerque para governar a India.

"Francisco de Sá era Vedor da Fazenda do Porto. Lionel Coutinho era filho de Vasco Fernandez Coutinho, e foy na naô *Flor de Rosa*. Ruy Freire era filho de Nuno Fernandez Freire, e foy na naô *Garça*. Jorge da Cunha na naô Magdalena. Rodrigo Rabello de Castelbranco na naô *Sta. Clara*. Bras Teixeira na *Ferroa*. Francisco Marecos em *S. Francisco*. Jorge Lopes Bixordo Armador na sua naô. Francisco Corvinel armador na sua naô, etc.

"Successo. De todas estes quinze naôs somente a de Francisco Marecos nam passou à India.

"O Marichal meteo de posse do governo da India a Affonço de Albuquerque, e Dom Francisco de Almeida se embarcou para o Reino por asy o mandar Sua Alteza.

"Depois de partido o Visorey para o Reino forão o gouernador e Mariçhal cõ toda a armada sobre Calicut onde desembarcarão, e tendo destrojda e saqueada a Cidade foy morto o Mariçhal, e mintos Capitães e soldados.

"No fim deste anno entregou o V. Rey a governança Affonço de Albuquerque, E se veyo para o Reino cõ tres Naos, e foy morto pellos Cafres, na aguada do Saldanha, este Visorey tomou por força de Armas duas Cidades populosas na India, fez tres Reys tributarios a Coroa de Portugal, e fez as primeiras quatro fortalezas de Pedra e cal, que os Portugueses teverão na India, Vençeo os Turcos de Soldão sobre a Cidade de Dyo e desbaratou a sua Armada: foy muy valeroso, Inteiro na Justiça, desprezador da fazenda e zelloso do Serviço de seu Rey."—Brit. Mus., Add. MS. 20902, fo. 12.

begged him, before he entered into the debate, of his graciousness to settle beforehand, between the two of them, what was the most proper course to pursue, so as not to go running any hazard at the caprice of four young captains who did not understand how to carry on a war.

Afonso Dalboquerque, in consideration of what had already taken place with the Marshal, told him that if he said this because he thought that he, Afonso, repented of what he had promised, as Manuel Peçanha had persuaded him to think, he must not believe it, for he had never refused to fight, much more was he desirous of fighting since he had two thousand Portuguese soldiers, a number sufficient to conquer the world, not to mention the Çamorin, whom indeed he was anxious to see overthrown. But, he added, so important an affair as this is, in which all the captains are going to adventure their persons, ought not to be undertaken without giving them an account of it, and it was for this reason that he had been induced to give orders for their assembling.

It appeared to the Marshal, by that which Afonso Dalboquerque said, that his whole mind was set upon thwarting this business, with the intent of not carrying it out, so he said that he considered it quite proper that an account of the proposed expedition should be laid before the captains, but it must be with the full understanding that, even if they thought it unadvisable, yet, for all that, the attack on Calicut should be made; for he had been informed that some persons were going about saying that it was against their duty to the King to undertake the business. Afonso Dalboquerque replied that, in matters of such importance, wherein many inconveniences might arise, it did not appear right to proceed to predetermination before careful consideration, but rather to discuss the matter, and to settle it to the satisfaction of all those who were to be employed in its performance; but, as for himself, he was so thoroughly convinced about it that no one could persuade him to the contrary.

And while they were thus discussing, the King of Cochim arrived, bringing with him the Brahmins whom he had sent as spies to Calicut; and these men stated that the King had gone into the interior country to a war which was raging there, but in the city itself there were few *Naires*, and on the *Cerame*, or jetty, they had made some wooden stages on which were placed six large bombards, and along the beach many holes had been dug, in order that the men as they landed should fall into them, and that on the side of the houses of the *Macuas*[1] there was not a single breastwork. And, owing to the delay caused by the arrival of the King, there was no time to relate the plan to the captains; so, after receiving all this information, Afonso Dalboquerque summoned them all to meet again on the following morning; and, when they had all assembled together, the Marshal told them that the King D. Manuel, their lord, had commanded him, in the instructions given to him, to destroy Calicut, and to embark in the undertaking, with the counsel and approbation of the Captain-General of India, who was there present. And, he added, according to news that had reached them, they understood that very few soldiers were left in Calicut, and all the people were paralysed with fear at the news which had reached them of his expedition against them. And since the Çamorim had gone into

[1] *Macuas;* Bluteau says:—"He o nome de certa gente da India, nas prayas do Reyno de Travancor, desde a fortaleza de Coulão, atè o Cabo de Comorim. Toda ella he Christaã, convertida pellos Missionarios da Companhia, desde o tempo de S. Francisco Xavier; aos quaes tem os Reys Gentios dado todo o poder sobre as seus Christãos, de sorte que elles sentenceão suas demandas, & julgão suas causas sem o Rey se entremeter nem no crime, nem no civil. Por todas aquellas prayas se vem Igrejas do verdadeiro Deos, & pela terra dentro ficão outras. (Viagem de Godinho, 171.)" Bluteau translates the word *Macuaria*, which occurs in Barros, as "a habitation of fishermen". Cf. *Matsya*, Arab., "fish".

the interior country, as was reported, he did not think that there were any serious obstacles in the way of attacking Calicut, and so he proceeded with his remarks, all directed towards the point in view.

When the Marshal had made an end of opening the matter in hand, various opinions were delivered in the Council; for Pedrafonso Daguiar, Lionel Coutinho, and Ruy Freire, and some others with them, considered that it was not advantageous to attack Calicut without its first of all being well spied, and without having better information of the state of affairs there than that which the Brahmins rendered. The Marshal was annoyed at this; and said to them that what they said seemed to be excuses of men who had not made up their minds, for the business they had in hand was one which admitted of no temporising,[1] if they really intended to carry it through. For, if the Çamorim with all his forces once came to the relief of Calicut, there would be no resisting him. And, as the rest of the captains were well content that Calicut should be attacked, Afonso Dalboquerque commanded everyone to be ready with all his people to set out on the last day of the month of December.

And when all the people were embarked, because already some rumours of this expedition had reached the ears of those in Calicut, in order to get more precise information thereof, the governors of the land had sent to beg a peace, dissemblingly, with Afonso Dalboquerque, by the aid of a Moor whose name was Cogebequi, who had always hitherto been on our side. And when he was now ready to embark, he ordered the Moor to go to his ship, for he would give him an answer there. He did this because the Moor could

[1] *Que aquelle negocia, pera se fazer, avia de ser assoprar e comer;* a phrase literally meaning "that that business, in order to perform it, had to be blown upon before it could be eaten, like very hot food which one has to eat up at once".

not then advise the governors on land of the determined attitude of the Portuguese; and when once the Moor was on board he was kept under guard; and after the Calicut business was over, Afonso Dalboquerque let him go to his own home again.

CHAPTER XIV.

How, when the great Afonso Dalboquerque was ready to set out, Vasco da Silveira arrived from Çocotora with a message from Duarte de Lemos, begging him to send ships and men; and what took place thereupon.

At the very moment that the fleet was ready to set out, and the greater part of the men on board, Vasco da Silveira arrived, coming from Çocotora in a vessel, to beg Afonso Dalboquerque, on the part of Duarte de Lemos, who had gone as chief captain on the Coast of Arabia, that he would send him some ships, for those he had were so decayed that he feared he should be unable to carry out his instructions with them only. And, as soon as Vasco da Silveira had arrived, he proceeded to Afonso Dalboquerque, and told him how Duarte de Lemos found himself in great need of ships, for two of his squadron had gone to the bottom with old age, and the others he had left were so completely eaten through that they would not float, and how he desired that some relief might be afforded to him in this respect before the departure of the fleet.

Afonso Dalboquerque replied, that he was now so pressed on all sides, that he had not time to put even his own shirt on; and even if he were willing to send him any help, there were no ships in readiness that he could send him, for all had been put out of order in the expedition made by the Viceroy against the Rumes,[1] and he had never had any op-

[1] "The Turks of Romania . . . pretended to be descendants of the Roman conquerors, and obtained from the Indians the name of Rumes

portunity of ordering their repair; but if it should please God to deliver him in the present enterprise he would then do what was asked of him. The reply of Vasco da Silveira to this was, that already in the year last passed, Duarte de Lemos had sent to the Viceroy begging of him two galleys and three ships that the King D. Manuel had by writing instructed him to deliver to Jorge de Aguiar, his uncle, to go in his company to the Cape of Guardafum and the Coast of Arabia, but he had not sent them to him, giving as an excuse that he was about to follow up the Rumes and could not therefore break up his fleet; and that since the Governors of India were unwilling to carry out the orders of the King, he would draw up a report to this effect and return to Çocotora, where Duarte de Lemos was stationed.

At this, Afonso Dalboquerque began to get into such a passion with Vasco da Silveira that the Marshal, who was witness to it, thought it best to take him away to his own house, for he was a very intimate friend of his father, and told him that he hoped he would not be annoyed, but the fact was he had come just at a time when they could not possibly carry out the one thing as well as the other, and that the needs of India were so great that there was no possible means left in her to carry out everything which the King wished to see done. But he promised him that as soon as the affair of Calicut was over, he would take care to give him some very material assistance. Vasco da Silveira became very much pleased at the words of the Marshal, and got the better of the passion he had been in, and offered himself to go in the Marshal's company in the projected expedition.

Now Bastião de Miranda, Fernão Perez de Andrade, and Simão de Andrade, his brother, were in dread lest Afonso Dalboquerque should treat them badly because they had

or Romans."—Note to Mickle's *Lusiad*, bk. 10. "Rumes Que trazido de Roma o nome tem."—*Cam. Lus.*, x, 68.

been opposed to him in his dissensions with the Viceroy; so when they became aware of the coming of Vasco da Silveira and of the object of his visit, they earnestly desired him to take them with him and get permission for them to accompany him. But when Afonso Dalboquerque heard of this, with his rare greatness of mind, he took no notice of their former conduct, but ordered them before him, and in the presence of some of the captains, he said to them that he was very desirous that they should not think that he owed them any ill-will on account of their having signed the remonstrance that was made to the Viceroy, nor for their having said some things in contempt for his person, because he knew very well that, as time and things were going then, they had been compelled to such a course of action. But they might now feel sure that he had quite forgotten all that had passed on that occasion. And he would beg them to serve the King well, and without any embarrassment tell him anything that they might think advantageous to the service of His Highness, for in the King's name he would always be thankful to them for such advice. And, he said, he would swear to them by the Holy Gospels, on which he placed his hands, that this was so, and that he spoke without any reservation. The captains told him in reply that it was quite true they had signed the remonstrance made to the Viceroy, because João da Nova and Jorge Barreto had deceived them, but as for having said anything against him personally, there was no one who could think of doing such a thing, and from that time henceforth they would serve the King in the manner they were desired to do.

And because Vasco da Silveira died in Calicut with the Marshal (as will be related further on), directly that Afonso Dalboquerque returned to Cochim, after completing the attack upon Calicut, he sent Diogo Correa in the same ship which Vasco da Silveira had come in, laden with provisions and stores for the fortress of Çocotora. And when Diogo Correa arrived there he recounted to Duarte de Lemos, who had only a few days before returned from Quiloa, the havoc that had taken place at Calicut, and the death of the Marshal, and of Vasco da Silveira his nephew, with many other fidalgos who there came to their end, and that on this account Afonso Dalboquerque could not send him ships nor galleys, for all had been routed, and there was need of time for repairs. But that a very large fleet was being made ready, to come and unite with him in the following summer, and then both should enter the Straits of the Red Sea, in accordance with the orders of the King D. Manuel, provided that the affairs of India would permit. Duarte de Lemos was not well pleased with this reply to his message, and very angry at the death of his nephew Vasco da Silveira; he therefore committed the captaincy of the fortress to Pero Ferreira, as the King had provided, and gave D. Afonso a ship in which to make his way to India, while he himself returned to pass the winter at Melinde.

CHAPTER XV.

How the great Afonso Dalboquerque and the Marshal set out for Calicut with their fleet: and of the council which they held respecting their disembarkation, and further proceedings.

When all the people of the fleet were gathered together —a fleet of twenty ships of war all told, besides *paráos* which were taken for use in disembarking, carrying two thousand Portuguese—they set out from Cochim on the last day of the month of December; and on the third day of January came to an anchorage in front of the port of Calicut. And, on their arrival, Afonso Dalboquerque with all the captains went on board the Marshal's ship and stayed to discuss the method to be pursued in landing the troops;

and when they had inspected the position and the nature of the sea, it was considered best to land in front of the houses of the *Macuas*,[1] for there the water was smoothest, and all could land with least trouble.

When this agreement had been arrived at, the Marshal declared he suspected, among so many captains and young men whom the fleet contained, there might be some one who imagined he would acquire honour in being the first to set foot on land [before he himself should do so], but he would swear to such an one, were he a captain or any one in his fleet, he would order his head to be struck off, but if such an one should be of the people of India and the Captain-General would not give a similar order, he would never speak to him again; and he said he would desire them earnestly not to disembark on the land before he himself should, but allow the boats to reach all together at the same time. And, because all his captains were not present there, he wrote to each one of them his written instructions with regard to the plan of action that had been determined; that they were not to plunder the city, nor set fire to it without his permission.

And on the following day, which was the fourth of the month of January, all went into the boats, and proceeded together to strike the land. But, because the current was running very strongly, Afonso Dalboquerque ordered the men in his boat to urge on their oars in order not to be taken with the current. And in front of him went Vasco da Silveira in one *parão* and Rodrigo Rabelo[2] in another; and in this order they reached the shore, and disembarked without gaining the spot which had been chosen beforehand for the landing. Afonso Dalboquerque, who was lying to on his oars within sight of shore, on the look out for the Marshal's disembarkation (—the current of the tide had

[1] See page 58, note.
[2] See page 56, note.

carried the Marshal further down where the sea broke very roughly—) as soon as he saw the men on land, and that they were beginning to march in a straggling line, he himself landed and ran along the shore to restrain them from starting off until the arrival of the Marshal, who had indeed by this time already landed. And whereas the men were in high spirits and eager to attack the *Cerame*,[1] or jetty, where the Moors had their stockades fortified with artillery, he could not keep them in check; but, when he beheld them marching along in such a disordered manner, without a captain, he went on behind them at a good pace, and with some, whom he took with him, arrived in the van of the men, who were already engaged in a combat with the Moors with lances; and they altogether pressed upon them so that they carried the stockades by force and put many Moors to death, while others fled to the city, and they also captured six large bombards which had been placed there.

Only two of our men were killed, and at this juncture came the Marshal with his men up along the shore, very tired, for they had landed far off, and could not bear the weight of their arms, by reason of the great heat. And as they thus arrived, a man-at-arms went up to him and told him to go on leisurely, for the *Cerame* was already captured. This news very much enraged the Marshal, and he allowed many words to fall from his lips, which I must omit. Afonso Dalboquerque quitted the *Cerame*, and proceeded along the beach in search of the Marshal, and he, when he caught sight of him, began to shout, and cried out that he had quite expected they would not keep all together in good and close order, and that the weakest always went in front. Afonso Dalboquerque answered him not a word of reproach, but commenced to explain the reason of his actions, saying how he had waited for him for hours without disembarking, in order to carry out the promises he had made, until at

[1] See vol. i, page 115, note.

last the men he had with him began to straggle, and Vasco da Silveira, his servant, had been the first to land; but he, Afonso, when he beheld the men marching without a captain, in order that they should not rush on their destruction, himself had disembarked to take the command of them, and the honour they had gained was all his own, for every one in the affair marched under his flag.

Without saying a word, the Marshal went on as he was, being in a great rage, and on reaching the *Cerame*, wished to march on at once straight upon the city. Then Afonso Dalboquerque told him that it would be best to rest the men there where they were for awhile, and after they had taken some little rest, that then they should proceed on the the march towards the city, burn the ships, and carry out whatever other plans should seem best to him. But the Marshal's mind was filled with distrust, and he replied to Afonso Dalboquerque in a very passionate manner:—"I know very well what this is that you want, that I am not to stir from here; but I mean to go on to the houses of the Çamorim, and destroy Calicut, before I take anything to eat, and let him who will go with me, go; and let him who will not, stay behind". And being seized with an unfortunate temerity of mind, he called out to Gaspar da India, and told him to lead the way, and take him to the king's palace.[1]

When Afonso Dalboquerque saw that the Marshal was of that determination, he told him that his reason for saying so was that it was excessively hot, the men were very tired and in want of food, the palace was a long way off, and he did not know how they would be able to reach so far; yet, if, in spite of all these reasons, he would go, he himself would not be one of the last of the party.

[1] *E o levasse aos paços do Rey;* in some places *paços* is used as equivalent to *passos*, roads or passes; but here, and often elsewhere, the word *paço*, in its plural form *paços*, is taken to signify a palace.

The Marshal answered nothing, but began to march on, with his flag unfurled before him; and Afonso Dalboquerque, although he was much opposed to this obstinate intention of the Marshal, followed him according to the promise he had made at first setting out. And as this was where the palisades begin, he gave word to D. Antonio de Noronha, his nephew, and to Rodrigo Rabelo, to take three hundred men and go and set fire to the ships, and to return to the same spot when they were burnt and remain drawn up in battle array with the men ready to assist wherever they should see any disorder.

CHAPTER XVI.

How the great Afonso Dalboquerque and the Marshal entered the City of Calicut, and proceeded to the Çamorim's houses, and our men were routed, and the Marshal killed, and further proceedings.

As soon as the Marshal, who was in the vanguard, had begun to force his way into the city, marching on towards the palace of the Çamorim, there came against him twenty or thirty *Naires*, armed with swords and shields, shouting aloud in their accustomed manner. When he caught sight of them coming against him he began to chuckle, and said to Gaspar Pereira who was close beside him:—"Is this your Calicut, that you terrify us all with in Portugal?" Gaspar Pereira replied that he would think differently before long; for he would wager that, if they could that day penetrate to the houses of the Çamorim, these naked little blacks would give them trouble enough. The Marshal replied:—"This is not the kind of people who will give me any trouble;" and, arriving at a mosque which stood at the entrance of the city, he commanded that it should be set on fire; but when he came close up to it he had already become so tired that it was necessary to help him along by two men taking him under the arms.

When our men found that they met with none to resist their entry into the city, they turned their attention to pillaging. But the Marshal, with those who remained with him, arrived at the palace, and immediately attacked a body of two hundred *Naires* who kept guard there, and pressed on them with their lances with such force that they routed them and killed eighty of them, and the governor of the city, and two *Caimais* of the Çamorim who were stationed there, while the rest took to flight. And following up this victory, the Marshal went into the palace through the gates, and reached as far as a spacious courtyard, which contained the houses; but he was so tired that as soon as he entered he sat down on a large block of stone,[1] and there remained for a long space of time without being able to stir. Then the people who had got in with him began to break open some doors which were fastened, and scattered themselves about, robbing whatever they found. But this courtyard, in which the Marshal was, had two gates facing upon two streets of the city; many *Naires*, therefore, began to arrive through them, coming to the succour and relief of those who were on guard at the palace, and these wounded many of our men with arrows.

Tired as he was, the Marshal collected the few that were with him, advanced to attack them, and fell upon them so severely that he made them retire. Afonso Dalboquerque, who was in the rearguard, as soon as he had arrived at the gate of the palace through which the Marshal had entered, rested quietly with his men in close order upon a broad terrace which was close to the palace. When the *Naires* perceived our men thus drawn up, they advanced to fight them, and with arrows wounded them so severely that

[1] *Poial*, or *poyal*, a small platform with steps, for mounting on horseback. Cf. *podium*.

Afonso Dalboquerque, in order to make them keep off from him, thought it advisable to tell Pedrafonso Daguiar to give orders to fire upon them with the small field gun[1] which he had brought up.

The *Naires* no sooner found themselves discomfited by the execution of the gun, than they withdrew outside, and began to set up loud shouts, which is their custom when they wish to collect a crowd. When Afonso Dalboquerque heard the shouting in the city, he sent word twice to the Marshal to retire. But he had not yet got over his fit of anger, so he paid no attention to the message, and allowed himself to get quite rested from his fatigue. Nevertheless, when Afonso Dalboquerque saw that the *Naires* were increasing in number, and that the Marshal was unwilling to withdraw, he left Gonçalo Queimado, who carried his flag, with his men, and went inside; and, being by this time worked up into a passion, told him to retire at once, for there was no longer any time for waiting, because the *Naires* were numerous and increasing in numbers every moment, and had already wounded some of his men, that it was a very long way to the ships, and that if they delayed a single hour longer all would be lost.

Then the Marshal immediately set to work to rally his men, who were scattered about, and went out on to the terrace; and when all had united, Afonso Dalboquerque said to him:—"Sir, how do you wish us to act? for these men require some one to lead the way for them and restrain them from straggling,—because the *Naires* are many, and the communication with the beach is broken, and I fear we shall have a bad account to give of ourselves to-day if we do not dispose ourselves properly." To this the Marshal replied, that since he wished it to be so, he, Afonso, should take the vanguard, while he himself would remain behind in

[1] *Berço;* peça curta de artilharia de fabrica antiga: hoje não se usa. —*Bluteau.*

the rear with his men. Then Afonso Dalboquerque began to march with his flag, taking Gaspar da India, who went on in front leading the way. And because all the way was palisaded on this side and on that, the natives began to crowd upon us, and from over the tops of the stockade handled our men very badly with arrows, stones, and hand-darts. Yet, although they were thus harassed, Afonso Dalboquerque ordered the men not to stay to attack them, but to take the most direct way back to the beach.

Before commencing his retreat, the Marshal, who was bringing up the rear, gave orders to set the palace on fire. The *Naires*, as soon as they perceived the flames, rushed up to extinguish them, and found the Marshal who was collecting his men as he went along, and began to attack the party. But as the *Naires* were freshly arrived and our men very much exhausted, after fighting for a considerable time, the *Naires* put them to flight and killed the Marshal, and his lieutenant, and Manuel Peçanha, Vasco da Silveira, Lionel Coutinho, and Filippe Rodriguez, in all ten or twelve of our principal men.

As soon as the news reached Afonso Dalboquerque that the Marshal was fighting, he wheeled round, but those who accompanied him were only very few, withstanding five or six hundred men; and in this manœuvre of turning round the natives wounded many of his men, and to him they gave a lance-thrust with a short lance, from the top of the palisade, in the left shoulder, and another wound in the shoulder-blade which made him fall down. But Diogo Fernandez de Béja, who was walking close beside him, with great difficulty saved him from being killed, and escorted him down to the ships borne on the backs of two men. In this manœuvre, too, the Moors killed Gonçalo Queimado, who carried Afonso Dalboquerque's flag; he met his end like a very brave cavalier, close beside his captain.

Immediately that D. Antonio de Noronha and Rodrigo

Rabelo perceived the discomfiture of our men, they brought up a body of soldiers to the entrance of the palisade to stay them in their flight, for there was no necessity for flying; and, had it not been for this fresh assistance, the rout would have been more disastrous. The *Naires* who were following hard upon our men dared not advance any further when they arrived at the place where D. Antonio and Rodrigo Rabelo were stationed, but withdrew. Our men were so thoroughly beside themselves, that on reaching the beach they threw away their arms and got into the water intending to take refuge in the boats. But Afonso Dalboquerque, who was suffering severely from the pain of his wounds and dared not venture to go up on board his own ship, commanded them to carry him to Antonio Pacheco's *caravela*, which was nearest to him, and there his wounds were dressed, and there he remained that night. And on the following morning he returned to his ship, and gave orders for all the fleet to set sail direct for Cochim, leaving behind him Jorge Botelho and Simão Afonso in their *caravelas* to lie to over against the port of Calicut, with orders not to allow any ship to sail away from that coast with spices.

CHAPTER XVII.

Of the behaviour of the Çamorim, when he learned that the Portuguese had entered the City of Calicut: and how the great Afonso Dalboquerque despatched Fr. Luis to Narsinga, to relate to the King what had taken place in Calicut, and further proceedings.

By the time that the great Afonso Dalboquerque and the Marshal had arrived with their fleet opposite Calicut, the Çamorim had been gone for some days already into the interior country close to the mountain-range, to war with a great lord, who was a vassal of the King of Cochim. But when news was brought to him that the Portuguese had forced their way into the city, he broke up his camp, and set off in the greatest haste by night without being perceived by the enemy. The Lord of the hill country, when morning broke, and he saw that the Çamorim's camp was broken up, and the Çamorim himself had gone away, hastened rapidly after him, burning and destroying everything in the land as he went.

It was not, however, until four days after the departure of Afonso Dalboquerque that the Çamorim reached Calicut; who, when he beheld the destruction of the city, and his mosque and palaces all burnt, and his *Catual*, the governor of the city, and two *Caimais* killed, as well as over three thousand of the native and Malabar soldiery dead, became very dejected; and, showing signs of the deep feeling which had seized him, he was unwilling to enter his palace, but ordered the principal Moors of the city to be summoned before him, and blamed them greatly for the excessive weakness they had exhibited in their defence of the city, and swore he would ruin them and cast them out of his kingdom. That which made him feel this destruction more deeply was the knowledge that there had not been killed more than eighty Portuguese.

Even these I believe would not have been killed if our men had not fled in so disorderly a way, without any body of *Naires* (who compose the principal body of soldiers that the King has) attacking them and throwing them into such a rout as to leave two chief captains and ten or twelve fidalgos who there met their death with them to be cut to pieces, and without turning to look behind them to see what imaginary danger it was from which they were fleeing. For had there been twenty men who had cared to rally themselves together, the Marshal would not have been killed, nor Afonso Dalboquerque wounded, for all the rest that were killed in that affair were men without any sense of shame, and careless of the general orders and proclamations that had been issued, and only going up and down pillaging in the houses. And because the *Naires* also busied themselves with robbing, if, in the house any of them entered, any Portuguese were found, the greater number overpowered the less, and in this manner some were killed, while the fire cut off others who placed themselves in positions that had not been preconcerted.

Afonso Dalboquerque was so deeply concerned at the death of the Marshal and the fidalgos who had been slain with him, that he determined to exact vengeance for their loss, so he wrote to the King of Narsinga (for his kingdom touches that of Calicut, and the two Kings were not very friendly), that if he would come with his army by land, he Afonso, would come by sea, and thus they would destroy the Çamorim; and to further the chance of success, he would endeavour to come to an understanding with some lords of the hill country to assist him. With this end in view, he dispatched Fr. Luis of the order of St. Francis with instructions as to what he was to say to the King (as is here given below in full); and the friar set out from Cochim in a vessel and reached Baticalá[1], and from that place made his way on land straight to Narsinga. And Afonso Dalboquerque also despatched Diogo Correa with a message to Duarte de Lemos, as I have already related.

Two days after they had set out, two vessels of the fleet commanded by Diogo Lopez de Sequeira arrived, and with them came Nuno Vaz de Castelo-branco, who related to him all that had taken place in Malaca, and how the Governors of the city had planned treachery against Diogo Lopez de Sequeira by order of their king, intending to seize him, and all who accompanied him on shore, at a banquet which he intended to give him, and afterwards to take the fleet; but this plan had not succeeded, for Diogo Lopez

[1] Baticalá. See page 53, note; and page 77; also Chapter xlviii.

de Sequeira had been warned by a *Jaoa*,[1] the lover of one of our mariners, who came by night swimming to his ship; and that the King, when he saw that the treason was discovered, had laid hands upon Ruy de Araujo the factor, and twenty other men who were with him on land attending to the collection of the cargo of the ships; and how he had ordered two of the vessels which composed the fleet to be burnt because he had not hands sufficient for their navigation, and sailed away; and how, when Diogo Lopez de Sequeira had arrived at Caecoulão, where he first heard that Afonso Dalboquerque was Captain-General of India, he had despatched him, Nuno Vaz de Castelo-branco, in these two vessels, to make their way to Cochim, for they were in a very leaky condition, and from that port, he, Diogo, had made his way to Portugal to the seaward of the Island of S. Lourenço.[2]

The Instructions which Fr. Luis carried.

"First of all you will say to the king of Narsinga, that I announce to him that I am now newly arrived as Captain-General of these parts of India by command of the King of Portugal; and that trusting in the confideuce which his ancestors possessed in him, I command you to visit him, and to offer to him the fleets and army of the King my Lord; for I know for certain that he, the King of Portugal, will be much gratified at my so doing, confiding in his friendship, his messages, and kindly offerings, which he has always received from the Kings his ancestors, and which were given to him in Portugal.

"You will tell him of the greatness and power of the King my Lord, and of the great fleets which he sends every year to India, and how the Indian seas are not navi-

[1] *Jaoa*; a woman of the Island of Jaoa, Jauha, or Java.

[2] Madagascar. See vol. i, page 25.

gated now without a safe conduct from him; and how the ships and merchandise of those who do not carry his safe conduct are captured; and likewise you will tell him how in my instructions the King of Portugal commands me to render honour and willing service to all the Gentile kings of his land and of the whole of Malabar, and that they are to be well treated by me, neither am I to take their ships nor their merchandise; but I am to destroy the Moors, with whom I wage incessant war, as I know he also does; wherefore I am prepared and ready to help him with the fleets and army of the King, my Lord, whensoever and as often as he shall desire me to do so; and I likewise for my part expect that he will help us with his army, towns, harbours, and munitions, and with everything which I may require from his kingdom; and that the ships which navigate to his ports may pass safely throughout all the Indian sea, and receive honour and good treatment at the hands of the fleets and fortresses of the King of Portugal.

"You will give him an account of the destruction of Calicut, and how I have been informed that he is its capital enemy, and desires to overthrow it; and therefore I send to inform him that its palaces and the city itself have been all burned and the inhabitants put to the sword, and all its artillery captured, and that the Çamorim did not venture to succour the city, but kept himself aloof in the hill country which is over against Calicut and on the borders of his kingdom, until he knew that we had withdrawn from the place.

"You will tell him that my determination is to take the Çamorim captive and send him to Portugal to the King my Lord, and that this can well be done if he, the King of Narsinga, will only come with his camp over against the hills of Calicut, whither the Çamorim withdraws when any one makes war upon him on the sea coast; and while he is marching his army through the interior country, I will come with a very large fleet along the shore, destroying all the ports and towns in such a manner that the Çamorim shall not be able to assist one side or the other with his army, and that we shall take him without his being able to escape. And so we shall drive out of Calicut the Moors, who are the people that furnish him with all the revenue that he requires for the expenses of the war, and depriving him of the people of the land, his ports will be left without trade, destroyed and undone; and after this is over, I shall give my attention forthwith to the affairs of Goa, wherein I can help him in the war against the King of Decan,[1] and from him will I take the trade in horses that comes to his kingdom, whereby he is enabled to carry on the war with him (the King of Narsinga).

"You will tell him, also, how Ormuz now belongs to the King my Lord; and if he wishes to obtain the King of Portugal's friendship and to send his ambassadors to Portugal to visit him with presents whereby he may show signs of true friendship, the King of Portugal on his part will send him many things that are in that kingdom. And that the horses of Ormuz shall not be consigned except to Baticalá, or to any other port he pleases to point out where he can have them, and shall not go to the King of Decan, who is a Moor and his enemy. And in order that our friendship be more firmly established, you will tell him that when he comes with his camp to these parts, I will proceed to visit him in person, and together we will arrange many matters that will benefit his service. And I again remind you that you are to labour as much as you possibly can to cause the King of Narsinga to send his ambassadors to Portugal, that they may visit the King, carrying presents of jewels and other things produced in that land.

"You will, moreover, speak to him to the effect that, in

[1] *Decan*, Dakhan, or Deccan, the name given to the great interior country in the South of India.

case it shall be to the advantage of the King my Lord that we should make a settlement and factory in any place within his ports between Baticalá and Mangalor,[1] he shall command that the King's men and fleets be received in those ports and be granted a space for erecting a strong house wherein his merchandise and people may be secured from any tumult of the natives which may arise, seeing that the distance is so great that his justices might not be able to arrive to succour them in time to retrieve their position if it were assailed. And if the King of Narsinga be willing to do this he shall hold securely all the trade in horses and every other kind of merchandise of Portugal which he may need in his land."

Of the Province of Malabar, and of some Customs which the People of Malabar practice.

The Province of Malabar commences at the port of Maceirão, close to Mangalor, and reaches as far as the Cape of Comorim[2] in the interior country, bounded by the great Kingdom of Narsinga; and all along this land there runs a very lofty mountain range which divides the Province of Malabar from the Kingdom of Narsinga. The greatest breadth of this land from the sea coast up to the range is about fifteen leagues. These ranges of mountains are so lofty that the natives of Narsinga say that in their country the east winds never blow, because they are prevented from passing over from the other side by reason of the great height. The length of the coastline of this Province would be about a hundred and thirty leagues. In it there are many kings, and all the people are heathens.

The sons of the kings do not inherit, but their nephews,

[1] Mangalor, or Mangalur, on the West Coast of India, 12 deg. 52 min. N., 74 deg. 50 min. E. See the plan and description of the fortress in Barretto de Resende's work, MS. Sloane, 197, fo. 188.

[2] The most southern point of the Indian Continent.

sons of their sisters, not the sons of their brothers, for they hold it to be a very doubtful matter if their sons are their own. Wherefore, if they have a sister, they give her to a Brahmin, who keeps her as his mistress, and the sons of this sister inherit the kingdom. And if they can get Brahmin *Patamares*,[1] who come from the Kingdom of Cambaya (and are held in these parts as a more noble race than any other), to them they give their sisters to take them from their earliest girlhood,[2] and with this charge they give the Brahmins large sums of money that they may be willing to take this trouble, which they perform very rigorously, and the sons of these sisters inherit the kingdom.

These Brahmins are a set of religious men (just as our priests among us here), who take care of their pagodas. They have among themselves a scientific language, which is like the Latin among us, that no one understands unless he is instructed in it. They are married to one wife only; they do not eat flesh nor fish, nor anything which may suffer death; their food is rice, milk, butter, and fruits, and their drink, water. And, in order that this kind of substance may never fail for the Brahmins, who were numerous, the ancient people of this land forbade that cows or bulls should be killed, under penalty of death; and this law was so strictly observed that, not only do they not kill them, but they worship them, and they are even held as objects of sanctity. They have knowledge of the Trinity and of Our Lady, whereby it appears that anciently they were Christians.

The *Naires* of this land are the military men and esteemed cavaliers, and the most honourable people of all the country; and it is said that in this province there would be about two hundred thousand of these men. They are very loyal to

[1] *Patamares*, among the Canarese, messengers, or runners.

[2] *Que as levem de virgindade.*

their king, and worship him; and it has never been found that a *Naire* has been guilty of treason.

They have physicians, whose method of cure is in this wise. To those who are suffering from fevers, they give meat and fish to eat, and purge them with the seed of the *figueira*[1] *de Inferno*, "the fig tree of hell", or give the leaves pounded to them in water to drink. If one suffers from diarrhœa, they give him to drink the fresh water of *cocos*,[2] and it is stopped immediately. If any are sick, they wash their heads for them with cold water, and the vomiting ceases. If wounded, they give warm oil three times a day, and cure them in this manner. In prolonged illnesses, the remedy which they give to the sufferers is to take musicians and make pilgrimages to their pagodas.

In the Province of Malabar, there are between Chetua[3] and Coulão many Christians of the time of St. Thomas, and there are many churches. Many other customs have they, concerning which I do not write, to avoid digression; but I leave the account of them to those who will write the history of India.

CHAPTER XVIII.

How the great Afonso Dalboquerque prepared his fleet with the intention of entering the Straits of the Red Sea: and of the council he held upon an expedition to Goa.

The great Afonso Dalboquerque was no sooner well of his wounds, although he continued to feel somewhat of the injury done to his arm, and could not lift it well up to his

[1] The *Ricinus communis*, sometimes *R. Palma Christi*, the castor-oil plant.

[2] The *Cocos nucifera*, or common coco-nut.

[3] *Chaitwa*, on the Western Coast of India, 10 deg. 32 min. N., 76 deg. 3 min. E.

head, than he set to work at once to order the refitting of all the ships, vessels, and galleys, which the Viceroy had left in a dismantled state at the time of his departure for Portugal. And when he had his fleet already fitted out with things necessary for the time that he should start, he summoned the captains and said to them :—" Sirs, now that the affairs of Malabar are in a quiet state and settled, as you perceive them to be, I have determined to go to Çocotorá and unite with Duarte de Lemos, in accordance with the orders I have received from the King our Lord, and thereafter to make our way to the Straits of the Red Sea in search of the fleet of the Grand Sultan; and, in case of not finding it in the Sea, to go on to Suez and burn it for him; for the best way is to go and seek them there and not let them get out and set foot in India, where for a certainty they would command the favour and assistance of the Moors against us. This has always been my policy, provided that we are to govern; and there are many reasons which I will give in support of my views, when I have more leisure to do so; and after this, we will go and complete the fortress of Ormuz, which I left just commenced. And I beg of you that, after well considering the one thing and the other, to advise me what I ought to do." And, after they had heard many propositions that were made concerning this matter, it was decided that he ought to make his way to the Straits of the Red Sea; and, with regard to Ormuz, time would show what he would have to do.

On this determination being arrived at, Afonso Dalboquerque left the fortresses of Cochim provided with captains, and men, artillery, gunpowder, and stores, and everything else that they required, and a fleet of vessels along the coast to rely upon in case anything should happen, and set out from Cochim on the tenth day of February in the year one thousand five hundred and ten with a fleet of twenty-three sail. And these were the captains :—Dom Antonio de

Noronha his nephew, Garcia de Sousa who had come from Malaca, Luis Coutinho, Jorge Fogaça, Jeronymo Teixeira, João Nunez, Diogo Fernandez de Béja, Jorge da Silveira, Simão Martinz, Fernão Perez Dandrade, Simão Dandrade his brother, Aires da Silva, Francisco Pantoja, Duarte de Melo, D. Jeronymo de Lima, Francisco Pereira Continho, Francisco de Sousa Mancias, Manuel de Lacerda, Bernaldim Freire, Jorge da Cunha, Antonio da Costa, and Francisco Corvinel, a Florentine by birth.[1] And sailing along the coast with all this fleet he made his way direct to Anjadiva,[2] from which point he had determined to steer across to the Cape of Guardafum.

And when he had progressed as far on his voyage as the port of Mergeu,[3] Timoja arrived in a *fusta* to parley with the ship of Afonso Dalboquerque. This man was a Hindoo by birth, very obedient to the interests of the King of Portugal; and being a man of low origin had as a corsair raised himself to a position of great honour. Timoja enquired of Afonso Dalboquerque whither he was bound with so powerful a fleet as this; and he replied that his intention was to proceed to the Straits in search after the fleet of the Grand Sultan, and to fight with it when found; and in case of not finding the enemies at sea, should he obtain correct information of their having by that time set out, then to go to Suez and burn all the ships and galleys for them that they had there. Timoja informed him that he was very much concerned at this idea, when he had the Rumes so near to him, of going to seek for them at Suez, and begged to acquaint him with the news that a captain of the Grand Sultan, with some Rumes who had escaped from the rout

[1] Compare these names with those in the note on page 56.

[2] *Anjadiva*, between Cape Ramas and Honawar, not marked in Keith Johnston's map, but its position is shewn in Pedro Berthelot's map in Barreto de Resende's work.—MS. Sloane, 197, f. 164.

[3] *Mergeu* is apparently *Mirjan*, 14 deg. 32 min. N., and 74 deg. 27' min. E.—The *Rio de Merzeu*, of Berthelot, as above.

inflicted upon them by D. Francisco Dalmeida, had arrived at Goa, and that the Çabaio[1] had made important overtures to this captain to the end that he should settle there, and among them there were carpenters and caulkers who had built ships and galleys after the model of those of Portugal; and that this same captain had written to the Grand Sultan to send him soldiers, because he hoped to establish himself strongly at Goa, inasmuch as it was a country wherein were plenty of supplies, and timber, and a good harbour, and with his help from that base of operations they would cast the Portuguese out of India, and then the spices would again go to Meca and Cairo as they used to go in ancient days.

In addition to this, Timoja informed Afonso Dalboquerque that the Çabaio, Lord of Goa, was dead, and Goa, being without him, was dead also, and the place was not very strong, and inside the city there were not men sufficient for resisting so great a fleet as this; and that the Hidalcão,[2] son of the Çabaio, was very young, and on account of the death of his father great divisions had arisen in the kingdom of Decan between the lords, and the opportunity now presented itself for laying hands upon the city, if he was inclined to attack it; and in the entrance of the bar there were about three fathoms and a half depth at full tide, whereby all that fleet could enter without danger. Afonso Dalboquerque thanked him excessively for this advice of his; but insomuch as in so great an undertaking as this which had been proposed he could not take any steps without giving an account of it to the captains and men of this fleet, because it had been decided to enter the Straits, he would lay the relation of this matter before them, and

[1] *Cabaio.* This word may possibly be connected with *sipahi*, Arabic, a soldier.

[2] *Hidalcão*; perhaps a proper name rather than a titular designation. The definite article is, however, always prefixed.

inform him, Timoja, of the conclusions at which they arrived.

As soon as Timoja had been dismissed with this reply, Afonso Dalboquerque convened a meeting of all the captains, *fidalgos*, and pilots of the fleet, and recounted to them all that had passed in his interview with Timoja. And after a prolonged debate, it was universally agreed that if Goa were really in the state described by this information, then the voyage to the Straits ought to be abandoned, and all should strive their utmost to capture the city and drive the Rumes out of it. After every one had delivered his opinion, Afonso Dalboquerque said to them that for all that the words of Timoja appeared to carry reason with them, still, as it was a doubtful matter after all, he would not yet swerve from the determination wherewith he had set out from Cochim, nor would he abandon his intention of making the voyage to the Straits, unless it were to strengthen the kingdom of Ormuz, which was quite as important as Goa, and very profitable to the service of the King our Lord. And when once they should reach Ormuz and refit her with supplies, she was a prize taken without any more fighting, and of this there could be no denial. But although he had his eyes upon Ormuz on account of the great trouble which she had cost him (for the captains who had deserted him had forced him to abandon the attack), nevertheless, if Timoja had spoken truly, he could not deny that if they omitted now to capture Goa, there would follow hereafter much trouble upon the affairs of India; and in addition to this it was very important to bear in mind that if the Rumes established themselves in Goa and fortified it, then the Çamorim, who was allied with the city, would never, in his opinion, withdraw from it; but would give much trouble to the King of Portugal if at any future time he should desire to take it. Nevertheless, he continued, in this that he said he was not finally determined on any plan of action—he was only representing to them all the reasons that could be adduced for and against the proposal. For in the whole of the fleet they had not a pilot who was better acquainted with Goa, its harbour, or its bar, than that Timoja stated that it had a good harbour and about three and a half fathoms of water in the bar at high water. But Timoja, he said, had promised him that he would return immediately with some more sure proofs of what he had told him, and when he had this further information before him, then he would make up his mind and lay his plans before them. And all agreed to this course of proceeding.

CHAPTER XIX.

How the great Afonso Dalboquerque set sail from the harbour of Mergeu, and took up his station in front of the Castle of Cintácora; and what passed with Timoja, and how sailing thence he went and anchored on the bar of Goa.

At the conclusion of all these debates, on a Monday, the twenty-fifth day of the month of February, the great Afonso Dalboquerque ordered all the fleet to set sail, and certain ships which were going in company with him to Chaul[1] to follow him, as he was of opinion that if he required these ships' boats for disembarking troops he could benefit by their assistance, and make use of everything else they contained. And they all made their way together and proceeded to anchor over against the Castle of Cintácora; and just as they were casting anchors Timoja arrived from Onor with thirteen *fustas* armed with a numerous body of men, and without delay had an interview with Afonso Dalboquerque, who was very much pleased at his coming, and enquired of him, through Gaspar Rodriguez, the interpreter, what trustworthy information he had of Goa.

[1] See vol. i, p. 222.

Timoja replied, that by means of messages and letters that he had received from certain influential Hindoos of the city he had been notified of the death of the Çabaio; and that in Goa there was a captain, named Melique Çufergugi,[1] who had in his pay a thousand men under arms, that were much enraged with him because he had not paid them, so that they were all dying of hunger; and that the river of Goa was of the same depth that he had formerly stated; and that this captain, after the death of the Çabaio, obeyed no one, and the people of the land were in great dissension one with another. Afonso Dalboquerque enquired of him the reason that had moved him to come and advise him to take Goa. Timoja answered, that the principal head-men[2] of the natives that were established in the land had written to tell him that the death of the Çabaio was certain, and that all were very well pleased at hearing of it on account of the numerous robberies and tyrannies which he had practised upon them, and that during the year last passed he had murdered and robbed more than two hundred merchants, and that on this account the whole land had risen up in mutiny and in quarrels one against another. "And," he continued, "if I wanted to possess myself of Goa, I have only to go there with my men and they would yield themselves up to me of their own accord."

Afonso Dalboquerque convened a general meeting of all at his ship, and gave them an account of everything that Timoja had told him, and begged them seriously to make up their minds, for they were wasting time without arriving at any action. And he ordered Timoja to speak first, who said that concerning the affairs of Goa he had nothing to say, for he had already stated all that had taken place; but that, as for himself, he was prepared with his *fustas* to accompany him by sea, and would send many of his men

[1] This is the Portuguese transliteration of a native name which I cannot identify.

[2] *Cabeceiras*, caboceers.

by land, and he would undertake to promise that, on the anchoring of the fleet in the harbour of Goa, the governors of the city would immediately order the keys of the fortress to be delivered up to him without any resistance.

When Timoja had made an end of stating his opinions, the captains debated about the business; and, after settling certain differences they had respecting the entering of the bar, it was agreed that they should fall upon the city. Hereupon Afonso Dalboquerque told Timoja to send his men by land to make their way, destroying the places which had been built along the sea front. And because this man's desires were that Goa should be captured for the sake of the profit that he hoped to make out of it, he sent by land two thousand men, led by one of his cousins and by a Moor who had been a captain of the Çabaio, whose name was Melique Çufecondal[1]—who had fled from Goa out of fear of the Çabaio, and had secreted himself in his house. As soon as our fleet had dropped anchor Timoja's men came up by land and fell upon the fortress of Cintâcora —which is on the bank of the river whereby the kingdom of Onor is divided from that of Goa, —in which fortress an alcaide was stationed with a body of men. And when they beheld our fleet all took to flight; so that Timoja's men found the fortress deserted when they reached it; and they threw down part of it, and set fire to the buildings, and collected some pieces of artillery[2] which the Turks had placed there. At the sight of this good fortune Afonso Dalboquerque hoisted sail with all his fleet and stood in and anchored inside the bar of Goa, a good distance away from it.

While Timoja was passing along the edge of the land in one of his *fustas* he captured a Moor, who was walking along the beach, barefooted and clad in the garb of a hermit, and he carried him before Afonso Dalboquerque, who

[1] The Portuguese equivalent of an Indian name.

[2] *Bombardas de cepo*, trunk-guns, perhaps mortars.

demanded of him what sort of a man he was and what he was doing there, and what news of Goa he could give. The Moor replied that he was a poor *jogue*[1] who lived there in the woods in a little house serving God, and that the news of Goa was that the Çabaio was dead and his son away in the interior country, and the captain that was at present in command had not more than a hundred Rumes in his company, but there were very many native soldiers, but all of them much opposed to the captain; and there were so many dissensions inside the city, one quarrelling with the other, that many prayed to God that the Franks would come against it and take it; and that there were twelve very large ships fitted out, built after the model of the *Flor de la Mar*, and many *fustas*, and watch-boats,[2] and four ships loaded with merchandise, two to go to Adem and two to Ormuz, and besides these Rumes who were stationed in the fortress, there were above a hundred in *paráos* and *fustas*, leading the life of pirates.

On the receipt of this information Afonso Dalboquerque summoned the captains to his ship, and told them that he had always been doubtful of undertaking this affair of Goa because he desired to comprehend the design and force of the enemy; but seeing that the affair was in the state that everybody declared, he was of opinion that it would be advisable to undertake it. But over and above this information which they had, they ought to order the sounding of the river first of all, for he did not wish to enter upon this business rashly. And all agreed in this, and that he should send Timoja on in front with his watch-boats.

[1] *Jogue*, an Indian word, *jôgi*, signifying an ascetic, or gymnosophist; for some account of their hideous practices and austerities of life, see Bluteau, tom. iv, p. 190, col. 2.

[2] See vol. i, p. 113.

CHAPTER XX.

How the great Afonso Dalboquerque ordered D. Antonio de Noronha and other captains to sound the river, and how they took the Castle of Pangij, which stands at the entrance of the bar, and further proceedings.

The morning of the day following that on which this council had been held, which was the twenty-eighth of the month of February, in the year '10, the great Afonso Dalboquerque ordered D. Antonio de Noronha, with certain pilots, to sound the bar, and Timoja to accompany them with two watch-boats. And they found two fathoms and a half depth at low water, and three at high water. When Dom Antonio had taken the soundings of the bar he returned and related to him what he had found. The captain of the city was fearful lest our men should capture one of the earthworks which were placed inside the bar when he saw them in progress of taking soundings, he therefore gave orders with great diligence to provide them with infantry and cavalry, and large and small pieces of artillery. And, because the principal of these fortifications was the tower of Pangij, which commanded the entrance of the bar, he sent a captain thither and ordered it to be reinforced with everything that was required for its defence.

And, although it had been determined with assent of all to enter with the whole of the fleet within the bar, yet Afonso Dalboquerque could not be persuaded to bring up his large ships into a river of which his pilots had no practical knowledge. And in this frame of mind he summoned a meeting of the captains to his ship in the night, and pointed out to them the anxiety which had troubled him with respect to this, and shewed how prudent an undertaking it would be for some boats first of all to go right over the bar inside to see how matters were going on there, and to sound the depth which the river had, so as not to find

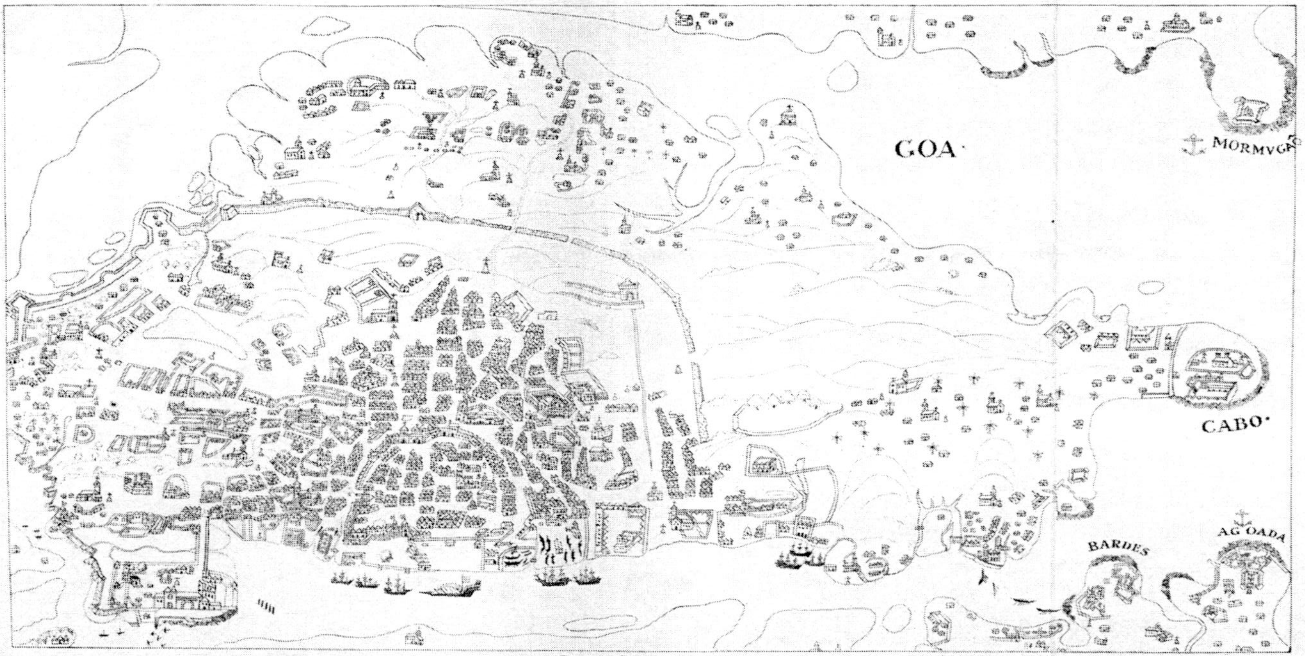

CHART OF GOA.

[*British Museum, Sloane MS.* 197, *folio* 248.]

themselves hereafter inside the bar with the large ships in any danger which they would be unable to remedy. Every one considered this advice excellent, so Afonso Dalboquerque commissioned D. Antonio de Noronha, his nephew, to get himself in readiness to take command of this undertaking as captain, and sent in company with him Jeronymo Teixeira, Simão Martinz, João Nunes, Garcia de Sousa, and Jorge da Silveira in their boats, and Simão Dandrade and Diogo Fernandez de Béja in two galleys whereof they were captains, and Timoja with his *fustas*. And on the following morning early they all set sail together and made directly for the bar, and shaped their course into the river straight to the fortress of Pangij, because it was close up by the entrance of the bar.

No sooner had D. Antonio de Noronha arrived with his fleet of boats and galleys in front of the fortress, than the Moors began to fire at him with the artillery they had with them, but as the guns were trained high, the shots passed overhead and did no injury to our boats. When the fury of the firing was over, D. Antonio thought a good opportunity offered itself for their disembarking, and he passed the word to the captains to order all the men to row right down upon the fortress, and jump on to the shore as soon as the prows struck the beach. And thus while the artillery began to open fire again without doing any harm, they all disembarked with a great and furious rush, and fighting bravely forcibly entered into the fortress through the loopholes of the bombards or by scaling the walls, and put many to death, as well those on foot as those on horseback, and even wounded the captain, who escaped, indeed, because he could not be distinguished from the others, and the rest of the men took to flight towards the city.

The Moors who were stationed in the earthwork on the land side perceived the overthrow of the fortress of Pangij, and every one of them fled away, because they were not sufficiently strong to resist any attack. Elated with this victory, D. Antonio ordered Timoja to proceed to the attack of the earthwork that stood on the opposite side; but when he arrived there he found it deserted, so he collected the artillery and everything that he found in it. And when D. Antonio had gathered all the spoil which he had gained from the Moors of Pangij, which consisted of a large number of lances, swords, shields, and eighteen pieces of artillery, he ordered the buildings of the fortress to be set on fire and betook himself again to the boats and made his way back to the ships.

On the arrival of D. Antonio with news of this unexpected success, Afonso Dalboquerque received them all with great approbation and delight, praising him very much for this deed of valour; and, being unable to brook any delay, seeing the benefits our Lord conferred on him, he again commanded D. Antonio to enter the river and go and reconnoitre the city with the galleys and boats which he had provided. And because he was afraid of the *fustas* that were in Goa, he ordered that the party this time should be reinforced with a few small vessels. And just as they were ready to set out on the following morning, two of the principal Moors of the city arrived in a *parão* with a message from the captain and inhabitants of Goa to the Captain-General, saying that all would put themselves under his orders and do everything that he should command, for they would rather become the vassals of the King of Portugal than of the Hidalcão, on account of the frequent tyrannies which the father of the Hidalcão had visited upon them.

Afonso Dalboquerque would not give them an immediate answer. And he ordered D. Antonio, notwithstanding this, to proceed on his expedition up the river to reconnoitre the city, and see how it was placed, and its walls, and its fortress; and especially to endeavour to find some places whereby the best means of entry could be effected. When D. Antonio had set out, Afonso Dalboquerque kept the Moors with him all that day; and when he thought that D. Antonio had already got on so far as to be opposite the city, he replied to them that they might tell the captain of Goa that he was the Captain-General of India for the King of Portugal, D. Manuel, his Lord, and provided that they on their part were willing to put themselves under obedience to him, and surrender to him the fortress of Goa, as they said they would, and deliver up to him all the Rumes and Turks in the city,—for these were his mortal enemies,—he, on his part, in the name of the King his Lord, would assure them their lives and treat them with every consideration, according to the instructions he had received from his Highness.

When the Moors had gone away carrying back this reply, Afonso Dalboquerque perceiving that the inhabitants of the city had virtually surrendered, like a prudent captain watching the victory which he had in his hands, without waiting any longer for news of D. Antonio, made ready all the boats and small vessels, and *paráos* of the ships of Cananor that were left with him, and set out at once behind the Moors with all this fleet, leaving the large ships outside the bar—for it was a matter requiring more leisure to get them over the bar,—and that same day he came up opposite the city, where he found D. Antonio de Noronha already at anchor in front of the fortress. The captain and governors of the city, terrified at this tumult of boats and armed host, sent immediately four principal Moors to beg a safe-conduct in order to treat for some settlement of affairs.

Afonso Dalboquerque replied that he would be happy to grant their request with the conditions which he had already conveyed to their consideration. The Moors returned forthwith with the answer that they would accept the safe-conduct that he would give them; and as all were willing to surrender the city into his hands, they begged him to be pleased to grant its extension as well to include certain Rumes and Turks who were there—strangers,—for it did not seem reasonable nor according to the laws of humanity to deliver them up. As Afonso Dalboquerque was unwilling to decide this point of his own responsibility, he called a meeting of the captains and recounted to them what the captain and governors of the city were treating for; and it was universally agreed that unless the Rumes and Turks were delivered up, the armistice should no longer be observed, but on the following morning the combat against the city should begin.

The Moors retired with this message, and a large part of the night was spent without any further negociation; and while Afonso Dalboquerque was considering what further proceedings he should enter into, and wondering what was the cause of the delay, there came to him by night a native —a relation of Timoja,—and informed him that the captain of the city had fled away, and that he had done so in order to avoid surrendering the Rumes and Turks, and had left the fortress stripped of everything, and that the people of the city were engaged in nothing but pillaging everything they could find. Although Afonso Dalboquerque was very desirous of getting these Turks and Rumes into his power, he was, nevertheless, pleased to get the city without any trouble or danger to his men, and ordered Garcia de Sousa and Dom Jeronymo de Lima to go forward in their boats in front of the gates of the fortress, and there station themselves on the watch until the morning, to prevent any Moors from going out or entering in by that gate.

Of the Site and Foundation of the City of Goa.

The kingdom of Goa belonged in ancient days to the Hindoos, and was tributary to the King of Narsinga; but at the time that Afonso Dalboquerque captured it, it had been freed for about seventy years, and no longer subject to that king. The principal centre of this kingdom was the city of Goa[1], which is situated on an island which all the Hindoos call Tiçuarij, surrounded on every side with lagoons of salt water and islands. And in some of the principal passes of this island they had built towers to prevent the incursions of the Moors of the mainland. And because the pass of Gondali was so shallow that it could be forded at low water, it was ordered that all those who were condemned to die by the hands of justice, and also any Moors who were captured in battle, should be cast into this part in order that the alligators that abound in these lagoons should come thither to seek for their carcasses—and these creatures were so numerous and so accustomed to assemble at this fattening place that the Moors on this account dared not attempt to pass over the ford,—and by means of this artifice, and with the rest of the towers that were built around the island, they lived many years without the Moors being able to get in among them.

The first population that occupied this island of Tiçuarij founded Old Goa, and from the appearance of its buildings it was a great place. The reason that the original founders established themselves there, and not where the city of New Goa now stands (if we may so call it)—granted that the harbour and river are much better,—was on account of the shallowness of the water on the bar, and the impossibility of ships and vessels passing over. But in course of time the water which comes down from the high land of the *Gate*[2]—which in the winter rushes down with great fury to the sea,—little by little enlarged the bar in such a manner that the depth of water increased so as to admit the passage of ships and vessels. When the inhabitants of Old Goa perceived that

[1] 15 deg. 27 min. N., 73 deg. 53 min. E. New Goa, or Panjim, is 15 deg. 26 min. N., 73 deg. 51 min. E.

[2] See page 95. Cf. *Ghaut*, or *Ghāt*.

this river and harbour were better, and that the bar had increased in depth so that ships and vessels could enter thereby without peril, they deserted the habitations of Old Goa, and came and founded the populous places where now stands our fortress, and there they built a very large city. And as they were a maritime race, and more inured to the hardships of the sea than all the other nations, they immediately began to build ships of great burthen, and navigated all the coasts of India. They were valiant men and good archers, and in this respect they performed good service to all their neighbours.

In the time of the Hindoos Goa was ever considered a very important place in those parts, and there were therein many soldiers, both infantry and cavalry, and by their aid the city defended itself for many years against the power of the King of Daquem.[1] The Hindoos had therein many venerable temples, of a very good style of architecture, wherein lived certain men, as religious persons; these they called Brahmans *(Bramenes)*, and there they keep the rites of their false worship. They had a custom that if any Hindoo died, the wife had to burn herself of her own free will; and when she was proceeding to this self-sacrifice it was with great merry-making and blowing of music, saying that she desired to accompany her husband to the other world. But the wife who would not so burn herself was thrust out from among the others, and lived by gaining, by means of her body, support for the maintenance of the pagoda of which she was a votary. However, when Afonso Dalboquerque took the city of Goa, he forbade from that time forward that any more women should be burned; and although to change one's customs is equal to death itself, nevertheless, they were happy to save their lives, and spoke very highly of him because he had ordered that there should be no more burning.

[1] *I.e.*, Deccan.

Through this harbour of Goa was always the principal passage to the kingdom of Narsinga and of Daquem; and for this reason it contained much merchandise, and large caravans of merchants came from the interior country in quest of it, and brought other commodities in exchange. And from this commerce which they had one with another the inhabitants of Goa grew so prosperous that it was said that Goa alone in those days had a revenue of two hundred thousand *pardaos*[1]. Between this kingdom of Goa and that of Daquem, on the side of the interior country, there runs a range of mountains, very lofty and very extensive, which is called the *Gate*,[2] and divides these two kingdoms one from the other. This range of mountains had certain passes by which it was entered, and in these the Hindoos had their towers with garrisons for their defence.

And, although the ascent to this range of mountains is very steep and rocky, yet as soon as the summit is reached the ground is quite flat for all the rest of the way in front, and densely peopled with very large towns, in such a manner that this range hangs over Goa and over the sea like an awning. I do not here give any further account of this land, for it is my intention only to treat of the way in which Dalboquerque gained possession of it from the Moors, and not how they made themselves masters of it. And after that the Moors had for many years gained the kingdom of Daquem from the King of Narsinga and were masters of it, although they always waged war with the Hindoos of Goa until the Çabaio became Lord of Daquem, they could never overcome them; but this prince carrying on the war with them was oftentimes overcome and as many times conqueror—finally, having seized the passes of the hill country by treachery, he came down with a great body of

[1] *Pardao*, an Indian coin equivalent to 370 *reis* Portuguese; *i.e.*, about 1s. 6½d. English. "Cem mil pardaos são noventa mil cruzados de nossa moeda."—Bluteau, *s.v.*

[2] See page 93.

men over against the island of Goa, and remained encamped before the city for so long a time until he got inside. And after the capture of the entire city, the rest of the kingdom fell without any further resistance, and thereupon became the principal city of both kingdoms. And when the old Çabaio perceived that the site of Goa was very good, and well supplied with water, and the island of itself very fertile and pleasant, he determined to take up his residence therein, and leave all the rest of his kingdom, out of liking for Goa; and lost no time in building palaces, very large and of excellent workmanship. And after finding himself settled there in security he became so well pleased with the harbour and the river, and the favourable position which it occupied for building large fleets, that he was constantly asserting to those who were his favourites that since fortune had bestowed Goa upon him, he hoped thereby to gain possession of the kingdom of Cambaya, and destroy the whole of Malabar, for these were always the most formidable opponents he had.

But when Afonso Dalboquerque took Goa, it would be about forty years, more or less, since the Çabaio had taken it from the Hindoos. As soon as the news got abroad that the Çabaio was Lord of the kingdom of Goa, owing to the great reputation which he had acquired in past times, everybody endeavoured all they could to enjoy his friendship, and the Xeque Ismael, and the Grand Sultan of Cairo, and the King of Adem immediately dispatched their ambassadors to his Court, making many overtures to him for his friendship. And because he used to give a greater payment to foreigners than any king of India, there immediately flocked to Goa many Rumes, Turks, Arabs, and Persians, and by the assistance of these people he wrested many places from the king of Narsinga and made himself the great lord of the kingdom of Daquem.

And after the Portuguese had gained a footing in India,

the people of Malabar, who were the principal enemies the Çabaio had, allied themselves with him and made him their captain-general, and offered him great sums of money and soldiers, and every other kind of assistance that he required in his operations against us. And towards the support of this enterprise the Çabaio had prepared a very large fleet of ships, vessels, and galleys in the river of Goa, which was just on the point of completion when the great Afonso Dalboquerque entered the city.

On the coast of the kingdom of Goa there are other harbours, in which, before it was taken by the Portuguese, there were ships and merchants, but there are none now by reason of their fear of our fleets, and also because Afonso Dalboquerque would not allow any trade along the whole of that coast except in Goa.

CHAPTER XXI.

How the Governors of the City of Goa delivered the keys of it to the great Afonso Dalboquerque, and of the spoils he found therein, and further proceedings.

As soon as D. Jeronymo and Garcia de Sousa had set out to watch the fortress (as I have already described), the great Afonso Dalboquerque remained quiet throughout the night waiting for the break of day, and advised the captains what course they should pursue if any resistance should be offered to them when entering the city. And just as the morning began to break he ordered the signal to be made to them, of which he had previously given them notice. When the captains heard the signal, they weighed anchor, and steered with all their people—about one thousand Portuguese and two hundred men of Malabar,—towards the galley where Afonso Dalboquerque was, and from that point commenced their course, and, arriving at the city when it was clear day, not meeting with any resistance, they entered in at the gate, with a cross carried in front of them; and there was the great Afonso Dalboquerque kneeling on his knees, who, letting fall many tears, gave thanks to our Lord for that loving-kindness which He had shewn him in delivering into his hands[1] so large and so powerful a city without trouble to, or death of any one. This cross was borne aloft by a friar of St. Dominic, behind it was carried the royal flag which was made of white satin with a cross of Christus worked in the centre, and in this order of procession they all went on up to the gate of the castle, where the principal Moors of the city, and the governors thereof, stood in expectation of their arrival. And these men casting themselves at the feet of our party, delivered up to them the keys of the fortress, and begged them earnestly of their kindness that they would respect the assurance of safety that had been given to them.

When Afonso Dalboquerque had entered into the fortress, because he perceived that many men of the city were following up behind him, he commanded Dom Antonio de Noronha to wait behind with fifty men at the gate, and not suffer any Moor to enter. The Hindoos who were inside approached him in their accustomed courteous manner, and told him that they wished to become vassals of the King of Portugal and to place themselves in obedience to him. He therefore received them with great affection and consideration, and ordered proclamation to be made, that under penalty of death for disobedience, no one should touch a single thing belonging either to the Moors or Hindoos who were in Goa, but treat them as vassals of the King of Portugal his lord.

As soon as this was over, he proceeded to inspect the fortress and the palace of the Çabaio, which was all made with joinery work, and had gardens and pools of water within it. And thence he went on to some large arsenals,

[1] See Camões, *Lusiada*, x, 42; quoted in vol. I, Introduction, p. i.

wherein he found many supplies, a great quantity of powder, and many materials for making it, and many weapons for the men, both infantry and cavalry, and a very large quantity of merchandise, and in some stables of large size, one hundred and sixty horses; and in divers parts of the city there were captured forty large field guns[1] and fifty-five howitzers[2] and of other lesser kinds of artillery a great quantity, and many other things which I do not write of, so that I may not tire the reader. To the shore there were moored forty ships, large and small, and sixteen *fustas;* and there was also there a great supply of ropes and cordage, and boltwork, and everything else that was necessary for them.

And there, too, Afonso Dalboquerque found all the women and children of the Turks and Rumes, whom they could not carry with them, by reason of the haste they made in fleeing away with Milique Çufegurgij. For when this man arrived at the pass of Gondali, intending to cross over to the mainland, so great was the thronging haste, that many fugitives were suffocated in the river, and others lost their horses and quantities of clothing which they were carrying, because there were no means of passing over the ford except by pieces of wood laid across one another. As soon as Afonso Dalboquerque had gathered the women and children of the Turks together, he ordered that they should receive proper attention, and be safely kept; and on the second taking of this city he converted them to Christianity, and married them to Portuguese men, as I shall show further on.

Now that the great Afonso Dalboquerque was already in possession of the city, he ordered that the captains of the ships of Cananor should be called together, and then he gave them permission to depart, and made them accept a part of the spoils that had been taken there. And when

[1] *Bombardas.* [2] *Falcões.*

these men had departed, he called Timoja, and told him he had information that there yet remained some Turks in the castle of Banda, and in other strongholds round about it; and as he was determined that there should not remain any of the seed of these people in the whole of the kingdom of Goa, he was desirous of ordering him to destroy those castles, and put them all to the sword; he would therefore earnestly desire him to send his cousin with some *fustas* to show our people the entries to the rivers, for they did not know them.

Timoja replied that he considered it a good plan to order the casting out of all the Turks from the island of Goa, and from the neighbouring places, for as long as they remained therein they would give much trouble, so he would make his cousin ready with the *fustas* which were necessary for that object. This having been agreed upon, Afonso Dalboquerque sent word to D. Antonio de Noronha, his nephew, to make ready the ship *Sancta Clara*, and the *Cirne*, and the *Flor de la Mar*, and the *Flor da Rosa*, which were stationed outside the bar (as I have already said), and three galleys, and go and overrun all those places and destroy them, not sparing the life of a single Turk or Moor whom they might find.

D. Antonio set out and drew up opposite the fortress of Banda; and as soon as the fleet had dropped anchor, he got into the galleys and ships' boats, and made his way up the river, taking with him in the front rank the cousin of Timoja with three *fustas*. When the Hindoos of the land perceived our fleet, inflamed with hatred against the Turks, they all rose up against them, and these, terrified at our men, deserted the fortress and fled away into the interior country, so that when D. Antonio de Noronha arrived, the Hindoos were already in possession of it, and their captain immediately had an audience with D. Antonio, and paid him homage for the fortress, promising to hold himself in obedience to the king of Portugal.

As soon as the news that Banda had surrendered ran along the coast, the Turks who were in the fortress of Condal—distrusting the Hindoos who were elated at the favourable treatment they had received from our fleet—deserted it and fled up the river. And when it was known in the land that the Turks had fled, a Hindoo captain came with a large body of men, and put himself into the fortress, and sent his submission to Afonso Dalboquerque, holding himself to be a subject of the king of Portugal, and D. Antonio returned to Goa, and passed up the river with the large ships, and gave an account of what had taken place to his uncle, and how he had set fire to four vessels which the Rumes had in the river at Banda.

CHAPTER XXII.

How the great Afonso Dalboquerque began to build the fortress of Goa: and what passed with the Captains and Timoja.

No sooner had the great Afonso Dalboquerque obtained complete information respecting the affairs of Goa, than he began at once to turn his attention to the fortification of the city, with the determination of repairing it, and strengthening his position therein, in order to be able to rely on the assistance it would give him in his trouble. And his first operation was upon the foundations and walls, with many people of the land who laboured at the work; and the captains with their men had their hours of work according as it came by turn to them, and so the work of fortification progressed with great rapidity by reason of the fear he had lest the Hidalcão should come up against him, and there he stood all day long, and at night slept with his clothes on upon a couch. And within the fortress he ordered them to lay the foundations of some very large stone rooms, in order that in them he might collect every year large quantities of corn and rice, that from these might be victualled all the other fortresses and all the fleets of India, making preparations that there all the business of India should be carried on, according to what he saw in the arrangement and situation of the city.

When he had put all this work into order, he called for Timoja to advise with him concerning the settling of the land, and told him that since the King of Portugal was lord of the land, it would not be right that he should get less revenue from it than other former lords; that he ought, therefore, to summon a meeting of all the Hindoos, and notify to them that from that time forward they would have to pay to the King their lord, from the property they held, the tribute which hitherto they had been accustomed to pay to the King and Lord of Goa.

Timoja replied that he would call them together and acquaint them of this matter. But nevertheless he was not pleased to find that Afonso Dalboquerque had resolved to retain Goa; for he had, some days before this, privately requested him to hand over the place to him, with all its lands, and he would pay a certain sum every year by way of revenue for it, sustaining and defending the place at his own risk. And Afonso Dalboquerque always made a point of deferring to give any reply to this request of his, without giving any account of it to the captains, by reason of the necessity he had of using Timoja's men for the work of the building. But when Timoja perceived that Afonso Dalboquerque would not give him any definite answer, he made up his mind to relate the affair to certain of the captains, in order to gain them over to take his part; and they, as people who were wearied with the war and the operations in Goa, gave him to understand that it would be very beneficial to the service of the King if Afonso Dalboquerque would hand over to him the possession of Goa.

When Timoja had gained over to his side these captains

with whom he conversed, he began to put greater pressure upon Afonso Dalboquerque for an answer to his request, and because this business soon leaked out between them, Afonso Dalboquerque, pretending to know nothing about it, ordered them all to be summoned to a meeting, and told them that they were well aware for how long a time Timoja had laboured in the service of the King of Portugal, and particularly what he had done towards the taking of the city, and how much reason there was that he should be rewarded, because, apart from its being very necessary that his services should be requited, it would also be an example to many others, urging them also to come forward and serve the King; and concluded by asking them to advise him what to do in the matter.

The captains, almost to a man, were of opinion that Goa should be given to him, alleging that Timoja was a lord over many people, and could maintain it, and defend it against the Turks; and that, notwithstanding all this, he would give twenty thousand *pardaos*[1] by way of tribute every year, and if he were to give this it would be more serviceable to the King than for them to maintain the place at their own cost.

When Afonso Dalboquerque saw the captains' intentions, he replied to them that he was very much surprised at their considering it right to give away so noble a city as Goa, and one so important for the service of the King of Portugal, to Timoja for no commensurate price which he would give for it, and not rather choosing to strengthen the city with a good fortress, because therein the governor of India ought to make his principal seat of government; neither ought the revenues to be farmed out to Timoja without first of all finding out to what sum they amounted, and being apprised of his intended manner of government, and whether, when

[1] 20,000 × 1s. 6½d. = £1541 13s. 4d., a large sum in the early years of the sixteenth century.

they had been so apprised of it, he would perform all things to the furtherance of the King's service. And, he continued, with regard to what they said concerning Timoja being sufficiently powerful to defend Goa from the Turks, he was much more surprised at this, that they were doing, by offering such advice, the very thing to make Timoja powerful enough to defend Goa from any one of the captains of the Hidalcão who might come against him, much more than from the Turks only. And the satisfaction due to him for his services should rather resemble that given to a spy who had bravely carried out the commands of his captain, or to a subject who had served his lord loyally, than that awarded to a man on whom the safety of every one depended. And they must not forget the services rendered by the King of Cochim, who indeed only received from the King of Portugal a yearly sum of five hundred cruzados, and was very well contented therewith.

The captains were so put to shame by this speech that Afonso Dalboquerque made to them, that they did not dare to reply to it. And when the meeting came to an end, he summoned Timoja before him, and told him that he had always desired to do him a kindness in the name of the King D. Manuel his lord in return for the numerous services that he had rendered in these parts; and as there was at present nothing that could be given to him, he would, in the King's name, make him a present of the whole of the revenue of the lands of Mergeu paid in the factory of Goa, and would appoint him to be chief *Aguazil*, and captain of all the people of the land; and that he begged him earnestly to be pleased to accept this offering, for the present occasion did not offer any possibility of recompense in any other manner; and with respect to his request, he could give no reply until he had in the first instance written to the King D. Manuel, but he would take care to carry out his Highness's wishes with regard to it.

Timoja was not pleased at this reply, for he had always entertained a hope that Afonso Dalboquerque would give Goa to him by reason of the promises that the captains had made to him, nevertheless he accepted the reward that had been offered, and returned home to his house a very rich man, because on the entering into the castle, Afonso Dalboquerque gave him two houses without ascertaining what he was giving, and it afterwards turned out that they contained a large quantity of merchandise and two *sambucos*, which Timoja loaded with the merchandise, and carried away with him. Three days after that Timoja had gone away, some Hindoos came to tell Afonso Dalboquerque that he was in the land of Salsete, and that as soon as he had got there every Hindoo had gone over to him and had come to a determination of going whithersoever he went and deserting the land. Afonso Dalboquerque knew that this was a piece of spite brought about by Timoja, but concealed his thoughts from the Hindoo messengers, and made as though he did not understand the drift of what they said.

When Timoja saw that Afonso Dalboquerque had not given any answer to the request of the Hindoos, he sent word to him by one *Naique*, his captain, that it had always been his desire to serve the King of Portugal, and for this reason, after he had set out, he had remembered that he had left him in Goa without anyone by his side to explain to him the manners and customs of the land, and therefore he would like to return again into the service of the King of Portugal, and do whatever was required of him. And thus Alfonso Dálboquerque, although he now knew him to be a worthless and ill-tempered fellow, seeing that he had now abandoned his former request, consented to his return, and agreed to receive him again in order to settle, with this man's co-operation, the affairs of Goa.

As soon as Timoja received the message of recall he returned without loss of time, and Afonso Dalboquerque commanded the principal Moors and Hindoos to unite together and go to receive him. And these took many trumpets and made a great deal of music, according to their custom, when they met him. And after performing this show of native courtesy, Afonso Dalboquerque told them that he had made Timoja chief *Aguazil* of the kingdom of Goa in the name of the King of Portugal, and had given him all the power of justice over the Hindoos and Moors, and that he was to provide for all things arising in the land, and everything that he might order was to be obeyed. And then he invested him with a drawn sword, ornamented with silver on the handle, and with a ring, for it was the custom of the country to give these things to those who were entrusted with any high position in the government.

The Hindoos were very well pleased with the consideration and honour that Afonso Dalboquerque had shown to them, and they set Timoja in a kind of sedan-chair, and carried him all round the city, with great merry-making and blowing of trumpets. And when this was over Afonso Dalboquerque farmed out to him the lands of Goa—reserving the island—for one hundred thousand cruzados, he agreeing to pay all persons and expenses necessary for its defence; and when all these matters had been arranged they became very friendly, and from that day forward Timoja began to attend to his duties.

CHAPTER XXIII.

How the Ambassadors of the Xeque Ismael, and of the King of Ormuz, who were in Goa, sent word to the great Afonso Dalboquerque, desiring an audience: and what took place with them, and how he sent Ruy Gomes to the Xeque Ismael.

A few days before the time that the great Afonso Dalboquerque had made his entry into the city of Goa, there had arrived two ambassadors, the one from Xeque Ismael, and the other from the King of Ormuz, each one by himself with his embassy suite and his present of horses, and silk stuffs, and gold, for the Çabaio. But whereas they found he was dead, after the fall of the city, although it was the intention of the ambassador who came from Xeque Ismael to proceed on his mission to the Hidalcão, the son of the Çabaio, according to the instructions he had received from his lord, nevertheless, in that he was a discreet man and understood the position of affairs, he took no notice of these instructions, but sent word to Afonso Dalboquerque begging that he would be pleased to grant him an audience. And when he had obtained this permission, he came before him offering the present he had brought, and told him that the Xeque Ismael his lord, in consequence of the events which he had heard regarding India, was desirous of maintaining a firm friendship with the King of Portugal; and whereas he had been informed that his lordship, Afonso Dalboquerque, had conquered the kingdom of Ormuz, he had therefore sent an ambassador to visit him with a present of horses, pieces of silver, and other valuables, but when the ambassador arrived at Ormuz, he found him already set out on his expedition to India, and the principal reason of his visit was the desire of gaining information and appreciation from his lordship; and if the King of Ormuz were unwilling to put himself under his orders, he, Xeque Ismael, would send a very great army against him in order to force him to do so; for as for men, both on horse and on foot, he would promise to supply as many as could possibly be required, and that this and much more the ambassador had been instructed to say to him at Ormuz.

Afonso Dalboquerque replied that, with respect to the affairs at Ormuz, he looked upon them as settled, and that he should not lose much time before he went there again, and that he was determined from that point to enter the Red Sea; and since the Xeque Ismael had always carried on war with the Turk and with the Grand Sultan of Cairo, it would be very necessary to the success of this policy that he should be in alliance with the King of Portugal his lord; because, apart from the supremacy over the Indian seas being in the King's hands, the royal fleets also ride triumphant in the Eastern Sea,[1] and he wages war with the Turk and with the Grand Sultan both on the one side and on the other. And, he continued, provided that the Xeque Ismael were desirous of confirming this friendly alliance with the King his lord, and of sending his ambassadors to visit him, and despatching his military forces against the house of Méca, there could be no doubt that the Turk and the Grand Sultan would lose their important positions, for the King of Portugal was very powerful upon the sea, and could bring immense fleets to the side of Xeque Ismael against them; and that for some time past he had been wishing to send an ambassador to him, to offer to him the kingdom of India in the name of the King his lord, but from having a great amount of business to transact he had omitted to do so, yet now he would send such an one in his company.

Then the ambassador began to dilate upon the grandeur of Xeque Ismael, and how very important a prince he was, a man of great fame, and desirous of extending his name throughout all the countries of the world; and, progressing with his reply, he proposed two things to Afonso Dalboquerque. The first was, that he should prevail upon the Moors of Goa to adopt the laws of Xeque Ismael, and perform their devotions according to his book in their mosques. The second, that he should issue an order for the coinage of the Xeque Ismael to pass current in Goa. To this Afonso Dalboquerque replied, that when the Moors surrendered to him the city of Goa, he had given them a royal safeguard in the name of the King of Portugal that they should live in liberty, and to put any compulsion upon them now in

[1] *Mar de levante.*

any matter, however small it were, would be in contravention of the promises that he had given to them, and a procedure which was not practised by Christian sovereigns. And, he continued, with regard to the currency of Xeque Ismael's money in Goa, he was greatly astonished at their entertaining the idea of such a thing, for kings were accustomed to value very highly their royal prerogatives, which consisted in their people and their subjects living in obedience to their laws, and in their coinage being received and current throughout their kingdoms at such value as the kings fixed upon it, and that a king would not on any consideration bring himself to permit any one to mint money in his land.

The ambassador answered that he had come to Goa with an embassy addressed to the Çabaio, and the instructions which he brought ordered him to speak upon these points; but, as he found the Çabaio dead, and his lordship Afonso Dalboquerque in possession of the kingdom of Goa, he had not exceeded his instructions in repeating to him the message of the Xeque his lord, for he was his ambassador; but if he had herein done anything wrong, he begged him of his graciousness to forgive him, for the first duty of ambassadors was to adhere faithfully to their instructions, and his duty in this case was to do what was most to the service of his King. And when this interview was concluded, the ambassador begged he would despatch his affairs, for he was desirous of setting out on his return journey.

Afonso Dalboquerque told him not to be annoyed, for he desired to make ready a messenger to be sent in company with him to the Xeque Ismael, and as soon as the ambassador had betaken himself to his house again, Afonso Dalboquerque sent word for the ambassador from the King of Ormuz, and enquired of him the reason of his coming, and what message it was that he brought for the Çabaio. The ambassador told him that Cogeatar had sent him, and the principal reason of his coming was to make an offer of the whole of the estate of the King of Ormuz to the Çabaio, begging of him assistance and co-operation against the Portuguese; and, relating to him how things had gone lately with Ormuz, he told him not to be surprised or annoyed at the conduct of Cogeatar, because the captains had been the cause of all the dissensions that had sprung up between them.

When this interview was over that Afonso Dalboquerque held with the ambassadors, he busied himself with despatching without delay Ruy Gomez, the servant of King D. Manuel—(he had been sent in banishment from the Kingdom of Portugal to India in the Marshal's fleet)—in order to send him to Xeque Ismael in company with the Xeque's ambassador, and through him he sent a letter to the Xeque, and another to the King of Ormuz, which are given here in full further on, and he also delivered him instructions as to what he should say to the Xeque Ismael on his part. And this Ruy Gomez was accompanied by an interpreter and a servant. As soon as Afonso Dalboquerque had arranged all the matters for the journey, he sent for the ambassador of Xeque Ismael, and shewed him much respect in the king's name, and then took his leave of them and gave them their pass, and the two embarked in two ships, whereof the captain and factor was Cogeamir, a noble Moor of Cananor, whom he found in Goa, and whom the Rumes had enslaved on the occasion of his coming in one of his ships from Ormuz with a cargo of horses and saying that he held a permit to navigate the Indian Sea from the King of Portugal and not from the Grand Sultan. And by this man Afonso Dalboquerque wrote a letter to Cogeatar, wherein he told him that if he would return to the obedience of the King of Portugal his Lord, and pay him the tribute which had been agreed upon, past troubles should be forgotten; and he begged him earnestly that this ambassador from Xeque Ismael should not be charged any duty upon his merchandize, and that he would provide Ruy Gomez, whom he sent in the position of an ambassador, with relays of horses, and with money and everything else that he or his should have need of; and that he desired that the merchandise which Cogeamir carried with him—belonging to the King his Lord, should be exchanged for horses; and that the ships which should sail from Ormuz to Goa should carry with them his signature to their papers, and all come to Goa and no other port, for unless they came there he would not hold them free.

Letter which the great Afonso Dalboquerque wrote, and sent by Ruy Gomez to the Xeque Ismael.

"Very great and powerful Lord among the Moors, Xeque Ismael: Afonso Dalboquerque, Captain-General and Governor of India, in behalf of the very high and very powerful King D. Manuel, King of Portugal and of the Algarves on this side and on that side of the sea, in Africa Lord of Guinea, and of the conquest, navigation, and commerce of Æthiopia, Arabia, Persia, and India, and of the Kingdom and Lordship of Ormuz, and of the Kingdom and Lordship of Goa: I give you to know that when I captured the city and kingdom of Goa, I found therein your ambassador, to whom I shewed great honour, treating him as ambassador of so great a King and Lord, and I looked to all his affairs just as if he had been sent to these parts to the King of Portugal. And whereas I am informed that the King D. Manuel, my Lord, would be pleased to have an understanding and alliance and intercourse with you; therefore I send to you this present messenger to whom you are to give credit in respect of all things which he shall relate to you on my behalf, for he is a knight and servant of the King my Lord, a man well-versed in military matters, bred up in arms according to our custom, and of all the affairs of the kingdom of Portugal he will be competent to give you a very good account.

"You are well-informed how it was that I gained the city and kingdom of Ormuz in accordance with the command of the King, my Lord, and how from that time forward I strove to gain information concerning your estate, power, and command, and desired to send messengers to you, if the business of Ormuz had not miscarried, which I hope to God will soon be re-established, for I am in expectation of going thither in person, and thence I will endeavour to have an interview with you on the coast of the sea and harbours of your kingdom; for the powers which I carry from the King my Lord, of ships and mariners, are for destroying and casting out the ships of the Sultan that may enter India and desire therein to establish themselves—which deed, with the help of God, we have brought to pass, for the Sultan's captain, Mirocem, and his fleet were routed at Diu,[1] and all his ships and artillery taken, and all his people killed, and

[1] Concerning this important event in the history of the Portuguese in India, spoken of in the early chapters of this Second Part of the *Commentaries*, Camões contains the following passage:—

"Qual o touro cioso, que se ensaia
Para a crua peleja, os cornos tenta
No tronco d'hum carvalho, ou alta faia,
E o ar ferindo, as forças exprimenta:
Tal, antes que no seio de Cambaia
Entre Francisco irado, na opulenta
Cidade de Dabul a espada afia,
Abaixando-lhe a tumida ousadia.

"E logo, entrando fera na enseada
De Dio, illustre em cercos e batalhas
Fará espalhar a fraca e grande armada
De Calecut, que remos tem por malhas:
A de Melique Yaz acautelada,
Co'os pelouros que tu, Vulcano, espalhas,
Fará ir ver o frio e fundo assento,
Secreto leito do humido elemento.

now I have put them to flight and gained the city of Goa and all its fleet and cast all the enemy out of it, as your ambassador will relate to you.

"And whereas I have been informed that he is your enemy and makes war upon you, I send you this news, offering to you for employment against him my person and fleet, and the men of the King my Lord, to help to destroy him, and I will be against him whensoever you shall require this of me. And if you desire to destroy the Sultan by land, you can reckon upon great assistance from the Armada of the King my Lord by sea, and I believe that with small trouble you must gain the lordship of the city of Cairo, and all his kingdom and dependencies, and thus the King my Lord can give you great help by sea against the Turk, and thus his fleets by sea and you with your great forces and cavalry by land can combine to inflict troublous injuries upon them.

"And in India he has great fleets wherewith he can help you. And thus you will gather that you ought to desire to obtain alliance and co-operation with so great a king as is the King my Lord by sea and by land, and you ought to send him your ambassadors, for he will be very glad to see any one who is competent to give an account of your kingdoms and your dependencies. And if God grant that this intercourse and alliance be ratified, come you with all your power against the city of Cairo and the lands of the Grand Sultan which are on the borders of your own, and the King my Lord shall pass over to Jerusalem and gain from him all

"Mas a de Mir-Hocem, que, abalroando,
A furia esperará dos vingadores,
Verá braços, e pernas ir nadando,
Sem corpos, pelo mar, de seus senhores:
Raios de fogo irão representando
No cego ardor os bravos domadores:
Quanto alli sentirão olhos, e ouvidos,
He fumo, ferro, flammas, e alaridos."

Lusiada, x, 34-36.

the land on that side. And for the sake of correct information with respect to your intentions in this matter, it is befitting that you should send your messengers, and through them get a reply from the King my Lord, and meanwhile let me be advised of what you wish me to do, or in what quarter the fleet of the King my Lord can proceed and inflict most injury upon the Sultan for your service."

INSTRUCTIONS WHICH THE GREAT AFONSO DALBOQUERQUE GAVE TO RUY GOMEZ, CONCERNING THAT WHICH HE WAS TO SAY TO THE XEQUE ISMAEL.

"First of all your journey is to be made by whatever method and manner that you can well perform it, direct to the place where the Xeque Ismael may be; and on your arrival before him you shall do him that reverence which is due to so great a king and prince.

"On your arrival at Ormuz you shall send a requisition to Cogeatar to supply you with the relays of horses that you require, and a requisition to him to give you all things necessary for your expenses, and for the despatch of your journey, in accordance with the advice which I have forwarded to him in my letters.

"In the journey which you are thus about to prosecute, you shall be ever under the orders, advice, and disposition of the Ambassadors of the Xeque Ismael in whose company you go, nor shall you ever detach yourself from him to go and see cities, strongholds, towns, streets, festivals, or games, nor shall you follow any other route than that which he takes, but be in all things under his orders, for you well know how the Moors desire to inflict upon us all the loss they can.

"You shall say to the Xeque Ismael, on my behalf, that I send this visitation to him on account of the greatness of his fame, lordship, and influence, and on account of the good and great qualities which he personally possesses, and also because he shelters the Christians, and shews favour and honour towards them.

"You shall tell him how my Lord will be pleased to come to an understanding and alliance with him, and will assist him in his war against the Sultan; and that I, in his name and on his behalf, offer him the fleet, and army, and artillery which I have with me, and the fortresses, towns, and lordships which the King of Portugal holds in India, and I will give him all this same help against the Turk.

"You will tell him that when he rises up and attacks the house of Méca, and is desirous of obtaining possession of it, I will enter the Red Sea and make my way to the harbour of Judá[1] with my fleet, and I will do likewise when he desires to go over the land of Arabia and Adem, and over the sea on the coast of Arabia, Bahrem,[2] and Catife,[3] and the city of Baçora;[4] and I will overrun all the coasts of the Persian Sea where I can come and see him; and I will do everything that I can for him.

"You will describe to him the greatness of the King my Lord, and of his kingdoms and dominions, and the extent of their richness and abundance; and speak of the greatness and beauty of the city of Lisbon, the edifices and costly houses that it contains, and of the great quantity and stores of silver, and gold, and riches, and number of people that are contained in the kingdom; and how the King my Lord has two gold mines which yield him every year a great

[1] See vol. i, p. 234, note 2, and the site of the "Cidade de Iuda" on Berthelot's chart, vol. i, p. 80.

[2] Baharem or Barem, "huma Ilha de Ormuz, onde se pesca o aljofar". See *Cam. Lus.*, x, 41, quoted in vol. i, p. 64, note; probably the Bahrein or Aval Islands, 26 deg. 10 min. N., 50 deg. 35 min. E.

[3] El-katiff, on the western side of the Persian gulf, 26 deg. 32 min. N., 50 deg 8 min. E.

[4] Bassorah, or Basra, in Irak-Arabi, Turkey in Asia, 30 deg. 31 min. N., 47 deg. 53 min. E.

quantity of precious metal; and you will relate to him the abundance of the ships that belong to the kingdom, their greatness, and the large fleets which he prepares every year for India; and how his fleets and subjects sail all over the world; and that he sends fleets to the East against the Turks.

"You will tell him how the King my Lord has acquired many towns, cities, and villages by force of arms in Africa; and how his power and dominion are rapidly progressing all along the sea-coast down to the Cape of Good Hope, and from that point inwardly as one enters the sea of India; and you will speak of the fortresses that are contained in this region, and the kings that are therein subject to his supreme authority.

"You will, moreover, tell him of the Queen my Sovereign Lady; whose daughter she is,[1] and how the king her father, and the queen, her mother, hold their kingdoms and dominions which border upon the kingdom of Portugal: and in this manner you will give him an account of her estate, and of the maids of honour who minister to her, that they are daughters of dukes, marquesses, and counts of Portugal; and how they appear clothed in brocades and cloth of gold, and in all sorts of different coloured silks, and adorned with much jewelry, and that on passing from the service of the queen, these maids are married to the grandees of the kingdom.

"You will mention the household estate of the king my Lord, how he is served, and in what manner he eats at his high table of four degrees, while all the great lords and fidalgos who frequent his court, stand at the table with their

[1] King Manoel, or Emmanuel "The Fortunate", married Maria of Castile, daughter of Ferdinand the Catholic, King of Aragon, and Isabella of Castile, in 1500. She was born in 1482 and died in 1517, and was the second wife of King Manoel who had previously married her elder sister, Isabella of Aragon.

caps removed from their heads until he has finished his repast and retired.

"You will tell him that he ought to send an ambassador to the King my Lord, with a view to procuring alliance and assistance, not only with regard to the war against his enemies, but also in the matter of the merchandise which can be sent into Persia from the kingdom of Portugal by way of Ormuz; and the King will help him against the Sultan, and against the Turk, by sea and by land, provided that he on his part will send to solicit his alliance, co-operation, and assistance.

"You will not omit to make mention to him of our Faith, and observe what his opinions are in this matter, and if he receives you well; and what you say to him in this respect shall not be more than what can be said without giving him any offence; and you will gather from the Christians of those parts if they practise the rites of our Faith, and believe truly that Our Lord was born of Our Lady, and died, and suffered on the Cross to save us; and you will take notice if any of these Christians exercise rites different in any way to ours, in the practice of their Faith; and see you if you can manage to bring some one of them back with you, that he may go to Rome to the Holy Father.

"You will inspect their churches and the ornaments therein, the altars, images, and saints; noting if they have Our Lord upon the Cross, and the image of Our Lady, and observing the manner of life among the friars and clergy, and their habits, and if there exist in this land any relics of the bodies of saints, martyrs, and apostles.

"You will relate to him minutely all the nature of the state of the King my Lord (although in a previous clause I have instructed you to touch but lightly upon these matters); nevertheless you will give him a detailed account of the greatness of the King of Portugal's feasts, the riches and brilliancy of his household officers and of his court, the beauty of his palace wherein they live; and of the expense of his feasts, and the treasures, precious stones, pearls, and jewels, that they wear of various fashions; and of the grandness of his Court and of the mounted soldiers who are continually going up and down on guard therein; and of the Ambassadors of the Kings his neighbours who are ever coming to his Court; and of all other particular matters which he may desire to hear of from you.

"You will tell him and assure him how loyally and truly affected towards their Lord the Portuguese are; and this you shall perform in such a manner that the Xeque may desire earnestly and endeavour to acquire the alliance, assistance, and co-operation of the King my Lord, and may so be minded to take upon himself entirely the obligation and good will of doing likewise whenever he shall be called upon to do so, either by request of the King himself or by that of the Captain General, made in his name.

"You will also give him an account of the power, and fleet, and men, and arms, and artillery which I have under my orders in India; and also the great quantity of artillery and its extent which the King my Lord has in his kingdom; and you will relate to him how the soldiers of Portugal march on horseback, and tell him of the trappings of silver and gold, the saddles and caparisons which they have on their horses, and also of their military arrangements and brilliant appearance, and how the men-at-arms march, and the fashion and manner of their arms.

"I command you that both you and the interpreter whom you have with you do minutely read these instructions, and you are to adjust your account with that of the interpreter in such a manner that there be no discrepancy in the relations which you are to deliver in respect of all these matters, but that you be ever unanimous and act in conformity with my letter which I write to him."

Letter which the Great Afonso Dalboquerque wrote to the King of Ormuz.

"Most honourable King Ceifadin, Abenadar, King of Ormuz, in the name of the most high and most mighty D. Manuel, King of Portugal and of the Algarves, on this side and on that side of the sea; in Africa Lord of Guinea, and of the Conquest, Navigation, [and] Commerce of Æthiopia, Arabia, Persia, and of India, and of the kingdom and dominion of Ormuz, and of the kingdom and dominion of Goa; I, Afonso Dalboquerque, Captain-General and Governor of India for the King D. Manuel my Lord, send you my greetings. Here in Goa I met with your messenger, and treated him with honour and befitting entertainment, out of my love for you. My departure from Cochim with the King's fleet was that I might make my way to your city of Ormuz to establish there a factory, and place therein certain persons whom the King has commissioned. You are to know that the Rumes prepared a fleet in Goa, but I came up against the city and captured it, and cast them out of it, and took all their fleet and artillery. If I can come and pass the winter with you in Ormuz, I will come; I have ordered a large quantity of provisions to be made ready against the arrival of the men composing my fleet, who are very numerous; I have forgiven and forgotten all that is past; I am your great friend; Cogeamir is going to you, he carries these two ships of the King my Lord, laden with his merchandise; I shall be glad if he is recognised and well greeted by you, as well as these messengers whom I send to you with a message from the King to the Xeque Ismael. I send my recommendations to you, and to your father and to your mother. Be well assured that in all your dealings I will assist you always like a true friend. Done at Goa, on the twentieth of March, 1510."

As soon as Ruy Gomez and Cogeamir arrived at Ormuz

they delivered the letters and messages which they carried from Afonso Dalboquerque to Cogeatar, who showed great attention and consideration towards Ruy Gomez. And after enquiring particularly of him after the present state of Afonso Dalboquerque, how he was, and after the state of affairs at Goa, he told him to retire to his lodging to get over the discomforts of the sea voyage, for he would set him on his return journey without delay. But, inasmuch as this same Cogeatar was still actuated with hatred towards Afonso Dalboquerque,—not only because of the favour which the Viceroy had shewn to him, but also because Duarte de Lemos, who occupied the position of chief captain of that coast, had apprised him that the King, D. Manuel, had not been pleased at the destruction which had been wrought upon that coast, and also because he was annoyed at the fresh alliance which Afonso Dalboquerque desired to enter into with the Xeque Ismael,—instead of remitting the dues in the case of the ambassador, he laid to his charge whatever he chose, and carried off from him as much as he carried: and he planned matters so that they killed Ruy Gomez by poison. When the servants saw that Ruy Gomez was dead, they made their way back to India, and Cogeamir continued to unload his ships and gathered together his merchandise and then returned to India, but did not go near Goa, as will be related hereafter. And thus it was that this embassy bore no fruit; and afterwards Afonso Dalboquerque sent Miguel Ferreira as ambassador to Xeque Ismael with this same set of instructions which he had given to Ruy Gomez, and in its proper place an account of his journey will be given.

CHAPTER XXIV.

How the great Afonso Dalboquerque ordered Francisco Pantoja to provide the fortress of Çacotorá with supplies, and what passed herein with Duarte de Lemos respecting a ship which he captured on the way.

On the departure of the ambassadors, the great Afonso Dalboquerque despatched Francisco Pantoja to the fortress of Çocotorá (for he had not received any news for a long time from D. Afonso, his nephew, the captain of the fortress,) with a ship laden with supplies: and through him he wrote and forwarded a letter to Duarte de Lemos, wherein he informed him that he had set out for Cochim with his fleet, with the intention of uniting himself to his (Duarte's) forces, in accordance with what he had before written and sent through Diogo Correa; but that when he had progressed on his voyage as far as Onor, Timoja had come up with him, and in consequence of the intelligence that the latter had given him with respect to the condition that Goa was in; and because the city could be captured without much trouble or peril to his men, he had altered his plans and gone up against the city and gained possession of it, more by the divine favour of Our Lord than by human force; and that he was now employed in strengthening its fortifications with an intention of maintaining them, because he was strongly of opinion that such a policy of maintenance would redound greatly to the service of the King of Portugal. But, he added, as soon as all this was arranged, he would come with a powerful fleet to fulfil the promises he had made.

And he also commanded Francisco Pantoja that, if it so fell out that Duarte de Lemos were in Ormuz, he should proceed thither to see him, and if he had any money in hand from the receipt of the tribute, that he should send it on to him, Afonso Dalboquerque, because he was very much in want of it on account of the expenses connected with the building of the fortress—(for the King, D. Manuel, had ordered Duarte de Lemos to assist Afonso Dalboquerque by every manner of means, and that the government of Ormuz was to be under obedience to his commands, as he would see by the letter which he sent him). And Afonso Dalboquerque further ordered Francisco Pantoja to say to D. Afonso [de Noronha], his nephew, if indeed he had not already set out on his voyage, that he was to come at once, because the King had sent word that he was to be appointed captain of Cananor, and Pero Ferreira, who was at Quiloa, to remain behind as captain in the fortress of Çacotorá, as he would have seen in the provisional instructions which had been forwarded through Diogo Correa.

Francisco Pantoja, after he had set out on his journey, was crossing over the great Indian Gulf towards Çacotorá, when he came upon a ship belonging to the King of Cambaya, which was called *Meri*,[1] and proceeding on its voyage laden with merchandise for Meca—a vessel of about six hundred tons, whose captain was a noble Moor of Cambaya, named Alicão.[2] And, although the Moor trusted in his numerous and stout men that he had on board, and put himself in an attitude of defending his ship with the object of saving the lives and property of all, nevertheless our party attacked them and fought so valiantly that the enemy surrendered and their ship was taken. And with this prize Francisco Pantoja sailed straight away to Çacotorá, where he found Duarte de Lemos who had come thither but a few days before from Melinde with four ships, in expectation of Afonso Dalboquerque's arrival, in order to accompany him

[1] This appears to have been a common name for a ship among the Arabs; for the description of another ship so called, captured by the Portuguese at Ormuz, see vol. i, pp. 113-115.

[2] This name seems to be the Portuguese translation of the name *Ali-Khan*.

in his entry of the Straits, according to the message which had come to him; and he found also Pero Ferreira acting as captain of the Fort S. Miguel, for D. Afonso de Noronha had sailed away in April last to India.

As soon as Francisco Pantoja had arrived and delivered his letters from Afonso Dalboquerque to Duarte de Lemos, the latter, observing the valuable nature of the ship, ordered him to deliver it up to the factory, and he would thereupon give orders to pay to him and his men whatever their share of the prize should amount to. But Francisco Pantoja being angered at this arbitrary proceeding on the part of Duarte de Lemos towards him, said that he did not belong to his division but to that of Afonso Dalboquerque, who was Captain-General of all those parts, and to him alone would it be right that he should deliver the ship; and hereupon he made a great show of remonstrance. But Duarte de Lemos did not desist from his demands, for he replied that he himself was the chief captain of those parts, and since the prize had been captured in waters subject to his jurisdiction, it therefore fell to him to superintend the management and distribution of the property; and without caring to hear any more about the matter, he gave orders to discharge the cargo, and took for himself all the share which belonged to Afonso Dalboquerque, without holding any ceremony with Francisco Pantoja, nor giving him anything of that which properly should have come to his share.

And having done this, and considering that Afonso Dalboquerque could no longer that season come to join forces with him, by reason of the successful operations at Goa, he made up his mind to spend no more time in waiting, but to make his way to India; and the more so because he had lost two ships, and the four which remained were so much out of repair that they could no longer render any service to the King in those parts. Therefore, after taking supplies and water he took leave of Pero Ferreira, captain of the fortress, and set sail, carrying with him Francisco Pantoja in his company, and the ship *Meri:* and without any adventures happening by the way, he reached Cananor on the last day of August, where he found Afonso Dalboquerque, who had arrived there from Goa but a few days before him, as will be related further on.

CHAPTER XXV.

Of the agreement which the great Afonso Dalboquerque entered into with Timoja and the principal men of the country, concerning the dues they would be required to pay each year, and how at their request he ordered coin to be struck.

After that Francisco Pantoja had sailed away, Timoja proceeded to the great Afonso Dalboquerque with the principal men and nobles of the land, as well Moors as Hindoos; and they told him that, in order that the course of things in Goa should remain in the same order and ancient custom in which they had always been hitherto, it would be necessary that all should understand the method which they were to practise in regard to the payment of dues. For, they alleged, the Çabaio, after he had become Lord of the kingdom of Goa, had doubled the amount of taxes, at which proceeding every one had been annoyed, and on this account many Hindoos had gone away to settle in divers parts; for anciently they used to pay a hundred and fifty thousand *xerafins*;[1] but afterwards the Çabaio had doubled this tax; and that they were afraid lest his Lordship, following this practice which he had found them labouring under, should oblige them still to pay this increased taxation; and that they begged him of his kindness to endeavour to arrange

[1] For the value of the *xerafim*, see vol. i, p. 82, note; 150,000 *xerafins* = (300 × 150,000 =) 45,000,000 *reis* = 45,000 *milreis* or dollars = £9,375 English money, and a very considerable sum in the years of this history.

this matter in such a manner that the people might be able to get their living, and yet pay something: for it was but reasonable to expect, now they had become the servants of so great a king as the King of Portugal was, that they should enjoy more liberty, in some respects, than they had hitherto possessed, when they lived under the rule of the Çabaio, a tyrant who had been ill-disposed towards them.

Afonso Dalboquerque replied, that his coming to Goa was not with the intention of visiting upon them the tyrannies of the Hidalcão, but on the contrary to shew favour towards them, and to honour them, and to give them increased means of living, provided that they, on their part, were willing to be true and loyal vassals of the King of Portugal, their Lord. And upon the condition that they would willingly remain in this obedience, he, on his part, would remit to them, in the name of the king, the taxes which the Çabaio had recently imposed upon them, and they should pay henceforth only as much as they had been accustomed to pay to the lords of the kingdom of Goa when they were of the Hindoo dynasties; but this remission should be in force only as long as they were in subjection to the King of Portugal and to his Governors of India. But that in case they should ever be called upon by any Governor of India and not respond to the call immediately, having no good grounds of excuse for such remissness, then they should be obliged to pay the same taxes that they had paid to the Çabaio.

Timoja and the others received, in the name of the people, the lands with these conditions that Afonso Dalboquerque laid down; but it had also to be stipulated that he should appoint over them a Tanadar,[1] and Hindoos to govern them.

[1] *Tanadar: Thânâdâr*, Hindostani; *Thânedâr*, Maráthí and Guzaráthí. Bluteau considers this officer equivalent to *Quæstor supremus*, or *Quæstorum maximus;* and translates it by *Almoxarife*, receiver of imposts, superintendent of royal demesnes. Wilson explains this word

Afonso Dalboquerque told them that he would promise not to appoint any Moor to the office of *Tanadar,* and he would give orders that the taxes should be collected by Portuguese in combination with certain Hindoos of the land to be appointed by Timoja, in order that everything should be done with least oppression of the people. And after having thus arranged the matter with them, Afonso Dalboquerque commanded that an oath should be administered to them, according to their heathen manner, that they would account for these taxes with him or the Governor of India for the time being; and he ordered that two *pacharins* [1] should be given to each one, for it was an ancient custom in the land to give these to these Hindoos.

On the conclusion of this business, Afonso Dalboquerque gave them permission to return to their houses and commence the collection of the taxes, according to the local registers of the lands. And they desired him to appoint over them certain *Tanadares,* who have the same office as our *Almoxarifes,*[2] to collect the revenue, and dispense justice among them. In order to content them, Afonso Dalboquerque nominated Bras Vieira over them as *Tanadar* of Cintacorá, and Gasper Chanoca to act as his secretary, and over all the other offices of *Tanadar* he appointed for them,

thus:—"An officer in charge of a *Thánd,* formerly, an officer under the *Faujdár* (criminal judge or magistrate), employed, with a small irregular force, in protecting the country and enforcing payment of the revenue." The *Thánd* was "a military post, or garrison, *a place,* sometimes with a small fort, where a petty officer, with a small irregular force, was posted to protect the country, preserve the peace, and to aid in making the collections."

[1] *Pacharim.* I am unable to fix the signification of this word with any satisfactory degree of certainty; but it probably refers to a sum of money.

[2] *Almoxarife;* the obsolete forms are *almosarifa,* and *almozarife,* a receiver of customs and imposts. Arabic, *almoshrif,* inspector.—See Engelmann's "Glossaire des mots . . . Portugais dérivés de l'Arabe", particularly the edition enlarged by Dozy.

as *Tanadares*, a number of honourable men, servants of the King, in whom he had complete confidence, to execute justice among them. And he ordered Timoja to appoint to each of these officers a Hindoo scrivener in order to show them the method to be pursued in collecting the revenue; and to each *Tanadar* he told off two hundred peons of the country to accompany them and carry out the instructions of their masters in the collection of the revenue. And he sent João Alvarez de Caminha, who was a very honourable man and possessed great authority, in order to set those things in action as they should be carried on, and to put them into working order; and to repose in him a confidence with regard to other greater matters; and to be his scrivener Antonio Fragoso was appointed; and a Hindoo servant of Timoja to show him the register-books of the lands, how they were held in separate occupation, in order that there should be no dishonesty. And João Alvarez de Caminha managed everything in such a manner that everybody was well pleased. The Hindoos who had fled out of Goa returned to their original dwelling places in the land immediately that they perceived that Afonso Dalboquerque had remitted to them a moiety of the dues which they had been accustomed to pay to the Çabaio, and had appointed natives over them to govern them.

As soon as João Alvarez de Caminha had gone with all the *Tanadares* to set them in their places throughout the lands, in accordance with the instructions contained in his papers, Timoja went, in company with certain principal Moors and Hindoos of the country, to Afonso Dalboquerque, and told him that the people of the city and the merchants were suffering from a great depression, not only in the government thereof, but also with respect to the merchant trade, because there was no currency of coin. And they begged he would of his graciousness grant a permission for coining some money, because it was impossible for the city to be well governed without a currency of coinage; and they alleged that he ought to order the price of gold and silver to be raised in order to prevent their exportation.

So Afonso Dalboquerque called a meeting of the captains, and laid open to them the matters which Timoja and the deputation of merchants had requested him in the name of the people to put into effect. And the captains, after debating upon the affair, unanimously agreed that the coinage of some money should be commenced. But Afonso Dalboquerque replied, that he was quite convinced by the reasons which Timoja gave, that it would be good to mint some money; yet, seeing that this was a novel proceeding, and one that had never before taken place in India, he would not venture to do so without first writing to the King his Lord, who should herein provide as best for his service, and thereupon he dismissed them.

However, after a few days had elapsed, Timoja returned, bringing with him the others who had formerly accompanied him, to discuss the previous requests that had been made, and, in presence of the captains, he begged earnestly that Afonso Dalboquerque would either give orders for the coinage of some money, because everything was going to ruin from want of it, and barter of merchandise could not be effected, or at least that he would permit the coinage of the Çabaio to pass current. The captains, after hearing the reasonable arguments which Timoja made in favour of the issue of a new currency, and listening to the relation of the inconveniences which resulted from the want of it, agreed to what they had said in the first assembly. So Afonso Dalboquerque, on consideration that the King of Portugal would hereby gain credit, renown, and profit, and that the kingdom was in his hands, agreed to give permission for minting money, and to write to the King respecting the circumstances of the case. And in order that the money should be produced in a befitting style, he called a meeting of the goldsmiths and some Portuguese experts whom he had with him, and Timoja and the principal men of the city, and commanded them to make a trial of the silver of the Moors, and every one found that it was of the same intrinsic value as our own. When this trial was concluded Afonso Dalboquerque appointed Tristão Dégа to be treasurer of the mint, and gave orders forthwith for the coinage of money in silver, and gold, and copper; and on the one side they were to stamp a cross of [the order] of Christus,[1] and on the other a sphere,—the device of the King D. Manuel,[2]—and the silver coin was to be equivalent in weight to a *bragani*,[3]—which is a Moorish weight equal to two *vintens*[4] Portuguese, and these he called *spheres*;[5] and he made another kind, which were smaller, and weighed one *vintem*, and these he called *half-spheres*,[6] and the copper moneys he called *leaes*;[7] and the other smaller copper moneys, of which three went to the *leal*, he called *din*-

[1] For the shape of this Cross, which resembles the heraldic *Cross pattée*, see the work on Portuguese Numismatics by Fernandes, cited below, note 5.

[2] "Teve El Rey D. Manoel por empreza a *Esfera*, que vulgarmente se chamava então *Espera*."—Manoel Severim de Faria, *Noticias de Portugal*, p. 186.

[3] *Bragani*: Cf. *Bargan*, or *burgun*, Hindostani; a partition, or share.

[4] *Vintem*, a penny, or twenty *reis* (*vinte* = *twenty*), of which fifty go to the dollar (*milreis* = *one-thousand reis*), or 4s. 2d. The English sovereign is equal to 4·8 dollars = 240 *vintens* = 4800 *reis*.

[5] *Esperas*. These copper coins, called here *Esperas*, and *Meas Esperas*, *i.e.*, spheres and half-spheres, must not be confounded with the gold coins called *Esfera*, struck by King Manoel, which on the one side had the device of a sphere, on the other the Latin inscription *Mea*, intending thereby to show that the sphere which King John II had given him for a device had been by him acquired by the glorious acquisition to the Portuguese Crown in the discovery and conquest of India and Brazil. See also a work by Manoel Bernardes Lopes Fernandes, in the "Memorias da Academia Real das Sciencias de Lisboa", 2a Classe, 1856, p. 121.

[6] *Meas Esperas*.

[7] *Leaes*, the plural form of *leal*.

heiros;[1] and in order that the gold coins should not be taken away out of the country, he ordered that the *cruzados* should be taken as equal to seventeen *braganis*.[2] And when these matters had been arranged, the coining of the money was commenced, and as soon as a large quantity had been made, on the twelfth of March, in the year one thousand five hundred and ten, Afonso Dalboquerque ordered that all the captains should be called together, with the fidalgoes and cavaliers, and all the noble persons of the fleet, and all the principal merchants among the Moors, and the Hindoo *chitins*;[3] and when these had assembled together in a large hall

[1] *Dinheiros*; *denarii*, Lat.; *deniers*, Fr.; *Dinheiro* is the generic name for all kinds of money, but in this case was evidently attributed to a certain very small coin.

[2] In order to put this novel system of coinage more clearly before the reader, I have constructed the following table. Very good notices on this coinage will be found in "Noticias de Portugal escritas por Manoel Severim de Faria", Lisbon, 8vo, 1791, tom. ii, pp. 68-72; and the work of Manoel Bernardes Lopes Fernandes mentioned in a previous note. The coins themselves are so rare, that they may almost be described as no longer extant, for this writer does not figure any of them.

Portuguese.		Goa Money.	Moorish.
	Copper.	*Dinheiro*, the smallest coin.	
		3 *Dinheiros* = 1 *Leal*, perhaps an adaptation of the word *real*, *rial*, or *rei* to Indian mouths; if so, twenty went to the *vintem*.	
1 *Vintem* . =	Silver.	1 half *Espera*, or *Mea Espera*.	
2 *Vintens* . =		1 *Espera*	= 1 *Bragani*.
[34 *Vintens*]	Gold.	= 1 *Cruzado* . . . . But cf. vol. i, p. 17, n. 1, for the Portuguese values of this coin.	= 17 *Braganis*.

[3] *Chitins*. "*Chitti*, or *Chetti*, more correctly *Sethi*, and corruptly *Chitty*. All members of the trading castes in the Madras provinces, either shopkeepers or merchants."—*Wilson*.

of the Çabaio's palace (wherein he used to live), that had been especially decorated for this occasion, Afonso Dalboquerque told them that he had given orders to mint silver and copper coinage, according to the arrangement that had been made, and in order to make the matter quite public it had been necessary to order proclamation to be made to every one of them throughout the city (for this was the native custom that used to be practised in the lands which the kings gained anew), for them to say if he should do so. And all declared that to them it appeared good that this should be done, since there were no other reasons to the contrary about it. And then, at this unanimous expression of favourable opinion, Afonso Dalboquerque immediately gave the word to take the royal flag, and the trumpets and kettledrums, and assemble all the men in the fleet, and ordered Tristão Déga to go and proclaim it; and he went with all this company of people all round the city, and at each proclamation that was made they scattered quantities of the new money over the heads of the crowds, which were great, and they went on proceeding in this manner all round the city.

As soon as this proceeding was over, Afonso Dalboquerque commanded that proclamation should be made, in the name of the King of Portugal, that no one from that day henceforward, under severe penalties, should keep any of the coinage of the Çabaio in his house, nor make any use of it, but whoever had any should carry it to the Mint, and there it should be exchanged for him with that of the King of Portugal; and whoever should break these regulations should incur legal penalties according as he Afonso Dalboquerque should think fit to impose upon him. The people were very much pleased with the money, and from that day henceforward they began to trade with their merchandise.

CHAPTER XXVI.

How the great Afonso Dalboquerque made ready to winter in Goa, and sent Diogo Fernandes from Béja to the fortress of Cintácora.

Inasmuch as the great Afonso Dalboquerque had made up his mind to maintain Goa and fortify his position therein, he determined, before winter should become more settled, to provide himself with all things necessary for that undertaking; and issued immediate orders for collecting together all the supplies that could be found. And all the horses that remained in the land were placed in some large stables which the Çabaio had erected in the fortress, wherein formerly they used to place the horses which the dealers brought from Ormuz to sell. And for this purpose the Çabaio used to have a *Xabandar,*[1] whose office corresponds to that of *Almoxarife da ribeira,* [superintendent receiver of the royal import dues,] whose duty it was to look to the care of the horses, and the people were obliged to bring hay, and corn, and *mungo*[2], which is a certain species of seed that they feed the horses with, in abundance. And to this *Xabandar,* in union with other Moors on which this charge devolved, Afonso Dalboquerque gave orders to look to the provender of these horses, and to see to all the other matters relating to the coast, with the intention of proceeding with his management of the affairs of Goa in the manner of his ordinances and government.

[1] *Xabandar;* a consul for merchants, a resident for affairs relating to commerce and trade.—*Vieyra.* From the text, it is evident that this officer is the *Zemindar* of the Indian continent, in his more ordinary capacity of responsible collector only of the revenues on behalf of the Government under the Mohammedan administration rather than as hereditary owner of the land he occupies. Wilson (pp. 562, 563) gives a concise account of this officer's position and duties.

[2] *Mungo;* a sort of pulse much used by the natives of India as an article of food. It is the *Phaseolus mungo* of Linnæus; cf. *Mung*, or *Mug*, Hindostani.

And seeing that the beginning of April was now come—when the winter commences in those parts,—Afonso Dalboquerque desired, before any more time should elapse, to acquaint the King of Cochim and the captain of the fortress and the officers of the factory, that he had made up his mind to pass the winter in Goa and complete the fortress that he had commenced, and that they must send him all the saddles they had among them, and certain stores.

Francisco Serrão set out immediately in a *caravela* [with this message], but he never went back with any reply: it appears that it was fear that prevented him from returning, although he gave it as an excuse that he was unable to get back on account of the weather;[1] but Afonso Dalboquerque would not accept the excuse at his hands, and when the events at Goa had gone by, and the expedition was returning to Cochim, he deprived him of the captaincy of his *caravela* and ordered him to be placed under arrest.

After Francisco Serrão had set out, Afonso Dalboquerque observing that the work of coining the new money progressed very slowly, and did not suffice for the demand upon it for the wages of the servants who were employed in the work of the fortress, nor for the maintenance of the fleet, at the rate of a *cruzado* a month, ordered the captains to provide food each one for his own people, and this he did for two reasons. The first reason was, because he had a large store of provisions now in the city and by means of them he could provide against this outlay, which otherwise could not be kept up at the rate of payment of a *cruzado* a month to every man, because the moneyers could not coin sufficient amounts to meet all demands. The second reason was, that he had been notified of the coming of the Hidalção, and desired to have all the men close by to withstand any attack that might be made upon them.

[1] *Por amor dos tempos.*

The captains were, however, tired with the labour that they had to undergo in constructing the fortress—for each one had his time of service arranged wherein he had to be at work with his men,—and were now desirous of going and taking their pleasure at Cochim; and also of shifting off their shoulders the additional trouble that would arise from having to provide food for their men; they therefore gave this advice to the soldiers, that they should not accept the eating in the captains' houses in place of money payments, but rather beg to be supplied with money for their own support; knowing all the while that from the great scarcity of money they could not be well provided therewith, and by reason of this check Afonso Dalboquerque would be compelled to abandon Goa and make his way to Cochim, which was what the captains occupied their thoughts about, and not whether the men were well or badly provided for.

Now, whereas Afonso Dalboquerque understood that the prime inciter of the people to disaffection was Jorge da Cunha, and that at his house Estevão Baiam and Francisco de Figueiredo had met and drawn up a list of many men who were to go and beg him, Afonso, to command that they should be paid their dues in money in order not to have to eat in the halls of their captains, he issued order to arrest Estevão Baiam and Francisco de Figueiredo as a punishment to them, and to prevent any further loss arising from this matter. And when those men who were mixed up in this conspiracy saw them arrested, they grew alarmed lest a similar fate should overtake themselves, and abandoned their intended requisition and went and took their meals in the captains' halls according to the arrangements that had been put in force. And in the judicial examination which was proceeded with in connection with this affair it was found that Jorge da Cunha was very much to blame, Afonso Dalboquerque therefore ordered the other two who were in durance to be released, and reprehended Jorge da Cunha on account of this, as well as on account of many other things which he had done. And Jorge da Cunha was so much disconcerted at the words which Afonso Dalboquerque addressed to him, that after a few days had elapsed he united with Jeronymo Teixeira, Luis Continho, and Francisco de Sousa Mancias (who were all of one way of thinking), and they went before him and besought permission to go away to Cochim; but as he would not grant this to them, from this time henceforth they carried themselves very passionately and angrily in their conduct towards him.

Nevertheless, Afonso Dalboquerque, on account of his great desire to complete the fortress out of dread lest the Hidalcão should come upon him unprepared, pretended not to notice them, and put up with all that they did. And he dispatched Diogo Fernandez de Béja, with sundry vessels and men, to proceed with the rebuilding of the fortress of Cintácora, and to remain therein as captain, lest, if the Hidalcão should come, any Moors should be placed therein with the opportunity of inciting the land to rise up against him. But when Diogo Fernandez arrived at Cintácora he found a large part of the fortress thrown down and ruined; and as winter had now begun to set in and there was no opportunity of beginning the work anew, he went back to Goa and reported to Afonso Dalboquerque the state in which he had found the fortress, and that a very great space of time would be required to repair it, and therefore he had returned.

CHAPTER XXVII.

How Mandaloy, Lord of Condal, wrote to the great Afonso Dalboquerque the news he had of the coming of the Hidalcão, and what was done respecting this information.

The affairs of Goa being in the state that I have described, Mandaloy, Lord of Condal, wrote a letter to the great Afonso Dalboquerque, wherein he informed him that

Balogi, Lord of the castle and lands of Pervaloy and of the kingdom of Sanguiçar, had put himself in communication with Roçalcão, a captain of the Çabaio, and with Melique Rabão, Lord of Carrapetão, and all three had sent their ambassadors to the Hidalcão, desiring him to furnish them with men, in order that, adding them to the forces they already had under arms, they might make a descent upon the territories of Goa and reduce them to obedience again; and that Balogi, who had been already in the interior at Banda with a large force, was there with two thousand men, raised at his own cost with the determined intention of defending that land on behalf of the Hidalcão, or to die in performing this service for his lordship; and earnestly begged him, Afonso Dalboquerque, to send him some reinforcement of men; and he, Mandaloy, on his part, would immediately deliver the lands to whomsoever should be sent, for he himself desired nothing more than a mere subsistence for the rest of his life.

As soon as this letter had been delivered to Afonso Dalboquerque, he called a meeting of the captains, and after having ordered the letter to be read in their presence, he told them that Timoja had offered to conduct an expedition at his own expense to the assistance of Mandaloy, and asked them whether he should entrust this business to him, or send some other person of greater authority. After debating for some time, it was unanimously agreed that Afonso Dalboquerque ought to send some captain who was a *fidalgo*, with a force of foot and horse soldiers by land and vessels by sea, to succour them. And having accepted this determination, Afonso Dalboquerque told off, for the conduct of this expedition, Jorge da Cunha, with sixty mounted men and several crossbow-men and musketeers, and in their company he sent Menaique,[1] one of the captains of Timoja, and Melique Çufecondal, with four

[1] Probably the man named *Naique* on page 105.

thousand native troopers, and Baldrez, the interpreter, and Diogo Fernandez de Béja with three vessels by sea, with instructions that he was to be under the command of Jorge da Cunha as soon as he came up with him.

And when all was in readiness, the expedition set out, and Jorge da Cunha reached the island of Divarij with the intention of passing over to the mainland on the following morning. But on that same night, which was the twenty-third day of the month of April, a native Canarese came to him with great haste, and brought him information that to the land of Banda[1] and of Condal there had arrived two of the Hidalcão's captains with a numerous body of men, and that it was reported that their intentions were to make good their entrance into the Island of Goa.

As soon as Jorge da Cunha had heard this news, he remained where he was, and would not permit Melique Çufecondal to pass over to the other side; but he sent the Canarese messenger with this news to Afonso Dalboquerque, who immediately sent him back again to Jorge da Cunha, with a letter telling him not to go any further, but to remain where he was in Divarij, and to permit none of Timoja's men to pass from the other side of the mainland until he had received fresh and more definite news of the army of the Hidalcão. And after having thus dispatched the Canarese messenger, Afonso Dalboquerque sent Diogo Fernandez as a guide,[2] with twelve mounted soldiers and

[1] *Banda.* 15 deg. 48 min. N., 73 deg. 53 min. E., near Goa.

[2] *Adail;* a Portugese word derived from the Arabic *ad-dalil*, guide or leader, according to Dozys Englemann. Bluteau derives from *delid*, "dux viæ" or "mostrador", and says:—

"O officio do Adail he mostrar, quando marcha o exercito, o caminho, não já publico, & manifesto, mas encuberto & não trilhado . . . Tocava ao Adail governor os Almocadens, & Almogavares, & a mais gente com que se fazião cavalgadas nas terras inimigas, & ter conhecimento da campanha, para levar com segurança as tropas."

Mirale[1] with him in command of a thousand Canarese peons, to pass over to the mainland, and see if they could come upon any interpreter who might give them any news of the coming of the Hidalcão.

Thereupon Diogo Fernandez set out, and without being perceived passed by night over to the mainland, and progressing in this manner, in the depth of the darkness he came up with the vanguard of the Hidalcão's army so suddenly that he was utterly routed, and just managed to escape on his horse, leaving behind him many of the native peons who were unable to save themselves, so that when he reached the city again not more than five hundred peons and the horsemen whom he had taken with him, accompanied him. And he related to Afonso Dalboquerque all that had taken place, telling him that he had been thoroughly discomfited and only saved himself by a miracle, and that the army of the Hidalcão was very large, and, in his opinion, the host was facing towards the quarter of Benastarim, with the intention of establishing their camp there.

Hereupon Afonso Dalboquerque, relying upon the relation that Diogo Fernandez had given him with regard to the approach of the Hidalcão, called all the captains together and earnestly desired them, seeing that this news was in every way trustworthy, to go armed every one of them, and keep their men in close quarters in order that they might be ready to rally wherever it should be necessary, if any assault should be attempted. And he sent word by a messenger to Jorge de Cunha that he was to return to the city. And at this very juncture there arrived a runner from Bersoré, King of Garçopa, bringing a letter for Afonso Dalboquerque, wherein was related that the King of Narsinga had written to him, King Bersoré, that the Hidalcão had sent to him a messenger to complain of the Hindoos (and chiefly of Timoja), who were his subjects, because they had assisted

[1] *Mir-Ali.*

the Portuguese to take Goa from him, and if this had not been done in accordance with his views, he begged him, the King of Narsinga, to help him to regain possession of that place; and that the King of Narsinga had replied that it was forty years since the Moors of Decan had taken from him the kingdom of Goa, and now it gratified him very much to see that it was in the power of the King of Portugal, whose brother and friend he had now become; and as for the assistance that he asked for retaking the city, he intended to give it, on the contrary, to the Portuguese for defending the place. And in the same letter the King of Garçopa sent word to Afonso Dalboquerque that he, too, was ready with his own body and all the resources of his kingdom to serve him against the Hidalcão whenever it was necessary, because he was very desirous of forming an alliance with him.

Afonso Dalboquerque despatched his messenger back, sending by him a letter in reply to the King of Garçopa, proffering him many thanks for the offers of assistance which he had made, and telling him that he would write to the King of Narsinga to get himself ready to fight the Hidalcão, and therefore he had not touched upon any matters concerning the latter, as contained in his present letter; but he had made up his mind to send him a messenger who would tell him all about the proceedings by word of mouth.

CHAPTER XXVIII.

How the great Afonso Dalboquerque, immediately upon hearing this news, provided the strongholds of the island with men and captains, and ordered the trial of the Xabandar, on account of the evil report he had of him, and further doings.

No sooner was this interview concluded that the great Afonso Dalboquerque held with his captains concerning the approach of the Hidalcão, than he remounted upon his horse, with as many people as he could gather together, and made an inspection of all the passes of the island, in order to provide them with everything that was required. And in Benastarim he placed Garcia de Sousa with a hundred Portuguese soldiers, and six horse-soldiers, and four pieces of artillery and gunners to man them, and impressed strongly upon him the need of taking care to cause them to search everybody who passed over to the mainland, lest they carried with them any letters of advice from the Moors in Goa to those in the camp of the Hidalcão; and thence he proceeded to Old Goa, and therein he placed Jorge da Cunha with sixty cavalry soldiers, under orders to hasten to the defence of the other passes if need should arise; and at the pass of Augij he stationed Timoja's cousin and Mirale, with his own company; and at that of Gondalij he placed Francisco Pereira and Francisco de Sousa Mancias, with at housand native soldiers; and in the dry pass he left Jorge Fogaça, with twenty of our men and twenty native soldiers; and in that of Agacij D. Jeronymo de Lima, with forty Portuguese soldiers and a number of natives. And in every one of these passes there were towers which had been constructed at the time when the Kings of Narsinga were in possession of Goa, Afonso Dalboquerque therefore ordered that the captains should be supplied with artillery, gunpowder, and gunners, for their defence in case the Hidalcão's men should shew any signs of attacking them; and that the boats of the ships should be kept close at hand in order to be able to take refuge in them if it were necessary.

As soon as Afonso Dalboquerque had arranged all those affairs in order, he betook himself again to the city, and ordered D. Antonio de Noronha to get ready the boats, galleys, *parâos*, and some small vessels, with men and guns, to pass up the river, visiting all these passes and reinforcing our men that were stationed in them. And while he was yet on the shore, ordering the disposition of all this fleet, Dinis Fernandez, the chief surveyor of the Navy, came up to him and told him that the *Xabandar* of the coast had despatched sundry *paráos* up along the river; and because he thought this was wrong and the crisis caused one to be very suspicious, he had told him not to send any *paráos* up, but down the river, towards the bar, whither already on occasions they had gone for necessary stores, but the *Xabandar* would not do so. Then Afonso Dalboquerque sent for the *Xabandar*, and asked him why he was sending the *paráos* up along the river, since he knew that the Hidalcão was posted there with a great force, intending to force an entry into the city; and the *Xabandar* replied that he did not know of the coming of the Hidalcão, and though he had sent the *paráos* up, it was in order that they should bring back stores required for the provisioning of the city, according to the instructions which had been given to him. But as the excuse was not a good one, and Afonso Dalboquerque had reason to suspect him, that he was sending the *paráos* to give a passage to the men under the command of the Hidalcão, he ordered his halbardiers to put him to death and throw his body into the river.

When D. Antonio had set out with the fleet which was ready by this time, a message was brought for him from Garcia de Sousa, stating that the Hidalcão had already arrived with all his men, and that he had pitched his camp before Benastarim, and, according to appearances, it was a very numerous force.

At the receipt of this intelligence Afonso Dalboquerque got on his horse, accompanied by all his captains and some people on foot, and made his way to Benastarim, and when he arrived, there was the Hidalcão already withdrawn with all his forces behind a hill, for Garcia de Sousa had killed some of them with his artillery. And in this spot where the Hidalcão had pitched his camp there stood a mosque and some houses in which the Moors could obtain shelter from the artillery of the fortress; so, for this reason, Afonso Dalboquerque ordered Garcia de Sousa to take the men that were under his command along with him, and burn the houses and throw down the mosque; and Garcia passed over from the other side and destroyed everything, and set fire to the mosque, and as it was all by the waterside he returned to his quarters again without suffering any injury at the hands of the Moors.

As soon as Garcia de Sousa had returned, Afonso Dalboquerque mounted again on horseback and proceeded with his inspection of all the passes where the captains were stationed, instructing them how they were to act; and then he returned to the city to see to the disposition of its fortifications and everything else that was necessary for the defence of the fortress and the city in case the Hidalcão should enter into the island. And when he was passing through the dry pass, Jorge Fogaça, who was stationed there as captain in command, delivered over to him a young man who had fled that morning from the camp of the Hidalcão. This young man was a Christian, a native of Crete, who had been captured by Camalo, a captain of the Turk, and a merchant had bought him with many others, and carried them to the kingdom of Decan, and given them to the old Çabaio. But as he was a Christian, and knew that they also were Christians who were there in Goa, he had fled away and betaken himself to them, and two others also had accompanied him in his flight, but he knew not what had become of them. And he gave much information concerning the camp of the Hidalcão and of the great numbers of men he had in it, and how he had fixed his determination to enter into the island by force. And two days afterwards the other two young men arrived; one of them was an Albanian and the other came from Russia.

CHAPTER XXIX.

How the Hidalcão sent João Machado, and a Venetian, who were with him, having turned Moors, with a message to the great Afonso Dalboquerque, desiring him to quit Goa, and of the reply he gave them.

As soon as the Hidalcão had pitched his camp, it occurred to him that when the great Afonso Dalboquerque knew the power of the army which he had raised, he would surrender Goa to him without any more armed opposition; in order, therefore, to sound his intentions, he sent him a message by means of a Portuguese and a Venetian, who were with him, having turned Moors. These men came up by night in an *almadia* to the pass of Agacij, whereof D. Jeronymo was the captain, and declared to him that they were the bearers of a message from the Hidalcão to the Captain-General of India, and they had been desired to demand a safe conduct for both of them, and a man who should remain in the camp as a hostage, in order that they might go and speak with his Lordship; and it might so turn out, they said, that their mission would prove very advantageous to all.

D. Jeronymo sent word immediately to Afonso Dalboquerque, relating all that had happened; and as he was very anxious to know who the Portuguese man was that had brought this message, he sent back a safe conduct at once for him, and appointed Baldrez to be lodged in the enemy's camp as a hostage; for this latter was very well versed in the native language, and on this account he was advised to listen to the deliberations and intentions of the Moors, yet not allow them to find out that he could speak any other language than Portuguese. When Baldrez had reached the camp, and the safe conduct come to hand, D. Jeronymo sent the Portuguese and the Venetian in his boat, and these two came up in it to the fortress on the first day of May, by night; and, in order that they should not enter into the fortress, Afonso Dalboquerque came down and waited for them at the gate which looked out on to the river, and when they arrived he enquired of them who they were. The Portuguese replied, that his companion was by nation a Venetian, who had been for a long time in the service of the Hidalcão, but he himself was called João Machado, and had come from Portugal in disgrace, in the fleet of Pedralvarez Cabral, and remained behind at Melinde, and from that place had passed over to the kingdom of Cambaya; but, as the King gave him very small wages, he had made his way to the kingdom of Decan and taken service, as a means of support, under the Çabayo, father of the Hidalcão. Yet, he said, for all that he had walked in such crooked ways, as his Lordship now perceived by this narrative, he had still retained his Christian religion, and believed truly that by Jesus Christ and by His Death and Passion he should be saved: and, although he had undertaken to deliver the message of the Hidalcão which he was now bringing, it really was in order to give him, Afonso Dalboquerque, certain information, and to tell him the truth concerning the enemy's army in whose company he had come to Goa.

Then Afonso Dalboquerque enquired of him if he desired to speak with him in private or in the presence of all who were there assembled. The Portuguese replied, that he would be glad to speak with him in private; and so Afonso Dalboquerque withdrew and took him aside, and João Machado told him that the Hidalcão was very desirous of obtaining his alliance, on account of the great name which he had acquired among the Moors, and that he was not surprised at the fall of Goa because he knew for certain that Timoja had intrigued with the Hindoos of the land to deliver up the city to the Portuguese, but that the Hidalcão now begged him earnestly to surrender the island and the lands of Goa, and in exchange he would give him another place of his own on the sea-coast, whichever he selected, wherein to erect a fortress: but if he, Afonso, were unwilling to carry out this that was asked of him, he was to know for a surety that the Hidalcão would on no consideration quit his military position until he had cast him out of the city, for the whole future of the State depended on this issue. And, he continued, since the Hidalcão was thus determined, his lordship, Afonso Dalboquerque, ought to take some means to arrange matters with him, for he was a young and powerful lord, anxious to obtain honourable reputation, and at the head of a numerous body of men of high caste who were highly esteemed and feared in these parts, and by whose means he had obtained the mastery over a large part of that kingdom, and of the other class of natives he could have as many as he required. And João Machado went on to say that he would advise Afonso Dalboquerque by no manner of means to repose any confidence in the inhabitants of Goa city, for they were ripe for revolution, and as soon as they should see four Moors from the camp get into the island they would all rise up at once against him, seeing that not a day passed that the Hidalcão did not receive letters from the Moors of the city, advising him to force an entry, that they were devoted to his cause, and ready to sacrifice their lives for him; but rather that he, Afonso Dalboquerque, should give orders for watching all the passes of the island, for he should know of a certainty that, wherever there was the most carelessness, at that place the Hidalcão would be sure to enter. And, he added, truly it appeared to him that Afonso Dalboquerque was not sufficiently strong to prevent the Hidalcão's entry into the island,—although that he did not say this as one who sided with that prince's army, but because it was his firm conviction; and he trusted in God that he might soon get back to Portugal and see the King D. Manuel, and give him a long account of the affairs of that land.

Afonso Dalboquerque replied, that he was much obliged to him for the good will he had shewn, and the advice he had given, and that he hoped it would please God to give him such knowledge of the truth that he might ultimately obtain true salvation,—and he was to carry back to the Hidalcão this reply, that he, Afonso Dalboquerque, had not taken Goa merely to lose it again, for Goa could only belong to him who had also the dominion of the sea, namely, the King D. Manuel, his Lord; but he would be very glad to come to terms of peace with him, seeing that hereby not only would the Hidalcão increase the stability of his own position, but he also would infuse great terror among the neighbouring states,—and this advice he gave as a man of sixty years of age and well experienced in arms, to him who was but a young man and badly advised. And, he continued, if the Hidalcão placed any reliance on his hopes of succour from the Grand Sultan, he had greatly erred, for the rout that D. Francisco Dalmeida[1] had inflicted upon the Rumes had been so thorough, that they could not be able to rally to his assistance at that juncture; but he begged the Hidalcão to be sensible enough to raise the siege and take himself off, and surrender Dabul, wherein he, Afonso, might erect a fortress, and on these conditions peace should be made, but if the Hidalcão did not choose to carry out all that had been laid down, it was no use talking any more in concert, for this would always be the ultimate answer that he would give him.

Then João Machado replied, that he was very much concerned at seeing affairs in such a desperate crisis that they could not be arranged, for the Hidalcão would certainly not agree to this settlement, because he would never give up a portion of his kingdom according to this proposal. And with this reply he took his departure, and Afonso Dalboquerque made him a present of sixty *cruzados*, and to the

[1] See note, page 112.

Venetian he gave forty, and so they returned in the same boat which had brought them, and on arriving at the camp they delivered the reply which they took back to Hidalcão; and he, on his part, sent Baldrez back again, telling him to say to Afonso Dalboquerque that he was much surprised at the rejection of the terms that had been offered to him, but he would promise him, before many days were passed, that he would be sorry for the message that he had sent. As soon as Baldrez arrived, he narrated to Afonso Dalboquerque the sayings of the Hidalcão, and told him how in the camp there were a numerous body of soldiers, both infantry and cavalry, and they were making ready large quantities of rafts, and fascines, in order to pass over thereby to the island; but the Turks, whose wives and families were in Goa, were unwilling that the Hidalcão should make any agreement with him, for they were all prepared to die or become again lords of Goa, and all that they talked about was that the attempt to regain the possession of the city might cost them a million of men.

CHAPTER XXX.

How the great Afonso Dalboquerque gave an account to Timoja of the message which João Machado had brought from the Hidalcão to him, and of further proceedings thereupon.

The great Afonso Dalboquerque, in this interview which he held with João Machado and the Venetian, became very much alarmed on account of what he was informed with regard to the Moors of Goa, although the information was not clearly expressed. And, in order to arrive at some determination in respect to his future actions in this matter, he sent for Timoja and narrated to him the message which he had received from the Hidalcão, and the reply which he had given. And after some conversation upon these subjects, he told Timoja that information had been given to the effect that certain of the chief Moors of the city were engaged in correspondence with the Hidalcão, and had communications with the Rumes who were in his camp, therefore he desired him to give him the benefit of his advice as a friend, as to the manner in which he ought to act in order to prevent this fire from bursting out into a flame.

Timoja replied, that he had now for some days ceased to repose any confidence in the Moors, because he had always considered that they were angry at beholding the city in the power of the Portuguese; and his advice would be, that Afonso Dalboquerque should order all the principal headmen, not only Moors, but Hindoos as well, to be collected together in the fortress, for in such times as these one ought not to confide in either the one or the other. Then Afonso Dalboquerque replied—for it was in order to get this advice out of Timoja that he had intentionally asked him this question—that he was very much indebted to him for such advice, and since his opinion was such, he, Timoja, as he was then governor, should be the first, in order to avoid disaffection among the one or the other, to take his wife and children to the fortress; for when the Moors and Hindoos should behold so important a man as he was, and one in possession of so much authority, performing this without any reluctance, he would be able to command every one else to do the same.

And although Timoja was now very sorry for the advice he had given, yet because he was the originator of this proposal, he was constrained to send off at once for his wife and a son whom he had, and placed them in the fortress. As soon as Afonso Dalboquerque had the wife of Timoja there in his power, he summoned a meeting of the principal Moors and Hindoos who governed the land, and told them to gather together all the noble Moors and Hindoos, as well of the island as those who lived in Old Goa, and to command them, on their own responsibility, to come on the following day with their wives and families to take up their abode in the fortress; for he was afraid lest they should receive serious injuries and efforts from the Turks, in case the Hidalcão should gain an entry into the island. In pursuance of this order, when the Moors and Hindoos knew that the wife and son of Timoja were already in the castle, they proceeded immediately to take up their quarters within it with their wives and families, although they were very much annoyed at this edict issued by Afonso Dalboquerque. And when these had been settled in their places, Afonso Dalboquerque issued similar orders for the gathering together of the women and children of the Turks who were engaged in the camp of the Hidalcão, and then sent word to them there in the camp, that unless within the space of six days they returned to the city, he would sell their wives and families into slavery, and they themselves should lose all their property.

Afonso Dalboquerque acted in this manner because he had given these Turks an assurance, which it will be remembered they had sent to demand of him, in order that they should come to him in safety; and he was thus compelled to keep to his word, and send notice first of all to them about his intention. But the Rumes, who were similarly employed in the camp of the Hidalcão, had no assurance of a like nature from Afonso Dalboquerque, so he ordered that their wives and children should be taken for slaves, being determined to make a terrible example of them, in order that throughout the whole of the land the people should observe the hatred which the Portuguese had to the people of the Grand Sultan of Cairo, so that no one of the rulers of India might dare to harbour them in their ports and villages.

And Afonso Dalboquerque ordered a large quantity of timber to be carried with the utmost despatch to Garcia de

Sousa, with the object of erecting a very strong stockade on the side towards the city, for he no longer placed any reliance upon the Moors of the city, and he feared lest they should gain an entrance into Benastarim by forcing themselves through the lines at that place; and Garcia de Sousa lost no time in building the stockade, and placed in it two large guns which had been sent expressly for that purpose by Afonso Dalboquerque, and a quantity of smaller artillery, and appointed Garcia's brother, Duarte de Sousa, to be captain of it, with a body of men under him to keep watch over the movements of the Moors who were in the city.

But when Afonso Dalboquerque was informed that the Hidalcão was determined to storm the island at the pass of Augij, where Timoja's men were stationed—who sometimes were inclined to desert the pass and go away—he told the chief to make ready four hundred of those men that had accompanied Jorge da Cunha, and then he sent them to the pass of Augij, where the other men were, and then without giving Timoja any explanation of his so doing he placed over them as captain an ambassador of the King of Onor, who happened to be with him, and in whom he reposed great confidence because he was one of the most illustrious men there, and a cavalier. And thus Afonso Dalboquerque, having provided all the passes with everything that they required, remained besieged for about the space of a month, sometimes being attacked by the Turks in many parts, in order that they might get into the island. But our men defended themselves very valiantly, and slew several of the Hidalcão's men in these engagements.

CHAPTER XXXI.

Of the message which Garcia de Sousa sent from Benastarim to the great Afonso Dalboquerque; and how the latter made an inspection of the passes of the island, and further doings.

While the passes of the island were in the state which I have described, a native peon arrived with a letter from Garcia de Sousa for the great Afonso Dalboquerque; wherein he informed him that the people who composed the besieging force of the Hidalcão were very numerous, and fresh supplies of men were coming up to swell its numbers every day; and that the soldiers who were on guard at the passes were very few, and although he had some native troops with him it was not right for him to put any trust in them, seeing that if they could turn traitors to their own fellow countrymen and their own sects, as they had done, they would be much more likely also to act in a similar manner towards the Christians: and that since they had not sufficient forces wherewith to withstand the Hidalcão's entry into the island, he was of opinion that his Lordship ought to order all who were engaged in defending the passes to withdraw into the fortress, in order that by fortifying themselves in it very strongly with barricades they might successfully oppose the power of the Hidalcão, who was coming against them; and that the fleet which was stationed in the river was sufficient for defending their passage and covering their re-embarkation, and thus everything would be arranged in a secure position.

Afonso Dalboquerque had become by this time so much irritated by the repeated importunities of his captains, that it was only his indomitable spirit which enabled him to bear up against the troubles which they continually brought upon him; so he sent back word in reply to Garcia de Sousa that he must keep good guard at Benastarim, which had been apportioned to his charge, and leave the management of affairs to him; for he had made up his mind to defend the island, yea, and the interior country also, if he thought necessary; and that there was no cause for alarm, because he relied upon the mercy of God to put his enemies to flight, seeing that he himself possessed sufficient bravery and confidence for every emergency. And together with this reply Alfonso Dalboquerque sent him a large gun to be placed in the stockade on the side where the Hidalcão had pitched his camp, and with the help of this he inflicted serious injuries upon the enemy.

At this juncture of events Diogo Fernandez de Béja returned with his fleet, that Afonso Dalboquerque had sent to Condal to act in concert with Jorge da Cunha, and related to him how all the land was full of the Hidalcão's soldiers; and, as he had no intelligence of Jorge da Cunha, he had made his way back because he thought his services might be required at Goa; and that in issuing out of the river many Moors came down against them and shot at them with matchlocks and arrows. Without any delay, Afonso Dalboquerque ordered him to sail up the river again immediately, with all his fleet, and co-operate with D. Antonio de Noronha in defending the passage against the Moors who were bent upon crossing over to the island.

And having arranged this matter, Afonso Dalboquerque mounted his horse, and accompanied by several people, both on horse and on foot, made his way immediately towards Old Goa, where Jorge da Cunha was stationed, carrying with him Melique Çufecondal whom he had met with on the road; and after having remained with him for some space of time he bade him look well to the guarding of that pass; and then he left and went on to the pass of Agacij, where on the water there were D. Antonio, Fernão Perez Dandrade, Luis Coutinho, Bernaldim Freire, and a large number of others with them, for there at that pass the

Hidalcão had stationed the greater part of his host. And when he took leave of these, he told them that he hoped they would of their goodness take care to keep strict watch and keep off the Moors from their attempts to cross over the river, for upon this the safety of everyone depended. And then he went on his progress to Benastarim, and stayed some time there conversing with Garcia de Sousa; and in the course of his interview he told him how on the road he had been informed by some Moors that Melique Çufecondal had entered upon an understanding with the Hidalcão, to the end the latter should attack all the passes of the island in the rafts and *paráos* that he could avail himself of, while the former was to rise up with all his men and put Jorge da Cunha and his companions to death, and as soon as these were dead to overrun all the stockades and get everything into their own hands, and therefore it was that he, Afonso Dalboquerque, was taking him unsuspectingly back with him to Goa to chastise him.

Garcia de Sousa told Afonso Dalboquerque that he was continually in dread of the people of the land, for they were all of the same mind as Melique Çufecondal; and that although his lordship had taken it in bad part that he had sent to remind him that the Christians were very few and the Moors many, yet he would assure him that through this pass that he had to defend none of the soldiers of the Hidalcão would enter whether he had many or few in his company. Afonso Dalboquerque told him that of a truth his intentions had been quite misunderstood; but that it was owing to the great confidence that he reposed in his person, and in the strength of his cavalry, that he had entrusted him with the command at Benastarim, which was the principal pass of that island of Goa.

And then, after staying a little while in conversation with him, Afonso Dalboquerque got again on his horse, and proceeded with his visit to all the other passes, and arrived at the city again when it was already night. And then he sent for Gaspar de Paiva, chief alcaide of the fortress, and to him he gave charge of Melique Çufe[condal] to keep in safe custody with the others, at which Melique Çufe[condal] became very much surprised, for he never had the least suspicion that he had been brought back a prisoner. As soon as Afonso Dalboquerque had returned to the city, Timoja told him that Mandaloi, Lord of Condal, had written him a letter, wherein he stated that as soon as he knew that the Hidalcão had come down against Goa with his host, he had gathered together four thousand men and overrun all the mountain passes, and captured from him the supplies that were proceeding to the camp, and that he was encamped at three leagues' distance from the Hidalcão, and if he, Timoja, would send word on what day he intended to fall upon the Hidalcão, he, Mandaloi, at the same moment would attack the camp with his men, for he felt it his duty to put himself in all things completely under the orders of the Portuguese. Afonso Dalboquerque told Timoja to write in reply that he owed him many thanks for his message, and he hoped to God that he should some day be able to repay him for the good intentions he had expressed of acting for the service of the King of Portugal, by making him lord of the lands of the Hidalcão in the name of the King; but that for the present he must keep quiet, and when the moment arrived he would send him word what he would have him do.

CHAPTER XXXII.

How the Hidalcão entered the island of Goa through the pass of Agacij, and proceeded to attack the city; and the great Afonso Dalboquerque retired to the castle with all his men, and what took place in continuation.

By this time the great Afonso Dalboquerque perceived that the Hidalcão was determined to enter into the Island of

Goa against him, without being deterred by any fear of the fleet that was riding in the river with its large number of soldiers and its artillery; yet he felt sure that this enterprise would never have been attempted had it not been that the Hidalcão was induced so to act by the intelligence which the Moors of the city had conveyed to him, according to the information which João Machado had given him. And as he had now some suspicion of certain native Moors of noble race, who were in correspondence with some of their relatives in the Hidalcão's camp, as soon as he arrived at the city he gave orders that they should be punished according to their deserts. And being very anxious about the security of the pass of Augij, on account of his suspicions concerning the men commanded by Timoja, he gave orders to his nephew, D. Antonio de Noronha, who was chief captain of the fleet in the river, to take up his station at that pass and keep very close watch over it.

The Hidalcão had by this time prepared his rafts, and on a Friday, the seventeenth day of May [A.D. 1510], there was a great and stormy sea running, for it was the winter season, when he gave orders to three hundred Turks to pass over from the mainland to the island by the pass of Augij. And because the tempest was at a great height, and the darkness of the night was very intense, D. Antonio failed to take care that the galleys should be ordered to stand well in to the shore, and thus the Turks had time to get across without being perceived, and then returned immediately on the same rafts and on others which they had already prepared for the occasion, and seven hundred Turks embarked on them and began to pass over. But as by this time the day was beginning to break, three of our boats, which were stationed close in towards the land, perceived them and signalled to D. Antonio, who immediately came up with all the ships, and with well-directed shot from his guns broke all the rafts to pieces and put all the Turks to the sword, so that none escaped except three who fled away.

The Hidalcão felt the death of these Turks on account of the great expenses he had been at to gather them together in his dominions. And while D. Antonio was engaged with his men slaying these Turks, a second party, to the number of two thousand, began to cross over from the other side through some lagoons of weed, all of them covered with mud, without being observed by the Portuguese, who were intently occupied with their own work; but Menaique, the captain of Timoja, who was stationed at Old Goa in company with Jorge da Cunha, caught sight of the Turks, when already a great part of them had got over, and proceeded on horseback to attack them with two hundred native peons who desired to follow him; the Turks, however, did not attempt to move, and Menaique, having come up with them, fell upon them in their van, and before they could free themselves from the mud, put thirty or forty of them to death. And when they began to rally and form in close ranks, and he saw that Jorge da Cunha rendered him very little support, he withdrew with his men and returned to Goa, taking with him the heads of those whom he had put to death.

Timoja's men, who had been placed at the pass, no sooner saw the Turks, than they went and united with them, and then all ran together in one body to Benastarim, where Garcia de Sousa held his position, and stormed the stockades and captured the great gun[1] that was therein, and some smaller guns[2], and put to death his brother[3] and four or five men, and set fire to the stockades. As soon as Garcia de Sousa perceived that he had no chance of resisting the Turks, he withdrew into a *parão* that was ready at hand and retired to Goa. Then Francisco de Sousa Mancias and Francisco Pereira Coutinho, who were on guard over the

[1] *Camelo.* [2] *Berços.* [3] Duarte de Sousa. See p. 150.

pass of Gondalij, retired from the tower at the approach of the Turks, leaving four guns[1] behind them, and took refuge in a boat at some stairs and came down into the city. And when Jorge da Cunha saw that our people were put to rout, and that the Turks had at length forced an entry into the island at many places, he began to withdraw with his mounted men, now very much in disorder, and three horsemen were killed.

As soon as Afonso Dalboquerque became aware that Jorge da Cunha was coming on with great difficulty, he sent Diogo Fernandez, the *Adail*,[2] with twenty horsemen and fifty rank and file, to go to his assistance and rally the party, which action he performed on that day like a very valiant cavalier as he was; for on this occasion, and in every other in which he was employed, he was always able to give a very good account of himself. And after that Diogo Fernandez had started off, Afonso Dalboquerque took horse, and went down to the market square with fifty armed men, in order to see if he could quiet the great demonstrations of joy which the Moors were making after the Turks had entered the island. And the Moors, like men who now had become thoroughly roused, no sooner caught sight of Afonso Dalboquerque, than they went up to attack him. And he, in order to more thoroughly prevail against them that were no longer awed by his presence, ordered fire to be set to the city in four places; and then, leading the people he had with him, he fell upon the enemy, and put to the sword every one of them that he found in the streets, without giving quarter to any one: and after having thus inflicted a very severe chastisement upon the Hidalcão's army, he began to pass along through the whole length of the city with all his people; and while he was thus passing along through one of the streets he caught sight of Timoja, who was also in progress of withdrawing, being hard pressed by certain

[1] *Bombardos.*

[2] See page 137, note 2.

Turks who were coming along in close quarters with him; and as soon as he saw them he charged down upon them, and so put them to discomfiture that they retreated.

And if it had not so happened that Afonso Dalboquerque had been there at that moment, Timoja, and some of his captains who were with him, would have lost their lives, and this would have afforded more satisfaction to the Hidalcão than the taking of the city. By this time, so numerous were the Moors of the Hidalcão's host that had penetrated into the city, that it was imperatively necessary for Afonso Dalboquerque to withdraw with all his army into the fortress, for there were already thirty of our men dead and many wounded. And as it was, this affair did not cost the Hidalcão so little as he suspected, seeing that upwards of two thousand of his men lay stretched out dead up and down the streets.

When Afonso Dalboquerque had entered into the fortress he found our people so full of fear at the enormous numbers whom the Hidalcão brought with him, that he began to encourage them, and on the following day, in the course of the morning, D. Antonio de Noronha arrived in the galleys and boats which he had under his command in the river, and his arrival infused a little courage into our people. And forthwith Afonso Dalboquerque despatched Jorge da Cunha with two hundred men in the boats to make for the shore and set fire to the ships that were drawn up in the dockyards, and to burn the magazine: but seeing that many Moors ran up in defence of the shore, Jorge da Cunha could not set fire to more than four, and to the magazine building, wherein were burned large stores of cordage, and all the dockyard apparatus, and then he returned. And on the next day, during the morning, the Hidalcão made his entry with all the men of his host into the city, with so much shouting and blowing of trumpets, that it was enough to terrify every one who heard it.

CHAPTER XXXIII.

How the great Afonso Dalboquerque determined to fortify himself in the fortress and maintain it; and of what passed with the captains thereupon; and of the message which the Hidalcão sent through João Machado, and what happened afterwards.

Directly that the great Afonso Dalboquerque had withdrawn with all his forces to the fortress, he commanded the captains to take up their positions in stockades on the wall, with the intention of fortifying himself therein and defending himself from the Hidalcão until he could get reinforcements from Cochim, for which he had determined to send. And in order to make up his mind thoroughly as to what course of action he should pursue, he called a meeting of the captains and told them that now that the Hidalcão had made good his entrance into the island and was now in possession of the city, owing to every one's fault, a good opportunity presented itself for them to retrieve the loss they had sustained by reason of the carelessness they had shewn in the matter, in maintaining this fortress. For in addition to its great natural strength,—it would not yield even to Rhodes itself in that respect,—there were therein a thousand Portuguese, against whom, if they defended themselves valiantly, all the power that the Hidalcão could possibly bring to bear would not be sufficient to force an entry, and meanwhile he would send for assistance from Cochim.

To these representations the captains replied, that the reason why the Hidalcão had been able to effect an entry into the island and take possession of the city was not the want of forces on their part nor any carelessness of which they had been guilty, but simply because the Moors were so numerous, and they themselves so few. And as for their desiring to defend the fortress and maintain it against the enemy, he ought not, they declared, to think any more of such a thing, because they were not sufficiently powerful to be able to ward off from themselves the attacks which the forces of the Hidalcão there stationed could make upon it; but he ought to withdraw to the ships and at any rate secure his fleet, for in this lay the safety of the whole of their Indian possessions. And this was the expressed opinion of all the captains, with the exception of D. Antonio de Noronha, and Gaspar de Paiva, chief *Alcaide* of the fortress, who, indeed, declared that Afonso Dalboquerque ought not to leave the fortress but rather secure it, and maintain their position therein, until they could ascertain the intentions of the Hidalcão, for they had the river behind them and could thereby make good their retreat whenever they so desired, without any risk of disaster.

But Afonso Dalboquerque, who was determined to fortify himself in the fortress and maintain it, would not give any opinion upon the state of affairs, and left the business in this state without arriving at any conclusion, and said that the remainder of the captains who were not then present must first of all come and then he would arrange what was needful to be carried out. The captains were, however, so dejected that they could not rest contented with this deferring of action, and each one by himself made his way to Afonso Dalboquerque, and requested him by various arguments to withdraw to the ships and give up possession of the fortress; but he always temporised with them, until at length one day all assembled in preconcerted union and told him he must withdraw because there was no longer any use in any further waiting, and if it should be that he were unwilling to do so, they at least were determined to retire and leave him.

Thereupon, Afonso Dalboquerque, who was afraid lest the fear which had fallen upon them should lead them into some fatal error, ordered D. Antonio de Noronha, his nephew, to proceed to the gate of the fortress that opened out on the riverside, and prevent any one from going out that way, or stirring forth thence, until he should see him in person, or receive a certain signal which had been arranged between them. And now finding himself surrounded by so much trouble, that in order to maintain possession of the fortress he was compelled to guard it from the Moors and from the Christians alike; and that the Hidalcão would become acquainted with the dissensions that were rife in their ranks by obtaining the information of two foreigners of the fleet, who had the day before cast in their lot with him; and that all of them would have to withdraw from their positions upon the wall at the instant of any serious attack, Afonso Dalboquerque came to a determination of his own accord to take refuge in the ships, in order that the artillery should not be lost that was on shore. To this end he dispatched Manuel Fragoso in a *fusta* privately by night to reconnoitre the state of the river, because he had received intelligence that the Moors had scuttled two ships of Malabar, laden with stone, in the bend which the river forms just below the docks, in order to stop up the passage, for that was the narrowest part of the course.

And when Manuel Fragoso had set out, Jorge da Cunha sent word to Afonso Dalboquerque that João Machado had arrived at his station, and brought him news that he desired another interview with Afonso Dalboquerque, who therefore enquired of the captains what he should do; and every one of them gave it as their opinion that he ought not to grant him any interview, for the suitable time for negotiating was now gone by, and all that they ought now to do was to re-embark. Nevertheless, Afonso Dalboquerque, at the last moment, said he would speak with this man, for he would not venture to go very far with the advice the captains gave; yet in order that João Machado should not perceive the disordered and disconcerted state in which our party were, he would not allow him to enter the fortress, but told Antonio da Costa to proceed with his boat and fetch the man and bring him to the galley of Simão Dandrade, while he himself got upon his horse and made his way as far as the gate of the city where the galley was stationed. And while he was there, João Machado arrived, when it was now the dead of night, and told him that he, for his part, had always been desirous that his lordship should come to some settlement with the Hidalcão, and that he could easily see that affairs were going very contrary to the way he should like them to go; and that since things were so, and his lordship could not hold the island against the power of the Hidalcão, much less could he defend the fortress, for in the Hidalcão's camp there was a large number of men and many military appliances ready to attack it; and so he went on alleging many other reasons in support of his argument. And while Afonso Dalboquerque stood thus conversing with João Machado, Francisco de Sousa Mancias came up, and speaking inopportunely asked what he should do, for the Moors were getting an entrance into the fortress, and the captains had sent him to beg that he, Afonso Dalboquerque, would re-embark, for if he would not consent to do so, they would quit their appointed stations.

This, that was thus said in the presence of João Machado, to whom Afonso Dalboquerque was, as it were, selling himself, and was evidently so contrary to the show of power which he was making, and so astonished him, that he sprang up in a passion and said to Francisco de Sousa Mancias:—"How is it, Francisco de Sousa, that you are so desirous of handing over this fortress to the Turks? Go, then, and give it up to them; and do as you wish." And then Francisco de Sousa, whose only anxiety was to extricate himself from the perils in which he found himself involved, made his way to D. Antonio de Noronha, and on coming before him said that his uncle had ordered that he was to surrender the fortress and withdraw. And thereupon D. Antonio, forgetting the orders his uncle had given him [concerning the appointed signal], and relying solely upon the words that Francisco de Sousa said, ordered his men immediately to set fire to one of the arsenals. And while the news was running through the station where the Portuguese forces were posted, our men came down in a confused mass to the gate on the waterside, with the intention of re-embarking. Afonso Dalboquerque heard the noise our men made, and thinking that it was caused by the Moors, because it was night, took his leave of João Machado, and got into a boat and made his way to the waterside gate, and there found the confused body of men who were crowding down to the banks with the object of betaking themselves to the ships; but he made them retrace their steps and dissembled his anger, for D. Antonio Noronha, his nephew, was more to blame in what he had done, than was Francisco de Sousa in what he had said. And when this was over, Manuel Fragoso returned from his mission to reconnoitre, and brought word that the Moors had sunk a Malabar ship laden with stone in the bed of the river, and the water which came down from the mountains had such force, and ran down with so great a fury, that it had broken out a new bed in another part much further up.

CHAPTER XXXIV.

How the great Afonso Dalboquerque quitted the fortress and proceeded to embark; and how the Hidalcão entered it, and what he performed.

The great Afonso Dalboquerque now perceiving that there was no remedy for these things, and being displeased at the vacillation of his captains, and convinced that they ought not to abandon the fortress without at least making an attempt worthy of its importance to hold it, made up his mind to withdraw to the ships, and commanded D. Antonio de Noronha to superintend the re-embarkation of all the artillery, not only our own but also that of the Moors which had been captured, and all the stores that could be collected, and the women and the children and merchants who were lodged in the fortress. And when everything had been collected, Afonso Dalboquerque commanded Gaspar de Paiva, chief *alcaide* of the city, to proceed to the fortress and order his men to cut off the heads of Melique Çufecondal and of a hundred and fifty principal Moors of the city, who had been detained therein in consequence of information which João Machado had given him, and to hamstring all the horses that were in the stables, and to set fire to the arsenals, wherein everything was consumed by fire that could be of any service to the Moors.

When this business was over, Afonso Dalboquerque gave word to his captains for each one to retire with his own men, for he intended himself to be the last of all. And our men were so anxious to see themselves out of the dangerous position that they then occupied, that they made such a great hurry and fell into such disorder in carrying out the order for re-embarking that, had it been done by day, any of the enemy's people who came up could have routed them. And when every one had quitted the shore, Afonso Dalboquerque betook himself to the ships on a Friday before daybreak, on the twentieth day of the month of May, in the year '10, and immediately ordered the whole fleet to set sail, and stood down the river in front of the fortress of Pangij, because there the river is wider, and there they would be safe from any accident befalling them, —with the intention of waiting there until the water of the bar deepened sufficiently to allow the ships to pass out with safety.

Without any consideration, and in contravention of the

orders which Afonso Dalboquerque had given, Francisco de Sousa Mancias,—who had been the first to set sail,—steered immediately with a rapid course straight towards the bar, but when Afonso Dalboquerque perceived this unauthorised manœuvre he sent Diogo Fernandez de Béja in the galley after him, and made him return, and when he was come back reprehended him seriously for daring to depart without permission, and deprived him of the captaincy of his ship, whereat he became very much displeased.

Directly that the Hidalcão observed that our fleet had sailed away, he despatched a brigantine to keep it in sight and take note of its intentions, while he himself entered into the fortress with all his Turks and Rumes with great joy, and many shouts and blowing of musical instruments, evincing thereby his great delight at having thus at length brought about a business for which he had so earnestly longed. But when he entered the castle and beheld in its courtyard all the principal Moors of the land decapitated, he became very sorrowful, and the outcries of all those who accompanied him were so loud that the Hidalcão was quite overcome at the sight of so much sorrow in a city which he had captured with so much satisfaction to himself.

And the Turks, too, and the Rumes as well on their part, when they did not find their wives and children, as they had expected, became very dejected, for it was this hope of recovering them that had induced them to undergo such great hardships in their efforts to effect an entry into the island. And while the Hidalcão was thus employed in this sorrowful task of consoling the fathers, the sons, and the relatives of those that lay there dead, the captain of the brigantine which he had sent out returned and reported to him how all the fleet of the Franks had dropped anchor opposite the fortress of Pangij, and how he thought it was its intention to establish itself there, because the chief captain had despatched a galley after one of the ships which had sailed away in the direction of the bar, in order to get away, and made it return again within the bar.

When the Hidalcão heard this, fearing lest Afonso Dalboquerque should capture Pangij, and fortify his position there, immediately sent João Machado (in order to temporise with him while he could in the meantime provide that fortress with means of resistance) in the same brigantine to go and treat for peace with him. And as soon as this man had been sent forth on his journey, the Hidalcão despatched a captain with four hundred Turks and two thousand native peons, and artillery and all necessary munitions, and sent them to the fortress of Pangij to guard it, and to do all the injury they could to our fleet, in order that it should be compelled to weigh anchor and go away, or at any rate to make some composition with him.

João Machado began to speak of terms of peace directly he arrived, and after a lengthy interview that they held upon this matter, Afonso Dalboquerque told him that at the time when he held the fortress of Goa then he would have forthwith entered into any peace and alliance with the Hidalcão; but now that he was no longer master of it, he would enter into no agreement without first of all being replaced in Goa and all its revenues returned to him, and the settled tribute paid to the King D. Manuel for the lands that he had taken from the Indians, and he, the Hidalcão, become his subject and use only his flag, and he would further have to give up Dabul[1] in order that a fortress might be constructed there; if he would perform all this, then he would agree to a peace with him, for Goa belonged to the King of Portugal and should ever remain so.

João Machado returned with this reply, and on the follow-

[1] Daiwal, in the Bombay Presidency, 17 deg. 23 min. N., 73 deg. 33 min. E.; not far from Caripatan, and north of Goa. See Berthelot's Chart, quoted in previous pages.

ing morning the Hidalcão sent again to desire of Afonso Dalboquerque a hostage in order that two Turks—chief men,—might proceed to speak with him. So Afonso Dalboquerque sent D. Antonio de Noronha in a galley to converse with the Turks, close by the fortress of Pangij, and Diogo Fernandez de Béja to remain on the land as a hostage. And when D. Antonio arrived at the appointed place he sent Diogo Fernandez on shore, and the two Turks came down to the galley to speak with him, and all three remained a long space of time in conversation without coming to any conclusion on any point, for of a truth they did not really desire anything except a procrastination of events, in order to gain time for the victualling of the fortress of Pangij, which they effected; and when they took their leave of D. Antonio they spoke with him in relation to the ransoming of the women and children of the Turks and Rumes, but D. Antonio undeceived them, for he did not intend to surrender them for any consideration in the world; and so it turned out, for Afonso Dalboquerque took them away with him when he departed, and on the occasion of the second taking of Goa he converted them all to Christianity, and found husbands for them, as will be related in due course of time.

And when the Turks had left, D. Antonio received Diogo Fernandez again and returned to the ships, and related to his uncle all that had taken place; and Diogo Fernandez told him that while he was on land the Turks had made him a great many grand speeches in Italian and in Castilian. Our people were still dejected at the past events, and when they perceived that D. Antonio had come to no arrangement with the Turks, they concluded that all was lost, and made their way to Afonso Dalboquerque and put urgent pressure upon him to sail over the bar, although they all knew very well that the winter season was at its height, and it was not the proper time to attempt to sail over any bar in India.

CHAPTER XXXV.

Of the council which the great Afonso Dalboquerque held whether he should sail away over the bar, and what happened thereupon; and how he sent away Fernão Perez Dandrade, who was cast away.

In order to pacify this uproar into which the captains had now induced all the people to enter, and in order to dissipate the disappointment which appeared to have taken hold upon them, the great Afonso Dalboquerque convened a meeting of the captains, masters, and pilots of the vessels; and when all were assembled, he told them that he was exceedingly astonished at their unreasonable conduct, for although they knew that it was not the proper time of the year to sail out over the bar, they were nevertheless exciting the men to make requisitions upon him to be gone, and that now they were all met together, masters and pilots, if they would tell him what they thought best for him to do, he would do it.

So whereas the captains were anxious to be gone, each one of his own motion began immediately to declare that the weather was favourable for sailing out over the bar, and it was his duty to proceed to winter quarters elsewhere, because he had a very short supply of provisions, and in these islands there were no means of their being able to lay in a fresh supply, for the Hidalcão had laid hands upon everything; and even if the weather should not permit them to reach Cananor or Cochim, they could at least pass the winter at Anjadiva;[1] and thus they rambled on, alleging various other

[1] Anjadiva. The position of this Indian seaport, now no longer marked on the maps, and apparently unknown to Pedro Berthelot when making his Indian charts in 1635, which are inserted into Pedro Barretto de Resende's work so often quoted in previous notes, is plainly marked in a very fine map of India contained in an atlas now in the Map Department of the British Museum, and formerly in the possession of Henry Chapman (? of Lisbon), from whom the Board of Admiralty

reasons in accordance with their own projects. But the masters and pilots, on the other hand, said that they were there in a broad and spacious place, with their ships securely moored, where the inhabitants of the city could not do them any harm, and even [if] this were not so, the bar was so dangerous to navigate now, that even a barque, let it be of ever so light a draught, could not go out over it; and even if it were taken for granted that they could pass out over it without incurring any danger, there was no place that they could pass the winter at; for Anjadiva, a place that had been proposed, could not admit of ships of so great a size and so deep a draught being able to remain there at that season of the year.

And at three or four assemblies which were held about this affair, the pilots and masters always arrived at the same conclusion, and the majority of the captains exactly the contrary opinion; and hereupon there were held many discussions, wherein they told Afonso Dalboquerque that all the people of the fleet were ashamed of him, and declared that he was anxious that they should all die of hunger there; and

purchased it in 1792. "This manuscript," according to a note on the first page, "appears to have been written in the year 1546, in the reign of John III, King of Portugal, when the Portuguese Nation had completed their Discoverys and Conquests in Africa, Asia, and America, at the time when their navigation and commerce was in the most flourishing state." The MS. is the work of Ferdinando Vaz or Fernão Vãz Dourado, and a very fine specimen of Portuguese illuminated hydrography of the middle of the sixteenth century. The places on the east coast of India apparently known to Portuguese navigators at this period are thus marked, commencing with the north—Gamdar, Baroche, Surate, *Damão*, Danu, Ilha das uaqas, *Agasai*, *Basaim*, Bombai, *Chaull*, Damda, Queleçi, Ceimado, *Dabull*, Zamgizara, Dobetelle, Ceitapor, Carapatão, O Pagodè, *I. Qeimadõ*, Bamda, *Goa*, Agasai, I. do Sall, *C. Daian*, Amgediua, *Onor*, Batecalla, Os Pumdes, *Barcellor*, Bacanor, I. de S. Maria, *Mangalor*, Momte Fermoso, Mamgesirão, Montedelli, Marabia, Baleapatão, *Cananor*, Tremapatão, Coulete, Challe, *Panane*, etc. The names in *italic* are in red ink, the others in black,—a distinction perhaps intended to shew Portuguese trade with, or possession of, the former class.

many other things they told him, which I suppress in order not to blame the dead nor shame those who are dead. When Afonso Dalboquerque perceived that in contrary spirit to the opinions of the pilots and masters the captains were ill-disposed to brook their present troubles and had quite forgotten that he was placed there as a governor over them all, he determined to venture the *St. John*, and ordered Fernão Perez Dandrade, who was the captain of this vessel, to proceed to Anjadiva, and, taking advantage of the first fair weather, bring back all the supplies he could possibly collect; and, in addition, he ordered Timoja to accompany him with two of his *fustas* to those ports, and bring away some of the supplies also. And when they were ready they set out and steered straight for the bar, but because the weather was very bad and the sea stormy, they dropped anchor just inside the bar and remained in that position all the night, and on the next morning at daybreak, when the weather began to moderate, Fernão Perez came to the resolution, with advice of his pilot, to make the attempt at getting over the bar.

When Timoja observed the resolution which had been taken, he told him on no account to weigh anchor, for even if the weather were to clear up, it was not a fit occasion for going over the bar, and if he endeavoured to do so he would be lost. But Fernão Perez was so anxious to execute the commands that had been delivered to him that he would not listen to Timoja's advice, but weighed anchors, and steered towards the bar, when it wanted but one watch to the ebb, and because the water ran strongly down from the mountains and the wind dropped, the ship grounded upon the shallows, where it was wrecked, and, being old, immediately went to pieces. As soon as Afonso Dalboquerque saw the ship was wrecked, he sent off help in boats to save the men, and every one was taken up, and the artillery and all the fittings were saved. And when the captains saw how the vessel had been lost, then at length they were convinced of the soundness of the advice which the masters and pilots had offered, and there remained our fleet for many days suffering great hardships.

CHAPTER XXXVI.

How the Captain who was stationed in Pangij began to harass our ships with artillery; and how the great Afonso Dalboquerque acted with our men thereat; and how he would not accept the present which the Hidalcão sent to him.

When the Hidalcão became aware that the great Afonso Dalboquerque would not reply to the proposition concerning an agreement of a peaceable nature between them, he hastened more than ever to send the captain and men whom he had told off for Pangij. And when this captain arrived at the fortress he ordered his men without loss of time to attack our ships with his artillery, and inflicted great damage upon us in this manner. There was one day when they struck us with fifty large cannon-balls, besides other smaller shot. Our men were so disconcerted and dejected at this new difficulty in which they were involved, that they began to imagine that the Moors would be able to take the ships by means of their rafts, and this fear seized them in such a complete manner that Afonso Dalboquerque dared not try to rouse them out of it by reprehension, lest he should drive them to despair. But, on the contrary, when they approached him for the purpose of giving him advice as to what was best to be done in order to extricate himself from the peril in which he was situated, he replied that he was quite of the same opinion as themselves with regard to everything they said, and that he would put it in action at once, and then he went straightway to his chamber and cast his eyes up to heaven and besought God to forgive his sins, for he felt that this dejection of the men could not be caused by fear, but a divine visitation on account of his sins, for he had the *Cirne*, and the *Flor de la Mar*,—two ships so powerful that they alone were sufficient to protect them from the power of the Hidalcão.

And while the men were yet in this state of dejection two of his men-at-arms fled away to the Moors, and told the Hidalcão of the plight in which our people were situated, and of the great numbers of the sick that were in the fleet, and how his artillery inflicted great havoc in our ships, and that there was so much starvation among them that for want of provisions they were eating up all the rats that could be caught in the ships, and taking off the skins from the leather-covered chests, and boiling them for food, and every day they were making urgent request to the chief captain to quit the river. But because Afonso Dalboquerque was not willing to come to any terms with him, the Hidalcão attached but little credit to this relation which the two Christian runaways told him; and in order to make certain that it was the truth, he made up his mind that he would send a present of sheep and chickens, and other fresh provisions from the land to Afonso Dalboquerque. And when the Moor, who was dispatched for this purpose, had set out in a barque with the present, he came alongside of Afonso Dalboquerque's ship flying a white flag; and Afonso no sooner perceived the barque and the things that were on board than he at once divined that this had been done because the young fugitives had told the Hidalcão of the great straits to which the fleet was reduced, and he had sent the present in order to make sure of the state they were in.

In order, therefore, to pay the Hidalcão out in his own coin, Afonso Dalboquerque ordered that the Moor should be detained on board the ship, and told the master to order the men to cut a barrel in two through the middle, and set it full of wine on the deck, and put all the biscuits that remained into a sail—there was but little of this, and he had reserved it for those who were sick,—and when all this had been made ready, he gave the word to introduce the Moor, who, when he had approached near to him, told him that the Hidalcão his master had been notified of the great need he was in from the lack of supplies, and because he desired to be on friendly terms, and to be at peace and in alliance with the King of Portugal (as indeed he had frequently sent to say), he had sent him these fresh provisions; and if he required any victuals he should say so, for he would then forward them to him; for, although there was war between them, yet he, for his part, did not wish to carry it on by hunger, but with the sword in the hand.

Afonso Dalboquerque told him to relate to the Hidalcão that he was greatly obliged to him for the remembrance which he had of him, but it was not his custom to accept presents from his enemies in the time of war, and with respect to the provisions that he sent to offer him, in the fleet there was so much biscuit and wine that all the ships were as well provided as he could see here for himself, and not enough men to make use of these victuals. With this answer from Afonso Dalboquerque, the Moor carried back the present he had brought, and related to the Hidalcão all that he had seen, and all that had passed in his interview with him.

CHAPTER XXXVII.

The council held by the great Afonso Dalboquerque respecting the attack upon the fortress of Pangij; and how he entered it, and of the slaughter he made of the Moors therein.

When the great Afonso Dalboquerque became aware of the great destruction which was inflicted upon his fleet by the artillery that was mounted in the fortress of Pangij, he determined, in spite of all obstacles that could arise, to attack the fortress, and for the effecting of this object to risk even life itself and all that remained. But in order to decide how he should act in this matter he called a meeting of all his captains, and told them that when first he found himself outside Goa he had come to the conclusion not to waste any more time in skirmishing with the Moors, for he who could relinquish the walls of a city so noble as that, ought not to care to be shooting arrows at a handful of negroes; but since it had so turned out that the artillery that was mounted in the fortress of Pangij compelled him to attack it, and he was thus forced to fight against his will, therefore he begged them of their kindness to tell him in what way he should act in order to achieve this object, for he was thoroughly set upon making the attack. And because in the deliberation which ensued there were numerous dissensions among the captains, and divers determinations were arrived at, Afonso Dalboquerque desired to be beforehand with them in everything before they could reply to him, so he said that he would not force any one to take part in this enterprise, but let them who were willing to follow him, upon hearing one of Timoja's trumpets sounded, assemble at his ship, for he intended, whether they were few or many, to take those whom he found ready with him, and go and fight the Moors who were stationed in the fortress, and relying upon the Passion of Our Lord he expected to take them into his hands.

The captains perceived his intentions, and replied that they would be with him in the projected enterprise, and without holding any more consultation on this behalf—for Afonso Dalboquerque was opposed to so doing, as he was by this time much annoyed at the course of affairs,—every one made his way to the ships to prepare himself, and that very night a young man fled away from the fleet and contrived to carry to the Hidalcão news of the council that had been held and of the intention which had been arrived at.

No sooner had the Hidalcão become possessed of the news which the young man had told him, than he summoned a meeting of his captains—and among them was João Machado,—and related to them all that the young man had said, and enquired of them whether or not it would be necessary to provide for Pangij a further supply of men and artillery. All the captains were of the opinion that the fortress contained a sufficient number of men for its defence, and that assistance could very easily be sent to it whenever any need should arise. But João Machado, who was the last to speak, said that he was not of that opinion, but thought, on the other hand, that some reinforcements should be sent there, because if the statement made by the young man, that the artillery placed in the fortress inflicted so much injury upon the Portuguese ships, were true, it was certain that they would make up their minds to take the place.

Then one of the captains, who had long been a rival of this man, declared to the Hidalcão, that all that João Machado had said was more like the opinion of a Christian than a Moor, and that if he considered Pangij were in danger of being weak in its defence, provided that he had five hundred Turks given to him he would undertake, in combination with the other men who were already there, to defend the position against the entire Portuguese force. João Machado replied that the reason he had given his opinion for reinforcing the place was that he knew well how determined the Portuguese were; and this captain was welcome to go, but he, João, would wager that if the Portuguese behaved as he expected they would, they would appear to this captain a sort of people whom one would be unwilling to attack with a small force only.

And as they then began to make use of angry words to each other, for they had now for long time been unfriendly, the Turkish captains interposed themselves between the disputants, and separated them; and the Turkish captain proceeded to take up his position in Pangij with the number of soldiers whom he had desired the Hidalcão to give him for this purpose, and it fell out that the reinforcement was made on the very day that Afonso Dalboquerque attacked the fortress. And the captain was received by those within it with loud shouts, and blowing of musical instruments, and bonfires, which were kept up all that night long.

Meanwhile, although the flight of the young man caused Afonso Dalboquerque to have some misgiving with regard to undertaking this expedition, it occurred to him that if the Hidalcão should be informed of his intentions, he would hasten to supply the fortress with as many soldiers as he had:—nevertheless, he would on no account withdraw from that which he had already determined to do, and therefore, when the time arrived, he ordered the trumpet to be sounded, and all came on board his ship, and set out from that point, on a Friday before daybreak, the fourteenth day of the month of June. And as soon as they came to land, Afonso Dalboquerque ordered Diogo Fernandez de Béja to take twenty men and go and seize that gate of the fortress which looked towards the city and remain there, for thither would all make their way to his assistance. And to Dinis Fernandez, chief superintendent of the dockyards, he gave orders that with fifty mariners and bombardiers he should take care to carry off the great gun[1] and all the rest of the artillery that was in the fortress to the boats; while he himself took up a strong position with a body of soldiers on the shore, ready to render assistance wherever it should be required.

When all this had been thus arranged, at the sound of the trumpets, the captains rushed with their men to attack the bulwark with such fury, that without any stoppage they entered into it, each one where he could best find a way. And Manuel de Lacerda was the first who mounted upon the top of the wall. The Moors, who were half asleep, and

[1] *Camelo.*

quite confident in the numbers of men they had, found our men already hand to hand with them when they wished to make use of their weapons; and when they perceived that they were cut off, they took to flight and made their way to the gate of the fortress at which Diogo Fernandez was posted. And this party would have been entirely routed, owing to the overwhelming numbers of the Moors, had it not been for Garcia de Sousa who came to their assistance, and on arrival he found Diogo Fernandez and the greater part of his men badly wounded, and three of them killed. Just at this moment the other captains came up following behind the Moors, and united themselves into one body and fell upon the enemy and immediately discomfited them, so that the fortress remained entirely evacuated by its defenders—a force of about four thousand Turks and Moors.

In this engagement a hundred and fifty Turks and a hundred Hindoo peons, and three captains of the Hidalcão were killed on the enemy's side; and of ours about five hundred Portuguese, all *fidalgos* and important men in the fleet, who, being few in number, then performed a deed worthy of the highest praise—for, in nobly born minds, the dread of infamy of defeat overcomes every peril and every fear.

And by this time Dinis Fernandez had carried away all the Moorish artillery to the boats, as well as the two *camelos*, which they had formerly taken from Garcia de Sousa at Benastarim, and five *falcões*, that had been taken in the tower of Agacij, and a quantity of bows, arrows, and lances; and then Afonso Dalboquerque withdrew with all his men and betook himself again to the ships. And when every one had retired the Hindoos came and burned all the dead bodies—according to their custom,—and by this victory, which our people obtained over the Turks, João Machado acquired greater credit than ever with the Hidalcão by reason of what I have said, and because his rival was dead.

CHAPTER XXXVIII.

How the great Afonso Dalboquerque sent Diogo Fernandez de Béja and the other captains in the galleys to reconnoitre the city and get true information respecting the fleet which was being made; and how D. Antonio, in succouring them, was killed.

After the great Afonso Dalboquerque had withdrawn with his forces to the ships, having obtained this victory—news having in the meantime reached him that the Hidalcão had built a fleet of twenty-five sails, of *paráos, fustas*, and watch-boats, armed with quantities of artillery and coiled cables, and painted flags,[1] and many men on board, with intention of setting fire to the Portuguese shipping—he dispatched Diogo Fernandez de Béja in a galley, and Afonso Pessoa and Simão Martinz in two others, to go and reconnoitre the city and observe whether this fleet that was reported was really being built. As soon as Diogo Fernandez and his companions had set out, Afonso Dalboquerque commanded Antonio de Noronha, his nephew, to make himself ready with all his captains in the boats belonging to their ships, in order to be able to render assistance to Diogo Fernandez, if it should be necessary to do so. And because, from the position in which the fleet was placed, neither the galleys nor the city could be seen by those on board—on account of their being hidden by a bend which the river makes there, —Afonso Dalboquerque gave orders to Diniz Fernandez to take up such a position in a *paráo* in the middle of the stream that he could observe both one and the other.

The Turks, who were by this time quite prepared, no sooner caught sight of our galleys, than they gave the word to weigh anchors and set off with the intention of rowing up to them. And then Diniz Fernandez, who had them in

[1] *Padeses.* It is difficult to fix the meaning of this word; it is possible that it may mean *flags* or *banners*.

sight, as soon as he saw that the fleet of the Turks was under weigh, made a signal to D. Antonio de Noronha, who started forth immediately, rowing with all his might and main,[1] in company with all his captains. And because the tide was full, they very soon came in sight of the fleet of the Turks, and as quickly as possible D. Antonio de Noronha called out to Diogo Fernandez and the other captains who were of his party to row on and attack two watchboats which were making their way in front of the fleet. When Diogo Fernandez and the other captains, who were now lying-to upon their oars, perceived the succour which was approaching them, they gave orders to row on more rapidly and keep on their course, gradually approaching to the fleet of the Turks, and began to fire upon them with their artillery; and it fell out that the shot from one of the guns that were in the galley of Diogo Fernandez struck the watch-boats, which were just ahead of them, and knocked them to pieces, and all the Moors were killed who were contained in them, some being killed by the discharges of the gun, and others being drowned in the river. And by this time D. Antonio and all the captains had come up and combined with Diogo Fernandez into one body.

Seeing the determination of our people, the Turks turned back towards the city, and Dom Antonio, with all the captains, continued to follow them up, until they ran aground at the dock, where many Moors were drawn up with the intention of resisting the fierce onset which our party was about to make; but when the ordnance on board the galleys began to tell upon them and killed several among them, they deserted the dock and retired to the city. D. Antonio, who proceeded towards one of our galeots which had remained on the stocks in progress of building, when the retreat took place, seeing that she was moored by cables on the land and without anyone on board, ranged up alongside of her in his

[1] *A voga arrancada.*

boat, and having landed, boarded her with his party, intending to launch her into the sea. And if all the others had acted likewise the galeot would not have remained on land, and he himself would not have been killed; but as it was, the Moors soon observed that D. Antonio was not well supported by our men, so they rallied round the galeot, and the contest raged on this side and on that in such a manner that three captains of the Hidalcão lay dead, and many of our people wounded, without their being able to dislodge the galeot, until at length they wounded D. Antonio with an arrow in the left knee, a wound which soon became so serious that he could not stand upon that leg, and being thus in very great pain, he left the galeot and withdrew into his boat again, and all the others lost no time in sheering off. And after this victory or disaster,—I know not which to call it, for there so rarely valiant a captain as D. Antonio was finished his days,—they all returned to the ships. But because he experienced great pain in his leg, he was unwilling that they should take him to his uncle's ship, so he went to the *Cirne*, of which he was the captain.

When Afonso Dalboquerque was informed of this disaster, he got into his skiff and went to see him, and found him already grievously stricken for death, and there were held many consultations as to the advisability of amputating the leg, but he would never consent, thinking that the evil was not so serious as to call for so severe a remedy, and thus he remained suffering great agony of pain until the eighth day of July, when he was attacked by a spreading inflammation,[1] which carried him off. And there was not a single person in the whole of the fleet who was not deeply affected, but especially his uncle, in that he had been deprived of him at a season when he most needed his personal assistance, his advice, and his knightly example. And then, letting fall many tears, Afonso Dalboquerque gave orders to bury him

[1] *Erpes.*

at the foot of a tree, and when Goa was captured for the second time, he ordered his remains to be removed to the principal church; and he himself, at his death, left directions in his will that they should be removed to his chapel of Our Lady of the Mountain, which he built in the city of Goa, as will be related hereafter.

D. Antonio de Noronha was the son of D. Fernando de Noronha and of D. Costança de Castro, the sister of Afonso Dalboquerque, and younger brother to D. Alvaro de Noronha. He was a very brave cavalier, and never found himself placed in any position which caused him any fear. He was very virtuous, and God-fearing, and very truthful. He was found side by side with Afonso Dalboquerque in every one of the troubles which up to the hour of his death had come upon him. He died at the age of twenty-four years, four having elapsed since he had set out from Portugal with his uncle in the fleet of Tristão da Cunha.

CHAPTER XXXIX.

The message which the Hidalcão sent to the great Afonso Dalboquerque, desiring that he would make peace with him, and further proceedings.

Inasmuch as the Hidalcão was far more anxious of making peace with the great Afonso Dalboquerque than of taking vengeance upon him for the defeat which our men had visited him with at the fortress of Pangij, after the space of a few days following this event, he sent two Turks, men of importance, to confer with Afonso Dalboquerque on the subject, and they, when they had come to the waterside opposite Pangij, began to make signals with their flags. Then Afonso Dalboquerque sent Gaspar Rodriguez, the interpreter, to land, to discover what they required.

The Turks told him to inform the chief captain that the

Hidalcão had sent them there to arrange terms of peace, and that he must send someone to confer with them. But as he was completely disgusted with their lying he would have nothing to say to them. Yet, nevertheless, in order that he might let no good opportunity escape him, he sent Pero Dalpoem in a boat well provided with men, to go and talk with them. Now whenever they came to discuss terms of peace, they always used to bring in their company certain Portuguese, who, having become Moors, were living among them, well dressed, and mounted on horses in accordance with their custom, and accompanied by canopies of state,[1] and these men used to give utterance to all manner of uncourteous words, and endeavoured to persuade our men to desert us and go to the Hidalcão—for besides gaining from him good wages thereby, they would spend there a very happy life, and become free of the troubles and shortness of food which they experienced with us.

Afonso Dalboquerque being angry at the vagabond behaviour of these Portuguese, and at the worthlessness of the Moors, in order to put an end to these shameful acts, told Pero Dalpoem to take with him a musqueteer, and if any of those vagabonds should come near them, he was to order his musqueteer to shoot him. Pero Dalpoem went off, and when he had arrived at the waterside, where the Turks were stationed, they began to discuss terms of peace, and there came up João Deiras, a Gallician—he formerly had been a mariner—who among our men served as a surgeon, together with others his companions, he being mounted on a horse very finely caparisoned, and clad in the attire of a

[1] *Sombreiros de Estado.* Bluteau describes at full length the *Sombreiro do pé alto*, which appears to have been a large kind of umbrella or canopy, used in India and China as a sign of nobility; and says "the men who carry this *sombreiro* are called in India *Boy*, and some of them are so dexterous in shading the sun, that running as fast as a horse, with the *sombreiro* in their hands, the sun does not ever strike upon their master's body."

Moor, with his servants and *sombreiro:* and he began to harangue in very discourteous terms. Then Pero Dalpoem seeing how João Deiras was proceeding with his wonted tales, told João Dilhanes, the bombardier, whom he had taken with him for this purpose, to shoot him, and he would hold him harmless. And as João Deiras was marching up and down, not far from the edge of the shore, putting his horse through its paces, and saying all kinds of things that came into his head, João Dilhanes, who was a very accurate marksman, fired off his matchlock, and down fell the vagabond dead upon the ground, whereat the Turks became very much alarmed.

But when Pero Dalpoem perceived how terrified they were at beholding the sudden death of João Deiras, he told them that the man had been condemned to death by just sentence, on account of his flight to the Moors, and consequently, in accordance with the law of the King of Portugal, any one could put him to death, wheresoever he might find him; he was sorry that it had taken place before their eyes, but he would beg them of their goodness, if henceforth they should come to talk about making peace, or about any other matter, not to bring in company with them any of those worthless fellows, for they made many very dishonourable speeches, but if they would continue to do so, it would be necessary to put them all to death.

The Turks replied that they were very sorry that at a time when they had met to talk of peace and friendship, these fellows should say anything to hurt the feelings of the Portuguese, and on this account, that which Pero Dalpoem had ordered to be done, had been done with very good reason, and there should be no more of these visits. And when these conversations were concluded, the Turks took their leave of Pero Dalpoem, and went away without having arrived at any conclusion, and Pero Dalpoem betook himself to the ship of Afonso Dalboquerque, and related to him all that had taken place.

CHAPTER XL.

How the Hidalcão sent one of his principal captains back again to speak with the great Afonso Dalboquerque respecting peace; and of the reply given to him, and what passed with him concerning Timoja.

Five days after the conclusion of this negotiation, which Pero Dalpoem had held with the two Turks, they began again to make signals with a flag from the fortress of Pangij. Afonso Dalboquerque sent to see what it was, and news was carried to him that there was a chief captain of the Hidalcão, whose name was Mostafaçāo,[1] desirous of an interview with him, if he would send a hostage to remain on land. But as Afonso Dalboquerque was greatly distressed at the death of D. Antonio, his nephew, he would not have any thing to say to this captain. Yet the Portuguese captains explained to him that inasmuch as the Hidalcão had sent a captain of so high a rank as this messenger manifestly was, it must be because he intended to perform all that was demanded of him, and therefore he ought to consent to see him and to hear what he had to say, for it was possible that he might propose some settlement which should meet with their universal approbation. And, thereupon, although it was against his will, at this opinion of the captains, Afonso Dalboquerque ordered them to get ready a *paráo*, all carpeted over with silken stuffs, and bade Gaspar de Paiva, and Diogo Fernandez de Béja, and Pero Dalpoem, to get into it and proceed to shore, and bring the captain to him; and with these he sent Francisco Corvinel,[2] and Diogo Fernandez, the *Adail* of Goa, to re-

[1] Evidently the Portuguese rendering of the Arabic *Mustafa Khan*.

[2] Francisco Corvinel was the *Armador* or *Armourer* of the fleet which accompanied Dom Fernando Coutinho to India in 1509. See page 56, note.

main behind as hostages, and Gaspar Rodriguez the interpreter to go on land also with the messages. And when the *parão* was ready, they set out; and having arrived in front of the fortress of Pangij, Pero Dalpoem sent Gaspar Rodriguez the interpreter to shore in an *almadia,* to inform the Turks that the great Afonso Dalboquerque had commanded him to come there in that *parão* in order to convey their captain to his ship, and that he had at the same time brought the hostages with the intention of leaving them on shore.

The Turks forthwith sent to reply to him that Mostafação was a man of the very highest rank, and one of the most superior captains in the service of the Hidalcão, and that he had in his retinue two Turks who were men of very great position; therefore if they brought D. Antonio de Noronha—it appears that they did not yet know that D. Antonio was dead—as a hostage to remain on shore, these three should go to Afonso Dalboquerque, but if not, they must go back again. Pero Dalpoem replied that Dom Antonio had not come with them, for he was very ill, but that two men of very high rank, servants and captains of the King of Portugal, had come for this purpose. And at this reply the Turks were quite contented and sent word for them to be landed.

Then Pero Dalpoem dispatched them at once in the *almadia,* and in it was conveyed back to him Mostafação, with the two noble Turks, who went on board the *parão,* and made their way to the admiral's flagship, where Afonso Dalboquerque was stationed with all the captains, *fidalgos,* and honourable persons in the fleet, on the quarter-deck of the ship, which had been decorated for this interview. And Afonso Dalboquerque stepped out to receive the envoy at the edge of the deck, and showed him much attention, and after much politeness had passed between them, Mostafação said that he wished to deliver a message to him from the Hidalção, but it could not be delivered before so large a concourse of persons.

Then Afonso Dalboquerque stood up, and withdrew with him and the two Turks into his private chamber, taking with him Cogebequi, and Lourenço de Paiva, secretary, and Pero Dalpoem, *Ouvidor*[1] of India; and when all were seated, Mostafação gave him many kind messages on the part of the Hidalção and of all his captains, saying that although war between them was still going on, it was the custom of captains in times of peace to send and receive compliments to and from one another; and proceeding with his remarks, he told Afonso Dalboquerque that the Hidalcão his lord, being very desirous of having peace, had sent him thither to perform everything that was desired of him; for he would be very glad if any kind of alliance could be arrived at between them; and that the Hidalcão would be very delighted to surrender Goa to him, so earnestly did he wish for his friendship, but the Turks would not permit him to give up the city; but he begged him earnestly that he would be pleased to take Cintácora, with all its lands and great revenue, for there was there a very good harbour, where he could construct a fortress if he desired.

Afonso Dalboquerque replied that he had no cause of complaint against the Hidalcão, for all the events of the war were guided by the will of Our Lord; and although for the present he had been driven out of Goa, yet a time would come when the tables would be turned; but as for everything else that he said he was determined on no account to accept any other thing except the island of Goa, with all its lands, and therefore if the Hidalcão chose to give it up, then they could become friends, but if not, then there was no use in talking any more about it.

Mostafação answered that the Hidalcão, his lord, would

[1] *Ouvidor*, a kind of Judge or Magistrate, here evidently *the chief magistrate*.

not surrender the island of Goa, because he had gained possession of it, and if he were to yield it up again, he would lose a great portion of his estate and his prestige; and then he went close up to Afonso Dalboquerque, and told him in the course of his conversation, that he thought that the Turks would consent to the surrender of Goa, if he would give up Timoja to the Hidalcão his lord. Afonso Dalboquerque was so affronted at the thought of Mostafação proposing such a thing as the betrayal of Timoja, that he answered sternly he was very much surprised at his daring to propose such a course of conduct as that to him, for Timoja had always been a very loyal servant of his lord the King D. Manuel, and for his services he was worthy of great consideration and honour; and let him say to the Hidalcão that the kingdom of Goa was a possession of his lord the King D. Manuel as long as his captain-general of India so chose; and he would promise him, before that summer should pass away, that he would be taking his rest again in the palace at Goa, and that he hoped to make Timoja a very great lord in the kingdom of Decan; and then the Hidalcão would learn whether the counsel which the Turks gave him was good or not; and then he took his leave of him, and he went back in the *parão* as he had come, and Diogo Fernandez and Francisco Corvinel, who had remained on shore as hostages, were brought back.

CHAPTER XLI.

How matters stood between the great Afonso Dalboquerque, at anchor in the river at Goa, and certain Captains, respecting the hanging of Ruy Diaz; and how he determined to send D. João de Lima with the sick men to Cochim.

At the time that the grand Afonso Dalboquerque was riding at anchor in the river of Goa, suffering all these hardships which I have detailed, with his forces prostrated by sickness and his supplies of food very much reduced, and all the while the weather remaining so foul that there was no means of any one of them getting over the bar, information was brought to him that for many days past a certain Ruy Diaz,[1] a man-at-arms, had been in the habit of entering into the apartments of the Moorish women whom he had taken prisoners in Goa. When he learned this, fearing lest Our Lord should visit him with some severe punishment unless he showed himself capable of appreciating the dangers of this situation, he summoned before him Pero

[1] This event, which is told in the Commentaries with the simplicity which characterises the whole of the text, has been thrown into, perhaps, unnecessary prominence by all the biographers of Afonso Dalboquerque, because Camões devotes considerable space to the case. The passage in the *Lusiad* is as follows:—

"Mais estanças cantara esta sirena
Em louvor do illustrissimo Albuquerque,
Mas alembrou-lhe huma ira, que o condena,
Postoque a fama sua o mundo cerque.
O grande capitão, que o fado ordena
Que com trabalhos gloria eterna merque,
Mais ha de ser hum brando companheiro
Para os seus, que juiz cruel, e inteiro.

"Mas em tempo que fomes, e asperezas,
Doenças, frechas, e trovões ardentes,
A sazão, e o lugar fazem cruezas
Nos soldados a tudo obedientes,
Parece de selvaticas brutezas,
De peitos inhumanos, e insolentes,
Dar extremo supplicio pela culpa,
Que a fraca humandade, e Amor desculpa.

"Não será a culpa abominoso incesto,
Nem violento estupro em virgem pura,
Nem menos adulterio deshonesto;
Mas c'huma escrava vil, lasciva, e escura:
Se o peito, ou de cioso, ou de modesto,
Ou de usado a crueza fera e dura,
Co'os seus huma ira insana não refrea,
Põe na fama alva noda negra e fea.

Dalpoem, the *Ouvidor*, and impressed very strongly upon him the need of privately obtaining information concerning the progress of this business (and to assist him he appointed

"Vio Alexandre Apelles namorado
Da sua Campaspe, e deo-lha alegremente,
Não sendo seu soldado exprimentado,
Nem vendo-se n'hum cerco duro e urgente.
Sentio Cyro que andava já abrazado,
Araspas de Panthêa em fogo ardente,
Que elle tomara em guarda, e promettia,
Que nenhum máo desejo o venceria:

"Mas vendo o illustre Persa, que vencido
Fora de Amor, que em fim não tem defensa,
Levemente o perdoa, e foi servido
Delle n' hum caso grande em recompensa.
Por força, de Juditha foi marido
O ferreo Baldovino; mas dispensa
Carlos, pai della, posto em cousas grandes,
Que viva, e povoador seja de Frandes."

Camões, *Lus.*, x, 45-49.

". . . Here with a sighful frown
The goddess paused, for much remained unsung,
But blotted with an humble soldier's wrong.
Alas! she cries, when war's dread horrors reign,
And thundering batteries rock the fiery plain,
When ghastly famine on a hostile soil,
When pale disease attends a weary toil,
When patient under all the soldier stands,
Detested be the rage which then demands
The humble soldier's blood, his only crime
The amorous frailty of the youthful prime!
Incest's cold horror here no glow restrained,
Nor sacred nuptial bed was here profaned,
Nor here unwelcome force the virgin seized;
A slave lascivious, in his fondling pleas'd,
Resigns her breast—Ah, stain to Lusian fame!
('Twas lust of blood, perhaps 'twas jealous flame;)
The leader's rage, unworthy of the brave,
Consigns the youthful soldier to the grave.
Not Ammon thus Apelles' love repaid,
Great Ammon's bed resigned the lovely maid:

as his scrivener Lourenço de Paiva to be secretary); and if they should find Ruy Diaz guilty, he bade them arrest him and proceed against him in accordance with the rules of justice.

Pero Dalpoem began to prepare his act of accusation privately, and discovered by the testimony of many persons that Ruy Dias had for some days been in the habit of entering the apartments of the women. And when he considered the nature of the crime, and the place and the occasion in which it had been committed, he adjudged that the perpetrator should be executed; so he ordered that he should be hanged in the ship *Flor da Rosa*, of which Bernaldim Freire was captain. And when the *Meirinho* proceeded to put the execution of this sentence in force, which the *Ouvidor* had ordered him to perform, there went out from the small galley—where they had all met together—Simão Dandrade, captain thereof, Fernão Perez his brother, Jorge Fogaça, Francisco de Sâ, and Bernaldim Freire, and passed alongside of the ship *Flor da Rosa*, where the *Meirinho* was hanging Ruy Diaz, and put on board her Bernaldim Freire and Francisco de Sá; and when these two had gone on board, Francisco de Sá went immediately with a drawn sword in his hand to the bowsprit of the ship, and cut the rope and drew him into the ship.

When the *Meirinho* perceived that they had rescued the prisoner, he began to cry in a loud voice for Afonso Dalboquerque to send him assistance, for they had rescued the delinquent. And Fernão Perez Dandrade, Simão Dandrade, and Jorge Fogaça in their *paráo* went up and down

Nor Cyrus thus reproved Araspas' fire;
Nor haughtier Carlo thus assumed the sire,
Though iron Baldwin to his daughter's bower,
An ill-match'd lover, stole in secret hour:
With nobler rage the lofty monarch glow'd
And Flandria's earldom on the knight bestow'd.

Mickle's *Lusiad*, bk. x.

among the fleet, and began to wave white cloths from one ship to the other, as signals, requiring the captains, on the part of the king, to forbid the execution of that man. The uproar, however, was so great throughout the fleet that they were not understood; and the captains, not knowing what was taking place, gave orders to haul their boats on board, and every one began to make himself ready to go and give help wherever it should be required. Afonso Dalboquerque perceiving the disturbed state of the fleet, and that the captains were making signals with white cloths, and having by this time received a message from the *Meirinho* that the prisoner had been rescued, got into his boat with fifty armed men, and proceeded to bear down upon the *parão* which contained Fernão Perez, Simão Dandrade, and Jorge Fogaça, with the intention of putting them down at once, and with them all those who had rallied at their outcries.

But when these men saw him in his boat, they ceased going from ship to ship, and went straight to meet him; and when they came up, Afonso Dalboquerque inquired of them what all the disturbance was about which they were making, for every one was terrified with a false report that it was the Turks coming to set fire to the fleet: and why they were calling out Murder,[1] for was not justice to be meted out to a man who had committed that crime at a season when it was more fitting to be sitting in sackcloth than undertaking such gallantries; and that he had commanded that execution to be performed on his own responsibility.

And while he was thus speaking, Jorge Fogaça leaped into his boat, and exclaimed that he ought not to have ordered such a sentence to be carried out in such a manner upon a man of so honourable a position as Ruy Diaz was, and he must at once produce the acts and testimony, and the power he possessed for acting in such a manner; and

[1] *E porque bradavam da parte del Rey.*

Fernão Perez Dandrade and Simão Dandrade concurred also in this way of thinking; only what they said was couched in more respectful terms of speech.

The great Afonso Dalboquerque determined to chastise these men, in order that this want of respect shown towards his personal authority should not pass without punishment according to its proper deserts, so he compelled them to go on board his own ship, and caused them to be taken below deck, loaded with irons, and ordered the *Ouvidor* to go to the *Flor da Rosa,* and at once give the necessary commands for hanging Ruy Diaz. Afterwards, in the formal inquiry which was made respecting these proceedings, Francisco de Sá was found to be deeply involved, therefore Afonso Dalboquerque commanded that he should be arrested, and put in irons below deck along with the others, and as for Bernaldim Freire, he only suspended him from the captainship of his vessel, for it was proved in evidence that he had been beguiled by Francisco de Sá.

When these captains had been arrested, the people in the fleet became more quiet and free from the uproars which had been going on every day, and the other captains from that time forward became more polite and frank in their conversation. And on the conclusion of all this, the fifteenth day of July being already come, on account of the numbers that were prostrated with sickness, and the want of proper supplies in the fleet for their cure, and the great need of supplies, Afonso Dalboquerque ordered D. João de Lima to make ready as chief captain of a squadron of four ships, whereof the captains were Nuno Vaz de Castelo-branco, Luiz Coutinho, Francisco Pereira, and Antonio de Matos, who were to force a passage out, and send him back whatever supplies they could gather up, loaded into two of the four ships; and if they were to find in Anjadiva any captain who had arrived thither from Portugal, to tell him, on the part of Afonso Dalboquerque, that he must make his way to the bar of Goa, and there anchor to help and succour him, and Nuno Vaz was to be sent on from Anjadiva with the sick men to Cochim; and he gave him a written note of instructions which he was to carry out, and where he was to wait for him: and he ordered Timoja to go in his watch-boats to Onor, where he could also get some supplies. And when all was prepared, the squadron set sail, and went straight towards the bar; but on account of the high wind the ships could not pass over the bar; so they cast anchor close to the bank, and there remained waiting for an opportunity to get out and prosecute their voyage.

CHAPTER XLII.

How the great Afonso Dalboquerque set sail with the intention of sailing away over the bar with the whole of the fleet: and the reason why he did not do so, and what further passed.

D. João had now set sail with the small vessels, and Timoja with his watch-boats, as I have already stated, and as the great Afonso Dalboquerque found himself every day insulted by the captains and the men with requisitions that he would get away from Goa, although it was not a proper season of the year to go to Cananor, nor to Cochim, nor was the bar sufficiently deep in water to enable them to force a way through, he decided, in order to arrive at a definite understanding with them all, and also in order to demonstrate to them that what they desired could not possibly be carried out, to give them an opportunity to have their own way. And consequently in five or six days' time—this would be about the twenty-first of July—he ordered the whole fleet to set sail, and proceeded to the bar, where they found D. João de Lima and Timoja still at anchor, because the weather was as yet not of that kind that they could get over the bar.

As soon as the Hidalcão discovered that our fleet was in full sail, he suspected that they were bound immediately for an outward voyage over the bar, and sent Roçalcão[1] with all the soldiers, both foot and horse, that he had in the city, to make the best way they could by land straight to the bar, and see if they could inflict any injury upon our ships as they were passing over. And on his arrival, Roçalcão lost no time in getting a large gun which he had in his train set up in position in a high wood on the side near to Bradez, which overlooks the entry of the bar, and from that place the enemy began to aim at our ships, and sent four cannon-balls into the side of the *Flor de la Mar*, and all the others were badly struck by the gun, and some men were killed. But because the weather again commenced to be very threatening, and our fleet was no longer secure in the position then occupied, they set sail back again to the old position which they had formerly occupied, and anchored there; and D. João, with his ships, and Timoja, with his watch-boats, also accompanied the fleet in its return.

When the news was spread in the city that Afonso Dalboquerque had returned to his old position within the bar, so great was the uproar and panic among those who had remained in the fortress—because it was entirely destitute of soldiers, every one having been taken to co-operate in the enemy's movements at the bar—that the Hidalcão fled away with his women and abandoned it. And after that all the ships had been moored, Afonso Dalboquerque, on account of the urgent necessity for provisions under which they laboured, sent orders forthwith to Garcia de Sousa to start that very night with the galleys, *parâos*, and boats, and make a descent upon one of the islands in the river of Goa, and endeavour as best he could to collect some provisions.

And all were ready for the expedition which started at

[1] The Portuguese transliteration of a native name, perhaps, *Rasul-Khan.*

midnight, and proceeded up the river, and attacked an island where some rice and a few cows, and *palmito*[1], and other fresh food were obtained, and the men took captive two daughters of a Brahman (*Bramindá*) of Goa, whom they found upon the island, and they set fire to the houses, and returned by the break of day; and Afonso Dalboquerque commanded that everything that had been obtained should be divided equally among all the people in the fleet, at which all were pleased.

After five or six days had elapsed, Timoja made his way to Afonso Dalboquerque, and told him that the Brahman, the father of the girls whom Garcia de Sousa had captured, had sent him word, saying, that on condition that his two daughters were restored he would give to the Portuguese information where there was a small *zambuco*, laden with rice and other native grain, and that they could also make a raid upon the island where it was. So Afonso Dalboquerque agreed to this, and delivered up the girls, and ordered Diogo Fernandez de Béja and Gaspar de Paiva to take their boats and go, in company with Timoja, to that cunningly planned rendezvous of the Brahman; and the appointed party did so, and went by night, and reached the island, where he was waiting for them, and there they took possession of the *zambuco* and fifty cows, and

[1] Bluteau gives the following account of the *Palmito*—"Toma-se por qualquer palma pequena; mas propriamente he o olho da palmeyra, e a parte interior, ou miolo do seu tronco, e finalmente o ponto, e como o centro donde sahem todos os ramos da arvore. He huã substancia alva como leyte coalhado, muito tenra, e de melhor gosto que os melhores doces; he alimento tão salutifero, que ainda que se coma muyto delle não offende. Dos palmitos de coqueyras, que tambem se chamão palmeyras diz o P. Fr. João dos Santos, no 3. livro da *Ethiopia Oriental*, cap. II. 'O olho destas palmeyras se come tambem, e he muyto excellente, e saboroso, ao qual chamão *Palmito*.' Quando querem comer estes palmitos, cortão as palmeyras pelo pé, e depois de lhe cortarem todas os palmas do olho, e a casca de fóra, fica o palmito limpo, alvo, e fermoso, de mais de hum covado, e de quatro, ou cinco palmos de roda."

Timoja gave him back his daughters whom he carried with him.

This done, the party re-assembled and returned before morning came; and as it was now the end of July, and small vessels could get out over the bar with less risk of danger, therefore Afonso Dalboquerque commanded D. João de Lima to set sail at once, and he told Timoja to go to Onor and make ready for him all the provisions that could be obtained, for he had made up his mind—having received information that the Hidalcão wished to depart—to wait where he was at Goa with his great ships for the fleet which was coming from Portugal.[1]

After that D. João de Lima had set sail, the captains,

[1] The expeditions from Portugal to India in this year are thus briefly tabulated in the "Armada da India", Brit. Mus. Add. MS. 20902, f. 13.

"Diogo Mendez de Vasconcellos, Cappitam môr.

Anno de 1510.

"4 Vellas a 12 de Março.

"Diogo Mendez de Vascosellos Cap. moor de quatro naos: partyo a doze de Março pera Ir conquistar Malaca: Capitães Balthazar da Sylua, Pero Caresma, Misser Serniche armador;* e no mesmo anno partio por capitão de tres Carauellas, João Serrão: Capitães Pero de Sousa, Gaspar Cão; e isto para descubrir a Ilha de São Lourenço e asentar nella feitoria que não teve efeito.†

"Neste mesmo anno Gonçalo de Siqueira Capitão moor de sete naos partio a desaseis de março:‡ Capitães Lourenço Moreno, João de Aueiro, Jorge nunes de Leão, Lourenço Lopez, Manoel da Cunha, que se perdeo Junto a Moçãbique, Diogo lobbo d'Alualade.

"Diogo mendes de Vasconselos não pasou a Malaca como lhe El Rey mandaua por lho impedir o Gouernador Affonso d'Albuquerque.

"Destas quatorze naôs as primeiras quatro de que era Cappitam

---

* Outra Relaçao lhe-chama Diniz Cerniche armador da naô em que hia.

† João Serram Cappitam môr de tres vellas, ou Caravellas partiu no mez de Agosto de 1510. Outra Relacão chama a Pero de Souza Payo de Souza, e não declara o nome do outro Cappitam, e só diz, que era Cavalleiro da Caza del Rey.

‡ Gonçalo de Siqueira Cappitam mór de 7 naôs partiu a 16 de Março, Manoel da Cunha era filho de Tristão da Cunha, perdeu-se—Jorge Nunes de Leam foy na naô *Sta. Anna* Enxobregas—João de Aueiro por ser muy sufficiente na Arte do Mar, servia tambem de Piloto na naô *S. Sebastiam* em que foy.

who by this time had divined the intentions of Afonso Dalboquerque, went to him and made many and earnest demands upon him to sail away out of the river, and go to Cochim, where he could refit his fleet, for there were not sufficient provisions on board if they were to remain where they were. And Afonso Dalboquerque replied that if they, the captains, felt themselves pinched by need of supplies, he himself also had not escaped the same, and that he earnestly hoped they would yet put up with troubles for a little longer, and rally the spirits of the men who had been kept in a constant state of alarm, for he had been credibly informed that the lords of the kingdom of Decan had risen up in rebellion against the Hidalcão, and his officers kept on sending him, day after day, letters and broken arrows, which were signs that his men were besieged; and thus the Hidalcão would be unavoidably compelled to go to their assistance, for should he not do so he would run a very great risk of losing his estate; and if the Portuguese remained in the river of Goa with their fleet, they forced the Hidalcão to keep there all his army; and in consequence of this proceeding that prince must lose either one thing or the other, viz., Goa or the rest of the kingdom.

Nevertheless, the captains, for all that they very well understood in what a position all these affairs stood, never ceased making their demands that he should go to Cochim

Môr Diogo Mendez de Vasconcellos hia a Malaca assentar nella trato.

"As sette de que era Cappitam Môr Gonçalo de Siqueira hiam para trazer a Carga da especiaria.

"As tres de que era Cappitam Môr João Serrão mandava El Rey descobrir a Ilha de S. Lourenço, e assentar com os naturaes della trato de Gengivre no Porto Matatana.

"Successos. Manoel da Cunha perdeu-se com toda a gente junto de Moçambique. Gonçalo de Siqueira vindo para este Reino invernou em Moçambique, e chegou no anno de doze."

and from that port return in such a manner that he would be sure of achieving whatever he desired. Yet, when Afonso Dalboquerque could not bring himself to abandon the attempt to regain possession of Goa, he begged the captains to wait there with him for a further space of fifteen days; and when these had passed, then he would do whatever they wished. For he knew of a certainty that the Hidalcão was anxious to return to his own lands, and indeed that he had been compelled to spend all that time at Goa more by the Turks than by his own will. And to see how true this statement was, they required no better proof than the many occasions on which the Hidalcão had sought to make peace, offering them lands and places for the purpose of erecting a fortress—provided only that it were not Goa—all the time that they remained in that river suffering so much trouble and so many hardships, as was well known.

Notwithstanding all these arguments, and others, which Afonso Dalboquerque laid before the captains, with the object of persuading them to wait and see what the Hidalcão intended to do, they maintained their own opinion, and continued to make many demands upon him to sail away. And thus, finding himself unable to count upon any assistance from the captains, and that he was compelled against his will to comply with their desires, he told them to get all in readiness, for on the very first opportunity when the bar should be in a fit condition, he would give them their own way, and set sail away from Goa.

CHAPTER XLIII.

How the great Afonso Dalboquerque sailed out of the river of Goa with all the fleet: and how he came up *en route* with Diogo Mendez, on the voyage from Portugal, and what passed between them.

It was not until the fifteenth day of the month of August, of one thousand fifteen hundred and ten, that the bar of Goa was in proper state for the fleet to pass over it, and then the order was issued to the captains to weigh their anchors and set their sails; and because on this day, on account of the lateness of the hour, they could not get over, the fleet proceeded to cast anchor upon the bank of the bar, and early in the morning of the following day they passed over, and sailed straight away to Anjadiva. And on that very day, at set of the sun, they caught sight of five sailing vessels, which stood in from the sea to observe the position of the land.

Thereupon Afonso Dalboquerque dispatched Antonio da Costa, captain of the vessel named *The Little King (Rey pequeno)*, and Duarte de Melo, of *The Great King (Rey grande)*, to go and speak with them, and discover what ships they were; and these two ships steered off in the track of the others, in order to reconnoitre them; but as the night was by this time come, they lost sight of them; but on the following morning the ships came up with our fleet. And then it turned out that it was Diogo Mendez de Vasconcellos[1], who had come from Portugal as chief

[1] A clerical error of both editions of the *Commentaries* gives this name here as Diogo *Fernandez* de Vasconcellos, but the texts, in the very next consecutive sentence, unconsciously correct themselves to Diogo *Mendez;* and the manuscript I have quoted at p. 196, substantiates the name of *Mendez*, which I have consequently here substituted for the erroneous reading. Diogo Mendez de Vasconcellos finds a place in the "Linhagens de Portugal" by Antonio de Lima Pereira.—Brit. Mus., MS. Lansd., 189, f. 304.

captain of four ships to go to Malaca, and Francisco Marrecos, Captain of the *Bretam*[1] (the *Briton*), one of the vessels belonging to the fleet of the Marshal[2], who had wintered in Moçambique.

Directly that Afonso Dalboquerque knew that it was Diogo Mendez, he ordered some persons to pay him a visit, and to tell him to shape his course for Anjadiva, and there they would have an opportunity of seeing each other. And on the seventeenth of the aforesaid month [of August] everyone came to an anchor off Anjadiva; and when all the fleet was riding at anchor, Diogo Mendez came with all his captains to visit Afonso Dalboquerque, and brought him news from Portugal, and of the fleet which had set sail that year, carrying as chief captain Gonçalo de Siqueira[3].

Afonso Dalboquerque told him he was very glad at the coming of Gonçalo de Siqueira just in the very nick of time, because he had deliberately come to the conclusion that he should return to the siege of Goa with all the forces he could possibly muster together, and attack the enemy, for he had been informed that he would easily be able to effect this object. And then he gave him an account of all that had taken place in Goa, and of the state in which its fortunes now were placed. And after that they had spent some time in conversing of these matters, Diogo Mendez took his leave, and returned to his ship, and on the morning of the following day came to Afonso Dalboquerque unaccompanied by anyone, and gave him a letter of the King D. Manuel, wherein he sent him his best remembrances, and commanded him to lose no time in setting Diogo Mendez quickly on his voyage, with the best dispatch of

[1] Francisco Marrecos, according to one account, was captain of the *S. Francisco*. See page 56, note.

[2] D. Fernando Coutinho.

[3] For the account of this expedition, see page 196, note.

his business, for such would be most serviceable to himself.

To this Afonso Dalboquerque replied that he would comply in every respect with the commands of His Highness, and besides the fact that he would thereby be only showing his obedience and respect to orders, yet out of kindly feeling also to him he would be happy to do all that lay in his power, and would give him pilots and everything else that was necessary. Diogo Mendez kissed the hands of Afonso Dalboquerque in token of gratitude for that willingness shown in his kindness towards him, and his offers of ready dispatch; and he said that if he would set him out on his voyage at once, he hoped, with the aid of God, to arrive again at Portugal before the ships of burden did; and he could assure him that, being actuated by a strong desire of reaching India at that time, and of doing all that he could to the service of the king, he had suffered great hardships in his voyage, because he had always endeavoured to carry as much sail as he could. He also brought a letter, he said, for Timoja, from the king, in which it was ordered that he should give him pilots for his voyage, and he should be glad if Afonso Dalboquerque would advise him what he ought to do in this respect. Afonso Dalboquerque replied that Timoja had no pilots whom he could give him; but nevertheless he would give him the letter, for he was sure to be very much pleased at the receipt of it; and he, Diogo, might return to his ship and make himself ready, for he had determined to sail away immediately in a straight course to Cananor; and these same instructions he sent round to all the captains, and that there would be a consultation when they arrived there.

On the night of that very day, which was the nineteenth of the said month [of August] all set sail and brought up in front of Onor. And when all had cast anchor, Afonso Dalboquerque sent a message to Timoja to come and converse with him; and there he found Bras Vieira, whom he had appointed as *Tanadar*[1] of Cintácora, with all the officers who had accompanied him from Goa, for he could not return to Goa on account of the Hidalcão's army; so he had made his way by land to Onor. As soon as Timoja received the message, he went at once to see Afonso Dalboquerque, and when he arrived, Diogo Mendez embraced him, and delivered the king's letter to him, with which he was very much gratified, and he declared that he was the subject of the King of Portugal, and would serve him in all things. And to Afonso Dalboquerque Timoja related that three days after he had passed out over the bar with his fleet, the Hidalcão had set out to return to his kingdom; and on the withdrawal of the hostile forces, all the lands of Goa and Saste, as far as Cintácora on the one side, and as far as Condal on the other side, had revolted, and the people had put to death all the Moorish *Tanadares* who had been appointed throughout the land to superintend the collection of the taxes.

Afonso Dalboquerque replied that he was much pleased at hearing this news, and begged and entreated him that he would maintain the natives in that hatred of the Moors until his return, which he hoped in God would be very soon, and that he would get ready a large quantity of supplies. And after spending the whole of that day in conversing about a variety of matters, he dismissed Timoja, and set sail with all his fleet, accompanied by Diogo Mendez with his ships; and on the twenty-sixth of the said month [of August] arrived at Cananor. But because it was late in the day when he arrived, he did not go on shore that day, but on the morning of the following day he disembarked, and on reaching the quay—where Rodrigo Rabelo, the captain of the fortress, with all his men, stood

[1] See page 125, note; and page 126.

waiting for him—they all made their way to the fortress, except Diogo Mendez and his captains, who had not disembarked. And when all were seated, discussing the present state of affairs, Rodrigo Rabelo told them he had received credible information from the Moorish merchants of Cananor to the effect that the Rumes had set out from Suez with an enormous fleet to reinforce Goa, and that in addition there had arrived there a ship, which had come from Diu, which had brought the same news.

As soon as Afonso Dalboquerque heard this information he declared to Rodrigo Rabelo, and to all the other captains who were there assembled, that Diogo Mendez, while he was at Anjadiva, had begged him to despatch him without delay, so that he might proceed on his voyage to Malacca; but now they ought to tell him whether they considered it well to allow Diogo Mendez to carry this voyage, which he had been ordered to perform, into effect, seeing that they were in possession of this positive news concerning the coming of the Rumes, or to detain him until the coming of Gonçalo de Siqueira. And after that Rodrigo Rabelo and all the captains had explained their own views in the matter, Garcia de Sousa said that by reason of what experience he had of the navigation of Malaca,—for he had been there with Diogo Lopez de Siqueira[1],—Diogo Mendez could not possibly lose his passage until the fifteenth day of September, but rather the weather would be better then for the navigation, and that Diogo Mendez ought to wait until that time, and then certain information could be acquired whether it would be more to the service of the king to take these ships with him to Goa, on account of the excitement which was then arising in India at the expected coming of the Rumes, or to suffer them to prosecute their voyage. The captains, after listening to Garcia de

[1] For notices concerning this expedition, and its result, see pp. 31 note, 45 note, and 73.

Sousa, concurred in his opinion, and Afonso Dalboquerque agreed with them.

CHAPTER XLIV.

How Afonso Dalboquerque reached Cananor, and had an audience of the King; and of the arrival of Duarte de Lemos and Francisco Pantoja: and what dealings Afonso Dalboquerque had with him.

A few days after this conversation, which the great Afonso Dalboquerque held with his captains, he sent word to the King of Cananor that he was very desirous of an interview with him, and that he begged him of his kindness that he would give him permission to do so; but whereas the king was already determined to come and visit him he sent word to Afonso Dalboquerque to remain where he was, for he would come and visit him on the beach outside the fortress.

And when this had been thus settled, the king commanded his men to furnish a tent on that spot, where the interview was to take place, all carpeted inside with very rich tapestries, and fitted with a sofa[1] covered over with a silken cloth, and having cushions of the same make, whereon he was to be seated. And as soon as everything had been prepared, the king came from the city to wait there for Afonso Dalboquerque, and brought with him Mamalle[2], and the *Alguazil* of Cananor, and the rulers of the land, and many other noble Moors, and his body-guard of five thousand *Naires*, all armed with swords and daggers. And on the arrival of the king, Afonso Dalboquerque set out from the fortress accompanied by all the captains very well appointed, and all the rest of the armed host, and made his way to the tent where the King of Cananor was sitting on the sofa; and behind the king there stood one page with a sword of gold, and another with a scimitar of gold; and

[1] *Catle*, for *Catre*, a couch or bed. [2] Mahomet Ali (?).

directly Afonso Dalboquerque arrived he went towards the king with great show of courtesy to kiss his hand, and the king, without rising from the sofa, received him with great attention and evident delight.

When the interchange of compliments was over, Afonso Dalboquerque ordered that the keys of the fortress should be presented to the king in a washhand basin, worked in the shape of bastions[1], and he took Rodrigo Rabelo, who was the captain of the fortress, by the hand, and told the king to give him those keys; and commanded the captains, who were there present, to perform whatever the king should order him to do, and ever to be obedient to his orders, because that fortress, with all the garrison that were within it, belonged to the King of Cananor by express wish of the King D. Manuel his Lord. And for this cause, he, Afonso, had always desired to be in his company and serve him, and that all his affairs should always be well assisted by him. And that he was so glad to see him, because now he considered the alliance ratified which he had made with the king his lord, and from that time henceforth he would serve him with all his fleets and men which there were in India.

The king returned him great thanks for those kind words, and declared that he truly desired that all Afonso Dalboquerque had said should be so performed, because of the great friendship which he had at heart with the King of Portugal his brother; and whenever it would help him in his affairs he, for his part, would place all his estate at his service every time it should be requested of him to do so. And as for the keys, he said, he would take them into his hands and deliver them to this captain of the king his brother; but on account of the waywardness of affairs lately he had not done so oftener, but, nevertheless he had not ceased to be a very good friend of the Portuguese; and that the captain

[1] *Bacio de agua ás mãos, lavrado de Bastiões.*

of the fortress, who was then present, knew very well how his officers carried on his business, and how he always strove to carry out everything that was asked of him. And from that time henceforward, he said, he would do the same with even greater willingness, because of the great pleasure which it gave him to see Afonso Dalboquerque, and because of the great renown which he had gained at the hands of the Moors. And as this was the first interview which had taken place between them, many things passed from one side to the other with great pleasure and show of much friendship.

On the conclusion of this interview the king took leave of Afonso Dalboquerque and went to the city, and made a present to the captains of three pieces of velvet and ten of camlet,[1] and Afonso Dalboquerque returned to the fortress. And after two other days were passed, Duarte de Lemos arrived, who had left the position of chief captain of the coast of Arabia, with four ships, and in his company came Francisco de Pantoja, who had gone to carry supplies to the fortress of Çocotorá, as I have already related.[2] And Duarte de Lemos brought with him the ship *Meri* which Francisco Pantoja had taken on his way. And when he arrived, Afonso Dalboquerque immediately caused a visit to be made to the ship by Antonio de Lis, who was his scrivener; and after two days had elapsed, Duarte de Lemos went on shore, and Afonso Dalboquerque went with all his captains to receive him on the beach, and they proceeded to the fortress.

After the usual preliminary courtesies had been given and received on both sides, Duarte de Lemos told Afonso Dalboquerque that his coming was occasioned by the great necessity he was in from not having vessels fit for carrying out the duties connected with his chief captainship, and those that he brought with him were merely kept afloat by

[1] *Chamalote*, a sort of stuff made of silk mixed with camel's hair.

[2] See chapter xxiv.

the constant use of their pumps, and he begged him earnestly of his goodness that he would grant him an early settlement of his affairs, and see to the ships which he would give him in order that they might be made ready. He related also to him how D. Afonso de Noronha, his nephew, had set out from Çocotorá, in the course of April last in the ship *Sancta Cruz*, and had taken with him Fernão Jacome, his cousin, and Diogo Correa, and the Reverend Father, Fr. Antonio, and many other persons; and after their departure he had never heard any more news of them; and since, up to the very present time he had never had any message from them, he concluded that they were lost.

Afonso Dalboquerque was very much cast down at this intelligence, for at that season—in consequence of the great difficulty in which the affairs of India were placed—it was a very great loss to him, and it caused him to renew the grief he had experienced at the death of D. Antonio de Noronha, his nephew. And after that he had recounted to Duarte de Lemos all that had passed in the city of Goa, and how he had quitted his position there, Afonso Dalboquerque said to him—in the presence of Rodrigo Rabelo, captain of the fortress, and the other captains who were there gathered together—that he begged him of his goodness not to put himself out about anything until the arrival of Gonçalo de Siqueira, for he had received information that this latter was on his way from Portugal as chief captain of a fleet,[1] in order that then he might come to a final determination with respect to the affairs of Goa, and the pacification of the Indian Empire, which was thoroughly excited with the news that had been spread concerning the intended coming of the Rumes.

Duarte de Lemos replied that the chief security of India lay in guarding the gates of the Straits of Méca, wherein there had been as yet no introduction of Portuguese power,

[1] See page 196, note.

although the King D. Manuel had given orders that it should be done. And the cause of this oversight, he declared, was that neither the Viceroy[1] nor he, Afonso Dalboquerque, had sent him the galleys which His Highness had, in his written instructions, commanded to be sent. And as for his remaining where he then was until the arrival of Goncalo de Siqueira, he would do so, he said, as it would be to the service of the king.

At the conclusion of this interview Duarte de Lemos begged Afonso Dalboquerque earnestly of his kindness to pardon Fernão Perez Dandrade and Simão Dandrade, his brother, and the other *fidalgos*, whom he had imprisoned, and order them to be released; and Afonso Dalboquerque, although they well deserved punishment for the deeds which they had done, yet out of desire to carry out the wishes of Duarte de Lemos, commanded that all these men should be set at liberty, and restored to them their captaincies, excepting only Jorge de Fogaça, for to this one, as ringleader of the insubordination which they had evinced towards him in the river [at Goa], he would not restore his office. After leaving them all in his house, Duarte de Lemos returned to his ship, and thither Afonso Dalboquerque ordered to be sent all that was required for his table, and for all those who messed with him, in the same style as he himself was served, and he always held him in high esteem and as one exercising the authority of chief captain of his fleet and men, with the understanding that he would help him in the Goa business.

When Duarte de Lemos had returned to his ship, Francisco Pantoja went to visit Afonso Dalboquerque, for he had not seen him since his arrival, and recounted to him the events of his voyage, and how he had on the way captured the ship *Meri* from the King of Cambaya, and on arriving at Çocotora, Duarte de Lemos had laid hands upon it and

[1] D. Francisco Dalmeida.

all it contained—which was very valuable—declaring that it belonged to him because it had been taken within the limits of his chief captaincy. And, he continued, although he had addressed many remonstrances to Duarte de Lemos with respect to this matter, to the end that he should neither meddle with the ship nor with the cargo she carried, because it appertained to his lordship [Afonso Dalboquerque] who was the Captain-general of the Indies, and under whose flag he, Francisco Pantoja, was sailing; nevertheless, Duarte de Lemos would not be convinced by these arguments, but he had taken the ship away from him, and her merchandise as well, and disposed of it all just as he pleased.

Then the Factor of Cananor, who happened to be present, said to Afonso Dalboquerque that the ship in question and her cargo with which she was loaded belonged to the king, and he hoped he, Afonso, would give orders for her to be delivered over to him, in order that he might arrange the proper distribution of it; because the officers whom Duarte de Lemos had placed in her would not attend to any of his orders. Afonso Dalboquerque replied that Duarte de Lemos had likewise deprived him, too, of the chief share of that ship which would have come to him by right, but that he should hold his tongue, in order to avoid coming to any rupture about it with him; and since Duarte de Lemos had already taken the best share of her, they must get on the best way they could, for there was an end of his interest in the matter, and he would have nothing to do with it. And whereas Duarte de Lemos was not in a very good humour when he arrived, because Afonso Dalboquerque had neither sent him the ships which he had applied for through Vasco da Silveira,[1] nor gone and effected an union with him according to the letter in which he had sent his word that he would do so, he grew very angry at

[1] See chapter xiv.

these words, which he was informed Afonso Dalboquerque had said to the Factor, although he pretended not to know anything about them.

CHAPTER XLV.

How an ambassador from the King of Cambaya arrived at Cananor to treat for peace with the great Afonso Dalboquerque; and the reply he received; and what passed upon this with Duarte de Lemos.

After the great Afonso Dalboquerque had concluded the matters with Duarte de Lemos which I have pointed out in the foregoing chapter, there arrived an ambassador from the King of Cambaya, who went immediately to the fortress, where Afonso Dalboquerque was expecting him, with all the captains and *Fidalgos*, except Duarte de Lemos, who was in his ship and remained there without coming to land. And when the ambassador delivered his messages to Afonso Dalboquerque from the King of Cambaya, he gave him also a letter of credentials, and told him that the king his lord was very desirous of having peace and alliance with the King of Portugal; and that many times already he had sent to say so; and that now he had been informed that his lordship, Afonso Dalboquerque, was making himself ready to pass through the Straits of Méca,[1] and if it were true, he begged him earnestly to arrange so that in his journey he should pass by his land, and he would come and converse with him in any of his ports that might be selected, and there they would settle the terms of their mutual alliances. And, he went on to declare, that the Portuguese captains had captured one of his ships, and he begged Afonso Dalboquerque of his kindness to order that it should be given back to him. And the King desired to

[1] See vol. i, p. 58, note 1.

acquaint him that he had under his protection a few Portuguese who had been wrecked in a ship which had run ashore on the coast in one of his ports, and he would immediately send them on to him.

And when he had made an end of his relation, the ambassador put into the hands of Afonso Dalboquerque a letter from the Christians who were there in captivity, wherein they showed how D. Afonso, his nephew, had sailed out from Çocotorá in the ship *Sancta Cruz*; and while they were making their passage across the gulf of India they took a very richly laden ship of Cambaya; and after having taken her, being as far advanced upon their course as the shallows of Padua,[1] so fierce a storm broke over them that they scudded along under bare poles, and at length reached a port of the Guzarates called Nabande,[2] and there they ran the ship upon some shallows, and it was wrecked. And, the letter continued, when the ship had struck,[3] D. Afonso and five or six men, thinking that they could save themselves by swimming because they were close to the shore, cast themselves into the sea on boards, and because the storm raged very violently, and the sea was running so boisterously, they were overwhelmed in such wise that all of them were drowned, while those who remained on board the ship—about fifty in number—waiting for the low tide, escaped with their lives. And when they had got to land, they were immediately taken prisoners in consequence of the representations of twenty Moors whom they had with them, men who had belonged to the ship which had been taken as a prize. This ship, in which Fernão Jacome was acting as captain, the same storm had driven to the country of the Hidalcão, and the Moors of the land had taken her and all

[1] See p. 218, note. [2] See vol. i, pp. 138, 139.

[3] *E que como a não tocára*, a misprint of the latest edition for *e que como a nāo tocára*, in which latter sense I have translated the passage; taken as printed in the text, it has no intelligible meaning. The quarto edition has *nao*.

the cargo she carried, putting Fernão Jacome and the Christians who were on board to death. And the letter went on to relate that when Gopicaiça, chief *Alguazil* of the King of Cambaya, was informed that the Portuguese were in captivity in those parts, and suffering ill-treatment at the hands of the people of the land, he had prevailed upon the king to send for them, and they were now dwelling in Champanel, and begged his lordship Afonso Dalboquerque to devise some plan whereby he might procure their release.

And in addition to this letter from the captives, the ambassador gave another to Afonso Dalboquerque from Gopicaiça, the text of which is here subjoined:—

LETTER FROM GOPICAIÇA, CHIEF ALGUAZIL OF THE KING OF CAMBAYA, TO THE GREAT AFONSO DALBOQUERQUE.

True friendship, such as I have in my soul, Afonso Dalboquerque! Chief Captain, may your good fortune ever be greater than that of Gopicaiça, who dwells in the city of Champanel; many times he recommends himself to you. After due commendations, I give you to know that one of your ships fought with a ship from Paverij, and took her, and carried her away to Cochim, and while they were on their voyage thither, a storm struck them, and your ship reached the shore in a harbour of Guzarate, where she was lost, and there came in her about sixty Portuguese more or less, and twenty persons belonging to the ship of Paverij. I was informed that the men of your ship had put to death certain persons of the ship of Paverij, which they had taken, and those who came with them told it to the people of the said harbour where your ship ran ashore, for which reason the people of the harbour desired to kill them; but I, when I heard this news, laid the matter before the king, and he issued a command that they should be immediately brought before him. Then Caixá, an *alcaide* of Nabande, sent them loaded with irons to the king, and I presented them to him, and he forthwith ordered their irons to be struck off, and commanded that they should be supplied with everything that was necessary for their maintenance; and your own people are writing letters to you whereby you will know that all this really took place. And know you, also, that in the kingdom of Guzarate a true friend of yours am I; and everything which shall be necessary between you and the king in respect of alliance and friendship that will I accomplish. It is necessary that you should send hither one of your people, a Christian and a trustworthy man, with an assurance that your ships shall not cruise about, ruining our maritime traffic and robbing in the seas; and then we will immediately give orders that your Christians be released, and your ships shall be able to go and to come unharmed to and from the ports of Cambaya, buying and selling in them, and all the ports of Cambaya shall be at your disposal; and this your man you can send in a ship to the port of Suret[1], and he might bring some good thing of service to the king, and I will present him to the king, and I will befriend him, and I will conclude matters with him in such wise that the ports of Cambaya be at your service, and you shall know that my friendship is true, and in this manner it will be augmented.

When Duarte de Lemos was informed by Jeronymo Teixeira and Francisco de Sá (who were the authors of all these dissensions which had arisen between him and Afonso Dalboquerque) that the ambassador of the King of Cambaya had arrived, and Afonso Dalboquerque had received his embassy—seeing that he already could hardly put up with his position, and by nature was of an obstinate and proud turn of mind—he came on shore and said to Afonso Dalboquerque, in the presence of Rodrigo Rabelo, that the boundary of his

[1] Surat, 21 deg. 10 min. N., 72 deg. 32 min. E.

captaincy extended as far as the coast of Cambaya, and for this reason the message from the King of Cambaya, and the letter of his *Alguazil*, belonged to him, and Afonso ought not to have received nor conversed with him without first of all having shown this courtesy to him.

When Afonso Dalboquerque perceived the direction which Duarte de Lemos was taking, he replied to him very dispassionately: "Sir, let us rescue the captives who are over there, and help me to punish thoroughly well the Moors of Goa who have disconcerted my plans[1], and let us for the present leave off thinking about these governments and commands; and it would be much better, since I have the power and the men of the king our lord, if you were to favour this business, and if we were to reply to the King of Cambaya in such terms, that we could get our Christians out of his power; and if you were not to be continually fostering dissensions with me."

Duarte de Lemos told him that, although he had the men and the power from the king, yet he himself was chief captain of the coast of Cambaya, and to him appertained these matters; for this reason, therefore, he ought not to have received the ambassador, but have remitted all the affair to him. And so he went on using very strong language and words full of pride, but Afonso Dalboquerque put up with everything, and at last replied: "Sir Duarte de Lemos, I well know the answer which these words of yours would have deserved, if I had not been captain-general of the Indies; but since it so happens that I am in that office, I wish I could prevail upon you to see things as I do, and I remember that which Tully said to Cæsar, when he begged him to pardon Marcellus, whom indeed he was unwilling to pardon, '*Vince te ipsum, qui vincis omnia!*'—Do thou, who conqueredst all things, overcome thyself also!"

And when Afonso Dalboquerque had spoken these words,

[1] *Que me quebráram a cabeça.*

he dismissed him, and Duarte de Lemos returned to his own ship, and remained in her ever afterwards with the title of Chief Captain, until Gonçalo de Siqueira arrived; and thither Jeronymo Teixeira and Francisco de Sá used to resort to set in motion their artful plans. And Afonso Dalboquerque wished to punish them for these disturbances, and for other matters which he had already for a long time experienced at their hands; but because he was desirous of utilising their assistance in the Goa enterprise, he left them alone unpunished until they should get to Portugal.

As soon as this difficulty had quieted down, Afonso Dalboquerque summoned before him the ambassador of the King of Cambaya, in order to set him on his way, and told him to relate to his king that he was busying himself in getting ready for a renewed attack upon Goa, and when he had brought that enterprise to a happy termination, he intended to pay him a visit, and settle the terms of an alliance, for the King of Portugal his lord would appreciate his alliance very highly; and whenever he might have need of his fleet and his soldiers, he would be prepared to serve him in all things; and then he begged him of his kindness to send back the captives who were there.

And having dispatched the ambassador, he treated him with every consideration in the king's name, and gave him this letter for Gopicaiça, by way of reply to the one he had received:—

Letter from the Great Afonso Dalboquerque to the Chief Alguazil of the King of Cambaya.

"Highly honoured and good cavalier, chief *Alguazil* of the King of Cambaya, I, Afonso Dalboquerque, captain-general and governor of the Indies and of the kingdom and lordship of Ormuz and of the kingdom and lordship of Goa, for the King D. Manuel our lord, send you my recommendations and my friendship. Your messenger reached me, and was well received and honoured; and he gave me your letters, whereby I was much pleased to know that the King of Cambaya, your lord, desires to have peace with the king our lord; and I saw as well in your letters that these men of the king our lord, and of this ship which was lost there, had been well received by the king, and succoured and well treated, and in like manner as this it is to be hoped that kings, who are such great lords and who possess such great authority and so much land and so many people as the King of Cambaya does, will do honour to the people of Portugal and of the king our lord. As soon as I received this news, which you wrote to me, I immediately commanded that due respect should be paid to the people who were taken in the ship *Meri*, which had been taken by one of my ships which I sent to Çocotorá; and the chief captain and governor of those parts, who is now here with me, brought her with him. Now let the king consider what he will command to be done to the ship and to the Moors, for I shall be pleased to serve him in everything; and so also will the chief captain of those parts do, who is here together with me. Your reply will find me along the coast as far as Goa, and I shall receive it from you as from one who is my friend. I should be very happy if the King of Cambaya would send me these Christians, for in all other matters I shall be happy to please him, and all shall be done according to his desire. Yea, would to God that an alliance were made between him and the king my lord, wherewith your king ought to be very greatly pleased, because he would have his harbours safe, and his ships and people could navigate the sea. And I trust that I shall arrive close to his territory, and I should be glad to receive a message from him to know with how good a will I forward his business, and how pleased I am to serve him in that which lies within my power. And should he make peace and alliance with the king my lord, I will assist him with all the king's power and people that I have in India. Look you well to your reply; and if you command anything of me, write to me about it. I shall be glad to have you for a friend. Written in Cananor, the sixteenth of September."

CHAPTER XLVI.

How the great Afonso Dalboquerque sent Simão Martinz, and Garcia de Sousa, to watch for the ships which sailed from Méca, that they might obtain certain intelligence of the coming of the Rumes; and of the request made to him by Diogo Mendez that he might be allowed to prosecute his voyage to Malaca.

After that the great Afonso Dalboquerque had set the ambassador of the King of Cambaya on his way, out of a desire to obtain exact information of the coming of the Rumes, and in order to make up his mind what line of action to undertake, and also in order that during these days which he had to occupy in getting his fleet ready to return against Goa, there should not pass any ships laden with pepper for the Straits, for it was now the sixteenth day of the month of September, which is the time in which the ships that set out from the Straits arrive off the coast of India—he made up his mind to send certain ships to cruise about in different parts, in order thereby to become more certainly informed of the coming of the enemy. And for this purpose he lost no time in forwarding Simão Martinz, in the position of chief captain of three vessels, and with him Francisco Marrecos, and Antonio de Matos, with orders to proceed to the *Monte de Deli*[1], and cruise about in that latitude until the close of the month of September; and if any

[1] This is the *Montedelli* of Fernão Vaz, 1546; apparently on the coast of India between *Mangalor* and *Cananor*. See page 169, note; also Lord Stanley's *Correa*, p. 145.

of them were to capture any ship from the Straits, he was to make his way at once with his prize to Cananor.

As soon as Simão Martinz had set forth with these vessels in his company, Afonso Dalboquerque sent for Garcia de Sousa, and told him that he had correct news of the departure of some ships from Méca, bound for Calicut, and that he was to get himself ready with three vessels, which would be put under his command, to cruise about from the shallows of Padua[1] to the Isles[2] of Panane; for in this crossing and latitude the navigation of the ships bound from the straits to Calicut was most likely to occur.

Thereupon Garcia de Sousa told him, that he was much astonished at his Lordship sending him on that undertaking, as he had already appointed Simão Martinz to be chief captain of three vessels which were to cruise in the same latitude, and that he would not go there, nor undertake such an enterprise as that one was, unless it was arranged that Simão Martinz should be placed under his orders and sail under his captaincy. But because this behaviour did not arise naturally from Garcia de Sousa, who was a very good man and a very brave cavalier, one who had served the King very well in all the undertakings in which he had been engaged, Afonso Dalboquerque replied that he begged him of his goodness to do this service for the King's sake and not to take any heed about rivalries, for Simão Martinz would cruise about in one place and he in another; and to be on his guard against the interested counsel of busybodies (for he was a man who could revolutionise India); and to bear in mind how bad he had always thought the underhand tales which João da Nova and the others who were of his party fostered between himself (Afonso Dalboquerque)

[1] The Padua Bank, or Munyal Par, Laccadive Islands, off the Indian Coast. 13 deg. N., 72 deg. 20 min. E.

[2] *Ilheo.* This word appears to signify a small uninhabited island, whereas *ilha* is an island in a more general sense, like the Latin *insula.*

and the Viceroy, and not to desire now to forfeit the honours he had already gained. And as Garcia de Sousa was desirous of serving the King, he performed all that Afonso Dalboquerque desired of him, and set sail with instructions how he was to act, wherein he was earnestly enjoined to cruise about and keep a sharp look-out, for information had reached him that in company with these ships of Calicut some of the Rumes also were coming.

Three or four days after Garcia de Sousa and Simão Martinz had departed on their voyages, Diogo Mendez came to land with his captains, and proceeded to the fortress where Afonso Dalboquerque was, and reminded him that he had promised, while at Anjadiva, to dispatch him, and give him pilots, and everything else that was necessary for him to make his journey to Malaca, as soon as they arrived at Cananor; and as there was now an opportunity, he begged him of his goodness to dispatch him, and give him permission to sail away. Afonso Dalboquerque replied, that after his arrival here he had been constantly occupied, not only with the King of Cananor, but also in dispatching certain captains whom he had sent to guard that coast; and on this account he had not had any time for communing with the captains: but now he would order them to be summoned to meet, and he would discuss with them this business of his, and would send him a reply in accordance with their opinions.

Diogo Mendez then said that matters which had been arranged by the King our lord ought not to be made to depend upon the opinions of any other persons, but all that remained to do was to comply with the commands of his Highness and his covenants and instructions; for, in so doing much was involved: and he desired of him, on the part of the King, to permit him to prosecute his voyage in accordance with the orders under which he had come out from Portugal. For, he said, in the covenant which the

King had made with him and the merchants, he had been all along exempted from the jurisdiction of Afonso Dalboquerque, as could be seen by an inspection of the papers which he there and then laid before him.

Afonso Dalboquerque replied, that he had no necessity to examine the papers, for the King would not exempt him, Diogo Mendez, from his own governor, if there should be any need in Indian affairs (as there was sure to be), and it was this very point that he desired to discuss with the captains. And when Diogo Mendez perceived that Afonso Dalboquerque was determined not to give him any answer until he had first of all communed with the captains, he no longer cared to insist upon being dispatched away, and returned to his ship.

CHAPTER XLVII.

How the great Afonso Dalboquerque deliberated with the captains, whether he should permit Diogo Mendez to go to Malaca or not; and what conclusions were arrived at, and what happened in regard to Diogo Mendez.

At the close of the interview which the great Afonso Dalboquerque held with Diogo Mendez, he gave an account to the captains (in the presence of Rodrigo Rabelo, captain of the fortress of Cananor) of all that had passed between himself and Diogo Mendez up to that time. And when they had discussed first one thing and then another, they agreed that in consideration of the events which had taken place with Diogo Lopez de Siqueira at Malaca,—who carried with him five ships and four hundred men,—and of the small strength of the fleet and men and other necessary things which Diogo Mendez brought with the intention of taking in hand so extensive an undertaking as that was which was contemplated, and also in consideration of the news of the coming of the Rumes, and that it was known for certain that there had set out from Suez fifty sail and ten thousand men,—in consideration, I say, of all these inconvenient events, they decided that Diogo Mendez ought not to go to Malaca, but that he ought to wait until the month of April, for by that time the affairs of India would have been reduced to their settled state.

And when this had been thus arranged, Afonso Dalboquerque ordered that Diogo Mendez and his captains should be called, and he told them that he had recounted the matter to Rodrigo Rabelo, captain of the fortress, and the rest of the captains, and all considered that it was very important for the service of the King that he should not be permitted to go, as well on account of the certain information respecting the coming of the Rumes, as also because the affairs of Malaca were so badly circumstanced that it required more force than that which he, Diogo Mendez, had brought from Portugal to pacify that country. For, he said, Diogo Lopez de Siqueira had returned from that region with his plans disconcerted[1] and sixty of his men killed or taken captives, and he himself had run great risk of losing all his fleet, if it had not been that he was advised in time of the treachery which had been arranged against him: and since the affairs of Malaca were in the state which he knew them to be, it was necessary that he should go to their assistance with sufficient forces, and undertake their settlement in such a manner that the powers there would be immediately compelled to make terms with him: and this it was, he declared, which would be more serviceable to the King than the mere loading of his ships well or badly. And, he continued, this reason alone was enough to make him think it unadvisable to carry out this journey at this time; not to mention another reason, of much greater weight, which was, the present state of Indian affairs, and the confirmed report of the coming of the

[1] *Com a cabeça quebrada; lit.*, with his head broken.

Rumes, and Goa risen up in successful rebellion, and the Kings of Cambaya and of Calicut, and the Rumes, all united in one body with that city against us, with many ships built all along the coast as far as Diu to co-operate with them against us. And therefore he would beg Diogo Mendez earnestly of his goodness to enter more heartily into this business at present in hand [the taking of Goa] than he had hitherto done, for thereby he would be really performing good service to the King our Lord, seeing that with India lost it would not be much use for the King to hold Malaca.

Diogo Mendez replied, that he was so desirous of performing the service of the King, that he would yield to no one in this respect; and, therefore, truly it appeared to him that nothing would so much conduce to this service as that he should be quickly dispatched to prosecute his voyage, in accordance with instructions which he had brought from Portugal. For, if he could not load his ships in Malaca, he could do so in Samatra or in Pegú, and therefore he would beg him of his kindness not to interpose difficulties in the way of his dispatch; because, although the affairs of Diogo Lopez had turned out as had been alleged, yet he hoped, with God's aid, that on arriving at Malaca he would be able to dispose his forces in such a manner that not only would he be able to get his ships laden, but he expected to rescue the Portuguese who were now in captivity there. And, he continued, seeing that the King in the letter which he had written to him, had especially dwelt upon the rapidity of his dispatch, Afonso Dalboquerque ought not to be so firmly set upon detaining him, because in India there were many ships and men, and the fleet of Gonçalo de Siqueira which was on the point of arriving, so that these ships of his might well be dispensed with.

The reply of Diogo Mendez somewhat exasperated Afonso Dalboquerque, and he said he knew very well the necessities that India was labouring under, and in respect of them he would undertake to give an account to the King his Lord, and therefore Diogo Mendez should not set his mind upon going to Malaca,—for it was now thus settled; but he would send him thither in April, and send in company with him four additional ships well supplied with arms and victuals, for in this wise he could go safely; whereas it was unsafe to attempt the voyage in four ships not much better than sides of bark, as his were, badly munitioned with everything that was necessary for the success of an undertaking like this. And this he said he would undertake to do for him, if the affairs of Malaca at that season were to improve their aspect.

Diogo Mendez answered that, as Afonso Dalboquerque had made up his mind not to suffer him to go to Malaca, he could certainly, in his capacity as Captain-General of the King of Portugal in the parts of India, exercise this power, but it would be against his will and that of his captains, for his only object in coming was for the service of the King; and, therefore, if Afonso Dalboquerque considered that by his remaining in India he would be doing better service, he would do so willingly. And so much cavilling about this could have been dispensed with; for he well knew that he would gain more by remaining where he was than by going to Malaca. And, on the conclusion of these debates, from that day forward, Diogo Mendez did not care to talk any more to Afonso Dalboquerque about his dispatch.

CHAPTER XLVIII.

How Lourenço Moreno, with two other vessels of the company of Gonçalo de Siqueira, reached Cananor: and how the great Afonso Dalboquerque ordered him to conclude peace with the Rulers of Baticalá; and of the letter which Afonso Dalboquerque wrote to Timoja through him.

While the great Afonso Dalboquerque was expecting every day the arrival of Gonçalo de Siqueira, with the intention of taking advantage of his coming to determine finally as to his return against Goa,—when it was now the eighth day of the month of September,—Lourenço Moreno, captain of the ship *Botafogo*,[1] arrived: he had come to be the factor of Cochim, and in company with him came João de Aveiro in the *Bastiaina*,[2] and Lourenço Lopez, nephew of Thomé Lopez, in another ship; and upon the same day that they arrived, Lourenço Moreno went immediately to land to see Afonso Dalboquerque, and after delivering to him a packet of letters which he carried from the King D. Manuel for him, he informed him that Gonçalo de Siqueira had set out from Portugal with seven ships, having very good soldiers on board; and as they were all sailing along in company at the *Cabo dos Correntes*,[3] so fierce a storm came upon them that it had scattered all the ships, and he himself indeed, with the two ships mentioned above, had run before the storm and reached Mozambique, and remained there for several days; but when they saw that Gonçalo de Siqueira

[1] *Botafogo*; a long stick with a match-rope fixed at the end to fire off cannon.—*Vieyra*. Perhaps here the best English equivalent is *Spit-fire*, from *Botar fogo*, rather than *Linstock*, which would be the more literal translation.

[2] *Bastiaina*; probably a feminine appellation signifying a woman of *Bastia*, the capital city of Corsica.

[3] Cape Corrientes, on the coast of Mozambique, 24 deg. 10 min. S., 35 deg. 12 min. E.

was still behind, and that the season was growing late, they had crossed over to India, but in consideration of the latitude wherein he had parted company with the others, and because the weather which had brought him to Moçambique was also favourable for their voyage, he was of opinion that it would not be long before they also arrived.

This news which Lourenço Moreno brought concerning the fleet which Diogo Lopez was conducting greatly pleased Afonso Dalboquerque, for he trusted to avail himself of its help in the Goa business. And after conversing respecting many occurrences in Portugal, Afonso Dalboquerque recounted to Lourenço Moreno the troubles which had happened at Goa; and how he was making himself ready to return against that city again. And when these conversations were over, he dismissed Lourenço Moreno to go and rest himself after the fatigues of the voyage; and with the object of not losing time in respect of what he had determined to do, he summoned Duarte de Lemos and all the rest of the captains, and informed them that when he was in Goa, Condanechatim[1] and Naodaquiçar[2], the rulers of Baticalá, had sent a messenger to him, saying that they desired to make peace with him, and to be in obedience to the King of Portugal, but up to that time he had sent no reply to them, because he had no ships which he could send to that place; yet now that Lourenço Moreno had arrived with two very large ships in his company, he could now go and settle this matter, and on the way take the ships laden with supplies for that fleet, which he was preparing for the renewal of the attack upon Goa; and therefore he would have them declare what they considered he ought to do.

Thereupon Duarte de Lemos, who was opposed to the policy of Afonso Dalboquerque, and other captains who were

[1] *Condane chatim—i.e., Condane*, the Merchant. See page 130, note 3.

[2] *Naoda quiçar—i.e., Nakhoda Quiçar;* Quiçar, the Captain. See vol. i, page 227, note 2.

also on this man's side, declared to him that with these ships of burthen he ought not to desire to do anything, except to send them on to Cochim to load, and depute Lourenço Moreno to superintend their loading, for he it was who was to be the Factor; and by no means to appoint him to the performance of so doubtful an enterprise as this was, for it might so fall out that the ships would not return in time to take in their cargoes. The other captains, however, said that since the ships would have to wait for Gonçalo de Siqueira, the lord governor could well send Lourenço Moreno to Baticalá to conclude the business, for there would be no time lost in so doing, and it would be very advantageous to have a treaty of peace with Baticalá, in order to be able to obtain from that place any supplies which might be required during the retaking of Goa.

In this latter opinion Afonso Dalboquerque coincided, so he sent for Lourenço Moreno, and sent him forth immediately to go and conclude this affair, and with him he sent also the two ships which had accompanied him from Portugal, and a Moor of Cananor, named Porcassem[1], as interpreter, to go on shore and negotiate the matter; and he gave to Lourenço Moreno written instructions of what he was to do, and certain memoranda of the conditions on which he was to conclude peace. Of these the principal articles were, that the rulers were to give him a house, built at their own expense, of stone and mortar, wherein the Factor of the King of Portugal could keep his merchandise secure; and they were also to pay in every year, by way of tribute, two thousand bags[2] of rice. And he ordered him that, having completed this business with the utmost alacrity, he was to proceed direct to Onor, and put himself in communication with Timoja, and deliver over to him Lourenço da Silva, and Fernão Vaz, whom he sent to that

[1] *Porcassem*, for *Abu'l-Casim*, softened into *Bul-Kāsim;* called *Pocaracem* in chapter li. [2] *Fardos*, each weighing forty-two pounds.

prince to occupy the position of captains of the Hindoos who were to wage war with those of Goa: and to these two captains he ordered that certain Portuguese should be delivered, to be carried with them, and saddles, bridles, and all other sorts of horse furniture, and he gave Lourenço Moreno this letter, which is given here below, to deliver to Timoja.

LETTER OF THE GREAT AFONSO DALBOQUERQUE TO TIMOJA.

"Honoured Timoja, chief alguazil and captain of the people of Goa, and lord of the lands of Cintácora, for the king our lord, I, Afonso Dalboquerque, captain-general and governor of the Indies, and of Persia, and of the kingdom and lordship of Ormuz, and of the kingdom and lordship of Goa, for the king our lord, send you my salutations. You know well my determination, which is to besiege Goa with your advice and help, and I trust in Our Lord that we shall quickly gain possession of that place. I should be glad if you would show favour towards this people who are engaged in war against those of Goa, and permit them to enjoy and consume the revenues of the land. To you I send Lourenço da Silva and Fernão Vaz, who are good cavaliers and captains, to command these people who are engaged in war: do you send them at once to the spot where the people are, and grant them some number whereof they may be captains, for they are good cavaliers; and I trust that they will perform their duty well. I shall soon be with you. I should be much pleased if you would send me, by one of your *fustas*, news of the way in which the land is going on, and what sort of army there is in Goa, and with what sort of soldiers you are able to help me. And as for those supplies which I desired you to get in readiness for me, do you order them to be delivered over to Lourenço Moreno, that he may bring them to me, for I am in need of them. Kiss for me the hands of the King of Garçopa, and tell him that I beg he will assist me with all his power, for I trust very quickly that we shall cast out the Moors from the land, and that I will help him with my person, my horses, arms, and people to gain much land from them, and I will make him a greater lord than all the others who are round about him; therefore I beg him of his goodness to favour this people who fight for us, and to have no fear of the Moors, for he shall soon see the Hidalcão destroyed, and all his estate ruined."

As soon as Lourenço Moreno had got his ships in readiness, he took leave of Afonso Dalboquerque, and proceeded to embark, and shaped his course straight for Baticalá.

CHAPTER XLIX.

How Simão Martinz captured a ship which came from Méca, richly laden, and brought her to Cananor; and of the news which two Jews, who were taken in her, related to the great Afonso Dalboquerque.

Five days after the departure of Lourenço Moreno for Baticalá, Simão Martinz arrived, whom Afonso Dalboquerque had sent to reconnoitre the ships which were coming out of the Straits (as I have already related), and with him he brought a ship which he had captured in the latitude of Monte de Deli,[1] bound from Méca to Calicut, laden with much merchandise. And, among other captives who were taken in her, there were two Castilian Jews, who declared for certain news that the Rumes were not able to set out that year, because the Grand Sultan had been engaged in serious dissensions with the governors of Damascus and Alepo, and there was no time for him to make ready.

Afonso Dalboquerque inquired of them whether many

[1] See page 217, note.

ships had sailed from the Straits for India, and they informed him that they knew nothing of any other ships than that one of theirs, and one other which was coming on behind, much more richly laden; for they had come by land to embark at the Island of Çuaquem[1], and there they had spoken with a Christian who was named Fernão Gomez,[2] and with a Moor who was in his company,—and Fernão Gomez had declared to them that his other companion was dead; and from that point he and the Moor set out on the road to Cairo; but after the lapse of a few days these returned again to Çuaquem; and because they could not agree respecting the road which they were to take, Fernão Gomez had separated himself from the Moor, and made his way to Judá,[3] and the Moor had turned into the interior parts of Çuaquem, and thenceforth nothing more was known of them.

Then Afonso Dalboquerque asked them what news they had of the Preste João,[4] and of his country. The Jews replied that they knew nothing more of him than that each year there went a caravan from Çuaquem, very near to the Red Sea, and it made its way to Mount Sinay, and thence straight to Jerusalem; and in company with this caravan there always went a captain with cavalry soldiers in his guard, on account of the Arabs;[5] and because the country is desert, and there are no means of obtaining supplies of food by the way, the members of the caravan took many camels loaded with victuals; and that into the Island of Çuaquem they imported many spices from India, and there

[1] *Cuaquem*, see *Suaque*, and the *Costa de suaque*, on the African side of the *Mar roxo*, in Berthelot's chart, vol. i, p. 80. It is now Suakin, in Lower Nubia, 19 deg. 6 min. N., 37 deg. 23 min. E.

[2] For the incidents relating to this journey of Fernão Gomez, see Vol. I, chapter liv.

[3] *Judá*. See vol. i, p. 234.

[4] Prester John, a favourite myth of Oriental voyagers and travellers from the days of Marco Polo and Sir John Mandeville.

[5] *Por amor dos alarves.*

they embarked in shallops[1] (which are a kind of barques *(barcos)*, like *caravelas*, which ply in the Straits), and were carried to Coçaer[2]—a port of the Red Sea—and from this port took them by land to Caná,[3] which is on the banks of the river Nile, about three days' journey from Coçaer, and there they took passage in barges *(barcas)*, and in a few days' time reached Cairo.

And these two Jews turned Christians: to the one of them was given the name of Francisco Dalboquerque, and to the other Alexandre Dataide. And Afonso Dalboquerque, as long as he lived, employed them as interpreters, especially Alexandre Dataide, because he knew many languages, and had a great aptitude for business. And after the death of Afonso Dalboquerque, they went to Portugal, in the time of the King D. Manuel, and from that country returned to India, and from India they proceeded to Cairo, where they again became Jews.

As soon as Afonso Dalboquerque had been informed of the other ship which was coming from Méca in company with this one, he ordered Simão Martinz to return again immediately, and cruise about in that latitude where he had fallen upon the ship which he had captured; and he ordered also Rodrigo Rabelo, captain of Cananor, to embark without loss of time in the ship which had been taken from the Rumes, and proceed to the sea-coast of the Monte de Deli, to look out for that ship, and in his company he sent Francisco Serrão and Alvaro Paçanha, in the two *caravelas*, and Afonso Pessoa in the *fusta;* and he commanded Rodrigo Rabelo that in case he should come up with Garcia

[1] *Geluas;* cf. *Jelua*, vol. i, p. 226, note.

[2] *Coçaer;* Coser, on the African side of the Red Sea, between *tera do egito*, and *aguada do dezafio*, in the chart of Fernão Vaz; now Kosseir, Kossayr, or Cosire, in Philoteras, Egypt, 26 deg. 5 min. N., 24 deg. 16 min. E.

[3] *Caná*, now Keneh, or Geneh, the ancient *Cænopolis*, 26 deg. 11 min. N., 32 deg. 45 min. E.; nearly opposite Dendera or Tentyris.

de Sousa and Simão Martinz, who were cruising about there, all three should take good counsel of what they ought to do, in order to get possession of this ship. And Rodrigo Rabelo set out, and seven or eight days afterwards he and Garcia de Sousa and Simão Martinz returned, and told Afonso Dalboquerque that along the whole of that coast there was no news of any ship which was coming from Méca, except only that one which Simão Martinz had already captured.

On the arrival of these captains at Cananor, because several days had elapsed, during which Diogo Mendez had not come to shore, Lourenço de Paiva recommended Afonso Dalboquerque to look well to the actions of Diogo Mendez, for Jeronymo Teixeira had told him that the captain was getting himself ready and had determined to make his way to Malaca. And Afonso Dalboquerque, who thought this was a true tale, immediately went that very night to the quay with the *fidalgos* and cavaliers who were with him, and ordered Rodrigo Rabelo to get into a boat manned with soldiers, and Pero Dalpoem, *Ouvidor* of India, in another, and to board the ship of Diogo Mendez, and summon him, on the part of Afonso Dalboquerque, and bring all his captains, masters, and pilots under arrest.

When Diogo Mendez reached the fortress, Afonso Dalboquerque said that he was very much surprised at his wishing to go away to Malaca with his ships and men, without permission, seeing that it had been decided in a council that the king's service required that he should remain in India, and not go to that port. Diogo Mendez replied that he had never imagined such a thing, but, on the contrary, he had told his captains and merchants who composed the expedition that he had to put himself at the obedience of Afonso Dalboquerque, and do all that should be required of him; and that he, Afonso, ought not to believe that a man in such a position as he was would attempt to do anything which would render it necessary to summon him in such a manner; and since he did not care to grant him permission to prosecute his voyage, he had better send and take possession of the fleet, and give an account of it to the king our lord; and that for the future he would be there under his orders, ready to do whatever was required of him. And at the end of all these arguments Afonso Dalboquerque required of him an oath of fealty, and commanded the *Ouvidor* to demand the same of the other captains in his company, that under the severest penalty they were not to depart from him without his permission; and every one promised, except Pero Coresma, who declared that Diogo Mendez was his chief captain, and he would not take an oath of fealty to anyone else but to him.

Therefore Afonso Dalboquerque ordered Pero Coresma to be imprisoned in the castle, and there he remained under arrest until the following day, when some of the captains begged his liberation, and Afonso Dalboquerque gave orders for his release and the taking of his oath of fealty like the others. And he ordered Pero Dalpoem to notify to the pilots and masters that under penalty of death and confiscation of their property, they should not stir from their quarters without his express orders. And when an official statement of all this affair had been drawn up, they returned to their ships.

And after the lapse of two or three days, Afonso Dalboquerque discovered that this which had been reported to him was untrue, and that Jeronymo Teixeira had concocted it because Diogo Mendez had fallen into disagreement with him. So when he knew this, he sent for Diogo Mendez, and earnestly begged his pardon for that which he had done to him, and declared that the fault really lay in his not informing him of the quarrelling of Jeronymo Teixeira; and he would promise him that when the Goa business was completed, he would set him out rightly on his voyage, and give him pilots and everything that he required for his passage. Yet with all these compliments, Afonso Dalboquerque did not cancel the oath of fealty which Diogo Mendez had taken, nor the penalty which had been imposed upon the pilots and masters.

CHAPTER L.

How Gonçalo de Sequeira reached Cananor; of the council held by the great Afonso Dalboquerque with the captains, respecting the return to Goa; and of the news he had concerning the death of the King of Cochim, and what he did thereupon.

When all these affairs which I have related had passed away, there arrived Gonçalo de Sequeira at Cananor, on the sixteenth day of the month of September, of the year 'ten:—he had set out from the kingdom of Portugal for India as chief captain of seven ships—and at his arrival, Afonso Dalboquerque was greatly pleased, and returned many thanks to Our Lord, because at the very juncture when he had determined to make another attack upon Goa, no less than fourteen ships had arrived in India, wherein were about one thousand five hundred Portuguese, with whom he could undertake anything, however great it might be. And of these fourteen ships the chief captains were Gonçalo de Sequeira, Diogo Mendez de Vasconcelos (as has already been related), and João Serrão, with three vessels which the King D. Manuel sent to examine and sound the entrance into the Straits of the Red Sea.

The same day that Gonçalo de Sequeira arrived he went at once to land to converse with Afonso Dalboquerque, who came down with all his captains and *fidalgos*, who were there, to meet him on the quay, and escorted him to the fortress. And after everyone had talked about the news from Portugal, Gonçalo de Sequeira gave to Afonso Dalboquerque the letters which he brought from the King D. Manuel for him, and one as well for Duarte de Lemos, which was immediately forwarded to him at the ship wherein he was; in which letter the King desired him to deliver over to Afonso Dalboquerque all his fleet and men, and to return to Portugal, and Afonso Dalboquerque, to give him a passage home in a ship for himself and his belongings.

At the receipt of this letter, Duarte de Lemos became more reasonably minded, and all his expectations were dispelled which Jeronymo Teixeira and Francisco de Sá had aroused in him, that he was to remain forsooth, after having fulfilled his term of duty, as Governor of India, seeing that he had succeeded to the chief captainship of the coast of Arabia upon the death of Jorge Daguiar his uncle, who would have became Governor of India if he had lived: but this was not so, for, as to the succession to the Government of India, D. Afonso de Noronha had the reversion of it, if he lived. After the day in which Gonçalo de Sequeira arrived had passed, whereas Afonso Dalboquerque thought of nothing else but the return to the attack of Goa, and was desirous of arriving at a conclusion of the business before any more time should be spent, on the following day he desired Gonçalo de Sequeira, Duarte de Lemos, and Diogo Mendez, and the rest of the captains who were there to meet; and when all were assembled he related to them everything that had taken place in Goa, and in the river during the time that he was there; and how, after he had sailed out of the river and arrived at Onor, Timoja had informed him that the Hidalcão had immediately departed with all his army, because all the lords of the kingdom of Decan had risen up in rebellion against him; and in consequence of the war in which the Hidalcão was engaged with these lords, he was prevented from coming to the assistance of Goa, and thus by this conjunction of events he, Afonso, could take it and make himself lord of it; therefore he begged that, as the Goa business was in this state, they would advise him what he should do.

Then the captains held their council concerning these propositions which Afonso Dalboquerque presented, and there were numerous discussions and many differences of opinion; for Gonçalo de Sequeira and Duarte de Lemos, and the captains who were about to return to Portugal, declared that it was more to the service of the King of Portugal that he should go and arrange the terms of peace with the King of Cambaya,—who was very desirous of it, and begged it with great show of reason,—than to return to Goa; that this enterprise was a very hazardous affair and one of great peril, and would result in no profit for the King of Portugal. But they gave these opinions in favour of avoiding the affair, because they were more anxious to load their ships and return to Portugal than to gain experience in their own persons of the hardships which their comrades had already undergone in the river of Goa.

Diogo Mendez and his captains, with all the *fidalgos*, and the rest of the Indian military staff, however, were of opinion that they should fall upon Goa again, because the Hidalcão was so far off that he could not relieve the place with sufficient rapidity; and even if he were to come, it would only be by the time our people had put an end to the affair; and if the matter did not succeed, as all hoped to God that it would, there would yet be time enough for them to proceed to Cambaya to interview the King and arrange terms of peace with him.

After it had been decided, by a majority of votes, that a renewed attack upon Goa should be made, Afonso Dalboquerque said to Duarte de Lemos and to Gonçalo de Sequeira that he begged them of their goodness to be pleased to go with him on his side in that enterprise, because, since Goa could not be relieved by the Hidalcão on account of the war in which he was engaged, very little time would be required by them for the re-capture, and thereby they would lose no opportunity for making their voyages. But they excused themselves, and gave their reasons, why they could not be with him in that business. But I well believe that when they saw the city was taken, they would have given much to have been found taking a part in the business, that they should not have returned to Portugal with such a bad name. Afonso Dalboquerque was not very well pleased with them; nevertheless, he commanded that his fleet should be made ready and everything which was required, with the intention of taking in hand the performance of this affair with the people whom he had now under his command, and to leave the rest to God, to direct as should be best for his own service.

And while Afonso Dalboquerque was occupied in this hasty way, there arrived a *Catur*[1] from Cochim with a letter from the King for him, wherein it was related that the King, the uncle of the present one, was dead, and that certain Moors, his enemies, and others, who styled themselves friends, had risen up in rebellion against him, and had gone over to one of his cousins, who desired to become king, all in consequence of the advice given by the King of Calicut, to put him in possession of the land; therefore he begged him of his goodness, if his affairs did not occupy him very much, that he would pay him a visit, because he had no one with whom he could take counsel, nor from whom he could derive assistance except him; because his cousin, who desired to become king, was at Vaipim, and all the lords who had come to see him had told him to go and put himself into his uncle's grave, and if he did not care to do so, his cousin would have to kill him; and the most powerful opponent he had was the King of Calicut; yet, with all these oppressions, he would never separate himself from the service of the King of Portugal, for he would always act in accordance with the policy of his uncle with regard to the

[1] See page 55, note 1.

troubles which the Portuguese experienced in India since it was discovered.

Afonso Dalboquerque related the contents of this letter to the captains, and all were of opinion that he ought to go and see to this matter without the least delay, before the King of Calicut took any more steps in it. Therefore, Afonso Dalboquerque determined to set out immediately, and commanded Gonçalo de Sequeira, with the ships of his own company, and the captains who had remained out of the fleet of the Marshal, to make themselves ready in order to set sail the next day in the morning with him to Cochim, and when there he would dispatch them to Portugal. And, forgetting the dissensions which he had with Duarte de Lemos, he left him in Cananor to act in his name with all the power and authority of Governor which belonged to himself in person.

CHAPTER LI.

How the great Afonso Dalboquerque set out for Cochim, and arranged the differences between the King and his cousin: and what passed with the captains while stationed at Cochim.

On the following day, which was the twenty-second day of the month of September, in the evening, the great Afonso Dalboquerque set out for Cochim, and took with him Gonçalo de Sequeira with all his ships, and those which remained of the Marshal's fleet to take in their lading and to set forth for Portugal, and the two galleys, and the ship lately taken from the Rumes, and disposed all the other fleet in a line along the coast to prevent any ship from entering into Goa, whether it should come from the Straits or from any other part, with supplies.

And he reached Cochim on the twenty-sixth of the said month, and immediately went on shore to visit the King, who was already in expectation of his arrival, with all the *Caimais*[1] of his court, and with many other persons, and so they all went to the fortress, and there the captain had prepared for him a house well furnished, where they sat down. And after the King had given him great thanks for that kindness and honour which he had shown him in coming at his request, he proceeded to relate all his troubles, and that the Brahmans told him, now that his uncle was dead, he would be obliged to place himself in the grave, for this was their ancient custom.

Afonso Dalboquerque then said to him, that as the King D. Manuel, his Lord, had caused him to be received as King upon oath of fealty during the lifetime of his uncle, therefore he should be king, and he need not trouble himself with his customs nor with that which his Brahmans had told him, for this should be so, and that he should be confirmed in his kingdom; for he and all the Portuguese who were there, and many others whom the King his Lord would send from Portugal, would spend their lives in his service, and in sustaining him in his estate; and therefore let him send word to his cousin—if he were still in Vaipim—to depart forthwith and to quit the island, because, if he were unwilling to do so, he was determined to fall upon him and destroy him and all those who should be found in his company.

And because Afonso Dalboquerque, as long as he was Governor of India, always made use of artifices with the kings and lords thereof, in order to instil terror into them and draw them over to his alliance and to preserve the authority of the state of the King D. Manuel, when he uttered these words he rose up out of his chair wherein he was seated, and drew out his sword, and declared to the King of Cochim that he ought not to be afraid of all the power of the King of Calicut, for he was his *Naire*,[2] and for him he

[1] See vol. i, page 3, note. [2] See vol. i, page 4, note.

would lay down his life, whenever it should be required of him; and that neither the King of Calicut nor his *pagodes*[1] would avail anything with his cousin against him; and as this was the true state of the case he would beg him of his goodness to remain for ever a true and loyal ally of the King D. Manuel, his lord, and to be grateful to him for the love and goodwill which he had evinced towards him by ordering his elevation to the throne, and to act in such a manner as not to lose this, because there was nothing which could destroy him except his ingratitude towards the King, his lord, in return for the kindness which had been shewn to him; and he would promise him that, on the conclusion of the business at Goa, he would afford him an opportunity of wreaking his vengeance upon the King of Calicut.

The King of Cochim replied, that he was the subject of the King of Portugal, and therefore he had nothing to say in the way of answer to these words of Afonso Dalboquerque, except that he would always perform whatever was required of him on the King's part. On the conclusion of this interview, the King of Cochim returned to his palace, and sent word to his cousin who was in Vaipim, on the part of Afonso Dalboquerque, to quit the island and get him gone without delay; for if he did not go, Afonso Dalboquerque would come up against him with all his army and destroy him. The King's cousin, as soon as he heard that Afonso Dalboquerque had arrived with the object of following him up and destroying him, quitted the island and desisted from the dissensions which he had kept up with the King of Cochim, and departed.

Now that these disturbances had been settled, Afonso Dalboquerque summoned to meet him Gonçalo de Sequeira, and all the captains and officers of the King who were in Cochim, and declared to them, that in all former councils which he had held concerning the business at Goa, he had

[1] *Pagodes*, Pagodas; here used figuratively for Brahmans or Priests.

not cared to declare his opinion, in order that they should not imagine that he desired to undertake that enterprise rashly and more out of vengeance for what had already taken place than because it was an important service for the King, his lord; but now he would assure them that if they did not succeed in taking Goa, and if the league which had been entered into between the Hidalcão and the Kings of Cambaya and Calicut flourished any longer, out of the expectation they had of obtaining the assistance of the Grand Sultan, it would be a very doubtful point whether the King of Portugal could retain India; and the principal motive which impelled him to take in hand this deed was the presence at this moment in India of so noble an army, so many captains, so many ships from Portugal, which encouraged him to do it; therefore he begged them of their goodness, before the officers of the King there present, that since at Cananor they had been of opinion, for reasons already given, that he should return again to attack Goa, to go willingly with him in the execution of his plans, for if they all went just as they then were, they would not lose the opportunity of making their voyage.

Then Gonçalo de Sequeira and the other captains began to declare that it would not be to the service of the King for the ships of burthen to proceed to Goa, and that it would also be reasonable to allow the men some opportunity of performing their engagements, since they had come to India with this object in view; and thus they went on adducing other arguments to excuse themselves from going with him. Thereupon, Afonso Dalboquerque said to them, that since they were searching out for inconveniences, to the end that they should not render the King any service in this enterprise, they might remain behind, for he had made up his mind not to take any against their will, but they must give an account of their conduct in Portugal to the King their Lord; as for himself, his mind was quite made up to go up against Goa with the army he had; and he trusted in the Passion of Our Lord, in whom he had placed all his reliance, that before they could sail away to Portugal, they would hear the news of how he was taking his rest at ease within the city of Goa, and an unfortunate creature must that Portuguese cavalier reckon himself, were such a good stroke of fortune to be gained, who should not be found taking part in this deed; and he intended to embark on the following morning, and let those follow him who chose to do so; but many allowed themselves to remain behind and would go no further.

So Afonso Dalboquerque set sail, leaving the cargo which was to proceed this year to this kingdom [of Portugal] already in proper order. And on arriving at Cananor he found Lourenço Moreno, who had arrived but two days before him, with the ships laden with supplies; and Lourenço Moreno related to him that on reaching Baticalá he had immediately sent Pocaracem[1] to land to converse with the rulers respecting the treaty which was to be concluded between them, but he found them quite changed in their opinions, and they had declared that they would do nothing without first of all finding whether the King of Narsinga, their lord, approved of it; and seeing that they were unwilling to come to any conclusion, he had laden his ships and sailed away and touched at Onor and given the letter to Timoja, who was busy getting himself ready, as well as the King of Garçopa, with all his people, with the intention of co-operating with him in the Goa expedition, and therefore he could proceed as soon as he pleased.

As soon as Lourenço Moreno had given to Afonso Dalboquerque an account of what had passed, he was sent off immediately with his ships to Cochim, to hasten the departure of the captains, and to see to the shipping of three

[1] The name apparently of a Mahometan, employed as an interpreter by the Portuguese, called *Porcassem* in chapter xlviii.

elephants, which he had left there, to be conveyed to the King D. Manuel in the ships which Afonso Dalboquerque had set aside for this purpose. And when Lourenço Moreno had set out, Duarte de Lemos besought Afonso Dalboquerque to provide him a transport for himself and his brother, for the purpose of proceeding to Portugal, since the King would have it so for his service. And Afonso Dalboquerque, forgetting all the ill-feeling which had now passed away, gave him all he required, and commanded every thing that was properly due to be paid to him and to his servants, and invested him with the chief captainship of seven ships, and supreme command over that fleet which he was to exercise after passing clear of the coast of India, and so dismissed him to make his way to Cochim. And when he arrived there, he fell into great dissensions with the officers of the factory, and did other things, which I pass over in silence, to have no murmurers who may say that I was not impartial. This Duarte de Lemos was a noble *fidalgo*, and was the largest man in Portugal, and very conceited, and had his front teeth inordinately long.

END OF THE SECOND PART.

THE COMMENTARIES OF THE GREAT AFONSO DALBOQUERQUE

BRIT. MUS., SLOANE MS. 197, FOLIO 18.
P. Barretto de Resende's Portrait of
DOM VASCO DA GAMA.

THE COMMENTARIES OF THE GREAT AFONSO DALBOQUERQUE,

SECOND VICEROY OF INDIA.

TRANSLATED FROM THE

PORTUGUESE EDITION OF 1774,

WITH NOTES AND AN INTRODUCTION,

BY

WALTER DE GRAY BIRCH, F.R.S.L.

SENIOR ASSISTANT OF THE DEPARTMENT OF MANUSCRIPTS IN THE BRITISH MUSEUM; MONORARY LIBRARIAN OF THE ROYAL SOCIETY OF LITERATURE; MONORARY SECRETARY OF THE BRITISH ARCHAELOGICAL ASSOCIATION, ETC.

VOL. III

..."Se as accoes d'Albuquerque fossem communs, e ordinarias; se as suas emprezas nao passassem as metas do possivel, nem a posteridade o collocaria na ordem dos Heroes, nem o seu nome chegaria a merecer o reverente pasmo dos seculos futuros."- Elogio por Fr. Xav. de Oliveira..

GYAN

Published by

GYAN

Gyan Publishing House
5, Ansari Road
Daryaganj, New Delhi-110002
Phone: 011-47034999, 9811692060
E-mail: books@gyanbooks.com

Distribution Network
gyanbooks.com
India, USA, Canada, UK, Australia, France

ISBN : 978-81-212-3261-6 (Set)
ISBN : 978-81-212-4807-5 (PB)
First Published, 1880

2nd Impression 2020

Printed at: Gyan Press, Delhi.

The Commentaries of the Great Afonso Dalboquerque Vol. III
Author: Walter De Gray Birch

THE

COMMENTARIES

OF THE GREAT

AFONSO DALBOQUERQUE,

SECOND VICEROY OF INDIA.

TRANSLATED FROM THE

PORTUGUESE EDITION OF 1774,

With Notes and an Introduction,

BY

WALTER DE GRAY BIRCH, F.R.S.L.,

SENIOR ASSISTANT OF THE DEPARTMENT OF MANUSCRIPTS IN THE BRITISH MUSEUM; HONORARY LIBRARIAN OF THE ROYAL SOCIETY OF LITERATURE; HONORARY SECRETARY OF THE BRITISH ARCHÆOLOGICAL ASSOCIATION, ETC.

VOL. III.

"Se as acções d'Albuquerque fossem communs, e ordinarias; se as suas emprezas não passassem as metas do possivel, nem a posteridade o collocaria na ordem dos Héroes, nem o seu nome chegaria a merecer o reverente pasmo dos seculos futuros."—Elogio *por Fr. Xav. de Oliveira.*

LONDON:

PRINTED FOR THE HAKLUYT SOCIETY.

M.DCCC.LXXX.

COUNCIL

OF

THE HAKLUYT SOCIETY.

LIST OF CONTENTS.

CONTENTS.

INTRODUCTION.

. . . . . o grande Cavalleiro,
Que ao vento vélas deu na occidua parte,
E lá, onde infante o Sol dá luz primeiro,
Fixou das Quinas santas o Estendarte.
E com afronta do infernal guerreiro,
(Mercê do Ceo) ganhou por força, e arte
O aureo Reino, e trocou com pio exemplo
A profana mesquita em sacro templo.
* * * *
O tempo chega, Affonso, em que a santa
Sião terá por vós a liberdade,
A Monarquia, que hoje o Ceo levanta,
Devoto consagrando a eternidade.
O, bem nascida generosa planta,
Que em flor fructo ha de dar á Christandade,
E materia a mil cysnes, que, cantando
De vós, se hirão comvosco eternizando.

De Christo a injusta morte vingou Tito
Na de Jerusalem total ruina:
E a vós, a quem Deos deu hum peito invitto,
Ser vingador de sua Fé destina.
Extinguir do Agareno o falso rito
He de vosso valor a empreza dina:
Tomai pois o bastão de empreza grande
Para o tempo que o Ceo marchar vos mande.

MALACA CONQUISTADA
pelo grande Affonso De Albuquerque.
Poema de Francesco de Sa' de Menezes.

THE Third Part of the COMMENTARIES OF THE GREAT AFONSO DALBOQUERQUE, a translation of which is given in this volume, maintains the interest in the Portuguese hero which was awakened by the previous

b

volumes. To the conquest of Ormuz and Goa, already published, we have here in continuation the second conquest of Goa, and the extension of the Portuguese empire to the Malay peninsula.

The volume opens with the return of Afonso Dalboquerque to Cananor, from which port he set sail with twenty ships, and put into Onor for supplies and water. Here he learned the imposing strength of the Hidalcão (about eight thousand Turks, Rumes, and Moors against seventeen hundred Portuguese), from Timoja and the friendly king of Garçopa, and then proceeded by way of Anjadiva to the river of Goa. A council was hereupon held, which resulted in an unanimous determination to attack the city at once, without relying upon the aid promised by the native chiefs. The forces were divided, but not without much opposition on the part of the captains, into three companies: one, commanded by Manuel da Cunha and Manuel de Lacerda, to attack the stockades near the citadel; another, under the leadership of Diogo Mendez de Vasconcelos, to storm the palisades near the sea; and a third, under the command of the Viceroy himself, to take the stockades in flank.

On the following morning, the 25th of November, 1510, with an effigy of their national patron, St. James the greater, carried in the van, a general assault was carried out, the stockades entered, and all who resisted the onward progress of the besiegers put to the sword; while of those who fled away in their panic over the numerous fords and passes an immense number were drowned. In this brilliant engagement seven of the Portuguese officers were killed, among whom the author of the *Commentaries* especially signalises D. Jeronymo de Lima, André de Afonseca, Antonio Graces, and Alvaro Gomez, while on the side of the enemy not less than two thousand, about one-fourth of the whole native strength, were estimated to have perished.

In the sack which ensued, besides the miscellaneous plunder, none of which Afonso Dalboquerque cared to appropriate, a considerable quantity of artillery, munitions, and horses were taken, and in accordance with the bloodthirsty laws which appear to have regulated such occasions, not only in India, but in other countries claiming to be far more civilised at the period, no quarter was given; none of the hated sect of Mahomet were spared; men, women, and children were mercilessly put to death; and as a punishment for the treachery of which the Moors had been guilty when Afonso Dalboquerque took the city for the first time, for four days incessantly the Portuguese and Hindoos poured out the blood of the Moors who were found therein; and it was ascertained that of men, women, and children the number killed exceeded six thousand.[1] On this occasion the Viceroy is stated to have perpetrated a very horrible act of vengeance against the enemy; a mosque was filled with Moors taken captive by the Hindoos and then set on fire; and among the people who thus perished was a deserter who had gone over to the Hidalcão and turned Mahometan when Goa was taken for the first time.

[1] Page 16.

No time was lost by Afonso Dalboquerque in fortifying the city, every one, from the highest to the lowest, had to take his share of duty, and the walls, towers, and ditches were completed in a marvellously short space of time, " where it now stands", for the plan of which the reader is referred to vol. ii, p. 88.[1] During the excavations a bronze crucifix was dug up in the course of demolishing some old foundations. Curiously enough, Correa[2] mentions a similar discovery in November 1512 in these terms: "Tambem o Gouernador n'estas naos mandou a ElRey huma caixinha de prata, e dentro metido hum corpo de crucificio, que foy achado per hum homem cauando pera fazer hum poço, e o achou tendo feito coua de tres braças, que se achou no inuerno, que foy d'esta maneyra: que cauando hum pobre homem pera fazer hum poço, tendo altura de tres braças, achou hum corpo de crucificio de grandura menos de hum palmo, aberto por detrás, muyto gastado, e o rostro bom e barbas, e o braço direito polo cotouello sómente, e o esquerdo inteiro e o corpo e pernas e pés enteiros, e feito de hum metal que ouriues e lapidairos nunqua souberão conhecer, nem com o buril o poderão descobrir, que nada entrava n'elle: o que fez grande espanto no Gouernador e todos os fidalgos, que caso podia ser em tal lugar terra de mouros de tantos annos,

[1] One of the most exhaustive works on Portuguese Goa is that entitled, " An Historical and Archæological Sketch of the City of Goa, preceded by a short Statistical Account of the Territory of Goa, written by authorisation of the Government, by José Nicolau da Fonseca, President of the 'Sociedade dos Amigos das Letras'." Bombay, 1878, 8vo.

[2] *Lendas da India*, 1, ii, p. 328.

sem auer memoria que nunqua n'ella ouvesse christãos." "The governor, Afonso Dalboquerque, also sent to the king in these ships a small casket of silver, and within it the figure of our Saviour from a crucifix, which had been found by a poor man who was digging the foundation for a well. This man found it when he had dug down as deep as three fathoms, and it was in the winter under the following circumstances. There was a poor man digging the foundation for a well, and at the depth of three fathoms he found the figure from a crucifix of the height of less than a palm, hollow behind, very worn, but the countenance and beard well preserved; the right arm broken off at the elbow, the left whole, the body, legs, and feet uninjured, made of a metal unknown to the goldsmiths and lapidaries, for it could not be scratched with the point of a graver. This excited great wonder in the governor and *Fidalgoes* how it could have chanced to get into such a place, for so many years the country of Moors, in which there was no remembrance of there ever having been any Christian inhabitants."

In return for this victory Afonso Dalboquerque made several presents to the convent of Palmela, the head of the military order of Santiago, and to the church of the same saint in Gallicia a lamp, and money to be invested for the supply of oil for the lamp. A similar gift of a lamp and provision for its oil was made by the viceroy on a later occasion, when he narrowly escaped death from a cannon ball.

The news of the fall of Goa effected a rapid change in the attitude of the Indian princes towards the Portuguese. The king of Cambaya set free D. Afonso de Noronha, nephew of Afonso Dalboquerque, and offered the site for a fortress at Diu, and the preparation of a Turkish fleet to operate against the Portuguese was countermanded by the Grand Sultan of Cairo. The letter sent by Dalboquerque to the Hidalcão announcing the capture of Goa, and offering the monopoly of the important trade in horses, also plainly shows the rapid exaltation of Portuguese *prestige* in consequence of this event. Not long after this, Meliqueaye, (perhaps the Portuguese equivalent of Melek Yahya,) was sent by the Hidalcão against the island, but he and his numerous army were routed without much difficulty, and the erection of the fortress, the colonisation of the newly acquired territory by Hindoo families (a race to whom Afonso Dalboquerque, throughout his career, always manifested great kindness), and the consolidation of the government of the province, for province indeed it was, proceeded rapidly and without interruption.

The advent of the royal Hindoo Merlao (or Milrrhau, as he is called in the latter part of this volume) enabled Afonso Dalboquerque to gratify the native Hindoos and Nequibares, and at the same time to ingratiate himself with them, by conferring upon him the farmer-generalship of the newly acquired territory for about thirty thousand pounds—a considerable sum in those days, and a welcome addition to the revenues of Portugal. But these matters did not cause the Viceroy to forget the other parts of his Indian jurisdiction, and in accordance with Royal instructions he dispatched

Diogo Fernandez de Béja with a fleet of three ships to dismantle the fortress of Socotra.[1]

The fall of the important city of Goa brought the Çamorin of Calicut to the feet of Afonso Dalboquerque for the time, and his offers of peace resulted in the mission of Simão Rangel, but on the arrival of that ambassador at the Çamorim's court that prince had somewhat recovered from his alarm, and his artifices succeeded in protracting negotiations, which were not to be crowned with success for a long time yet to come,

[1] The island was taken possession of by the Portuguese in 1507, but passed from the possession of Portugal to that of the Sultan of Keshin, a small territory on the opposite Arabian coast. This island is off the gulf of Aden, situated about 150 miles N.E. from Cape Guardafum, and extends about seventy or eighty miles from west to east, with an average width of fifteen or twenty miles. It contains 1,300 square miles, consisting chiefly of a table land, which is between 700 or 800 feet above the level of the sea. North and south of the table land are two plains. The northern plain is not so low as the southern, nor so level, the surface being intersected by flat valleys in many places. The western districts of this plain, though less sterile than the southern plain, are more adapted for pastures than for cultivation. The eastern districts have a superior soil, which is a reddish earth, covered in certain seasons with abundant grass, and well adapted for the cultivation of grain, fruit, and vegetables. In most of the northern plains water is found at a depth of from 8 feet to 10 feet below the surface. The climate is sultry. During the north-east monsoon there is an almost daily fall of rain. The island is exposed both to the north-west and north-east monsoons, rendering the anchorages unsafe. There are about 5,000 inhabitants, consisting of two distinct races—namely, Arabs who have settled on the island, and the aboriginal inhabitants, who are Bedouins, wandering from one part of the island to another with their flocks and herds. The principal commercial products are aloes of the finest quality, the dragon's-blood tree, tamarinds,

and Afonso Dalboquerque contented himself with a blockade of Calicut by a small and probably inefficient fleet, which was compelled by the disastrous turn of affairs at Goa to hasten to the relief of the besieged garrison there.

Another Indian potentate, whose policy was manifestly disturbed by the Portuguese successes, was the King of Narsinga, to whom Fray Luiz had been accredited by Afonso Dalboquerque in the previous year.[1] This king hastened, after some tergiversation, to conclude an alliance with the Portuguese commander, but Fray Luiz did not live to return, being murdered at the reported instigation of the Hidalcão.

After putting the local government of the city and island of Goa into a satisfactory condition, dedicating the principal church to the patronage of St. Catherine,

tobacco, and various fruits and gums, besides some cotton and indigo. Sheep and goats in the western districts constitute the principal wealth of the inhabitants; the oxen are small. The civet cat and chameleon are found all over the island. Turtles are found on the southern coast. Fish abound on several parts of the coast, and many families live on the produce of their fishing. The capital is Tamarida, with only 100 inhabitants, built not far from the northern shores.

As the island lies almost directly in the line of our communication with India from the Red Sea, it has acquired additional importance by the construction of the Suez Canal, and this consideration has, without doubt, determined the action of the Indian Government, which, in 1876, entered into a treaty by which, for a small subsidy, the Sultan engaged never to cede Socotra to any foreign power, nor to allow any settlement to be made on it without the consent of the British Government. The Indian Government has lately re-occupied the island, and the British flag was rehoisted there not long ago.

[1] See vol. II, ch. xvii.

on whose auspicious feast day he had gained the victory, appointing various officers, munitioning the fortress, assisting by beneficent measures the colonisation of the lands, and re-establishing the currency, it was Afonso Dalboquerque's intention to have proceeded without delay to the Red Sea; but two events had transpired which caused him to change his mind, and this change was productive of unexpectedly great and glorious achievements, which added new lustre to the already brilliant career of the Viceroy.

One of these was the circumstance of the continued captivity of Ruy de Araujo and his companions in Malaca against the advice of Ninachatu (or Ninapam, as Correa calls him), the Hindoo adviser of the king of that country, the other the natural desire of Diogo Mendez de Vasconcelos, who had come from Portugal under special orders to effect the release of these prisoners, to make his way thither without delay, although Afonso Dalboquerque, in the exercise of his undoubted authority, desired to put off this undertaking for a more convenient opportunity, when a more imposing force than that which Diogo Mendez de Vasconcelos commanded could be mustered for the service. The determined intention and endeavour of Diogo Mendez to separate from the fleet of his superior officer, in direct opposition to orders, did not succeed at the time, yet this act undoubtedly operated with some weight in influencing the subsequent movements of Afonso Dalboquerque, who, finding the winds adverse to his intended voyage to the Red Sea, reversed his course, and after a brief stoppage at Cochim, shaped his way as straight as he could for Malaca, and brought up his fleet at Pedir, on the northern coast of Sumatra.

At this port the hopes of the Portuguese were raised in a remarkable degree by the unexpected meeting with João Viegas and eight other members of the little band under the headship of Ruy de Araujo, that had escaped from their durance at Malaca. These men pointed out to Afonso Dalboquerque the complicity of the Moor Naodabegea or Naodabeguea in the plot to destroy Diogo Lopez de Sequeira and his retreat to Pacé, a neighbouring port at which the Portuguese fleet touched, and made ineffectual efforts to get him into the hands of the commander. But on the advance of the fleet towards the waters of Malaca the Moor was overtaken in a *pangajaoa*, and after a sharp encounter, in which the enemy were worsted, the curious spectacle of the fugitive Naodabegea, severely wounded and nearly dead, but without any blood flowing from his mangled body, presented itself to the astonished eyes of the Portuguese. This apparently unaccountable circumstance was explained by the finding of a bracelet made of the bones of the animal called *cabal*, a word which appears to be related somewhat too transparently with that signifying *horse* in many European languages. The peculiar power possessed by this bracelet of preventing the flow of blood from any wounds which the wearer should experience recalls the incident of the magic scabbard of King Arthur's sword, *Excalibur*. In the *Morte d'Arthur* we read: "'Well,' said the damsel, 'go ye into yonder barge, and row yourself unto the sword, and take it and the scabbard with you'......So King Arthur and Merlin alighted, tied their horses to two trees, and so they went into the barge. And when they came to the sword that the hand held, King Arthur took it up by the handles, and took it with him......and so came to the land and rode forth. King Arthur looked upon the sword and liked it passing well. 'Whether liketh you better,' said Merlin, 'the sword or the scabbard?' 'Me liketh better the sword,' said King Arthur. 'Ye are more unwise,' said Merlin, 'for the scabbard is worth ten of the sword, *for while ye have the scabbard upon you ye shall lose no blood, be ye never so sore wounded, therefore keep well the scabbard always with you.*'" This strangely gifted bracelet was sent by Afonso Dalboquerque to the King of Portugal, but was lost on the voyage, with other unwonted evidences of his prowess, and rare trophies of Portuguese valour over the unknown races of the Eastern world.

After the incident of capturing a junk, on board of which was the King of Pacé, who was evidently making the best of his way to Malaca to warn the king of the propinquity of the hostile Armada, Malaca was reached, and negotiations were immediately commenced for the restitution of the Portuguese captives, and for satisfaction of the insult done to that nation by their detention; but this only resulted in the king temporising with Afonso Dalboquerque while he secretly made extensive preparations to withstand his demands. At this point the author of the *Commentaries* breaks off for the moment the thread of his narrative, and devotes a chapter to a historical digression upon the site and foundation of the kingdom and city of Malaca, and another chapter to a description of the customs and government of the city. We may here, in like manner for the moment so far digress, as to glance at the impression made by Malaca, in its present phase of existence, upon the learned Mr. Wallace, in his most interesting work on the Malay Archipelago. Writing in 1869 the author says:—

"At present[1] a vessel over a hundred tons hardly ever enters its port, and the trade is entirely confined to a few petty products of the forests, and to the fruit which the trees planted by the old Portuguese now produce for the enjoyment of the inhabitants of Singapore. Although rather subject to fevers, it is not at present considered very unhealthy.

"The population of Malacca consists of several races. The ubiquitous Chinese are perhaps the most numerous, keeping up their manners, customs, and language; the indigenous Malays are next in point of numbers, and their language is the Lingua-franca of the place. Next come the descendants of the Portuguese—a mixed, degraded, and degenerate race, but who still keep up the use of their mother-tongue, though ruefully mutilated in grammar; and then there are the English rulers, and the descendants of the Dutch, who all speak English. The Portuguese spoken at Malacca is a useful philological phenomenon. The verbs have mostly lost their inflections, and one form does for all moods, tenses, numbers, and persons. *Eu vai* serves for 'I go', 'I went', or 'I will go'. Adjectives, too, have been deprived of their feminine and plural terminations, so that the language is reduced to a marvellous simplicity, and, with the admixture of a few Malay words, becomes rather puzzling to one who has heard only the pure Lusitanian.

---

[1] Alfred R. Wallace, *The Malay Archipelago.* London, 8vo., 1869, pp. 41, 42.

"In costume, these several peoples are as varied as in their speech. The English preserve the tight-fitting coat, waistcoat, and trousers, and the abominable hat and cravat; the Portuguese patronise a light jacket, or, more frequently, shirt and trousers only; the Malays wear their national jacket and *sarong* (a kind of kilt), with loose drawers; while the Chinese never depart in the least from their national dress, which indeed it is impossible to improve for a tropical climate, whether as regards comfort or appearance. The loosely-hanging trousers, and neat, white half shirt half jacket, are exactly what a dress should be in this low latitude."

The testimony also of the gifted author of a recent work upon the Straits of Malaca may be here perused with advantage, for its characteristic touches upon the state of the settlement in 1875. Mr. J. Thomson says:—

"I paid a passing visit[1] to Malacca, but finding it neither an interesting nor a profitable field, I made but a short stay in the place. Malacca is a quaint, dreamy, Dutch-looking old town, where one may enjoy good fruit, and the fellowship and hospitality of the descendants of the early Portuguese and Dutch colonists.

"Should any warmhearted bachelor wish, he might furnish himself with a pretty and attractive looking wife from among the daughters of that sunny clime; but let him make no long stay there if indisposed to marry, unless he can defy the witchery of soft dark eyes, of raven tresses,

---

[1] J. Thomson, F.R.G.S., *The Straits of Malacca, Indo-China, and China.* London, 1875, 8vo., pp. 52, 53. For further information upon Malacca and the adjacent countries and islands, the reader may consult with advantage the work by J. H. Moor, on *The Indian Archipelago*, Singapore, 1837, 4to.; Newbold, *British Settlements of Malacca*, 1839; Crawford, *Dictionary of the Indian Archipelago.*

and of sylph-like forms. It is a spot where leisure seems to sit at every man's doorway; drowsy as the placid sea, and idle as the huge palms whose broad leaves nod above the old weather-beaten smug-looking houses. Here Nature comes laden at each recurring season with ripe and luscious fruits, dropping them from her lap into the very streets, and bestrewing the byeways with glorious bananas on which even the fat listless porkers in their wayside walks, will hardly deign to feed. It is withal a place where one might loiter away a life, dreamily, pleasantly, and uselessly. These are but passing impressions, and Malacca may yet, after all, develop into something in every way worthy of the straits which bear its name."

In this chapter also the author of the *Commentaries* has put on record some carly and interesting information concerning the inhabitants of Lequea, or the Loo-choo Islands, who are there called Gores and maintained considerable trade with the Malay settlements in the peninsula. These islands have lately become somewhat prominent in Asiatic politics, in consequence of the disagreement between China and Japan, produced by the forcible seizure of them by the latter power.

The *Politische Correspondenz* gives an official review of the dispute between China and Japan regarding the Loo-choo Islands, in a letter from Shanghai dated July 18, 1879. It says:—

"The Japanese Government took possession with a military force of the Loo-Choo Islands last April, and transported its Governor, who called himself a King, and yearly paid tribute both to China[1] and Japan, to Yeddo. He

[1] With respect to the relations of the Loo-Choo Empire to China, it is proved from Chinese historical works that even in the earliest times, during the reigns of the Emperors of the dynasty

here received the rank and income of a Japanese Prince. At the same time he was replaced by a Japanese Governor, and the whole country placed under Japanese control; the paying of tribute to China was stopped, and the Chinese system of a calculation of time was replaced by the Japanese calendar.[1] All these changes were so well prepared, so quickly carried out, that they were only known after they had actually taken place, although at the time doubted. Everybody was curious to know what steps the Chinese would take in the matter.

"The little Loo-Choo Empire extends between 20 and 30 degrees of latitude, in a north-eastern direction, from the northern end of Formosa to the southern end of Japan. It is composed of over three hundred little islands, and divided into three large groups, called Tshung-shan, Shan-nan, and Shan-pei. This geographical arrangement is also the political arrangement, as the three groups form the three provinces of the Empire, which are again divided into thirty-five districts, and these into 378 parishes. The capital town, at the same time the former residence of the Prince, is Ewang, on the Tshung-shan. Of the number of the inhabitants nothing positive is known, but they are a peace-loving people, cultivating their land and carrying on cattle breeding. Their habits and dress are similar to those of the Chinese. They write in Chinese characters, but the common dialect is similar to the Japanese. Regarding the real history of the people nothing at all is known.

"The Loo-Choo Islands were the causes of continual

Han, the Princes of the Loo-Choo Islands paid their tribute to China. In the nineteenth year of the reign of the Emperor Kanghi (1681), the tribute to be sent was settled as follows:—12,600 catties of sulphur, 3,000 muschels, and 30,000 catties of copper. One cattie is 1 1-3lb. English.

[1] Since 1372 of the Christian calculation, the Chinese calendar has been in use on the Loo-Choo Islands, the years being named and numbered according to the Chinese Emperors.

quarrel between China and Japan in earlier times, the latter having repeatedly tried to annex this little island-empire. In the nineteenth year of the reign of the Emperor Wan-li (1592), a number of the inhabitants of the Loo-Choo islands were delegated to China to complain of Japan's attempts to annex the islands by force. These efforts, as well as others made in 1606, were frustrated. Yang-Tsung Ye, the Chinese Commander-in-Chief of the province Chekiang, brought (also in Wan-li's reign in 1613) the Prince of the Loo-Choo Islands, who governed then, and who had been forcibly carried off by the Japanese, back again into his kingdom.

"It is not to be doubted that, although the Chinese are able to prove historically a certain Suzerainty over the Loo-choo Islands, the Japanese can also do the same; in fact, both Empires have hitherto considered the Loo-Choo islands a state dependent on them; both the Emperors of China and of Japan style themselves Suzerain of the Loo-Choo Islands, and it will have to be proved which of the two is able to prove supremacy and to keep it.

"When the news of the seizing of the Loo-Choo islands by Japan reached Pekin, great surprise and dissatisfaction was shown among the supporters of the Government. A few days earlier the new Japanese Ambassador at Pekin had presented his credentials without taking advantage of the occasion to say a word. On Prince Kung and the Ministers of the Tsungli-Yamen appealing to him regarding the action of his Government, he replied that he was, with regard to this question, without any instructions whatever. The Japanese Government, in answer to the Chinese Ambassador's appeal at Yeddo, replied that they were ready to prove at any time their right to the Loo-Choo Islands, and that a giving up of them could never be thought of. Japan, who only would yield what she had taken by force of arms, to do which China has not the means, having neither money, an army, and, least of all, a fleet.

"From authentic quarters it is affirmed that Prince Kung conferred with ex-President Grant, who visited

Pekin lately, on this question. Prince Kung begged his intervention. General Grant may have given his word to introduce this subject in a private conversation, but not officially, as the General in his retired position would undoubtedly avoid even exercising a seeming influence on the politics of the present Government of the United States.

"In Pekin,[1] according to the latest news, the excitement seems to be on the increase; the Ministers of the Tsungli-Yamên speak of war between China and Japan, but they at the same time make it known that they will first call in the intervention of the Foreign Powers, hoping thus to attain restitution of their original position. But whether such an intervention, in case of hostilities really breaking

---

[1] I have extracted this from the *Standard*, which, at the time, published the following remarks upon the situation of affairs:—"The cloud which arose six months ago between China and Japan, in consequence of the seizure by the latter of the Loo-choo Islands, has not yet cleared off. In fact, it may be said that, despite the hope prevailing among the European communities in the far East, it has grown thicker in the months that have elapsed since the Loo-Choo question first attracted attention. Nor does this afford any just ground for surprise. For centuries the Chinese have exercised rights over the Prince of those Islands; neither Japan nor any other Power has ever challenged them; but suddenly they discovered that the Mikado of Japan had taken possession of the islands, deposed the Ruler, and nominated a Governor of his own. He has since justified the seizure by asserting that the Loo-Choo Islands have always been tributary to the Prince of Satsuma, the great feudatory of Kinshin, who was finally overthrown in 1877. The Manchu dynasty has never been remarkable for its indifference, nor, indeed, has any of its predecessors upon the Throne of Pekin, to the rights which it has acquired; and the Japanese Government took this step at a moment when the Chinese had given signal proof not only of their determination not to abate one jot of their pretensions, but also of their ability to enforce them. It is true that months have passed since the tidings reached China that a Japanese garrison held Loo-Choo, and that a Japanese fleet was riding in the roadstead of Napa-

out, would be granted is difficult to predict. Anyhow, the attitude of China to England in the serious difficulties between China and Japan some years ago regarding Formosa is too fresh in people's memory not to be profitably used at the present time.

"The inhabitants of the Loo-Choo Islands are said to have sent a deputation to Pekin to beg her direct help in their favour. The Japanese consuls in the Chinese ports have received orders by telegraph to seize the members of the deputations on their appearing and send them back to Japan. A Japanese corvette is now at Shanghai, and two other Japanese men-of-war are cruising about in Chinese waters. In case of this news being true, the deputation

---

kiang without beholding a Chinese fleet and army being despatched to reassert the Imperial authority. But it is not in accordance with Chinese habits to be precipitate, even if the supposed efficiency of the Japanese fleet were not an additional incentive to caution. The latest official announcement is one fully in consonance with the train of thought of the official Chinese mind. A despatch has been sent to the Mikado informing him that, unless the Japanese forces are withdrawn, and Loo-Choo restored to its old state of semi-independence and double vassalage to China and Japan, within the space of three months, he must take the consequences. The Japanese are anxious to have the matter submitted to either a mixed Commission or to an arbitrator, knowing well that Europeans, and Englishmen in particular, have little sympathy with the claims China possesses, and periodically advances, over most of the States of Eastern Asia. The Tokio authorities perceive that, in the eyes of most foreigners, China's grievance with regard to Loo-Choo is sentimental, for the Pekin Government does not demand the surrender of the islands. Far from that, it wishes to ensure their autonomy, only demanding the perpetuation of the nominal tie and of the fluctuating tribute which have constituted Loo-Choo in its eyes a portion of the Celestial Empire. There are deeper motives behind, and underneath all this talk about the past there is a very clear perception of the fact that the Loo-Choo question is one of practical importance."

may have succeeded in landing on some place on the coast, and making their way to Pekin,[1] where, however, they have not yet arrived. Leaving aside the question of the right of possession, it is not to be denied that the Japanese have shown great skill and energy in carrying out their purpose, and an exact knowledge of Chinese affairs. China will be

[1] "At Pekin it is evident that the Japanese occupation of the Islands constitutes a grave danger to China. An insult of such a venial character to the Imperial dignity might be tolerated; but a menace to the nation must be grappled with, so that it shall not develope into an actual peril. It is on this point that something may, with advantage, be said at the present time, when various circumstances are calculated to put the Japanese view so prominently forward that the Chinese claims may be lost sight of. The gist of the difference lies in the question, why is the Japanese occupation of Loo-Choo dangerous to the peace of China. Between China and Japan there has been for centuries a rivalry, not very dissimilar to that which existed for a long time between France and England. The introduction of Western ideas, arts, and manufactures into the two countries, far from allaying the keenness of the rivalry, had rather the effect of embittering it. The very eagerness shown by the Japanese to acquire gun-boats and improved weapons was a grievance in the eyes of the conservative Chinese, for they felt that their neighbours would test their naval and military efficiency either upon them or against some of their outlying possessions. The example set by the Japanese proved contagious, however, and there is good reason for believing that the Celestials have now, mainly through the energy of the Viceroy Li-Hung-Chang, caught up with their progressive neighbour, so far as the purchase of men of war, rifles, and improved artillery can be said to constitute progress. For military purposes the two States may be admitted to be much on an equality, provided the numerous responsibilities of the Pekin Government do not detract from its vigour at the critical moment. At the same time, the advantage of position undoubtedly lies with Japan, and this would enable her fleet to prosecute an offensive war on the exposed seaboard of China with very considerable effect. The occupation of Loo-Choo further improves that posi-

quite as incapable of taking the islands from Japan as she was in preventing her from seizing them. Even Japan may, after these first successful efforts, at no very distant time take steps to occupy Formosa, where new sources of wealth, exhausted in her own country, are to be found in rich abundance."

---

tion, for the excellent harbour of Napakiang in its sheltered bay provides the Mikado's fleet with a station on the flank of the Eastern and Yellow Seas, within two days' steaming of the coasts of Fuhkien and Chekiang. But it has further advantages which have not been mentioned, and prominent among them must be held to be that the possession of the Loo-Choo Islands carries with it that of the little-known Madjicosemah group. This latter lies off the east coast of Formosa, and has enjoyed in the eyes of the neighbouring countries a semi-sacred reputation, not widely different to that held by the Hesperides in the mythology of ancient Greece. The two largest of the group are Pachuran and Typinsan; and the coast of Formosa is less than one hundred and fifty miles distant from the former. It thus appears that the apparently harmless act of the Japanese in deposing the king of Loo-Choo has resulted in their acquisition of two groups of islands, representing a tract of territory as large as England and Wales, and having a commanding position in waters which have always been considered to be Chinese. A glance at the map will suffice to show that the Mikado has now obtained possession of two admirable halting-places on the road to Formosa and the China coast. By the acquisition of Napakiang he has supplemented the value of his own western harbours, and there is no reason for supposing that Pachusan does not contain convenient bays and safe roadsteads. These facts should show that the Loo-Choo question is one not of sentiment alone to the Chinese, but of serious practical import. Unfamiliar as the names of these places may be to us they are well known in the history of China, and the Pekin rulers are aware that as they have in past times exercised considerable influence on the result of wars between China and Japan, it is quite probable that they would do so again in any future struggle.

"The hostile policy which Japan has always pursued towards

Negotiations with the King of Malaca having failed, Afonso Dalboquerque made extensive preparations for resorting to force, and, as a preliminary step, attracted to his side a merchant fleet of five Chinese junks, having a force on board which the King of Malaca was about

China, her intrigues in Corea, and expeditions to Formosa, have kept the vigilance of the Celestials constantly on the alert. Li-Hung-Chang now beholds the Mikado, strong in his new freedom and liberated from the dread of his arrogant Daimios, stretching out his hand to the north and to the south for the purpose of extending his influence and curtailing that of China. Within the last few months Japan has committed two acts which will further incense her rival. The one is the occupation of the Loo-Choo and Madjicosemah Islands, which brings her close to Formosa, the Chinese Ireland, and the other is the signature of a Treaty with the King of Corea, which gives Japanese subjects special privileges in that country. The Mikado has thus not restricted his aggressive policy to the sea. His alliance with the ruler of the peninsula of Corea gives him a foothold on the mainland, which acquires special significance from the remembrance of the siege of Nankin and triumphs on the Yangtse by the Japanese in the sixteenth and seventeenth centuries. These considerations, and others of a similar kind, make it very improbable that the Chinese will acquiesce in the most recent achievement brought about by the aggressive policy of Japan. To them it will appear to be a bad policy to show weakness with regard to Loo-Choo. The Japanese are the aggressors. They have no sufficient excuse for their seizure of this group, and they have for years followed a systematic policy which would, if China continued as indifferent as she is now counselled by some of her friends to remain, lead to the loss of every island she possesses beyond the immediate vicinity of her shores. If Sir Thomas Wade, or some other leading authority on the spot, cannot induce the Japanese to withdraw, the Chinese will, beyond all question, take the matter into their own hands, and at the fitting moment endeavour to expel the Japanese from the islands which they have seized." —*Ib.*

to employ in military operations against the King of Daru or Aru,[1] a state on the coast of Sumatra, nearly opposite the port of Malaca, with which he was at war.

On the feast day of St. James the Greater the storming of the bridge or pier was made, under circumstances narrated in the text, and a great part of the city fired. These operations, although they did not result immediately in the fall of the city, severely harrassed the enemy, and crippled his resources. The author of *Malaca Conquistada* records the subsequent attack upon and destruction of the city by fire in these stanzas.

> "Em tanto das janellas, e terrados,
> Que para aquella parte respondião,
> Mil frechas, mil pelouros desmandados
> Sobre a gente Christã mortes chovião:
> Mas, chamando Albuquerque aos esforçados
> Lima e Caldeira, áquelles que região,
> Lhes mandou que de fogo as mãos armassem,
> E que as vizinhas casas abrazassem.

> "Manda tambem o Malavar valente
> Que com os seus adustos tiradores
> Impida o assomarse a imiga gente
> Ás partes, que lhe ficão superiores.
> Da empreza o forte barbaro contente
> Os seus incita a bellicos furores:
> Mil, e mil frechas logo os ares calão,
> Troços de breados cabos fogo exhalão.

---

[1] The initial "D" here, as in *Dupe* lower down, is plainly only the Portuguese preposition *de* in combination. The place appears as *Daru* in the Portolano of Fernão Vaz Dourado, and as *Aru* in the map given by the Dutch translator of João de Barros.

"Dão ao mandato effeito: pega o fogo
Na disposta materia: com tremenda
Furia vibrantes pontas sobem logo
Aos ares, e de fumo nuvem horrenda:
Grita a misera gente; porém rogo
Não admitte a voraz chamma, contenda
Com as nuvens horrisona travando,
As esféras mais altas ameaçando.

"Eolo neste ponto desatava
Da formosa Orithia o bravo amante,
Com que o incendio cruel mais se esforçava,
Com horrivel estrondo crepitante.
Contra o fogo remedios mil buscava
A Pagã gente, mas nenhum bastante,
Que c'o vento de casa em casa prende,
E, consumindo aqui, já lá se accende.

"Edificio, em grandeza, e valor raro,
Sobre secretas rodas se movia,
Finge a materia o marmore de Paro
Illustre c'o metal, que Arabia cria.
Nelle, se lhe não fora o fado avaro,
Da Infante as bodas celebrar queria
O Rei, e com alegre variedade
Carro triunfante dar vista á cidade.

"Á nupcial casa, de delicias chêa,
Tambem se atreve o vingativo lume,
E na materia rica assi se atêa,
Que em leve fumo, e cinza em fim a resume:
Della a mesquita, onde com torpe e fêa
Adoração, e barbaro costume,
Ao vil Mafoma hourava a gente cega,
A flamma ardente em consumir se emprega.

"Á mesquita esquadrão confuso acode,
E procura atalhar o fogo. Em tanto
Vendo o prudente Affonso que não pode
Cansada a gente com trabalho tanto;

Porque o intentó ao possivel se accommode;
Em quanto o incendio dura, e crece o pranto,
A artilharia embarcar manda ganhada,
E a que em terra ficou deixa encravada.

"O esquadrão militar logo começa
A ir, e vir, despojos embarcando,
Como no estio com fervente pressa
Multidão de formigas, saqueando
De trigo as eiras, montes atravessa
Por entre ervas, e espinhos, sustentando
Na boca o grão pezado, até encerrallo,
E na estreita caverna enthesourallo.

"As barbaras catervas offendidas,
Quando tanto despojo embarcar virão;
A dar e recebir novas feridas
Bramando vingativos acodirão.
Torna de novo a morte a troncar vidas:
Aqui appellidão Marte, alli suspirão;
Em fim effeitos crus de dura guerra
No mar ostentão, porém mais na terra.

"Rios correm do sangue derramado;
Que, nas ondas entrando, em sanguinosa
Mudão a cor cerúlea: de ira armado
Se vê o mesmo furor, vista espantosa!
Mas já fim dava ao dia o Sol dourado
Do grande Oceano visitando a esposa:
Torna-se ás naus a baptizada gente;
A Agarena o elemento apaga ardente."

Liv. ix, st. 134-143.

The Javanese headman, Utemutaraja, who administered the suburban district of Upe or Dupe,[1] made overtures of service, and for the time, but not without showing suspicions, which were afterwards verified,

[1] See p. xxii.

Afonso Dalboquerque accepted his services. In the end, probably out of political necessity quite as much as proved guilt, this prince was convicted of treachery, and executed with his son and son-in-law, as an effectual means of restoring quiet in, and manifesting the Portuguese power over, the city. The Chinese, who had come for trading purposes in their junks, seized this opportunity of renewing their request for permission to depart on the prosecution of their voyage to Siam, and the Portuguese commander gladly availed himself of the occasion to send Duarte Fernandez as ambassador to Siam in their company.

After a characteristic speech, setting forth the Imperial policy of the Portuguese king, Afonso Dalboquerque again pushed forward in full strength, assaulted the bridge, and made good his position upon it. From that hour the fate of Malaca was sealed, and soon fell an easy prey into the hands of the commander, who thus captured in a city extending three miles along the shore, and of great depth inland, an incredible amount of plunder and three thousand pieces of artillery, and added to Portugal a territory considerably larger than the mother kingdom. But the King of Malaca, although in full flight, was yet in hopes of rescuing his patrimony from the foreign invader, and dispatched his own uncle, Tuão Nacem Mudaliar, to the King of China, an empire at that period in close alliance with the Malay king, to beg for assistance. Tuão Nacem made his way to Canton, and from that port was conveyed, according to custom, to Pekin; but the King of China, who had heard of the friendly treatment accorded by Afonso Dalboquerque (for this very political object) to the Chinese merchants at Malaca, was unwilling to act, and Tuão Nacem Mudaliar, partly out of chagrin for the failure of his mission, and partly dispirited at the untimely death of his wife, did not live to convey the news of his repulse by the Chinese court to his royal nephew, but died on the return journey at Yang-chow-fu or Yang-cheu-fu, near Nanking.[1]

A manuscript Report, in which is embodied a succinct historical relation of the principal European embassies to China, now preserved among the Wellesley papers in the MS. department of the British Museum, very justly attributes to Afonso Dalboquerque the design of establishing friendly relations with the Chinese empire. This design was probably suggested to him in the first place by the intercourse he had with the Chinese merchant junks in the port of Malaca at the time of the siege. The following passage describes briefly the first dealings of Portugal and China :—

"Alphonso Albuquerque (from whose wise administration, while Viceroy in the East Indies, Portugal derived such advantages) formed the design of opening a communication with China, though he did not live to see it attempted. In consequence of intelligence sent by him to the Court of Portugal, a squadron sailed from Lisbon, in 1518, to convoy an Ambassador to China. The Abbé Raynal's account of this Embassy is as follows :—

---

[1] Yang-cheu-fu, in Kiang-su, 32 deg. 26.32 min. N., 117 deg. 4.13 min. E., was, in 1277, under the Mongols, a *lu*, or chief town of a district. Marco Polo is said to have been governor of this town for three years. He cites it under the name of Yanju. But see Col. Yule's *Marco Polo*, ii, 138, etc.

"As soon as the squadron arrived at the islands in the neighbourhood of Canton, it was surrounded by Chinese vessels, who came to reconnoitre it. Ferdinand Andrada, who commanded it, did not put himself in any posture of defence, he suffered the Chinese to come on board, communicated the object of his voyage to the Mandarins that presided at Canton, and sent his ambassador on shore, who was conducted to Pekin.

"Whatever may have been the state of China when the Portuguese landed there, as they had no other object in view than to draw riches from thence and to propagate their religion, had they found the best kind of government established in this country, they would not have profited by it. Thomas Perez, their Ambassador, found the Court of Pekin disposed to favour his nation, the fame of which had spread itself throughout Asia. It had already attracted the esteem of the Chinese, which the conduct of Ferdinand Andrada, who commanded the Portuguese squadron, tended still further to increase. He visited all the coasts of China, and traded with the natives. When he was on the point of departure, he issued a proclamation in the ports he had put into, that if any one had been injured by a Portuguese, and would make it known, he should recover satisfaction. The ports of China were now upon the point of being opened to them. Thomas Perez was just about concluding a Treaty, when Simon Andrada, brother to Ferdinand, appeared on the coast with a fresh squadron. This commander treated the Chinese in the same manner as the Portuguese had for some time treated all the people of Asia. He built a fort, without permission, on the island of Taman, from whence he took opportunities of pillaging and extorting money from all the ships bound from or to the ports of China. He carried off young girls from the coast, he seized upon the Chinese, and made slaves of them; he gave himself up to the most licentious acts of piracy, and the most shameful dissoluteness. The sailors and soldiers under his command followed his example. The Chinese, enraged at these outrages, fitted out a large fleet; the Portuguese defended themselves courageously, and escaped by making their way through the enemy's fleet. The Emperor imprisoned Thomas Perez, who died in confinement, and the Portuguese nation was banished from China for some years. After this the Chinese relaxed, and gave permission to the Portuguese to trade at the port of Sancian, to which place they brought gold from Africa, spices from the Molucca Islands, and from Ceylon elephants' teeth, and some precious stones. In return they took silks of every kind, china, gums, medicinal herbs, and tea, which has since become so necessary a commodity to the northern nations of Europe.

"The Portuguese contented themselves with the huts and factories they had at Sancian, and the liberty granted to their trade by the Chinese Government, till an opportunity offered of establishing themselves upon a footing more solid and less dependant upon the Mandarins, who had the command of the coast.

"A pirate named Tchang-si-lao, whose successes had made him powerful, had seized upon the Island of Macao, from whence he blocked up the ports of China, and even proceeded so far as to lay siege to Canton. The neighbouring Mandarins had recourse to the Portuguese, who had ships in the harbour of Sancian; they hastened to the relief of Canton, raised the siege, and obtained a complete victory over the pirate, whom they pursued as far as Macao, where he slew himself.

"The Emperor of China, informed of the service the Portuguese had rendered him on this occasion, bestowed Macao upon them, as a mark of his gratitude. They received this grant with joy, and built a town which became very flourishing, and was advantageously situated for the trade they soon after entered into with Japan.

"The author of *L'Idée Générale de la Chine*, published at Paris in 1780, adds to his account of this transaction (which agrees with the above) that the behaviour of the

Portuguese ambassador confirmed the Chinese in their aversion to foreigners,[1] against whom they had always shut their empire. And speaking of the Emperor's edict permitting the Portuguese to settle at Macao, he says, 'but the restrictions with which the Chinese accompanied this favour, and the manner of forming the settlement, as well as the shackles imposed on the liberty of the Portuguese, give to Macao rather the appearance of a place besieged than of a free commercial city'."[2]

The Viceroy of Canton has just lately expressed himself in cordial terms towards the Portuguese nation, and expressed the necessity of drawing still closer the relations between China and Portugal, which was the first of the European nations to possess commercial establishments in China.

The construction of a powerful, in fact to the Malays an impregnable fortress in the heart of their capital was a natural consequence of the Portuguese victory. The bird's-eye view of this fortress, which has been reproduced for this volume from Correa's invaluable *Lendas da India*, and the plan of the same, also reproduced for this volume from the equally precious manuscript of Pedro Barretto de Resende's *Livro do Estado da India Oriental* (by kind permission of the trustees of the British Museum), show sufficiently the imposing nature of this stronghold. Next in importance to the

[1] This author adds in a note—"Ammian Marcellin qui écrivoit dans le quatrième siècle de notre ère, parle de cet éloignement des Chinois pour les étrangers."

[2] Add. MS., 13,875, fo. 24: "Report of Embassies to China, presented to the British Museum by the Representatives of the Marquess Wellesley."

fortress were reconstructive measures of the victors, as for example the rearrangement of the currency upon a more scientific basis, and the repression of sedition with that iron hand, for which some historians and biographers have been so unnecessarily severe upon Afonso Dalboquerque. Before we condemn this prominent trait in the character of the Portuguese commander we must take into consideration the somewhat ungentle spirit of the age in which he lived, the brutalities practised by Asiatics upon such unfortunate Europeans as fell into their hands, and the absolute necessity that a comparatively small band of men were under to repress unsparingly any and every measure likely to injure their tenure of a territory so far from the natural basis of their operations. Viewed in this light, the execution of Utemutaraja, and the carrying out of the sentence passed upon Ruy Diaz, were measures calculated to procure the security of the whole body, rather than instances of supreme gratification of personal antipathy towards the sufferers.

The incidents of the dispatch of Duarte Fernandez to the court of Siam with specific instructions—an event which helped greatly to elevate the position of Portuguese politics in the east of Asia—the subsequent mission of Antonio de Miranda de Azevedo to the same country, the interchange of presents and friendly compliments, similar courtesies exchanged with the kings of Campar and Java, and the sending forth of a party to explore the Moluccas, then known as the Clove Islands or Mace-apple (*i.e.*, nutmeg) Islands, combine to elevate in a considerable degree the career of Afonso Dalboquerque from that of a vulgar freebooter or licensed adventurer (as some will have him to be) to that of an earnest and scientific pioneer, anxious that his nation, his own followers, and himself also should—

"αἰὲν ἀριστεύειν καὶ ἔξοχον ἔμμεναι ἄλλων."

After detailing the arrangement made by Afonso Dalboquerque for the government of the newly-conquered territory, the author of the *Commentaries* introduces an interesting ORATION, delivered by the illustrious Roman orator, Camillo Portio, before Pope Leo X. This oration, although it introduces notices of some events beyond the scope of the *Commentaries*, is of value, as showing the way in which the Papal court, and probably all Christendom, viewed with admiration and emulation the marvellously rapid successes which had fallen to the arms of Portugal in her dealing with the infidel nations of the East.

The remaining portion of the present volume reverts to India and Goa, and the events which had transpired during the absence of Afonso Dalboquerque in the Malay expedition. Milrrhau or Merlao, the duly appointed Governor of Goa, was conducting the affairs of the city peaceably, when Pulatecão, in command of a force mustered by the Hidalcão, came down from the inland territory of that prince, and took up a strong position in Benastarim, or Benestarij,[1] a fortress on

[1] The variation in the orthography of this fortress is interesting, and shows the peculiar proclivity of the Portuguese language for a nasal sound at the termination of words. Many of the names of persons and places which occur in the text of the *Commentaries*,

the mainland due west of the Island of Goa; but in so disposing his forces he appears to have exceeded the instructions which he had received from the Hidalcão. This prince therefore appointed Roçalcão, called by some historians Rasul Khan, to supersede Pulatecão (or Fulad Khan), and by means of the Portuguese under Diogo Mendez de Vasconcelos (who had been liberated by the people to succeed Rodrigo Rabelo as Captain of Goa, when that officer fell in a skirmish with the Turks, in preference to Francisco Pantoja, to whom the succession rightly belonged), Roçalcão got possession of the fortress of Benestarim, and immediately disconcerted the little garrison of Goa, by making a formal demand for the surrender of the city.

While these events were transpiring, Afonso Dalboquerque had set sail from Malaca in the *Flor de la Mar*, but suffered shipwreck off the dangerous coast of Sumatra, and only reached Cochim with great difficulty some time in the month of January 1512. This disaster was felt all the more keenly by the Viceroy because he afterwards learned that had he visited the Maldive Islands,[1] according to his original intentions during this voyage, he would have fallen in with Mafamede Maçari, the merchant of Cairo—an enemy with whom he was particularly anxious to measure

terminate in -ij, and it is probable that they were all pronounced with a nasal sound at the end of the word. Hence we find Pangim or Pangij, and Augim or Augij; just as in the ordinary language, *assi*, *perú*, *mui*, and other words have a nasal, not written, but always pronounced at the end.

[1] Pedro Barretto de Resende gives a plan of the Portuguese fortress on one of these islands.

his strength. This man was the chief upholder of the policy of bringing over the Rumes to assist the Çamorim in driving the Portuguese out of Malabar. He however feared that Afonso Dalboquerque would get him into his power, so he fled from Calicut (when the break in the blockade happened by the recall of Manuel de Lacerda to the assistance of Goa against Pulatecão) towards the Straits, but was caught in a storm and wrecked at the Cape of Guardafum, and thence made his way, carrying with him Simão Rangel (who had been captured on his voyage from Cochim to Goa) into slavery to Candaluz, in the Maldives, where he imagined himself safe, and out of the possibility of capture by the Portuguese cruisers, who had hitherto kept to more northerly latitudes.

The welcome arrival of the fleet with the great commander on board gave the signal for heartfelt rejoicing throughout the Portuguese settlements of India, and from January to August 1512, Afonso Dalboquerque busied himself with the expedition of necessary business which had no doubt accumulated in his absence during the past year. But fate had not ceased to "weave the crimson web of war" for Afonso Dalboquerque; the relief of Goa was the uppermost feeling in his heart, and he hailed with the greatest satisfaction and delight the arrival of two annual fleets sent out from the mother kingdom in 1511 and 1512 respectively, for the reinforcement of the Indian colonies. These fleets, the one commanded by Dom Garcia, or Gracia, de Noronha, his nephew; the other by Jorge de Mello Pereira and Gracia de Sousa, added no less than seventeen ships of war, with their men and stores, to the sadly diminished number of serviceable vessels and fighting men at the disposal of the Viceroy. But the joy he experienced at receiving these welcome reinforcements was quickly dispelled by the orders sent out to him from the king of Portugal for discussing the question of retaining or abandoning the possession of Goa.

Afonso Dalboquerque very prudently abstained from mentioning this matter until he had re-established the liberty of the city by the operations which led to the recovery of the dominating fortress of Benastarim, for he doubtless felt that had he divulged the king's orders to his captains and officers before they had driven the Turks into the interior, the movements in aid of the besieged city and island would have been carried out without heartiness and spirit, or perhaps even neglected and refused. But when the fortress had yielded to the Portuguese, the spirits of the populace raised by the dispersion of the enemy, and the martial feelings of the army elated by the easy victory, then it was that the commander felt that a fitting opportunity at length had arrived when, although he could no longer with propriety withhold the contents of the Royal dispatch, the general consensus of opinion would lean towards that course which he so ardently desired to carry out.

The surrender of Benastarim was accomplished with practically little trouble, for Roçalcão seems to have been, after all, but half-hearted in the task of its defence. He appears, however, to have tried as far as he could to shield the Portuguese renegade deserters from a fate which he probably knew only too well would overtake them if they fell into the power of their irate master; but the excuse which he made, that it was contrary to the law of his country and the principles of his religion[1] to give them up, availed nothing with Afonso Dalboquerque, whose ferocity (particularly if all that Castanheda and Correa state be true) towards the ill-fated wretches can hardly be paralleled with any other relation out of the whole range of history.

The settlement of Fernão Lopez, the ringleader of these renegades, upon the uninhabited Island of Saint Helena, is of great interest to the political geographer. Correa, whose phrases seem to indicate that he commiserated the unfortunate man, says of him: "Fernão Lopez[2] managed to get on board a Portuguese vessel homeward bound, for he had left his wife and children in Lisbon, but the ship stopped at the Island of St. Helena to take in water, and there this Fernão Lopez remained in hiding, and when he was found missing out of the ship the crew set out and searched for him, but they could not find him, so they left him a barrel of biscuit and some pieces of hung beef, and dried fish, and salt, and a fire and some old clothes, which

[1] See MS., Sloan. 1820, a closely written folio work, seventeenth or eighteenth century, in Portuguese, apparently unpublished, entitled "A Seita dos Indios Orientais, e principalmente dos Malavares", in eight books, treating of the history and mythology of the religious sects, manners, and customs, of the people inhabiting Malabar.

[2] See the extract on pp. 240-242 for the Portuguese text.

each one contributed; and when the vessel set sail, they left a letter for him, that in case of any ship putting in there he was to make signs to show whether he were alive or dead, and shew himself in order that they might supply him with whatever he required. Then the vessel set sail, and Fernão Lopez, seeing the ship had left, went out of the wood and took possession of the things which he found left for him, and kept up the fire so that it should not go out, and set to work to find stones which he beat one against another, and he saw that they struck fire and he kept them. Thus, with the four fingers of his left hand, and with the stump of his right hand which had been cut off, as God helped him in his great mercy, he dug a hollow in a bank wherein he made a small grotto, and enlarged it within, where he lived in retreat and used to sleep, and he filled up the mouth of the grotto with prickly bushes. He found tender herbs which were savoury to eat, and he boiled them with salt in two saucepans which they had left for him. And while he was living in this way during the next year a ship touched at the island, and when he saw the ship he hid himself.

"The crew of the ship, going on shore, when they saw the grotto and a straw bed whereon he slept, and the bags, and the staves of the barrel which had been left with biscuit for him, and the saucepans, and coals for the fire, were amazed, for they thought that some negroes were living there in hiding from another ship, but when they beheld the clothing they agreed that it was a Portuguese man. So they took in their water, and did not meddle with anything, but, on the contrary, left him biscuits, and cheeses, and things to eat, and a letter bidding him not to hide himself, but when any ship should touch there he should speak with it, for no one would harm him. And the ship set sail, and, in spreading her sails, there fell overboard a cock, which the waves carried to the shore, and Fernão Lopez caught it and fed it upon some rice which they had left behind for him, so that the cock became on such loving terms with him that it followed him wherever he went, and at night it roosted with him in the hole. This cock remained with this man for many years, it would come at his call, for, as time went on, this man used to show himself and converse with the people of the ships which passed by, and all gave him things to plant and to sow, so that he cultivated a great many gourds, pomegranates, and palm trees, and kept ducks, hens, sows, and she-goats with young, all of which increased largely, and all became wild in the wood.

"This man lived for many years alone in this island, leading this remarkable life, and when it was related to the king he was very desirous of seeing him, for they said that he was like a wild man; therefore, the king sent word to beg him of his own accord to come to Portugal. This he did, and he went and secretly disembarked in the house of the captain of the ship, and thence went by night to converse with the king and the queen, who gave him a hermitage and houses of friars wherein he might remain; but he would accept nought of this, but obtained permission of the king and went to Rome, and confessed himself to the Pope, who was pleased to see him, and gave him letters to the king that he would send him back again to the island. This likewise the king performed. This man stayed on this island for upwards of ten years without any one ever seeing him, for he used to hide himself.

"In this island there lived a fugitive Javanese youth, who also stayed with him many years. This youth was the one who revealed him to a ship which touched there. For the captain, Pero Gomez Teixeira, who had been Auditor-General in India, threatened the black man so much that he went and pointed out the place where Fernão Lopez was hidden. And when he found that he was taken he made loud outcries, thinking that they were going to take him on board. But Pero Gomez consoled him, and talked for a long time with him, and assured him that he would not carry him away, and gave him many things, although he did not care for them, but very earnestly besought him to take the youth with him in the ship. Pero Gomez, therefore, took him on receiving a promise from Fernão Lopez that he would not hide himself from the crews. And when this had been agreed to, Pero Gomez left with him a paper, signed and sealed, wherein he desired all captains who might touch there of their kindness not to use any force in desiring to carry him to Portugal against his will, for it was from fear of this that Fernão Lopez used in by-gone times to hide himself. Therefore, he gave him a safe-guard in the king's name, and swore to it, that no one should carry him away from the island against his will. And then Fernão Lopez felt assured, so that he used no longer to hide himself, and spoke with all comers, and gave them of the produce of the island, which yielded in great abundance. And in the island he died, after living there for a long time, which was in the year 1546."

The blockade of Calicut, which was commenced anew by D. Garcia de Noronha; the mission of Diogo Fernandez, Adail of Goa, with the returning ambassador of the Hidalcão, to arrange the terms of peace; the dispatch of the Cambayan ambassador, in whose company Tristão Déga went to demand leave to erect a fortress in Diu; the dispatch of a messenger from Miliquiaz of Diú; the mission of Gaspar Chanoca to Narsinga; the reception of an ambassador with presents from the king of Vengapor, an inland territory bordering on the kingdom of the Zabaim; an interview of a fruitless nature with Roçalcão; and other similar business, naturally occupied Afonso Dalboquerque for some time after his return to Goa. But an event occurred about this period to which he devoted considerable interest, and attached great importance. This was the arrival of an envoy, named Mateus or Matthew, the brother of the Patriarch of Abyssinia, from the little known and mysterious kingdom of Prester John, with a present of a piece of the Wood of the True Cross from the Warden of the Franciscan Friars of Mount Sion, Jerusalem, to the king of Portugal, and an offer of alliance by marriage of the children of the Prester John with the Royal Princes of the kingdom.

Afonso Dalboquerque forwarded this ambassador and his sacred present with great *éclat* to the king of Portugal, but in the eyes of many of the Portuguese Mateus was looked upon as an impostor whom the Viceroy favoured for his own glorification. The king treated him with honour, and sent him back in 1520 with D. Rodrigo de Lima, a Portuguese ambassador, but Mateus died on the way at Bisam,[1] on the 23rd of May, 1520, and D. Rodrigo prosecuted his journey, a relation of which,[2] by Father Francisco Alvarez, translated from the Portuguese and edited by the accomplished Portuguese scholar Lord Stanley of Alderley, is now being published by the Hakluyt Society. Students of Portuguese history, who are already under a debt of gratitude to the noble translator of Vasco da

[1] According to the work mentioned in the next note; but from the *Commentaries*, p. 254, he appears to have died at Maçua, or Massowah, an important city on the African side of the Red Sea; cf.

> "........... e as melhores
> Povoações que a parte Africa tem,
> Maçua são, Arquico, e Suanquem."—*Cam. Lus.*, x, 97.

Mateus, the ambassador, appears to have been of an irritable disposition, and this was perhaps the cause of the dislike shewn to him by the Portuguese with whom he came into contact.

[2] The title of this rare book, a fine specimen of early Portuguese typography, is: "Ho Preste Joam das Indias. Verdadera informaçam das terras do Preste Joam, segundo vio e escreveo ho padre Francisco Aluarez Capellã del Rey nosso senhor. Agora nouamẽte impresso por mandado do dito senhor em casa de Luis Rodriguez liureiro de sua alteza." The colophon states that the book was printed in 1540.

Gama from Correa's *Lendas da India*, will look forward to the appearance of this narrative of the Portuguese embassy to Abyssinia in 1520 with the greatest interest.

After making disposition for the projected fortress in Calicut, if the Çamorim should really grant the site —a fact which Afonso Dalboquerque seems to have despaired of at last—an assembly of the principal Portuguese personages was held, and the King's articles read. The debate which ensued resulted in the determination to hold Goa at all hazard; and the letter which Afonso Dalboquerque addressed to the King, a characteristic specimen of the fearlessness of the great commander,[1] concludes this volume.

The portrait of Dom Vasco da Gama, which is placed as a frontispiece to this volume, and that of Diogo Lopez de Sequeira, which is set to face page 254, are derived from the MS. of Pedro Barretto de Resende, in the Sloane Library of MSS. at the British Museum. They have been reproduced by the autotype process, with permission of the Trustees of the British Museum, to whom the thanks of the Hakluyt Society are due for this favour.

The interesting plan of Malaca fortress and settlement comes from the same MS. The map of the

[1] The phrase, "*e não me tome cada anno conta do que faço como a Almoxarife*", in Afonso Dalboquerque's letter, seems clearly to point to a certain necessity on the part of those who have had to govern India for occasional use of large sums of money for secret political objects. The history of Warren Hastings and Lord Clive in later centuries afford examples of the disasters attendant upon this necessity.

Malay peninsula has been reproduced in a reduced form with great care from a chart contained in a most valuable Portolano executed by the Portuguese hydrographer, Diego Homem, in 1558. This MS. is preserved among the additional MSS. in the British Museum. (*Add. MSS.*, 5415 A.) For the permission to trace these, I desire to record my thanks to Mr. E. M. Thompson, F.S.A., keeper of the manuscripts in the British Museum. The bird's-eye view of Malaca has been reduced by photo-lithography from the frequently cited *Lendas da India,* a work of very great value for collation with other historical narratives of the Early History of Portuguese India.

CHRONOLOGY OF PART III.

PAGE		A.D.
1.	Afonso Dalboquerque assaults Goa . .	25 Nov. 1510
1.	[Sails for the Straits	. Feb. 1511]
207.	[Dom Garcia de Noronha sails with six ships from Portugal .	25 March and 8 April 1511]
101.	Afonso Dalboquerque assaults Malaca on St. James's Day	[25 July 1511]
207.	[Builds the fortress of Malaca . .	August 1511]
164.	Antonio Dabreu sails to explore the Moluccas	During November [1511]
195.	[Afonso Dalboquerque, shipwrecked on the voyage from Malaca to India, reaches Cochim	During January 1512]
195.	[Dom Garcia de Noronha reaches Moçambique	Beginning of February 1512]
208.	[Jorge de Mello Pereira sails with twelve ships from Portugal	. 25 March 1512]
208.	[João Chanoca sails for Portugal . .	13 July 1512]
207.	Arrival of the Fleets of D. Garcia D. Noronha, and Jorge de Mello at Cochim . .	20 Aug. 1512
210.	Afonso Dalboquerque sails from Cochim for Goa	10 Sept. 1512

208. [The Fortress of Calicut built by the Portuguese During the Year 1512]

255. Dom Garcia de Noronha blockades Calicut During Jan. [1513]

256. But rejoins Afonso Dalboquerque at Goa 10 Feb. [1513]

172. Oration of Camillo Portio before Leo X During Oct. 1513

COMMENTARIES

OF THE

GREAT AFONSO DALBOQUERQUE.

COMMENTARIES

OF THE GREAT

AFONSO DALBOQUERQUE

WHO WAS

CAPTAIN-GENERAL OF THE EAST INDIES

IN THE TIME OF THE VERY POWERFUL

KING D. MANUEL,

THE FIRST OF THIS NAME.

PART III.

LISBON:
IN THE ROYAL PRINTING OFFICE,
ANNO MDCCLXXIV;
With Licence of the Royal Board of Censors, and Royal Privilege.

TITLES

OF THE

CHAPTERS CONTAINED IN THIS THIRD PART.

WHEREIN IS CONTAINED AN ACCOUNT OF WHAT THE GREAT AFONSO DALBOQUERQUE PERFORMED IN THE CONQUEST OF THE KINGDOM OF GOA FOR THE SECOND TIME, AND OF THE KINGDOM OF MALACA: AND ALL THE REST THAT HE DID UNTIL HIS DEPARTURE TO THE STRAITS.

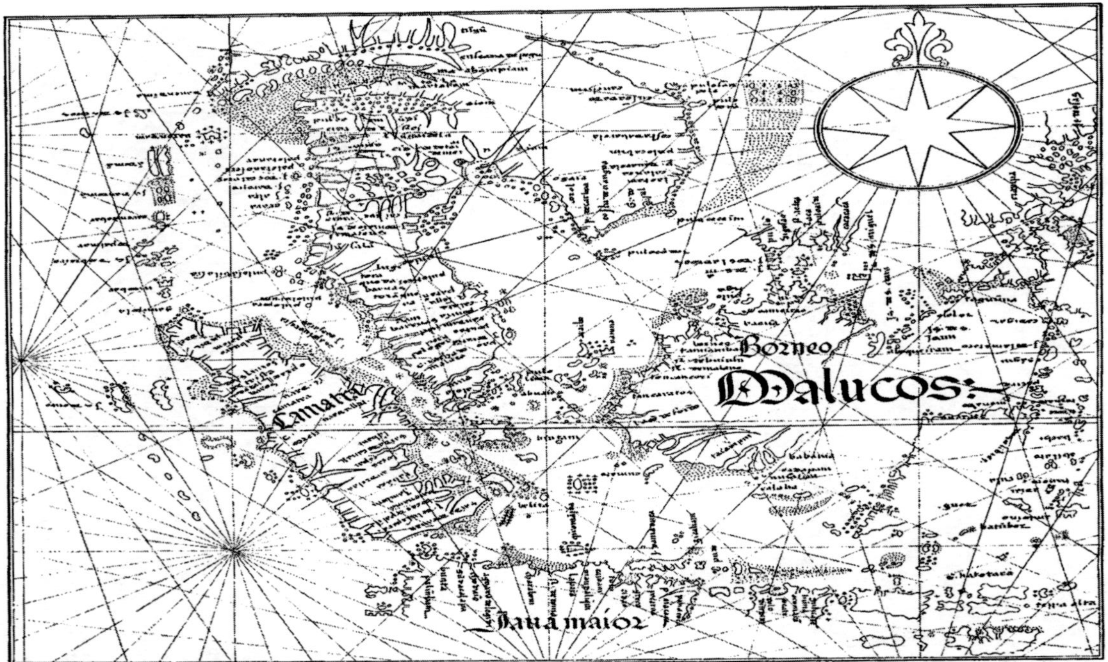

CHART OF THE MALAY PENINSULA, &c., FROM THE PORTOLANO OF DIEGO HOMEM, A.D. 1558.

(*British Museum, Additional MS.* 5415 A, folio 19.)

PART III.

WHEREIN IS CONTAINED AN ACCOUNT OF WHAT THE GREAT AFONSO DALBOQUERQUE PERFORMED IN THE CONQUEST OF THE KINGDOM OF GOA FOR THE SECOND TIME, AND OF THE KINGDOM OF MALACA: AND ALL THE REST THAT HE DID UNTIL HIS DEPARTURE TO THE STRAITS.

CHAPTER I.

How, after his fleet was ready, he set out for the harbour of Cananor: and what passed with the King of Garçopa and Timoja concerning the entry of the river of Goa.

When the interviews were concluded, which the great Afonso Dalboquerque held in Cochim with Gonçalo de Sequeira and the other captains, he set out towards Cananor, where he found ready the fleet and all the things which he required for his voyage. And without making any delay, he set sail with a fleet of twenty-three vessels, containing about two thousand Portuguese: and of them there were the Captains Manuel de Lacerda; Fernão Perez Dandrade; Simão Dandrade, his brother; Bastião de Miranda; Afonso Pessoa; Ruy de Brito Patalim; Diogo Fernandez de Béja; Jorge Nunez de Lião; Francisco Pereira Pestana; D. João de Lima; D. Jeronymo de Lima, his brother; Manuel da Cunha; Duarte de Melo; Pero Dafonseca; Gaspar de Paiva; Simão Martinez; Francisco Pantoja; Antonio de Matos; and Diogo Mendez de Vasconcelos, who was going to Malaca; Dinis Cerniche, Balthezar da Silva, and

Pero Coresma, who were to accompany [Diogo Mendez de Vasconcelos]. And so the whole fleet went along the coast and stood over against Onor to take in fresh supplies and water.[1]

As soon as the King of Garçopa and Timoja were informed of the arrival of Afonso Dalboquerque at the port, they went to talk with him, and after the customary greetings were over, he asked them what news they had of Goa

[1] It is useful to compare with this list that of Gaspar Correa, who gives the following names of captains accompanying Afonso Dalboquerque against Goa :—

*Joam de Lima.
Jeronymo de Lima, his brother.
Manuel de Lacerda.
Fernam Peres d'Andrade.
Simão d'Andrade, his brother.
Diogo Fernandes de Béja.
*Manuel da Cunha.
Duarte de Mello.
Francisco de Tavora.
Vasco Fernandes Coutinho.
*Garcia de Sousa.
Gaspar Cão.
Lopo Vaz de Sampayo.
Ayres da Silva.
Dinis Fernandes de Mello.
Joam Serrano.
Diogo Mendes de Vasconcellos.
Pero Coresma.
Baltesar da Silva.
Micer Vinete Cerniche [called Dinis Cerniche in the *Commentaries*].
Antonio Raposo.
*Simão Martins.
Gaspar de Paiva.
Francisco Pantoja.
*Bastiam de Miranda d'Azevedo.
Afonso Pessoa.
Jorge Martins de Lião [called Jorge Nunez de Lião in the *Commentaries*].

in twenty-eight ships, and 1,700 Portuguese. The names marked with asterisks are among those who gave an opinion at the council of war just before. Correa also mentions the following as being with Afonso Dalboquerque in the attack on Goa:—

Fernam Gomes de Lemos.
Nuno Vaz de Castello Branco.
*Jorge da Silveira.
Ruy de Brito.
Luis Coutinho, brother of Vasco Fernandez.
Simão d'Andrade, brother of Fernam Perez.
Gonzalo d'Almeida.
Simão Martins Henriquez.
Payo Rodriguez de Sousa.
Diogo Pirez de Miranda.
Duarte de Mello.
Alvaro Peçanha.
Luis Preto.
Pero Dafonsequa.
Antonio de Matos.
Antonio Diniz, and others.

Lord Stanley's *First Voyage of Magellan*, pp. xxiii, xxiv.

and of the Hidalcão? They told him that there were in Goa three captains, who had about four thousand men in the garrison, all Turks, Rumes, and Coraçones,[1] with certain peons of Balagate, who were archers; and there were about an equal number of native Moors. And they declared that, if he had come with the intention of attacking the city, it was just at the very nick of time, for the Hidalcão was prosecuting a war with the Guazils of the Kingdom of Decan, who had wrested from him a great part of his lands, and he was now so far advanced into the interior of the country, that it was impossible for him to return and relieve Goa. They said, too, that they were ready with all their people, as they had already notified to him, to serve him by land in that expedition.

Afonso Dalboquerque received the promises they made, and thanked them heartily for them. But, although it seemed to him to be a doubtful thing to attack Goa, held as it was by so many forces and now become so much on the alert, as these persons had declared to him, nevertheless he made up his mind to blockade it with all his forces, and to attack the enemy; and with this determination he set sail with the whole of his fleet, and bore up for Anjadiva, where he remained for eleven days without forming any resolutions of future proceedings. For when he arrived there, he was advised not to place any reliance upon the promised offers of the King of Garçopa and of Timoja, because they were in fear lest things should not turn out well for them, and they did not wish to be in worse relations to the Hidalcão than they were already. And thus the great Afonso Dalboquerque, perplexed by all these doubts which were conveyed to him, set out from Anjadiva, and proceeded to cast anchor over against the bar of Goa, and ordered Manuel da Cunha, with six ships, to enter through Old Goa, and make his way to Agacij, and to the land of Saste, to co-operate with the army

[1] Inhabitants of the Khorassan.

of Timoja, who would have to approach by that direction. And Manuel da Cunha, as soon as he reached the pass of Benastarim and of Agacij, fired a gun and remained quietly in the river waiting for the army to arrive.

No sooner had Manuel da Cunha set forth, than Afonso Dalboquerque summoned the captains to his ship, and told them they were well aware of the promises made to them by the King of Garçopa and Timoja, but that he himself, from what he had heard in Anjadiva, and also because they had delayed in their journey, very much doubted if these people meant to keep their word. He therefore begged them to decide whether he should undertake this matter without counting very much on the support of the native army which had been offered, or whether they should first go to Cambaya and there settle the terms of peace. The captains listened to the arguments of Afonso Dalboquerque, and were all unanimously of opinion that he ought to attack Goa; for if that city were once taken, the King of Cambaya would consent, they said, to carry out all the conditions they might require of him; and what was more, he would not delay releasing the captives whom he had in his power. This advice appeared good to Afonso Dalboquerque, who sent immediately a message to Manuel da Cunha to return and rejoin the fleet. And, as soon as he arrived, all weighed anchor, and stood in up the river and reached a pass about as far from the city as a falconet would carry a shot, where the Turks had sunk three Malabar ships laden with stones, in order to impede any further passage of our vessels up the river. But this artifice, which the Turks thought to avail themselves of, turned out exactly the opposite of what they intended; for, instead of blocking the river, the force of the water that ran down was so great, that it opened two channels much deeper than the one which they had blocked up.

When Afonso Dalboquerque arrived at this spot, he

ordered the small vessels to go up through these new channels which the river had made, and told the captains to strain every nerve to reach the fortress as quickly as they could; and, as it was now late, there was not time for great vessels to make the passage. But, as soon as morning broke, Afonso Dalboquerque got into a boat, and proceeded to the station where the small vessels were at anchor, with all the rest of the fleet which followed him, and there he settled himself, and sent Duarte de Lemos, Gaspar de Paiva, and Diogo Fernandez de Béja, to man their skiffs and reconnoitre the condition of the fortress. These three got up in front of it, and examined it very closely, and reported to Afonso Dalboquerque that it was very strong, fortified with many trenches and bulwarks, and embrasures flush with the water,[1] with much artillery therein, and a very large ditch. So Afonso Dalboquerque, on receipt of this intelligence which the captains reported, and on consideration of the number of the forces within the city, came to the conclusion that it was a very perilous undertaking to attack it; yet, nevertheless, confiding in God to help him, he sent on in advance Bastião de Miranda, Afonso Pessoa, and Ruy de Brito Patalim, to make their way with their galleys to the other side of the fortress; and as they were perceived they were plied with the artillery contained in it, but our Lord protected them, so that they sustained no injury. And, although all these things rendered the business of attacking the city more hazardous, yet, in order to be more completely informed on all points, he ordered Diogo Fernandez de Béja to seize by night upon some native interpreter; and by means of a Moor who was thus taken, he learned that the Turks had a great quantity of artillery both large and small, and many foot soldiers and cavalry, and many stores; and that Moors, the natives of the land, had promised the Hidalcão that they would all die in defending the city from the

[1] *Ao lume da agua*, "between wind and water".

entry of the Portuguese; and that the Turks, in addition to this promise which they had made, out of fear that if any troubles came upon them the Moors would rise up against them, had given orders that all the women and children of the principal persons of the land should be placed in the fortress.

CHAPTER II.

Of the council which the great Afonso Dalboquerque held with the captains concerning the attacking of the city, and the remainder of the events connected therewith.

For three days after the great Afonso Dalboquerque had acquired this information concerning the ready state of the city he remained without coming to any determination whether he should wait or not for the King of Garçopa and Timoja, from whom the only help he expected was that they would come and stir up the Hindoos against the Moors, and prevent their furnishing the latter with supplies or paying the duties for the land which they were bound to pay. And at this juncture, while he was thus delaying himself, without making up his mind what to do, the Turks made some very strong stockades of timber, filled in with earth, with their ditches full of water, along the banks, and in these they stationed many pieces of large artillery, and appointed a captain with his men to defend them.

But when Afonso Dalboquerque perceived that the Turks, out of the excessive confidence they had in their fortress, were constructing stockades outside to ward off the attack upon their ships, and prevent their being burned, and were quite certain of the safety of everything else, he summoned the captains and all the *Fidalgos* and cavaliers of the fleet, and laid before them the opinion he had of these doings of the Turks, and desired it to be debated whether they should first of all attack the stockades, or set themselves forthwith in battle array and storm the fortress. And when this had been discussed, at length every one agreed that the fortress should be attacked before the stockades; because, although it might be the stronger, it was there that they all desired to accomplish the wishes they had of taking vengeance of what had already befallen them. For after they had once taken the fortress, there was nothing more for them to do.

But Afonso Dalboquerque and Diogo Mendez de Vasconcelos were not with them in this way of thinking, but rather considered that they should first destroy the stockades, and when these were overcome, they would get in [to the fortress] with the enemy pell-mell; and that this ought to be put into practice immediately, because all the rest of the time they spent there without doing anything was but weakening more and more their chances of succeeding in this matter; and in this opinion of Afonso Dalboquerque everyone concurred, but they agreed to wait three days longer for the King of Garçopa. For Afonso Dalboquerque told them that as they were clearly minded to attack the city, they had no time now to look for any other help beyond that of our Lord Jesus Christ, which would not fail them, seeing that they fought for his Holy Faith, which he for his part truly believed in; and that the detention of the King of Garçopa and Timoja had all been brought about by the Turks by the great force of bribes which they had given them not to come; and that Timoja was so artful that he was sure to keep up his dissembling and not arrive until after the fall of the city, for he saw very well that it was like to cost much blood in the taking; and therefore they ought not to lose time in waiting for his support.

And with this settlement of the matter he dismissed the captains to their ships to make ready for the next day, in the morning, when all were to proceed to attack the stockades, and when they were once captured, the circumstances of the victory would point out how they should proceed. So he divided all his forces into three companies in order of battle; that is to say, Manuel da Cunha, Manuel de Lacerda, D. João de Lima, D. Jeronymo de Lima, his brother, Gaspar Paiva, Gaspar Cão, Fernão Feyo, Pero Dafonseca, and many others, into one company, which was to go and attack the stockades near the fortress. And in the second company he set Diogo Mendez de Vasconcelos, Baltezar da Silva, Dinis Cerniche, Pero Coresma, who carried with him his son Jorge Coresma (who is now superintendent of the royal ovens), who, though he was but a child, gave a very good account of himself that day; and Ruy de Brito Patalim, and Jorge Nunez de Lião, with many other soldiers, to attack the stockades on the sides near the ships; while he himself, with the remainder of the forces and captains, would go and take the stockades in flank by a road which led from Mandovij by a branch upwards which he knew of, for if he went there he would be placed between the Moors and the city, and if he took their stockades in flank they could not fail to make great havoc among them.

And because there were in that road, which Afonso Dalboquerque determined to explore, certain palisadings of very strong timber, in order not to be delayed by anything when he should get there, he ordered Dinis Fernandez, the master of his ship, to go in advance in charge of thirty mariners to cut them down, and he was not to allow anyone to set fire to the ships which were on the beach, unless they were entirely discomfited in the endeavour to take the city. But, whereas the captains still adhered to their opinion, they returned again forthwith by night to talk with Afonso Dalboquerque, and laid before him many reasons why he should attack the fortress before the stockades; and he on his part unfolded to them many others, to show where he disagreed from their conclusions. And there arose so many discussions on one side and the other about this, that Afonso Dalboquerque, in spite of his own opinion, and in order to content them, desisted from what he had arranged to do, and allowed himself to be convinced by their arguments. And when the Turks perceived this delay, for it was now seven days that our men had been there without doing anything, they began to grow audacious, and built some stockades still closer to our fleet, wherein they placed six large bombards, and began to fire them against us.

Afonso Dalboquerque was annoyed at the little account the Turks made of him, and with grave and opportune consideration, he sent word to the captains to make themselves ready, and on the following day, in the morning, to come on board his ship, for his intention was, in spite of all the discussions that had been held, to attack the stockades and fight the Turks, for he could not brook their vain-glorying; and each one was to fight in the place which had been marked out for him.

CHAPTER III.

How the great Afonso Dalboquerque attacked the city of Goa, and took it by force of arms, when some of our side were killed; and of the great havoc that was made of the Moors.

And now that the great Afonso Dalboquerque had made all arrangements to attack the city, as I have said, on the following day, before morning broke, which was the day of St. Catharine,[1] the 25th day of the month of November,

[1] "Na luz, que sempre celebrada, e dina
Será de Egyptia Sancta Catharina."

CAM., *Lus.*, x, 43.

See Vol. I, Introd., p. i, for the context and Fanshaw's quaint translation.

of one thousand five hundred and ten, the captains, who were already prepared, arrived with all their men, and boarded the flag-ship; and they found Afonso Dalboquerque already gone on board his skiff, and a *parão* with a hundred and fifty soldiers waiting for them. And after a general confession had been made by all of them, they arranged themselves in three companies of attack, according to the instructions already promulgated, and proceeded against the city, for the day had now fully dawned; and, on their arrival, without any further consultation, they went on to attack the stockades, each company taking up the position that had been marked out for it.

The Turks, who were stationed therein, defended themselves for a long time, and prevented any entry of the enemy, and Afonso Dalboquerque, with the men he had in his company, on arriving at the palisades which Dinis Fernandez had already cut down, went up along the edge of the ridge at the double. The Turks, because they did not fear any attack from that side, as soon as they felt themselves harassed by people at their back, after making a long resistance, began to retire from the stockades. The captains, when they perceived that the enemy were beginning to become embarrassed with the arrival of Afonso Dalboquerque, fell upon them so valiantly, carrying in their van the Apostle Sanctiago [Saint James the greater], who was going with them as their guide, that in a short space of time they got into the stockades, and with the enemy in flight made their way pell-mell as far as the gates of the city, without looking behind them, killing and maiming many Turks and Rumes, all of them of superior class, and many well attired in silken habits and brocades.

Manuel da Cunha, Manuel de Lacerda, Dom João de Lima, D. Jeronymo de Lima, his brother, and others in their company, which were in advance, on arriving at the gate, experienced great resistance from the Turks; but, nevertheless, animated by the victory which our Lord pointed out to them, they entered into the city by force of arms, and behind them entered Dinis Fernandez, who had come up by this time with the men whom he had taken to cut down the palisades. And so all these being united together kept on pursuing the Moors as far as the gate of the fortress, and then they fought a great battle with them; so well fought indeed was it on one side and the other, that for a long space of time each side thought that it had gained the victory. The Turks, however, who were stationed within the fortress, came up at once on horse to succour their men, and so put our men to rout. But just at this moment there arrived Diogo Mendez and Jorge Nunes de Lião, with all the *Fidalgos* and men they had in their company, and found a great number of our men already wounded and put to great straits; but on their arrival, the new comers shouted out to them to fall again upon the Turks, and they would follow them up.

With this fresh relief our men fell upon the Moors on foot and on horseback, and one and all closed so desperately with them, that they routed them, and all together entered pell-mell through the gates of the fortress; some of our party being left behind already dead or wounded. Manuel de Lacerda, who was marching along wounded in his face by an arrow, just as he entered by the gate encountered a Turk upon a horse, and killed him, and mounted the horse, and performed a great feat in continuing to go on, for he had a piece of broken arrow fixed in his face, and all his armour was smirched in the blood which ran down from it. At this time Afonso Dalboquerque was making his way with his company at the back of our men, going at a quick march, in order to give succour whenever he should perceive they had need of it. But the Turks, when they became aware that they had been invaded by our men, who were following them up, collected together to the number of five hundred, including a hundred mounted men with their own captain, and rallied and turned back, and fought with such vigour, that our soldiers tried hard for a long time without being able to make them yield.

When Afonso Dalboquerque was informed of the peril our men were in, he bore down to this spot at full speed, with all the soldiers in his company, to reinforce them, and on coming up to them, some among their company made such fierce havoc among the Turks with their lances, that they routed them, and killed many; among them being two chief captains out of three whom the Hidalcão had there. As soon as Manuel de Lacerda beheld Afonso Dalboquerque, he dismounted his charger and presented it to him. And when Afonso Dalboquerque saw him with his armour all smirched with blood, he embraced him, and said:—"Sir Manuel de Lacerda, I declare to you that I am greatly envious of you, and so would Alexander the Great have been, had he been here, for you look more gallant for an evening's rendezvous than Arelhano".[1] And when Afonso Dalboquerque mounted on the horse, all the captains took horses which the Turks had abandoned, and followed up after the enemy, and these, without making any further resistance, turned their backs and fled out of the gate of the fortress. And many others there, just wherever they chanced to be, threw themselves down from the walls, in order to shorten their journey.

As soon as the fortress had been abandoned, Afonso Dalboquerque gave orders that the gates should be shut that led to the city, and a good watch kept over them, in order that our men should not follow the Moors, nor disband themselves to plunder. For he feared that as the enemy were very numerous, they would unite together, and bring

[1] The Emperor Aurelian, whose reign presents a succession of brilliant exploits which restored for a time their ancient lustre to the arms of Rome. In a war against the Sarmatians he was believed to have slain forty-eight of the enemy in one day.

about another catastrophe like that which befel the Portuguese at Calicut.[1] So he gave orders to all the captains to take up positions in the walls of the fortress; for he had made up his mind to fortify himself in it. The Turks indeed were so dismayed, that those who managed to escape from the fury of our soldiers made their way in flight over towards Benastarim, with the object of passing over from that place to the opposite side of the mainland. And they went on so excited by fear, that without waiting for any vessel of transport they swam across the river, and thereby many of them were drowned and many horses were lost.

The city had now been entered, and when Afonso Dalboquerque perceived that the fortress was strongly fortified with artillery, and the embrasures covered with clay outside, in order to deceive our people if they attacked them, he offered up many thanks to our Lord for thus delivering them from the dangers which had been prepared against them, had they operated against the fortress, as the captains had thought they ought to have done. Out of our party, one hundred and fifty soldiers were wounded; and of the *Fidalgos* and captains, Manuel de Lacerda, who was the first who went in at the gate and the first who received any wounds (for thus I found it written), and Gaspar de Paiva, Manuel da Cunha, D. João de Lima, Gaspar Cão, Simão Dandrade, Dinis Fernandez, and all the rest who were in the advance guard. And seven were killed, of whom one was D. Jeronymo de Lima, who was mortally wounded at the entry of the gate of the fortress. And while he lay on the ground so severely struck that he could not survive, his brother, D. João de Lima, who was wheeling round with others, came upon him; and when he beheld him in such a condition, with his head leaning against the wall, he exclaimed, with many tears :—"What is this, brother? how art thou?" D. Jeronymo replied :—"I am on the point of

[1] See vol. II, p. xix.

finishing this journey; and I am glad, as it has pleased our Lord to require this service of me, that it has been completed here in his service and in that of the King of Portugal."

D. João de Lima desired to remain in company with him; but he said:—"Brother, there is no time for you to remain with me; go and perform what is required of you, I will remain here and finish my days, for I have no longer any strength left." So D. João de Lima left him, and went on, following after the Moors; and when the fortress had been captured and the Moors driven out, he returned to seek after his brother, and found him already dead. I should be very glad to have been either one of these two brothers; but I know not how to decide which one of the two I most envy,—whether D. João de Lima, because he went to fight where such another one as himself could be met with, or D. Jeronymo de Lima, who did not desire to remedy his wounds, although they were mortal (it being a very natural thing for men to desire to live), but rather sought to advance his brother's honour, and would not consent to his remaining behind with him at a time when the other *Fidalgos* and cavaliers were carrying on the fight with the Turks within the fortress. The decision of this I leave to those who read the lessons of this history; let them judge whether of these two brothers best performed his obligations.

They killed also André de Afonseca, Antonio Graces, and Alvaro Gomes, son of the *almoxarife*[1] of Alenquer, and others, whose names are not known. But they who died and they who remained alive so performed their task, not only in the attack on the city, but in all the other conflicts in which they found themselves this day engaged with the enemy, that it is worthy that they should be held in great remembrance; for, in thus gaining Goa, the possession of India became secured [to Portugal].

[1] *Almoxarife*, a receiver of customs or dues for commodities imported or exported. Arabic, *Al mochrif*, an inspector.—Engelmann.

Nor should anyone forget Diogo Mendez de Vasconcelos and those of his company, for the alacrity and powerful efforts with which he relieved our soldiers, when a great number of them had already been wounded, contributed in a great measure towards the capture of the fortress. And, indeed, Afonso Dalboquerque was so very well aware of the powerful efforts and discretion of Diogo Mendez, that he often declared to him, when they were at variance respecting his voyage to Malaca :—"I abhor the life that I lead, Sir Diogo Mendez, for my tenure of the supreme office here has done you harm." Thus it was that if our soldiers, after the first capture of this city, were considered to have been ill-advised to evacuate it, in this second capture they recovered their *prestige* in returning to take it by force of arms, putting to death, besides many other natives of the city, two thousand men, whites, Turks, Rumes, and Coraçones, which produced, indeed, a terrible dread throughout all the land, on account of the great confidence that had hitherto been reposed in their invincibility.

CHAPTER IV.

How the great Afonso Dalboquerque gave the soldiers permission to sack the city: and, of the crucifix which was found in some old walls from which stone was taken for the fortress: and of the miracle which Our Lord performed for our side on the day of the battle.

Directly it was reported in Cochim that the great Afonso Dalboquerque had taken Goa, the captains who were there loading their ships to set out for Portugal, calling to mind how he had told them that before their departure they should have news of the taking of Goa, became very sad and full of shame, when they knew of it, because they had not been with him in that enterprise.

After having commanded the captains to take up their

positions and guard the fortress, Afonso Dalboquerque gave permission to the soldiers to sack the city, and free right to keep everything they took; but as for his own share, he cared for nothing more than the contentment derived for having been enabled to keep his word, which he had given to the Hidalcão when he was in Goa, as has already been related.

In the city were captured a hundred large guns *(bombardas)* and a large quantity of smaller artillery, and two hundred horses, and many supplies and munitions of war. All these were ordered to be delivered to the factor for the king. And after the city had been pillaged, Afonso Dalboquerque told the captains to reconnoitre the whole of the island and to put to the sword all the Moors, men, women, and children, that should be found, and to give no quarter to any one of them; for his determination was to leave no seed of this race throughout the whole of the island. And he did this, not only because it was necessary for the security of the land that there should be none but Hindoos within it, but also as a punishment for the treachery of which the Moors had been guilty when he took the city for the first time. And for four days continuously they poured out the blood of the Moors who were found therein; and it was ascertained that of men, women, and children, the number exceeded six thousand.

The Hindoos, also, for their part, by reason of the hatred in which they held the Turks, because they had been deprived there of the lands whereon they lived, as soon as they heard the news of the fall of Goa (the principal men, with their dependents, having fled up into the mountain country), descended, and cut off the Moors' retreat through the passes, as they were flying from the fury of the Portuguese. And when they had taken from them all they carried, they put them all to the sword, without saving any lives. Now, in the company of these Turks they killed one who was the treasurer and paymaster of the Hidalcão's forces; and from him they took all the money he had. And Afonso Dalboquerque ordered that a certain mosque should be filled with some Moors whom the Hindoos had taken prisoners, and then set on fire, and in this body of people was a renegade Christian who deserted to the Hidalcão when Goa was taken for the first time.

As soon as the despoiling of the land had been accomplished, Afonso Dalboquerque turned his attention without delay to the fortifications of the city, and ordered that a great quantity of cement should be prepared, and all the sepulchres of the Moors thrown down, in order to obtain plenty of stone for the works, and to all the captains and *fidalgos* he appointed a regular turn of duty, and so made great haste to complete the work; for he was fearful of the arrival of the Hidalcão, and would not that he should find him in an unprepared state. And, as he hoped to establish in Goa the principal seat of the Governors of India, he so arranged the plan, that the palace of the Çabaio remained within the boundary, because the edifices of it were very nobly designed, a work of great beauty and finely built. And by reason of this great diligence, in a very short time he completed the fortress where it now stands, with its towers and ditches, with their breastworks, for the defence of the harbour and anchorage of the ships.

At this time some men were progressing with the destruction of some old walls, in order to get stones for the works of defence, when they discovered in the foundations[1] an image of the crucifix in copper. When the news of this ran through the city, Afonso Dalboquerque came down at once with all the people and clergy who were with him, and they carried the crucifix, with great devotion and many tears, to the church. Great wonder was there that then

[1] *Alicerces;* also found as *alicesse* and *alicece*, from the Arabic *al-aças*, the cement of a building.

seized upon all beholders; for within the memory of man there was no record of any Christians ever having been at that place, and they believed that our Lord had sent down that sign from Heaven, in order to shew that it was his will that the kingdom should belong to the King of Portugal and not to the Hidalcão, and that their mosques should become houses of prayer,[1] wherein his name should be worshipped. For whereas the city was very strongly garrisoned and provided with artillery and arms, and all other things necessary for its defence, our people had not been sufficient —being so few in number—to take it, had there not been within it this signal of the Cross whereon our Lord suffered, which called upon them as it were, and gave them the power to attack the city; had it not been also for the Apostle Sanctiago, who helped them, whereof the very Moors bore good testimony, to the effect that after the fall of the city they inquired of our men what manner of man was that captain with shining armour and a red cross, who marched with the Christians, striking and killing the Moors, for it was he alone that had taken their city from them.

And Afonso Dalboquerque, not only from the great devotion which he had for this saint, but because he was a knight of the order of the saint, did not forget this favour which he had received from him; and he sent to the convent of Palmela[2] a staff of the length of six palms and of the thickness of a lance,[3] all overlaid with gold, with inlaid work,[4] and the hand of the staff covered with pearls and

[1] Isaiah lvi, 7; Math. xxi, 13; Mark xi, 17; Luke xix, 46.

[2] Palmela, a town in Portugal, south of Lisbon, 38 deg. 34 min. N.; 8 deg. 57 min. W. Bluteau gives an interesting account of its history. The convent is the head of the Military Order of Santiago, and is kept by Brethren of the Rule of St. Augustine.

[3] *Arremeção.*

[4] *Lavrado de Tauxia; Tauxía* or *atuxía*, damaskeening or inlaying of one metal upon another; from the Arabic *at-tauchiya*, to colour, to render

rubies, and a penitential scourge of very large beads of gold, and a shell[1] of gold of good size, with many precious stones in it, placed upon a hat of crimson satin; and at his death he bequeathed to the Apostle Sanctiago of Galiza[2] a very large lampstand of silver, and a hundred thousand *reis*[3] in cash for oil.

When this news of the taking of Goa reached Cambaya, and it became known that Afonso Dalboquerque was fortifying himself therein, with intent to maintain his position, the king perceived that his own league was destroyed, and therefore ordered the liberation of the prisoners whom he had captured when D. Afonso Noronha, the nephew of Afonso Dalboquerque, had been taken prisoner, and also offered to give up Diu for the site of a Portuguese fortress; and from that time forward the king continually sent ambassadors to treat for peace. And Mirocem,[4] captain of the fleet of the Grand Sultan, who was in Cambaya (with some of the forces that had escaped from the rout inflicted upon them by the Viceroy[5]), where he was awaiting the relief for which he had sent to Cairo, in order to refit his forces at Goa, no sooner learned that Goa was taken (and that, too, with great havoc among the Turks), than he gave up all hopes of bringing his mission to a fortunate termination, and obtained permission from the King of Cambaya to go to Judá,[6] where he remained for some days, and from that port set out for Suez by sea in a shallop,[7] where he found

beautiful; in Portuguese the word has the more limited meaning given above.

1 *Vieira*. This word gives the name to a large number of Portuguese families. Among others who have borne it, is the author of the well-known Portuguese Grammar and Portuguese-English Dictionaries.

2 Gallicia.

3 About £20 16s. 8d. of English money,—a large sum in those days.

4 See vol. i, p. 222; vol. ii, p. 112.

5 At Diu. See vol. ii, pp. 112, 113, note.—*Lusiada*, x, 34-36.

6 Djeddah. See vol. i, p. 234.

7 *Gelua*. See *jelua*, vol. i, p. 226, note.

the fleet in progress of preparation. And when Mirocem thus arrived at Cairo to impart this news of the taking of Goa to the Sultan, orders were given to stop the building of the fleet, and no more trouble was taken about it. The ambassador of the King of Cambaya was thereupon despatched with orders to report that on the completion of the fortress, Afonso Dalboquerque would come and visit the king and arrange the terms of peace. And because Afonso Dalboquerque was desirous of sounding the wishes of the Hidalcão relative to an alliance, he wrote the following letter to him, with certain grandiloquent ideas[1] involved in it; for, as long as he governed India, he always availed himself, first of one thing, then of another, in his intercourse with the kings.

Letter which the great Afonso Dalboquerque wrote to the Hidalcao as soon as Goa had been taken.

"Very honourable and good Cavalier Milohau! the great Afonso Dalboquerque, Captain-General of India and of the Kingdom and Lordship of Ormuz and of the Kingdom and Lordship of Goa, for the very high and very powerful D. Manuel, King of Portugal and of the Algarves, on this side and on that of the sea, in Africa Lord of Guiné, and of the Conquest, Navigation, and Commerce of Ethiopia, Arabia, Persia, and of India, I send you my greeting. You must well know how the Çabayo, your father, used to take the ships of Malabar out of the ports and harbours of the King my Lord; wherefore it was that I was constrained to go against Goa, and take the city, and there it is that I am occupied in building a very strong fortress. I wish most sincerely that your father had been living, that he might know me to be a man of my word: out of regard for him, I shall be ever your friend, and I will assist you

[1] *Rebolarias*, an uncommon word, probably derived from *rebolar*, to roll about.

against the King of Decan, and against your enemies; and I will cause all the horses[1] that arrive here to be carried to your stations and your marts, in order that you may have possession of them. Fain would I that the Merchants of your land would come with white stuffs and all manner of merchandize to this port, and take to yours in exchange merchandize of the sea and of the land, and horses, and I will give them a safe conduct. If you wish for my friendship, let your messengers come to me with your communications, and I will send you others on my part, who shall convey to you my communications: if you will perform this which I write unto you, by my aid shall you be able to gain possession of much land, and become a great Lord among the Moors. Be desirous of performing this, for thus it shall be well with you, and you shall have great power; and for all that the Çabayo, your father, be dead, I will be your father, and bring you up like a son. Let your messenger bring back immediately to me a reply, and let the merchants of the land come under safe-conduct to Goa; and as for the Merchants who bring merchandize and come under your letters of safe conduct, signed by your hand, I will be responsible for their safety."

CHAPTER V.

How the Nequibares sent to request a safe conduct from Afonso Dalboquerque, in order that they might come and live at Goa; and how our forces put to rout Meliqueaye, the captain of the Hidalcão.

When the Nequibares, who were stationed on the mainland, perceived that the great Afonso Dalboquerque was establishing himself firmly in Goa, they sent to desire a safe

[1] The horse trade was a great source of employment and revenue on the Indian coast.—See vol. ii, pp. 76, 77, 107, 111; see also Col. Yule, *Marco Polo*, vol. i, pp. 84, 88, 324, 333, etc., and Index; 2nd edition.

conduct from him in order that they might come over with all their people and live in the city. These Nequibares were the principal men and captains of the people. Now, whereas Afonso Dalboquerque was anxious of gathering together into the city all the native Hindoos of the land, he was very glad of the offers of these Nequibares, for he was in hopes that they would help him in the construction of the fortress, so he sent them the safe conduct which they had desired him to give; and when they arrived in Goa he gave them houses and possessions according to each one's station of life on the mainland. And after he had sent messengers to this effect to the Nequibares, news reached him that Meliqueaye,[1] captain of the Hidalcão, had arrived with a large body of men at Condal, and at Bandá, with the intention of forcing an entrance into the island of Goa. And although Afonso Dalboquerque was fully occupied in the work upon the fortress, because he felt so strongly the necessity of finishing it as quickly as he could, nevertheless he could not endure that a captain of the Hidalcão should come and besiege the lands of Goa while he was in the island; he therefore lost no time in despatching Diogo Fernandez de Béja to sail into the River of Bandá, and dispute the passage with Meliqueaye in the lands of Antuge and Saste. And with him he sent also, as captains of the vessels, Aires Pereira, Antonio Dabreu, Gaspar Cão, and Antonio de Matos, with two hundred men.

Diogo Fernandez, as soon as he was ready, set out with his people, and reached Bandá, and went up the river, and without any further consideration disembarked immediately. When Meliqueaye perceived that our men had disembarked, he proceeded to attack them, relying upon the numerous bodies of Turks who were under his command, and Diogo Fernandez waited for them with great bravery, and plied

[1] The first part of this name is *Melek*, Lord. See vol. ii, pp. 85, 86, for names similarly formed.

the enemy so fiercely with lances, that the Turks, disconcerted by the determined resistance with which our people awaited them on foot, took to their horses and retreated in so disorderly a manner, that many threw themselves down over the ravines and there ended their days.

With this victory, Diogo Fernandez returned to Goa, and related to Afonso Dalboquerque all that had taken place, and declared how Meliqueaye was making his way in the direction of Divarij, in order to cross over into the island [of Goa] in that direction. With this news of the intentions of Meliqueaye, which Diogo Fernandez brought him, Afonso Dalboquerque forthwith dispatched Gaspar de Pavia to proceed to guard that pass, and in company with him there went Afonso Pessoa, Martim Guedez, Vasco Fernandez Coutinho, and many others. Meliqueaye, finding himself discomfited by the inability of his people, withdrew with the shattered remains of his forces, and made his way to essay the entrance to the island by the pass of Divarij. But, on arriving there, although he went carelessly, with the idea that he would not find anyone there to resist him, inasmuch as he was by nature very proud, nevertheless he made up his mind to lay siege to the stockades which Gaspar de Paiva had by that time constructed, and drew up his forces, both infantry and cavalry, in battle array, with himself in the front rank, and made his way to attack them.

But Gaspar de Paiva, who had already received notice of the approach of Meliqueaye, awaited the attack with great readiness, and at the first encounter his matchlockmen slew some of the mounted Turks; and these, according to their custom, used to ride fastened into their saddles with straps, so that the horses, having no longer any riders to govern them, ran among their own people and threw them into disorder. As soon as Gaspar de Paiva observed that the Turks were thrown into confusion, he sallied out of his trenches and lost no time in falling upon the enemy, and routed them, and followed up after them for a good space. Vasco Fernandez Coutinho, although at that time he was but a lad of eighteen years of age, encountered a Turk on a horse, and taking him by the reins, raised up his caparison and stabbed him with a sword; and when the horse fell down dead, he fell upon the Turk, and cut off his head, and thus at that day of the fight shewed himself to be a son worthy of his sire, a descendant worthy of his ancestors.

When the affair was thus terminated, Gaspar de Paiva withdrew to his stockade, and Meliqueaye, finding himself sorely pressed by our men on both sides, no longer ventured to attack them, but withdrew with his men two leagues away into the interior country, to a place which is called Diocalij, and there he pitched his camp, making some very strong stockades of wood for its defence, in case he should be attacked there. As soon as Afonso Dalboquerque perceived that Meliqueaye was thus put to rout and it was probable, in case of his being attacked at once, that this chief might easily fall into his hands, he proceeded himself to seek for him, in the place where the camp was pitched, with one thousand Portuguese, and two thousand natives commanded by their own captains, and passed over to the mainland in the galleys and boats. And as soon as the force had disembarked, Afonso Dalboquerque divided it into four battalions, and stationed them in certain passes, about the distance from the edge of the sea of a shot from a matchlock, and there he arranged an ambush, and ordered the captains of the Hindoos to take their soldiers and run to the enemy's camp, and in case any Turks should issue out after them, they were to retreat in the direction of the place where he had placed the ambush.

The captains of the Hindoos, as soon as they came in sight of the camp, found Meliqueaye outside the stockades, drawn up on a lofty hill with his army, like a man who was well aware of the trap laid for him by Afonso Dalboquerque.

But as he was a good captain, and well versed in the art of war, he remained perfectly quiet, and would not attack the Hindoos. So when the captains observed that Meliqueaye did not care to meddle with them, they withdrew to the place where Afonso Dalboquerque was waiting (for he had given them the order to do so in this case), and related to him the position of the affair as they had found it. And Afonso Dalboquerque, perceiving thus that Meliqueaye had become aware of his plan, proceeded to the Island of Divarij, and therein he left Rodrigo Rabelo and Manuel de Lacerda, with soldiers, and then he went on to the city.

After the lapse of a few days, Meliqueaye, who found himself not sufficiently strong to be able to resist our people if they were to desire to invade him, sent a messenger to Afonso Dalboquerque desiring peace with him. But Afonso Dalboquerque demanded of the messenger whether Meliqueaye held a permission from the Hidalcão to enter into negotiations for peace or not. The messenger replied that the only message he carried was from Meliqueaye, who was a captain of the Hidalcão, and could not enter into peace without the permission of the Hidalcão. Afonso Dalboquerque therefore dispatched the messenger back without any reply, for it appeared to him when he reflected upon the disorganised proceedings of Meliqueaye, that his stay there could not be in accordance with the wishes of the Hidalcão.

CHAPTER VI.

How Merlao came to Goa, and the Nequibares desired Afonso Dalboquerque to give him to them for their governor, and what took place thereupon; and how he ordered Diogo Fernandez de Béja to destroy the fortress of Çacotorá.

For some days past, a messenger from the King of Onor had been staying in Goa, seeking to conclude an alliance with the great Afonso Dalboquerque; for this king had usurped the kingdom and ejected from it Merlao, to whom it belonged by right of being the elder brother; and therefore the king was very much in fear that Afonso Dalboquerque would favour Merlao in opposition to him, in consequence of the undertaking which he had given to the Portuguese to help them in their first enterprise against Goa. As soon as Merlao (who at this period was in Baticalá with the king, his uncle, in possession of soldiers on foot and horse, with the intention of setting out to recover his kingdom if he could) became aware that his brother was negotiating with Afonso Dalboquerque, in order to benefit himself by such an alliance, he sent a messenger with letters informing Afonso Dalboquerque of the position in which the matter stood, and telling him how his brother had risen up against him, and deprived him of the kingdom by force, begging Afonso Dalboquerque to help him with his alliance, and stipulating that he would serve the King of Portugal in all that might be commanded of him. And Afonso Dalboquerque accepted his offers, not only because his fame was great as a brave cavalier, but also because he was a captain whom the Hindoos held in great esteem. And this he did with the intention of conferring upon him the government of the lands of Goa; for he had been brought up there, and had always made war upon the Turks, and on two occasions, when he had been besieged by them, with his Hindoos alone he had defended the city like a very valiant cavalier; and with this determination, because it seemed to him to be very conducive to the service of the King Dom Manuel to re-establish Merlao and shew him favours, Afonso Dalboquerque sent to Baticalá the galleys for him, with some vessels for the transport of his men and horses. And he also sent two Portuguese captains, with two thousand Hindoo soldiers, to go by land and receive him at Cintácora, carrying letters to the Tanadares[1] and people of the lands of Goa, ordering them to receive him and obey him as they would Afonso Dalboquerque himself. And all these people did so with great delight, by reason of the estimation in which they held him, for they were desirous of being governed by him.

The brother, who was in Onor, being informed that Merlao had come to Cintácora to embark, immediately sent some of his people to Caribal and Ancola (two places which lie in front of Cintácora, on the opposite side of the river, where the Kingdom of Goa is divided from that of Onor), to labour to prevent his passage, promising them great rewards if they captured him; for he was alarmed lest Afonso Dalboquerque should assist him in his attempt to cast him out of the kingdom. But, notwithstanding all these endeavours which his brother made, Merlao conducted himself with such skill, that he passed over without any conflict with the soldiers of his brother, and reached Goa (taking with him a captain of the King of Narsinga, who was called Icarao, who for days past had been in his company, in discord with the king), where he was received with great pleasure by Afonso Dalboquerque, who ordered that he should be lodged in the principal houses of the city, and instructed the factor to supply him with everything he or his people should require.

The Nequibares were so delighted at the arrival of Merlao, that it was not many days before they went to Afonso Dalboquerque [and begged him] to give him to them as their governor, for all the people desired him. And Afonso Dalboquerque was very glad at this proceeding on their part, because this was the principal reason why he had extended his assistance to him; so he told the Nequibares that for his own part he was glad of it, and he would talk with Merlao and then give them a reply. And, on the following day, in the morning, Afonso Dalboquerque caused

[1] See vol. ii, p. 125, note.

Merlao to be summoned before him, and told him that he was desirous of letting him hold the lands of Goa at a yearly rental, and of giving him the government of them, provided that he would pay every year to the King Dom Manuel, his Lord, or to his governors of India, forty thousand *pardaos*,[1] in four payments, just as the people had to pay, in addition to a payment for three months, which the land still owed to the Hidalcão; for they had to be demanded on the part of the King, his Lord. Merlao was very well pleased.

And when the agreements which were made about this matter had been drawn and signed, Afonso Dalboquerque summoned before him the Nequibares and all the principal men of the Hindoos, and took Merlao by the hand before them, and told them that he gave him to them to be their governor, for he knew how much they desired to have him, and how well they would be treated by him; and they received Merlao with great pleasure and much festivity and blowing of horns, in accordance with their customs. And, in two or three days' time, Merlao set out, and crossed over to the mainland, taking with him five thousand peons and fifty horsemen, and commenced at once to farm his *Tanadarias*.[2]

Now, seeing that the fortress of Goa was already in so advanced a state that it would withstand all the power of the Hidalcão, Afonso Dalboquerque sent Diogo Fernandez de Béja, as chief captain of three ships, to dismantle the fortress of Çacotorá (as the King D. Manuel so often had ordered to be done), and he gave him a set of instructions how he was to act in this business, and there he was to remain until the fifteenth day of the month of May, for he

[1] For the value of the *pardao*, see vol. ii, p. 95. Forty thousand *pardaos* is somewhat more than £3000.

[2] *Tanadaria* is rendered by Vieyra *Cabeça de Comarca*, the principal city or town of a *Comarca* or district; in this passage the word appears to apply to the office or appointment of a *Tanadar*.

might be enabled to come to him, if the affairs of India permitted it, as late as this; but if it were to fall out that Afonso Dalboquerque could not be with him by that time, then Diogo Fernandez de Béja was to proceed to Ormuz, with his letters and powers which he carried, in order to receive the tribute, for Cogeatar had sent word to say that he was willing to pay it; and when this had been done, he was to make his way in the month of August by the route to India, and unite with the fleet of Manuel de Lacerda, who was to remain as chief captain of the sea while he himself (Afonso Dalboquerque) sailed away from India, and the two united were to cruise off that coast, for so, if Goa fell into any trouble, they could succour the city; and in order that Diogo Fernandez might be the better entertained by Cogeatar, Afonso Dalboquerque gave permission to all the ships of Ormuz that were in Goa to carry spices, and gave them a safe conduct to be enabled to pass, giving them to understand that they were to come back direct to Goa with the horses they were to bring with them.

And because Afonso Dalboquerque was in certain respects impeded and prevented from carrying out his intended expedition in this direction, Diogo Fernandez de Béja, after he had destroyed the fortress of Çacotorá, and the appointed period of time had elapsed, made his way to Ormuz, and received the tribute, and from that port set sail for India, and found Goa besieged by the forces of the Hidalcão, as will be related hereafter.

CHAPTER VII.

Of the ambassadors whom the Çamorim, after the fall of Goa, sent to the great Afonso Dalboquerque, desiring peace with him; and how Simão Rangel was sent upon this business, and what passed concerning it.

Whereas the Çamorim had been informed that the great Afonso Dalboquerque had captured Goa, and was fortifying himself in the city with the intention of retaining possession of it,—no longer relying upon the league which had been made between himself and the Hidalcão with the object of ejecting the Portuguese from India; and whereas, too, he was aware that the King of Cambaya, another member of the league, had sent back to Afonso Dalboquerque the Portuguese who had been prisoners in his territory; he ordered his ambassadors to repair to Afonso Dalboquerque, and they set out from Calicut in a *parão*, and in a few days reached Goa. And when they had arrived they sent word to Afonso Dalboquerque that they had come to his Lordship with an embassy from the Çamorim, and begged him of his kindness that he would grant them a hearing.

So in order to give a greater air of importance to this business, Afonso Dalboquerque ordered Francisco Pantoja, chief alcaide of the fortress, to proceed to the ambassadors and bring them; while he himself waited in the hall of reception with all the captains and *Fidalgos*, and received them with great expressions of delight and demonstrations of being well pleased with their friendship.

The ambassadors, after shewing him the accustomed courtesy according to their manner, told him that the Çamorim, their Lord, had sent word by them to inform him how happy he would be if he could have been able to converse with him, so that he could shew him the pleasure he felt in the capture of Goa by the Portuguese; and that in consequence of his desire of friendship with the King of Portugal he had sent to make him an offer of all his estate, if it would please him, and a site in the kingdom for the construction of a fortress, for thus would his friendship be more truly manifested; and begged that a person of great confidence might be sent to him to arrange this matter on a proper footing.

Afonso Dalboquerque replied to them that he accepted those offers of alliance made by the Çamorim in the name of the King of Portugal, his Lord, and on these conditions he himself would serve the Çamorim with all his fleets and soldiers that were stationed in India, whenever it were required, and that he would send without delay, in their company, a servant of the King, his Lord, to treat of that matter of theirs that had been proposed. And whereas for some time Afonso Dalboquerque had been desirous of setting foot in Calicut and constructing there a fortress with peace and friendship (seeing that he never could get the better of the Çamorim in the war which he had carried on against him), when three or four days had passed after Afonso Dalboquerque had related to the captains all this business, and all of them had arrived at the conclusion that it would be very conducive to the service of the King of Portugal that a fortress should be constructed in Calicut, he dispatched the ambassadors and shewed them every attention in the name of the King; and in company with them he sent Simão Rangel, servant of the King, in a *fusta*, with written instructions concerning the way he was to proceed.

As soon as Simão Rangel arrived at Calicut, he went on board the *caravela* of Simão Afonso which was riding at anchor in the harbour, and there he awaited the answer of the King, for Afonso Dalboquerque had so commanded him to act. When the ambassadors had come before their king, they related to him how Afonso Dalboquerque was in Goa with great strength of soldiery, and how he was fortifying himself in that city, and how the Portuguese had discomfited a captain of the Hidalcão, who had come down upon the lands of Goa; and that Afonso Dalboquerque had sent in their company a servant of the King of Portugal to ratify the terms of peace.

The Çamorim, knowing that Simão Rangel was on board the *caravela*, and was not likely to come on shore, commanded the governors of the city to commune with him, and they had many conversations relative to the terms of the peace, without being able to arrive at any definite conclusion; for the king was willing only to grant a fortress in Chale, whereas Afonso Dalboquerque ordered in his written instructions that he was not to accept any site unless it were in the harbour of Calicut in front of the king's own landing-stage.[1] And it turned out that, after all, they came to no agreement, for the king would not grant any site for a fortress in his own land; but only wanted to keep the matter open with dissimulations, to the end that, at this same season, the Moorish merchants might dispatch their ships, which they had laden, for the Straits; but this they could not do as long as the *caravelas* of the Portuguese fleet were lying there at anchor in the harbour.

When Simão Rangel perceived the object of these delays, and that it was all owing to the bad temper and dissimulation of the king, he ceased to communicate with the governors, and went on board the *fusta*, and shaped his course for Goa, where he arrived and gave an account to Afonso Dalboquerque of what had taken place, and related the dilatory way in which the Çamorim had carried on the negotiations with him. And he declared, too, that in his own opinion the king would never, of his own will, grant permission to erect a fortress in any site in his land, for all that he might offer them a site in Chale.

But, inasmuch as Afonso Dalboquerque was by this time

[1] Or jetty, *Cerame*; see vol. i, p. 115.

ready with his fleet to sail away and cruise off the straits [of the Red Sea]—which projected expedition he afterwards abandoned for the voyage to Malaca, as will be related further on—he left this matter open and in the position it now stood, until his return from Malaca, and desired Manuel de Lacerda, who was under orders, to remain as Chief Captain of the Fleet on that coast [of India] to continue ever cruising off the harbour of Calicut, and to harass it in every possible way, and prevent any ships from getting out.

But while Afonso Dalboquerque was away at Malaca, the Turks came down to besiege Goa, and thereby Manuel de Lacerda was compelled to quit the coast of Calicut and proceed to the assistance of Goa. And at this very time the Moors had an opportunity of dispatching their ships, laden with spiceries, to the Straits: and these, when they were so far advanced as the Island of Çacotorá, between the Cape of Guardafum and Magadoxo,[1] encountered a storm so fierce that it wrecked two of them, and the others were wrecked in that gulf; and Mafamede Maçari,[2] who was sailing in that company reached the Maldive Islands.[3]

When the Moorish merchants, who lived in Calicut, perceived that their trade navigation was thus cut off, they departed with their wares, some to Cairo, others to Cambaya, others to Ormuz and to other parts, in such wise that very few who were not natives of that place were left remaining in Calicut, and these used to come from Çufim,[4]

[1] On the coast of Somali, in Africa.

[2] Mafamede Maçari, evidently a corrupted form of the name Muhammed.........

[3] In the Indian Ocean, 5 deg. N. lat., 73 deg. 30 min. E. long.

[4] Çufim, also called by the Portuguese Azafic, and by the natives Asfi, is evidently Safie, on the coast of Barbary, 32 deg. 17 min. N., 9 deg. 8 min. W. There is a valuable account of this great city in *Le Grand Dictionnaire Géographique* of M. Bruzen de la Martiniere. Paris, folio, 1768.

from Ourão[1] from Tremecim,[2] and from Tripoli,[3] with their wares, to Cairo, and from Cairo they used to make their way to Judá, and from Judá to Calicut, with ready money, and there they used to build new ships, and load them with spiceries, and so returned to their own lands.

On one occasion, Afonso Dalboquerque enquired of a Moor of these people who had been taken in one of their ships which had come from the Straits, how it was that they ventured to come from so far off to trade in Calicut, seeing that it stood between two of our fortresses, and that they were obliged to pass over the very place where our fleets were stationed. The Moor replied that the profits were so great that they would run all risks to get there; for, for every *cruzado* laid out in Calicut, they used to make twelve or thirteen in Judá and in all the places that stood within the mouth of the Straits; and he stated it was in consequence of this profit being so great, and the trade in pepper being so extensive, that the Moors who were established in Calicut laboured to prevent the Çamorim from granting permission to the Portuguese to erect a fortress in his territory, for if this were granted to them the merchants would be left without any trade navigation to the Straits.

[1] Ourão, now Oran, on the north coast of Africa. See vol. i, p. 120.

[2] Tremecim, also called Tremecem, Telemicen, Telmsen, Tlemecen, or Tlemcen, and anciently Timisi, a town fifty miles S. W. of Oran, 34 deg. 52 min. N., 1 deg. 18 min. W. See K. Johnston's *Dictionary of Geography*; Ritter's *Geographisch-Statistisch Lexicon*, by A. Stark, Leipzig, 1865; and M. Bruzen de la Martiniere's work quoted above, where there is an interesting notice of the site.

[3] Tripoli, on the north coast of Africa.

[4] Jidda. See vol. i, p. 234.

CHAPTER VIII.

How the King of Narsinga sent his ambassadors to visit Afonso Dalboquerque concerning the capture of Goa; and of the news which Fr. Luiz communicated to him, and what passed thereafter.

After that the great Afonso Dalboquerque sent Fr. Luiz to Narsinga,—following the disaster of Calicut (as I have already related),—he never received any news of how things had fared with him in respect to the instructions which he carried with him; but when Goa had been taken for the second time, as soon as the news reached Narsinga the king immediately ordered his ambassadors to pay a visit to Afonso Dalboquerque, and by means of them Fr. Luiz wrote to him, relating the manner of his arrival at Narsinga, and stating that, in other letters which he had written he had described how he had been well received by all except the king; and, on this occasion, he desired to inform Afonso Dalboquerque that the King of Narsinga was getting himself ready with five thousand men on foot and two thousand on horse, for an expedition against one of his vassals who had risen up in rebellion and seized the city of Pergundá,[1] (the rebel) declaring that to himself belonged the kingdom itself by right; and that directly he had taken the rebel the king would proceed with all this force of men to his places situated on the edge of the sea, and he (Fr. Luiz), for his part, could not understand the drift of this, but as Goa was so close by he would advise Afonso Dalboquerque to keep up friendly communications with the king, and by no means to place any reliance upon the King of Garçopa, nor upon Timoja, for they were men of such bad dispositions that they had even written to the King of Narsinga that, if he wished to regain possession of Goa,—for it had

[1] Pergundá, perhaps Purkundi, in the Bengal Presidency, 30 deg. 28 min. N., 79 deg. 4 min. E.

anciently belonged to the ancestors of the king—he must send them both infantry, and cavalry, and elephants, and then they would deliver the city over to him before the Portuguese could fortify their position therein. And, he went on to say, that he had received trustworthy news that the Hidalcão had set forth with a large force to attack the city of Calbergate,[1] the Guazil of which was an Abyssinian eunuch, a servant of the King of Decam,[2] by name Melique Distur,[3] and, as it could not withstand the siege, after two months it had surrendered upon certain conditions; and there had risen up against the Hidalcão four of the principal Guazils of the kingdom (for the Hidalcão carried back with him the King of Decam a prisoner, deprived of all his command), who had gone up against him with a numerous force in hopes of destroying him; and when these Guazils arrived at a certain watercourse which they could not pass they let themselves rest and there remained; but the Hidalcão, out of fear of them, had sent for the soldiers who were on duty in guarding the lands of Goa.

And Fr. Luiz went on to declare that there had also arrived news to the King of Narsinga that the principal Hindoos of the city of Bilgão[4] (as soon as they had heard of the capture of Goa and fortification of it by the Portuguese) had broken out into rebellion against the Hidalcão, and had cast the Moors out of the city, and put themselves under the command of the king [of Narsinga], for this city had

[1] *Kulburga*, *Golburga*, or *Calberga*, in the Nizam's dominions, Bengal Presidency, 17 deg. 20 min. N., 76 deg. 52 min. E. The latter part of the name, according to the Portuguese rendering, may be intended to signify *Ghaut*.

[2] The Deccan.

[3] This is manifestly the Portuguese rendering of *Melek Distur*. The first word has been frequently explained before. The word *distur* is of Persian origin, and is used both in the Persian and Arabic languages to signify a *minister*; here, however, it appears rather as a proper name than as a title.

[4] *Belgãon*, *Belgaum*, or *Belganw*, in the Bombay Presidency, 15 deg. 50 min. N., 74 deg. 31 min. E.

formerly belonged to him, but the Hidalcão had taken it from him.

Bilgão is a very large city, and there is in it a very large fort, and it is a pass and principal port from the kingdom of Decam to Goa. There is a very extensive mountain range which overlooks the lands of Goa, just as the range of Algarve [in Portugal] looks over the plain of Ourique, and when this range has been crossed the kingdom of Decam lies all along flat table-land, like the same plain. And because the principal reason why the old Çabayo had obtained possession of Goa was that he had captured this fortress by treachery of the Hindoos who used to hold it, Afonso Dalboquerque used to say very often, when he found himself annoyed by the recalcitration of the Hidalcão, that if the king D. Manuel desired to keep the kingdom of Goa safe, he ought by all means to try all in his power to take this fortress, for by holding it he would secure all the estate he had there. And as for the nogotiations which his instructions ordered him to carry out, he had presented them many times without getting any answer to the purpose, but always had been put off; but at last he had told him, that he was very much disconcerted at the orders for attacking him, and he might build a fortress in Batacalá, for he said that he was very desirous of his friendship at the very time that he knew that it had been entered into with the Hidalcão, but that did not agree with the offers that he had made to help him in taking the kingdom of Decam, which had been his of old. And when these interviews with the king were over, the king sent for the governor of the city, and blamed him very much for desiring this alliance with the Hidalcão. And that King of Garçopa had written him a letter by virtue of which he could take him and destroy him if he liked, but as they were now very friendly, he had not done so; but that if this were done for money, which he had promised to give him every year, the Hidalcão would show towards them that true faith which his father had shown towards the King of Narsinga when he took him in battle, but released him on his promise to serve him for ever.

At the receipt of this intelligence, which Fray Luiz wrote of matters which had passed with the King of Narsinga, and with his governor, Afonso Dalboquerque became somewhat in suspense when he saw that he was withdrawing from that which he had so often declared, namely, to help him against the Hidalcão. But as he knew how this came about, he dissembled with him, and wrote to Fray Luiz by the same ambassador who had brought him the letter, to take his leave of the king with as much dissimulation as he could, and return immediately; and he put himself in communication with the Hidalcão, declaring that he desired friendship with him. For, in order that the affairs of India should progress satisfactorily, as was convenient to the King of Portugal, Afonso Dalboquerque always laboured to make each one of these lords understand that he desired to have peace and friendship and the trade in horses with him, which was what they claimed; for, whereas he held the key of their position at Goa, he desired by means of this artifice to sow dissensions among them.

After he had written to the Hidalcão, he sent off to the ambassadors of the King of Narsinga, sending word by them that a year ago he had sent certain conditions to him through Fray Luiz, but as he had not yet received any reply to them, he could not come to any conclusion with regard to the messages that had been sent. The ambassadors set out, and when they arrived at Bisnaga, they found Fray Luiz was dead, for a Turk had killed him, and it was reported that the Hidalcão had ordered his murder; and they delivered the message which they brought from Afonso Dalboquerque to the king, and told him that while at Goa they had discovered that he was communicating with the Hidalcão. So alarmed was the King of Narsinga at hearing of this alliance, for he knew that the Hidalcão had the horses which was the principal strength of his army, that he immediately sent back the two ambassadors to the great Afonso Dalboquerque with very full powers to conclude a treaty of friendship, and to arrange the terms of the trade in horses.

CHAPTER IX.

How the great Afonso Dalboquerque set in order certain matters in the city, and established a Mint there, and of what followed.

The great Afonso Dalboquerque was so desirous that Goa should return to the state of trade which it had always enjoyed when under the rule of the Çabayo, that so soon as the fortress was on the point of completion he dispatched several captains along the coast with orders to compel all the ships they met with to go into port at Goa, and this he did for two reasons. The first was, that he might benefit the harbour and re-people the city to its former number of population; and that the caravans of Narsinga and of the kingdom of the Decam, with their merchandise, might come to Goa in search of horses as they used of old to come (for the horses of this region are much esteemed and fetch a great price, because, apart from the need of them for military purposes, the captains and principal lords are in the habit of carrying their wives about on horses). The other reason was, that he might ruin the harbour of Baticalá, which had become very noble through the horse-trade and the quantity of merchandise which flowed into it from Ormuz. For he considered that if the horse-trade were established in Goa, there would always be in the city from four to five hundred horses belonging to the merchants which he could make use of in case of urgency. And in consequence of the diligence which Afonso Dalboquerque set about this matter, and because he had ordered that houses in the city should be given to the principal merchants for the better arrangement of their merchandise, merchant ships began immediately to flock from many quarters to the harbour of Goa, some coming from Ormuz with horses. And with a view to improving this state of business, he gave orders for the construction of some great stables, and organised a service of three hundred peons of the district, whose duty it was to transport grass, hay, and supplies for horses. And with the object of providing return cargoes for the merchants, so that they should not be compelled to seek a cargo in any other port, he commanded the Factor and officials to take care always to have in the Factory pepper, cloves, and ginger, and all the other kinds of merchandise which the merchants were likely to require, and in the clearing papers which they delivered with the cargoes whenever the merchants desired to set sail, it was to be set forth that the ships were to be bound for Ormuz and to no other port, for it was Afonso Dalboquerque's desire to destroy the commerce of the Straits.

In consequence of the liberty which the Moors had of loading their ships with spices at Goa, all the merchants came there to settle their trade. And in one of these ships which brought horses Cogeamir[1] was found, to whom Afonso Dalboquerque, on the occasion of his taking Goa for the first time, had given two ships laden with merchandise to make the voyage to Ormuz. This man was now bringing back horses in exchange for his merchandise, and when he arrived at India and learned that the Moors of Goa had risen up against Afonso Dalboquerque, and had driven him out of the city, he had made his way to Dabul and gone to make a present of the horses to the Hidalcão. But when Afonso Dalboquerque was informed that this man was arrived, he ordered his people to arrest him because of the treachery he had been guilty of, and with him

[1] See vol. ii, p. 110.

was taken also one of his sons, and they were put in chains, and all their goods seized, among them being twenty-five horses, which were forthwith put into the Factory.

After having arranged all these matters, Afonso Dalboquerque established a chief office wherein could be coined money of silver, gold, and copper, of the same standard which had been settled with the people and the merchants of the city when Goa was captured for the first time.[1] And with this end in view, he commanded that all the Moorish money should be brought to the Mint and be stamped with the dies of the King of Portugal, and he gave to these coins the same names that they had, as has been declared already.[2] This Mint was farmed out to a Chetim[3] from Baticalá, at the rent of six hundred thousand *reis*;[4] and Alvaro Godinho, a married householder of Goa, was appointed Treasurer of the Mint, and all the other offices were filled up with chief men who were married, with a view to encouraging the people to marry and people the land.[5] For, already at this time there were in Goa about four hundred and fifty married men, all servants of the King, and of the Queen, and of the Lords of Portugal: and those who desired to marry were so numerous, that Afonso Dalboquerque could hardly grant their requests, for he did not give permission except for the men of proved character to marry. But in order to favour this work, as it was entirely of his own idea, and also because they were men of good character, and had deserved by their good services that this privilege should be granted to them, he extended the permission to marry far beyond the powers which had been assigned by the king D. Manuel, for the women with whom they married were the daughters of the principal men of the land.

And he granted this favour, among other reasons, in

[1] See vol. ii, p. 128.
[2] See vol. ii, pp. 129, 130.
[3] See vol. ii, p. 130, note 2.
[4] About £125.
[5] See vol. ii, p. 99.

order that when the Hindoos observed what he did for their daughters, and nieces, and sisters, they might with better willingness turn Christians; and for this reason he would not suffer any of the women to be enslaved, but ordered that they should all be taken away from the masters who had possession of them; and he divided among all the married ones, the lands, houses, and cattle, and everything else that there was, to give them a start in life; and if the women whom he thus gave in marriage asked for the houses which had been in possession of their fathers or their husbands, he ordered that these should be so given, and therein they found many jewels and gold-pieces which had been hidden underground and abandoned when the city was captured. And as for the landed property which, according to information he obtained, had been in possession of the Moorish mosques and the Hindoo pagodas, he gave them all to the principal church of the city, which he dedicated to the protection of *Sancta Catherina*, on whose feast-day Our Lord had given him the victory over that city.[1] But in this matter of giving permission for marriages, Afonso Dalboquerque experienced much opposition, for there were many who disapproved of his thus maintaining Goa. The chief opponents in this were Lourenço Moreno, the Factor of Cochim, and Antonio Real, Chief *Alcaide*, and Gaspar Pereira, and Diogo Pereira, who, not content with meeting together and taking counsel upon this business, even went so far as to write to the king D. Manuel, setting forth their arguments how that the king ought to give orders for its prevention. And the principal reason they gave, was that it created many expenses, for they thought that if it were shown to entail loss of state property the king would be stirred to more rapid action in this matter.

And Afonso Dalboquerque appointed as captain of the fortress Rodrigo Rabelo, who was a very brave cavalier;

[1] See vol. i, Introduction, p. i.

and Francisco Pantoja, chief *Alcaide;* and Francisco Corvinel, a Florentine by birth, factor. The scriveners of the Factory were João Teixeira, son of João Paçanha of Alenquer (who accompanied Afonso Dalboquerque in the first capture of Goa), and Vicente da Costa (son of Master Afonso who had been chief physician to king D. Manuel), married in Goa. And he laid down rules for the inhabitants of the city, with regard to the appointment of judges, municipal officers,[1] and superintendent of weights and measures,[2] every year.

And when all these things have been thus ordained (as well as others which I omit, to avoid seeming unnecessarily long), the great Afonso Dalboquerque began to make his fleet ready, with the intention of not passing the winter in Goa, because of the dearth of supplies therein, and because there was not enough money to pay his men. And he determined to set forth in that direction where he could be of most service to the king. And he left four hundred soldiers to guard the fortress of Goa, and a great quantity of artillery, both large and small, gunpowder, saltpetre, and sulphur, and a machine in working-order for making as much as might be required, and eighty mounted men, married and settled in Goa. Duarte de Mello was appointed chief captain of the sea, with four ships and three galleys, under orders to cruise along the coast and provide the city with whatever was required; and when Manuel de Lacerda should arrive, whom Afonso Dalboquerque would leave to be chief captain of a fleet in Cochim, with all his powers, then Duarte de Mello was to obey him as if he were Dalboquerque himself. And for payment of all these people and fleets, he assigned the twelve thousand *cruzados* which Merlao had undertaken to pay for the rent of the island.

[1] *Vereadores.*

[2] *Almotaceis:* there is an older form, *almoçabel; al-mohtasib*, Arab.

CHAPTER X.

Of the proceedings of the Bendará, Governor of Malaca, when he heard that Goa had been taken, and of the news which Ruy de Araujo, who was in captivity there, wrote to the great Afonso Dalboquerque.

Inasmuch as Goa was very much renowned in all the parts and kingdoms of India, the news soon spread through the merchants of Calicut, informing all the kings how the great Afonso Dalboquerque had taken the city and driven the Turks out of it. When this news reached Malaca, the Bendará who governed the kingdom for the king his nephew, fearing lest Afonso Dalboquerque should determine to come to Malaca and exact vengeance for the treason and spoliation which had been practised upon the Portuguese,[1]—with his accustomed dissimulation and subtlety,—lost no time in providing his city with quantities of supplies, and went to Ruy de Araujo and the other captives who had been put into a house and very badly treated, and told them, without saying anything about the current state of affairs in India, that the tumult which had arisen against the Portuguese had not been brought about by his design nor by his orders, but that the Guzerates and Jaos had planned it without his knowledge, because they were afraid that the Portuguese would treat them badly whenever they went out of their port, and he further declared that it was his intention to punish these people severely, because he desired very much to be on friendly terms with the Portuguese, and to see them carrying on a trade with Malaca.

When this interview was at an end, the Bendará gave orders to take the prisoners into a house outside the city, which was not so dismal as the one they had occupied. When Ninachatu, a Hindoo resident of Malaca, who had

[1] See vol. ii, pp. 73, 74.

frequently performed many good services to our people during their captivity, heard this news of the taking of Goa, he made his way to the Bendará, and told him that if Goa had been taken by the Portuguese—as the report went—he was afraid that the Governor of India would desire to come to the land [of Malaca] to take vengeance for what had been done therein to the Captain of the King of Portugal; and therefore it was his opinion that it would be advisable to order the liberation of Ruy de Araujo and his companions, and to treat them very kindly, for it might even be that a time might come when they would be glad to use these men for mediation. This advice, which Ninachatu gave, pleased the Bendará, and he gave orders for the release of the Portuguese, and gave them a house wherein they might live, and ten thousand *calains*[1] worth of Cambayan stuffs, of that which had been taken from the fleet of Diogo Lopez de Sequeira,[2] to trade with, and support themselves from their profits, for this was the custom of the king with his slaves; and it was signified to them that this property was assigned to them for their support, but when the Portuguese ships should arrive, then their accounts should be settled, and all the loss that they had sustained there should be made good. This time-serving[3] policy, which the Bendará used in his dealings with Ruy de Araujo and his companions, was not only the result of the entreaties of Ninachatu, but also because there was a junk ready to set sail for India, and he wanted the news to be taken there by it how well he was treating the Portuguese whom he had captured; and so said some Moors, who were his friends, to Ruy de Araujo. But they said also that as soon as the junk had set sail, all that the Bendará had granted to them would be taken away again, and they would be again cast into prison, and even if the Bendará did not do so it would be solely out of fear

[1] *Calains.* The word *Calaim* signifies a very fine kind of Indian copper.

[2] See vol. ii, page 74.

[3] *Viztude.*

of what he had heard of the progress of Afonso Dalboquerque.

When Ruy de Araujo came to know this, he determined to send word to Afonso Dalboquerque of all that had taken place in Malaca, and arranged his plans with a Moor who was named Abedalla,[1] and through him he wrote that he would have Afonso Dalboquerque to know there were nineteen Portuguese alive, and the Bendará had tried many times to force them to turn Moors, and did many cruel things to them on this account, and behaved very cruelly to them on this account. But the Bendará was in a great dread, lest he (Afonso Dalboquerque) should make his way to Malaca, for he was not liked by any of the kings whose territory was contiguous to his own, and all were obliged to oppose him because he was a great tyrant and practised constant robberies upon the merchants who had any intercourse with that port. And if he (Afonso Dalboquerque) should make up his mind to go to Malaca, then it ought only to be with the greatest fleet possible, to the end that the sea and land both should obey him when they beheld the great power of the King of Portugal in those regions; and if any junk should be captured in their passage for Malaca, no cruelty ought to be done to the people taken in them, only they should be kept captive, and on arriving at the port he ought to send some of them on land with orders to convey to the Bendará the message that he (Afonso Dalboquerque) was not minded to make war upon Malaca nor to take any of her possessions, provided that the king would make a treaty of peace and friendship with him, and deliver up the Christians, and put himself under the orders of the King of Portugal; for the Bendará had determined, directly he should be informed of the arrival of our fleet on the coast, to send all the captains off immediately four leagues' distance up into the interior country, until terms

[1] Cf. Abedalá, vol. i, p. 121.

could be arranged, for he was afraid that if they remained on the spot they would give Afonso Dalboquerque intelligence of many events. But as for past events, after that day of his misfortunes, and of the departure of Diogo Lopez de Sequeira from that port, he would not write too minutely, for all was overwhelmed by the bad treatment they had received from the Bendará in their captivity up to the present day. It was true, indeed, that the Bendará had thought good to give them a home in which they were all living, and ten thousand *calains*[1] worth of merchandise, whereof they were to support themselves by the profits, declaring that he was ready, on his part, to make good to them all the loss they had received when Afonso Dalboquerque, on his part, should reimburse him for the loss, on the other hand, which he had experienced from the attacks made by Portuguese ships on his junks; and declaring, too, that he had punished the Guzerates and Jaos who had been guilty of treason, in such a manner that henceforth they would never again dare to do so, for (said the Bendará), he was very desirous of the friendship of the King of Portugal, and wished to become his vassal. And (Ruy de Araujo continued) as for these things and many more of which he did not write, as he did not take any notice of them, the Bendará every day made a thousand excuses; but he himself, and all his fellow captains with him, begged him (Afonso Dalboquerque), for the love of God, to keep them in remembrance, and rescue them out of this captivity, and to cause to be given to the Moor, the bearer of the letter, twenty *cruzados* out of his effects, for he had lent it to the captives to buy food, and to show him kindness; for, besides his always helping them and accompanying them, he had consented, with very little persuasion, to undertake the journey, seeing that he ran a very great risk of his life if he had been discovered, but he trusted in the kindness

[1] See p. 45.

which Afonso Dalboquerque would shew him for it; and that Ninachatu took the opportunity to beg him, of his great kindness, that he would not let the Moors of Cochim know what he had done for the captives in Malaca, for he feared lest they should write to the Bendará and do him an injury for it; for it was Ninachatu who had given the captives an opportunity of writing, and of despatching the Moor with the letter; but if it were so disposed that his Lordship, Afonso Dalboquerque, could not possibly get to Malaca by any reasonable manner, then that he would send them word of it as secretly as he could, before the Moors could get intelligence of the impossibility of his going, for he trusted that Our Lord would grant them a means of going from that to some other place safe and free to make their way back again to India.

CHAPTER XI.

How the Captains of the Fleet of Diogo Mendez requested him to set out for Malaca; and of what passed with them, and how he begged Afonso Dalboquerque to grant him permission to go; and of the reasons wherefore it was not granted.

The captains of the fleet of Diogo Mendes, seeing that the fortress of Goa was quite finished, and the affairs of the city continuing to become more and more in order, and being desirous of performing their voyage, went to him and declared to him that their ships were those of merchants who had struck a contract with the king D. Manuel, to go to Malaca, and take in a cargo, and that up to that present time there had always been some excuse for the delay of their setting sail because the monsoon had not yet come; but now that they were having this wind, and the business of Goa was finished, in which, indeed, all had served the king very well, they ought to proceed.

Diogo Mendes replied to them that he liked their advice very much, but it was necessary to give an account of the proposed starting to Afonso Dalboquerque, not only as a compliment, but in order that the opportunity might be taken to get him to supply the ships with some things which were necessary for that voyage, and they had given their fealty to him, and could not sail out of that port with his licence.[1] Dinis Cerniche, like a foreigner, and one who had more regard for his profit than for his honour, replied that those compliments might be dispensed with, for in the contract which the merchants made with the king he had therein given them exemption from the jurisdiction of Afonso Dalboquerque and all other governors of India. But inasmuch as Diogo Mendez was an experienced man, although in this matter he erred in what he did by advice of the captains, masters, and pilots of his fleet, dismissing from his mind the arguments advanced by Dinis Cerniche, he went to Afonso Dalboquerque and told him that while they were in Cananor he, Afonso Dalboquerque, had said that on the completion of the Goa undertaking, and on arrival of the time of the monsoon, permission should be accorded for his departure to Malaca, and he would give him everything that he required for his voyage; and that as Our Lord had given him the city thus gained with so much honours for himself, and he, Diogo Mendez, was no longer required there, therefore he begged him very much of his kindness to dispatch him, and give him licence to set forth, for when he looked into the conditions whereby the merchants had contracted with the king, he found he could not put any hindrance in the way of their performing their voyage, but on the other hand his captains would murder him if he did not go; and they made every day formal requisitions to him that they might set out, but he did not wish to do so without Afonso Dalboquerque's consent.

[1] See vol. ii, pp. 232, 233.

Afonso Dalboquerque replied that it was true he had promised at Cananor to dispatch him directly the business of Goa was completed; but when he had made that promise he was not aware of the condition in which the affairs of Malaca were, and that it was but a few days since he had received a letter from Ruy de Araujo, giving him an account of the state of that country, and declaring that in case he had to navigate to those parts it must be with so powerful a fleet that everything should yield to it; and when he considered this, and saw in how difficult a position the affairs of Malaca were placed,[1] he must beg him of his kindness not to be desirious of risking his vessels and the people he had brought with him, for should any disaster happen to them both would have to bear the blame, since it was plain, from what had happened to Diogo Lopez de Sequeira,[2] that they could not open up any commerce with Malaca except by exchange of lance-thrusts,[3] and this could not be effected by four rotten ships and two rusty swords. And there were two reasons why he could not help him with his soldiers and his fleet:—the first, because affairs at Goa were, as he could see for himself, in so delicate a condition; the second, that there was news of the coming of the Rumes, which had set the whole of India in an uproar; but when these disturbances were over he promised he would help him, as he had already promised. After many conversations with Afonso Dalboquerque, who was determined not to grant him permission to go, Diogo Mendez took leave of him discontented, and when he arrived at his ship the captains came on board to hear what had taken place, except Baltezar da Silva, who remained behind ill at Cananor. Diogo Mendez gave them an account of what had been said by Afonso

[1] *Os negocios de Malaca estarem de má desistão.* The latter word is equivalent to *digestão*, and the phrase signifies "of a hard, indigestible, untractable character". [2] See vol. ii, pp. 31, 73, 74.

[3] *A troco de lançadas.* There is here a play on the word *troco*, which also signifies "exchange" in a commercial sense.

Dalboquerque, and with this reply all came to the determination of setting out without making any further demand for permission to do so.

CHAPTER XII.

How Diogo Mendez, by the advice of his captains, hoisted sail to pass over the bar, and the great Afonso Dalboquerque sent after him, and they made him turn back, and the rest which took place.

Now inasmuch as the captains were ill pleased because the great Afonso Dalboquerque had denied them the permission to depart which Diogo Mendez had begged of him, and as they held firm to their opinion that he could neither demand their submission to his orders nor could they profess it to him, because they had come out under exemption from the orders of the Governor of India, they therefore determined to set their sails and shape their course in a straight line for Malaca. And because they had some misgiving about sailing out over the bar at night, Manuel Pirez, who held the office of pilot and captain of Baltezar da Silva's ship, declared that he could lead all the vessels out over the bar, even if it were at midnight, and could take them to Malacca, and return to Portugal without touching at India at all on the return journey.

At this declaration made by Manuel Pirez, immediately on the fall of night all set their sails except Pero Coresma, who was not in this plot and kept quietly aloof. Now Manuel Pirez, whose vessel could sail very well on a bowline, found no difficulty in sailing at once right over the bar, but the others kept on tacking until the morning broke. As soon as Afonso Dalboquerque was informed that Diogo Mendez had gone off, he immediately sent after him Duarte da Silva and James Teixeira in two galleys, and Manuel de Lacerda along the shore with a party of mounted men, to make their way to the bar and take up and get into any boats that might be there, and force him to stop; and he gave instructions both to one party and the other, that in case the fugitives would not give heed to this, their command, then they were to sink them all.

On coming up with Diogo Mendez, James Teixeira required him, on behalf of Afonso Dalboquerque, to return, but the former, who was still fully resolved to go, would not yield when called upon to do so. So when James Teixeira perceived that he would not pay any attention to the commands of Afonso Dalboquerque, he called out to Martim Afonso, who was the pilot of the fugitive vessel, to give orders for taking in their sails, but he replied that only if Diogo Mendez, who was properly his chief captain, should order him to do so would he do it. So perceiving that neither by fair nor by foul means could he prevail upon Diogo Mendez to return, he aimed a shot at him, high up over the rigging, and then ordered another shot to be fired; but at this juncture there arrived Duarte da Silva in the other galley, and fired a shot at the fugitive ship and struck her on the halliards, and down fell the main yard all at once.

When Diogo Mendez perceived that his mainsail was disabled, he signalled to the others to take in their sails, and he let go his anchor. As soon as Manuel Pirez saw that the flagship of this fleet had struck her sails, he came up alongside of her and asked Diogo Mendez for further instructions; and he replied that all he could do was to shorten sail, and then they must all go back and pay the penalty for what they had done, in accordance with the advice given by him and the other captains. And while the matter was in this state Pero Dalpoem, Auditor of India, came up in a *parão*, and when Manuel de Lacerda saw him he proceeded to unite with him, and they took Diogo Mendez and all the other captains, pilots, and masters, and carried them back as prisoners to the city.

Afonso Dalboquerque, who had already received intelligence of the progress of the affair by a messenger, whom Manuel de Lacerda had despatched by land, caused Diogo Mendez to be brought into his presence, and told him that he was exceedingly astonished to think that he should thus break the word of honour which he had given, and disobey his captain-general before all the ambassadors of the kings and lords of India, who were in that place, by the advice of four lunatics[1] in his fleet, when it had been already decided that it was not advantageous to the service of the king that he should be permitted to go to Malaca. And Diogo Mendez replied that he had done this, not with the intention of acting disobediently towards him, but because his honour had compelled him to do as he had done, for he, being a man accustomed to very great deeds, had been sent out, like an ordinary esquire, with two boats to reinforce the Island of Chorão,[2] upon which the Turks had made a descent.

Afonso Dalboquerque told him that that was not a valid excuse, for no honourable man who was a cavalier like himself would think of feeling dishonoured at being ordered to fight for the service of his king, and he reminded him that he had despatched on that same expedition to Chorão Manuel de Lacerda, the chief captain of the king's fleet, with other boats, and he had not thought it any affront to be engaged in it. And, he continued, this affair was very serious, and of such a character that he should not be performing his duty if he failed to visit it with its just punishment, which he for his part intended to carry out to the full; and there and then he sent him under arrest to the keep of the castle.[3] And as for the other captains, pilots, and masters, he

[1] *Sandeos.*

[2] One of the many islands that lie near that of Goa, and make up the Goa territory.

[3] *A torre de menagem.* See vol. i, p. 45.

ordered them to be put into chains, and in solitary confinement, and gave orders to Pero Dalpoem to draw up, as briefly and quickly as he might, a formal account of this affair, for there were in Goa at that time ambassadors of the king of Narsinga and of other kings of India, who had witnessed the disobedience which had been shown to Afonso Dalboquerque; and he did not wish that they should depart without first of all observing the punishment which he should visit upon them in consequence.

And when the final inquiry had been made, and all was drawn up, Afonso Dalboquerque commanded that all the captains should be summoned; and, having taken notice of the charges brought against them by the Auditor, it was adjudged that Diogo Mendez be sent back in disgrace to Portugal, to appear and answer to the acts of accusation for his misdeeds in person before the king D. Manuel, and Pero Coresma was also to be sent back in disgrace to Portugal, although he was not in the plot, because he did not divulge the intended flight of Diogo Mendez; and Dinis Cerniche was condemned to be put to death by decapitation, and Martim Afonso, chief pilot, and Manuel Pirez, pilot and captain of the ship of Baltezar da Silva, and Diogo Fernandez, master of Dinis Cerniche's ship, all three to be imprisoned in their ships, of which they were but lately masters and pilots; and these sentences upon them were carried out forthwith that very day; and when Afonso Dalboquerque ordered the execution of Dinis Cerniche to be carried out, the ambassadors of the King of Narsinga came and begged him to forgive him, which he did, commuting this punishment into transportation to Portugal in disgrace, there to answer in person the formal charges of misdeeds brought against him.

CHAPTER XIII.

How the great Afonso Dalboquerque set sail for the Straits of Méca with his fleet, and finding he could not cross the shoals of Padua, stood off Goa and made his way direct to Malaca.

Although the king D. Manuel had very often written to the great Afonso Dalboquerque to go up the Straits of the Red Sea and erect a fortress in Adem, the affairs of Goa occupied so much of his time and thoughts that he never yet had any opportunity before now of taking this enterprise in hand. And although the letter which Ruy de Araujo wrote concerning the state of affairs at Malaca had greatly embarrassed him in his proceedings (as has already been related), nevertheless, trusting to the mercy of God, he made up his mind to proceed to the Straits and accomplish the desires of the king D. Manuel; and having his fleet ready with men, supplies, arms, artillery, and everything else that was required for the undertaking of this enterprise (leaving Goa in good order), he set out, but when he had made his course so far forward as the shoals of Padua,[1] and found that he could not get beyond them because the season was now so far advanced, he put back again into harbour, and came to an anchor with all his fleet over against the bar of Goa, and after having dropped anchor, he ordered Rodrigo Rabelo, captain of the city, to be summoned, and told him that on account of the adverse state of the weather, and because the monsoon of the Straits and Ormuz was already gone by, and there was no longer any opportunity of navigating to those parts, it was his intention to go and winter at Malaca and see if he could in any way chastise the Malays for the treason which they had practised upon Diogo Lopez de Sequeira; therefore he

[1] See the B[aixos] de Padua, 13 deg. N. lat., on Fernão Vaz Dourado's Map of India, vol. ii, p. 1.

greatly commended to him the charge of taking care of the city, for the city was always the uppermost thought of his heart,[1] dreading lest the Hidalcão should attack it again; and from that port he went on to Cananor, and leaving the fortress provided with more men than it had, he set out again for Cochim.

As soon as the king learned that Afonso Dalboquerque was on the bar, he lost no time in visiting him on board his vessel, and gave him a long list of reasons why he ought not to go to Malaca, for, he said, the affairs of Goa were still in so critical a state, that it required him personally to control them; and in addition to this, the Çamorim of Calicut was in such a state of disaffection, that he for his part should not be surprised if he broke out into open treason directly he heard of his departure from India. But although this statement by the King of Cochim had a great show of reason in it, yet in it he did not express his own sentiments, but the design of causing Afonso Dalboquerque to abandon his voyage to Malaca was conceived by the advice of Chirinamercar and Mamalemercar, two Moorish merchants, men full of all kinds of evil and worthless designs.

Now the principal cause of their giving this counsel was, that they feared lest Afonso Dalboquerque should capture the ships which they had sent to Malaca; and if Malaca were taken, they would be left without any means of trading in the whole of that archipelago, from Cape Comorim eastwards, for they were the richest merchants in the whole of Malabar. And although Afonso Dalboquerque clearly perceived that those merchants had deceived the poor king in persuading him to turn aside from the course he really wished to pursue, yet because the king was friendly to us, Afonso Dalboquerque dissembled with him and pretended not to see through the plot, and told him that his mind was now quite made up to accomplish that voyage, because the

[1] *Porque a levava atravesada na garganta.*

season would not permit of his passing over to the Straits in accordance with the orders he had received from the king D. Manuel, his lord; but, he said he trusted in God that the king of Cochim would very soon hear news of how thoroughly he had taken vengeance for the treason which had been practised in that city of Malaca upon the Portuguese; and that Goa was in so strong a condition that he should not be afraid even if all the power of the Hidalcão were brought to bear against the city.

When this conversation was over which Afonso Dalboquerque held with the king, he took his leave of him, and sent for Manuel de Lacerda, whom he found there, and because his fleet was but small he reinforced him with four small ships more, and two large ships, men, and munitions of war, with instructions that in the month of August he was to proceed to unite with the other ships which he would then find cruising off the bar of Goa; and he gave him also plenary jurisdiction over all the other captains who should come there, that they should obey him, as though he represented Afonso Dalboquerque in person; and he was always to cruise along that coast in order to be able to render assistance if the affairs of Goa required it; and then Afonso Dalboquerque dismissed him to get his fleet in readiness, while he himself gave orders to his captains to lift their cables and set sails.

CHAPTER XIV.

How the great Afonso Dalboquerque set sail from Cochim, and made his way direct to Malaca, and of what passed thereupon.

The great Afonso Dalboquerque, having thus taken his leave of the King of Cochim and dispatched Manuel de Lacerda, who was to remain behind as chief captain of that coast, set sail with all his fleet, which consisted of eighteen sailing vessels, three of which were galleys. The captains were—D. João de Lima; Fernão Telez Dandrade; Gaspar de Paiva; James Teixeira; Bastiam de Miranda; Aires Pereira; Jorge Nunes de Lião; Dinis Fernandez de Melo, chief *Patrão;* Pero Dalpoem, Auditor of India; Antonio Dabreu; Nuno Vaz de Castelo-branco; Simão Dandrade; Duarte da Silva; Simão Martinz; Afonso Pessoa; Simão Afonso; and Jorge Botelho; and, proceeding on their way, when they had got as far forward as Ceilão (Ceylon), they caught sight of a ship.

Afonso Dalboquerque gave orders to chase her, and they took her, and he was very glad to find it belonged to the Guzerates, as he felt his voyage would now be carried out safely, for the Guzerates understand the navigation of those parts much more thoroughly than any other nations, on account of the great commerce they carry on in those places. And while the fleet was in this latitude a storm arose, during which the galley which was commanded by Captain Simão Martinz, was lost; for, without his knowledge, the ship had been loaded with copper, and she sprung a leak at the prow, and the force of the storm drove her over on her side, and she foundered, but all the people were saved, for Duarte da Silva stood by the ship in his great galley, which was all ready for the emergency. And when all the men had been brought off the wreck, Afonso Dalboquerque led the whole fleet, and brought up at anchor in the harbour of Pedir,[1] having in his company five Guzerate vessels which he had captured on the voyage.

And there he found João Viegas and eight Christians of the company of Ruy de Araujo, who had arrived thus far in their flight from the city of Malaca, and João Viegas recounted to him how the King of Malaca had endeavoured to force them to become Moors, and had ordered some of

[1] A harbour on the northern coast of the Island of Sumatra, 5 deg. 24 min. N. lat., 96 deg. 4 min. E. long., a little to the east of Acheen.

them to be tied hand and foot and circumcised; and they had suffered many torments because they would not deny the faith of Jesus Christ. And one night, when they were all ready to flee away, they were discovered, and Ruy Daraujo and those who were now with him were left behind, because that they were unable to escape. And he declared further that with the King of Pacé there was a principal Moor of Malaca whose name was Naodabegea,[1] who had been the chief author of the treason which had been plotted against Diogo Lopez de Sequeira; and this man had fled from Malaca because he and the Bendará, whom the king killed, had laid a plan to kill the king and take possession of the kingdom.

On hearing this news Afonso Dalboquerque immediately took his leave of the King of Pedir, and made his way to Pacé,[2] which is the principal port of the Island of Samatra, and as soon as he arrived there he sent João Viegas to pay him a visit, and to declare to him that it had come to the knowledge of Afonso Dalboquerque that in the city of Pacé there was a Moor who was fleeing from Malacca who was implicated in the attempt to murder certain Portuguese, who belonged to some ships which the King of Portugal, his lord, had sent to the port of the city of Malaca, and that

[1] The Edition of 1576 reads Naodabegea, that of 1774, Maodabegea; but from the recurrence of the name on p. 62 there can be no doubt that this latter is a typographical error. For the meaning of the first part of this word, see vol. i, p. 227.

[2] Pacé, a harbour a little to the east of Pedir, on the northern coast of the Island of Sumatra. Barretto de Resende gives "Passen" and "Porto de Passen" in Pedro Berthelot's map dated 1635, in the Sloan. MS. 197, fo. 390, on this site. K. Johnston, in the "Royal Atlas", spells the place "Passier" and "Pasier", and assigns the position of 5 deg. 2 min. N., 97 deg. 10 min. E. to the former; and that of 5 deg. 10 min. N., 97 deg. 22 min. E. to the latter place. There can be no doubt that this is a mistake. The spelling adopted by Berthelot is an illustration of the peculiar nasality introduced into the sound of final vowels by the Portuguese.

he begged him of his goodness to cause this Moor to be delivered over to him.

The King of Pacé replied that it was quite true that the Moor had been there, but at present he had no news of him, but he would cause very diligent search to be made after him, and when he was found he would hand him over to Afonso Dalboquerque. And when the king had sent this reply to Afonso Dalboquerque he advised the Moor to go straight at once to Malaca and give the king notice of the approach of the Portuguese, for when he heard this news he would pardon him, and reinstate him in his good favour. As soon as the king had arranged this he sent to Afonso Dalboquerque to say that he had ordered search to be made for the Moor but he could not be found, and he thought he must have fled away, for he could not learn any news of him anywhere throughout the city. But as Afonso Dalboquerque perceived that all this was deception on the part of the king he would not hold any further communications with him, but, not breaking off his friendship, he sailed away.

CHAPTER XV.

How the great Afonso Dalboquerque set sail from the port of Pacé, and at sea he sighted a sailing vessel which was carrying the Moor who was flying from him, and how he sent after the vessel, and what further took place.

As soon as Afonso Dalboquerque had taken his departure from the King of Pacé he ordered the fleet to set sail, and in this manner so sailing along all together with a favourable wind, they caught sight of a *pangajaoa*.[1] This is the name

[1] The latter part of this word is clearly the Portuguese fem. adj. for Javanese. The *Pangajaoa* was a sort of boat impelled by oars. Bluteau calls the *Pangajoa* a kind of rowing boat, used in India. It appears to be different from the *Pangaio*, a sort of small boat composed

of a kind of long vessel, very fast sailing, used in that country; and as the wind had dropped by this time, and Aires Pereira, captain of the *Taforea*, was nearest to it, Afonso Dalboquerque signalled to him to give chase. Aires Pereira got into his boat with some soldiers and set out in pursuit. And the Moors who were on board of the vessel defended themselves with so much spirit that they wounded Aires Pereira and a considerable number of his people without their being able to get in.

Not content with thus defending his vessel the captain, although he was severely wounded, leaped down to Aires Pereira in his boat, and they fought with cuts and blows at each other, and there was at length despatched; and then our people boarded the *pangajaoa* and put to death all the Moors who sought to make any defence, and took seven or eight prisoners, and gathered themselves together again in their boat, and there they found the Moorish captain half dead, without any blood flowing from the numerous wounds he had received.

Aires Pereira commanded the mariners to throw him into the sea just as he was; but when they perceived that he was richly clothed, they sought first of all to strip him, and then they found on his left arm a bracelet of bone, set in gold, and when they took this off all his blood flowed away and he expired. Aires Pereira was so surprised at this that he took the bracelet and the captive Moors to Afonso Dalboquerque, and recounted to him all that had passed, and Afonso Dalboquerque inquired of the Moors who that Cap-

of boards tied together with cords only. "Navigium Pangaio, e levi et raro ligno constructum, non nisi funibus colligatum est, nullo omnino clavo ferreo infixo" (*Hist. Ind. Orient.*, p. 220). Camões calls it *sutil*, "lightly skimming", in the line—

"Os Pangayos sutis da bruta gente."—I, 92.

Although narrow and lightly built, the Pangaio is capable of carrying a considerable burden.

tain was, and what was the use of that bracelet to him which he wore; and they replied that he was a principal Moor of Malaca, whose name was Naodabeguea,[1] and he was on his way to warn the king of the coming of the Portuguese, and the bracelet was formed of the bones of certain animals which were called *cabals*,[2] that are bred in the mountain ranges of the kingdom of Siam, and the person who carries those bones so that they touch his flesh can never lose his blood, however many wounds he may receive, so long as they are kept on him. Afonso Dalboquerque was much moved at the death of the Moors from whom he had hoped to obtain information concerning the state of affairs at Malaca, and he prized the bracelet very much for its virtues, and kept it to send it to the king D. Manuel.

When Aires Pereira had returned into his own ship, the whole fleet went back along the coast in the same order as they had first come, and when they were in the latitude of the Powder Island[3] they sighted two very large junks, and gave chase to them. One of these, which was from Choromandel,[4] struck immediately; the other, from Jaoa,[5] would not do so; Afonso Dalboquerque therefore ordered Pero Dalpoem to go up close and call upon her to surrender, and if she would not do so, then to attack her at close quarters; and as it happened that, in the act of boarding the junk, our own men were closely pressed, the Javanese wounded

[1] Called Maodabegea, on p. 59, *n.*

[2] *Cabais.* João de Barros, in *Decad.*, ii, f. 139, col. 23, relates a similar circumstance to this here described; no description of this fabulous creature is recorded by Bluteau, who mentions the passage.

[3] Polvoreira, shown in Barretto de Resende's copy of Pedro Berthelot's map as Polverera, an island in the Straits of Malaca. MS. Sloan, 197, f. 390; Keith Johnston does not mention it.

[4] Coromandel, or Karimanal, Madras Presidency, 13 deg. 24 min. N., 80 deg. 19 min. E.

[5] Java.

several of the men with arrows, and hampered the gear of the mizen-sail[1] and the bowsprit.[2]

When Pero Dalpoem perceived that his rigging was thus destroyed, he disengaged his ship from the junk, and drew off from her. But Afonso Dalboquerque, who was the nearest to him, as soon as he saw Pero Dalpoem disengaging himself, drew up close and demanded the surrender of the junk, which was about six hundred tons burden, very well supplied with arms, and carrying three hundred fighting men on board; and fearing lest her men should set her on fire as soon as he had grappled her—a custom which the Javanese have when they find themselves overcome by the enemies—Afonso Dalboquerque ordered the master[3] of his ship to take the ship's boat, ready with a cable through the ship's hawses,[4] with orders to the effect that he was to arrange so as to be able to cast off the cable whenever he wished, if the Javanese should set fire to the ship.

When this had been set in order, Afonso Dalboquerque drew up close alongside the junk and began to fire into her with his bombards; and as the enemy would not even yet yield, although there were already forty of them killed and a great number of the others wounded, he got ready to board her. As soon as the Javanese perceived that they were overpowered by the ship, the *Flor de la Mar,* which was built with very lofty castles, they set fire to the junk.

[1] *Traquete.* Jal interprets this rightly as the *Voile de misaine*, or mizen sail; it was also called the *traquete davante.* Moraes wrongly defines it to be *a vela do mastro mais alto do navio.* It is the *trinchetto* of the Italians. Bluteau calls it the "*Vela pequena, atada à peça mais alta do mastro grande.*"

[2] *Goroupés;* also *gouroupêz* and *gurupês.*

[3] Mestre, probably *mate*, through Maître, *Fr.*

[4] *Esconvês*, an indeclinable plural, sometimes written *escovêns* and *escouves.* Jal quotes the passage in more than one place in his *Glossaire Nautique*, as *escouves*; but the misprint of *esconves*, if it is one, is found in the early edition, as well as the later one, of the *Commentaries.* The word appears to be derived from *excubiæ*, Lat.; *écubier*, Fr.

It was not until the flames reached the ship that Afonso Dalboquerque gave orders to the mate to unhook his ship and cast off from the junk, and draw away out from between the vessels. The Javanese no sooner observed the shadow of the towering ship passing away from over them, than they set to work to extinguish the fire in their own vessel, but as it had by this time become very extensive, they could only do so, with very great difficulty, and this compelled them to surrender.

The junk having now surrendered, Afonso Dalboquerque discovered that the King of Pacé was on board, and so he sent for him, and when he saw him he begged his pardon very earnestly for this unfortunate affair which should not have happened if he had known of his Royal Highness being on board, and he showed him those ceremonies and that good treatment which is due to a personage of such dignity; and when he had entertained him and taken care for some of his servants who had got badly wounded in the fight, the king gave him an account of his misfortune, setting forth how he was on his way to the King of Java, who was his relative, to ask his assistance with soldiers and a fleet against one of his governors who had risen up in rebellion with the kingdom against him, but if he, Afonso Dalboquerque, would undertake this enterprise and reseat him in his estate again, then he would become a vassal of the King of Portugal, and pay him tribute.

Afonso Dalboquerque, considering that the trade of Pacé would be of great importance to Malaca, if he took it, on account of the great quantity of pepper that the Island contains, told him that he was now engaged on an expedition for settling accounts with the King of Malaca for an injustice which he had done to a captain of the King of Portugal his lord, who had reached that port under the royal safeguard, but when this had been completed he would promise that upon his return voyage to India he would replace him in the possession of his kingdom. The king thanked him very much for his promises of assistance, and declared he would remain there in the ship with him, and ordered those who were in the junk to follow him. And when the fleet was now close to Malaca, Nuno Vaz de Castelo-Branco captured a very rich junk which had just sailed out of the port, bound for the kingdom of Siam, and from the Moors who were taken in her Afonso Dalboquerque learned that Ruy Daraujo and the Portuguese of his company were alive, and that the king already knew of his coming.

So numerous were the ships that they passed on that voyage, that had it not been Afonso Dalboquerque's determination to go to Malaca, they could have taken the largest prize that was ever beheld in those parts; for it was just the time of the monsoon when the Moors navigate to the kingdoms of India which lie to the east of Cape Comorim, but during the other monsoon they make their way direct to the Straits of Méca, laden with all sorts of different spices which are brought to Malaca. But inasmuch as Afonso Dalboquerque desired to have secure peace and friendship with all the kings and Hindoo lords who have their territories on the South, and to trade in their ports—as the King D. Manuel had ordered that the commerce of Malaca should not be destroyed,—he treated all the ships which he passed on the way with good will and entertainment, and to their captains he shewed every kindness in the name of the king of Portugal, and gave them safe conducts, enabling them to navigate—provided they did not go to the Straits—and at this they were very well pleased.

CHAPTER XVI.

How the great Afonso Dalboquerque reached the port of Malaca, and the king sent immediately to visit him, and the rest that took place.

When the great Afonso Dalboquerque had taken the king of Pacé into his ship, he continued his course and sailed up to the shoals of Capacia[1], and entered the twelve fathom passage, and reached the harbour of Malaca one day at evening with all his fleet decked with flags, and the men sounding their trumpets, and ordered them to salute the city with all the artillery, and proceeded to cast anchor in front of the harbour. And when the fleet had thus anchored, the king immediately sent a Moor with a message to Afonso Dalboquerque, asking what was the object of so great a fleet; whether he came for war or for peace, for he did not wish for anything else than peace with the king of Portugal; and giving him to know that his Bendará had been put to death by his orders on account of his complicity in the rising which had taken place against the Portuguese captain (Diogo Lopez de Sequeira) who had come to that port, and resulted in the murder of the Christians who were in the land, but this was no fault of his.

Afonso Dalboquerque listened to this artful apology, and dissembled with him, in hopes of getting Ruy de Araujo and the other Christians who were there in his power again, so he replied that he was well aware how little the king of Malaca was to blame in the matter of the treachery shown to the captain of the king his lord, and now that the king had at length avenged the death of the Christians whom the Bendará had put to death, by cutting off his head, he begged he would of his favour cause those who were left alive to be

[1] In the Straits of Malaca, to the north of the city.

delivered up, and pay, out of the property of the Bendará, for all the goods which had been seized.

The king lost no time in sending the Moor back to declare to Afonso Dalboquerque that they should make peace first, and then he would send back the Christians and make satisfaction for all that had been taken. Afonso Dalboquerque replied that he would not make peace until the Christians had been sent back and all the king's property restored, according to the terms of his first answer sent through the same Moor, and when he had received everything, there would be time to talk of peace, for this was what the king his lord desired, and it was for this object that the King of Portugal had sent him thither, for this fleet had not come in search of a cargo, but to make war upon the king of Malaca, if he would not come to terms of peace with the king his lord.

Notwithstanding all this, the king still refused to deliver up Ruy de Araujo and the Christians without first making peace, for he thought by this means to curb the spirit of Afonso Dalboquerque; but he, on his part, determined not to come to any terms until the Christians were first of all restored to him, as well as all the property which had been detained, and so these negotiations went on from one side to the other until the king of Malaca began to put into practice some of his artifices, and ordered a fleet of launches[1] to issue out of the river, and when they had made a good muster with men and artillery they withdrew again; with these trickeries[2] and follies they thought to get the advantage of Afonso Dolboquerque, but he put up with everything in hopes of getting Ruy de Araujo into his

[1] *Lancharas.*

[2] *Biocos*, a word employed chiefly in the phrase *andar a biocos*, said of women that walk about with a cloak that covers the greater part of their faces and one eye, so that they can see other people without being known.

hands again, for he remembered how the Viceroy had sent him in company with Diogo Lopez de Sequeira in disgrace to Malaca, on his account.[1] And being informed by Ruy de Araujo that the king was causing certain stockades of very great strength to be erected along the seaboard, Afonso Dalboquerque sent word to the King of Malaca to say, that it did not look like a sign of good friendship when he would not send back his Portuguese but ordered the erection of stockades, like one who rather desired war than peace; and how differently, he said, had the king of Pacé behaved to him, for as soon as his port was reached he immediately sent back nine Portuguese who had got away so far in their flight from the bondage in which he, the king of Malaca, had held them; but it seemed, indeed, as if there was no arriving at any settlement with him. The king, in spite of all these arguments, still determined not to surrender the Christians without first of all making a treaty of peace.

Afonso Dalboquerque saw through this design of the king; and in order that he should not think that he had produced any effect by this display of launches in the river which were making a great show there every day according to the king's orders, he decided to undeceive him, and so he gave orders that an expedition of four boats well armed with fighting men and artillery should be got ready, and make their way along the bank and throw some shots from their bombards into the city. When the Moors perceived the boats setting out from the ships, they came out to wait for them, beyond the river's mouth, in a fleet of twenty *pangajaoas*, armed with many men. No sooner had Afonso Dalboquerque perceived them than he ordered a number of boats to be sent to reinforce the four first sent. This disconcerted the Moors, who observed the movement, and

[1] For the circumstances concerning the carrying of Ruy de Araujo to Malaca, see vol. ii, p. 45.

withdrew themselves back again into the river with their fleet. And when they had retired the king again sent the accustomed messages, full of deceit and specious words and falsehoods, to Afonso Dalboquerque.

And Afonso Dalboquerque again listened to them with great patience, always hoping to avoid having recourse to war, and explaining to the king how his coming to Malaca was for the preservation of the port, and for the making of a treaty and ratiying friendship with him, and by no means for the purpose of destroying him. But as there were Moors of many races in the city, all of whom were anxious to prevent a peaceable solution of this matter—to the end that our people should not get a footing in the land—they led the king to believe that Afonso Dalboquerque would never dare to attack the city, but as soon as the monsoon should spring up he would have to be gone without waiting any longer. And a similar thought was in the minds of his own captains. Those who most laboured to prevent peace being made were the Guzarates, for all the trade of Cambaya lies at Malaca, and they offered to help the king with six hundred whites, all well armed, and forty bombards.

And besides all these designs which the king entered into, with the aid of the Moors both native and foreign, Ruy de Araujo sent word to Afonso Dalboquerque that the stockades were fast approaching completion, and the king was making ready for his defence; and the Turks, Guzarates, Rumes, and Coraçones were the principal ones who were advising him to make no agreement, but to forbid our people to make any settlement in the land; and in order to carry out their designs they were giving large bribes to the king and his governors; and they had also on their side the Cacizes,[1] who made long harangues to him,

[1] Cacizes, priests whose duty was to recount with dramatic vehemence in high places, and public concourses, the circumstances of the death of the Prophet.

declaring that the Portuguese were renegades and thieves, desirous of lording over the whole world, and that he would be sorry for it if he allowed them to come into the city. And Ruy de Araujo went on to say that the Xabandar[1] of the Guzarates, who was the mainstay of all the merchants of Cambaya—a man of great credit with the king—had gone to the king and begged him very earnestly not to make friendship with the Portuguese nor come to any terms of peace with them, for their ships and those of the Moors could not navigate in one and the same course in one and the same monsoon, neither could they take in their cargoes all together in the same port, for, if this was a matter of keen competition, even when all engaged were of one nation, how much more difficult would those things be, seeing that these on the one hands were Moors, and the Portuguese, on the other hand, Christians, desirous to destroy them and procuring the destruction of them all; and the Xabandar declared that he gave him this advice because he was very desirous of doing him a service, and preserving the kingdom; and he ought to temporize with the chief captain of that (Portuguese) fleet, and keep up negotiations with him, for when the monsoon should come, he could not remain there any longer.

The king was well pleased with the advice given by the Xabandar, and discussed it all with his governors, and they all were of opinion that such a policy should be carried out; therefore he ordered that his fleet should be repaired immediately, to the end that it might be prepared for anything that might happen, and that the work of the stockades should be pressed on more quickly.

[1] See vol. ii, p. 132. The meaning of the term is "Lord of the Shore".

CHAPTER XVII.

Of the site and foundation of the kingdom and city of Malaca.

The kingdom of Malaca[1] on the one side is co-terminous

[1] Camões makes the prophetic Siren sing:—

"Mais avante fareis, que se conheça
Malaca por emporio ennobrecido,
Onde toda a provincia do mar grande
Suas mercadorias ricas mande.

"Dizem que desta terra, co'as possantes
Ondas o-mar entrando, dividio
A nobre ilha Samatra, que já d'antes
Juntas ambas a gente antigua vio:
Chersoneso foi dita, e das prestantes
Veas d'ouro, que a terra produzio,
Aurea por epitheto lhe-ajuntaram,
Alguns que fosse Ophir imaginaram.

"Mas na ponta da terra Cingapura
Verás, onde o caminho ás náos se estreita
Daqui, tornando a costa á Cynosura,
Se encurva, e para a Aurora se endireita:
Vês Pam, Patâne, reinos, e a longura
De Sião, que estes e outros mais sujeita;
Olha o rio Menão, que se derrama
Do grande lago, que Chiamai se chama."

x, 123-125.

"MALACCA, see before where ye shall pitch
Your great Emporium, and your Magazins:
The Rendezvouz of all that Ocean round
For Merchandizes rich that there abound.

"From this ('tis said) the Waves' impetuous course,
Breaking a passage through, from Main to Main,
SAMATRA's noble Isle of old did force,
Which then a Neck of Land therewith did chain:
That this was CHERSONESE till that divorce,
And from the wealthy mines, that there remain,

with the kingdom of Queda,[1] and on the other with the kingdom of Pam,[2] and would have about a hundred leagues of coast, and in breadth, across the land up to a chain of mountains where the kingdom of Sião[3] stops, it would be about ten leagues. All this land of old was subject to the kingdom of Sião, and it would be about ninety years,[4] a little more or less—when Afonso Dalboquerque arrived there—since it became a kingdom of itself. And the kings of this kingdom became in time so powerful, that they were called *Coltois*, a word used among them for "Emperor." Now, because it is necessary, for well understanding these commentaries, to look a little further into the foundation of Malaca, I will relate here whence this kingdom derived its first beginning.

At the time when Malaca was founded, there reigned in the Island of Jaoa a king who was called Bataratamurel,

The Epithite of GOLDEN had annext:
Some think it was the OPHYR in the Text.

"But at that Point doth CINGAPUR appear:
Where the pincht Streight leaves Ships no room to play.
Heer the Coast, winding to the Northerne Beare,
Faces the fair Aurora all the way.
See PAN, PATANE (ancient Realms that were),
And long SYAN, which These, and more, obey!
The copious River of MENAM behold,
And the great Lake Chiamay from whence 'tis roll'd!"

Fanshaw.

[1] Queda, or Kidah, 7 deg. 6 min. N., 100 deg. 33 min. E.; on the western side of the Malay Peninsula.

"Quedá, que he só cabeça
Das que pimenta alli tem produzido."

Lus., x, 123.

[2] Pahang, 3 deg. 35 min. N., 103 deg. 17 min. E., on the eastern side of the Peninsula.

[3] Siam.

[4] See notes derived from Col. Yule's *Marco Polo*, at end of this chapter.

and in the kingdom of Palimbão[1] which lies within the Island of Jaoa, there reigned a Hindoo king whose name was Parimiçura, and as there were many dissensions between them they at length came to an understanding that Parimiçura should marry one of the daughters of Bataratamurel, who was called Parimiçuri, and continue paying a certain tribute to the king of Jaoa his father-in-law. This king Parimiçura, when a few days had elapsed after he had made this agreement, repented of it, and rose up and threw off his promise of obedience, and would not pay the tribute to his father-in-law, and in order to do this he conferred with some of his relatives, and put his intentions into practice.

When Bataratamurel perceived that his son-in-law had risen up in rebellion against him, and was unwilling to pay the tribute, he came against him with a large force and overcame him, and took away his kingdom from him; and Parimiçura, seeing that he was worsted and fearing lest he should fall into the hands of his father-in-law, fled away with his wife, his children and his slaves, and some few remnants of his forces, in a junk, and reached Singapura,[2] which was a very large and very populous city—as is witnessed by its great ruins which still appear to this very day—before the foundation of Malaca, and put himself under obedience to the king of Sião.

Singapura, whence this city takes its name, is a channel through which all the shipping for those parts passes, and signifies in the Malay language, "*treacherous delay*"; and this designation suits the place very well, for sometimes it happens that when ships are there waiting for a monsoon there comes so fierce a storm that they are lost.

When the king Parimiçura had arrived at this port, the captain of the city, whose name was Tamagi, seeing him coming in this plight, entertained him in his house, and

[1] ? Palembang, in Sumatra island, 2 deg. 46 min. S., 104 deg. 50 min. E. See note at end of chapter.

[2] Singapore.

showed him many honours. But Parimiçura, as a payment for the good treatment he had received, out of covetousness for the richness of the land, murdered him with a creese a week after his arrival, and became Lord of the Channel and population that there were in it.

As soon as it was known in the kingdom of Palimbão how prosperous Parimiçura had become, three thousand natives of this kingdom made their way to the king, and these he kept with him, and he lived in the city of Singapura for five years, robbing every one who passed through, for he had a numerous fleet of launches on the sea. The Lord of Patané,[1] who was Tamugi's brother,[2] when he learned that Parimiçura had murdered his brother, and had made himself lord of the channel, made ready and fell upon him with a large force, and being assisted by those of the country who owed him a grudge on account of his rapacity, overcame him.

Parimiçura being now overcome fled away and went up into the river of Muar, where he found some fishermen who lived in poverty, and commenced again to get land into cultivation to produce bread[3] for his subsistence, and with a little fish which the fisherman used to give him he lived there for some time; and some people whom he carried with him led no other life than roving as robbers over the sea in launches which they found.

At this time there lived also in the port, where now the population of Malaca is located, twenty or thirty fishermen, who supported themselves sometimes by fishing, and at other times by robbing; and they hearing that king Pari-

[1] Patani, in the Malay Peninsula, 6 deg. 56 min. N., 101 deg. 2 min. E.

[2] Note the altered form of this name.

[3] *E começou a fazer terras de pão pera se manter;* it may be that there is here a play on the word *terra* in the phrase *terras de pão*, lumps of bread, as it were, instead of the expanse of territory he had formerly held sway over.

miçura was settled at Muar, with the reputation of being a cavalier and man of spirit, made their way to him and told him that in the country where they were, three leagues' distance along a river, there was a plain which was called Bintão,[1] very fertile, wherein large crops of rice could be grown, as well as all other things required, and well supplied with water for drinking; that he ought to remove

[1] Bintang. "An Island called *Pentam*, a very wild place. All the wood that grows thereon consists of odoriferous trees."—*Marco Polo*, Ed. Yule, ii, 261.

Of this island, situated in 1 deg. 10 min. N. lat., 104 deg. 30 min. E. long., Col. Yule writes as follows:—"Pentam is no doubt the Bintang of our maps, more properly Bentan, a considerable Island at the Eastern extremity of the Straits of Malaca. It appears in the list published by Dulaurier from a Javanese inscription, of the kingdoms conquered in the fifteenth century by the sovereigns reigning at Majapahit in Java. Bintang was for a long time after the Portuguese conquest of Malacca the chief residence of the Malay Sultans who had been expelled by that conquest, and it still nominally belongs to the Sultan of Johore the descendant of those princes, though, in fact, ruled by the Dutch, whose port of Rhio stands on a small island close to its western shore. It is the Bintão of the Portuguese, whereof Camoëns speaks as the persistent enemy of Malacca." The passage is as follows:—

"Mas despois que as estrellas o chamarem,
Succederás, ó forte Mascarenhas,
E, se injustos o mando te tomarem,
Prometto-te que fama eterna tenhas!
Para teus inimigos confessarem
Teu valor alto, o fado quer que venhas
A mandar mais de palmas coroado,
Que de fortuna justa acompanhado:

"No reino de Bintão, que tantos danos
Terá a Malaca muito tempo feitos,
N' hum só dia as injurias de mil annos
Vingarás co' o valor de illustres peitos:
Trabalhos e perigos inhumanos,
Abrolhos ferreos mil, passos estreitos,
Tranqueiras, baluartes, lanças, settas,
Tudo fico, que rompas e sobmettas."

x, 56, 57.

thither, and if he would make his settlement there, they would serve him and become his tributaries.

Parimiçura, having received this information which the fishermen had given to him, went and viewed the site, and was very much pleased with it and with all that territory; and returning to Muar embarked with all his household and followers, and went to live at Bintão, and began to make extensive sowings of grain, and orchards of fruit, and made some very large palaces for his occupation, and became so well pleased with this land that he created the fishermen to be Nobles and Mandarins of his household out of recompense for their services in having shown him the situation; and because the harbour was commodious and very deep with good water, in the space of four months after Parimiçura had first gone thither, there was a population of a hundred inhabitants where the city of Malaca now stands.[1]

The robbers who used to go about pirating over the sea in launches that made a practice of putting into the port of Malaca for water, appreciating the favours and good entertainment that they received from the king Parimiçura, began to take up their abode there, and carry thither the goods they had stolen, and a great development began to take place, so that within two years there was a population of two thousand inhabitants, and they began to acquire a steady trade. This Parimiçura gave the name of *Malaca* to the new colony, because, in the language of Jaoa, when a man of Palimbão flees away they call him *Malayo;* and since he had come to that place fleeing from the kingdom of Palimbão, of which indeed he once was king, he gave the place the name of *Malaca.* Others say that it was

[1] From this text it would appear that the city of Malaca was built on the *plain of Bintão.* If the statement of the *Commentaries* is correct, Bintão can hardly be identified with the Island of Bintang, as above. Very possibly there were several sites thus named. Bantam, on the West Coast of Java, is another example of the name.

called Malaca because of the numbers of people who came there from one part and the other in so short a space of time, for the word *Malaca* also signifies to *meet*, and therefore they gave it the name of city in contradiction. Of these two opinions let each one accept that which he thinks to be the best, for this is the truth of the matter.

Batara Tamurel, having perceived the rapid growth of affairs at Malaca, and the prosperity which attended his son-in-law, reconciled himself with him again and sent him a great many supplies at his expense; and because the king Parimiçura was a man of good nature and treated with kindness those who visited that port, the inhabitants of Pacé and of Bengala[1] began to trade with those of Malaca, and seven years after Parimiçura had begun this population of Malaca, he died, and left behind him a son whose name was Xaquendarxa, who, though he was a Hindoo, married a daughter of the king of Pacé, but it would not have been very difficult to make him turn Moor, for when they were married, either by reason of the entreaties of his wife, or from the admonitions of his father-in-law, very few days elapsed before he became a Moor. And this king Xaquendarxa, after having several sons, desired to go and see the king of China, saying he wished to go and see a king who had for his vassals the Javanese, and the Siamese, and people of all other known lands; so he set out from Malaca, taking with him a present for the king of China, and occupied three years in the journey, and became his vassal, and brought back with him a half seal in sign of vassalage, and obtained permission to coin small money of pewter, which money he ordered to be made as soon as he reached Malaca; and to it he gave the name of *Caixes*,[2] which are like our *ceitils*, and a hundred of them go

[1] Bengal.

[2] Cf. "Aos quaes se davão *duas Caixas*, que sam *tres reis* da nossa moeda" (*Hist. de Fern. Mend. Pinto*, 128, col. 4). *Bluteau.*—The Chinese

to the *calaim*, and each *calaim* was worth, according to an appointed law, eleven *reis* and four *ceitils*.[1] Silver and gold was not made into money, but only used by way of merchandise.

And when the king of China had taken his leave of Xaquendarxá, he sent with him a captain who was to accompany him back to Malaca, and in consequence of the

Le (? Portug., *Re*) is the European *cash*; 100 *Le* = 1 *Candarim* (? Portug. *Calaim*).

[1] We here obtain the value of the *Calaim* (as a coin), which is mentioned above, at p. 45. But, on the other hand, Bluteau quotes from the *Decadas* a passage where the word is used as equivalent to *estanho*, and calls it a fine kind of Indian pewter. According to the above, the monetary system of Malaca, as arranged by Xaquendarxa, would be—

1 *Caixe*, or *Cash*, Malay = 1 *Ceitil*, Portuguese.
100 *Caixes* = 1 *Calaim* = 11 *Reis*, 4 *Ceitils*.
∴ 1 *Rei* = $8\frac{8}{11}$ *Ceitils* or *Caixes*.

But from Bluteau's description of the *Ceitil*, which I translate below, the correspondence between the *Rei* and *Ceitil* is different from this deduction. "*Ceitil*, or *Seitil*, as though one said *Sextil*, for of old it was a coin which was equal to the sixth part of an *adarme* ($\frac{1}{16}$ of an ounce). Others say that *Ceitil* is derived from *Ceita*, understanding thereby that this coin was taken from the city of *Ceita*. Others will have it that the coin was called *Ceitil*, as though for *Settil*, because *seven* of them go to the copper *Real*. Francisco Soarez Toscano says, in his *Parallels*, p. 129, that king D. João I, in remembrance of his conquest of the city of Ceita, ordered copper money to be struck, which he then called *Septil*, now *Ceitil*, of which *six* go to the copper *Real*, although they are no longer current in this kingdom, and, indeed, in the time of the said author they were only current in Guimaraens, where flax was bought and sold by the *Ceitil*. On one side of this coin, the said king ordered to be placed the arms of Portugal; on the other, a city along the water side," etc. For the best information upon the native currency, the reader will do well to consult "Recherches sur les Monnaies des Indigènes de l'Archipel Indien et de la Péninsule Malaie, par H. C. Millies; Ouvrage Posthume, publié par l'Institut Royale pour la Philologie et l'Ethnographie de l'Inde Néerlandaise. La Haye. M. Nijhoff, 1871," 4to. For figures of these coins, see the work of Manoel Bernardes Lopes Fernandes, entitled "Memoria das moedas correntes em Portugal", etc.; among the "Memorias da Academia Real das Sciencias do Lisboa, 2*a* classe", p. 96, etc.

great friendship which sprung up between them on their road, Xaquendarxá married one of his daughters,[1] by whom he had a son whose name was Rajapute, from whom are descended the kings of Campar[2] and Pam. And a few days after his return to Malaca he died, and his eldest son, whose name was Modafaixa, reigned after him.

When Modafaixa came to the throne he again confirmed the treaties of peace which his father had made with the king of China, and of Sião and of Jaoa, and greatly ennobled Malaca, and always kept a fleet on the sea, and conquered many lands, and took the kingdom of Campar and of Pam, and of Dandargiri, and made [the kings of] them Moors by force and married them to three daughters of his brother[3] Rajapute. When he had done this he took the name of Sultan Madofaixa,[4] and soon after died, and one of his sons, named Sultan Marsusa, became king after him.

This king when he began to govern his kingdom built upon the mountain of Malaca great palaces in which he lived, and because he was afraid lest his uncle Rajapute, who was at Bentão, should rise up against him and deprive

[1] The text is "casou-o Xaquendarxá com huma filha sua", "Xaquendarxá married him to one of his daughters"; but from the context and pedigree, there is no doubt that the author of the *Commentaries* has translated wrongly here from some original account. The article should not be enclitic; the sentence will then become "Xaquendarxá married", etc., as I have given it; and this is borne out by the reading of the edition of 1576. "Casou ho Xaquendarxá", etc.

[2] "Vês, corre a costa que Champá se chama,
Cuja mata he do pao cheiroso ornada."—*Lus.*, x, 129.

"Here (mark it!) runs the Coast that's called CHAMPA,
Whose groves smell hot of Calambuco wood."—*Fanshaw.*

See also Yule's *Marco Polo*, ii, 248, Book III, chap. v: "Of the Great Country called Chamba"; which the learned editor identifies with "the whole coast between Tongking and Kamboja, including all that is now called Cochin China outside of Tongking".—*Ib.*, p. 250.

[3] See pedigree at the end of the chapter.

[4] Note this variant form of the name.

him of his kingdom by force, he went to that place and killed him with a creese, although he was now of an advanced age.

As soon as the kings of Pam and Dandargiri were informed of the murder of his uncle which had been committed by Sultan Marsusa they conspired against him, but as he was a cavalier he went up against them and overcame them, and compelled them to pay a double tribute, and married them with his two sisters, and he himself married a daughter of the king of Pam. These marriages produced great amity among them all, and by this daughter of the king of Pam the sultan had a son who died by poison; and afterwards the sultan married a daughter of his Lassamane,[1] by whom he had a son called Alaoadin. On the death of Sultan Marsusa, Sultan Alaoadin became king and married a daughter of the king of Campar, and this king was so rich and amassed so much gold out of the revenues of the port of Malaca, that it was estimated at a hundred and forty quintals[2] of gold.

He now contemplated his wealth and determined to go to the temple of Méca, and made ready many junks for the passage, intending to carry with him the king of Campar and the king of Dandargiri, whom he kept in his court because they were inclined to revolt, not permitting them to return to their own lands, and he had become lord over all that land because he was very powerful on the sea and very rich. And in this king's time Malaca became so noble a city that it was said to contain forty thousand inhabitants, amongst whom were people from all parts of the world. This Sultan Alaoadin married a daughter of his

[1] For the signification of this word, see next chapter.

[2] The *quintal* is equal to 4 *arrobas*, of 32 *arratels* each. The *arratel* contains 2 *marcos*, of eight *onças* each. The *quintal* is represented as equivalent to 58.7428 *kilogr.*, Fr. 140 *quintals* = 8824 *kilogr.*, nearly; that is, upwards of eight tons avoirdupois, English. At £3, English, to the ounce, this would amount to upwards of £860,000.

Bendará, who had been Quelim[1] in the time of his father, whom he loved very dearly, and by her he had a son who was called Sultan Mahamet, and by the daughter of the king of Campar he had a son whose name was Sultan Celeimão, and to this latter the kingdom appertained by right, because he came of the lineage of the kings.

When Alaoadin was ready to set out for Méca, he died of poison, and it was said to have been given to him by the intrigues of the kings of Pam and Dandargiri, because he tried to carry them away against their will. On the death of Sultan Alaoadin, a great dissension arose in the kingdom, because the daughter of the king of Campar, who was queen, wished that her son should inherit the kingdom, for it belonged to him by right. But the Bendará, who was very powerful, and had command of large sums of money, favoured the grandson of his brother who had been Bendará before him, and the kings of Pam and Campar favoured the former. At last the Bendará seized the kingdom for his relative; and as soon as Sultan Mahamet was in possession of the kingdom, he threw off the yoke of Sião and Java, and submitted himself to the king of China.

When the king of Sião found that the king of Malaca would not obey him, he came down against him with a fleet of a hundred sail. The king of Malaca getting knowledge of this, sent his Lassamane to intercept the fleet on the way, and the Lassamane proceeded to wait for him off the island of Pulapicão,[2] and routed the whole of the fleet. And from that time until Afonso Dalboquerque took Malaca[3]—twenty-two years after—they never came again.

[1] This word appears to be a titular designation and of Chinese origin.

[2] ? Panjang, or Pulo Panjang Island, in the Gulf of Siam, 9 deg. 9 min. N., 103 deg. 25 min. E.

[3] Col. Yule, in his Second Edition of *The Book of Ser Marco Polo*, gives the substance of the following notes in vol. ii, p. 263, 264, which are necessary to understand this chapter.

Singapura was founded by an emigration from Palembang, itself a

This king Sultan Mahamet was very vain and very proud, and made a quarrel with his father for wishing to go to the temple of Méca, for he used to say that Malaca was the right Méca; and, being suspicious of his brother, Sultan

Javanese colony. It became the site of a flourishing kingdom, and was then, according to the tradition recorded by De Barros, the most important centre of population in those regions. The Malay chronology, as published by Valentyn (v, 352), ascribes the foundation of Malaca to a king called Iskandar Shah, in A.D. 1252, fixes the reign of Mahomet Shah, third king of Malaca, and first Mussulman king, from A.D. 1276-1333, and gives eight kings in all between the foundation of the city and its capture by the Portuguese in A.D. 1511, a space, according to those data, of 259 years. As Sri Iskandar Shah, the founder, had reigned three years in Singapura before founding Malaca, and Mahomet Shah, the loser, reigned two years in Johore after the loss of his capital, we have 264 years to divide among eight kings, giving thirty-three years to each. This certainly indicates that the period requires considerable curtailment.

Again, both De Barros and these *Commentaries* ascribe the foundation of Malaca to a Javanese fugitive from Palembão, called Paramiçura, and the latter makes Xaquendarxa (Iskandar Shah) the *son* of Paramiçura, and first convert to Mahomedanism. *Four* other kings (see pedigree here following) reign in succession, the last of them being Sultan Mahamet (Mahomed Shah), who was expelled by Afonso Dalboquerque in 1511.

The historian, De Couto, while giving the same number of reigns from the conversion to the capture, places the former about A.D. 1384. And these *Commentaries* allow no more than some ninety years from the foundation of Malaca to the capture of the city by the Portuguese. This would place the foundation about A.D. 1421. There is another approximate check to the chronology, afforded by a Chinese record in Amyot's *Collection*, vol. xiv, where we read that Malaca first acknowledged itself tributary to the empire in 1405, the king being *Sili-ju-eul-sula* (?). In A.D. 1411 *Peilimisula* (Parimiçura) came in person to the Court of China to render homage; and in 1414 the Queen Mother of Malaca came to the Court, bringing her son's homage. Now this notable fact of the visit of a king of Malaca to the Court of China, and his acknowledgment of the Emperor's supremacy, is also recorded in these *Commentaries;* wherein, it is true, the visit is attributed not to Parimiçura, founder of Malaca, but to his son and successor Iskandar Shah. This may be a question of title only, perhaps borne by both; but, we seem entitled to conclude with confidence that Malaca was founded by

Celeimão, he murdered him with a creese, and in like manner he murdered seventeen of the principal men, all of them his relatives, without any cause, and even killed his own son and heir, because he had asked him for some money to spend. The Moors, indeed, used to say that it was in retribution for these crimes that Afonso Dalboquerque deprived him of his kingdom.

a Prince whose son was reigning, and visited the Court of China in 1411. And the real chronology will be about midway between the estimate of De Couto and of the *Commentaries*; that is, the commencement of the fifteenth century.

PEDIGREE OF THE KINGS OF MALACA,

According to the "Commentaries".

Bataratamurel, king of Java.

PARIMIÇURA, king of Palimbão, and 1st king of Malaca. = Parimiçuri.

A dau. of the king of Pacé. =(1) XAQUENDARXÁ, 2nd king of Malaca. =(2) A dau. of the king of China's Captain.

Rajapute. = ...

Three daus. married to the kings of Campar, Pam, and Dandargiri.

.... = SULTAN MODAFAIXA, 3rd king of Malaca.

A dau. of the king of Pam. =(1) SULTAN MARSUSA, 4th king of Malaca. =(2) A dau. of the Lassamane.

A son, poisoned.

A dau. of the king of Campar. =(1) SULTAN ALAOADIM, 5th king of Malaca. =(2) A dau. of the Bendará.

Sultan Celeimão.

SULTAN MAHAMET, 6th and last king of Malaca.

And when these men were dead, he seized all their property, amounting to about fifty quintals of gold, and took all their wives and daughters to be his concubines—about fifty women of great price. Thus there were in Malaca, from the first king who founded the city to the time of Sultan Mahamet, in whose time Afonso Dalboquerque took it, six kings, that is to say, Parimiçura, Xaquendarxá, Sultan Modafaixa, Sultan Marsusa, Sultan Alaoadim, Sultan Mahamet. And Malaca became so noble that they used to say, when Afonso Dalboquerque took it, that the city and the suburbs contained about a hundred thousand inhabitants, and extended a good league's length along the sea.

CHAPTER XVIII.

Of the customs and government of the city of Malaca.

This port of Malaca is very safe; there are no storms to injure it, and never was a ship lost there. It forms a point where some monsoons commence and others end, so that the inhabitants of Malaca call those of India people of the West, and the Javanese, Chinese, and Gores,[1] and all other of those Islanders, people of the East; and Malaca is the middle of all this, a sure and speedy navigation, such as Singapura never had, for in the shoals of Capacia many a ship has been lost. And those which come from the east to the west find here western merchandize, and carry it away with them, leaving that which they bring of theirs here instead, and in like manner do they who come from the west. By these means Malaca gradually increased to so great an extent, that whereas the place used once to be a village of Pacé, Pacé became at length a village of

[1] These are described further on in this chapter.

Malaca, for most of the Moors of Pacé came thither to settle.

Every year there used to come to Malaca ships of Cambaya, Chaul, Dabul, Calicut, Adem, Méca, Xaer,[1] Judá, Choramendal, and Bengala, of the Chinese, Gores, and Javanese, of Pegú, and all those parts. But those of Sião did not come to Malaca with their merchandize, because they were continually at war with the Malays. And I verily believe, according to information which I have obtained concerning the affairs of Malaca, that if there were another world, and another navigable route, yet all would resort to the city, for in her they would find every different sort of drugs and spices which can be mentioned in the world, by reason of the port of Malaca being more commodious for all the monsoons from Cape Comorim to the East, than any other ports that exist in those parts. But I do not describe particularly the other advantages that are possessed by this port of Malaca on account of the monsoons, which enable a navigable intercourse to be maintained in those parts independently of the shallows of Capacia, in order that I may not make too long a digression.

The Malays are proud men by nature, and esteem themselves highly for killing men adroitly with stabs of the creese.[2]

[1] Xaer, or Shehr, a port on the coast of Arabia, between Adem and Dofar, 14 deg. 44 min. N., 49 deg. 40 min. E.

[2] Bluteau describes the *Crîs*, or Creese, the national arm of the Malays, as a kind of dagger, with a flat blade, sometimes undulating at the sides, and poisoned. The poison is applied in two ways, either by steeping the weapon in the juice of herbs, and so applying the poison whenever it is required to use it; or, by incorporating the poison into the temper of the blade, in order that the metal may be thoroughly imbued with it. Of this latter kind, there are some specimens which cost as much as a thousand *patacas* (piastres), for the makers spend much time in their manufacture, using many superstitions and observing certain periods for the tempering. They strike a certain number of blows on certain days of the month for the forging, and sometimes the ceremony of this work lasts, with mysterious interruptions, for more than a year.

They are malicious, generally of little truth, yet the Gores always used to be truthful because they held it to be a high honour that men should trade with them, for they are a noble race, and one of good customs. The Malays are gallant men, they wear good clothing, they will not allow anyone to put his hands on their heads, nor on their shoulders. All their delight is in conversing about military matters, and they are very courteous. No one is allowed to wear yellow colours under pain of death, except only the king of the land, unless he be a person to whom the king gives permission to do so in order to show him honour. The Fidalgos, when they speak to the king, have to stand off from him at a distance of five or six paces.

In the hot season the poison which is communicated by the *cris* is so subtle, that, from a light prick or a mere scratch, it reaches the heart and kills. The only remedy is for the wounded person immediately—*comer do seu proprio esterco.*

Mr. H. Syer Cuming, F.S.A.Scot., whose collection of ethnographical objects is very extensive, has kindly given me the following notes concerning this weapon :—"The *Kris* may be regarded as the typical or national weapon of the Malays of Java and Sumatra. It is a dagger with a waved or serpentine double-edged blade, varying from less than eleven to full fourteen inches in length, and gradually widening from the point to the grip, where it has a rather sudden expansion, which is always more or less richly decorated on one side with a perforated device. This device occasionally takes the form of the head of a serpent, the body of the reptile constituting a sort of mid-rib, running nearly the whole length of the blade; which, it is well to state, is of fine watered or damasked steel, and it is a common practice to dip this blade in poison before going into action.

"The hilt, or grip, of the *kris* has a singular curve or bend on one side, and is generally wrought of a beautiful rich brown wood which takes a high polish; but ivory is sometimes employed. The grip is almost constantly carved; the decorations, however, vary from a few slight cuttings to elaborate designs.

"The wooden sheath of the *kris* is also of peculiar fashion, having a broad wing on one side to receive the sharp projecting portion of the blade, and it further serves as a support to the weapon when worn in the waist-girdle."

The lords who are adjudged to suffer penalty of death have the honourable privilege of dying by the creese, and the nearest relation of the sufferer is the one who kills him. If any man of the people die without heirs, his property goes to the king; and no one can marry without permission from the king or the Bendará. If anyone take his wife in adultery, he may kill within his house both of the parties, but not outside the house, neither can he kill the one without the other, but he must accuse them before the judge. In the case of a fine for injuries, when it has been imposed, the kings used to take half of the money, and the injured person the other half. In Malaca there were divers manners of administering legal punishment, according to the nature of the crime: some were thrust upon spits, others struck forcibly on the breast;[1] some hanged, others boiled in water; others roasted and given as food to certain men who are like wild men, from a land which is called Daru, whom the king brought to Malaca to eat those condemned to this death. And of every man who dies at the hands of the law, the king takes the half of the property when there are heirs, and the whole of it when there are none.

There used to be in Malaca five principal dignities. The first is *Pudricaraja*, which signifies Viceroy, and after the king this one is the greatest. The second is *Bendará*, who is the Controller of the Treasury, and governs the kingdom. Sometimes the *Bendará* holds both of these offices of *Pudricaraja* and *Bendará*, for two separate persons in these two offices never agree well together. The third is *Lassamane*; this is Admiral of the Sea. The fourth is *Tamungo*, who is charged with the administration of justice upon foreigners. The fifth is *Xabandar*; and of these there were four, one of each nation—one of China, another of Java, another of Cambaya, another of Bengala. And all the lands were

[1] *Acotovelados nos peitos*; lit., elbowed, or struck with the elbow.

divided among these four men, and every one had his portion, and the *Tamungo* was Judge of the Custom House, over all these.

One may well and truly say that Malaca, in point of fact, and merchant trade, is the most extensive place in the world, and her laws were always very strictly obeyed, and the city had need of great persons to govern it, as well in the administration of justice as also in the management of the public property, for it deserves this; but had the city been fairly well governed, Malaca had never ceased to be as it was of old. Yet I do not speak here of the numerous lands, islands, kingdoms, and provinces that lie round these parts, although I had certain information of them in the letters which I used to see from Afonso Dalboquerque to the king, D. Manuel, wherein he gave him account of all those parts of the world, for my intentions are to write only of the labours and conquests of Afonso Dalboquerque, and all else I leave to him who will do it better than I can. I will only here make mention of the Gores, as it is necessary I should do so for the sake of this history.

As for the Gores, according to the information which Afonso Dalboquerque [obtained] when he took Malaca—although now we have more correct accounts concerning them, at that period it was reported that their province was on the mainland—the general opinion of all is that their land is an island, and they navigate from it to Malaca, whence come every year two or three ships. The merchandizes which they bring are silk, silk-stuffs, brocades, porcelain, a great quantity of corn, copper, rock alum, and *frusseria*;[1] and they bring a great deal of gold in little cakes, stamped with the seal of their king. It could not be ascertained whether these little cakes were the money of that land, or whether they impressed them with that mark to show that it was a

[1] *Frusseria;* gold or silver dust in its native state, as obtained from washings at the river mouth, or in mines.

thing which had passed through the port whence they brought it, for they are men of very reserved speech, and do not give anyone an account of their native affairs. This gold comes from an island which is close to theirs; it is called Perioco, and in it there is much gold.

The land of these Gores is called Lequea;[1] the men are fair; their dress is like a cloak[2] without a hood; they carry long swords after the fashion of Turkish cimetars, but somewhat more narrow; they carry also daggers of two palms' length; they are daring men and feared in this land [of Malaca]. When they arrive at any port, they do not bring out their merchandize all at once, but little by little; they speak truthfully, and will have the truth spoken to them. If any merchant in Malaca broke his word, they would immediately take him prisoner. They strive to dispatch their business and get away quickly. They have no settlement in the land, for they are not the men to like going away from their own land. They set out for Malaca in the month of January, and begin their return journey in August and September. The usual course of their navigation is to beat up the channel between the Islands of Celate and the point of Singapura, on the side of the mainland. At the time when Afonso Dalboquerque set sail for India, after having captured Malaca, there had arrived two of their ships at the gate of Singapura, and they were coming on to Malaca, but by the advice of the Lassamane, who was the king of Malaca's admiral of the sea, they remained where they were, and would not pass up, having learned that Malaca had been taken by the Portuguese; but when the governors of the land were informed of their position, they

[1] Lew-Chew, or Loo-Choo, Islands, in the Chinese Empire, 26 deg. 30 min. N., 127 deg. E.

[2] *Balandrois;* the *balandrão* is an ample cloak used by several religious fraternities in Portugal.

sent a safeguard for them, and a flag of truce, and then they came on immediately.

This Lassamane was a man of eighty years of age, a good soldier, and of good repute and great knowledge: when he perceived that the king of Malaca was lost, he went and settled in Singapura, and after Afonso Dalboquerque was in possession of Malaca, he came down to the River of Muar and sent to ask a safeguard, declaring that he was desirous of returning to live at Malaca and serving the king of Portugal. Afonso Dalboquerque sent him the safeguard; nevertheless he would not come, and it was thought that some of the Moors of Malaca, hoping to gain favours from Afonso Dalboquerque and obtain the government of the land, had written something to this Lassamane, whereby they had prevented his coming, for they feared that as he was a man of uncommon capabilities, Afonso Dalboquerque would seize the opportunity to make use of him for the governing of Malaca.

CHAPTER XIX.

Of the message which the great Afonso Dalboquerque sent to the king of Malaca, and of the council which he held with his captains concerning the letter which Ruy de Araujo sent him.

The great Afonso Dalboquerque perceiving the pride of the king, and the little dread he had of the Portuguese fleet,—remembering, too, the events which had happened to Diogo Lopez de Sequeira,—became very despondent when he reviewed the course of this business, looking at the falsehoods and deceit which the king of Malaca was practising upon him. And contemplating all these things, Afonso Dalboquerque sent word how he had many times begged that the Christians might be surrendered, for the king had no right to detain them forcibly, because they had not been taken prisoners in fair war nor by way of reprisals, but rather, on the other hand, under cover of his safeguard and that of his governors; for when they were walking in the city unarmed, the king had ordered them to be put to the sword in the very streets by any who chose to kill them; and although the king had declared that he had ordered his Bendará to be put to death because he had been the cause of the murder of the Portuguese, yet he, Afonso Dalboquerque, had received information that this man had been condemned to death on account of a treasonable offence, of which he had been guilty, in plotting to stir up a revolution against the kingdom; and this was the truth, for all that the artful excuses about it had for the time been accepted, for after the death of the Bendará, the king himself had given orders for the Christians to be put to the torture, to the end that they should be compelled to become Moors, and some among them, who would not bear their sufferings, had renounced the Faith of Jesus Christ by force, yet he had pretended to take no notice of all these things, and put up with them to see whether it was possible to make a good peace and friendship with him. But since the king was so obstinate as to desire no kind of termination to this business, he, Afonso Dalboquerque, would have him to know that none of the men in the fleet could bear to stay there day after day, without having wreaked their vengeance upon the treason which had been done in that city towards the captain and soldiers of the king of Portugal, whom the king of Malaca had ordered treasonably to be put to death.

Along with this communication which Afonso Dalboquerque sent to the king of Malaca, he also wrote a letter to Ruy de Araujo, wherein he said how well aware he was of his obligation, and that of the captains and all the rest of the forces in the fleet, to die for the service of the king D. Manuel, his lord, and much more so in a war so just wherein he had frequently justified himself; but that the king of Malaca had apparently obstinately made up his mind neither to deliver up the Christians nor to receive the peace and friendship which were offered to him on the part of the king of Portugal, for which reasons it was advisable to lay hold upon him, Ruy de Araujo, without any further delay; but if this state of affairs should grow more serious, they must put up with their hardships and bear them with patience, for he on his part was bound, insomuch as it was to the advantage of the king of Portugal's estate, to make an end of this business and match his forces against those of the enemy, and the longer he delayed, the more time they had for fortifying themselves.

Ruy de Araujo replied, God grant that neither the fleet of the king of Portugal, nor his Portuguese themselves, should receive any affront or discomfiture in order to make his life secure, for he was also on his part bound to die for the service of God and of his king, and for the liberty of his countrymen, and he held it to be a good fortune for him that Our Lord had placed him in a state where he could die for his Holy Faith; and, as for himself and his companions, he should not fail to do what was best for the service of the king of Portugal, for they were now quite resigned to anything that would happen to them; and he would have Afonso Dalboquerque to know that the king of Malaca was making ready as fast as was possible, and that it was the Guzarates who were at work day and night upon the fortification of the stockades, for these were the principal people who could not bear that the Portuguese should get a footing in the land; and if the Portuguese attack upon the city should be decided upon, it ought to be put into execution as quickly as could be, without wasting any more time in discussing the terms of agreement, or making demands for the surrender of the Christians; for he must know for certain that the king would not restore them to the Portuguese, except under compulsion; and he was now become so puffed up with pride when he surveyed the great number of foreign soldiers that he had, that he thought of nothing less than actually capturing the Portuguese fleet.

On receiving this reply from Ruy de Araujo, Afonso Dalboquerque summoned a meeting of all his captains on board of his own ship, and gave them an account of all this which was contained in the letter, and seeing that the king of Malaca was fixed in this determination, he desired them to declare to him whether an immediate attack should be made upon the city, or a further exchange of complimentary negotiations be carried on. The captains replied to him, that for days past they had not thought it right for him to be so long-suffering towards the king; for since the very day of their arrival, the replies of the enemy had always clearly indicated that they did not desire to come to any understanding or friendship with them, and all these delays which had been set up were to enable them to make their preparations and fortify themselves, as Ruy de Araujo had indeed often declared in his communications.

CHAPTER XX.

Of the requisition which the great Afonso Dalboquerque ordered to be made to the king, signed by himself and all the captains; and how the king sent him Ruy de Araujo and his companions whom he had there.

Notwithstanding the above-mentioned opinion of the captains, the great Afonso Dalboquerque thought right, for the better qualification of these proceedings in the sight of God, and of the kings of all that land (that they should not say the Portuguese were tyrants) that he should first of all order a final and formal demand to be drawn up, and signed by him and by all the captains, and after this certain improvised attacks with a show of battle; and this demand was forthwith forwarded to the king of Malaca by the hands of a Moor, who was employed in going backwards and forwards with these negotiations.

The substance of the communication was to the effect that the king D. Manuel, his lord, had sent to the port of Malaca a captain, with certain ships, which came bearing more of merchandize than of men, out of a desire which he had of establishing peace and friendship with him; but, in violation of the safeguard which both the king and his Bendará had granted to this captain, they had notwithstanding stolen all the property and murdered or imprisoned the Portuguese—as had already been the subject of complaint—and laboured as much as they possibly could to seize his ships, but miraculously Our Lord had delivered them from their hands, the king of Malaca should therefore know for certain that unless orders were issued for the immediate release of the Christians and restitution of the property which had been captured in the ships, that he (Afonso Dalboquerque) would certainly destroy him, and take his city away from him, and he held God to be judge between them that he and his governors were the cause of their own destruction; for, by following the advice of the Guzarates—deadly enemies to the Portuguese—he (the king of Malaca) would not take any steps towards concluding terms of peace with him; and, as for the present fleet which he had now with him, it had no thoughts about the monsoon—as the Guzarates had pretended to the king—neither was it losing any season of voyage; nor was it searching for a cargo; for the ships of which it was composed belonged to the fleet which the king of Portugal employed for the government of India, and it was of no consequence to them whether they remained one year or ten in that harbour; and the king of Malaca should rest quite sure that unless he gave up all thoughts of prosecuting the war which he wished to make upon the captains and men of the king of Portugal, he would very soon lose his estate; and, as a material sign of all these things being in this position, Afonso Dalboquerque gave this token, that he shifted a ring he wore from one finger to another; which he did forthwith in presence of his messenger, who took this declaration to the king.

And the king of Malaca lost no time in sending the messenger back again to declare that his heart was good and sound, and he did not remember about Ruy de Araujo and his Christians; that the reason of not sending them was that he was having some clothing made for them; and that he desired Afonso Dalboquerque would order his ships to withdraw from right in front of the port, in order that there might not arise any disputes between the Christians and the Moors, who had their ships there.

Therefore, although Afonso Dalboquerque was well aware that this was only an artifice of the king, nevertheless, in order not to give him an opportunity of taking hold of anything for future complaint, he ordered the small vessels to withdraw and lie off outside the port; and told the Moor, his messenger, that he was waiting for Ruy de Araujo and his companions, and unless they were returned to him immediately, he should not trouble himself with any further parley or communications. The Moor went back with this message, and six days passed away without his returning with any reply to this. Afonso Dalboquerque, seeing this delay, would not wait any longer, and sent ten boats, with armed men in them, to set fire to some houses which stood close to the edge of the shore; and to burn the ships of the Guzarates, in order that they should lose all hope of returning to their land so soon with a cargo, because they had taken so much trouble to prevent the settlement of differences between him and the king of Malaca; and to burn also all the other ships that lay in the port, except only those which came from ports to the east of the Cape of Comorim, if they belonged to Hindoos.

When these boats reached the houses they set them on fire immediately, and did the same to the ships. The king, now having experienced the determination of Afonso Dalboquerque, lost no time in sending back Ruy de Araujo and the Christians, and with them a Moor to treat for terms of peace, asking him to send back detailed statements of his complaints, and he would do whatever was desired of him. But although Afonso Dalboquerque knew very well that this would not produce any effect, nevertheless he sent back certain statements of his demands, and told the Moor to declare to the king that these were the conditions on which only he would make peace and establish himself in the land.

The king considered the articles, and conceded those of which Afonso Dalboquerque was most doubtful (which did not seem to him to be a good sign), viz., that he would agree to grant a site in the city on which to erect a fortress, and would pay in ready money for everything that had been taken from Diogo Lopez de Sequeira. Afonso Dalboquerque, employing artifices also on his side against the king, replied that although he attached greater importance to the other articles which he had sent than to those which the king had conceded, nevertheless he would consent to accept these concessions, that it might not be said that he was a hard man to please.

To this reply no answer was ever sent back from the king, but some Moorish spies came disguised like merchants, and brought for sale musk, chickens, and other things; and at other times there came the Moor who had been employed to convey the communications between the king and the Portuguese, discoursing of matters which were nothing to the purpose. He pretended that he came to apprise Afonso Dalboquerque of many junks that were approaching from various parts, armed and with forces on board favourable to the king of Malaca, and of the great preparations for war that they carried. And when the Moor went off, there came out of the river a number of armed *paráos* making show of desiring to come to combat with our fleet; yet with all this, Afonso Dalboquerque bore with it for some days, to see if they desired to follow good advice. But when he saw their stockades bedecked with flags, and everything arranged in order of battle, and that the king, being a tyrant who was anxious to keep up his position at all risks, and spending a great deal of his treasure to keep up his power, and to maintain it, was so blind that he did not see the danger that he ran of losing his kingdom, he considered with himself that this was a judgment that had come upon the king, and that Our Lord desired to make an end of him for good and all, and to cast the Moors, and the very name of Mafamede, out of the land, and to have his Gospel preached in those regions, and their mosques transformed into houses of God's praise by means of the king D. Manuel and by the labours of his subjects, so he gave orders for an attack with armed boats and two barges with heavy bombards, with the object of viewing the men who rallied at the alarm, and seeing where they had stationed their artillery, and how they managed their defence.

CHAPTER XXI.

How the Chinese merchants, who were at Malaca, made their way to the great Afonso Dalboquerque; and of what passed with him; and of the council which he held with the Captains, Fidalgos, and Cavaliers of the Fleet to attack the city.

Among the foreign ships which were in the port of Malaca, to which Afonso Dalboquerque would not have any injury done when he ordered those of the Guzarates to be burned, were five Chinese junks, whose captains and crews the king of Malaca had detained for some days past, intending to avail himself of them against the king of Daru, with whom he was at war, and this was their condition when Afonso Dalboquerque arrived with his fleet. But the king of Malaca, confident that the Chinese would never dare to fly away for fear of the Portuguese in the port, and also because he had quite enough to do to look after himself and his country, ceased to think about them.

When the Chinese perceived that they had greater freedom than before, they sought a means of escape, and gathered themselves together in their junks. The crews, who were left on land, seeing their captains in safety, a few at a time, each one as best he might, made their way to them, and these captains, when they had reassembled their men, being thoroughly indignant against the king for the robbery and tyranny which he had exercised upon them in respect of their merchandise, and also in order to obtain security for themselves, came and offered themselves to Afonso Dalboquerque with their crews and ships, to help him in his war.

He thanked them very much for their offers of help, but would not accept any assistance from them except the barques[1] of their junks, to be used for disembarking his men on land, for should their business not succeed in the way he hoped in Our Lord that it would, if the Chinese were in opposition to the king of Malaca in the matter, they might hereafter be ill treated by the king for the part they had taken.

The Chinese replied, that seeing he would not accept their services, they begged him very much of his kindness to grant them permission to go away to their own land, and wherever they might encounter Portuguese, those should be ever remembered for the favour he had done

[1] *Barcas.*

them in letting them depart at liberty and get away from such a bad set of people as the Malays were; and if Malaca should fall into his power, they would undertake that every year more than one hundred junks should come there with great quantity of merchandise; and with very courteous words they told him to take very good advice before he attacked the city, for there were inside it more than twenty thousand fighting men, Javanese, Persians, and Coraçones, men in whom the king reposed the greatest confidence; while of the natives, the king could have as many soldiers as he wished; and he had twenty war elephants, with their castles well armed, and plenty of artillery and arms of every kind, which the Guzarates had brought for him from Cambaya, and as for all other things necessary for the war, he was not in need of anything; and unless the city were taken by starvation (though the inhabitants had provided even for this contingency), by stopping the supplies which came to her from Jaoa, they thought it very doubtful if any victory could be obtained against her; therefore they told him this, because they would be very sorry to see him in any peril.

Afonso Dalboquerque told them that he thanked them very much for their advice, but he was already quite determined to undertake the matter; and even if the king of Malaca's power were great, still greater was the power of God, for whose faith they were fighting; that he begged they would stay there a few more days to see what end came to Malaca, and then carry news to the king of China of all that might take place; and he would send them a galley in which they could be drawn up close by the place of disembarkation, so as to see the great spirit with which the Portuguese would attack the city, and their manner of fighting. The Chinese did as Afonso Dalboquerque ordered, and, with great concern that he would not have them serve him in that enterprise, went away to their ships and sent him the barques.

As soon as the Chinese had gone away, Afonso Dalboquerque summoned a meeting of all the captains, fidalgos, and noble persons of the fleet, and recounted what had passed between him and the Chinese, and told them how much he took it to heart that these Chinese had declared to him that they looked upon the impending undertaking as of doubtful result, and, in order to get over his affront, he had made up his mind to attack the city before they set out for China, and erect therein a fortress of convenient dimensions, with determination to maintain it, for this was what would conduce most to the service of the king their Lord; because, if they did not accomplish this, it was of little profit to stake very much upon the chance of capturing the city, seeing that Malaca was the principal seaport of the whole world, and thither resorted Moors from all parts in search for spiceries, especially from Cairo and Méca; as well as all the inhabitants of places to the eastward of the gates of the Straits. And these Malays were the people who did the most harm to the trade of India, so much so that the ships of Portugal, that were thither bound, ran great risk of being lost, unless it were a fleet of very large numbers, well provided with men and munitions of war. At all these things he begged them to look, and tell him, when their minds were quite made up, what they would have him do; because, if they did not consider it advisable to construct a fortress, he would not jeopardise the life of a single cabin-boy for all the Moors that there were in Malaca.

The captains, after many debates held concerning this matter, declared to him that they did not doubt that the service of the king would be furthered by their constructing a fortress in Malaca, with a view of securing the commerce of those parts, but the business would have to be undertaken when he had everything ready that was required, so that he could accomplish it in a short space of time; and that his plan should be to attack the city and inflict a punishment upon the king for his misdeeds, and overcome that pride which he had manifested; and, if after the capture of the city, the necessary materials for the construction of the fortress could be got together, they then could make it, provided that they did not let the proper time slip away for their returning to the assistance of India.

Afonso Dalboquerque approved of this opinion which the captains had arrived at, and dismissed them to their ships to make ready against the time when he should let them know the day he had selected for the attack upon the city.

CHAPTER XXII.

How the great Afonso Dalboquerque, on the morning of St. James's day, attacked the city of Malaca, and what passed thereupon.

The great Afonso Dalboquerque was so devoted to the Apostle St. James, that after it had been agreed by all that the city should be attacked, he delayed the completion of his preparations for some days, with the object of putting his hands to this work on that saint's day, for he trusted that through the prayers and merits of the saint, Our Lord would give them victory over it, as He had done in the capture of Goa. And when the time was come, he summoned the captains and declared to them that he was determined to attack the city upon the following day, which was the day of the Apostle Saint James, and it was necessary, before doing so, to discuss where and in what order they must disembark, in order that every one should know what duty was assigned to him.

The captains began to give their opinions, but as there were various opinions among them, so that some said the attack should be made on one side and others on the other, Afonso Dalboquerque desired, before any final decision should be made, that Ruy de Araujo, who had considerable experience concerning the land,[1] should give his opinion.

Ruy de Araujo declared that in his opinion they ought first to attack the bridge before anything else, for if they took that and made themselves strong in it, our people would be placed just between the city and the inhabitants of Upe, and the power of the king divided into two parts; for one could not render any assistance to the other except by means of the bridge, which one hundred men, with small barricades that they could set up in it, could defend against every forcible attempt of the Moors that might be made; but if the attack upon the city were made at any other parts, as some of the Lords who were there present advised, Malaca was of such a size and possessed so many fighting men in her population, that he, for his part, held the matter as very doubtful of success, and all would run a risk of being lost.

Without listening to any further advice, as soon as Afonso Dalboquerque had heard Ruy de Araujo's words, he agreed with the opinion he gave, and immediately gave orders that the captains, with their men in two battalions, should proceed to attack the bridge. D. João de Lima, Gaspar de Paiva, Fernão Perez Dandrade, Sebastião de Miranda, Fernão Gomez de Lemos, Vasco Fernandez Coutinho, and James Teixeira, with other fidalgos and soldiers of the fleet, to disembark on the side of the mosque; while he himself, with Duarte da Silva, Jorge Nunes de Lião, Simão Dandrade, Aires Pereira, João de Sousa, Antonio Dabreu, Pero Dalpoem, Dinis Fernandez de Melo, Simão Martinz, Simão Afonso, and Nuno Vaz de Castelo-branco, with all the rest of the armed forces, would disembark on the city side; and after an entry had been effected through the stockades, one and all were to rush on towards the middle

[1] Compare this with what is written of Ruy de Araujo at the end of chapter xxiv, p. 111.

of the bridge, until they could estimate the strength of the enemy and in what direction their spirit led them, for in an affair of which they had not yet seen the result, he could not come to any other determination than ordering this only, that where they saw his flag flying, there all should concentrate themselves.

Having given these orders, he dismissed the captains to go and get ready, and on the following day, when they heard a trumpet sounded, come on board his ship so as to set forth therefrom.

Two hours before the break of day Afonso Dalboquerque ordered the trumpet to be blown, in order to awaken them, and they embarked immediately with all the rest of the men-at-arms and went on board his ship, and when a general confession had been made, all set out together and came to the mouth of the river just as morning broke, and attacked the bridge, each battalion in the order which had been assigned to it.

Then the Moors began to fire upon them with their artillery, which was posted in the stockades, and with their large matchlocks[1] wounded some of our men.

As soon as the first fury of their artillery was spent, the great Afonso Dalboquerque gave order for the trumpets to be blown, and with a war-cry of "Sanctiago", *i.e.*, "Saint James", they all, with one accord, fell upon the stockades of the bridge, each battalion in its proper place, and from on this side and on that an infinite number of Moors rushed up, some with bows and arrows, and others with long lances, and shields like those of Biscay, blowing their horns[2] and trumpets, and for a good space of time they fought very bravely, and defended the stockados; but our men, who had disembarked on the side of the mosque, by dint of arms

[1] *Espingardões;* the *espingardão* was probably a large kind of *espingarda*, or matchlock, a word of frequent use throughout the text of the *Commentaries*.

[2] *Anafis.*

*

forced their way through them;[1] and at this very moment the king of Malaca came up mounted upon an elephant, and his son upon another, with a body of armed men, and elephants armed with wooden castles, containing many warlike engines, and compelled the Moors to return to the stockades which they had deserted.

D. João de Lima, Fernão Perez Dandrade, and all the others who were in that company were inspired with fresh vigour at the sight of the king, and without any fear of his elephants attacked the Moors in so spirited a manner, that they got possession of the mosque immediately. Afonso Dalboquerque, who remained on the side nearest to the city with all the other captains and men, attacked the bridge on that side, and although his division met with great resistance by reason of the presence there of a large part of the force which had accompanied the king, very well armed, many of them with bows, others carrying blowing tubes[2] with poisoned arrows, wherewith they wounded a great many of his men, nevertheless anxiously emulating the captains of the other battalion who had by this time become masters of the mosque and the head of the bridge, they fell upon the Moors so bravely that they got into their stockades by force of arms, and killed many of them, and put them to flight. On our side many were wounded, and some died of the poisoned arrows.

[1] ...... *e defendêram as estancias; mas os nossos, que eram daquella banda da mesquita, por força darmas os entráram*; there is probably a typographical error in the latter part of this extract, for the *os* before *entráram* refers to *estancias*, and should be *as* to agree with this word.

[2] *Zarvatanas com setas ervadas;* this word is also written *Sarabatana*, and *Zaravatana*, by Vieyra, who calls it "a sort of speaking trumpet".

CHAPTER XXIII.

How Tuão Bandão, captain of the king of Malaca, perceiving the dispersion of the Moors, went to their assistance with a body of soldiers, and what passed thereupon; and how the king took to flight, and our men pursued him.

No sooner did Tuão Bandão, captain of the king of Malaca, who held a stockade on the bridge, bedecked with flags of his colours, perceive the discomfiture of the Moors, than he sallied out with seven hundred Javanese, and other two captains with him, and went to reinforce the bridge on the city side, with the intention of falling on our men in the rear. When Afonso Dalboquerque caught sight of them coming along one of the principal streets of the city, he dispatched from his company João de Sousa, Antonio Dabreu, and Aires Pereira in command of their men, with orders to fall upon the advancing body, and this they did so rapidly, that before the Moors could get up as far as the stockades, they fell upon them with the lance with such impetuosity that they made them turn and fly.

D. João de Lima, and other captains who were on the side of the mosque, when they saw these Moors, ran up to attack them in front, and there and then killed several of the body. The others, perceiving themselves cut off in front and in rear, all threw themselves into the sea. And the mariners, who were in the boats, came up without a moment's delay and put them all to death, so that not a single man was left, their captain, Tuão Bandão, being already dead, as well as the two captains who had set out with him; and when they had accomplished this business they went back to the stockades.

D. João de Lima, and the others who formed his company, seeing, after they had established themselves in the stockades, that the king was retiring by a side path up the hill, set out in pursuit after him, fighting with the Moors at every step. The king and his son, who were mounted upon their elephants, saw that they were pursued by our men, turned back again with two thousand men whom they carried in their company. The Portuguese captains awaited their coming at the head of a street, and with great efforts and brave determination fell upon the elephants with their lances, as they were coming on in the vanguard, and it is related that Fernão Gomez de Lemos was the foremost in this action; and whereas elephants will not bear with being wounded, they turned tail and charged the Moors behind them and put them to rout. The elephant on which the king was riding, mad with the mortal wound which it had received, seized the black man who was guiding it with its trunk, and roaring loudly, dashed him in pieces, and the king being already wounded in the hand, sprang out of the castle, but escaped because he was not recognised; and thus he and his son, and the king of Pão,[1] his son-in-law, who had come to Malaca but a few days before to marry one of the king's daughters, retreated to the back of the city.

Afonso Dalboquerque, with the rest of his men,—having forced an entrance through the stockades,—followed up after the Moors along a street which led to the bridge, and killed many of them; but because the men of the city, who were fighting in the streets with our forces, were very numerous, Afonso Dalboquerque, fearing lest his party should begin to straggle, made them rally towards the bridge, and ordered them to erect a palisade on the city side; and gave charge over it to Jorge Nunez de Lião and Nuno Vaz de Castelo-branco, with orders for them to command one of the principal streets leading to the bridge with their artillery.

When the Moors saw this they gathered themselves to-

[1] This word is written *Pam* in the previous chapters.

gether in the other streets of the city, and Afonso Dalboquerque feeling himself at length free of them, gave orders that another palisading should be erected on the side towards the mosque, starting from the river to reach up to the mosque, in such a manner that the bridge remained in the middle [between this palisade and the one mentioned above]. And while these palisadings were in progress of formation, he sent Gaspar de Paiva with a hundred men to set fire to the city from that side as soon as the sea-breeze should begin to blow, and Simão Martinz with another party of a hundred men, to set fire to the king's houses which stood at the side of the mosque. When the fire gained possession of one part and the other, it raged so fiercely that it destroyed a great part of the city. As soon as the Moors beheld the flames, they retired a long way off from our men.

Here was burnt a wooden house, of very large size and very well built with joiners' work, about thirty palms breadth solid timber, all inlaid with gold, built up on thirty wheels, every one of which was as large as a hogshead, and it had a spire, which was the finishing-point of the building, of great height, covered with silken flags, and the whole of it hung with very rich silken stuffs, for it had been prepared for the reception of the king of Pão and his bride, the daughter of the king of Malaca, who were to make their entry through the city with great blowings of trumpets and festivities; and in the houses of the king, and the other houses round about, which were burned, there was consumed by fire a great store of merchandise and other things of great price, which the king had in his palace. And when this was completed, they returned again to the bridge where our men were stationed; and it was about two hours after midday, and as yet the men had not eaten anything.

The captains, to whom Afonso Dalboquerque had entrusted the duty of constructing the stockades, went to him and told him that the men, being tired, and suffering from the great heat, were by this time quite out of heart with their work, and they recommended that they should withdraw and take some rest. Afonso Dalboquerque put them off, for he hoped to get the barricades completed, and so pass the night there; but because they came again with more earnestness to press this, he made a virtue of the necessity; and, the sun being now gone down, he began to draw off his men to the boats. When the Moors perceived that they were withdrawing, they began to open fire with large matchlocks, arrows, and blowing-tubes, and wounded some of our men, yet with all the haste they made Afonso Dalboquerque ordered the men to carry off with them fifty large bombards that had been captured in the stockades upon the bridge; and when the men had returned to the ships, he ordered the wounded to be attended to—about seventy in number—but of those who were struck with the poisoned arrows, none escaped but one, Fernão Gomez de Lemos, who was burned with a red-hot iron directly he was struck, so that ultimately God spared his life.

CHAPTER XXIV.

How the king of Malaca, after the Portuguese had withdrawn to their ships, began to reconstruct the stockades and fortified his position on the bridge; and of the message which Utemutaraja sent to the great Afonso Dalboquerque.

Directly that all had retired into the ships, the king ordered that the stockades should be reconstructed, and made stronger than they had been before, and placed in them double the quantity of artillery, of which there was a great supply in Malaca, as will be related hereafter, and ordered the bridge to be divided into sections with very strong palisades, and erect others in one of the principal streets leading from the city to the bridge, and in them he placed much artillery, and on the other side of the mosque he did just the same, and on the shore side, where the landing-place was situate, he ordered his men to throw down many *chevaux-de-frise*, full of poison,[1] to prick our men when they made their landing. And because the Javanese, who composed the principal soldiery under his command, were discontented at not receiving their pay, in order to content them, he ordered that they should be paid all that was due to them of their pay, and three months in advance as well, for he was in great dread lest Afonso Dalboquerque should return again to attack the city. And while he was thus occupied with the fortifying of his stockades, a Javanese headman, who was called Utemutaraja,[2] who lived in the settlement of Upe, and had about five or six thousand Javanese slaves of his own or of his sons and sons-in-law, a very rich man, and one who traded very extensively to all parts of the world, sent a present of sandal woods to Afonso Dalboquerque, and secretly begged a safeguard for himself and for all that settlement wherein he lived, declaring that he desired to have peace and friendship with him, and to serve the king of Portugal in all that lay in his power.

Afonso Dalboquerque accepted his offer of friendship, and sent him the safeguard and sometimes some presents, always striving to keep him on our side. Now, although the agreement which had been made with this man stipulated that he should give no assistance, and show no favour to the king of Malaca, after three days, Afonso Dalboquerque sent and told him that he had been informed that after

[1] *Mandou lançar muitos abrolhos, cheios de herva*, etc. The word *herva* is used in the concluding sentence of the previous chapter in the signification of *poisonous juice of herbs;* but in this passage, although I prefer the translation I give above, there is a possibility of the word being used in the sense of grass or prickly brushwood.

[2] The latter part of this name is evidently the titular designation *rajah*.

he had sent him the safeguard, he was nevertheless helping the king with his men to make the stockades on the bridge, which was not the thing that they both had agreed upon, neither was it according to the law of friendship for him to favour his enemies against him. Utemutaraja replied, that it was true he was rendering certain assistance of men to the king for constructing the stockades, but it was insignificant, and he only did so to put him off his guard, for by no other means could he live in this, to him, a foreign land, unless he performed this service.

But with all this provocation, Afonso Dalboquerque did not cease to adhere to his promise of safeguard, and ordered his captains that upon the inhabitants of the territory of Utemutaraja they should make no requisition; and this he did, not because he had deserved any better treatment than the others, but in order to have a fewer number of enemies in the city. And so also he gave the foreign Moorish merchants to understand, that he had not ordered a sacking of the city out of regard for them; yet, nevertheless, if the king would not give way in his opinions, he, on his part, could not restrain his men from destroying the city when they made a second attack upon it. And so from that time henceforward the merchants were the men who counselled the king not to desire war, but to come to terms, and make peace with Afonso Dalboquerque. But, as the king was now obstinately bent on his purpose, he did not fall in with their opinion, but told them that only a few days back they had given him exactly the opposite advice.

When a few days had elapsed, Afonso Dalboquerque, seeing that the king had not sent him any reply, though he had already tasted the power and capability of the Portuguese, became anxious, for he was forcibly compelled for a second time to risk his men in a danger like the past, to the end that he might achieve the taming of the king's pride; and he had not in the land any means of building a fortress

—which it was his chief intent to do—neither could Ruy de Araujo give any advice on these events, for all the time he had been in captivity he had been shut up in a house. And, on the other hand, he saw that leaving Malaca in the power of the Moors meant total destruction to the trade of India and to our ships. And with these perplexed thoughts, which were constantly present in his mind, not knowing in what kind of conclusion this enterprise against Malaca would result, he placed everything in the hands of Our Lord, for this was always the best remedy that he could find in all his affairs; and, putting his trust in Him, he began to give orders and make himself ready in some matters which were needful for the second attack upon the city.

CHAPTER XXV.

How the great Afonso Dalboquerque prepared himself for renewing the attack upon the stockades which the king had set upon the bridge: and how the Chinese desired of him permission to return to their land: and of the ambassador whom he sent with them to the king of Sião.

When Afonso Dalboquerque perceived that the king, because of the little account he made of the Portuguese—not taking to heart the lesson of experience which he had had the first day they attacked the city—was again setting up stockades on the bridge, with men and artillery for its defence, he determined in his invincible mind to attack it again, and break their pride; and, with this object in view, he prepared a large junk, with many men and artillery,—because these vessels are very lofty,—and it was to be placed in a position overtowering the bridge, in order that our men might avail themselves of its shelter, and more securely be able to attack the stockades which the Moors had built. And he appointed Antonio Dabreu captain of the junk, and ordered him to arrange in it lodging-places for the soldiers, and provisions and all other things that were necessary for that affair. For, if any great rain-storm should occur, they could take shelter in it, and the supplies, of which they were in great need, would not be lost. And for guard over this junk he appointed a *caravela*, whereof Simão Afonso was captain, and the great galley in which Duarte da Silva went as captain, for its protection. And when all this was ready he told Antonio Dabreu to sail up along the river and pass over a spit of sand which lay before the bridge, while he himself, with all the rest of the men, would follow up close behind. But because the junk drew very deeply in the water, and could not pass over the spit on account of the neap tide, Afonso Dalboquerque desired, in order not to lose any more time, to send another junk with less draught of water, but this also could not pass over, so he was compelled to wait for the spring tide.[1]

When the king of Malaca saw that the junk could not pass the sand-bank, and that for all that it remained there, and did not go back again, he sent four barges full of firewood, and pitch, and oil, to set it on fire, and as soon as the tide began to run down they set them on fire, and let them go on the turn of the tide down the river straight towards the junk, and this they did for nine successive nights.

Now, as Afonso Dalboquerque observed the order in which the Moors arranged themselves for the burning of the junk, he ordered the captains, when they had withdrawn each night, to make their arrangements for sleeping close by him in their boats, and with bowsprits and harpoons hung with iron chains to turn the fire-ships out of their course as they came on in flames, so as to prevent the junk from catching fire; and they carried out this order so well that this design of the Moors was of no effect. And while this delay was going on, waiting for the spring tides, Afonso

[1] Spring tides rise 11 feet, neaps 8½ feet, at Malacca in the Roads.—*China Sea Directory*, vol. i, p. 79, 1878.

Dalboquerque ordered the iron-smiths, whom he had brought from Goa, to set up their forges and begin to repair some weapons which were out of order, and they made a magazine for the crossbows, for they were in much need of it. And he ordered the Factor of the Fleet to get ready barrels,[1] hatchets, hoes, picks, and all that was requisite, in order that when they had gained the bridge they might immediately set up stockades therein, and to arrange for the construction of mantlets, to the end that under shelter of them our men might go in better security from the enemy's bombards, and when all was completed and ready, to cause everything to be embarked on board of the large barques and junks which he had taken.

And because Afonso Dalboquerque had been informed that the King had determined, as soon as our men disembarked, to send down a number of watchboats and many launches by night to set fire to our Fleet, he ordered Pero Gonçalves, the Chief Pilot, with all the mariners, to go and sleep on board the ships every night, and he would give orders for a good look out to be kept over them, for if any alarm should occur he could render assistance if required.

While Afonso Dalboquerque was engaged in arranging all these matters the Chinese Captains went to him and begged his permission for their departure, inasmuch as the season of their monsoon had arrived, and they begged also that he would of his kindness give permission likewise for their taking a little pepper which they had in their ships belonging to a Moorish merchant, a native of Malaca, from whom they had received very good treatment; and to do them a kindness he granted this permission, and gave orders that they should have given to them all the supplies which they needed for their voyage, and made them a present of a few things which he yet had left from Portugal, and desired them (seeing they were bent on going), to shape

[1] *Pipas.*

their course for Sião, for he wished to send in their company a messenger with letters for the King.

They were very happy at this result, and promised him that they would present the messenger to the King and return very soon with the reply, and would highly extol the prowess of the Portuguese and the little dread they had of encountering the enemy's bombards.

Afonso Dalboquerque lost no time in making ready Duarte Fernandez, who had been in captivity with Ruy de Araujo and knew the language very well, and by him he wrote to the King of Sião of the events which had taken place in Malaca, and how his determination was to destroy the city and build therein a fortress, and cast the Moors out, and how pleased he would be if the people of his land [of Sião] would come and live it, and that the King D. Manuel, King of Portugal, his Lord, having been informed that he was a Hindoo and not a Moor, had much affection for him and desired to have peace and friendship with him, and had ordered him [Afonso Dalboquerque], as to all the ships and people of that kingdom desirous of trading in his ports, that he was to grant them all the safeguard that they found necessary. And by this Duarte Fernandez he sent the King of Sião one of our swords, all mounted in gold and precious stones, made after our fashion; and Duarte Fernandez having been thus despatched, the Chinese set forth for their own land highly pleased with Afonso Dalboquerque.

CHAPTER XXVI.

The speech which the great Afonso Dalboquerque made to the Captains and men of the Fleet for the second attack upon the city, and what passed thereupon.

When the great Afonso Dalboquerque had all things ready that were necessary for attacking the city again, it was reported to him that there were some among the Captains who were in the habit of saying that they did not think it of service to the King for them to maintain the city nor to build a fortress within it. On being apprised of this he ordered them to be called to his ship, with all the Fidalgos and Cavaliers of the Fleet, and said to them :—[1]

"Sirs, you will have no difficulty in remembering that when we decided upon attacking this city, it was with the determination of building a fortress within it, for so it appeared to all to be necessary, and after having captured it I was unwilling to let slip the possession of it, yet, because ye all advised me to do so, I left it, and withdrew; but being ready, as you see, to put my hands upon it again once more, I learned that you had already changed your opinion: now this cannot be because the Moors have destroyed the best part of us, but on account of my sins, which merit the failure of accomplishing this undertaking in the way that I had desired. And, inasmuch as my will and determination is, as long as I am Governor of India, neither to fight nor to hazard men on land, except in those parts

[1] Correa's version of this speech, which is given in the *Lendas da India*, vol. ii, pp. 232-234, is worthy of perusal here as showing how the two reports of the same event, each professing to be derived from authentic sources, differ from each other: "Senhores capitães, e nobres fidalgos, bem sabem vossas mercês que todo o estado d'El Rey nosso senhor depende e está posto nas vossas mãos, em que está muy seguro de nom receber quebra, nem falta, em quanto as vidas tiverdes nos corpos; do que darão bom testimunho os que viverem, e eu, que o tenho bem visto com meus olhos, nunqua poderei dizer os grandes vossos merecimentos ganhados com vosso sangue e tantos trabalhos, a que El Rey nosso senhor vos he em muyta obrigaç o, e satisfação que Sua Alteza nom faltará. Bem sabem vossas mercês que nós hiamos pera o estreito de Meca, a que nos Sua Alteza mandava hir, com intento de sequar aquella navegação, e passagem da pimenta e drogas que os mouros lá passavão, que lhe fazem grande avesso a seus tratos; ao que nos hiamos com toda' vontade, e polo querer de Nosso Senhor tivemos contrastes de ventos que nom consentirão que lá fossemos, e arribamos com tanto trabalho, e porque se nom perdesse o gasto que era feito n' armada, per

wherein I must build a fortress to maintain them, as I have already told you before this, I desire you earnestly, of your goodness, although you all have already agreed upon what is to be done, to freely give me again your opinions in writing as to what I ought to do; for inasmuch as I have to give an account of these matters and a justification of my proceedings to the King D. Manuel, our Lord, I am unwilling to be left alone to bear the blame of them; and although there be many reasons which I could allege in favour of our taking this city and building a fortress therein to maintain possession of it, two only will I mention to you, on this occasion, as tending to point out wherefore you ought not to turn back from what you have agreed upon.

"The first is the great service which we shall perform to Our Lord in casting the Moors out of this country, and quenching the fire of this sect of Mafamede so that it may never burst out again hereafter; and I am so sanguine as to hope for this from our undertaking, that if we can only achieve the task before us, it will result in the Moors resigning India altogether to our rule, for the greater part of them—or perhaps all of them—live upon the trade of this

conselho de vossas mercês bem atentado, foy assentado, pois tinhamos tempo, que viessemos esta viagem a Malaca, pera livrarmos os cativos, e tomar vingança d'esta cidade, dos mortos, e roubos que erão feitos; onde Nosso Senhor aquy nos aportou, e sobre bons conselhos avidos cometemos esta guerra, que está no esta do que vedes, com que bem certos estaes que a cidade será nossa polo querer de Nosso Senhor. Mas parece que averá algumas pessoas que farão duvida que sendo tomada nom será possivel fazer n'ella forteleza e a sostermos, o que se assy nom fosse logo El Rey nosso senhor ficava com toda a perda, que são muytas; a saber: o gasto d'armada, perda de sua gente, e sobre tudo estas perdas sem nenhum fruito, que será grande sua perda, porque esta cidade he o celeiro de todolas drogas e riqas mercadarias, que os mouros de todas as partes da India e do estreito de Meca aquy vem buscar, e levão suas naos carregadas, e passão per antre as ilhas, e se colhem ao estreito muy seguro de os toparem nossas armadas, e as drogas que levão, que he grande soma, correm polo Cairo, e a Veneza, e d'ahy a ponente e levante, com que dão muyto abatimento ás drogas da casa da India, que vão ter a Frandes. Outras drogas passão a India, que nos vendem por tresdobro

country and are become great and rich, and lords of extensive treasures. It is, too, well worthy of belief that as the King of Malaca, who has already once been discomfited and had proof of our strength, with no hope of obtaining any succour from any other quarter—sixteen days having already elapsed since this took place—makes no endeavour to negotiate with us for the security of his estate, Our Lord is blinding his judgment and hardening his heart, and desires the completion of this affair of Malaca: for when we were committing ourselves to the business of cruising in the Straits [of the Red Sea] where the King of Portugal had often ordered me to go (for it was there that His Highness considered we could cut down the commerce which the Moors of Cairo, of Méca, and of Judá, carry on with these parts), Our Lord for his service thought right to lead us hither, for when Malaca is taken the places on the Straits must be shut up, and they will never more be able to introduce their spiceries into those places.

"And the other reason is the additional service which we shall render to the King D. Manuel in taking this city, because it is the headquarters of all the spiceries and drugs

do que aquy as comprão a troco de roupas de Cambaya que trazem; do qual trato de tantos anos os mouros de toda a India são grandes em muytas riquezas com que são senhores nas terras, e dos corações dos Reys e senhores, com a qual possança nos tem feitos tantos malles em Calecut, e por todolas partes da India, que se o poder grande d'estes mouros nom fôra, dormindo tiveramos a India debaixo dos pés. Pois que mór serviço podemos fazer a Nosso Senhor em favor de nossa santa fé senão punirmos estes mouros, e seus tratos aquy os confundirmos e apagarmos, que percão este tamanho bem como lhe aquy tomamos? E pois está tão manifesto que este serviço nom faremos, indaque tomemos esta cidade chea d'ouro, se a nom deixassemos segura com segura forteleza, que durasse pera sempre este tamanho serviço de Nosso Senhor, e d'El Rey, e seus vassallos que n'estas partes militamos; tomaremos estes tratos, com que nos faremos riquissimos assy como o estão os mouros, e com lhe assy tomarmos seus proveitos os hiremos deitando fóra da India, que será quando a Nosso Senhor aprouver.

"E pois tomando nós agora esta cidade, com sua tanta riqueza, será pera nós grande honra e proveito, e d'El Rey nosso senhor, que nos

which the Moors carry every year hence to the Straits without our being able to prevent them from so doing; but if we deprive them of this their ancient market there, there does not remain for them a single port, nor a single situation, so commodious in the whole of these parts, where they can carry on their trade in these things. For after we were in possession of the pepper of Malabar, never more did any reach Cairo, except that which the Moors carried thither from these parts, and forty or fifty ships, which sail hence every year laden with all sorts of spiceries bound to Méca, cannot be stopped without great expense and large fleets, which must necessarily cruise about continually in the offing of Cape Comorim; and the pepper of Malabar, of which they may hope to get some portion because they have the King of Calicut on their side, is in our hands, under the eyes of the Governor of India, from whom the Moors cannot carry off so much with impunity as they hope to do; and I hold it as very certain that if we take this trade of Malaca away out of their hands, Cairo and Méca are entirely ruined, and to Venice will no spiceries be conveyed except that which her merchants go and buy in Portugal.

mantêm, e sostem nossas gerações, e com seu tanto gasto aquy somos aportados com esta armada, e com os poderes d'ella ganhâmos, e El Rey tudo ficaria perdendo se lhe nom dessemos premicias do seu gasto e nossa obrigação, que lhe forçadamente devemos, que ha de ser aquy lhe fazermos sua forteleza com nossos trabalhos, porque possamos dizer que ganhámos esta cidade ás lançadas com nosso sangue, e lhe entregamos arrematada pera sempre em seu serviço, pedindolhe que este tamanho serviço nos pague a nossos filhos e gerações, do que elle se nom poderá escusar; tudo, senhores, vos he presente, porque cada hum por seu assinado me ha de dar sua determinação, pera me eu livrar ante Sua Alteza de quem me accusar. Pera que sem duvida lhes affirmo que indaque n'esta hora Malaca se me entregasse, com toda sua riqueza, a não tomaria se n'ella nom ouver de fazer a milhor, e mais forte, e possante forteleza que ouver n'estes partes; pois Malaca he a mais populosa cidade da India, que está no meo e estremo de todolas riqas mercadarias e tratos que por ella correm. E pois, senhores, tudo lhe tenho apresentado, vossas mercês agora se determinem no que façamos, porque eu nada hey de fazer, senão o que per elles for assentado."

"But if you are of opinion that, because Malaca is a large city and very populous, it will give us much trouble to maintain our possession of it, no such doubts as these ought to arise, for when once the city is gained, all the rest of the Kingdom is of so little account that the King has not a single place left where he can rally his forces; and if you dread lest by taking the city we be involved in great expenses, and on account of the season of the year there be no place where our men and our Fleet can be recruited, I trust in God's mercy that when Malaca is held in subjection to our dominion by a strong fortress, provided that the Kings of Portugal appoint thereto those who are well experienced as Governors and Managers of the Revenues, the taxes of the land will pay all the expenses which may arise in the administration of the city; and if the merchants who are wont to resort thither—accustomed as they are to live under the tyrannical yoke of the Malays—experience a taste of our just dealing, truthfulness, frankness, and mildness, and come to know of the instructions of the King D. Manuel, our Lord, wherein he commands that all his subjects in these parts be very well treated, I venture to affirm that they will all return and take up their abode in the city again, yea, and build the walls of their houses with gold; and all these matters which here I lay before you may be secured to us by this half-turn of the key, which is that we build a fortress in this city of Malaca and sustain it, and that this land be brought under the dominion of the Portuguese, and the King D. Manuel be styled true king thereof, and therefore I desire you of your kindness to consider seriously the enterprise that ye have in hand, and not to leave it to fall to the ground."

When the great Afonso Dalboquerque had brought his harangue to an end in the words which I have recounted, the Members of the council held among themselves divers opinions, some leaning to this, and others to that side, and the result of the meeting was that the majority again declared that it would be of service to the King to take the city of Malaca and cast the Moors out of it, and build a fortress therein. The others were of a contrary opinion, and declared that the city ought not to be again attacked, for it was very doubtful if the undertaking could be accomplished, and that the vengeance which had been meted out to the Moors for their treatment of Diogo Lopez de Sequeira and his men was sufficiently severe, and even if they had all things necessary for the construction of the fortress there was not time enough for its completion, for they were already at the beginning of the monsoon, and it was absolutely necessary to support India, for no one could tell how affairs at Goa had gone on since they had set out from that city.

Afonso Dalboquerque, perceiving these differences of opinion which were held in the council, yielded to the majority and resolved to attack the city and fortify himself in it, and as for all other doubts which were raised by the opposite party, to put them into the hands of Our Lord Jesus Christ that He might order them all as best to his service, and he commanded that a formal resolution should be drawn up by the Secretary, whereunto he put his signature, as did also all the Captains, Fidalgos, and Cavaliers who were there.

CHAPTER XXVII.

How the great Afonso Dalboquerque again attacked the city according to the resolution which had been arrived at, and how he entered the bridge by force of arms and fortified himself on it.

Having taken the opinions of the Captains, Fidalgos, and Cavaliers of the Fleet, under their signatures, as I have related, the great Afonso Dalboquerque made up his mind to attack the city, and taking it, by the aid of our Lord, to fortify himself therein. And because the Moors were in an advanced state of preparation, and had arranged a better system of defence than they had on the first occasion when our men made an entry into the city, he decided with all the Captains to attack the bridge with his whole force in one company.

Having agreed upon this method of attack, all went away to their respective ships to get ready, waiting for the day when it would be high water in the spring tides, so that the junk could get up to the bridge; and when the time was come—on a Friday, two hours before morning—Afonso Dalboquerque gave orders for the signal which he had agreed upon, to wake them, and they, as they were already prepared, came on board his ship, and from it set forth all together in their boats; and when Antonio Dabreu in the junk had now arrived within a crossbow-shot from the bridge, the Moors began to open fire upon him from one side and the other with large matchlocks,[1] blowing tubes, and poisoned arrows; and with bombards which threw leaden shot as large as an *espera*[2] they swept the decks of the junk from one side and the other, and as Antonio Dabreu did not seek therein any place of safety where he could avoid the shots which they kept on pouring into the junk, he was the first who was hit with a bullet from a large matchlock, which struck him on the jaw and carried away many of his teeth and part of his tongue.

Afonso Dalboquerque, who was in his boat close by the junk, seeing Antonio Dabreu wounded, ordered him, more by force than by his own wish, to be taken to the ship to have his wounds dressed, and appointed Pero Dalpoem to go on board the junk and act as Captain of it until Antonio Dabreu was well again. When the delay that had thus arisen had

[1] *Espingardões.*

[2] *Espera* or *Esfera*, an ancient kind of artillery—*Bluteau*, s.v. But see also vol. ii, p. 129, note 5.

passed away—not much time having been wasted—they went on again a second time with the junk leading the way, in the order which they had appointed, and when the junk drew up alongside, as it was very lofty and quite overhung the bridge, as I have already said, the Moors, not being able to bear the severe handling which our men gave them from the round top of the mainmast[1] with many canisters of gunpowder, and darts,[2] and matchlocks, fled, deserting the bridge, and withdrew to the stockades which they had on the bridge, on this side and that.

Afonso Dalboquerque, perceiving that the Moors were beginning to fall into confusion, ordered the Captains to press on more quickly at the oars, and all united in a body set to work to fall upon the stockades, according to the preconcerted arrangement. And although they found behind them a great force of Moors, who defended them for a considerable space of time with signal bravery, nevertheless our men got into the stockades and routed those who held them. In this affair of entering, many of our men were wounded and two or three killed, but it was at the cost of many Moors, who there lost their lives; and Afonso Dalboquerque, seeing himself now master of the bridge, remained where he was quietly with his flag and a part of his force, and gave orders to certain of the Captains to go and take the mosque, and to others to attack some palisades which the Moors had set up at the mouth of a street which led to the bridge, and that neither the one party or the other should leave their stations without his express orders.

When the Captains arrived at the palisades, although they met with some amount of resistance, yet they bore themselves so valiantly that they discomfited the Moors and got possession of the works. The others, however, to whose lot it fell to assault the mosque, found they had a heavy and

[1] *De cima da gavea;* see Jal, *Glossaire Nautique*, s.v. *Gavea.*

[2] *Lanças de arremeço.*

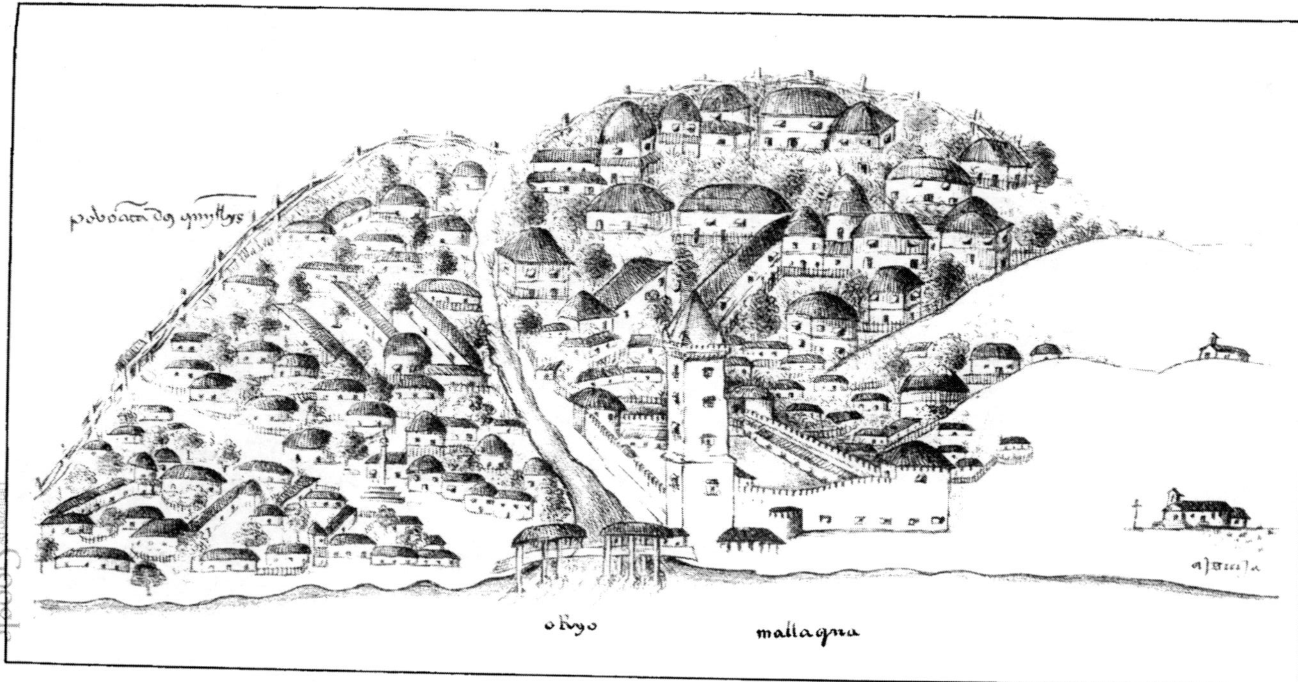

VIEW OF MALACA.
FROM CORREA'S LENDAS DA INDIA.

troublesome task before them, for in that place of defence there was the King with a large body of men and elephants, and the defence was maintained so vigorously that a considerable space of time elapsed without our men being able to get in. Afonso Dalboquerque, seeing from the bridge the circumstances in which our men were situated, made his way with all haste at the head of all his forces to succour them, and because at the mouth of a large street which led to the mosque, where he was, there were many Moors pressing on the flanks of certain Captains that were following the King, who was in flight with three thousand men armed with shields, he stayed himself there with his flag and his men, and sent the Captains word to remain quiet and rally towards the position he had taken up, for there were yet many Moors on their flanks, and then they withdrew at once; and as soon as the junction of these forces had been carried out, Afonso Dalboquerque left in charge over the mosque and stockades Jorge Nunez de Lião, Nuno Vaz de Castelo-branco, James Teixeira, and Dinis Fernandez de Melo, with some of the men, while he himself, with the rest that remained, returned towards the bridge; and he ordered the Captains who were stationed on one side and on the other to stay where they were and not fight with the Moors, even if they came on and attacked them, until he had fortified the bridge; and ordered four large barques which he had, with great bombards, to pass over to the other side and sweep the field on one side and on the other, and cause the Moors to keep off so that the men could more securely work at the stockades; and having arranged this he ordered them to take out of the junk all the munitions which he had brought, and began upon the stockades; and as all went to work with willing hands, in a short space of time he had made two very strong palisades, one on the side of the city, the other on the side of the mosque, with barrels filled with earth, and wood, and he arranged in them many guns: and ordered that the bridge and the junk should be covered with palm leaves, for the benefit of the men, for the sun was very strong and he was fearful lest they should all fall ill from the hard work they had to perform.

CHAPTER XXVIII.

How the great Afonso Dalboquerque ordered relief to be given to our men who were stationed at the mouth of the street which led to the bridge: and how Utamutaraja and Ninachatu, and other merchants, seeing the overthrow of the city, came and placed themselves in his hands.

While the great Afonso Dalboquerque was thus occupied in this eagerness to complete the fortification of the stockades which he was making upon the bridge, he saw that the Captains whom he had ordered to take up positions at the mouths of the streets were undergoing, rather than disobey his commands, much discomfort from the attacks made upon them by the Moors with bombards which they had placed upon the terraces of their houses, and with matchlocks with which they were firing upon them, so he dispatched with great haste Gaspar de Paiva, Fernão Perez Dandrade, Pero Dalpoem, Antonio Dabreu, who was now by this time well of his wound in the jaw, to go and succour them with their men, along one of the streets of the city, and D. João de Lima, Aires Pereira, Simão Dandrade, Simão Martinz, and Simão Afonso, along another street which led up to a place where the Moors where at lance-thrusts with our men, and to patrol through all the city and not to give quarter to a single person they met, while he himself would come on behind them in support, with his royal standard; and although the Moors were very numerous, the Captains fell upon them so valiantly that, not being able to resist the fury of the onset with which they were attacked, they turned their backs and threw themselves into flight, and some, indeed, among them, who were nearest to our men, cast themselves into the sea, thinking that thereby they ensured their safety.

The mariners, whom Afonso Dalboquerque had ordered to man the skiffs and row up and down the river, came up at once and put to death every one whom they could get at; and when it was sundown the Captains withdrew to the bridge, where they now had their stockades very strongly built on one side and on the other, and Afonso Dalboquerque took up his quarters in the middle, and they passed the whole of the night on the watch. And he ordered the Captains of the barques that were stationed in the river to keep up a continual fire upon the city all through the night with their bombards, and Pero Gonçalvez, chief pilot, to take all the seamen to the ships to sleep there, and carry out the same instructions regarding the cannonade, and in this manner they remained all night. And it was a terrible thing to look at the city, for on account of the constant firing it seemed as if it were all on fire.

When morning came, the Moors, terrified at the unexpected misfortune which they witnessed, dared not appear in the streets, and this went on for a period of ten days running without any cessation by night or by day, and during this time our men were continually spilling the blood of the Moors, for inasmuch as the hunger they suffered was extreme, they risked their lives to go and look for food in the city, and there they lost their lives. And when they perceived the troubles that had fallen upon them, and the great peril they were in of losing their lives, and the hopelessness of their case, some began to come to Afonso Dalboquerque and beg for mercy; and the first who came were the Pégus, and these he received very kindly and gave them a safeguard to enable them to prosecute their voyage, and permission to carry with them their property, and in like manner he allowed all the merchants who came from Cape Comorim to the eastwards, who had no ships there, free exportation of their merchandize, and they began to start their trade again, and revive the navigation from their lands to Malaca, and this was the principal reason why he did so.

Utemutaraja, as I have already said, who had a safe-conduct from Afonso Dalboquerque, seeing the destruction of the city, and fearing that he should incur displeasure because his son had gone over to the assistance of the King against our men—although indeed he was well rewarded for it, for he was severely wounded and many of his men were killed—came and made excuses for the behaviour of his son, making a show of being highly delighted at the ruin which had fallen upon the King. He received him with benignity, but nevertheless gave orders to the Captains to go always armed with all their men, and keep a good look out, for there could be no reliance placed upon him. Ruy de Araujo, remembering the kindnesses which he and the other christians had received at the hands of Ninachatu, a Hindoo by nation, during their captivity, brought him to Afonso Dalboquerque, begging that he would show him favour and honour him, for he could not repay him in any other way for the kindness of the treatment he had experienced. Afonso Dalboquerque entertained him, and told him that he would promise, before he left for India, he should be rewarded in accordance with what Ruy de Araujo had said of him.

And when Afonso Dalboquerque found himself less troubled by the uproars which the Moors caused by day and night, and that there was no longer in the city any force which could resist them, and as a recompense for past labours, he gave permission to everyone to sack the city, and free power to keep or dispose of everything they took, only warning them not to touch the houses or the subterranean storehouses[1] of Ninachatu. When the city had been sacked, certain merchants, who had fled away to their country houses, seeing the kind way in which Ninachatu had been treated, sent and begged a safe-conduct from Afonso Dalboquerque that they might come to the city; and he granted this to all, except the Malays, who were natives of the country, for as to these he gave orders that all should be put to death wheresoever they were found.

In this second time of taking the city, many of our men were wounded, and some of those who were wounded with poison died, but all the others were cured, because Afonso Dalboquerque took very good care to give orders for their cure, and of the Moors, women and children, there died by the sword an infinite number, for no quarter was given to any of them. Three thousand pieces of artillery were taken, and among them there were about two thousand in bronze, and one very large gun which the King of Calicut had sent to the King of Malaca. The rest were of iron, of the fashion of our *berços*, and all this artillery had its proper complement of carriages, which could not be rivalled even by that of Portugal. Large matchlocks, poisoned blowing tubes, bows, arrows, armour-plated dresses,[2] Javanese lances, and other sorts of weapons, it was marvellous what was taken, besides much merchandize of every kind.

[1] *Gudões.* Storehouses or rooms built partly above and partly under ground. For example, in Correa's account, when Afonso Dalboquerque laments that the fire will destroy the riches of the city:—"Se o fogo nos der a cidade, elle levará todo o bem que ella tem de riqueza, com que a gente ficaria com trabalho e sem proveito." Ruy d'Araujo lhe dixe: "Senhor, posto que se queime Malaca, inda o milhor ficará, que está nos gudões, *que são casas de pedra fortes e meas feitas debaixo do chão.*"—*Lendas da India*, tom. ii, p. 236. And again, during the progress of the sacking: "Os capitães, com suas quadrilhas de seus navios, ajuntavão e metião fato em grandes casas pera depois o mandarem embarquar. Estas fazendas estavão em casas *que tinhão meas feitas debaixo do chão, per cyma argamassadas por resguardo do fogo.*"—*Ib.*, p. 247.

[2] *Laudeis de laminas.*

All this, and more which I leave, not to be prolix, Afonso Dalboquerque ordered to be divided among the Captains and among all the people of the Fleet, without taking anything for himself, except six large lions in bronze which he took for his tomb, and the bracelet, which I have already described,[1] and young girls of all the races of that country, and some toys, all which he took to send them to the King D. Manuel and to the Queen D. Maria, but they were lost in the ship *Flor de la Mar*, on the voyage back to India, as I shall narrate hereafter.

Let not those who read this writing be astonished when I say that in Malaca were taken three thousand guns, for Ruy de Araujo and Ninachatu declared to Afonso Dalboquerque that there were eight thousand in Malaca, and this may well be believed, for in Malaca were much copper and much tin, and the gun founders were as good as those of Germany; on the other hand, the city was a league in length, and when Afonso Dalboquerque disembarked they aimed at him from on all sides, whence it appears that even this number was insignificant in comparison to what was required for the defence.

CHAPTER XXIX.

Of how, after the Prince of Malaca had withdrawn from his father, he came to the river of Muar and fortified himself therein with a number of stockades, and the great Afonso Dalboquerque sent a force against him, and put him to flight.

The great Afonso Dalboquerque, being desirous of setting the affairs of Malaca in order, determined to appoint Ninachatu, because he was a Hindoo, Governor of the Quilins[2]

[1] See pp. 61, 62.

[2] In the view of Malaca given by Correa, *Lendas da India*, vol. ii, p. 250. The "povoacã dos quyllȳs" is marked on the left of the city, and separated from it by a palisade. See also *supra*, p. 81, note 1.

and Chetins;[1] and in order to make the Moors more secure he made Utemutaraja their principal chief, and with these two men, as they were prominent persons, the people began to settle down quietly, and merchants, a few at a time, returned to the city; but with all this Afonso Dalboquerque did not put too much confidence in them, especially in Utemutaraja, and in order to get rid of this suspicion which he had, he tried all he could to get the king into his hands, and with this end in view he sent many boats up the river and along the coast to see if they could take him.

The king, owing to the constant alarms which arose every day, and knowing the desire which Afonso Dalboquerque had of getting possession of him, fearing lest his own people should deliver him up, drew himself off from the city, a day's journey, taking with him some Malay merchants and his captains and governors of the land, with the intention of keeping in that neighbourhood, waiting for his Lassamane, the Admiral of the Sea, whom he had sent to the Island of Lingá,[2] to convey to them a numerous fleet with many men, and in their company the King of that Island who was called Rajalingá,[3] who was subject to him, with determination of returning against the city; but this did not come to pass, for the Rajalingá, knowing that Afonso Dalboquerque was in possession of the city, did not dare to come; and the King of Malaca, being of the opinion that Afonso Dalboquerque simply meant to rob the city and then leave it and sail away with the spoil he might get out of it, kept about that place for a space of ten days, in expectation of the issue of these events. But when he was informed that Afonso Dalboquerque was beginning to establish a fortress of timber[4] wherein to shelter himself, and so

[1] See vol. ii, p. 130, note 2.

[2] Linga Island, Sumatra, 0 deg. 10 min. S., 104 deg. 45 min. E., lying to the south of Singapore.

[3] This name is evidently but a title, "The Rajah of Lingá".

[4] See p. 135.

acting as to shew his wish to make a settlement in Malaca with the intention of maintaining possession of it, terrified at this news, and not deeming himself safe in the locality where he then was, he went further off into the interior country, a distance of two days' march; and because the party was sharply pressed for want of provisions the Prince separated himself from his father and set out to pitch his settlement close to the river, and there he marked out some very strong stockades, and barred the river with a quantity of timber, so that our boats might not pass up to the place.

As soon as Afonso Dalboquerque was informed that the Prince of Malaca was fortifying his position on the river, he despatched Fernão Perez Dandrade, Simão Dandrade, his brother, Gaspar de Paiva, Francisco Sarram, Aires Pereira, Ruy de Araujo, and Jorge Nunez de Lião, with four hundred Portuguese soldiers, and six hundred Javanese who were given for the purpose by Utemutaraja, and the Pégu Captains with three hundred of their men, to take boats and launches up the river and put to rout that nest of robbers which was beginning to form itself there, and they did so; and when the expedition reached the stockade which the Prince had constructed, they began to root it up with machines which they took with them for this purpose, and when they had rooted it up, they pressed on to attack the enemy at their fortifications.

The Prince, when he saw the fleet and the determined spirit with which the men came on, struck his camp, without making the least show of resistance, and fled away to the place where the King was, which was about a day's journey distant, and our men entered in pell-mell into their buildings, and captured all that had been stored there which the Prince had been unable to remove; among their spoil his palanquins, very rich and gilded, and painted, and seven elephants, with their castles and housings; and having obtained this victory the force returned to the city.

When the Prince reached the place where the King his father was, there arose differences between them concerning the loss of Malaca, each one seeking to put off the fault from his own to the other's shoulders, and this dissension ran so high, that being thus divided in plans, and suffering also from the discomforts of famine, they departed and shaped their journey for the kingdom of Pão, through a region desert and marshy, mounted upon their elephants with their wives and children, taking with them fifty men whom they forced to accompany them in their flight.

CHAPTER XXX.

How the King of Malaca, after the Portuguese had gained the city from him, withdrew to the kingdom of Pão, and dispatched an Ambassador to the King of China, begging for succour.

The King of Malaca, having arrived at the kingdom of Pão, and seeing that there was no remedy for his misfortunes, determined to dispatch an Ambassador to the King of China, begging for succour, that he might be enabled to recover the city which he had lost, reminding him, with the object of obtaining a favourable reply to this request, of the ancient friendship which the Kings of Malaca had always kept up with those of China, and of the obedience which they had shown them as their vassals; and in order to give a greater appearance of authenticity to this embassy, he desired that it should be accompanied by one of his uncles, whose name was Tuão[1] Nacem Mudaliar, in whom he reposed the highest confidence; and he, after receiving his order to depart, went and proceeded to embark at the river of Muar,[2] whence he set sail in a junk with his wife, accompanied with certain Moors in his retinue; and when he

[1] This is the common Malay word for Lord or Master.

[2] The river in Malaca, on which the city of Pahang or Pão is built.

reached the city of Cantão,[1] which is the port of China whither all those who sail to those parts are accustomed to make land, the Governors of that city—in accordance with the ancient custom which they keep up—immediately sent off a messenger to the King, who was in the interior a distance of a hundred and eighty leagues, giving him notice of the arrival of the Ambassador of the King of Malaca, and asking that word of the King's pleasure as to what should be done might be sent, for the custom of China is that not a single stranger can pass beyond that port nor go to the King without his permission.

The messenger whom the Governor despatched reached the city of Pequim,[2] where the king was, and delayed on the journey two months, and then returned with the reply to the Governors, to the effect that they were to permit the ambassador, with the retinue in his company, to pass through the kingdom, and to give them everything that they required for their journey. When the ambassador received this reply, he lost no time in making his preparations, and set out with his wife on the road for the Royal Court, and kept continually traversing along the bank of a river[3] where there were very noble cities and very sumptuous edifices, of which I do not treat because it has nothing to do with this history. On the arrival of the ambassador at the Court, he was very well received by all the Lords and Governors of the land; and after some days had elapsed the King desired to receive him in person, although this was not his usual custom, for no one sees him, and business is transacted by the men who govern the land. And after the ambassador had performed his courtesy to the King after

[1] Canton, or Quangtung, 23 deg. 12 min. N., 113 deg. 17 min. E.

[2] Pekin, or Shun-tien, China, 39 deg. 53 min. N., 116 deg. 29 min. E.

[3] This probably refers to the Yang-tsze-kiang, which is connected by the Yun-ho, Sha-ho, or Grand Canal, with the Yun-ho, or Eu-ho River, on a branch of which the city of Pekin is built.

the manner and custom of the Chinese, he threw himself at the King's feet, and with many tears begged him that he would be pleased to assist the King his lord in his present trouble, for in him he placed all his confidence.

The King ordered him to rise, and told him to relate all the history of the affair in order. He related it to him, for he had been an eyewitness of it all, and told him that the King his lord, after he had been overcome, had retired to the kingdom of Pão, and there he remained waiting, in the hopes that he (the King of China) would turn a favourable ear to him, and assist him, with men and a fleet, to recover possession of the kingdom, to be revenged for the affronts which the Captain of the King of Portugal had given him; and although the King of China had already been informed, by the Chinese who had come from Malaca, of all that had taken place, he was glad to hear the ambassador, and he enquired very particularly of him concerning the person and authority of the great Afonso Dalboquerque and of the Portuguese, what sort of men they were, and what was their manner of fighting.

The ambassador, as he was a discreet man, gave him a very good account of everything, whereat he was very well satisfied. And when these conversations were over, the King told him to go and enjoy himself, for he would dispatch him and do everything that he wished, but really he was unwilling to give his word that he would help the King of Malaca, for his intentions and desires were to keep on friendly terms with the King of Portugal and with his Captain Afonso Dalboquerque, and to send some persons to visit him, as well because of the great news which he had of his person, as also because of the good treatment that he had shewn to the Chinese whom he had found in the port of Malaca, and his desire to open the commerce in his land. And one thing which greatly helped this policy of the King of China was the complaints which the Chinese merchants made of the tyrannies that the King of Malaca had practised upon them in the matter of their merchandise, in the time when they were in his territory.

The ambassador spent a long time at the Court without being able to get dispatch of his business, and during this time his wife died; and after some days had elapsed the King replied to him, through the officials, excusing himself from granting the succour which was asked of him, and giving his reasons why he could not do it, and the chief reason was the war that was on hand against the Tartars. With this reply the ambassador set out without loss of time, and when he arrived at the city of Janquileu, and bethought himself of the unfortunate result of his mission and of his departed wife, he died of sheer grief, having given orders to build a chapel for his interment in the outskirts of the city, and therein he lies buried in a sepulchre surrounded by steps of lateen, on which he ordered an inscription to be placed, which reads: "*Here lies Tuão Nacem, Ambassador and Uncle of the great King of Malaca, whom death carried off before he could be avenged upon the Captain Afonso Dalboquerque, lion of the sea robbers.*"

CHAPTER XXXI.

How the King of Malaca, having arrived at the kingdom of Pão, died; and how the great Afonso Dalboquerque began to build the fortress; and the inscription which he placed over the gate after it was finished, and what passed hereupon.

As disasters kept following this ill-fated King of Malaca, Fortune not being content with placing him in the position of losing his city, wife, children and people, disheartened and deeply chagrined at his losses, after he had arrived but a few days at the kingdom of Pão, he died. When the King was dead, all the Moors of honourable estate, who had followed his fortune, scattered themselves through the forests there, and after the lapse of some days came down, seeking to get to the sea coast, and sent to beg permission from Afonso Dalboquerque that they might return to their city; and to some of them, who were men of principal power, he granted permission, for he considered it was more prudent to have such men as these within the city, than that they should be going about outside, stirring up assemblies and inciting the merchants not to come to the port; he therefore commanded the Javanese to band themselves together and scour the land, and bring back captive all the Malays found in the woods there, to work at the building of the fortress which he was anxious to begin; and if among these captives any one should chance to be found who could be recognised as having taken a guilty part in the massacre of the men forming the company of Diogo Lopez de Sequeira, Afonso Dalboquerque commanded that proper punishment be meted out to him, and that the others, with iron chains upon them, should serve at the work.

And in company with them there were brought to him one thousand five hundred slaves who had belonged to the king, with their women and children, and he took them all as captives of the King D. Manuel, just as they had been of the King of Malaca, and ordered that they should be supplied with wages and provisions when they worked at the building, in accordance with the native custom; and when they were not thus required to serve they worked for their own advantage, for after this manner they had been compelled to serve the King of Malaca; and when he had thus arranged these matters, he ordered them to take off from the fortress the timber[1] and woodwork which it carried for the protection of the men who were employed on the work, and to make ready lime, stone, and masonry for a beginning; and although Ruy de Araujo never expected to be able to find sufficient stone to build the fortress, yet

[1] See p. 129.

as it was the will of our Lord that the Portuguese should make good their settlement in that city, and that His name should there be worshipped, so great a quantity of stone and masonry was discovered in some ancient sepulchres of bygone kings, which were situated on the land beneath the surface of the ground, and in the mosques that were thrown down, that two fortresses might well have been constructed; and now, as there were plenty of helping hands to begin the work, and many labourers, Afonso Dalboquerque gave orders to open out the foundations, and he founded a very strong fortress, the foundation filled in to the depth of a war lance, for the position of the ground required it to be so, with two wells of very good water within the precincts for drinking purposes, that were there already built with worked stone masonry.

And in order that our men, who were within the fortress, might be able to rally together for defence, if it were necessary, whenever they so desired, without the enemy being able to cut them off, he laid the foundation of a keep[1] of four storey's height along the sea, so that also from its height they might with their artillery defend a hill which the fortress has over against it, which commands its position.

Now because it may be that some who read this history may find fault with building a fortress in an enemy's country with such a weak point, the answer is that Afonso Dalboquerque put up with the commanding position of this hill because there was not in the whole of the city a more commodious place for the security of the captain and the forces that might be placed therein, for alongside of this tower one of our ships of two hundred tons burden could come whenever it was desired. And they called the fortress "*A Famosa*", *i.e.*, "The Famous." And as I have been told by many persons who have seen it, it seems to have been very appropriately so called; but I do not give a

[1] *Torre de Menagem;* see vol. i, p. 45.

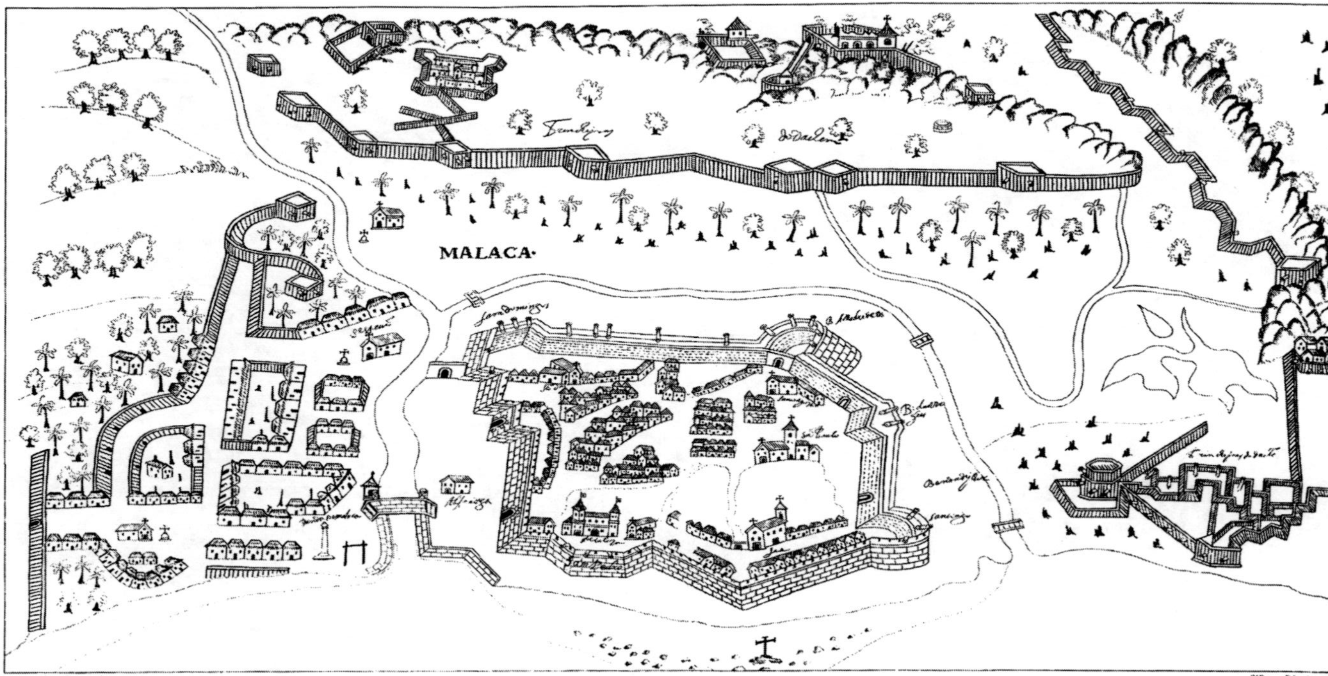

PLAN OF THE PORTUGUESE FORTRESS OF MALACA.

[*British Museum, Sloane MS.* 197, folio 382.]

special account of its details of construction because it is very much frequented by our Portuguese. And because Afonso Dalboquerque was very much devoted to Our Lady he ordered the men to build a church, to which he gave the name of "*Nossa Senhora da Annunciada*", *i.e.*, "Our Lady of the Annunciation." . And in order that the memory of the persons who had taken part in the conquest of this kingdom and foundation of the fortress might remain for ever, he ordered them to make a very large stone slab, upon which were inscribed the names of all the principal men. But, the Portuguese are by nature envious of honour, they would not, therefore, suffer Afonso Dalboquerque to make more account of one than of another, seeing that all were equally meritorious in the work, and in the conquest of that city; and he, in order not to give them cause for displeasure, and yet not to abandon that which he had done, gave orders that the stone should be set up over the gateway with the inscribed names turned to the wall, and on the back of the slab that verse of David, which says: "LAPIDEM QUEM REPROBAVERUNT EDIFICANTES," that is, "The stone[1] which the builders refused."

CHAPTER XXXII.

How the great Afonso Dalboquerque, at the request of the Governors and people of the city, ordered money to be coined; and of the value thereof, and of the rest that was done thereupon.

While the affairs of Malaca were in this state, Ninachatu came to the great Afonso Dalboquerque with the Governors of the land, and declared to him that the people were suffering great inconvenience from the want of a currency, and they begged he would of his graciousness give orders for some system of coinage; and although he had already for

[1] Psalm cxviii, 22 (cxvii *Vulg.*).

many days desired this himself, yet, as the work of building the fortress occupied the whole of this time, he had put this matter off to a more fitting opportunity, when he should have less to occupy his attention; yet because the necessity which they represented to him was very urgent, and the people could not improve their condition without a currency, he desired to set to work and arrange the matter without loss of any more time, as well because it was a royal privilege of the King, D. Manuel, and of his victory in a kingdom newly acquired, whereof he was by right the king[1], so also in order to withdraw and suppress the coinage of the Moors, and cast their root and their name out of the land.

Having made up his mind concerning this, Afonso Dalboquerque ordered that all the merchants, governors, and principal men of the city should be called together, and held a conversation with them respecting their desires expressed to him; and after many different opinions had been given by them all, they agreed to the opinion of all the captains who were there present, that a coinage should be made, and that out of two *caixes*,[2] which was a pewter coin of the King of Malaca, should be struck a coin with the *sphere*[3] of the King D. Manuel, to which they gave the name of *dinheiro* (*i.e.*, money), and another, of greater size, which was worth ten *dinheiros*, they termed *soldo*,[4] and others, which weighed ten *soldos*, they entitled *bastardos*; and all this money was of pewter, which is found native in the land of Malaca, and the mines of this metal he made direct Crown property of the King of Portugal.

And because there was not in Malaca any gold or silver coinage, but trade was carried on by barter of one kind of merchandise for another, they agreed that there should be

[1] Maimonides, Gezelah, 5. "Ubicunque numisma alicujus regis obtinet, illic incolæ regem istum pro domino agnoscunt." Quoted by Farrar, *Life of Christ*, ii, 232, *n*.

[2] See p. 77.

[3] *Espera*, see vol. ii, p. 129.

[4] Cf. Lat. *Solidus*; Fr. *Sou*.

such a coinage; and after much disputation concerning the value that should be assigned to it, the opinion which found favour with everyone was that the gold coin should weigh a quarter of a *tundiá*, which is worth among us a thousand *reis*, and to this they gave the name of *Catholico*; and the silver coin the merchants thought well to be that of Pegú, which is somewhat less than that of Castelete, but upon this point there were several opinions given on both sides; but Afonso Dalboquerque appointed that this coin should be made of merchantable silver, so that if the Kings of Portugal should desire to send silver for sale to Malaca, on account of the high value it would fetch, they could do so.

The merchants, although this high value of the silver was against them, assented to the opinion expressed by Afonso Dalboquerque, and agreed that the silver coin should be called *Malaqueses, i.e.*, Malaca pieces, and should have the same value of a quarter of *tundia;* and in order that currency of the coinage of the Moors might be immediately stopped everywhere, especially that of pewter, which was the most common in use in the land, Afonso Dalboquerque gave orders for the establishment of a house for the mint, and that all the Moors who held coin of the King of Malaca should convey it thither without delay under pain of death; and so great a quantity of money was thus carried there out of fear of the penalty which had been appointed to them, that the officers could not dispatch their business fast enough, and in a short time a great quantity of silver, gold, and copper had been recoined.[1]

[1] Correa's description of the coinage differs in some respects from this text. He says:—"Em Malaca nom corria nenhuma moeda d'ouro nem de prata, porque todo se compraua, e vendia, as mercadorias humas a troqo d'outras, e as miudezas do bazar de comer se comprauão per huma moeda d'estanho, a que chamauão calayns. O Gouernador mandou laurar d'esta moeda assy miuda, e outra de dez soldos, a que pôs nome bastardos, e de hum lado a espera e de outro hum A grego. Fez moeda d'ouro de valia de mil e corenta reaes, e n'ella huma mea fegura de Rey

When Afonso Dalboquerque had been informed by the officials as to the quantity of coin which they had in hand, he ordered the Governors of the land to be summoned, and told him that he had given orders for minting a large sum of money, in accordance with the advice of every one, and that it was necessary to send forth a proclamation concerning it throughout the city with that solemnity which belonged to the estate of the King D. Manuel his lord. The Governors agreed that upon the morning of the following day the change in the currency should be proclaimed, and all the principal men of the people met together, and made their way to the fortress, where Afonso Dalboquerque was with

com coroa, e huma espada na mão, e letras que dizião derrador, COM ESTA CONQUISTADA E GANHADA, e da outra parte o escudo das quinas, e letras derrador que dizião, GLORIA PERA SEMPRE MEMORIA. A esta moeda pôs nome catolica, e d'esta fez meos catalicos de preço de quinhentos e vinte reaes, a que pôs de huma parte a espera com letras que dizião, ESPERA EM DEOS PERA MAIS, e da outra banda o A grego, e letras que dizião, O ESCRAVO GANHA PERA O SENHOR. Estas moedas lauradas erão muy fermosas, de que mandou laurar huma soma. E fez moeda de prata de setecentos e vinte reaes, de huma banda as quinas sem coroa, e da outra banda espera com as mesmas letras, que chamou reaes brancos, e meos reaes."—Tom. ii, p. 256. From this extract we get the following values:—

10 *Soldos* = 1 *Bastardo* (pewter).
1,040 *reaes* = 1 *Catholico* (gold).
520 *reaes* = 1 half *Catholico* (gold).
720 *reaes* = 1 *real branco*, *i.e.*, white *real* (silver).

SCHEME OF THE PORTUGUESE COINAGE OF MALACA, deduced from the foregoing text.

PEWTER.

2 *Caixes*, or Cash = 1 *Espera* = 1 *Dinheiro*.
10 *Dinheiros* = 1 *Soldo*.
10 *Soldos* = 1 *Bastardo*.

SILVER.

1 *Malaquese* = $\frac{1}{4}$ *Tundia*.

GOLD.

1 *Catholico* = $\frac{1}{4}$ *Tundia* = 1000 *Reis* (Portuguese).

all the Captains, Fidalgos, and Cavaliers of the Fleet, and from that place they began their procession in the following order.

There went first, in front of all the people, one of the principal Governors of the City mounted upon an elephant with his castle caparisoned with silk, and carrying in his hands a flag of the arms of the King of Portugal upon a long spear, and behind him went all the people on foot on one side and the other, as it were in a procession; and in the midst of these people there went a Moor mounted upon another elephant, likewise caparisoned with silk, making the proclamation; and behind this one came the trumpets; and after them the Governors of the City, and all the Merchants, and principal men thereof; and at the rear of this throng there went Antonio de Sousa the son of João de Sousa of Santarem, and the son of Ninachatu, both together upon a large elephant, which had been kept for the King's own use, with his castle caparisoned with brocaded cloths, and they carried with them a large quantity of gold, silver, and copper coin, which they kept on throwing out over the heads of all the people at each publication of the proclamation which the Moor made. The crowd was so great that the streets could scarcely contain it, and with many songs and blowing of horns, according to the native custom, the people gave great praise to Afonso Dalboquerque for giving orders for this distribution of money by the advice and in accordance with the opinions of their natives.

When the publication of this money was finished the Pegús begged permission of Afonso Dalboquerque to depart to their own country, and he granted it to them, and shewed them great honour and kindness, whereat they were very pleased, and gave him great thanks for what he had done for them when the city was sacked, in not permitting that their houses and merchandise should be robbed, which indeed was of no small importance, for it amounted to a thousand *miticaes*[1] of gold, apart from the sums of gold and silver which they had concealed.

When Afonso Dalboquerque had taken his leave of them, they set forth promising him that they would very soon return to that port with much merchandise, and would endeavour to bring him a very large junk, which was being built in their country for the King of Malaca. And there remained behind in Malaca one of the sons of the Pilot, a youth of good breeding, with a hundred Pegús, and he learned our Portuguese language; and he was so curious to see everything that the principal reason why he stayed behind was to see our fortress completed, and he was always at work upon it with his men, whom Afonso Dalboquerque ordered to be liberally repaid for their labour.

Of this gold which I have spoken of above as coming to Malaca, the larger part comes from a mine of Menamcabo, which is at the extremity of the island of Samatra, on the southern side, fronting opposite to Malaca, a sea voyage of six days' distance, and it also comes from the kingdom of Pão, and in all the islands round about Malaca there is gold, but only a little. The Gores and the Chinese also bring it. The silver comes from the kingdom of Sião, and from the

[1] Roquette, who gives the forms—*Matical*, *metical*, *medegal*, and *metigal*,—considers this to be an Asiatic weight of one drachm and a half for pearls, amber, etc.

Bluteau describes the *Matical* or *Metical*, as a coin or weight of gold, current in Mozambique, and worth 480 *reis*, according to João dos Santos in the *Ethiopia*, fol. 53, col. 3; and records that in the same place the above historian speaks of "quatorze maticaes que são seis mil e seis centos reis"; from this latter passage we may deduce nearly 472 *reis* to the *metical*. Under *metical*, Bluteau quotes two passages from Portuguese authors: (i) João de Barros, *Decada* i, 68, 2, to the effect that 30 *meticals* are equal to about 14,000 *reis*. This would give only 466½ *reis* to the *metical*. (ii) Damião de Goes, fol. 23, c. 4, that each *metical* is worth 240 *reaes da nossa moeda*. If the *real* is equal to two *reis*, this value of the *metical* agrees with that assigned to it above by João dos Santos.

kingdom of Pegú, where there are many mines of it, and its quality is as good as that of Castelete.

CHAPTER XXXIII.

How the merchants and all the noble Moors of the city complained to the great Afonso Dalboquerque of the tyrannies which Utemutaraja exercised in the land, and how he had in his power all the supplies, and of many other things which he did.

When some days had elapsed, after the fortress was raised to such a height that it could defend itself against its enemies, they came from time to time to declare to the great Afonso Dalboquerque that Utemutaraja was planning some treachery in concert with the King Alaoadim, who had succeeded to the kingdom after the death of his father King Mahamet, who had died in Pão, as I have already related, with the intention of rising up in conjunction against us, and for the better proof of this matter they gave him a letter which the Utemutaraja had written to the King, and the reply to it.

The substance of this letter was Utemutaraja's excuses to the King for the friendship he had made with Afonso Dalboquerque, and the obedience he had shown to the same, giving many reasons and excuses for the course he had pursued, and offering in it his own person and his men to help the King if he is determined to attack the city of Malaca, with all his household and possessions, relatives and friends, making very light of this business because of the smallness of our forces. Afonso Dalboquerque kept this within himself without giving account of it to any one, and from that time forward showed to Utemutaraja much good-will; and Utemutaraja, considering this favourable treatment which he experienced, and vainly imagining that Afonso Dalboquerque was not cognisant of the treachery in which he was engaged, began to act with some little effrontery in the government of the land, and gave opportunity to the Moors who lived in his district of Dupe to make use of their own coinage, and prevented ours from being current; and although Utemutaraja had been present, in his position as a principal personage, when it was agreed that this coinage of money should be made, nevertheless neither he, nor his sons, grandsons, nor relatives, would be present at the formal proclamation of the change of currency; wherefore it was that Afonso Dalboquerque did not place any very great reliance on his protestations of friendship, but began to act very cautiously in his dealings with him, and appeased the Moors, who complained every day of the robberies practised upon them by Utemutaraja, who was constantly leading his men in little bands about the country, robbing the people who had returned to settle in the city in consequence of the safeguard held out to them by Afonso Dalboquerque. And not content with this, Utemutaraja had even given orders for seizing all the slaves of the King and his Mandarins, and of the Merchants, and began to take possession for himself of certain estates in the interior country, which had been deserted by the Governors of Malaca when they had fled with the King, without anyone being able to compel him to relinquish any of the things which he had seized.

And because the merchants and people of the city came again to pour out their complaints against Utemutaraja to Afonso Dalboquerque, and because also he had intercepted all the cargoes of rice that had arrived, and would not suffer a single merchant to purchase any of them, in order to have them all in his own hands, so that on this account there was a great scarcity of provisions, Afonso Dalboquerque sent word to Utemutaraja, through Ruy de Araujo, temporising with him, that certain merchants were complaining of the bad government of the land; but it must surely be without any reason, for they were a difficult class to be made happy, yet he begged earnestly that he would give orders for an inquiry to be made into the matter. But Utemutaraja took so little heed of this hint to mend his ways, that Afonso Dalboquerque again sent word to say that on an occasion when a certain *Naire*,[1] who had turned Christian—a man in the employment of the *Meirinho*[2]—was walking in the district of Dupe, he had ordered his arrest; and when the *Meirinho* with very gentle words desired him to look well to what he was doing, for that man was a Christian and not subject to his jurisdiction,—but if he had done anything wrong it ought to be reported to Afonso Dalboquerque, who would order him to be severely beaten,—he (Utemutaraja) had given no reply, neither had he given up the *Naire*, but from that time forward he began to construct in Dupe strong stockades surrounded with ditches.

Ruy de Araujo, who observed these evident signs of effrontery on the part of Utemutaraja, made his way to Afonso Dalboquerque, and related to him all these things that had taken place, little thinking that he was well aware of them all, and told him that unless that Javanese (Utemutaraja) were once and for ever put to silence, he felt sure that as soon as the Portuguese sailed away for India he would be the cause of a great deal of trouble to the fortress, and to the men who were left behind in it; and this very same opinion was given to Afonso Dalboquerque by the merchants, who begged him very earnestly not to depart from Malaca without first of all casting Utemutaraja out of the country, for he was a traitor, and an evil man, who had always been an opponent of the late king, and had even endeavoured several times to rise up in open rebellion

[1] See vol. i, p. 4.

[2] *Meirinho*, an officer whose duty it is to apprehend criminals and malefactors.

against him; and they declared that they dared not stay in the land if Utemutaraja remained therein; and they gave very good reasons for all this, alleging that Utemutaraja was not only an old man, and of very ancient family, and one to whom much faith was attached in that country, but also he had many sons and grandsons, and was very rich, and had many retainers. And beyond all these arguments which the merchants laid before Afonso Dalboquerque, he himself had certain information that the principal reason why this Javanese practised these doings was because he could not bear that the Quilins and Chitims, who were Hindoos, should be out of his jurisdiction, or have a governor and a system of judicature set apart for themselves, for it was Ninachatu who ruled them, and framed his government in accordance with their native Hindoo manners and customs. And another strong motive which influenced this matter was that Afonso Dalboquerque greatly favoured the Hindoo merchants, because they were men much employed in trading, and richer, and possessed of greater estates than the Moors; and in their hands lay all the commerce and business of Malaca, and they, too, were under the obligation of causing six hundred families of the richest inhabitants of Choramandel to come and settle in Malaca; and this favour which Afonso Dalboquerque showed to the Hindoos, and the great trouble he was at to root out the Moors from Malaca, was the cause of Utemutaraja's entering into a confederation with King Alaoadim to rise up in revolt against our people.

CHAPTER XXXIV.

How the great Afonso Dalboquerque, on account of the corroboration which he received concerning the treason which Utemutaraja was planning against him, determined to seize him, and his son, and his son-in-law; and the rest that took place, and what passed with the wife of Utemutaraja.

The great Afonso Dalboquerque, being thus aware of the conspiracy in which Utemutaraja was engaged together with the King Alaoadim, intending to rise up in revolt against him, and having information that he had bought up all the rice in the markets, which formed the staple article of food for the inhabitants of the city, and fearing that this business would entail great trouble upon him if he bore with Utemutaraja any longer, determined to seize him and his son, son-in-law, and grandson,[1] and on several occasions caused them to be summoned, that he might take counsel with them concerning the government of the land, but they always made excuses for absenting themselves, and were unwilling to come at his summons, whereat Afonso Dalboquerque began to be more displeased than ever with them; nevertheless, he continued to dissemble his real feelings towards them.

But when the time came for Afonso Dalboquerque to set sail for India, and he saw he could not bring this affair to a conclusion except by some open acts of force, veiling his real intentions he said to Cojeabrahem,[2] a Moor, by nation a Persian, who was a great friend of Utemutaraja, who was constantly requesting him to give him the official position

[1] "Tinha elle hum filho valente caualleiro, e tinha hum seu genro, casado com huma filha, de que tinha hum neto valente caualleiro, todos homens muy poderosos e riqos."—*Correa*, p. 258.

[2] *Coge Abraham*, *i.e.*, Master Abraham; for the first part of the word, which is a titular designation, see vol. i, p. 227.

of *Quitoal*,[1] that he had determined not to confer the offices of the city upon any one without the counsel and advice of the principal inhabitants of it, and therefore they must all be convened, and if they were agreed then he would give him the office in their presence.

Cojeabrahem, seeing by this a means for the accomplishment of his aspirations, so managed that he brought them together and conveyed them to the fortress where Afonso Dalboquerque was with all the captains; and when they had gone in, without any further parley with them, Afonso Dalboquerque ordered that their arms should be taken away from them, and then gave orders to Ruy de Araujo to read to them before the whole assembly certain articles which he had against Utemutaraja and his son, son-in-law, and grandson, concerning many things which they had done against the service of the King D. Manuel, their lord, and among others the letter which Utemutaraja had written to King Alaoadim.

Utemutaraja confessed to certain of the articles, but denied others, and as for the letter, he said it was true that he had written it, but it was not his intention to revolt against Afonso Dalboquerque, but rather to get the king into his own hands, so as to deliver him up to the Portuguese; and as for the rice which they alleged he had bought up and kept in hand, he had indeed bought it to make profit by the transaction, for this was the business by which he made his living, and he had not done this for any other or for any bad purpose; but these were matters which the Hindoos had trumped up against him out of the ill will they bore him because he would not take part in their peculations.

[1] Correa gives the signification of this native title by the paraphrase:—"Que andaua em requerimento com o Gouernador que o fizesse *gozil e guarda do mar*"; *i.e.*, governor of the port, and warden of the sea, p. 259.

When this examination was over, Afonso Dalboquerque gave orders to put all four of the prisoners into a cellar of the keep, and to maintain good watch over them, and to throw down the stockades and fill in the ditches which Utemutaraja had constructed in his district; and to Pero Dalpoem, who held the office of *Ouvidor*,[1] order was given forthwith to take judicial notice of their deeds, and to act in strict letter of law against them. As soon as the merchants and principal inhabitants received the news that Afonso Dalboquerque had captured Utemutaraja and his sons, they came and asked him to make just restitution of the great quantity of property of which that prince had robbed them. Therefore he gave instructions to the *Ouvidor* to cause restoration to be made to them of everything that should prove to have been obtained by robbery; and beside many other things which were thus caused to be restored to these merchants and to the people of the city, there were five hundred slaves whom Utemutaraja had seized by force. And when all the forms of the judicial process had been executed, and when everything was at an end, waiting for the passing of the sentence, Afonso Dalboquerque gave orders for the summoning of all the captains, and in their presence told the *Ouvidor* to read the indictment of the crimes of the prisoners; and having heard them, they adjudged the prisoners to suffer capital punishment[2] by decollation.

As soon as the sentence had been pronounced, Afonso Dalboquerque gave orders that there should be set up a lofty scaffolding in the middle of the square, that the execution might be witnessed by all the populace. Now when the wife of Utemutaraja knew that her husband and children were condemned to death, she sent to Afonso Dalboquerque a Javanese named Patequitir, to beg he would have pity on

[1] Chief magistrate.

[2] *Julgáram que morressem morte natural;* a curious Portuguese phrase, probably to be accounted for on euphemistic principles.

her and pardon her husband and her children, and she would take them away with her and go and live in her own country (for she was a native of Java), for she was never happy at their living in Malaca, and on this condition she would give, towards defraying the expenses of the works at the fortress, seven *Bahares* of gold, each one of which contains four *quintals*.[1] Afonso Dalboquerque replied that the custom of the Portuguese was not to sell justice for gold, that for his part he was very sorry to find them guilty and to have to give orders for justice to be meted out to them, but that he would allow that their bodies after death should be delivered over to them that they might bury them according to their own rites. When the scaffold was ready he ordered the *Ouvidor* to go and execute justice upon the prisoners, taking with him in his train all the guards, and a large body of other men armed, because these criminals were men of considerable importance; and when they were on the scaffold and the executioner desired to execute the sons first, Utemutaraja said to him that he should begin upon him, for he was an old man, and could not bear to see them come to such a fearful end. The bodies remained where they were from the morning until the evening, in sight of all the people of the city, who could not bring themselves to believe that these men had been executed.

This spectacle of the punishment of these Moors was a special permission of Divine Providence, for in this very

[1] Correa's account of this proffered gift involves a curious typographical error in his text. The passage is as follows:—"E por ysso dariào sete báres d'ouro e meo, que erão trinta quintaes, por cada hum dez," p. 260. "And they would give seven and a half *báres* of gold, which was thirty *quintals*, for each one *ten*"; a manifest error for *four*.

The *Quintal* is equivalent to four *Arrobas*, or 58.7428 kilo, French. Vieyra's description of the *Bahar* is somewhat confused. He gives three values, 386 lbs. avoird., 625 lbs. and 6250 lbs. for different Eastern localities. Bluteau quotes a passage from Damião de Goes, fol. 60, col. 3,......"Que faz cada *Bahar* tres quintaes, tres arrobas, e desouto arrates do nosso peso".

same square, where Afonso Dalboquerque ordered these men to be decapitated by the sword of the justice of the King of Portugal, two years ago the King of Malaca had determined to kill his chief captain, Diogo Lopez de Sequeira, and all those who accompanied him to that country, in a banquet which was given to them, had it not been for a woman of Java, who by night swam off to the ships to warn one of the mariners who was her friend.[1] The wife of Utemutaraja, after having performed her rites of sepulture upon those devilish corpses,[2] conferred with Patequitir and gave him seven or eight *miticaes*[3] of gold, and desired him to gather together all her slaves, who were very many, and to take vengeance for her upon the *Quilins*[4] and *Chitins*,[5] who had been the cause of the death of her husband and her sons.

When Afonso Dalboquerque knew of this, he came up with some soldiers and fell upon this band, and put them all to the sword in the very streets of the city, killing a great number of them. Patequitir, finding himself worsted, and seeing that he had no power to carry out what was desired of him, took the wife of Utemutaraja, and all the property he could carry off, and struck out into the interior of the country, and set fire to a large number of country houses of *Chitins* and *Quilins*, and carried on this rebellion for ten or twelve days; but when he reflected that this enterprise of his could not possibly come to a good end, he sent to Afonso Dalboquerque to give him a safeguard, and this was granted according to his request, but he would not return to live in Malaca.

This Utemutaraja was by birth a Javanese Hindoo, and it was many years since he had become a Moor. He was about eighty or ninety years of age, of the lower class; he was poor when he came to Malaca, and he had lived about

[1] See vol. ii, pp. 73, 74.
[2] *Aquelles corpos de Satanás.*
[3] See p. 142.
[4] See p. 128.
[5] See vol. ii, p. 130 *n*.

fifty years there: he prospered well with his merchant trade, and became exceedingly rich; he was very proud, excessively tyrannical, restless, rebellious, and so was he always in the time of King Mahamet; and he had so much power and so much authority in Malaca, that had he not been got rid of he would certainly have caused very great trouble to us. For Afonso Dalboquerque very often used to say (when he observed how quiet the country remained after the death of Utemutaraja), that if he had carried out a similar policy in Ormuz, in regard to Cogeatar,[1] that one also would never have raised up rebellion against him, nor practised so many impostures upon him.

This son of his, who was put to death with him, was the one who stood ready with the dagger in his hand to murder Diogo Lopez de Sequeira; and he it was, too, whom the King of Malaca had appointed Captain, after the fall of Diogo Lopez, to seize the ships of the Portuguese, with a large body of his own and his father's retainers; but Our Lord would not that he should accomplish this crime, but, on the other hand, willed that he should pay the penalty which such an undertaking merited.

CHAPTER XXXV.

How Duarte Fernandez, and the Chinese, whom he carried in his company, reached the city of Udiá, where the King of Sião lived, and gave him the message which he carried from the great Afonso Dalboquerque; and of the ambassador whom the King of Sião sent to him.

When Duarte Fernandez had set sail from Malaca in company with the two Chinese captains, bearing the message of the great Afonso Dalboquerque to the King of Sião, as has already been mentioned, in a few days they

[1] See vol. i, p. 108, etc.

stood off on the other tack and reached the mouth of a large river which leads to the City of Udiá,[1] in which the King of Siam lived; and when the King heard of the arrival there of some foreign people he sent thither a Captain with two hundred launches, to learn what people they were and whence they came.

As soon as the Captain reached the harbour where the Chinese had remained, he enquired of Duarte Fernandez the purpose of his journey, and by whom he had been sent. Duarte Fernandez replied that he was the messenger of a great Captain of the King of Portugal, who was established at Malaca with a large fleet, and that he had been sent thither by the orders of that Captain to visit the King of Sião and carry a letter to him. On receiving this intelligence the Siamese Captain sent to the King an account of the people, who they were, and with what object they had come, and asking that instructions should be sent how he desired him to proceed in this matter.

The King, having already had some information of the arrival of Afonso Dalboquerque at Malaca, was very much gratified to know that this messenger came from him, and ordered the Captain to bring the messenger to him immediately. When the King's reply was received the Captain embarked in the launches with Duarte Fernandez and the Chinese Captains, and they all proceeded up the river[2] as far as the City, and when the party disembarked the Captain with all his men escorted Duarte Fernandez to the Palace, where the King was waiting for them in a large hall, all hung round with brocades and upholstered with very rich

[1] Udiá, called by Bruzen de la Martiniere *Juthia* or *Judia*, the capital city of the kingdom of Siam, corrupted from the native name *Si-yô-thi-yâ*. Pedro Barretto de Resende, in MS., Sloan, 197, fol. 380, shows on Berthelot's map of 1635, the "Cidade de India, metropolli do Reino de Siam". Keith Johnston, in his Royal Atlas, places *Yuthia* or *Ayuthia*, a little to the north of Bangkok, 14 deg. 24 min. N., 100 deg. 27 min. E.

[2] The river Menam, see p. 71 *n*.

cushions, the King himself being seated on a lofty chair, habited in the Chinese fashion, and close to him, on the right and left, all his wives and daughters, seated, clad in brocades and silken clothes, with a great display of golden ornaments and jewellery, and lower down on each side many other women of noble birth, dressed after the same manner, so that it was a very grand spectacle. The women of this country are somewhat short of stature, but yet they are very handsome. And there were also present there all the principal lords of the country, very richly attired.

After Duarte Fernandez had entered the hall he made his obeisance to the King after the Hindoo manner, and went up to him and gave him Afonso Dalboquerque's letter and the sword, which the King received with many words of acknowledgment, asking him about the doings at Malaca, and the King of Portugal, and the state and power which he possessed. Duarte Fernandez, being a man of considerable ability, gave a very good account of everything in his replies to the King's enquiries. And when this interview was over the Captain was commanded to take him to his own house and to entertain the Chinese Captains in a very good manner, and on the following day the King ordered that all the City should be shown to him in order to do him honour, and also that he should see a white Elephant which he had, at which the Chinese became very greatly struck with amazement; and indeed had it been a thing which could be purchased, they would have given a large sum of money for it in order to carry it to the King of China.

After some days had elapsed the King granted a farewell audience to Duarte Fernandez, sending in company with him an Ambassador to Afonso Dalboquerque, with a letter to the King D. Manuel, and a ring set with a ruby, and a crown and sword of gold, and they set out from the city of Udiá and in seven days got as far as the other side of the Coast of Samatra and reached Taranquè, which is a city belonging to the King of Sião, and from that point they kept along by his towns as far as the shoals of Capacia, and on their arrival at Malaca they found the walls of the fortress already with a great part of the battlements and towers complete, and much artillery set up in them, and all the city in obedience to Afonso Dalboquerque.

The Chinese Captains, who had all along fancied that he would be ruined in that enterprise of his against Malaca, when they beheld the fortress finished and the peaceable state of the city were very much astonished, and very much ashamed of the way in which they had behaved towards him before their voyage. When Afonso Dalboquerque learned that an Ambassador of the King of Sião had come in company with Duarte Fernandez, he gave orders that he should be received by all the Captains, and he treated him with great honour and entertained him. The Ambassador delivered to him a letter which he had brought, and another for the King D. Manuel, with the present. The letter for Afonso Dalboquerque was the reply to that which had been sent to the King by Duarte Fernandez, and in it the King said that he was much pleased with the messenger and with the declaration of friendship, and offered him his kingdom and person for the service of the King of Portugal, and supplies and men and merchandize for his country, as much as was required, and that for a long time he had desired to be on friendly terms with him on account of the great things which he had heard reported of the Portuguese done against the Moors, and that he hoped he would take vengeance for him upon that tyrant the King of Malaca, for as yet he did not know that the city was taken.

CHAPTER XXXVI.

How the great Afonso Dalboquerque dispatched the ambassador of the King of Sião, and in company with him sent Antonio de Miranda de Azevedo with instructions how to act, and of the present which was sent through him.

As soon as the great Afonso Dalboquerque had concluded his interviews with the Ambassador of the King of Sião, he determined—being just on the point of setting sail for India—to dispatch him back again, and to send in company with him Antonio de Miranda de Azevedo, as Ambassador to the King, and ordered him to make ready to sail in the junk of the Chinese who were waiting there for him; and this was the instruction given to him as to what he was to say:—

"You shall declare to the King of Sião how the King of Portugal, my lord, sent me to this port of Malaca to take notice of the treason which the king and his governors did to a certain one of his chief captains and to his men, who had been sent to treat as to terms of friendship, and that he had killed them in face of a safeguard which had been granted to them, and thrown into captivity in that country a great part of the men.

"You shall declare to him that, after I had arrived at this port, I had sent many times to beg of the king to give an account of his proceedings, and order the release of the Portuguese whom he had thrown into captivity, and make good the property which he had taken; but he, with his unmeasured pride, never gave answer to this proposal, nor desired to be on friendly terms, nor make a treaty of peace with me, but shewed favour to the Moors of India (who had their ships there) in opposition to the service of the King of Portugal.

"You shall declare that when I beheld his determination to be false I attacked his city and entered into it by force of arms, and overcame the king (who escaped with a wound only) and his people and his elephants; but, in order that I should not destroy the city, I re-embarked, and so remained for the space of fifteen days in expectation of his repentance; and the king, having had experience of the dashing spirit of the Portuguese cavaliers, had nevertheless not abandoned the intention of risking all at any price upon the hazard of war, rather than wishing to have an agreement of peace and friendship arranged between myself and him.

"You shall declare to him that, in order to repress this contumacy which he shewed, I again attacked the city and overthrew it, killing many people and even some of his captains; and I took his elephants and I burnt his palaces, but I forgave his people and his merchants, so that the city might not be destroyed nor the trade of the country; and that I give the King of Sião hereby this notice of it, because I know for certain that he will be well pleased at hearing of the overthrow of this king, for he has always been at war with him.

"You shall declare unto him that the King of Portugal, my lord, will be greatly pleased if the ships and people of Sião trade with Malaca, and that this was the principal reason why I was glad when it was taken; and, if he should have any need of the fleets or armies of Sião for the preservation of his estate, I, as his captain general, will make use of them in everything that he orders me to do."

And with these instructions Afonso Dalboquerque gave him a present for the king, to be given to him in the name of the King of Portugal, consisting of some breast-pieces of crimson velvet; a long corselet with complete suit of arms; a helmet with the chin-piece very richly garnished; a buckler of buff,[1] with its cordings very richly made and set

[1] *Adarga danta.* The Anta, according to Vieyra, is an animal found in the East Indies, like a little cow, without horns. The hide is much valued to make buff small-clothes.

in a brocaded guige;[1] three cloths of arms made of velvet and satins of various colours, stamped in patterns and trimmed with gold tassels. These had belonged to the King of Malaca, and had adorned the wooden house wherein the King of Pão, his son-in-law, was to go in procession through the streets of the city (as I have related already[2]); and a basin for washing the hands, with bastions;[3] and two double-handed vases[4] of the same pattern; and a small kettle of fine workmanship; and two cups with bastions, all of silver; and a cross-bow, with its furniture;[5] and four branches of coral, very thick and of fine quality, because of its great value in that country; and a piece of scarlet; and he made a present of some articles to the King of Sião's ambassador, whereat he was much pleased.

Antonio de Miranda, as soon as he received his letters of credence for the King, embarked on board the Chinese junk, and proceeding on the voyage in a few days reached the city of Taranque, which belongs to the King of Sião, and there he parted from the Chinese and made his way through the country with horses and draught oxen, straight to the city of Sião, where he was very graciously received by the King who was reigning there.

This kingdom of Sião is very narrow on that side where the Chinese make their navigation. It possesses some harbours and villages, and from thence it is a ten days' journey to the coast of Tanaçarij,[6] and Taranque, and Savião, and on the other side of the sea of Samatra he has also many harbours and villages, and he is lord of a large population. These are Hindoos, and in the country are many Moorish merchants from numerous parts of the world. The Chinese keep up in this country their establishments, for they repose

[1] *Funda*, a sling, strap, or *guige*, by which the shield is slung over the shoulder. [2] See p. 107. [3] See vol. ii, p. 205.

[4] *Albarradas.* [5] *Almazem.*

[6] Tenasserim, 12 deg. 2 min. N., 98 deg. 55 min. E.

great confidence in the people. The King of this land was always at war with the King of Malaca, and therefore he was not sorry to see him overcome.

There are many things which I could have written about this kingdom of Sião, but my purpose is not to write any more about the countries than that which is necessary for the understanding of this history.

CHAPTER XXXVII.

How the great Afonso Dalboquerque dispatched the ambassadors of the Kings of Campar and Java, and ordered the exploration of the Island of Maluco.

The King of Campar having received intelligence of the discomfiture of Malaca, and of the state in which the affairs of that kingdom were, and fearing that because he was his son-in-law the fury of the Portuguese would be brought to bear also against his own country, embarked in ten launches, and came down to the river Muar, which is in the kingdom of Malaca, a distance of eight leagues from the city, opposite to the kingdom of Pão, and when he had arrived at this river he sent a messenger to Afonso Dalboquerque with a present of eight packages[1] of *lenhonoe*,[2] of very fine quality, and two of a mass which is made of the blood of the dragon,[3] which serves as a varnish for painted

[1] *Fardos*, bundles or bales. The *fardo* in India is a definite amount of forty-two pounds weight Portuguese.

[2] *Lenhonoe;* perhaps the *len-hae*, considered by the Rev. Dr. Mason of Burmah to be the *Acorus Calamus*, the root of which is very fragrant. See J. F. Watson's *Index to the Native and Scientific Names of Indian and other Eastern Economic Plants*, p. 342, fol. London, 1868, Indian Museum. Cf. *lenholoes*, chapter xliii.

[3] *Dragrão*, a typographical error for *dragão*. The *sangue do dragão* is the resin of a tree known to botanists as *Calamus Draco*. Bluteau writes of the *Sangue de Drago*:—" He huma especie de goma, que por incisão destilla em licor, e logo em se levantando o sol, se endurece, e se congela

articles, and sent word to say to Afonso Dalboquerque that this was a specimen of the fruit that was gathered in his country, and that he very greatly desired his friendship, and to become a vassal and a servant of the King of Portugal, and that he was not culpable in any way for the doings of his father-in-law.

Afonso Dalboquerque sent to thank him sincerely for the present, and for the desire to serve the King of Portugal, his Lord, which he had shown, and he sent him also certain things in return for his present, and offered him men and a fleet whenever he might need them; and when this messenger from the King of Campar had set forth on his return journey, Afonso Dalboquerque dispatched another, who many days ago had arrived there from the King of Java, bringing with him for a present a dozen lances of very great length with their slings of wood fastened into the iron, and a very long piece of cloth, whereon was painted a representation of the manner in which the King goes to battle, with his car-

em humas pequenas lagrimas friaveis, e vermelhas como sangue. O sangue de Drago com estas qualidades he o melhor dos tres, que se vendem nas boticas. Mana de huma arvore do tamanho de pinheyro, que dà muyto ramo, e lança humas folhas da feyção de espadas; os frutos se parecem com ginjas, e formando huns como cachos, de amarellos se fazem vermelhos, e de vermelhos azues, e azedinhos ao gosto. Disserão alguns, que, tirada deste fruto a pelle, apparece a figura de hum drago, donde lhe veyo o nome; porèm a mais commua opinião tem esta circunstancia por fabulosa.

"A outras duos gomas, que tem alguma semelhança com esta, se dà o nome de sangue de Drago; huma se tira de humas plantas das Ilhas Canarias, a qual dà folhas como de pereyra, a outra tem folhas como de ginjeyra, e dizem que huma e outra se cria na Ilha de S. Lourenço...... Disserão outros que o sangue de Dragão era huma certa especie de vermelhão, muyto fino, e apurado. O que tamhem he falso, porque o verdadeyro vermelhão he mineral, on artificial, e o sangue de Dragão, que se usa nos boticas, he licor congelado a modo de resina, que se destilla das arvores, as quaes...se chamão Dragoens. Sangrão os moradores da terra estas arvores, dandolhes golpes na casca, onde acode a humidade que tem, e alli se coalha, e faz em resina, vermelha, dura, e transparente."

riages, horses, and elephants armed with their wooden castles, and a figure of the King therein painted, riding in certain wooden erections placed above the carriages, and all this very beautifully depicted; and he sent him also twenty little bells, of which their music consists, and players who could play upon them with carved sticks, and they harmonised very well and gave a very pleasant sound; and he sent him two very large bells, which they strike in battle, for they can be heard a long way off; and the King desired to offer him men and supplies, and all other things that might be necessary for the war in Malaca. The reason of this was that the King of Java was very much opposed to the King of Malaca, on account of the frequent tyrannies which were continually practised upon his native subjects whenever they went thither.

Afonso Dalboquerque dispatched the ambassador, and with him he sent to the King of Java one of the elephants which had been captured in Malaca, for in that country they are held in very great esteem, and a piece of scarlet, and another of velvet crimson, and granted him free passage for himself and for the transport of the elephant. And just at this very juncture there arrived at Malaca three *pangajaoas*[1] from the kingdom of Menamcabo, which is at the point of the island of Çamatra on the other side of the south, and brought with them a sum of gold, and they came to seek for cloths of India, for which there is a great demand in their country. The men of this kingdom are very well made, and of fair complexion; they walk about always well dressed, clad in their silken *bajus*,[2] and wearing their *crisis* with sheaths adorned with gold and precious stones in their girdles. These are a people of good manners and truthful character; they are Hindoos; they

[1] See p. 60 *n*.

[2] *Baju*, a kind of garment worn by the Indian ladies.—*Vieyra.* "Camisa de meyo corpo."—*Bluteau.*

have a great veneration for a certain golden head-dress[1] which, as they relate, Alexander [the Great] left there with them when he conquered that country.

Now that Afonso Dalboquerque had dispatched all these messengers, he determined to send a party to explore the islands of Maluco, and all the others of that archipelago,[2] for he had been informed that there were many of them; and he made ready three ships, of which he conferred the chief captaincy upon Antonio Dabreu, of whom I have already written how he was wounded in the junk with which he attacked the bridge at Malaca,[3] and he indeed quite deserved this honour on account of his dashing spirit and chivalrous character. And of the other two ships he gave the captaincy to Francisco Serrão and Simão Afonso; and for pilots he appointed Luis Botim, and Gonçalo de Oliveira, and Francisco Rodriguez, a man of youthful age, who had always had employment in India as a pilot, and knew very well how to set up a memorial monument[4] if it were required, and this indeed was the object of Afonso Dalboquerque in sending him there. And with them he sent two native pilots; and as factor João Freire, servant of the Queen D. Leonor; and Diogo Borges, servant of the King D. Manuel, to be the scrivener. And he prepared a junk laden with various kinds of merchandise, whereof he gave part to Ninachatu, and to a Hindoo whose name was Cogequirmani,[5] whose wife and children were settled with

[1] *Carapuça de ouro.*"

[2] It is doubtful whether this refers to the group of Moluccas or Spice Islands, 0 deg. 0 min., 127 deg. 30 min. E., as Borneo lays between them and the Malay peninsula. Probably the term was employed generally for the multitudinous groups of small islands lying on the equator between Asia and Australia in the Pacific.

[3] See p. 121.

[4] *Padrão*, a post or pillar on which was engraved an inscription, set up in accordance with the custom usually adopted by the discoverers of new countries.

[5] *i.e.*, Khoja Kirmânî, the "Merchant of Kirman", or Kerman, one of the provinces of the Persian Empire. Here, as frequently is the case

him in Malaca, and this one went as captain of the junk. And because there was very little to do in getting the junk ready he set out two or three days before our fleet.

And the instructions which Afonso Dalboquerque gave to Antonio Dabreu were, on no account whatever on that voyage to take any prizes, and to go on board of no vessel whatever, nor to consent to any of his men going on shore, but in all the harbours and at all the islands at which he might touch to give presents and gifts to the kings and lords of the country, and for this purpose he ordered that there should be given out many pieces of scarlet and velvets of Méca, and many other kinds of merchandise; and, further, he gave orders that the captain should not interfere with a single ship of Malaca or of the other parts (whether they belonged to the Moors or to the Hindoos) which he might meet with in these Clove islands[1] or Apple islands[2] taking in cargo, but rather shew them favour and give them as much assistance as he possibly could; and, in the same way that such ships as these negotiated for their cargo, so also in like manner was he to act for his cargo, observing all the customs of the respective countries. But whatever might happen not one of the captains was to go on land, except only the factor and scrivener with two or three to accompany them.

These ships carried a hundred and twenty Portuguese and twenty captive slaves to work at the pumps; and they went very well supplied with provisions and artillery, and had on board plenty of tow and pitch, and caulkers, in order that if necessity should arise they might go and overhaul their ships at the cape of a large island (which lies at a distance of four days' sail from the clove islands), which is

throughout the *Commentaries*, the Portuguese interpreter appears to mistake the title or designation of the individual for his proper name.

[1] *Em essas Ilhas do Cravo.* The Molucca Islands are known even now under the name of the Spice Islands.

[2] *Ou das Maçans.*

called Amboino,[1] for we have already a knowledge of the rise and fall of the tide there. And when they were all quite prepared they set out in the month of November.

And as soon as Antonio de Abreu had set sail, Afonso Dalboquerque gave orders to make ready a very large new junk, of which he gave part to Ninachatu and the other merchants of Malaca, and he ordered that it should be laden with much merchandise of Cambaya, which had been captured on the voyage from India to Malaca, and that the vessels should go to Pacé[2] to take in a cargo of pepper to be stored up in the fortress, in case of the Chinese, or Gores (whose arrival he was expecting) coming in search for a cargo. And all the other merchants and chitins of Malaca began to prosecute their trading voyages, and to arrange their commercial undertakings in such a manner that in a very short space of time the brisk trade which was carried on in Malaca began to be very celebrated. And at the report of the good treatment which the great Afonso Dalboquerque had ordered to be shown to all the shipping which touched Malaca with merchandise, they began to make their voyages thither from all parts, and every one of them found something in the way of a cargo to carry back to their own country.

[1] *Amboino;* Amboina Island, 3 deg. 45 min. S., 128 deg. 15 min. E.; a little to the south of the island of Ceram. Amboina is a high island, eleven leagues in extent N.E. and S.W., the largest of those called the Clove Islands. The great bay extends about seven leagues into the island, separating it nearly into two parts. Amboina Bay is formed at the entrance by two high points, that of Allang on the west side, and Noessaniva Point to the eastward; they are steep-to; situated in lat. 3 deg. 47 min. S., long. 128 deg. 6 min. E., and bear nearly E. and W. of each other, distant six miles. About three cables' lengths from Noessaniva Point, in a S.S.E. direction, there is a narrow bank of sand, stretching E. and W., having soundings of fifteen to twenty fathoms on it, upon which a ship might anchor when calm. The tides in the bay are very irregular, being governed chiefly by the winds, and rise about six or seven feet.—Horsburgh, *India Directory*, vol. ii, p. 714. Eighth Edition. London, 1864.

[2] *Pacé;* see p. 59 *n*.

CHAPTER XXXVIII.

Of the Council which the great Alfonso Dalboquerque held with the Captains respecting the order in which he should leave the management of affairs at Malaca, and some ordinances which he made for the government of the country before his departure for India.

When the great Afonso Dalboquerque had concluded his dispatch of all the matters which I have related, he ordered that a meeting of all the captains, *Fidalgoes*, and servants of the King throughout the fleet should be convened, and then he told them that the fortress of Malaca was now completed in the way in which they beheld it, with plenty of artillery within it, capable of defending itself successfully against all the powers of the Kings of these parts who could come against it: that the monsoon favourable for a voyage to India was now blowing, and that it was very necessary for them to set sail, for the condition of affairs at Goa was so unsettled, that he could not tell in what state they were; therefore he desired them earnestly to declare to him the policy which he ought to carry out concerning the government of Malaca, and what number of men, and how much artillery he ought to leave in the fortress, and how many vessels, and whether he should appoint a captain of the sea or not, or whether one alone would be sufficient on sea and on land, and whether or not he should remove certain principal Moors of the city of whom there was some suspicion.

In the Council there arose different opinions, and at the end of all it was arranged that there should be a Captain in the Fortress and a Captain of the Fleet in the Sea, and that the Captain of the Sea should be under the orders of the Captain of the Fortress (this was so arranged to avoid the shameful deeds done in India, which had then already taken place, but Afonso Dalboquerque always punished them with great rigour as long as he was Governor of that country), and that he should take an oath of homage to the Captain of the Fortress to obey him in all things, and all the Captains do so, as it were to the proper person of his Lordship; and if it should happen that God should dispose of the Captain of the Fortress, then the Captain of the Sea should succeed to be the Captain of it, until provision could be made.

As soon as this had been agreed to by all, Afonso Dalboquerque appointed Ruy de Brito Patalim, Captain of the Fortress, and Fernão Perez Dandrade, Chief Captain of the Sea, and as Captains of the vessels which were to remain under his orders, Lopo de Azevedo, who was to be Vice-Captain, Christovão Graces, Aires Pereira, Antonio de Azevedo, Pero de Faria, Christovão Mascarenhas, Vasco Fernandez Coutinho, and João Lopez Dalvim. And Antonio de Abreu also had orders to remain there with his Captains, whenever he returned from Maluco. And he appointed Ruy de Araujo—owing to the great obligation which he was under to him—Factor and Chief *Alcaide* and Overseer of the Fortress; and Francisco de Azevedo and Pero Salgado, Scriveners of the Fortress; and João Jorge, Receiver (*Almoxarife*) of the Supplies, and Jacome Fernandez his Scrivener; and Francisco Cardoso, *Almoxarife* of the Armoury, and Bras Afonso his Scrivener; and as Manager for the Defunct and of the Hospital, Christovão Dalmeida, and Diogo Camacho for his Scrivener, and Bastião Gallego, *Meirinho* of the Fortress. And he also appointed Governors of the land (not, however, beyond the superior jurisdiction of the Captain of the Fortress), of the Hindoos, Ninachatu; and of the Moors a *Caciz*[1] of his; and of the Javanese of the district of Dupe, Regunecerage, a Moor; and of the other part of the city, Tuão Calascar, a Javanese by birth; and he appointed Ruy de Araujo to be decider of their disputes and differences, and whenever the course of justice

[1] *Caciz*, see p. 69.

required the action of a higher court, the Captain of the Fortress was paramount over all.

This having been thus arranged, when the merchants of the country received information that Afonso Dalboquerque was firmly resolved to set sail for India, they made their way to him, and one among them, in the name of them all, declared to him that they had learned how his Lordship desired to set sail and leave them, for they were astonished beyond measure that he should leave an undertaking so important and so rich as was the City of Malaca and go away, for the well-being of the city without him at its head could not be maintained. And since he had in his hands the government of the largest city there was in the world, he ought not to leave it to destruction in favour of any other undertaking, but if he was going to do so from want of money, they, for their part, would give him as much gold, silver, and merchandize as he had need of, yea, and they would spend all the rest of their property in the service of the King of Portugal, and in his service, and therefore they begged him earnestly that he would not quit the city until its affairs had become more settled.

Afonso Dalboquerque thanked them very much for their offers, giving them certain reasons why it was necessary that he should return to India, but he would promise that he would quickly return to visit them, and for the security and defence of the city he would leave the fortress provided with plenty of artillery, and many Portuguese Cavaliers to defend it against any power in the world; and for the security of the sea and for protection of their merchant trade, a Fleet with many *Fidalgoes* and Cavaliers. The merchants replied that when he was in Malaca his name alone was sufficient for its defence and maintenance for a hundred years, and therefore they begged he would not leave them, and so they went on enlarging on their subject with good words and praises of his character.

Again, Afonso Dalboquerque thanked them for the confidence which they reposed in him, and told them that for his own part he would be very glad to remain there to perform what they desired of him, but that he was compelled to go to India, because the fortress of Goa had yet to be completed, and he did not know how affairs had gone since his departure.

As soon as this audience which he held with the merchants was over, being now quite ready for his departure, he was detained yet another day; for the King of Pacé, whom he had captured on the voyage from India (as I have already related[1]), and kept in his own house, treating him with all the courtesy and ceremony which was due to his rank, had secretly disappeared for two days, and no one knew whither he had gone.

Afonso Dalboquerque, after using all diligence to get him into his hands again, and perceiving that it was an useless search, took leave of the captains and all those who were to remain behind, and proceeded to embark in the ship *Flor de la Mar*,[2] and Pero Dalpoem, auditor of India, in the ship *Trindade;* and Jorge Nunez de Lião in the ship *Enxobregas;* and Simão Martinz in a large junk which was going to sail laden with many kinds of merchandise which had been taken at the sacking of the city. And Simão Martinz took with him in the junk thirteen Portuguese and fifty men of Malabar from Cochim to form the guard; and sixty Javanese carpenters of the dockyard, very handy workmen, whom Afonso Dalboquerque carried with their wives and children to serve the King of Portugal at Cochim in repairing the ships, because they were very much needed in India.

The Governor of Pacé, who had risen up in rebellion

[1] See p. 64.

[2] "Partio o Governador de Malaca em primeyro de Dezembro d'este anno [1511].—*Correa, l.c.*, p. 258.

against the king (as has been already related), hearing that Malaca had been taken by the Portuguese, full of fear of Afonso Dalboquerque, submitted himself to be a vassal of the King of Portugal; and Afonso Dalboquerque received him, because the rightful king would not accept his offers, and from that time forward the governor was always at the service and under the orders of Afonso Dalboquerque.

CHAPTER XXXIX.

Oration which Camillo Portio made to the Pope Leo the Tenth in praise of the capture of Malaca; and of the victories gained by the Portuguese in their conquest of India.

This kingdom having now been taken, and a fortress built in the city of Malaca, the great Afonso Dalboquerque immediately apprised the King D. Manuel of the state in which its affairs were placed; and the king, in order to render them of greater importance (because this *Golden Chersonese*[1] is greatly celebrated by all authors both ancient and modern), wrote letters[2] to inform the Pope Leo the

[1] See p. 71.

[2] "In hujus anni [1513] exitu Rex Emmanuel tres legatos ad Leonem decimum Pontificem Maximum, cum muneribus regia magnificentia dignis, instituit. Princeps legationis Tristanus Cugna fuit. Collegæ duo jurisconsulti magnæ apud Lusitanos auctoritatis extitere. Unus Jacobus Paciecus, alter Joannes Faria nominabatur. Per illos Pontifici sacras vestes ex auro, cum multis gemmis opere excellenti perfectis dono misit. Vasa præterea ex auro, atque monilia maximi ponderis et pretii vestibus adjecit. Opus erat ejusmodi, ut cum materia nihil pretiosius excogitari posset, artificium tamen ipsam materiam multis partibus superaret.

"Misit præterea elephantum Indicum miræ magnitudinis, quem non solum Romæ, ubi homines, post inclinatum Romanæ majestatis amplitudinem, illud animal nunquam oculis aspexerant, sed quacumque gradum inferebat, nemo circumfluentem undique turbam, admiratione obstupefactam, submovere poterat. Panthera etiam venatica missa fuit, quod munus hand scio, an olim Romæ Ædiles, cùm ludos magnificentissimos apparabant, et præter alias immanes beluas, pantheras etiam in

Tenth. And when he had been notified by João de Faria, the Portuguese Ambassador who was then at Rome, of the great victories of the Portuguese which they had gained in those parts of the world by the assiduity, valour, and spirit of this great Afonso Dalboquerque, he ordered that a solemn Procession[1] should be made in which he himself took part;

publicis spectaculis exhibebant, præstare potuerint. Ea namque mansuefacta, non in circo cum bestiariis, sed in sylvis cum apris atque cervis prælium committebat, et principibus qui venationibus oblectantur, plurimum voluptatis afferebat. Ea insidebat equi Persici tergo, integumentis auratis eleganter instrati. Equum regebat Persa venator eximius, qui ad id munus obeundum ab Armuzii rege cum equo et Panthera missus fuerat.

"Tristanus Cugna cùm esset vir et nobilitate, et auctoritate, et existimatione non vulgari præditus, tum propriis sumptibus eam legationem exornandam susceperat. Ducebat autem secum tres filios et cognatorum copiam, amplamque familiam quibus stipatus non abjecti Principis speciem præ se ferebat. Legationis scriba, Nicolaus Faria, qui equis Regiis curandis præerat, agebat equum pulcherrimum, ephippiis aureis, et phaleris aureis, emblematis et gemmis maximi pretii distinctis instratum et ornatum, qui etiam Pontifici donandus erat."—*Hieron. Osorii de Rebus Emmanuelis Regis. Col. Agr.*, 1574, fol. 297 *b*. Ciaconius, in his *Vitæ Pontificum* (tom iii, A.D. 1513, cols. 328-9), repeats this with an interesting anecdote of the sagacity of the elephant mentioned in the foregoing extracts.

[1] "Such a concurrence of great and prosperous events induced the Pope to direct the celebration of a public thanksgiving in Rome, which was accordingly observed with extraordinary pomp and splendid processions to the churches of S. Maria del Popolo and S. Agostino; in which the pontiff appeared in person, and by the propriety and decorum which always distinguished him on public occasions, gave additional dignity to the ceremony. At the same time he ordered Camillo Portio to pronounce, in the pontifical chapel, a Latin oration in praise of the character and actions of the King of Portugal, who had communicated to him his success, and testified his dutiful obedience to the Roman Court, and his personal attachment to the supreme pontiff.

"This mutual interchange of civility and respect between the King of Portugal and the pontiff was, however, rendered much more conspicuous by a splendid embassy from the Portuguese monarch, which soon afterwards arrived at Rome, to the great delight and astonishment of the inhabitants. The chief ambassador on this occasion was the celebrated Tristano Cugna, who had himself held a principal command in the ex-

and, on returning to the Sacred Palace, Camillo Portio,[1] in the presence of every one, made him the following

pedition to the East, and had acquired great honour by his conduct and courage in its prosecution. He was accompanied by Jacopo Pacheco and Giovanni Faria, professors of the law, of great eminence and authority. Three sons of Cugna, with many others of his relatives and friends, accompanied the procession, which was met at the gates of the city by a select body of cardinals and prelates, who conducted the strangers to the palaces appointed for their residence. But the respectability of the envoys was of less importance in the eyes of the populace than the singular and magnificent presents for the Pope by which they were accompanied. Among these were an elephant of extraordinary size, two leopards, a panther, and other uncommon animals. Several Persian horses, richly caparisoned, appeared also in the train, mounted by natives of the same country dressed in their proper habits. To these was added a profusion of articles of inestimable value; pontifical vest-

[1] Camillo Portio, Porcio, Portius, or Porcarius, must not be confounded with another personage of the same name, who flourished later in the sixteenth century. He was a Roman of noble birth, a canon of St. Peter's, Rome, and appointed by Pope Leo X, on the 4th March 1517, Bishop of Teramo (Theramum or Aprutium), the episcopal city of the Abruzzi. He is celebrated as a poet and orator. (See Tiraboschi, *Storia della Letteratura Italiana.* Modena, 1792, 4to, tom. vii, pt. 3, p. 1015.—*Nuova Biblioteca Populare; Opere di C. Porzio,* P. Giordani Torino, 1852, 8vo, p. 13.—Ughelli, *Italia Sacra*, vol. i, p. 371, "Vir varia literatura clarus".—Richard et Giraud, *Bibliothèque Sacrée*, vol. xxiv, p. 427.) According to Giordani, Camillo Porcio died in 1521. Ughelli and Richard place his death in 1522. The following note is of interest:—

"Camillus Portius, ut meos quoque cives, in scenam hanc inducam, quantæ fuerit celebritatis, ignorat nemo, sive ille Romanam cathedram magno omnium stupore, et admiratione decoraret, sive pro rostris declamaret, ut nihil ejus dictione suavius, nihil jucundius, nihil expolitius, haberetur. Is tamen simulac ab Leone Decimo Pontifice Maximo Aprutinæ est Ecclesiæ præfectus, acerbissimâ diuturni cujusdam morbi, nulli medicorum cogniti, correptus inclementiâ, postquam miserabili cruciatu menses plurimos decubuit afflictatus, morbi demum ejus truculentiâ, et totius corporis doloribus oppressus, virente adhuc ætate animam egit, incredibili apud omnes sui relicto desiderio."—*Joannis Pierii Valeriani Bellunensis de Literatorum Infelicitate Libri Duo.* Amstel., 1647, p. 15.

ORATION in October of the year one thousand five hundred and thirteen:—

"If ever at any time, Most Blessed Father, the Christian people had reason to give thanks to the Lord, and magnify his strength and power for an undertaking begun with bravery and daring, and brought to a fortunate end, this year stands forth on this account as the most brilliant

ments, adorned with gold and jewels, vases, and other implements for the celebration of sacred rites, and a covering for the altar, of the most exquisite workmanship. A herald, bearing the arms of the Portuguese sovereign, led the procession. On their arrival at the pontifical palace, where the Pope stood at the windows to see them pass, the elephant stopped, and, kneeling before his Holiness, bowed himself thrice to the ground. A large vessel was here provided and filled with water, which the elephant drew up into his trunk and showered down again on the adjacent multitude, dispersing no small portion of it among the more polite spectators at the windows, to the great entertainment of the Pontiff.

"Six days afterwards the ambassadors were admitted to a public audience, on which occasion the procession was repeated. The Pope, surrounded by the cardinals and prelates of the church, and attended by the ambassadors of foreign states and all the officers of his court, was addressed in a Latin oration by Pacheco, at the conclusion of which Leo replied to him in the same language, highly commending the king for his devotion to the Holy See. Of this opportunity the Pontiff also availed himself, to recommend the maintenance of peace among the states of Europe and the union of their arms against the Turks, expressing himself with such promptitude, seriousness, and elegance, as to obtain the unanimous admiration of the auditors. On the following day the presents from the king were brought into the conservatory of the gardens, adjoining the pontifical palace, where, on the introduction of animals proper for that purpose, the wild beasts displayed their agility in taking, and their ferocity in devouring, their prey: a spectacle which humanity would have spared, but which was probably highly gratifying to the Pontiff, who was devoted to the pleasures of the chase. The Portuguese monarch had intended to have surprised the Roman people with the sight of another and yet rarer animal, which had not been seen in Rome for many ages; but the rhinoceros, which he had brought from the East with this view, unfortunately perished in the attempt to get him on board the vessel prepared to transport him to Italy."—William Roscoe's *Life and Pontificate of Leo the Tenth.* London, 1846, vol. i, pp. 362, 363.

example which has as yet occurred, wherein our Lord God, by reason of his profound pity for his people, has deemed it right to increase their pleasure with fresh joy, and their prosperity with new and universal occasions of rejoicing. For in addition to His elevation of your holiness this year to the majesty of the pontifical throne, more for the universal profit of Christendom than for any particular benefit to your own self, He yet further made your holiness the sole refuge and safeguard in matters almost hopelessly ruined, and at a time when the whole world is occupied in the prosecution of wars, in order that with greater rejoicings his new choice might be inaugurated. At this very juncture it was that He gave to the most puissant and very fortunate and invincible King D. Manuel of Portugal so many and such great victories and triumphs over his enemies, that one may easily believe that the Lord is fighting on our side; and indeed that in this last brilliant enterprise, which was fought out victoriously in His name, He has given us a sign that from this day forward we should have confidence in Him to confer upon us signal victories, if we will only make up our determination to use that prestige which belongs naturally to us, and which is so universally admitted and dreaded among barbarian nations.

"Is it possible that there may haply be some one who is capable of deeming as works performed by the hands of men those deeds which have lately been accomplished by the Portuguese in India, under the captainship of the valiant Afonso Dalboquerque? So many cities of unmeasured wealth and immense strength entered by force of arms? so many various nations conquered? so many tribes overcome in battle? and this, too, with a very disproportionate number of soldiers, who were always able to come victoriously out of every enterprise to which they had devoted themselves. Yea, and more than this, they compelled many kings to become tributaries, after having been reduced to the state of subjects by the valour of the arms of Portugal: and even those who were not reached by the perils of the war, in order to secure their immunity from him, either came in person or sent their ambassadors with great earnestness to sue for peace and alliance. And for this reason the noble nature of these victories is greater and more excellent, because they are justly celebrated, not for the slaughter and destruction which was so frequently dealt out to the enemy, but for the notable Portuguese spirit, whereby they were gained; and it was to this spirit that God thus showed His favour; that the victories of the present age should put those of the past ages out of remembrance in such a manner that the spoils of the one should exceed the spoils of the other, and yet with these victories there should be added so many kings conquered, and all the other potentates who were unwilling to measure their strength against the intrepidity of the Portuguese arms, compelled to enter into an alliance.

"Wherefore, Most Blessed Father, your holiness proceeds with great prudence and Christian zeal, like all the rest in this respect, when for a victory of so much importance as this is (and I know not if any one could wish for a greater one), which at such a happy season our Lord has been pleased to grant to the most Christian King D. Manuel, you order solemn processions to take place, and accompany them in your own person, in order that due thanks may be given to the Lord, and to all the saints for such a great mark of His mercy as this is.

"For this is not a victory which has been gained over a warlike tribe, or over a fortified and obstinately defended city, but over that great and celebrated land of India, wherein, after the subjecting by Portuguese arms of the exceedingly rich kingdoms of Goa and Ormuz, and making them tributary, in such a manner that from the hands of the valiant Captain Afonso Dalboquerque, in the name of the King of Portugal, his lord, these kingdoms received the persons who were appointed to govern them, now, as a result of these great victories by sea as well as by land, there lies overthrown that most fertile and rich kingdom of Malaca, called by the ancients, on account of its enormous wealth, *Golden*,[1] for they desired by this appellation (given never to any other land) to signify the great extent of its immense sources of wealth; and not only in the conquest of these kingdoms is our mind occupied with the greatness of them, but (and this is of no small importance in these present times in which we live) we have to bear in mind that as for the barbarians whom before this event the report of our prowess had not reached, now, I say, the peril of these kingdoms terrifies those barbarians to whose lands we have opened the roads, and of whom up to the present time we have had no knowledge whatever.

"Thus, for example, there is thrown open to us by the conquest of the kingdom of Ormuz the road whereby the Holy House of Jerusalem (the country in which our Saviour was born) can again be recovered and rescued from the hands of those infidels who tyrannically and unrighteously possess it, for into their hearts we have instilled a dread which makes them fear lest they be compelled to share in the peril which has befallen their comrades. And in all these matters I am at a loss to decide to which of two facts I ought to give the greater praise, to the zeal and good fortune of the most puissant King D. Manuel, who with so much trouble and expenditure of treasure has desired to extend the name of Christ to the regions so far distant, and to nations foreign to our intercourse, with the intent that where the law of Christ had never before been in force there might he plant the flag of His Holy Cross; or to the spirit, understanding, and bravery of Portuguese minds, which with an effort of daring never before witnessed, and with a thoroughly determined eagerness to augment the Christian

[1] See p. 71.

religion, have passed over into climes so different from their native land, and there have been compelled to do battle, not only with cruel and inhuman enemies, but also with hunger itself, thirst, cold, and heat insufferable: and yet with all this to despise every one of the troubles that could possibly supervene, in order to accomplish the obligations which, at the orders of their king, they had cheerfully undertaken to perform.

"And in these enterprises those who will take the trouble to look into the matter may easily perceive the extensive nature of the Lord's mercies, when they bear in mind the smallness of the heroic band which gained possession of the whole of India. For although there were not so many as three thousand Portuguese souls in the whole of the fleet, they overcame so many kingdoms of that country and took them by force of arms; and so many kings, who were so terrified at the fame of the Portuguese, that they came in humble guise to beg for peace, while those who were unwilling to accept the terms of peace had to receive by force the laws imposed upon them by the hands of their conquerors: yea, and some among them, whom it pleased the Lord to enlighten, received baptism and embraced the Christian faith, in such a way that, even in climes so remote as these are, Christians were found with Christians: and as the ultimate result of these victories, gained by means of the same limited number of men, and even fewer still,—for they were obliged to detach some of the number to form the garrisons of the kingdoms that had been captured—we behold Malaca taken, her King conquered, and put to flight with a small remnant of his army that could barely manage to follow him, the greater part of it having met their death by the sword; and thus is this city of such noble fame, the capital of such a rich kingdom, in the power of Christians. This, Most Blessed Father, is that *Golden Chersonese*[1]

[1] See p. 71.

which lies at the other end of that great gulf wherein the River Ganges discharges her waters into the sea, so famous for her immense wealth, that on account of the very many kinds and very great worth of her merchandize, which is imported thither from different countries, as well as on account of the no less rich materials which are exported therefrom, she stands in estimation of being the noblest place of the whole of India; and this is but reasonable, for there is not a single thing of those which are desirable in this life, whereof she does not contain a very great abundance.

"There reigned in Malaca a King, who was, as to his faith, a Moor, as to treasures, rich and powerful, and possessed of a navy, and a very bitter enemy of the Christian name, especially of the Portuguese, for about two years previously he had treacherously sought the death of a noble Portuguese Captain who had arrived at this port, and the celebrated Captain Afonso Dalboquerque—(a name deserving of all praise for his illustrious deeds)—who at that time, in the name of the most puissant King D. Manuel, governed India, having pacified and established in security the other kingdoms and their fortresses of which in that country on this side of the Ganges, or as the Portuguese call it 'inside the cape of Comorim', he had gained possession, made up his mind to avenge the treason which the King of Malaca had practised towards the Portuguese, and by way of satisfaction for this deed to deprive him of his kingdom; and thus having arrived in good season at Malaca, he put himself in array to attack the city, not only by land but also by sea.

"The King of the country, who had never allowed his thoughts to be disturbed by the idea of such an event, perceiving himself not to be so well prepared as he wished to be for defending himself, thought it right to resort to artifice, and sent a message of peaceful import to Afonso Dalboquerque, the spirited avenger of the treason which had been shewn to the Portuguese, and began with dilatory proceedings to lengthen out the time for the settlement of the measures for peace, for which he was pretending to treat, and to temporise with him while, at the same time, he continued to fortify himself; but these measures of precaution did not escape the notice of the Portuguese, who put themselves in position for attacking the city; and manning their small craft, with breasts inflamed with a spirited valour, swooped down upon the coast; and bringing into action the artillery they carried with them, began to disperse the Moors so that they might effect an entrance into the city with less danger to themselves.

"The King of Malaca, finding himself thrown into this difficulty, and that he was now driven into a position in which he was compelled to defend himself by force of arms, and that now artifices were no longer of any avail, sets in order his defence with his men behind their stockades, while he himself mounted upon an elephant keeps on going up and down among them urging them on, and calling upon them that they must not think of failing their country in its present need, and in the supreme necessity which had fallen upon it. And now the Portuguese, with a spirit overjoyed and animated, had reached the wall, and the guns along the shore were pouring forth their fire, when the inhabitants of the city began to grow alarmed, their heart failed them, and deserting their stockades, which they had maintained for a short time only, commenced their flight; the Portuguese pursuing them with victorious exultation, and following closely pell-mell in the pursuit after the routed enemy, got into the city, and reached the very heart of it, where, upon a bridge which stood over a river along which the shipping enters, running through the midst of the city, the King had made his last stand, and posted the main force of his army, and strengthening the defences of the stockades here more and more, he rallied in it those who were in flight; for as the river could not be forded by the Portuguese, he fortified himself on the bridge.

"Here it was that the contest grew sharper, nevertheless the Portuguese, favoured with the hope of victory (the enemy being somewhat dashed with dread of the Portuguese arms) fought so fiercely with the infidels, that taking no precautions against their arms, and caring nought for their elephants with the castles full of archers, and despising the difficulty of the ford, with their swords carved out an open way through the midst of the enemy, some of whom out of sheer despair threw themselves upon the weapons of the Portuguese, while others cast themselves into the river to gain safety; finally, after the space of a few hours, all were in full flight, and the King, wounded as he was, along with them.

"The city was then entered and pillaged, a large number of the enemy put to death. In it was found an immense quantity of gold and silver, and they found also very many stores and munitions of war, among which there were two thousand pieces of artillery. Among the spoils there were taken seven elephants, caparisoned for battle, with their castles and their harness woven with gold and very richly garnished; so that not only the human beings, but even the brute beasts, of that kingdom were put under obedience to the Portuguese empire.

"O good God, O mighty Lord, Thine is the power,[1] Thine the might;[2] Thy right hand hath conferred the valour; Thy right hand exalted us: for how could so strongly fortified a city as this have been entered, and

[1] "Thine, O Lord is the greatness, and the power, and the glory, and the victory, and the majesty."—1 Chron. xxix, 11; cf. also 1 Chron. xxix, 12; Matth. vi, 13.

[2] "Rulest thou not over all the kingdoms of the heathen? and in thine hand is there not power and might, so that none is able to withstand thee?"—2 Chron. xx, 6.

so powerful a King be cast out from it, if Thou hadst not given us Thy help and Thy favour. Not unto us, Lord, not unto us, but unto Thy name give glory. Thou hast broken the strength[1] of the enemy. Thou hast made the races subject unto us, and hast put them under our feet.[2] Thou didst send forth thine arrows,[3] and overcamedst them, with Thy lightnings Thou didst scatter them, Thou wert the Captain,[4] Thou the Counsellor,[5] Thou didst strike fear into our enemies, Thou madest them flee away. Not for our sakes, Lord, not for our sakes, but for the glory of Thy name.

"But wherefore do I thus dwell so much upon the capture of Malaca, for what was done with the ruins of the city after it was taken is no less worthy of narration. Of it and of its mosques there was immediately constructed a fortress, strong enough to act as a check upon that turbulent people, and Governors were appointed over them every year, under whose government they might live, and laws whereby they might be upheld, in the dispensation of justice, and after this treaties of peace were concluded with many kings of countries adjacent to it, as, for example, the Kings of Pegú, Samatra, Pedir, Pacé, the Javanese, and lastly, even the Chinese of the far distant East, so celebrated on account of their merchant wares.

"And in order that there should not be wanting to the Portuguese an occasion of consolidating their forces, and by means of them extending that empire which had been by their employment acquired, the illustrious Afonso Dalbo-

[1] "I will destroy the strength of the kingdoms of the heathen."—Hag. ii, 22.

[2] "He shall subdue the people under us, and the nations under our feet."—Ps. xlvii, 3.

[3] "His arrow shall go forth as the lightning."—Zach. ix, 14. "Cast forth lightning, and scatter them; shoot out thine arrows, and destroy them."—Ps. cxliv, 6.

[4] "God himself is with us for our captain."—2 Chron. xiii, 2.

[5] "Who hath been his counsellor."—Rom. xi, 34.

querque, having sailed away from Malaca,[1] returned to Goa; and how shall I describe the victory which he gained? For it does not appear to be so much a victory as a Divine dispensation which would have affairs turn out thus; for this illustrious captain, having gained possession of the island and kingdom of Goa by force of arms upon two occasions, leaving it, at the time of his setting out, in the most fortified condition that he could, while he prosecuted his voyage to Malaca, and visited the remaining fortresses of India. The Hidalcão, who had been lord of this city, seeing that Afonso Dalboquerque was no longer at hand to defend it, came down and besieged it with a great force of soldiers on foot and horse, and built a fortress close to an arm of the sea, which runs up into the land and surrounds the island; and so causing his men to pass over to the island, he instructed them with constant skirmishes and surprises to tire out the Portuguese who were left in the fortress, and these, besieged as they were by so powerful an enemy, found themselves in great straits and necessity. But in accordance with our Lord's will, at the very time while they were in this difficulty, the fleet, which was returning from Malaca with the honour of such a great victory, came into sight; and at its coming so great was the fear of the enemies, that without waiting for the Portuguese forces to disembark, they raised the siege and hastened away with as much haste as they had first shown at their coming.

"We read concerning that great Alexander, Prince of Macedon, that when he arrived at the country of India, and had assaulted a fortified city well defended by its inhabitants, he held it to be of such great importance, and it appeared to be so successful a matter to have captured the place, that his soldiers did not fail to declare that he was

[1] From this paragraph to the end of the oration, the orator deals with events connected with Portuguese rule in India, which the *Commentaries* are about to describe in the succeeding chapters of the volume.

more valiant than Hercules. If this be so, what triumphs, what sovereign honour is due to the King D. Manuel, who has subjects by whose hands and might he has not only conquered by force of arms a city of India, but with a continued round of his victories kept on going about India itself—a country never beheld by the Romans, unknown to the Goths, and in vain assailed on many occasions by the famous Sesostris,[1] King of Egypt, Cyrus,[2] and Semiramis.[3]

"When Augustus Cæsar had become monarch he esteemed it as the greatest happiness he could enjoy, among his other pleasures, to be visited by the kings of India with presents, and that they sent him their ambassadors to ask for peace.

"Who can well recount the great services which have been offered to the all-unconquered King D. Manuel by the kings of India? the tribute which they have paid him? the amity which they have besought of him? and, lastly, the

[1] "Sed Germanicus....... visit veterum Thebarum magna vestigia: et manebant structis molibus literæ Ægyptiæ, priorem opulentiam complexæ: jussusque e senioribus sacerdotum patrium sermonem interpretari, referebat, 'habitasse quondam septingenta millia ætate militari: atque eo cum exercitu Regem RHAMSEN,* Libya, Æthiopia, MEDISQUE et PERSIS et BACTRIANO ac SCYTHA, potitum'," etc.—Tacit., *Annal.*, ii, 60.

[2] This refers to the inheritance by Cyrus of the territory of his uncle Cyaxaras, who thereby became master of nearly all Asia. His empire included Babylon, Assyria, the Medes, the Persians, and Asia Minor.

[3] Semiramis, Queen of Assyria, subjugated Arabia, Egypt, part of Ethiopia and Libya, and the whole of Asia as far as the Indus; but, having experienced a check on the banks of that river, did not push her conquests any further in that direction.

---

* Valpy's Delphin edit. of 1821, has the following note here, to shew the identity of Sesostris and Rameses: "Eadem dicuntur de Sesotride a Diodoro. 'Armais' apud Josephum, unde hos Reges depromsit Eusebius frater Sesothios, ipso fratre expeditionem in Asiam faciente, invasit regnum Ægypti, etc. Iste SESOTHIOS trinominis fuit, teste Manethone. Vocatus enim est RAMESSES et præterea ÆGYPTOS. Sed Josephus hæc nomina permiscuit. Nam SESOTHIS Josephi est SESŌSTRIS Herodoti et SESOŌSTIS Diodori."

terms of vassalage which almost all of them have been compelled to accept at the hand and by the might of this illustrious captain? For apart from those who by force of arms Afonso Dalboquerque had rendered tributary, there remained not a single king of India by whom he was not approached with services of an infinite importance; by the King of Cambaya, by the powerful King of Narsinga, who when he was apprised of the victory of Malaca transmitted by his ambassadors a cup of gold, and a golden sword, with a ruby of inestimable value set in the handle, and sent word to beg that Afonso Dalboquerque would think fit graciously to make use of him and of his kingdom. But wherefore do I tarry in relating the gold and the precious stones, and articles of value which the infidels sent to him? I will pass on to what is of far greater importance. The celebrated Preste João, lord of the whole of Ethiopia which lies below Egypt, in order to gain him over as his friend, sent him not gold, nor precious stones, but he sent him that which he held in much greater estimation, and which Afonso Dalboquerque himself valued far more highly, and this was a large piece of the wood of the True Cross;[1] and with it he sent word to say that he felt he was justified in thus sending him that part of the True Cross[2] wherein we have been redeemed, because he had by force of arms unfolded the banner of the Holy Cross so far away from his fatherland.

"Historians write that Demetrius, the son of Antigonus, who was the successor of Alexander in the lordship of Macedonia, on account of his assiduity in capturing cities, was called Poliorcetes, which in the Greek language signifies the taker of cities. What name shall we give then to the excellent captain, Afonso Dalboquerque, since he has taken

[1] *Vera Cruz.* This adjective is very rarely used, except in connection with Cruz, and not always then, as below.

[2] *Verdadeira Cruz.*

so many cities, conquered such kingdoms, dispersed so many armies? What happiness is there which can be compared to that of a king who is the lord of such a subject, who by force of arms destroyed the most powerful kingdom of Calicut? Did he not compel the King of Narsinga, mighty as he was, with all his vassals, and the treasure of kingdoms, and abundance of elephants, to come and sue for peace from the King of Portugal? Did he not force the King of Cambaya to accept terms of peace? Did he not restore their kingdoms to the Kings of Cochim and Cananor after that he had beaten them in battle? Did he not deliver from their heavy thraldom the Christians who lived in India? Did he not gain the kingdom of Ormuz? the kingdom of Goa? the kingdom and Island of Ceylon? And, lastly, not satisfied with so many victories, did not the powerful King Dom Manuel send him to prosecute the war against the grand Sultan of Egypt, and pass the Red Sea? And in order that there should not be any parts of the world to which his victories did not extend, did he not take the noble city of Çafim[1] in Africa?

"All which victories and most auspicious successes of the most invincible King Dom Manuel are just so much the more worthy of praise and honour, in proportion as we ourselves deserve the opprobrium of mankind, for he labours for no other object than to extend throughout the world the Faith of Christ, which has been entrusted to us as the righteous and universal aim of all our exertions, while we are all occupied and overburdened in our attempts to avenge private injuries: he attacks infidel enemies, we are fighting against one another: he acquires for himself new kingdoms and provinces, we by our remissness are losing

[1] *Cafim*, or *Saffi*, the ancient *Rusupis*, a walled town and port of Morocco, to the north of Mogador, taken by the Portuguese in 1508, and abandoned in 1641. See Osorius, lib. v, *ad init.*, for the narrative of the events connected with the Portuguese conquest of this town.

what we already possess, and we shall lose more and more if we do not listen to the Lord, who calls us every day, and cries out to us to awaken.

"Consider, lords, I entreat you by your faith, how many and how serious losses has the Christian religion suffered for the last sixty years in these parts. Are they, peradventure, things that we can possibly forget? Can we recall them to mind without great pain? What of Constantinople?[1] What of Negroponte?[2] What of Lepanto?[3] What of Modon?[4] What of Durazzo?[5] What of the other cities,

[1] Mahomet II, son and successor of Amurath, who was raised to the Ottoman throne in the twentieth year of his age in 1451, conceived the design of achieving the conquest of the Greek Empire, by the taking of Constantinople. He succeeded in overcoming all the difficulties which obstructed this enterprise, in which several of his predecessors had failed. At the head of an army of 300,000 combatants, supported by a fleet of 300 sail, he appeared before that capital, and commenced the siege on the sixth of April, 1453. The besieged, having only from 8,000 to 10,000 men to oppose the superior force of the enemy, yielded to the powerful and redoubled efforts of the Turks, after a vigorous defence of fifty-three days. The city was carried by assault on the 29th of May, and delivered up to the unrestrained pillage of the soldiers. Constantine, the last of the Greek emperors, perished in the first onset, and all the inhabitants were carried into slavery. In the short space of six or seven hours the Turks had cleared the city entirely of all its inhabitants. This conquest was followed by that of Servia, Bosnia, Albania, Greece, and the whole of the Peloponnesus or Morea, as well as most of the islands of the Archipelago. The Greek Empire of Trebizond, on the coast of Asia Minor, submitted in like manner to the law of the conqueror in 1466. *Koch.*

[2] *Negroponte*, the ancient *Eubœa*, wrested by the Turks from the Venetians in 1470.

[3] *Lepanto*, the ancient *Naupactus*, west of Athens, on the northern side of the Gulf of Lepanto. The Turks besieged the city in 1475 without success, but obtained possession of it in 1498. The city was reconquered by the Venetians in 1687, but they lost it again in 1699.

[4] *Modon*, the ancient *Methone*, a fortified town in Messenia, on a rocky projection into the sea south-west of Tripolitza. It has an octagonal tower built upon an isolated rock. A Venetian possession, probably captured and held by the Turks at this period.

[5] *Durazzo*, the ancient *Epidamnus*, and *Dyrrachium*, a maritime town

which to our deep disgrace are in the power of the Turks? What do we look for? except that they should take us asleep, and destroy us while we are unprepared, and kill us before we can put ourselves on our guard. Even now they are making an entry into Hungary; even now they are making war in Sclavonia; even now they scour the sea unchallenged; even now they are seeking to sieze upon Italy.

"Now, therefore, Most Blessed Father, for you have come, as it were a star of salvation in the midst of this unsupportable misery, take precautions against this, pacify these discordant motives, which actuate the Princes of Christendom, put down for ever this miserable war which is raging among them, for no possible good can come of it; put aside all animosity, so that when all are as friends again the arms which one party have prepared against the other, combined together, may be turned against the common enemy,[1] to the end that when he is overcome, and we have recovered the Holy House in union with the King Dom Manuel (who is sending twelve thousand men under command of the Duke of Bragança, his son-in-law, over to Africa), if we turn out victorious we may lift up unto the Lord a trophy of the victory which he has given to us over barbarous nations, and those may be put to confusion who worship idols, and

of Albania, to the south of Scutari. In the middle ages this town was the seat of a Duchy held by the house of Anjou-Sicily. The Sultan Bajazet II (1481-1512), reunited it to the Turkish Empire.

[1] In an assembly held by Pope Pius II at Mantua in 1459 he had, upwards of sixty years before the delivery of this oration, proposed a general association among the powers of the West against the Turks. A crusade was published by his orders, and he was on the point of setting out in person at the head of the expedition when he was suddenly cut off by death, in 1464, at Ancona, where he had appointed the general rendezvous of the confederate troops. This event, added to the terror which the arms of Sultan Mahomet II had created among the Western nations, disconcerted the plans of the crusaders, and was the means of dissolving their confederacy.

put their trust in vain gods, and that they may know the name of the Lord, and admit that He alone is the Mighty One over all the world." Amen.

CHAPTER XL.

The proceedings of the Portuguese in Goa with the Captains of the Hidalcão, who came and besieged the city after the departure of the great Afonso Dalboquerque for Malaca.

The Hidalcão having recalled to mind that which the great Afonso Dalboquerque had sent to declare to his father (while that commander was lying in the river of Goa, as has been already related, when he was no longer able to restrain his temper) that he should yet see his words come to pass, and the city in the power of the Christians, and Milrrhao,[1] the Hindoo, carrying on the government, and farming the revenues of the mainland districts; and having brought himself to imagine that the season was favourable to get possession of his city again, on account of the departure of Afonso Dalboquerque for Malaca, he sent one of his captains, who was called Pulatecão,[2] with a force of infantry and horsemen, to make their way down against Milrrhao, and cast him forth out of the country, and endeavour as much as he could to capture Timoja, who was in company with Milrrhao, and as soon as he had got them into his hands to remain

[1] *Milrrhao;* the latter part of this name is the title *Rao*, used by the Hindoos for a chief or prince, probably derived from *Raja*. Among the Mahrattas it is a title for distinguished persons, whether military or civil, and is assumed by a caste of Sudras pretending to be derived from the primitive *kshatriya*, or military caste. He is called *Merlao* in the early part of this volume. See chapter vi.

[2] *Pulatecão;* here, as is frequently the case in this work, the name and title of the person are combined. *Pulad*, or *Fulad*, are not unknown as personal names in Oriental literature; *Cão* is *Khan*, a title borne by Mohammadan nobles, especially when of Persian or Pathan descent; it is also a common adjunct to Afghan or Pathan names.

quiet as he was, and wait until he should receive instructions how to proceed. Pulatecão, having set forth on his expedition with his camp, as soon as Milrrhao received information of his intended attack, he proceeded to get ready and wait for him with five thousand native peons and fifty mounted men, and sent forward Hicarrhau[1] to defend a pass in the mountain range which the enemy had to traverse, but he was so slow about this that when he reached the pass he found that Pulatecão had already taken possession of it; and Pulatecão with all his men fell upon him, and routed him, and, pursuing him hotly, killed him in his flight, and a large portion of the men who were with him; and, just as he was, without waiting for anything, he fell upon Milrrhao's camp, and put him to rout without any loss of time. And Milrrhao, perceiving himself to be thus worsted, and having no hope of any succour, at the advice of Timoja would not return to Goa, but turned his steps towards Narsinga, and when he arrived at Bisnaga, where the King of Narsinga lived, he met with a very favourable reception, and there it was that Timoja died, shortly after arriving there; and Milrrhao, after the lapse of some days, having received a report from Onor that his brother, who had risen up and taken possession of that kingdom, was dead, begged permission of the king to depart, and proceeded to take possession of that kingdom, and always remained a staunch adherent of the King of Portugal.

Pulatecão, when he found that he had gained this victory, and was in possession of the lands of Goa, forgetting all that the Hidalcão had ordered him to do, desired to follow up his good fortune, and prepared certain rafts and boats which he found at hand, and without meeting with any resistance, crossed over to the Island of Goa, and fortified his position in Benastarim, which position Rodrigo Rabelo, who was the captain of the city,[2] either from carelessness or from

[1] *Hicarrhau;* he is called *Icarao* in chapter vi. [2] See p. 42.

being occupied with other matters, which he considered more necessary, had not fortified, although Afonso Dalboquerque had commanded him to do so before his departure, for it was a place of passage, and a principal pass leading from the mainland to the Island of Goa.

As soon as Pulatecão had fortified Benastarim, with the determination of maintaining the military position there, he made an incursion through the neighbouring Hindoo villages, destroying and burning everything that he found there. But when Rodrigo Rabelo was informed of this he sallied out of the city with thirty mounted men, and the aged Alguazil of Cananor with four hundred Naires arrived with drawn swords and shields, whom Diogo Correa had sent up to his assistance, when he heard the news of the coming of the Hidalcão's forces, fell upon Pulatecão very valiantly and worsted him, and killed fifteen hundred of his Turks and Coraçones. Nevertheless, this sudden accession of good luck caused Rodrigo Rabelo to despise the enemies whom he had overcome, and he set himself in hot pursuit after them with his mounted men. The Turks finding themselves pressed by ours, rallied a party of about sixty at some old ruins of walls, which were on a hill, in order to escape the onrush of our men. Rodrigo Rabelo got up to them, and engaged them, but as the place where they stood was somewhat uphill, and difficult to enter on horseback, the Turks defended themselves with such success that they killed him and Manuel da Cunha who were in the van.

When the remainder of the Portuguese force saw they were left without a captain, they returned again with news of this sad disaster to the city, in which there arose much sadness for the death of Rodrigo Rabelo, because he was a very daring Captain, and of singular bravery. And Pulatecão, with the remainder of his forces, retired back to Benastarim, determined to make war upon the city. The greater number of our party, who did not wish that Francisco Pantojo, who was entitled to the succession because he was chief *Alcaide* of the fortress, should become Captain, after some dissensions had amongst themselves elected as their Captain Diogo Mendez de Vasconcelos, whom Afonso Dalboquerque had left captive in the keep[3], for the reasons already narrated. As soon as this election was made, they all proceeded to the castle, and loosed him, and delivered over to him the government of the city, with an oath which they all took before him, that they would obey him as the representative of the proper person of Afonso Dalboquerque, until he himself should make such arrangements in this matter as should seem best; and as soon as Diogo Mendez de Vasconcelos was in possession of the captainship, he wrote to Manuel de Lacerda, who was making his way as chief Captain of a fleet against Calicut,[3] giving him an account of all that had occurred, and desiring him to come back to help him.

CHAPTER XLI.

How the Hidalcão, on learning that his Captain had made an entry into the Island of Goa and taken Benastarim without permission, ordered Roçalcão to take it from him, and what passed thereupon.

Directly that Manuel de Lacerda received news from Diogo Mendez of the trouble in which he was involved, he left off guarding the coast of Calicut, and came on with all his fleet and people to relieve Goa, and there he found all the city in great alarm at the news that was going about of the approach of Roçalcão, principal Captain of the Hidalcão; with a numerous force of men, and much artillery. And in order that they should not be taken unprepared, and at a disadvantage, they hurried on with great rapidity the

[1] See p. 43. [2] See p. 53.
[3] See ch. ix, at end.

fortification of the city, and removal of the stockades, and collection of provisions, before winter should come on, and at this juncture there arrived Diogo Fernandez de Béja with his fleet and forces, whom Afonso Dalboquerque, just before he sailed to Malaca, had sent off to Ormuz, and this greatly inspirited our men.

The Hidalcão, when he heard how Pulatecão had entered into the Island of Goa, and was in possession of Benastarim, fearing what he might do next, because he was a restless character, who, after the loss of Goa, had risen up in rebellion against him, and would not obey him, as he always used to do in respect of the revenue of the land, sent one of his principal Captains, in whom he had great confidence, who was called Roçalcão, with a large force of men and guns against Goa, with orders to do his best to eject him.

Pulatecão was not pleased at the arrival of Roçalcão, but considered himself deeply injured by the Hidalcão sending another Captain upon that business, when he himself had gained the entry into the island; and what provoked him more than all was that it was Roçalcão, with whom he was not on very friendly terms, and on this account he would not obey his orders. Now, as Roçalcão was a discreet man, and perceived that this matter could not be managed by forcible means, he made up his mind to make use of our people to gain his purpose, and with a most profound dissimulation availed himself of the following artifice.

There came in his retinue João Machado[1] with fifteen Portuguese who had been taken prisoners with Fernão Jacome, when his ship went ashore wherein he had set out from Çacotorá, as has been already narrated, and among the company of these captives came one Duarte Tavares, esquire of the Count of Abrantes, whom the Turks took prisoner in the Island of Choram,[2] and because this Duarte

[1] See vol. II, ch. xxxix.

[2] See vol. II, Introduction, p. cv.

Tavares was a man of credit with them, Roçalcão sent him with a communication to Diogo Mendez, Captain of the Island of Goa, to declare to him that the Hidalcão, his lord, greatly desired to have peace and friendship with the King of Portugal, and was very much annoyed at what Pulatecão had done, and had therefore sent him thither with a force to get him into his hands; but, on arrival at Benastarim, he had found him out of his reach, and in the attitude of one who had risen up in rebellion; therefore Roçalcão desired him graciously to assist in casting him out, for the Hidalcão did not wish to make war upon the Portuguese, but desired peace and friendship.

Diogo Mendez, not bearing in mind that the King of Portugal would be better served if he assisted Pulatecão, who was a man with an adventurous spirit, a Turk by birth, who had risen up in rebellion against the Hidalcão (for, had he been assisted by our party, he might have been persuaded to undertake some proceedings against him), and trusting also in the words of Duarte Tavares, who came quite deceived of the true state of affairs by the artifices of Roçalcão, agreed with all the *Fidalgoes* and cavaliers to help him, and immediately made ready the boats and galleys, and ordered Diogo Fernandez de Béja to proceed with two hundred men up the river to assist the operations made by Roçalcão; and thus by means of our assistance by water, while Roçalcão himself manœuvred on the land, they fell upon Pulatecão, and routed him; and when Pulatecão saw that he had lost the day, he fled to the mainland of Goa, where he died of poison.

As soon as Roçalcão had got possession of Benastarim, and fortified it, and provided it with a large force of men, and artillery, and munitions of war, after the lapse of a few days, he sent a message to Diogo Mendez, begging him greatly of his kindness to admit him into the city, for it was the chief city of the kingdom of the Hidalcão, his lord, which could not be established in any other locality. At the receipt of this message Diogo Mendez became very downcast, and discovered the error into which he had fallen, and those who had given their assent to his policy were discomfited, and from that time forward Roçalcão began to make war upon him, and kept the city closely besieged during the whole of that winter, so that our people underwent many hardships, hunger, and misfortunes—far too many for me to relate them here—up to the time when the great Afonso Dalboquerque returned from Malaca, which was just at the very height of these troubles, when already there was a good space of the wall of the fortress thrown down to the ground, which had fallen during the severe wintry weather.

When João Machado saw that some of the Portuguese went over to Roçalcão, out of despair of the city being able to hold out any longer, he left his wife and children, who were there with him, and came over to our side with ten or twelve Christians who desired to accompany him, and this incident greatly inspirited our men, because it was in so opportune a crisis. This João Machado had married a Moorish woman, who became a Christian, and by her he had three or four children, whom he himself baptised secretly.

CHAPTER XLII.

How the great Afonso Dalboquerque, having set sail from Malaca, steered for the channel by which he had entered when he came from India: and how he was wrecked on some shallows off the Coast of Çamatra, and miraculously saved, and the rest that took place.

The great Afonso Dalboquerque, having set out from Malaca, steered so as to reach the channel by which he had entered when he came from India, and when he had passed over the shoals of Capacia he ordered the captains of the ship *Enxobregas* and the junk to keep close together, because they sailed well in company, lest the Javanese, who were on board the junk, should plan any treason against them, while he himself and Pero Dalpoem sailed as convoy to each other; and thus proceeding with their voyage, when they had gone as far forward as the Powder Island,[1] the Pilots of Afonso Dalboquerque's ship not being on their guard concerning certain shallows which were situated off that part of the coast of Çamatra, just opposite to the kingdom of Darú,[2] ran the ship *Flor-de-la-Mar* ashore upon them in the night, and the vessel, being by this time very old, broke up into two parts directly she struck.[3]

Pero Dalpoem, who was on the outer hand, let go his

[1] See p. 62, *note* 2.

[2] Darú is marked neither by Berthelot in Pedro Barretto de Resendé's MS., to which I have already so frequently referred, nor by Keith Johnston in his *Royal Atlas*. The Portolano of Fernão Vaz Dourado, described in the Introduction of vol. ii, marks Darú on the western side of Sumatra.

[3] The parallel account of the shipwreck of Afonso Dalboquerque from Correa, p. 269, is very graphic:—"Assy vindo, lhe deu hum tempo trauessão tão forte que nom pôde al fazer senão sorgir, que foy com huma ancora grande e huma amarra de rótas, que são canas delgadas moçiças, que trócem, e fazem d'ellas fortes amarras. E tambem sorgio Pero d'Alpoym, que era á sua vista, que os outros nom parecião, que correrão áuante, porque erão mais metidos no mar; mas çarrando a noite, o tempo e o mar se tanto aleuantou que foy tromenta desfeita, em tal maneyra que conueo ao Governador cortar todos os mastos, porque a nao trabalhaua muyto com o mar por proa; e mandou que todo ficasse amarrado á nao, e de todo fizessem jangada, porque a nao se hia ao fundo com a bomba que nom podião vencer. Polo que toda a gente se meteo no trabalho da jangada fortemente, em que alguns morrerão, porque o mar era grande, vendo que nom tinhão outra saluação. E porque a jangada se desfazia na nao, então a mandou o Gouernador largar por popa, e homens que defendião 'os negros que se hião meter n'ella com trouxas, que seus senhores mandauão meter. O Gouernador mandou meter os doentes no batel por popa da jangada, e fallou a toda a gente que elle em ciroulas e jaqueta se auia de meter na jangada; que por tanto soubessem certo que d'outra maneyra ninguem n'ella nom auia d'entrar;

anchor immediately that he heard the cries of the crew and understood that the ship was lost, and remained where he was all the night long in a fierce gale at the mercy of the cable; and when morning broke the boats of the ships *Trindade* and *Flor-de-la-Mar* having been lost (being staved in on board the ships on account of the heavy seas breaking over the decks), Afonso Dalboquerque gave the order that a raft should be prepared with boards placed upon some timbers, and he got upon it, clad in a grey jacket, and lashed to the raft with a rope, lest the waves should sweep

pedindo a Deos misericordia das almas, porque das vidas ninguem fizesse conta.

"Então o Gouernador per huma corda atada pela cinta se deitou no esquife, e com elle os homens que couberão, e se foy a jangada em que se meteo, e o esquife tornou á nao tantas vezes até que nom fiqou nenhum homem portuguez; e o Gouernador nom consentio na jangada nenhum negro, nem negra, que todos deitou ao mar, e ficauão pegados á jangada. Estando n'este trabalho, a nao se quebron polo conúes em dous pedaços, e se foy ao fundo; em que se perdeo a mór riqueza d'ouro e pidraria que nunqua se perdeo em nenhuma parte da India, nem nunqua perderá. E porque a madeira da nao vinha fazer mal na jangada, se aleuantarão, e 'agoa os foy leuando pera terra, onde tornarão a sorgir com huma ancora que leuaua o batel, e assy estiuerão com as almas nas boquas pedindo misericordia a Deos, até que amanheceo, que o vento e mar era menos.

"Quando amanheceo, que da nao de Pero d'Alpoym nom virão a nao do Gouernador, e virão a madeira polo mar, a derão por perdida, e a gente morta, ou que se fôra a terra. Polo que deu a vela, e hindo pera terra ouverão vista da jangada, porque aleuantarão panos nas pontas das lanças que meterão na jangada pera defensão dos negros; em que a nao foy sorgir perto da jangada, que todos bradauão; 'Senhor Deos, misericordia!' As que logo Pero d'Alpoym mandou o batel, em que se meteo o Gouernador com a gente que pôde, e tambem o batel, com a gente que descarregou na nao se tornou á jangada áte que a descarregou; e todavia ouve homens que saluarão muyto ouro derrador de sy. Dom João de Lima pôs a sua nao ao pairo, e abrio tanta agoa que correo ao som do mar, e pôde fazer caminho porque era muyto afastado da terra, que nada soube da perdicão da nao do Gouernador, e como o tempo abonançou, andou com pouqa uela aguardando polo Gouernador, que bem sabia que ficaua atrás; e assy andando, d'ahy a dez dias o Gouernador foy ter com elle, e seguirão seu caminho pera Cochym, onde chegarão com grande trabalho de bomba, meos perdidos, já em janeiro de 1512."

him off, and two mariners with him, who with oars improvised out of some pieces of boards rowed the raft: and so in this plight, and by these means, and also by help of ropes which by Pero Dalpoem's orders were thrown out, tied to buckets, with infinite difficulty he reached the ship *Trindade.*

The men who were left in the wreck of the *Flor-de-la-Mar*, seeing themselves already come to the last day of their lives, began with loud cries and complaints to shout after Afonso Dalboquerque, who was making way on the raft, and he, touched with profound pity at the sight of them in this sad state of misery, told them not to be alarmed, but to put all their trust in our Lord, for he would promise them that he would not desert them, even if he ventured to lose his own life and the other ship and all her company in saving them; and he desired them, in the meantime, to construct another raft, for he would come back without delay for them.

While the shipwrecked men were making their raft, the junk, which was commanded by Simão Martinz, came up on her land-tack, very close to the spot where the remains of the *Flor-de-la-Mar* were with our men clustering upon them, and those on board the junk clearly perceived the plight in which they were, and then she tacked again and stood out to sea, and they never saw her again. The reason of this was, that the Javanese, who were on board this junk, on account of the careless conduct of Jorge Nunez de Lião (although Afonso Dalboquerque had especially cautioned him in this respect, and also because of the severe illness of Simão Martinz), rose up in mutiny, and killed all the Portuguese on board, without any escaping, except four mariners who took advantage of the confusion of the outbreak and got into an *almadia*, and made their way to Pacé, where the Governor, who had risen up in rebellion and taken possession of the kingdom, received them with hospitality and shewed them great honour, and sent them forward on the way to India in a ship which had put in there coming from Malaca bound for Choramandel; and just as they were about to set out, the junk's barge came in crowded with Javanese, and they declared that the junk was lost.

As soon as Afonso Dalboquerque had reached the ship *Trindade*, after a great deal of difficulty—our Lord having been pleased to save him miraculously, because, by all human reason, on account of the sea running so high, it was impossible for him to have been saved,—he remembered the promise which he had given to those who were left behind on the wreck, and lost no time in commanding Pero Dalpoem to set sail so as to get up to them and take them on board. But the crew of the ship *Trindade*, thinking more of themselves than of the danger and trouble in which their companions were, made many objections and requests that he would not order the ship close in to the shore, for it was shelving rock, and the wind was very high, and they also would be wrecked.

Afonso Dalboquerque, considering that he could not with any sense of duty fail to save those persons who had accompanied him in his labours, would not listen to these murmurings, but rather reprehended the crew for the little remembrance which they had of the frequent occasions when they had been protected by these very shipwrecked companions in the reverses which they had experienced in the Malaca enterprise, and determined, at all hazards, to save them; and creeping in shore under sail to reach the raft which the wrecked crew had put together out of the mast and the yard, with all the company of the ship upon it, he saw that it was not riding to its cable (some of the mariners declared afterwards that the cable had been cut but they did not know who it was that did it); and because both wind and sea were contrary for the raft to get towards the ship, but drove her towards the shore, without those who were on her being able to make any use of the pieces of oars with which they tried to row, in order to accomplish that which he had promised them he would do, although he had no longer any hopes of being able to save them, he ordered the crew to set all the sail they possibly could in order to catch up the junk before she struck on the coast, and to get ready two anchors so as to cast them if need should arise; and he ordered the pilots to keep on sounding the bottom with their lead in their hands, and, as the turn of the tide was just beginning, and the sea filling, in a very short space of time they reached the raft, and cast the anchors immediately in three and a half fathoms, which was the depth which the ship required with proper precautions; and with ropes tied to buckets and empty barrels which they let out of the ship, they took the junk with great trouble, and when they had drawn the people up on board, they remained where they were all that night with a great gale blowing behind them, trusting in the Lord's mercy, which did not fail them; for, just before dawn of day, there sprung up a little land breeze which enabled them to draw off and proceed with their voyage.

CHAPTER XLIII.

Of what was lost in the ship *Flor-de-la-Mar:* and how the Great Afonso Dalboquerque, after having collected his people together on the ship *Trindade*, proceeded on his route to Ceilão: and of what took place on the voyage until they arrived at Cochim.

In this ship, *Flor-de-la-Mar*, and in the junk which mutinied against us, there were lost the richest spoils that ever were seen since India had been discovered until that moment; and besides this, many women who were greatly skilled workers in embroidery, and many young girls and youths of noble family from all those countries which extend from the Cape of Comorim to the eastward,[1] whom Afonso Dalboquerque was carrying to the Queen D. Maria. They lost the castles of woodwork, ornamented with brocades, which the King of Malaca used to carry upon his elephants, and very rich palanquins[2] for his personal use, all plated with gold, a marvellous thing to behold, and great store of jewellery of good and precious stones which he was carrying with him in order to send it as a present to the King D. Manuel. And they lost a table with its feet all overlaid with plates of gold, which Milrrhao presented to Afonso Dalboquerque for the king, when the lands of Goa were delivered up to him. For when he arrived at Cochim, with the intention of leaving this table with the Factor, who could forward it to Portugal, so great was the hurry to embark, in order to save the monsoon which was getting well forward in its season, that it was forgotten, and then he took it with him. And all our men also lost a great quantity of their own things. And this so extensively, that of all that was on board, both in the ship and the junk, nothing was saved except the sword and crown of gold, and the ruby ring which the king of Sião sent to the King D. Manuel; but that which Afonso Dalboquerque grieved for most of all in this loss was the bracelet[3] which had been found upon Naodabegea, for he brought it with great estimation in order to send it to the king, because the efficacy of it was so very admirable. So also he felt very much the loss of the lions, which he brought because they were found on certain ancient sepulchres of the kings of Malaca, and he took them with the intention of placing them on his own tomb in Goa as a memorial of the achievement of taking Malaca; and, of all the spoils which were then taken, he reserved only these two things (the

[1] Cf. Chapter xxxix, áquem do Ganges, a que os Portugueses chamão *do Cabo do Comorim pera dentro.*

[2] *Andores.*

[3] See p. 62.

bracelet and lions) for himself, for as they were of iron they were [not] of great value.[1]

In this return journey of crossing over the Indian Ocean to Ceilão they would have perished for want of water and supplies if Our Lord had not succoured them by means of two large Moorish ships which they overtook on the voyage, bound from Çamatra and laden with pepper and silk, sandal wood and wood aloes.[2] For as soon as Afonso Dalboquerque

[1] *Que por serem de ferro eram muito pera estimar;* I am inclined to consider that *não* has dropped out before *eram* in this passage, in both editions.

[2] *Lenholoes; i.e., lignum aloes.* Cf. the note on *lenhonoe*, page 159. As very little appears to be now known of the *wood-aloes*, or *Calamba*, the following note will be read with interest:—"Calamba, Calambâ, ou Calambuco; na 1 Decada, f. 17, col. 3, João de Barros lhe chama *Lenholoè*, aonde diz, 'passado este Reyno Camboja, entra outro Reyno Chamado Campâ, nas montanhas do qual nace o verdadeiro *Lenholoè*, a que os Mouros daquellas partes chamão *Calambuc*'. Com J. de Barros se conforme A Academia Francesa no *Diccion. das Artes*, p. 90, donde diz que os boticarios chamão ao Calambà *Lignum Aloes*. Segundo as noticias que me derão Antonio de Mello e Castro, Viso Rey que foy da India, e Manuel Godinho de Sá, Capitão da Nao *Milagres*, que assistio em Macáo 32 annos, *Calambâ* na lingoa da terra, que o produz, val o mesmo que *doença da arvore*. A rezão desta nome he, que na Cochinchina, e nos Reynos de Champâ, e Camboja, ha grandes devezas de arvores, muy espessas e enmaranhadas, e metendose entre ellas alguns Gentios practicos, encontrão huma certa casta de arvores, e às vezes vem alguma dellas, que se vay murchando, e dizem logo comsigo, 'esta arvore parece que tem doença'; poem na devesa suas balizas, e vindo da hi a alguns dias por ellas, achão a tal arvore murcha toda, e cortando-a bem rente do chão, achão no amago da cortadura do tronco, hum como nó, mais preto, que, à maneira de cancro, chupou, e chamou a si o succo e oleo da tal arvore, que unido e junto nelle, tem o suave e precioso cheiro, que experimentamos, e quanto mais vigor havia na arvore, mais oleoso e precioso he o Calambuco; e se a arvore tinha pouco alento, não ha nella o Calambuco prezado, senão secco, e sem oleo, e val muy pouco......o ditto Capitão Manoel Godinho provava o Calambâ desta maneira. Tirava com huma faquinha huma migalhinha deste pao, e a metia na boca, e andava com ella entre os dentes, e se ella se-lhe-ajuntava, e amassava entre os dentes como cera, tinha-a por boa; e esse dia andava ordinariamente com dores de cabeça, porque he cousa muito quente, e de cheiro muito penetrante; e desta especie tem muito pouca a Europa,

caught sight of them he gave orders to chase them, and took them, and out of their stores he furnished himself with provisions and water, which enabled him to make his way to Ceilão. And because the Moors declared that the ships came from Chaul and from Dabul, he ordered Simão Dandrade with a prize party, and Dinis Fernandez to remain on board of them until he could learn the truth of it.

The Moors who formed the crew of the ship of Chaul, to which Simão Dandrade was appointed, found out that he did not know his latitude, nor yet the course they were sailing on, so they steered their course for the Maldive Islands,[1] and succeeded in reaching Candaluz[2] (which is the

porque tem grande preço em Japão, donde dizem, que val mais de outenta mil reis o arratel. Com este precioso aroma perfumão os Japoens as cazas e os vestidos. Usam delle os Chins nos accidentes de Paralysia, e na falta dos espiritos vitaes. Feito em pó, e tomado em vinho, ou em caldo, corrobora o estomago, veda os vomitos, e sara as dysenterias. Dizem que a arvore, que o produz, he algum tanto mayor que oliveira, com que tambem se parece. As vezes se achão humas pequenas porçoens deste pao nas margens do Ganges, por isso lhe-chamão alguns *Lignum Paradisi.*

"Escrevem algums modernos que tambem se acha Calambâ, ou Calambuco, nas Ilhas Maldivas......os Padres Missionarios da Companhia no seu livro *Summarias noticias da Cochinchina* mostrão que ha sómente nas terras del Rey da Cochinchina, o qual como faz todos os gastos no descobrimento, tem todo o proveito da conquista. Usam muito os Japoens delle para perfumes," etc.—*Bluteau.*

[1] Navigators in general are not aware, more particularly those coming from Europe, that the whole group of the Maldiva Islands are inhabited by a civilised race of people, who carry on a considerable trade with India, more particularly Bengal, Ceylon, and the Malabar coast, as also to the Red Sea, and are expert sailors. They are an inoffensive, timid people, and there appears far less crime among them than with more polished nations; murder is not known among them, nor is theft or drunkenness; being strict Mussulmans, they are forbidden the use of spirituous liquors, which could be easily made from the fermented juice of the coco-nut

[2] *Candaluz;* this island is marked (as *Camdalus*) in the map from the Portolano of Fernão Vaz Dourado, a facsimile of which is given in vol. ii, facing chapter I.

principal island in this group), and there all the Moors fled away from him; and from some Moors of Cananor whom Simão Dandrade found in that place, he learned that Mafamede Maçari,[1] a merchant of Cairo was there, and he was one who always maintained the policy of the Rumes with the Çamorim, and tried hard to bring them over to India; but when Afonso Dalboquerque was in Malaca, out of fear

tree, which they have in abundance. The men, in appearance, are of a dark copper-colour, rather short, and in person not unlike the natives of Ceylon and the Malabar coast, but their language is totally different; their women are not pretty, and are extremely alarmed at the sight of strangers. The group consists of a range of innumerable low islands and rocks, extending nearly on a meridian line (as shewn in the map referred to above) from latitude 7 deg. 6½ min. N. to latitude 0 deg. 42 min. S.; the larger islands abound with coco-nut trees, and are generally inhabited, but many of the others are only sandbanks or barren rocks. The greatest breadth of the range is about twenty leagues, and the islands are formed in large groups or clusters, sometimes double, which are called by the natives *Atolls* or *Atollons*. These Atolls appear to be the summits of submarine coral mountains, rising very abruptly to the surface of the sea, and having an almost unfathomable depth of water outside of them, but enclosing within the crater-like ridges which bound them, banks of soundings of various depths, from ten to thirty or forty fathoms. The islands of each Atoll generally lie in a continued chain on the barrier ridge which bounds it, although there are many on the interior banks, which, in addition to the islands, are generally studded with rocky patches and banks. There are nineteen Atolls, with several detached islands or rocks in the channels that separate them. Although these islands have long been thought to present an impenetrable barrier of four hundred and seventy meridional miles to ships bound to Ceylon, or the southern parts of India, and have consequently been dreaded and avoided by modern navigators, yet the early traders from Europe to India appear to have been much better acquainted with them than we until lately were, and, like Afonso Dalboquerque on his return voyage from Malaca to Cochim, often passed through some of the wider and safer channels which separate the Atolls, without apprehension of danger. Horsburgh, from whose work the above notes are derived, does not mention any island with a name at all resembling Candaluz, except Karndoo-doo, the northern island on the western side of the Collomandoo Atoll; whereas the position of Candaluz in Fernão Vaz Dourado's chart seems to point to the island now called Cardiva in the Cardiva Channel of this group.

[1] See p. 33.

which he had, lest, if we gained the victory, the Çamorim would deliver him up to Afonso Dalboquerque (for this had long been a subject of secret negotiations, but the Çamorim had always temporised with it and screened him with lies), and dreading lest some day the Çamorim should tell the truth about him, he set out from Calicut with three ships laden with spiceries, and, having his wife and children and all his property on board; and, when he had progressed on his voyage as far as Çacotora, sailing close in shore between the cape of Guardafum[1] and Magadaxo,[2] he encountered so fierce a storm that he was driven ashore, and in that tempest lost two of his ships, and he himself in the one he sailed in with his wife and children ran to the Maldive Islands and managed to get to Candaluz, and there he capsized his ship, but saved some of his spiceries and bought a *candura*, which is a kind of small vessel with which they navigate those islands.

And when the proper season of the year came on, he sailed away with the remainder of his spiceries that he had managed to save, taking Simão Rangel, whom he had bought, and made his way to Calayate,[3] where the *candura* was lost, and from that port he sailed away in a ship bound for Ormuz, and got to Aden.

In this storm many ships were lost which had set out for the Straits [of the Red Sea] while Afonso Dalboquerque was at Malaca; and, on account of this great destruction which the Moors of Calicut suffered in their ships because they were large ships, and every one that was lost caused them to suffer heavily—for they dared not venture to sea except in the winter for fear of our fleets,—from that time forward they built small vessels, and, rowing them about, navigated all the Straits of the Red Sea.

When Afonso Dalboquerque, after his arrival at Cochim,

[1] See map, vol. i, p. 80. [2] See chapter VII, and vol. i, p. 45.

[3] See vol. i, p. 62.

learned that Mafamede Maçari had visited the islands, he felt his unfortunate shipwreck much more, for he had come with the determination of sweeping through them with his squadron and keeping on the course used by the Moors in their navigation of these islands; and so it might have turned out that he would have fallen into the hands of the Portuguese with all his property, and this was what Afonso Dalboquerque was very desirous of happening.

Simão Rangel was a very honourable man, a servant of the King D. Manuel, and Afonso Dalboquerque had made use of his assistance in many matters because he was a man who knew how to perform everything very well; and when he was at Cochim—Afonso Dalboquerque being at Malaca—he and some of the others began to disagree about some proceedings done by Lourenço Moreno, Antonio Real, and Diogo Pereira to the disservice of the king, so they sent him in a *catur* to Goa, and on the voyage the *paraos* of Calicut took him captive. And this Mafamede Maçari bought him and took him with him, whereat Afonso Dalboquerque was very much annoyed and desired to punish Lourenço Moreno, who was the Factor; but, as all were to blame, he left the matter alone, and wrote to the King Dom Manuel of all that they had done while he was in Malaca, and of the carelessness they had been guility of in failing to victual Goa when it was besieged.

CHAPTER XLIV.

How the great Afonso Dalboquerque reached Cochim; and of the news which they gave him concerning Goa, and of the coming of the Rumes, and of the fleet which arrived from Portugal.

As soon as the great Afonso Dalboquerque reached Cochim, inasmuch as up to that moment there was no news of him nor of the events which had taken place at Malaca, there was a great excitement and all were filled with pleasure, for at his arrival the Moors of India abated in some degree the excitement they had fallen into at the news of the coming of the Rumes. And Lourenço Moreno, Antonio Real, and Diogo Pereira became very much ashamed of themselves for having written to the King D. Manuel, and set on foot throughout India a rumour that Afonso Dalboquerque was lost, and all his fleet with him; although this great captain was so much dreaded by the Moors, and such authority was attached to his person among them, that by means of his presence only, frustrated as he was, wrecked, and clad in the same grey jacket which he was saved in at the wreck, the mere knowledge that he had returned to India, made all the kings of that land disband and withdraw from that conspiracy which they had set on foot against the Portuguese.

And Afonso Dalboquerque disembarked on the very day of his arrival, and from the dock where the captain stood with all his company ready to receive him, they took him up under a brocaded canopy to the church, the vicar of it standing at the door with the reliques awaiting his coming; and, after prayer made, and many thanks given to our Lord for having delivered him from the perils which he had passed through, he went to the fortress accompanied by every one, and after giving them a great reception he took his leave of them at the gate, and remained behind alone with the captain and the king's officers. And after having given them an account of the doings at Malaca, and of what had taken place during his voyage, he asked them concerning the king's property and the ships which had sailed away laden with Oriental produce to Portugal that year. For, although military affairs occupied much of his thoughts, yet he never wanted time to look after the property of the king. And when he inquired after the state of affairs at Goa—for this was the matter which occupied the chief position in his thoughts even while he was at Malaca—they related to him how during all that winter the city had been besieged by three captains of the Hidalcão with a large army, and they showed him all the hardships which the siege had brought upon our people, both by war and by famine, and that they were quite undone from the fact that a considerable length of their wall had fallen from the severity of the winter; they told him, too, that the Captain and Manuel da Cunha were dead.

Afonso Dalboquerque felt these deaths very keenly; that of Rodrigo Rabelo because he was a brave cavalier, and that of Manuel da Cunha because he was not on very good terms of intercourse with his father Tristão da Cunha on account of the disagreements which arose between them respecting his journey when they went to India; and whereas there was nothing which he felt so earnestly as the safety of Goa, he sent off a *catur* without delay, carrying a message to Diogo Mendez, with an account of his coming; and he wrote to the judges and aldermen[1] of the pleasure it would give him to revisit them, and that he was getting himself in readiness to be with them immediately, and that he relied upon God's mercy to give him a good revenge upon the Turks of Benastarim, and he sent them a warrant for Manuel de Lacerda to be captain of the city, and Duarte de Melo chief captain of the sea until his own arrival.

As soon as the arrival of Afonso Dalboquerque was known in Goa, there was general rejoicing throughout the city, and a great ringing of bells and firing of salutes, for every one looked upon himself as redeemed from death. When the *catur* had sailed off, there arrived a message from Diogo Correa, Captain of Cananor, to report that the merchants brought news that a great fleet of Rumes had set sail from Suez, coming to help the Hidalcão against Goa, and this had been prepared as soon as it became known that Afonso Dalboquerque had sailed away to Malaca. When he heard

[1] *Vereadores.*

this, Afonso Dalboquerque became very unhappy, because he had a very small fleet which would serve for going in search of them, as he had originally intended;[1] and while affairs were in this condition, and he himself undecided which undertaking he should enter upon first (viz., the relief of Goa or attack on the Rumes), on the 20th day of August, in the year [fifteen hundred and] twelve, D. Garcia de Noronha, who had set out in the preceding year with six ships, and wintered at Mozambique, arrived;[2] and Jorge de Melo

[1] See p. 55.

[2] This expedition and its results are thus briefly tabulated in the "Armada da India", Brit. Mus., Add. MS. 20902, f. 14:—

"Dom Gracia de Noronha Cappitam môr.
"Anno de 1511.
"6 naôs a 25 de Março, e a 8 de Abril.

"Dom Gracia de Noronha Capitão mor de seis naos, partio a vinte çinco de Março: Capitães Dom Ayres da Gama, Pero Mascarenhas, Christouão de Brito, Jorge de Brito, Manoel de Castro Alcoforado: Foy Capitão mor de mar Dom Gracia de Noronha, e destas seis Naos sò tres passarão a India, E a Nao de Jorge de Brito descobrio o penedo de São Pedro.

"Neste anno tomou Affonso de Albuquerque Malaca, e em Agosto fez a fortaleza, de que foy o primeiro Capitão Ruy de Brito Patalim, a que pos nome "Nossa Senhora da Assumpção."

"Pedro Mascarenhas foy na não *Santa Eufemia*, Jorge de Brito em *Santa Maria da Luz*, Manoel de Castro Alcoforado em *S. Pedro*, Christovam de Brito em *Santa Maria de Belem*, D. Ayres da Gama em *Santa Maria da Piedade*.

"Destas seis naôs sò tres passaram â India, a saber as duas de Christovam de Brito, e D. Aires da Gama, que partirão deste Reino doze dias depois do Cappitam môr, e Pedro Mascarenhas, que o mesmo Cappitam môr mandou de Moçambique (aonde chegou com muito trabalho) â India para tirar de confuzam aos que nella estavão com sua chegada.

"Successo.—Seguindo Dom Gracia sua viagem, e nam podendo dobrar o Cabo de Sto. Agostinho, quiz o seu Piloto fazerse na volta de Guiné para tomar outra mais larga sobre o mesmo Cabo, na qual travessa se ouvera de perder em hum penedo, que acharam no meyo daquelle Golfão, no qual de noute foy dar a nâo *S. Pedro*, Cappitam Jorge de Brito, que fez farol âs outras, que vinham na sua esteira, por razam do qual perigo, e do nome da naô, que deu no penedo, elle ouve o que hoje tem de S. Pedro."

Pereira, who had set sail that year from the kingdom of Portugal, as chief Captain of eight ships,[1] with a large body of men on board, whom the King D. Manuel sent in consequence of his belief that Afonso Dalboquerque was lost,

[1] The expedition here referred to, is thus tabulated in the "Armada da India", Brit. Mus., Add. MS. 20902, f. 15:—

"Jorge de Mello Pereira Capitam môr de outo naos, e Gracia de Sousa Capitam môr de quatro naos, que fazem as 12 em duas Capitanias.

"Anno de 1512.

"12 velas a 25 de Março partiu a mayor parte dellas.

"Jorge de Mello Pereira Capitão moor de oito naos, e Capitão môr Gracia de Sousa das outras quatro: partio a Vinte e çinco de março: Capitães Jorge de Albuquerque, Gonçalo Pereira, Loppo Vãz de Sampayo, Gaspar Pereira, Dom João d'Eça, Jorge da Silueira, Simão de Mirãda, Francisco Nogueira, Antonio Raposo de Beja, Pero de Albuquerque; A Nao de Francisco Nogueira se perdeo nos baixos de Angoya, E saluouse a gente.

"Jorge de Albuquerque filho do João de Albuquerque na Nao *Nazarê* = Gonçalo Pereira filho de Gonçalo Pereira na *Conceiçao* = Jorge da Silveira no *Botafogo* = Simam de Miranda nas *Virtudes* = D. João d'Eça, ou de Sâ (como diz outra Relação) na *Magdalena* = Francisco Nogueira em *S. Antonio* perdido = Loppo Vaz de Sampayo em *Santa Cruz* = Pero de Albuquerque filho de Jorge de Albuquerque na *Bastiana* = Antonio Raposo de Beja em......, Gaspar Pereira que era para servir de secretario de Affonso de Albuquerque, como o tinha sido de Dom Francisco de Almeida, na naô *Santo Antonio o Grande*.

"Neste anno se fez a fortaleza de Calicut a que se pos nome *N. Senhora da Conceição*, de que foy primeiro Capitão Francisco Nogueira.

"Successos.—A naô *Santo Antonio*, Capitam Francisco Nogueira, se perdeu nos baixos de Angoxa, onde morreo quasi toda a gente, e elle por nam saber nadar se deixou ficar com dous filhos seus sobre o que apparecia da naô, e na baxamar esprayou tanto que a pê enxuto se recolheu a huma das Islas de Angoxa, onde os Mouros o tomarão, e depois derão pelo seu Xeque, que Antonio de Saldanha cativou, quando foy vingar as mortes que os Mouros daquellas Ilhas tinham dado a alguns dos nossos, que a ellas forão buscar mantimentos.

"No Mesmo anno de 1512

"1 Navio a 13 de Julho.

"A 13 de Julho partio hum Cavaleiro por nome João Chanoca em hum navio a buscar a carga da Naô *Galega*, que, por nam estar para navegar, descarregou em Moçambique."

and the invasion of the Rumes certain to take place, in accordance with that which Lourenço Moreno and Antonio Real had written to him from India.

And at the arrival of these two fleets Afonso Dalboquerque became very greatly pleased, and returned many thanks to our Lord that this had fallen out at that very time, and much more was he pleased at the arrival of his nephew D. Garcia, as well on account of the good qualities of his person, as also because he would help him in the Indian troubles which grew heavier every day, and the King D. Manuel wrote that he ordered him to be Chief Captain of that fleet, and if there should arise any necessity of his presence to assist Afonso Dalboquerque, then he was to remain in India as Chief Captain of the Sea; and because Lorenço Moreno, Antonio Real, and Diogo Pereira, had written to the King D. Manuel, showing how Goa was besieged, and declaring the little need there was of the position, severely censuring Afonso Dalboquerque's wishes to maintain that city, for they thought that thus they would be revenged upon him for his reprehensions of their vices, and the malpractices of which they had been guilty in their offices, against the service of the King; therefore, in view of this information the King wrote to Afonso Dalboquerque that it would please him very much that he should discuss this question [of retaining possession of Goa] with his captains and officers; and if it should be universally admitted advisable to withdraw from Goa, then he was to destroy it, yet he never would be blind to the fact that Afonso Dalboquerque had on two occasions gained it from the Moors with so great a labour and personal risk, for by so doing he had done him great service.

Afonso Dalboquerque, perceiving that all this was prompted by Duarte de Lemos and Gonçalo de Sequeira, who, being ashamed at not having been with him at the taking of that city, seized this opportunity of screening themselves, put off for a time this business, without mentioning it to any one, and when the attack upon Benastarim was accomplished he did what the King ordered him to do, as will be related hereafter.

CHAPTER XLV.

How the great Afonso Dalboquerque set out from Cochim with the intention of going in search of the Rumes; and how he proceeded to besiege the fortress of Benastarim.

At the receipt of this intelligence of the coming of the fleet of the Rumes, the great Afonso Dalboquerque hastened on his departure more rapidly; and, although his fleet was not so great as to be able to resist the power which it was reported the Rumes were bringing, because the principal ships that were in India—and of which he could avail himself—were found to be in a very decayed condition when he arrived from his voyage to Malaca, on account of the carelessness which the King's officers, who were stationed at Cochim, had shewn in looking after them; nevertheless, buoyed up by the hope which he had of Our Lord's assistance, he set out for Goa on the tenth of September, in the year [fifteen hundred and] twelve, with a fleet of sixteen sail, and four which he was to take up at Goa, with the intention of going in search of the Rumes; but when he reached Cananor, somewhat late on account of the adverse state of the wind, he found the report of the coming of the Rumes looked upon as somewhat uncertain, and hereupon he sent two of the ships from among those which had come from Portugal and accompanied him thither, to return to Cochim and take in their cargo; and then he set sail from Cananor, and sailed over the bar of Goa, with determination of putting his hands upon the Captains of the Hidalcão who were in Benastarim; and by means of some

Moors whom he captured in a ship which came from Adem, he was informed that no fleet of the Rumes would come to India during that year, for it was reported that they intended first of all to take Adem and so secure the countries along the Straits [of the Red Sea], in order that our fleet might not be able to navigate there.

Having therefore cast anchor on the bar, Afonso Dalboquerque declared to the Captains that he had made up his mind to go up against Benastarim before the Hidalcão could know of his arrival, while they went to the city with all their fleet, for he desired to make for Old Goa, in order to forestall the pass over the sea before the Hidalcão could besiege it by land; and although the peril was considerable, he was determined to force a way through the artillery of the Turks, and isolate them in such a manner that no succour could possibly reach them, for the river had sufficient depth of water in it for the ships to draw up quite close to the fortress, and even to ram the bulwarks.

As soon as this had been arranged, Afonso Dalboquerque gave orders for the disembarkation of all the men-at-arms who were on board the vessels, for they were to accompany him, and in their place he shipped a hundred mariners and bombardiers picked out of the whole fleet, and furnished them with the best artillery he had, and plenty of powder and shot, and appointed to the captainship over them Tristão de Miranda, of the ship *S. Pedro;* Pero de Afonseca, of the *Sancta Maria da Ajuda, i.e., Saint Mary of the Aid;* Vicente Dalboquerque, of the small *Ajuda;* Antonio Raposo, of the ship *Ferros,*[1] *i.e., Irons;* Garcia de Sousa, of a Malabar ship;[2] and Aires da Silva, of the ship *Rosairo, i.e., Rosary,* whom he made chief captain of all these ships, and Afonso Dalboquerque himself went in a *catur.* When all was in

[1] This was one of the ships brought by Jorge de Mello in the 1512 fleet from Portugal.

[2] Garcia de Sousa had commanded the *São Gidão* in the above fleet.

readiness, he commanded D. Garcia [de Noronha] to make his way with the rest of the whole fleet to Goa, and get ready against his arrival all the things that were necessary to proceed by land to Benastarim, and not to allow any one of the inhabitants of the city to go forth without his special permission; and then he himself set sail and made good his entrance into Old Goa; and as soon as he reached in front of the fortress of Benastarim he sent word to Tristão de Miranda to stand in with his ship *S. Pedro* until he was at the distance of a gun-shot from the fortress, while he himself with the other captains of these ships would follow him up, and there they all remained until the artillery of the Turks somewhat abated from the fury with which they had begun their fire.

When our men had lost their fear and alarm at the continued firing of the enemy, Afonso Dalboquerque commanded the Captains to draw yet a little nearer with their ships, and Garcia de Sousa to lay his ship athwart between the fleet and the fortress, for it was a very large vessel, and would serve in that position as a shelter for the other vessels. But the Turks, who were not altogether pleased at the proximity of our ships to them, fired so many shots at them, and so furiously, that they swept clean across the decks. And as our men were just in the line of fire of a *basilisk*,[1] which the Turks had mounted upon a rampart flush with the water-line, Afonso Dalboquerque made ready a barge with a gunmetal *camel*,[2] and ordered his Constable to take six bombardiers and go by night and anchor it close to the Turkish bulwarks in front of their guns, and try their best to silence the basilisk.

The Constable was so brave a soldier that, without the least fear of the danger he ran, carried out the orders which Afonso Dalboquerque had given him, and when morning

[1] *Bazalisco*; an ancient kind of cannon, of large calibre, and very long, carrying a ball of a hundred and sixty pounds weight.

[2] *Camelo*; see vol. i, p. 73.

broke he began to fire the camel with round shot, and it was Our Lord's will that one of the shots struck the basilisk on the mouth and broke it, and killed two of the renegade bombardiers, one of whom was a Gallician, the other a Castilian, who had fled away at the first entry of the Portuguese into Goa and gone over to the Moors.

Aires da Silva, who found himself in the line of the basilisk, ordered his ship to be hauled more forward, but the mariners managed these operations so badly that they ran the ship athwart the enemy's guns. And the Turks, perceiving the embarrassed state of our men, fired at them with so many guns broadside that they almost dashed them to pieces; and it happened that one of the shots went through the ship's prow, and striking three barrels of powder that were in that place they blew up, and part of the hatchways, the castles, and the deck were destroyed, and two planks close upon the water-line were blown off, although no other casualty occurred among the crew beyond the burning of three cabin boys, but the crew were so alarmed that they all jumped overboard, and Aires da Silva was left alone in the ship. When the Turks beheld the misfortune of our men they raised a great shout and blew their trumpets.

But Afonso Dalboquerque, when he saw Aires da Silva in this predicament, got into a skiff with four men, and under the fire of the Turks he got up to the ship and called out to the crew who were swimming away to return to him, reproaching them with leaving him thus unprotected, and using towards them words of reprehension for deserting their captain in so shameful a manner. And when the mariners saw him in his skiff passing along under fire in front of so many guns, they grew ashamed of what they had done, and took courage and turned back again to the ship; while he, although the guns of the enemy did not cease to fire, called out to his mate, who was coming on in a boat, to go and haul at the poop of the ship so as to draw her off from the guns' mouths; and as soon as the ship had thus been hauled off, he ordered a number of caulkers, with hides and all other necessaries, to go to the ship and cover over the holes made by the explosion on the water line.

While the caulkers were thus occupied, Aires da Silva with the mariners baled out all the water which the ship had made; but, as the repairs could not be finished on that day, so soon as night came on Afonso Dalboquerque gave orders to draw off, and that Tristão de Miranda should cause the ship *S. Pedro* to be hauled in front of the small ships, and the latter at nightfall ordered his cables to be strengthened, because in the daytime not a boat dared venture out.

When the Turks saw the ship they began at once to fire a very large gun at her, and at the very first shots swept her decks clean from one side to the other. And although our men underwent danger with considerable risk of their lives, yet the Turks did not get off easily, for our artillery had killed a great many of their men and many horses inside the fortress, and had thrown down all the wall in such a manner that Roçalcão and his captains dared not go into the keep because of the danger of going along towards it, and he ordered his men to repair during the night the wall which our artillery knocked down during the day.

CHAPTER XLVI.

How the great Afonso Dalboquerque ordered the stockade, wherewith the Turks had surrounded the fortress in order that our ships should not go inside, to be pulled up; and how he went to the city after having put them inside, and what further took place.

While affairs were thus situated the great Afonso Dalboquerque, in order to completely cut off all chance of the Turks receiving their wished-for reinforcements, sent a message to D. Garcia de Noronha that he should send him two small ships and a barge with their *arrombadas*[1] very strong, and artillery, and order them to pass through the shallow pass,[2] in order thereby to assault the fortress upon that side; and he was to have in readiness many waggons laden with cannon balls, and gunpowder, and many mantelets, benches,[3] gabions,[4] pickaxes, and large and small artillery on carriages, and everything else that was needed to attack the fortress by sea and by land, and the captains of the trained-bands to have their men ready, for as soon as he had the ships within the stockade he would be with him.

At receipt of this message Dom Garcia ordered his ships to be made ready, with their *arrombadas* made of coco-nut fibre[5] and barrels, and the barge to be prepared and fur-

[1] *Arrombadas;* cables lashed round a heavily laden ship, with empty barrels on the water's edge, to give additional buoyancy in shallow places.

[2] *Passo seco.* The city of Goa had no walls of its own, though at the time when Linschoten and others visited it the ancient walls existed, but without gates. It was protected not only by the fortifications raised for the defence of the harbour, but also by the long wall covering chiefly the eastern side of the island. This began with a fort in the north-east part of the island at Daugim, and extending from that point to the church of São Braz, was joined there to an old Muhammadan fort which had been rebuilt by the Portuguese; thence it proceeded to Benastarim, where it met the fortress of São Thiago. It then took a southern direction to the fort of Mangueiral, and thence to that of S. João Baptista. This wall had three principal gates, at which sentinels kept watch day and night, and as people passed through them in crossing over to the Muhammadan territory on the mainland, they were called *passos.* They corresponded with the three forts abovementioned—the *passo* of Daugim, to the north-east; the *passo secco,* shallow pass, or ford of São Braz, to the east; and that of Benastarim to the south-east. This last was most frequented by the people, especially as articles of daily consumption were carried through it from the mainland to the city.—J. N. da Fonseca, *Sketch of Goa.* Bombay, 1878, p. 153. See also the coloured plan of Goa in MS. Sloan. 5027A, folio 52.

[3] *Bancos de pinchar;* an heraldic term, explained by Bluteau. Here it appears to signify a three-legged stool or bench used in storming operations.

[4] *Cestos.*

[5] *Com suas arrombadas de cairo e de pipas. Cairo* is the outer or fibrous shell of the coco-nut, with which in the Maldive Islands, and other parts of India, all ships' cordage and rigging is made.

nished with a large gun; and he conferred the captaincies of these ships upon Fernão Gomez de Lemos and Antonio de Matos, and that of the barge upon João Gomez; and as soon as they were ready they proceeded on their way up the river, and when they tried to pass over the shallow pass, the ship which Antonio de Matos commanded, being larger than the others, took the ground, and it was necessary to remove from her the *arrombadas* with which she was supported in order to pass over, and because the weight of the artillery which she carried upon her deck was very great the ship canted over and capsized.

Nevertheless, Fernão Gomez de Lemos and João Gomez passed over, and on arriving at the fortress fixed immediately upon a bulwark which was on that side, and berthed themselves so close to it that the Turks from the top of it shot some of their crew with matchlocks and with arrows, and swept the vessels through and through with their guns; but, notwithstanding this, like men of courage they stuck to their post and would not quit it. And when Roçalcão saw that an attack was made upon him on that quarter also, he issued immediate orders that four large guns should be conveyed to that part of the fortifications; and in the lower part of the curtain of the wall, and above also, he commanded that guns should be placed, and by these means he shot through our ships from one side to the other, but our party, with all this danger, did not fail to pay him out for it in the same coin.[1]

And when Afonso Dalboquerque had made sure that no reinforcement could possibly reach the enemy from that quarter, either of troops or supplies, he made up his mind to pull up a stockade with which the Moors had encircled the fortress, and to berth the ships inside the space in order to have their decks flush with the walls, and ordered Tristão de Miranda and Aires da Silva, who were with him in the

[1] *Não deixavam de lho pagar na mesma moeda.*

ship, because the ship of the latter captain remained outside for the reasons already shewn, to drive the ship *S. Pedro* against the palisades in order to overthrow them, and so make a large hole through which they could get in, for that which the Moors had left for convenience of getting to the fortress was very narrow. And behind these he sent Pero de Afonseca, Antonio Raposo, and Vicente Dalboquerque to do likewise; and all the while that these captains were running their ships with great courage close up to the stockade it was not without great risk, for they were well plied with the enemy's artillery, arrows, and gunshot. And, as soon as night fell, Afonso Dalboquerque went up to them, and thus they destroyed a large quantity of the stockade.

When this had been accomplished he commanded Tristão de Miranda to lay out an anchor beyond the palisades and haul in the ship *S. Pedro* upon the cable as far up inside the space thus thrown open as he could, and the other ships to follow after. And as soon as the Turks perceived that our side were occupied by night with getting the ships into positions inside the stockade, they threw down burning trusses of straw to the foot of the wall, and taking aim at our men by means of the bright light thus afforded, fired their guns at them; and our men being now opposite to the very mouths of the guns, and Afonso Dalboquerque running great risk in the skiff which he used, the captains begged him earnestly to withdraw outside the palisade, because in thus exposing himself to danger the whole of the enterprise might be put in jeopardy; for he ought to take rest, they said, while they carried out in the best and bravest possible manner the undertaking which he had appointed them to do.

But Afonso Dalboquerque, with his accustomed invincible spirit, replied that he could not remain at rest while he saw them in their present dangerous position, but they must do what he had ordered, for he did not intend to leave them without knowing in what condition they were left. And when he had got the ships inside the stockade all ranged in order so as to attack the fortress, he retired outside with the intention of going to the city to make ready to bring up a reinforcement by land, and, as he withdrew, the enemy picked off two of the black men who were rowing in his skiff; and when he got outside he made his way to the *paráo*, and from it despatched two Canarese peons to go to the mainland and take captive some one who could speak the native tongue and give news of the Hidalcão; so they went and caught two Moors who were coming to the fortress of Benastarim, and from them he learned that Içufularij[1] was on the march with two thousand men to relieve the fortress, and that within the fortress there was a combined force of about six thousand Turks, Rumes, and Coraçones, and of the other troops there were about three thousand, including a hundred musketeers and three hundred horsemen.

On hearing this news, Afonso Dalboquerque appointed Aires da Silva chief captain of the ships, and attached to his service a *paráo* to act as a tender for supplying water and necessary provisions, and told him to attack the fortress on the side of the sea with his forces directly that he (Afonso) fell upon them on the land side. And having arranged this plan he set sail for the city in the *catur* which had brought him. This operation went on for eight days and eight nights, and, during the whole of the time, the Turks never ceased firing their artillery, whereby our ships were well riddled because they were close to the ramparts, and in the direct line of the guns. And our people who were engaged in this enterprise used to say that, during these eight days, the Turks fired more than four thousand times at them with guns of large bore, beside the smaller

[1] This is probably the Portuguese rendering of the Arabic name *Yusuf-ul-Araj*; *i.e.*, "Yusuf the Lame".

shot, and from the top of the wall used to fire at them with arrows and matchlocks, whereby they wounded a great many of our men. The masts, yards, and shrouds of the ships were so thickly covered with arrows which had stuck into them that it was a terrible thing to behold them.

Tristão de Miranda and Vicente Dalboquerque, although at this time they were but youths, bore themselves very bravely in those days, and became so stunned with the continual roar of the Turkish artillery and our own (for their ships were in the vanguard all through the affair), that for a long time afterwards they could not hear anything. Aires da Silva, also, on his part, performed the deeds of a very valiant cavalier; and the accident which happened to his ship was owing to the fact that he thought little of warps and of kedges,[1] but only cared to be the first of all to make an end of anything, for he did not know what fear was. And after Afonso Dalboquerque had departed for the city, Aires da Silva, learning that on the other side of the mainland a caravan of draught oxen had arrived with a supply of provisions for the fortress, started one night with the men he had with him in his ships, and fell upon them and burnt their houses, and killed a great number of the Moors, and captured all the provisions, and those who were left alive took to flight. Pero de Afonseca and Antonio Raposo also on their part fought with great bravery, and without any fear of the enemy's guns laid out their anchors.

As for this enterprise thus taken in hand with so many guns and so many of the enemy's forces in a fortress, I do not believe there was ever seen or heard such another in those parts of the world, for very often Afonso Dalboquerque used to chide our men for not considering the risks in which they placed themselves, both body and life, for the ships were so battered all over by the artillery of the Turks, that there was not a place left in which they could have

[1] *Nunca curou de rageiras nem de proizes.*

secured themselves, had it not been our Lord's will to preserve them in that peril.

CHAPTER XLVII.

How the great Afonso Dalboquerque arrived at the city [of Goa], and of the great reception with which the inhabitants met him, and of the rest which passed with the Turks.

After that the great Afonso Dalboquerque had succeeded in cutting off the Turks who were in the fortress from any succour which could have reached them, he made his way by water to Goa in the *catur* which had brought him to the fortress; and when he had reached the quay—seeing that this was the first time that he had entered the city since his return from Malaca—the inhabitants came down to receive him at the gate of Saint Catherine, where his disembarking was conducted in the following manner.

D. Garcia de Noronha, with all the crews of the fleet; Manuel de Lacerda, captain of the city, with all the *Fidalgoes* who inhabited it; and Pero Mascarenhas, with the trained bands; and the judges and aldermen, and the rest of the native population in their company. And they had prepared for him a young mare, on which he was to ride, with a caparison of brocade, and stirrups, and all the rest of the housings of very finely chased silver, and a canopy of brocade, which the aldermen of the city were to carry; and, on arrival at the gate, they made him an oration, the substance of which was the great delight that all had felt at his return, and their joy at the victory which our Lord had given him against the power of the king of Malaca.

And when the harangue was finished, Manuel de Lacerda drew near and delivered up to him the keys of the fortress. And after all these ceremonies had been performed, Afonso Dalboquerque spoke to all present with great love and kindness, and, riding upon the young mare, which they had provided for his use, surrounded by all his retinue, he began his procession direct to the church, all going in front of him on foot; and, while he was yet in the middle of the way, the clergy came to receive him with a cross raised up aloft, and no sooner did Afonso Dalboquerque perceive it, than he got down off his horse, and, falling down on his knees before the cross, he declared to those who carried the canopy that they ought rather to take the cross under it, for such an honour ought not to be shown to anything except that cross, which resembled the one upon which our Lord had suffered, and in this manner they all followed after it up to the church. And when the sermon was ended, Afonso Dalboquerque again mounted upon the young mare, and attended by the canopy, made his way to the palace of the Çabayo, wherein he lodged, and immediately began to attend to the affairs which were necessary in order to go by land against Benastarim.

And when he was ready to set forth, with the determination of conducting a vigorous storm against the fortress, and so making a broad passage way whereby a body of soldiers might enter, news was brought to inform him that Roçalcão had quitted the fortress and was on his way, marching with a large force of infantry and cavalry in order of battle to challenge the city. And Afonso Dalboquerque, as soon as he received this intelligence, ordered Manuel de Lacerda, captain of the city, to be mounted by break of day —for it was then night—and Pero Mascarenhas, Antonio de Saldanha, João Machado, Fernão Caldeira, Manuel Fernandez, João Cabeceira, Lourenço Prego, and Diogo Fernandez the *Adail*,[1] to go with him, and reconnoitre the enemy.

On the following day, early in the morning, these went out by the gate, and proceeded to the heights over a valley

[1] See vol. ii, p. 137.

where Roçalcão was bivouacing with his forces; and as soon as Manuel de Lacerda caught sight of the enemy he sent word to Afonso Dalboquerque of the position occupied by Roçalcão, and that the probable number of the enemy were estimated at three thousand men. At receipt of this intelligence, Afonso Dalboquerque commanded a sally by Ruy Gonçalvez and João Fidalgo, with three hundred men of the train-bands, crossbowmen, and musketeers, and some with pikes, to go along the direct path and unite themselves with Manuel de Lacerda by way of reinforcement; and behind these he sent thirty more mounted men, with a message to Manuel de Lacerda to maintain his position, supporting the trained band, but not to engage in battle with the Turks; and, if he observed that they were determined to fight, then he was to send him word.

When Roçalcão perceived that our men were few in numbers, he came on with his men in battle array. But Manuel de Lacerda remained where he was, and would not fight with him. Then Roçalcão, seeing how determined our men were, halted, and dared not advance any nearer upon them. And while the two were in this position, João Machado was running to the city, and he told Afonso Dalboquerque how Roçalcão was on the point of offering battle, and it was for him (Afonso) to say what he desired to be done. And at this news he summoned all the captains and narrated to them the state of affairs. And as soon as João Machado began to affirm that Roçalcão was desirous of fighting, the opinion of all was that the Portuguese ought to sally out in a body with all their men, and go and fight him.

Afonso Dalboquerque replied to them that since they had decided already to go and attack the fortress by land, as they had already blockaded it by sea, and to cast the Turks out of it, it did not seem to him to be good counsel to go about all over the country skirmishing about with the Moors, but rather they ought to seek the victorious conclusion of their undertaking with hearty good will, for the Moors were good archers, and their soldiers always in open order, and lightly armed, and could close up and open out their ranks whenever they thought fit, whereas our men could not do so, for they were all heavily armed, and far too much encumbered to manœuvre in skirmishing order with the Turks in the field; but over and above all these objections, they all again affirmed that he ought to sally out and fight the Turks.

Thereupon, Afonso Dalboquerque finding himself compelled by the weight of this counsel, ordered the advance to be sounded, and the gates opened, and he sallied out into the open country with the whole of his forces, having divided it into three companies.

In the van (B)[1] he sent Pero Mascarenhas, with orders to unite with Ruy Gonçalves and João Fidalgo, and to take charge of the train-bands. And in the main body (C) D. Garcia [de Noronha], accompanied by Pero Dalboquerque, Lopo Vaz de Sampayo,[2] Antonio de Saldanha, Francisco Pereira Pestana, Jorge Dalboquerque,[2] Jorge Nunez de Lião, Gonçalo Pereira,[2] D. João Déssa,[2] Diogo Fernandez de Beja, D. João de Lima, Gaspar Pereira,[2] Jorge da Silva, Ruy Galvão, Pero Correa, João Delgado, Manuel de Sousa, Jeronymo de Sousa, and many other *Fidalgoes* and Cavaliers; while he himself and the rest of the forces followed in the rear-guard (D); and so, marching in this order of battle, in sight of the Turks (A), Roçalcão began to push on his battalions towards ours.

When Afonso Dalboquerque saw this he ordered Pero Mascarenhas to wheel round the train bands so as to face the enemy (B 2), and D. Garcia to keep on his way in quick march to their right (C 2), while he bore on to their left, and improved his position going up a valley, taking the Turkish

[1] See plan.

[2] See p. 208. These came in the fleet of Jorge de Mello, A.D. 1512.

army in flank (D 2); but as D. Garcia got on considerably faster than he could, he sent him word to halt and keep his ground until he himself should reach the head of the valley, for the place was one of very great strategic opportunity

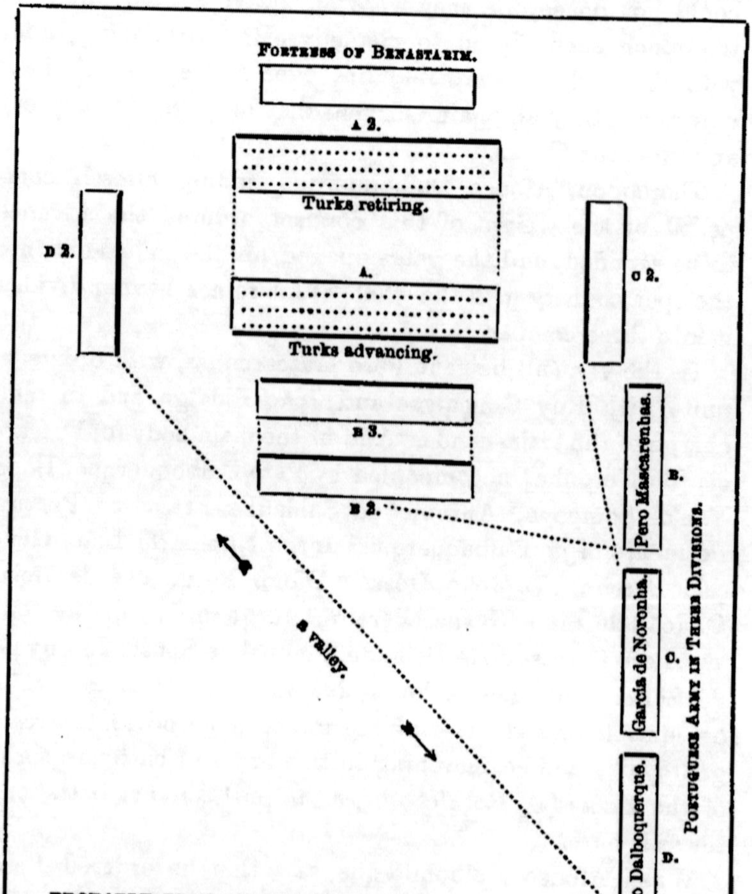

PROBABLE PLAN OF THE OPERATIONS
mentioned on pp. 223-225.
The thick lines shew the front of the columns.

for attacking the Turks. Roçalcão perceiving how eager our men were to give him battle, halted, and ordered his forces not to advance any further.

But Afonso Dalboquerque, as he was an experienced

soldier, soon observed that the Turks desired to retreat, like people who had changed their original intention, so he ordered Pero Mascarenhas to press them somewhat more vigorously (B 3), and D. Garcia de Noronha to follow them along his line, and Manuel de Lacerda to support the train-bands with the cavalry, according to the instructions he had already received, and then the Turks, finding themselves with the train-bands in front of them, fell into disorder and turned round (A 2) and faced towards the fortress.

CHAPTER XLVIII.

How Roçalcão was put to flight, and the great Afonso Dalboquerque followed in pursuit after him up to the very walls of the fortress of Benesterij, and of what further took place.

When the great Afonso Dalboquerque perceived that Roçalcão was facing to the fortress he ordered Manuel de Lacerda to fall upon the Moors with his mounted men; and as our men were closing up with them one thousand native Canarese peons became separated and went up along a rising ground. Afonso Dalboquerque, seeing that they marched along in disorder, detached from his army a body of soldiers who were to manœuvre so as to get in between these peons and the main body of the Turks, and when these peons saw that they were cut off, they quitted the road on which they were travelling and made their way to the ford of Gondalij, because it was the nearest, and crossed over the river, and many of them were drowned in the passage.

During this event Pero Mascarenhas with the train-bands had already come up with the Turks and was engaged with them, and D. Garcia de Noronha on the right hand was rapidly coming on; and both the one party and the other, for they were all now so very close to the fortress, again fell upon the Turks so courageously that they caused them to lose all their horses, and the enemy being in great dread of our own men in this onslaught, they all got in in a crowd inside the fortress, they then shut the gates, leaving a great many outside, who with great trouble saved themselves with headgear which those who were inside threw over to them; others ran along the side of the fortress and made their entry good on the other side, and many of these stuck in the mud and were stifled to death; others again, who preferred to throw themselves into the river, were intercepted and put to death by Aires da Silva and other captains, who came up in the boats, and got out at the foot of the wall with their men protected with shield work, for they thought that the time had arrived at which Afonso Dalboquerque had ordered them to do so.

As soon as the Turks saw our men at the foot of the wall they threw down so many stones, and shot bows and arrows, and muskets at them so continuously that they were compelled to retire with a great number of the detachment severely wounded. The other part of our forces, which was stationed on the land side, finding themselves close up to the wall of the fortress, tried which way were easier to be done; whether, as some did, upon the top of pikes, or, as others, jumping on foot (for the wall on the side of the city is lower and less strong than on that of the river), and as there were some *Fidalgoes* and Cavaliers on the top, Roçalcão came up with a body of Turks and essayed to throw them down off the wall, and wounded many with arrows, musket shot, powder-cans, and blazing bundles of hay, without getting any advantage over them; and as for the Captains whom Afonso Dalboquerque was expecting to help him in rallying his men, who were on that side, these were they who were working very hard to get up, helping each other up by the leg; and the first who got up this was Pero Mascarenhas, who was in command of the trained bands, whom Afonso Dalboquerque after the rally embraced and kissed on the face, whereat some were scandalised, although they had no need to be, for besides his actions that day like a brave cavalier, Afonso Dalboquerque was under an obligation to him, for he had left the Fortress of Cochim, of which he was Captain, and had come to serve the king in that war.

Francisco Pereira Pestana, who was the one who was most concerned at this, went up to the wall, and striking it with the palm of his hand (and this he did not without hurting himself), said, "I should like to know if the women pedlers of Lisbon will say that Francisco Pereira was in this affair". Afonso Dalboquerque reproved him, saying he was astonished that he could do such a thing at so inopportune a moment. And Francisco Pereira, as he was a passionate man and of irritable nature, began to exchange angry words with Afonso Dalboquerque, and the strife went so as for him to say, "Why do you pick quarrels with me, and not with Duarte de Lemos, because he showed you his teeth, I suppose?" To this Afonso Dalboquerque replied with great forbearance, for in all his dealings he was always a pattern of patience, "He may well shew them, for he has very large and very long ones";[1] and without saying another word he turned his back upon him, for but a few days before, when they were at high words, Afonso Dalboquerque had borne with Francisco Pereira and omitted to punish him, and said to him on that occasion, "I vow by my life, Francisco Pereira, I am so angry that I could tear myself," and then he took hold of a slashed scarlet cloak which he was wearing, and tore it.

D. Garcia de Noronha, with all the rest of the forces who were posted on the right hand side, owing to the unmanageableness and kicking of the horses which the Turks had abandoned in order to save themselves on the top of the wall, fell into such confusion that the enemy prevented them

[1] This refers to vol. ii, p. 242, where the unusual length of Duarte de Lemos' teeth is mentioned.

from getting to the wall or to the gate, and had enough to do as it was to defend themselves; but the Turks also, before they could get up on the wall, were severely handled by our men, who killed many of them. And in this hurried action, in which all were engaged in pursuit of the Turks, Roçalcão thought he was entirely overthrown and the fortress entered; and, indeed, there would not have been much doubt of this if our men had only been prepared for such an event.

Afonso Dalboquerque, with his body of men who were on the left wing, began to assault a bulwark where Miliqueaye,[1] the second captain, was posted with a large body of men, and defending it with great bravery; notwithstanding this, our men were confident that they could have prevailed over the enemy in such a manner as to get upon it so that Afonso Dalboquerque could have easily placed his flag upon the wall at that place if he had had any hope of being supported on the other sides; but, as Benestarij was a very large town, and he had not any artillery at hand with which he could make a breach in the wall, he ordered the men to retire. And, although our soldiers on that day did not do more than what I have related, it is well worthy of praise that so many cavaliers and noble people, loaded with heavy arms and during the intense heat, should march from Goa to Benestarij, a distance of two leagues, on foot, and succeed in laying hands on the wall, and with so much courage have it in their power to enter into a fortress in which were stationed so many Turks, who knew very well how to defend it.

In this engagement they wounded Manuel de Lacerda, Pero Dalboquerque, Jorge da Silva, Lopo Vaz de Sampayo, Ruy Galvão, Pero Correa, João Delgado, Ruy Gonçalvez, captain of the trainbands, Diogo Fernandez de Béja, Manuel de Sousa, Jeronymo de Sousa, and many others of noble

[1] *Miliqueaye;* perhaps for *Melek Yahya*, the second word being equivalent to *John*.

degree who had accompanied their captains and fought very valiantly, not fearing the fire nor the powder-cans, muskets, lances, arrows, and stones with which they had to contend. And besides these above-mentioned, we had a list of wounded amounting to a hundred and fifty soldiers who served with the artillery, for they were posted close to the foot of the wall. But this was not without its reward, for of the Turks there were a great many killed and wounded before they could retire into the fortress; and of the peons who were left outside when the gate was closed there were many killed, as well as two Hindoo captains, one called Miralle,[1] the other Conaique.[2]

CHAPTER XLIX.

How the great Afonso Dalboquerque rallied his people, and went back to the city; and how he returned again with all his battle array to besiege the fortress, and of what passed with Roçalcão.

When our forces had withdrawn from the foot of the wall, the great Afonso Dalboquerque drew up in front of the fortress, in a spot where none of the enemy's guns could reach him, and stood there a long space of time with all the captains, *Fidalgoes*, and Cavaliers, surveying the manner of action which ought to be carried out in order to be able to get in; and when all had been carefully examined he set off for the city with the whole army, and there he remained for several days attending to the wounded and resting the unharmed from the labours which they had gone through on that day. And he gave orders for the immediate preparation of all the artillery,

[1] *Miralle;* probably for *Mir Ali*, a title and name frequently adopted by the descendants of the Prophet, through the Khalif *Ali*, his son-in-law.

[2] *Conaique;* I am unable to suggest the probable equivalent of this name.

scaling ladders, *bancos pinchados*,[1] mantlets, empty barrels for the stockades, and everything else that could be collected in the city for such an enterprise; and when all was in order and on the route, after a lapse of two days he ordered the trainbands to sally out, with all the crossbowmen and musketeers, to convoy these munitions and wait for him at the *Two Trees* (which is the half-way mark from Goa to Benestarij), and there they were to pitch his tent; and on the following day, in the morning, he set out with the whole of the army, to the number of about three thousand five hundred men; and when they had reached the *Two Trees*, he pitched his camp, surrounded on all sides by artillery, and there he stayed for two days waiting for the supplies of which he had given charge to Bastiam Rodriguez, his dependent, who is now Warden of the Balance at the Mint of this city of Lisbon. And when he had arrived, Afonso Dalboquerque put himself on the march with all his array in three companies, and ordered Pero Mascarenhas to lead the trainbands in the vanguard with all the artillery, and erect some stockades in which he could plant the guns.

As soon as our men came in sight of the fortress the Turks commenced to fire at them, and Afonso Dalboquerque, in order to pay them out in their own coin, ordered Pero Mascarenhas to fire at them in like manner. But when our artillery began to play, the Turks, who showed themselves on the top of the wall, withdrew inside. Thus having cleared the wall, Afonso Dalboquerque dismounted from the young mare which he rode and made his way on foot to the spot in which Pero Mascarenhas had imparked his artillery, and as night fell he ordered it to be advanced more towards the fortress, in front of a certain place which João Machado had pointed out to him as having the wall weaker there than elsewhere, for his intention was to throw down a portion of it so as to be able to send into the breach

[1] See p. 215, n. 3.

a strong storming party whom the Turks could not withstand. And on that day which they arrived they did no more than pitch their camp all round about the fortress, and on the morning of the following day Afonso Dalboquerque returned and placed himself in a spot where his back was against a rock to see what our men were doing.

The Turks, who felt their pride wounded by Afonso Dalboquerque's being able to stop there, began to train their guns towards that part more frequently, and at this juncture Diogo Mendez de Vasconcelos came up; but when he perceived how unsafe it was to remain in that situation, and how continuously the balls were coming against them, he begged Afonso Dalboquerque to step behind the rock, for in the place where he then stood he ran great risk of being hit; and although Diogo Mendez and Afonso Dalboquerque were not on very friendly terms, yet the latter did as he was advised, and just as they were going behind the rock a ball came and killed a man who was conversing with him, and he was covered with blood. Afonso Dalboquerque gave many thanks to our Lord that he had saved him from that peril, and ordered that the ball should be preserved and be plated with silver and taken care of against his funeral obsequies, and carried to Our Lady of Guadelupe[1] with a very large lamp of silver and a collar of gold set with very rich stones, and he contributed a hundred thousand reis in cash to be invested for the purchase of the supply of oil for the lamp, and all this was performed by Pero Correa, who became his executor.

When this incident was over, Afonso Dalboquerque commanded D. Garcia de Noronha to push forward his stockades nearer to the wall during the night, for he was somewhat too far off; and he set to work about this with such diligence that before morning broke he had made a stockade of greater strength than the original one, with a number

[1] A church in the Island of Goa, to the south of the town.

of barrels and baskets full of earth, and all the artillery arranged in their proper positions, and Afonso Dalboquerque was on his mare all the night long seeing after the progress of the work. And at daybreak, when Roçalcão beheld our stockade brought much nearer to his fortress, he made ready four hundred Turks and ordered them to assault it.

Pero Mascarenhas, Ruy Gonçalvez, and João Fidalgo, who were in command of the trainbands stationed in a hollow, in order to be out of the range of the Turkish artillery, came up at once on hearing the alarm of the attack, and Dom Garcia de Noronha came up on the other side and fell upon this party with such impetuosity that before the Turks could withdraw a number of them were left stretched upon the field. As soon as the Turks had retired our artillery began to play upon the wall with such fury from the morning until the evening that there was not a single Moor who dared to shew himself between the battlements.

And because we had in our camp some very powerful guns, and the gunners were very skilful at their work, they began to breach the wall in several places. So when Afonso Dalboquerque saw the state of the walls, he gave orders to the captains to hold themselves in readiness to assault the fortress on the morrow in the morning, and take the Turks by force of arms; but he said he would not appoint them the place, only that every one was to be on the alert, and where they saw him thither everyone was to repair; and he also ordered the gunners to approach yet nearer to the fortress with the guns. Roçalcão, finding himself pressed so hardly on the sea side, as well as on the land, and having no hope of any relief, sent for Miliqueaye—the second captain, who was a native Coraçone—and all the principal Turks of the fortress, and made them a speech, in which he declared that they could well see for themselves how closely they were besieged, and cut off from all succour, and a great portion of the wall thrown down, and how greatly they were in want in supplies and gunpowder, and all other munitions needful for its defence, and how slender were the chances they had of being freshly supplied with them therefore, as they could no longer hold out successfully by their arms, they ought to secure themselves by some arrangements of peace, which they must make with the Christians.

Miliqueaye and the other Turks, after considering the arguments of Roçalcão, and drawing a lesson from their recent experiences, came to the conclusion that he ought to beg for truce, with the intention of afterwards treating for an agreement upon terms of peace. And as soon as they had been agreed upon, early in the morning of the following day, Afonso Dalboquerque still adhering to his intention of storming the fortress, they hung out a white flag on the wall; and when he caught sight of it, he sent João Machado immediately to speak with Roçalcão and learn what he wanted; and João Machado went to the foot of the wall, and Roçalcão came down and conversed with him, and told him to say to the captain general that he must give him a safe conduct, for he would perform whatever was demanded of him. Then Afonso Dalboquerque, who thought it more important a matter to preserve the life of a single Christian whom he imperilled in the fight than to encompass the death of the whole of the Turks who were in the fortress, was very pleased, and sent word to Roçalcão that he must hand over to him two of the principal men of the Turks as hostages, and then he would send him a statement of what he would have him do. João Machado returned with the message, and as Roçalcão was anxious to make peace, he lost no time in sending him back again with the Turks who had been demanded.

CHAPTER L.

Of how the great Afonso Dalboquerque debated with the Captains and Fidalgoes who were there the terms offered by Roçalcão; and of the agreement which was made; and how he set out for Goa.

No sooner had João Machado returned with the two Turks who were to remain as hostages until the conclusion of the negotiations for a treaty of peace, for which Roçalcão sued, as I have related, than Afonso Dalboquerque summoned all his captains and *Fidalgoes* who were in that camp, and shewed them how the Turks of the fortress of Benẹstarij were already on the point of surrender, for Roçalcão, the principal Captain, had sent to discuss terms of peace, and had promised to do whatever was required of him, therefore it was necessary that all should declare to him their opinions, in order that he might send the reply to this the request of the enemy.

The reply of the captains was that they had offered themselves there at great risk of their lives, willing to suffer death for the service of God, and of the King Dom Manuel; and as they had so large an army there, with such a high spirit of victory, he ought not to entertain the proposals made by Roçalcão, but storm the fortress and enter it by force of arms, and get Roçalcão into his power; for that the enemy should sue for peace, while all the time he had with him in the fortress twice as large an army of Turks as there was of Christians outside it, was really because his condition was far more desperate than they all had any idea of, and therefore for these reasons, and for many others, they were of opinion that he ought not to enter into any treaty with him.

But inasmuch as Afonso Dalboquerque and D. Garcia, and others, were of the opposite opinion, he replied to these arguments that the best things the Turks had in the fortress were the artillery and the horses, for as for the men, even if he took them all prisoners he would not give twopence for the whole of them, and he certainly would never allow them to set foot inside the city, for there was a great scarcity of provisions there; and if they thought that by giving them battle they would take Roçalcão prisoner, as they alleged, it was very doubtful whether they could do so or not, and it would very likely cost them the lives of four or five *Fidalgoes*, or perhaps even twenty, seeing that every one was anxious to be the first in; for eight thousand Moors, surrounded, and cut off, without any hope of relief, would of necessity spill much of their assailants' blood before they could be quite beaten down; and therefore it was his opinion and firm resolve, that if Roçalcão would surrender him the fortress with all its artillery and the horses, and everything else that it contained, and deliver up to him the renegades, then he would let them go, even if he had to build them a bridge of silver to enable them to pass over to the mainland.

Having settled this, Afonso Dalboquerque sent word to Roçalcão, through João Machado, that, provided he agreed to the conditions which I have related, he would make peace with him, and let him go freely away; but if he would not accept these terms, then he must know of a certainty that he would not spare his life, nor the life of a single person who was left in the fortress. And as Roçalcão was very desirous of peace, he agreed to every condition; but as for the renegade Christians, who were in his host, he begged Afonso Dalboquerque not to make any special demand for them, for he could not surrender them, seeing that it would be contrary to the law of the country.

To this Afonso Dalboquerque replied that the principal point of all which he required to be conceded was the surrender of the renegades, and unless this were adhered to he would not listen to any further proposals; Roçalcão therefore, perceiving how determined he was, and being very desirous of feeling himself free and out of the toils in which he was involved, desired rather to ameliorate the necessity of his condition than comply with the obligations of his law; so he told João Machado to declare to the great Captain that as he made so great a matter of the renegades he would surrender them on the condition that Afonso Dalboquerque would spare their lives.

This Afonso Dalboquerque granted, and sent back a safe conduct for him and for all the Turks and Moors, provided that they carried away nothing with them except only the clothing in which they stood up. And as soon as Roçalcão received the safe conduct, he lost no time in sending his wives over to the mainland; and when they were all over on the other side, he and Miliqueaye (who was the second in command of the fortress), fearing lest Afonso Dalboquerque should violate his safe conduct, crossed over immediately, forgetting all about the promises which they had made to the Turks that they would not quit the fortress without, first of all, seeing them safely out of it.

CHAPTER LI.

How our men entered the fortress, and wanted to pillage the Turks, if the great Afonso Dalboquerque had not prevented them; and what passed with the renegades, and how he set forth towards Goa.

As soon as the news ran through the camp that Roçalcão and Miliqueaye had crossed over to the mainland, our people, eager to sack the fortress, came on in a confused mass and got inside it, and began to pillage it, and illtreat the Turks, many of whom, out of fear, cast themselves into the river and were drowned. But when Afonso Dalboquerque perceived this disturbance he went up to the gate to hinder the people from going in until it was completely evacuated by the Turks; nevertheless, after he got to the gate he was compelled to go in, in order to adhere to the pledge of safety which he had given them, and only with great difficulty could he prevent our men from killing and robbing them.

And as the Moors were very numerous, and there were no means of passing them on to the mainland so expeditiously as Afonso Dalboquerque desired, in order to make an end of this business of casting them out, he ordered the boats belonging to the ships to be brought up, along with some watchboats which he had there, and by these means he began gradually to reduce the numbers of people who stood on the shore. Notwithstanding this, so numerous were the Persians, Turks, Coraçones, and other people of the country, that they took two days in passing over. And it fell out that on the very next day in the morning after all had passed over to the other side of the mainland, Içufularij, Captain of the Hidalcao, arrived to relieve Roçalcão with a great body of men and a large quantity of supplies; but inasmuch as Benestarij was by this time surrounded, both by land and sea by our men, it was perfectly impossible for them to get in, and Içufularij, when he saw the fortress in the hands of the enemy, and no help for it, returned with the army which he had brought back again to his own lands, very much discouraged, and throwing great blame upon Roçalcão for surrendering a fortress which contained so many people for its defence.

The Turks, too, feeling themselves safe, waited for nothing else, but went away immediately under their Captains, with a large number of whites, into the interior country. And as soon as the fortress was entirely clear of the enemy, Afonso Dalboquerque gave orders that all the horses and artillery which it contained should be collected together, and the dilapidations of the fortress be repaired in the strongest manner that was possible, and replenished with more artillery and munitions of war, and he appointed a captain with a retinue of soldiers to guard it.[1] And after he had completed his provision of these matters he commanded them to bring up before him Fernão Lopez and the other renegades; these men, when they found themselves in his presence, fearing that he would not keep the promise he had made them of sparing their lives, threw themselves at his feet, and with many tears besought him to have mercy on them. But Afonso Dalboquerque, who could not break his word, kept the promise which he had made of not taking their lives, according to the promise given to Roçalcão, so he ordered that their right hands, and the thumbs of their left hands, and their ears and noses should be cut off in memory and as a terrible example of the punishment meted out to them for the treason and wickedness which they had committed against God and their king.[2]

[1] The fort of Benastarim became very famous in the annals of Goa after the Portuguese conquest. Pietro della Valle makes especial mention of it, as also the house in which the commandant of the fort then resided, from the balcony of which a splendid view of the surrounding country could be enjoyed. In this fortress there was a very large gun which had been taken from the Mahammadans, and which was, until lately, preserved as an historical reminiscence.—*J. N. da Fonseca*, Sketch of Goa, Bombay, 1878, p. 153.

[2] Castanheda, in his account of this horrible cruelty (a foreshadowing perhaps of the tortures invented by the Inquisition at Goa in later years), attaches even more horrid details to this great blot upon the otherwise magnanimous character of Afonso Dalboquerque. He says that the hair of the wretched men's heads and beards was torn out by the roots, and the raw places smeared with mud. He adds some interesting information respecting the life of Fernão Lopez, whom he himself saw in the island of St. Helena. The passage is as follows:—

"E ho principal que ho moueo a fazer isto, foy por ser exemplo a outros que não fizessem outro tanto, e tambem por não ficar sem castigo hum crime tamanho como aquelle foy. E a justiça foy com lhes mandar pubricamente e com pregão cortar narizes, orelhas, mãos dereytas, dedos das ezquerdas, e entregalos aos moços que lhes depenassem os cabelos das barbas e das cabeças, e que os enlameassem, e injuriassem, e a Fernão Lopez sobre todos porque era de mais qualidade: e por derra-

This Fernão Lopez, who was the ringleader of the renegades, set out on his return to Portugal after the death of Afonso Dalboquerque, but when he had got so far forward on the voyage as the Island of Saint Ilena, he made up his mind to stay there with a slave who belonged to him, and there he ended his days. He was the first who made a habitation in this island, establishing a Hermitage, and planting many trees, and he bred a great number of hogs and goats, so that the site became a very commodious place

deiro foy degradado pera Portugal, e eu ho vi na ilha de santa Helena, onde por seu rogo ho capitão da nao que ho leuaua ho deixou sò: e ali viueo muyto tempo, seruindo a nosso señor arrependido do peccado que fizera. E disseramme que assi ele como muytos dos outros sofrerão estes tormentos com muyta paciencia dizendo que mais merecião polo graue peccado que cometerão."—*Castanheda*, lib. iii, ch. xciii.

Correa gives even a more revolting account of this punishment, which was spread out over three days, and resulted in the death of more than half the number of the victims. He says:—"Depois de os mouros serem deitados fóra da ilha de Goa, o Gouernador proueo e afortelezou os passos da ilha, como dito he. Logo entendeo com os arrenegados que estauão com o Roçalcão, os quaes, com baraços nos pescoços e mãos atadas detrás, forão leuados á picota fóra da cidade, com pregão que dizia: 'Justiça que manda fazer ElRey nosso senhor, que manda bascamar estes homens, porque forão trédores a sua ley e a seu Rey; e a morte lhes he perdoada por amor do Hidalcão.' E chegados á picota negros algozes e moços do pouo lhe depennarão e arrancarão quantas barbas tinhão, até as sobrancelhas, e lhe tirarão com lama fedorenta de chiqueiros de porcos, que pera ysso já estaua prestes, aos rostros e olhos, onde os fizerão taes que lhe nom parecião os rostros; com que forão tornados á prisão, em que jazião deitados com correntes de ferro nos pés e pescoços, e algemas nas mãos, e assy como jazião mijauão e sayão por sy. Então ao outro dia, assy d' esta maneyra como estauão, os tornarão a leuar á picota com o mesmo pregão, onde lhe cortarão as orelhas rentes e os narizes, e os tornarão á prisão, onde os meterão como estauão assy nas correntes de ferro sem serem curados. E ao outro dia assy os leuarão á picota com seu pregão, onde lhe cortarão as mãos direitos e os dedos polegares das esquerdas; com que forão tornados á prisão, e forão curados de suas chagas. De que na prisão morrerão mais d' ametade delles, e os que ficarão forão soltos, que liuremente se fossem por onde quigessem; o que assy fizerão, que todos desappareçerão."—*Correa*, pp. 315, 316.

of shelter for our ships which touched there on the homeward voyage from India.[1]

[1] Correa's account of this unfortunate man, whose adventures are worthy of record here because he is believed to have been the first settler upon the island of St. Helena, is as follows:—

"Fernão Lopes se meteo em huma nao do Reyno, que em Lisboa tinha molher e filhos, a qual nao foy apartar na ilha de S. Elena, onde tomarão agoa; onde este Fernão Lopes fiqou escondido, o qual achado menos na nao o forão buscar, e o nom achando lhe deixarão hum quarto cheo de biscoito, e tassalhos de carne, e pexe sequo, e sal, e fogo, e roupas velhas que cada hum deu; e a nao se partio, e lhe deixarão huma carta que vindo ally ter alguma nao désse sinaes de sy se era morto ou viuo, e se mostrasse pera o prouerem do que ouvesse mester; e a nao se partio. Fernão Lopes, vendo a nao partida, sayo do mato e tomou o que achou, e acendeo o fogo que se nom apagasse, e logo buscou pedras, que bateo humas com outras, e vio que ferião fogo, e as guardou. Assy com os quatro dedos da mão esquerda, e com o cotinho da direita que tinha cortada, como Deos lhe ministraua por sua grande misericordia, cauou em huma ribanceira, em que fez huma lapa, que dentro fez grande, em que se recolhia e dormia, e a boca da lapa tapaua com tojos. Achou heruas tenras, que erão gostosas de comer, que cozia com sal em duas panellas que lhe deixarão. Assy estando, o outro anno foy hy ter huma nao, e elle vendo vir a nao se escondeo.

"Os da nao, sayndo em terra que acharão a lapa, e cama de palha em que dormia, e os sacos, e as duellas do quarto em que lhe deixarão o biscoito, e as panellas, e os caruões do fogo, ficarão espantados, e crerão que erão negros que ficarião ally fógidos d'outra nao; mas vendo o fato assentarão que era homem portuguez. Tomarão sua agoa, nom bolirão em nada, antes lhe deixarão biscoito, e queijos, e cousas de comer, e huma carta em que lhe dizião que nom se escondesse, que quando nao ally portasse fallasse, que ninguem lhe faria mal. E a nao se fez á vela. Em largando as velas da nao cayo as mar hum galo, que as ondas trouxerão a terra, que o F. Lopes recolheo, e lhe daua arroz que lhe deixarão, com que o galo fiqou com elle em tal amizade que sempre o acompanhaua onde andaua, e de noite se recolhia com elle á coua. Este galo esteue com este homem muytos annos, a que elle chamaua; que depois passando a tempo este homem parecia, e fallaua com a gente das naos que passauão, e todos lhe dauão cousas pera prantar e semear, em que fez muytas aboboras, romãs, palmeiras, ades, galinhas, porcas, cabras prenhes, que tudo se fez em muyta criação, e tudo se fez brauo do mato.

"Este homem esteue muytos annos só n'esta ilha fazendo esta espantosa vida, o que sendo dito a ElRey desejou muyto de o vêr, porque lhe dizião que era como homem seluagem; polo que ElRey o mandou rogar

Afonso Dalboquerque, after having provisioned the fortress with everything that was requisite for it, made his way to the city with all the army, and there they were received by the entire populace with a great procession at the city gate, and from that gate they marched straight to the church, to return thanks to Our Lord for the great victory which he had given them over their enemies; and when all these ceremonies were over, he immediately established a hospital of very large size, with beds and everything that was necessary for the care and cure of the wounded, who were very numerous; and he commanded Garcia de Sousa to take certain ships and cruise off the bar of Dabul, and not permit a single vessel to go into, or out of, the port, with the object of making war upon the Hidalcão wherever he was able to prevail against him.

que por sua vontade fosse ao Reyno. O que elle fez, e foy, e escondido desembarqou em casa do capitão da nao, d'onde de noite hia fallar com ElRey, e a Raynha, que lhe dauão hermedys e casas de frades em que estiuesse; o que elle nada quis aceitar, mas ouve licença d'ElRey e se foy a Roma, e se confessou ao Papa, que folgou de o vêr, e ouve cartas pera ElRey que o tornasse a mandar á ilha. O que assy o fez ElRey. Esteue este homem n'esta ilha passante de dez annos, sem nunqua o ninguem vêr, porque se elle escondia.

"N'esta ilha fiqou hum moço jáo fogido, que assy esteue com elle muytos annos. Este moço foy o que o descobrio a huma nao que hy foy ter, em que hia por capitão Pero Gomez Teixeira, que fôra ouvidor geral na India, que fez tantos medos as negro que o foy descobrir onde estaua escondido; que vendose tomado fez grandes prantos, cuidando que o querião leuar na nao; mas P. Gomes o consolou, e com elle muyto fallou, e segurou que o nom leuaria, e lhe deu muytas cousas, postoque elle os nom queria e muy aficadamente lhe rogou que leuasse o moço. O Pero Gomes o leuou, com F. Lopes lhe prometter que se nom esconderia á gente. O que assy concertado o P. Gomes lhe deixou hum seu assinado em que pedia por mercê a todos os capitães, que ally chegassem, que nom fizessem força ao querer leuar ao Reyno contra sua vontade, porque todos os tempos passados que se escondia era com esse medo que tinha; polo que lhe dera seguro em nome d'ElRey, e lho jurára, que ninguem o leuaria da ilha contra sua vontade. Com que o F. Lopes fiqou seguro, com que se nom escondia, e fallaua com todos, e daua do que nacia na ilha, que foy em muyto crecimento: e na ilha morreo depois d'ahy a muyto tempo, que foy no anno de 1546."—*Correa*, pp. 316-318.

As soon as Garcia de Sousa had set sail, Afonso Dalboquerque prepared a large supply of lime, stone, and masonry, in order to fortify the fortress of Benestarij, and strengthen the island passes, which had great need of it; and he renamed the fortress *The Castle of St. Peter*, because of the name of the ship which had there been broken to pieces in front of it. And he appointed Manuel Fragoso to the command of the outwork of Pangij and the tower of the island of Choram; and to Bastião Rodriguez, cavalier of the king's household and the present warden of the balance in the Mint of the city of Lisbon, he gave command of the tower of Divarij, and because this latter officer was a householder of Goa, he conferred also upon him the office of chief Alcaide of Goa during his life. And because these passes were the principal ones, and of very great importance for the security of the transit from the mainland to the island, he made the completion of them a matter of great urgency, for his real intention was to penetrate the straits of the Red Sea, and take Adem, if it were possible; but of this enterprise he had given no account to any one, that his voyage thither might not be suspected. Yet, because the time of the monsoon was now at hand, and he had a number of matters which he had to put in order, before entering upon them he determined first of all to dispatch the ambassadors of the kings of India who were awaiting him at Goa. Pedro Mascarenhas also, seeing that the siege of Benastarij was over, begged permission to return to his fortress of Cochim, but Afonso Dalboquerque, anxious to leave him in office as Captain of Goa, out of great confidence in his courage and discretion, desired him earnestly of his goodness to be pleased to remain where he was to superintend the completion of the towers, for which, indeed, all things were by this time ready prepared, for in so doing he would advance the king's service much more than by returning to, and staying in, Cochim.

CHAPTER LII.

How the great Afonso Dalboquerque sent D. Garcia de Noronha, his nephew, with a fleet against Calicut; and how he dispatched the ambassadors who were waiting for him at Goa, and the rest which took place.

Now, inasmuch as the great Afonso Dalboquerque was very angry with the Çamorim because he had broken his word, in respect of the peace which he (Afonso) had sent by ambassadors to conclude while he was on the way to Malaca, in which embassage Simão Rangel went; therefore, when the proceedings against Benestarij were finished, Afonso Dalboquerque, out of a desire to be revenged on him, sent D. Garcia de Noronha, his nephew, to go up against Calicut, and do as much harm as he could to the Çamorim, and blockade the coast in such a manner that not a single ship should leave the port with spices for Méca. And, because certain ambassadors of the kings of India had been for a long time waiting in Goa, as soon as D. Garcia had set sail, Afonso Dalboquerque occupied himself upon their dispatches, and ordered the secretary to lay before him all the papers and letters of the Hidalcão; and when he had examined them, he sent for the ambassador of this prince, and told him that if the Hidalcão desired to be at peace and have friendship with the King of Portugal, his Lord, he himself would be very much pleased, but the articles which he had brought were not similar in their import to those which the Hidalcão had frequently written; and therefore, in order to clear up this matter, he had determined to send him back with an ambassador in company with him.

The ambassador of the Hidalcão replied that there was no variation whatever in the articles; but if he desired to send to the Hidalcão a messenger from the Portuguese, and any delay should arise from this circumstance, he would desire him earnestly that during the period of time consumed in arranging the articles of peace, he would be pleased to command his captains to open the port of Dabul,[1] and give free ingress to the ships which were thither bound with merchandise and provisions. Afonso Dalboquerque was so desirous of coming to some conclusive understanding with the Hidalcão, that he lost no time in sending word to D. Garcia de Sousa, who was watching the port of Dabul, to set free the shipping of the port, provided that no prohibited merchandise were carried; and if the Moors should desire permission for a free navigation of their ships, they were to be sent to apply for it at Goa.

Having therefore dispatched this ambassador, Afonso Dalboquerque sent, in company with him, to treat for peace, Diogo Fernandez, *Adail* of Goa, and the son of Gil Vicente as his scrivener, and João Navarro as his interpreter, and six complete services of horses, and a native captain with twenty peons to attend them on the way. And when Diogo Fernandez had set out on his journey, Afonso Dalboquerque dispatched the ambassador of the King of Cambaya, who had been going up and down Goa for some time; but his departure was prolonged as much as possible, for as the Portuguese fleet, which was in course of preparation, was very large and being prepared very carefully with everything that was requisite to perform any undertaking, however important it might be,—although he had not yet given any account to anyone of the route he intended to follow,—he was fearful lest the Moors should surmise that he was preparing to enter the straits of the Red Sea, and, by the medium of Cambaya and Miliquiaz (who was very cunning), his enterprise should come to be known before he could start, so that Adem, which he was determined to attack, should get ready to withstand him. And what made him believe this more than ever was, that just at this juncture

[1] See the map of Fernão Vaz Dourado, vol. ii, p. 1.

there arrived unexpectedly another messenger from the King of Cambaya, who gave out that he had come to hasten forward the settlement of the treaty. The principal reason why Afonso Dalboquerque delayed concluding this dispatch was because he was very desirous of having a personal interview with the King of Cambaya, and as it was now very late in the season, and they were like to lose the monsoon for the Straits, and D. Garcia de Noronha, who was to accompany him, could not possibly join him in time to perform the two enterprises [of going to Cambaya and the Straits], because he had so many things to attend to in Cochim and Calicut, Afonso Dalboquerque finally dispatched the ambassadors with the intention that when he was tacking for the Straits he would make his way to Cambaya and visit the king, provided that there were time enough for it.

And when he had examined the articles and conditions which the King D. Manuel had appointed as a basis of peace, he determined to send in company with the ambassador, Tristão Déga as ambassador to the King, and João Gomez as his scrivener, with a present of articles from Portugal and India; and the instructions which our ambassador carried were to demand leave to erect a fortress in Diu, for the security of the subjects and property of the King of Portugal; and that the merchants of that kingdom should send their merchandise to Goa and not to any other part, and there they would find everything they required by way of a homeward-bound cargo; and that the king should not receive any Rumes or Turks into his kingdom, because they were capital enemies of the Portuguese.

And after this Afonso Dalboquerque dispatched a messenger who had come from Miliquiaz to visit him as long ago as before his arrival at Malaca, and before this one returned, orders were given that he should be taken round to inspect the king's arsenals, which at that time were full of artillery, saddles and horse gear, weapons, and all kinds of munitions and material of war, and all the stables filled with horses, and a general review of all the crossbowmen and musketeers was ordered; there were a great number of these, for every householder of Goa, whether married or single, was obliged to carry a crossbow or musket, not only for the defence of the city, but also in case of the occurrence of any unforeseen event.

And Afonso Dalboquerque likewise commanded that this messenger should inspect Benestarij, which the Turks had built very strongly with ramparts, and see the place where our ships rammed it, and took it by force of arms from the Turks, not dreading in the least the numerous guns which were posted on these ramparts. And Afonso Dalboquerque also desired that he should be taken into the fortress and see the destruction which had been wrought within it, in order that he might tell his lord not to place much confidence in the ramparts of Diu, if the King of Portugal were to command him to take it; and by means of this policy, which Afonso Dalboquerque knew well how to carry out both in peace and war, as long as he was Governor of India, Miliqueaz never felt himself very safe in Diu, although he was very crafty in dissembling this fear.

CHAPTER LIII.

How an ambassador from King Vengapor arrived at Goa, and how the great Dalboquerque bore himself with Roçalcão, and what passed with them.

When Tristão Dega and the ambassadors of the king of Cambaya had set out in one of the ships belonging to Miliqueaz which had come to Goa laden with provisions, the great Afonso Dalboquerque dispatched Gaspar Chanoca to go to Narsinga, for he had been sent thither when the expedition to Malaca was just about to start, and had returned with the answer, bringing back in his company an ambassador from the king of Narsinga with a present for the king D. Manuel, and this ambassador finding that the Portuguese had not returned from Malaca, went back, and this was the reason why Afonso Dalboquerque sent Gaspar Chanoca back again with similar instructions to the king, giving him an account of the siege of Benestarij; and among many other matters which he was to relate to the king there was this, that inasmuch as all the kings of India had granted a site in their harbours for the construction of a strong house wherein the property of the king of Portugal might be preserved, and he was very desirous of being on friendly terms with the king, therefore he ought to grant him such a site in Baticalá; and, in return for this, he would willingly forward all the horses that came to market at Goa to Narsinga, for he would be much more pleased to send them to him than to the Hidalcão; and although Fr. Luis had written to Afonso Dalboquerque not to place much reliance upon this king's friendship, nor to trust in his words, yet, as long as the king of Garçopa was living, Afonso Dalboquerque was content to temporise with him, for the king D. Manuel had frequently sent word to him to strive to keep on good terms with him because he was a Hindoo.

Three days afterwards, there arrived an ambassador from King Vengapor to congratulate Afonso Dalboquerque on his return from Malaca, and his success at Benestarij, and brought for him a present of sixty horse trappings, with their covers and tail pieces, of very beautiful workmanship and finish, with twenty-five saddles with their stirrups and furniture,[1] and sent word to propose to Afonso Dalboquerque that he should be appointed to the government of the

[1] "*Sessenta cubertas de cavallo com suas testeiras, e colas, obra muito bem feita, e acabada, com vinte e cinco sellas com seus estribos e guarnições.*" Cf. "Ephippia, frontalia, phaleras, et tegumenta."—*Osorius*, p. 263.

lands of Goa, and for them he would pay a certain specified rent, and that he might be allowed to take three hundred horses, of which the king was in great need.[1]

Afonso Dalboquerque received the ambassadors with very great kindness, and commanded that the horses which he required should be supplied to him at his own price, and he added many things for the king in return for the present, always making much of him, for besides his seeking after the friendship of the king of Portugal, and offering himself in person, and his forces to aid in the war at Goa against the Turks, his kingdom is a veritable and safe road to Narsinga, and well supplied with provisions, and in it they make caparisons and saddles, and everything required for horses, so that Goa could very well avail herself of all these things whenever need of them should arise.

When this affair was over, Roçalcão, who was waiting quietly in the territories of Goa, on the other side of the river, after the rout of Benestarij, very often sent word to Afonso Dalboquerque that he would be glad to have an interview with him, and it could take place whenever he liked; and when Afonso Dalboquerque excused himself from this, Roçalcão knowing that he was ready to set out from Goa, became more importunate in his requests. Afonso Dalboquerque being wearied with him, and considering that no harm would be done to the treaty of peace, which was being negotiated with the Hidalcão, if they communed together, appointed a meeting in the river of Benestarij, and met

[1] "Rex Vengapor (est autem Vengapor Regio mediterranea, cum Zabaimi regione continens), legatum ad Albuquercium de pace misit. Nomen enim illius per omnes illas terras cum hominum admiratione vagabatur, et multi ob eam causam Regis Emmanuelis imperium sequi volebant, ut in illius tutela constituti, aliorum Principum tyrannidem declinarent......Hoc autem postulabat, ut liceret sibi equos trecentos precio, ut alii faciebant, persoluto, ex urbe singulis annis educere. Fuit huic postulato satisfactum, et legatus honorifice dimissus."—*Osorius*, p. 263. From this it appears that the horses were to be delivered yearly.

him, but nothing passed except compliments made to him by Roçalcão, with expressions of desire of his friendship, and to be at the service of the king of Portugal.

By this interview Afonso Dalboquerque plainly perceived that Roçalcão did not feel himself very safe in the position which he then occupied, and that the Moors, who observed how small a force he had left under him, and how he was out of favour with the Hidalcão, were thinking of raising a quarrel with him; and that it was because he might avail himself of the power of the king of Portugal, for he dreaded lest the Hidalcão should come against him, that he was so desirous of being on friendly terms with the Portuguese.

Therefore Afonso Dalboquerque would not accept the offers of Roçalcão, but treated him with uncertain words, that he might have nothing to complain of, until it could be seen what position the Hidalcão would take up in the treaty of peace. And when the interview was over, Afonso Dalboquerque inquired of Roçalcão for news of the Hidalcão; and he replied that there was a serious dissension in his camp, for the Persians and Coraçones were opposed to the Turks and Rumes because they had put to death Camalcão, one of the chief captains of the court, and the governor of his property, who was by birth a Persian. And so when they had conversed upon these events and others, Afonso Dalboquerque took his leave of Roçalcão and returned to Goa without coming to any agreement with him.[1]

[1] Correa, at p. 324, says that Afonso Dalboquerque excused himself from any interview with Roçalcão, "O gouernador se escusou de fallar com elle, somente lhe mandando palauras d'amizades".

CHAPTER LIV.

Of the arrival of the embassy of the Prestes João at Goa, and of the manner in which he was received; and how the great Afonso Dalboquerque sent him to Portugal, and the rest which took place.

When the great Afonso Dalboquerque reached the city he found therein Estevão de Freitas, who had come back from Dabul with a message for him from D. Garcia de Sousa, in which he notified that at that port there had arrived a ship from Zeila bringing an ambassador from the Prestes João,[1] king of the Abyssinians, to the king of Portugal, and the governors of the land had detained him, and he desired to know what he ought to do, for, as he had received commands to raise the blockade of the port until further orders, he did not dare to meddle with him.

This news very much gratified Afonso Dalboquerque, for the king D. Manuel had often written to him to do his utmost to obtain information concerning the Prestes João and the men whom the king D. João before his death had sent to that country by land.[2] He, therefore, lost no time in sending back Estevão de Freitas in the *fusta* which had brought him, with message to D. Garcia de Sousa that he should send the ambassador to him. And when Garcia de Sousa received this message he sent word to the governors of the land that the man whom they had detained was an envoy from the Prestes João to the king of Portugal, and that the captain-general of India hearing of his arrival had written for him to be sent on, therefore he begged them of their kindness to hand him over for that purpose, and that the matter would not admit of any doubt. The governors, although they had at first determined not to allow this man to go on any further without hearing from the Hidalcão—

[1] See vol. I, chap. liv.

[2] See vol. II, Introduction, p. viii; and chap. xlix.

to whom they had sent word of his arrival—nevertheless, dreading lest Garcia de Sousa should maltreat them, changed their mind and delivered him up. And as soon as Estevão de Freitas had got him into his possession, he hastened the man's preparations for his departure, and supplied him with provisions and everything that he required for his voyage. And as soon as he reached the bar of Goa Afonso Dalboquerque commanded all the *Fidalgoes* and Captains to proceed to meet him in their boats. This ambassador brought with him a piece of the Wood of the True Cross for the king D. Manuel. Afonso Dalboquerque, therefore, went to the beach to receive him, with all the clergy and inhabitants of the city, with crosses in procession, and there they took up the Wood under a canopy to the Cathedral Church, and after all had given great thanks to Our Lord because he had shewn them so desirable a thing as this was, the opening of a road whereby communication could be made with the Prestes João, Afonso Dalboquerque ordered that the ambassador should be entertained and supplied with all necessary things for the expenses of himself, his wife, and a young man and woman of Abyssinia who were in his suite.

The ambassador's name was Mateus; he was a white, and of good bearing, and stated that he was the brother of the Patriarch of Abyssinia. And although our people doubted whether he were really dispatched by the Prestes João or not, and declared that he was a Moor, a spy sent by the Grand Sultan, yet he conversed upon matters of the Faith like a man who had been brought up among Christians.

What an astonishing thing it is that our people should have doubted this man to be a true ambassador from the Prestes João, and decided hastily that he was a Moor, for not small was the fame of the name and power which the King D. Manuel had acquired in those parts of the world; not small was the reputation of the constant war which he was waging with the Moors, that a king so seriously dedicated to Christianity, and so desirous of being in communication with Christians, and within twenty days' sail of India, should never trouble himself to learn what manner of men, and what sort of people Christians were, although he had in his own territories Portuguese whom D. João the Second had sent thither; and that although he had Jerusalem so near to him, whither his own subjects were continually journeying to visit the Holy Sepulchre, they should doubt whether the Warden of [the Friars of the Order of] St. Francis of Mount Sion had sent him a piece of the Wood of the True Cross! These are the works of Satan, who ever seeks to exercise his influence in the quarter where he perceives he can do the greatest injury.

Two days after this, Afonso Dalboquerque commanded that the ambassador should be brought before him; and in the presence of Pero Dalpoem, the secretary, and Alexander de Ataide, the interpreter, enquired of him what route he had taken, and how it was that the Prestes João had sent him in this manner, without sending also with him some of the Portuguese who were in that country, and what message it was that he brought with him for the King of Portugal. The ambassador replied that he had come by way of Zeila, and that only in the same hour in which the Prestes João had summoned him to depart, had he disclosed also to him his route, without giving notice of it to anyone, and had then put into his hands the letters for the King of Portugal without saying anything to him beyond this, that he was to make his way to India, and beg the Captain-General to give him a passage to Portugal; for had he not started on his journey with these precautions, and had it been known in the Court of the Prestes João that he was setting forth with a message for the King of Portugal, in no wise could he have passed through the country of the Moors without great peril. The message which he brought was that the

Prestes João, his Lord, sent word to desire the marriage of his children with those of the King of Portugal, as it were in exchange; and to offer him troops and supplies for the destruction of the House of Méca and the Grand Sultan of Cairo, and all these he would order to be conveyed to, and delivered at, any port of his country, whichever he might select; that the Wood of the True Cross which he brought was sent to the king by the Warden of Jerusalem, with whom he was in friendly communication; and all these matters which he had asserted could be proved to be true by the letters.

Afonso Dalboquerque declared that it was not his custom to open letters which were directed to the king of Portugal, nor to make trial of the ambassadors who were on their way to him; but he would dispatch him on his journey immediately, so that he might make the passage in the ships which were just on the point of sailing for Portugal. And in order that this Wood of the True Cross might go with greater ceremony and reverence before the king, Afonso Dalboquerque ordered a casket of gold to be made for its reception. And as he was now very anxious to set out on his journey for the Straits, he sent this ambassador to Jorge de Melo Pereira, captain of Cananor, with orders to grant him a passage in the ship of Bernaldim Freire, or of Francisco Pereira, whichever was best suited for him, and to supply him with everything necessary for his voyage.

But at Cananor the captain and everybody held this ambassador to be a buffoon and a spy sent by the Grand Sultan; therefore, no sooner had Bernaldim Freire, in whose ship he took his passage, set sail, than he received very bad treatment at that captain's hands, and at Mozambique, where the ship watered, he was even put in irons by advice of Francisco Pereira, and they did many other things (thinking thereby to injure Afonso Dalboquerque), which I will not repeat now, because they are dead.[1]

And when they arrived at this kingdom of Portugal, although Bernaldim Freire, with the hopes of justifying what he had done, said a great many terribly bad things against the ambassador, notwithstanding all, the king D. Manuel, in accordance with Afonso Dalboquerque's letters, gave him a very good reception, and always treated him in the manner due to an ambassador. And when the ambassador himself had lodged his complaints with the king concerning the treatment which he had experienced at the hands of Bernaldim Freire and Francisco Pereira, the king ordered that these men should be thrown into prison in Lisbon Castle, and there they remained until the ambassador set out for India, well provided, and in company of D. Rodrigo de Lima, who was sent by the king D. Manuel, as ambassador to the Prestes João. And when Diogo Lopez de Sequeira,[2] Governor of India, was entering the Straits with a fleet, and just going into Maçua,[3] Mateus the ambassador died, but D. Rodrigo proceeded upon his embassy, whereof I do not give any account, because it did not take place in the time of Afonso Dalboquerque. And in these same ships which made their voyage to Portugal that year,

[1] These actions, which are so magnanimously passed over unrecorded by the author of the *Commentaries* are thus clearly described by Correa. "......meterão o embaixador em ferros, e lhe dormirão com as molheres, e esbofetearão e depenarão as barbas, defamando que era truão, falso, e espia do Turqo, que Afonso Dalboquerque que nom o soubera conhecer, e o queria fazer embaixador do Preste com enganos per ElRey por se fazer grandioso," etc.—Page 327.

[2] Diogo Lopez de Sequeira, whose portrait is given, from Goa, by Pedro Barreto de Resende, in Sloan. MS., 197, p. 15, succeeded Lopo Soarez de Aluergaria [the successor of Afonso Dalboquerque] in A.D. 1518, and gave place in 1521 to Dom Duarte de Menezes. For some biographical memoranda of this governor the reader is referred to the above MS., and vol. ii, pp. 31, 45.

[3] *Maçua*, on the African side; see Map, vol. i, p. 80.

BRIT. MUS., SLOANE MS. 197, FOLIO 15.

P. Barretto de Resende's Portrait of

DIOGO LOPES DE SIQUEYRA.

there came an ambassador from the king of Ormuz, of which I will make mention in his place.

CHAPTER LV.

Of the arrival of D. Garcia de Noronha at Cochim; and how, after settling the order in which the vessels were to be arranged, and dispatching the ships which were to sail to Portugal during that year with their ladings, he set sail for Calicut with all his fleet, and what took place there.

D. Garcia do Noronha having arrived at Cochim, and having given orders to the vessels concerning the cargo which they were to carry that year to Portugal, and arranged those which he was to take with him, set sail for Calicut with all his fleet; and when he got in front of the city harbour, the prince, brother of the Çamorim (who was friendly to us), sent word to say that his brother the Çamorim was desirous of being at peace with the king of Portugal, and would be happy to grant a site in Calicut for the erection of a fortress, and would pay him tribute. Nevertheless, on account of the delays and artifices which had been practised upon Simão Rangel, D. Garcia would not give any reply to the proposals, but went on with the war, and blockaded the coast in such a manner that not one ship of all those which were ready laden to sail for the Straits ventured out; and there he remained during the whole of the month of January, until Afonso Dalboquerque wrote to him to quit the coast and come away, disclosing to him secretly how he intended to sail into the Straits of the Red Sea, whereby they would be more certainly enabled to capture those ships with all their goods than at Calicut.

As soon as D. Garcia received this intelligence from his uncle he quitted the coast and proceeded to Cochim, and prepared all the ships which were already repaired, and set sail with them, and reached Goa on the tenth of February, and gave an account to Afonso Dalboquerque of all that had passed with the Çamorim, and declared how, at the last moment, the prince of Calicut had written him a letter wherein he stated that the Çamorim was sorry that he had not come to terms of peace with him, and was now willing to grant him the site he had requested for the erection of the fortress, but up to the present time he had not so granted it, because the Moors who were settled in Cairo had prevented him; and he had not carried on the matter any further because of his recall.

At the receipt of this information, Afonso Dalboquerque waited at Goa for four or five days, and dispatched Francisco Nogueira with instructions (for it was the will of the king D. Manuel that if a fortress were built in Calicut he was to become the captain of it, and Gonçalo Mendez was to be the factor), that both these should go and conclude this business, because of his earnest desire to set his foot in Calicut. And Afonso Dalboquerque further commanded them on no account to accept any site for the fortress unless it were within the reef in front of their landing pier, in the harbour pool; and gave him letters for the captains and officials of Cochim and Cananor containing orders for them to contribute everything that was required for the work.

Francisco Nogueira having thus taken his leave of Afonso Dalboquerque set sail for Cochim to make his preparations, and delivered his letters to the captain and the king's officers; and from that port he sailed for Calicut to set to work about the construction of the fortress in accordance with the instructions which he had received from Afonso Dalboquerque. But when the Çamorim knew that Afonso Dalboquerque had sailed away from Goa, and that there was not sufficiently strong a fleet left on the coast to prevent ten ships from setting forth laden with pepper for the Straits, he temporised with Francisco Nogueira and lengthened out the negotiations with complimentary communications. And Francisco, finding he was deceived by the Çamorim, returned at length to Goa, and remained there, waiting for the return of Afonso Dalboquerque; and, after he had set sail, the Moorish ships which had their cargoes on board ventured out and began their voyage, but when they had gone so far on their course as the latitude of Çacotorá towards Cape Guardafum, a squall struck them, of so tempestuous a character, that some foundered, and others ran before it and tried to put in to some of the ports of Cambaya as far back as Dabul. And when Afonso Dalboquerque came from the Straits, cruising along that coast, he captured them all, and took them into Goa; and at the loss of these ships the merchant Moors of Calicut were utterly ruined.

CHAPTER LVI.

How the great Afonso Dalboquerque gave an account to the captains and officers of the King concerning the letter which the King had written to him respecting the surrender of Goa to the Hidalcão, and what was agreed to in this behalf.

When these affairs were over, the great Afonso Dalboquerque ordered an assembly of all the Captains, and certain of those *Fidalgoes* who were more anciently connected with India, and the king's officers, and to each one separately he caused an oath upon the Holy Evangelists to be administered, that they would not divulge to anyone that which he desired to unfold to them; then he declared to them how some days ago he had received from the King D. Manuel a letter ordering him to discuss with them whether it were to the good of his service that Goa should be maintained or not, but as a heavy press of business had occupied his attention ever since the arrival of the letter, he had not given them any account of it, nor of certain articles, sent to him also, which, in his opinion, were the work of Gaspar Pereira, Lourenço Moreno, Antonio Real, and Diogo Pereira, for he had long ago observed that they, not being pleased with the war, were engaged in these underhand tricks and conspiracies; and, inasmuch as he was of opinion that it would be very prejudicial to the estate and credit of the king to hold a public council over this matter, he had thought right to hold it in such a manner as would be least injurious to the king's service, and therefore he begged them of their goodwill to inspect the articles—which he there and then laid before them—and to write to His Highness what their opinions were concerning this matter, in order that he might send back their answers in the ships which were just about to start on the voyage to Portugal.

Letter from the great Afonso Dalboquerque to the King of Portugal concerning the maintenance of Portuguese power in Goa.

"Sire, I captured Goa, because your Highness ordered me to do so, and the Marshal[1] had orders to take it in his instructions; I took it also because it was the headquarters of the league which was set on foot in order to cast us out of India; and if the fleet which the Turks had prepared in Goa river (with a large force of men, artillery, and arms, specially assembled for this object) had pushed forward, and the fleet of the Rumes had come at this juncture, as they had expected, without doubt I should have been utterly discomfited; yea, even if ever so great a fleet had come from Portugal they would not have allowed it to make good its arrival in the country. But when once Goa was conquered, everything else was at our command without any further trouble, and when Goa was taken, that one victory alone did more for the advancement of Your Highness' *prestige* than

[1] D. Fernando Coutinho; see vol. II, chap. xiii.

all the fleets which have come to India during the last fifteen years. And if Your Highness, in deference to the opinions of those who have written this advice to you, thinks it possible to secure your dominions in these parts by means of the fortresses of Cochim and Cananor, it is impossible; for, if once Portugal should suffer a reverse at sea, your Indian possessions have not power to hold out a day longer than the kings of the land choose to suffer it; for if one of our men take anything by force from a native, immediately they raise the drawbridge and shut the gates of the fortress; and this causes Your Highness not to be Lord of the Land, as of Goa, for in this territory the injury which is done to Moors or to Portuguese does not reach beyond the Captain of the Fortress. Justice is yours, and yours the arm, yours the sword, and in the hand of your Captain-General reposes the punishment, and before him lies the remedy for the complaint of every one; and if today there be any improvement in regard to the obedience shewn by the natives of the land, it is plainly to be referred to the fact that the taking of Goa keeps India in repose and quiet; and the fact that the island has so frequently been attacked by the Turks, as those who wrote to Your Highness assert, and so valiantly defended by the Portuguese, enhances the credit which the progress of affairs in these parts deserves. And I have so completely disheartened the members of the league against us, that the King of Cambaya, powerful prince as he is, lost no time in sending to me his Ambassadors, and restoring to me all the Cavaliers and *Fidalgoes* who were shipwrecked[1] with D. Afonso de Noronha, my nephew, on their voyage from Çacotorá, without my sending to ask this of him, and even offered me permission to build a fortress in Diu,[2] a matter

[1] See vol. ii, p. 211.

[2] For a coloured plan, and description of the extensive fortifications made by the Portuguese in later times at Diu, see Pedro Barreto de

of such immense importance that even now I can hardly believe it; and I am now importuned by the Çamorim of Calicut, who desires to grant me a site to build a fortress in his city, and is willing to pay a yearly tribute to the Crown. All this is the result of our holding Goa, without my waging war upon any of these princes.

"And I hold it to be free from doubt, that if fortresses be built in Diu and Calicut (as I trust in Our Lord they will be)—when once they have been well fortified, if a thousand of the Sultan's ships were to make their way to India, not one of these places could be brought again under his dominion. But if those of your council understood Indian affairs as I do, they would not fail to be aware that Your Highness cannot be lord over so extensive a territory as India by placing all your power and strength in your marine only (a policy at once doubtful and full of serious inconveniences); for this, and not to build fortresses, is the very thing which the Moors of these lands wish you to do, for they know well that a dominion founded on a navy alone cannot last, and they desire to live on their estates and property, and to carry their spiceries to the ancient and customary markets which they maintain, but they are unwilling to be subject to Your Highness, neither will they trade or be on

Resende's MS., Sloan. 197, ff. 166 *et seq.* Mr. T. W. H. Tolbort, in his paper on "The Portuguese Settlements in India" (*Proc. Asiat. Soc., Bengal*, June 1874, p. 131), says Diú is the most interesting of all the Portuguese settlements after Goa, but the one least known to Englishmen, as it lies so out of the way. The passage from Daman to Diú in a sailing vessel takes, on an average, three or four days. The island of Diú lies to the south of Káthíwár. Its length from east to west is about seven miles; its average width from north to south scarcely a mile. It is separated from the mainland by a narrow arm of the sea, the eastern access to which is easy for ships of considerable burden, while the western access is obstructed by shallows. A portion of the Portuguese territory, including the village of Gogola, lies on the north of the inlet adjoining the mainland. The fortress or citadel of Diú, built by the Portuguese in 1535, a formidable and imposing structure, is at the ex-

friendly terms with you. And if they will not have any of these things, how is it likely that they will be pleased to see us establishing ourselves in this city of Goa, and strengthening its defences, and Your Highness lord of so important a port and bar as this is, and not labour with all their might to hinder us from accomplishing our intentions? And if it seems a hard matter to those who have written about this to Your Highness that the recovery of Goa should have been so many times attempted, how much harder must it have been to gain the country from so powerful a king as the Hidalcão, lord of so many armies, who is not likely to refrain from straining every nerve to recover the possession of it and striking a decisive blow at our *prestige*, if he could do so? And whenever any one of his captains shall come up against this city, are we to surrender it immediately without first of all measuring our forces against him? If this be so, Your Highness may as well leave India to the Moors, and seek to maintain your position therein with such extraordinary outlays and expenses on the navy, in ships as rotten as cork, only kept afloat by four pumps in each of them.

"As for the extraordinary expenses connected with the maintenance of Goa, of which these idle fellows write to

treme east or north-east point of the island. The fortifications are constructed of stone dug in the island, and the town or Praça is intersected by the numerous quarries thus excavated. The stone somewhat resembles the laterite of the Malabar coast, but is darker in colour and much stronger in substance. Three great events have made Diú memorable in the history of Portuguese India:—1. The death of King Bahádur of Cambay, followed by the siege of Diú, in 1537-8. 2. The second siege of Diú, in 1546. 3. The sack of Diú by Arabs from Maskat, in 1668. The two former are amongst the most glorious incidents of Portuguese history, and may be compared to the defence of Arkát or to that of Lakhnau in the history of British India. The third event was a sad contrast to the two former, and, with other contemporary disasters, marked the decadence of Portuguese power. Correa has preserved a sketch of the fortress in his days, about 1561.

Your Highness, the mere dross of India is so great, that if the Portuguese possessions be properly farmed by your officers, the revenue from them alone would suffice to repay a great part of these expenses to which we are put, and if they say that the reason why I desire to keep possession of Goa is because it was I who took it, Your Lordship may rest assured that if I were a Portuguese of such a character as they are, I would be the first, if you ordered me to destroy it, to put the pickaxe into the walls, and to fire the barrel of gunpowder under the keep,[1] if only for the pleasure of seeing the cards of the game of India shuffled for a new deal;[2] but as long as I live, and while it remains my duty to send an account to Your Highness of Indian affairs, Goa must not be dismantled, for I would not that my enemies should exult in the contemplation of any serious disaster to this estate; and I must sustain it at my own cost, until they get their wishes and another Governor be sent to rule over it.

"If this that I say does not agree with the ideas of some of those who are half-hearted about this matter of Goa, Your Highness may know for certain that as yet there is one man who is governing it: and old and weak as I am, I will accept the government of this conquered territory at Your Highness's hands, if it may be permitted me to confer the lands of the Moors upon the Cavaliers and *Fidalgoes* who have assisted me to gain them. But do not require of me every year an account of what I am doing as if I were a taxgatherer, because four ill-mannered fellows, who sit at home like idols in their pagodas, have borne false witness against me; but honour me, and thank me, for I shall be happy to complete this enterprise, and spend what little I have upon it: and, in conclusion, all that I have to say is, that if Your Highness either now or at any other

[1] *Torre de menagem.*

[2] *Por tal que este jogo da India se tornasse a baralha.*

time surrender Goa to the Turks, then plainly Our Lord desires that the Portuguese dominion in India should come to an end;[1] and, as for me, Your Highness may be sure that, so long as I am Governor, although I be put to much trouble, I shall not at any rate send you painted pictures of fictitious places, but rather kingdoms taken by force of arms from their masters, and fortified by me in such a manner that they may give a good account of themselves in all time.

"This is my opinion concerning this question of Goa, which Your Highness commanded me to discuss with its captains and officers."

Articles which the King sent to Afonso Dalboquerque concerning Goa.

"That Goa was very unhealthy, and was the cause of unnecessary expense, of no use except to give trouble to the soldiers.

"That therein there must always be a continued war, for the Hidalcão was so powerful, that he would be sure to try his utmost to recover it, because it was the capital of his dominions.

"That the revenues of the mainland, upon which Afonso Dalboquerque laid great importance, were impossible to be

[1] Compare these sentiments with the peculiar ideas of a writer who has lately visited Goa:—"Portuguese India is, thank Heaven, only a strip of about seventy miles long which they would do much better to sell to the British Government; for of all the God-forgotten, deserted holes, one thousand years behind the rest of Creation, I have never seen anything to equal Goa. Do not let the residents who read this fancy that I am touching them in any way. I only remember them as charming, kindly, gentle, hospitable people, whom I pitied for having to live there. I have lived in sandy deserts, and in primæval forests, and have suffered hunger and thirst, cold and heat, fatigue, privations, and danger, and thought it charming; but I hated the life at Goa. It is *dead*, and nothing rewards one."—*Arabia*, *Egypt*, *India*, by Isabel Burton. London, 1879, p. 300.

collected, except by maintaining a great number of people with heavy expenses for collection of this revenue, because the Hidalcão himself could not collect them without the assistance of a large army.

"That the Hidalcão would be glad to agree to any proposal, and become tributary to His Highness, provided that Goa were restored to him."

After all had examined these articles, they wrote to the king that they were amazed at His Highness desiring to surrender, in pursuance of the advice of men who had never donned a suit of armour for the sake of experiencing the trouble it would involve, a place so commodious and so important to his cause as Goa, which had been acquired at the cost of so much Portuguese blood. When the king read the letter of Afonso Dalboquerque, and the opinion of the captains, he wrote in reply that he considered it of great importance to retain Goa, and thanked him very much for the way in which he had conducted this matter. And as soon as the Turks had been cast out of Benestarij, a feeling of relief gradually came over Goa, and the city began to flourish, and those who had written to the king advising its demolition became very much ashamed of ever having written such a thing. And it was on this account that Afonso Dalboquerque often used to say that he deserved more thanks from the King D. Manuel for defending Goa for him against the Portuguese, than he did for capturing it on two occasions from the Turks.

END OF THE THIRD PART.

APPENDIX.

DESCRIPTION OF MALACCA, FROM PEDRO BARRETTO DE RESENDE'S "LIVRO DO ESTADO DA INDIA ORIENTAL".

Sloane Manuscript, 197.

MALLAQUA.

DESCRIPSAM DA FORTALLEZA DE MALLAQUA.

A FORTALLEZA de Mallaqua esta plantada na costa oriental F. 383.
de Iuntana entre ho rio Panagim, e Muar em altura de dous graos e vinte menutos da Banda do Norte foy conquistada e fundada pello insigne Afonso de Albuquerque em quinze de Agosto de mil quinhẽtos e onze esta oje feyta Çidade que tem a fortalleza dentro, e a Çidade sercada de hum muro de pedra e cal de altura de vinte pés e a largura comessa embayxo em doze e arremata emsima em sete palmos. Tem seis balluartes em que entra ho que chamã Courassa cada hum chamado com o nome que nelles estam escritos. Todos os muros com seus parapeytos; e cada balluarte tem de prassa vinte passos. E o que chamã Madre de D[eo]s a tem dobrada de man[ei]ra que apenas pode ser defendido e lauado dos mais Balluartes: o sircuyto de todo este muro he de quinhentos e doze passos entrando tambem hõ lugar que ocupam os Balluartes: do Balluarte do Ospital athe Sam Domingos ha contramuro e do de Sanctiago athe Madre de Deos com entulho no meo ficando tudo de largura de catorze palmos, a artilharia que ha nestes Balluartes sam quarenta e huma pessas de doze athe quarenta e quatro liuras de pillouro de ferro. Todas sam de bronze, tirado noue que sam de ferro pera a qual hâ bastante poluora

e monisõis nos almazeis de sua Mag^{de}., destas, estam lansadas no chã doze das grossas, sem repayros dedicadas pera ho forte da ilha das naos que se esta fazendo, e tambem estam algumas das outras pessas rebentadas =

Os cazados branquos que hâ nesta Çidade sam duzentos sinquenta, os quaes teram dous mil negros catiuos de diferentes nasõis, que todos sam de armas, e as tem bastantes pera elles: porque raro he ho cazado que nam tem seu cabide de lansas, e sete, oyto, e des mosquetes ou espingardas de pederneyra com monisõis bastantes para ellas: porem destes duzentos e sinquenta cazados branquos, os çento viuem da outra bando do rio que chamã a banda de Mallaqua. A respeyto de ho piqueno sircuyto qua fica dentro nos muros estárem tres Conuentos que ho ocupam quazi todo; o de Sam Paulo, Sam Domingos, e Sancto Agostinho e viuem os ditos cazados em cazas de palha arriscados a hum jnsendio = He esta banda muy fresca de pumares, e ortas de diuersos fruytos = Viuem fora de Mallaqua muytos cazados Christãos da terra todos muy boa gente de armas e as tem de toda sorte particullarmente espingardas porque tirã com ellas muyto bem. Estes em toda ocaziã de gerra sam muy prestes e dellegentes: os mais delles andã buscando sua vida: sam tam arriscados que por muy pouco dão com hum cris pella barriga ferida que tem pouco, ou nenhuma cura porque alem de serem estas armas pella mayor parte de pessonha, o modo de seu feytio acollebrinado mostra bem o dano que fara, alem de que a pesonha basta so tirar sange para matar.

A fortalleza que esta dentro nesta Çidade onde viue o Capitam he huma torre de sinquo sobrados, e no segundo viue o Capitã em huma caza de quadro como ho he a torre que tem cada pano de parede vinte passos. Nos outros
F. 383b. agazalha o Capitã ospedes e se tem a poluora. No primeiro se guardauã quatro mil candĩs de arroz que agora nã hâ. Tem huma serca de muro da mesma altura do da çidade e largura.

Ao liuel do segundo sobrado da torre vã correndo humas cazas onde se agazalha a famillia do dito capitã. Nã hâ aquy artilharia mais que a referida que fica nos Balluartes = =. Tem esta Çidade a renda do hum por sento aplicada pera as obras da fortificassã, que no tocante hâs do muro estam ja acabadas. O Rey da terra dentro onde esta esta fortaleza de Mallaqua he ho Rey de Jor e Pam, e grande amigo dos Portuguezes, he senhor de mais de çem legoas de costa, e nã se estende muyto pella terra dentro; no mar he tãbem senhor de hũa corda de ilhas que hâ neste destrito a mayor parte dellas abitadas; a gente sam Malayos, a ley que professã he de Mouros o poder que tem hê de athe doze mil homẽs de armas, e brigã com artilharia, mosquetes, azagayas, paos tostados que chamã salligas, espadas, rodelas, arcos, e frechas: crises de que se tem feyto mensã, e sompitas que sã hũas frechas piqueninas de pessonha que metem em zaruatanas e tiram com asopro cõ ellas e basta tirarẽ sangue para matarem loguo: Christandade nã hâ nas suas terras. E pello Rio asima de Mallaqua tem os cazados della muytos e muy frescas ortas cõ muyta diuersidade de fruytas que has hâ nesta terra muy boas alem de toda a sorte das que se dam na India muytas outras; e he muyto para notar que com esta cidade estar quazi debayxo da linha he de ares muy sadia e de aquas exsellentes, e muy fresca e fertil de tudo ho que lhe semeã: onde choue quazi todos os dias e noytes= Tem os cazados de Mallaqua muytas legoas de terra de que sã senhores. De huma banda athe o Cabo Rachado e da outra athe o Rio Fermozo, e tambem muytas legoas pella sertã, porem tudo despouoado sem quem ho cultiue, sendo terras muy fertĩs e que derã muyto arroz= Confina pella terra dentro cõ hos Manamcabos Mouros de huma terra que chamã Rindo, vassallos delRey de Pã, e junto delles estam sinquo ou seis mil tambem dos mesmos Mouros Manancabos, vassallos de sua Mag[de]. que tem hum Portugues cazado em Mallaqua que hos go-

uerna, que chamã Tamungam, offissio que da ho Vizorrey: a este obedessem: e morrendo algummo Mouro destes sem filhos erda-o este Tamungam, e tendo-os se conserta cõ elles: de todas as couzas que julga tem des por çento. Oje serue hum Portugues em vida este offissio= Laurã estes Mouros grandes terras de que se sustentã e particullarmente com muyto betre: comprã Callaym aos da terra dentro que vem trazer a Mallaqua= O Rio desta Çidade e porto de Mallaqua he de agoa dosse de hum tiro de pedra de largura: de bayxamar tem ho canal da barra palmo e meo de agoa e em conjunsã de agoas viuas so quatro dedos que apenas cobre a vaza de que he o fundo= e de preamar em agoas viuas huma brasa e quatro palmos; e em mortas de sinquo para seis palmos, e logo pouqua distansia pera sima vay estreytando e tem quatro e tres brassas e em partes o
F. 384. seu fundo sera de huma sem faltar em vazantes nem enchentes de mare: Tem muytos lagartos grandes e carniseyros por cuja cauza e ser de vaza se nam vadea= Por este Rio e terra dentro ha muytas ortas assỹ de cazados Portuguezes como dos da terra em que viuem com suas famillias laurando as terras cõ grande proveyto= ha muytos tigres que antigamente erã muy carniseyros e depois que hum bispo os excomungou ho nã sam tanto: Todos estes cazados tem suas armas= Mea legoa pollo Rio asima se atrauessa de noyte ho mesmo Rio cõ hum pao prezo em huma cadea e fechado cõ hum cadeado ao pee de huma guarita onde asiste hum Portugues que a Çidade proue e lhe paga cada mes seis cruzados por não leuarem nem trazerem fazenda defeza has naos grandes que ficã aynda ao mar da ilha das naos: a cujo respeyto se tem mandado fazer hum forte nesta ilha, a qual esta nã bem de fronte da Çidade senã hum pouco perabayxo distansia de mil e quinhentos passos da Çidade, e o canal que vay pello meo he piqueno, e nã capas de embarcasõis grandes, de bayxamar fica cõ muy pouca agoa e fundo de vaza:—Tambem fica outra restinga de area mais ao

mar e entre ella e a ilha hâ canal de seis brassas a ilha he mais cõprida que larga ves e mea: tera em roda sessenta brassas quazi da figura de huma ferradura de cauallo. Tem hum outeyro leuantado montuoso quatro pera sinquo brassas = O forte que se fas aquy pera que ja estã feytos aliserses he couza piquena de trinta passos de prassa em quadro pera que esta separada a dita artilharia: o effeyto pera que se fas he para defender as embarcasõis grandes que nã podem estar a sombra da artilharia da fortalleza e nã tem oje mais que hos aliserses ficandose ajuntando todos os materiais em Mallaqua pera se acabar todo de huma ves: porque indo se fazendo pouco a pouquo o pode vir senhorear o enemigo e huma ves ocupado por elle sera de grande detrimento a Mallaqua = = =

A ponte que se mostra na planta tem dous pegõis cada hum de dous brassas e mea de altura, e de outro tanto de comprido e cõ muy pouca largura cõ que se nã pode cuydar hos que algũs praticauã de serem estes pegõis couza donde se pudesse offender a Mallaqua: a ponte que esta em sima delles he de madeyros grandes e fortes que cadaues que se quizer cortar se pode fazer = = dos soldados do prezidio se tiram todos os annos sinquenta athe sesenta pera andarem embarcados em tres, quatro, athe sinquo jaleas que andam de armada nesta costa sayndo em Mayo a Pulopinã ou aonde se determina, a esperar os couzas de Goa para auisar aonde estã os enemigos, e ajudar o liurar: e em setembro a Junsalã a esperar as de Negapatam, sam Thome, e tambem de Goa: e em dezembro ao estreyto de Sincapura a esperar as da China, e Manilla pera ho mesmo fim = Ao Capitam Mor se da huma ajuda de custo de çem cruzados: e nam se da aos soldados e capitãis das jalleas por se embarcarem quartel nenhum senã so se-lhe-pagam os mantimentos comque todos se dam por satisfeytos = e sam as capitanias das jalleas muy cobissadas e pretendidas porque susede muytas vezes nas muytas perdisõis que hos Olandezes cauzam has

nossas embarcasõis que vã de todas as partes leuarem as
F. 384b. jaleas o melhor e ho pior hê que sem ho tornarem a seus donos, o que susede particullarmente no que vem da China pella muyta vallia do que saluam que he ouro, sedas, e almiscar: e tambem se nam pode negar que saluã estas jaleas muytas embarcasõis e fazendas: mas conuem muyto andarem em pessoas muy desynteressadas, ou ao menos de boa consiensia que tam raramente se acha em soldados = Os mais gastos que fazem as jalleas sam de marinheyros porque trazem de sinquenta pera sima a respeyto de remarem vinte e tres por banda, hum mais ou menos, a fora os dous que gouernam a popa e proa, leuando tãobem algũs de sobreselente pellosque podem adoeser ou cansar, dasse a cada marinheyro huma para de arros que he pouco mais de hum alqueyre cada mes e hum cruzado de quatroçentos e sesenta rés todo o tempo que andam embarcados = e como huma jalea destas he de sinquoenta palmos de comprido pouco mais ou menos = e de menos de sinquo de largo, e quatro de altura de pontal, remada cõ quarenta e seis remos, fica a mais ligeyra embarcassã que anda no mar; que para auisos, socorros, e se poderem desuiar dos enemigos, seruem muy bem; e quantas mais ouverã milhor seruisso fizeram = Mandã se tambem algumas outras embarcasõis de Mallaqua com algũs auizos como Bantĩs muyto mais piquenos que jallêas que nam fazem gasto mais que ho dos marinheyros que fica dito e os mantimentos dos soldados que como em terra lhos pagã tam poucas vezes se embarcã por elles com muyta vontade; porque tambem quando as vezes se vam a alguma parte como a Pera e outros portos guanhar hum quartel dos mercadores, nem por isso sam lansados do presidio, nem deyxa de se-lhes-dar a sua paga, senam se entretanto la andã Iefes; porque de outra sorte nenhum soldado aturara na fortaleza com tam poucas pagas delRey sendo huma terra tam cara: e antes se pode estranhar auer aynda assỹ soldados que asistam nella = = =.

Huma couza se pode referir das molheres cazadas desta terra de grande louuor, e hê que nenhuma pede a seu marido nada pera ho gasto de sua caza que he ho conduto; porque ellas por sy ho buscam com couzas que fazem pera comer, que sam as estallagẽis que hâ nesta Çidade o que de ordinario andam suas escrauas vendendo pellas ruas = e logo desde pequeninas as vã suas mãnis criando neste exersisio de maneyra que nã ha filha nenhuma em caza de seu pay que nam tenha seu cabedal tambem separado pera isto: e assỹ quando na India se nã resseam tanto filhas a respeyto de hos homẽs andarem muy desemparados e se acomodarẽ com muy poucos dotes pessoas muy benemeritas; Tem este Vzo mayor forsa nesta terra pellas rezõis apontadas = = =.

As fazendas que hâ nesta fortalleza de Mallaqua quanto has que produze a terra sam muy poucas; e muytas as que vem de fora. As que ha na terra sam a prinsipal Callaym algumas pedras bazares e de porquoespim aguilla braua. O que tudo vem da terra dentro, e algum japam que he hum pao vermelho pera tintas pouquo menos que ho do Brazil; e vem lhe todas as drogas do sul e fazendas da China e tambem as roupas de Çambaya e costa de Choramandel e ahy as hiã buscar todas as nasõis do sul a troco de fazendas que traziã com que ficaua sendo o comersio muy grande, e nã menos os rendimentos o que esta quazi de todo extinto: porque nenhumas ou raras sam as nasõis que F. 385.
vem a Mallaqua a buscar nada: tendo tudo o que ha mister nos olandezes = mas aynda cõ este pouco se fazem viagẽis para muytas partes de Mallaqua = As prinsipais sam para a China, Manilla, CochimChina = e as de menos porte sam para Patane, como Sião esta oje de gerra: e quando nã, se nauega muy ordinariamente pera Camboja, Champa e pera todas estas partes se nauega pera o sul que comessa a ventar em Mallaqua de vinte da Abril athe todo Agosto: o que se leua pera estas partes he ho seguinte = Para Patane roupas assy de Cambaya como de toda a costa de Chora-

mandel que sejam a seu modo porque cada nassã do sul tem seu modo de roupas = e de Patane se trazem pataquas, algum ouro, boas pedras bazares, arros, carnes, legumes, asucar preto de cana, azeytes, e todo o genero de mantimentos, has milhores gallinhas e capõis de todo o sul.

Este reyno de Patane nã se gouerna senã por molher por costume muy antigo: Esta çento e sinquoenta legoas de Mallaqua por Costa e assỹ se pode vir por ella sem mousã de norte: particullarmente em balôs que sam como nauios darmada nã tam compridos mas de mais bojo cõ dous mastros e seus remos com dous lemes que chamã Camudes; e em galles Malayos que sam menores que as nossas Panchelõis que nã sam gales, nem balôs, e mais paressem ballos que gualles, cõ seus remos, e Bantĩs do tamanho de huma Manchua grandemente ligeyros com remos e dous mastros: que sã hos em que mais ordinariamente se nauega na costa de Mallaqua com marinheyros Malayos de Malaqua Christãos que leuam suas espingardas e panellas de poluora =.

De Camboja onde hâ igreja e padres da Companhia, e o Rey muyto amigo dos Portuguezes, e hâ muyta madeyra de Angellim muyto grossa, se tras muyto bom Bejoim amendoado muyta bom lacre de formiga: Muyto arros milhor e mais barato que ho de Bengalla; a mayor parte da gente que aquy asiste sam Japõis Christãos, e Chinas Valhaquos que lansaram de Manilha os Castellanos peresses, ou elles fogirã; e assỹ sam hos mayores enemigos que temos: ha tãbem neste reyno muyto Callamba e aguilla = Na costa de Champa hâ dous ou tres portos a que vam os Portugueses comersear, leuã boyõis pretos da China, e algum fio de ouro; e resgatã pao preto muyto mayor e milhor que ho de Mosambique: hâ aqui Igreja e Christandade cõ hum padre da Companhia =.

Esta adiante o reyno de Cochim China e antes de entrar em seu porto junto delle esta huma Ilha donde os padres da Companhia tem Christandade que se chama Pullo Cambim: e entrando no dito porto tem nelle os ditos padres Igreja e Christandade.

Alem da dita Ilha = hâ dous portos neste reyno onde comerseã os portuguezes: hum em que esta O Rey: e outro que chamã Turam. Tem muyto milhor a colheyta que nenhum outro; leuã se pera estes portos muytas roupas de sua sorte (oje esta o contrato por la quebrado pellas forsas do Capitã de Mallaqua, e assÿ nam se vay la senã da China). Vem do dito reyno alguma calamba, e muyta aguilla, muyta cantidade de cobre que trazem Malayos e Japõis = =. As mais breues viagẽis que se fazẽ de Mallaqua sam pera Pam F. 385b.
que he hum porto oytenta legoas de Mallaqua do dito Rey muyto amigo dos Portuguezes que ho he tambem de Jor e das ilhas maritimas = a este porto nauegam de Malaqua todos sem proybesã, leuã lhe roupas e anfiam, e de la trazem ouro em poo da mesma terra e em moeda, pedras Bazares, e de porquoespim, muyto arros, aguilla da costa, e algumas drogas que hos naturais do sul lhe trazem per nam querer vir a Malaqua =. Ha na mesma terra mais dous rios do mesmo Rey: onde se vay comersear e selleua e tras o mesmo = de fronte ao mar esta a Ilha de Pulo Timã piquena montuoza, e muyto pouoada de Malayos: hâ nella muyta Cassa de pombos: hũs animais como corsas muyto bõns e gordos que chama Palandos: muyto bom peyxe fresco: ribeyras de agoa exsellente; muytos figos; e breu = o fundo junto della he de Vinte e sinquo brassas da banda de terra = da ponta da Romania pera dentro esta o porto de Jor que ja se vay pouoando outra ves, em que se fazem oje muytos galles e outras embarcasõis: hâ nelle muyto mantimento, aguilla, e breu =.

Da outra banda naquella corda das ilhas de Bintam = esta a çidade de Bintam outra ves pouoada de nouo cõ muyta gente e muytas fortificasõis por amor de Achem. Deste Rey de Jor e Pam ha outras Ilhas per aquy pouoadas, de pouca considerasã, e nellas mesmas junto ao estreyto de

Sincapura esta o porto de Bullã muyto pouoado de Malayos, frequentado sobre maneyra de muytos mercadores de todo sul onde vem vender suas drogas de que rezulta grande rendimento a ElRey de Pam, o que fazem sem vir a Mallaqua pellas grandes tiranias que hos capitãis daquella fortalleza vzam com elles em lhe tomarem as fazendas por presso muy ynferior ao que corre na terra e assỹ lhe fazerem tãobem leuar a sua moeda muy ordinaria em todas as çidades e fortallezas deste estado e que as tem chegado a igual mizeria de que hos mesmos Olandezes; e hê tanto assỹ em Mallaqua que hos Christaos que vã a estes portos resgatar algumas destas fazendas lhas toma o Capitam por perdidas cõ muytas afrontas: e algũs porisso as metem de noyte em caza e auizã ao Veedor da fazenda para pagarẽ os direytos, cauza poronde se desencaminhã muytas = = =.

Da outra banda desta Ilha na costa da Samatra esta ho porto de Yambe Rio caudallozo, fundo e de apressada corrente, onde os Olandezes sam muy ressebidos e tem sua feytoria e resgatam gram copia de pimenta = Logo mais para Mallaqua pouqua distãsia deste porto esta o grande Rio Andregy donde tambem tiram os Olandezes gram copia de pimenta = ha mais outros Rios em que hâ escalla de pimenta, e aguilla em que se nã falla particullarmente por ser de pouca cõsiderassã = = Junto ha Ilha de Sâbam que esta mais pera Mallaqua esta o porto de Siaca tambem de Malayos onde todas as Luas nouas e cheas ha grandes feyras de todas as couzas do sul, ouro, pedras de presso, e Bazares, Aguilla, Calamba, e outras muytas couzas, e mantimentos = deste porto por hum Rio que vem sayr de fronte de Malaqua esta a boca de Bancalles na Samatra da outra
F. 386. banda de Mallaqua aonde ha todas as Luas a mesma feyra que alem das couzas referidas tem muyta carne de porquo fresca e salgada; e de hũas ouas de peyxe sauel que chamã Trubo de que ha em Mallaqua grande expediente pera todas as partes, Esta aquy na boca de Bancalles o rio

das galles de que de tudo he senhor ElRey da Pã que foy sempre emperador do sul. O estreyto de Sinquapura em que atras fallamos que he onde os Olandezes vem esperar as embarcasõis dos Portuguezes que vem da China, Manilla, Macassa e de todo o Archipellago de Maluco tem muytos canais e tam estreytos que em partes vam as embarcasõis tocando cõ as vergas nos aruores da terra onde as correntes das mares sam grandissimas: a agoa posto que funda muyto clara de maneyra que vem as peyxes andar nella os quais os mercadores que vam nas embarcasõis comprã aos Salletes que são os que abitam este estreyto yndo o peyxe nadando na agoa, e elles o vendem, e vam logo em ballõis muyto lygeyros em que viuem cõ suas famillias e fisgã ho peyxe e o trazem. Sam este Saletes gente pessima e particullarmente contra os Portuguezes; sã velhacos e traydores as mayores espias que tem hos Olandezes porque onde quer que esteja a nossa embarcassã das muytas paragẽis que aly hâ dam logo auizo aos Olandezes e os leuã e encaminhã a ella: de sorte que tem cauzado as mais das perdesõis das nossas frotas; e isto respeyto de os Olandezes lhe-darem grandes datos de tudo ho que assỹ apanhã. E assỹ conuem muyto que as nossas armadas de jaleas e nauios que vam a estes estreytos esperar as ditas frotas fassam toda a gerra possiuel a estes Salletes para os enxotar destas paragẽis ==.

As viagẽis de mais importansia que se fazem de Mallaqua sam como fica dito pera a China, aonde se leuauam de Mallaqua todas as drogas do sul; que ja oje nã vam mais que alguma pimenta e pouco ou nenhum crauo que a nos, e massa, esta em poder dos Olandezes: sendo senhores das Ilhas de Banda de donde deytarã hos proprios naturais que andã vagamundos por todo o sul dezeijando alguma ocaziam pera se vingarem e recuperarem suas terras == O mais que leuam pera a China he ho que lhe vay da India, e juntamente pera Manilla ho que se tras de la ja fica dito == He regimento de Mallaqua que nenhuma embarcasã que venha da Banda do dito estreyto passe sem tomar Mallaqua e fazer aly direytos de tudo ho que trouxer de que pagã des por çento, e dous a Çidade pera forteficassam e artilharia: ė ja ouue algumas que passando sem tomarem esta fortalleza forã julgadas por perdidas ==.

Fas-se tambem viagem de Mallaca pera o Macasa que he huma Ilha que esta trezentas legoas de Mallaqua ao Veste, de hum Rey Mouro que sabe muy bem fallar Portugues, e tem muytos em suas terras e hê grande seu amigo, o que lhe leuam nã sã mais que roupas; e se trazem as drogas que aly vem vender os naturais do sul, tendo a terra em sý muyto mantimento, e tartaruga, e daquy he de que prinsipalmente se proue Malluquo; para esta Ilha se fas tambem viagem de todo ho estado: ha nella Igrejas cõ padres que administrã os sacramentos aos Portuguezes que aly asistem e vam e vem= Tem este Rey prometido de nã dar porto em sua terra a Olandezes como foy e assỹ tem em sua terra Denamarcos, e Ingrezes= Sendo este Rey e todo seu
F. 386b. reyno gentios mandou pedir a Mallaqua hum padre para lhe mostrar o que era a ley dos Christaos porque se lhe paresesse bem a tomaria: dizem que tardou em yr mais do que premetia couza tam ymportante= e assỹ quando tinha chegado primeyro hum marinheyro de hum pataxo que chamauã Lucar Mouro que lhe ensinou a sua ley e lhe pareseo tam bem que logo a tomou ==.

De Mallaqua a Pera sam quarenta legoas por costa pera a banda de Leste foy este Rey vassallo de Sua Magde muytos annos, e pagaua de pareas hum grande cantidade de callaym ha tres annos que lhe negou as pareas a que responde que ho liurem do Achem e que entã pagara ás pareas e sera vassallo de Sua Magde porque com as muytas armadas cõ que ho Achem anda de ordinario nestes mares da de ordinario nas terras deste Rey ho destroe, e lhe catiua sua gente de maneyra que responde ho Rey que muyto bem conhesse de quanta mais ymportansia lhe sera ser sogeyto a Sua Magde do que ao Achem: mas que nam tem poder pera rezistir a este tirano, e a muyta forsa que tem, e nã lha dando Sua Mag.de forsado ha de procurar ho remedio de seus reynos com se-lhe-auasallar e pagar as pareas que pagaua a Sua Mag.de E aynda assỹ teue com que rezester a hũa armada nossa que ho hia castigar = Tem em seus reynos grandes minas de Callaym que he ho metal que fica dito de sorte que sayrã dellas todos os annos de sinquo para seis mil quintais de Callaym; os quais antigamente vinham todos os mais delles pera Mallaqua e oje nam vem a tersa parte ho mäis vam pera ho Achem donde os Olandezes o leuam, e o trazem para a India cõ grandes ganhos =.

A feytoria que ho capitam de Mallaqua tinha em Pera era donde tiraua o mayor ynteresse que oje nã hâ: e por estas e outras couzas descahio tanto esta fortalleza e capitania, que nã ouue prouido que quizese entrar nella no anno de seisçentos trinta e tres: e assỹ foy entrar hum capitam mandado pello Visorrey.

DESCRIPTION OF THE ISLAND OF GOA, FROM PEDRO BARRETTO DE RESENDE'S "LIVRO DO ESTADO DA INDIA ORIENTAL".

Sloane Manuscript, 197.

ILHA DE GOA.

DESCRIPSAM DE ILHA DE GOA E TODAS SUAS ANEXAS.

F. 219. ILHA DE GOA Metropolly e cabessa de todo ho estado da India de que Sua Mag^{de}. he senhor esta em altura de quinze graos e quarenta e sinquo menutos. Tem de comprimento duas legoas de sircuyto e de largura huma e em partes pouco mais. Esta pegada cõ a terra firme do Concam do Ballagatte he muy fresca e chea de muytas ortas e palmares com agoas muy boas e comerseada de todo oriente, porque como cabessa concorrem a ella por mar e terra todas suas fazendas e riquezas, e della se espalham por todo o mundo. E antes que entremos em dar mais particullar rezã desta Ilha e Çidade de Goa sera bem que ho fassamos dos fortes passos com que na sua entrada e por toda ella esta forteficada :—

DESCRIPSAM DO FORTE DE NOSSA S[ENH]ORA DO CABO.

Entrando pella ponta de Nossa Senhora do Cabo pera dentro da barra de Goa se a de afastar alguma couza da dita ponta porque lansa ao mar huma restinga de pedras cuberta de agoa pouco mais de mea legoa, fica da banda do sul o outeyro aonde esta a Igreja de Nossa Senhora do Cabo no mais alto delle, de frades Capuchos Recoletos o qual esta leuantado da superfisie do orizonte setenta brassas ficando a dita Igreja em hum terreyro de sinquoenta de roda na qual ha tres sisternas que leuam trinta mil pipas de agoa ;—fica afastado da rais do outeyro pera sima da banda do mar distansia de vinte brassas hum forte pera onde se vay por huma estrada cuberta que comessa em huma calheta que fica detras do mesmo monte da banda de dentro, de mil passos de comprido athe chegar a huma porta do dito forte por onde se entra a hũa plataforma de çem passos de comprimento e vinte sinquo de largura sercada pella banda do mar de hum parapeyto de seis palmos de altura com seis lugares para outrastantas bombardas: e pella do monte que lhe fica muyto alto e sobranseyro tem hũas sete cazas de sobrado cubertas de terrados bastantes pera viuer nella qualquer pessoa que possa seruir de capitam = E embayxo tem no andar da dita prassa doze cazas em que podem viuer soldados piãis, e bombardeyros: e nemhumas das ditas cazas està aynda de todo acabadas = Nam asiste neste forte que chamã "Nossa Senhora do Cabo" Capitam nem soldado algum, e so tem hum negro que ho vigia: e tem na ditta plataforma quatro pessas de bronze em seus repayros de quinze athe vinte libras de pillouro de ferro = E como a vigia dos frades emsima he continua tem no dito Conuento monisõis bastantes pera as ditas quatro pessas de artilharia.

Auisam de qualquer couza que paresse ao mar pera se F. 249b.
prouer logo de capitam bombardeyros e gente como se faz porem nam deyxa de estar este forte offeressido a se arroynar com a muyta agoa que pello ynuerno desse do dito monte que fica arroynando as paredes das ditas cazas.

* * * * *

FORTALLEZA DE PANGIM.

Pello Rio asima hum quarto de legoa do forte de Guaspar Dias esta o Castello de Pangim no qual se fizerã apozentos pera os Visorreis estarem quando vam a barra despedir as armadas e naos do reyno por ficarem mais perto e quando he nesesario em qualquer ocaziã de enemigos estarẽ mais perto da barra = Estam feytos apozentos a borda do Rio e cazas muy bastantes e hum cais onde desembarcã pera as mesmas cazas e posto que ElRey quando se fizerã na era de

seis çentos e quinze se ouue por mal seruido e mandaua que
as pagasse o Visorrey dom Jer[ony]mo de Azeuedo = despois
o ouue por bem paressendo huma das melhores couzas que
tinha o estado como de feyto o hê aonde quando os Visorreis
la nã estã, tem a Çidade hum homem Portugues por ter cuy-
dado das ditas cazas e conserto dellas a que pagã seis X.es
cada mes = Estam em Pangim obra de trinta cazas entre
terreas e de Sobrado algũas muyto grandes e fermozas de
Portugueses de Goa e outras dos que fazem aly sua abitassã
de que tambem parte estã ao longo do Rio cõ ortas e pal-
mares de recreasam e rendimento e assỹ vã continuando
algumas cazas athe Sancta Inis que esta mais pera a barra
e dahy athe Nossa Senhora do Cabo aonde estã oyto cazas
assỹ de moradores de Goa: como de algũs velhos ermitõis
Treseyros da Ordem de Sam Françisco; que estam e viuem
F. 250. aly retirados a sombra dos Recolletos do dito Conuento =
Ha em Pangim doze ou treze almadias compridas e estreytas
que leuã des e doze remos por banda que seruẽ de leuar
auiso a qualquer parte e prinsipalmente ao norte, e tam-
bem pessoas e fazendas de pouco vollume porque por sua
muyta ligeyreza nauegam sem armadas porque nam vam
sogeytas a paros posto que ja acontesseo tomarem algumas.
O gasto que esta fortalleza de Pangim fas a fazenda real, a
qual nã he mais que hũa torre antigamente alta que oje esta
no meo das cazas em que nã ha artilharia nẽ couza defensa-
vel he o seguinte, etc.

* * * * *

PASSO DE RIBANDAR.

Adiante de Pangim fica huma ponte que a Çidade de
Goa mandou fazer por mandado do Conde de Linhares
Visorrey pera passagem de hum brasso de Rio do caminho
que vay de Goa feyta sobre vinte e oyto arcos de pedra e
F. 250b. cal muyto forte e fermoza: da qual sa vay continuando hum
fermozo cais, ou caminho por meio do Rio de quazi huma

legoa de comprido obra insigne cõ que fica o dito camynho muy fassil pera qualquer ocaziã apressada como ordinariamente acontese o que nam era antigamente antes de se fazer esta obra porque se nam podia yr senã por mar em manchuas que primeyro que se achassem pera qualquer suseso apresado; Era nessessario pera isso muyto tempo; e tambem se ficam cobrando hũs pedassos de varzeas muyto grandes que ho Conde de Linhares Vizorrey aplicou pera sustento do Ospital da Piedade que elle edificou e ynstetuhio.

Esta neste porto e paragem de Ribandar hum passo cõ hum balluarte piqueno de des passos de comprido e seis de largo onde esta somente hum sino de vegia que como a artilharia aquy nam serue mais que pera hos da terra se pode por cada ues que for nessessaria = ficam lhe pegadas as cazas do Capitam ou tanadar, e muytas outras ha roda em que viuem Portugueses e Canarĩs cõ huma Igreja que por todos serã passante de vinte, e muytos palmares de huma e outra banda.

* * * * *

PASSO DE DAUGỸ.

Passando pella Çidade de Goa indo pello Rio asima de propia parte em terra da mesma Ilha esta ho passo de Daugim chamado por outro nome da Madre de D[eo]s: pello mosteyro que lhe-fica peguado de Capuchos Recolletos: F. 251.
Nã he este passo mais que humas cazas grandes sobradãdas onde mora ho capitam ou tanadar do dito passo = Nã hâ nelle artilharia nenhuma mais que hũs de pee de Çeylã, fazendo conta de se-lhe-por quando for nessesaria, porbayxo tem huma porta por onde entrã e saem os que passam pello dito passo de huma para outra parte em manchuas que ha de vigia e almadias pera passagem da gente e para fazerem chegar todas as embarcasõis a registar no dito passo se acazo o nam querem fazer = De fronte da porta do dito passo a borda do Rio pegado na agoa esta hum balluarte

razo coadrado que tem perto de duas brasas de altura, e de roda tem vinte e sinquo pasos andantes no qual se poem artilharia quando he necessaria pera qualquer ocaziã = E da ponta das cazas do passo comessa o muro que vay correndo pella Ilha em roda ao longo do dito Rio muyto grande espasso athe de fronte de Sam João Bautista onde se afasta do Rio e vay cõtinuando pella terra dentro da Ilha como se vera da planta = Tem este muro de altura em partes tres brassos e em partes menos, e em outras mais cõ seus balluartes a espassos pera defenderem os panos de muro que hâ entre hũs e outros posto que de Sam Joã Bautista athe de fronte de Barganỹ onde ja chegaua ho dito muro esta muy ymperfeyto e com muytas quebradas = E nam foy esta obra mais por diante por se entender era de pouco effeyto assỹ por ho sircuyto ser muy grande e descomprasado hauer mister mais de sinquoenta mil homẽs pera ho defenderem como por ficar muy destante da Çidade e aynda dos mais afastados arrabaldes della e tem se alcansado que com ho dinheyro que se gastou nesta obra se pudera ter forteficado a Çidade muyto bem e alem della a Ilha toda em roda quero dizer naquellas partes onde tinha nesesidade de forteficassam e assỹ foy dinheyro perdido o que nella se gastou = Tem este passo de Daugỹ capittam Portugues e fidalgo a quem se paga seu soldo e vensimento: mas ho que ho sustenta he os prois e percalsos e lagimas que lhe importã muyto =

* * * * *

F. 251b. PASSO SECO CHAMADO DE SAM BRAS.

Passado ho passo de Daugỹ indo correndo a Ilha de Goa a roda ao longo do Rio e muro se segue o passo sequo chamado de Sam Bras = Tem hum balluarte grande de pedra e cal pegado no dito muro: onde estam tres pessas de artilharia de Bronze em seus repayros huma de desoito liuras e as outras de des de pillouro de ferro este passo he muy perigozo e chegado hâs terras do Idolcam e de mare vazia se pode passar a pee enxuto e a este respeyto tem a guarda e vigia que abayxo se vera a quem se paga da fazenda real o que se segue, etc.

* * * * *

PASSO DE SANCTIAGO POR OUTRO NOME BENASTARIM.

Continuando ao longo do mesmo Rio e muro adiante a F. 252.
vista deste passo seco esta ho passo de Sanctiago o qual tem no mesmo muro hum balluarte muyto forte e bem feyto em que estam sinquo pessas de artilharia huma de ferro mourisca muyto grande que tira pillouro de pedra de disforme grandeza: e as quatro de bronze que forã dos galleõis de doze athe desoyto liuras de pellouro de ferro = Pera se sayr ao Rio se hã de passar por sinquo, ou seis portas que estam debayxo da Abobada das cazas do capitam ao longo do dito balluarte que todas em tempo de gerra erã de Rastilho, ou alsapã que se fechã do alto da Abobada parabayxo cayndo por encayxes de pedra; e se abrem leuantandose do alto da abobada com mollinetes com que ficaua fortissima a entrada do dito passo, etc.

* * * * *

PASSO DE SAM JOÃ BAUTISTA: POR OUTRO NOME CARAMBOLLIM.

Ao passo de Sanctiago em roda da Ilha de Goa se segue outro passo que chamã sam Joã Bautista e por outro nome Carambollim porque esta em hũa aldea deste proprio nome o qual nam tem Balluarte nem artilharia alguma fazendo conta de se-lhe-leuar e por no muro quando seja nessessa- F. 252b.
rio = para sua guarda e vegia, tem hum Tanadar que he o mesmo que capitam soldados naiques e piãis cujo numero e o que a cada hum se paga da fazenda real se segue, etc.

* * * * *

PASSO DE SAM LOURENSO POR OUTRO NOME AGASSAYM.

Adiante do passo de Sam Joam Bautista muyto grande distansia pello Rio abayxo quazi de fronte da barra de Mor-Mugã e Ilha de Salsete esta o passo de Sam Lourenso que por outro nome se chama Agassaym porque esta em huma aldea do mesmo nome e he o por onde se passa para as terras de Salsete. Tom por fortalleza hũas cazas de sobrado em que viue o capitã sem outra defensa de balluarte, muro, nem artilharia: fica muyto desuiado da Çidade porque esta quazi no fim da Ilha de Goa, etc.

* * * * *

F. 253. ILHA DE JUÃ.

A Ilha de Juã esta entre a Ilha de Goa e a terra firme pera a banda Nordeste, he de pouco menos de huma legoa de comprimento; e hum tiro de falcã de largura onde mais = Tem na cabessa que comessa da banda de Goa noue moradas de cazas de Portuguezes de pedra e cal, muy boas e fermozas que sam de moradores de Goa = Junto a ellas esta a Igreja de Sancto Esteuam que he fregezia, onde asiste por vigario hum clerigo de casta Canarim = como sam todas as mais das Igrejas da Ilha de Goa e suas adjasentes = Excepto algumas que hos tem frades de Sam Domingos, ou de Sancto Agostinho: e as de Bardes dos de Sam Francisco = E as de Salsete de padres da companhia de Jesus = Perto da esta Ilha de Juã hâ mil e dusentos Canarĩs entre os quais os oytoçentos sam de armas, e a milhor gente de todas as demais Ilhas, e da de Goa: e acodem cõ ellas todas as veses que sam chamados:—Esta Ilha, a de Diuar, Choram, e a das mãgas sam sogeytas ao capitam de Naroa.

ILHA DE DIUAR.

A Ilha de Diuar fica de fronte da Çidade de Goa pera a banda do Norte a qual fas o mesmo Rio cõ outro brasso que a serca, tera de comprimento huma legoa, e de largo hum quarto e em partes menos, esta nella o castello e passo de Naroa de que abayxo se fara mensã da banda de Leste da terra firme dos Mouros: Tem este Ilha em sӯ passante de quatro mil moradores entre os quais auera dous mil de armas e as tem, e os mais destes se ocupã em cultiuar as terras : e outros sam pescadores mas todos Christãos hâ nella tres freguezias cõ seus Vigarios cõ as ordinarias que adiante se dira.

PASSO DE NAROA.

Passando pella Çidade de Goa indo pello Rio asima voltando sobre a mã esquerda na ponta da Ilha de Diuar que fica de fronte da terra firme dos Mouros como atras se dis esta hum castello antigo que chamã Naroa, pegado ao qual F. 253b.
estã as cazas do Capitam bastantes pera se agasalhar cõ sua famillia = Ao pee do castello ou torre esta huma caza no Rio fundada sobre arcos onde se vegia de mais perto as embarcasõis que passã = A artilharia que tem este torre sam quatro falçois e hum berso porque tambem ella nâ he capas de artilharia de mais porte = Estam junto a este passo des cazas de pedra e cal terreas = onde viuem cazados Portuguezes, etc.

* * * * *

ILHA DAS MANGAS.

A Ilha das Mangas he hũa ilheta que esta entre esta Ilha de Diuar e a terra firme dos Mouros e a Ilha de Juã tem de comprimento hum tiro de pessa e pouco menos de largo = Nã tem mais que palmares e mangueyras tem humas cazas cõ hũas torrinhas do dono della que lhe seruẽ de fortes e oytenta canarĩs Christãos que a cultiuã e guardã: e nam tem Igreja.

ILHA DE CHORAM. F. 254.

Peguado ha Ilha de Diuar deuedida so por hum brasso de Rio fica a Ilha de Choram pera a banda de Noroeste a qual tem huma legoa e hum quarto de cõprido e mais de duas de roda: muyto mais abitada que a de Diuar e assỹ chega a ter perto de quinze mil almas dos quais sam de sinquo para seis mil homẽs de gerra sam todos pescadores e lauradores e algũs marinheyros; nam tem esta Ilha de Choram fortalleza nem balluarte algum que a defenda mais que a mesma gente que he a mais rica, e luzida de todas as Ilhas. Tem em sy duas Igrejas = e muytos palmares, mangas, e terras de arros.

CIDADE DE GOA.

A Çidade de Goa esta lansada ao longo do Rio que fas Ilha comessando as cazas della de Panellim athe Madre de D[eo]s em que entrã hos arrabaldes neste comprimento que sera de dous tersos de legoa: A largura he desde ho Rio athe Nossa S[enh]ora da Lus lansando aynda algumas cazas mais adiante the junto ao outeyro de Barganỹ: que serão mil seisçentos passos de largura e pellos outros dous lados da banda do comprimento, fica o grosso da Çidade entre os dous outeyros de Sancto Agostinho, e Nossa S[enh]ora do Monte que ficão Leste Oeste hum do outro, Sancto Agostinho para a banda de Veste e Nossa S[enh]ora de Monte para a de Leste, e dista hum do outro por linha recta dous mil passos e pello oblicar cõ as dissidas e sobidas dous mil e trezentos cada hum destes outeyros fica caualleyro ha çidade de forma que estando artilharia em qualquer delles a poderã com fassillidade arrazar = Os fogos que hâ nesta Çidade de Goa dentro nos ditos lemites sam tres mil e quinhentos a fora os Conuẽtos dos quais os oytoçentos sam de Portuguezes cazados que hũs por outros tem dous escrauos que possã tomar armas = sendo que conhessy muytos que tinhã a desaseis e a vinte: mas tãbẽ algũs nã tinhã nenhũ: Os mais delles sam Cafres, e de outras nasõis da India = Halem destes tem hos ditos Portuguezes cazados oyto pessoas entre escrauos Inutẽis que chamã Bichos e escrauas, ou negras = aduertindose tambem que posto que ha muytos que não tem pessoa nenhuma destes Inutẽis = hâ caza em que ha vinte escrauas e mais = Todos os ditos cazados tem muytas armas com que ornam suas cazas, assỹ cabides de lansas, azaguayas e partazanas como tambem espingardas de pederneyra e murrã de maneyra que tem armas pera sỹ F. 251b. e seus escrauos e so lhe podera faltar poluora e ballas que nã tem de portas a dentro = O mais numero de fogos que hâ nesta Çidade sam de cazados prettos Christãos Canarĩs e de outras nasõis da India que tambem tem algũs escrauos de armas que sempre sera a metade do dito numero muytos destes sam offissiais mecanicos: hos dous mil delles homẽs de armas: e posto que algũs delles por sua pobreza as nã tenhã de seu cõ tudo ha outros que sam ricos e tem muytas = Hâ entre este numero de fogos tambem muytos Gentios moradores, e offissiais Canarĩs, e Guzarates que se sustentã do que tirã e ganham dos Portuguezes; como do mantimento que leuã do terreyro de Goa, acarrettado, e trazido cõ as Armadas que por este effeyto se fazem = Teram este dous mil cazados pretos que hâ em Goa tres mil e quinhentas para quatro mil pessoas em suas cazas Inutẽis e de nenhum prestimo pera nenhuma couza do seruiso delRey; Antes se sustentã assỹ do que ganhã com hos Portuguezes como do mantimento que as armadas trazẽ de fora =

Os soldados Portuguezes e filhos seus que hâ em Goa que se embarcam nas armadas, nam se pode saber nem apontar numero serto: porque ora sam mais e ora menos conforme vem do reyno, de maneyra que as vezes sam mil e as vezes mais e se for como estes annos de seisçentos e trinta para qua em que faltarã dous annos areo naos do reyno; e ouue as mais mortes e mayores doensas que nunqua se viram na India: seram tanto menos quanto o exprimentou o Conde de Linhares que para recuperar Ceylam e Mombassa em tempo de tantas callamidades lhe foy nesessario para tam grandes emprasas vallerse de Canarĩs e Cafres = e quando logo chegam do reyno os consomem muyto as doensas como tambem a todo o forasteyro que chega a esta Çidade de Goa que ou morrem ou chegam ao ultimo que tal he ho clima della que nam perdoa a ninguem; e em particullar aos mais gordos e de mais carnes porque em lhe dando a doensa em quatro ou sinquo dias os acaba. E posto que a cantidade de fogos referidos e mais abitadores que se declara nesta descripsã da Çidade de Goa seja do numero que se tem visto foy ja tanto mayor do que oje hê que se mostrã muytos bayrros seus despouoados cõ a mayor parte das cazas caydas e as que aynda estã em pee desabitadas; de maneyra que tirado as rellegiõis que oje estam em mayor aumento do que nunqua estiuerã nã tem a Çidade de Goa a tersa parte dos moradores que ja teue = e os que oje hâ mais pobres do que nunqua forã como se vera pello comersio que antigamente tiuerã; e pello que oje tem:—

A Ilha de Goa da grandeza que temos referido tem em sỹ muy boas agoas e muytas fazendas de palmares, e varzeas de arros, e outros legumes e fruytos que possuem a mayor parte os Canarĩs naturays ja todos feytos Christãos sendo tambem muytas fazendas de Portuguezes = hauera aynda por toda a Ilha de Goa quatro mil Gentios moradores
F. 255. nella pouco mais ou menos fora os da Çidade e seus arrabaldes hos mais dos Canarĩs Christaos que viuem pella entre os quais ha muytos que chamã gancares, que sam como offissiais da Camara, sam gente de armas, e conforme a lista que deu o Tanadar Mor que he capitam desta gente sam tres mil e sesenta e dous, has armas de que vzam sam espingardas, espadas, e rodellas, lansas, e arcos e frechas: e todos estes Canarĩs da Ilha de Goa estam debayxo da jurdissã do Tanadar Mor = = Sam estes Canarĩs naturais de Goa muyto dados a papeis e demandas; porque alem de terem grande natural pera escreuerem, hos que se dam a isso fazem muyto exsellente letra por onde hâ mais de mil

escreuentes na Çidade de Goa e por toda a Ilha: posto que hos mais delles no que escreuem aynda que se-lhe-dem copias poem mil negradas, sendo que ha outros que escreuem muyto serto = Sam tantas as demandas que trazem hũs cõ outros ajudando tambem has que hos Portuguezes exersitã: as quais cõ seus modos de requerimentos e trapassas estendem por muyto largos tempos: e paresse a Çidade de Goa mais academia de letigantes, que escolla de armas, nem fortalleza, e Çidade fronteyra e cabessa de hum tam dellatado estado = E podesse afirmar que ha oje em Goa mais escriuãis: sollessitadores: aduogados: e demandistas: que soldados e capitãis que cursem as armas e o seruisso dellas = E em concluzã sam mais de seis mil as demandas que de prezente andam correndo em Goa: e so no Juizo dos feytos auia em Mayo deste anno de seisçentos trinta e sinquo concluzos de muytos annos a esta parte mil e quinhentos feytos a que se nam podia dar vazã alem dos que andauã correndo e por aquy se vira os que aueria nos mais juizos =

Os Mosteyros que ha nesta Ilha de Goa = o primeyro chamado a Madre de D[eo]s que esta ja fora dos arrabaldes da Çidade da banda de Leste junto ao passo de Daugim de Capuchos Recoletos tem de ordinario de trinta e sinquo pera quarẽta relligiosos nam tem ordinaria alguma da fazenda real porque se sustentã de esmollas e nem por isso passam pior que hos outros: Tem estes frades quinze negros que hos seruẽ: e muytos destes frades forã soldados como tambem o forã grande parte dos das outras relligiõis = e quando vã nas armadas por capellãis ou passageyros susede muytas vezes nas ocaziõis de brigas pellejarem cõ tanto vallor os frades como os soldados, ou as menos exortarẽ-nos a isso com crussefixos nas mãos = Esta outro conuẽto fora da Çidade que chamã Nossa S[enh]ora de Pillar, tambem dos mesmos Recolletos Capuchos obra de m[e]a legoa da Çidade onde de ordinario asistem athe des relligiosos = sustentã-se de esmollas como os outros sem

padesserem faltas de tudo ho que lhes he nessessario = = Esta mais nesta Ilha de Goa o Most[ei]ro de Nossa S[enh]ora do Cabo da mesma ordem dos Capuchos Recolletos onde asistem de ordinario athe quinze relligiosos que tambem se sustentã de esmollas a caza esta na paragem que se tẽ referido da qual athe Goa auera duas legoas por terra := Na mesma Ilha de Goa em huma Igreja chamada Sancta
F. 255b. Barbara que he fregezia obra de mea legoa da Çidade esta hum Conuento de P[adr]es de Sam Domingos onde asistem de ordinario, oyto, athe des relligiosos a que elles chamã a sua Recolleta tem de ordinario por anno sete mãos e mea de azeyte para alumiar a lampada do sanctissimo sacramento = Nas terras de Bardes esta o Conuento ou Collegio dos Reis Magos que he da ordem de Sam Fran[cis]co onde asistem athe sete relligiosos da dita ordem = Neste conuento ha tambem hum Collegio de meninos pretos e branquos, onde lhes ensinã Latim e ler e escreuer aos que ho nam sabem: Neste Conuento se apozentã hos Vizorreis quando desembarcã das naos em quanto se prepara ho que he nesesario para entrarem em Goa e tambem vã a elle outras muytas vezes = Tem este conuento de ordinaria por anno ho que no titollo das Igrejas de Bardes fica declarado :—

RIBEYRA DOS NAUIOS, GALLES, E MAIS MAIS EMBARCASÕIS DE SUA MAG[DE].

Tem esta Çidade de Goa huma ribeyra de Sua Mag[de] a que chamã a Ribeyra Grande onde mora o Veedor da fazenda e estam os nauios de remo que seruẽ nas armadas, artilharia e fundissã della, ferraria, e dous Almazẽis de prouimentos de toda sorte que sam nessessarios para as armadas = Os nauios que Sua Mag[de] oje tem em Goa serã athe oytenta, entre nauios sanguiseis, e galleotas = Os sanguiseis carregam sinquoenta athe sesenta candĩs: que cada candil he como vinte alq[uey]res de Portugal = Os nauios athe oytẽta nouenta candĩs, e as galleotas athe çento e sinquoenta = os mais destes nauios e sanguiseis se fazem em Bassaym por contrato que se fas cõ hos capitãis pella muyta mad[ey]ra, offissiais e mais petrechos que pera isso aly hâ: e de presente porque ho presso da mad[ey]ra tem cresido como em todas as mais couzas; se fas cada sanguisel por quatro çentos e sinquoenta patacõis: e cada nauio por seis çentos e sinquoenta: mas nẽ cõ isso o capitã de Bassaym que ho contratou se ouue por pago antes moue demanda a Sua Mag.^{de} por ficar notauelmente lezo = E posto que estes nauios durem sinquo e seis annos a todo mais: cõ tudo vam para Mascate, Mallaqua, Sam Thome e outras partes = Aonde ordinariamente ficã quazi todos: e alem disto os sucesos da gerra em que de contino andã sam muy varios e gastã-nos muyto e assỹ he nessesario refazerẽ-se muytas vezes as armadas de nauios nouos e as que escapã durã algũs annos e custa o concertar porque em quazi todos os portos em que entrã tem nessesidade de conserto = Tem mais Sua Mag.^{de} huma gualle real muyto grande e fermoza a que chamã Sam Miguel e outra mais piquena que arribou indo para Mallaqua = E no porto de Panellim oyto galleõis dos quais se aparelharã quatro pera sayrem cõ dous que este anno vierã do reyno e ficam no estado: e dous que estam prinsipiados no cais de Sancta Cri[stin]a que vem a ser doze por todos e isto a fora a armada de Mascate, Dio, e Mallaqua, que sam do numero de nauios que em a discripsã de cada hũa das ditas fortallezas se aponta = Mais seis nauios de remo que hão de yr cõ hos galleõis cõ seu Capitam Mor e capitãis debayxo das ordeñs do capitam geral dos ditos galleõis.

A artilharia que ho estado tem em Goa de prezente sam somente çento e sinquoenta pessas nos galleõis = sete pessas no forte da Agoada = quatro pessas no forte de Nossa S[enh]ora do Cabo. Tres pessas no forte de Sam Bras do passo seco = Sinquo pessas no forte e passo de F. 256.

Sanctiago = No forte de MorMugã seis pessas de bronze= desaseis sagres para ho forte de Gaspar Dias e Bardes= No paso de Naroa quatro falcõis e hum berso = huma pesa de ferro de quatro liuras sinquo pessas na galle real = Tres pessas na outra galle mais piquena = Noue pessas nouas na Ribeyra auera mais athe sasenta sagres que andã nos nauios das armadas = Vinte falcõis meios falcõis e bersos = quinze falcõis meios falcõis e bersos no almazẽ que sam por todas trezentas e quatro e a grande falta de cobre que hâ no estado da India he cauza de nã auer muyta conforme trabalha nisso o Conde de Linhares VizoRey mas vay ho buscando por todos os modos, e cõ ho fauor de D[eo]s fundira muyta em seu tempo se estiuer mais annos na India =

A Barra desta Çidade de Goa he depois de entrar da ponta de Nossa S[enh]ora do Cabo e da fortalleza da Agoada pera dentro distansia de mea legoa pello Rio asima de fronte do forte de Guaspar Dias: onde esta hum banco de area que a atrauessa com hum canal de des brassas de largura = e sinquo brassas e mais de preamar de agoas viuas = O Rio no prinsipio entre as ditas pontas tem de largura huma legoa: e entrando para dentro vay fazendo hũa enseada pera detras de Nossa S[enh]ora do Cabo com que fica a largura do Rio mayor e depois vay estreytando pera dentro da forma que na planta se vee = Antes de chegar este Rio ao banco e barra lansa hum braso pera a banda do Norte a que chamã Nelur = o qual vay distansia de huma legoa pellas terras de Bardes dentro e nã torna a fazer sayda neste Rio se uã meter muytos nauios dos que hâ em Goa de trato = Passando de Pangim fas este Rio dous brassos hum para o Sul e outro para o Norte: o do Sul vay athe Sancta Crus e nam passa mais adiante nem tem sayda para outra parte, O outro brasso que lansa para a banda do Norte vay fazendo as Ilhas de Choram, Diuar, e Juã: e nem por isso deyxa ho Rio de Goa de ter fundo bastãte para estarẽ nelle surtos e yrem e virem athe as naos de reyno que sam as mayores embarcasõis que nauegã o mar = = A barra de Goa a Velha tem tambem hum banco de area que a atrauessã; por meo do coal esta o canal de çem brasas de largura e sinquo de fundo de preamar: e seis de agoas viuas: o canal de Goa demanda ao Veste; e o desta barra ao Sul: por onde se entra nella aynda com Sul como fizerã muytas embarcasõis cõ ho ynuerno = e quando as naos ou galleõis se recolhem a Mormugã se ficam seruindo desta barra de Goa a Velha por lhe ficar em direytura =

A costa desta Ilha de Goa corre ao mesmo rumo de Norte a sul que a de Damã; Bassaym; e Chaul: nam prefeytamente metendo mais pera susueste e nornordeste e quanto mais se vay pera o Sul mais vay a costa metendo pera o susueste = Os ventos que cursam nesta costa sã hos mesmos que temos dito atras, ha nella athe o Cabo dõ Comorim = As correntes tambem sam quazi as mesmas que temos dito da costa do Norte tirado que como esta Goa F. 256b.
desuiada de Cambaya e çem legoas nam lhe alcansa ja as correntes furiozas de suas mares = =

As viagẽis que se fazem de Goa sam muytas porque se nauega para ho reyno e para todo ho estado com toda sorte de embarcasõis = A prinsipal viagem e de mais porte que se fas de Goa he pera Portugal em naos de quatro cubertas que sam as mayores em que se nauega no mar salgado = Onde se leuã e trazem grande copia de toda sorte de fazendas = As que vam de Portugual sam as milhores e de mais ganho, ouro, e prata; porque alem dos sinquoenta por çento que se ganha de Portugal para a India se ganha mais a cresensa que as pattaquas vallem mais de oyto tangas, que de presente vallem noue tangas e mea = e aynda mais e assӯ vay tambẽ o ouro cressendo ao mesmo theor = Cauza por que forã cressendo as fazendas e tudo ho mais que neste estado se compra com ouro e prata, a tanto que ja raramente se pode ter ganho nellas; ao que nã hâ poder se buscar remedio = porque como o ouro e pratta hê fazenda por todo este estado, vay cressendo e abayxando conforme a falta delle hâ = Trasse de Portugual muyto coral, assỹ em ramos : como redondo = panos de vestir de toda sorte de lã : e a mesma lã = e tambem pano de linho branquo, muytas esmeraldas, robĩs, perolas, e aljofres grandes = que posto que estas tres ultimos espessies se leuaram da India pera Portugal; com tudo cresserã depois tanto em presso na India que se tornarã a trazer a ella cõ grandes ynteresses; e assỹ tambẽ outras pedras preciozas de diferentes sortes: assỹ soltas como feytas em joyas. Todo ho genero e sorte de couzas de comer e beber tirado pam e vaca, que se nam pode trazer por veniaga: e quaisquer pessas ricas e curiozas que hos Reis deste oriente comprã = folhas de espada largas e estreytas porque as estreytas seruẽ pera os Portuguezes, e tambem as largas porem estas comprã mais comũmente os naturais, e particullarmente os Mouros, e tambem artilharia, e com mais commodidade a de ferro que se viera muyto alem do muyto que se ynteressa nella se ganhara muyto mais em ficar todo ho estado prouido cõ ella para defensa de suas Cidades fortallezas e embarcasõis = e em effeyto athe pedras de atafona se trazem de Portugual e com grande ganho sendo hum dos milhores lastros que podem trazer as naos = Todas estas fazendas que vem de Portugual nam pagam direytos nenhũs sendo os ganhos dellas has vezes exsesivas: e na prata e ouro assỹ em pessas, como em moeda sempre passa de sinquoenta por çento: couza porque as naos vem a custar tanto ha fazenda real e renderem tam pouco = = =

O que leua da India sam muytas couzas porem nas mais dellas ha oje muyto pouco ynteresse; pellos Olandezes e Ingrezes encherem toda a Europa de roupas: em que auia, e nas drogas, o prinsipal ganho deste comersio e aynda assỹ leuam pimenta por conta delRey,—e algumas roupas de Cambaya: caras e roĩns: porque tãbem estas sã tam ynferiores; e so menos do que antigamente que aynda que nã estiuerã tam sobidas de presso, e os Ollandezes e Ingrezes as nã leuarã aynda assỹ em grande copia forã hos ganhos muy piquenos = F. 257. Leuã se tambem algumas roupas de Tutocorim que nam estã tam vesiadas: mas tambem nestas ha pouco ganho = pessas de eruas de Bengalla = porque as cassas ja nã sam de nenhum ynteresse = Leuanse tambem algũs enricollados e Ballachos de Negapatã e pimenta de Canara e costa do Mallauar, e canella de Ceylão = e desta se nã partessipã os Olandezes e tambem alguma do mato = e no tocante hâs mais drogas, nos, e massa, ja nam vem a nossos mãos, e crauo muy pouco o qual tambem se leua pera Portugual; e todas as fazendas de Chyna como sedas em pessas e em rama: porem estam oje em tã alto presso que nã se leuã ja para veniaga pello pouco ganho, ou nenhum que pode auer nellas = Hia antigamente muyto anil de Cambaya: Ja oje pello leuarem Ingrezes e Olandezes nem na India esta em presso pera se poder leuar, nem em Portugual tem expediente= Alem destas fazendas se leuã outras de pouco momento como huma fruyta que chamã Coca, e por outro nome Matapeyxe = Courama = Cayxaria dourados de Japã e China = Escritorios e contadores de Dio, e de todo o Norte = colchas lauradas e camas de Dio, Chaul, Bengalla, e China = e Caurim por outro nome Buzio = athe couseyras pera portas se leuã da India: muyto pao preto de Mosambique e muyto arros que alem de ser mantimento he veniaga em que se ganha mais que em muytas das outras = e por remate de tudo se leua e tem leuado muytos diamantes das minas nouas que se abrirã, e ouue nao que leuaua duas arrobas de diamantes: porem oje sam ja muyto menos e assỹ pellas ditas cauzas esta este comersio de Portugual muy acabado: sendo que se nauegaua nelle mais de dous milhõis de ouro; e oje apenas andarã trezentos mil cruzados: de sorte que nem os offisiais tem quem lhe carregue, nem elles com que carregar seus gasalhados = O tempo em que costumã partir estas naos da India pera ho reyno hê desde o prinsipio de

Dezembro athe meo do Março: porem em passando des, ou doze de Feuereyro = se nã vam athe Mosambique cõ a Mousã dos Leuantes com que partem as embarcasõis que vam para esta fortalleza: passam cõ trabalho o Cabo de Boa Esperansa: e quando chegam a costa de Portugal he ja quazi ynuerno em que padessem tambem ygoais detrimentos assỹ naos, como gente, e fazendas = = =

As viagẽis depois das do reyno que se fazem de Goa de mais considerassã sam para Mosambique e sam estanques que se dam por despacho: e sem trabalho rendem ao dono des, e doze mil X.^{es} conforme as embarcasõis que vam de tres, quatro, athe sinquo Pataxos: leuam roupas como fica dito: e todo ho genero de mantimentos o que tudo se declara no titollo de Mosambique: Onde se pos tãbem ho tempo em que vã e vem: ho muyto que as vezes trazem estas embarcasõis que ordinariamente sam pataxos de quinhentos athe mil Candĩs = e andara neste comersio melhoria de hum milhã = = = As viagẽis de Goa pera Mombassa e toda aquella costa sam de pouco momento que em Goa nã hâ as roupas que nella so vallem. E assỹ estas se fazem de
F. 257b. Dio, Damã, e Chaul: e quando de Goa vay alguma galleota, leua prouimentos e algumas teadas e se tras sera, escrauos, marfim, e ambre = Vam, e vem no mesmo tempo que a Mosambique = Andara neste comersio de Goa des athe doze mil X.es = = =

As viagẽis que tambem se fazem de Goa de ymportansia sam as de Mascate e Basora, porque quem vay a Bassora, primeyro ha de yr a Mascate, e nem sempre as embarcasõis que vam a Mascate passam a Bassora senã as que querem pagar direytos do que leuam em Mascate: o que selleua ja atras fica dito e os tempos em que nauegã onde andam pataxos e galleotas e nauios de remo = Trarsehâ empregado neste comersio quinhentos mil X.es = e as vezes mais, e menos = a mayor copia que de Mascate vem emprezado pera Goa hê em aljofar de Baharem em que hâ muyto ganho porem de nenhum se paga direytos porque como he couza de pouco volume fasilmente se esconde = Nauegasse de Goa pera ho Sinde leuando marfim: cocos = copra = calaym que hê hum metal da cor de estanho alguma couza mais duro, e todas as drogas de pimenta: crauo: cardamomo: canella: gengiure: e nos: e massa: Vay se em galleotas de quatro çentos athe quinhentos candĩs no mesmo tempo em que vam para Mascate = e assÿ tãbem ha vinda trazem roupas de toda sorte de mais dura que as de Cambaya e athe as camizas e ciroulas feytas pello pouco que custã hos feytios, e esta gente do Sinde ser particularmente dada a cozer e laurar de sorte que athe couros vem de la laurados muyto curiozamente de seda que sam de muyta dura e estima = andarã neste comersio empregados de oytenta athe çem mil X.es = o que se yntende so nas embarcasõis que vam e vem pera Goa = = = As viagẽis que se fazem de Goa para Cacha e Nagana nam sam ordinarias de todos os annos senam quando se offeresse; vam e vem em galleotas de remo, e pataxos, no mesmo tempo que ao Sinde e Mascatte posto que em galleotas de remo sam muy arriscadas, pellos muytos paros que vam aquella enseada: e os Sanganes tambem andarem roubando como fica dito = o que se leua, e tras fica referido ja em seu lugar: e quando se fazem as viagẽis a saluamento dam muyto proueito e ynteresse = Andam neste comersio de vinte athe trinta mil X.es =

A nauegassã que se fas de Goa para Dio nã he em rezam do comersio de considerassã porque em Dio, nã hâ mais que ho que fica dito: senã por respeyto do prouerẽ esta fortalleza do nessessario: e assÿ nã se vay lâ senã com a armada que leua a Cafilla pera Cambaya pera onde de Goa hiã todos os verõis duas Cafillas com grande copia de nauios de remo que as uezes chegauam a trezentos: porem oje pellas rezõis apontadas apenas hâ cõ que poder yr huma e os nauios de Cafilla nã chegam a quarẽta e esses aynda vem descarregados: nam tendo mais ynteresses que ho que leuã de

fretes e aynda em copra, cocos, areca, marfim, e callaym e algumas drogas posto que poucas = e assỹ andando antigamente neste comersio empregados mais de dous milhõis: nã chegam a andar oje çento e sinquoenta mil Xes: donde se deyxa bem vir a grande perda e descayda que so nesta
F. 258. terra derã as Olandezes e Yngrezes a este estado =

Para a banda do sul se fazem de Goa muytas viagẽis e nauegasõis as primeyras sam para o Canara com armada que leua e tras quatro Cafillas huma mais ou menos todos os verõis de arros e trazer pimenta para as naos em que andã ora çento, ora çento e sinquoenta nauios entre grandes e piquenas que chamã parangues, e trazem tãbẽ de Onor e Cananor a madeyra de mastros e vergas, nessessarios pera a ribeyra de Sua Magde Anda neste comersio do arros a fora a pimenta mais de trezentos mil Xes = = =

A armada do Cabo de Comorim leua e tras a Cafilla de Cochim duas vezes cada verã = A primeyra com a Cafilla que vay buscar a pimenta pera as naos do reyno e a cayxaria courama e mais fazendas de roupas de Sam Thome, Negapatam e Tutocorim em que andauã de trinta pera correnta nauios de Remo e oje a penas chegam a doze = Andarã neste comersio empregados a fora a pimenta sesenta athe oytenta mil Xes = = = A segunda vez que vay a armada a Cochim chega athe o Cabo de Comorim onde antigamente hia esperar as embarcasõis da China, Mallaqua, e Bengalla, que ja agora sam quazi nenhũas mais que algumas de Mallaqua: de Bengalla muy poucas, e menos da China = Tras esta armada as embarcasõis da Costa do Travancor, Coulam, e Cochim afora os moradores de Tutocorim e as fazendas que aly vam parar de Bengalla, Mallaqua, China, e Manilla: Era esta Cafilla antigamente de sinquoenta e mais nauios: hoje nã chegã a des = Andarã neste comersio de quarenta para sinquoenta mil Xes e quando as vezes vem embarcasõis do sul hum nauio tras esta contia sô = O tempo em que custuma yr he em Feuereyro; e uir por todo

Mayo: e tambem costuma trazer a Goa arros das fortallezas do Canara = = =

A nauegassã que se fas de Goa para Ceylã he em pataxos ou galleotas de remo: Vam por todo Setembro quatro, ou sinquo pataxos; ou des ou doze galleotas pera trazerem a canella que oje corre so por conta de Sua Mag^{de}. e assỹ nenhum vassalo ynteressa neste comersio mais que hos fretes porque lhe fretam as ditas embarcasõis as quais tambem leuã algũs prouymentos pera a dita Ilha de gente e o mais que lhe he nessessario pera sustento de seus moradores = A cantidade de canella que trazem sam dous mil athe tres mil bares = que cada bar sam em Goa tres quintais e des arratẽis = Importou esta canella a Sua Mag^{de}. o anno de seisçentos trinta e tres por yndustria do Conde de Linhares çento e sinquoenta mil X^{es}. de que se tirarã hos gastos: Trazem tambem estas carauellas, e pataxos, os Ellefantes de Ceylã pera em Goa se venderem por conta de Sua Mag^{de}. ho numero he conforme se cassã: que ordinariamente hê de sete athe des = o presso por que se vendem tambem nã he serto, porque he conforme a grandeza, e a boa ocaziã = porque hâ Ellefante por que se dã dous e tres mil pagodes, de noue çentos rẽs o pagode = E outros tãbem valiem menos. He animal que custa muyto a embarcar e trazer por sua grandeza; e tãobem morrem muytos — Trazem as ditas embarcasõis muytos cocos por F. 258b. lastro e as curiozidades de Ceylã de cabides de lansas, alabardas, ymagẽis de marfim, pessas de cristal, esteyras e chapeos de palha que sam de muyta estima =

A nauegassã que antigamente se fazia de Goa pera a China era tirado a do reyno a mais rica; e de mayores cabedais que auia neste estado = porque so a primeyra nao que chamauã a da prata que tomarã os Olandezes aos Portuguezes na India = a primeyra promessa que se lhe fes de partido porque alargassem, forã mil pãis de ouro que cada pã tem tres quartas de arratal = e oje ha anno em que apenas hâ quem queyra carregar huma galeota de trezento pera quatro çentos candĩs pella continua asistencia cõ que os Olandezes estam esperando no estreyto de Sincapura estas embarcasõis que vam de Goa para a China ou pera Manilla e de la passã ha China = O que leuã para Manilla sam vinhos = azeites = escrauos = amendoas = farinhas = pimenta = cordoalha = roupas de cachas, e algumas beatilhas, e canequĩs = e o mais que se leuaua nos primeyros tempos erã muytas joyas de diamantes de que a fazenda real nam tinha nenhũs direytos ymportando grandes contias: Mas foram tantos que ja oje la tem menos vallia que em Goa = e assỹ nas embarcasõis que vam e vem a China e Manilla andaram de duzentos e sinquoenta para trezentos mil X.es prosupondo como atras fica dito que estas embarcasõis sam esperadas nas monsõis da vinda no estreyto de Sinquapura: de quatro sinquo e seis, entre naos e pataxos Olandezes muy bem artilhados e so cõ ho lastro pera ficarem mais ligeyros = Onde tomando as nossas empachadas e carregadas sem artilharia; ou muy póuco para se defenderem sam tomadas e vendo o pouco meo que ha para lhe escaparem os que vem nellas dam cõ as galleotas, ou pataxos a costa e âs vezes os queymã: saluando o ouro que he sustansia de tudo: e alguma pedraria de rubĩs e aljofres, e almiscar: por cuja cauza, o mayor ou quazi todo o emprezo he nestas duas couzas: sendo o lastro e mais carga de muyta menos ymportansia: Mas como as fazendas da China sam todas de muyta vallia: nunqua deyxam de ser de muyta considerassã quaisquer que hos enemigos tomã: porque nunqua podem deyxar de ser ao menos = Tutunaga que he hum metal mais preto que estanho: e Calaim muyto mais duro: lancoas que he por outro nome galangas = lousa de toda sorte e a milhor que ha no mundo: pao da China = asucares boñs e muytos branquos = em fim muyta seda assỹ em pessas como em rama: muytos dourados: que qualquer destas couzas sam de grande presso e a falta dellas as fas aynda sobir mais = O que vem de Manilla sam asucares que a mesma terra dá tam bõs como os da China = sapã que he hum pao que tambem aly nasse que serue de tintas = crauo = tartaruga = e algum ouro tambem da terra = Os tempos em que vam estas embarcasõis para Manilla e China hê desde Março athe todo Mayo: e quando vem na monsã do sedo he em Dezembro: chegando a Goa em Janeyro = e na do tarde em Feuereyro: e chegam a Goa em Março, Abril, athe Mayo = = = F. 259.

A nauegassam de Goa para Mallaqua se fas no mesmo tempo que para a China e Manilla e alem disso tambem em Setembro = Esta este comersio ja quazi de todo acabado: porque como em Malaqua nam auia mais que as fazendas do sul de que as prinsipais erã drogas de pimenta, crauo, senos, massa = e todas as tinhã os Olandezes e Ingrezes senhoreado; e os Jaos e Mallayos nam vinhã buscar a Mallaqua as roupas de que se vestem pellas terem pellos Olandezes. Esta esta fortalleza oje tam falta de comersio, e trato: que sendo huma das tres da India, nam ouue em Setembro de seisçento trinta e tres prouido que quizesse yr entrar nella por onde se mandou capitam por Sua Mag^de^ mas aynda vam huma; e duas embarcasõis de quinhentos para seisçentos candĩs: e trarã neste trato em Callaym, que he sô o que oje hâ em Mallaqua, e algum crauo, e tartaruga, que lhe vem do Macassa sinquoenta mil X^es^ empregados a fora algumas miudezas que nam sam de momento.

Vem a Goa alem das partes referidas huma nao mourisca todos os annos piquena do Rey de Carem do estreyto de Meca = que esta em pas cõ ho estado que tras ensenso, e azeure; e algũs chamallottes = = = Das Ilhas de Maldiua e de Mamale vam tambem muytas gundras que sã hũs nauios de remo piquenos e malfeytos pellos quais se dis que a palmeyra poem hum nauio ha vella: porque ho casco he do mesmo pao da palmeyra, cozido cõ ho cayro dos seus cocos: a carga dellas he ho mesmo cayro dos cocos = Ho mantimento da gente destas embarcasõis os mesmos cocos, e a agoa delles mesmos = os mastros, e as virgas das palmeyras = as vellas de esteyras de palma = As de Mamalle nam trazem mais que cayro, e destas vem mais todo pera a ribeyra de Goa = As de Maldiua vem raramente a Goa; e trazem cayro = ou buzio e destas Ilhas he todo ho que hâ neste estado = peyxe sequo que chamã comballamas: algum ambar, tartaruga = e coco que chamã de Maldiua ou das Ilhas que se tem por grande contrapessonha muytas esteyras e cocos ordinarios que inda que piquenos se tem por de milhor carne que hos mais da India = O tempo em que vam e vem he desde Setembro athe Mayo: em quanto dura o verã = Trara o comersio da nao do Rey de Cayxim e destas gundras empregado ao redor de trinta mil X.es =

De tudo ho referido se collige que andã nos comersios e nauegassõis da Çidade de Goa dous milhois; oyto çentos e sinquoenta e dous mil X.es, porem ha se de considerar que as vezes o mesmo cabedal que anda em hum comersio, anda tambem em outro, ou parte delle, como nos comersios da costa de Goa pera Cambaya, ou pera Cochim = e tambem parte destes dous milhõis he de gentios que hũs sam vassallos de Sua Mag.de e outros nam: e que muytos embarcasõis de todas as partes fazem naofragio: ou sam tomadas dos enemigos Ingrezes, ou Olandezes que com grandes escoadras de naos ocupã estes mares: e nã menos de muitos paros: que tem feyto e fazem muyto dano = e assỹ que contra todos estes empedimentos e outros muitos sendo nam menos os castigos do Çeo de tromentas: fomes: pestes: e outros malles: hâ de andar sempre preuenindo remedios quem tem âs costas apezado gouerno deste estado.

F. 259b. O Rey da terra dentro com quem confinã estas nossas de Goa: Bardes: e Salsette se chama o Idalcam, ou Idalxá: capitam antigo que foy do Rey de Bisnaga e se lhe leuantou com esta parte das terras que gouernaua: de Gentio se fis

Mouro: como se fizeram deste Oriente = O seu reyno por costa he desde o Rio do Mar athe Merizeu que sam sesenta e duas legoas de costa e pello sertã dentro se estendera neste distrito a doze legoas = A mayor parte de seus vassallos sam Mouros mas aynda tem algũs Gentios = A gente que pode por em campo chegou ajuntar o anno passado em Vijapor que he a sua corte sinquoenta mil homẽs de cauallo pera se defender do Mogor que lhe pos serco nella, afora hos de pee de que nam fazem numero como ja fica dito: porem estes cauallos sã hos mais delles guadaras: e entre oyto ou des se achara hum bom arabio ou partio, porque os da terra aynda que nassã delles ja não sam couza de considerassam, donde tambem se pode ver ho que sera dos homẽs. As armas de que se vzam sam todas as que se vzam em Europa e sobre ellas muytos arcos e frechas hos de pee = e assỹ tambem vzã de artilharia prinsipalmente em defensa de suas fortallezas = A forma de pas que guarda cõ ho estado he ser ho Idalcã amigo de amigos e enemigo de enemigos: porem nam guarda elle isto tam pontualmente: porque tem comersio com ho Dachem onde manda naos de Dabul Çidade sua que esta no Norte, nam se lhe dando do nosso feytor Portugues que esta na dita Çidade como atras fica dito: e ha Persia nauios hũs e outros sem cartazes: e em outros muytos particullares nã guardam os capitãis e gouernadores do Idalcã os capitallos das pazes fazendo algumas semrezõis aos vassallos de Sua Mag.[de] Christandade nenhuma tem os naturais do Idalcam = antes acolhendose os escrauos dos Portuguezes de Goa, ou os mesmos Portuguezes para sua terras os deyxa viuer em que ley querem: e ordinariamente os escrauos renegam e os Portuguezes viuem muy fora da ley que professã = He costume e capitallo das pazes que tenha sempre o Idalcam hum embayxador na corte da Goa como ordinariamente asiste posto que algumas vezes falta; e a despeza que faz he a custa de seu Rey, so as cazas lhe da ho estado = e nas fazendas que aprezenta na alfandega se lhe quitam mil e quinhentos Xes. por contrato.

As fazendas que hâ nestas terras do Idalcã nam sam outras mais que algumas roupas que chamã beatilhas; argarĩs; pacharĩs; teadas; pedras bazares; grande copia de diamantes de minas que a quinze annos se descobrirã de nouo nas terras do Rey de Golconda que chamã Cotumaxa que confinã com estas do Idalcam: e desde o descobrimẽto das ditas minas athe o prezente se tem empregado mais de des milhõis nos ditos diamantes com nenhum, ou muy pouco ynteresse da fazenda real = a cuio respeyto o Conde de Linhares Vizorrey tem criado o offissio de Corretor Mor da pedraria com que se tem esperansa poder a fazenda real ter
F. 260. mais proueyto da muyta deste estado:—Vem mais das terras de Idalcam para Goa toda a sorte de mantimentos cauza porque hos Mouros tem com este estado algũs maos termos paressindo-lhe que nos tem o sustento em suas mãos particullarmente trigo, e carnes, e legumes de que comem os cauallos: e muyto mais que tudo isto os marinheyros dos nauios de remo = =

As fazendas por que se resgatam todas as que vem das terras do Idalcam que lhe vem desta Çidade de Goa sam todas as drogas do sul, e as mais das que vem do reyno prinsipalmente prata, ouro, coral = e muytas da China como seda, ouro, lousa, pao: e o que com mais yñstansia procurã e leuam os vassallos do Idalxa, sam os cauallos Arabios que se trazem de Mascate: e algũs Cachĩs de Cache: posto que estes nã com tanta vontade: e assỹ nã dam tanto por elles: como pellos Arabios— Tem esta Çidade de Goa huma caza de poluora ao longo do Rio hum pouco afastado do Amago da Çidade a qual tinha prinsipiada o Conde da Vidigueyra e a acabou o Conde de Linhares com grande trabalho e asistensia custando-lhe muyto de sua fazenda, he huma das melhores obras e mais bem trassada que ha na India porque tem muytas cazas entre as quais ha tres patios pera ficarẽ as offissinas tam distantes hũas das outras que auendo desastre de fogo em hũa nã possa empesser hâs mais dentro neste sircuyto ha hũa fonte de agoa muy boa e moem continuamente oyto moynhos cõ mullas =

* * * * *

As armadas que ho Estado da India lansa sam a primeyra pera a costa do Canara que coñsta athe quinze fustas entre nauios e sanguiseis a segunda he pera ho Norte de athe vinte nauios = a outra pera o cabo de Comorim de huma galle e des nauios = outra armada que se chama dos auentureyros que coñsta de athe vinte nauios esta nam sirue mais que de andar buscando paros dos Mallauares, etc. F. 260b.

EPISTOLA

POTENTISSIMI, AC INUICTISSIMI EMANUELIS REGIS PORTUGALIÆ & ALGARBIORUM. &C. DE VICTORIIS HABITIS IN INDIA & MALACHA. AD. S. IN CHRISTO PATREM & D'N'M NOSTRUM D'N'M LEONEM. X. PONT. MAXIMUM.

[*Woodcut of arms of Portugal ensigned with a crown.*]

S Anctissimo in Christo Patri, ac beatissimo Dño Dño nostro E. S. additissimus filius Emanuel Dei gratia Rex Portugalliæ & Algarbior*um* citra ultraq*ue* mare in Affrica Dominus gui nee & conquiste nauigationis ac cõmertii Ethiopiæ, Arabie, Persiæ, atq*ue* Indiæ, humillima beatorum pedum oscula. Quantum Deo Opt. Max. q*uan*tum & tibi gratulari debeamus Beatissime Pater, vel ex nuntio q*uo*d nostra Indica Classis proxime attulit satis apparet. Quod enim te Pont. Max. te S. Ro. Ecclesiæ & Christiano Orbi presidente tam admiranda in Dei laudem ac gloriã gesta tam ex uoto successerint tua certe laus tua gloria censeri debet, Iure itaq*ue* uisum est que in India Dei suffragio ad ipsius cultum spectantia nostris armis modo facta sint ad tuam Sanctitatem, utpote totius Christiane Reipublice Caput & orthodoxe religionis normam, carptim ac summatim, ne stilum Epistolarum excedamus prescribere, ut pro rerum dignitate cuncta pensari, summoq*ue* deo accepta referri ualeant, ac indies sui san ctissimi nominis gliscentem laudẽ xpĩaniq*ue* dogmatis propagationem facile speremus. Igitur paccata post plures dubii Martis ui ctorias non sine labore & sanguine partas, India relictis in ea opportunis presidiis Al phonsus de Albiecherq*ue* protho capitaneus noster ut iacturã, quã superioribus annis nr̃i fecerant, iniuriãq*ue* ulcisceretur auream Cher sonesum, Malacham accole appellant con- tendit, ea est inter sinum magnum et Gange ticum sita Vrbs mire magnitudinis, utq*ue* ui gintiquinq*ue* millium & amplius larium cen seatur terra ipsa fecundissima, ac nobilissima rum, quas fert India mertium feracissima ce lebratissimum ob id Emporium, ubi non modo uaria aromata & omnigeni odores, sed Auri quoq*ue*, Argenti, Margaritarum ac preciosorum lapillorum magna copia af- fluit: Hanc Rex Maurus gubernabat ea- tenus uires suas Maumetica Secta proten- dente, cætera Gentiles tenent: Huc itaq*ue* cum instructa Classe applicuisset Alphon- sus Vrbem oppugnare destinat: Quod pre- sentientes Sarraceni bello, se multis Mu- nitionibus, & Armis præparauerat, sed frustra: nam commisso bis prælio, nostri omnia ad bellum contra catholica fidei hostes opportuna: militum exercitus: armorum ac cõmeatus præsidia ultro offerat: præsertim si mare rubrum suo coniunctum dominio ura classis traiiciat: ubi cõmodissime utriusque uires iungi possent. Haud exiguũ adorande & uere crucis lignum ad nos mit tit uiros uafros & industrios poscens quorum ingenio & artificio a Sulcani territorio & Regione Nilũ deflecti aliqua diuerti posse existimat: aderant tunc apud nostrũ prefectum a Narsingue Rege legati, Rege Genti li adeo potentissimo, ut mille & quingentos belligeros Elephantes armatorum equitũ qua draginta millia præter innumerũ peditũ nu merum suo arbitrio in aciem paruo negotio proferre tantũque agri possidere perhibeatur quantũ semestri itinere uix emettiri possit, huic plures Reges ac Satrapes parent, quorum nõ nulli maritimis oris proximi nobis sunt tri butarii. Apud Alfonsum & Cambaye Regis legatus, terra marique potentissimi, atque in ter Mauros maximi. Item a Zabayo Goe quondam dño, atque a Rege Grosapa, Aliique complures Regum Satrapumque legati a no stro prefecto fedus pacemque ultro exorantes ac sua munera singuli afferentes, in hac etiã quæ proxime appulit classe ab Armuzii Re ge legatus cum multis margaritarum rerumque pretiosarum donis, in signum uidelicet fide litatis & recognitionis ad nos uenit: Hunc Regem Alfonsus idem urbe oppulẽtissima & præcipuo emporio Armusio ui capto quin decim millium Seraphinorum, ea est aurea moneta ducatis equiualens, annuum nobis tributarium effecerat. Inter hos successus Pater Beatissime Diuino suffragante numine per uniuersam Indiam plurimi Spiritus sancti gratia igneq*ue* afflati depositis gẽtilitiis erroribus indies ad nostram religionem cõ uersi ueram dei fidem agnoscunt, obq*ue* Deo Opt. Max. summæ gratiæ sunt merito refe rendæ: quod tam procul a nostro orbe, in tam remotis regionibus, quo ne fama quidẽ sui sanctissimi nominis penetrauerat, nostra nunc sedula opera, suam ueram fidem cultumq*ue* celebrari, publicari, ac propagari dignatus sit: unde proculdubio diuina fauen te clementia sperandũ est, cum nunc Prefectus noster ad mare rubrũ ut eius ostio occupato Sarracenis ear*um* partiũ cõmertia interdicat relictis in India oportunis presidiis ingenti classe properat ut ibi coniunctis sub Crucis uexillo presbyteri Ioannis nostrisq*ue* uiribus maximum dei obsequium, & Mau metice secte detrimentum & ignominia sequatur, extremaq*ue* Orientis ora, quo & sacras Apostolor*um* uoces, intonuisse compertum est occidentali nostræ propediem iungatur, & ad ueri dei cultum ipsius suffragante numine traducatur. S. Sedi Apostolicæ ac tuæ sanctitati ut optimo pastori Christia ni gregis more debitum obsequium & obe dientiam oblatura. Bene ualeat Beatitudo tua, quam pientissimus Deus diu ac felicissime conseruare & augere ad uotum dignetur. Dat. in Vrbe nostra Olisipone. 8. idus Junias Anno Dñi. M.D.XIII.

Romæ impressum per Jacobum
Mazochium. 9. Augusti.

THE
COMMENTARIES OF THE GREAT AFONSO DALBOQUERQUE

AFOSO·DALBOQVERQVE

THE COMMENTARIES OF THE GREAT AFONSO DALBOQUERQUE,

SECOND VICEROY OF INDIA.

TRANSLATED FROM THE

PORTUGUESE EDITION OF 1774,

WITH NOTES AND AN INTRODUCTION,

BY

WALTER DE GRAY BIRCH, F.S.A.,

A SENIOR ASSISTANT OF THE DEPARTMENT OF MANUSCRIPTS IN THE BRITISH MUSEUM; MONORARY SECRETARY OF THE BRITISH ARCHAELOGICAL ASSOCIATION, ETC.

VOL. IV

"..Agora: pois que tendes apprendid
Trabalhos que vos facao ser acceitos
As eternas esposas, e formosas
Que coroas vos tecem glorioss:
Podais vos embarcar; que tendes vento
E mar tranquillo para a patria amada."
Cam. Lus., x, 142.

GYAN

Published by

GYAN

Gyan Publishing House
5, Ansari Road
Daryaganj, New Delhi-110002
Phone: 011-47034999, 9811692060
E-mail: books@gyanbooks.com

Distribution Network
gyanbooks.com
India, USA, Canada, UK, Australia, France

ISBN : 978-81-212-3261-6 (Set)
ISBN : 978-81-212-4808-2 (PB)
First Published, 1875

2nd Impression 2020

Printed at: Gyan Press, Delhi.

The Commentaries of the Great Afonso Dalboquerque Vol. IV
Author: Walter De Gray Birch

THE COMMENTARIES OF THE GREAT AFONSO DALBOQUERQUE,

SECOND VICEROY OF INDIA.

TRANSLATED FROM THE

PORTUGUESE EDITION OF 1774,

With Notes and an Introduction,

BY

WALTER DE GRAY BIRCH, F.S.A.,

A SENIOR ASSISTANT OF THE DEPARTMENT OF MANUSCRIPTS IN THE BRITISH MUSEUM; HONORARY SECRETARY OF THE BRITISH ARCHÆOLOGICAL ASSOCIATION, ETC.

VOL. IV.

"... Agora: pois que tendes apprendido
Trabalhos que vos fação ser acceitos
As eternas esposas, e fermosas
Que coroas vos tecem gloriosas:
Podeis vos embarcar; que tendes vento
E mar tranquillo para a patria amada."

CAM. *Lus.*, x, 142.

LONDON.
PRINTED FOR THE HAKLUYT SOCIETY.
M.DCCC.LXXXIV.

COUNCIL

OF

THE HAKLUYT SOCIETY.

LIST OF CONTENTS.

INTRODUCTION.

Olhai que ledos vão por varias vias,
Quaes rompentes leoens, e bravos touros,
Dando os corpos a fomes, e vigias,
A ferro, a fogo, a settas, e pilouros,
A quentes regioens, a plagas frias,
A golpes de idolatras, e de Mouros,
A perigos incognitos do mundo,
A naufragios, a peixes, ao profundo.

Cam. *Lus.*, x, 147.

The present volume contains the translation of the Fourth and last Part of the Commentaries of the Great Afonso Dalboquerque, as written by his son. The interest in the career of the hero is sustained throughout, and a short summary of the principal events recorded herein may with propriety be introduced at this part of the work. The portrait which is placed as a frontispiece to this volume is a reduced photographic facsimile from that given in Correa's *Lendas da India*, at the place which treats of that period in the history of Portuguese India when the Lusitanian sceptre was practically swayed there by this great man. Its value as a contemporary portrait is undoubtedly great, and it may be compared with the portraits derived from other sourçes which have illustrated the previous volumes of this translation.

After setting affairs in order at Goa, under the chief captaincy of Pero Mascarenhas, Afonso Dalboquerque set sail on the 7th of February, A.D. 1513, with a body of seventeen hundred Portuguese and eight hundred natives, in twenty ships, intending, in accordance with instructions which he had received from the King of Portugal, to make the voyage to Adem, with a view of capturing that site, of the importance of which, from a military and strategic point of view, he was fully aware. The passage to Socotra was made without difficulty; and while lying off the island a native vessel from Chaul was captured and forced to accompany the fleet, to prevent it carrying news of the presence of a powerful Portuguese force in Arabian waters. On the way differences of opinion as to the best manner of proceeding in the contemplated attack arose among the leaders. One party thought that negotiations should be entered into with the rulers of Adem before the attack was made; the other —and among these was Afonso Dalboquerque—considered that an immediate endeavour to gain possession of the city should be made. This was finally agreed upon. Sighting Abedalcuria, the fleet coasted along until near Meyet Island, and crossing the mouth of the Red Sea Straits, came up in sight of Adem at sunset, and avoiding a ruse artfully planned for the destruction of the ships, then proceeded to work in to the harbour. Communications were opened with Mira Merjão, governor of the city, but this man was not slow to discover the real intentions of Afonso Dalboquerque, although they were at first veiled under the pretext of an expedition to Suez. The next day, Easter Eve, preparations were made to storm the city, and some large boats of very small draught of water were seized, with a view of disembarking the men as expeditiously as possible.

At this point the author gives a long and interesting account of the situation of the city of Adem; and the view of Adem, as it appeared to Correa at the time when the attack was being made, will be found useful for comparison with a view of the same exploit, published from the original contemporary woodcut in the British Museum, by Col. H. Yule, C.B., our President, in his 2nd edition of the *Travels of Marco Polo.*[1]

The first attack upon the city, which is graphically described in chapter iii, appears to have failed, principally on account of the defective scaling-ladders then employed in the assault. It resulted in the Portuguese withdrawing their forces from off the city walls, upon which some of the more adventurous had

[1] The great reduction in scale which has been made in that view prevents the reader from making out some part of the inscription in the upper right-hand corner. It is as follows:—

"¶ Dese machteghe eñ grote stat Adē genoemt die gelege is int coniсrijc vā Persē in den wech vā mecha was bestormt eñ beuochtē vā Alfonso Dalburkerke capitein generael van dē hogē eñ machtegē edelē conīc vā portegael heer Emanuel mz drieduist vijfhōdert volcx die welke vochtē drie vrē lāo tsegē die ɪ de stat warē, dese bataelge gesciede up dē heiligē paeschauōt int iaer ōs heerē ih'u cristi als mē screef . M. CCCCC. XIIJ . Eñ als dese edele eñ wel gemoedde capitein mz sinē volcke ald warē vechtēde tsegē die ongelouige hondē eñ viandē ons heerē ih'u cristi wies den hoop der morē so seere ɪ grotē getale die binnē der stat warē dat dese edele capeteyn mz sinē volke moeste vliē tsinē scepē waert mz groter last eñ forcē al vechtēde eñ dootslaēde seer veel vā diē moren, die hem ooc groot scade dedē onder sijn volc als elckerstē mensche wel beclaghen mach."—Vol. ii, p. 438.

mounted, to the ships again, after losing, among others, Jorge da Silveira, one of the captains, and Garcia de Sousa, another, the details of whose gallant fate are related more particularly at length. As the Portuguese retired, Mira Merjão endeavoured, from his position on the island of Cira, to harass them, and did so for a time; but Dom Garcia de Noronha assaulted the tower on the island, and drove out the native forces. Shortly after this escalade, Afonso Dalboquerque received intelligence of a revolt at Cairo, the fears of the Sultan at the rumoured entry of the Portuguese into the Red Sea, and the doings of the Xeque Ismael.

Sending forward the small ship of Chaul, lately captured by João Gomez, the Portuguese commander set sail for the Straits of the Red Sea, and quickly sighted the large, lofty, and apparently barren island of Jebel-Zukur, and put in to a port on the Abyssinian side of the Red Sea, where he found some Arabs collecting slaves. These he rescued, and punished their captors in the customary barbarous manner then so frequently practised in that part of the world.

Here follows a chapter devoted to a description of the shores, winds, tides, and currents of the Red Sea, probably useful in the highest degree at the time when it was written, to those whose navigation led them into those treacherous waters. In the middle of this digression the author records two unaccomplished resolves of Afonso Dalboquerque—the diverting of the River Nile from Cairo, by piercing a range of hills, so as to throw the water into the land of Prester John; and, secondly, the landing of a small body of horsemen on the Arab coast, so as by making a dash to get possession of the body of Mahomet.

Proceeding up the Red Sea, the Portuguese fleet stood off Luya, or Loheyyah Bay, where the flag-ship grounded, but after great exertion was fortunately floated off uninjured. The next day the fleet made its way in safety to Camarão, intending to proceed to Judá, or Djiddah, but the wind proved adverse; and during the forced delay a miraculous cross—an illustration of which is given from the Portuguese text—was seen in the heavens, not only by Afonso Dalboquerque, but by all who accompanied him. After a stay of two months—June and July, 1513—at Camarão, he weighed anchor and proceeded to Ras-Zebid, a watering-place on the Arabian coast, with the intention of inquiring after certain Portuguese captives wrecked in a brigantine commanded by Gregorio da Quadra. João Gomez, who had been sent to reconnoitre the pearl-fishery on the islands of Dalaca, or Dahalak, returned with unfavourable news of the refusal of the natives to trade with the Portuguese.

At this time Afonso Dalboquerque despatched a messenger overland, by way of Cairo, to the King of Portugal, carrying news of the doings of the Portuguese in India; and on the very day after the messenger set out, a miraculous ray of light, probably a shooting star or electric ball, fell down from the sky, to the dismay of the fleet and the terror of the natives.

The author of these *Commentaries* here introduces

a relation of the wanderings of Gregorio da Quadra, whose vessel, a brigantine, in the fleet commanded by Duarte de Lemos, had broken away from her anchorage on a dark and stormy night off the coast of Melinde, the whole crew being taken prisoners next morning, opposite Adem, by the natives. The ruler of Adem appears to have been content to keep them in captivity, without exercising the cruel tortures upon them so frequently inflicted upon Europeans whose misfortune placed them in the power of Oriental princes at that time; and Gregorio da Quadra, becoming in course of time proficient in Arabic, made a stealthy visit to Medina, inspected the sepulchre of Mahomet, and after nearly perishing in the inhospitable deserts of Persia, finally reached Busrah, or Baçora, where he embarked for Ormuz, and there D. Garcia de Coutinho, the captain of the fortress, received him with great kindness. The wanderer at length returned to Lisbon, and became a Capuchin friar.

Leaving Camarão on the 15th July, A.D. 1513, the Portuguese commander explored the Island of Perim, in the Red Sea Straits, to which he gave the name of *Ilha da Vera Cruz*, and sending two vessels forward to Zeila—an expedition which bore no fruit, on account of the refusal of the natives to have any communication with the Portuguese—bore up opposite Adem, and lost no time in skirmishing with the natives, burning the shipping on the shore, and exchanging shots with forces in the towers along the beach. On the 4th of August 1513, Afonso Dalboquerque weighed anchor—abandoning for the time all further attempt to effect an entry into Adem—and ran in to Diu, where the native authorities received him with an apparent friendliness, which did not, however, deceive the Portuguese commander. From that point the voyage was continued to Chaul, whither Tristão Dega had just returned from his mission to Cambay. Setting forward again, he stopped for a short time at Dabul, where three ships under Lopo Vaz de Sampayo were left to blockade the port in order to compel the surrender of several native ships, which had left Calicut with produce against the commands of the Portuguese. By this and similar means every one of the native vessels that had left Calicut for the Straits fell into the hands of Afonso Dalboquerque, who at length reached Goa, where he was received with great joy by everyone.

Francisco Nogueira, who had been commissioned to build the Portuguese fortress at Calicut, about this time gave the commander an account of the abortive circumstances attending the building. I have been able to reproduce at p. 72 a contemporary view of the fortress from Correa's *Lendas da India* bearing the following inscription :—

"O . Rey . de . Caleqvv . cõ . temor . qve . os . nossos . tomariã . dele . vingança . da . morte . do . marichal . cõ . mvitos . rogos . Afonso . Dalboqverqve . lhe . asentov . paz . fazendo . esta . forteleza . a . sva . cvsta . qve . esteve . em . mvita . paz . ate . o . ano . de . 1525 . qve . dõ . Joam . de . Lima . sendo . capitam . alevãtov . gera . e . se . desfez . esta . forteleza . em . tenpo . do . governador . dom . anriqve . de . meneses ."

The Portuguese commander was, however, determined to bring this important matter of establishing a powerful fortress on the West Coast of India to a successful issue, and sent forward his nephew, D. Garcia de Noronha, to Calicut, to interview the Çamorim, while he himself proceeded to Cochim, and after a stormy interview with the king, which showed him how little advantage he was likely to gain by negotiations, despatched secret instructions to a brother of the Çamorim of Calicut, advising him to poison the ruler, his brother, with a view to succeeding to his power. This was effected, and the new Çamorim, owing his elevation to the Portuguese (whose influence in this proceeding admits of no palliation), showed his gratitude by conceding a site for the Portuguese fortress, which was immediately commenced, in a position which commanded the entry into the port. This fortress, invaluable as it was in all respects to a nation whose policy was to hold the coast by means of superior military organisation, was not long destined to stand, for it was destroyed in 1525, by order of D. Anrique de Menezes, the governor, to prevent it falling into the hands of the natives.

Having thus carried out successfully an undertaking calculated to overawe the races on the coast of central India, Afonso Dalboquerque sailed away to Cananor, where he received news of the unsettled state of Cairo, Suez, the Red Sea, and the coast of Arabia and Northern India. Hereupon, Pero Dalboquerque was despatched to Cape Guardafum and Adem, to acquire more precise information of the proceedings of the

Turks, who were reported to be organising an attack upon the Portuguese in India.

In December 1513, Afonso Dalboquerque sailed to Cochim, and sent Miguel Ferreira to the Xeque Ismael by way of Dabul; and, after making provision for refitting the Portuguese fleet, proceeded to Goa, whither he arrived in the beginning of January 1514. Miguel Ferreira arrived at Tauriz, and eventually reached the Xeque, who received him well, and sent him back with costly presents for Afonso Dalboquerque, and with a good impression of the Court of that potentate. The calamitous condition of the Portuguese at Malaca, reported to Afonso Dalboquerque at Goa by Manuel Fragoso, the Portuguese envoy to the Court of Siam, demanded immediate succour, which was at once sent, and arrived out just in time to reinforce the fort. The little garrison was in hourly expectation of attack by a large fleet of ninety junks, carrying 10,000 men, that arrived off the fortress a few days later; but, overawed by the three large Portuguese vessels that lay off the shore, the enemy drew off, and suffered considerable loss at the hands of Fernão Perez Dandrade, who fell upon them as they fled. To the Court of Cambay, Diogo Fernandez de Béja and James Teixeira were sent, with instructions to obtain a site for a fortress in Diu. This expedition, which, like the others, was unsuccessful, is related at considerable length in the *Commentaries*.

Pero Dalboquerque, in pursuance of the instructions he had received, cruized about off Socotra for the summer, and at the end of May bore away for Ormuz, where he was visited by the king, and after in vain attempting to recover possession of the fortress by negotiations, landed some merchandise under charge of two factors, and sailed into the Persian Gulf in July, explored it as far as Barem Island, returned to Ormuz on the home voyage (to India) in August. His endeavours to obtain the payment of tribute by the king were ineffectual; he therefore sailed away, after embarking his factors and merchandise, and reached Goa on the 28th of September 1514.

The account of the condition of Ormuz which Pero Dalboquerque was enabled to lay before his uncle Afonso Dalboquerque, incited the Portuguese commander to make his way thither with a fleet without losing any time; and after receiving visits of diplomatic importance from the ambassadors of the King of Narsinga, who desired to enter into an alliance with the Portuguese to attack the Hidalcão (a matter put off for the time by Afonso Dalboquerque), and from the Hidalcão on his own behalf, who was desirous of maintaining peaceful relations with the Portuguese, he summoned Jorge Dalboquerque from Cochim, and sent him on to Malaca with four vessels and two hundred men, to relieve that distant colony. Thus, intending to winter at Ormuz, four galleys were to be built and sent on to him at that port, with a view to their taking part in the intended expedition, during the ensuing summer, to Adem and the Red Sea Straits.

On the 25th of February 1515, a council was held at Goa by the captains of the twenty-six vessels composing the Portuguese fleet, having on board fifteen hundred Portuguese and seven hundred Malabarese. At this meeting Afonso Dalboquerque unfolded the Portuguese policy, and, after some opposition on the part of the captains, it was decided to sail to Ormuz and establish themselves in that city. On Ash Wednesday, the 21st of February, the fleet sailed out of Goa harbour, and on the 25th of March drew up opposite Curiate, on the Arabian side of the Gulf, and proceeding along the coast, anchored off Mascate, where news was obtained of the condition of the city of Ormuz, the king of which had been virtually a prisoner for the last two months in the hands of Reys Hamed, a Persian Moor.

Sailing away in a direct course, the Portuguese fleet arrived safely opposite Ormuz, where Miguel Ferreira, on his return from the embassy to the Xeque Ismael, rejoined the ships and gave Afonso Dalboquerque a detailed account of his journey. The intrigue of Reys Hamed, which appeared likely to become successful, was more than counterbalanced by the astuteness of the Portuguese governor-general, who brought about the deliverance of the king and his chief councillor Rexnordim, or Reys Nordim, by the assassination of the rebellious Reys Hamed, to whom the success of the Portuguese in getting possession of the fortress of Ormuz, on the 31st March, or 1st April, 1515, was especially galling, as interfering with his intention of usurping the royal authority in that city.

The reception of the ambassador from the Xeque Ismael in Ormuz was conducted by Afonso Dalboquerque with great pomp and magnificent ceremonies, which delighted the Oriental mind, to which such things are dear; and it was no doubt calculated to impress upon the king and the inhabitants of Ormuz the importance of the Portuguese influence in that part of the world. The author of the *Commentaries* gives a long and detailed description of these proceedings. The disarming of the inhabitants of Ormuz, and the prompt seizure of an opportunity which arose for getting possession of the enemy's artillery, were master-strokes of policy, and tended effectually towards the preservation of that territory in Portuguese hands. The inhuman treatment of the runaway Portuguese, who were burned in a boat in the principal square of Ormuz, cannot be defended. It is a typical instance of Oriental cruelty—and other instances will be met with by the reader of these *Commentaries* —probably instigated in this case by the desire on the part of Afonso Dalboquerque to make a terrible example of those who proved traitors at a time when the utmost peril would have been brought upon the whole body if any serious defection had arisen. The settlement of affairs at Ormuz; the despatching of Fernão Gomez de Lemos to the Court of the Xeque Ismael with terms of a treaty; the departure of D. Garcia de Noronha for Portugal; the reception of several native envoys; and the building of the Portuguese fortress, are among the most notable events successively chronicled in these *Commentaries* immediately previous to the supervention of the illness to which the great commander succumbed. Appointing Nicoláo Ferreira to keep guard over the King of Ormuz, and Pero Dalboquerque, his nephew, to be governor of the newly erected fortress, Afonso Dalboquerque sailed away, dangerously ill, in the *Flor da Rosa*, captained by Diogo Fernandez de Béja, on the 8th of November 1515. The disorder with which he was afflicted was aggravated by the report which reached him of the appointment of Lopo Soarez de Albergaria in his stead by the King of Portugal. On Sunday, the 16th of December, he died on shipboard at anchor off the bar of Goa, to the extreme grief of the inhabitants of Goa, who, indeed, owed their all to his bravery and forethought. The work ends appropriately with an account of the funeral obsequies; the text of the king's letter to Lopo Soarez, limiting that governor's powers in India, and continuing Afonso Dalboquerque in his office, with the exception of the fortresses of Cochim, Calicut, and Malaca, which were placed under Lopo Soarez absolutely; a well-written panegyric upon the character and achievements of the dead hero, including a review of the condition of India at the time of his death; an account of the circumstances attending the translation of the remains of Afonso Dalboquerque to the Chapel of Our Lady of Grace, at Lisbon, in April, and their final sepulture in May 1566; and a summary of the pedigree of the family, derived from Dom Dinis, King of Portugal, and Dom Sancho, King of Castile.

The Appendix will be found to contain some important information of little known Portuguese-Indian places and fortresses, as well as other matters relating to the text of the *Commentaries*.

The Index which has been compiled for the four volumes will be found useful as containing a variety of references not usually, perhaps, placed in an Index. The references to names of persons are under the Christian name or first name—a plan laudably adopted by many authors, and notably so by Barbosa Machado in his *Bibliotheca Lusitana*.

CHRONOLOGY OF PART IV.

PAGE		A.D.
1.	Afonso Dalboquerque sets sail with a fleet for Goa	7 Feb. 1513
8.	Stands in to Adem Harbour . Good Friday	[25 Mar. 1513]
10.	Prepares to attack Adem Easter Eve	[26 March 1513]
45.	Lies off Camarão, in the Red Sea, with his fleet during	June and July 1513
54.	Sails for Camarão to Perim Island, *en route* for Adem	15 July 1513
58.	Leaves Adem and proceeds to Diu . .	4 Aug. 1513
80.	Sails to Cochim	December 1513
89.	Reaches Goa . .	Beginning of January 1514
109.	Pero Dalboquerque cruizes off Socotra .	In the Summer 1514
109.	Pero Dalboquerque visits Ormuz .	End of May 1514
114.	Pero Dalboquerque sails to explore the Red Sea	7 July 1514
115.	Pero Dalboquerque returns to Ormuz .	6 Aug. 1514
118.	And arrives at Goa	28 Sept. 1514
133.	Afonso Dalboquerque embarks on board the fleet at Goa for Ormuz	20 Feb. 1515
136.	Sails for Ormuz	21 Feb. 1515

136.	Stands off Curiate	25 March 1515
147.	Takes possession of the fortress of Ormuz	31 March or 1 April 1515
179.	D. Garcia de Noronha sails from Ormuz for Lisbon	29 Aug. 1515
188.	Afonso Dalboquerque informs the captains of his illness	26 Sept. 1515
192.	Sails from Ormuz for Goa	8 Nov. 1515
196.	Arrives off Goa	15 Dec. 1515
196.	His death	16 Dec. 1515
200.	Letter from the King of Portugal to Lopo Soarez	20 March 1516
211.	Remains of Afonso Dalboquerque conveyed to Lisbon	6 April 1566
211.	Their burial	19 May 1566

COMMENTARIES

OF THE

GREAT AFONSO DALBOQUERQUE.

COMMENTARIES

OF THE GREAT

AFONSO DALBOQUERQUE,

WHO WAS

CAPTAIN-GENERAL OF THE EAST INDIES

IN THE TIME OF THE VERY POWERFUL

KING D. MANUEL,

THE FIRST OF THIS NAME

PART IV.

LISBON:

IN THE ROYAL PRINTING OFFICE,

ANNO MDCCLXXIV;

With Licence of the Royal Board of Censors, and Royal Privilege.

TITLES

OF THE

CHAPTERS CONTAINED IN THIS FOURTH PART.

WHEREIN IS CONTAINED HOW THE GREAT AFONSO DALBOQUERQUE ENTERED THE STRAITS OF THE RED SEA, AND WHAT PASSED AFTER HIS RETURN TO INDIA, AND WHAT HE DID IN THE SECOND TAKING OF THE KINGDOM OF ORMUZ, AND HOW HE DIED, AND WHOSE SON HE WAS.

PART IV.

WHEREIN IS CONTAINED HOW THE GREAT AFONSO DALBOQUERQUE ENTERED THE STRAITS OF THE RED SEA, AND WHAT PASSED AFTER HIS RETURN TO INDIA, AND WHAT HE DID IN THE SECOND TAKING OF THE KINGDOM OF ORMUZ, AND HOW HE DIED, AND WHOSE SON HE WAS.

CHAPTER I.

How, after making his fleet ready, he took counsel with his captains and pilots respecting the voyage: and how it was determined to enter the straits of the Red Sea, and what passed in the course until they reached Adem.

After the great Afonso Dalboquerque had agreed with the Captains and Fidalgoes of India concerning the affairs of Goa, and had writtten to the King D. Manuel explaining his opinions in that matter, he sent Jorge Dalboquerque, as Captain, to Cochim; for Pero Mascarenhas, who at this time held that office, was to remain in Goa as Captain, as I have related; and when this had been arranged he proceeded to embark on the seventh of February, in the year [fifteen hundred and] thirteen, and ordered the captains and men to assemble in their ships, to the number of about one thousand seven hundred Portuguese and eight hundred Malabars and Canarese in all.

And after that all had embarked, the whole fleet being now outside the bar of Goa, before sails were set he caused all the captains to be summoned to a meeting. These were:—

D. Garcia de Noronha,
Pero Dalboquerque,
Lopo Vaz de Sampaio,
Garcia de Sousa,
D. João de Sâ,
Jorge da Silveira,
D. João de Lima,
Manuel de Lacerda,
Diogo Fernandez de Bejá, Captain of Afonso Dalboquerque's ship
Simão Dandrade,
Aires da Silva,
Duarte de Mélo,
Gonçalo Pereira,
Fernão Gomez de Lemos,
Pero de Afonseca de Castro,
Ruy Galvão,
Jeronymo de Sousa,
Simão Velho,
Antonio Raposo, and
João Gomez, Captain of the caravela.

And when they had all assembled together he declared to them that the King D. Manuel, his lord, in every letter which he had written, made it a very great point that he should endeavour to capture Adem and make his way into the straits of the Red Sea; and that now, in letters brought by D. Garcia, his nephew, there present among them, this matter was still further insisted upon; but for some proper precautions which he had taken, he had as yet given them no explanation of his determination, as well also because now that the course of their proceedings had been arranged and decided by His Highness, it was no part of their duty to put to the vote whether they should act upon their orders or not, unless it should so happen that so much opposition should be shown to the orders that he would be compelled to adopt another plan. Therefore, he would beg them of their goodness if they had any objections to urge, to the end that it would not be to the service of the King to undertake the proposed expedition, to state them to him. And after much debate had ensued, it was unanimously agreed that Afonso Dalboquerque must make an entry into the straits, seeing that now the affairs of India afforded him an opportunity of effecting it.

When the council meeting was over, every one rejoined his ship, and on the morrow morning Afonso Dalboquerque ordered a gun to be fired as a signal for setting sail, and all anchors were weighed, and thus, with a favourable wind for a good voyage, they shaped their course direct to the Cape of Guardafum;[1] but, in the Gulf, the winds were so boisterous, that they lost more time than could have been anticipated by any one for that voyage, and this caused the store of water to run out; and because there was no watering place at the Cape of Guardafum for so many ships, and it seemed likely that, if delay of some days should arise on account of taking in water, the Moors of Adem might obtain information of the arrival of the Portuguese fleet, Afonso Dalboquerque ordered the whole fleet to stand in to Çacotorá,[2] and anchors were cast in the port of Çoco,[3] where our fortress used to stand. In this place, there were already about fifty Fartaquins,[4] who had begun to repair it, but as they had not yet any means of defending it, as soon as they saw the fleet they all fled to the mountain range opposite Calaceá,[5] which is a port

[1] See vol. i, p. 80.

[2] See vol. i, p. 19.

[3] Súk, on the N. coast in Tamarida Bay.

[4] See vol. i, p. 58.

[5] Ghubbet Gollonsier, *i.e.*, Gollonsir Bay, at the N.W. corner of the island. Col. Yule calls this place *Colesseeah*, and sees in it a resemblance to *Ecclesia*.—*Marco Polo*, 2nd edit., ii, 402.

situated on the other side of the island. But the native Christians came down to parley with Afonso Dalboquerque, and he ordered a present to be given to them of some cloths and rice, and all the houses belonging to the Moors to be thrown down, and set on fire everything they possessed therein.

As soon as this had been done, Afonso Dalboquerque ordered the whole fleet to take in water, and sent João Gomes to cruise along the coast in his *caravela,* round the island as far as Calaceá, for he was in fear lest there might be there some barque belonging to the Fartaquins, or some Moorish vessel, watering; which, when it passed over from the other side for Fartaque and Dofar,[1] would carry intelligence of the coming of the Portuguese. João Gomes searched all the island, and entered the port, without finding a single barque or vessel, and then set out to return, but as the winds were easterly, and contrary for returning to the port of Çoco, where our fleet had remained, he was compelled to tack, and, while he was tacking out to sea, he fell in with a ship which was on its way to the straits, and took possession of her and brought her along with him. But as she came from Chaul, with which we were at peace, and brought no spices, although there was no safe conduct among the ship's papers, Afonso Dalboquerque would not take anything out of her, but brought her in his company, in order to avail himself of the pilot in that voyage, for there was not one with him who knew the coast.

After that João Gomez had thus returned, the whole fleet having already laid in a supply of water, Afonso Dalboquerque, before setting out, discussed with all his Captains, Fidalgoes, and Cavaliers of the fleet, the manner in which they should proceed to attack the city of Adem. In this debate various different opinions were delivered.

[1] See vol. i, p. 58.

For the greater number of voices declared that on reaching the city they ought to parley with the Moors before making any attack upon it, demanding to know whether they were willing to stand in obedience and service of the King of Portugal: on the other part, others declared that without holding any further communication, they ought to attack the city.

Afonso Dalboquerque was of the latter opinion, for he said, that in important undertakings, which, like this city of Adem, had help so close at hand, it was not fitting, when they were at the crisis, to be taking counsel as to what they must do, but rather to make up their minds thoroughly to attack it; for to wish to negociate with the inhabitants was the same as giving them time to get themselves into a better condition of defence than they now were in, and opportunity for help to come to them from some other quarter, if any necessity for succour should arise; and if only the inhabitants were suffered to equip themselves for defence, then the Portuguese would have to run the risk of their lives, and put out their whole strength; therefore his opinion was that as soon as they reached Adem, without holding any further communication with the Moors (provided nothing untoward should arise), to attack the city at once, for the best advice he could give them was to forestall events which might happen, and not in the midst of peril be seeking for a remedy; for the Moors of that land would not pay tribute in consequence of philosophical arguments, but only after much blood had been spilt among them. And every one agreed with him in his opinion.

CHAPTER II.

How the great Afonso Dalboquerque set sail from Çacotorá, and reached Adem; and the reason why he did not immediately attack the city as he had intended, and the rest that took place.

As soon as this debate was over, the great Afonso Dalboquerque gave orders that all the fleet should set sail direct to Adem; and because the wind began to drop, all proceeded to warp in as much as possible, in order to get well in under the lee of the Cape of Guardafum, which lay to the windward of the fleet; for from that point, no matter from which direction the wind came, they would have it in their power to make the mouth of the straits, and notwithstanding that they altered their course from one rhumb-line to another, yet they touched in shore at a place to the leeward of Abedalcuria,[1] and from that point onward sounded the coast as they proceeded along it, with the intention of crossing over from Mete[2] to Adem. But inasmuch as the currents were contrary to the wind, and the sea ran high, our fleet experienced great difficulty for the space of three days, so that all the *caturs*, which hung at the prows of the ships for use when the fleet had entered the straits, were lost. And when the pilots made out their position to be ten leagues from Mete, they determined to cross over to Adem. But because if once they missed the port they could not make it again on account of the easterly winds, they ordered the fleet to steer a north-westerly course, so as to be continually to the leeward, and with this course they held on all that day and night, under very little sail,

[1] See vol. i, p. 199.

[2] Meyet. This is the present course. "Vessels bound to Aden during the S.W. monsoon should keep along the Somali coast until off Meyet island, when they should stretch off from it for the Arabian coast."—*Gulf of Aden Pilot*, 1882, p. 52.

and when dawn broke they were between Canacani[1] and a mountain range called Arzina[2] and on that day they made their way along the coast. But when night fell, Afonso Dalboquerque, not wishing to pass the port of Adem, ordered signal to be made for all the fleet to stop; and all the vessels lay to under bare poles until morning, when they made sail again, and at sun-down they came in sight of Adem. And as they were not acquainted with the land, and the fleet was very large, and the ships might dash one against another if they anchored, every one was of opinion that it would be well not to try and enter the port in the night, but to lay out cables with the intention of remaining in their present position for that night. And being thus minded, Pero Dalboquerque came in his boat to the ship of Afonso Dalboquerque and told him how he had found a bottom in thirty-five fathoms. On receipt of this intelligence which Pero Dalboquerque had given him, he ordered a signal to be made to the ships to weigh anchor, and with sounding[3] and leads[4] in their hands they made their way through that reef until the lead showed fourteen fathoms, very close in to the harbour of Adem. The Moors, who had already for some time had our fleet in view from a very high ridge of mountains which overlooks the whole of that sea, made fires to entice it upon a point of land which is just opposite the straits after passing Adem, thinking that our men would steer their course toward the fires, because if they had once made their way to that side they could not make the harbour again as long as the east wind blew.

But Afonso Dalboquerqe, with his accustomed caution,

[1] Called the Islands of Canicani, on the Arabian coast, N.W. of Socotra, and N.E. of Aden, in Barretto de Resende's Map. See vol. i, p. 80.

[2] Darsina, between Aden and Canicani Islands on the same map.

[3] *Traquetes*.

[4] *Prumos*, *i.e.*, Plumbos.

fearing for some unexpected event, ordered the whole fleet to come to anchor, and remained there thus at anchor during the whole of that night. On the following day, in the morning, which was Good Friday,[1] they set sail and started with intention of anchoring in the eastern harbour, but as there were many Moorish vessels already lying in the harbour, so as to occupy the whole space, our vessels remained a little way off outside.

Our men, however, being all under arms, and apparelled in all respects for disembarking, in accordance with the arrangements already concerted, desired to lose no time in getting to land, and falling upon the city. And although Afonso Dalboquerque was very desirous of gratifying their wishes, because it was Good Friday, the day of the Passion of our Lord Jesus Christ, to whom he was very devoted, and in whom he reposed all his hopes, yet seeing that the necessity of the situation somewhat altered his plans, he desired rather to insure the safety of the fleet and place the vessels where they would not be one in another's way, and strengthen their cables, with the end that if any very fierce wind should suddenly arise, no untoward event should take place; and so indeed it fell out, for after the ships had cast anchor, the east wind blew so fiercely that some of his ships had to lay out three, and others four cables.

After the burst of wind had passed over, Mira Merjão, Governor of the city, sent a message to Afonso Dalboquerque, by a Moor of Cananor who was in Adem, asking what it was that he wanted, and what it was that he had come to seek for with that fleet? Afonso Dalboquerque replied that he was the Captain-General of the King D. Manuel, King of Portugal and Lord of the Indies, that he had been on his way to Judá[2] in pursuit of the Rumes,[3] and not finding them there, had determined to go to Suez to discover

[1] *Sesta feira de Endoenças.*

[2] See vol. i, p. 234.

[3] See vol. ii, p. 60.

if the report was true that the Sultan of Cairo was daring to fit out a fleet against the power of the king his lord.

The Moor returned to land with this reply, and Mira Merjão sent him back immediately with a present of fowls, sheep, lemons, and oranges, and sent with him a message that the city of Adem was the King of Portugal's, and everything that king wished or ordered concerning it should be carried out. Afonso Dalboquerque replied to this, that it was not his practice to receive presents from lords with whom he was not in a settled state of peace, let him therefore look to his own words, for he would accept the presents on that condition only; and the Moor was told to declare to Mira Merjão that inasmuch as he was willing to be in obedience to the king his lord, he must give orders for opening the gates of the city, and must receive the Portuguese flag and soldiers in the same; and as for the Moorish merchants whose ships were there, he (Afonso) would grant them safe-conduct, and they must apply to him for the permission. Afonso Dalboquerque did this with the object of drawing these merchant ships out of the city, so as to have fewer enemies arrayed against him.

When Mira Merjão perceived by this last communication from Afonso Dalboquerque, that he liked deeds better than words, he sent him a message by two of the principal Moors of the city, that he (Mira) was the servant of the Xeque, lord of all that land, and had no permission to allow the Portuguese to enter within the city; but if he desired anything further let him come and discuss the matter at the water's edge with twenty men, and he on his part would bring the same number of men to the interview. Afonso Dalboquerque replied that he begged to be excused from taking part in any meeting between them in any other place except within the city. The two Moors thereupon returned, bearing this reply, and no further intercourse transpired, neither did the merchants take care to come and get safe-conduct for their ships, and upon this matter there was no more correspondence nor counsel. And because on account of the want of the *caturs* which were lost on the voyage, Afonso Dalboquerque was not provided with the means of disembarking the men so rapidly as was necessary, he ordered the ships to collect together some large barges[1] that drew very little water, which were used by the Moors there in the lading and unlading of their vessels, with the intention of attacking the city on the following morning before daybreak, which was Easter Eve.[2]

Of the Situation of the City of Adem.

Adem[3] is a city seated on the coast of Arabia in twelve and a half degrees of north latitude. Its circuit would be greater than that of the city of Evora, but the population is not so great. It contains very beautiful houses, very lofty, all made of stone and mortar. The city is situated at the foot of a very lofty mountain range, and along the road at the summit[4] there are many castles and towers, which seems to be a thing made more for the sake of beautiful appearances than profitable for defence.

The city lies in the mouth and fairway of the straits of the Red Sea, and close alongside of it there pass by the ships which set sail from India to the straits in the months of November, December, January, February; but those which set out in the month of March hug the coast of the Cape of Guardafum and keep always in sight of the land of Barbora[5] and Zeila,[6] but do not catch sight of Adem, for at that season of the year the west winds already begin

[1] *Barcaças.*

[2] Easter Eve in A.D. 1513 fell on March 26th.

[3] See Appendix. The best chart of Aden that I have seen is that of Commander Haines.

[4] *Comiada.* [5] See vol. i, p. 58. [6] See vol. i, p. 58.

to blow. This city is stronger on the side of the land than on that of the sea. There are two places where an entry may be effected. From this mountain range which overlooks the city comes a wall of very steep ascent,[1] reaching down to where the sea touches the city wall, which would be about the same length as in Lisbon from the Golden Gate to the gates of the dockyard. And this wall lies opposite to the harbour which the Moors call Focate,[2] which is the road whither all the ships proceed to lie at anchor, and there are two towers there with a bastion, wherein the Moors had artillery and a catapult.[3] In this harbour lies a little island of sharp rock, with not a green blade of grass upon it, separated from the city, and this the Moors call Cira;[4] the which has a mole or mass of wall crossing the harbour and sheltering the ships under it from the east wind, which, when it comes, is so furious that they suffer greatly from its effects. And at the head of this mole they have a tower and a bastion, both very strong.

When Afonso Dalboquerque returned hither after his coming from the straits he found this island surrounded with a wall with many towers made in it, that Mira Merjão had caused to be made, fearing lest our men should take it, and fortify themselves in it, when they returned to these parts, but this availed him very little, as I shall show further on. Neither in the island nor in the city is there any water except that which is brought into them by carriage, and two or three years often pass without any rain. On the back of the city, behind this mountain range, lies another harbour, which they call Ujufu,[5] sheltered from

[1] *Talhado a pique.*

[2] Bay of Hokát, south of the old town of Aden in Haines' chart.

[3] *Trabuco*, a military engine for throwing large masses of stone against the enemy.

[4] Sirah, or Fortified Island, to the east of the town on the same chart.

[5] Ras Hejáf, or Heyof, on the N. coast of the Peninsula of Aden, facing the entrance of the inner bay.

every wind. It has a bottom in which very large ships can lie at anchor, and into this harbour there runs a very narrow creek, which at low tide has but little water. Over it passes a bridge made in ancient times by the inhabitants of the city, because it formed the shortest route from Zebir[1] to Adem, where the king spent the greater part of the time. And along this road runs a stream of water, in a conduit which passes at the side of the bridge, and discharges itself into a large tank built of masonry, at a league's distance from the city, and it is to that spot that the camels are taken for water.

The water which issues out from under the arches[2] is spread over the country below in pools or lagoons, and if the inhabitants of this city had not this bridge, they could not go round in a single day so many pools as there are spread forth over those fields. And beyond this water service of the bridge, there is a broad plateau, which reaches from the interior country plain to a gate which is formed in the mountain range, having two strongly fortified towers, and by means of it they used to supply the camels with water at the very time when our fleet lay in the harbour, for from our ships and boats our people used to see them going and coming laden along the plateau and entering the gate of the mountain range.

The breadth of this isthmus, from one sea to the other, is about a quarter of a league, whence it may clearly be seen that Adem is not an island, although in ancient times it was always so held to be. But Afonso Dalboquerque, hoping hereafter to return again and attack it, desired to obtain better information about this, and ordered Manuel

[1] Perhaps the village of Biyar Ahmed, site of the Sultan's residence, to the N.W. of Aden on the chart. But from chapter ix, it is more probably Zebid, N.W. of Aden, near the Arabian coast of the Red Sea.

[2] The remains of this aqueduct are marked on the chart as still existing. Total breadth, 54 ins.; water channel, 19 ins. deep, 16 ins. wide; wall, 19 ins. on each side.

de Lacerda, Simão Dandrade, Pero de Afonseca, and Simão Velho, to take their boats and explore all this and examine it very carefully. For he often used to say that had he seen Adem he would not have attacked it on that part where he did attack it.

In front of this mountain range, on the other side of the land, lies a place which is called Rubaca, in which there lived twenty fishermen, all poor people, in straw huts, and in this district there are many pools of good drinking water and a small palm grove.

The King of Adem has about fifteen hundred cavalry soldiers, and a large force of infantry. His principal revenue, which, indeed, maintains him, is from the madder,[1] which grows in his country, of which there is a yearly crop of about twenty-five thousand bales. No one may purchase this except only the king of the land. The growers give it to him at six *xerafins*[2] the bale; and he sends it on to Cambaya, where it is used in dyeing cloth, being sold there at twenty-two [*xerafins*] the bale. All his other sources of revenue are insignificant.

This harbour of Adem was anciently a very small settlement, but after the discovery of India by the Portuguese and their navigation to that place, it began to increase, and at length became a large mart of all the kinds of merchandize which enter the mouth of the straits [of the Red Sea] inwards. The reason of this is, because the fleets which the King of Portugal always maintains on the Indian coast do not allow the ships of the Moors to make their way to those parts [which lie inside the straits] in their proper season, for these ships, to avoid capture, set out on their voyage without waiting for the monsoon, and go and discharge their merchandize at Adem, selling them to the native merchants, and then buying other goods,

[1] *Ruiva:* called in Vieyra's *Dictionary* "*Ruiva dos tintureiros*".

[2] See vol. i, pp. 43, 82, 170.

which they take back with them to India, and then, when the monsoon is come, the merchants of Adem send this merchandize to Judá, to Meca,[1] to Suez, and to other sites which lie within the straits. For this reason it was that many merchants came to settle at Adem from Cairo, from Judá, and from India, and from other such places, with large possessions. This made Adem the noble place it is to-day, being reputed to be the richest district that there is on all that coast.

CHAPTER III.

How the great Afonso Dalboquerque attacked the city of Adem, and what passed in this first attack.

When Friday was passed, the whole day being occupied in fastening the ships together with cables, as I have already said, on the following night the great Afonso Dalboquerque sent for all the captains and told them that, although it had been agreed by all that an attack should be made upon the city, the extent of the wall was so long that they had neither sufficient men nor ladders to invest the whole of it; therefore, it seemed good to him that all must unite together to make an assault upon it at one spot, so as to get a double line of men up to the wall, who could thereby succour each other; and when once they had forced their entrance into the city, they must be careful to take up such a position in respect to the Moors as to get possession of the gate of the mountain range which led towards the interior country, for if they failed to take that, they would fail to obtain any real advantage, and the Moors could place as many reinforcements as they

[1] See vol. i, p. 58.

liked inside the city, so that the Portuguese would be compelled after all to retire to their ships, and this would be a great disaster and failure for them. Therefore, it was very important for all of them to fight like cavaliers, and labour to the utmost to gain possession of the gate.

The captains began to feel somewhat disconcerted, and replied that he need not be under any misapprehension, nor bring himself to abandon undertaking the assault, for they on their part were quite ready to give him their assistance in the enterprise. This having been, therefore, thus arranged, Afonso Dalboquerque decided that D. Garcia, with the greater part of the soldiers, Fidalgoes and Cavaliers whom he could muster, were to proceed to assault the wall with their scaling ladders, on the left hand side, where the Moors had posted the larger number of their forces. For on that side there was a gate, concerning which they have a prophecy that through it the city of Adem must be captured. This gate D. Garcia endeavoured to break in, but he found it was walled up inside. Meanwhile, Afonso Dalboquerque himself, with the rest of his people, were to attack on the right hand side, and João Fidalgo, the Captain in command of the train-bands, was to take up a position between the two, having with him a very broad scaling-ladder, by means of which six men could mount abreast. At the same time Anrique Homem, with a party of a hundred ordnance soldiers, were to cross the summit of a rock which ran level with the wall, for by this means he could easily descend into the city. And as soon as our people had reached the top of the wall they were to leap down inside.

When all had been instructed in the different duties which they were to carry out, they returned to their ships, and, when there wanted two hours to daybreak, Afonso Dalboquerque ordered a trumpet to be sounded; then all came on board his ship immediately, and from it they set out just as the dawn was breaking, making their way to reach the wall. But, as the bottom of the water was very shelving, with *parcel* rocks, the boats were compelled to come to a stop about the distance of a cross-bow shot from shore, and this gave our people great trouble, for they all were forced to wade through the water, and the musketeers wetted the powder which they were bringing with them. But not the less on this account did the captains and all these servants of the king, like valiant cavaliers, take the scaling ladders on their backs, each one in the company in which he was placed, and set them up against the wall, with great efforts.

The captains who formed Afonso Dalboquerque's company, placed their scaling ladders and mounted up to the walls by means of them without any further consideration, which caused Afonso Dalboquerque great concern, for although this was a deed of daring worthy of cavaliers, it resulted in the ranks of the men of their company becoming at once disordered, with the exception of a few Fidalgoes and Cavaliers who went up the ladders at the same time with the captains, and so eager was the haste which every one made to mount, each exerting himself to be the first, that with the weight of numbers the ladders broke down.

When Afonso Dalboquerque perceived that the ladders of his party were broken, and all the rest of the men hastening towards that one which was under command of João Fidalgo, Captain of the train-bands, he was under the apprehension that they would break it also in like manner as they had done his, so he ordered the halbardiers of his company to hasten to the spot to try if, by means of their halbards, they could prop up the scaling ladder and protect it from being broken. But, notwithstanding this, the ladder broke down under the great weight of the

Adem

men, and the halbards were broken in pieces, and some of the halbardiers killed and others badly wounded.[1]

D. Garcia, also, during this time, with the assistance of the captains who were in his company, had placed his scaling ladders in position; and, although the Moors had posted a large body of men to oppose him, nevertheless, our men had manœuvred in such a manner that a great number of them had climbed to the top of the wall, and had cleared everything from off it, and planted their banner upon it. And it is declared that Garcia de Sousa was the first to plant his banner upon one of the turrets.[2]

The remainder of the men forming the company of Afonso Dalboquerque, envious at the sight of their companions who had got on the top of the wall, repaired to the scaling-ladder under charge of D. Garcia, with a view to ascending also, and so great a number of men thronged together there, one upon the other's heels, that all the scaling-ladders were broken; and D. Garcia himself was wounded, together with a large number of those under his command at that place. And when he saw that the scaling-ladders were broken, and that he himself could do nothing, wounded and in evil plight as he was he ran along the top of the wall, with the men whom he had with him, and made his way to Afonso Dalboquerque, to learn from him what was to be done. When Afonso Dalboquerque saw him in this sorry condition, streaming with blood, he said to him: "Sir nephew, do not excite yourself, for this orchard cannot produce any other kind of fruit than this; and, although these Moors now get the best of us as we have broken our ladders, I trust in Our Lord that at some

[1] See the early woodcut of this escalade in the British Museum Map Department, reproduced in Col. Yule's *Marco Polo*, 2nd ed., 1875, vol. ii, p. 438.

[2] *Cubelo.* Cubello, a sort of tower formerly erected upon the walls of a town or fortress.

other time we may be revenged upon them. Then he ordered him to make his way along the wall with his men and see if he could burst open any porthole or embrasure, so as to let some twenty or thirty cross-bowmen or musketeers pass through it, in order to help those of our forces who were on the top of the wall, and fortify themselves in the turret which they had already taken, while he himself mended some of the scaling-ladders in order to make a second attempt to get up.

D. Garcia, as soon as he arrived at the embrasure, burst it open; and inside it was about the height of a man standing upright. When our men saw the embrasure cleared, they all ran up to it so as to make good their entry through it. But D. Garcia, in accordance with the orders which Afonso Dalboquerque had given him to admit none but cross-bowmen and musketeers, tried hard to prevent any other but these from entering; yet, by this time, João de Ataíde, and some soldiers, had already forced their way in. The Moors, perceiving so small a number of our men on the wall, and the scaling-ladders broken, swarmed up at the mouth of the embrasure, intending to prevent our men from entering in; and, with great store of lighted straw, and earth, and stone, which they cast in, soon covered up the embrasure again, most of our party of cross-bow men and musketeers being by this time dead, and many others wounded, for they could not get in on account of the suffocating smoke; while our other party, who were on the top of the wall, not being provided with lances, could not drive away the enemy who were engaged in closing up the embrasure, for when they had climbed to the top of the wall the only weapons they carried were short swords and bucklers.

CHAPTER IV.

How Jorge da Silveira, with some Fidalgoes who were on the wall, leaped down inside and went to attack the Moors; and the rest that took place.

When the Captains, Fidalgoes, and Cavaliers, who were on the top of the wall—that is to say, Jorge da Silveira, Aires da Silva, D. João de Lima, Vicente Dalboquerque, D. João Déssa, Ruy Galvão, João de Meira, Ruy Palha, João de Ataíde, Manuel da Costa, João Gonçalvez de Castelo-Branco, Tristão de Miranda, Garcia de Sousa, D. Alvaro de Castro, Lourenço Godinho, Gil Simões, and other servants of the king—perceived that the Moors were barking at them below, piqued at the little account in which they were held by them, and without waiting for any further reinforcements, they leaped down at them, and, with brave endeavours, came to close quarters with them, and, pursuing them as they ran, they got in, altogether in a confused mass, inside the palisades which had been set up at the mouths of the streets leading to the market square, until they reached a terrace, where they slew very many of the enemy.

Mira Merjão, the Captain of the city, who was watching the train-bands, which Afonso Dalboquerque had stationed on the edge of the mountain range, to see that they did not make any movement of coming down, for, if they had come down, they would have fallen upon him in the rear, and, in that case, would have inflicted a severe blow upon him, saw that they did not make any move, so he sallied out, with a band of about a hundred Moors, and fell upon our party from the wall. These showed him a very good front, killing some of his men and wounding Mira Merjão himself. But, while this was being done, so many Moors rallied together to support him, that our men were compelled to retire up against the wall, Jorge da Silveira having been killed, and some of the soldiers wounded in the encounter.

Meanwhile, Garcia de Sousa, Duarte de Mélo, Gaspar Cão, Diogo Estaço, Diogo de Andrade, João de Sousa, André Correa, and a mulatto man, belonging to Garcia de Sousa, fortified themselves in a turret; and the others watched on the wall for the Moors who were following up in close pursuit after them. These, when they arrived near to them, were handled very severely (the ground being on a level with this landing) with darts[1] and arrows; for our men had no lances which would have enabled them to attack the enemy from the top and drive him away. Afonso Dalboquerque, who was on the outer side, close up to the wall, seeing them thus hard pressed, gave orders to reconstruct, out of the splinters of the broken scaling-ladders, another one, lashed together with cords, whereby they could get up and rally to the support of those on the wall. No sooner had this newly made scaling-ladder been set up against the wall—every one being desirous of mounting it, and failing to make way for those who were above to descend by means of it—so large a body of men got upon it that it was again broken into pieces. Anrique Homem, who was drawing off with train-bands party under his command, ashamed of being the cause of this disaster, and of the careless way in which he had acted in this attempt to succour our men, made an endeavour to get down the ladder again; but, because there was no longer any time to do it, Afonso Dalboquerque ran up in haste and reproved him, and made him turn back, and then returned to D. Garcia, whom he had left mending a scaling-ladder and ropes so that our men might drop down from the wall. But because the ladder was a little too short, most of our men slid down the ropes in safety, and, at length

[1] *Zagunchos.*

none were left in the turret on the top of the wall except Garcia de Sousa and one more, his mulatto man. Then Garcia de Sousa, seeing that all had deserted him—some of them, indeed, with such haste that they broke their legs—began to call out aloud to Afonso Dalboquerque: "Sir, order some men to come up here, to help me in defending this turret, for those who were with me have deserted me." Afonso Dalboquerque, in a great rage at seeing affairs turning out thus, without any means of improvement at his hands, replied: "I know not what to do for you, all the scaling-ladders are broken, and we have nothing wherewith we can make any more. The hour of Adem is not yet come, so I beg you to save yourself by these ropes, just as these other Captains and Cavaliers here with me have done."

Garcia de Sousa made no answer to this, but turned himself to the Moors, who were working their way to get in at him in the turret, and said to his mulatto man: "Do thou save thyself, for I shall die here, for never would God have it that I should go down except by the same way which I went up. Thou shalt take this, my buckler, to the king, our lord, in order that it may be a witness before him how I have met my end here in his service." Then he took out a piece of the Wood of the Cross, which he wore round his neck, and gave it to the mulatto man. By this time the Moors had already got on the top of the wall close to the turret, and he and his mulatto man defended themselves so stoutly that none of the enemy could get into it, until at length Garcia de Sousa was struck with an arrow on the head, which laid him low, after he had made great havoc among the Moors.

When the mulatto, who was already severely wounded, saw his lord was dead, he took the buckler and let himself slide down by the ropes. This buckler was made after the fashion of those of cowhide, which are used by the Malabar people, and on this account it was thick with arrows. The combat lasted from daybreak until midday, at which time our men withdrew. I do not blame Garcia de Sousa because he rashly refused to do that which the other Fidalgoes and Cavaliers had done, neither do I blame those of whom he complained, for deserting him, for all the scaling-ladders were broken, and the wall was very lofty, and there was no means of scaling it, nor place where the artillery could fire against it so as to effect a breach, because the tidal water came up close to the spot. Let him who reads these Commentaries decide the matter for himself.

CHAPTER V.

How the great Afonso Dalboquerque, after having collected all his forces together, and made ready to embark, commanded D. Garcia to capture the artillery placed in the Island of Cira, with which the Moors were firing upon him.

The great Afonso Dalboquerque having all his forces collected together for re-embarking, Mira Merjão ordered an attack to be made upon him with the artillery which he had in a tower upon the Island of Cira, with the result of killing some of our men and wounding many. Seeing the damage which the large guns of the enemy inflicted upon him, and that he could not resist them because he had no scaling-ladders nor means of getting to close quarters with them, and his people much exhausted with their labour, and the excessive heat of the weather, Afonso Dalboquerque proceeded to embark—the high tide being already close up to the foot of the wall—much against every one's wishes, for they were desirous of returning again to the combat, and wanted Afonso Dalboquerque to order the heavy guns to be taken out of the ships and put on shore and trained on the wall, so as to effect an entry under cover of their fire.

But Alfonso Dalboquerque, who was well aware that this could not be carried out, on account of the difficulty which I have already spoken of, with respect to the tide, and also because the east monsoon was beginning to fail, and a single day more spent at Adem would put the fleet to the hazard of being lost for want of water, and to turn back would be equivalent to the loss of two months and a half, and if they wished to enter the straits [of the Red Sea], the east wind was just on the point of ceasing to blow, would not undertake this, but withdrew to the ships with all his forces; and, on the following day in the morning, ordered D. Garcia de Noronha, his nephew, with all his men, to go and take possession of the tower and bulwark of the Island of Cira. On his arrival at the foot of the tower, with the force that accompanied him, D. Garcia bore himself so bravely in the attempt, that he took it with very little damage on our side. As for the Moors, they could not stand against the onset with which we fell upon them; many threw themselves down from the wall, others fled into the city, and those who were left were all put to the sword. There were taken in this tower and bulwark thirty-six cannon,[1] of the size of our *camelos*,[2] and others somewhat smaller. D. Garcia, with this victory, kept himself stationed there until Afonso Dalboquerque desired to set sail for the straits, bombarding the city and throwing down many houses in it.

When D. Garcia had returned to the ships, Afonso Dalboquerque ordered all the masters of the ships to refit them with rigging and shrouds, and all other things that they had need of, out of the ships of the Moors which were lying in the harbour; and the captains and soldiers in the fleet to strip them of all the merchandise which they carried, and gather together all the provisions they could find. And when the Moorish ships were thus sacked and despoiled

[1] *Bombardos*, mortars.

[2] See vol. i, p. 73.

of all their contents, Afonso Dalboquerque ordered that they should be set on fire, and thus all were consumed without a single one remaining.

All that can be said concerning this attempt upon Adem is, that the Captains, Fidalgoes, and Cavaliers engaged in it, attacked the city with great bravery and fierce onset, but Fortune, envious at seeing them at the point of gaining with such great honours a city of such importance as that was, under the very beard of the Grand Sultan, would have it that the scaling-ladders should be broken all at the same time; for without contradiction they would have taken the city had it not been for this unexpected accident, seeing that there was no force of the enemy who could dare to fight at close quarters with our men in the streets of the city, notwithstanding that three days had already elapsed since our fleet had been sighted from the heights of the mountain range of Arzina[1] ere it arrived before the harbour of Adem. It would have been, indeed, a very creditable deed for Portugal, and highly advantageous towards the security of India, if we had gained possession of Adem and fortified ourselves in it.

Afonso Dalboquerque, indeed, often used to say that for the preservation of India, and the prevention of troubles arising from that territory to the Kings of Portugal, there were four things, of which their possession by the Portuguese must be made very strong and very sure. These were: Adem, in order to have dominion over the Straits of Méca, before the Grand Sultan could forestall them in their seizing it; Ormuz, so as to have supreme rule over the Straits of Baçorá; and Diu and Goa, for the sovereignty of all the other districts of India. And with these four places assured to Portugal, and fortified with very strong fortresses, she could avoid many other unnecessary expenses to which she was now subject.

[1] See p. 7; Camões calls this Arzira, see p. 30.

A fortnight after the day when Afonso Dalboquerque had reared the scaling-ladders against the walls of Adem, news reached Cairo by the camel-post sent from the Xeque of Adem to the Grand Sultan, to the intent that he would have him to know that the Portuguese had effected an entrance into the Red Sea, and intercepted the route of the pilgrimages to Méca. The reply sent back was to the effect that if the Christians had made good their entrance into the straits, the Xeque must keep a good guard over his harbours and his lands, just as he himself intended to do the same over his. The reason of the Grand Sultan's reply being couched in such dry terms was that a few days ago he had sent a message to the Xeque desiring that he would hand it over to him, for it had belonged to his father and his ancestors; but the Xeque's answer to this demand had been that he was not aware that Adem ever had any other lord than himself. And the Moor who brought back this reply also gave intelligence that Judá was being depopulated of all the women and children, out of fear of our fleet; that in Cairo a great revolt had broken out because it was reported that the Christians were coming up against Alexandria, and the Xeque Ismael, with a great army, against Aleppo; that the Grand Sultan, upon hearing of the entry of our fleet within the straits, had fallen into a great state of alarm, because he was of opinion that this was part of a preconcerted plan made by everyone to effect his destruction; and that the same Xeque had ordered the execution of Amirquebir, Udaquebir, and Mircelaquebir, the three principal captains of his kingdom, on account of the suspicion which he had that they were privy to this conspiracy against him, and had summoned to his presence the Governor of Damascus, who would not go at his command, because he feared lest he should be subjected to the same death which had overtaken the others at the Xeque's orders. All this news was corroborated afterwards before

Afonso Dalboquerque, by an Abyssinian[1] who came off with Ruy Galvão in Zeila on the return voyage out of the straits.

CHAPTER VI.

How the great Afonso Dalboquerque set out from the harbour of Adem with his fleet, and made sail direct for the straits.

When the great Afonso Dalboquerque was now quite ready to set forth, and all the fleet supplied with everything necessary for the sureness of their voyage, he sent forward, in advance of the vessels, a ship of Chaul, which João Gomez had captured in Çacotorá, having on board twenty Portuguese and a Jew for interpreter, giving them directions to take a pilot for him at the entrance of the straits out of the number of those who dwell there, for he was afraid that if they were to see our whole fleet they would flee away, and he would be left without a pilot. The ship had no sooner arrived at an island which lies at the mouth of the straits than one of these pilots came up and hailed her, and came on board, asking if there was need of a pilot. Then our people came out of their hiding as soon as they had the pilot on board, and laid hands upon him. These pilots are called Rubães; they live at the entrance of the straits, in the island of which I have already made mention. They conduct the navigation from that point inwards, and have great experience of all the shallows and harbours of those parts; and the ships which are making for port inside the straits call at that island for a pilot, paying thirty cruzados for his services as far as Judá.

As soon as this Chaul ship had gone forward, Afonso Dalboquerque ordered the whole fleet to be towed out of the harbour, and set sail direct for the straits, and in two days' time reached the mouth. And as they were the first

[1] See further on, chapter xi.

Portuguese who had ever reached that point since the discovery of India, the great Afonso Dalboquerque ordered that the ships should be dressed with their flags, and all the artillery fired, and great rejoicing made; and they proceeded to anchor in the eastern harbour which lies just inside the gate of the straits. When the fleet was anchored, our men (who had gone forward in the Chaul ship) came back, bringing with them the pilot whom they had captured; and, although Afonso Dalboquerque carried three whom he had taken in some ships from Zeila which had reached the harbour of Adem, he was very much pleased at the sight of this one, and gave him a very good reception. On the morning of the following day, an inward-bound Moorish ship hove in sight, making for the passage, but as soon as she caught sight of our fleet, she hauled down her sails and went and anchored behind an island lying in the mouth of the straits, which they call Mium,[1] and as she lay to windward of us, she was saved.

Afonso Dalboquerque, seeing that the time was passing quickly, and that his great need of water had put him into considerable difficulty, not knowing where he could get it if the Moorish pilots had not said that they would be able to furnish it for him in Camarão, would not allow himself to be detained any longer, and on the next day set sail, shaping his course through the broad sea which is in the middle of the straits. Keeping the coast of Arabia and of the Preste João always in sight, the Portuguese fleet drew along in front of an island which lies in the middle of this passage called Jebelzocor,[2] but could not put in that day;

[1] Perim Island, sometimes called Meyún, a bare rocky island, rather flat, about three miles long and one and three-quarters broad, close to Cape Bab-el-Mandeb.

[2] Jebel Zukur, lying on the parallel of 14 deg. N., is by far the highest island in the Red Sea, and may perhaps be considered a small mountain. It is twenty-eight miles in circuit, and nearly nine miles long from north to south, composed of a series of lofty hills of barren aspect.

and as the land was new to them, which they had to explore with the lead-line in their hand, and the sun was nearly set, Afonso Dalboquerque told the pilots to show him a harbour, and they caused the fleet to draw up opposite the Arabian coast, and then proceeded to take it to a headland, where he remained under shelter from the east wind; there the fleet cast anchor, riding in a bottom of from eight to twelve fathoms. In this harbour there were found four ships from Barbora and Zeila, laden with supplies for Judá and Méca, and in it were taken some Abyssinian women and youths, whom the Moors were carrying to sell in Judá. But as this was the land of the Preste João, Afonso Dalboquerque would not allow them to be made captives; but of the Moors they took only a few, for most of them saved themselves by swimming off, and those who remained, he punished by cutting off their hands, ears, and noses, because they were subjects of the Xeque of Adem, and ordered them to be put down on their own land; and in like manner he served all those whom he took inside the straits, except those of Camarão, because he had determined to make a treaty of peace with that land.

CHAPTER VII.

Description of the lands adjacent to the harbours of the Red Sea Straits inwards.

The gates of the straits, which the Moors call Babelmandem, are exceedingly narrow. They lie in a latitude of twelve degrees and two-thirds, and in the very mouth of the straits there lies an island extended right across it which the Moors call Mium, and on one side stretches the territory of the Preste João called Jazem by the Moors, and on the other lies the mainland of Arabia. Between this island

and terra-firma runs a passage or canal about one league only in breadth, through which pass all the ships of the Moors bound to Suez and all the other parts thereabouts, for they come with the east winds, and they lie to on the Arabian side of the land, which forms a very sheltered harbour for them. And in front of this island of Mium, in the same harbour and shelter from the east wind, lies a small islet,[1] to which at low tide one can walk dry-shod on to terra-firma. It is in this island that the Rubães live, who are the pilots of the straits. In the middle of this canal the soundings are about twelve fathoms, and in the harbour sheltered from the east winds the soundings vary from seven to nine fathoms. In these two islands there is no fresh water, neither is there any in the harbour of shelter from the west winds, but it is brought there from terra firma on camels; and behind the island of the Rubães, just before the entrance to the gates of the strait, on the side of terra firma there is a good harbour of shelter from the west winds, which has water at some little distance from the sea-shore. Between the island of Mium and the land of the Preste João[2] runs another canal, which has about seventy-five fathoms' depth of water, and is about two leagues in breadth. Few ships navigate this canal, although it is wider and deeper than the other, and the reason of it is that it possesses no harbour of shelter from the east winds wherein they can ride at anchor, if there is any necessity to do so.

The Moors divide their navigation of the Red Sea[3] into

[1] Sheikh Malu, or Oyster Island on Lieut. Gray's Chart of Perim Island, 1874.

[2] See vol. ii, p. 229.

[3] Camões makes the prophetic siren sing :—

"O cabo vê já Arómata chamado,
E agora Guardafú, dos moradores,
Onde começa a boca do affamado
Mar Roxo, que do fundo toma as cores :

three partitions, and take for their fundamental basis this. that in the breadth of the Red Sea there are twelve *gemmas*,

Este como limite está lançado,
Que divide Asia de Africa ; e as melhores
Povoações, que a parte Africa tem,
Maçuá são, Arquico, e Suanquem.

"Vês o extremo Suez, que antiguamente,
Dizem, que foi dos Héroas a cidade,
Outros dizem que Arsinoe, e ao presente
Tem das frotas do Egypto a potestade:
Olha as aguas, nas quaes abrio patente
Estrada o grão Moysés na antigua idade:
Asia começa aqui, que se apresenta
Em terras grande, em reinos opulenta.

"Olha o monte Sinai, que se ennobrece
Co'o sepulchro de sancta Catharina:
Olha Toro, e Gidá, que lhe fallece
Agua das fontes doce, e crystallina:
Olha as portas do estreito, que fenece
No reino da secca Adem, que confina
Com a serra d' Arzira, pedra viva,
Onde chuva dos ceos se não deriva.

"Olha as Arabias tres, que tanta terra
Tomam, todas da gente vaga e baça,
Donde vem os cavallos para a guerra,
Ligeiros, e feroces, de alta raça.
Olha a costa, que corre até que cerra
Outro estreito de Persia, e faz a traça
O cabo, que co'o nome se appellida
Da cidade Fartaque alli sabida.

"Olha Dofar insigne, porque manda
O mais cheiroso incenso para as aras," etc.

Lusiadas, x, 97-101.

"The Cape which Antients 'Aromatic' clepe
Behold, yclept by Moderns Guardafú;
Where opes the Red Sea Mouth, so wide and deep,
The Sea, whose ruddy bed lends blushing hue:
This as a bourne was far thrust out to keep
Asia distinct from Africk, and a few

that is, three daily courses,[1] containing about thirty leagues in the widest part of the straits, and these they divide in the following manner; that is to say, four *gemmas*, or one *sangradura*, of foul sea, islands, shallows and parcel reefs, along the Arabian coast as far as Suez; and other four

Of the best markets Negro sea-boards claim
Arquico are, Masuá and Súanquem.

"View extreme Suez where, old annals say,
Once stood the city hight Hero'opolis;
By some Arsin'oe called, and in our day
She holdeth Egypt's fleets and argosies:
Behold the watery depths, where clove his way
Moses, the mighty, in past centuries:
Asia beginneth here her huge extent
In regions, kingdoms, empires opulent.

"See Sinai mountain, with her boast and pride,
The silver bier of saintly Catherine:
See Toro-port and Gidá, scant supplied
With fountain-water soft and crystalline:
Behold the straits which end the southern side
Of arid Aden-realms, that here confine
With tall Arziran range, nude stone and live,
Whence soft, sweet rains of heaven ne'er derive.

"See threefold Ar'aby, cov'ring so much ground,
Where tawny peoples vague o'er vasty space;
Whence come the Rabytes* best for battle found,
Light-limbed, high-fettled, noble-blooded race.
Behold the coast that trends to bind and bound
Yon other Persian Strait, where sight can trace
The Headland proud the potent name to own
Of Fartak-city, erst to fame well-known.

"Behold insign Dofar that doth command
For Christian altars sweetest incense-store," etc.

Burton.

* Arab horses.

---

[1] *Sangraduras.* The *Sangradura*, or *Singradura*, is the way or progress made by a ship during the space of twenty-four hours.

gemmas of foul sea, as already described, along the territory of the Preste João as far as Çoar,[1] which lies nearly north and south with Otor,[2] close to Suez; and other four *gemmas* are of clear sea, which runs in the middle of the straits; and in these two repartitions which the Moors make of the foul sea, the soundings vary from eight to twelve fathoms; the bottom is parcel reef, and with the lead-line in hand, one can heave-to and get under weigh as much as one likes, and ride at anchor where one wills. But for the navigation of this rough sea pilots are taken at the gates of the straits; for if the weather prove unfavourable they can take a ship into port between the islands and shallows from any one part to any other.

The çanal which leads to the middle of the straits, which the Moors call broad sea, has a depth of from twenty-five to forty fathoms, and for its navigation ships have no need of taking the pilot, for whereas they come in settled weather, the same winds which bring them enable them to navigate this broad sea, and pass by the island which is called Jazelzocor,[3] that lies, as I have already said, in the midst of the straits; and beyond this, opposite Judá,[4] lies another island which they call *Sertão*,[5] and they ride at anchor off these when they think fit, for they have very good roadsteads there. And in spite of all the absurdities[6] which have been anciently reported about this foul sea, our ships can navigate it from one side to the other securely by day with proper precautions, but not by night; and they can navigate the middle of the straits by night or by day without any embarrassment, anchoring at will, provided they are furnished with strong cables.

[1] See vol. i, p. 84.

[2] Tór, for the initial letter here is the Portuguese article, as in Oporto; see plan of Tór on the Admiralty chart, No. 8*a*, Red Sea, sheet 1.

[3] See p. 27, where the name of the island is given as Jebelzocor.

[4] Here probably Eïd.

[5] Kurdumyat (island) or Çurdomeate.

[6] *Biocos*, see vol. iii, p. 67.

The straits have no fresh water, neither are there rocks sunken below the water, just a wash covered by the sea, as the Moors of those parts used in ancient times to declare, only so that no one should dare to navigate them. There are no storms there, nor contrary winds, nor thunderings:[1] the winds that blow in the spring are always easterly, and those that blow in the winter westerly; but sometimes for an hour, immediately after nightfall, when the east winds drop, there is a land breeze. It is a hot land:[2] the Moors call these straits of the Red Sea, in their language, Bahar Queixum, which means in ours "the enclosed sea", and, in my opinion (not following the ideas of those who have written the history of India, but following in this respect the opinion of Afonso Dalboquerque, who was the first after its discovery to penetrate through the gates of the straits), this name Red Sea, or Vermilion Sea, is more suitable to it than any other, and he who first called it by this name had very good reason for it, because all the straits of the Red Sea are full of many spots as scarlet as blood.

And when Afonso Dalboquerque was riding at anchor, with all his fleet, off the point of the straits in the harbour of shelter from the west winds, being then already on his return voyage to India, he saw from the masthead of his ship a streak of sea of a very crimson colour, discharging itself through the mouth of the straits in an outward direction, and running down opposite Adem, and extending within the straits as far as a man could stretch his sight. Afonso Dalboquerque, being terrified at this, asked the Moorish pilots what was the meaning of that great expanse

[1] Hurricanes or heavy storms are almost unknown in the Red Sea, but fresh gales and close-reefed topsail breezes are of constant occurrence.

[2] The climate of the Red Sea, with exception of that of the Persian Gulf, is perhaps the hottest in the world. At the end of June the temperature is about 98 deg. Fahr., rising to 105 deg. in August in the shade.

of vermilion colour in the sea. They told him not to be alarmed, because the revolution which the tide made in the waters, as the bottom was so rocky, and of little depth, together with the flow of the tide, were the causes of that vermilion colour, and it is principally at the ebb that the waters run out of the straits more rapidly, for within the straits there would not be any current of waters; and when the winds are high, the water would run a little with the wind, especially when it blows from the west, for then the waters run more strongly out of the straits, and the sea is even of a deeper vermilion colour. These reasons seemed good to Afonso Dalboquerque, and he was convinced that this was the way to account for these things, and that the cause of this redness was the nature of the soil at the bottom of the sea. From the head of the straits, that is, from Suez, to the Levant Sea [of the Mediterranean], is a very short road; and, according to that which the Moors have recorded in their writings, when Alexander conquered this land, he formed an intention of uniting this sea to the Levant by using the River Nile; and the Moors, with whom Afonso Dalboquerque conversed, told him that traces could yet be seen where this work had been commenced, which is a road of sandy desert, running from Cairo to Jerusalem, which the Moors call Ramilá.[1]

Setting out from the gates of the straits along the coast of Arabia as far as Camarão,[2] all the land is under the domination of the Xeque of Adem, and along the sea there is not a single town nor first-rate harbour; there are only villages and points of land jutting out into the sea, which shelter the ships that stand in and anchor there from the east and west winds: and from Camarão as far as Judá belongs to the Xerife of Jazem. Judá belonged to the

[1] Ramleh. Traces of this canal are to be seen in the Wady túmilat lately traversed by our troops from Ismailijeh to Tel-el-Kebir.

[2] Kamarán Bay, below Loheyyah. See plan of Kamarán on Admiralty chart, No. 14.

Xerife Parcati, but at the time that Afonso Dalboquerque arrived there, it was subject to the Grand Sultan of Cairo, who had placed there a factor with twenty Mamelukes to collect the taxes upon the spiceries and all other sorts of merchandise which reached the port. It was a small place, and the greater part of the houses were built of straw. But when D. Francisco de Almeida overcame the Rumes,[1] Mirocem came to live at Judá, and encircled it with a wall and built towers on the land side for fear of the Alarves who live there in those deserts as far as Méca (which would be about a day's journey), for they come down and rob the inhabitants of the land; and on the side of the sea there was nothing to fear. This harbour of Judá is girt with sharp-pointed ridges of rock like little islands, and close to the land it has hidden banks. It is sheltered from all winds. There are no provisions in the land; they procure all they require from Barbora and Zeila[2] and Alaca[3] and Meçua.[4] And in those days, when Afonso Dalboquerque stayed within the straits, the inhabitants suffered great privations, for the Moors did not dare to make the voyage.

From Judá all the way to Otor there live many bands of Alarves. Otor is a city of Christians. From Acintura,[5] and so on as far as Suez, throughout the interior country, they are all Alarves who live in those deserts, nearly as far as Jerusalem, spreading themselves along the sides of the range of Mount Sinai, between the Persian Gulf and the Red Sea. Between Judá aud Otor, along the shore of the sea, there lies a harbour which is called Liumbo,[2] and from that

[1] See vol. ii, p. 16.

[2] See p. 10.

[3] Ras Alargah, near Jebel Hasan (Aden).

[4] Massowah, or Musawwá Island, the port of Abyssinia, in the northern extremity of Harkiko Bay.

[5] Ras Sedour, in the Gulf of Suez, on the Arabian coast between Suez and Tor.

[6] Liumbo, now Yenbo, the port of entry for Medina, on a low sandy shore on the northern side of an inlet of the sea. The entrance to the

place, two days' journey into the interior country, lies the city of Midina, where the body of their false prophet is preserved.

Afonso Dalboquerque had made up his mind to carry out two important undertakings if death had not prevented him (or, to speak more accurately, if the King D. Manuel, listening to the counsel of his enemies, had not ordered him home from India). The first was to pierce through a very small range of hills which runs along the side of the River Nile in the land of the Preste João, so as to divert its waters into another bed, and destroy the irrigation of the lands of Cairo. It was for this object that he sent many times to beg the King D. Manuel to forward to him workmen from the Island of Madeira, accustomed to cut the rocks, so as to make trenches, with which they used to water the sugar-canes in that island. This undertaking could be carried out very easily, for the Preste João was very desirous of accomplishing it, but had no means of carrying it out; and if this had been done (as I believe it could have been done if Afonso Dalboquerque had lived), the land of Cairo would have been entirely destroyed. For, if the Alarves who lived in the desert between Caná[1] and Coçaer[2] were powerful enough to break through the bank, and divert the rising of the Nile whenever they quarrelled with the Grand Sultan, as I shall describe further on, it is clear that it would have been far more easy for Afonso Dalboquerque to do so, with the aid of the Preste João.

The other enterprise was that, on his return entry into the straits of Méca (as he hoped with the help of God to ac-

harbour lies in lat. 24 deg. 4 min. 30 sec. N. There is a loopholed wall, formerly of considerable strength, now in ruins; the houses also are falling into decay.

[1] Keneh. See further on in this chapter.

[2] Kosair, in lat. 26 deg. 6 min. N. There is a caravan route to the river Nile, four days' journey to the westward, formerly used by passengers travelling overland between Europe and India.

complish very soon), he had a mind to fit out an expedition of four hundred horsemen in *taforeas*, disembark them in the harbour of Liumbo, march rapidly to the temple of Méca,[1] and strip it of all its treasures, for they were, indeed, many; taking as well the body of its false prophet, and conveying it away, with a view to ransoming the Holy Temple of Jerusalem in exchange for it. This could have been carried out very easily, for it is but a day and a half distant from Midina, where his bones lie, and that is but a small place, with no one in it except a few Moors who are accounted saints, with painted finger-nails,[2] and maintained by alms sent to them from Cairo and from the Xeque Parcati, who used to be lord of that territory. For, with three hundred horsemen of the Alarves, without arms, none would dare to attack our party, and to get succour from Cairo would take them thirty or forty days, for they would have to get ready a large transport service of caravans of camels carrying water and provisions for their men, because the country round about is nothing but sand and desert, and without water. Much less could help be obtained, for by the time that the news of our entry into Midina had reached Cairo, we should have all returned to the port of Liumbo, and re-embarked.

From the Island of Mium, which lies at the entry of the straits, as I have already said, as one goes along the shore of the territory of the Preste João as far as Dalaca,[3] two

[1] Méca here must be an error for Midina or Medina. Jiddah or Judá is the port of Mecca, and the body of Mahomet does not lie in that city, but at Medina, of which city Liumbo, that is Yenbo, is the proper port.

[2] *Com as unhas alfenadas.* The *alfena* is considered by Vieyra to be the privet plant. Perhaps a stain was made from the juice of the berries. The expression is clearly one of contempt; the last word, however, may be connected with *alfenim* a long and slender roll of sugared paste used in Arabic pharmacy; hence the term *homem de alfenim*, a slender, delicate, or dainty man.

[3] Dahalak Bank and Islands, lying between the parallel of 15 deg. 25 min. N. and 16 deg. 38 min. N.

Moorish lords are rulers of the country, one of whom is called Azali, and the other Dancali. From Dalaca, as far as Maçuá,[1] Çuaquem[2] and Arquico,[3] lies the land of the Preste João, whose lordship is extended along the coasts of the interior country of Magadoxo and Çofala; on this further side of the Red Sea, it is extended over against Cairo as far as Çuaquem; and in the interior it is bounded by Nuba,[4] and the land of the Moors called *Ajaje*,[5] from which site comes the gold to Çuaquem, in little square blocks like dice. The Abyssinians only call the Preste João by the name of Elati, which is the name of "Emperor".

From Çuaquem, as far as Coçaer, the land is inhabited by bands of Alarves, a people rich in horses, and most of them armed. Coçaer lies on the shore of the Red Sea; it is a large city,[6] but depopulated, with old buildings of masonry, and ruins, churches having marks of crosses on the walls, and inscription in Greek letters, from which it appears that at some time or other it was inhabited by Christians. On the road from this city of Coçaer, which is situated, as it were, just at the top of the Red Sea, a distance of three days' journey[7] through the interior to the Nile, lies a village, with a few houses called Canaa,[8] through which at that

[1] Not the same as above, Massowah, but Macowa or Makawwa Island, lat. 20 deg. 44 min. N.

[2] Suakin or Sawákin.

[3] Argeego, or Harkikó Bay.

[4] "Ve Méroe, que ilha foi de antiga fama
Que ora dos naturaes Nobá se chama."—*Cam. Lus.*, x, 95.

[5] *Aji* is the most powerful of the Somali tribes, S.E. of Abyssinia.

[6] See plan of Kosair on the Admiralty chart, No. 8*b*, Red Sea, sheet 2.

[7] Four days, according to the *Red Sea Pilot*, 2nd ed., 1873, p. 61.

[8] This is the place called Cana a little further back in this chapter. It is Keneh or Kenopolis. Of it, Ebers, in his *Egypt*, vol. ii, pp. 223, 224, says:—"Keneh......has long since supplanted the ancient Koptos (now Kuft) as the starting-point of the caravans travelling from the Nile to the Red Sea and the harbour of Koseyr. In former times great quantities of corn were exported from Egypt to Arabia by this route, but now the grain destined for Djiddah is more commonly sent round

time the Portuguese and Castilian Jews used to make their route to India. The reason of choosing this route, in preference to that through Judá, was that they were terribly afraid of passing through Méca.

In the interior of this country, between Coçaer and Canaa, there live many Alarves, horsemen and foot soldiers, and, when they were at variance with the Grand Sultan, they used sometimes to cut the bank of the Nile when the waters were rising, and let out the waters along some extensive valleys of their land, in order to be revenged upon him. The Sultan, in order to prevent their doing so great an injury to Cairo, as it would be if he were deprived of the irrigation of certain high-lying lands, which were cultivated round about Cairo, laboured sometimes with the lance in his hand, and at other times with presents, to maintain their friendship, and draw them over to his side.

At the top of all these straits lies Suez, which is a village built with straw houses, wherein there used to live thirty Mamelukes, whom the Sultan maintained there to keep watch upon the hulls of his galleys, so that the Alarves should not burn them, for they used to come down and attack the Mamelukes sometimes; and also to keep these hulls well watered every day in the morning, so that the joints should not open under the heat of the sun, which beats down very fiercely there. This village of Suez shows, by its great buildings, now thrown down and in ruins, that in ancient times it had a great population, and that it must be the site of Sião Gaber,[1] of which the Bible makes mention.

by Suez. The traffic between Keneh and Mecca is still very considerable at the season of the pilgrimage, for many pilgrims from Upper Egypt, Nubia, the Soodan, and the Mohammedan provinces of Central Africa, prefer the route by Keneh and Koseyr, and Djiddah is easily reached from that port by sailing or steam vessels."

[1] A mistaken reference to Ezion Geber, N. of the Gulf of Akabah, not Suez. Cf. Dr. Shaw, *Travels*, p. 322; *Numb.*, xxxiii, 35; *Deut.*, ii, 8, etc.

CHAPTER VIII.

How the great Afonso Dalboquerque set out from that harbour for Camarão, and how he was like to have been wrecked on the way.

On account of the necessity which the fleet had for fresh water, the great Afonso Dalboquerque did not remain in that harbour beyond that night, and, having collected the provisions and burned the ships which he took there, he set sail at daybreak, shaping his course for Camarão; and, when he had made his way as far on as the Island of Jebelzocor, he told the pilots that it would be well to stand in to shore, for it was getting late, and the fleet would not make the island until the night was far advanced, and even then he did not feel sure that all the ships could anchor in the harbour. They replied that they had no need to put in at any other harbour except the island to which they were bound.

Afonso Dalboquerque, however, insisted that, notwithstanding this, they must point out a harbour to him, for the wind would drop during the night, and they could not reach the anchorage in such time that the fleet could get well moored. The Rubães then gave the word to stand in to the shore, and proceeded to take up their quarters close to the Arabian shore in twelve fathoms, and there the ships remained during the night. But, when morning was come, they set sail again, and passed close under the Island of Jebelzocor; and one hour before sundown, Afonso Dalboquerque, again ordered the Rubães to take him into harbour, for at those times he was very careful to put in to shore lest any evil chance should happen to him at night.

The Rubães set all the fleet in order, so as to stand in, over against a place called Luya,[1] where there is a large

[1] Loheyyah, or Loheia, in lat. 15 deg. 43 min. N., on the Arabian coast. See plan on Admiralty Chart, No. 8*b*, Red Sea, sheet 4. From the *Red Sea Pilot*, it does not appear that there is good anchorage for ships.

bay, with a headland jutting out into the sea, and behind it a very good harbour sheltered from the east wind. As they were proceeding thus on their course in full sail, one of those Rubães, to show that he had better knowledge than his fellows, told Afonso Dalboquerque to order the fleet to luff[1] as much as possible, for, if they kept on in the tack they were now sailing upon, they would not be able to double the point of the reef; so he ordered the pilot of his ship to keep on sounding with the lead-line in his hand, and steer the ship as was suggested. And the pilot thus making way and sounding at the same time, the ship touched the ground at eight fathoms, and then struck again in four fathoms and a half; and on this reef the ship beat three times.

As soon as the ship touched the bottom, the pilot gave the word to strike all the sails at once,[2] and cast an anchor, and the ship swung back immediately upon the cable, and fell back into five fathoms and a half. At the sight of this accident, which had befallen the flag-ship, Lopo Vaz de Sampaio, D. João Dessa, Pero de Afonseca, Simão Velho, and Fernão Gomez de Lemos, furled their sails and cast anchors, and came up at once in their boats. The other captains, who were out more to seaward, held on their course a good way off, for they were more to leeward, and proceeded to take up a good position where D. Garcia had berthed his ship.

The pilot, finding that the ship held by the cable, got down into his skiff and took soundings all round her; and finding a good bottom, proceeded to lay out a towing-rope to the *Madanella*, which had cast anchor in sixteen fathoms. And, as the bottom where the ship had grounded was ribbed with sand, in a very little space of time they

[1] *Que mandasse ir a Armada toda á orsa quanto podesse.* See Jal, *Gloss. Naut.*, s. v. orza.

[2] *Amainar de ramania;* "*Toute de suite*", Jal, s. v.

managed to float the ship off the bank, but not without great exertion on the part of Diogo Fernandez de Béja, the captain of the ship; for, although he had been severely wounded by a musket shot, which struck him on the breast at the attempted entry into Adem (of which he carried the ball until the day of his death, for it could not be extracted, and was therefore compelled to use a leaden tube, by which a large discharge was kept up), he worked very hard on his part to save the ship; and all the Fidalgoes and Cavaliers that sailed in her helped him, for on such occasions as this all the mariners are looking after their own treasures. The ship, however, proved to be water-tight, and without the least leak, for the strokes which she made on the sand were but slight; and when everything had been set right again, they all set sail, and stood in for the anchorage where D. Garcia was already berthed. He, indeed, knew nothing of this accident, for he had gone on in advance.

All that night the fleet rode at anchor in this harbour, and when morning was come, set sail again and reached Camarão; and just as the ships were standing close in to the harbour some shallops[1] were sighted, sailing out of the port. As soon as they were caught sight of, Afonso Dalboquerque ordered D. Garcia to go in chase of them, thinking it was a ship from Dabul, which was keeping along in front of him. D. Garcia reached the shallops, and found they were barques carrying persons from the island to the mainland, who were flying in fear of our fleet; so he made them strike their sails, and took out of them certain Moors, both men and women, as well as a Principal Xeque, who had hidden himself for fear of the King of Adem. The whole fleet, then, stood in under sail, and anchored in the harbour, where we found a ship belonging to the Grand Sultan, and another to the merchant, without crews—for they had all fled—and two ships drawn up on the beach. The next day after their ar-

[1] *Geluas*; see vol. i, p. 226.

rival the easterly winds dropped, and the west winds began to blow, whereupon Afonso Dalboquerque became very much alarmed, for he saw that it was no longer in his power to get to Judá nor to Suez, as he had hoped to do, for, in the straits, the only winds that blow are east and west.[1]

CHAPTER IX.

How the great Afonso Dalboquerque determined to set sail from that place to Judá, and what happened on the way; and of the sign which he beheld in the heavens.

After many days had passed, while the great Afonso Dalboquerque lay to off Camarão, because of the west winds that were blowing, one day during the night the east wind began to blow, so he, desirous as he was of performing the voyage that he had set out upon, sent word immediately to the captains to make themselves ready, for on the following day he was determined to set sail; and when morning was come they all weighed anchor and made sail, and steered out of the harbour between some islands and sand banks—a very narrow passage for ships so large—shaping their course for an island which lies in the broad sea; but just as they arrived off this island the west wind began to blow again, so they all anchored there in a bottom of from fifteen to thirty fathoms, where they remained for many days. Afonso Dalboquerque, annoyed at this westerly gust of wind, and anxious to know what was going on in the open sea, despatched João Gomez in the *caravela,* and Domingo Fernandez the pilot with him, to make their way to an

[1] This is scarcely correct of the winds that now are met with in the Red Sea. See *Red Sea Pilot, l.c.*

island lying in the midst of the straits, called Ceibão,[1] so as to see what sea and what wind there might be there, for he could not believe that this was owing to anything else than his sins.

They proceeded on their way, and in tacking once, in and out, they reached the island; and, after taking the soundings all around it,[2] returned forthwith to the place where our fleet was at anchor, and declared to him that they found out there just the same kind of calm weather as there was with the fleet, and the same soundings around that island, but no current in the sea from one side to the other, only the ebb and flow. Afonso Dalboquerque was pleased at the news brought by João Gomez, for as there were no currents in the sea he was in hopes of being able to make one tack out and in again, so as to reach Judá, or, at least, some harbour on the land of the Preste João; but this was impossible, for in the straits one cannot sail by tacking, on account of the shallows, whereat he became much alarmed. The Rubães,[3] seeing him in this state of mind, begged him not to be alarmed, for a change of wind was a very natural thing in the straits; and when a certain star, called Turia, appeared on the south side, two or three days of east wind would ensue, and this would carry them to Judá. With this ray of hope which the Rubães[3] offered him, Afonso Dalboquerque permitted himself to rest there a few more days, and while they were all there lying at anchor, waiting for the favour of our Lord, there appeared over against the land of the Preste João a cross in the heavens, very clear and resplendent, just as is here depicted; and when a cloud passed over it, it was rent into several parts without

[1] Saba, or Zebayer, Island, lying in 15 deg. 5 min. N. lat., N.W. by W. of Jebel Zebáyir, and between Jebel Teir and Cape Bab-el-Mandeb, about half a mile over and nearly round, consisting of a sandy plain with two remarkable hills on it, each of which has a crater.

[2] See Admiralty chart, Red Sea.

[3] Rudães, a typographical error in the text.

touching the cross, or covering its clearness. This cross was beheld by everybody in the fleet, and all with many tears fell down on their knees and worshipped it.

Seeing that sign in the heavens, Afonso Dalboquerque came to the conclusion that our Lord was minded that they should shape their voyage to the land of the Preste João and not to Judá, since it was towards that land that He had shown them the sign of His Holy Cross, and he determined to tack towards the land of the Preste João; but the people in the fleet, like men of little faith, caused him much inconvenience in hope of preventing this. Afonso Dalboquerque, however, commanded that an examination should be made throughout all the ships concerning this sign which was seen in the heavens, and all declared that they had seen a Cross in the heavens, very clear and resplendent, for a considerable space of time. Whereof a document was drawn up which he sent to the king D. Manuel.

When this incident had passed, the want of water being still felt in the fleet, Afonso Dalboquerque, finding himself quite in despair of ever making the intended voyage (as it was now the end of May), ordered all to set sail, and they set out towards Camarão, where they remained during the months of June and July, without rain once during the time, nor having any bad weather when a boat could not pass all over the straits. During the time that he remained there he lost many men by disease, for it is a very unhealthy land; and he ordered that all the ships should be refitted in anticipation of the time that was coming when they should shape their course for India. Now, because the Island of Dalaca[1] is very celebrated in those straits on account of the seed-pearl fishery which is carried on therein, he ordered João Gomez, captain of the *caravela*, to go and see what kind of thing it was, and use the best endeavour he could to get possession of a shallop, so as to learn news

[1] See p. 37.

of Judá and of Suez, giving him a Rubão of the same land, and Domingos Fernandez, the pilot, to accompany him.

As soon as João had started, Afonso Dalboquerque determined to proceed to Zibit,[1] which is a chief city where the Xeque of Adem always stays, intending to parley with him concerning certain Portuguese captives still in his power, who were wrecked in a brigantine which accompanied Duarte de Lemos[2] when he went as chief captain of a fleet on the Cape of Guardafum (whereof Gregorio da Quadra was captain, as I shall relate hereafter so as not now to interrupt the thread of my history), and in order the better to accomplish this business he sent also a Moor, who had been taken out of the Grand Sultan's ship, with his wife and children, a merchant, who had been formerly a captive, and gave him a letter for the Xeque of Adem and another for the captives who were there, promising at the same time that on the restoration of the captives he would give him his wife and children again and set him at liberty.

The Moor replied, that if only he would put him on shore he would do all that was demanded of him; and when he reached Zibit, where the Xeque lived—seven days' journey from Adem—he delivered the letters which he carried, and the Xeque received them; but on the following day the Xeque sent back the Moor without delay to the harbour wherein the vessel which had brought him was lying, escorted by certain men in charge of him, and then he declared to our people, without saying a word about the captives, that if Afonso Dalboquerque chose to restore to him his wife and children, he would give two hundred

[1] Called Zebir in chap. ii, but from the context, there is little doubt it is the same place. Rás Zebid, on the Arabian coast, in lat. 14 deg. 6 min. N., has an excellent spring of fresh water emptying itself into the sea, and is still used as a watering-place on the voyage from Kamarán to the Straits of Bab-el-Mandeb.

[2] See note of his character in vol. ii, p. 242.

pardaos;[1] but he said no more, for the Moors who escorted him would not allow him to speak any further, although they showed him a place where he could send off some fresh stores from the land, and from that place they returned to the Xeque, without any further intercourse.

Three days after the vessel had returned with this reply, João Gomez arrived, and recounted to Afonso Dalboquerque how he had reached the Island of Dalaca,[2] and anchored outside the shallows which encircle the harbour, and gone in his skiff to shore; and that the Xeque of the island had sent word to him by two mounted Moors asking what it was that he wished; and he had replied that he came thither in obedience to the orders of the Captain-General of India, who was anchored off Camarão with a great fleet, seeking to know if they would purchase any merchandise in exchange for seed-pearl;[3] and the Xeque had sent in answer to say that there were no merchants in his land, but only men-at-arms; and on receipt of this reply he did not care to hold any more converse with the Moors, but withdrew and sailed all round the island, which lies in sight of the land of the Preste João—just as do the fields along the banks of the river Tagus opposite Lisbon—but he had not crossed over to it, for he carried no definite orders empowering him to do so; and he had met with a shallop in the sea, fishing for seed-pearl, but when he got up close to her, she took to the shallows and sandbanks close by, whither the *caravela* could not follow her, and so got away.

Afonso Dalboquerque was somewhat cheered up at this news, for when the weather should turn out favourable for the navigation, he was determined to sail away to the land of the Preste João with all his fleet. And being thus minded, there came a man-at-arms to him, who said, if his lordship desired to send to the King Dom Manuel an account of what had been done in that part of the world, he would

[1] See vol. ii, p. 95. [2] See p. 37. [3] See vol. i, p. 235.

essay to make good his journey to Cairo, and so proceed from that city to Portugal. At this, Afonso Dalboquerque asked him how he could hope to accomplish such a journey when he did not know the language of the country? The man-at-arms replied, that he had been a Moor, but at Azamor[1] he had joined the Christians, and therefore he could make that journey in safety, for he was well acquainted with the Arabic tongue. Seeing that he ran no risk in this matter, and that it would be a great happiness for the King Dom Manuel to know how the Portuguese were faring in the straits, Afonso Dalboquerque accepted this man's voluntary offer, and ordered that he should be supplied with money for the journey, telling him how to conduct himself, and then gave orders that he should be set upon the main-land in front of Camarão with iron fetters on his feet, so that it should be seen that he was a fugitive from the fleet.

This man reached Portugal in due course, and the king was very much pleased with the news which he brought, and made use of him to carry back the reply. On that very night in which he set forth, while the heavens were quite clear, there came down from the side of the Preste João's land a ray of fire,[2] very broad and very long, which spreading itself along the sky fell down at last in the direction of Judá and Méca, causing great dismay throughout the fleet. The Xeque, also, and all the Moors who were captive there became terrified, for they regard it a prophecy that the Preste João shall give his horses provender within the temple of Méca. This Xeque allowed Afonso Dalboquerque free intercourse with all his people up to the day of sailing, and shewed him many favours.

[1] A town and district on the N.W. coast of Marocco.

[2] A sudden ray of fire in the clear sky is a common form of mediæval wonder, both in European and Oriental chronicles.

CHAPTER X.

How Gregorio da Quadra and the others, his companions, who were captive in the power of the King of Adem, escaped from their captivity; and what he went through until his arrival at this kingdom of Portugal.

Inasmuch as I have just declared that I would give some account of the Portuguese captives in the power of the Xeque of Adem, who would not take any ransom for them, and would relate how they escaped out of the captivity in which they lay, I thought it fit that I should first of all narrate how they were wrecked. It was in this way. At the time when Duarte de Lemos, chief captain, was lying at anchor with his fleet off the coast of Melinde, a great darkness and storm fell on them one night, and one of his brigantines was driven from her moorings, but no one knew whether the cables snapped accidentally or whether they were cut by design. The captain of this vessel was Gregorio da Quadra, an honourable man, servant of the king D. Manuel. The great current of water,[1] which at that time was running direct towards the entrance of the straits, brought the ship down with it, and when morning broke the crew found themselves opposite Adem.

When the natives of the land saw the brigantine, and perceived that there were Christians on board, they fitted out two *fustas* and took her, and all those who were on board, and carried these men forthwith before the King of Adem, who dwelt in the city of Zebit,[2] the capital city of his kingdom. As the king was an ill-conditioned fellow, and accustomed to treat his captives with cruelty, he gave orders that they should be thrust into a dry cistern, where he kept many other captives of different nations. They had

[1] The currents sometimes have a rate of forty miles a day.—*Red Sea Pilot.*

[2] See p. 46.

already been eight years in captivity, and all were dead, except five when Afonso Dalboquerque was at anchor off Adem. Gregorio da Quadra, being a sensible man, lost no time in learning the Arabic tongue, and could speak the language very well, so much so that the people could not believe that he was not a Moor. And he became a tailor, and there in the cistern he used to make caps; and at length he became so clever in the fashioning of them, that the Moors used to bring him dates and raisins, wherewith all the captives were supported, for the custom in that land is to wear these caps.

A few days after Afonso Dalboquerque had returned out of the straits, making his voyage to India, one of the principal Moors of the city of Zebit rose up in rebellion against this king who held these men in captivity, claiming that the kingdom belonged to him, and came down against the king, and routed his forces and took from him the city of Zebit, setting free the captives in the cistern, and giving them their liberty to go wherever they pleased. And as he had vowed, should Mahomet give him the victory, to make a pilgrimage to his shrine, after all the affairs of the kingdom were set in order again, he made ready to set out in fulfilment of this pilgrimage. Gregorio da Quadra, being determined to go to Méca and wait there for the caravan which comes from Damascus every year, intending to proceed from that city to Baçora,[1] and from Baçora to Ormuz, besought the new king to take him in his company, and he, looking upon him as a saint, was delighted with the idea of his desiring to be of his company, and gave him a camel to ride on, and paid all his travelling expenses.

As soon as they arrived at Medina, where Mahomet lies buried in a sepulchre in the midst of the temple, surrounded with iron gratings, the king and all those who accompanied him began to march around it, reciting their prayers. But Gregorio da Quadra, who was with them,

[1] Basra, or Bassorah, at the head of the Persian Gulf.

remembering the Faith of Jesus Christ, in which he had been brought up, and finding himself in that position, shedding many tears, cried out, "Prophet of Satan, if thou art that one whom these dogs adore, manifest to them that I am a Christian, for I hope, by our Lord's mercy, that I shall yet behold this, thy house of abomination, become a church for His praise, like as is that of our Lady of Conception at Lisbon." And he uttered these words with so many tears, that the Cacizes[1] who were standing by, astounded at his sanctity, begged him very earnestly to take up his abode with them for some days.

Now, as the Damascus caravan had set out just two days before this party arrived at Méca, Gregorio da Quadra decided to cross the desert and try and overtake it, and if he failed to do so, then to trust to the mercy of our Lord to direct him towards the straits of Ormuz. So he told the king that he was desirous of going to pay a visit to the Temple of Mahomet's grandchildren who are buried in Persia, and therefore he would beg royal permission for this journey. The king, who was pleased to have him in his company, took this very much to heart, and said to him: "Whither dost thou desire to go? There is nothing there but desert; and even the birds of that country cannot hold any communication with the birds of this land." Nevertheless, Gregorio da Quadra took leave of the king, and set out upon his journey, not knowing where he was going, travelling for many days along those deserts, with not a blade of grass in them, only heaps of loose sand; and when he had consumed the slight store of provision which he had taken with him, he used to eat locusts and other winged creatures. As he carried no clothing upon himself, except only a piece of common cloth to hide his nakedness, and the sun was fierce, he became blistered in such a dreadful manner that long stripes burst open all down his body, and

[1] See vol. iii, 69.

he became so raw that he could not lie down to sleep, but used to make a pit with his hands in the sand, of considerable depth, and then getting into the middle of it so slept standing. When he felt himself at length thoroughly weakened, and all his energy gone, so weak, in fact, that he could walk no further, he crawled to the foot of a hill of sand and fell upon his knees, and, casting his eyes up to the heavens, besought the mercy of God, saying: "Lord, seeing that I am Thy creature, redeemed with Thy precious blood, and that Thou hast permitted me to escape from the captivity in which I lay, have mercy upon me, and be not willing that I should come thus miserably to my end here in these deserts." Then he began to confess his sins to God, begging Him to bear his soul in remembrance, having quite made up his mind to bring his journeyings to a close at that spot. But while he was uttering these words, and many others of the same kind, he was lifted up off the ground, and borne up on to the top of the sand hill, where those who bore him left him without his seeing who they were; and, remaining in this state, he looked down and beheld a camel, and going a little further he caught sight of a Moor; then, making his way towards him, he came up with the caravan, which had halted at that spot to take in water, for this spot happened to be one of the watering places of the route.

The Moors of the caravan were astounded when they saw, as they thought, men in those deserts, and decided that he must be a saint; they took him in among them, and healed the raw places with which he was afflicted, his body being entirely covered with open sores; then they gave him a garment to cover him, and inquired of him whence he came, and how he had come to be in that place. Gregorio da Quadra replied with a narrative of all that he had gone through, showing how he was engaged on a pilgrimage to the sacred bodies buried in Persia. So when the caravan party had accomplished their taking-in of water, they set forth again on the journey, and reached Babylonia, and there they parted company with him, and made their way to Damascus. Gregorio da Quadra, however, reached Baçora, and embarked in a *terrada*[1] (or small Indian man-of-war), which was bound to Ormuz, in company with other Moors; and when he arrived at the gate of our fortress, he asked what day it was. He was told that it was Thursday in Passion week.[2] Then he threw himself down on the ground, and shedding many tears, gave thanks to our Lord who had brought him safely to the land of Christians on that day. D. Garcia de Coutinho, captain of the fortress, when he saw him, was very much astonished, and inquired of him the way he had taken. Thereupon, Gregorio da Quadra recounted all that had taken place with him; and that before Afonso Dalboquerque had arrived off Adem with his fleet, he had tried to escape with four companions—for all the others were dead by that time—in a shallop; but when they got out to sea they were retaken, and something was given them to eat which intoxicated them; and while they were insensible for three days, the sign of the Moor had been wrought upon them;[3] and at the time of Afonso Dalboquerque's departure they were at Zibit, and he knew nothing more of what had happened to them. D. Garcia treated him with great kindness, and embarked him for India with all necessaries for the voyage; and when he arrived at length at this kingdom of Portugal, he became a Franciscan friar in the Capuchin Order, and so ended his days with holiness.

[1] See vol. i, p. 105.

[2] *Quinta feira de Endoenças.*

[3] *I.e.*, they were circumcised.

CHAPTER XI.

How the great Afonso Dalboquerque set sail out of the harbour of Camarão for India, and what took place on the voyage.

The great Afonso Dalboquerque, having carefully gathered together all the information he could obtain concerning the affairs of the straits, and being now very desirous of performing his voyage to India, commanded the captains to get themselves ready, and on the fifteenth day of the month of July, in the year [one thousand] five hundred and thirteen, warped his ships out of Camarão harbour, and without touching land anywhere, steered his course direct to the gates of the straits; and having passed through, proceeded to cast anchor with all the fleet behind the island,[1] which lies athwart the mouth of the straits, as I have already shown. And, in order that he might leave nothing unexplored in this voyage, he desired also to find out what islands these were, and what harbours there were in them. One day, therefore, before sunrise, he got into his boat with Domingo Fernandez, the pilot, and D. Garcia de Noronha, Lopo Vaz de Sampayo, and D. João de Lima in theirs, and all together in a party made their way to a harbour which the island possesses, looking towards the land of the Preste João, that makes a large bay,[2] eating away, as it were, part of the island, and making within itself three smaller bays;[3]

[1] Perim or Meyune.

[2] Perim Harbour, on the south-west of the Island of that name, is small, and divided into two branches, each about eight or nine cables long. The entrance is four cables and a half broad, and has a depth of ten or twelve fathoms, extending to within half a cable's length of each side; the north-east arm is considerably obstructed by shoals; the north-west one is better to anchor in as it is clearer. Anchorage may be obtained in it in five or six fathoms, as the *Commentaries* proceed to shew. The bottom is sand and coral, with plenty of room for a ship to swing.—*Red Sea Pilot*, p. 127.

[3] These three bays are well shown on the Admiralty Chart of Perim Island.

the mouth of the harbour being so situated that when it has been entered the land appears to close in around it in such a manner that the open sea can no longer be seen. This harbour has an inside depth of from six to twelve fathoms, and would contain two hundred of our ships. It is sheltered from the winds on all sides.

When Afonso Dalboquerque found himself within the harbour, he disembarked with all his captains and explored a great part of the island, which he found covered with loose stones, large and small, with not a single tree, nor a green blade of grass in it. In a sandy valley, which lies on the Red Sea side, they found a very ancient cistern, built after the manner of a tank, without a covering, choked up and without any water, and a pond also choked up with earth, but they could only see the mouth of it. This island has a lofty knoll opposite the entrance of the straits, and upon it Afonso Dalboquerque ordered that a cross should be set, large and very tall, formed out of a mast, and he inscribed upon it the name ILHA DA VERA CRUZ, *i.e., Island of the True Cross,* in remembrance of the sign which he had seen when he was in the straits. When he had made an end of seeing everything on the island, he withdrew to the boats, and so returned to the ships; and on the following morning dispatched Ruy Galvão in his ship, and João Gomez in the *caravela*, to proceed to Zeila, and endeavour to open communication with the Moors of the land, and observe the nature of the place, and of its people and its trade; but if they found any ships in the harbour, and the Moors would not treat their overtures with respect, then they were to set the ships on fire, and return to Adem and look out for the fleet, for he would lie off and wait there for their return.

As soon as Afonso Dalboquerque had despatched these off, he set sail, and proceeded to cast anchor in front of the city, where were found a large number of great ships; the island of Cira having been fortified with a wall and many more towers upon it than there used to be. But, in order that the Moors should understand the foolishness of their idea that these preparations added at all to the greater security of their position, without any delay he placed D. Garcia de Noronha, his nephew, in charge of a large party to attack the island, and told the constable to train two *camelos*[1] in two of the principal ships which lay closest to the walls of the island, and from that position to fire, and do as much injury as could be done to those of the enemy who were inside. D. Garcia led off his company of men, and assaulted the bulwarks, bearing himself so bravely against the Moors who defended them, that in a very short space of time he overcame them, and took possession of the island. As soon as he was established within it he ordered his men to set up a *camelo* on the principal tower, and from that point began to fire upon the city, throwing down a great part of the houses. Now, because a catapult, which the Moors had set upon the top of the mountain range, was doing considerable harm to our men who were stationed in the tower, D. Garcia gave João Luiz, artilleryman in charge of the *camelo*, orders to fire as fast as he could at the Moorish catapult, and destroy it, if possible. João Luiz, angry that one of his gunners had been killed by the enemy, opened fire upon the catapult, and got so good a range, that at the second shot he broke it down, and the Moors, to shelter themselves from his fire, built up a high wall of stone and mortar. The merchant strangers, who had ships in the port, perceived the destruction of the houses which was going on within the city, and fearing that Afonso Dalboquerque would give orders that their ships too should be set on fire, sent word to him, that they would ransom them at whatever price he would set upon them; but his answer was that he would not take any price for

[1] See vol. i, p. 73.

them, except only the liberation of the captive Christians in power of the Xeque of Adem, and if this were not complied with he would not save a single ship that should not be burned.

As these merchants never came back with any further offers, Afonso Dalboquerque determined to fulfil his threat that he would set fire to them, so he gave an account of what he had said to the captains; but because the setting fire to them could not be carried into execution without some danger to our men, the captains were all of opinion that it ought not to be attempted, and that it was not worth while to jeopardise the life of a single man in a matter of so little importance, for the Moors were possessed of a great store of artillery, trained upon these ships in order to protect them, and that business could not be carried out so easily, but that it would be like to cost us dearly. When Afonso Dalboquerque noticed all these excuses made by half-hearted men, he determined to execute the business by the sailors alone—whom he indeed always spoke of as "my cavaliers." So he ordered Fernão Afonso, master of his ship, and Domingo Fernandez the pilot, to prepare in readiness for him a hundred men, for with their aid he intended to perform this undertaking and thereby to put to shame all the captains, fidalgoes, and cavaliers of the fleet. So when all were in readiness, this party embarked in the boats, and Afonso Dalboquerque got into his skiff, intending to encourage them with the trumpeters. It was on a Friday at midnight, when the Moors were not on the watch, they ran the boats on shore, and running for a considerable distance along the water side, fell upon thirty Moors who were keeping guard over the ships and killed the greater number of them, and set the ships on fire. But as they were all sodden with water, only three were destroyed. When this was done, the party returned to the boats, and made their way to the ships, highly pleased with their adventure, without any misfortune happening to any one of them. And when all had returned with this unlooked-for victory, the captains and men-at-arms became so ashamed that they begged Afonso Dalboquerque to give them permission to go and burn the ships which remained, but he would not allow them to do so because the Moors were now on the watch for them.

That very morning Ruy Gonçalvez and João Gomez returned, bringing word how they had reached Zeila, and explored the entrance of the harbour, yet when they desired to open communication with the people of the land, they could get no reply; but some of the mounted men began to skirmish, endeavouring to draw them on, and when they perceived this they would not be provoked, and avoided any conflict; nevertheless they burnt twenty of the native ships, which lay in the harbour, of great size. It was there that the Abyssinian fled off from shore, with Ruy Galvão (as I have already related),[1] and Afonso Dalboquerque sent him to the king D. Manuel to carry information concerning those parts, for he was a man of considerable ability and could give a very good account of these things, because he had been always attached to the Factor of the Grand Sultan.

CHAPTER XII.

How the great Afonso Dalboquerque set sail from the harbour of Adem for India; and of what passed in the way until his arrival at the city of Goa.

When all these matters had been brought to an end, the great Afonso Dalboquerque gave orders to his captains to weigh anchor; and thus he set sail away from the harbour of Adem, on the fourth day of the month of August, and with all his fleet hove in sight of Cape Guardafum, and

[1] See p. 26, end of chap. v.

from that headland tacked over to the other side, and bore up opposite Diolocindi,[1] and from this point ran along in sight of the coast, and so at length arrived at Diu, where Miliqueaz[2] received them very kindly, and offered them many presents, which he gave to all the captains. Afonso Dalboquerque remained in this port for six days, and took the opportunity of repairing the ships' boats, which had become very much dilapidated from constant service. At his arrival, Miliqueaz came down at once to pay him a visit on board ship, and they both conversed on matters of no importance.

Afonso Dalboquerque told him that he wished to leave in the port a ship laden with merchandise for sale, and begged him earnestly to order that the Portuguese factor and officers who remained with it should be well treated. Miliqueaz, who was not very well prepared with excuses, replied with ample offers, and Afonso Dalboquerque paid him in the same coin, and then took his leave with many marks of friendship. And when the Portuguese ships had taken in their store of water, he set sail, leaving behind the ship *Enxobregas*[3] with all the merchandise which she carried, appointing to the duty of factor for this business Fernão Martinz Evangelho, and Jorge Correa for his scrivener. When the fleet had got out to sea, Afonso Dalboquerque sent forward Ruy Galvão to proceed to Goa in his ship, and apprise the captain of the city of the coming of the whole of the fleet; and Jeronymo de Sousa to go on to Cananor and Cochim to do the same; and he himself, with all the other vessels, made his way to Chaul, where he found

[1] Probably the latter part of the word indicates that Diolocindi is on the coast of Scinde. See Dr. G. P. Badger, *Travels of Varthema*, p. 104, Cheo, Joah, Joaah, or Kow, one of the estuaries of the Indus.

[2] See vol. iii, pp. 244-246.

[3] *Enxobregas.* The name of this ship appears to be derived from that of a village near Belem, one of the suburbs of Lisbon.—See *Castanheda*, II, chap. cxii, p. 355.

that Tristão Déga[1] had reached that port two days before, and an ambassador of the King of Cambay in company with him. Tristão Déga recounted that he had been very well received by the king, and gave him a letter for Milecopi, one of the principal Moors of that kingdom, manifesting a desire to serve the King of Portugal; for when he arrived at Cambay (he said), he found that the king had gone to the furthest limit of the kingdom of Mandao,[2] with a large array of men, horses, and artillery against the king; and, therefore, he awaited the king's return at Champanel,[3] and there gave him the two letters sent with him, but the king had answered coldly with respect to the matter of Diu, and it seemed that he would not grant the request concerning it, for, after conversation held between them in this business, the king had offered certain other islands along the coast wherein we might build a fortress and make a settlement, but he would not accept them on the part of the Portuguese, because he held no orders from Afonso Dalboquerque to do so. He had, however, learned from Milecopi that Miliqueaz was at the bottom of all this, being annoyed at finding himself kept out of Diu, and as for the business of the Rumes, the king would not allow them to enter his territory again.[4]

After Tristão Déga had given an account of all these matters to Afonso Dalboquerque, the ambassador for the King of Cambay came to pay him a visit, and delivered his credentials, declaring at the same time that the King of Cambay sent word asking earnestly for his favourable consent that he would give permission to him to send a trading company of Guzarates[5] to Malaca, and also a safe-conduct

[1] See vol. iii, p. 245.

[2] Manda, or Mandoo, south-west of Indur, 22 deg. 21 min. N.; 75 deg. 22 min. E.

[3] Champaner, north-east of Baroda, 22 deg. 29 min. N.; 73 deg. 29 min. E.

[4] See vol. iii, p. 245.

[5] *Hum estante dos Guzarates.*

for the Cambayan ships to navigate towards those parts; and complaining that the Portuguese had captured the ship *Meri*, which belonged to him,[1] but now he desired earnestly that Afonso Dalboquerque would give orders for its restitution, because it had been captured from him while he was at peace with the King of Portugal.

Afonso Dalboquerque replied that the king, his lord, was very desirous of peace and friendship with the King of Cambay, and of trading in his territory, and for this reason he (Afonso) had never made war upon him, nor burned his villages, nor bombarded his fortresses; but if his ships or his men had received any hurt at the hands of the Portuguese, it must be on account of his having always taken the part of the kings and lords with whom the King of Portugal, his lord, was at war, principally the King of Malaca and the King of Ormuz, to whom he had supplied many ships laden with arms and filled with men; but he (Afonso) had always pretended to be unaware of it, so as not to break off relations with him. And to Milecopi, Afonso Dalboquerque wrote many thanks for the care he had taken in the affairs of the king, his lord, leading him to indulge in hope of a great reward for his services, and that as for the ship *Meri*, which the king begged to be restored, he had caused her to be refitted at Cochim, and would return it to him through his ambassador. The ambassador thereupon wrote to the king an account of all that had taken place with Afonso Dalboquerque, sending the letter by one of his servants, and that he himself would accompany the Portuguese, in order to convey the ship back; and thus it happened that when he reached Goa he set sail in her for Cambay.

Now, inasmuch as Afonso Dalboquerque had received information that the ships for Calicut, which had set out that year as usual for the straits [of the Red Sea], being

[1] See vol. i, pp. 113-115; ii, p. 122.

very late in their departure, had been struck by a storm, which compelled them all to run for shelter into the port of Cambay, as far down as the Mount of Deli,[1] and one of them had even entered in at Danda, in the territory of Chaul; as soon as he entered the harbour, he sent word to those on land to surrender the ship to him, for it belonged to the Meceris of Cairo, the enemies of the king, his lord, and the Governor of Chaul accordingly ordered that it should be immediately delivered to him. The ship proved to hold about three thousand *quintals* of pepper and ginger. Then Afonso Dalboquerque set sail again and stood off Dabul,[2] where he sent word to the governors to deliver up to him two other ships which were lying in the harbour. But as they began to make excuses, and Afonso Dalboquerque could not delay his voyage, he left Lopo Vaz de Sampayo to keep guard over them with three ships, giving him orders to blockade the port, and prevent any commerce from going on in it until the ships were delivered up to him. In a few days after Afonso Dalboquerque had sailed away, the ships were surrendered with all their cargo of spices.

And because, also, Afonso Dalboquerque had received information that yet another ship of Calicut was in the harbour of Baticalá,[3] he sent Antonio Raposo in a galliot to make his way to that place, and if he should find the governors of the land would not surrender it, then he was to stop the navigation of the place; and Fernão Gomez de Lemos, in another *fusta*, to proceed to Mangalor, where, according to information received, he knew that there were two more ships, and to do the same. By means of this diligent search, Afonso Dalboquerque obtained possession of every one of the ships which had set out from Calicut for the straits that year, and this caused a great loss to the

[1] See vol. ii, p. 217. [2] See vol. ii, p. 166.
[3] See vol. ii, pp. 53, 73, etc.

native merchants. And having thus dispatched these captains, he himself set sail and proceeded to Goa, where everybody received him with great joy; and there he found a present which one of the Ambassadors of the Xeque Ismael, one of the Court of the Hidalcão, had sent him by a servant, who had started from Goa with the intention of returning to see him on his homeward voyage from the Red Sea, before setting out for Persia.

CHAPTER XIII.

How Francisco Nogueira gave an account to the great Afonso Dalboquerque of all that had taken place with the Çamorim respecting the erection of the fortress; and of the council which he held with the captain relating to this, and of what was decided upon.

The great Afonso Dalboquerque having at length reached Goa was received by the captain and people of the city with joyful demonstration. Afterwards, Francisco Nogueira, whom he had left, at the time of his sailing away, with instructions to build the fortress of Calicut (as I have already shown), gave him an account of how, on arrival at Calicut, he had delivered his letters to the Çamorim; but in discussions with that potentate on certain occasions, respecting the building of the fortress, he had found him always unwilling to entertain the idea, making the excuse that he could not prevail upon the Moors of the land to consent to the building of it in the position which was asked for, but he would give him Challe for its site; he would not, however, accept this site, and, even if a site had been conceded to him in Calicut, it would have been impossible to build a fortress in it, unless he himself (Afonso) had been there in person, on account of the conduct of the captains and king's officers, who, although they had received orders to assist him with all their power and aid in carrying out the work, yet had secretly worked against the undertaking with the desire of gratifying the Kings of Cananor and Cochim.

Afonso Dalboquerque, who was determined to plant his foot firmly in Calicut, was highly incensed at the duplicity of the Çamorim, and at finding him, as it were, entering into a new line of policy; and so, desiring to come to a final determination of what should be carried out, he ordered that the captains and king's officers should be summoned, and then and there recounted to them everything that Francisco Nogueira had transacted with the Çamorim, and how, in the ships which had come that year from Portugal, the king had written to him to say that, in respect of the affairs of Calicut, he must so bear himself, that the King of Cochim should have no cause of complaint; and that the reason of the king's writing in this manner to him must be owing to certain baseless statements which the officers of Cananor and of Cochim had sent to Portugal concerning that matter, while it was all the time really owing to them that the affair was in a critical state, from their seeking to gratify the kings of those places, who were greatly cast down at thought of this settlement, which the king D. Manuel desired to establish in Calicut; for His Highness was, indeed, under an obligation to the King of Cochim to maintain him in his estate, and pay him the appointed price for the purchases of pepper, but not to maintain his customs and paganisms, nor to make war on Calicut whenever that king wished him to do so.

After listening to these arguments, which Afonso Dalboquerque put before them, everyone carefully discussed the matter. D. Garcia and the captains, on the one hand, declared their opinion that a fortress ought to be erected in Calicut, provided that the king would assent to it by way of friendship and mutual arrangement, for, in a city of such a great size as Calicut was, and one which could be so rapidly reinforced, a fortress could never be built by force unless it were at the cost of much blood. The king's officers, on the other hand, held a different opinion, and maintained that it was not to the interest of his service that a fortress should be built at Calicut, because it could not be sustained without heavy expense, which Afonso Dalboquerque ought to avoid as long as possible (for it was economy that the king desired him more than all to practise), but it would be quite sufficient to prevent and destroy the navigation of the Calicut ships if it were decided to cruise off the coast with a fleet, and so intercept the trade; and so they went on, with other reasons, all based upon the abandoning of the intention of building a fortress.

After D. Garcia and the other captains had given their opinions in this business, Afonso Dalboquerque, perceiving how the excuses, that the king's officers were alleging against the erection of a fortress in Calicut, were evidently preconcerted with the wishes of the Kings of Cananor and Cochim, declared that he would never think of carrying on a dilatory warfare with the Çamorim, but would determinedly enter into it in such a manner that he would be able to completely accomplish it, for any other policy would simply result in keeping the Indian fleet always occupied in blockading Calicut, without being free to undertake any other enterprises; but for the fleet to gain any real advantage, it was very necessary to keep peace and friendship with the Kings of Calicut and Cochim, and endeavour the utmost that they should remain friends, and continue to be so, for in these two ports they would always find the spices packed in the way that they liked best for lading the ships homeward-bound to Portugal; and this friendship could neither be lasting nor secure, especially with the Çamorim, unless the king, our lord, had a fortress in Calicut; for, apart from the fact that by its building they would gain great prestige with the Moors, on account of the extensive repute which this war with us had acquired among them, we should drive away out of the land the Moorish agents from Cairo, for they are really the cause of all these troubles; and we should once for all remove the continual bickerings with the Çamorim, which are of no use except only to redound to the credit of the Moors, and to cause infinite trouble to the Governors of India. And if those persons, he said, who write to the king, our lord, to the effect that it is not beneficial to his service to build this fortress, would only take the trouble to march through the sea with their weapons on their backs, bombarding the Moorish ships which sail away laden with pepper to Méca, as we have done, they would be delighted enough that we should not have these bickerings. And, he continued, although Lourenço Moreno and Antonio Real had written to the King of Portugal that the building of this fortress would greatly increase the expenses of Portugal in India, yet the sums obtained for the safe-conducts of native ships bound to Calicut for their cargoes would amount to quite as great a sum, if they were closely looked after, so that half this source of revenue would be sufficient to pay the expenses of the officers and men who would have to be stationed there. "Much more," said he, "do I trust in our Lord that when we go to Calicut we shall settle this matter in such wise that, on account of the competition of these two Princes, the merchants of Cochim will come to give pepper in exchange for merchandise, and thus a great service to the king will be brought about."

And to these arguments, which Afonso Dalboquerque advanced, there was not one among his hearers who had any reply to make, for, in a matter so clearly stated, nothing more remained to be said. And, in order no longer to delay putting into practice the matters already finally decided upon, Afonso Dalboquerque forthwith ordered a fleet to be made ready, so that he might go in person and conduct this business. He wrote, also, to the king, sending his letter by the ships of burden which that year reached Portugal, relating all that had taken place, and pointing out the determination at which they had arrived. The king replied that he had considered the arguments advanced in favour of building a fortress in Calicut, and not carrying on that desultory warfare (which he had often written that he ought to do), and that he now approved of this intention, and that must be done which seemed best for the service; for, as he had a very good experience of what had been already performed, this would of itself be good reason to look upon the counsel now offered as more valuable than that of any one else, even if he (the king) had been in India, and much more so as he was far away from that country, although the reports he had received enabled him to form a very good idea of the position in which the matter stood.

CHAPTER XIV.

How the great Afonso Dalboquerque set sail for Cochim, and sent D. Garcia de Noronha to Calicut to settle the terms of peace; and what passed with the King of Cochim on this matter.

Now that all the captains had decided that a fortress must be built in Calicut, for the reasons already detailed, the great Afonso Dalboquerque made up his mind to set sail for Cochim with the fleet, which he had already in preparation, and from that place make a settlement of the business in hand as best could be to this end: and he ordered D. Garcia de Noronha, his nephew, to proceed to Calicut and learn from the Çamorim what course he intended to pursue, and to request him to perform four conditions.

The first was to grant space in the roadstead in front of his *Cerame*,[1] on which to build a fortress, capable of re-

[1] See vol. i, p. 115.

ceiving our men and protecting them from troubles, such as they had suffered in the past.

The second, that he must give whatever pepper was required for the lading of the ships bound to Portugal, in exchange for merchandise of various kinds, according to the weights and prices current in Cananor; and that the factor of the king, his lord, must be allowed to purchase the ginger, which the producers are in the habit of bringing down for sale to the market-place, in accordance with the custom of the country.

The third, to repay all the property which the Moors had taken from the Portuguese in times past.

The fourth, that he must pay a yearly tribute towards the expenses of the fortress, and those who are in charge of it, equivalent to one-half of the payments compulsory on the Moorish merchants, for the safe-conduct of their shipping.

A few days after D. Garcia had set out for Calicut, Afonso Dalboquerque sailed away to Cochim; and as soon as he arrived, the king came down and paid him a visit; and in the interview between them, which was held in the presence of Gaspar Pereira, Diogo Pereira, and Lourenço Moreno, officers of the factory, the king began to complain loudly that he had not given him any account of this new friendship which he was striking up with the Çamorim, and brought out some letters which he (Afonso) had written to him, and the replies. But, as there was nothing contained in them which the king of Cochim could find fault with, Afonso Dalboquerque flew into a great passion, and said to him: "These letters are, indeed, mine; I will not deny them; and you ought to have the sense to perceive that, in accordance with the charge with which I am entrusted, I should reply in the name of the king, my lord, both to friends and to enemies, especially to those who send word to me to make peace and friendship, and are willing to give me a fortress in their ports, as the Çamorim does. I know, too, very well how you are plotting to draw over to your side both friends and enemies, and casting about in every possible manner to maintain your kingdom and your lands in security, although you do not tell me anything about it, nor do I ask you to do so, although it would have been a sensible act on your part to have sought to interest me in these matters, for in all your difficulties you seek my assistance; and bear in mind, when the death of your uncle took place,[1] with what haste I came at your call, although my fleet was all cleared for immediate sailing to undertake the enterprise against Goa; and if you are to be at liberty to do what pleases you best, how is it that you do not think it equally right for me to learn from the Çamorim what it is that he desires of me, and to reply to his letters, for all that he is an enemy of the King of Portugal, my lord; and besides that, not to be at peace with him, when it pleases me, for it is in my hands to keep peace with him if I choose, and to make war with him if I choose, and burn his ships if I choose, and destroy all his ports if I choose?[2] But if either of us has any thing to complain of I am the one, and not you; for if I have not destroyed the Çamorim, it is solely because you, and the King of Cananor, whenever you see he is worsted, help him with your forces, and send him ships laden with supplies, sailing under safe-conduct from the king, my lord; for you wish that this argument should be always going on; but if both of you really desire his destruction (as you have often given me to understand that you do), and had ranged yourselves on my side, and on that of the marshal,[3] in the attack on Calicut, he would have been entirely destroyed."

The King of Cochim, somewhat disconcerted at this turn in the conversation, and at the impetuosity with which

[1] See vol. ii, p. 236.

[2] Note the passionate repetition of *se quizer* at the close of these periods.

[3] Dom Fernando Coutinho. See vol. ii, chaps. xii-xvii.

Afonso Dalboquerque put the case before him, replied that he had always been the servant of the King of Portugal, and that all the members of his family, ever since the Portuguese had made their entry into India, had died in his service; and inasmuch as the King of Calicut had been the principal cause of this, it was not likely that he would now turn round and help that king against the Portuguese; and the reason why he had not assisted the Portuguese in the Calicut enterprise (as was alleged by Afonso Dalboquerque) was because he had not desired more help from him than that which formerly the marshal had requested from him, the day when he gave him an account of the matter.

Afonso Dalboquerque answered that the King of Cochim ought to bear in mind that the differences which the Portuguese had in times past with the Çamorim were all caused by their defending for the king his kingdom of Cochim, which the Çamorim claimed to belong to himself; and if his relatives had died in the service of the King of Portugal, so likewise the Marshal,[1] and all those who came to their end at Calicut, died in defending his honour and estate for him, and even he himself had been maimed in the left arm, so that he could not easily raise it to his head.[2] And he would have him to know for certain that if he (the King of Cochim) and the King of Cananor had made up their minds beforehand to support the Çamorim henceforth, as they had hitherto done, so also he on his part was determined not to wage war upon him any longer, so let every one look after his own interests.

When this interview was over, the King of Cochim took his leave of Afonso Dalboquerque, not well pleased at these and other things which he had heard; but notwithstanding

[1] For a review of the historical circumstances here alluded to, see vol. ii, pp. 63, 64.

[2] For account of Afonso Dalboquerque's wound, see vol. ii, pp. 70, 71.

this, both he and the King of Cananor, in order to obstruct this business, did not break off their communication with the Caimais[1] and the lords of the Malabar territory. All this Afonso Dalboquerque learned afterwards from the aged Alguazil of Cananor who lived in Calicut.

CHAPTER XV.

How D. Garcia de Noronha sent a despatch to the great Afonso Dalboquerque of what had passed with the Çamorim, and what was done in consequence of this; and how he went to Calicut and built a fortress therein.

Now, while the relations between the King of Cochim and the great Afonso Dalboquerque were in the condition recounted above, each one endeavouring to improve his position as best he could, there arrived a despatch from D. Garcia for Afonso Dalboquerque, wherein was set forth that on his reaching Calicut he had laid the appointed conditions before the Çamorim, but up to the latest hour no reply to it had been received; and, indeed, he did not think that the Çamorim intended to take the necessary steps to bring the matter to conclusion, for delays were continually brought forward, and every day showed a new aspect of the affairs, so that he had no name to give to these procrastinations.

Afonso Dalboquerque knew very well from which quarter all this proceeded, and determined to cut short this malice as well as he could; and because the Çamorim was encouraged by the native Moorish merchants to continue to delay this business, he thought it wise to make use of the Prince, brother of the Çamorim, who was a devoted servant of the King of Portugal, and consequently wrote to him pri-

[1] See vol. i, p. 3.

vately a letter, in which he said that if he really desired the friendship of the King of Portugal (as he had oftentimes declared that he did), now was the time to give effect to this desire by ordering the Çamorim to be poisoned; and when he was dead, then they would take counsel together in the manner which he liked best. The Prince, who was desirous of peace, and greatly disgusted with the Moors of Cairo, who had taken up their abode in Calicut, because they made it their business to advise his brother the Çamorim not to comply with the Portuguese demands, and being also actuated by a desire of reigning, put into execution the suggestions which Afonso Dalboquerque made to him.

As soon as the Çamorim was dead, the Prince was raised to the throne, and, being in possession of the kingdom, took to himself the aged Alguazil who had come from Cananor, whom his brother would not countenance because he was a true and loyal servant of the King of Portugal; and after the lapse of a few days, the new Çamorim sent word by one of his Caimais to D. Garcia desiring him to write to the Captain-General of India that his brother the Çamorim was dead, and he in possession of the kingdom; and that he would be happy to make peace with the King of Portugal, and give him a site in Calicut to build a fortress whenever he liked; and that he had not, however, given any notice of this affair to the principal Moors of the land, a course which had caused great difference between them, for they all desired to maintain the policy of inflexibility and contumacy shown by the late Çamorim. But as the Prince was a true man, and influenced by his wife, whom he loved very dearly (for although it was the custom of that country to have many wives, and for their sons not to become their heirs, he had only this one, and the children which he had by her had been declared his heirs), and she very desirous of maintaining peace and friendship with the

CALEQVV

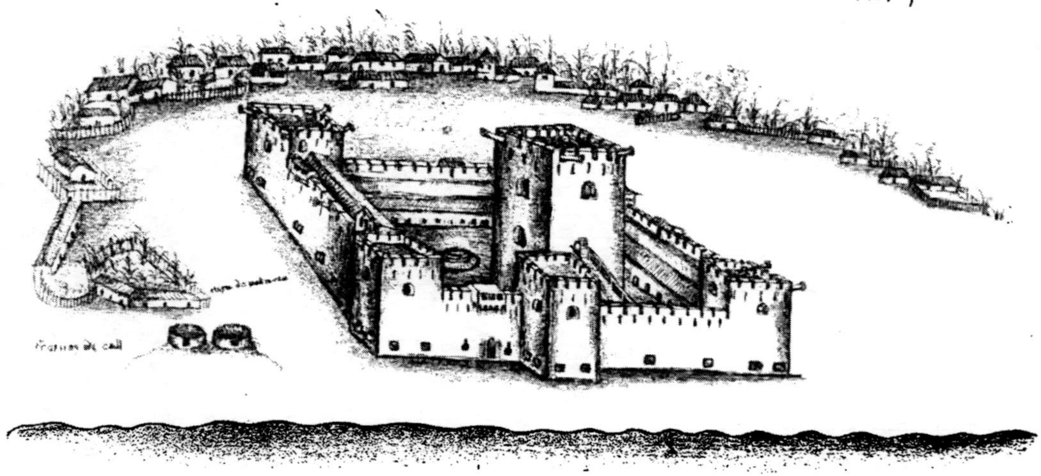

O REY DE CALEQVV CÕ TEMOR QVE OS NOSOS TOMARIA DELE VINGANÇA DA MORTE DO MARICHAL CÕ MVITOS ROGOS · AFONSO DALBOQVERQVE LHE ASENTOV PAZ FAZENDO ESTA FORTELEZA A SVA CVSTA QVE ESTEVE EM MVITA PAZ · ATE O ANO DE 1525 QVE DOM JOAM DE LIMA SENDO CAPITAM ALEVATOV GERA E SE DESFES ESTA FORTELEZA EM TENPO DO GOVERNADOR DOM ANRIQVE DE MENEZES

Portuguese, which was a great reason why the native Moors of the country yielded to this agreement of peace. As for those who could not be induced to yield, he ordered them to be killed before him to gratify his wife; while, as for the foreign Moors, he gave shipping for them, their wives, children, and property, to go away out of his kingdom. As soon as these troubles, which arose on account of the Moors, had become settled, D. Garcia concluded peace with the Çamorim on the basis of the articles which Afonso Dalboquerque had drawn up, and wrote to that commander of what had transpired, and he, immediately on receipt of the intelligence, set sail for Calicut. After an interview with the Çamorim, wherein great compliments of friendship passed between the parties, he commenced to give his attention to the building of the fortress, which had its foundations laid in the water within the reef, and close to the anchorage for the shipping.

The size of this fortress[1] corresponded to that of Cochim, with two towers on the side towards the sea, and between them, in the length of the wall, he set a wicket-gate,[2] in order that by means of it they could receive assistance whenever it was necessary, without the Moors of the land being able to prevent them. And in this same length of the wall was made a keep[3] of three storeys, very large and very strong; and on the side of the city they built two others, very strong, and having between them the principal door of the fortress, with a bastion for its defence. And when the work had so far progressed in height that it could be defended without difficulty, he delivered the custody of it to Francisco Nogueira, with men in sufficient force for its guard, and made Gonçalo Mendez the factor and paymaster of the works, and João Serrão scrivener of the factory.

[1] See a drawing of it in Correa's *Lendas da India*, vol. ii, p. 330.

[2] *Postigo*, a postern, or small door set in a larger one.

[3] *Torre de menagem*. See vol. i, p. 45.

And as it had now become necessary that he should set sail to put certain affairs in forward condition which had been left over waiting for completion, he took his leave of the Çamorim in a very friendly manner, leaving the fortress well stocked with guns, powder, and supplies in abundance, and sailed away for Cananor; and the Çamorim sent in company with him two ambassadors, who were to go that year to Portugal with a present for the king, D. Manuel, and through them he sent the king a letter of peace, signed by himself and the principal men of his kingdom, and sealed with a golden seal, begging that he would, on his part, send him another in return, confirming the treaty of peace which he had made with Afonso Dalboquerque, and a royal safe-conduct for all his harbours. The ambassadors reached this kingdom, and were very well received by the king, and in far better manner sent back on their way home.

Three things were thus performed by the great Afonso Dalboquerque in this year of [fifteen hundred and] thirteen, whereby he excited the greatest wonder and amazement among all the kings and lords of India.

The first was his entry into the Red Sea, which they held to be a very difficult enterprise, and this caused them infinite vexation.

The second was the delivery to him, when he came from the straits down to the ports of Cambay, as far as the Mount of Deli, of all the Moorish ships which had put into them on account of the storm, laden with spices, which had set sail that year from Calicut to Méca.

The third was this fortress which he made in Calicut, because that was the principal mart of the foreign Moors who traded in India, and by its building their voyages were cut short; and the King of Narsinga used to declare, when he heard of it, that since the Çamorim of Calicut had assented to the building of a fortress in his land by the Portuguese, the Captain-General of India might as well build another in Bisnaga, if he pleased. This fortress, D. Anrique Menezes,[1] when he was Governor of India, badly advised by his captains, ordered to be thrown down, being besieged by the Moors, and after it had been destroyed he was very sorry; for I thoroughly believe, had this happened in the time of Afonso Dalboquerque, that it would never have been destroyed, even if it had been overrun by the Moors, as was Goa, for to have one foot on the neck of the Çamorim of Calicut, was the principal object which moved him to labour so intently to carry out the scheme.

CHAPTER XVI.

How the great Afonso Dalboquerque set sail for Calicut, and proceeded to Cananor: the news which Fernão Martinz Evangelho wrote to him from Diu: how he sent Pero Dalboquerque with a fleet to explore the Persian Straits, and the rest which took place.

When the great Afonso Dalboquerque had taken his leave of the Çamorim, he proceeded direct to Cananor, with the intention of not sailing away from India that year—not, indeed, in order to gain rest from his past troubles, but to arrange and remedy certain irregularities which the Royal officers had been guilty of in regard to the king's property during the time when he was away from India. And having in due course of time reached Cananor, in a few days a dispatch came to his hands from Fernão Martinz Evangelho, who was at Diu, wherein he had stated that a shallop in the

[1] Seventh Governor, 25th Dec. A.D. 1524, to 23rd Feb. 1526. See his portrait, and sketch of his life in P. Barretto de Resende's *Livro do Estado da India*, Brit. Mus., Sloane MS. 197, folio 19: "Em seu tempo se desfes a fortaleza que hos Portugueses tinhã em Callecut por nã ser de proueyto Auendo padessido grandissimos sercos pello Samorim = sendo sempre muy bem socorrida do governador."

port had arrived from the straits [of the Red Sea], with a messenger from the Cadi of Cairo on board, bringing apparel for the King of Cambay and for the Hidalcão,[1] and for all his governors,[2] with blessings and excuses in great number, encouraging them, with many words, to make war upon the Christians.

This Cadi of Cairo is one of the principal persons there, like the chief priest[3] of Méca; for the grand Sultan of Cairo confirms the election when a new cadi is chosen, and the cadi in turn receives the confirmation direct from the Grand Sultan himself. News was brought by the same, also, that at Suez there was nothing left but the hulls of the galleys, and in Cairo itself the pestilence was raging to so great an extent that twenty thousand persons died every day of it (and this is not very marvellous, seeing that it is affirmed that there are in that city twenty-five thousand streets); that after his lordship (Afonso) had set out from Adem, a shallop had got away out of that port and made its way to Zeila, and related there that the artillery of the Portuguese ships had killed a large number of persons in the city; that the Xeque of Adem had written to the King of Zeila that he must send all the ships which were in his harbours, and all the fighting men whom he could muster for hire; but the king had answered that he must look elsewhere for assistance, because he required all the men and ships he had for the protection of his own land. After this shallop there arrived a *terrada*,[4] coming from the Furtaque coast,[5] and Meliqueaz, after consulting with the Moors who made the passage in her, had recommended them not to tell the news to any one, but he (Fernão), by means of friendly Moors whom he had attracted to his cause, had learned that the King of Adem was advising all the Moors of his king-

[1] See vol. ii, p. 101.
[2] *Guazis*.
[3] *Caciz.* See vol. iii, p. 69.
[4] See vol. i, p. 105.
[5] See vol. i, p. 58.

dom who were at Diu to get out on the first opportunity, for he had certain information that the Portuguese Captain-General of India was getting ready to renew the attack upon him, and, as it was, he had already collected a body of six hundred Furtaquins, taking them by force out of certain ships which had put into his harbour; that the King of Furtaque, on account of this forcible proceeding, was determined to help his lordship (Afonso Dalboquerque) with some men against the king, if he went there; that Miliqueaz had set out to the King of Cambay's court in regard to the affair of Diu, carrying a considerable quantity of silver and gold, jewels and rich cloths, and two hundred horses, to entice the king and his governors; carrying also, as a present for the king, the sword which his lordship had at a former time presented to him; and that a ship from Ormuz had arrived, bringing news of the death of Cogeatar, who, at the last moment of his life, had counselled the king and his governors to accept the cap of Xeque Ismael and grant his prayer permitting the Portuguese to erect a fortress in Ormuz, for, unless these two things were done, he had great doubts that the king's estate could be maintained.

At receipt of all this news which Fernão Martinz Evangelho sent, Afonso Dalboquerque became greatly alarmed, when he considered that his entry into the straits had in so short a space of time effected so great a number of changes. He therefore made ready a fleet of four ships to go to Cape Guardafum and Adem, if weather would permit of gaining any information of what was going on there. And as soon as he had fitted out these ships in all that they had need of, he appointed, as chief captain of them, Pero Dalboquerque, his nephew, and, as captains of the other ships, Ruy Galvão, Antonio Raposo, Jeronymo de Sousa, and, as factor, Tristão Déga, and João Teixeira, scrivener; and gave them written orders that, in case of weather permitting, they were to go and have a look at Adem, and proceed to winter at Ormuz, and demand of the king the fortress which he (Afonso) had left already begun, in order to store up in it the merchandise which he brought, and also to demand of him the tribute money that had fallen due to the Portuguese last year; and, having finished doing this, to go and explore the straits of Persia, and from that point to make their way to India. As soon as Pero Dalboquerque received the order, he took leave of his uncle, and shaped his course, with his captains, direct for the Cape of Guardafum; and further on I will give an account of his voyage.

CHAPTER XVII.

Proceedings of the great Afonso Dalboquerque with the Alguazil of Cananor concerning certain things which he did prejudicial to the service of the King of Portugal; and how he set sail for Cochim; and of the message which the ambassador of the Xeque Ismael who was in Dabul sent to him: and how Miguel Ferreira was sent in company with this ambassador, on an embassy to the Xeque Ismael.

When Pero Dalboquerque had sailed away, the great Afonso Dalboquerque began to examine into certain irregularities which the king's officers were in the habit of doing in regard to the royal property, and reprimanded them for the careless manner in which they had attended to their charge; and, after having arranged every thing as it ought to be done, being aware that the Alguazil of Cananor was also in the habit of doing certain wrong things prejudicial to the service of the King of Portugal, and of speaking much that was ill of him, because he would not countenance his tyrannous and wicked conduct, and also because he (Afonso) was favourable to the old Alguazil, living in Calicut, whom, indeed, the present

Alguazil had caused to be cast out of Cananor because of his adherence to our side, he summoned the new Alguazil before him, and gave him a golden chain, which hung round his own neck, saying, at the same time, that he would give it to him in spite of the many ill things that he was constantly saying of him; but as for the affairs which related to the service of the king his lord, he would beg him earnestly to carry them out in such a manner that the king's officers should make no more complaints of him, and also not to be sowing discord between the King of Cananor and the captain of the fortress, for if these matters were not set right it would be necessary to punish him with the rigour that his faults deserved; and he must remember, also, that he had been forgiven for his harsh conduct towards Pocaracem the Moor,[1] in depriving him of his horses when he had no better excuse for so doing than that Pocaracem was on friendly terms with the Portuguese.

The Alguazil was not particularly well pleased at hearing these words of reprimand, which Afonso Dalboquerque said to him, and replied that he was greatly devoted to the King of Portugal, and that in all the matters which his lordship had been concerned in with the King of Calicut, he, on his part, had ever laboured to turn matters towards the king's service; and, in so far as related to the horses of Pocaracem which had been mentioned, the fault lay at the doors of the officers of the King of Portugal's factory, and not at his. Afonso Dalboquerque, however, although he had very good information that this Moor was a very bad man, and very inimical to the king's service, dissembled with him because he was just then in high favour with the King of Cananor, and so they managed to remain friendly towards one another.

Just at this juncture of events there arrived at Cananor the messenger from the Ambassador of the Xeque Ismael,

[1] See vol. ii, p. 226.

who was in the Hidalcão's Court. I have already spoken of this man as having come to Goa with a message to Afonso Dalboquerque while he was in the straits of the Red Sea.[1] The gist of his message was to beg a safe-conduct so that he might pass on to Ormuz, and to ask Afonso Dalboquerque to send in company with him an ambassador to the Xeque Ismael. But as Afonso Dalboquerque desired that the man should have an opportunity of inspecting all the Portuguese fortresses in India, and especially that one which was being erected in Calicut, he set him on his way, telling him to travel on to Calicut, and then to make his way to Cochim, for he would send him home from that place, for it was also Afonso Dalboquerque's desire that the messenger should see the numerous ships of burden which had that year arrived from Portugal,[2] and their size, and all the rest of the fleet which was being refitted, and the busy scenes in the dockyards. For, although Miguel Ferreira (afterwards) carried in his instructions orders to point out all these things to the Xeque Ismael, Afonso Dalboquerque nevertheless desired this messenger to be as well an eye-witness of the greatness of the King of Portugal.

And, in a few days after his departure, Afonso Dalboquerque set sail for Cochim in the middle of December in the year 'thirteen; and, when he arrived, he prepared in readiness Miguel Ferreira, servant of the King D. Manuel,

[1] See p. 63.

[2] "Sendo vinte e dous dias de Setembro d'este anno, chegarão á barra de Goa tres naos do Reyno, e por Capitão mór d'ellas João de Sousa de Lima, e outra Anrique Nunes de Lião, e João d'Abreu, da Ilha da Madeira. Estas tres sómente; e outra nao de guerra Capitão Francisco Correa, filho de Braz Afonso Correa, corregedor de Lisboa, que partindo de Moçambique pera a India se apartou da companhia, se perdeo que nunqua mais apareceo; e porque a nao era noua e boa de vela, e nom ouve tromenta n'esta travessa, se presumio que podia auer desastre de fogo."—Correa, *Lendas*, vol. ii, p. 361.

with four changes of saddle-horses, to go as ambassador to the Xeque Ismael, carrying instructions in the terms which he had given on a former occasion to Ruy Gomez, whom he sent on the same journey—as I have already related in the account of the first taking of Goa,[1]—although it did not produce any good result, because, when he reached Ormuz, Cogeatar, Governor of the kingdom, gave orders to have him poisoned.

When Miguel Ferreira had been thus provided with instructions with due care, Afonso Dalboquerque ordered passage to be provided for him and his followers until they reached Dabul, for from that port he would have to go in company with the ambassador of the Xeque Ismael who was waiting for him, and he showed favours to the Xeque's messenger, whereat he was very much pleased. In fact, the man was so struck with the personal appearance of Afonso Dalboquerque, that he desired a life-size portrait of him to be painted, which could be carried to the Xeque Ismael.

The ambassadors then set out together, and Miguel Ferreira with them, but Afonso Dalboquerque still lingered behind a few days in Cochim, attending to various needful arrangements; and when he had set everything in order, he left D. Garcia de Noronha, his nephew, to attend to the dispatching of the ships of burden which were to set sail that year for Portugal, desiring him with earnestness to entertain the ambassadors of the Çamorim in a fitting manner, who were to make the voyage to Portugal in these ships, and to give orders for the refitting of all the fleet that lay in Cochim, so that in the spring it might sail whithersoever the service of the King of Portugal should require its presence; and so he sailed for Goa.

[1] See vol. ii, p. 114.

CHAPTER XVIII.

Of the ambassadors whom the Xeque Ismael sent to the King of Cambay, and to the Hidalcão; and of the origin of their embassies.

Inasmuch as the Xeque Ismael was very greatly desirous of drawing all the Kings of India over to friendship with him, and of persuading them to follow his religious tenets,[1] he frequently sent his ambassadors, in pursuance of this policy, to the King of Cambay, and to the Çabayo,[2] for he knew that if these two, being of superior power and great estate, could only be persuaded, all other rulers would yield without demur to that which he wished to accomplish. Hence it was, that in the year '13, when Afonso Dalboquerque penetrated the straits of the Red Sea, the Xeque again sent his ambassadors to the same kings as before, each one of them being equipped with a hundred saddle horses, and with very richly-furnished tents for their lodging, and silver services of plate for their tables. The instructions which were carried by these ambassadors were to the effect that the kings must accept his cap,[3] [and so acknowledge his supreme power], and cause the especial book of prayer which he used to be read in their mosques. With a similar request he sent another ambassador to the King of Ormuz; and this one, acting upon the advice given to him by Cogeatar—as I have already shown—and also on account of the circumstance that Rexnordim,[4] the Governor of the land, was a Persian by birth, had little trouble in persuading the king in the matter of the acceptance of the cap and the prayer of the Xeque Ismael, and the admission of his supremacy.

The ambassador who was sent to the Hidalcão reached

[1] *Cepta.*

[2] See vol. ii, p. 82.

[3] *Carapuça.*

[4] See vol. i, p. 132.

the city of Calbergate,[1] where he found that potentate, carrying for a present to the same certain horses caparisoned with very rich housings, and brocaded cloths, and Persian silk-stuffs, and some pieces of gold and silver, and emeralds, and a bowl[2] of ordinary turquoise which Diogo Fernandez, *Adail*[3] of Goa, whom Afonso Dalboquerque had sent there, and he happened to be present at the time, declared was quite a marvel to look upon. When the ambassador reached the city, he lost no time in sending a messenger to pay a visit to Afonso Dalboquerque at Goa, as I have said in a former place. The Hidalcão received the ambassador very favourably, and after the lapse of a few days sent him back, giving him a reply to the effect that he might report to the Xeque Ismael how gratified he was at the offer of friendship, but he could not accept any other law or any other prayer than those in which he had been brought up, and gave him some jewels as a present for the Xeque Ismael, and so sent him on to Dabul, so that he might embark at that port; and it was when he arrived there that he sent to Afonso Dalboquerque the messenger of whom I have just given an account.

The other ambassador, who went to the King of Cambay, reached Champanel, and was very well received by the king, but his departure did not end very favourably on account of a misadventure that happened to him in the following way. At the very time when this ambassador reached his

[1] I am not certain if this place is to be identified with Kolapoor, or Kolhapur, an important town in Bijapur, now in Bombay Presidency, lat. 16 deg. 43 min. N.; long. 74 deg. 13 min. E. In that case *Gate* refers to the Ghauts or ridge of mountains along the coast, beyond which lies the city of Kolapoor, to the N.E. of Goa. Kalberga, also called Calberga, Golburga, and Kulburga, appears to be too far distant in the Deccan, although the form of the word is very similar to Calbergate of this text. It lies in lat. 17 deg. 20 min. N.; long. 76 deg. 40 min. E.

[2] *Porcelana.*

[3] See vol. ii, p. 137.

destination, it was but a few days that there had arrived at the Court the eldest son of the King of Mandao, accompanied by certain of his subjects who had wished to follow his fortunes, begging military assistance [from the King of Cambay], so as to be enabled to cast out of his kingdom one of his younger brothers who had risen against him on the death of their father. The ambassador fell into conversation with this young man when he was at Court, and frequently invited him to an evening banquet; and it chanced that one night when they were alone, after the banquet was over, the youth being a handsome fellow, the ambassador laid hold of him, and treated him rudely (for these Ishmaelites are more given to this, if report be true, than any other Moors in those parts of India). The young man began to cry out, and all his people immediately ran in to help their master. The ambassador, when he perceived the uproar, pushed the yonng man out, and barricaded himself in some houses, and began to defend himself from the people who were attacking him. When the news of all this reached the King of Cambay, he sent all his guard and put down the rioting, but not before seventy or eighty people on one side or the other had lost their lives. The son of the King of Mandao, ashamed of what had taken place, went away to the Reys Butos,[1] who border on his realms, and they afforded him assistance against the rebel brother; and, when this man had been cast out of the kingdom, he recovered possession of it.

This kingdom of Mandao[2] also borders on that of Cambay. The people are very warlike, and in all the rajah's towns and villages there are men in garrisons. The former king, father of this youth, used constantly to carry about with him for show seven or eight thousand women riding on horses, with their bows and arrows. They used to go a hunting with him, but in war he did not make use of them.

[1] See p. 106.
[2] See p. 60.

As soon as the son was in possession of the kingdom he abandoned this custom, and would not have them any more with him. The King of Cambay, disgusted at the proceedings of the ambassador, made haste to send him away, having very soon shown him that it was no use to try and obtain those things for which he had come thither; but he gave him two elephants, and an animal which is called *ganda, i.e.*, a rhinoceros, and many other articles, in return for the gifts which he had brought, and gave orders to a captain to carry him to Çurrate,[1] and from that port to put him and his baggage on board a ship.

When the party reached Çurrate, the ambassador wasted no time in getting on board a ship, which was just on the point of setting out for Ormuz. As soon as he had set out, the servants made a ship ready, in which they embarked the elephants, and the beast, and all the baggage; but the Moors of the land, not being very well pleased with the request for a ship which the ambassador had brought to them, put a faulty mast into the ship; and, hence, when the ship got out a little way from shore, and felt a somewhat stiff breeze, which struck it, the mast broke, so they were compelled to put back into Çurrate, and from this circumstance the king got his present again. The ambassador, however, at length, made his voyage in another ship, not much pleased, it is true, with the sorry entertainment which the King of Cambay had given him, and somewhat less pleased when he learned the trick which the Moors had played with his servants.

[1] See plan of Surat, or Surrate, in Pedro Barretto de Resende's MS., British Museum, Sloane MS., 197, f. 182.

CHAPTER XIX.

How Miguel Ferreira, who went as ambassador to the Xeque Ismael, arrived at Tauriz, and of the reception which he experienced, and of what took place until his return to Ormuz.

Miguel Ferreira, who had set out for Cochim, reached Dabul, where the ambassador of the Xeque Ismael remained, as well in expectation of the arrival of his messengers, as because he was very desirous that the great Afonso Dalboquerque should send some one to visit the Xeque Ismael, his lord. And inasmuch as this Portuguese ambassador was also accompanied by an ambassador of the Hidalcão, the man was highly gratified at their arrival, for he cared for nothing else than to see his court thronged with ambassadors of all the kings in the world. A few days after Miguel Ferreira's arrival, they all embarked in a ship and made their voyage to Ormuz, where the king showed them much entertainment; and from that city they shaped their course straight to Tauriz,[1] where the Xeque Ismael was staying, and he had been already advised of the coming of Miguel Ferreira by a letter from his own ambassador and by the ambassador of the Hidalcão, who was, indeed, on the same journey. The Xeque Ismael, very desirous of gaining the friendship of Afonso Dalboquerque, because of the great fame which was reported about him, desired to show honour to Miguel Ferreira, and ordered the Lords of his Court, and all his military men, to go and receive him, and bring him into the royal presence before the ambassador of the Hidalcão was introduced. This caused the ambassador of the Hidalcão to become very angry, because the reception which they gave him was not so grand as that with which Miguel Ferreira had been honoured.

[1] Perhaps Taurie, on the Persian Gulf, 27 deg. 41 min. N. lat.; 52 deg. 27 min. E. long.

When Miguel Ferreira was brought before the Xeque Ismael, he delivered the credentials which he carried from Afonso Dalboquerque; and these the Xeque received with many speeches and demonstrations of amity. But Miguel Ferreira had become very ill; that day, therefore, he could not hold any further converse with the Xeque Ismael beyond delivering the letters and begging permission to go and recruit his health; and this was accorded to him, and the Chief Physician was commanded to attend upon him and do his best to restore him to health, under penalty of being beheaded if he did not succeed. In a few days' time, Miguel Ferreira's health began to grow a little better, and the Xeque Ismael sent for him again, and inquired concerning the estate of the King of Portugal, and of the Queen, and whose daughter she was, and of our manner of using arms, and how we conducted our war, and with whom we were at war, and if there were many horses in Portugal; and he asked, also, about the ships and navigation of India, and many other details of the power and estate of the king, D. Manuel, in foreign parts.

To all these inquiries, Miguel Ferreira made reply in accordance with the instructions he carried; and the messenger who had been sent to Afonso Dalboquerque, and who was also present at this interview, showed the Xeque Ismael Afonso Dalboquerque's portrait, which he had brought, and spoke in high terms of praise of the greatness of his Indian fleet and of his ships of burden, and how the kings of those parts of India durst not send their ships outside their harbours without safe-conduct of the King of Portugal. The Xeque Ismael was very much gratified at hearing these things, and at his conversation with Miguel Ferreira, because of the excellent account which he gave about everything, and, ere he dispatched him back home, caused him to be summoned before him on many occasions, and conversed with him upon the estate of the King of Portugal, and on the affairs of India, and the desires which he cherished of the destruction of the Grand Sultan, and the house of Méca, even offering to devote his own person and estatè towards the accomplishment of this purpose.

After many days had in this manner been spent by Miguel Ferreira in the Court, he entreated the Xeque Ismael to dispatch him back with an answer, because Afonso Dalboquerque, Captain-General of the Indies, being desirous of gaining information respecting his royal person, had ordered him to return as quickly as he could. The Xeque Ismael was so pleased with Miguel Ferreira, that it was greatly against his inclination that he consented to allow him to return, and in company with him he sent back the same messenger who had come with him, as ambassador to Afonso Dalboquerque, bearing a present of many clothes of silk stuff, and brocades, and horses caparisoned with very rich housings, and several coats of mail, and other arms, which the Persians are wont to use, and two suits made of brocade, trimmed with golden buttons, wherewith they are clothed, and a girdle, target, and short broadsword, and other objects, all made of gold, and half an *alqueire*[1] of turquoises, just in the same condition as when they came out of the mines.

This present, which was of great intrinsic value, Afonso Dalboquerque divided among all the captains, without retaining a single thing for himself, except only the horses, and these, which he kept for the King D. Manuel, he ordered to be delivered up into the keeping of the officers of his factory. But, as the pieces of gold seemed to him to be good, and he looked at them in the light of mementoes of so powerful a prince as the Xeque Ismael, he redeemed them of the captains at his own expense, and sent them to the King of Portugal by the hands of D. Garcia de

[1] The Portuguese *alqueire* is believed by Vieyra equivalent to one peck, three quarts, and a pint, in English.

Noronha, his nephew. When Miguel Ferreira had received his letters of dispatch, he took his leave of the Xeque Ismael, and then, taking the ambassador with him, they both set out and made their journey to Ormuz, being entertained all the way in great style by all the villages which they passed through; and, having at length reached Ormuz, they were well received by the king and by Rexnordim, his governor. And it was while they were staying there, waiting for a good wind to enable them to pass over to India, that Afonso Dalboquerque arrived, with the intention of putting in order the affairs of this kingdom; and he also gave them a very cordial reception.

CHAPTER XX.

How the great Afonso Dalboquerque reached Goa; and of the news which reached him from Malaca, and the succour he sent thither; and how Fernão Perez Dandrade gained a victory over the Javanese fleet.

At the beginning of January, in the year [fifteen hundred and] fourteen, the great Afonso Dalboquerque reached Goa, and there he found ambassadors from the Kings of Pegú and Siam, and another from the king's mother, with presents of very rich things, and letters of many compliments, showing in them how much they desired the friendship of the King of Portugal, and wished to make arrangements for carrying on in peace the trade in Malaca; and as he was, on his part, also desirous that the commerce of this state should be widely celebrated among all the kingdoms of those parts, he was much pleased with their mission to him, and treated the ambassadors with great entertainment.

In the company of these ambassadors came Manuel

Fragoso, whom Afonso Dalboquerque had sent with Antonio de Miranda[1] to the King of Siam, to prepare for him a written report of all the matters, merchandise, dresses, and customs of the land, and of the latitude of their harbours; and this report Afonso Dalboquerque sent immediately, together with the presents, to Dom Garcia de Noronha, in order that he might convey them to the King D. Manuel, in the ships of burden that were ready to set sail for these kingdoms [of Portugal]. This Manuel Fragoso delivered to Afonso Dalboquerque a letter from Ruy de Brito Patalim, captain of the fortress of Malaca,[2] wherein he rendered an account of the state of that settlement, and showed how Patequitir had risen up in rebellion with the slaves[3] of Utemutaraja's widow, numbering about six thousand, and with some of the native armed men, who determined to follow his fortunes; and they had constructed a fortress, with very strong palisades, so as to be able to use it as a base for their hostile operations, by co-operation of the Lassamana,[4] or Admiral of the Sea, who was cruising about in the straits of Sabão,[5] intercepting any provisions from reaching the city; and, seeing this, he had dispatched Fernão Perez Dandrade with his fleet, by sea, and Antonio Pessoa, with armed men by land, to attack the palisadings; and although, in forcing an entry through them, they had been exposed to great danger, because of the naturally strong position of the place itself, nevertheless the position was attacked with so much vigour that they got into it by force, after killing many of the enemy; and when Pate-

[1] See vol. iii, p. 156.
[2] See vol. iii, p. 166.
[3] See vol. iii, p. 151.
[4] See vol. iii, p. 87.
[5] The Straits of Sabon and Mandol are very intricate, and, according to Horsburgh, p. 210, are never attempted by European navigators. The former is contiguous to the west sides of False-Durian, Sabon, and the Great Carimon. As both these straits are bordered by reefs, with shoal water in some places, they appear to be only navigable by proas or small vessels.

quitir perceived that he was worsted, he had retired along the River Muar,[1] into the interior, and had sent to beg for assistance from the King of Java, promising, in recompense, to make him Lord of Malaca.

After Afonso Dalboquerque had read this letter, he gathered from Manuel Fragoso how Antonio de Miranda had reached Malaca, and how, when he found that settlement in this difficulty, he had decided to remain there himself, sending forward Antonio de Miranda, with the ambassadors who had accompanied him in the voyage thither; and, at the moment of his setting out, there arrived Antonio Dabreu, who had gone to explore Maluco,[2] and Mendafonso, with all their party quite safe except Francisco Serrão, who had lost his [ship] in the Island of Ternate,[3] and remained there with those who were saved with him, and that he had also fallen out with the natives whom the king of those islands governed, of which, however, I do not give any account, because the end of it happened after the death of Afonso Dalboquerque.

Afonso Dalboquerque having thus, through Manuel Fragoso, received the latest and truest account of the necessitous condition of Malaca, gave orders to fit out immediately three vessels, with a hundred and fifty soldiers, and a large quantity of warlike stores; and of these ships he made Francisco de Melo, Jorge de Brito, and Martim Guedez, captains, for it was his opinion that these, with the larger reinforcement which had already arrived there under Antonio Dabreu,[4] would be sufficient until he could provide

[1] See the Mua River on the chart of Diogo Homem at beginning of vol. iii; also vol. iii, p. 131.

[2] See vol. iii, p. 162.

[3] See *L. de Varthema*, p. 245, Hakl. Soc. Edition.

"Vê Tidóre, e Ternáte, co' o fervente
Cume, que lança as flammas ondeadas."
(Cam., *Lus.* x, 132.)

[4] See vol. iii, p. 162.

the fortress with a captain.[1] These reinforcements arrived in due course at Malaca, and were joyfully received by those who were in the fortress; for, by means of this timely succour of new strength, they were reassured and relieved from the apprehension which the hourly-expected arrival of the great fleet of the enemy produced upon them. It was but a few days later, that one day, at sundown, Pateonur came in sight with a fleet of ninety sail against the harbour of Malaca, bringing with him ten thousand men, not counting the large junks which he left in the Muar River; and in company with him came Patequitir and the Lassamana, and they all cast anchor close to our fleet.

Patequitir, when he beheld the number and powerful armament of the ships, and saw such an unexpected number of fighting men, changed his mind, and gave up the intention for which he had come, which was to disembark and fall upon our fortress, and went to Pateonur and [the] Lassamana, and told them that it was his opinion that it was not the moment for attacking the city, for if they were to disembark all their forces on land, the Frangues, *i.e.*, the Portuguese, would remain supreme on the sea, and could easily set fire to all the fleet; and if the fleet were destroyed in that manner, then they were indeed all as good as ruined; therefore it would be well-advised for them to rally again at their rendezvous on the Muar River, and from that position as their base, wage war upon Malaca. Inasmuch as this advice seemed prudent to them all, an hour before daybreak they weighed anchor and set sail. Fernão Perez Dandrade, who was keeping a watch over their movements, no sooner espied their retreat, than he made a signal to slip the cable of all his fleet, and gave chase to them, and before they could reach Muar River fell upon them, and sent many of their ships

[1] According to Correa, Jorge Dalboquerque was sent as Captain of Malaca.—*Lendas*, ii, 381.

to the bottom, and put to death a large number of their people, many of our own men being wounded, and some killed in the engagement.

Pateonur, being in the van, had time, while our men were engaged in conflict with his fleet, to retreat with the greatest possible haste, and as soon as he reached the Muar River, embarked on board his junk, and set sail right away to Java, not at all well pleased at the result of this enterprise; and the Javanese were so dejected and terrified at this defeat—for it is indeed one of the glorious actions that we can tell of in those parts of the world—that they never dared to return again to Malaca. Patequitir and the Lassamana sailed up the river in the same ships which had brought them from Malaca, and saved themselves by taking to the interior country; and Fernão Perez Dandrade returned to Malaca elated with this victory, being there received with great joy by the captain and the rest of the people in the fortress. Of this victory, and of many others which Fernão Perez gained over the Moors, what time he held the appointment of chief captain in those parts, I do not give a detailed account, because there are others who have written a good deal about that commander.

CHAPTER XXI.

How the great Afonso Dalboquerque sent Diogo Fernandez de Béja and James Teixeira as ambassadors to the King of Cambay: and how they arrived at Çurrate, and set out from that place to the King's Court.

The great Afonso Dalboquerque, at the news which Fernão Martinz Evangelho wrote of the journey of Miliqueaz to the King of Cambay's Court, became very disappointed, and was much afraid that the proposed affair of building a fortress in Diu would not be productive of any material success, and that Miliqueaz would injure the matter even in a greater degree by his visit in person than he had already done by his letters, although up to this time he (Afonso) had great hopes of succeeding if he could trust the intelligence which Milecopi had announced to him through Tristão Déga. And with the intention of carrying out this policy, he sent Diogo Fernandez de Béja and James Teixeira, as ambassadors to treat of this matter with the king; and through them he sent as a present to the king, a collar of gold, enamelled, and a dagger with its sheath all gold and niello-work,[1] and a creese of gold and ten *covados*[2] of black velvet, and a piece of green brocade from Persia, and two other pieces from China, and a washhand basin with its double-handled ewer,[3] all very well gilded. And to the end that this embassy should possess greater authority than the others—so desirous was Afonso Dalboquerque to make a footing in Diu—he sent as a present also twenty horses and their harness, and silver vessels for the service of his table, and many native peons to attend the members of the embassy, and he drew up also written instructions which they were to observe.

As soon as Diogo Fernandez and James Teixeira had set out on their voyage, they sent on before them in advance Pero Queimado and Ganapatim,[4] a Hindoo, who was very well acquainted with the Guzarate language, to go and beg safe-conduct from the King of Cambay, that these two

[1] *Anilado.*

[2] See vol. i, p. 176.

[3] *Albarrada*, a flower-pot with two handles.

[4] See Correa's *Lendas*, vol. ii, p. 868, where a parallel account of this expedition is recorded. The name of the Hindoo is there given as Ganda Chatim, and a note in the same page refers to Castanheda, book iii, chap. 127, where the name is written Anagapatu; and, chap. 131, Ganapatu.

ambassadors might come to visit him; and as the weather was very adverse, they delayed a long time on their voyage, that they did not reach Çurrate until the fifteenth day of the month of March. But as Pero Queimado had not yet come back,[1] they sent to ask Desturcão,[2] ruler of the city, for a safe-conduct, in order that they might disembark. But as he had already been ordered by the king (who from Pero Queimado knew of their coming) to receive them with rejoicing, he sent them a safe-conduct, and Meacoja, and Meababu, captain of the King of Cambay, and a brother of Milecopi—in whose house they were to be lodged—were instructed to receive them, with many relays of riding horses for them and their servants, and waggons[3] for their baggage. As soon as they disembarked they proceeded without delay to the house of Desturcão to pay him a visit, for he was lying ill on a bed; and after an exchange of courtesies with him, they all remained in conversation one with another, until two *cabayas* (or native dresses of silk), were brought, which Desturcão had sent for, in order to present them to Diogo Fernandez and James Teixeira, for it is a custom of theirs to do this. Diogo Fernandez said to him that ambassadors of the King of Portugal, in whose name they had come thither, were not accustomed to accept anything except from the kings to whom they were accredited, but as Desturcão considered

[1] From Champanel, Correa, *Lendas*, ii, 368, where the details of these journeys are somewhat difficult to reconcile with the account here given in the *Commentaries*.

[2] Correa, *Lendas*, ii, 369, calls this man Deruscão; Castanheda, iii, chap. 131, calls him Destrocão. The final syllable is the title *khan*.

[3] Of these *carretas*, Correa, *l.c.*, says:—"As carretas, em que elle e os Portuguezes forão, erão de muytos lauores, e paramentadas de pannos de seda, cubertas do sol, e as carretas de tal andar, porque a terra he campinas muyto chãs, que a gente n'estas carretas vão dormindo tão assassegados como no chão." Correa gives a long and very minute account of the grandeur of this embassy and of the festivities in which Diogo Fernandez indulged.

himself thereby injured, because of the need which they had of him, in order to show him honour, they accepted these things of him; and then, taking their leave, they proceeded to take up their quarters in the houses of Melecopi's brother, which had been already prepared for their reception. And on the following day, in the morning, they sent, by the hands of Duarte Vaz and Ruy Paez, certain articles to Desturcão, which he also at first declined to accept, but finally accepted. Three or four days more elapsed, and then Desturcão sent them word that he had received a letter from the king his lord, ordering him to give them everything they required for their journey, and asking them to send him word of the time when they wished to set out, so that he might have everything ready for them. And because at this juncture Pero Queimado came back, bringing them news that Milecopi was out of the Court, and out of favour with the king, and in the instructions which these ambassadors carried they were enjoined to do nothing without him, they dissembled about the time of their starting, and sent word by Duarte Vaz to Desturcão that the man who had gone forward to obtain the safe-conduct for them had declared that the king had set out for the city of Patané,[1] making war upon the Reys Butos; and as Afonso Dalboquerque had commanded them in their instructions to return and winter in Goa, and the monsoon was now spent, and there was now no longer opportunity of doing either one thing or the other, therefore they had decided upon returning therefrom, and on the commencement of the next monsoon they would return at an easier pace. Desturcão replied upon this, through Meababu, that as they had already obtained their safe-conduct, and everything they required for their voyage was now in readiness, they did not seem to him to be acting courte-

[1] Pattan, Puttun, or Anhulwar Pattan, in the Gaikwad's dominions, Bombay Presidency, 23 deg. 47 min. N.; 71 deg. 56 min. E.

ously in failing to make their way to the king; neither could he feel certain of his own safety, if he were to allow them to go back without first seeing the king, for it was to this end that they had come, and it would be necessary to acquaint the king first of all of this alteration of their intentions, and on receipt of his reply then they could do as he should command them.

When Diogo Fernandez de Béja and James Teixeira perceived the firmness of Desturcão, and felt they could do nothing except what he wished, in order to put a good front to their remaining, they sent word in reply, that as he thought it good, they would comply with his desires, for the Captain-General of the Indies would look upon it all as for the best, and therefore they wished to set out immediately on their journey to the Court. Desturcão thereupon gave orders that they should be supplied with all they required, and he appointed Meacamadim, captain of the king, with thirty peon archers, to go with them and arrange their halting places. Thus they set out on their journey from Çurrate on the twenty-eighth day of the month of March, and reached Champanel[1] on the fourth of the month of April, and proceeded to take up their quarters in a vegetable garden close to the city, where they clothed themselves in their best, and made themselves smart, to go and see Melecopi who was at that time in Champanel.

When Melecopi learned their arrival, he sent one of his sons in charge of a large body of men on horse and on foot, with a great company of trumpeters, to receive them, and there they passed the night, being richly entertained and nobly banqueted by Melecopi, to whom Diogo Fernandez de Béja delivered the letter which he had brought from Afonso Dalboquerque, and with it a present, and gave him an account of the business for which he had come, for in this way he had been instructed to act. Melecopi told them

[1] See p. 60.

that Miliqueaz, after the departure of Tristão Dega, had gone to the king's Court, and spoken frequently with the king, advising him by no means to grant a fortress in Diu to the Frangues; for, if they wished to build it there, it was in order to wrest his kingdom eventually from him; and so the king had strongly fortified Diu, and now had no apprehension that any power in the world could prevail against it.

After long conversations held upon this matter, Melecopi on his part giving them advice how to conduct themselves, and pointing out to them the position which they ought to take up in the business, they took their leave of him, and set out on their way to Madoval[1] where the king lived, and Melecopi sent with them one of the principal men of his household, with six horsemen in his train, in order to accompany them, and told them on no account to lodge anywhere except where this man of his indicated to them.

CHAPTER XXII.

How Diogo Fernandez de Béja and James Teixeira reached Madoval, and the reception which they experienced there; and what passed with Çodamacão, Chief Alguazil of the King of Cambay, in reference to dispatching them.

Diogo Fernandez and James Teixeira having set out from Champanel, before they drew near to the city of Madoval, where the king was, sent word to Meacamadim, who was occupied in arranging the places for their lodging, to go forward to Çodamacão, Chief Alguazil, and acquaint him of their coming; and he sent word back telling them to lodge on that day in a vegetable garden which belonged to him, just outside the city. And on the following day, in the morning, he sent one of the principal men of his household, a Turk by birth, with thirty

[1] See description of this town further on at end of chapter xxiii.

attendants mounted on horses, and a large number of footmen, furnished with many trumpets and horns, to accompany them by way of ceremony to a banquet in his house; and when all had arrived at the door of his courtyard, Melique Coadragui, the son of Desturcão, who was one of the king's pages, came out to receive them, and there they alighted and entered into a large chamber where Çodamacão was waiting in expectation of them, and by him they were received with great cordiality and honour, and there forthwith Diogo Fernandez presented to him the present which he had brought for him, giving him at the same time a letter from Afonso Dalboquerque. After spending a little time in conversation, he told them to go and take their rest, and when the king should return—for he was gone a hunting—he would go to the palace and acquaint him of their arrival, and learn from him when he would choose to give them audience; and he ordered that they should be entertained in one of the rooms of his house, where all were taken in comfortably.

On the following day, in the morning, the Çodamacão went to the palace, and from that place sent word to Diogo Fernandez and James Teixeira, telling them that the king had returned and desired that they should be brought before him immediately; and, for a body guard, he sent them Melique Coadragui with all the mounted men of the Court, and with a large body of horn-blowers, who arrived just as Diogo Fernandez and James Teixeira and all their party had finished dressing themselves. Thereupon they got upon their horses and proceeded direct to the palace; and after they had alighted, and passed through many houses and courtyards, they came to a very large one where the king was seated upon a low sofa,[1] with all the captains of the kingdom in rows against the wall, each in due place according to his precedence; and they went up to the king

[1] *Catle.*

(carrying before them the present which Afonso Dalboquerque sent him, for this is the custom with them), and made obeisance before him, according to our fashion, and the king received them with great kindness, manifesting that he was much pleased at their coming; and after that all the members of the company he brought had kissed the king's hand, Diogo Fernandez presented to him the letter which he brought from Afonso Dalboquerque, and he read it forthwith, for it was written in Arabic; and, after he had read it, Diogo Fernandez told him that Afonso Dalboquerque, Captain-General of India, sent him his salutation,[1] and an offer of the whole of the fleet of the King of Portugal to serve him therewith.

The king thanked him very much for his offers, and inquired of him how Afonso Dalboquerque was, and how they themselves had borne the fatigue of their journey. After this was over, Melique Coadragui drew them aside to the top of the courtyard, and there brought them two *cabaias*[2] of brocade for Diogo Fernandez and James Teixeira, and others of coloured velvet for the rest of the party. And when they had attired themselves in these new robes, they made another obeisance to the king after the native fashion, and he told them to go to their lodging, and of the business for which they had come they could give an account to Çodamacão, for he was instructed to dispatch them back without delay.

Next day, after dinner, Çodamacão caused them to be sent for, and told them to lay before him all that they desired the king to do for them, because he had received orders to dispatch them immediately. Diogo Fernandez declared to him that the principal cause of his coming was to request a site in Diu upon which to construct a fortress, so that therein the men and the property of the King of Portugal might be assured against harm; for Afonso Dalbo-

[1] *Calema.*

[2] See p. 95.

querque, Captain-General of India, was hoping to carry on a great trade in the kingdom of Cambay, and in this manner the king would have the Portuguese nearer at hand to serve him, and the native custom-house would produce twice as much revenue as heretofore. Çodamacão replied that up to that moment no mention had ever been made about a fortress except at Bacar,[1] which he had conceded to Tristão Dėga when he was there; and truly as far as maintaining friendly relations with the King of Cambay and trading with his kingdom, Bacar would be quite sufficient, for the very name of fortress was distasteful.

Hereupon Diogo Fernandez declared that the King of Portugal's men and property could not be put into Bacar, but only in a very strongly fortified fortress, so that it should not be exposed to robbery, nor the men to slaughter, things which it was notorious had been perpetrated in Calicut, Coulão, and Malaca; but if the Portuguese had only had fortresses therein when those events took place, as now they have them, all would have been safe, and peace and friendship would never have been broken. And it was because the King of Portugal desired to maintain friendship on a true basis with the King of Cambay, that he was now sending to request him to cede the site for a fortress in Diu; and besides these reasons, many further advantages were dwelt upon which would arise out of a satisfactory settlement of the business. Çodamacão answered, that out of kindness to Afonso Dalboquerque he would lay before the king all the reasons which had been urged upon him, and he would take all the trouble he could to dispatch them on their homeward voyage as quickly as he could.

Three days elapsed, when Çodamacão sent for them again

[1] Bakar, or Bakkur, Island and Fort in Sinde, lat. 27 deg. 45 min. N.; long. 68 deg. 50 min. E., according to K. Johnston's *Royal Atlas*. It appears to be Béka, of the *West Coast of Hindostan Pilot*, 1880, p. 226; but the position given at p. 338 varies considerably from Johnston.

at night (for the houses ran one into the other by communicating passages), to deliver them the despatch which the king had dictated; in which it was shown, how, in consideration of the friendship which he desired to maintain with the King of Portugal, and also, because Afonso Dalboquerque, Captain-General of India, had sent an embassy to request it of him, he would be happy to grant him a site for a fortress in any one of the following places at his pleasure, to wit, Beroche,[1] Çurrate, Maim[2], Dumbes,[3] or Bacar, and let him send him word in his despatch as to which of these places he would desire to accept; but if he would not accept these terms, he should consider that the heart of the Captain-General was not good. Diogo Fernandez replied that he carried no instructions from Afonso Dalboquerque enabling him to accept any other fortress than in Diu, and seeing that he (Çodamacão) was so important a personage, and one in whom the king reposed great confidence, he ought to consider very seriously how much honour and profit he would acquire if the King of Portugal's people were to carry on trade in his land, for by these means the kingdom of Cambay would again become noble, and greatly improve her revenues beyond their present condition, and her ships would perform their merchant voyages in safety without any one doing them any injury. Çodamacão, how-

[1] Beroche, Bharuch, Baroach, and Broach, in the Gulf of Cambay, lat. 21 deg. 44 min. N.; long. 72 deg. 58 min. E. Vessels of one hundred tons can ascend the Nerbudda at high tide to the town of Broach, nearly thirty miles from its mouth, but skilful pilots are necessary.

[2] See plan and description of Mayme in P. Barretto de Resende's MS., Brit. Mus., Slo. MS. 197, f. 202. It is now called Méhim. See *West Coast of Hindostan Pilot*, p. 175, on the North Konkan coast, close to Salsette Island.

[3] Near Surat, called Domus in the *West Coast of Hindostan Pilot*, p. 183. Formerly the channel was deepest here and used by ships going over the bar to Surat. It took a direction on the east side of the bank towards the village Domus on the eastern shore, but is now only navigable by boats at half tide.

ever, asked him if, provided that the king kept on terms of peace and friendship with the Portuguese, they would hinder the Cambay ships from making their voyages to the straits [of the Red Sea] and to Adem, on condition they did not carry spices. Diogo Fernandez replied that it would not be reasonable for the ships of Cambay to make voyages towards those parts, because they belonged to nations with whom the King of Portugal was at war, whereas true friendship must hold friends of friends for friends, and enemies of friends for enemies. Çodamacão then said that, inasmuch as according to this rule the ships of Cambay would be unable to make their voyages in security to the Straits and to Adem, which were the principal centres of their commercial traffic, what profit would the King of Cambay gain by an alliance with the King of Portugal? and as for the request which the Captain-General of India had made, he had already given it to his slave Miliqueaz; and if the terms of this despatch were unwelcome to them, he could not undertake to broach the subject any more to the king. The answer of Diogo Fernandez was, why were not the Guzerates content with making their voyage to Malaca, Pegú, Martabane,[1] Bengála and Ormuz, and all other places which were under the service of the King of Portugal, and allied in peace with him, without seeking to visit the Straits and Adem, where he was carrying on war? These very places the Captain-General of India had determined to visit with his fleet, and destroy, and then, when he had made a settlement of the affairs of those parts, the Cambay ships might go thither with their merchandize. But as he had declared that he would not trouble the king any further with the matter, let him send him the despatch, couched in the terms mentioned, so that he might give an account of

[1] In Pegú.

himself to Afonso Dalboquerque, for they were determined to be gone. And at the conclusion of this conversation they returned to their house.

CHAPTER XXIII.

How Diogo Fernandez, and James Teixeira took their leave of the King of Cambay, and journeyed away: and what passed until their arrival at Goa.

After a lapse of three days, the Çodamacão sent word to Diogo Fernandez and James Teixeira, that they were to go and take their leave of the king, for he had already drawn up their despatch; and just as they were ready to go, Melique Coadragui came up with a large body of mounted men, as they had done at first, and entering the Palace all of them were presented with *cabaias,* which they put on, and daggers and swordbelts,[1] with which they girdled themselves, and in this manner they proceeded to kiss the king's hands, and he told them that they must look to Çodamacão, for he would deliver the despatch to them, speaking at the same time words of friendship, which they were to repeat on his behalf to Afonso Dalboquerque. Being thus despatched, they visited Çodamacão at his house, and he handed over to them a letter from the king for Afonso Dalboquerque, and gave them a present of Cambay productions, and a certain animal[2] because it was a monstrous

[1] *Camarabandes.*

[2] According to Correa, this was a *Ganda* or Rhinoceros, "que desembarcando em Goa fez espanto sua vista. Esta Ganda, ... mandou o Gouernador a ElRey. E porque assy era espantosa a vista da ganda, ElRey a mandou ao Papa; que era alimaria mansa, baixa de corpo, hum pouqo comprido, os coiros pés e mãos d' alifante, a cabeça como de porquo comprida, e os olhos junto do focinho, e sobre as ventas tinha hum corno, grosso e curto, e delgado na ponta; comia herua, palha, arroz cozido."—*Lendas da India*, pp. 373, 374.

thing, never before beheld in those parts. This creature was in Champanel, and he intended to forward it for them to Çurrate. And when they had thus received their despatch from the Çodamacão, they took their leave of him, and went home to their house, where there were already prepared for them waggons and horses; and thence they set out on their journey, reaching Çurrate on the eighth day of the month of May. But because the weather had by this time become very boisterous,[1] so that they could not venture on the voyage, they wintered there. When the winter was over, they desired Desturcão to supply them with a transport, in accordance with the king's orders to him, for they were anxious to get away; so he caused three *cotumbas*, (which are a certain kind of small vessels) to be given to them, and in these they had their baggage embarked, and the creature which had by this time arrived at Çurrate; this at length was brought to this kingdom of Portugal, and the King D. Manuel sent it to the Pope, but on the voyage the vessel which had it on board was lost.

After their baggage was all placed safely on board, they took their leave of Desturcão, and set out accompanied by two captains of the King of Cambay, until they reached the quay where they were to go on board, and taking leave of these they sailed away, shaping their course for India, and reached Goa on the fifteenth day of the month of September; and there they found Alfonso Dalboquerque in a great state of alarm, for he had given them written instructions, wherein he expressly ordered that they should on no account in the world winter in Cambay, and up to that day he had received no news of them. Diogo Fernandez and James Teixeira related to him the details of all that had

[1] "Although southerly winds prevail greatly after the middle of May, the stormy weather and rain usually do not set in until the dark nights, sometime between the 8th and 15th June."—*West Coast of Hindostan Pilot*, p. 18.

taken place, pointing out that the king was very far from granting them a fortress in Diu, for Miliqueaz was intriguing against it by means of corrupt bribes, which he was constantly giving to Bilirrane, the king's chief wife, who ruled him; and that, as for the sites which were offered for the fortress, the letter which they brought would indicate these to him.

This kingdom of Cambay was anciently in possession of the Hindoos. It borders on one side with the territories of the Reysbutos[1], by the harbour of Barapatane, and with the kingdom of Decam by a port which lies between Chaul and Maim. Its coast line extends for about a hundred and thirty leagues. Its form is as it were pointed (at the base), and in the interior country its width is about sixty leagues. The surface is flat, very fairly well supplied with provisions, and containing a great number of very valuable horses. It is bounded, in like manner, on the interior, by the kingdom of Delij,[2] and with the kingdom of Mandou, which are ruled by two very mighty kings. When the Portuguese discovered India, it had already been held for two hundred years by the Moors; and this fell out in the following manner.

Cambay possesses an island close into the mainland, with very steep rocks, called Betexagor,[3] in which the Arabian and Persian Moors, resorting thither to trade their merchandize with the Hindoos, settled a colony and began to form alliances with them; and as the Hindoos, in accordance with their creeds and religion, may not keep arms in their houses, the Moors found a way to dispose of them, and with little trouble became lords of all the villages and harbours on the sea side, and from those points began to invade the

[1] The Rajputs of Rajputana, north of Cambay. [2] Delhi.

[3] Bate or Bet island, in the Gulf of Cutch, about five miles long. The whole island still abounds with temples and shrines in honour of Crishna; the population, being for the most part Brahmins, is mainly supported by the pilgrims who resort here.

mainland, and in a very short space of time found themselves lords of the whole country; then they began to build keeled ships, wherein they performed voyages to all parts of India. The second king of this Moorish dynasty at Cambay, a great conqueror, sent certain ships to the coast of Melinde, and from that place they stood away to the Cape of Good Hope, intending so to make their way to these parts [of Europe]; but when they got to the Cape, they found the weather so contrary that they stood in to land, and reached the Island of São Lourenço (*i.e.*, Madagascar); and as their ships were no longer seaworthy they stayed in that island, and colonized some of the harbours; and it is believed that the advent of these ships originated the population of Moors in the island of São Lourenco, and as this kingdom of Cambay is plentifully supplied with all sorts of merchandize, there was a constant trade of ships to it from all parts of India.

The king who was on the throne when Diogo Fernandez reached the Court, was a man of forty years of age, married to a Reybuta, a woman of great worth and estimation, called Belirrane, and besides her he had five hundred others. He was a great falconer, and when he went to the chase he was always accompanied by three hundred huntsmen on horses. The King of Cambay is accustomed to spend most of the time in the city of Madoval,[1] because it is contiguous

[1] There is little doubt that this city of Madoval is none other than Ahmadabad, the chief city of Cambay. The Portuguese writer has cut off the initial *a*, mistaking it for the definite article; but I can only explain the final *d* becoming *l* by a typographical error. The latitude is 22 deg. 2 min. N., longitude 72 deg. 32 min. E. Father Clemente Tosi, in his *L'India Orientale*, Roma, 4to., 1676, vol. i, pp. 20, 21, recites: "E tirando verso settentrione s'incontra Amadabat Metropoli, e cittá, che à verun'altra cede frà quelle dell' Imperio del Mogol. E di circuito niente inferiore à Londra girando lo spacio di sei miglia. E situato in una amenissima pianura lungo le rive d'un fiume. E assicurata da una buonissima fortezza, da un muro, che la ricinge valido, e sedo. Le strade, e le piazze sono ampie, e selciate con gli edifitij dall' uno, e l'atro

to the mountain ranges of the Reysbutos, with whom he is contantly carrying on war.

This city is about a good league in length; it is very luxuriant, and supplied with plenty of fresh water, many entertaining sights, and many palatial houses, and it is for this reason that the king spends most of his time there; but all his treasure, artillery, and munitions of war are kept in the city of Champanel, because of its great strength. This latter city has a fortress on a height, where there are certain principal men in whom the king reposes the greatest confidence, always on guard with a large standing force of cavalry. In this kingdom of Cambay, at the time when Diogo Fernandez and James Teixeira made their journey there, were four principal lords who maintained the king's courts of justice and governed his property. The chief of these was Çodamacão, who had been his tutor and taught him to read,—a Turk by nation. The other three were called Dabiadastur, Asturmaleque, and Asturcão.

CHAPTER XXIV.

How Pero Dalboquerque fared on his voyage to Cape Guardafum; and how the King of Ormuz came to visit him.

After Pero Dalboquerque had set sail from Goa (as I have already related), he proceeded on his voyage straight to Çacotorá, with intention of taking in fresh supplies of water there; and in his passage across the sea he sighted three ships and boarded them; but as they proved to be bound from Calicut, carrying letters of safe-conduct from Afonso Dalboquerque, he let them go and left them to follow their

lato molto bene intesi. Fiorisa di mercantie, e gli habitatori sono molto industriosi. Puó in un tratto mettere insieme da sei mila cavalli in circa," etc.

voyage. On board of these ships were all the merchant Moors who had been carrying on their business in Calicut, and with them their wives, children, and property, for the the king had decreed their expulsion, as has already been shown. Pero Dalboquerque, after letting these ships go, shaped his course for Çacotorá, and cruised about in the adjacent parts for the whole of the summer, during which time he took ten very richly-laden Moorish ships, which were bound for the straits. And as the season was now far advanced, and the favourable winds would not hold out sufficiently long to enable him to go and have a look at Adem, as Afonso Dalboquerque had instructed him, he tacked out and stood over to Ormuz, at which port he arrived at the end of May; and as soon as he had cast anchor in the bay, the King Terunxa, who was then upon the throne,—for his brother Ceifadim[1] had died of poison—sent Hacem Ale, a Moor born at Grada, to pay him a visit on board ship; and by him he sent word to say that the city was at the service of the King of Portugal, and that he considered himself that king's vassal.

Pero Dalboquerque shewed great signs of pleasure at this visit, and declared how happy he was to find the king in this frame of mind; and on the following day, in the morning, he sent Tristão Déga on shore, accompanied by Francisco Dalboquerque, the converted Jew, as interpreter, with the letter sent by Afonso Dalboquerque to the king, and with instructions to declare that Afonso Dalboquerque, his uncle, Captain-General of the Indies, having been informed of the death of King Ceifadim (his brother), had sent him thither to ratify the peace with him, which had been concluded between the Portuguese and the late king, and to beg him to order payment to be made of the tribute due for the last two years; and inasmuch as the ships which he had brought were deeply laden with merchandize,

[1] For the account of this king, see vol. i, p. 228.

he begged him of his kindness to deliver up the fortress which his uncle had left already commenced, in order to store up the goods safely in it; and also that the people who should be left behind with them might be secure from any misfortune arising out of the affairs of Ormuz.

The king replied, that as for the fortress, he could not surrender it, for it was placed close to the palace, and as it was also set close to the sea, there was nothing which he took a greater delight in than it, therefore let him look about and see if there were any other place near the sea, or within the city, where the property and persons of the Portuguese could be placed in security, for he would order it to be immediately placed at their disposal; and as for the tribute, his late brother, just before his death, had sent an ambassador to the King of Portugal, bearing a present of pearls and other things of great value, begging him to remit the dues of the past years, and he was yet awaiting the reply; and if the tribute were not remitted, he would undertake to pay all that was owing; and as for the ratification of peace, he was ready to perform everything that Afonso Dalboquerque desired.

Tristão Déga returned with this answer, but as Pero Dalboquerque was not pleased with it, he sent him back to say, that he had never demanded the surrender of the palace, but only the house and the fortress which had been begun by his uncle, at the cost of the King of Portugal's property, and with the consent of the king's late brother and his governors, as was manifestly shown in the letter containing the articles of peace drawn up between the two parties; therefore he begged him earnestly of his goodness to command its surrender to them, for within its walls he was desirous of discharging his cargoes, and beginning to sell his merchandize, for indeed by these means no little profit would accrue to the native custom-house; and as for his assertion that the fortress ran close up to the palace, this was the very thing that the king ought to wish, for the nearer he had the Portuguese to himself by so much the safer would his royal person be against the designs of his enemies, and he would maintain his kingdom more peacefully, and his harbour would become more frequented, and full of all the riches of the world.

The king replied that it was true his brother had granted a site whereon a fortress might be built, but without considering the inconveniences which might arise from this grant; but after it had been commenced, and Cogeatar, Governor of the kingdom, perceived the loss which the palace would sustain on account of it, he would not allow it to be completed, and this had been the chief cause of the differences which arose between Afonso Dalboquerque and the late king his brother; and that the fortress was in sight of his palace, and for this reason, as well as many others, he could not yield up the building; and inasmuch as he had offered to build another fortress in any place they chose to select, at his own expense, his offer ought to be accepted, and the matter not insisted upon any more, for in the letter which the Captain-General of India had written to him, this alternative was conceded.

Tristão Déga replied that, as the king desired to stand by the terms of the letter, and to give another site for the building of a fortress, Pero Dalboquerque, Chief Captain of the Fleet, would accept no other than the hospital or the custom-house, for in either of these two Afonso Dalboquerque had provided for the fortress to be constructed, in order that it might be closely adjacent to the palace, where the men and merchandize of the King of Portugal could be more safely housed,—if he was determined not to give him back his own. The king replied, that the hospital, which Pero Dalboquerque sent to demand of him was a house of prayer, which his ancestors had founded for the reception of the sick, and the pilgrims who come to Ormuz, and it would be a shameful thing for him to give up a house which had been dedicated to God, for the purpose of converting it into a fortress; and as for the custom-house, that was a house wherein were paid of old the customs and dues of the Kings of Ormuz, and to take this would be the same as to take the sight of his eyes away from him; in no possible manner therefore could he part with either of these buildings, but he would give him any other that he chose to select, as he had already declared. And with this final answer Tristão Déga went back, and related to Pero Dalboquerque all that had passed with the king.

CHAPTER XXV.

How Pero Dalboquerque, seeing that the King of Ormuz would not give him the fortress, nor a site for building another, sent to beg for a house wherein he could discharge his cargo; and then sailed away to explore the straits of the Persian Sea.

Pero Dalboquerque being now well aware of the delays which the king was practising, and finding that he had already been there for some days without achieving any result, sent word to him by Tristão Déga, that as it was his intention, in concert with his Governors, not to surrender the fortress which the great Afonso Dalboquerque had begun, nor grant any other of those sites which he had pointed out for the building of another, he must then, at least, order that some house should be given, in which he could discharge the cargo of his ships, so that the sale of the merchandize could be commenced. The king, demonstrating great pleasure at this new point of the business, ordered that the same house should be given to the Portuguese in which the factory of the King of Portugal had formerly been established, on the occasion of Afonso Dalboquerque's first visit to Ormuz, and in it were found still remaining certain things which there had not then been an opportunity of removing, and these were, at the orders of Rexnordim, delivered to Tristão Dega and João Teixeira.

When the houses had been handed over to the Portuguese, the disembarking of the cargo was immediately proceeded with. And as soon as the ships had been unloaded, Pero Dalboquerque ordered them to be set on fire, for although in so doing a considerable sum of money was wasted, which the Moors would have willingly given for them, he gained greatly by their not thus having these ships for their navigation. When this event was over, he appointed Tristão Dega and João Teixeira to remain behind on land as factors of the merchandize, and Christovão Cercado, and Vasco Pirez, scrivener of the fleet, to be their scriveners, and then he made ready with his fleet to go and explore the straits of the Persian Sea (*i.e.*, the Persian Gulf), in accordance with the instructions which he had received from Afonso Dalboquerque; and just as he was on the point of spreading his sails to start away, the king sent word to him by Hacem Ale, begging him earnestly not to undertake the voyage, for his ships were too large and the straits full of shallows and islands;[1] for he was dreading lest any misfortune should arise to them in their voyage. Pero Dalboquerque replied that he was very much obliged to him for this piece of advice, but he could not omit the performance of the voyage, for the Captain-General of India had instructed him to explore the whole of the straits; and had

[1] The soundings in the gulf are deep where the land near the sea is high, and where it is low, the depths are less. The gulf is studded with islands of various sizes. They are commonly of volcanic origin, in part at least. The navigation in a sailing vessel requires great attention. The winds, as in most inland seas, are very uncertain and blow occasionally with great force down the gulf; and in winter, also, in the opposite direction. They set in without much warning.—*Persian Gulf Pilot*, 1870.

also ordered him to find out whether Barem[1] was still in obedience to his commands, and as he was bound thither he (the King of Ormuz) should consider if he could do him any service while he was there, for with that fleet of the King of Portugal he was quite ready to do him any service, and indeed Afonso Dalboquerque his uncle had so ordered him to act; and he would beg him earnestly to get ready the tribute and the golden letter, for as soon as he returned he would have to sail away again in a direct course for India.

When the King of Ormuz saw that Pero Dalboquerque, in spite of the advice he had given him, was determined to enter the straits, he commanded that two pilots should be given to him, who were well acquainted with the navigation of those parts, and letters for his use on the voyage, whereby to procure other pilots, and all other things needful for him; and desired him earnestly to show favour to a certain one of his captains who was journeying thither. And thereupon Pero Dalboquerque sailed away on the seventh of July of this year, and entered through the straits of the Persian Sea, and explored all the harbours, islands, and villages which are contained in it, as far as an island called Lulutem;[2] and when he was as far advanced as Bárem, the winds being now westerly, and the season getting late for returning to India, in accordance with the instructions which he carried, he tacked about and stood along in the tack for

[1] Barem, celebrated for its pearl fishery, is on the Arabian side, now called Bahreïn island, about twenty-seven miles long, north and south, by ten in breadth. The principal town is Manámeh at the north-east corner, the capital of the chief of the great Uttúbí tribe. Captain Kemball, late Political Resident in the Persian Gulf, estimates the total population of the islands at 50,000.

[2] The only island with a name at all approaching this is Húlúl, almost in the middle of the waterway, seventy-two miles S.E. by E. ½ E. from Ras Rekkem, barely one mile across; the highest peak being 180 feet, visible fourteen to fifteen miles. There is a good landing-place, but the island is quite barren. It is visited by the pearl boats; the edge of the Pearl bank being just outside the island.

a two days' voyage and reached Raxel,[1] where he found Mirbuzaca, captain of the Xeque Ismael, who had captured twenty *terradas*[2] from a captain of the King of Ormuz.

Pero Dalboquerque getting information of this, sent word to him that the great Afonso Dalboquerque had sent him to those parts in the service of the King of Ormuz, therefore he begged him of his goodness to order the restoration of the *terradas* which he had taken from this captain. Mirbuzaca, who had no fleet capable of offering any resistance to ours, ordered the surrender of the *terradas* and all the rest which he had seized. And after the captain had received the *terradas* again, Pero Dalboquerque sailed away to Ormuz, where he arrived on the sixth day of the month of August, and the king immediately sent Hacem Ale to visit him, giving him great thanks for the result of the affair with Mirbuzaca respecting his *terradas*. Tristão Dége and João Teixeira also, came off shore immediately, to see him on board, and related to him how that the king had not paid them the tribute, nor prepared the golden letter, which he had told the king he must do, before he sailed away.

Two days elapsed after this, and then Pero Dalboquerque sent a message to the king through Tristão Dége, João Teixeira, and Vasco Pirez, scrivener of the fleet, after the manner of a formal demand, stating that as he would not surrender the fortress which Afonso Dalboquerque had commenced, he must send back in writing the reply to this demand, and he must order the tribute to be paid to them, for he did not intend to return to India without it. The king was unwilling to make any written reply, but he sent back a verbal answer to the effect that as for the fortress, which they were beginning to talk about again, he had already shewn the reasons why he could not give it up; and as for the tribute, he was a poor man; on account of the

[1] This seems an imperfect word for Ras-el-...... or Ras-al-.......
[2] Small vessels used for purposes of war.

great expenses to which he had been put; therefore he begged him to consider him in this respect, as well as in all the rest which he had told him about the expected return of his ambassador [from Portugal], and this reply he could give to the Captain-General; and thereupon Tristão Déga took his leave of the king.

CHAPTER XXVI.

How Pero Dalboquerque again endeavoured to compel the king to pay the tribute, and what passed upon this matter with him; and how he set sail for India and arrived at Goa.

Pero Dalboquerque became so angry at this reply of the king, that he immediately sent Tristão Déga back again to tell him that as he had requited him so badly for the service which he had rendered him in procuring the restitution of his *terradas*, he might rest assured that he did not intend to go out of the harbour without first of all being paid all the debts which were due to him. Tristão Déga delivered this message to the king, and then, without waiting for any further reply, returned to the ships. The king and his Governors, seeing the determination of Pero Dalboquerque, and fearing that if he remained in this humour he might perhaps set fire to some seventy merchant vessels in the port, which were on the point of setting out for the straits (but having received intelligence that he was cruising about with his fleet at the Cape of Guardafum, they had put in at Ormuz), unanimously agreed, that in order to remedy this state of affairs, they ought to use their best endeavours to pay all they could of the tribute that was due. So the king sent word immediately by Hacem Ale, that as he would not take cognisance of his necessity, nor wait for the return of the ambassador sent to Portugal for a reply, he would therefore seek for a loan of some money so as to pay him, but this would be all he could do. Three days afterwards the king sent by the hands of Hacem Ale, ten thousand *xerafins*, begging him earnestly to pardon him for not sending a larger sum, for the merchants were so poor (as they dared not make their voyages out of fear of the Portuguese fleet), that the collection of that sum had only been effected with great trouble; and as for the golden letter, it was being prepared, and when it was finished he would send it to the Captain-General of India.

Pero Dalboquerque, finding the season would not allow him to delay any longer, on account of the monsoon, accepted the ten thousand *xerafins*, and gave orders for gathering together the goods which still remained on land for sale, and re-shipping it; and when it was all collected together, and the fleet ready provided with supplies and water for the voyage, he sent word to the King by Tristão Déga and João Teixeira that Afonso Dalboquerque had learned that the Xeque Ismael was very desirous of getting possession of Ormuz; therefore he, on his part, begged the king of his goodness—since the King of Portugal recognised the necessity of protecting him—not to consent to any armed men of the Xeque Ismael entering into his lands, and to cause it to be proclaimed that no person coming from Persia could pass through to India, for Afonso Dalboquerque ordered that every one taken in this sea, on his way to that country, should be put to the sword; but merchants could go safely, as many as pleased. And in case any ambassador from the Xeque Ismael should reach Ormuz on his way to any king in India, he must not be allowed to take in his company more than fifty persons, for all above that number were to be detained as captives. And because the King of Portugal had given order for the dismantling of the harbour of Baticalá, and desired all the horses from Arabia and Persia to be landed at Goa, therefore he begged him of his goodness to order all the ships carrying horses, to proceed direct to Goa, for there they would find all the merchandise they required for their return journey; and if this were conceded, he on his part would undertake not to give a safe-conduct to any ship to make a voyage except to Ormuz with merchandise; and he could rest assured that every ship which was not bound for Ormuz, would have its cargo seized, and its crew put to death.

The king replied, that he was quite content that the merchants should go to Goa, but it would have to be on two conditions. The first was, that the above-mentioned penalty should only apply to those who were clearly convicted of abandoning Goa in order to visit other ports. And the other, that he should give orders to treat the merchants with every honour, bearing in mind how dear horses were in Ormuz, and to what great expenses those who shipped them were put. If these two conditions were observed, and the merchants could obtain such a price for their merchandise that they could get a profit out of it, all the merchants would be delighted to go to Goa, without there being any necessity of fixing a penalty to compel them to use that port only.

With this reply, Tristão Dóga and João Teixeira took their leave of the king; and, as soon as they got on board, Pero Dalboquerque immediately sent word to the captains, giving them notice that he was about to set sail; and, on the following day in the morning, they all spread their sails, and he shaped his course direct for India; and without anything taking place on the voyage worthy of notice, he arrived at Goa, with all his fleet, on the twenty-eighth day of September in the year [fifteen hundred and] fourteen, and there he found the ambassador of the King of Ormuz, who had arrived from Portugal a few days before in the ships which came from that kingdom that year;[1] and at the news of the arrival of Pedro Dalboquerque, great was the rejoicing in the city, for it was already known that he had taken some valuable prizes. And, as soon as he reached the land, he went immediately to visit his uncle Afonso Dalboquerque, and gave him an account of what had taken place on the voyage, showing him how the King of Ormuz had accepted the cap of the Xeque Ismael, and ordered his prayer to be recited in all the mosques, and that Rexnordim ruled everything, and had sent orders for all his sons to come thither from Persia; and that a captain of the Xeque Ismael, called Mirbuzaca, was cruising about with a fleet lording it over all the Persian Straits.

Afonso Dalboquerque, happy as he was at the safe return

[1] The British Museum *MS. Add.* 20,902, gives, at f. 17, the following account of the ships sent from Portugal to India in 1514:—

"Anno de 1514.

"Christovão de Brito, Capitam Môr.

"Christovão de Brito, Capitão moor de çinco naos partio a Vintasete de Março; Capitães Francisco Pereira Rusticão; Manoel de Mello, Luis Dantas, João Serrão; E neste anno se fez a fortaleza de Coulão, a que se pos nome Sancthome. E foy primeiro Capitão, e feitor Heitor Rodriguez. 5 Vellas a 27 de Março.

"E em dous de Julho do mesmo anno partio Sebastião de Sousa por Capitão moor de tres Navios de que forão Capitães Luis Figueira e Pedr' Aluares Françes para fazerem feitoria na Ilha de São Lourenço que não teue efeito. 3 Vellas em 2 de Julho do mesmo anno.

"*Successos das cinco nãos.*—Luis Dantas chegando â India primeiro, que os de sua companhia, foy por mandado de Affonso de Albuquerque a Cambaya carregar de algumas merçadorias para ajuda da Carga, aonde se perdeu, salvandose a gente."

The marginal note to the first paragraph of this extract is:—"Outra Relação diz, que partiu a 9 de Abril com estes Capitães = Mel. de Melo, em *Sat Ma da Luz* = Franco Pereira Coutinho em *Sta Maria da Ajuda* = Luis Dantas, perdido = João Serrão."

"Esta mesma Relãçao diz, que depois de partida a Armada das 5 naôs partirão mais 2 vellas a 11 de Junho para na Ilha de S. Lourenço assentarem trato, e feitoria de que eram Capitães Luis Figueira, e Pedreanes Francês." Cf. Correa, *Lendas*, p. 385.

of his nephew, whereby the needs of India would be supplied, felt displeased when he learned the condition of affairs at Ormuz, and was not slow in making up his mind privately to himself, to go that very year and set the affairs right again, before the Xeque Ismael could set his foot there; and he lost no time in beginning to make himself ready, giving out openly, indeed, that this preparation was being made with a view to penetrating the Straits of Méca. The prize which Pero Dalboquerque brought, was valued at about forty thousand *cruzados* for the crown, as well as a ship laden with merchandise, which could not be sold, and besides the ten thousand *xerafins* which the King of Ormuz had paid as tribute. And although Afonso Dalboquerque was advised by the king's officers to lade a ready-money cargo for Portugal, because the cost would be less, yet, remembering the necessity of his people, he would not do it, but ordered them to set out a table in the public square, and pay every one in cash and merchandise all that was due to him for his wages and subsistence up to that very hour; whereat everyone became very happy.

But before this payment was concluded, it had happened that Afonso Dalboquerque had been very much importuned by a Lascar to give orders for the payment of his wages, for he was dying of hunger; and Afonso Dalboquerque, finding himself unexpectedly left without any cash wherewith to pay him, pulling at his beard said, "I swear by the life that I am living, what would you have me do for you? Here, take these hairs of my beard and go and pawn them." The Lascar had kept these hairs, and when it fell out that he saw the others were being paid openly, he made his way to Afonso Dalboquerque and cried out: "See, here are the hairs of your beard, send and take them out of pawn and pay me." Afonso Dalboquerque embraced the man, and said that one who had so carefully preserved the hairs of his beard, ought with good reason to be well paid; but as all the public money belonging to the King of Portugal had been paid away, he ordered him to be paid out of his own private purse, and from that day forward they used to call the man Afonso Dalboquerque's Lascar.

CHAPTER XXVII.

Of the arrival of the ambassador of the King of Narsinga, and of the reception which the great Afonso Dalboquerque gave him; and how he sent him back with a despatch, sending in company with him Antonio de Sousa and João Teixeira to settle the business for which he had come.

With the receipt of this intelligence, which Pero Dalboquerque brought, of the present condition of affairs at Ormuz, the great Afonso Dalboquerque made up his mind to go thither that summer with a well-armed fleet, to complete the fortress which he had left already commenced, and to take possession of the kingdom before ever the Xeque Ismael should busy himself about it; and to this end he began to make secret preparations, without acquainting anyone with his intention, giving out openly that his voyage would be to the Straits of Méca, because the King D. Manoel had given him orders to that effect. Just at this juncture of events there arrived an ambassador from the King of Narsinga, called Retelim Chetim, Governor of Bracelor,[1] and of the villages on the edge of the sea, who was a principal man of the royal household, and held in great esteem by the king, accompanied by a large number of native peons, that ministered to him by the way.

Afonso Dalboquerque, having received information of his coming, and of the high position to which his rank entitled

[1] See "Plan and Description of the Fortress and Town of Barsilor" in P. Barretto de Resende's MS., Brit. Mus., *Slōane* 197, fo. 284.

him, commanded Pero Mascarenhas, captain of the Fortress, with a large guard of mounted men, to go and await his coming outside the city. And when he arrived before him, he made a salutation, coming accompanied ceremoniously with many men on horseback, and a captain in command of a body of native peons. And he brought in front of his train four elephants with their castles made of wood covered with silk, and in each of them there sat a Hindoo personage of honorable rank, holding washhand bowls of silver gilt, wherein they carried pearls and jewelry of precious stones and other richly made articles of native manufacture, which the king sent to Afonso Dalboquerque as presents. With all this apparatus they arrived at the Çabayo's palace, where Afonso Dalboquerque was stationed, waiting for the new comers in a large saloon, richly hung around with trophies of arms, and having a canopy of brocade with a throne of crimson velvet, whereon he was seated, and all the captains, Fidalgoes, and noble personages who were in Goa standing up along the walls; for, although the great Afonso Dalboquerque lived on familiar terms with our own people, yet before the Moors and Hindoos of India he always maintained his authority, whence it happened that every one evinced towards him a great esteem and high consideration.

When the ambassador first entered the hall, Afonso Dalboquerque, having regard to the quality of his person, went down to the middle of the hall to receive him, and from that spot both proceeded to the places where it was appointed that they should sit. Thus, the ambassador standing up, delivered to him the present which he had brought, giving him at the same time a letter of credence from the King of Narsinga, in which he earnestly begged him to despatch the ambassador at an early moment. Afonso Dalboquerque told him to go and refresh himself from the hardships of his journey, while he looked at the letter and arranged the terms of his despatch, ordering that he should be supplied with all he and his people required at the cost of the Portuguese. On the following day, Afonso Dalboquerque ordered the ambassador to be called before him, and told him that the King of Narsinga had written, desiring him to give credit to all that he had written on his part, therefore he desired to know the business on which he had come, so that he might despatch him.

The ambassador replied, that the King of Narsinga, his lord, was very desirous of maintaining the peace and friendship which had been concluded with the King of Portugal, and for this reason, knowing the differences which were standing between him and the Hidalcão, he had determined to go to war with the latter; therefore, if he was still thus minded as he had been, let him send him word by a messenger, for if both were of one mind in this war, it would cost them very little trouble to destroy the Hidalcão. The letter also made mention of the trade in horses; but because the King of Narsinga, after Afonso Dalboquerque had sent Manuel Fernandez and Gaspar Chanoca to press him to a union for them both to make war upon the Hidalcão, was always making excuses without coming to any settled purpose; he also desired to delay the acceptance of this proposal until the king should understand that he had it in his power to destroy him by taking away from him the trade in horses, and giving it to the Hidalcão; therefore he told the ambassador that he would carefully consider the matter, and give him an answer at a future time.

The ambassador lost no time in informing the King of Narsinga of this diplomatic reply which Afonso Dalboquerque had made, and the king, when he perceived that Afonso Dalboquerque did not hasten with alacrity to announce to him that he was prepared to begin the expedition into the territory of the Hidalcão, being a business which he had often pressed him to undertake, came to the conclusion that he (Afonso) must have received some communication from the Hidalcão, so he immediately sent a messenger to his ambassador, telling him to hasten forward his dispatch more quickly than ever, and that he was to say to Afonso Dalboquerque that the king was already on the road with all his military array awaiting his reply.

But when Afonso Dalboquerque saw that the King of Narsinga was leaving no stone unturned to hasten matters to a crisis, like one who desired to bring his business to a decisive issue, from the dread he had of the Hidalcão, he gave the ambassador his dispatch, and fitted out Antonio de Sousa and João Teixeira with ten mounted men and fifty native peons to minister to them on the way, and sent them in company with the returning ambassador to settle the terms of the friendship which was to be struck up between them; and in the instructions which he prepared for them to declare to the king on his part, he said that if he, the king, really desired the help of the Portuguese in their projected invasion of the territory of the Hidalcão, he would give it on the condition that the wages of all the men whom he sent for that purpose should be paid by the king; and as for the trade in horses, he would have to pay, on this point, an annual sum of thirty thousand *cruzados*, and undertake to send for the horses to Goa and pay the dues upon them, and to Baticalá or Bacalor, whichever of these places Afonso Dalboquerque liked best to assign for the purpose. These and other things they were instructed to press upon the king, for Afonso Dalboquerque considered that the time was now come, when he could make an advantageous bargain with the king; for sometimes it happens that a lucky juncture of events is enabled to produce better results for an undertaking, however great it may be, than all the power of a king. When these, then, were ready, they set forth on their way, and by them Afonso Dalboquerque sent a present of very rich articles for the king, which Pero Dalboquerque had brought from Ormuz, as well as others which had come from Portugal.

CHAPTER XXVIII.

How, after the departure of the ambassador of the King of Narsinga, another ambassador came from the Hidalcão to treat for peace and the trade in horses, and yet another from the Hidalcão's mother, who came to hasten forward the matter: and what Afonso Dalboquerque did thereupon.

The Hidalcão, knowing that the King of Narsinga had sent his ambassadors to the great Afonso Dalboquerque, and that he was making preparations with a large force to invade his territory and make war upon him, fearing lest Afonso Dalboquerque and the king should strike up a bargain about the horse trade, which was the principal spring of his defensive policy, sent a messenger with letters addressed to his ambassador, who had been in Goa for several days past (for he had come with Diogo Fernandez, the *Adail*, and João Teixeira, as I have already related,[1] whom Afonso Dalboquerque had sent there, and they returned without coming to any definite conclusion), to hasten forward the matter more than ever, and to declare to him that, since it had been agreed between them that as long as they maintained the treaty of peace, he would not prevent the coming of the Moorish ships with their merchandise to Dabul, he begged him of his kindness to give orders for the punishment of his captains, because, in contravention of the terms agreed upon between them, they were capturing every ship bound for Dabul; for he on his part desired (as he had oftentimes sent word to him through his ambassadors) to maintain a state of peace and friendship with the King of Portugal, and to arrange the trade in horses, and they ought not to take away these [horses] to give them to the King of Narsinga. The ambassador gave a relation of all this, which the Hidalcão wrote to him, to Afonso Dalboquerque, begging

[1] See p. 83.

to be dispatched away; for, he said, the Hidalcão, his lord, imagined that it was owing to his negligence that the matter was left unheeded. But, as it was the determination of Afonso Dalboquerque to dally with him, until he could find out whether the King of Narsinga wished to come to a conclusion, in respect of the propositions which had been laid before him, or not (for Afonso Dalboquerque preferred this one's amity, as he was a Hindoo, if with an honest intention he would busy himself with the conquest of the kingdom of Decam, to that of the Hidalcão, who was a Moor, with whom there never could be any lasting relations of peace because of the intrigues of the Turks who advised him not to keep on good terms with the Portuguese), he replied that he would dispatch him.

After the lapse of a few days, the Hidalcão's mother, who governed that prince, perceiving that the ambassador was delayed, and being desirous that her son should have a treaty of peace with Afonso Dalboquerque, sent word to him through one of her female servants (a woman of great authority, who was married to a Moor who governed the royal household of this queen-mother), with a letter to treat concerning this agreement for peace, making many offers and begging him to dispatch her son's ambassador, who had already been waiting for some time to receive his dispatch, and also that he would give permission to her said servant to purchase a few horses, of which she had need—for in that country all the noble women go on horseback, and for this reason, apart from the necessity they have of them for military purposes, they are highly valued. Afonso Dalboquerque gave the desired permission to buy the horses, and dispatched the servant immediately, telling her to declare to her ladyship that he was busy about a great many important matters, and therefore at present unable to dispatch the ambassador of the Hidalcão, her son, but he would dispatch him as soon as he could.

But because the ambassador strove hard with Afonso Dalboquerque in the matter of obtaining his dispatch, and Antonio de Sousa and João Teixeira had not returned with any message from the King of Narsinga (who was waiting to decide finally what reply he would make), and the time of Afonso Dalboquerque's departure for Ormuz was at hand, he at length dispatched the Hidalcão's ambassador, intending on his return from Ormuz to come to an understanding with that one who would accede to the most favourable terms; and in order to entertain the Hidalcão in the meantime, he sent in company with this ambassador João Gonçalvez de Castel-Branco, very nobly accompanied with attendants on horse and foot; and through him an answer was sent, showing that out of a desire to cultivate his friendship and to be neighbourly towards him, he would give him all the horses that found their way to Goa, on condition of his surrender of the mainland [adjacent to Goa] and the pass of the land of the *Gate*[1]—for the military position of Goa would thereby be rendered more secure—and he promised that the king D. Manuel, his lord, would give all the assurances he could wish for, so that he might rest certain that the king would not send orders to make war with him, nor thwart his policy to the advantage of the King of Narsinga; but in respect of chastising the Portuguese captains who had taken his ships when bound for Dabul, in contravention of the articles agreed upon between them, this had been perpetrated by a galley that had mutinied there, and he was powerless to mete out the just punishment merited by these Portuguese, who, armed with a safe conduct, were robbing the ships of the Moors; for out of fear of being banished by him they would flee to his (the Hidalcão's) camp or headquarters, and there he felt sure they would be very well received by him; and, indeed, it was but a few days ago that four Lascars had seized upon a ship from Cananor, and finding shelter in his

[1] *I.e.*, *Ghaut.*

land, he [Afonso Dalboquerque] could not get at them to punish them as they deserved, therefore it were better (he thought) to leave them to rob the the Moors' ships. This artifice which Afonso Dalboquerque invented was so successful, that no sooner had the ambassador arrived than the Hidalcão wrote letters to the Tanadars[1] of all his lands to seize all the Portuguese they could lay their hands upon in them, and send them to him, even if they were already married and settled in the country; and when Afonso Dalboquerque was at Ormuz, these men were carried away to Goa and delivered up to the captain of the fortress.

The true cause of this complaint made by the Hidalcão was, that Afonso Dalboquerque, irritated at his conduct in giving shelter in his kingdom to certain Portuguese of low degree, and treating them with great honour and liberal entertainment, sent a secret message to Duarte de Sousa, who was cruising off Dabul in a galley, as I have already narrated, that, acting as though he had mutinied, he was to take possession of all the ships of the Moors which might put into that port, even if they carried the Portuguese safe-conduct; and in order that certain Portuguese soldiers, who had risen up in revolt on account of the great inducements which the Hidalcão had held out to them, should not be tampered with, he ordered one of them to be arrested, who, according to information, was going about declaring his intention of deserting to the Hidalcão unless a certain grievance which he had were settled in his favour; and as this man was a clever workman and knew how to cast guns he was ordered to be hanged, the public crier on the occasion declaring that "they are hanging this man because he supposes that he is useful for some purpose". In the meantime, Afonso Dalboquerque had arranged beforehand privately with the Vicar of Goa to come before him with all the clergy, and beg that the man's life might be spared, and

[1] See vol. ii, p. 125.

on the way to the place of execution they turned him back to prison, and the soldier, having by this time repented of his intention, was ordered to be released, and when the ambassadors returned with the Hidalcão's answer to all this, they found that Afonso Dalboquerque was dead.

CHAPTER XXIX.

How D. Garcia arrived at Goa with the vessels which he had caused to be refitted at Cochim; and how the great Afonso Dalboquerque made his fleet ready to set sail, and sent away Jorge Dalboquerque to be captain of Malaca, and what happened on the voyage.

A few days after these ambassadors had set out, D. Garcia de Noronha arrived with the ships which he had been keeping behind to repair at Cochim, and on his arrival the great Afonso Dalboquerque immediately began to fit out his fleet. And inasmuch as the King D. Manuel had laid great stress upon the duty of leaving all matters relating to the protection of any place, on the occasion of the governor leaving India to go to any other place, in such a condition that that place should be able to give a good account of itself if any cause of trouble should arise—(for to preserve what one has gained is more important than to make new gains)—he busied himself about providing all the fortresses of India with men, artillery, and supplies, and everything else that was necessary, in profusion; and commanded D. Garcia to make ready the fleet.

When this was done, he summoned Jorge Dalboquerque to come to him from Cochim, and dispatched him with a fleet of four sail, carrying two hundred men, and all manner of munitions of war that could be required, to go as Captain to Malaca, arranging that Pero Mascarenhas was to return to Cochim and finish his proper term of service, and he conferred the Captaincy of Goa upon D. João Déssa. Now as Afonso Dalboquerque had made up his mind to pass the winter at Ormuz, intending in the ensuing summer to go and capture Adem and penetrate the straits of the Red Sea, he ordered that four galleys should be built and sent on to him at Ormuz as soon as they were finished, fitted out with every thing that was needful for them.

Just as they were now all ready to set sail, the Çamorim sent to ask permission that he might despatch two ships to Adem, but Afonso Dalboquerque made an excuse for not granting permission by saying that it would be contrary to the agreement to which both parties had consented, and that he himself was now on the point of making a voyage to Adem, and did not wish that these two ships should go before him and acquaint the king of his coming. Notwithstanding all these reasons, and others which were given, the Çamorim became more urgent in his request, and when Afonso Dalboquerque perceived this, he made a virtue of necessity and sent word to say that he would be very happy to give them permission for what they desired, provided they did not carry pepper—seeing that they were going to a country hostile to the King of Portugal, his lord—and on condition that the merchants of Calicut should make for him, at their own expense, two large galleys, and this he desired so as to justify his excuses. Nevertheless the merchants, considering the great gain they would make by sending their merchandize to the straits, were happy to make these galleys; and in order to get them made the more speedily, Duarte Barbosa was left to be manager of the works, and a Portuguese carpenter, with a gang of native artificers were set to work upon them, for the intention of Afonso Dalboquerque was, after his entry into the straits of the Red Sea, to convert all the fleet of India into galleys.

Jorge Dalboquerque, having now got his fleet in perfect readiness to set out, took leave of Afonso Dalboquerque, and sailed out of the harbour of Goa on a Saturday in the morning, and without any notable event taking place during the voyage, he arrived at Pacé just at the moment when the king—who was a devoted adherent to the King of Portugal—was in readiness with his army to give battle to a certain lord of the land who had risen up in rebellion against him. The king, learning the arrival of Jorge Dalboquerque, sent immediately to pay him a visit, desiring him to take his side in the coming attack, for he trusted with the help of the Portuguese to gain a victory over his enemies. Jorge Dalboquerque sent word back to him that he would serve him with a very good will, but it must be on condition that he was left alone with his men to attack the enemy, for he trusted in God's mercy to give him vengeance on them, and the king must post himself on a lofty knoll with all his array, every man with a branch in his hand, for from that spot he would see how the Portuguese could fight.

This having been thus arranged, Jorge Dalboquerque disembarked with all his fighting men, and proceeded to attack the enemy, who were posted in a low lying site, the king and all his people lying behind them. And he fell upon them with such an onslaught that they were dispersed and put to flight, and an innumerable quantity of them slain. Then he rallied his men at the harbour where he had anchored the fleet. The king thereupon commanded his soldiers to follow up after the flying enemy, while he came down to see Jorge Dalboquerque and gave him great thanks and much praise for the achievement—for it was indeed one of the great victories which were gained in those parts of the world, considering the small number of our men who were engaged in it.

Jorge Dalboquerque then took his leave of the king, offering to serve him whenever he had need of his assistance, and proceeded to embark, and made his way straight to Malaca, and on his arrival he took charge of the fortress; and Ruy de Brito Patalim embarked in the same fleet and returned to

India, but when he reached Goa he found that the great Afonso Dalboquerque was dead. Besides that Jorge Dalboquerque was a great Cavalier, he was so very conscientious a man that on the first voyage which he made to Malaca as captain he took ten thousand cruzados, and on his second voyage of return he brought twelve and took ten [thousand] which is not done now!

CHAPTER XXX.

Of the Council which the great Afonso Dalboquerque held concerning the voyage he should make; and how it was decided that he should go to Ormuz; and of the news which reached him when he arrived at Mascate.

The great Afonso Dalboquerque having thus arranged all the affairs of India, and supplied the fortresses with all things they required, and having a fleet ready prepared of twenty-six sail, of which were captains the following:—

D. Garcia de Noronha,
Pero Dalboquerque,
Lope Vaz de Sampayo,
Diogo Fernandez,
Aires da Silva,
Simão Dandrade,
Duarte de Melo,
Vasco Fernandez Coutinho,
Antonio Ferreira,
Fernão Gomez de Lemos,
Antonio Raposo,
Ruy Galvão,
Jorge de Brito,
Jeronymo de Sousa,
Silvestre Corço,

Manuel da Costa,
Pero Ferreira,
João Pereira,
Fernão de Resende,
Francisco Pereira,
João Gomez,
João de Meira,
Nuno Nunez Raposo,
Pero Corço,
Fernãodianes, and
Vicente Dalboquerque,

who was captain of the ship *Nazareth*, having his uncle Afonso Dalboquerque on board,—proceeded to embark on the twentieth day of February of the said year, and after they were embarked, he summoned all the captains to his ship, and with them D. João Déssa, captain of the fortress of Goa, and D. Sancho de Noronha, chief *Alcaide*, there being present also Nicoláo Ferreira,[1] ambassador for the King of Ormuz, who had arrived in September[2] last from Portugal, bearing the king's reply to his mission.

And when all were met together, Afonso Dalboquerque shewed them that he had gathered together that fleet, made ready with all the provisions and munitions which he could procure, and as far as he could gather from the muster rolls of the land there were on board about fifteen hundred Portu-

[1] Of this man Correa gives the following notice:—"Veo n'estas naos (*i.e.*, the fleet of Christovão de Brito) hum embaixador que ElRey d'Ormuz, e Cojatar, tinhão mandado por terra a ElRey com suas cartas de vassalagem, pedindo a ElRey que lhe confirmasse sua paz pera sempre: que pagaria cad'anno, com fortaleza que daria, com condicão que nunqua lhe mais pedissem outra nenhuma cousa. O qual messigeiro era homem ganicero de nação, homem auisado, que deu a ElRey muy larga conta de todo o feito d'Ormuz, e d'outras muytos cousas da India e Turquia, que ElRey lhe fez mercê e a rogo d'ElRey se fez Christão, e se chamou Nicoláo de Ferreira."—*Lendas*, pp. 386, 387.

[2] Correa gives the date of 22nd August.

guese and seven hundred Malabars; and the King Dom Manuel had written to him year after year that it would be to his service if they entered the Red Sea, and built a fortress in Adem, and that very year he had written a letter to him wherein he reminded him of the same duty; and also the King had signified to him how pleased he would be if the affairs of Ormuz were set on a proper footing; and that he had it for certain intelligence that the King of Ormuz, after the death of Cogeatar, had accepted the cap and prayer of the Xeque Ismael, which was a beginning of his coming in time to be lord of the kingdom, and this Nicoláo Ferreira, his ambassador, who was there present, knew better than he did. And, he continued, inasmuch as the King D. Manuel had written to him in a pressing manner upon these two points, he, on his part, desired to gather from them, which of the two enterprises would be most to the service of the country for the fleet to undertake, whether in fact to penetrate into the Red Sea and build a fortress in Adem, or to make sure of Ormuz in such a manner that the Xeque could not possibly maintain his footing in it.

When Afonso Dalboquerque had thus made an end of setting all these things before the meeting, there arose differences of opinion between the parties; for some thought it a better policy to penetrate into the straits [of the Red Sea] and to erect a fortress in Adem, while others thought it better to finish the fortress of Ormuz, which had already been commenced. And in order to avoid these differences, Afonso Dalboquerque desired, before any determination was arrived at, to learn the opinion of Nicoláo Ferreira, who declared that the King of Ormuz, his lord, who had sent him as ambassador to the King of Portugal was dead, and the present governor was a native of Persia, vassal of the Xeque Ismael, having under his command within the City of Ormuz seven or eight nephews who ordered everything, and these had it in their power, whenever they thought fit, to put the reigning king to death (just as indeed they had served the late king, his lord), and to deliver over the kingdom to the Xeque Ismael; and when once the Xeque was in possession it would be a difficult matter to put him out; therefore as this affair was in so serious a situation it was his opinion that the fleet ought rather to go to Ormuz and make sure of it, for by so doing the service of the King of Portugal would be better advanced.

When Nicoláo Ferreira had made an end of expressing his opinion, Afonso Dalboquerque declared that he on his part had no doubt that the shutting up of the straits was the most important undertaking that could be performed throughout the whole of India, followed by the destruction of the Grand Sultan and the temple of Méca, if a fortress were built in it; but this project must be put off until a time when the necessities of India were not so imperative as to compel the Portuguese to change their policy; and reinforcements could not be got from the mother country under two years' time. And, apart from this, the thing which, more than any other, compelled him to be on the alert to perform his obligations, was the information that the King of Ormuz had accepted the cap of the Xeque Ismael and his prayer, and that Reys Nordim,[1] his governor, was a Persian by birth, a covetous old man in whose power all the treasure and property of the king lay,—having as he had, on his side many sons, and also when he observed the ambassadors of the Xeque Ismael, who were continually traversing India, and the affairs which they were beginning to transact with the kings and lords of that country, and the presents which he used to send them, for it was owing to these proceedings and for many other reasons which he would not mention on that occasion, that in his opinion they ought to determine to go and make a final settlement of the affair of Ormuz, for in that city they would gain large sums

[1] This name has hitherto been written "Rexnordim" in the text.

to pay their necessary expenses, and a set-off for the men's wages, and when this were once carried out to a successful issue, from that time forward he would get more ease and opportunity for penetrating the Red Sea and destroying the fleet of the Sultan, and temple of Méca.

And inasmuch as the rest of the captains were of the same opinion, Afonso Dalboquerque ordered a formal document of assent to be drawn up, which was signed by every one; and after João Déssa, captain of the city [of Goa] had taken his leave, on the following day, which was Ash Wednesday, the twenty-first of the said month of February, Afonso Dalboquerque set sail with all his fleet, and on the day [of the Annunciation] of Our Lady in March, they were over against Curiate[1] and there they found a fleet belonging to the King of Ormuz, which was cruising about to guard the coast of the Nautaques, and this, when it perceived our fleet, stood off on the other tack. But Afonso Dalboquerque kept on his course direct to Mascate[2] and cast anchor there, to take in supplies and water. The rulers of the land, when they saw our fleet, remembered the lesson they had learned[3] and came down at once to pay him a visit, with a fine present. He asked them for news from Ormuz, and they told him that about a month or two back, Reys Hamed, a Persian Moor, nephew of Reys Nordim, who was governor of the kingdom, had risen up in rebellion, and seized the fortress and the king's palace, and made the king a prisoner, together with Reys Nordim and his sons, and was now in absolute possession of the land; and that certain letters which had reached that port, had come already under seal of the new ruler, who had in Ormuz five hundred Persian archers and his three brothers as well; and as for nephews and cousins-german there would be in Ormuz as many as five-and-twenty families, whom he had caused to come and live there from

[1] See vol. i, p. 67. [2] See vol. i, p. 72.

[3] See vol. i, chap. xxiii.

Persia. At this news which the rulers gave him, Afonso Dalboquerque became somewhat disconcerted, because it seemed to him that the affairs of Ormuz were not so easy to arrange as he had thought, particularly when he bore in mind he had written to the King D. Manuel that he would take in hand and finish the affairs of Ormuz, for it was now like to be lost if he did not hasten up and save the city.

CHAPTER XXXI.

How the great Afonso Dalboquerque set out from Mascate and reached Ormuz; and of the messages which he sent to the king, and of the rest which took place.

After the great Afonso Dalboquerque had been informed by the Rulers of Mascate of all these affairs which I have mentioned, he ordered that some pieces of stuff which he had brought with him should be given to them, and having taken in water and supplies, he took his leave of them and sailed away direct to Ormuz without touching at any other place. On arrival he ordered that a salute should be fired in honour of the city, with all the artillery. Reys Hamed became so alarmed at the sight of the fleet and the soldiers on board the shipping, that he lost no time in sending Hacem Ale to pay a formal visit, on the part of the king, with a present of provisions; and in company with this personage came Miguel Ferreira, whom Afonso Dalboquerque had sent as ambassador to the Xeque Ismael, as I have already related. This Miguel had been staying there for some days, as well as an ambassador of the Xeque Ismael, who had accompanied him, waiting for favourable weather to make the passage to India; and after Miguel Ferreira had given a detailed account of his journey, Afonso Dalboquerque asked him how affairs were going on at Ormuz, and he corroborated all that the Governor of Muscate had told him, and that Reys Hamed, as soon as he caught sight of the Portuguese ships in the harbour, had given the king more liberty and set free Reys Nordim and his sons from the prison in which they had been confined by his orders; and that only a few days back there had arrived at Ormuz Abrahem Beque, one of the principal captains of the Xeque Ismael, accompanied by six or seven serving men, leaving the rest of his party and his horses on the other side of the land; and on enquiring of the ambassador of the Xeque Ismael wherefore this his captain had come, he had declared that it was with the intention of sending from that port a messenger with twenty horses and some letters to the king of Cambay.

Afonso Dalboquerque stored up in his memory this artfully planned arrival of Abrahem Beque. Like a prudent commander he was not careless of what it behoved him to perform, but sent orders secretly to keep guard all round the Island with the galleys and brigantines which he had in the fleet, in order that no stranger should get into Ormuz, and he told Miguel Ferreira to return to shore and stay with the Xeque Ismael's ambassador, until he should send him word what he was to do. Having thus dismissed Miguel Ferreira, Afonso Dalboquerque called for Hacem Ale and sent him to the shore, accompanied by Duarte Vaz, a servant of the King D. Manuel, very well conversant with the native tongue, bearing a message to the king and to Reys Nordim, wherein there was no mention of Reys Hamed. Duarte Vaz had an interview with the king, and declared to him, on the part of Afonso Dalboquerque, that the ambassador, whom King Ceifadim, his brother, had sent to the King of Portugal, was there with the Portuguese, bearing letters and a reply to his mission; but inasmuch as he had returned to the religion in which he had been brought up, and had arrived only to find the king and Cogeatar dead who had formerly sent him, he dared not come to land unless they first sent the son or nephew of Reys Nordim to him to remain in his hands as a hostage, and then he would send him his ambassador to give him the message with which he was charged; and he hoped to be excused for asking for hostages, because the King of Portugal, his lord, had so ordered him to act; and also, in order to avoid trouble he had commanded a watch to be set upon the island, so that no armed force might get into the city; and therefore he desired that this fact might be announced by public crier, because every fighting man who was found there without permission would be put to death by decapitation, and this he had done for the good and quiet of the land; and as for the other things which he had to discuss with him, he would send word about these after he had received the message which the ambassador had brought for him from the king, his lord.

The king replied to Duarte Vaz, that he was greatly delighted with the return of his ambassador, but as for the man's having turned Christian without permission, he could not pronounce any opinion until he had consulted with his governors, but he would send them without delay an answer of what they decided about it; and on the next day he sent one of the sons of Reys Nordim, a youth, as a hostage to the ship; and when the youth had arrived, Afonso Dalboquerque sent Nicoláo Ferreira, with a very imposing company, and Pero Dalpoem, secretary for India, with him, and Alexander de Ataíde, the interpreter; and when Nicoláo Ferreira had gone through the ceremony of giving the king the letters which he brought, and the reply of Portugal to the mission, he returned to the ship. During the space of time which the youth was awaiting the return of Nicoláo Ferreira, Afonso Dalboquerque asked him how the affair of Reys Hamed was progressing. The boy was so dispirited, and in so great a fright, that he did not dare to say a word; and seeing him thus so terrified, Afonso Dalboquerque would not hold any further communication with him, but sent him off as soon as Nicoláo Ferreira returned.

After Pero Dalpoem and Nicoláo Ferreira had related all that had passed, Afonso Dalboquerque asked them about Reys Hamed, what sort of a man he was. They told him he was a man of fair complexion, a young man of about thirty years of age, of good carriage, and a noble presence, and accounted to be a man of strength of mind, and a great lover of military things, and he always stood (they said) close beside the king's chair, holding a short sword, with one hand placed on his dagger, and that the king would never answer any more than what this man told him. Afonso Dalboquerque, who would not brook delay, and knew that Reys Hamed was determined to defend Ormuz, ordered the captains to be summoned to his ship, and declared to them that inasmuch as the King of Ormuz, by the letter which the King D. Manuel had written, had seen his determination to set to work at once to grapple with the affairs of Ormuz while they were yet in a pretty simple condition, let them therefore tell him how or in what way he should make a beginning with the king. And after discussing first one thing and then another, for some time, D. Garcia at length declared in the name of them all, that there really was no need of saying anything in the matter, for since the fortress which had been left after its commencement was still lying in the same condition there, and in the whole of the city there was not any other position more suitable than it was for the king's service; therefore one ought to claim to be allowed to complete it, rather than undertake other new enterprises, for they would take a long time to achieve; and therefore he ought to send and beg the king to grant a lodging-place, in the city, for the captains and men needed to be left on shore, to be a guard for the workmen who would be told off to perform the work.

The captains therefore, having come to this determination,

Afonso Dalboquerque sent Diogo Fernandez de Béja, Pero Dalpoem, the secretary, and Alexandre de Ataíde, the interpreter, to shore, to tell the king that he would be pleased to parley with his governors, in order to arrange certain matters which would redound to his service; therefore be begged him of his goodness to order these governors to make their way to a parley with him, carrying with them the text of the contract which had been originally made with King Ceifadim and Cogeatar, for he was desirous of taking his part. When this message had been delivered to the king, Reys Nordim replied in the king's name—for Reys Hamed was so proud that he never would hold any conversation with, nor receive any message from, Afonso Dalboquerque—that the King of Ormuz considered himself to be, as it were, the son of the King of Portugal, and the city and all the rest of his kingdom to be in his hands, and he would do everything he desired; but that it would be necessary to give an account of this policy to his governors, which he would do that very night. And on the morrow morning he would send the answer to Afonso Dalboquerque. And when morning came, Hacem Ale came off to Afonso Dalboquerque's ship, and in the presence of all the captains declared to him that the king had discussed with his governors what answer should be sent to the Portuguese terms, and in truth he desired to show him all the service he could, and especially that which the King of Portugal had ordered him to do; and he was aware that to ask for the surrender of the fortress which had by this time been incorporated with the [king's] houses, was certainly forcing him to adhere strictly to the agreement which he had made, but nevertheless he must beg him earnestly of his goodness to let him keep it, and he would give him any other site he should select on which to make another fortress, and for this end there was no need of making any formal contract.

Afonso Dalboquerque and the captains, after holding some

conversation upon this matter, agreed that they would waive the claim to the fortress, on condition that the king would give them as hostages for the performance of his promises two of the sons of Reys Nordim; and with these terms of reply Afonso Dalboquerque sent to shore Pero Dalpoem, Manoel da Costa, and Alexander de Ataíde, interpreter, who always accompanied the parties sent with messages. The king replied that in order to comply with the demand of Afonso Dalboquerque for hostages, it would be necessary in the first case to know the place whereon he desired to build the new fortress; and with them came Hacem Ale to learn the intentions of Afonso Dalboquerque, and he told him, speaking somewhat angrily, to declare to the king and his governors that he could not understand their way of conducting business, for they had sent word to say that if the fortress were suffered to remain in the king's possession, they would give him any other site that he chose, and then, when he asks for hostages to ensure the performance of this condition, the reply is made that he must first specify the position of the place, and then the hostages would be given; therefore let him tell the king that he had made a contract with his brother and with Cogeatar, his governor, and according to the terms of it he intended to stand; therefore let him send Reys Nordim to discuss matters with them, and bring the text of the contract with him, as he intended to carry it out to the very letter; for he did not want his houses nor his mosque, but only that which had been begun at the cost of the King D. Manuel, his lord; and he might rest certain that if this were not surrendered he would destroy Ormuz, and on this issue he and all the Portuguese who were there were prepared to risk their lives.

CHAPTER XXXII.

How the King of Ormuz sent Reys Nordim to parley with the great Afonso Dalboquerque concerning the surrender of the fortress: and of what took place about this matter.

Hacem Ale reached the shore, and related to the king and his governors all that had passed with the great Afonso Dalboquerque, and the reply which he had received, wherewith the king and all of them were much astonished, when they perceived the determination of the Portuguese. And the king lost no time in sending Hacem Ale back again with a message, begging him not to be angry, for he would send Reys Nordim, his governor, immediately, to consult with him, and would agree to everything in accordance with the wishes of his lordship; but as Reys Nordim was an old man and subject to gout, and would be unable to get up into the ship, he would desire him of his goodness to be pleased to come and see him in a galley, and send some Portuguese hostages to remain on shore.

On the following day, therefore, in the morning, Afonso Dalboquerque embarked on board the great galley, Captain Silvestre Corço, accompanied by all the captains, and stood close into shore, and ordered Lopo Vaz de Sampayo, Simão de Andrade, Aires da Silva, Pero Dalboquerque, Duarte de Melo, and Vasco Fernandez Coutinho, to take their boats to shore and convey Reys Nordim to the galley, taking with them Diogo Fernandez de Béja, who had been selected to remain behind as a hostage. When the captain reached land, Diogo Fernandez was delivered up to a captain of the King of Ormuz, and Reys Nordim went up into the boat which Lopo Vaz de Sampayo had brought, and with him went Reys Mudafar, brother of Reys Hamed, and two servants of Reys Nordim, and thus they went altogether to the galley, where

Afonso Dalboquerque was, and when he caught sight of Reys Nordim he embraced him and shewed him great favour, and after they had been seated, they conversed for a while upon the matters which had taken place on the first occasion of his visit to Ormuz.

When this talk was over, Reys Nordim asked him if there must needs be a king in Ormuz? Afonso Dalboquerque replied in the affirmative, and added that the king must also be in obedience to the King D. Manuel, his lord, and adhere to the treaty which he had made. Reys Nordim thereupon told him that the king, who looked upon him as a father, as it were, had sent a message asking him to waive his claim to that building which had been erected close to the palace, and in order to show him consideration he had granted this request. Yet, because the additional materials necessary for the construction of another would be troublesome to collect in so short a time as he wished, therefore the king would be pleased, after all, to surrender him his fortress which had been commenced, and that he might finish it in a short space of time, for Ormuz, and all the kingdom belonged to the King of Portugal. And thus each of them in this business used this sort of diplomatic action, for Reys Nordim, being alarmed at Afonso Dalboquerque's demand for the hospital, which was a building of great veneration among them, preferred to give up the fortress which had been commenced, rather than the hostages which they demanded. And Afonso Dalboquerque in like manner demanded the hospital in order to compel them to give up the fortress; for it was situated in the best position in the city, and looked towards two of the principal harbours, the one on the east and the other on the west. And after having agreed upon this point, Reys Nordim told him that the King of Portugal, in the reply to the letters of the mission from Ormuz, had left everything to the Portuguese commander; therefore he begged him of his goodness, as this was so, that he would swear in the name of the King of Portugal to keep the contract which he had made, and he on his part would also swear to maintain it in the name of the King of Ormuz. Then Afonso Dalboquerque laid his hand on a book, and swore to perform everything that was mentioned in the contract, and Reys Nordim took out another from his breast, a little one, written in Arabic letters, gilded on the top, and in his king's name he swore to be always in obedience to the King of Portugal and his governors.

When the taking of these oaths was over, Afonso Dalboquerque ordered that a robe *(cabaia)* of brocade, with gold buttons, and a spray of very large beads of gold, should be given to Reys Nordim, and to Reys Mudafar another of crimson satin with gold buttons, and through Nicoláo Ferreira he sent to the king a very rich collar of gold and enamel, begging his pardon very earnestly for not sending so valuable a present as his royal personage really deserved. And he made a gift to Hacem Ale of fifty *cruzados*, and five ells *(covados)* of scarlet stuff; and he told Reys Nordim to acquaint the king that he begged him earnestly of his goodness to give orders immediately to close up the door of the fortress which led into the palace, and to open out another which led to the shore, and to grant him lodgings in the city for his people until the completion of the fortress; and as sign of peace and friendship let him command that a flag should be run up over his palace, which he there and then delivered to him, bearing the arms of Portugal, that it might be known to every one that it wac in obedience to the King of Portugal.

Reys Nordim told him that all he wished should be carried out, and desired him to give a safe-conduct in order that the Moors might come from the mainland with provisions and merchandise to the city; and this he granted them on condition that there should not come in company with them any fighting men, for if such should be found he would not spare the life of a single one of them; and as Reys Nordim was taking his leave, Afonso Dalboquerque was desirous of enquiring after the affairs of Reys Hamed, how his intrigue was progressing, but he had no opportunity, for Reys Mudafar would never give him the opportunity of speaking to him privately. Then Reys Nordim returned to shore, accompanied by all the captains, in the same way as he had come, and Diogo Fernandez returned to the Portuguese ships. And the king immediately commanded his people to fly the Portuguese flag from the loftiest pinnacle of his palace; and when those on board the fleet caught sight of it they fired off a salute of all the artillery.

When Reys Nordim had made an end of giving the king an account of what had passed with Afonso Dalboquerque, the king ordered that the gate of the fortress which communicated with the palace should be closed, and that the other which led to the strand should be opened. And as soon as this had been carried out he sent word to Afonso Dalboquerque that the gate of the fortress was now open, therefore he might take possession of it whenever he chose. Then Afonso Dalboquerque ordered D. Alvaro de Castro and Lopo de Azevedo, with the train-bands, to go and take possession of the fortress; and this took place on Palm Sunday, the last day of the month of March,[1] in the year one thousand five hundred and fifteen, with great demonstration of joy and a grand discharge of artillery. And when night fell, Afonso Dalboquerque, accompanied by D. Garcia, his nephew, and certain of the captains, proceeded to inspect the fortress, and at the entrance of the gate he fell down on his knees, and shedding many tears gave thanks to Our Lord for having given him his house without war and without loss of his men; and on the following day he commanded them to make a palisading of fascines filled with earth, along the beach, and between them to arrange the artillery; and he

[1] Palm Sunday fell on the 1st of April in A.D. 1515.

placed within the palisading certain wooden huts, in order that the gunners and the working parties and some men of the train-bands might withdraw into them for shelter. And when this was all settled, after the lapse of a few days, Afonso Dalboquerque came and lodged in the keep,[1] which was half finished, and ordered that the train-bands should be lodged in the hospital.

CHAPTER XXXIII.

How Reys Nordim sent, through Alexandre de Ataíde the interpreter, an account of the intrigue of Reys Hamed, and of what passed thereupon.

When all these things were passed, the great Afonso Dalboquerque sent a message to Reys Nordim, through Alexandre de Ataíde the interpreter, saying he had learned that Reys Hamed, his nephew, was actually in possession of the king's palace, and of all his treasures, and held the king himself as it were in captivity; therefore he begged him earnestly to send word secretly as to the exact condition in which affairs stood. Reys Nordim, although out of fear of his nephew he dared not open his mouth, nevertheless, being, as it were, disconcerted at having his honour involved in the question, sent word to Afonso Dalboquerque, that after King Ceifadim was dead he had set up this king who was now reigning, and out of a desire for the safety of his estate he had placed over all the palace, from the gates inwards, his nephew Reys Hamed and his two brothers; and because he was left, as it were, chief of the household of the late king, after the death of Cogeatar, he was carrying on the government, for the present king was but a youth; and after one year had elapsed since he had come to power,

[1] *Torre de menagem.*

Reys Hamed had begged the king to bestow on him the post of the government which had been held by Cogeatar, as well as his houses which he used to inhabit; and the king had put him off several times, commanding him, in order to divert his mind from this object, to make ready certain *atalaias*, or watch boats, for it was his intention to send him out as captain of them, against the Nautaques; and after they were ready the king had paid the crews who were to go with him a month's wages beforehand, and then caused him to embark, but Reys Hamed, after going to sea, had disembarked, and returned with greater pride than ever to the king's palace; and one night, when it was raining, with the connivance of his brothers, who had their apartments within the palace, he effected an entrance with the crews, and penetrated to the very bedchamber where the king was sleeping with his wife, and catching hold of him by the hand, had drawn out a dagger, calling out and asking him if he recognised at length that he was in his power, and he could kill him.

The king, perceiving his enemy standing over him, in fear of his life, threw himself at his feet and begged him not to kill him, for he would do whatever he liked; and thereupon Reys Hamed had got power over all his household and his treasures, and being countenanced and assisted in this enterprise by his brothers, he had got him and his sons completely in his power; and on the same day that his lordship (Afonso Dalboquerque) had reached the harbour he had let the king go free, as indeed he could not resist doing, for he was in bed very ill with an attack of gout; but that Reys Hamed, when once he had got the king under his power, had never more let him go, carrying him about like a prisoner, not even allowing him to speak with any one except in his own presence, which caused the captive king great sorrow, for he was unable to give away anything to any one out of his own property, seeing that

Reys Hamed had the keys of all his treasury, only allowing him a hundred *xerafins* yearly, and spending all the rest just as he liked; and thus it was that the king was no longer in possession of his own kingdom, and he himself out of the government, and Reys Hamed lord of all.

Alexandre de Ataíde repaired with this account to Afonso Dalboquerque, who became very much alarmed at the intelligence (for he had left Reys Nordim acting in concert with the late king), and sending back the messenger at once, he ordered him to declare to the king that the ambassador of the Xeque Ismael had sent to him to say that he wished to pay him (Afonso) a visit, but before having an audience with him it would be necessary for him to speak with Reys Nordim, and therefore he begged him of his goodness that he would come and converse with him there in the fortress; and he ordered Antonio Raposo, Nuno Martinz Raposo, and Pero Dalpoem, secretary, to go and bring him, and thus he came, accompanied by all the merchants and principal men of the land, and in his company came also Reys Mudafar, brother of Reys Hamed.

Afonso Dalboquerque showed every one great honour and courtesy, and administered to each one the oath that they would always remain faithful vassals of the King of Ormuz, and if it were needful to spend their fortunes and even their lives for his service, that they would do so; and so, also, he made them swear that they would not recognise as governor on the part of the king and kingdom any other person than Reys Nordim, to whom he had delivered the government of the other king who had just lately died; and he said that in like manner he, too, would swear to keep and maintain them in justice, and to defend the king from his enemies; and the same oath he administered to Reys Mudafar, that he would not be obedient to the commands of any other governor of the land than the king, unless it were to Reys Nordim; and for all that he desired to evade the taking of this oath, yet notwithstanding at last he performed that which Afonso Dalboquerque commanded him to do.

When this was concluded, Reys Nordim took his departure, and just as he was on the point of leaving, Afonso Dalboquerque drew him aside, by himself, to the far end of the house, with the secretary and Alexandre de Ataíde, the interpreter, and there Reys Nordim told him the same which he had already sent him word about, and begged him earnestly of his goodness to honour his white hairs and not permit that at the close of his old age he should be vexed and deprived of his honourable position, for he had always been loyal to the King Ceifadim, his lord, and to this one with whom he was now living. Afonso Dalboquerque bade him not to be troubled, for he would promise him he would very quickly put Reys Hamed out of Ormuz, and the king should become free again, and he himself in possession of all his honour which he had always enjoyed hitherto.

CHAPTER XXXIV.

How the ambassador of the Xeque Ismael went to pay a visit to the great Afonso Dalboquerque; and of the reception which he met with; and of the events which took place thereafter.

After the great Afonso Dalboquerque had been properly established in our fortress, the ambassador of the Xeque Ismael sent word to him, through Miguel Ferreira, that he desired to come and deliver the message which he had brought to him from his lord.

Afonso Dalboquerque sent back word to say to him that he could not see him on that day, for he had certain business that must be dispatched, but on the following day he would attend to his wishes. Then he gave immediate orders to make ready, in front of the fortress (which led directly on to one of the principal streets of the city), a large platform of timber with three stages, all carpeted over with carpets, and adorned round about with quantities of cloth stuff and a canopy of brocade, and some cushions of green velvet placed on the platform, and two chairs of the same colour, fringed with gold.

And he ordered the captains of the train-bands to make ready their men, with their arms, all in good order—to the number of about six hundred men—and the crossbow-men and musqueteers, and to draw up all this body of men along the beach; and he ordered all the other soldiers, carrying lances and targes, that they also should be there drawn up in order at a closer range to the platform, in such wise that they formed a very long passage; and beside this body of men whom he had all thus drawn up in array, there were many other bodies of men who went about disbanded, and all the populace of Ormuz—a wonderful sight to behold. And all the captains, Fidalgoes, and servants of the king had to be present on the platform with Afonso Dalboquerque, very smartly attired and accompanied by the pages, who carried their arms.

All being, therefore, arranged in this manner, on the following day, after partaking of some food, Afonso Dalboquerque sent D. Garcia de Noronha, his nephew, with all the captains, Fidalgoes, and cavaliers to go for the ambassador and bring him to him. The King of Ormuz was standing at a window of his palace which looked out on the sea-front, with all his governors, witnessing this triumphal ceremony; and when Dom Garcia arrived at the place where the ambassador was lodged, he showed them great courtesy, as was right should be shown to the ambassador of so great a prince, and then they began to form a procession in the following order.

In front of all came two Moors on horseback, hunters who used trained ounces, or panthers, each one with his ounce on the crupper; and after them came six horses in single file, saddled with their saddle-cloths of great richness, and head-gear of steel and caparisons of mail on their flanks; and behind these, twelve mounted Moors richly attired, carrying golden jewellery, pieces of silk stuff, and brocade in silver washhand basins; and immediately after these the trumpeters of Afonso Dalboquerque, and people playing drums, and all the captains and Fidalgoes following them in order, one row on one side and one on the other; and last of all came D. Garcia with the ambassador, and in this order they reached the place where Afonso Dalboquerque was waiting for them.

Our fleet, which was all bedecked with flags, as soon as the ambassador reached the fortress, fired off a salute of all the guns, and it seemed as if the whole world had blown up; and as he went up the last step of the platform, Afonso Dalboquerque rose up from the chair on which he was seated and went forward two or three steps. Then the ambassador made a courteous salutation according to his native fashion, and gave him a letter from the Xeque Ismael for the King of Portugal, and Afonso Dalboquerque took it, cap in hand, and he remained thus uncovered as long as he held it; and he gave him one in return for himself, which Afonso Dalboquerque handed over to Pero Dalpoem, secretary, who was standing close beside him. Having by this time made an end of giving him the letters, with some words which he made him, he presented him the gift which he brought, of which I do not here make mention, for I have already given an account of what it consisted.

Afonso Dalboquerque received the present with great demonstration of pleasure and satisfaction, and, after giving orders for it to be gathered together, he stood in conversation for a little space with the ambassador, inquiring of him about the Xeque Ismael, how he was, and where he was staying, and how he himself had borne the fatigues of the journey. And when this interview was over, Afonso Dalboquerque bade him go and recruit himself, and he would talk with him more at length on a future day. D. Garcia de Noronha then conducted him back again to his house with the same ceremony as that which had been observed at his coming, and there Afonso Dalboquerque ordered that he should be supplied in plentiful abundance with everything that he or his party required for their maintenance.

Two days afterwards, Afonso Dalboquerque ordered that the ambassador should be summoned before him, and in the conversation which took place between them he declared the desire of the Xeque Ismael to become personally acquainted with and be in close friendship with the King of Portugal, and of utility to his lordship; and offered his great thanks for the entertainment and good treatment which his ambassadors had received at the hands of the Portuguese in India, offering him certain places in his kingdom, if he would be pleased to accept them, and that he would be happy to make him a lord therein on account of the fame of his personal character which had reached him.

When this interview was over, the ambassador laid before him four points which he brought in the instructions of his mission.

The first was that the dues which were levied upon the merchandise coming from Persia to Ormuz should belong to the Xeque Ismael.

The second, that shipping should be supplied for the passage of his people to the land of Arabia, which is on the coast whereon lies Barem[1] and Catife.[2]

[1] See p. 114.

[2] Al-Katif, on the Arabian coast, an important town now, nine-and-a-half miles S.W. from Ras Tanureh. There is a minaret eighty to a hundred feet high in the south part of the fort, and the citadel in the north-west corner is said to have been built by the Portuguese. There is plenty of water in the neighbourhood.—*Persian Gulf Pilot*, 1870, p. 123.

The third, that he would assist the Xeque, with his fleet, to capture a place called Guardaré;[1] for the King of Maçaram,[2] his vassal, had risen up in rebellion against him and seized it. This Guardaré lies between Diolicindé[3] and the land of Jasque,[4] which forms part of the kingdom of Ormuz, where the Nautaques for the most part of the year make their refuge, and from that place prey upon the ships which are making their way to Ormuz.

The fourth, that he should have a harbour in India for the Persian merchants to trade their merchandise, and permission to establish a factory house in Ormuz.

When the ambassador had presented these articles, Afonso Dalboquerque replied that matters of such importance as these required to be carefully considered, therefore he would consider them and dispatch him as quickly as he could.

CHAPTER XXXV.

How the great Afonso Dalboquerque related to the captains all that had taken place with Reys Nordim, and the condition in which the king's affairs stood, and what was determined upon concerning this: and how the king came to pay him a visit at the fortress, and Reys Hamed was killed.

When the great Afonso Dalboquerque had been informed by Reys Nordim of the king's condition, he sent for D. Garcia de Noronha, his nephew, and all the captains, and related to them all that had taken place at the interview, desiring them each, one by one, to tell him how he should proceed in this business. All were unanimous in declaring

[1] Perhaps Tárát island, large and fertile, opposite Al-Katif.

[2] The Mekran or Persian coast in the Persian Gulf. See the chart by Brucks and Haines, 1829.

[3] See p. 59.

[4] Jaskh, on the Persian side of the Persian Gulf. See *Persian Gulf Pilot*, p. 140.

that he ought to deliver the king out of the power of this tyrant, and command the same to leave the kingdom immediately with his brothers. This, then, having been agreed upon, whereas Afonso Dalboquerque had made up his mind that Reys Hamed should be put to death, although he had not communicated his intention to any one except to D. Garcia, his nephew (for, in any affair that was known to many, there could be no secret), he cast about to see if, by any way, with as little disturbance as might be, he could get him into his hands. Therefore, it was that from time to time he used to send him word, couched in gentle and mild language, that he was desirous of seeing him, and conversing with him. But Reys Hamed was never without an excuse for not coming, declaring that when the king went to see Afonso Dalboquerque, then they could have an opportunity to see and converse with one another; for it appears that he, too, cherished the idea, if opportunity should prove favourable, of killing Afonso Dalboquerque, and for this end he, had already in readiness a large number of men-at-arms within the city. Afonso Dalboquerque, however, accepted his excuses without apparently perceiving their object, and from that time forward began to make arrangements so as to bring about a visit from the king; for if Reys Hamed were to accompany the king in the visit, he could the more easily be enabled to put his determination into effect. Therefore it was, that he sent word to the king by Pero Dalpoem, secretary, that he was very desirous of seeing him, begging him earnestly to appoint, at his own convenience, a time and place for an interview.

The king replied that he would consult with his governors and send him word of their decision. And, on the following day in the morning, word was sent by Hacem Ale to Afonso Dalboquerque, that the king, also actuated by a desire for an interview, would order a tent to be pitched at the gate of his palace, and there they could see one another. But Afonso

Dalboquerque, perceiving that this was merely an artifice of Reys Hamed, answered angrily that when he came to that port on a previous occasion, as chief captain of four ships, King Ceifadim, his brother, had come to pay him a visit in a pier[1] outside his palace, and now that he had become Captain-General of India, and possessed of far more power and authority (as he could see), it seemed to him an undignified course to go and visit the king at his own house, but the interview must be conducted in the manner which he desired. Hacem Ale returned with this answer; but the king and Reys Nordim, who were desirous of seeing themselves freed from the subjection in which they were lying, declared that it seemed good to go and visit Afonso Dalboquerque in the fortress, and the other governors of the city also concurred with them in this opinion. But Reys Hamed, who was a proud man, maintained that it was not honourable nor dignified in the King of Ormuz to go and visit a captain of the King of Portugal in his house; and, after the interchange of many messages between the two parties, in reference to this matter, Reys Hamed at length consented that the king should go and see Afonso Dalboquerque, for he was of opinion that in some of these interviews he would have an opportunity of putting his diabolical intentions into practice; so he sent word, on the king's behalf, by Hacem Ale, that, on the following day in the morning, the king would come and see him, but in the house wherein the interview was to take place he must not place any person except the Portuguese captains, and these without any arms, for those who accompanied the king would also come without any arms.

Afonso Dalboquerque sent word to say that he was so anxious to see the king that he would comply with these conditions, but all the rest of his men, who would be on duty outside, must be under arms, for this was always his un-

[1] *Cerame.*

changing custom. These preliminaries having been agreed to, Afonso Dalboquerque gave orders to fit up a large reception-room, built of prepared earth, which had just been finished, and hung it with cloth, and set up a brocaded dais, furnished with two chairs of crimson velvet, fringed with gold, and benches all round them, covered with cushions, for the captains and governors of the land who were to accompany the king; and he also ordered the men-at-arms, crossbow-men, and musqueteers, to be stationed under arms, close outside the gate of the fortress which looked towards the sea; and the captains of the train-bands, who were lodged in the hospital, to be in readiness, and when they heard a gunshot, as a signal, they were to march out by the street on the right hand and form up in front of the gate of the fortress leading to the city, and make themselves masters of it; and to the other captains orders were given that they were to be prepared for the reception of the king on the following day, putting on weapons secretly, and having their daggers hidden, so as to be able to avail themselves of them if occasion should arise and they should have need of them; and he also told D. Garcia de Noronha to select a body of fifty trusty men and take care of the gate, and as soon as the king, Reys Hamed, and Reys Nordim had entered, to close it, and not permit any other person to enter.

All being thus put in proper order, on the morning of the next day, Afonso Dalboquerque sent word by Pero Dalpoem and Alexandre de Ataíde, the interpreter, to tell the king in what manner he was expecting him. And as soon as they reached the king with his message, he immediately made himself ready with all the lords and governors of the land on foot, and he himself riding on a horse, surrounded by many archers as a body-guard, and so came to the fortress where Afonso Dalboquerque was waiting. Reys Hamed, who came with the intention which I have already referred to, brought all his party armed in coats of mail, with short swords[1] under their dresses,[2] and he himself carried a short sword and dagger, and a shield, and in his hand a long iron mace. And when he had proceeded so far forward as to be close up to the gate of the fortress, he told the king to remain still where he was, for he would go inside first of all and see how the buildings were placed; and when he had gone in he made his way to Afonso Dalboquerque, who treated him with respectful recognition, and told Alexandre de Ataíde to ask him why he came with weapons in his hands when the agreement had been made that neither party should carry arms. Reys Hamed, like an overbearing and insolent man, as he was, answered: "This has nothing to do with me", and turned round to go back to the spot where he had left the king, with the intention of returning home, for he did not think it was a favourable opportunity of putting his intention to effect; and he quickly came up with the king, who had begun to go in through the gate, and when he came up with him he told him not to go in any further, for Afonso Dalboquerque had a number of men with him, all of whom were armed. Thereupon Alexandre de Ataíde, who stood by and heard these words, said to him, "Come this way, and I will go and show you how all the things are arranged." And he took him by the hand and led him up to Afonso Dalboquerque, who bade him put away his weapons, for it was wrong to have brought them. Reys Hamed thereupon began to lose his temper, putting his hand to his short sword. Afonso Dalboquerque, perceiving him in this discomposed state, and feeling that the opportunity was come to put him to death, in accordance with the determination already arrived at, called out to Pero Dalboquerque, who had already been instructed how to act, "Lay hold of him then." And Pero ran up at once and placed himself between Afonso Dalboquerque and

[1] *Tarçados.* [2] *Cabaias.*

Reys Hamed, and just at that moment Reys Hamed laid hands upon a tag of velvet which he was wearing. Then Afonso Dalboquerque pushed him away from him and said to Pero Dalboquerque, "Kill him." And in an instant he received so many dagger-thrusts that he was dead before he had time to call out; and in order not to look on him, Afonso Dalboquerque turned his back, and began to walk on towards the spot where the king was, and said in reply to Dom Garcia and the other captains who followed that leader, "It is nothing; all is over."

As soon as Dom Garcia had left the king with Afonso Dalboquerque, he ran back quickly to the gate to prevent any one from making his way in, and this task he performed not without great difficulty. The king, when he beheld Reys Hamed lying dead—for he never intended to bring his death about, but only cast him out of the kingdom—became beside himself, dreading lest the Portuguese intended to visit the same treatment on himself. And there were around him there Reys Nordim, and Reys Xarafe his son (who has been here in Portugal), and Hacem Ale; and when Afonso Dalboquerque cast his eyes upon him, he made his way to him cap in hand, smiling, and desired him not be under any apprehension, for he should be king of Ormuz in the name of the king Dom Manuel, his lord; and then he set him in one of the chairs beneath the canopy of the dais, and paid him all the ceremonial deference which is due to one of kingly rank, desiring him earnestly of his goodness to pardon him for venturing to perform such a deed as this had proved to be in the presence of his royal person; as for Reys Hamed, he had been put to death because he was too proud a man, for when he had entered the house, he had laid his hand on the sword which he carried, and when he came up to him he had laid hold of the velvet tag, and because he (Afonso Dalboquerque) had been informed that the man kept him (the king) prisoner, and was in possession of all his kingdom and treasures. This was all said with his cap in his hand, with many courteous expressions, which Afonso Dalboquerque on occasions such as these knew very well how to use.

The king thanked him very much for all that he had done, declaring to him that he looked upon him as a father, and that all he had done was very well done, and that he would acknowledge the receiving of the kingdom from his hand in the name of the King of Portugal.

CHAPTER XXXVI.

How Reys Mudafar and his brother, on hearing of Reys Hamed's death, set out with all their host to attack the king's palace, and fortified themselves therein; and of what further happened.

The brothers of Reys Hamed, who found themselves put out of the business, with their people (although what with the blowing of trumpets and beating drums incessantly, because they had been ordered so to do, they had perceived nothing of what had happened indoors), nevertheless, on account of the suspicions which they experienced, drew near with axes, intending to break the doors in, and force the entrance. But Afonso Dalboquerque, desirous of preventing this, ordered a gun to be fired. This was the signal which he had preconcerted with the captains of the train-bands; and as soon as they heard it, they made their way directly to the gate, and compelled Reys Hamed's brother and all his people to withdraw. And when they began to skirmish with these, Dom Garcia came up and bade them, on the behalf of Afonso Dalboquerque, to take care what they were about, for there were adherents of the king and of Reys Nordim mixed up with these Moors. Afonso Dalboquerque also, with the intention of pacifying all this uproar, commanded Don Alvaro da Silveira, Ruy Galvão, and Diogo Fernandez de Bejà to make their way to the men of the train-bands, and induce them to be quiet; and ordered all the captains to arm themselves, and he left D. Garcia with the men, and went up upon a terrace with the king and Reys Nordim, and there he ordered that a carpeted platform should be set out, upon which he sat for a long time, in sight of all the Moors, who thought that he had been killed. When the brothers of Reys Hamed beheld him, they demanded of him with great vehemence what had become of their brother; and they were so persistent in this, that Afonso Dalboquerque sent word to them by Alexandre de Ataide, the interpreter, that he would order Reys Hamed's head to be delivered to them if they desired it.

When they heard this, they became aware that Reys Hamed was dead, and then began to threaten the king, declaring that they would make their way to the fortress and set up one of the sons of the late King Ceifadim to be king. And in this furious state of mind they rushed away to the palace, and closed the gates, and made ready all their guns, with the intention of maintaining their position in it. Now, inasmuch as it was advisable that all those of the faction of Reys Hamed should be pacified without loss of time, before any of the people outside could combine with them, Afonso Dalboquerque sent to the ships for a number of scaling ladders which he had brought with him, and made ready all his people, with intention of getting in by force; and ordered that certain pieces of artillery should be carried up to the terrace, so as from that point to assault the fortress. Reys Nordim begged him to suspend any active measures against them, until the king should send some one to parley with them and learn their intention, for it was impossible that they really desired to raise that man to the sovereignty; and he sent a message to his

Mulás (*i.e.*, Mollahs), who went backwards and forwards twice without coming to any determination.

When Afonso Dalboquerque perceived that he should never come to any practical end if he went on in this way, he sent word for Abraham Beque, captain of the Xeque Ismael, and his ambassador, and through them he sent a message that unless by sundown every one had gone out of the fortress and embarked for the mainland, they might rest assured that he would not spare the life of one of them. Abraham Beque, who was the chief instigator of this uproar, spoke with the rebels, and easily persuaded them to evacuate the palace and retire to the furthermost point of the city, and then to send and beg of Afonso Dalboquerque the body of Reys Hamed, their brother, with the intention of carrying it away for interment in his own land, and a vessel to enable them to pass over to terra firma with their wives and people, for there were in all about seven hundred fighting men. This request Afonso Dalboquerque granted; but as for the body of Reys Hamed, he said he could not grant it, for those who were traitors to their lords ought not to have sepulture of a certainty where they could be laid.

That very night every man of the party embarked and crossed over to the opposite side; and when there was yet the space of an hour to sundown, Afonso Dalboquerque rode out, accompanied by the king and all our people, and made his way through the midst of the city as far as the palace, taking along with them in advance the train-bands, with all the trumpeters and drummers, while Dom Garcia and Reys Nordim came along in the rear with all the captains and noblemen of the fleet on foot. Great was the delight in the city when the bystanders beheld their king, and still greater was the gratification every one felt to find himself freed from the thraldom of Reys Hamed, and boundless the praises given to Afonso Dalboquerque; and this with much reason, for though he had under his hand the king and his palace, which was the principal fortress of Ormuz, and all his treasures, yet he did not wish to lay hands on it, but, as a prudent man, he always bore himself towards the king with great authority, showing him that he had come to Ormuz simply to serve him and maintain his estate, willingly foregoing this splendid opportunity of seizing the power, to avoid the stigma of being called a tyrant. And in this triumphal procession the king reached his palace at length, which Afonso Dalboquerque delivered up to him and to Reys Nordim in the name of the King of Portugal, in the presence of the ambassador of the Xeque and Abraham Beque, his captain, in order that when they returned to Persia they might be trustworthy witnesses of this grand exploit of Afonso Dalboquerque.

CHAPTER XXXVII.

How the King of Ormuz again paid a visit to the great Afonso Dalboquerque in the fortress, and what passed between them; and the punishment which was visited upon seven Portuguese who fled away to the Moors.

A few days after the death of Reys Hamed, when the King of Ormuz reflected how much it was owing to the great Afonso Dalboquerque that he had been rescued from the hands of that tyrant, he determined to pay him another visit, and brought with him as a present several pieces of gold ore, and rich objects of native manufacture, to give to him and his captains, and sent word to him by Reys Nordim that he was very desirous of seeing him, and hoped that a day for an interview might be arranged; for on the former occasion when he visited the fortress there had been no time or opportunity of conversation between them, because of the events which had then arisen. Afonso Dalboquerque replied that it was a great favour and honour which he was showing him in thus desiring to visit him; but as it was his wish, let him come and pay him a visit in the building where he had been delivered from the power of the traitor. Reys Nordim returned with this reply, carrying with him to the king a sword richly ornamented with gold, a present from Afonso Dalboquerque.

On the Tuesday fixed by the king for the interview, the trumpeters and drummers of Afonso Dalboquerque went out to form an escort for the king, who came on horseback, accompanied by Reys Nordim and all the lords and governors of the land on foot, bringing a present, according to the native custom, carried in advance.

Afonso Dalboquerque, with all the captains, awaited the royal arrival in that building richly adorned with tapestry; a canopy and two silk-covered chairs being set for themselves, and a circle of cushioned benches set around for the captains and the people who accompanied the king. As soon as the king arrived, Afonso Dalboquerque proceeded to the entrance with all his captains to receive him; and, after the exchange of mutual courtesies, the king declared that the favour he had received at the hands of Afonso Dalboquerque in being delivered from the thraldom of that bad man would always remind him of his duty, and that he would remain in obedience to the King of Portugal, for it was in his name that he held the kingdom of Ormuz. Afonso Dalboquerque replied that he was his servant, and would never fail to assist in maintaining him in his position; and so he recommended the king to all his men who stood by, that they should always serve him and risk their lives and property for him, as they were in duty bound to do. And after spending some considerable space of time thus in conversing of the disorders which Reys Hamed had wrought in the kingdom, Afonso Dalboquerque, who was anxious to forbid the practice of carrying arms in the city, in order to get more complete mastery over the land, made use of the following artifice with the king, and told him that a few days ago he had given orders for putting to death that traitor Reys Hamed (as he knew), who had brothers and relatives, and in the city there were yet lurking certain of his creatures, of whom there was not one who, despising death, would not shoot him with an arrow; therefore he would beg him of his goodness, in order to avoid these difficulties, to give orders that no person in Ormuz should carry arms; and since the obligation of guarding the city belonged to him, it was sufficient for its defence that the Portuguese alone should go armed; by this means, too, all possibility of a conflict between the natives and the Portuguese would be prevented. The king was so dispirited by the cruel manner in which Reys Hamed had treated him, that when this proposal was made, he replied that he quite approved of it, and he would order it to be promulgated forthwith. And when this conversation was over, he took leave of Afonso Dalboquerque and made his way back to his palace, very much pleased with him.

On the following day, in the morning, the king sent orders immediately to the public crier to proclaim, that no Moor, of whatever position he might be, should bear bow, arrow, or any other weapon, in the city, by day or by night, under penalty of death, except only the archers of the royal body-guard, whom Afonso Dalboquerque had permitted to go armed. By these means it was that he proceeded with his plan for obtaining the mastery little by little over the land, while the king, for his part, never ventured to do anything without first of all sending to inquire whether he should act or not. And on that very day, in the evening, the king sent word to inform Afonso Dalboquerque that one of the native captains, stationed in a fortress on the mainland, had written to him of the arrival there in the morning of seven Portuguese and a negro in a small boat; but when he endeavoured to lay hands on them, they had set themselves in an attitude of self-defence with the matchlocks which they carried, and as they were Portuguese he had forbidden his men to kill them. Afonso Dalboquerque made inquiry respecting the flight of these men, and learned that a certain Antonio Fernandez, called De Alvito, who had lived a long time in Persia, being a Moor, had prevailed on them to accompany him, and was taking them to the Xeque Ismael. Having gained knowledge of this, he sent back word to the king, begging him of his goodness to lose no time in sending off a party of men to seek them and to bring them back to him, dead or alive, as well as the boat which they had taken with them. The king sent out letters to all his captains ordering them to strain every nerve to capture the fugitives, declaring that if they failed to do so he would cut off their heads. And besides this action of the king, Afonso Dalboquerque fitted out Jeronymo de Sousa in a galley with an armed force, and sent them to the mainland; and also Nicoláo Ferreira in a *parao*, for he knew the native language, in order to get hold of the fugitives.

The king's captains, as soon as the royal message reached them, sent out a large body of searchers in different directions to look for them, and at length they fell in with them at a distance of fourteen leagues up in the interior country, accompanying a caravan which was travelling to Persia, and had taken the clothing of the fugitives from them; so they were all taken, except one, a Gallician, whom they killed because he would not surrender himself. And just as they had been captured, with the weapons that had been taken from them, so they were delivered up to Jeronymo de Sousa, who returned with them to the city.

As soon as they arrived, Afonso Dalboquerque gave notice to the *ouvidor*, to take proper proceedings in this business. And after the trial was over they were condemned to be burned to death in the very boat in which they had made their flight; and Pero Dalpoem, who was *ouvidor-general* of India, ordered that the boat should be conveyed to the principal square of the city, and there all the culprits were publicly burned alive, except João Afonso, and Antonio Fernandez, a seaman, whose lives Afonso Dalboquerque spared, because it was declared that these two had saved his life in the shield[1] at Calicut, when that affair with the marshal took place[2]; so he commuted their punishment to degradation in the galleys. On account of the rapid manner in which this meting out of justice was accomplished by him, a much greater fear of Afonso Dalboquerque was experienced from that time forward.

CHAPTER XXXVIII.

Of the message which the great Afonso Dalboquerque sent to the king concerning the forces of Reys Hamed; and of certain other matters which were ordained for the security of the kingdom; and how Abraham Beque, Captain of the Xeque Ismael, returned to his own land.

Now, as the great Afonso Dalboquerque had received information that there was in the fortress of Monejão, as captain, one of the brothers of Reys Hamed, and also in all the other villages and fleets his adherents and his captains were distributed; and being desirous, as he was, of rooting up all that man's seed out of the kingdom, he sent word to the king, through the secretary, to order every one of those people to quit the country immediately, and if they would not go away of their own free will, then he (the king) must send those who would put them out by force;

[1] *Padez*, a word equivalent to *pavez*, a pavese, or pavise, a large shield to cover the whole body, or a cloth screen used in fighting-ships.

[2] See vol. ii, p. 70.

and as for all the captains and adherents of Reys Hamed, who were at present engaged in a fleet against the Nautaques, and scattered up and down throughout the towns and villages of the kingdom, he must order them to be forthwith discharged and cast out of the country.

The king replied that he would send out thither his *Muluás*, or religious men, and if these could not prevail upon the persons objected to that they should quit the kingdom, then he would do as Afonso Dalboquerque desired, and he would also take care for the future to have no dealings with them. Reys Hamed's brother, on receiving the king's message, replied that if the sum of twenty thousand *xerafins* were paid to him, he would yield up the fortress; and after a long course of negotiation upon this point, finally he declared that he would accept four thousand *xerafins* to go away. The king, to save himself trouble, ordered that this sum should be paid, and the captain surrendered the fortress and went away.

When Afonso Dalboquerque found out that the king had given this sum of money to Reys Hamed's brother for the surrender of the fortress, he sent a message to Reys Nordim to make immediate reprisals on two of their ships which had arrived from India laden with merchandise, so as to thereby repay himself the money of which he had thus been deprived, and Reys Nordim did so. And when this had been done, the king issued letters throughout all his kingdom to his captains, to the effect that all the soldiery who were found in the fortress belonging to Reys Hamed should be stripped and banished, and never more set foot in the kingdom, under penalty of death; and he ordered the fleet to be recalled from its cruise against the Nautaques, and dismissed the captains and men of Reys Hamed who were serving in it. By these active measures it was that Afonso Dalboquerque caused the country to be pacified from the numerous uproars and robberies that used to take place therein.

And as, also, he had been informed that there was a public place of prostitution of men[1] in the city, he sent word to Reys Nordim to order that such persons should be immediately banished throughout the kingdom, for he would not dare to remain in a land where a sin so heinous against God was so publicly practised; and he declared that if from henceforth any persons were found guilty of such crimes he would order every one of them to be burned alive in the middle of the market square. Reys Nordim ordered these persons to be driven out, and none dared to return, with the dread of this punishment hanging over them.

When all these matters had been arranged, Afonso Dalboquerque took in hand the affairs of the merchants, and granted them a safe-conduct for their shipping, to make the voyage to India to take in merchandise, and permitted the caravans to come from India to Ormuz, and gave them such privileges and powers that friends and enemies alike were delighted to come to Ormuz with their merchandise, as in former times, for they placed confidence in his words, and if anyone had received any injury at the hands of the Portuguese, the offenders were severely punished; and on account of these measures and others which were put in force, many merchants came from abroad to settle in Ormuz, which now began to grow great on a noble scale. But with the person of the king, and in the government of the kingdom, Afonso Dalboquerque would not meddle (leaving everything to him and his governors), but he treated the king always with the greatest consideration and deference, and this went a great way towards effecting the pacification of the country.

When all these matters had been set at rest, Abraham Beque, captain of the Xeque Ismael, who was in Ormuz, as I have already mentioned, perceiving all his plans were defeated by the death of Reys Hamed, begged permission

[1] *Mancebia publica de homens.*

of Afonso Dalboquerque to retire to his own lands, which were situated upon the borders of the Persian Sea, and this was granted. And as Afonso Dalboquerque always dissembled his affairs, for he did not wish to be at variance with the man, because he was the principal captain of the Xeque Ismael, and a neighbour to the territory of Ormuz, he showed him much kindness in the name of the king, whereat he was greatly pleased, and when he reached his own lands he wrote an account of the greatness of Afonso Dalboquerque, and specially a relation of the affair of Reys Hamed, to the Xeque Ismael.

As soon as Abraham Beque had set out, Afonso Dalboquerque ordered that representations of his needs should be made to the king and Reys Nordim, his governor, and also that the protests should be shown to them which had formerly been made to King Ceifadim and to Cogeatar, respecting the fortress which had been commenced, but taken from him by them when he visited Ormuz for the first time—and in this enterprise he had laid out a large sum of money and lost much property, not to mention other losses occasioned by the rebellion of their officials on land—therefore it was that he begged them earnestly to look well into this matter, and give orders that payment should be made in ready money of all that was found to be due to him, for he was in need of money for the completion of the fortress and for the expenses of his fleet.

After some time had been spent in several messages from one to the other on this matter, the king at length sent word that he would be very happy to pay everything that was due, provided that a set-off was made in the account for five thousand *xerafins* which the Viceroy D. Francisco Dalmeida had received from his brother; and that as for the property, which, it was alleged, had been taken from him, Reys Nordim had already restored a great part of it to Pero Dalboquerque when that commander visited

Ormuz in the past year, and he had the papers to verify the fact; and as for the balance of the account, let them discuss it with Reys Nordim, and all that was due should be paid. On the following day, in order to lose no time, Afonso Dalboquerque sent Pero Dalpoem, Alexandre de Ataide, the interpreter, and Manuel da Costa, the factor, to Reys Nordim's house, and after examining the accounts, it was found that there was a sum of one hundred and twenty thousand *xerafins* due, and this the king ordered to be paid by days, wherewith the fabric of the fortress was made, and the other expenses settled. Thus was at length terminated the grumbling of the captains at the time when Afonso Dalboquerque ordered this claim to be made upon Cogeatar, as I have already related.

CHAPTER XXXIX.

How the great Afonso Dalboquerque, on account of the news which he received concerning the coming of the Rumes, sent to beg the king to lend him his artillery, and what passed thereupon; and how, after having obtained possession of it, he paid the king a visit in his house.

The affairs of Ormuz being now in the state and quiet which I have described, and the fortress being already advanced to a considerable height, there arrived a Moor from Calayate with news for the great Afonso Dalboquerque, informing him that when he left that port, news had just come in from Adem that the Rumes were making themselves ready in Suez with a large fleet, to come up against Ormuz; and although it seemed to him that this news had been circulated by the brothers of Reys Hamed, out of a desire to set the country in an uproar, Afonso Dalboquerque turned it to a good advantage in making it serve the purpose which he had for days past been desirous of effecting, which was to get the whole of the king's artillery into his hands by some means which should not cause any scandal. And, in order to give a better air of importance to the matter, he ordered Dom Garcia de Noronha, his nephew, to go with a message to the king, accompanied by certain of the captains and an escort of men-at-arms—for this was the fashion at Ormuz—and give him an account of the news which had arrived concerning the coming of the Rumes, and to acquaint him with the determination of the Portuguese to attack them on the seas, and therefore he begged the king of his kindness to sanction the lending of all his artillery, in order to mount it in the fortress, for his own was required for furnishing his fleet, and was not sufficient for both of these requirements.

When D. Garcia reached the palace with this message, he found the king in company with Reys Nordim and other principal Moors; and as Afonso Dalboquerque had instructed him to take up a dominant position in the palace immediately upon entering it—for if the artillery were not delivered up to him he must take it by force—as soon as he had gone in he stationed a captain with some soldiers on guard at each portal, making show of doing so out of politeness, to avoid bringing armed men to the place where the king was; and when he came up with the king, D. Garcia delivered him the message with which Afonso Dalboquerque had entrusted him.

Reys Nordim replied to the effect that the king looked upon the Portuguese commander as a father, and would do everything that was required of him, and that there was no need of so great a personage as D. Garcia coming upon such a business, when the least person of his household would have sufficed to convey the message, and the king would send him all the artillery for the fortress. Now, whereas D. Garcia had been instructed by his uncle not to return without first bringing the artillery before him, he replied to Reys Nordim, that seeing that the king would willingly grant that service to Afonso Dalboquerque, let him therefore be so good as to order the immediate delivery of it, for Afonso Dalboquerque had made arrangement for getting ready the fleet that very night, so that if the Rumes were to come, they should not be taken unprepared.

Now Reys Nordim regretted that he had assented to the request of D. Garcia, and became anxious to see him return and take away with him from the palace the armed escort, so that when they had gone he might have time to reflect and consider what to do; therefore he began to temporise, and declared that the man who kept the keys of the magazine had gone out. But Dom Garcia, who was determined not to quit the palace without taking the artillery with him, told him that in matters which were likely to be imperilled by being put off, it was not right that there should be any delay, for he did not intend to go away without the artillery. Reys Nordim, therefore, perceiving that he would gain nothing by his pretended artifices, made a virtue of necessity, and gave orders for taking the fastenings from the doors of the storehouses where it was, and the bombardiers, with their gunners, forthwith began to set up the guns on carriages; and it was about three hours after nightfall when at length all had been put out on the shore (and a beautiful sight it made); and on the next day Reys Nordim wrote the captains of Mascate and Calayate to send him all that they had in their charge; so that by June a galley and a brigantine arrived with it on board, and Afonso Dalboquerque ordered that all should be gathered together and mounted on the walls of the fortress, and thus he secured for himself all the artillery of Ormuz. In this way it turned out that if the news brought by the Moor of the coming of the Rumes was pretended, at any rate it cost him dear.

Two days after the conclusion of this affair, Afonso Dalboquerque thought it well to go and see the king, to put him into a good humour; and when he reached the palace, Reys Nordim came forward to receive him on a large terrace, from which they both proceeded to an audience with the king; and on arriving at the door of the chamber, Reys Xarafo, chief officer of the king's guard, came up to speak with him, and declared that it was Afonso Dalboquerque to whom he owed the enjoyment of that office, and that he was there as a slave to serve him; and while this talk was going on the king came to the door.

As soon as Afonso Dalboquerque caught sight of him, he went up to him, cap in hand, and desired to kiss his hand The king would not give him his hand, but embraced him and kissed his head—an honour customarily reserved for personages of such dignity—and having thus embraced one another, they went into a chamber built with a carved ceiling, and fitted up with a dais, on which were two chairs, one covered with china silk stuff, for the king, the other, of crimson velvet, for Afonso Dalboquerque, and two cushions of the same suite, on which they placed their feet. And as soon as they seated themselves, they talked for a while upon friendly business, and the king declared that it was the happiest day of his life; and Afonso Dalboquerque replied that it would give him the greatest pleasure and happiness to do any service to those whom he could benefit, and he begged the king to send for the sons of King Ceifadim that he might see them, for they were two youths, each about eight or nine years old, to whom he showed great respect, remembering whose sons they were, and begged the king and Reys Nordim to bring them up very carefully. When the conversation was over, Afonso Dalboquerque took his leave of the king, and Reys Nordim accompanied him as far as the gate of the fortress, and then returned.

CHAPTER XL.

How the great Afonso Dalboquerque despatched the Ambassador of the Xeque Ismael, and sent Fernão Gomez de Lemos to go in his company; and the present which was sent to that prince through him.

At this juncture, the ambassador of the Xeque Ismael, perceiving that Afonso Dalboquerque was making preparations to fight the Rumes, begged that he might receive permission to return, for he had been waiting there for several days; so Afonso Dalboquerque lost no time in despatching him, and caused Fernão Gomez de Lemos, brother of Duarte de Lemos da Trofa, to get ready, for he intended to send him in the party as ambassador to the Xeque Ismael; and Gil Simões, page of the King D. Manuel, as scrivener of the embassy, and fitted him out with eight saddle horses to accompany him, all of them caparisoned with silk after our fashion; and also made ready to send to the Xeque, as a present, several things, namely, two çuirass-bodies, one of crimson velvet, the other of brocade; a head-piece and chin-piece, ornamented with gold; a suit of harness embroidered with all its parts; four bracelets of gold and rubies; very rich rings and other very rich jewellery of gold and precious stones; and a short cannon (*berço*), and a gun (*cão*) of metal; and half a dozen matchlocks, and as many cross-bows; and sent him copper, tin, and a small quantity of all the spices of India. And it was to be intimated to the Xeque that he could make use of all that kind of thing whenever he desired, but as he (Afonso Dalboquerque) was always at sea, and brought nothing with him except arms and provisions, therefore he had not sent him a specimen of many other things which there were in Portugal, but of the products of India he had sent that collection, with which he hoped he would be pleased.

And the instructions which were sent were to the effect

that he was to declare to the Xeque Ismael, that if he desired to maintain useful and friendly relations with the King of Portugal his lord, he must send his ambassadors to Portugal, for by means of the Portuguese he would be enabled to destroy the Grand Sultan and the house of Méca; and if the King of Portugal's sanction were given to the fleet, he (Afonso Dalboquerque) would be very well able to help him, for he had now settled himself in Ormuz. But if the Xeque Ismael should be unwilling to send his ambassadors, on the pretext of the great distance (as he had said to Miguel Ferreira), the Portuguese ambassador was instructed to point out, that if the Xeque had need of the friendship of the King of Portugal, he ought not to fear the trouble which the journey would cost one man, who would be taken great care of and well entertained in the vessels going to Portugal. He was also to describe to the Xeque the grandeur of the King and Queen of Portugal, and the incessant wars which they waged against the Moors of Africa and of India, as well as against the Turk and Sultan of Cairo.

When Fernão Gomez was quite prepared to start, Afonso Dalboquerque caused the ambassador to be summoned before him, and told him that in respect of the four things demanded of the Portuguese on behalf of the Xeque Ismael he had looked to them.

As for the first, demanding the dues upon merchandise coming from Persia, payable at Ormuz, they must be his; for the expenses that the King of Ormuz was compelled to spend upon his army and fleet, for the maintenance of his kingdom, were so great (besides the tribute-money paid to the King of Portugal his lord), that were it not for the dues upon the merchandise coming from Persia and other parts, the King of Ormuz could not support himself, for all the remainder of the revenue of his kingdom was but little (as the Xeque knew very well), therefore he could not surrender this part of the revenue to the Xeque.

As for the second, which was a demand of a water-passage for the conveyance of his people to the land of Arabia, he would be very much pleased to accede to this, and give him all the vessels he stood in need of, provided that the Xeque Ismael would give sufficient security to the King of Ormuz that no untoward event should be perpetrated in his lands nor in the island of Barem.[1]

As for the third article of the demands, that, namely, of help by means of men and fleet against the King of Maçaram (who was his vassal, and had revolted against him in the city of Guardaré), he would help the Xeque with all the fleet and forces of the King of Portugal (who had ordered him thus to act), but this would have to be associated with one condition, that the merchandise coming from Persia to Ormuz be not conveyed away thence.

As for the fourth, which consisted in the request of a port in India where the merchants of Persia might carry on their trade, and have permission to establish a factory-house in Ormuz, to this request Afonso Dalboquerque would be exceedingly pleased to assent, but the selected port of India must be Goa, and the entry at Ormuz; for in every other district of India wherein merchants from Persia should be found, they should lose their merchandise and be made subject to the greatest penalties which he could inflict.

And having thus replied to the demands of the ambassador, Afonso Dalboquerque desired him to declare to the Xeque Ismael that he ought to look upon the lands which were thus offered for him to accept as a valuable gift, and to gladly receive the desire of the Portuguese to make him a great lord in his country, on condition that he would preserve it and defend it against its enemies, for he (Afonso) had gained many territories in those parts for the King of Portugal his lord, and hoped yet to subject many others to Portuguese power, and all for the sake of doing the Xeque

[1] See p. 114.

a good turn; and as for the friendship and good assistance which Afonso Dalboquerque desired to proffer him, he was glad to do so to so great a prince; and also he would be highly pleased to order all the soldiers of the Xeque's own faith, who were to be found in India, to be sent to him to enter his service, in accordance with his express desire; and he hoped in God very soon to return to Ormuz, wherein he looked to have leisure to meet him in some one or other of his towns on the coast of the Persian Sea; and to this end he had sent in his company a *Fidalgo*, one of the chief personages of the household of the king his lord, as ambassador to the Xeque Ismael, and begged he might be well received there.

When these interviews were over, Afonso Dalboquerque made him a present of jewels, and dresses, and pepper, for which he asked, and wherewith he was very much pleased. And now, having everything in readiness, the party set out together on the tenth of August in the year fifteen hundred and fifteen. But I do not make any relation of what happened to Fernão Gomez in his embassy, for he did not return until after the death of Afonso Dalboquerque.

CHAPTER XLI.

How the kings of all parts sent their ambassadors to visit the great Afonso Dalboquerque: and how D. Garcia de Noronha begged permission to return to the kingdom of Portugal, and the rest that happened.

After the setting out of these ambassadors to the Xeque Ismael, D. Garcia de Noronha, perceiving that there was but little work yet remaining to be done upon the fortress, begged permission of the great Afonso Dalboquerque, his uncle, to go to Portugal, but as Afonso Dalboquerque found himself indisposed with a very weary illness, and also because he felt the great value of his personal assistance and service, he was unwilling to accede to the request; nevertheless, D. Garcia, being very greatly desirous of returning, urged his suit so strongly that at length it was granted, but very unwillingly. So he dispatched him on the twenty-ninth day of August of the said year [1515], furnishing him with all authority to load his vessel, and with him he sent to the king D. Manuel a basin, cup, and drinking vessel, and a belt and dagger of solid gold, which had formed part of the present sent to him by the Xeque Ismael, and some caparisons for a horse, made of crimson plates, with the head-piece ornamented with gold inlaying-work, and a saddle ornamented with silver, and a skirt of mail, and a piece of felting cut out and coloured, which although of little price was a fine thing to look at; and in his company he sent fifteen blind kings who were in Ormuz with their wives, children, and servants, with orders to deliver them up at Goa to the captain, who was to keep them under safe guard, giving them everything they required for their maintenance. Afonso Dalboquerque did this with intention of putting an end to the line of kings of Ormuz, and preventing them from being scattered over many parts and so in future times causing troubles to the kingdom.

And he dispatched Antonio de Afonseca, with ten thousand *xerafins*, as factor, and Aires de Magalhães for his scrivener, to make ready for him in Goa a large quantity of provisions and munitions of war, and to repair the vessels that might be in India, and complete the fitting out of the galleys which had been begun when he left Goa, and he wrote to Duarte Barbosa to take care that the two galleys of Calicut should be ready finished for his use, for he had made up his mind that in the following spring he would fit out a large fleet to take Adem and fortify himself

N 2

in that place, and force the entry of the Red Sea Straits, and make a settlement in the land of the Preste João.

But God ordered all this according to his own wish, for, when Afonso Dalboquerque reached Goa, he died (as I shall proceed to relate); and if he had not died, Lopo Soarez was on his way to be Governor of India, so that these his wishes could not have been accomplished. And D. Garcia sailed away in the ship *Belém*, and reached Cochim, where, as he was getting ready to sail to Portugal, Lopo Soarez arrived, and some differences arose between them.

As soon as D. Garcia had set out, Afonso Dalboquerque began to feel a little better of his illness; and just at this moment there arrived certain ambassadors from the kings neighbouring upon the kingdom of Ormuz, to visit him, namely, the King of Lara, bringing him a horse for a present, and a letter making a great show of offering him everything that there might be in his country. Lara is three leagues from Ormuz; it is a very large city, situated in Persia, and under the sovereignty of the Xeque Ismael. Afonso Dalboquerque replied to the letter, and caused a visit to be made to him by Fernão Martinz Evangelho, whom he charged with the purchase of horses, for there are many in that land.

After this ambassador there came another from Mirbuzaca, captain of the Xeque Ismael, who lived at Raxel, on the Persian shore of the sea, as I have already related, and he also brought for Afonso Dalboquerque a horse, and a letter of grand offers, begging him to be so kind as to help him by sea to capture the ports and islands lying in the straits of the Persian Sea, then he would be a faithful adherent of the King of Portugal, and pay him tribute for these conquests, and give him all the horses and supplies that he required.

Afonso Dalboquerque would have nothing to do with this request of Mirbuzaca, for he intended to write to the king an account of it, and to act in the matter in accordance with his wishes, but he wrote in reply a great many thanks for these offers, putting off any movement in the business until his return to Ormuz. And of all the kings and lords of that Persian coast, ambassadors were in waiting, whom Afonso Dalboquerque dispatched with copious expressions of thanks, and presents, which he sent to them, as also to the Moors of Persia and Tartary; and from all the parts of the interior country so many were they who came daily into the fortress in order to look upon Afonso Dalboquerque, that our people could not keep them back; and although his illness prevented him from going out very often, they begged those who were on guard at the doorway of the fortress to at least permit them to get sight of him, for they had come from their own country for this sole purpose. And if at any time he rode on horseback, so large a crowd of people followed after him along the streets, that he could hardly make his way through them; and as the fame of his person, and his greatness, was the topic of all those parts, and in consequence of the news which the ambassadors whom the Xeque Ismael had sent to him had circulated, they sent their servants to him with orders to draw his portrait to the life.

CHAPTER XLII.

How a Captain of the Xeque Ismael came to Ormuz to see the great Afonso Dalboquerque, and the news which he gave him, and the rest that took place.

A few days after D. Garcia de Noronha had set out on his voyage, there arrived from Persia a caravan with many merchants from Tartary, and Russia, and all that part of the world, with their merchandise, whereby the city began to grow very much ennobled; and in company with them came a captain from the Xeque Ismael, who had set out from the Court with the object of seeing the great Afonso Dalboquerque, on account of the great reputation which he had there, whereat he was highly delighted.

And because it was but a little time past since the Xeque Ismael had had a fierce battle with the Turk, in which this captain had taken part, he asked him all about the engagement; and he told him that the Turks came down with thirty thousand horse, and a large force of infantry, to attack a pass in the mountain range, so as to be enabled to pass through it to Tauriz,[1] and the captains of the Xeque Ismael who were in the van first reached the mountain, and took up a commanding position on it and withstood the passage of the enemy. But when the Xeque himself came up he was angry that they had not allowed the Turk to pass through, and ordered his captains to abandon the pass. When the Turk saw that the pass was no longer threatened, he crossed the mountain and, resting his rear upon it, fortified himself there with a large number of gun carriages chained together, by which means he had encircled the whole of his camp and fifteen thousand musketeers all drawn up in battle array, with determination of there awaiting the attack of the Xeque Ismael, for he had not ventured to go and attack him where he was; and the Turks kept so good a look out in their camp that the Xeque Ismael could never learn in what condition it was; so, like a man who made no account of the Turks, he fell upon them with twenty thousand cavalry. The Turks divided their army into two battalions and came out of the fort that they had constructed, to wait for the onset. When the Xeque Ismael fell upon the Turks, he put them at once to flight, and followed up hotly the pursuit after them until he entered into the camp itself; but as he did not know

[1] See p. 86.

anything about the artillery, nor how it was mounted, nor in what position it commanded, he strove very gallantly to get in along with his adversaries. When the Turk perceived that the Persians were in confusion, he gave the word for firing the artillery, which on the one flank, and the musketeers on the other, made so great a havoc that the Xeque Ismael seeing that he was beaten and a large part of his army killed, retreated rapidly to Tauriz, which lies distant about twenty leagues; and the Turks followed him up rapidly, and, meeting with no resistance, entered the city of Tauriz, and took all the treasure of the Xeque Ismael that there was in it. And while he lay there with the determination of fortifying himself in the city, news was brought to him that the Christians were already on their way to besiege Constantinople, and on this account he abandoned the undertaking and returned in great haste, and the Xeque Ismael reorganised his forces and returned to Tauriz. But certain captains whom the Turk had left behind in the city, as soon as they were apprised of his return, deserted the city and fled away, and when the Xeque Ismael arrived there, he ordered punishment to be inflicted upon all the chief men of the land, because they had allowed the Turks to enter the city without a struggle.

When Afonso Dalboquerque heard all this news he declared (one day when the captains were conversing with him about the enmity which the Xeque Ismael had towards the Turk and the Grand Sultan, concerning differences of their law) that the Xeque Ismael had been a thunderbolt sent down by God upon the sect of Mahomet for the preservation of India, although the Xeque himself was not aware of it; for when he was but a youth of eight years of age, and not holding any influential position, or having any distinction in the kingdom, he had risen up in rebellion, in the year that the admiral[1] discovered India, and being favoured by the assist-

[1] See vol. i, Pref., pp. xv *et seq.*

ance of his uncle had gained possession of Turcomania, Persia, the kingdom of Khorassan, Camarcand, a city of the Tartars, the kingdom of Aquilam,[1] and all Lower Armenia, and many other provinces of the Turks and Tartars, burning all the Moorish mosques, but sparing the Christian churches; and doing all this when only eight years old, what would he not have effected when now twenty-four years old, if God had not ordained that he should have two such powerful enemies as the Turks and the Grand Sultan of Cairo?

And as Afonso Dalboquerque was a great conqueror, and very successful in his method of performing great deeds, he wrote many times to the King D. Manuel to concert with all the Christian Powers that they should be on terms of friendship with the Xeque Ismael, for if he were on their side, they would have no difficulty in ruining the power of the Turk and the Grand Sultan; and to ask the permission of the Pope to send him master workers to make guns for him, for this was the only thing wanting to enable the Xeque to destroy his enemies. The captain of the Xeque Ismael, who had now spent several days in Ormuz, having come simply for the sake of seeing Afonso Dalboquerque, begged permission to return, and Afonso Dalboquerque made him a present of many very valuable lumps of gold, and commanded his people to show him all the artillery that there was in Ormuz, and told him to declare to the Xeque Ismael that by means of that, and much more in Portugal, he would serve him in the name of the King of Portugal against his enemies in any way most convenient to him.

[1] Cf. Gilam, p. 186. Ghilan, or Gilán, a province of Persia, on the South shore of the Caspian Sea. The initial letter A here is only the Portuguese feminine article.

CHAPTER XLIII.

Of the situation of the city of Ormuz and of its commerce.

There are three places in India which serve as marts of all the commerce of merchantable wares in that part of the world, and the principal keys of it.

The first is Malaca,[1] which lies in three degrees [N. lat.] at the entry and exit of the Straits of Singapara, of which I have already made mention.[2] The second is Adem, which is situate in the twenty-first degree of [N.] latitude, in the entry and exit of the Straits of the Red Sea, and of this place I have related all that has come to my knowledge.[3] The third is Ormuz, which is in fifteen degrees [N. lat.], and at the entry and exit of the Straits of the Persian Sea. This city of Ormuz is, according to my idea, the most important of them all. And if the King of Portugal had made himself master of Adem, with a good fortress, such as those of Ormuz and Malaca, and so held the sway over these three Straits which I have specified, he might well have been called the lord of all the world—as did Alexander when he penetrated to the Ganges—for with these three keys in his hands he might shut the doors against all comers. And well do I believe that if death had not cut off Afonso Dalboquerque, all these would have been in his hands. There is much which I could write upon this point, but as it is not my intention to point out the mistakes of others, I must revert to the thread of my narration.

Ormuz is a very ancient place, and by reason of its commerce and navigable position is very much renowned throughout the whole world; but I could not learn the history of its foundation, for it is impossible to believe that it sprang from a band of robbers who scoured the seas for

[1] See vol. iii, pp. 71 *et seq.*

[2] See vol. iii, p. 73.

[3] See the early chapters of this volume.

their prey (just as Corinth began its history), for it is an island of three leagues, all consisting of rock salt, very deficient of water, and dependent on the mainland for all its water-supply. If, on the other hand, it is considered that it was built in the first instance by fishermen who resorted thither in pursuit of their occupation (as was the case with Malaca),[1] this also cannot be the fact, on account of the want of water; which I have just shown. But be this as it may, and let each one attribute to its foundation whatever origin he pleases, nevertheless, the Moors hold Ormuz to be such an important place that they say, "The world is a ring, and the jewel in it is Ormuz"; and so it may well be, for thither pour in all the merchantable commodities of Tartary, Turcomania, the kingdom of Gilam,[2] of Bagadá,[3] and Cairo, and of all the parts of India; and in Ormuz can be obtained every desired kind of merchandise.

There is no country in that part of the world better supplied with provisions, although none whatever are produced in it. In the market of Ormuz may be found every kind of fruit, dried or fresh, just as in Spain. Ormúz, indeed, is so exacting in these things, that at the time when Afonso Dalboquerque was there, the people used to bring snow for sale from a distance of thirty leagues into the interior of Persia. From Ormuz are carried many horses to India, of great price, for they are of the best breed of all. The Straits of the Persian Sea are thickly populated with villages and islands on both sides, chiefly on the Arabian side, where stands the city of Baçora,[4] at which a river rising at the distance of two days' journey from Méca debouches, and divides the whole of the land; and on the Persian side is the Province of Raxel,[5] which contains many

[1] See vol. iii, p. 74. [2] See note, p. 184. [3] Baghdad.

[4] Basrah Town, the port of Mesopotamia. The entrance lies in 30 deg. 32 min. N. lat.; 47 deg. 51 min. E. long.

[5] See the map at vol. i, p. 80 (*Rexil*). Cf. vol. iv, p. 115.

villages and fortresses along the sea, engaged in a flourishing trade, and accustomed to import all kinds of Persian merchandise; and at the head of all this strait lies the city of Bagadá,[1] which used to belong to the lords of Armenia, but the Xeque Ismael took it from him, and now the Turk is lord of it. Three great rivers[2] unite into one there; one is called Euphrates, the other Tigris, and the third Fizam; and it is said that they come from a great lake lying in the interior of Persia, and at the spot where this enters the sea the Moors call it Xerdebaudá, and the water has an immense force.

From this city of Bagadá, there used in the ancient days to come various merchantable wares to Ormuz, but this trade is now forbidden by the King of Portugal. The Straits also contain an island called Barem,[3] noted for its large breeding of horses, its barley crops, and the variety of its fruits. And all around it are the fishing grounds of seed pearls, and of pearls, which are sent to these realms of Portugal, for they are better and more lasting than any that are found in any other of these parts. Besides these principal places the whole shore on the Persian side of the sea is filled with numerous little villages having a small trade, and, indeed, the whole sea is overrun with small vessels of light draught on account of the frequent shallows: and all these places supply Ormuz with a great quantity of silk, which is exported to India. The greater number of the inhabitants of this island are Persians, and the language which is most commonly employed there is the Persian. This island,

[1] Baghdad.

[2] At Kurnah, to the N. of Basrah, or Bassorah, is the meeting of the three great rivers, Euphrates or El Frát, Tigris or El Imarah, and Kerkhan or Hawiza. To the S. of Basrah, on the W. side, is the River Karun. After passing Basrah the stream is called Basrah River or Shatt El Arab. See Gen. F. R. Chesney's *Narrative of the Euphrates Expedition*, 1835-7. London: 1868 (Map).

[3] See p. 114.

too, contains many sulphur mines, and in the summer, on account of the sun's great heat, it is somewhat unhealthy. Its dominion extends as far as Goader,[1] a large city which lies in the land of the Noutaques.

CHAPTER XLIV.

How the great Afonso Dalboquerque, on account of his illness, held a conversation with the captains with regard to the succession in case of his death; and what was agreed upon on this behalf, and how he sailed away to India.

Now, inasmuch as the great Afonso Dalboquerque never went away from work, by day or by night, in the hopes of making an end of the building of the fortress with rapidity, and as the heat was great, and he himself old and in a bad state of health, the illness he suffered from began again to attack him with greater vehemence, and for eleven days he had not gone out of doors, nor had any one seen him except his own intimate friends. But, as it was thought strange that the people had not seen him, it began to be rumoured through the city that he was dead; so that he was compelled, in order to allay the apprehensions of the Moors and our own people, to show himself in public; and from that time forward he permitted some of the captains to see him, although his illness was so great that it would scarcely allow it. Every day he became worse, and felt so weak that at length, on the twenty-sixth day of the month of September, he summoned all the captains to his house, and in the presence of Pero Dalpoem, the secretary, declared to them that he was an old man, and attacked with an illness which might prove fatal at any moment. Nevertheless,

[1] See map at p. 80, vol. i—Guadel district, and Guadel port, to the east of Ormuz; and the earlier map at p. 1, vol. ii—Guadel, on the coast of the Noutaques.

because, if it were our Lord's will that his career should be finished, he was desirous of leaving the affairs of the kingdom in proper order, and the fortress that he was engaged upon finished, to the advantage of the king, his lord's service, therefore he desired them of his goodness to give him their oaths of fealty that they would obey that person to whom he, before his death, should delegate his powers, until the king D. Manuel could make provision in this case in accordance with his own desires.

The captains answered him with many tears, hoping that our Lord would grant him that good health which every one desired him to enjoy, and that it was proper for the preservation of the King of Portugal's estate in that part of the world that he should do what he pleased, for they would all be very happy to do his bidding, and to obey him to whom he should entrust his authority. Afonso Dalboquerque, with many kindly words gave them many thanks for their good wishes for his health, and received from every one an oath of allegiance, which they made at his hands, that they would submit themselves in the king's name to him whom he should nominate; and of this proceeding he ordered Pero Dalpoem the secretary to draw up a record, which was signed by every one.

When this was over, Afonso Dalboquerque finding himself daily growing more seriously ill, made his will, and turned his attention to religious matters. And after having thus put himself right in the sight of God, confessed, and communicated, and performed all the acts of a Christian, on the twentieth day of the month of October he called Pero Dalboquerque his nephew, son of Jorge Dalboquerque his cousin-german, and told him that as he was of such a character that the men would be glad to remain in the fortress with him; and also because the King of Ormuz had always evinced a great regard for him, and expressed a wish that he should always remain there; and, further, as he deserved it by reason of his knightly prowess and nobility of birth, he would appoint him to the charge over the fortress in the name of the King of Portugal, with four hundred thousand reis and two hundred quintals of pepper as well, for salary every year; and from that time forward he must give his attention to the construction of the fortress, for he had no longer any desire, either of body or mind, to interest himself in any other thing except only the account which he must render to God for the bad services that he had rendered; let him therefore order the artillery to be mounted in the appointed places, for the fortress had already reached a height sufficient to enable its defence to be maintained, and call it Nossa Senhora da Conceiçao, "Our Lady of the Conception," and give orders for the collection of all the supplies that were outside in the house of the Almoxarife, or receiver of customs. And he told him that he would leave Nicoláo Ferreira as chief guard of the King of Ormuz, and would strongly recommend him to a favourable reception; and then he ordered the two sons of King Ceifadim to be brought before him, and delivered them up into the care of Pero Dalboquerque, telling him that he begged him earnestly to look to their care, and keep them with him as a curb upon the king, whom indeed he was leaving in Ormuz against his will, for he had killed his brother, King Ceifadim, and risen up and usurped his kingdom, but he (Afonso Dalboquerque) had dissembled with him thus far because these two youths were not sufficiently old to conduct the government.

Pero Dalboquerque, after kissing his hands in token of thanks for the gift he had made to him of the fortress, told him that he would rather that he would select from among so many captains, fidalgoes, and cavaliers, some other one for that position (for everyone of them deserved it more than he did), but whatever benefit could arise to him from being the commander of the fortress, in all things he would act in obedience to his commands. As soon as it was known that Pero Dalboquerque was appointed captain of the fortress, many became discontented, (for each one of the captains thought himself would be chosen); but they were unreasonable, for he was a man of rare qualities and showed his spirit well in the account he gave of himself during the time that he held that position. And from that time forward he busied himself on the erection of the fortress and preparation of all that was required. Afonso Dalboquerque then appointed as factor, Manuel da Costa, son of Master Afonso, chief physician of the king D. Manuel and as scriveners of the factory, Manuel de Sequeira, page of the Duchess of Braganza, and Diogo Dandrade, page of the Royal Chamber.

And when all this had been arranged he ceased to trouble himself with any other business, and would not be consulted upon any other affairs; and ordered Diogo Fernandez de Béja to get the ship *Flor da Rosa,* of which he was the captain, ready for him, that he might sail away to India, with all the ships which were to go in his company. And thus having settled the manner of his departure, he sent word to the King of Ormuz by Pero Dalpoem and Alexander de Ataide, that he was desirous of going away, for it was absolutely necessary for him (dead or alive) to go and set the affairs of India in order; therefore he begged him earnestly to forgive his not having taken a personal farewell, for his illness had increased to so great a degree that it gave him no opportunity of doing so, but he trusted in God that he would be able very soon to return and visit him; and that he would leave Pero Dalboquerque his nephew as captain of the fortress, and he was assured that that commander would serve him very well. The king replied to Pero Dalpoem that he must declare to his father how grieved he was at his departure, but he would be supported by the hope of speedily seeing him again.

Thereupon Afonso Dalboquerque, being so eagerly desirous of setting out on the way to India, took his leave of Pero Dalboquerque, and the captains who were to remain behind, and went on board on Thursday the eighth day of the month of November of the same year [1515], about six o'clock, that no one might take notice of him, and immediately set sail and brought up again at anchor about a league's distance from the city, and there he remained waiting for the two great galleys and the caravela of João Gomez, and the brigantine *Sanctiago* which were to accompany him in the passage. And on Saturday morning Hacem Ali arrived with two native war-boats (*terradas*) laden with refreshments sent to him by the king; so he ordered him to be brought into the chamber where he was. And after Hacem Ali had delivered the king's message, Afonso Dalboquerque replied, thanking him very much for his visit, and saying that he had felt better after he had got out to sea; and that now he was no longer present in Ormuz, he begged the king would pay better attention to the work of the fortress, for it was the best thing he could have in the kingdom for the preservation of his state; and then he bade him farewell, giving him thirty *xerafins*, and to the Moors who navigated the *terradas* forty, and a good supply of wine to drink, which pleased them more than the money did. And as soon as they were gone he set sail and steered away direct to India.

CHAPTER XLV.

How the great Afonso Dalboquerque, by means of a war-boat which he captured on the way coming from Diu, learned that Lopo Soarez had come as Governor of India; and how he died on reaching the bar of Goa.

Directly that Hacem Ali had taken his leave, the great Afonso Dalboquerque bade Diogo Fernandez de Béja to clap on all sail, and having now got clear out of the throat of the Straits of Ormuz, as far advanced as Calayate,[1] one day in the morning a Moorish *terrada* or native war-boat hove in sight, under full sail; and as Afonso Dalboquerque was very desirous of knowing some news from India, he told Diogo Fernandez, captain of the ship, to send the brigantine *Sanctiago* after her, who chased her so close that she struck sail. And after he had gone on board, Diogo Fernandez enquired of them whence they came? The Moors replied that they came from Diu. Afonso Dalboquerque thereupon ordered that the captain, master, and pilot should be brought before him; and when they were there, he commanded Alexandre de Ataíde, the interpreter, upon his oath, to conceal nothing from him that these Moors should reveal, nor any of the news of India that they might give. The Moors craved pardon of Afonso Dalboquerque because they had not struck sail immediately the brigantine bore down upon them, alleging as an excuse that they did not know that he himself was in the ship. But as the disease with which he was suffering was hastening him to his end, and the mere act of conversation wearied him, he desired Alexandre de Ataíde to make very searching inquiries of them concerning Indian news, and to what port they were bound.

The captain of the *terrada* confessed that Cide Ale, and

[1] See vol. i, p. 213.

an ambassador of the Xeque Ismael who was at Diu, had dispatched him with letters for his lordship (Afonso Dalboquerque), and in these they might see for themselves the news of India. Then Afonso Dalboquerque ordered Alexandre de Ataíde to read the letters at once. That written by Cide Ale stated that twelve[1] ships had come from Portugal, and with them Lopo Soarez as captain major of India, and Diogo Mendez as captain of the fortress of Cochim, and other captains for all the other fortresses, as they were therein named, and that Miliqueaz had not written to him because he was very much offended at the king having ordered him to leave India.

And in the letter sent by the ambassador of the Xeque Ismael to Afonso Dalboquerque it was written, that inas-

[1] The British Museum MS. 20,902, f. 18, gives the following account of the fleet of *fifteen* ships that sailed from Portugal to India in A.D. 1515:—

"LOPPO SOARES DE ALBERGARIA, Governador da India.
"Anno de 1515.

"15 Naôs, a 7 de Abril.

"O Gouernador Loppo Soares Capitão Mor de quinze Naos, partio a sete de Abril, Capitão Dom Guterre de Monroy, Castelhano, Simão da Silueyra, Aluaro telles, Diogo Mendes de Vasconcellos, Jorge de Brito, Copeiro mor del Rey, Fernão Peres de Andrade, Dom Aleixo de Meneses, Christouão de Tauora, Dom João da Silui[a], Aluaro Barretto, Franco de Tauora, Simão dalcaçeva, Antonio lobbo falcão, Jorge Mascarenhas, Dõ Aleixo foi por Capitão mór do Mar, Sobrinho do Gouernador e nas absençias tinha poderes de G[ouernad]or."

"João de Barros diz, que foram somente treze naôs, e não conta mais, que os treze capitães seguintes nesta forma=D. Gutterre de Monroy Castelhano na *Piedade*=Simam da Silveira en *Sto Antonio*= Christouão de Tavora=Alvaro Tellez Barreto em *S. Gião*=Frco de Tavora em *S. Christovão*=D. João da Silveira em *Sta Maria da Serra*= Jorge de Brito Copeiro Mŏr del Rey=Alvaro Barreto=Simão de Alcaçova=D. Aleixo de Menezes=Diogo Mendes de Vasconcellos Capam e Feytor de Cochim=Fernam Peres de Andrade."

From this latter paragraph it appears that the number of ships, according to Barros, was *thirteen*. Correa says twelve *naos* and three *navios*, and gives his own list of captains, etc.—*Lendas*, ii, 463.

much as the King of Portugal so badly recognised his knightly deeds and his services, he advised him to take service with the Xeque Ismael, for he was sure the Xeque would appreciate his services by making him one of the greatest lords of his land; and he desired a safe-conduct to bring his merchandise to Ormuz and so take it to Persia.

When Afonso Dalboquerque learned that another governor had come out in his stead, and saw how his enemies were in favour with the king, he lifted up his hands, and gave thanks to Our Lord, and cried: "In bad repute with men because of the king, and in bad repute with the king because of the men. It were well that I were gone." And having said so he ordered that all the letters which the Moors were carrying to Ormuz should be taken from them, wherein it was advised that if a fortress had not already been given to Afonso Dalboquerque, that it should not be now granted, for another governor had been appointed who would do anything they wished. And in order that those letters should do no harm to the building of the fortress he caused them all to be burned, and bade the Moors begone, and remained alone with his secretary; and having already made his testament, wherein he expressed a desire to be interred in his chapel that he had built in Goa, which he had taken from the Moors, he added a codicil whereby he ordered that his bones, after the flesh had been consumed, should be carried to Portugal; and other matters not necessary to be written here.

And when this was done he wrote a letter to the king D. Manuel after the following words:—"Sire, I am writing this letter to Your Highness while I am suffering from a spasm which is a signal of my dissolution. In the kingdom of Portugal I have a son, and I beg Your Highness to ennoble him for my sake, as a reward for the services which I have performed for Your Highness in accordance with my condition of being your servant; for I command him on pain of forfeiting my blessing to ask this at your hands. And as for the affairs of India I say nothing, for they will speak for themselves and for me."

At this time he had become so weak that he could not stand, ever desiring Our Lord to take him to Goa, and there do with him as should be best for his service; and when the ship was yet distant three or four leagues from the bar, he ordered them to summon Fr. Domingos, the Vicar-General, and Master Afonso, the physician. And as he was so weak that he could not eat anything, he ordered his attendants to give him a little of the red wine which had been sent that year from Portugal. And when the brigantine had sailed away in advance to Goa, the vessel proceeded to cast anchor on the bar, on Saturday night, the fifteenth day of the month of December. When they told Afonso Dalboquerque that he was at the end of his voyage, he lifted up his hands and gave many thanks to Our Lord because he had vouchsafed to grant him that mercy which he had so earnestly desired, and thus he remained all through that night (with the Vicar-General, who had already come off from the shore to the ship, and Pero Dalpoem, Secretary of India, whom he constituted his executor), embracing the crucifix and continually talking; and he desired the Vicar-General, who was his confessor, to recite the Passion of Our Lord, written by St. John, to which he was always devoted, for in it, and in that Cross which was made in the likeness of that whereon Our Lord had suffered, and on his Wounds, he rested all the hope of his salvation: and he commanded them to attire him in the habit of Sanctiago, whereof he was a "Commendador", that he might die in it; and on the Sunday, one hour before the morning, he rendered up his soul to God; and there finished all his troubles without seeing any satisfaction of them. And we may well believe that one who thus finished his life could not have so many errors of commission laid to his charge that the king whom he had served very loyally should command him to return to Portugal without rewarding his services; but whereas Afonso Dalboquerque had enemies in the King's Council who were envious of his greatness and of the glorious victories which Our Lord had granted him in those countries, they prevailed upon the king D. Manuel to command his return, and they did not fail to allege reasons for this according to their intent, and to send Lopo Soarez as Governor of India. But when the king perceived his mistake, and the need he had of Afonso Dalboquerque's personal presence in India, he wrote a letter to Lopo Soarez, which I have given further on in my work, having ordered it to be transcribed from the original which I found among my papers.

CHAPTER XLVI.

How the body of the great Afonso Dalboquerque was carried to burial in his chapel, and the great mourning which was made for him; and of his life and manners.

Now that the great Afonso Dalboquerque had expired, before any one came from the city he was immediately enshrouded and clothed in the habit of Sanctiago, with some buskins on his legs, and spurs on the boots, and a sword in his belt — after the customary manner of burying the Commendadors—and on his head was placed a velvet cap, and at his neck a stole of the same. And when the body had been thus attired, Pero Dalpoem gave orders to lay down carpets on the quarterdeck of the ship, and there they set out the body upon a bier covered with a pall of black velvet, with a cushion of the same material at the head. And Diogo Fernandez de Béja, who was the captain, ordered a boat to be made ready wherein the body was to be conveyed to land; and when morning came, the people of the city began to assemble in boats with a great outcry to accompany him, but when they heard that he was dead, so great was the crying and weeping on all sides that it seemed as if the very river of Goa was being poured out; and because the people were in a great throng he was immediately put into the boat and so carried to the city.

And when the quay was reached where D. Goterres,[1] captain of the city, and all the Fidalgoes and Cavaliers, and all the populace and clerks and friars were waiting, the body was taken out of the boat to the land on the biers on which it had rested, and thereupon uprose another fresh outbreak of lamentations. And after praying for him, which the clerks and friars could not do without weeping, the Fidalgoes who were standing by took up the bier on their shoulders and beneath the pall bore him to his chapel of "Our Lady of the Conception", where he was interred, while there accompanied the procession all the people of the city, not only Christians but Hindoos and Moors, who filled the streets, demonstrating by the profusion of their tears the great sorrow they felt at his death. As for the Hindoos, when they beheld his body stretched upon the bier, with his long beard reaching down to his waist and his eyes half open, they declared, after their heathen notions, that it could not be that he was dead, but that God had need of him for some war and had therefore sent for him. And thus, after this order and with these lamentations and outcries, all arrived with the body at the chapel which he had founded over against the city gate, where he entered when he took the city from the Moors, and there were performed the last rites of the Church over him with a sermon of which I could gladly say much. And for the support of this chapel, he left in Goa an ample revenue in ground rents of houses to be paid for the performance of daily Services, and the remainder to be given away for alms every

[1] D. Goterre de Monroy; *Correa.*

Friday to orphan boys, sons of Portuguese parents. And when his son Afonso Dalboquerque desired to remove his bones to Portugal he obtained permission by a Papal Bull to sell the property, and built a hospital for pilgrims in Azeitão and a church adjoining it with the money, leaving in Goa property which renders forty thousand *reis* for a daily mass in the said chapel, in accordance with the express provision of the Pope's Bull.

When the funeral ceremonies were over, Pero Dalpoem caused a monument of three steps covered over with black velvet to be placed over the grave, and the chapel to be hung with black cloth; and he ordered to be suspended over the grave the royal flag which Afonso Dalboquerque always carried before him to battle, for it had been sent to him by the king D. Manuel from Abrantes (for the plague was ripe at Lisbon) to the port of Belem, when he was on the point of departure. This is now preserved in the principal chapel of Our Lady of Grace where his bones are interred.

This great captain was a man of middle stature, with a long face, fresh coloured, the nose somewhat large. He was a prudent man, and a Latin scholar, and spoke in elegant phrases; his conversation and writings showed his excellent education. He was of ready words, very authoritative in his commands, very circumspect in his dealings with the Moors, and greatly feared yet greatly loved by all, a quality rarely found united in one captain. He was very valiant and favoured by fortune. The king D. Fernando [II], King of Castile, said to Pero Correa, when he was Portuguese ambassador to the court, that it was a very astonishing thing that the king D. Manuel his son should have ordered Afonso Dalboquerque to return from India, seeing that he was so great a captain and so fortunate in his wars. He always gained the victory in his battles, both at sea and on land, against the Moors, sometimes indeed being wounded, for the places where he was posted were not very secure. He was very prompt in the performance of any undertaking when he had once determined upon it, and his name and his successes are so celebrated among all the kings and princes of Europe and Asia, that the Grand Turk when conversing with D. Alvaro de Sande, captain of the Emperor Charles V, whom he held in captivity, concerning the state of India, laid his hand on his breast and said that Afonso Dalboquerque had been a very remarkable captain. He was a man of the strictest veracity, and so pure in the justice he administered that the Hindoos and Moors after his death, whenever they received any affront from the Governors of India used to go to Goa to his tomb, and make offerings of choice flowers, and of oil for his lamp, praying him to do them justice. He was very charitable to the poor, and settled many women in marriage in Goa. For he was of such a generous disposition that all the presents and gifts which the kings of India bestowed on him—and they were numerous and of great value—he divided among the captains and Fidalgoes who had assisted him in obtaining them. He was very honourable in his manner of life, and so careful over his language, that the greatest oath which he ever took when he was very much enraged was this: "I abhor the life that I live." He died at the age of seventy-three years, having governed India for ten years.

CHAPTER XLVII.

How the king D. Manuel repented of having ordered the return of Afonso Dalboquerque from India and sent word that he was not to come back; and of the letter which he wrote thereupon to Lopo Soarez the Governor of India.

Lopo Soarez having set sail for India in the capacity of Governor during the month of March in the year 1515, in the following August news reached the king D. Manuel by way of Venice (for he always received news from that city of the movements of the Grand Sultan and from his ambassador at Rome), that the Grand Sultan of Cairo, annoyed at the Portuguese having entered the Straits of the Red Sea, had caused a large fleet of galleys and galleons to be made ready at Suez, with a large body of fighting men and artillery to proceed to India, principally to the kingdom of Ormuz, to prevent Afonso Dalboquerque from getting possession of it. The king, disappointed at this intelligence, and sorry at having recalled him, made up his mind to act vigorously in the way of supporting his Indian forces as quickly as he could, and ordered the immediate preparation of a fleet, so as to be able in March of the year 1516 to draft a large body of them to India; and he wrote to Lopo Soarez the following letter, telling him all this news which had come to hand of the projected fleet of the Sultan, and telling him what to do to confine himself to his proper sphere of duty if he had already entered upon his office in India:—

"Lopo Soarez, friend, we, the king, send you our hearty greeting. Because not many days past news has reached us that the Grand Sultan is preparing a fleet in Suez for his service in India, we hereby acquaint you of the manner in which you must proceed in case the fleet of the Sultan shall have passed into Indian waters, though we trust in Our Lord that this is not the case; for we ought to provide against and counteract a thing so prejudicial to our service, and one calculated, as we fear, to bring about the complete subversion of Portuguese influence in that part of the world. And in consideration of that which should result in the greatest security, and give the best grounds of success, it has seemed best for our service, in case the said fleet of the Sultan shall have entered into Indian seas and Afonso Dalboquerque still be there, to order him not to make any new arrangements for his return to these kingdoms as we had ordered him, but to remain with you in our service, and that you—because Cochim and Calicut are places of such great and manifest importance, and inseparably bound up with the preservation of our estate in India—remain therein (in India) as captain major and governor, Malaca being also subject to your command; and that you take command of four hundred of the men who went out with you, choosing those whom you prefer, to keep them with you, over and above those going on service in the said fortresses, and all the fleet on duty at Malaca and Cochim, and that you take up residence in whichever of the said fortresses of Cochim and Calicut that you prefer, and in which you perceive it most advantageous to the security and good of our service. And we hold it good that the lading of the vessels going to India every year, and returning with spices, be under your control without the intervention of any one therein except only the factor and officers of the factory.

"And we will that all the other fortresses, soldiers, fleets, and forces, as well of sea as of land, remain under the command of Afonso Dalboquerque for our service and in expectation of eventualities, and in order to render aid by reinforcements when required at any place where difficulties may arise in respect of the said fleet of the Sultan; and he is to labour to destroy it (as we trust in the Lord he will destroy it); and we have written to him at length to this effect.

"And although we repose entire confidence in you, that you will serve us in this business with the great bravery and with the knightly deeds which you are accustomed to perform, yet in an affair so new and untried, and of so great a need, it does not appear to us that you would be able to cope with it unassisted, if the Sultan's fleet were once to gain an entry into India; for it is impossible that you should be endowed with qualities such as we know are possessed by Afonso Dalboquerque, for the advancement and security of our state in those parts of the world, because of his experience during many years, and because of his acquaintance with the kings and lords who are our true friends and servants, and also because of his knowledge of those who are not so, but opposed to us, and of his knowing the heart and disposition of each one, having been so long among them, and had dealings with them and made trial of them, and also because of the matters in which he can exercise his care, and his ability to destroy those combinations in which he dare not hope to find perfect fidelity of action towards our service, so as thereby to prevent the enemy from combining with one another against us. And for all these reasons and others which may arise, it is expedient that we take advantage of the especial as well as of the general experience which he possesses not only in naval but also in military matters; and principally we regard the great victories with which Our Lord has ever favoured him in those parts, in all the things to which he has set his hand and which he has undertaken: for we trust in His mercy that He will give him the victory even in this enterprise; for albeit that many men are available for many things, and in him we ought to have entire confidence, as we have in you, not only for this matter but even greater matters, (although it may turn out to be nothing after all but an idle rumour), by making use of his services, whom Our Lord has already assisted in these very enterprises, it seems likely that the business may thereby be better carried and completed, especially when one knows the method of carrying them on as Afonso Dalboquerque does.

"And because this is a matter which so closely appertains to, and is involved in, our service, honour, and estate, as you will easily perceive, we recommend you and command you by especial orders in no wise to resist this which we desire you to do, but to assist us in the manner herein described.

"And because the military operations which ensue upon the entry of the Sultan's fleet into India will undoubtedly entail upon us considerable expenditure, we command the officials of Cochim, Calicut, and Malaca, in case Afonsŏ Dalboquerque requires any money or supplies from our stores, to send them to him immediately without the least delay in accordance with the provision which we have on this behalf dispatched to the said Afonso Dalboquerque. We do also notify this to you that you may know in what way we order it, and that you may not prevent it, but rather we desire you heartily to exercise in this matter all the attention possible, in order that all that Afonso Dalboquerque may require in respect of this matter may be thoroughly performed.

"Done at Almeirim, the twentieth day of March, in the year 1516."

CHAPTER XLVIII.

The state in which the great Afonso Dalboquerque left India at the time of his death.

The great Afonso Dalboquerque perceiving the desires of the king D. Manuel for universal peace in India, which he had indeed frequently expressed in his letters, for if a perpetual warfare were maintained it could not be well prosecuted because of the great expenses which it produced, laboured earnestly as long as he lived to maintain peace with all the kings and Hindoo lords of those parts, maintaining with them a constant intercourse, sending his messengers to them and offering to place at their disposal the fleets of the King of Portugal for the destruction of the Moors, and the casting them out of the country, which indeed they had wrested from the native rulers, especially the King of Narsinga, to whom not once but many times he sent Portuguese ambassadors, desirous of procuring his friendship and begging him to turn his attention to operations calculated to crush the Hidalcão and the King of Decam; and with all the other Hindoo kings from the Cape of Comorim up into the interior country, not only along the sea-shore, but also into the midland tracts, he also held friendly relations with a view of attracting them to be on peaceable terms with the King of Portugal, sending ambassadors to them in that king's name, and offering them his fleets and his forces.

This policy was carried out so consistently, that everyone endeavoured to be on terms of the greatest friendship with Afonso Dalboquerque; some showed it by their obedience, which they sent to assure him of by their messengers; others by the tribute which they rendered to him out of their revenues; others listened to the kind and peaceable expressions which he employed when he negotiated with them; and others again were attracted by the jewels and presents which he sent to them on the part of the king D. Manuel; others also offered him sites in their harbours for the erection of fortresses, actuated by a desire to maintain trade and friendship with the Portuguese, for they looked upon them at this time like Indian neighbours. And if death had not carried him off, the magnanimity of his spirit was such, that the King of Portugal would have become, by his assistance, lord of the whole of India; for, putting aside all thought of the Hindoos (whom he knew very well how to manage), the Moors feared him so greatly (because in his manner of conducting wars he was so fierce and dashing), that the Hidalcão, great lord as he was, and at the head of a large force, occupying a commanding position over against Goa which Afonso Dalboquerque had forcibly dispossessed him of, frequently made overtures of friendship to him, fearing lest he should invade his territories. And indeed it would not have been very difficult to carry out such an invasion, if the King of Narsinga had operated in conjunction with him on the interior border, as he had often sent word he would do if required, and sent him many messengers and presents; and even his mother, whose influence was paramount in that country, interposed as a mediator towards the settlement of this friendship, offering him all her forces against anyone whom he wished to attack.

At the time of Afonso Dalboquerque's death peace was universal from Ormuz to Ceylon; and all the kingdom of Cambay, Chaul, Dabul, Goa, Onor, Baticalá to Mount De Deli, Cananor, Cochim, Caicoulão to the Cape of Comorim,—all the kings, lords, and marine merchants,—and the interior lands he left so quiet and well-ordered that there was never a nation left so completely conquered and subdued by force of arms as this was. And the land had by this time become so pacified, that the Portuguese used to carry on their merchant business in every place, without being robbed of anything, or being taken captive; and they used to navigate the whole of the Indian sea in their ships, vessels, small and large *zambucos*, and used to cross the sea in safety from one part to the other; and the natives on their part used to visit Goa with their wares without any molestation being offered to them. And from the Cape of Comorim eastward Afonso Dalboquerque left the kings of those countries in perfect peace and friendship with the King of Portugal, sending to them ambassadors bearing presents in his name, and they sent similarly to him. Among these I may name the King of Pegú, the King of Bengála, the King of Pedir, the King of Siam, the King of Pacé, and the fortress of Malaca in repose. He remained also in the closest terms of peace with the King of China, and the King of Java, the King of Maluco, with the Gores, and all the other neighbouring princes were kept by him in a state of submission and tranquillity.

The principal means by which India was tranquillized, and the spirit of its kings and lords tamed, was that they perceived the intimate relations which the great Afonso

Dalboquerque held with the Xeque Ismael, with intention of overcoming the house of Méca and destroying the Grand Sultan, and all the Moors, sending his ambassadors to them with presents; and also with the Preste João, desiring him to cut through a range of hills and divert the course of the Nile into another bed so as to ruin Cairo; and that they saw him also erecting powerful fortresses in India; they saw him provided with plenty of artillery, plenty of shipping vessels and galleys; they saw him surrounded with numerous Portuguese households, youths and girls born in their land; they saw houses of stone and mortar erected; orchards planted; arable lands cultivated, and the increase of all kinds of stock; they saw his commerce flourishing both on sea and on land; they saw everywhere around them order and justice and good government prevailing, and many other matters of civilization belonging to the people who were settling in the land and intended to establish their progress therein.

The fame of this ran through all the lands of India, Persia, Cairo, and Turkey. The Grand Sultan used to enquire if there were many families established in India, and the Hidalcão how many young men and girls there were in Goa, for they were not afraid of any hurt the Portuguese could do them on the sea, but only of the colonization which this people desired to effect in the land. And when the Moors beheld the [apparently] limited power of fleets and fighting men belonging to the King of Portugal in India, they looked upon all these conquests and successes as nothing less than miracles. Afonso Dalboquerque, with that greatness of spirit which always characterised him, frequently used to say, that he trusted in Our Lord for taking Adem and establishing the Portuguese therein, so as to be thereby enabled to close the Straits with a powerful fortress, to the end that the Grand Sultan should finally abandon his hope of becoming chief lord of India; and when this had been successfully carried out then only to return again to Portugal for a short rest, to lean a little while on the handle of the hoe.[1] But Our Lord in his divine providence cut all this short when he took him to himself.

At the time of Afonso Dalboquerque's death he left in Malaca—twice captured by his arms from the Moors—a very strongly fortified fortress, with ample supplies of artillery and plenty of men to keep it. He left another in Ormuz, completed, and furnished with a large body of soldiers and great quantity of guns, and all that kingdom under the obedience of the King of Portugal—this, too, he had captured on two occasions from the Moors. He left a fortress in Calicut, of great defensive strength, provided with men and guns. He left the fortress of Cochim finished and in the same condition as it now stands—he had commenced to build it on the occasion of his first visit to India—furnished with seven very large elephants employed in the ship-yard on the beach. He rebuilt the fortress of Cananor with stone and mortar, for up to that time it was built with mud.[2] He left fleets attached to all these fortresses for their protection and maintenance. He left the City of Goa fortified with many castles set around the island for its safety;—this too had been taken twice under his assault from the Moors. He left therein many Portuguese families, many Hindoos converted to Christianity, and a large body of mounted men. He left many armourers, and officers employed in the setting of jewels and precious stones, saddle-makers, buckler-makers, blacksmiths, stone-masons, gun-founders, master-workmen skilled in the manufacture of matchlocks, ships' carpenters, caulkers; and the greater part of these Portuguese, the rest native Christians, as true vassals and subjects of the King of Portugal as though they were natives of Portugal.

[1] *A repousar hum pouco sobre o cabo da enxada*, evidently a proverbial expression.

[2] *Taipa.*

He left the magazines of Goa supplied with large quantities of weapons, many caparisons for horses, many saddles, much store of gunpowder, cannon balls, and all other kinds of necessary munitions of war. He left in the harbour a fleet of fifty sail, counting vessels, ships, and galleys, and *fustas*—a large assembly for those days—besides the *paráos* and merchant vessels not taken into consideration in this estimate. He ordered money to be struck at Goa and Malaca in the name of the King of Portugal; and this was current throughout the whole of India. He was the first captain of the King of Portugal who penetrated the Straits of the Red Sea. "*Y quien mas hiziere passe a delante*", "And let him who does more than all this take precedence of him," which is the inscription that the Count Fernão Gonçalvez ordered to be set up on his sepulchre, which stands at the entry of the door of the monastery church where he lies buried.

CHAPTER XLIX.

How the bones of the great Afonso Dalboquerque were conveyed to Portugal: and how they were carried to [the church of] Our Lady of Grace.

The great Afonso Dalboquerque having made and ratified his testament, wherein he left orders that he should be interred in his chapel of Our Lady which he had built in Goa, on the occasion of returning from the conquest of the Kingdom of Ormuz, and leaving behind a fortress built in that city, as has been already related, he added a codicil to it, in these words: "I declare, that in case of my death in these parts of India—which may Our Lord of His mercy not permit—for certain just causes which move me to this end, and for the rest of my soul, I command that after the flesh is consumed, my bones be conveyed to Portugal and interred [in the church of] Our Lady of Grace, of the Order of St. Augustine, where my ancestors lie." A matter thus earnestly desired by Afonso Dalboquerque, the conveying of his bones to Portugal (as is shown by these words in the codicil), it would have been carelessness on the part of his son to let fifty-one years pass away without fulfilment; but as this duty was incumbent upon Pero Correa, and being executor he was bound to perform it, the son remains excused, for this very Pero Correa frequently desired the king D. Manuel to give him permission to get them conveyed away, but the king never would consent, declaring that as long as he had the bones of Afonso Dalboquerque safe in Goa, India was secure. But, on the death of Pero Correa, this duty devolved upon his son as his heir, who strove hard with King John the Third to obtain this permission; nevertheless it was always denied him, by reason of the constant representations made to the king by the inhabitants of Goa, and, indeed, of all India, not to yield in the matter. When this king died, however, and Queen Dona Catharina[1] our Lady was ruling these kingdoms for the king D. Sebastião her grandson,[2] he renewed his endeavours to obtain his desire, but several years passed without attaining his wishes, for it was necessary to obtain a Papal bull, couched in terms of greater excommunication against the inhabitants of Goa, to prevent their hindering him. It seemed, indeed, that the fitting opportunity had not even then arrived. At length, having succeeded in getting the necessary permission from the Queen our Lady—for there was now no longer any one there to prevent their carrying out the design,—and on the timely arrival of D. Antão de Noronha[3] in India as Viceroy, who

[1] Daughter of Philip I of Austria; Regent of Portugal, A.D. 1557.

[2] Posthumous son of John, King of Portugal, born A.D. 1554.

[3] See *British Museum Add. MS.* 20,902, p. 67; *MS. Sloane* 197, fol. 38*b*, portrait and life.

did all in his power to expedite the business, the removal to Lisbon was carried out, and the remains reached the port on the sixth day of the month of April 1566. They were then taken out of the ship in which they had been brought, and carried to the *Casa da Misericordia*, or House of Mercy, under the directions of Ruy Lourenço de Tavora, *Provedor*, or chief officer, accompanied by a large body of Fidalgoes; and there they remained for several days, the funeral car being draped with cloth of crimson velvet, in charge of many of the clergy, who accompanied the body, and these sang mass daily for his soul, while the order was being drawn up for the removal to the principal chapel of Our Lady of Grace, which his son endowed with a competent rental for the interment of the remains.

When all matters had been put in readiness, on a Sunday, the nineteenth day of the month of May, all the lords and fidalgoes in the court assembled in the *Casa da Misericordia* to accompany the remains; and from that place they set out in procession, preceded by the flag of the Misericordia, and all the brotherhood behind this, the Franciscan friars and the Austin friars, and all the clergy of the city, each one with a torch in his hand; and at the close of the procession the Chapter of the See on the one side, and D. Afonso Anriques, *Adaião*[1] of the king, and all the staff of the chapel on the other side, and behind these the bier on which were the bones, carried by the brethren, covered over with a large pall of cloth of gold; and in front of the coffin went the *provedor*, with his wand in hand, and Afonso Dalboquerque, son of the departed Viceroy, on the one side, clad in a mourning cloak, with bare head, and on the other side André Dalboquerque, his nephew, in similar guise; and behind the bier the Duke of Aveiro and his sons and brothers, and all the rest

[1] The *Adaião* is probably the same as the *Adail*, already described. *See* Glossary.

of the lords and fidalgoes and prelates who were in attendance at the court at the time. The crowd of people was so great that the streets would not hold them, and in this order the procession made its way; and as each church was passed the bells that were being rung redoubled their peals, until at length the chapel of Our Lady of Grace was reached. And in the High Chapel there had been prepared a lofty platform with two tiers of steps, which took up almost all the floor, enclosed on all four sides, set with numberless torches, and draped with many carpetings, and thereon they deposited the coffin in which the bones had been laid, bordered with gold tissue, surrounded with a company of his servants, every one dressed in mourning. And over this coffin were hung three flags of the colours and devices of the three kingdoms which the great Afonso Dalboquerque had gained from the Moors in India. Over these flags floated the royal flag which the king D. Manuel had sent to him, as I have already narrated, now very much torn and ragged, for it had been delivered to him on the sixth day of the month of April, in the year 1506. And thus, sixty years after he had set out on his journey, his bones were at length brought back to the monastery of Our Lady of Grace, of the order of St. Augustine, replete with many victories which he had gained in India under that very symbol of the Cross, in the reign of the king D. Sebastião our lord. And when all was quiet Master Fr. Sebastião Toscano[1] began his preaching, of which I say nothing in these commentaries, not only so as not to increase the bulk of my volume, but also because it is already printed.

[1] See Barbosa Machado, *Bibliotheca Lusitana*, vol. i, p. 702, for an account of Fr. Sebastião Toscano, and the title of the oration here mentioned, which was printed in Lisbon, 1566.

CHAPTER L.

Of the pedigree of this excellent Captain Afonso Dalboquerque, his origin, and parentage, and an account of the way in which he spent his youth, until his first voyage to India.

Inasmuch as I have written an ample discourse, collected from the Chronicles and genealogical works of Portugal and Castile, concerning the genealogy of the Alboquerques, their antiquity, and the origin and derivation of the name, which descends by the direct line of the kings of Portugal, Leon, and Castile, for the information of those who are descended from the family, I will not say here more than is necessary for the understanding briefly whence this great Afonso Dalboquerque is descended, and whose son he was.

It is in this way that the pedigree stands.[1] The King D. Dinis,[2] King of Portugal, had by Dona Aldonsa de Sousa, a court lady of high quality,[3] native of Galicia, a natural son, who was called D. Afonso Sanches, and married Dona Tareja Martinz, granddaughter of the king D. Sancho of Castile,[4] surnamed the Brave, and had with her for her dowry the town called Villa de Conde, in Portugal, and many lands in Castile, and Castle Dalboquerque, which he rebuilt, and laid the foundation of the town below it, surrounding it with a wall, tower, barbican, and moat, and peopled it with Portuguese and Castilian families; and then he took up his abode, and over the principal gateway of the town he placed a shield of his arms, which are here figured.

[1] See Appendix for further particulars of the pedigree.

[2] A.D. 1279-1325.

[3] Infansona, for Infançoa, a feminine form of Infanção, a royal page.

[4] Sancho III, A.D. 1157-1158; or Sancho IV, A.D. 1284-1295.

These are the arms that the Alboquerques descended from him ought to bear, and not those which they do bear.[1]

On the same door he put up the following inscription :—

> EM NOME DE DEOS SEJA TUDO . AMEN . EU DOM AFONSO SANCHES SENHOR DESTE CASTELLO.DALBOQUERQUE COMECEI ESTE LAVOR FERIA QUARTA AOS QUATRO DIAS DO MEZ DE AGOSTO DA ERA DE . 1314 . O QUAL SEJA PERA SERVIÇO DE DEOS E DE SANCTA MARIA SUA MADRE SALVAMENTO DE MINHA HONRA ENDEREÇAMENTO DA MINHA FAZENDA PORQUE AS COUSAS QUE A DEOS SÃO FEITAS TODAS ADIANTE HÃO DE IR . E AS QUE SEM ELLE SÃO TODAS HÃO DE FENECER .
>
> ---
>
> E POREM PRAZA A DIOS QUE HAJA BOA GLORIA O MESTRE PEDREIRO QUE FEZ ESTE CASTELLO.

[1] Viz., those figured on the title-page of this edition of 1774. The arms figured in the text above are a very charming example of the herald's art as practised in Portugal, where the principal and eponymic charges of the ROYAL HOUSES, LEON and CASTILE, are arranged alternately

In God's name be everything. Amen. I, Dom Afonso Sanches, Lord of this Castle Dalboquerque, began this work on Wednesday, the fourth day of the month of August, in the year 1314 *of the [Spanish] Era*[1] [A.D. 1276] ; *and may it be to the service of God and of Saint Mary His Mother, the salvation of my soul, augmentation of my honour, and improvement of my estate, for all those things which are done to God's glory shall prosper, and all those things which are done without God must perish.*

May it also please God that the Master Mason who built this Castle attain to the glory he merits.

This D. Afonso Sanches Lord Dalboquerque had a son by his wife, named D. João Afonso Dalboquerque, who inherited his estates and became a great lord in Castile, being the first who took this name of Dalboquerque. He built the Castle-keep [*Torre de Menagem*] of Codiceira, and over

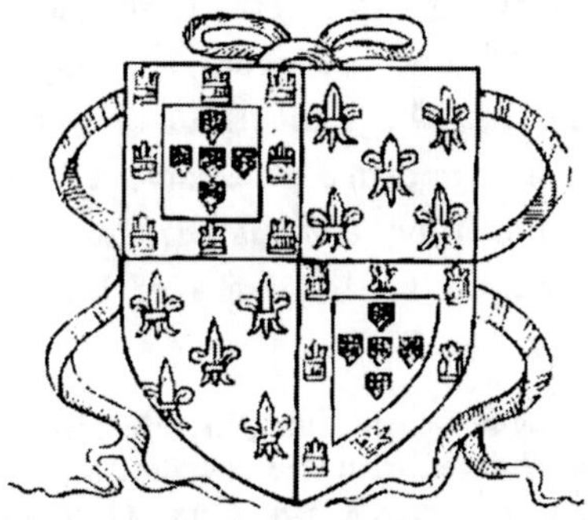

on a cross, cantoned with the ROYAL ARMS of PORTUGAL. The arms which are figured on this page, viz., those used by the son of this Afonso, are simply those of PORTUGAL and FRANCE (five fleurs-de-lis in saltire, by error for semé-de-lis).

[1] This Era is calculated from the Conquest of Spain by the Emperor Augustus, B.C. 38. It prevailed in Portugal as late as A.D. 1415, if not later. The fourth of August fell on Tuesday in A.D. 1276. *Era* is, however, occasionally used for *anno*, and may be so used perhaps in this passage. But the day of the week does not correspond.

it placed the shield of his arms, which are represented at the beginning of this book, mingling with the *quinas*[1] of Portugal, the fleurs-de-lis which were borne as the arms of his mother, who was descended from the Royal Family of France, and these the Alboquerques now bear.

From this D. João Afonso descends the great captain Afonso Dalboquerque, who was the second son of Gonçalo Dalboquerque, Lord of Villa Verde, and of Dona Leonor de Menezes, daughter of D. Alvaro Gonçalvez de Ataide, first Count of Atouguia and of the Countess Dona Guiomar de Castro, his wife. When he was quite a lad, he was brought up in the household of D. Afonso the Fifth,[2] and when this king died, he went to Arzila,[3] and after a few years returned to the service of the king Dom João the Second, his son, and held the office of *Estribeiro mór*,[4] chief equerry to the king. When King João died,[5] Afonso Dalboquerque returned to Arzila, accompanied by his brother, who fell fighting against the Moors; and in consequence of this bereavement he returned to Portugal to the service of the king Dom Manuel,[6] and entered the royal body-guard. Then he accompanied the fleet that operated at Taranto, and took part in the capture of Graciosa,[7] and in fact was present in all the military actions that happened in his day in these kingdoms, up to the time of his first voyage to India.

[1] From *quina*, a cinque or quincunx, in reference to the *five* escutcheons in cross, each charged with *five* roundles in saltire, in the shield of arms of PORTUGAL, which are thus blazoned:—*Argent*, five escutcheons in cross *azure*, each charged with as many plates, on a border, *gules*, seven castles, *or*. *See* p. 215.

[2] A.D. 1438-1481.

[3] Arzilla, or Acila, in Morocco, stormed and taken in A.D. 1471, by Alphonso V of Portugal, but retaken by the Moors, and again captured by the Portuguese.

[4] Called *Estaleyro Mor* in vol. i, p. x.

[5] A.D. 1495.

[6] A.D. 1495-1521.

[7] Island of Gratiosa, off the west of Morocco.

Afonso Dalboquerque never married, but he had a natural son,[1] whom he appointed inheritor of all his property, as well as of the services which he had performed towards three kings of these kingdoms; and the king D. Manuel desired—because of the obligation he was under of making a formal acknowledgment of his father's merits—that his name should be changed to that of Afonso Dalboquerque, his father. This son married Dona Maria de Noronha, daughter of the Lord D. Antonio, first Count of Linhares, who was very well disposed towards him, and of the Countess Dona Joanna da Silva, daughter of D. Diogo da Silva, first Count of Portalegre. And after his marriage the king sent him in the fleet of Savoy as captain of a galleon, with the infante, Dona Beatriz, his daughter. And on his return from his voyage, hoping that the king D. Manuel would at length reward him out of satisfaction for the services done by his father, and in accordance with the promises that had been made to his father-in-law, the Count of Linhares, he found him dead, and thus he was left without the recompense that the services of his father richly merited, not only because of the little care his parent took to prosecute his own interests, but also because of the altered aspect of the times.

[1] See vol. i, pp. xlvii-l.

END OF THE COMMENTARIES.

APPENDIX.

A.

TITLE-PAGE, DEDICATORY EPISTLE, AND COLOPHON

OF THE FIRST EDITION OF THE COMMENTARIES, FROM THE UNIQUE COPY IN THE SUNDERLAND LIBRARY. SALE NO. 3657.

COMMENTARIOS de Afonso Dalboquerque capitão geral & gouernador da India, collegidos por seu filho Afonso Dalboquerque das proprias cartas que elle escreuia ao muyto poderoso Rey dõ Manuel o primeyro deste nome, em cujo tempo gouernou a India Vam repartidos em quatro partes segũdo os tempos de seus trabalhos.

Com Priv[i]legio Real.

* * * * *

AO SERENISSIMO PRINCIPE | DE PORTUGAL DOM BASTIAM NOSSO SENHOR

Duas rezões principalmēte antre outras muytas me obrigarão (Serenissino Principe) a copillar esta historia dos grandes feytos Dafonso Dalboquerq' capitã geral & gouernador da India: áqual pus nome Cõmētarios, polos colligir dos proprios origináes q' elle no meyo dos acõtecimētos de seus trabalhos escreuia a el Rey dõ Manuel vosso. visauoo, q' nosso Senhor tẽ na sua gloria. A primeyra, pera q' V. A. veja neste pequeno volume, cõ quanto sofrimento & trabalho de sua pessoa este seu capitã conquistou os reynos & senhorios da India (q' V. A. sucederá depois de largos annos de vida del Rey dõ Joam o terceyro nosso senhor vosso auó), & a obrigaçã que tem aos netos & parẽtes daquelles q' nesta conquista acabarã seus dias. A outra foy, ver eu como os q' escreueram a historea da India (cõ tanto trabalho & louuor de seus engenhos) ou por terẽ hũa occupaçam geral em contar tudo o q' aconteceo aos Portugueses naquelles partes, des o principio de seu descobrimẽto, ou por falta das informações q' teueram, passarã breuemente por muytas cousas q' Afonso Dalboquerq̃ passou nesta conquista. E nam deũe de ter menos credito & authoridade ante A. V. estes seus Cõmentarios polos eu colligir sendo seu filho, do q' Cesar tẽ polo mũdo escreuendo de sy mesmo ha tantos annos. E porq̃ tratar aqui de seus louuores (em q' auia muyto q' dizer) seria fazer outra obra mayor que a sua, nã direy mais q' aquelles q' vão semeados por este liuro, & o q' dizia hum Pero Gomez homẽ antigo na India, o qual sendo já muyto velho (vendo as desordẽs della depois de sua morte) se ya em Goa cõ hum páo na mão á sua sepultura, & dizia. O grande capitão, tu me fizeste quanto mal podeste, mas eu nam te posso negar que foste o mór cometedor & sofredor de trabalhos que ouue no mundo, aleuantate q' se perde o que tu ganhaste. V. A. açeite, de mym este pequeno seruiço q' lhe faço nesta sua primeyra jdade, pois jaa a não tenho palhe poder fazer outros, mayóres. E se o estillo da historea nã for tam elegante como sua grandeza merecia, desculpo (*sic*) o atreuimento q' tiueem lha offerecer cõ o pouco q' aprendi da reitorica, & cõ escreuer *ueste* (*for* neste) estillo rudo a verdade do que passou.

* * * * *

Foram jmpressos estes Com- | mentarios Dafonso Dalboquerque capitam geral & go- | uernador da India na cidade de Lixboa, por Joam | de Barreyra jmpressor del Rey nosso senhor. | Acabaranse de jmpremir vespera de sam Se- | bastiã, dezanoue dias de mes de Ianeyro | da era de mil & quinhentos & cinco- | enta & sete annos, em cujo dia | o Principe dõ Bastiam nosso | senhor a quem esta obra | vay offerecida, fez | tres annos. |

B.

PEDIGREE OF AFONSO DALBOQUERQUE,

AND GENEALOGICAL NOTES OF THE FAMILY.

Lansdowne MS. 189, f. 55.

TITULO DOS ALBUQUERQUES SEGUNDO SE ACHA NO LIVRO ANTIGUO DAS LINHAGE'S E CHRONICA D'ELREY DOM DINIS.

§ El-Rey Dom Dinis de Portugal entre os filhos bastardos que teue, houue dous, de hũa Dona Chamada Mor Afonso. § Dom Afonso Sanchez, De que trataremos, e Martim Afonso Chichorro, segundo achamos em hũ liuro das lembranças da torre do tombo, por hũa carta que dise ser tirada dos Registros do año de 1439, E a carta no año de 1450.

§ Dom Afonso Sanchez foy o prinçipal filho bastardo de todos os d'ElRey Dom Dinis, E mais estimado delle, foy Conde, e senhor d'Albuquerque, e de Codiçeyra, e de Villa de Conde e de outras terras, e mordomo mór d'ElRey seu Pay, e a quem o dito Rey quis grande bem, e lhe foy tão affeiçoado, que lhe assacarão, que o queria fazer Rey; E sobre isso, e por amor delle, teue ElRey grandes differenças, e guerras, e arroydos, e mortes de parte a parte, com o Infante seu filho herdeyro, que despois Reyno, e foy Rey Dom Afonso o 4º.=foy cosado com Dona Tareja mỹz filha do Conde Dom João Afonso telo de Meneses senhor d'Albuquerque, Polo qual casamento foy senhor d'Albuquerq' e lhe ficou por appellido de sua linhagem=Da qual Dona Tareja houue Dom João Afonso d'Albuquerque, que disserão o Bom, senhor d'Albuquerque, e de Medelim, e de outras muytas terras.

§ Este Dom Afonso Sanchez, e a Condessa Dona Tareja Mĩz sua molher, fizerão, e dotarão o Mosteyro de Sancta Clara de Villa de Conde; E a pouoa de Dom Martim, e outros lugares, e muitas Rentas, e lugares, como se ve na Instituição, que fizerão, e ordenarão. O qual mosteyro edificarão no Castello, e Paços de sua morada; E assy estão sepultados na Capella que chamão dos Senhores, os quaes mudou da Galili, onde d'antes estauão sepultados para esta nobre Capella onde agora estão=Este Dom Afonso Sanchez se foy, e desnaturou para Castella com rreceo da má vontade do Infante seu Irmão Dom Afonso; De que Portugal ficou perdendo Albuquerque, e Codeseyra, e para sempre ficarão a Castella.

§ Don João Afonso o Bom, Senhor de Albuquerque, a que as Chronicas de Castella chamão o bom de Portugal, filho deste Dom Afonso Sanchez Senhor d'Albuquerque herdou, e foy Senhor da casa de seu Pay. Da parte que tinha em Castella, foy senhor d'Albuquerque, de Melinde, de SeyraZagala, e Alconchel, e outras muytas Villas, terras, e lugares, e foy hũ dos grandes Senhores de Castella em seu tempo. E foy Ayo, e Mordomo mor d'ElRey Dom Pedro o Cru. Este foy o que andou em tempo d'ElRey Dom P^{o}. com os grandes de Castella, como se ve na dita Chronica, foy casado com Dona Isabel de Meneses filha de Dom Telo de Meneses, que foy filho do Infante Dom Afonso de Molina, e de Dona Maria filha do Infante Dom Manoel Irmão d'ElRey Dom Afonso o X^{o}., E da Infanta Dona Costança d'Aragão filha d'ElRey, como se mostra no liuro das linhagẽs no tit^{o}. 24, § 3°. e no tit^{o}. 21, f^{as}. 57. De que houue Dom Martim Gil d'Albuquerque Adiantado de Murçia, que ElRey Dom P^{o}. o Cru mandou matar com poçonha, sendo moço, e estando em rrefẽns, como se conta na Chronica do dito Rey de Castella no anno 4°. no cap^{o}. 23. folh. 22.

§ E houue bastardos Dom Fernando d'Albuquerque, e a condessa Dona Britis de Albuquerque, molher que foy de Dom Afonso Telo de Meneses Conde de Barcellos Irmão da Raynha Dona Leonor, e filho de Martim Afonso Telo de

Meneses, o que matou ElRey Dom P$_o$. de Castella em Touro, E a condessa Dona Maria d'Albuquerque molher de Dom Gonçalo telo de Meneses Conde de Neyua, e de Faria, e Senhor de Cantanhede.

§ Dom Fernando Afonso d'Albuquerque filho bastardo de Dom João Afonso o bom Senhor d'Albuquerque, e de Medelim se veo para Portugal, onde foy Mestre de Sanctiago.

Lansdowne MS. 189, f. 581*b*.

TITULO DOS ALBUQUERQ'S DE GOMIDE, QUE AGORA HA EM PORTUGAL.

§ G^{co}. L^{co}. de Gomide foy f^o. de Nuno Mĩz de Gomide natural de Portalegre, e este he o de Portalegre vẽ de dous Irmãos.

§ Foy hũ homẽ m^{to}. honrrado em tempo d'ElRey Dom João o 1°, E seu Escriuão Da Puridade, e m^{to} priuado foy s^r. de Villa Verde, e outras heranças q' deixou em Morgado, e foy Alcayde Mor d'Obidos. foy casado cõ Jnes Leytoa f^a. de Vasco Leytão ou de Gil frõ o fariseu. De q' houue João Gl'z de Gomide, e M^a. Gl'z molher de Lopo da Cunha Veedor do Infante Dom Anrrique f^o. do dito Rey Dom João e Dona Isabel Leytoa molher de Ruy Mẽz Cerueyra. O qual Gonçalo L^{co}. Jaz sepultado no cap^o. de nossa S^{ra}. da Graça de Ls^a. E este, ou hũ seu Irmão dizem que fez os Morgados dos L^{cos}. de Miranda, de Guimarães, os quaes trazem por armas hũz gomiz q' trazião os Gomides. E dizẽ q' deixou este seu Morg^{do}. a hũ sobr^o. O qual deuia ser G^{co}. Caldr^a. q' foy Escriuão da Cam^a. d'ElRey Dom João o 1°. E seruia pollo dito G^{co}. L^{co}. E este so soube o segredo Da tomada de Cepta, e no dia q' a tomarão chegou este G^{co}. L^{co}. com 400. homẽs de sua Libre, e a mor parte de sua Criação e pedio alli a ElRey o fizesse (como fee) caualr^o. sendo nisso o prim^{ro}.

§ João Gl'z de Gomide f^o. deste G^{co}. L^{co}. foy senhor do Morgado de Villa Verde e foy casado com Leonor d'Albuquerq̃ fª. de Gᶜᵒ. Vaz de Mello o moço Sʳ. de Castanhrª. e Pouos. De q' houue Gᶜᵒ. d'Albuquerque, e João d'Albuquerque-azeyte, e Pᵒ. d'Albuquerque azeyte, e Lopo d'Albuquerque dos Olivães, e Dona Isabel molher de Fernão de Sousa Alcayde Mor de Leyria fᵒ. de Diogo Lopez de Sousa o velho Mordomo Mor d'ElRey Dom———.[1]

CAUSA PORQ' OS GOMIDES SE CHAMÃO DE ALBUQUERQUE.

§ Estes se chamão d'Albuquerque polla may q' era neta de Vᶜᵒ. Mĩz da Cunha o velho, e de Dona Tareja d'Albuquerque sua molher 2ª. q' foy fª. do Mestre de Sᵗ.tiago Dõ Fernando Aᵒ. d'Albuquerque. O qual foy fᵒ. de Dom João d'Albuquerque, como vereis no titᵒ. dos Albuquerques.

§ Gᶜᵒ. d'Albuquerque fᵒ. de João Gl'z de Gomide foy sʳ. do Morgado de Villa Verde e foy casado com Dona Leonor de Mñs fª. de Dom Aluʳᵒ. Gl'z d'Atayde 1ᵒ. Conde de Atouguia. De q' houue Fernão d'Albuquerque, e Aᵒ. d'Albuquerque, e Aluʳᵒ. Gl'z d'Atayde q' foy clerigo, e Prior de Villa Verde, e Martim Gl'z d'Atayde q' os Mouros matarão em Arzilla, e Dona Costança de Castro, molher de Dom Fernando de Noronha Guouernador q' foy da Exª. Senhora e Dona Isabel d'Albuquerque molher de Pᵒ. da Silva Relle, Alcayde Mor de Porto de Mos, e outras freyras.

§ Fernão d'Albuquerque fᵒ. 1ᵒ. deste Gᶜᵒ. d'Albuquerque herdou o Morgᵈᵒ. de seu Pay e foy Vedor do Mestre de Sanctiago Dõ Jorge fᵒ. bastardo d'ElRey Dom João o 2ᵒ. foy casado com Dona Cⁿª. da Silva fª. de Diᵒ. da Silva thrᵒ. Mor d'ElRey Dom Aᵒ. o 3ᵒ. e Irmão do dito Pᵒ. da Silva Relle. De q' houue Dona Guiomar d'Albuquerque molher de Dom Martᵒ. de Noronha, fᵒ. de Dom Pᵒ. de Noronha Mordomo Mor d'ElRey, Dom Joãa o 2ᵒ. e-Comen-

[1] Blank in the MS.

dador Mor de S^{t}.tiago, e Dona Joana d'Albuquerque molher de Jorge barreto de Crasto Comendador de Crasto Verde e por este casam^{to}. veo este Morgado de Villa Verde aos Noronhas.

§ O Grande A^{o}. d'Albuquerque f^{o}. deste G^{co}. d'Albuquerque, e Irmão deste Fernão d'Albuquerque, foy Estribr^{o}. Mor d'ElRey Dom João o 2°. Capitão Mor, e Guouernador da India, onde tomou aos Mouros Ormuz, Goa, e Malaca, onde Jaz sepultado. E dahi o mandou trazer seu f^{o}. E fez outras m^{tas}. Cousas de q' estão os da India cheos, E o Liuro q' de seus feytos compos seu f^{o}. bastardo A^{o}. d'Albuquerque. E não foy casado.

§ A^{o}. d'Albuquerque f^{o}. natural deste grande A^{o}. d'Albuquerque foy casado com Dona M$_{a}$. de Noronha f^{a}. de Dom Ant^{o}. de N^{ra}. Conde de Linhares. De q' houue Ant^{o}. d'Albuquerque, q' falleceo moço, E Dona Joana d'Albuquerque molher q' foy de Dom Fr^{co}. de Castro o magro Capitão d'Evora e Comendador de ——[1]. E della não houue geração. E casou 2°. vez cõ Dona C^{na}.de Mñs. f^{a}. de Dom M^{el}. de Mñs, q' viue em Almada Camareyro Mor q' foy de s^{r}. Dom Dr^{te}. Condestable de Portugal, e Duque de Guimarães. De q' não houue geracão, e houue bastardo João A^{o}. d'Albuquerque.

§ P^{o}. d'Albuquerque d'alcunha azeite f°. 2°. de João Glz' de Gomide, e Irmão de G^{co}. d'Albuquerque foy casado com Dona Guiomar de S^{t}. Payo f^{a}. de Amadis Vaz de S^{t}. Payo Juiz da Alfandega de Ls^{a}. De q' houue Lopo d'Albuquerque azeyte, e Jorge d'Albuquerque, e Fran^{co}. da Cunha, e Dona Leonor d'Albuquerque Prioressa do Saluador de Lisboa.

§ Lopo d'Albuquerque azeyte f°. 1°. deste P^{o}. d'Albuquerque foy casado com Dona Isabel f^{a}. de P^{o}. Botelho Juiz da Alfandega de Lisboa. De q' houue Vte. d'Albuquerque, Dona Joana, e Dona C^{na}. Freyras no Mostr^{o}. do Saluador.

[1] Blank in the MS.

§ Vte. d'Albuquerque f^{o}. deste Lopo d'Albuquerque azeyte andou na India em tpo do Grande A^{o}. d'Albuquerque.

§ Jorge d'Albuquerque f°. 2°. de P^{o}. d'Albuquerque azeite, e Irmão de Lopo d'Albuquerque foy casado com Dona C^{na}. f^{a}. de Jan Alz' (Aluarez) da Porta de Mancos de Samtarem dalcunha Rabo d'ovelha hũ homẽ honrrado do Campo. De q' houue P^{o}. d'Albuquerque.

§ P^{o}. d'Albuquerque f^{o}. deste Jorge d'Albuquerque, foy o 1°. Capitão d'Ormuz, q' o fez A^{o}. d'Albuquerque seu thio. Não casou. E houue bastardo Ant^{o}. d'Albuquerq'.

* * * * *

C.

DESCRIPTION OF LOPO SOAREZ

(Successor of Afonso Dalboquerque).

FROM PEDRO BARRETTO DE RESENDE'S "LIVRO DO ESTADO DA INDIA ORIENTAL".

British Museum, Sloane MS. 197, f. 13*b*.

Lopo Soares de Albergaria filho do Chanseller Mor Rui Gomes daluarengua segundo Gouernador e Treseýro no gouerno do Estado da Jndia: Partio de Lisboa em sette de Abril de mil quinhentos e quinze e chegou a Goa em oýto de Setr^{o}. delle auendo tomado Mossambique=Guouernou tres Annos—foý em huma Armada ao Mar Roxo, destrohio Zeýla Çidade de Mouros porq' lhe querião empedir a Agoa e Mantimentos: edificou as fortallezas de Coulã e Collumbo e fes ho Reý tributario—Em seu Tempo se descobrio a Enseada de Bengalla e a Costa de China athe a Çidade de Cantam q' he a prinsipal das provĩsias della por Fernão peres de Andrade tambem se descobrio o Reýno Sião e outras partes do Sul: Leuou de Lisboa para a Yndia hum

Embajxador do presto João q' Afonso De Albuquerq' auia mandado=Acabado o seu gouerno se foẏ para o Reẏno em quinhento e desanoue. As Armadas q' em seu Tempo passarã de portugual ha Jndia se seguem:

ANNO DE 1515. ARMADA 17ª.

TREZE NAOS.

Em sete de Abril do Anno de Mil quinhentos e quinze despedio ElReẏ Dom Manoel Pera a Jndia huma Armada de Treze naos de q' forã por Capitãis: Sr. Lopo Soares De Albergaria gouernador=Simã da Silueẏra filho de Nuno Mĩz da Silura. Sõr de Gois=Dom Guterre de Monrroẏ filho de Dom Afonso de MonRoẏ Cauallejro q' foẏ da Ordem De Alcantara em Castella=Christouã de Tauora filho de Lourenso Pĩz de Tauora Aluaro Telles Barretto filho de João Telles=Franco. de Tauora filho de Po. Lourenso de Tauora sr. do Moguadouro=Dom Joam da Silueẏra filho de Dom Martinho da Silura. Jorge de Brito copeẏro Mor delReẏ Dom Manoel filho de Artur de Brito Alcaẏde Mor De Beẏa=Aluaro Baretto de Montemor ho nouo=Simã de Alcasoua filho de Po. de Alcassoua em huma Nao de Mercadores em q' Fernã Peres de Andrade Auia de Ir por Capitão Ao descobrimento da China cõ quem Auião de Ir Jorge Mascarenhas filho de Joã glĩz Montañt=E Joanes Impolle Mercador Aos quais Lopo Soares auia de dar Nauios na India=Dom Aleẏxo de Menezes por Capitam mor do Mar da Jndia Anto. Lobo Falcã=e Diogo Mendes de Vasconcellos=Embarcarã nestas naos Mtos. fidalgos e Mil e quinhentos homẽs de gerra chegarã a Goa em oẏto de Setro. cõ hos dous Nauios q' ho Anno atras auiã partido em demanda da Ylha de Sam Lourenso destas Naos ficarã Algumas na Jndia seruindo e as mais tomada Carga em Cochim derã a Vella para o Reẏno em Janro. do anno de Mil quintos e desaseis e nellas por Capitã Mor Dom Garsia de Noronha em falta de seu Tio. Afonso de Albuquerq' a quem ElReẏ mandava Jr nellas pera o Reẏno, depois de Entreguar ho gouerno a Lopo Soares: o qual era fallessido.

ANNO DE 1516. ARMADA 18ª.
SEIS NAOS.

Em Vinte e dous de Março do anno de Mil quinhentos e desaseis despedio ElRey Dom Manoel P. A Jndia huma Armada de seis Naos de q' erã capitãis Sr. Joam da Silueẏra Capitam Mor q' foẏ ter a Quilloa cõ hos mastros quebrados=Anto. de Lima q' se perdeo em Sam Lço.=Fransisco de Souza Mansias em Nossa Sora. da Lus q' se perdeo mas saluou a gente Afonso Lopes da Costa Garsia da Costa seu ẏrmã=e Diogo de Vnhos A dar auizo da armada do Soldam do Caẏro q' estaua em Sues As que nam se perderã forã a India em fim de Outro. o Capitam Mor depois de consertar os Mastros foẏ no Anno seguinte a Yndia=os dous Jrmãos com a[s] suas naos e outras das q' Andauã no seruiso do Estado dos Annos atras Partirã para ho Reẏno depois de tomarem Carga em Janro. de mil quinhentos e desasete: e com boa Viagem chegarã a saluamento=Diogo de Vnhos Capitam e pilloto de hum Nauio em q' foẏ dar Auizo da Armada do Soldam como fica dito: com partir des dias depois das naos teue tam bom tempo e fortuna q' chegou hum mes primeẏro q' ellas a Jndia e em breue tempo tornou a Voltar ao Reẏno.

ANNO DE 1517. ARMADA 19ª.
OYTO NAOS.

Em noue de Abril do anno de Mil quinhentos e desasete despedio ElReẏ Dom Manoel pera a Jndia huma Armada de Oẏto naos em duas capitanias ou escoadras=Da primra. q' era de seis Naos erã Capitãis Sr. Pinto. de Saldanha Capitã Mor, em Nossa Sora. da Serra=Tristam de Menezes filho Bastardo de Dom Rodrigo de Menezes Afonso Enrriques de Sepulueda filho de Fernã de Sepulueda=Mel. de Larserda em Sanctiago q' hia para Capitam de Calecut Fernã de Alcasoua q' foÿ o prº. Veedor da fazda.=e Pº. Correa: ou Coresma pera feÿtor de Cochim.

E para Malluquo duas Naos e Capitãis dellas erã Sr. Dom Nuno Manoel Capitã Mor=e Rafael Castanho=Esta Armada chegou a Jndia em desasete de Setro. o Capitam Mor Anto. de Saldanha ficou nella pera seruir de Capitã Mor do Estreÿto de Meca como ja outra Ves ho auia sido na era de mil quinhentos e quatro e as quatro naos q' auiã de voltar depois de ÿrem tomar carga a Cochim partirã pero ho Reÿno em Janro. de mil quintos. e desoÿto Aonde chegarã a saluamto. Neste Anno foÿ a primra. Armada para a China e se leuantou ho primro. Mouro Mallauar cosario a Roubar por mar cõ Nauios.

D.

ACCOUNT OF CURIATE.

British Museum, Sloane MS. 197, f. 115.

DESCRIPSAM DA FORTALLEZA DE CURIATE QUE HE A PRIMEŸRA DO ESTREŸTO DE ORMUS ANTES DE MASCATE.

A fortalleza de Curiate esta doze legoas Antes de Mascatte pa. o Cabo de Rosalgate sitta na Costa braua a Borda da Praÿa Onde nã ha Rio nem enseada nenhuma mais q' hum Ilheo pegado e continuo com a terra q' he somte. Ilheo em lansar ao Mar hum Outeÿro piqueno ho qual em Agoas Vivas fica em nado Neste lugar se abrigã Algumas Embarcasõis de pescadores do Sul e Sudueste porque pera grandes nã ha fundo ao longo delle: Esta neste Ilheo hum Balluarte Couza piquena do tamanho de huma Caza de des passos andantes de prassa Em quadro que se fes pera jugar daquy Artilharia pera ho Campo e Mar: oje nã tem nenhuma= A fortalleza de Curiate em q' fallamos esta aborda da praÿa he Em coadro nam Prefeẏto senã hum pouco mais comprida q' larga. Tera de Comprim[to]. nos dous Lansos de Muro q' vam da praya pera Terra sinquoenta passos Andantes, e de Largura Trinta. O Muro he de Adobes Como todos os mais da Arabia q' fizerã Mouros como a estes de quatro brasos e mea de Altura e tres palmos de grosura, nã tem parapeẏtos maĩs q' seteẏras. Tem quatro Balluartes nos q[tro]. quantos quadrados cõ des passos andantes de Vam cõ seus sobrados e hum delles serue de Viuenda do Capitam portuges q' nelle asiste: E os outros dos Lascarĩs q' nesta fortalleza e em outra mais Interior e no Balluarte do Ilheo estã q' são por todos oẏtenta=hâ mais dentro nesta fortalleza hum Almazem para mantimentos; Outro para Munisõis: hum posso de Agoa sem mais Outra Couza=A fortalleza q' dizemos esta mais Interior desta fica hum tiro De falcã pella terra dentro entre hũs palmares para hos defender he em triangullo, Cada Lanso de Muro de des passos andantes de comprimento tres brasas e mea de Alto: e dous palmos e meio de grosso de Adobes sem parapeẏtos, e cõ seteẏras. Estam duas pouoasõis de Arabios e Baluços pella terra dentro quatroçentos passos distantes huma da Outra de Trezentos Moradores cada hũa pescadores e soldados q' tambem Acodem a defender As terras, Estão sercados cõ seus muros, e Balluartes pera se defenderem: forã estas fortallezas DelReẏ de Ormus onde elle Asistia depois de se perder Ormus quis Entregallas e por essa Cauza as mandou senhorear Ruẏ Freẏre q' Ja nã pode ser sem gerra. He esta Terra de Coriate fresquissima com muẏtos palmares q' fazem quazi todo ho gasto de fortallezas, e se proue Mascate de muẏta Verdura e Mantimentos=Nã hâ aquẏ nenhuma Artilharia mais q' Espingardas dos Lascarĩs q' bastam pera os da terra e tambem em Auendo Gerra se manda logo Vir de Mascatte:—o gasto q' esta fortalleza fas a sua Mag[de]. he o seguinte:—

* * * * *

E.

DESCRIPTION OF ORMUS.

British Museum, Sloane MS. 197, f. 157.

Da fortalleza de Ormus nam trateÿ de fazer descripsão por não ser oÿe do Estado E somente lhe pus aquy a Planta[1] da forma q' era pera memoria, pera q' se algũ Dia D's premitir q' torne a ser do Estado se saber o q' Auia sido, porq' em nosso poder Nam teue Nunqua A Caua aberta de todo como agora tem comessada sÿ : mas como se Nam Cuÿdou q' lhe susedesse Nunqua tal nam tratarã Nunqua de lhe abrir: porq' se lha tiuerã aberta Como o disse Afonso de Albuquerq' puderã dormir seguros Mas a Confiansa dos portuguezes he m^tas. vezes Cauza, e seus descuÿdos, dos maos susesos q' ham tido : O persa lhe mandou Abrir a Çaua e fazer ponte Leuadissa Com Balluartes na porta e pontes da Caua cõ que estã seguros e sera Nessesario hum serco muy dillatado e sem elle se pode perder a esperansa de se tornar a tomar.

Dista Ormus de Mascate sesenta legoas em Altura de Vinte e sete graos : Tinha ElRey de Ormus nesta Ilha huma Çidade muy populloza Onde Elle Reyñia com hos seus fidalgos : Abitada de Christãos e Mouros q' por todos seriam Oÿto Mil Almas = Era muÿ frequentada de Mercadores, Persios :—Turcos = Arabios :—Mogores = Armenios gentios = Tinha sua Mag^de. nella huma Alfandega q' lhe Rendia cada anno duzentos mil pardoas e lhe pudera Render muÿto mais se ouuera ter conta cõ sua fazenda = Era huma dos boas fortallezas q' Auia no Estado, e muy bem Artilhada cõ dous engenhos de poluora e huma Ribeyra de fustas e galleóttas pera as Armadas daquelle Estreÿto = Auia na-

[1] See vol. i, p. 112.

quella fortalleza afora a See e a Mizericordia hum, Conuento de sancto Agost°. com vinte Rellegiozos = Ha Ilha Piquena nã tem mais em sȳ de comprido q' huma Legoa : e de Largo hum quarto de legoa nã tem mais em sȳ que sal, enxofre : e sisternas de Agoa da Chuua : e hum Cano de Agoa q' ElRey de Ormus Achou em Tambaque na põta da Ilha q' he muy sallobre : cõ tudo isto era muẏ prouida e abundante de tudo ho nessesario mais q' outra deste Oriente :— De fronte de Ormus na terra firme da Persia na fralda do mar q' era toda DelRey de Ormus estaua á fortalleza do Bandel do Comoram q' mais he huma Caza forte q' fortalleza Onde hiam Parar todas as Cafillas da Persia, de Lara, e outras Partes.

F.

DESCRIPTION OF BASSORA.

British Museum, Sloane MS. 197, f. 161.

DESCRIPSAM DE BASSORA E VIAGẼIS Q' DE MASCATE SE FAZEM A ELLA.

Fasse tambem Viagem de Mascate pera Basora em todo ho anno em a qual vão tomar huma Ilha q' chamão a da Carga q' esta çento e sinquoenta Legoas de Mascate. E nesta Nauegassã se vam sempre Vendo as terra da Persia Prayas, ou Serras, pera se liurarem da forsa dos ventos Noroestes : Nem viuem Na dita Ylha da Carga mais q' pillotos que seruem de Leuar as embarcasõis a Bassora Onde se vaẏ cõ ho prumo na mão athe entrar os Medõis q' he hum parsel de Lama de tres brasas de fundo : Brassos de Rios com que vẽ Ao Mar o Eufrates cõ Alguma distansia hũs dos Outros em q' hos mesmos pillottos se embarassem nam sabendo has vezes por q' Rio vam e susede Irem m^{tos}. vezes seis e sete dias por hum Rio dentro e como nã Vem huma Balliza q' chamão as Bafras que os sertefica ýrem Pello Rio de Basora tornão a desandar com o Corrente da Agoa a o Buscar he hâ pillotos tam destros q' Pello Cheýro da Lama conhessem ho Rio de Bassora pello qual se vaý doze Legoas athe a Çidade de Bassora a qual esta situada a borda do Rio cõ hum fortalleza muý fermoza e aberto hum Riacho a mão q' A serca q' chamão Sete Larobo dentro do qual se vaý estendendo a Çidade m^a. Populloza e grande em Numero de Cazas com algũs quinze mil Vezinhos q' viuem m^to. juntos e pello Campo muýtas tendas De Arabios das Cabildas da dezerta= He Este Reýno de Bassora do gram Turco porem O Xa q' hoýe o gouerna lhe esta aleuantado cõ Elle Vam a Elle pataxos de athe mil candĩs porq' ho Rio he muýto fundo e todas as mais Embarcasõis piquenas athe Terradas: Leuasse pera Bassora ho mesmo que para a Persia e o q' la Val mais he todo o genero de Drogas, e a Roupa mais fina e presioza porq' se tratã todos muý custozos e o q' se tira he Muýta Tamara, Muýto Alýofar: e muýta Ruýua e toda a fazenda da Persia q' trazem alý os persas a vender aos portuguezes : Vem a Bassora grandes Cafillas de Alepo com m^ta. fazenda de Europa de q' se tras grande soma pera a Yndia=A Cafilla q' vaý de Mascate pera Bassora nã leua mais ordinariam^te. q' hum soo nauio de Armada q' A gouerne porq' guarda não tem nesesidade por nam passarem La os Enemigos de Europa; e na terra não hos Auer mais q' Niquillas que nam sam de momento pera poderem fazer mal hâs Embarcasõis dos portuguezes q' forem com Vigia=He tam grande a Escalla de Bassora q' si todas quantas Embarcasõis forem darão Carga e acharâo Venda porem Ora cõ pouco ora com muýto ganho: como susede em couzas de Mercansia:—Sam hos Arabios De Bassora diferentes de todos os Outros da Arabia porq' sam muý Corpullentos, brãcos, e fracos, e puzillanimes:— Tem ho Baxa quatroçentos homẽs de sua guarda De Espingardas, Achas, e Machadas; Tem dous Mil Agáas q' sam os seus parentes e senhores da terra: Em seis Çentos Vinte e Noue Vindo o Cam de Xiras sobre elle aÿuntou quinze mil homẽs de Armas, porem os mais gente fraquissima E assÿ nam Acabou de tomar Bassora por Morrer o Xa: e a cauza porq' o nam tomara tam de Pressa he porq' Vindo ho Exersito do Xa por terra ha de Vir pella dezerta: e depois ao Longo do Rio por lhe nam faltar Agoa, e quando tornarse ho Turquo trouxer seu Campo ha de Alcansallo no Caminho: e por Mar vindo em Terradas quatro Nauios nossos o podem destroÿr=Sam hos Arabios de Bassora muy dados ao Nefando com terem as Molheres m[to]. fermozas posto q' Algum tanto as desfea pera cõ nosco as Arrecadas e ganchos De prata e ouro que trazem nas Narizes, e tambem algũs persas sam tocados deste Visio. He a terra de Bassora fresquissima de todas as fruÿtas de Portugual: e com grande Copia de Vinhos, de Mais e milhores Vuas q' as do Reyno: Trasse de lâ m[ta]. Marmellada pera a India: pellos Marmellos dalÿ serem milhores q' hos da Persia: Estimão tanto a Algallia por ser o cheyro de q' mais vzão: as Molheres q' dam por hum gato de Algallia hum ginette;

Estam pello Rio asima de Bassora tres Ilhas huma dellas muÿto grande de seis legoas de Comprimento e mais de Legoa e Meia de Largura em Paragẽis Abitada de Bidũis Arabios muÿto fresca e chea de muÿta diuersidade de aruores donde vem a maÿor parte da fruÿta a Bassora chamase Quidre: as outras duas sam piquenas huma dellas de hũa legoa quazi, Alagadissima, e como he de Agoa dosse Viuem nella Moradores nos Altos: A outra esta a Vista De Sete Larabo Ilha mais piquena porem fertellissima de tudo ho q' nella se semea de seuada e Arros, e chea de Pumares= A forma da pas q' tem ho Baxa de Bassora Com ho Estado he de toda a boa Amizade, e a guarda muÿ bem, tirado q' as vezes obrigados das semRezõis q' nos lhe fizemos e forsados dellas nos fazem muÿtas Vexasõis: Aÿudamos a este Baxa de Bassora cõ nossa Armada c[tra]. ho persa: Mas he gente tam puzillanime e Coÿtada q' nenhuma satisfassã da de considerasã ao muỳto q' por elles fazem os soldados e Capitãis de sua Mag[de].=A Alfandega de Bassora he a mais fauorauel pera os portuguezes q' outra nenhuma nem nas suas mesmas terras, em tanto q' leuã os Mercadores as fazendas pera sua Caza e La lhe vã abrir os fardos; e depois quando se querem vir vão a alfandega e pagam, E alem do grande fauor na[1] baxado porq' se vender a fazenda Descontã aos Mercadores e lhe dã huma pessa cõforme a contia do q' pagou hâ Alfandega=Temos em Bassora duas Igreiỳas huma de Carmellitas, Outra de Agostinhos Exercitando os sacramentos cõ hos portuguezes e mercadores e passageỳros de toda a nasã Christãos e cõ hos catiuos destes em q' fazem m[to]. seruico a D's pella acolheỳta q' tem aquỳ depois de fogidos pera os Mouros: como vam m[tas]. vezes donde forsados cõ alguma nesessidade tornã pera nos achando nestes Padres tudo ho nesessario athe q' hos tornã A Entregar a seus Donos: Estã aquỳ m[tos]. Armenios Christãos q' se sogeỳtã a estes Padres Cuỳas Molheres comungam Cada Domingo muỳtas dellas=Esta Vezinho a Este Reỳno de Basora O Reyno de Bombareca Ja oỳe sogeito Ao Persa o qual posto q' ho Rey he Mouro os mais doz seus Vassallos sam Christãos de Sam João que seguem a Leỳ de Christo Nosso Sõr porem com m[tos]. Erros e particullarmente porq' ho Bautismo o fazem pello Rio dizendo dizendo[1] quando Lansã a Agoa sobre a Cabessa Eu te bautizo Assỹ Como Sam João Bautizou a Christo e não tem Missa nem nas nossas terras a Ouuem: Viuem muỳtos em Bassorâ embayres[1] Apartado dizem q' querem Vir para ho Estado da India obedesser a Igreiya Romana sam muỳ soberbos com serem todos offissiais de Ouriues Carpentr[os]. ferreỳros e espadr[os]. Sam As Molheres todas Castissimas mas particullarmente As Cazadas. O modo de cazarem he leuaremnos ao Rio despidos da sintura pera sima e pera baỳxo quando muỳto A Molher cõ hum pano branquo muỳ delgado e singello, e

[1] *Sic*, MS.

juntando os cachassos lhe dam com hum Caẏadinho humas pancadinhas na cabessa cõ pallauras de seremonias e depois estam Ambos deuedidos hum do outro hum mes ao Cabo do qual tempo os tornã a leuar ao Rio Onde lhe dizem Outras pallauras sem se ajuntarem e depois se lhe consede o Aẏuntam^{to}. Carnal: Serão todos trinta mil: ho Rey de Bombareca folga m^{to}. q' se lhe vão de seu Reẏno porq' por serem tantos se teme delles e os despede tomandolhe As Armas= Esta gente escreueo e mandou seus embayxadores Ao Conde do Linhares Vizorrey da India pera q' desse Ordem pera se poderem Vir pera este Estado a qual elle mandou logo a Mascatte e com ella Veo logo huma pouqua desta gente e parte delles ficarã em hũa das fortallezas do Estreẏto q' ho Conde lhe mandou dar pera elles a pouoarem e Viuerem nella: E a outra passou a India e o Conde os mandou a Çeẏlam e a outras partes do estado pera Verem as terras determinando de hos passar qua todos pera ter gente pera as gerras e Armadas porq' he boa gente de Armas: e sera de prestimo na India=De Bassora ha hum Brasso de Rio q' chamã ho Rio de Catifa q' sem saẏr ao Mar vaẏ dar A esta Çidade q' esta situada ao Longo de hum Riacho q' no fundo he lamarã e neste Lama tẽ de pedra mea Legoa como Ilha: Ao Longo do Mar La fora de Ordinario Carregam e descarregam as Embarcasõis grandes pera Vazias poderem entrar pelo Riacho, e nelle ficarem em seco em sima da dita Lama a Ilha de fora tem hum forte Couza piquena q' se chama Tanora=Catifa esta na Arabia Felix de fronte dos baẏxos de Verde, q' estã ao Sul antes de Basora Mais de oẏtẽta Legoas=He esta Escalla de Catifa mediana de fazendas porq' dous Nauios q' Vam de portuguezes a enchem aonde. he so mercador o Baxa e seus dous filhos per onde fica ho trato muẏto Roim e nã ha mercador q' compre duas corẏas de panos saluo estes, ou outros q' vem de fora q' sempre andam atemorizados e escondidos porq' em sabendo tem Alguma Couza Logo lha apanham o Baxa e seus filhos=

As fazendas q' se leuam sam Roupas prettas do Sinde e de Cambaya poucas fazendas e poucas sortes dellas : As que se tirã sam muytos e muy fermozos ginetes os Milhores de Todo Oriente q' nam passa o Milhor de duz^tas. Pataquas e daly para bayxo muytos athe sinq^ta. e sesenta pataquas : muyto e imnumerauel Alyofar grosso e meudo quazi todo o de Barem q' Aly passa em Rezam dos pescadores q' ho vam pescar serem destas prayas : Esta hê a sustansia Da fazenda q' Aly se vay buscar em q' se trazem empregados m^tos. Mil Cruzados q' por se não poderem leuar todos em fazenda pella terra a nã guastar hos leuam em dinheyro de Pratta de Larĩs e Abessis de q' atras fallamos : Tras-se tãobẽ Tamara de q' ha na terra Abundansia mas não tam boa como ā de Bassora : fas-se tambem Congo q' he a Tamara tanto q' comessa a picar de Vermelho a tirão e cozem no fogo em grandes Caldeyras de Agoa e depois a Lansã na praya a enxugar nos Areais athe q' fiqua muy dura : e dura m^to. tempo desta sorte e se tras a India e se pode Leuar ao Cabo do Mundo he este Congo de Catiffa mais meudo, e mais duro, Vermelho e mais dosse q' ho de Mascate e de mais duro= Ha grandes Cabildas de Arabios pella terra dentro q' he a dezerta onde viuem separados com seus capitãis=Ha huma fortalleza pella terra dentro a q' chamã Lassa de donde saem os prefeitos ginetes de q' se atras falla : O modo dos Casam^tos. dos Naturais da terra a dentro hê deste modo= qualquer homem q' tem filha e he Requerido per Algum mansebo solteyro q' lha de em Cazam^to. por molher o pay sae cõ ella Ao Campo Onde a poem em hũa tenda e sae o q' a Requere tambem ao Campo, e se poem em som de Batalha ; e de ordinario tem Competidores q' lhe contradizem ho tal Cazam^to: Ou pella quererẽ tãobẽ ou por lhe acharem a elle defeytos E assỹ se desafiam e se poem em pees sobre Camellos Ligeyros e com seus Cayados nas mãos trauã battalha da qual sae vensedor o que mais forte, ou destro foy ou teue milhor fortuna esse leua a Noyua saluo ouuer outro q' lhe contradiga porq' ha de venser athe nã ter contradissã E assỹ fica Onrrado e Rico porq' lhe ficão hos despoẏos de todos q' venseo :—O Baxa de Catifa obedesse ao Turco porq' ho he de Nassam, Mas não se fia delle, nem lhe vaẏ pessoalm[te]. obedesser senão manda filho ou quem lhe paresse dar a obediensia.

G.

DESCRIPTION OF SINDE.

British Museum, Sloane MS. 197, f. 167*b*.

NAUEGASÕIS E VIAGEIS DO SINDE E SUA DESCRIPSAM.

De Mascate se fas Viagem pera O Sinde desde Outobro athe quinze de Março com Ventos Vestes, e Noroestes e Suis: q' sam çento e Trinta Legoas Esta O Sinde na Costa da Persia=A Barra do Rio Indo q' por aquẏ desemboca Ao Mar de Marca ao Nordeste Sudueste por entre hum banco cõ a boca da Barra de fundo de duas brasas e mea de Baxamar e de preamar sinquo e de Largo hum Oẏtauo de Legoa e daquẏ se vaẏ estendendo este banco pera ho Leste athe A Restinga de Doba tam nomeada o parsel sera de tres athe sete Brasas de fundo, tanto q' entra Março he hum Ynferno neste Banco cõ hos trauesõis mas aynda Assỹ se sae da Barra, e entra athe Junho=Tem outra boca este Rio Yndo q' vem a hũas Ilhas q' chamã As Monaras tres legoas da outra para o Noroeste a qual esta oẏe entupida Mas Nã Pera Embarcasõis piquenas—Nem pera surgirem em enseadas as Embarcasõis grandes mas nam pera ẏrem dentro=A causa de se entupir a dita barra foẏ por os portuguezes entrarem por ella a dar hum grande asoute em huma Çidade mas com Embarcasõis piquenas podem ẏr dentro a fazer Resgate.

Tem ho Rio jndo outro brasso por onde entra no mar oÿto legoas do Sinde Pero Ho Leste a q' chamão Daraÿa. Esta barra esta na cabessa da Restinga de Debâ Tem hum grande Parsel a boca do Rio de mais de tres quartos de Legoa na Entrada de huma brassa e quarto de fundo per onde he muÿ dificultozo entrarem embarcasõis saluo forem fustas e essas muÿto piquenas porq' he de Area muÿ Perigozo=Hâ Nauegassã deste Rio pera a Entrada de Cacha e Nagana em Nauios piquenos q' chamã Cotias muÿ frequente e de proueÿto por este se vaÿ tambem ao Reÿno do Sinde= O grande e prinsipal de q' tratamos fas seis ou sete voltas q' fazem quatro legoas athe chegar cõ Ban Ar Bandel aonde esta a Alfandega em q' hos nossos Nauios vam Anchorar e Lansar, e tomar Carga: Vam a este porto muÿtas embarcasõis de toda a costa da India desde a ponta do proprio Sinde athe o Cabo de Comorim; deste Bandel onde hâ hũa Pouoassã muÿto grande e estendida e huma fortalleza piquena fraca e caÿda, Ao Reÿno do Sinde ha doze Legoas de Caminho por terra em q' tem tres Passagẽis de proprio Rio Indo q' em Coracol vim correndo por Estas terras onde hâ muÿtas Aldeas de considerassão: pello Rio asima se nauega em embarcasõis piquenas q' leuam estas fazendas ao dito Reÿno pera La se guastarem. O Reÿno he huma Çidade m^to^. grande com mais de çento e sinquoenta mil vezinhos de Cazas meudas de pedra e cal com grandes terrados; mas o ordinario he serem todas de Varichas cubertas de Barro podre amassado cõ palha q' ho fas muÿ duro: Viuẽ muÿ juntos q' se ouuerão de Abitar como os portuguezes nem sinquo tanto do campo da dita Çidade lhe bastaria: He gente muÿ fraca dellicioza, e superstisioza e Mentiroza: Mouros e gentios Viuem todos misturados=Foÿ o Reÿno antigam^te^. de hum Reÿ gentio, de cuio ospissio e emparo se veo valler o Rey Mogor antigamente e depois pello tempo adiante lhe fez traÿsã, e tomou ho Reÿno cuio oÿe hê: e por elle he gouernado com seu Nababo Mogor cõ muýtos capitãis Mogores e he o Reýno do Sinde em sỹ tam rico q' vem a elle capitam q' vense de quartel quinze mil pataquas e dalý para baýxo athe oýto, e quatro: e destes Muýtos: He hum Cano o Sinde por onde se enche o Reýno do Mogor de muýto Alýofre e perolas de Barem; e de grande Cantidade de ouro e de prata: Muýtas drogas do Sul: muýta Tamara, Congo; Cocos; Copre e Algodam q' lhe leuam os portuguezes e as mais nasõis q' la uã: porq' týrã somente Roupas; Anil, Asucar: e Anfião:—

A terra he muý fertil de mantim^tos^. Trigo: Arros: gerzellim; Milho; Mango; Seuada, e todas as carnes tirado porco: m^tos^. Carn^ros^. e muý boñs: Mas nã da ho Reýno do Sinde Bastante Algodam pera hos m^tos^. offissiais q' tem: porq' so na Çidade Referida hâ trinta mil Teares, e dahý pera sima e assỹ se val do Algodam de Cache e Nagana: E he tam grande o trato desta terra q' a quantos Nauios e Embarcasõis forem a ella a todas dara Carga cõ auer nauio de Portuguezes q' leua em pratta, ouro, e Alýofre quatroçentos mil pataquas de Cabedal, e destes hâ m^tos^: E athe da moeda se paga direýtos cõ grandes tiranias na Alfandega a tres e meio por çento q' A uallia em dobro e aýnda mais da Vallia das fazendas. Com q' vem a pagar a sette e mais por çento—Mas como os Mogores q' aquý asistem sam muý leuados do Interesse cõ qualquer couza se lhe tapa a boca nos grãdes descaminhos q' hos portuguezes lhe fazem do q' leuã—

Vam aquý nas Monsõis muýtas Embarcasõis de portuguezes e se juntarão em seisc^tos^. trinta e tres vinte e huma embarcasõis entre galleotas pataxos fustas cõ algũs duzentos portuguezes porq' como pera estas partes, e pera ho estreýto nã hâ Ladrões Mallauares nem dos naturais, andam cõ muý poucos soldados: Tem ha dita Çidade grande do Sinde huma Igreiýa dos padres Carmelitas descalços muý bem ornada e consertada: q' posto q' se nã fassa Christã nenhum natural porq' nenhũ se fas Christã na terra, senã quando os leuamos fora della porq' entã he muý fassýl, cõ tudo he muý grande auxillio p^{a}. os portuguezes e mais christaõs: porq' viuerã ja e viuem portuguezes cazados na dita Çidade, e de ordinario Jnuernã em quanto se nã fas nauegassã algũs portuguezes em sima e embayxo na qual ýgreiýa, ha de ordinario dous padres Carmellitas q' se sustentã das Esmollas dos portuguezes cõ q' viuem muý bem= e na Era de seis Çentos Trinta e quatro emfadados os Mouros do tanger do sino desta igreiýa a derrubarã e tomarã tudo ho q' nella auia de ornamentos e mais fabrica: Mas depois tornarã a dar tudo e a fazer a igreiýa=:—

Como ho dito Rio he muy caudallozo e vay tanto pella terra a dentro Nauegam por ella asima m^{tas}. embarcasõis de quatroç^{tos}. Candĩs com todas estas Fazendas pera os Reýnos do Mogor pondo muýto tempo a ýda pellas grandes Correntes, e muý pouca a Vinda. He gente esta q' em hum Cazamento de hum gentio gastã quatro e sinquo Mil Rupias: e cada Rupia tem M^{a}. [*i.e.*, meia] Pataqua; e has vezes quarenta e sinq^{ta}. mil conforme os cabedais andando em perpetuos Banquetes, e deýxam perder grandissimos contratos por hũa festa a q' chamã Tamaxa, comendo muýto e muý porcamente e tanto he assỹ q' m^{tos}. perdem as Mõsõis da Embarcassã e nauegassã por se Darem a suas festas: Vem as ditas embarcasõis do Rio carregados de m^{to} anil Asuqueres e Jagra e gasta a terra todos os annos mais de des mil Candĩs de Manteýgaa=:

No bandol de Baýxo temos onde esta a Alfandega huma Ygreiýa em q' viuem dous Rellegiozos Agostinhos A quem paga sua Mag^{de}. mas ho seu sustento prinsipal he das Esmollas dos portuguezes posto q' lhas nam Dam com tanta Largueza, como aos Carmellitas: Viuem Ao Redor da Igreiýa hos Portuguezes em cazas de Aluger: ondi tambem viuem as Molheres publicas. e hum tiro de falcã pera a Terra dentro esta a pouoassã de Mouros e gentios Todos misturados: Sam aquý tratados os Portuguezes muýto mal com grandes perrarias de q' elles mesmos sam a Cauzą porq' fazem çem mil Asintes, e semRezõis aos Naturais, dandolhe muÿtas pancadas athe chegarem a mattallos de q' tudo se limã Com dinheÿro e athe aos mesmos a quem fazem ho mal, os fazem callar cõ qualquer couza q' lhe dam Porq' he gente muÿ baÿxa e amiga de Interesse=Amarrã hos portuguezes os fardos de Roupa, e mais fazendas em suas cazas a q' vem ver e escriuer os Menistros Mogores: da qual amarrassã lhe passã Lista, e chapão os fardos cõ suas Chapas a q' depois vem hos mesmos amarradores a noÿte, a tornar a encher os fardos de outras sortes de Roupas melhores; e quando pella menham vem tornar a ver as chapas as acham muÿ boas com q' furtã muÿtos direÿtos na Alfandega pellas grandes aualliasõis q' nella lhe fazem q' ordinariam[te]. he mais da a metade.

Tem no Sinde Sua Mag[de]. feÿtor q' serue de Aquiatar todas as Alterasõis, e couzas q' se mouem entre nos, e os Naturais, porq' lhe tem muÿto Respeÿto: Nam tem ordenado da fazenda de Sua Mag[de]. senã humas Liberdades de quarenta por çento q' lhe dam hos Mouros menos do q' leuã aos mais portuguezes e isto so nas suas fazendas: Mas elle adquire muÿtas cõ q' vem a fazer hum ordenado conueniente=Tem Liberdade de poder fazer Vinho q' como he contra A leÿ dos Mouros tem muÿto proueÿto, por lho Virem cõprar de Noÿte =O vinho he de Jagra, e de huma casca de huma Aruore q' chamã Joto: mas o mais de q' Viue o feÿtor he de sua Mercansia e Nauio porem cõ a lÿberdade de feÿtor espanca Mouros, e da em todos e vaÿ gritar em caza do gouernador estando em ÿanta de gouerno: E Ronca q' ha de mandar vir Armada: E assÿ he obedessido=E entrando hum Pataxo Olandes em Jan[ro]. de seisçentos trinta e dous no Sinde com prepozitto de Alÿ fazer Comersio e feÿtoria pera nos tirar dalÿ entrando com muÿtas Drogas e grandes pessas de dattas: Ao q' ho nosso feÿtor encontrou fazendo grandes gritas e couzas e ameasando os Mouros q' logo se sahia dalÿ cõ todos os portuguezes : E com todos se foẏ ao Nababo e disse q' era ẏmpossiuel q' portuguezes e Olandezes asestissem Alẏ q' visse quais lhe estaua milhor chamando muẏtos oprobrios aos Olandezes q' elles sofrerã e se pos o feẏtor cõ ho Nababo em tal estado que pedio o Nababo Ao feẏtor q' lhe desse firmã pera q' hos portuguezes nã fizessem mal ao dito pataxo dos Olandezes : E contudo Auizou ao Capitam geral Ruẏ freẏre a Mascate : O qual não mandou a Armada sobre elle : porque naquelle Rio estão debaẏxo da seguransa do Reẏ Mogor, E seria quebrar ho Porto e dar mao trato aos Mercadores porem os olandezes se foram logo muẏ enfadados da Ma ospedagem q' lhe fizeram e de ver quam mais estimados alẏ erão hos portuguezes do q' elles podiam Vir a ser E na Verdade o sõr deste porto do Sinde q' he Asefacã grande priuado do Mogor os estimara alẏ muẏto : Mas ho Nababo de Surratte lhe disse cõ muẏta liberdade q' se consentia nelle olandezes, ou Ingrezes Avia de perder logo ho grande comersio de Surratte porq' se lhe auiam La de passar : Ao q' teue o Mogor muẏto Respeẏto porq' entendeo ser assẏ Verdade e a esse Resp[to]. os nam acolherão no Sinde.

H.

DESCRIPTION OF CHAUL.

British Museum, Sloane MS. 197, f. 236.

DESCRIPSAM DA FORTALLEZA E ÇIDADE DE CHAUL.

A fortalleza e Çidade de Chaul esta Çita na costa da Terra firme do Reyno do Decam em Altura de Oẏto graos e dous terços da Banda do Norte na Entrado de hum Rio de Agoa salgada : Hum quarto de Legoa da boca delle pera dentro posta ha borda da praẏa da banda esquerda quando se entra toda sercada de Muro com Noue Balluartes e quatro Reuezes nos mesmos Balluartes os quais estam na forma seguinte= Ho Balluarte Sam Pedro q' cahe sobre ho Rio tem hum Camello de Marca mayor pedreyro q' tira balla de desoyto Liuras—O Balluarte Sancta Crus q' se segue a este nã tem nenhuma Artilharia e esta por entulhar=O Balluarte Sam Paulo q' vay cõtinuando estão (*sic*) bem por entulhar e sem Nenhuma Artilharia=O Balluarte Sanctiago q' se segue a este tem duas pessas s^r^. (*i.e.*, saber) hum Canhão Reforsado q' tira balla de sesenta e sinquo Liuras=e hum Camello q' tira desaseis de pillouro de pedra=Tem hum Reues este Balluarte aonde esta huma pessa de ferro=No Balluarte q' esta De fronte de Sam Paulo esta hũa pessa de Bronze por dentro ferrada de ferro Collebrina Joga desaseis Libras de balla= Este Balluarte tem dous Reuezes hum tira para ho Balluarte Sanctiago cõ duas bombardeyras em huma dellas esta huma pessa de bronze=O Balluarte Sam Denis q' se vay segindo a este nã tem nenhuma Artilharia: No Reues q' tem q' cae pera a praya esta hum Pedreyro de ferro de Catorze Liuras =O Balluarte Sam Fran^co^. q' fica sobre o mar pera A Costa braua tem tres pessas de Metal. S^r^. huma Aguia q' tira quarenta Liuras De Balla: hum Canhão Reforsado q' tira sinq^ta^. Liuras: hum Leão q' tira outras sinq^ta^. todas de Pillouro de ferro=O Balluarte Sam Domingos q' se vay seguindo a este nã tem pessa Alguma=O Balluarte q' esta sobre a porta dos Cazados tem hum Canhã de Metal que joga balla de Vinte e quatro Liuras de ferro=No Cais junto ha see estão duas pessas de Metal, huma he Canhão de catorze Liuras de pillouro, e a outra da mesma forma=Toda esta Artilharia q' sam treze pessas estão em seus Repayros: porem bẽ claro se vee quam falta esteya esta Çidade de Artilharia estando m^tos^. Balluartes e Reuezes sem ella e auendo tambem mister os q' A tem alguma Mais :=:—

A Altura destes Muros hê muy Varia porq' pella banda de terra pella m^ta^. gerra q' por ella costuma ter são muyto mais Alto q' pella do Mar e Rio: e assy̆ tem quatro Brassas e m[a]: athe sinquo: de des palmos Cada brassa e pella do mar e Rio tres brassas athe tres e m[a]: cõ seus parapeÿtos de sinquo athe seis e sete palmos: A grossura destes Muros hê des palmos na Rais e vem Acabar em seis: Nam tem entulho nenhum pella banda de dentro, nem Caua pella de fora porq' nesta Çidade sam hos Arrabaldes m[to]. largos e quando ha gerra se defendem todos=Os Balluartes sam de diferentes formas e não estam aÿnda prefeÿtos nem no Entulho nem na Altura Cuÿas obras estam Remetidas por ordem de sua Mag[de]. Aos padres da Companhia=O Capitam Viue dentro dos Muros em huma serca de Ladrilho como a de Bassaÿm aonde esta o Tronquo=A gente q' mora dos Muros a dentro desta Çidade sam duzentos Cazados portuguezes em Cazas muÿ boas todas de pedra e Cal: e sinq[ta]. pretos Christãos da Terra q' hũs e outros tem cada hum seu Escrauo que possa tomar Armas q' são as prinsipais espingardas e toda a mais sorte dellas. E a cauza de serem os Escrauos tam poucos he por fogirem todos pera a Terra firme dos Mouros=E Viuem alem destes nos Arrabaldes Referidos e em muÿtos palmares e ortas dos portuguezes q' estão pouqua distansia da Çidade e quazi debaÿxo da Artilharia de seus Muros quinhentos homẽs cazados pretos Christãos e Gentios, e os mais delles offissiaÿs de offissios mecanicos, e athe os chaudarĩs q' sam os q' sobem hâs palmeÿras a Colher os Cocos e fruÿto delles nos seruirã ja na gerra cõtra os mesmos Mouros naturais, e senhores da Terra=

Ha nesta Çidade dous almazẽis hum de sua Mag[de]. outro da Çidade os quais estam prouidos Bastantemente de poluora e Monisõis e petrechos pera qualquer ocasiã de gerra athe se prover de Goa: como sam todas as fortallezas e Çidades do estado nas gerras e couzas extra Ordinarias=Ha nesta Çidade de Chaul dos Muros a dentro seis Igreiÿas. S[abe]r. A see:=Mizericordia=Sam Paulo q' he Conuẽto dos Padres da Companhia=Hum Most[ro]. de Sam Domingos=Outro de Sam Fran[co].=outro de Sancto Agóstinho os quais sustenta

Sua Mag^de. pagando a Cadahum e ao Capitam e mais offisiais o q' se Vera nas cõtas adiante=A barra desta Çidade de Chaul he a mais Bem guardada q' hâ neste Estado pella Courassa do Morro q' Atras dissemos fica sobre ella Com q' nam pode entrar nem saÿr nenhuma couza senã por baÿxo das pessas da misma Courassa. Tem a barra hum Banco de Area q' a atrauessa pello M^o. do qual fica o Canal q' demora ao sueste de baÿxamar nã tem fundo mais q' oÿto, e noue palmos: e em agoas Viuas tem tres brassas=E em entrando da barra pera dentro fica ho Rio mas largo e cõ fundo bastante pera Estarem nelle m^tas. Embarcasõis sem auer couza q' lhe fassa dano=A Costa desta fortalleza Corre Ao mesmo Rumo q' a de Damã de Norte a Sul mais alguma couza para o Sueste=As Correntes sam tambem as mesmas tirado q' como fica mais afastado Da Enseada de Cambaÿa não sam as Mares cõ tanta furia como as q' temos Referido= E as Monsõis de Ventos sam tambem as mesmas=

As Viagẽis q' se fazem deste porto de Chaul sam m^tas. e pera m^tas. partes porq' como Estes Moradores nam tem fazendas de q' possam viuer, Como os de Damã e Bassaym dãose mais ha mercansia: E viuem puram^te. do trato e Nauegassam=Fasse Viagem de Chaul pera Cambaÿa em Nauios de Remo: e posto q' podem Ir e Vir em Todo ho Tempo não Andão senã em Cafillas em Companhia da Armada q' lhe da guarda a Respeÿto dos m^tos. paros de q' Aquella Costa anda sempre chea pello Verão: E assÿ nam fazem mais q' Duas Viagẽis em Verão: Ho q' leuã sam ao maÿor parte Cocos, Areca, Canilha, Pimenta, e todas as mais Drogas do Sul: Crauo, Nos Masta; e tambem as do China como Pao, Lousa, Tutunaga, o q' trazem sã Roupas, Anfiam, e Anil=Fasse tambem Viagem de Chaul pera Mascate e dalÿ pera Bassora; Leuando ho prinsipal Arros, e Roupas de Cambaÿa Cocos e Copra q' sã hos mesmos cocos passados ao Sol: de q' se Vza m^to. neste Oriente, e o mais q' atras fica Referido=A jornada he nos tempos q' temos apontado nas descripsõis de Damã E Bassaÿm As embarcasõis sam pataxos e galleotas: o q' se tras de la tãobem fica ja atras Referido=Nauegasse tambem de Chaul pera Mossambique pera onde vaÿ hós mais dos Annos hum pataxo cõ Lisensa do dono da Viagem em Janeÿro athe os prim^{ros}. de Feu^{ro}.=Leua Roupas de Cambaÿa das q' seruẽ pera os Cafres q' são Canequĩs pretos a q' chamão Serqueÿra e muÿta contaria q' lhe vem de Ballagatte q' sao hũas Continhas de Vidro q' costumã trazer os Cafres em q' hâ m^{to}. grande ganho por cuÿo Resp^{to}. he Esta Viagem so do Capitam; ho q' de la se tras he Marfim, Ouro, e Cafres=Vam tambem embarcasõis de Chaul pera Manilla e Chÿna leuão pera a China algumas Roupas de Cambaÿa e de Norte como Canequĩs e Teadas e algũas couzas de Mascatte como amendoas passas de Vuaâs, Ensenso; pucho q' he hum pao q' vem de Cambaÿa e serue pera Lâ=e o mesmo pera Manilla Acresentando Muÿtas farinhas de trigo, Anchoras, e ferro: de q' ja se dise q' em Chaul auia Muÿto q' lhe vinha da terra adentro do Ballagate de q' tambem se fazem falcõis de ferro Batido: partem pera Estas Viagẽis desde fim de Março athe todo Maÿo=He este ferro de Chaul alguntanto grosso e assÿ ho mais pera q' serue he pera Estas obras grossas de Anchoras e falcõis: não deÿxando tã bem de seruir pera pregadura. Chaul de sima q' dizemos paga Vinte mil Larĩs de pareas he hũa pouoassã de Mouros q' esta hum quarto de Legoa da nossa Çidade pera a banda de Leste q' he a do Sertão em q' viuẽ m^{tos}. offisiais Tessilõis de sedas q' se fazem na dita pouoassã de toda sorte e Marseneÿros de obras de Escritorios e Marchetaria de q' tãobem hâ m^{ta}. abundãsia e outros offissiais e tãobem hâ m^{tos}. Mouros de gerra e sera a dita pouoasã de tres mil Vezinhos mas sem Muro nem fortalleza alguma.

I.

DESCRIPTION OF THE FORTRESS OF ONOR.

British Museum, Sloane MS. 197, f. 285.

DESCRIPSAM DA FORTALLEZA DE ONOR.

A fortalleza de Onor Esta na terra firme do Concani do Ballagatte desoÿto legoas de Goa para o sul Em Altura de Catorze graos e vinte e noue Minutos foÿ conquistada e feÿta pello Vizorreÿ Dom Luis d'Ataÿde que depois foÿ Conde da Atouguia, No Anno de quinhentos sesenta e oÿto=Esta plantada esta fortalleza hum quarto de Legoa da Barra de hum Rio de Agoa salgada q' Vem saÿr ao Mar, em Sÿma de huma Rocha toda sercada do Muro de tres Brassas de Altura e quatro palmos de Largura cõ seus parapeÿtos: Tem em Roda quatro ç^{tas}. Brassas: dentro dos quais Muros fica a pouoassã dos Cazados e Moradores q' sam Trinta Branquos=Tem esta Pouoassã e Muros Onze Balluartes em Roda feÿtos em forma Redonda e são estes Balluartes por sima cubertos de Telha em hos quais estã Repartidas quatro pessas de Artilharia Tres de Bronze e hũa de ferro—Huma de doze e outra de des e outra de seis liuras de Pillouro de ferro: e hum Camello pedreÿro de desoÿto Libras de pillouro de pedra=Tem mais oÿto falcõis=dous Bersos, e hum Canhão tudo de Metal: que para a copia dos ditos Balluartes e grandeza delles paresse Couza Muÿ desconforme porem como esta preuensã não foÿ feÿta pera os Enemigos de Europa de q' oÿe mais nos tememos, ouueram que bastaua para os da Terra: hum dos ditos Balluartes he Caualleÿro a todos os outros=He esta fortalleza de Onor muÿ fresca sadia e de Bons Ares, e tem muÿto boas Agoas de Maneÿra q' se tem pella melhor nestas Couzas q' hâ neste Estado porq' dos Muros a dentro tem os Cazados Napulle piqueno destrito muÿtas ortas em suas Cazas q' lhe dam Muÿ boas Vuas e fruÿta de Espinho exsellente=Não ha Alfandega em Onor porq' nam tem nenhũ Comersio, e so viuem aquelles Cazados dos quarteis de Sua Mag[de]. e de Algumas Terras De Arros q' semeão fora dos Muros: e Palmares q' tem: porq' A terra como fica dito he muỳ fertil: e so lhe Vem de fora algumas gundras das Ilhas de Maldiua com Caurim caỳro, e Cocos: Tirase desta fortalleza e suas terras algum Arros: m[to]. menos q' de nenhuma outra fortalleza do Canara, alguma madeỳra de Mastros e Vergas de q' Abunda o Mato da Terra dentro mas cõ Lisensa do Reỳ della sobre q' nam deỳxa de auer algũs incõuenientes, Alguma Aleca e Cato e Algumas Beatilhas q' se fazem pella Terra dentro=o q' mais se tira desta fortalleza e Terras Vezinhas he m[ta]. pimenta a melhor q' hâ na India q' se compra por Contrato a o Reỳ da Terra o qual he de Nassão gentio chamado o Reỳ do Equerỳ, ou Çanara como se ỳntitulla Esta provinsia de q' he sõr e por Nome proprio Vira Bador naỳque o qual todos os Reỳnos de q' he sõr na dita prouinsia erdou ha seis annos de seu Avoo Vintapa naỳque q' hâ trinta e dous Annos as cõquistou Desde o Rio de Merizeu athe o Canharotto q' sam trinta e seis Legoas de Costa tomando os aos Reỳs cuỳos erão e os tizouros fazendolhe m[tas]. Tiranias com q' tinha ayuntado grandissimas Riquezas=E hâ seis annos q̃' por morte de seu Auo se lhe leuantarã Todos os Ditos Reis com quem tiue m[tas]. Batalhas e Encõtros ora de perda ora de ganho athe q' hũ seu Tio foỳ leuantado por Reỳ chamado Virapa naỳque o qual estando ja em posse do Reỳno Morreo em breue dizem q' por negoseasã deste Virabadar naỳque o qual tornando a tomar posse do Reỳno foỳ conquistando seus Enemigos athe q' hâ dous Annos os acabou de Venser e fazer se sõr de tudo o q' lhe deỳxou seu Auô=Tem o estado asentado pas cõ Este Reỳ de amigo de Amigos, e enemigo de Enemigos e que todos os seus portos nos serã muỳ franquos para Tirarmos delles Todo o mantimento q' ouuer por q' hos do Canara sam donde vem Todo o Arros q' sustenta Esta Çidade de Goa e seus Contornos: porem Como Este Reẏ esta muẏ soberbo pellas grandes Vitorias q' tem alcansado nam guarda isto como esta obrigado particullarmente pella fortalleza q' ho Conde de Linhares Vizorreẏ fes a seu pezar Na Ilha do Cambollim=

O poder q' Este Reẏ tem oẏe he de quarenta pera sinq^{ta}. Mil homẽs Canaras q' se tem por huma das Milhores gentes de Armas q' hâ neste Estado, e Raramente Tĩuemos gerra cõ Elles q' leuassemos o Milhor=Mas nã sam traẏdores para de Baẏxo de fee e pallaura de pas fazerem a sua: como alguñs Naturais deste Oriente=A leẏ q' professã he gentillica como hȯ seu Reẏ de q' hâ Muẏta diuersidade, e sam Raros os q' se conuertem a Nossa sancta fee Cathollica e assẏ̃ Nenhuma Igreiẏa Temos em suas Terras nem ho Reẏ se entende as consentira=Nã se sabe q' este Reẏ tenha athegora comersio nem Commonicassã cõ nassã Alguma Estrangeẏra fora dos portuguezes, q' Como Vassallo do Idalcam e q' lhe paga pareas: paresse q' ho Imita nisto: posto q' nam sabemos ser athegora cometido cõ a dita Comonicasã=A Barra desta fortalleza de Onor he de hum Rio de Agoa salgada q' vaẏ m^{to}. pella Terra dentro atrauesa a pello meo hum Banco de Area como a todas as deste Estado pello m^{o}. Do qual tem Hum Canal de sinquo Brassas de Largo, e doze athe quinze palmos de fundo por onde nam podem entrar por elle embarcasõis q' ho demandem maẏor senão em Ocazião de Agoas viuas: e dentro no Rio hâ fundo de Vinte e sinquo athe trinta palmos. Nã hâ nesta Costa mais Correntes, Ventos, e Monsõis q' hos q' temos dito no prinsipio della, de Terrenhos e Virasõis: Corre o mesmo Rumo de Norte a Sul metendo alguma couza pera ho susueste e Noroeste=Tem esta fortalleza de Onor Offissiais e presidio q' se vera abaẏxo e o q' se lhe paga de prezente e o q' se lhe pagaua antigam^{te}. q' he ho seguinte=

* * *

J.

DESCRIPTION OF THE MALDIVE ISLANDS.

British Museum, Sloane MS. 197, f. 377.

A Planta que se segue he das Ilhas de Maldiua Vaẏ aquẏ como Outras Muẏtas q' não sam do Estado. Escriuem Muẏtos Autores q' e huma Corda de Onze mil Ilhas Intitullase Reẏ dellas hum Dom Phellipe q' asiste em Goa Mas nellas Reẏna Outro Gentio q' dizem se leuantou ha Muẏto cõ ho Reẏno em tempo do Auo Ou Paẏ deste Dom Phellipe e goza o senhorio dellas sendo q' Aỹda Vem ao dito Dom Fellipe alguma Couza posto q' Pouqua do Rendim^{to}. de Algumas E a sua Iñstansia e pedimento foẏ de Portugal Ordem Ao Conde de Liuhares sendo Vizorreẏ Da India pera q' Mandasse huma Armada has ditas Ilhas=E o dito Vizorreẏ Mandou Em Abril de '631: ho Capitam Mor da Armada do Canara Domingos Ferreẏra Belliago cõ hũa Armada de quinze Navios o qual foẏ em demanda da prinsipal das Ilhas aonde o Reẏ Abita q' Esta leuantado cõ Ellas: Mas Elle foẏ auizado da ẏda da Armada e quando ella chegou estaua Muẏ bem forteficado: e hũa so entrada q' há pera a dita ẏlha estaua tapada cõ nauios cheos de pedras de forma q' era empossiuel entrar por ella e m^{to}. mais ẏmpossiuel entrar por outra nenhuma parte por ser Toda sercada de Rochedo e arresifes como da planta se pode Ver E o modo Em q' Estaua forteficada: e depois de a dita Armada estar Algũs dias sobre ella jugando as bombardadas Vindo q' era ẏmpossiuel podella entrar e q' era Tempo perdido Todo ho q' Alẏ gastasse se Volto para Goa Trazendo esta planta q' Eu lhe auia pedido me Trouxesse q' Pus aquẏ da mesma forma:—

INDEX.

B.

G.

GLOSSARY

OF

REFERENCES TO FOREIGN AND UNUSUAL WORDS.

Provedor, *iv*, 211
Prumo, *iv*, 7
Pudricaraja, *iii*, 87

Q.

Quina, *iv*, 216
Quintal, *ii*, 49 ; *iii*, 80, 150
Quitoal, *iii*, 148

R.

Ramadão, *i*, 234
Rebolaria, *iii*, 20
Reis, *iii*, 41
Relogio de mar, *i*, 25
Rea, *iii*, 140
"Repousar sobre o cabo da enxada", a proverb, *iv*, 208
Ruiva, *iv*, 13

S.

Sandeo, *iii*, 53
Sangradura, or Singradura, *iv*, 31
Satia, *ii*, lxx
Satiawati, *ii*, lxxi
Sembah, *ii*, lxxiv
Sesta Feira de Endoenças, *iv*, 8
Slendang, *ii*, lxxiv
Soldo, *iii*, 138, 140
Sombreiro, *ii*, 182
Sphera, *iii*, 138
Sudra, *ii*, lxxi
Swarga, *ii*, lxxi

T.

Taforea, *i*, 18, 54 ; *iv*, 37
Taipa, *iv*, 208
Talhado, a pique, *iv*, 11
Tamungo, *iii*, 87
Tanadar, *ii*, lxxvii, 125 ; *iv*, 128
Tarçado, *iv*, 158. *See* Terçado.
Tauxia, *iii*, 18
Terçado, *i*, 137. *See* Tarçado.
Terrada, *i*, 105 ; *iv*, 53, 115, 192, 193
Titiran, *ii*, lxxiv
Torre de Menagem, *i*, 45 ; *iii*, 136 ; *iv*, 73, 147, 215
Trabuco, *iv*, 11
Traquete, *iii*, 63 ; *iv*, 7
Travessa, *ii*, xviii
Tuão, *iii*, 131
Tundea, *iii*, 139

V.

Vara de Coromandel, *i*, 41
Veador, *ii*, xvi
Vereadores, *iii*, 43, 206
Vintem, *ii*, 129
Virtude, *iii*, 45
Voga arrancada, *ii*, 179

X.

Xabandar, *ii*, lxxviii ; *iii*, 87 ; the description at, *ii*, 132, is incorrect
Xerafim, *i*, 43, 82, 129, 170 ; *ii*, 124 ; *iv*, 149, 168, 170, 171, 192, *etc.*

Z.

Zaguncho, *iv*, 20
Zamboa, *i*, 100
Zambuco, *i*, 29 ; *iv*, 206
Zamorim, *i*, 1. *See* Çamorim.
Zarvatana, *iii*, 104